ENGLISH-KONKANI DICTIONARY

ENGLISH-KONKANI DICTIONARY

ANGELUS FRANCIS XAVIER MAFFEI

GYAN

Published by

GYAN

Gyan Publishing House
5, Ansari Road
Daryaganj, New Delhi-110002
Phone: 011-47034999, 9811692060
E-mail: books@gyanbooks.com

Distribution Network
gyanbooks.com
India, USA, Canada, UK, Australia, France

ISBN : 9788121243278 (PB)
First Published, Mangalore, 1883

2nd Impression 2020

Printed at: Gyan Press, Delhi.

English-Konkani Dictionary
Author: Angelus Francis Xavier Maffei

AN

ENGLISH-KONKANI

DICTIONARY

BY

ANGELUS FRANCIS XAVIER MAFFEI

OF THE SOCIETY OF JESUS

MANGALORE

PRINTED AT THE BASEL MISSION PRESS

1883

PREFACE

In presenting this Dictionary, the first attempt of its kind in Konkani, to the public, it would, the Author conceives, be sufficient claim to their indulgence to state that the bulk of the work is the fruit of an extremely short acquaintance with English, and of a still shorter one with Konkani. But it should further be borne in mind that the Author has had no written materials whatever to assist him in his work. The Konkani language hitherto has existed only in the mouth of the people, and it has been part of the Author's task, first, to pick up the language by personal intercourse with them, and secondly, to endeavour to reduce it to method and uniformity. Moreover, circumstances have rendered it impossible for him to carry the manuscript, at least the English-Konkani portion of it, through the press himself, so that he has been debarred from correcting faults which he would otherwise have seen proper to correct in the course of publication.

In spite of these drawbacks, however, the Author would call attention to the fact that all the words given in the Dictionary as Konkani, with the exception of a few expressly marked, are really such. It may be urged in opposition to this statement, 1) that many of them are, if not identical with, at least very like the Canarese or Tulu equivalents; 2) that, as a matter of fact, many of them are not understood by the people themselves; 3) that the meaning of certain words, in familiar use with the common people to express certain material objects, have had their meaning extended, and been used to express analogous abstract ideas; and lastly, that words have been compounded and given in the Dictionary, which did not exist as such before. To the first objection he would answer, that such words cannot be considered purely Canarese or Tulu, since they are to be found in both the Dravidian and Gaurian languages. The second objection may be met by the following considerations; that the reason why some words are not understood by the people themselves, is, not that those words are not Konkani, but that the language embraces so great a variety of dialects, that what is understood by some is not understood by others, and what is spoken in one place is not spoken in another. The Author has not confined himself in his researches to one particular district or to particular classes of men. It is quite true, however, that not all the Konkani words that exist, have been inserted, nor are all those inserted equally good or correct. A selection, perhaps, will have to be made later on. As to the third and fourth objections, it should be remembered that either no equivalent at all, or a Sanskrit or Marathi one, which very few, if any, would have understood, had to be given for such words. The Author may reasonably justify his adoption of these methods on the ground that they seemed to him the only means calculated to raise the tone and enrich the vocabulary of a long neglected language. As regards the compound words more particularly, he would remind his readers that this manner of compounding words is not alien to, but in conformity with the spirit of Konkani. Moreover, all such compounds have been carefully tested and examined with the assistance of different native gentlemen.

As regards the use of the Dictionary, frequent references have been made throughout to the Author's Konkani Grammar, lately published, which it presupposes, and of which indeed it is the proper completion. To show the proper use of a word, the most important part of a Dictionary, a literal second translation of the Konkani word or phrase, instead of an example, has been given; the reader will choose that which corresponds to the meaning he requires. The different meanings of the English words have been established chiefly according to the Dictionary of Smith; to the different English meanings, some of which are rather rare, different Konkani words or expressions have been assigned, distinguished, for clearness' sake, by numbers; where only a semicolon distinguishes them, the words or expressions are simply or nearly synonyms. To the Konkani translation of an English word, words in brackets have sometimes been added; the reader must use his judgment as to when the sense requires the addition of the bracketed words, when not.

Finally, the Author offers his hearty thanks to all who have assisted him in his work; among others to the Rev. Fr. A. Coelho, who, after a careful inspection, was pleased to declare in writing his full approbation of the work. He would more especially express his gratitude to His Excellency Mountstuart Elphinstone Grant Duff, Governor of Madras, for according to him the assistance of Government in the printing of this work; as also to J. Sturrock Esq., Collector of South Canara, for the sincere interest he has evinced in its promotion. Above all, the Author gives thanks to God, the Giver of all good, to Whose special help is due whatever is good in this Dictionary.

Cannanore, October 1883. *A. F. X. M., S. J.*

Application of Roman characters to the Konkani Alphabet.

ă = a closed a, *often* nearly ó.
a = a common a.
ā = a long a.
b = a common b.
bh = the same aspirated.
č = a soft c, *as* ch *in* chapter.
čh = the same aspirated.
d = a common d.
dh = the preceding aspirated.
ḍ = a cerebral d.
ḍh = the preceding aspirated.
e = a short e.
ē = a long e.
f = a common f.
g = a hard g, *as* gh *in* Latin.
gh = the same aspirated.
gn = ny *in* banyan.
g-ṇ = gn *in* Ignatius.
h = h aspirated, *as in English*.
i = a short i.
ī = a long i.
j = a soft g, *as* j *in English*.
jh = the same aspirated.
k = a hard c, *like* c *in* calendar.
kh = the same aspirated.
kṣ̌ = x *in* appendix.
l = a common l.
ḷ = a cerebral l.
m = a common m.
n = a common n.
ṇ = a cerebral n.
ñ = a nasal, indistinct sound.
o = a short o.
ō = a long o.
p = a common p.
ph = the same aspirated.
q = a common q.
r = a common r.
s = an English s *as in* salute.
š = an English sh.
ṣ̌ = an English cerebral sh.
t = a common t.
th = the same aspirated.
ṭ = a cerebral t.
ṭh = the same aspirated.
u = a short u.
ū = a long u.
ụ = a half vowel.
v = a common v approaching u.
y = y *in* yam.
z = z *in* wizard.
zh = the same aspirated.
′ upon a vowel *shows* a closed vowel, *e. g.* é *is pronounced as* a *in* tale; è *is pronounced as* e *in* well.
″ *shows the accent of the preceding syllable.*

The diphthongs are pronounced according to the Roman alphabet, viz. by joining the original sounds of the compounded vowels; thus au is like ou in house; ei as in Latin *mei*, *etc.*

Directions for the use of this Dictionary.

1. The accent is generally upon the last syllable: where not, ″ is put after the accented syllable.

2. Of the nouns, the Nominative and Original cases are given.

3. Of verbs, the root is given, which generally is found in the Imperative singular; in some rare cases the 3rd person singular is given, to be known by the literal translation. In order to secure uniformity, the Imperative has been put, even when the meaning would have required the 3rd Person Indicative, *e.g.* Succumb = pă̤ḍāu ză *instead of* pă̤ḍāu zātă.

4. Of the adjectives of three terminations, the masculine singular has been given.

5. The negative forms given under **Im** and **Un** are generally not used by common people: they rather use the affirmative form with a negative verb or in a negative construction.

6. The construction of Konkani phrases is generally hinted at in their literal translation. Thus, if in the literal translation of the Konkani word corresponding to an English transitive verb, a verb and a noun with a Genitive occurs, this shows that the Genitive must be used instead of the English Accusative, provided nothing else is stated.

See further explanations in the Directions prefixed to the Konkani-English Dictionary.

Abbreviations.

a. or *adj.* = adjective.
Acc. = Accusative.
ad. or *adv.* = adverb.
anal. = analytical.
App. = Appendix.
approx. = approximate.
Art. = Article.
bet. = better.
c. v. = causative verb.
Cn. or *Can.* = Canarese.
ch. = chapter.
ch. cs. = change construction.
Comm. or *Cm.* = Communicative case, *i.e.* Original *with* lāgiñ *or* kăḍe.
com. = commonly.
conj. = conjunction.
comparat. = comparative degree.
crc. = circumlocution.
D. or *Dat.* = Dative.
decl. = declinable.
Dim. = diminutive.
e.g. = for example.
esp. = especially.
emph. = emphatic.
ex. = exactly.
F. or *f.* = feminine gender.
fg. = figurative, *i.e.* meaning.
fr. = foreign word, *i.e.* of European origin, especially Portuguese; sometimes this *fr.* has been omitted.
fut. = future.
G. = Genitive.
G. M., *G. F.*, *G. N.* = Genitive masculine, Genitive feminine, Genitive neuter; *see* Gram. p. 11 and 51.
Gram. = Grammar.
H. K. = used especially by Hindu Konkans.
h. w. = high word.
Hind. = Hindustani.
Imp. = Imperfect tense.
ind. art. = indefinite article.
indecl. = indeclinable.
Instr. = Instrumental.
int. = interjection.
It. or *Ital.* = Italian.
Kan or *Kn.* = Kanarese.
Konk. = Konkanism.
l. = literal, *i. e.* translation.
Lat. = Latin.
Loc. = Locative case; *see* Gram. p. 10.
M. or *m.* = masculine gender.
mn. = meaning *or* it means.
Mr. = Marathi.
mt. = metaphorical, *i. e.* meaning.
n. or *N.* = neuter gender.
N. or *Nom.* = Nominative.
n. c. = not common, *i. e.* not in common use: this sign has been sometimes omitted.
n. u. = not used: sometimes this sign has been omitted.
n. v. = neuter verb.

Necess. = Necessary mood.
neg. form = negative construction.
Or. or *O.* = Original case.
obj. = object.
obs. = obsolete.
ol. = old *or* obsolete word.
opp. = opposite.
P. = Part.
p. = page.
part. = participle.
pass. = passive.
perh. = perhaps.
phil. = philosophically.
pl. = plural.
Postp. or *Pstp.* = Postposition.
poten. = potential mood.
pr. = proper meaning as opposed to figurative.
prep. = preposition.
pron. or *pro.* = pronoun.
Prs. = Person.
pr. fg. = properly and figuratively.
r. = rare word.
rl. or *rel.* = religious word.
rs. = resolve into.
s. = substantive.
Sans. = Sanskrit.
Sb. = Subject.
sing. = singular.
superl. = superlative degree.
tr. = transitive verb.
v. or *vrb.* = verb.
var. = variety, *i.e.* of pronunciation, *etc.*
vl. or *vlg.* = vulgar.
w. = word.

See these abbreviations further explained in the Konkani-English Dictionary.

ENGLISH-KONKANI

DICTIONARY

A

A, an, *ind. art.* yek; *see* Gram. p. 80.

Aback, *ad.* pāṭi.

Abandon, *v.* 1. sōḍ, *e.g.* a town, a poor man; (sōd = seek; zōḍ = obtain, clasp); sānḍ, *e.g.* a house.

2. vāṭer ghāl, *or* sóḍn vāṭer ghāl = put on the way, *fg.*

Abandoned, *part. a. see v.* nirādhāri = having no help; upāi nātullo = having no means.

Abandonment, *s.* 1. soḍni, -ne, *f.*

2. nirādhār, -rā, *m. see adj. and v.*

Abase, *see* **Humble.**

Abash, *v.* lăzăi, *c. v. of* lăz; lăjek ghāl = *l.* put to shame.

Abate, *v.* 1. uṇo kăr = *l.* make less, *tr.*; uṇo zā, *n. v.*; hăḷu kăr = *l.* make light, *fg.*

2. deuñ, *n. v.* devoi, *c. v.*, *e. g.* price, fever.

Abatement, *s.* 1. devāp, -pā, *n.*

2. haḷuāi, -ye, *f. see v.*; uṇepoṇ, -ṇā, *n. see v.*

Abbess, *s.* (mādrinči) voḍiln, -lni, *f.* = *l.* superioress (of nuns), *fr.* (kănyāstriānči) voḍiln, -lni, *f.* = *l.* superioress (of nuns).

Abbey, *s.* móṭ, -ṭā, *m.* (*not applied to Christian converts*).

Abbot, *s.* moṭāādhipăti, -ti, *m. or* -voḍil, -lā, *m.*

Abbreviate, *v.* moṭvo kăr = make short; uṇo kăr = make less.

Abbreviation, *s.* 1. moṭvepoṇ, -ṇā, *n.* = *l.* shortness: *bet. rs. v.*

2. sănkšép, -pā, *m.* = abridgment.

3. zōḍakšer, -rā, *n.* (in writing).

Abdicate, *v.* sōḍ = *l.* leave, *e.g.* an office, a kingdom; rāji di = give resignation, *obj. Dat.*

Abdication, *s.* soḍni, -ne, *f.*; rāji, -je, *f.*

Abdomen, *s.* pòṭ, -ṭā, *n.*
Abduction, *s. rs. v.* kāḍ *or* kāḍn kāṇe *or* kāḍn voḍ.
Aberration, *s.* 1. tsuk, -ki, *f.*= *l.* error, deviation.
2. vāṭetsuk, -ki, *f.*=*l.* mistake of the way.
3. vānkḍi vāṭ, -ṭe, *f.*=*l.* crooked way.
Abet, *v.* (vāiṭāk) kumok kăr= *l.* make help (to evil).
Abettor, *s.* (vāiṭāk) kumok kăr-tolo, *or* vāiṭākumki, -kiā *or* vāiṭākumkegār, -rā, *m.*
Abeyance, *s. rs.* khāli āsā=vacation is; *or* sădiāk rāvāp, -rāupā, *n.*
Abhor, *v.* kānṭāḷ, *e.g.* sin; *see* **Hate.**
Abhorrence, *s.* kānṭāḷo, -ḷeā, *or* kānṭāḷ, -ḷā, *m.*; hăgeñ, -geā, *n.*=*l.* hatred; jiddu̥, -dā, *n.* =*l.* enmity.
Abide, *v.* 1. rāu=*l.* remain; vās kăr=*l.* make residence.
2. rāk=*l.* wait for, expect.
3. thirzāun rāu=remain constant.
Ability, *s.* šăkăt, -kti, *f.*; sāmărthi, -rthe, *f.*; trāṇ, -ṇā, *n.* *see* **Cleverness.**
Abject, *a.* uṇo, *e.g.* ab. man; kirkoḷ=*l.* low, wretched; hălko=*l.* low, corrupted; ăṇvo=*l.* of low state.
Abjectness, *s.* uṇepoṇ, -ṇā, *n.*; hălkepoṇ, -ṇā, *n.*; kirkoḷāi, -ye, *f.* *see adj.*
Abjuration, *s.* pārmāṇār soḍni, -ḍne, *f.* *or bet. rs. v.*
Abjure, *v.* pārmāṇār sóḍ=*l.* leave on oath.
Able, *a.* šăktivont; trāṇ āsullo; zāṇto=clever; *rs.* tānktā= power is, *or* 'tānk āsullo'.
Able (Be), *see adj.*
Ablution, *s.* duvāp, duupā, *n.*; snān, -nā, *n.* (*H. K.*)
Abnegation, *s.* āpli inkāri, -re, *f.*=reşistance to oneself.
Aboard (Go), tārvār tsăḍ.
Abode, *s.* biḍār, -rā, *n.*; ṭhikāṇeñ, -ṇeā, *n.* = residence, place; vās, -sā, *n.*; ṭhāṇeñ, -ṇeā, *n.*
Abolish, *v.* dānk *or* dāmp=*l.* shut, *fg.*, *e.g.* ab. a school; mokup kăr; kāḍn ghāl, *e.g.* an order=*l.* drawing put; kāḍn uḍāi.
Abolition, *s.* mokup, -pe, *f.*; răddu̥, -dā, *n.*=*l.* nullity; *rs. v.*
Abominable, *a.* 1. kānṭāḷeātso *or* kānṭāḷo fāvo zāllo; khoṭepoṇātso=wicked.
Abominate, *see* **Abhor.**
Abomination, *s.* 1. kānṭāḷo, -ḷeā, *m.*=act of abhorring.
2. khoṭepoṇ, -ṇā, *n.*=object of 'kānṭāḷo'.
Aborigines, *s.* mulvāsi=*l.* radical inhabitants.
Abortion, *s.* voḷauṇeñ, -ṇeā, *n.*
Abortion (Cause), *v.* voḷāi, *e.g.* āvoi burgeāk voḷāitā=the child is miscarried.

Abound, *v.* 1. bhòr = *l.* be filled, from 'bhór = fill'; *see* Gram. p. 276. 6; sompurṇāi āsā; bhòrn āsā.
2. tsăḍ, *or bet.* tsăḍ āsā = be too much, *or also* be much.

About, *ad. prep.* 1. sumăr, *Lat. circiter* (more or less).
2. băhuša = *l.* nearly, almost (a little less).
3. višyānt = as, speak ab. God.
4. bountăṇiñ = *l.* around.
5. thăiñ = *l.* as regards, *e. g.* ătmeā th. = as r. the soul.
6. *by 1st Loc., e. g.* ab. the neck = găḷeānt.
'Come ab. = găḍ'; 'bring ab. = găḍăi *or* kăr *or* kărăi'.

Above, *prep.* 1. *2nd. Loc.*
2. voir.

Above, *ad.* 1. voir; unts, *e.g.* look above.
2. prăs, vorn, *with Comparat. see* Gram. p. 65.
'Be ab. = bepārvo kăr = *l.* make contempt, be unwilling to condescend, *G. M.*

Abrade, *v.* 1. kāḍ *or* pusun kāḍ.
2. pus = clean, *e. g.* a black-board.

Abrasion, *s.* pusāp, -spā, *n. or rs. v.*

Abreast, *ad.* 1. hārin = *l.* in a line.
2. lāgiñ = close.

Abridge, *v.* sănkšép kăr, *G. M.*; moṭvo kăr = make short.

Abridgment, *s.* sănkšép, -pā, *m.*; gošvāro, -reā, *m.*

Abroad, *ad.* 1. bhāir = outside, out.
2. părgāvānt = in a foreign country.

Abrogate, *see* **Abolish.**

Abrupt, *a.* 1. aučit = sudden.
2. lāganātullo = *l.* unconnected; *see* **Steep.**

Abscess, *s.* fōḍ, -ḍā, *m.*

Abscond, *v.* lipăi, *c. v. of* lip, *n. u.*

Absence, *s.* găirhāzri, -ri, *f. or rs. a.*

Absent, *a.* găirhāzăr; 'be ab. in mind = motir nāñ'.

Absent, *v.* disānāñ = does not appear.

Absinth, *s.* 1. mănpătri, -tri, *f.*
2. if used *fg.*, kāzro, -reā, *m.* = *nux vomica,* (*used as a term of comparison*).

Absolute, *a.* 1. ăšertātso *or* asă-rtātso = *l.* unconditional.
2. sotăntrụ āsụllo *or* sotăntrā-tso = *l.* having absolute power, independent.
3. *Often rs., e.g. into* 'purteñ = fully', *or* 'sompurn = perfect', *etc.*

Absolution, *s.* 1. absolusāuñ, -sāvā, *n.* (*rl.*), *fr.*; bogsāṇeñ, -ṇeā, *n.* = forgiveness.
2. suṭka, -ke, *f.* = acquittal.

Absolve, *v.* absolusāuñ di = *l.* give absolution (*rl.*); bogsi, (*old form* 'bogos'); māp kăr

= excuse, overlook; sóḍ = acquit, *pass.* suṭ; *see* Gram. p. 134. 4.

Absorb, *v.* 1. girăi, *c.v.* of gir, *n.v.* (*var.* jirăi), *e.g.* a sponge absorbs; voḍ = *l.* draw, *fg.*

2. giḷ = *l.* swallow.

'He is absorbed in meditation = to niyāḷānt buḍlā'.

Abstain, *v.* 1. tsukăi, *c.v.* of tsuk, *e.g.* pātak tsukăi = ab. from sin; *by neg. gerund in* '-tanañ' *and* 'rāu', *e.g.* khāināstanāñ rāu = ab. from eating.

2. jinzvār dovor = keep fasting, *fr.*; upāsi rāu = remain fasting.

N. B. There is no word in common use to distinguish true fasting from simple abstinence.

Abstemious, *a.* 1. hăḷtān piyeuntso = drinking moderately.

2. soro piyenātullo = not drinking liquor.

Abstinence, *s.* 1. tsukouṇeñ, -ṇeā, *n.*

2. *vlg.* jinzvār, -rā, *m.*, *fr.*; mās khăunk nozo, *vlg.*; upās, -sā, *m.* = true fasting.

3. māsāsoḍăp, -ḍpā, *n.* = leaving of meal, *n. u.*

Abstract, *v.* 1. kăḍ *or* vóḍ.

2. *fg. ch. cs.* as, 'ab. your heart from the world = tumčeñ kāḷiz săuñsār tsukoundi', *or* 'tujeñ kāḷiz humboḷ = *l.* root out your heart'.

3. *phil.* vingăḍ čint.

Abstraction, *s.* 1. *phil.* vingăḍ kărči čintnā, -tne, *f.*

2. *in other mn. rs. v.*

Abstruse, *a.* guṭātso *or* gupit = secret, *fg.*; somzanātullo = *l.* not understood; somzanāñso; tăzvizitso = maliciously ab., *n. c.*; kănṭiṇ *or* kăṭiṇ = difficult, *e.g.* to be learnt.

Abstruseness, *s.* 1. kăṭiṇăi, -ye, *f.*

2. kāḷok, -kā, *m.* = *l.* darkness, *fg.*, *n. c.*

Absurd, *a.* 1. *vlg.* nozo = is impossible; 'this is ab. = yeñ nozo'; lāgānātullo = not connected.

2. nākāzāllo = nonsensical; vāreāvelo = windy, *fg.*, *e.g.* ab. words.

Absurdity, *s.* 1. virodhāi, -ye, *f.* = *l.* contradiction; virodhpoṇ, -ṇā, *n.*

2. nākāzālli văstų = *l.* nonsensical thing; nākāzāllo, -leā, *m.* = nonsense.

Abundance, *s.* sămpurṇāi, -ye, *f.*; păripurṇāi, -ye, *f.*; *vlg. rs.* tsăḍ = much.

Abundant, *a.* sămpurṇ, *e.g.* ab. crop; păripurṇ, *e.g.* ab. crop; dădos *or* dādosi, *e.g.* ab. crop.

Abuse, *v.* 1. gāḷi săng *or* g. sou = say abuses; ăulăkṣ kăr, *n. c.*

2. ălăkṣa kăr, *e. g.* ab. time, *n. c.*; pāḍ kăr = spoil; beparvo kăr = *l.* contempt, *fg. G. M.*; nisprăyog kăr, *G. M.* = *l.* make abuse, *n. c.*

3. mekoa, mirua = *l.* trespass, *e. g.* podvek m. = abuse power.

Abuse, *s.* 1. gāḷ, -ḷi, *f.*; ăulăkṣ, -ṣā, *n. c.*

2. nisprăyog, -gā, *m.* = wrong use; uksam, -mā, *m.*, *n. c.*; *rs. v.*

Abusive, *a.* ăkmānātso; 'ab. words = gāḷi'.

Abyss, *s.* gunḍi, -ye, *f.*

Academy, *s.* vidyesāl, -le, *f.*

Accelerate, *v.* 1. lāgiñ kăr = make near.

2. vegiñ kăr, *or bet.* ăusăr kăr = make haste; vegiñ tsălăi = cause to go fast; vegiñ tsăl = go fast; *ch. cs.*, *e.g.* ac. death = jiṇi moṭvi kăr.

Accent, *s.* 1. tāḷeābhār, -rā, *m.* = heaviness of voice, weight of voice; tāḷeābhed, -dā, *m.* difference of voice.

2. tāḷeābhārātso gurtu, -tā, *m.* = sign of weight of voice.

Accent, *v.* tāḷeābhār ghāl.

Accept, *v.* 1. kāṇe *or* kānghe *or* ghe; mānuă = please, *Sb. Dat.*; vopun kāṇe = consenting take; vopsun kāṇe = consigned take.

2. meḷăi = aggregate.

Acceptable, *a.* mogāḷ = dear; ăpurbāyetso = amiable; mānvontso = pleasing.

Acceptable (Be), mānuă = *l.* please; '(āuñ) săntos pāutāñ . . . thăiñ = I feel pleasure in . . .'

Acceptation, *s.* 1. ghevāp, -pā, *n.*; mānuāp, -pā, *n.*, *e. g.* of a present.

2. meḷouṇeñ, -ṇeā, *n.* = aggregation.

Access, *s.* rig, -ge, *f.*

Accessible, *a.* rigatso *or* votsayet ăsullo.

Accessory, *a.* uṇeñ gărjetso = less necessary.

Accident, *s.* 1. grātstsār, -rā, *m.* = fate; găḍāp, -ḍpā, *n.* = event.

2. tsuk, -ki, *f.* = *l.* mistake.

3. sārkeñ, -keā, *n.* *opp. to* sār = substance.

By ac. 1. tsukon = by mistake.

2. grātstsārān *etc.*

3. apsents = by itself.

Accidental, *a.* 1. grātstsārātso; găḍpātso.

2. aučit = *l.* sudden, unexpected.

Acclamation, *s.* hogḷāp, -pā, *n.*

Acclivity, *see* Slope.

Accommodate, *v.* 1. lāyek kăr = make fit.

2. zāgo di = give place.

'ac. yourself to the will of = *G.* khušie pārmāṇe tsăl'.

Accommodation, *s.* 1. bori suāt, -te, *f.* = good place; boro zāgo, -geā, *m.* = good place.
2. sămādhān, -nā, *n.* = concord, peace; rāji, -je, *f.* = ac. between litigants.

Accompaniment (of marriage), hóru, -rā, *m.*; dibbăn, -ṇā, *n.*

Accompany, *v.* pāvoi = *l.* cause to reach, *fg.*; *or*...sāngātā vots = go with....

Accomplice, šāmil, -lā, *m.*; vānṭeli, -liā, *m.*; sāngāti, -tiā, *m.*

Accomplish, *v. vlg.* kābār kăr = finish, *fr.*; tirsi, *tr. v.* tirsa, *n. v.*; phăḍča kăr.

Accord, *v.* săma poḍ = fall right; vop = agree.

Accord (With one), yekā motin *or* yekā budin.

Accordance (In acc. with), 1. *rs.* zātā = is fit.
2. părmāṇe āsā, *e.g.* in acc. with the order.

Accordingly, *ad.* tăr, dekun.

Account, *s.* 1. lèk, -kā, *n.* (*also* statement, importance).
2. *fg.* kārāṇ, -ṇā, *n.* = cause; săbāb, -bi, *f.*; *rs.* pāsun *or* pāsvot = on account of; 'give acc. = lèk di'; 'call to acc. = lèk duinčeāk āpoi'; *see* **Value, Importance, Profit.**

Account, *v.* 1. kārāṇ dākăi = show the cause, acc. for; săbāb di = give reason, acc. for.
2. lèk di = give account.

Account-book, *s.* lekāčeñ pustak, -kā, *n.*

Accumulate, *v.* rās kăr, *Acc. or G. F.* = make heap; tsăḍăi = increase; meḷăi, *e.g.* acc. sins; zomăi *or* zomo kăr; punzăi, *e.g.* acc. money.

Accumulation, *s.* rās, -si, *f.*; zomo, -meā, *m.*; punzo, -jeā, *m.* (of money).

Accuracy, *s.* zāgrutāi, -ye, *f.*

Accurate, *a.* zāgrut = *l.* awake, *fg.*; sārko = *l.* exact.

Accursed, *part. a.* širāp poḍullo.

Accusation, *s.* 1. firiyād, -di, *f.* = criminal acc.
2. kăifet, -ti, *f.* = civil acc.
3. dur, -rā, *n.* = private acc.

Accuse, *v.* 1. firiyād di *or* f. sāng, *2nd Loc.*
2. kăifet di *or* k. sāng.
3. guniāukār kăr = make guilty; duruăi, *c. v. of* duruā; siṇ ulăi = say complaint.

Accuser, *s.* 1. muddăi, -dăi, *m.* *opp. to* muddăyāle, -le, *m.* = accused, criminal.
2. vādi, -di, *m. opp. to* prătivādi = civil acc.

Accustom, *v.* sóvói kăr, *G. F. tr. v.*; s. zā, *n. v.*

Acerb, *a.* 1. hărvo (not ripe).
2. āmboṭ = *l.* acid.

Acerbity, *s.* 1. hărvāi, -ye, *f.*
2. āmsāṇi, -ṇi, *f.*; koḍsāṇ, -ṇi, *f.*
3. *fg.* kăṭiṇāi, -ye, *f.* = severity.

Ache, *s.* 1. duk, -ki, *f.*; phoḍāpoḍ, -ḍi, *f.*; *rs. v.* duk-tā: 'I have a headache = māteñ duktā'.

Achieve, *see* **Accomplish.**

Acid, *a.* āmboṭ.

Acidity, *s.* āmsāṇ, -ṇi, *or* āmboṭāi, -ye, *f.*

Acknowledge, *v.* 1. vop, *or* voppigi kăr, *e.g.* 'āuñ mozo gunyāuñ voptāñ = I ack. my fault'; voḷok kăr, *G.F. or* voḷkā = recognize.
2. lek, *or* lekun ghe: 'ack. the receipt = răšid lekun ghe'.

Acknowledgment, *s.* 1. voḷok, -ḷki, *f.*; voppigi, -ge, *f.*
2. răšid, -de, *f.*

Acquaint, *v.* kăḷāi (*c. v. of* kăḷ = know); zāṇāi (*c. v. of* zāṇa = knows).

Acquaintance, *s.* voḷok, -ḷki, *f.*

Acquainted (Be acq. with), *G.* voḷok āsā; *rs.* voḷkitso, *e.g.* 'tāči voḷok mākā āsā, *or* to moje voḷkitso.

Acquire, *v.* zōḍ; jik; meḷtā = is found, *fg.*, *sb. Dat.*

Acquirement, *s.* 1. zoḍ, -ḍi, *f.*
2. zāṇvāi, -ye, *f.* = knowledge.

Acquit, *v.* soḍ = dismiss innocent; *pass.:* suṭ; *see* Gram. p. 134.4. *see* **Behāve.**

Acquittal, *s.* suṭkā, -ke, *f.*

Acrid, *a.* 1. khār; lāstso = burning; tik; koḍu = bitter.
2. *fg.* ništur = cruel.

Acrimony, *s.* 1. koḍsāṇ, -ṇe (-ṇi), [*f.*
2. *fg.* kăṭiṇāi, -ye, *f.*

Across, poltăḍi = *l.* beyond, *opp. to* 'āltăḍi = on this side'.
'I come acr. a person = yeklo mākā meḷtā'.

Act, *s.* kāryeñ, -yeā, *n.*, *e.g.* of the mind; *also* an action out of the common run, *e.g.* a dinner to guests; kărni, -ne, *f.*

Act, *v.* 1. kăr = do.
2. tsăl = behave.
3. bădli poḷe *or. G.* suāter tsălăi = act for.
4. guṇāk poḍ = *l.* fall to effect, *e.g.* a medicine.

Acting, *s.* bădli, -liā, *m.*; *G.* suāter tsălăitolo.

Action, *s* 1. kărni, -rne, *f.*
2. kāryeñ, -yeā, *n. see* **Act.**
3. kărtueñ, -tueā, *n.* (*or* kărtuā, -ye, *f.*) = great action.

Active, 1. tsurk; sudāḷ = agile; suḍsuḍāyetso = agile; ušār = clever.
2. boḷādik = *l.* strong, *e.g.* a [medicine.

Activity, *s.* 1. tsurk, -rkā, *n. or* tsurkpoṇ, -ṇā, *n.*; sudāḷāi, -ye, *f.*; suḍsuḍāi, -ye, *f.*; ušārāi, -ye, *f. see adj.*
2. boḷ, -ḷā, *n. see adj.*

Actor, *s.* nāṭakār, -rā, *m. or* āṭāgār, -rā, *m.* (in a drama).

Actual, *a.* 1. khărots = real.
2. ātāntso = *l.* of now.

Acute, *a.* 1. dhār āsullo, *or* dhāritso = having a fine edge; domsātso = pointed.
2. *fg.* bārik, *e.g.* eyes, mind.

Acuteness, *s.* 1. dhār, -ri, *f.* 2. domos, -msā, *m.* 3. *fg.* bārikāi, -ye, *f. see adj.*

Adage, *s.* gād, -di, *f.*

Adamant, *see* **Magnet.**

Adapt, *v.* 1. lāyek kăr, *tr. v.* 2. zātā *or* sāztā, *n. v.*=is fit.

Add, *v.* 1. āniki ghāl *or* ā. di= put *or* give more; 'āni' *with the required verb, e.g.* 'ā. tin di=add three'. 2. kuḍsi, *e.g.* a wing to a house. 3. tāče šivāi sāng=say besides.

Addict, *v.* 1. lāi=*l.* apply, *tr. v.* 2. lāg = *l.* be applied, *n. v.*; bhāl=devote oneself wholly to.

Addicted, *part. a.* lāgullo, *e. g.* piyeunčāk *or* piyeunk=*l.* ad. to drinking.

Addition, *s.* 1. tsăḍāu, -ḍāvā, *m. or* tsăḍāp, -ḍpā, *n. or* tsăḍoṇi, -ṇe, *f.* 2. kusri, -sre, *f.*=extra measure or weight given to purchasers.

Additional, *a.* tsăḍāvot; by 'šivāi *or* khărit=beside' *with the required verb.*

Address, *v.* 1. *Cm.* ulăi=speak with. 2. *Dat.* borei=write to; *G.* nāvār borei, *e.g.* a letter; melviḷās borei = write the address.

Address, *s.* 1. melviḷās, -sā, *m.*= ad. of a letter. 2. uloṇeñ, -ṇeā, *n. or rs. v.*

Adduce, *v.* dākăi.

Adequate, *a.* lāyek; kāmāk poḍtso (*or whatever other word the sense requires*).

Adhere, *v.* 1. lāg, *e. g.* pān pānāk lāgtā=leaf adheres to leaf. 2. *fg.* vop=*l.* agree, *e. g.* to a proposal.

Adherence, Adhesion, *s.* lāgāp, -gpā, *n.*

Adherent, *s.* pāṭlāugār, -rā, *m.*= follower; păkšegār, -rā, *m.* partisan.

Adjacent, *a.* lāgsilo *or rs. v.*, *or rs.* lāgiñ.

Adjoin, *v.* yekkoṭ kăr = make union; meḷăi *or* kuḍsi.

Adjourn, *v.* bāki dovor, *or* pāṭi ghāl.

Adjudge, *v.* tirp di = *l.* give decision.

Adjure, *v.* āṇ di *or* āṇ diun māg.

Administer, *v.* tsălăi=*l.* cause to walk, *fg.*

Administration, *s.* kārkāno, -neā, *m.*, *e. g.* adm. of an establishment; kārbār, -rā, *n.*, *n. c. in this mn.*

Administrator, *s.* kārkāneāgār, -rā, *m.*; . . . tsălăitolo=causing to walk. . . *fg.*; kārbāri, -riā, *m.*

Admiral, *s.* tārvāñmukedam, -mā, *m.*

Admiration, *s.* ăjāp, -pā, *n.*; ătsăryeñ, -ryeā, *n. used also for* 'miracle'.

Admire, *v.* āuñ ăjāp pāutāñ *or* ăjāp zātāñ, (*Acc.*) *n. v.*

Admission, *s.* rig, -ge, *f.* = *l.* entrance, *or rs. v.; see* **Acceptation.**

Admit, 1. ghe = *l.* receive; *past.* ghetlo; milākăt di = give audience.
2. kobul kăr *or* kobuli di = *l.* make *or* give consent, *Dat.;* vop = *l.* acknowledge, *Dat.*
3. rigunk răjā di = *l.* give leave to enter; rigăi.

Admonish, *v.* 1. bori bud sāng = *l.* say good advice; beşţăi = *l.* reproach.
2. kăḷăi = warn.

Admonition, 1. bud, -di, *f.*
2. beşţăuṇeñ, -ṇeā, *n.*
3. sikoṇi, -ṇe, *f.* = *l.* instruction.

Adopt, *v.* 1. posko kăr *or* posko kărn ghe = *l.* make adoptive; dhărmaputrų kărn ghe.
2. *fg.* vintsun kāḍ = choose.
3. vop = *l.* consent, *e.g.* ad. an opinion.

Adoption, *s.* poskepoṇ, -ṇā, *n.* *from* 'pos, *v.* = feed'; *rs. v.*

Adoptive, *a.* posko; dhărmātso, *or* dhărmāk kāṇeillo = *l.* of charity *or* taken to charity; dătta (putrų).

Adorable, *a.* nămăskār fāvo zāllo, *or* nămăskārātso.

Adoration, *s.* nămăskār, -rā, *m.* *with non-Christians*=salute; vondaneñ, -neā, *n.*, *n. c.*; părnipāt, -ti, *f.*; bhăzăn, -zne, *f.* = adoration (*of idols chiefly*); sămarāṇ, -ṇā, *n.*

Adore, *v.* 1. nămăskār (*or* vondaneñ) kăr; bhăz; sămarāṇ kăr.
2. māg, *l.* supplicate, *prs. Cm.*

Adorn, *v.* 1. surungār (*or* ălănkār) kăr, *G. M.*; neţăi, *c. v.* *of* neţ = adorn thyself.
2. bhor = *l.* fill, *e.g.* ad. with grace; sobăi, *c. v.* *of* sob = get beautiful.

Adornment, *s.* 1. surungār *or* ălănkār, -rā, *m.*
2. nēţ, -ţā *m.* *or* neţoṇ, -ṇi, *f.*
3. sobitāi, -ye, *f.* = *l.* beauty; *or* sobāi, -ye, *f.*

Adrift (Be), upe.

Adroit, *see* **Skilful.**

Adulation, *s.* fuslāuṇeñ, -ṇeā, *n.*; foţkireñ hogḷāp, -pā, *n.* = *l.* deceiving praise; tonḍāčeñ hogḷāp, -pā, *n.* = *l.* praise of mouth.

Adult, *a.* voḍlo = *l.* big; prāyetso = *l.* of age.

Adult, *s.* mānāi, -yā, *m.*

Adulterate, *v.* bórsi = *l.* mix; pāḍ kăr = *l.* spoil; kuţ ghāl (= ad. gold).

Adulterer, *s.* prăduvari, -riā, *m.*

Adulteress, *s.* prăduvariṇ, -ṇi, *f.*

Adultery, *s.* prăduvar, -rā, *n.*

Adumbrate, *v.* 1. sāuḷi kăr, *tr.* = make shadow.
2. ăbiprāi kăr = *l.* make a summary description; risko kāḍ, *fr.*; năkša kāḍ.

Adumbration, *s.* ăbiprāi, -ye, *f.*

Advance, *v.* 1. mukār ghāl *or* m. voḍ=*l.* put *or* carry before; bădti kăr=*l.* make promotion (to higher offices).

2. boro kăr; mukār vots *or* m. tsăl=go before.

Advance (In), mungăḍ *or* mubādlo (*indecl.*), *e. g.* 'āuñ yek rupoi m. ditāñ=I give a rupee in ad.'; săñčigār=earnest (part paid before as a pledge).

Advanced in age, tsăḍ prāyetso =*l.* of much age; mālgoḍo=*l.* eldest, ancestor; utăr prāyetso.

Advancement, *s.* băḍti, -te, *f.*=(promotion); 'get ad.=b. meḷtā'.

Advantage, *s.* fāido, -deā, *m.*; upkār, -rā, *m.* (=benefit); ādāi, -yā, *m.*; lāb, -bā, *m.*; jikāp, -kpā, *n.*

Advantageous, *a.* ādāyātso; upkārātso.

Advent, *s.* ādvent, -tā, *m.*, *rl.fr.* yeṇeñ, -ṇeā, *n.*=*l.* coming.

Adventure, *s.* 1. ădrušṭ, -šṭā, *n.* (fate) (*var.* ădrăšṭ); grātstsār, -rā, *m.*; găḍāp, -ḍpā, *n.*=event.

2. mosāčeñ kām, -mā, *n.*

Adversary, *s.* dusmān, -nā, *m.* veiri, -riā, *m.*; virod mănis, -nšā, *m.*; dušṭ, -šṭā, *m.*

Adverse, *a.* virodhi *or* virodh āsụllo.

2. *fg.* kăšṭāntso.

Adversity, kăšṭ, -šṭā, *m.*=*l.* difficulty, pain; āpad, -dā, *n.*; upădrụ, *m.*, *ol. rl.*; ākānt, -tā, *m.*

Advertise, *v.* kăḷāi, *or* kăḷit kăr=*l.* make known; zāṇāi; părgăṭ kăr=*l.* make public; dākăl kăr=*l.* make known; vărtamān di=give news; kăbār di (*pass.* k. āik)=*l.* give news.

Advertisement, *s.* istyār -rā, *m.* *used esp. for adv. of public authorities;* vărtamān, -nā, *n.*; kăbār, -bre, *f.*; vordi, -de, *f.*

Advice, *s.* bud, -di, *f.*

2. āločen, -ni, *f.*=opinion.

3. kăbār, -bre, *f.*=news.

Advisable, *a.* kărtso=to be done; lāyek,=*l.* fit, suitable; boro=good; buditso=of wisdom.

Advise, *v.* 1. bud săng=*l.* say advice.

2. kăbār āḍ=bring news; kăḷāi =make known.

3. āločen kăr=*l.* deliberate.

Advocate, *s.* văkil, -lā, *m.*

Advocate, *v.* *see* **Plead.**

Adze, *s.* tāsṇi, -ṇe, *f.*

Aerial, *a.* vāreātso.

Aerolite, *s.* ākāšātso fātor, -trā, *m.*

Aerometer, *s.* vāreāčeñ māp, -pā, *n.* (vereāmāp).

Afar, *ad.* pois.

Affability, *s.* 1. mogāḷpoṇ, -ṇā, *n.* from 'mogāḷ = dear'.
2. măryād, -di, *f.* = *l.* urbanity.

Affable, *a.* mogāḷ.
2. măryāditso.

Affair, *s.* 1. kām, -mā, *n.*
2. kārbār, -rā, *n.* *seldom used:* 'tujeñ k. kăseñ āsā? = how are your affairs?'

Affect, *v.* lāg = *l.* be attached; 'lāg' *is the most general equivalent, but different words are often employed, e.g.* 'I am affected with pains in the feet = pāi duktāt *l.* the feet feel pain', *etc.* 'The sermon affected me = sermāuñ monānt boro riglā', *l.* the sermon entered good in the heart, *or also* 'sermāuñ lāglo'.
2. sevoṭ āsā = *l.* aim is.

Affectation, *s.* kăpăṭ, -ṭā, *n.* = *l.* simulation.

Affected, *a.* 1. kăpṭi.
2. *rs.* with 'lāg' (*see v.*).

Affection, *s.* 1. vondoṇ, -ṇe, *f.* *or* vondouṇeñ, -ṇeā, *n.* = *l.* inclination, *e. g.* ăntăskārnāči vóndoṇ = incl. of the heart'; khuši, -še, *f.*; ăpurbāi, -ye, *f.* = amiability, fondness; mōg, -gā, *m.* = love.
2. sălgi, -ge, *f.* = fondness, (*ex.* familiarity).

Affectionate, *a.* mogāḷ: 'tsākor dhăniyā thăiñ mogāḷ āsā = the servant is affectionate to his master'; *often rs. v.*

Affiance, *see* **Betroth.**

Affidavit, *s.* pārmāṇ, -ṇā, *n.*

Affiliate, *v.* meḷăi = *l.* cause to be united.

Affinity, *s.* 1. săirik, -ke, *f.* (*pr.*)
2. sămănd, -dā, *m.* (*fg.*)
3. vondouṇeñ, -ṇeā, *n.* = chemical af., *l.* inclination.

N.B. băile isili seirik = affinity; băpăi isili seirik = consanguinity; *l.* relation in the direction of the woman, or father.

Affirm, *v.* voi moṇ = *l.* say yes; khăṇḍit (*or* khăṇḍit zăun) sāng = *l.* say positively; kăbul kăr = make consent.

Affix, *v.* lăgăi *or* lăi, *c. v. of* lāg.

Afflict, *v.* dukăi, *c. v. of* duk; duk di, kăšṭ di = give sorrow, pain; kăšṭăi, *c. v. of* kăšṭā.

Afflicted, *a.* dukest, *or* khăntišṭ.

Afflicting, *a.* dukouutso, *or* lāgtso, *e.g.* aff. words.

Affliction, *s.* 1. kăšṭ, -šṭā, *m.*
2. duk, -ki, *f.*
3. khănt, -ti, *f.*; ăsăntós, -sā, *m*; săntāp, -pā, *m.*

Affluence, *see* **Abundance.**

Afford, *v.* di = *l.* give.

Affront, *v.* 1. mukār vots, *or* m. rāu, *or* m. poḍ = *l.* go, *or* fall, *or* remain in face.
2. ăkmān (*or* ăpamān) kăr = *l.* make offence.

Afoot, *ad.* pāivāṭen; 'he goes af. = to p. vetā *or* tsăln vetā *or* p. tsăltā'.

Afraid, *a.* 1. bhizuḍ, *Lat. timidus.* 2. bhiyātso; phukkela.

Afraid, (I am af.) 1. 'mākā bheñ distā = *l.* to me fear appears'. 2. āuñ bhiyetāñ = *l.* I fear.

Afresh, *ad.* 1. portun = again; āni yek pāuṭi = once more. 2. āileāvăr = lately.

After, Afterwards, *prep., ad.* 1. uprānt (*var.* uprānteñ); māgir. 2. pāṭleān, *e.g.* 'tāčeā pāṭleān vots = go after him, *Lat. sequere eum*'.

After, (Immediately af.) *ad.* teā farā uprānt = *l.* after that moment; teāts fara *or* teā farats = in the very moment; tăkšăṇ = in that moment; pāṭleānăts; phuḍeñ, *e.g.* 'āileā phuḍeñ = as soon as he came'; *or* 'farāk', *joined to the participle, e.g.* uṭleā farāk.

After all, 1. tări = nevertheless. 2. sekiñ = finally. 3. ăseñ = thus, *or* ăseñ zāleār = things being so. 4. săkăṭ čintun = all considered.

Again, *ad.* 1. āni yek pāuṭi = *l.* once more. 2. portun *or* porteān. 3. punotin. 4. ag. and ag. = portun portun.

Against, 1. *2nd Loc.* in 'čer' *e.g.* šāstrăčer = ag. religion. 2. *2nd Loc. and* āḍ, *e. g.* 'to šāstrăčer āḍ uleitā = he speaks ag. religion'. 3. āḍ (*Dat.*), šāstrāk āḍ = ag. religion. 4. porto (*or* portun), *Dat.*

Age, *s.* 1. prāi (*or* pirāi), -ye, *f. Lat. aetas, e.g.* 'tuji prāi kiteñ? = what is your age?' 2. kāl, -lā, *m.* (epoch), *e.g.* 'teā kālār găḍlāñ = it took place at that time'; 'advanced age = săbār pirāi', *or* 'utăr pirāi = declining age'.

Aged, *a.* 1. mātāro. 2. prāyetso.

Agency, *s.* dălālpoṇ, -ṇā, *n.*; dălālkāri, -re, *f.*

Agent, *s.* dălāl, -lā, *m. G.* muttālgi, -giā, *m.* (commercial); 'suāter tsăltolo = acting in the place of. . .'

Aggravate, *v.* 1. bhār kăr *or* bhār -di = *l.* give weight; zăḍ kăr = make heavy. 2. *fg.* tsăḍăi = *l.* increase; *see* **Oppress.**

Aggravation, *s.* zăḍāi, -ye, *f.*; bhār, -rā, *m.* = *l.* weight.

Aggregate, *v.* 1. meḷăi, *c. v. of* meḷta = if together. 2. yekṭai kăr = make union; rās kăr = accumulate.

Aggregation, *s.* 1. meḷ, -ḷā, *m.*, *e.g.* agg. of Christians. 2. mėḷouṇeñ = the act of aggregating. 3. rig, -ge, *f.* = admission; *see* [**Acceptance.**

Aggression, *s.* zulum, -lme, *f.* = violence; bōḷ, -ḷā, *n.* = violence; āngārpoḍāp, -ḍpā, *n.*

Aggressive, *a.* 1. zulmetso *or* zulum kărtso = *l.* making violence; āngār poḍtso = *l.* falling to life.
2. *fg.* mosātso *or* risketso = dangerous.

Aggressor, *s.* āngār poḍtolo = *l.* falling on body; zulmegār, -rā, *m.*

Agile, *a.* sudāḷ; suḍsuḍāyetso; tsurk = *l.* active.

Agility, *s.* sudaḷāi, -ye, *f.*; suḍsuḍāi, -ye, *f.*; tsurkāi, -ye, *f.*

Agitate, *v.* 1. hālăi = *l.* cause to move (*pr.*), *c. v. of* hāl; phāphud.
2. kuṭ kăr = *l.* make plots (*fg.*); tănḍ kăr (*fg.*) = make parties.

Agitation, *s.* 1. tsāḷāp, -pā, *n.*; hālāp, -lpā, *n.*
2. *fg.* kuṭ, -ṭā, *n.* = plot.

Agnate, *s.* (bāpā isileān) săiro, -reā, *m.*

Ago, *ad.* adiñ = *l.* before, *e.g.* some years ag. = thoḍeañ vărsañ adiñ.

Agony, *s.* mornăčeñ thănḍ, -ḍā, *n.* = *l.* cold of death; āṭeviṭe, *plur. m.*, *and* voḷvoḷe, *m. both mn.* pains of a mortal sickness; mornăčeo voḍi, *pl. f.* = *l.* convulsions of death; gărgăr, *pl. m.*, *or* găr, -ri, *f.*

Agree, *v.* 1. vop = *l.* consent, *Dat.*; kăbul kăr = *l.* make consent, *Dat.*, *or* kobul zā = *l.* get consenting; kărār kăr = *l.* make an agreement (*It. andar d'accordo, accordarsi*).
2. zātā = *l.* becomes, *e.g.* yeñ mākā zāināñ = it does not suit me, agree with me.
3. săma zāun āsā = *l.* is equal, *i.e.* is in conformity.

Agreeable, *a.* 1. khušālāyetso; săntós āsullo *or* săntósātso = *l.* having joy; boro = *l.* good.
2. lāyek = *l.* suitable.
3. *rs.* zātā = it suits.

Agreement, *s.* 1. kărār, -rā, *m.* (contract); guttigeñ, -geā, *n.*; gutto, -teā, *m.*
2. sămādhān, -nā, *n.* = *l.* concord, *fg.*; yekoṭ, -ṭā, *m.* = *l.* union.

Agriculture, *s.* buiñsāgoḷi, -ḷe, *f.*

Ague (fever), *a.* šeḷitso (tāp) = *l.* of cold (fever).

Ah *int.* ye! *or* o! *or* ah!
2. abbā (for admiration).

Aid, *s.* ādhār, -rā, *m.*; kumok, -mke, *f.*; măzăt, -ti, *f.* = intercession; săhāi, -ye, *f.* = *l.* assistance.

Ail, *v.* duk = *l.* feel pain; sos = *l.* suffer.

Ailing, *a.* piḍest = sick; bolāikinātullo = not healthy.

Ailment, *s.* = piḍā, -ḍe *f.*; asoukāsāi, -ye, *f.*

Aim, *s.* sevoṭ, -ṭā, *m.* = *Lat. 'finis'*; zăbāb, -bi, *f.* = *l.* motive.

Aim, *v.* 1. zok (*Acc.*); ponteri kăr (*Acc.*); nōṭ kăr; nōṭ dăr; *e. g.* aim with the gun.
2. sevoṭ āsā = *l.* is aim, *e. g.* tuzo sevoṭ kiteñ? = at what do you aim? disṭ dóvór = *l.* keep the sight; prăyătăn kăr = make effort, *with another verb, according to the meaning, e. g.* he aims at heaven = to sărgār votsunk prăyătăn kărtā; dhăn mòn dovor.

Air, *s.* vāreñ, -reā, *n.*; hăvo, -veā, *m.* (climate).

Air, *v.* vāreñ ghāl = *l.* put air.

Airy, *a.* vāreātso.

Aisle, *s.* bólkāuñ, -āvā, *m. fr.*; *see* **Wing.**

Akin, *a.* săiro (*mn.* related): 'he is akin to me = to mākā (săiro) lektā.

Alacrity, *s.* tsurkāi, -ye, *f.*; suḍ-suḍāi, -ye, *f.*; ušārāi,- ye, *f.*

Alarm, *s.* ăvăntăr, -rā, *n.*; bheñ, bhiyā, *n.* = trepidation; ā-kānt, -tā, *m.*, *e. g.* ākāntiči-ghānṭ mārleā = the alarm bell was rung.

Alarm, *v.* ăvăntăr kăr.

Alarum, zāgounčeñ āid, -dā, *n.* = *l.* instrument for awakening; zāgounčeñ ghăḍiyāḷ = *l.* awakening clock.

Alas, *int.* ye!

Alcohol, *s.* mădyāsār, -rā, *m. n. c. from Cn.*

Ale, *s.* bir, -ri, *f.*

Alehouse, *s.* gudki, -ke, *f.* (*mn.* any house in which liquor is sold); găḍăng, -gā, *n.*

Alert, *a.* zāgrut.

Algebra, *s.* ăkšerāgăṇit, -tā, *n.*

Alienate, *v.* părādin kăr, *or* părasuādin kăr, *e. g.* al. a house.
2. *fg.* mòn pois kăr = *l.* make far the heart.

Alienation, *s. rs. v.*; 1. părādin, -nā, *n.*, *n. u.*
2. *fg.* nāñkhuši, -še, *f.* = *l.* no will.

Alight, *v.* deuñ = *l.* descend.

Alike, *a.* săma.

Aliment, *s.* khāṇ, -ṇā, *n.*; grās, -sā, *m.*; ahār (*var.* hār), -rā, *m.*

Alimentary, *a.* khāuntso = *l.* eatable; postso = nourishing.

Alive, *a.* 1. jivo, *pr.*
2. ušār, *fg.*

All, *a.* 1. săkăḍ (= each, whole, all).
2. sămest = all, (*Lat. universi*).
3. yekyek = each, (*var.* yeyek).
4. sărvu = *Lat.* '*universi*', (*com. in pl. but sometimes also in sing.*)
5. săgḷo = whole, *Lat.* '*integer*', *but in pl. mn. also Lat.* '*omnes*'.

All (At), purteñ = *l.* fully, *or* păripurṇ; bilkul, *Lat. prorsus;*

usually expressed by the emph. -ts (Gram. p. 81), *e.g.* I have nothing at all = moje kăḍe kāints nāñ.

Allay, *v.* 1. thănḍ kăr = *l.* make cold, *fg.*; nivăi = *l.* make cold, *fg.*
2. uṇo kăr = *l.* make less, diminish.
3. hăḷu (*or* hāḷu) kăr = *l.* make light, *e.g.* pain.
4. sămādhān kăr, *or* soukāsāi kăr = make peace; nidān kăr = make quiet.

Allegation, *s.* 1. dāklo, -leā, *m.* *e.g.* al. of a text.
2. nib, -bā, *n.* = *l.* excuse.

Allege, *v.* 1. khănḍit sāng = *l.* affirm, tell as certain.
2. dāklo di, *G. M.* = *l.* give an example.
3. nib sāng = *l.* say excuse.

Allegory, *s.* vopār, -re, *f.*; guṭ, -ṭā, *m.* = *l.* a secret, *fg.*

Alleviate, *v.* 1. hăḷu kăr = *l.* make light.
2. *fg.* bhuzăi = *l.* console.

Alleviation, *s.* 1. hăḷuāi, -ye, *f.*
2. *fg.* bhuzoṇ, -ṇe, *f.* = *l.* consolation.

Alliance, *s.* 1. sollo, -leā, *m.*; iṣ̌ṭăgăt, -ti, *f.* = *l.* friendship.
2. *fg.* yekoṭ, -ṭā, *m.* = union.
3. sămănd, -dā, *m.* = *l.* connexion.

Alligator, *s.* (Amerikāči) sisăr, -sri, *f.*

Allot, *v.* vānṭ = make parts and give; di = *l.* give; vopsun di = *l.* assign.

Allotment, *s.* vāṇṭo, -ṭeā, *m.*

Allow, *v.* soḍ = *l.* leave, permit; răja di = *l.* give leave; vop = acknowledge; di = *l.* give.

Allowance, *s.* 1. bāteñ, -teā, *n.* (al. including food and clothes); póḍ, -ḍi, *f.* (al. including only food).
2. răja, -je, *f.* = *l.* permission; kobul, -li, *f.* = consent.

Allowed (It is), *v. by the poten. mood of the verb, e.g.* kăriet = it is allowed to do it; kāideātso *or* nāyātso = lawful.

Alloy, *v.* borsi = *l.* mix.

Alloy, *s.* borsilleñ loha, -hā, *n.*

Allude, *v.* săr kărn dākăi *or* săr kăr, *Dat.* = *l.* comparing show, *or* comparison make.

Allure, *v.* voḍni di = *l.* give allurement; tāḷnio ghāl = put temptations; nāḍi kăr; fuslāi; piso kăr = make mad, *fg.*

Allurement, *s.* voḍni, -ḍne, *f.*; fuslāuṇeñ, -ṇeā, *n.*; umaḷāi, -ye, *f.*

Allusion, *s.* săr, -ri, *f.*

Ally, *s.* iṣ̌ṭ, -ṭā, *m.* = *l.* friend; solleāgār, -rā, *m.*

Almanac, *s.* pănčăng, -gā, *n.*

Almighty, *a.* sărvụpodvedār; sărvesvăr; sărvụhukumdār = all-commanding.

Almond, *s.* bădām, -dmā, *n.*

Almost, *ad.* tsăḍ-uṇeñ = *l.* more (or) less; sumār = nearly, about; lāgiñ lāgiñ = *l.* near near; *it corresponds to the Latin 'paene'*, *e.g.* almost 30, *i.e.* something less than 30; *whereas the preceding ones correspond to the Lat. 'fere'*; băhuša (*the same as* lāgiñ lāgiñ).

Alms, *s.* izmăl, -lā, *n. fr.*; bhik (*fully:* bikṣa); dhărm, -mā, *m.* = *l.* charity (work of charity).

Aloe, *s.* kānṭekuvór, -ri, *f.*; loḷisăr, -rā, *n.* (*H. K.*)

Aloft, *ad.* unts (*ad.*), untsāi, -ye, *f.* (*subst.*), *e.g.* yek fātor unts uḍăi = throw a stone al.; divo untsāyer umkăḷtā = a lamp is suspended in the space aloft.

Alone, *a.* 1. yekăts (*emph.* Gram. p. 81).

2. āpleā-itleāk = by itself, alone (*see* Gram. p. 134); yeksuro = solitary.

3. *rs.* mātrụ *or* făkăt = *l.* only.

Along, *ad. prep.* kăḍe *or* lāgiñ, *or* sărsiñ.

Aloof, *ad.* pois.

Aloud, *ad.* 1. voḍleān = *l.* with great (voice), *e.g.* voḍleān ulăi = speak aloud.

2. sóṣṭ = *l.* distinctly.

3. hāk, *used only with vbs. signifying* make a noise, by crying out, striking a thing violently, *etc.*, *e.g.* yemkoṇḍānt ătme hāk āni bob mārtāt.

Alphabet, *s.* ăkṣărāñmālā, -le, *f.* (*Cn. Mr.*) = *l.* series of letters.

Already, *ad.* poilots, *emph. of* poilo = first: *hence it is declined, e.g.* to poilots gelo = he has gone already'; 'ti poilits geli = she has gone already'; *sometimes* -i, *but this ex. mn.* also, even; *it is often omitted.*

Also, *ad.* 1. -i *joined to the modified word*, *e.g.* āmkāñ-i = to us too. (Gram. P. III. ch. ix.)

2. legun (*put after the modified word*): 'āmkāñ legun = also to us'.

3. săit (*put after the modified word*): 'āmkāñ săit = also to us'.

Altar, *s.* āltār, -ri, *f.* (*var.* -rā, *m.*); piṭh, -ṭhā, *n.* (*H. K.*)

Alter, *v.* 1. bădăl (*obj. with* thăiñ), *tr.* = change, *also* falsify money (nāṇeñ) *or* alter the face (sārkeñ bădăl).

2. bădăl zātā, *n.v.* = *l.* it changes; *or* bădăl; *see* Gram. p. 279.

Alteration, *s.* bădlāp, -pā, *n.* = *l.* change; *rs. v.*

Altercate, *v.* zăgăḍ (*var.* zăgḍa); *see* **Quarrel**; ārenji.

Altercation, *s.* zăgḍeñ, -ḍeā, *n.*

Alternate, *a.* ădălbădăl; parăspăra, *n. c.*; sărten.

Alternate, *v.* ădălbădăl.

Alternately, *ad.* ădălbădăl zāun.

Alternative, *s.* vintsāp, -tspā, *n.* 'there is no alt. = dusro upāi nāñ'.

Although, *conj.* zărităr, *compound of* zărtăr = if, *and* i = also: *hence it may be resolved* (*see* Gram. Part II. Conjunct.); -i *joined to the Conditional, e.g.* tuveñ yeñ keleāri = alth. you did it; *but this form may be used only when the vb. has a conditional meaning.*

Altitude, *s.* ubārăi, -ye, *f.*

Altogether, *ad.* 1. voṭṭu, *e.g.* the expenses alt. amount to.
2. purteñ = *l.* fully; păripūrṇ; kēvăl; ăgdi; bilkul.

Alum, *s.* phăṭki, -ke, *f.*

Always, *ad.* 1. sădāñ, *or emph.* sădānts.
2. sădănkāl = *l.* (at) time of always.

Amalgamate, *v.* meḷăi; borsi = mix.

Amanuensis, *s.* gumost, -stā, *m.*; borăitolo = *l.* he who writes, *or* bărpi, -piā, *m.*; năkălvis, -sā, *m.* = copyist.

Amass, *v.* 1. zomăi *or* zomo kăr, *G. M., from* 'zomo = multitude', *used both of people and things.*
2. rās kăr = *l.* make a heap, *e.g.* duḍu rās kăr = am. money; punzăi, *c. v.* (am. money).

Amazed (Be), ăjāp zā *or* ăjāp pāu = *l.* admire; zim *or* jim zātā.

Amazement, *s.* jim, -mā, *n.*

Ambassador, 1. rāibāri, -riā, *m.* rāyădut, -tā, *m.*
2. muṇiyāri, -riā, *m., e.g.* am. of J. C.

Amber, *s.* trănagrāhi, -he, *f. Cn.*; *vlg.* ambar (*also H. K.*).

Ambiguity, *s.* dubāubăruānso, -seā, *m. or* dubāubăruānseā-čiñ utrañ; gūḍārth, -thā, *m.*: 'to guḍārthān ulăitā = he speaks ambiguously.

Ambiguous, *a.* dubāubăruānseā-tso; guḍārthātso.

Ambition, *s.* ăhānkār, -rā, *m.*; mānăša, -še, *f.*

Ambitious, *a.* ăhănkāri *or* ăhăn-kārātso; mān āšetolo.

Ambulance, *s.* phirti-āspătri, -ri, *f.* = *l.* moveable hospital, *n. c.*

Ambush, *s.* 1. nāḍ, -ḍi, *f.* = trick.
2. lipči suăt, -te, *f.*

Ameliorate, *v.* boro kăr = *l.* make good, *e.g.* a garden; kurt kăr; sārko kăr = *l.* make exact.

Amelioration, *s.* kurt, -tā, *m.*; guṇ, -ṇā, *m.*: *the 1st is used esp. of material* am., *the 2nd esp. of mental improvement.*

Amend, *v.* săma *or* sārko kăr, *e.g.* errors; boro kăr = *l.* make good; bădăl = *l.* change, *e.g.* a life.

Amends (Make), fārikpoṇ di = *l.* give satisfaction.

Amenity, *s.* khušālăi, -ye, *f.*; rāmayata, -te, *f., n. c.*; săntos,

-sā, *m.*=*l.* joy; sukh, -khā, *n.*=happiness.

Amiable, *a.* mogātso *or* mogāḷ; ăpurbāyetso; prititso *or* pritimogātso.

Amidst, *see* **Among.**

Amiss (Take), vāiṭāk vor=*l.* take to evil; păščātāp kāṇghe=*l.* take sorrow.

Amnesty, *s.* sărvụmāf, -fe, *f.* (*or* -māfi, -fe, *f.*); bogsāṇeñ, -ṇeā, *n.* = *l.* forgiveness; māp, -pi, *f.* (*or* māf) = *l.* excuse, pardon (granted).

Among, *prep.* 1. păiki, *or.*; modeñ=*l.* in the middle; *yet used also for* am.; bităr=*in Latin* '*in*' *or* '*inter*'; *by* 1*st Locative.*

Amount, *s.* 1. răkkăm, -kmā, *n.*; ăivoz, -zā, *m.*, *e.g.* am. of money; lek, -kā, *n.*=*l.* account.

Amount, *v.* lēk zātā, *e.g.* yek hăzār rupoi lēk zātā tākā = *l.* it amounts to 1000 Rs. to him.

Ample, *a.* vistārlolo=*l.* extended; rund=*l.* broad.

Amplify, *v.* vistār, *tr. n. v.*; rundăi, *e.g.* a road.

Amputate, *v.* kātăr.

Amulet, *s.* măntrăčeñ āid, -dā, *n.* = *l.* article of charm.

Amuse, *v.* khušāl kăr, *tr.* = *l.* make joyful.
2. khušāl zā, *n.* = *l.* get joyful.
3. khiāḷ (*or* khéḷ)=play.

Amusement, *s.* 1. săntós, -sā, *m. or* khušālāi, -ye, *f.*=joy.
2. kheḷ, -ḷā, *m.*=*l.* play.

Analogy, *s.* sārkeñ, -keā, *n.*=*l.* similitude; vopār, -re, *f.*

Analysis, *s.* 1. vingăḍāi, -ye, *f.*=*l.* resolution, separation.
2. părikṣa, -kṣe, *f.* = *l.* examination.
3. vingăḍ kārči čintna, -tne, *f.*=*l.* thought separating; *rs. into v.* vingăḍ kăr *or* bhed kăr.

Ananas, *s.* ānās, -nsā, *n.* (*perh. corrup. of* 'ananas', *Mr.*)

Anarchy, 1. rāinātulleñ rāz, -jā, *n.*=*l.* kingdom without king; anădikār, -rā, *n.*; *or rs.*
2. *fg.* gusăp, -pā, *m.*=confusion.

Anathema, *s.* sărgiširāp, -pā, *m.*; igărješirāp, -pā, *m.*

Anatomy, *s.* āngāsodnā, -ne, *f.*=*l.* inquiry into body.

Ancestor, *s.* mālgoḍo, -ḍeā, *m.*; pitra, -rā, *m.*; purvoz, -zā, *m.*

Anchor, *s.* nāngor, -rā, *m.*: 'nāñgorār=at an.'

Anchor, *v.* nāngor ghāl = cast an.; nāngorār āsā=is at an.

Anchorite, *s.* sănyāsi, -siā, *m.*; vănavāsi, -si, *m.*=Christian anc., *n. u.*

Ancient, *a.* 1. porno, *used of things;* purvillo.
2. ādiñ āsụllo *or* ādlo=anterior. In anc. times = ādiñ purviñ.

And, *conj.* āni (*vlg.* ānik): *often omitted* (*see* Gram. P. II. ch. xii.)

Anecdote, *s.* kătā, -te, *f. or* lān k. = little story; kāṇi, -ye, *f.*; kuḷakăta, *n. c.*

Anew, *ad.* portun *or* porteān; āniyek pāuṭi = once more.

Angel, *s.* boḍvo, -veā, *m.*; ānj, -jā, *m. fr.*
 Guardian A.=rākoṇbóḍvò, *from* rāk = keep, guard.

Angelus (Domini), *s.* = amori, -re, *f. corrup. of Ave Maria;* tinsān, -ni, *f.* (evening ang. when it begins to get dark); 'am. mār = *l.* beat ang. (ring a.)'

Anger, *s.* rāg, -gā, *m.*; kród, -dā, *m.*; kōp, -pā, *m.*

Angle, *s.* 1. gări, -ye, *f.* = fishing tackle; sintāri, -re, *f.* (for fishing).
 2. konso, -seā, *m. pr. and fg.* (= corner).

Angle, *v.* māsḷio dhăr = *l.* catch fishes; pāg.

Angry, *a.* rāgiṣṭ.

Angry (Get), *Dat.* rāg ye = *l.* anger come; rāgār zā = *l.* get in anger; rāgān rāu = *l.* remain in ang.; kōp kăr: 'dusreānk rāg āḍăitāñ = I cause to get angry'; 'dusreāntso rāg āilā = I got ang. with others'.

Anguish, *s.* kăḷvăḷo, -ḷeā, *m., e. g.* of a mother for a sick child; săntāp, -pā, *m.*

Anil, *s.* niuḷičeñ zāḍ, -ḍā, *n.*

Animadversion, *etc. see* **Reproof, Censure, Consideration.**

Animal, *s.* 1. jiuzāt, -ti, *f. or* jivāḷ, -ḷe, *f.* (any living creature), *exact, but n. c. words, from* 'jiv = life'; prāṇi, -ṇi, *f., n. c.*
 2. monzāt, -ti, *f.* = beast *or* irrational animal.

Animate, *v.* 1. *pr.* jīv di = *l.* give life; *or* vāntsăi.
 2. dăirāvont kăr = *l.* make courageous; dhăir di = *l.* give courage.

Animated, *a.* 1. jivo = *l.* living, *pr.*; prāṇ asullo.
 2. *fg.* ušăr = lively.
 3. dhăirādik = courageous.

Ankle, *s.* khubo, -beā, *m.*

Anna, (a coin) *s.* āṇo, -ṇeā, *m.* '¼ a. = pāvāṇo, -ṇeā, *m., or* săkās = 6 kās, *m., or* deḍki, -ke, *f.*'; '⅓ a = poiso, -seā, *m.*'; '1/12 a. (pie) = ruvi, -ye, *f.*'; '½ pie = res *or* kās, -sā, *m.*'; 'tāru, -re, *f.* = 2 pies'; 'tsăkru = 4 annas'.

Annals, *s.* vărsānčeo kobro = *l.* news of years, *n. c.*; *h. w.*

Anneal, *v.* hăda kăr, kāmăi.

Annex, *v.* meḷăi, *c. v. of* meḷ, *n. v.* = be united'; găḍsi.

Annihilate, *v.* 1. nānts kăr = *l.* make not at all (*Konk.*); (purteñ) nāš kăr = *l.* destroy, ruin (completely); nirastăi = *l.* cause not to be, *n. c.*; antarăi = cause to finish, *n. c.*

Anniversary, *a.* vorsātso.

Anniversary, *s.* vorsātso dis = *l.* day of the year (of death).

Annotate, *v.* tsătrāio kăr = *l.* make notes; šero kăr (šăro?).

Annotation, *s.* tsătrāi, -ye, *f.*; šero, -reā, *m.*

Announce, *v.* khăbār āḍ = *l.* bring news, *or* k. di; părgăṭ kăr *or* părgăṭăi = *l.* make public *or* known; kăḷit kăr *or* kăḷăi = make known; zāṇăi, (*c.v. of* zāṇā) = cause to know, *n. c.*

Annoy, *v.* kărkăr kăr, *tr.*; k. zātā (mākā) = I get annoyed; dós, *tr.*; bezār kăr; tondre kăr.

Annoyance, *s.* kărkăr, -rā, *m.* (*used commonly in pl.*)

Annoying, *a.* kărkărātso, *or* bezārāyetso, *or* bezār kărtso.

Annual, *a.* *see* **Anniversary.**

Annul, *v.* răddu păḍsi, *c. v.*; r. kăr, *e. g.* ann. a sentence; *see* **Annihilate.**

Anoint, *v.* kuḍir tēl lāi = *l.* apply oil on the body; mākh, *n. c.*

Anointment, *s.* mākhāp, -pā, *n.*

Anomalous, *etc.* *see* **Irregular,** *etc.*

Anon, *ad.* 1. ātānts.
2. thoḍe pāuṭi = sometimes.

Anonymous, 1. nāuñnātullo.
2. tăḷḷi, *e.g.* ano. letter; *ex. it mn.* deceitful (*Cn.* tāḷāṭōḷi = deceit).

Another, *a.* 1. āniyek = *l.* one more (and one); āniyeklo, *pron.*
2. dusro.

Another (One), yekāmekā; *see* Gram. P. II. ch. iv., *Recipr. Verbs.*

Answer, *s.* zăvāb *or* zăbāb (*vlg.* zāb), -bi, *f.*

Answer, *v.* zăvāb *or* zăbāb di = *l.* give ans., *e. g.* reply to a letter; 'I get an ans. = mākā z. meḷtā'.

Ant, *s.* mui, -ye, *f.*; 'white a. = vāḷăi, -ḷie, *f. sing. and pl.*

Ant (Black), kānṭmui; ant of sugarcane = domḷo, -ḷeā, *m.*

Ant (Red), umḷo, -ḷeā, *m.*

Ant (Very small), *s.* urnā, -rne, *f.*

Antagonism, *s.* virodhāi, -ye, *f.*

Anterior, *a.* 1. ādlo, *from* 'ādiñ = before' (in point of time).
2. mukāvelo, *from* 'mukār = in front' (*esp.* in point of place).

Anthem, *s.* āntifon, -nā, *n.*; kirta, -rte, *f.*, *n. c.*

Anticipate, *v. pr.* ādiñ kāṇe, *or* ā. kāḍ, *or* ā. poḷe *or* ā. somzā; *but as this verb is vague and may have many meanings, according to the context, that verb must be chosen, which best suits the case, e.g. in* 'he was anticipated by death while brooding over his plans'; 'kāḍlā *or* dhārlā = he has been caught' *might be used for* 'he was anticipated'.

Antidote, *s.* 1. vokāt, -ktā, *n.* = *l.* medicine, *fg.*
2. upāi, -yā, *m.* = counteraction, preventive.

Antipathy, *s.* nāñkhuši, -še, *f.*; *rs.*, *e. g.* mojeñ mon tāče thăiñ boreñ năiñ = my heart is not good towards him; dusmānkāi, -ye, *f.* = enmity; hăgeñ, -geā, *n.* = hatred.

Antiquity, *s.* 1. ādlo (*or* porno) kāl, -lā, *m.* = *l.* old age.
2. ādiñ āsụlle mănis *or* ādle mănis = *l.* men who have been before.

Anvil, *s.* boḍountso (*or* dāḍāuntso *or* bettso) fātor, -trā, *m.* = *l.* beating-stone; ăḍigal, -lā, *m.*, *n. c*, *Cn.*

Anxiety, *s.* husko, -keā, *m.* (sigh); čintnā, -ne, *f.* = *l.* thought, *fg.*; bezārāi, -ye, *f.* = *l.* tiredness, *fg.*; ākānt, -tā, *m.* = *l.* distress.

Anxious, *a.* 1. čintest.
2. bezāri *or* bezār.

Any, *a.* kăsolo-i (*see* Gram. p. 75), *e.g.* I am satisfied with any kind of. . . .; *it corresponds to the Italian 'qualsiasi' both in interrogative and non-interrogative sentences.*

Anywhere, *ad.* sărvụ thăiñ; săgḷeān (*Instr. of* săgḷo).

Apart, *ad.* vingăḍ: 'take a. = v. dóvór'.

Apartment, *s.* 1. māḷăi, -ḷiye, *f.*
2. kuḍ, -ḍā, *n.* = *l.* room.

Apathy, *s.* bepārvāi, -ye, *f.* = *l.* carelessness.

Ape, *s.* vāndor, -drā, *m.*

Aperture, *s.* 1. fuṭ, -ṭi, *f.* = chink.
2. iḍeñ, -ḍeā, *n.* = opening.

Aphorism, *s.* gād, -di, *f.*; văčan, -nā, *n.*

Apocryphal, *a.* foṭkireñ nāuñ āsullo, *or sometimes only* foṭkiro.

Apologetic, *a.* 1. sāmbāḷtolo *or* sāmbāḷtso = *l.* defending.
2. udārăṇ sāngtso = giving explanation.

Apologize, *v.* māp māg = *l.* ask pardon (*or* māf māg); udārăṇ kăr (*or* u. sāng) = exculpate oneself *or* give explanation of what has been done; fārikpoṇ di = *l.* give satisfaction.

Apology, *s.* udārăṇ, -ṇā, *n.*

Apoplexy, *s.* răgtāči piḍā, -ḍe, *f.* = *l.* sickness of blood.

Apostasy, *s.* bāvāḍtāsoḍni, -ne, *f.*

Apostate, *s.* bāvāḍt soḍụllo (*or another word instead of* 'bāvāḍt', *according to the kind of apostasy meant*).

Apostatize, *v.* (bāvāḍt) soḍ = *l.* leave (faith); *see* **Apostate.**

Apostle, *s.* ăpostlụ, -lā, *m.*; J. Kristā muṇiyāri, -riā, *m.* = *l.* ambassador, minister of J. Christ.

Apothecary, *s.* voktāñ iktolo = *l.* he who sells medicines; voiz, -zā, *m.* = native physician; *vlg.* potkeri, -ri, *m. fr.*; găndsărkāgār, -rā, *m.* (= native apothecary).

Apparatus, *s.* sāmān, -nāñ, *pl. m.*

Apparel, *s.* mustāigi, -ge, *f. see* **Dress**; sāmagri, -re, *f.*; sărănjām, -mā, *n.*; surungār, -rā, *m.* = *l.* decoration.

Apparent, *a.* 1. distso.
2. sošṭ = *l.* distinct, clear.
3. foṭkiro = deceiving, *e. g.* ap. happiness (*opposite to* real); sāuḷetso = of shadow.

Apparently, *ad.*, *rs. into a.*; *rs.* distā mātrụ = *l.* only it appears; *by* -so (*see* Gram. p. 160).

Apparition, *s.* dišṭ, -ṭi, *f. joined to the verb;* dišṭipoḍāp, -pā (*or* -ḍpā), *n.* (*used absolutely*).

Appeal, *v.* 1. metsăi.
2. māg = *l.* request, *Cm.*
3. sākši moṇ āpoi; vitsār = ask.

Appeal, *s.* metsouṇeñ, -ṇeā, *n.*

Appear, *v.* 1. dis; dišṭi póḍ = *l.* fall in sight, *used of visions*, *e.g.* Somi J. C. Pedruk dišṭi póḍlā.
2. hāzăr āsā = (*Lat. adest*), *l.* is present; *or only* āsā.

Appearance, *s.* 1. disāp, -spā, *n.*
2. sārkeñ, -keā, *n.* = similitude, *e.g.* ap. of bread; rup, -pā, *n.* = figure, *e.g.* what is the ap. of that man?
3. *as opposed to reality*, *rs. into verb*, distā mātrụ; *or* sāuḷi, -ḷe, *f.* = *l.* shadow, *fg.*

Appease, *v. see* **Allay**; *moreover*
1. movāḷāi = *l.* make tender; fārikpoṇ di = *l.* give satisfaction.
2. fuslāi (pacify quarreling persons, a crying child *etc.*; *l.* caress).

Append, *see* **Add, Annex.**

Appendix, *s.* tsăḍāp, -ḍpā, *n.* = *l.* addition; *or* tsăḍāu, -vā, *n.*

Appertain, *v.* 1. fāvo zā, *e.g.* the book appertains to me.
2. lāg = *l.* be attached, *fg.*, *e.g.* things appertaining to this life.

Appetite, *s.* 1. ruts, -či, *f.* (of food); bhuk, -ke, *f.* = *l.* hunger.
2. *fg.* khuši, -še, *f.* (any desire); āšā, -še, *f.*

Applaud, *v.* hógóḷsi (*or* uboḷsi).

Applause, *s.* hogḷāp, -pā, *n.*

Apple, *s.* bòr, -rā, *n.* (*of this country*).
Ap. of the eye = bāuli, -le (*var.* māuli, -le), *f.*

Applicant, *s.* ărjegār, -rā, *m.*

Application, 1. *s.* lāgāp, -gpā, *n.*
2. māg-ṇeñ, -ṇeā, *n. or bet.* ărji, -je, *f.* = *l.* petition; sādān, -nā, *n.* = (act of applying), *l.* effort.

Apply, *v.* 1. māg = *l.* ask praying (*Acc. of thing and Cm. of person*); *e.g.* sărkārā lāgiñ yek kām māg = apply for an office to the magistrate; ărji kăr.
2. lāg, *e. g.* oneself to study; *or also* be applied, *e. g.* words of the Bible.
3. lāi *or* lāgăi, *e.g.* ap. a boy to study.
4. ghāl = *l.* put, employ, *tr.*

5. zā = *l.* suit.
6. săr kărn dākoun di = *l.* make allusion, showing give, *e.g.* these words are to be applied to us; *or bet.* 'lāi = apply' in this *mn.*, *e.g.* yeñ săt āmkāñ lāun poḷeyā = see this truth applied to us.

Appoint, *v.* nemsi, *e.g.* to an office; nomiyār = *l.* nominate; kărn dóvór, *e.g.* J. C. appointed St. Peter.

Appointment, *s.* mokruri, -re, *f.* *e.g.* mākā yek mokruri zāli = I got an ap.; nemăk, -kā, *n.*

Apposite, *a.* lāyek.

Appreciate, *v.* mānd, boreñ čint = *l.* think well, *e.g.* of a man; ăpurbāi kăr (of things); khuši pāu *or* săntos pāu (*Nom. of pers.*, 1*st Loc. of thing*); mòl voḷka = acknowledge the price, *e.g.* of the grace.

Apprehend, *v.* 1. dhăr = catch; sāmpaḍāi.
2. somzā = *l.* understand; voḷka = know; kăḷ = grasp.
3. bhiye = fear.

Apprehension, *s.* 1. bhirānt, -ti, *f. or* bheñ, bhiyā, *n.* = *l.* fear.
2. čintnā, -tne, *f.* = *l.* thought, idea; *see* **Idea** (*in* 1*st mn.*)

Apprehensive, *a.* bizuḍ (= timid).

Apprentice, *s.* umedvār, -rā, *m.*

Approach, *v.* lāgiñ pāu = *l.* arrive close.

Approbation, *s.* mănjur, -re, *f.*; păsănd, *not used as noun*; metsoṇi, -ṇe, *f.*

Appropriate, *v.* 1. dovor (*Dat. or with* 'passun') = *l.* keep for.
2. āpṇāk kāṇe = *l.* take for oneself.

Appropriate, *a.* 1. fāvo zātolo *or* fāvo = *l.* belonging (*bet. rs.*)
2. lāyek = *l.* fit, suitable; *rs. into* 'zātā = is ap'.
3. *by the G.* (peculiar).

Approval, *see* **Approbation.**

Approve, *v.* 1. păsănd kăr = *l.* make approval, *Acc.*
2. metsva (*or* metsvo), *with N. of pers. Acc. of thing; or N. of thing, Dat. of pers., e. g.* āuñ yeñ metsvotāñ = I like it.
3. metsoṇi kăr = *l.* make approval.

Approximate, *a.* lāgsilo, *or* lāgiñ āsullo, *or rs. ad.* lāgiñ.

Approximate, *v.* lāgiñ pāu = *l.* reach close.

Approximation, *s.* lāgiñpāvāp, -pāupā, *n.*

Apron, *s.* mukāveleñ lugāṭ, -gṭā, *n.* = *l.* anterior cloth.

Apt, *a.* lāyek.

Aquatic, *a.* udkāntlo.

Aqueduct *s.* udkātso tōḍ, -ḍā, *m.* = *l.* canal of water.

Arbiter, *s.* 1. pănčāyetdār, -rā, *m.*; mădest, -stā, *m.*
2. melpănčāyetdār = head arbiter.

Arbitrary, *a.* khuše pārmāṇe āsullo = *l.* according to the will; sotāntrātso; *bet. rs. into v.*

Arbitrate, *v.* pāñčāyetdār zāun tsāl = *l.* behave as an arbiter; niščeisi = *l.* decide; tīrp kār; mādesti kār.

Arbitration, *s.* 1. kārār, -rā, *m.* = *l.* agreement.
2. pāñčāyetdārāčeñ phāisāl, -lā, *n.* = *l.* sentence of an arbiter; tīrp, -pā, *n.* = *l.* decision.

Arbour, *s.* 1. moḷo, -ḷeā, *m.* = *l.* bower.
2. māṭou, -ṭvā, *m.* = *l.* shed.

Arcade, *s.* varānd, -dā, *m.*

Arch, *s.* 1. ārk, -kā, *n. fr.*; gompru, -rā, *n.*
2. doṇu, -ṇvā, *n.* (*also* geometrical figure): 'doṇu poḍlāñ = rainbow appeared'.

Archangel, *s.* arkanj, -jā, *m.*; šreṣṭboḍvo, -veā, *m.*; melboḍvo.

Archbishop, *s.* arčbisp, -pā, *m.* ('sāib = Lord', *is usually added*) *rl. fr.*

Archeology, *s.* porneañ kālānči vidya, -dye, *f.* = science of former times.

Archetype, *s.* nāmuno, -neā, *m.*

Architect, *s.* bāndpi, -piā, *m.* bāndpāpāṇḍit, -tā, *m. or* bāndpānāmuneagār, -rā, *m.*; šilpišāstri, -ri, *m.*

Architecture, *s.* bāndpāvidya, -ye, *f.*; šilpišāstru, -rā, *n.*

Archive, *s.* dāfterakhāno, -neā, *m.*

Ardent, *a. pr.* 1. lāstolo, *from* lās = burn.
2. umāḷātso = *l.* boiling, *fg. used*; zāḷtso; *see* **Hot.**

Ardour, *s. pr.* 1. gārmi, -me, *f.* (= heat); vōt, -tā, *n. or* vāt (= heat of sun *etc.*), *e.g.* votāk ghāl.
2. *fg.* khuši, -še, *f.* = desire.
3. suḍsuḍāi, -ye, *f.* = fervour.
4. umāḷo, -ḷeā, *m.*

Arduous, *a. pr.* 1. ubār = high, *fg.*
2. kāñṭiṇ = difficult (*var.* kāṭiṇ).

Area, *s.* voileñ āng, -gā, *n.* = *l.* surface; suāt, -te, *f. or* zāgo, -geā, *m.*; melbhāg, -gā, *n. is sometimes used; yet it mn.* surface, *l.* part above; 'āñgāṇ, -gṇā, *n.* = open surface before house'; māidān, -nā, *n.*

Areca-nut, *s.* phopāḷ, -pḷā, *n.*

Areca (tree), *s.* māḍi, -ye, *f.*

Argil, *s.* āvo, -veā, *m.*; čikolmāti, -ye, *f.* = *l.* dirty earth; kumbārāmāti, -ye *f.*

Argue, *v.* tārk kār = *l.* make discussion; dākāi = *l.* show.

Argument, *s.* 1. ruzvāt, -ti, *f.* (proof).
2. dāklo, -leā, *m.* (= proof of documents).
3. vivor, -rā, *m.* (= explanation).
4. tārk, -kā, *n.* (= discussion).
5. *vlg.* ārment, -tā, *n.* (*an old school-term*), *fr.*

Arid, *a.* suko.

Aridity, *s.* sukidād, -ḍi, *f.* (*Lat. siccitas*).

Arise, *v.* 1. tsāḍ *or* unts vetā = *l.* mounts aloft.
2. uṭ = *Lat. surge.*
3. ude, *e.g.* sun arises.
4. zā = become, happen.
5. *fg.* ubzā = *l.* proceed.

Aristocrat, *s.* 1. voḍlo mānis, -šā, *m.* = *l.* great man.
2. prābu, -bu. *m.* (*var.* porob, [-rbu).

Arithmetic, *s.* ānkeānči vidya, -ye, *f.* = *l.* science of numbers; gāṇit, -tā, *n.* (*Cn., Mr., Sans.*); lèk, -kā, *n.*

Ark, *s.* 1. ārk, -kā, *n.*
2. Noha-tāruñ, -rvā, *n.* = *l.* ship of Noah.

Arm, *s.* bhuz, -zā, *n. pr.*; bāuḷo, -ḷeā, *m.* = upper joint; rāṭṭo, -ṭeā, *m.*

Arm, *v.* 1. *tr. v.* hātyārañ di = *l.* give arms.
2. *n. v.* hātyārañ kāṇe = *l.* take arms.

Arm-chair; *s.* hāt āsulli bāska, -ke, *f.* = *l.* chair having hands.

Armorial, *see* **Escutcheon.**

Armpit, *s.* kāk, -ke, *f.*

Armistice, *s.* hātyārañrāvāp, -pā (*or* -rāupā), *n.*; zuzārāvāp, -pā (*or* -rāupā), *n.*

Armoury, *s.* hātyārañgār, -rā, *n.*

Armour, *s.* kuḍičeñ rākṇeñ, -ṇeā, *n.*

Arms, *s.* hātyār, -rā, *n.*

Army, *s.* lāskār, -rā, *n.*; fouz, -ji, *f.*; sāin, -nā, *n.*, *n. c.*; sipāiānči pāṭlām, -mi, *f.* = *l* battalion of soldiers, *vlg.*, *fr*

Aroma, *s.* pārmāḷ, -ḷā, *m.*; pār māḷāči vāstu, -tu, *f.* = *l.* a good-smelling thing.

Aromatic, *a.* pārmāḷātso.

Around, *prep. ad.* bountāṇiñ *or* bountiñ.

Arouse, *v.* utsāmboḷ kār *or* utsāmboḷāi, *c. v.* = cause to get excited; uṭāi, *c. v. of* 'uṭ *e.g.* ar. to virtue.

Arrack, *s.* soro, -reā, *m.* (*divided into* 'rās, -si, *f.*', 'dobrād, -dā', *and* 'tibrād, -dā, *m.*').

Arraign, *see* **Accuse.**

Arrange, *v.* mānḍ = put in order, *e.g.* ar. matters; sāma kār = *l.* make right, *or* sāma ghāl = *l.* put right.

Arrangement, *s.* 1. tāyārāi, -ye, *f.* = *l.* preparation.
2. mānḍāvoḷ, -ḷi, *f.* (good disposition).
3. *often rs.*

Array, *v.* 1. tāyār kār.
2. mānḍ = arrange.

Array, *s.* mānḍāvoḷ, -ḷi, *f.*; krām, [-mā, *n.*

Arrear, *s.* bāki, -ki, *f.*: 'mojer bāki kiteñ? = what are my arrears?'

Arrest, *v.* dhār = *l.* catch; sāmpḍāi *or* sāmpḍāi, *also fg.*; kāidānt ghāl.

Arrest, *s.* kāid, -dā, *n.*

Arrival, *s.* 1. yeṇeñ, -ṇeā, *n.* (= coming).
2. pāvāp, pāupā, *n.*

Arrive, *v.* pāu.

Arrogance, *s.* gărv, -vā, *n.* = *l.* pride; săḷ, -ḷā, *n.*=obstinacy; ăhănkār, -rā, *m.*; hăṭ, -ṭā, *n.*

Arrogant, *a.* gărvi (*var.* gărvišṭ); săḷišṭ; āpleā vādeātso = *l.* of his own will.

Arrow, *s.* bhāli, -ye, *f.*

Arrowroot, *s.* kuveāčeñ piṭ, -ṭā, *n.*

Arsenic, *s.* pāšāṇ, -ṇā, *n.*

Art, *s.* 1. vidya, -ye, *f.* = *l.* science; sikāp, -kpā, *n.*=*l.* learning; sāmārthi, -the, *f.*
2. hikmăt, -ti, *f.*=*l.* industry.

Article, *s.* 1. sărăk, -kā, *n.* (goods).
2. ārtig, -gā, *m.* (*more commonly*, -ge, *f.*), *e.g.* of the creed, *fr.*
3. sāmān, -nā, *m.*=*l.* furniture; *see* **Joint, Item.**

Articulate, *a.* sošṭ=*l.* distinct.

Articulate, *v.* sošṭ utsār=*l.* express with distinction.

Artifice, *s.* 1. čămătkār, -rā, *m.*
2. tăntrụ, -rā, *n.* (=magic ar.)
3. nāḍ, -ḍi, *f.* = *l.* trick.
4. hikmăt, -ti, *f.* = *l.* industry.

Artificial, *a.* hikmătitso, *e.g.* ar. fire.

Artillery, *s.* 1. nāḷi=guns.
2. nāḷisipāi, *pl. m.*

Artisan, *s.* āčāri, -riā, *m.* (*esp.* carpenter).

Artist, *s.* 1. sāmārthigār, -rā, *m.*
2. udyogist, -tā, *m. or* uddeogār, -rā, *m.*

As, *ad., conj.* 1. *a term of comparison,* bări, *e.g.* to Pedru bări kărtā (*Lat. instar*).
2. zăseñ = in that way in which (*e.g. sicut dicit Isaias*); *or* tăseñ = in that way.
3. *causat. particle* (because): *a.* dekun (Gram. P. IV. Ch. ii. Art. vii.) *placed at the end: b.* pāsvot *or* pāsun *with the participle,* (*Lat. propter*); *c.* kiteāk moḷeār.
4. moḷḷeā jinsār = (*Lat. quatenus*), *l.* on the said way, *e.g.* Deu mănšāčeā moḷḷeā jinsār pātkiāk kānṭāḷnāñ = God does not hate the sinner as man, *l.* God does not hate the sinner in the way called man.
5. moṇ, zāun; *in sentences like these:* 'he came as a governor; he is called prophet'.
6. kārn, *e.g.* accept him as a father.

As—as, *correlative ad.* 1. bări (*or* pori), *e.g.* he is as wise as you = to tumče bări budivont.
2. zăso — tăso, *or* kăso — tăso, *e.g.* kăso tuñ budivont, tăso to budivont = as you are wise, so he is wise.
3. kitlo—itlo *or* titlo, *e.g.* kitlo vo budivont, titlo to budivont.

N.B. All these words are declined (*see* Gram. p. 82).

As **if,** bări, *e.g.* he speaks as if he were a fool = piša mănšā bări ulăitā = *Lat. loquitur stulti hominis instar*; *some times this* 'bări' *is preceded by* 'moḷḷea', *while the principal verb is put in the tense required by the meaning; e.g.* live every day as if you were to die on the same = ăseñ jiyezāi teāts disa mortoloi moḷḷea bări; *about this* 'moḷḷea' *see* Gram. p. 313.

As **far as,** 1. titleñ *put after the verb*, *e.g.* mākā kăḷtā titleñ = as far as I know; *see* Gram. pp. 236-237.

2. tăseñ *or* teā jinsiñ = thus *or* in that way.

As far as possible, 1. tānki părmāṇe = according to the power; *or* tānktā titleñ = *l.* is possible as much, 'kitleñ' *being understood*, *thus*: (kitleñ) tānktā titleñ = *Lat. quantum possibile est, tantum*; *see* Gram. *l.c.*

As **much as,** *ad.* kitlo—itlo = *l. Lat. quantus tantus.*

As **soon as,** kšaṇ = moment, *followed by* 'uprānt', *e.g.* teā kšaṇa uprānt = *l.* after that moment. *Where* a. s. a. *introduces a verb, the participle of the verb is used with* 'kšaṇa' *or* 'făr' *in the Dat. or Or. without postp.*, *e.g.* as soon as they had gone out, the house fell = te băirgellea farāk, ghăr poḍleñ = *l.* in the moment (in which) they (had) gone out, the house fell.

As **to,** višyānt *or* thăiñ = *l.* about, *ch. cs.*: 'as to what you write = tumiñ borăilleā višyānt = *l.* about the... written by you.'

As **follows,** tășeñ *or* ăseñ = *l.* thus; kiteñ moḷeăr.

N.B. For the use of all these phrases see Gram. *esp.* P. II. Ch. iii. P. IV. Ch. ii. Art. iii.

Asafœtida, *s.* hing, -gā, *m.*

Ascend, *v.* tsăḍ *e.g.* a mountain; unts vetā = *l.* goes aloft, rises, *e.g.* the thermometer rises.

2. khāḍuñ ghāln tsăḍ = climb with a rope, *l.* putting rope ascend, (as is the practice here in some parts of Kanara).

Ascendency, *s.* podvi, -ve, *f.*; ădhikār, -rā, *m. see* **Influence.**

Ascension, *s.* sărgārtsăḍneñ, -neā, *n. or* sărgiñtsăḍneñ, -neā, *n.*

Ascent, *s.* tsăḍneñ, -neā, *n.*

Ascertain, *v.* 1. niščeisi, *e.g.* asc. news = khăbār n.

2. kăḷăi = *l.* cause to know, *Dat.*; zāṇăi, *c. v. of* zāṇā = knows.

Ascetic, *a.* 1. ătmeătso = *l.* of soul, *mn.* spiritual.

2. devasponātso, *e.g.* a book.

Ashamed (Be), lăz; loje, (ăuñ 1.); lăz distā = *l.* shame appears

Sb. Dat.; šermetāñ, *n. v.* (āuñ š.).

Ashes, *s.* 1. gobor, -brā, *m.*; 'as. with fire(embers)=murmuro, -reā, *m.*'
2. sinz, -ji, *f.*, *rl.*, *fr.*

Ash-Wednesday, *s.* sinjitso budvār, -rā, *m.*

Ashore, *ad.* tăḍi; 'go a.=tāḍi vots'.

Aside, *ad.* vingăḍ.

Ask, *v.* 1. māg, *mn.* a. with prayers, request (*Lat. roga*), *Prs. Cm.*
2. itsār *or* vitsār = question, *Cm. Prs.*; nimgi, *v.* = ask, *Cm. Prs.*

Askance, (**Look a.**) vānkḍea jinsiñ poḷe = look in a crooked way; *or only* 'vānkḍeñ poḷe'.

Asleep (Be), nid *or* nidlā, *perf.*

Asleep (Fall), nid poḍ = *l.* sleep fall, *Dat. Prs.* (*esp.* at night *or* bed-time); nid yetā (*esp.* at extraordinary times).

Asleep (Put), nidāi, *c. v.*; gāṇa gā = cause (children) to sleep by singing in a low voice.

Aspect, *s.* 1. rūp, -pā, *n.* = *l.* figure; *rs.* distā (*e.g.* boreñ) =looks (*e.g.* well); tònḍ, -ḍā, *n.*; tsāro, -reā, *m.* (*Ital. ciera*).

Asphalt, *s.* dāmbor, -rā, *m.*

Aspiration, *s.* uskār, -rā, *m. pr. fg.* umed, -di, *f.*

Aspire, *v.* ăpekṣi = *l.* desire; lāle.

Asquint, *a.* tirso: 'look asq. = tirso poḷe'.

Ass, *s.* gāḍāuñ, -ḍvā, *n.*

Assail, *v.* āngār poḍ = *l.* fall on body; zulum kăr = *l.* make violence.

Assassin, *s.* khunigār, -rā, *m.*

Assassinate, *v.* khuni kăr=*l.* make assassination; jiusi mār=kill.

Assassination, *s.* khuni, -ye, *f.*

Assault, *v.* zulum kăr = *l.* make violence; zomp mār=pounce.

Assault, *s.* zulum, -lme, *f.*; zomp, -pi, *f.*; uprāḷi, -ḷi, *f.*

Assemblage, *s.* 1. mēḷ, -ḷā, *m.*; zomo, -meā, *m.*
2. rās, -si, *f.* = *l.* heap, *fg.*

Assemble, *v.* 1. *tr.* meḷāi, *c. v. of* meḷ, *n. v.*; zomo kăr *or* zomāi.

Assembly, *s.* zunt, -tā, *m.*, *fr.*; mēḷ, -ḷā, *m.*=meeting; yekoṭ, -ṭā, *m.* = union; săbha, -bhe, *f.* = council.

Assent, *s.* kăbuli, -le, *f.* (*var.* koblāt, -ti, *f.*)

Assent, *v.* kăbuli di, *or* kăbul kăr = *l.* give consent, (*or* kăbul āsā = is consenting); vop.

Assert, *v.* khănḍit (zāun) sāng = *l.* say certainly; moṇ = *l.* say.

Assertion, *s.* khănḍit utsār, -rā, [*m.*

Assessment, *s.* tirvo, -veā, *m.* *see* **Valuation.**

Assets, *s.* āst, -ti, *f.*; jindigi, -ge, *f.*

Asseverate, *v.* khănḍit zāun sāng.

Assiduity, *s.* *rs. into* khăḷanāstanāñ = without intervention, *ch. cs.*; zāgrutāi, -ye, *f.*

Assiduous, *a.* zāgrut.

Assiduously, *ad.* khăḷanāstanāñ; thāmbanāstanāñ = *l.* not ceasing.

Assign, *v.* 1. di = *l.* give.
2. mokruri kăr, *Acc. of thing Dat. of pers. l.* make appointment.

Assignation, *s.* mokruri, -re, *f.* (= appointment).

Assignment, *s.* hăvālo, -leā, *m.*

Assimilate, *v.* 1. sārko kăr = *l.* make like, *or* sār kăr.
2. bădăl = change ('into = thăiñ').

Assist, *v.* ādhār (*or* kumok) kăr = *l.* make help; pāu; săhāi di *or* s. kăr.

Assistance, *s.* săhāi, -ye, *f.* = help; kumok, -mke, *f.* = help; ādhār, -rā, *m.* = help.

Assistant, *a. s.* kumki (*a.*); *or* kumkegār, -rā, *m.* (*s.*)

Associate, *v.* 1. sāngāt kăr = *l.* make company; sāngāti zā = *l.* become companion; yekoṭ kăr = *l.* make union.
2. *fg.* zā = *l.* suit.

Associate, *s.* sāngāti, -tiā, *m.*; iṣṭ, -ṭā, *m.*

Association, *s.* mēḷ, -ḷā, *m.*; yekoṭāi, -ye, *f.* = union; yekoṭ, -ṭā, *m.* = union.

Assort, *v.* thăra thărāk vingăḍ kăr.

Assortment, *s.* thărāvoḷ, -ḷi, *f.* = *l.* variety.

Assume, *v.* 1. kāṇe = *l.* take.
2. *fg.* lék = consider, *e.g.* ass. for granted.
3. vopsun ghe, v. kāṇghe = consigned take upon oneself.

Assumption, *s.* 1. ghevāp, -pā, *n.*
2. sărgiñrigāp, -gpā, *n.*, *rl. mn.*

Assurance, *s.* 1. ghăṭ āločen, -ne (*or* -ni), *f.* = firm conviction.
2. pātiyeṇi, -ṇi, *f.* = confidence.
3. khănḍit sāng-ṇeñ, -ṇeā, *n.* = positive declaration; tirmāṇ, -ṇā, *n.* = solemn declaration, decision.
4. ăumăryād, -di (-de), *f.* = want of modesty.

Assured (I feel), niščei zāun (sāngtāñ).

Asterisk, *s.* ful, -lā, *n.* (fula, -le?).

Asteroid, *s.* lān graha, -hā, *n.*

Asthma, *s.* lăs, -si, *f.*: 'tākā lăs mārtā = he suffers from asth.'

Astonish, *v.* 1. ăjāp kărunk lāi, *or* ăjāpăi, *tr. v.*

Astonished (Be), ăjāp zā; zim zā (be astonished, with fear).

Astonishing, *a.* ăjāpātso.

Astonishment, *s.* ăjāp, -pā, *n.*; zim, -mā, *n.* (ast. with fear).

Astray (Go), āuñ vāṭ tsuktāñ = I miss the way.

Astrict, *v.* 1. bānd = tie; ărnun bānd.
2. dāmb = press (in order to astrict).

Astringent, *s.* bănd kărčeñ vokāt, -ktā, *n.*

Astrologer, *s.* jotis, -sā, *or* jotisgār, -rā, *m.* (zoti).

Astronomer, *s.* joyiṣ, -ṣā, *m.* (*H. K.*); neketrāñpăṇḍit, -tā, *m.*

Astronomy, *s.* jotis, -sā, *n.* (*H.K.*); neketrāñvidya, -ye, *f.*

Asylum, *s.* āsro, -reā, *m.*

At, *prep.* 1. *by 1st Loc. Lat.* '*in*'.
2. *by 2nd Loc. Lat.* '*in*', *and* '*super*', *used for time and space.*
3. *by Cm. Lat.* '*apud*'.
4. *by Acc. or Or. to show time.*
5. *by the Or. case of the fem. derived adjective* (*showing time*).
6. *Dat.* (*to show price*); *see Gram. passim for all these cases. Examples of each case:* 1. 'to ghărānt āsā = he is at home'; 2. 'fānteār = at daybreak'; 'modeñ rātir = at midnight'. 3. 'Trebia kăḍe zālli lăḍāi = the battle at the Trebia'. 4. 'at noon = donpār *or* donpāra'. 5. 'rātičeñ = at night'. 6. 'at what price = kitleā molāk? (*bet.* tāčeñ mol kiteñ?)'

Atheism, *s.* nāstikamăt, -tā, *m.* (*Mr. Sans. Cn.*), *n. u.*

Atheist, *s.* nāstik, -kā, *m.*, *n. u.*

Athwart, *see* **Across.**

Atlas, *s.* bhuiññăkṣa, -ṣe, *f.*

Atmosphere, *s.* vāreñ, -reā, *n.* = *l.* air; ăntrăḷ, -ḷā, *n.* = sky; ākāš, -šā, *n.* = sky.

Atom, *s.* 1. lān lān kuḍko, -keā, *m.* = *l.* very little piece; kuskuṭ, -ṭe, *f.*
2. kăṇi, -ye, *f.* = *l.* a piece of grain; tus, -sā, *n.* (of rice, corn).

Atone, *v.* fārikpoṇ di = *l.* give satisfaction; prăčit kăr = *l.* make penance (*G. N.*)

Atonement, *s.* fārikpoṇ, -ṇā, *n.*; prăčit, -tā, *n.*

Atrocious, *a.* bhăyănkărātso = *l.* dreadful; *or bet.* biyānkuḷ; khoṭepoṇātso = *l.* wicked; niṣṭur = *l.* cruel; ghātki = traitor; mhāru = cruel.

Atrocity, *s.* khoṭepoṇ, -ṇā, *n.* = *l.* wickedness; niṣṭurāi, -ye, *f.* = *l.* cruelty; mhārupoṇ, -ṇā, *n.*

Attach, *v.* 1. *tr.* lāgăi *or* lāi, *c.v. of* lāg, *n. v.* = be attached.
2. *fg.* dhăr = *l.* seize.

Attachment, *s.* 1. lāgāp, -gpā, *n.*; *bet. rs. v.*
2. *fg.* mōg, -gā, *m.* = *l.* love, *fg.*; sălgi, -ge, *f.*, *e.g.* of a son to the mother; ăpurbāi, -ye, *f.* = fondness.

Attack, *v.* āngār poḍ = *l.* fall on body; zulum kăr = *l.* make violence; *where the verb is used figuratively, other Konkani verbs should be used, according to the context, e.g.* be attacked by disease = piḍa tākā lāgtā, *or* p. t. zātā; att. an opinion = inkār kăr = *l.* resist; virodh ulăi.

Attack, *s.* 1. zulum, -lme, *f.*; bōḷ, -ḷā, *n.*

2. *fg*., *e.g.* att. of a disease; *rs. into v.*

Attain, *v.* 1. *n.* pāu=*l.* arrive.
2. *tr.* zóḍ = *l.* obtain; jik = *l.* gain.

Attar, *s.* gulobāčeñ tèl, -lā, *n.*; attār, -rā, *n.*

Attempt, *v.* 1. prăyătăn kăr=*l.* make effort, *pr.*
2. zulum kăr = *l.* make violence, *fg.*

Attempt, *s.* prăyătăn, -tnā, *n.*

Attend, *v.* 1. sāngāta vots=go with; pāvoi=cause to reach, *fg.*
2. hāzăr āsā=is present; āsā=is, *2nd Loc.*
3. rāk=await.
4. čit di=give attention.
5. tsākri kăr=serve, *G. F.*; *see also* **Follow.**

Attendance, *s.* 1. tsākri, -re, *f.*
2. *rs. v.*

Attendant, *s.* sevok, -kā, *m.* *or* tsākor, -krā, *m.*

Attention, 1. kān diunčeñ, -čeā, *n.*; čit, -ti, *f.*; zāgrutāi, -ye, *f.*; tsătrāi, -ye, *f.*; mon, -nā, *n.*=*l.* heart, *fg.*, *e.g.* pray with attention.

Attention(Pay), 1. kān di *or* čit di; zāgrut rāu=*l.* remain awake.
2. tsătrāi kāṇghe=take heed; kăbărdār rāu=take heed.

Attentive, *a.* zāgrut, *or rs. v.*

Attest, *v.* sākṣ̌ sāng *or* s. di.

Attestation, *s.* sākṣ̌, -ṣ̌i, *f.*=evidence.

Attitude, *s.* stiti, -ti, *f.* *or* āngāčeñ āsāp, -spā, *n.*=situation of the body, *n.c.*; rūp, -pā, *n.*

Attorney, *s.* văkil, -lā, *m.*; kārbāri, -riā, *m.*; *G.* kām tsălăitolo=*l.* managing the business; muttālik, -kā, *m.*

Attract, *v.* 1. vóḍ.
2. *fg.* voḍni di *or* fuslāi; *see* **Interest.**

Attraction, *s.* voḍni, -ne, *f.* *or* vondouṇeñ, -ṇeā, *n.* *or* vondoṇ, -ṇe, *f.* *pr.*, *fg.*; fuslāuṇeñ, -ṇeā, *n.*

Attribute, *v.* *see* **Ascribe.**

Attribute, *s.* 1. guṇ, -ṇā, *m.*, *e.g.* att. of God; lăkṣ̌ăṇ, -ṇā, *n.*, *e.g.* Devāčiñ lăkṣ̌ăṇāñ; *Neuter of the Adj.*, *e.g.* it is an att. of man=mănšāčeñ, *as Lat.* '*hominis est*'.

Attrition, *s.* bhirāntiči duk, -ki, *f.*=*l.* sorrow of fear.

Attune, *v.* (tāḷo) săma kăr=*l.* make right (the tune).

Auction, *s.* lăilāuñ, -lāvā, *n.*

Audacious, *a.* 1. dhăirāvont = *l.* courageous; zobor.
2. lăzbanḍo=*l.* impudent.

Audaciousness, *s.* 1. dhăir, -rā, *n.*; zobordăst, -ti, *f.*
2. lăzbanḍpoṇ, -ṇā, *n.*=*l.* impudence.

Audience, *s.* 1. bèṭ (*or* bheṭ), -ṭe, *f.* = *l.* visit; milākăt, -ti, *f.*; 'he got aud.=tākā beṭ meḷḷi, tākā milākăt meḷḷi'.
2. āikap, -pā, *n.* (= act of hearing).

Audit, *v.* poḷei = *l.* look; tănki kăr, *e.g.* aud. accounts.

Auditor, *s.* tănkidār, -rā, *m.*

Auger, *s.* burmo, -meā, *m. for making large holes;* rum, -mā, *n. for boring holes in wood for nails.*

Augment, *v.* tsăḍăi, *c. v. of* tsăḍ.

Augment, *s.* tsăḍāp, -pā (*or* -ḍpā), *n. or* tsăḍouṇi, -ṇe, *f.*

Augur, *s.* bolmeñ sāngtolo, -leā, *m.* = *l.* saying augury; bolmegār, -rā, *m.*; *or* bolmegārn, -ni, *f.* [charm.

Augur, *v.* bolmeñ sāng = *l.* say

Augury, *s.* bolmeñ, -meā, *n.*

Aunt, 1. māusi, -se, *f.* (maternal aunt).

2. ākăi, -kăi, *or* māvoḷn, -ni, *f.* (paternal aunt).

3. māmi, -ye, *f. or* āi, -ye, *f.* (*term of respect, or address*); Gram. p. 157.

Aurora, *s.* fānteñ *or* phānteñ, -teā, *n.*; *it seems to be used only in the 2nd Loc.*, phānteār = at aur.; uzuāḍ, -ḍā, *m.* = *l.* light: 'uzuāḍ zālo (*or* u. distā) = it is aurora'.

Auspices, *s.* bolmiñ, *pl. n.*

Austere, *a.* kăṭiṇ (= severe); kăḍḍụ (*sounded like* kărd), *e.g.* aus. superior.

Austerity, *s.* 1. kăṭiṇăi, -ye, *f.*; nibărāi, -ye, *f.*, *e.g.* aust. of penance; tsălounči nibărāi, -ye, *f.* (=rigour); kărdāi, -ye, *f.* = rigour.

2. khănt, -ti, *f.* = melancholy.

Authentic, *a.* khărots (*emph. of* khăro = true).

Author, *v.* kărt, -tā, *m.*, *n. c.*; ... kello, *or rs. v.*

Authoritative, *a.* podvi āsullo = *l.* powerful; ădikāri, *e.g.* auth. answer; podvetso.

Authority, *s.* 1. podvi, -ve, *f.* = *l.* power; hăkkụ, -kā, *n.* = *l.* right; sotăntrụ, -rā, *n.* = absolute power; ădhikār, -rā, *m.*, *e.g.* auth. of the church.

2. sărkār, -rā, *m* = public authority, government.

3. pātiyeṇi, -ṇi, *f.* (grounds for believing).

Authorize, *v.* podvi di = *l.* give power.

Autocrat, *s.* sotăntri, -riā, *m.* = having absolute power.

Auxiliary, *a.* ādhārātso *or* kumki.

Avail, *v.* (use) 1. prăyóg kăr = *l.* make use (*G. M.*): 'av. yourself of the opportunity = săndrāp ghe *or* kāṇe, = *l.* take the opportunity'; upăyogsi.

2. upkārāk poḍ = *l.* fall to benefit; *see* **Use.**

Avarice, *s.* 1. surāt, -tā, *m.*

2. ăbsuārt, -tā, *m.*, *rl. w. Not a few of the natives of Kanara understand by* 'ăbsuart' 'gluttony'.

Avaricious, *a.* surāti; imṭo, *stronger and more comprehensive than* surāti.

Avenge, *v.* fārikpoṇ kāṇe = *l.* take satisfaction, revenge, *G. N.*

Average, *s.* sumār, -rā, *n.* = not much, nor little; sărāsăr, -ri, *f.*

Averse, *a.* nākhušetso; *bet. rs.*

Aversion, *s.* nākhuši, -še, *f.* = *l.* not will; ăpaprit, -ti, *f.*; kānṭāḷo, -ḷeā, *m.* = *l.* abhorrence; vonkāro, -reā, *m.* = nausea.

Avert, *v.* pois kăr *or* p. dóvór = *l.* keep far.

Avidity, *s.* 1. khāugepoṇ, -ṇā, *n.* (for eating).

2. *fg.* tsaḍ khuši, -še, *f.* = *l.* great wish, *or* āša, -še, *f.*; urbā, -be, *f.* (zeal).

Avoid, *v.* 1. tsukăi (*or* tsukon kāṇe), *c. v. of* tsuk = be missing.

2. vāṭāi (vāiṭāntlo); *also used in the meaning of* 'exchange money'.

3. pois kăr = *l.* make far, go far from.

Await, *v.* rāk, *Acc.*

Awake, *v.* zāgăi, *c. v. or* zāgo kăr (*n. v.* zāgo zā); uṭăi, *c. v. of* uṭ = rise.

Aware (I am), (mākā) kăḷtā = *l.* to me is known; zāṇāñ = I know.

Away, *ad.* peleān: 'take aw. = p. kāḍ'; *it is often untranslated; e.g.* go away = vots *or* tsăl.

Awe, *s.* zim, -mā, *n.*

Awful, *a.* bhăyănkărātso = *l.* dreadful, *or* bhiyānkuḷ; tărtărountso; poḷenātullo = not to be seen.

Awkward, *a.* tārifetso.

Awl, *s.* (*Lat. subula, Ital. succhiello*) dăbbăṇ, -ṇā, *n.* = instrument for boring holes in leather.

Axe, *s.* 1. kurāḍ, -ḍi, *f.* (*var.* [kuḍār).

2. mōtsụ, -tsā, *m.*

Axiom, *s.* văčan, -nā, *n. mn.* evident truth; ărămbăčeñ săt, -tā, *n.* = *l.* fundamental truth, *or* mukhya s. = chief truth; *see* **Aphorism.**

Axle, *s.* pārăi, -riye, *f.*

Azure, *a.* niḷso *or* nīḷ rongātso = *l.* blue *or* of blue colour.

B

Baby, *s.* burgeñ, -geā, *n.*; bāḷšeñ, -šeā, *n.*; bāḷok, -kā, *m.* (*used of* J. C.) = child J.

Babble, *s.* boḍboḍneñ, -neā, *n.*; phandḷo, -ḷeā, *m.*

Babble, *v.* boḍboḍ.

Bachelor, ānkuār, -riā, *m.*; kāzār-nātullo.

Bachelorship, *s.* ānkuārpoṇ, -ṇā, *n.*

Back, *s.* pāṭ, -ṭi, *f.* = *Lat. dorsum.*

Back, *ad.* pāṭi, *e.g.* go back = p. vots; *or* pāṭleān = *l.* behind.

Backbite, *v.* tsāḍio sāng = *l.* say backbiting.

Backbiting, *s.* tsāḍi, -ye, *f.*

Backbiter, *s.* tsāḍiyegār, -rā, *m.*

Backbone, *s.* pāṭikāṇo, -ṇeā, *m.*

Backwards, *ad.* pāṭleān.

Bacon, *s.* ḍukrāčeñ mās, -sā, *n.* = *l.* meat of pig.

Bad, *a.* pāḍ; vāiṭ (physically *and* morally); khoṭo = wicked; tākā vāiṭ kārtā = he is sick'; 'to vāiṭ kārtā = he commits evil'.

Badge, *s.* billo, -leā, *m.*, *e.g.* of a peon.

Bad-hearted, *a.* ušṭo.

Bag, *s.* 1. čil, -lā, *n.* (*general name*); póti, -ye, *f.* = small b.; poteñ, -teā, *n.* = b. of leather, *as* a school-boy's satchel; thāili, -le, *f.* = money-bag; goṇi, -ye, *f.* = *l.* sack.

Baggage, *s.* sāmān, -nā, *m.*

Bail, *v.* 1. zāmin zā = *l.* become security; zāmin di = *l.* give surety.

Bail, *s.* zāmindār, -rā, *m.* = *Lat. vas.*

2. zāmin, -ne, *f.* = *Lat. vadimonium.*

Bailiff, *s.* kārbāri vitātso, *or* k. itlātso = administrator of property; āmin, -nā, *m.*

Bait, *s.* 1. dūd, -dā, *n.* (māḍāčeñ d. = b. of palm, *used as* an astringent to stop blood flowing).

2. khāṇ, -ṇā, *n.* = food; tsārāḍu, -dā, *n.* (to catch fishes with); buko, -keā, *m.*; kānni, -ne, *f.*

Bait, *v.* khāṇ *or* khāunk di (monzātink poiṇ kārčeā veḷār) = *l.* give food (to animals when they are on a journey).

Bake, *v.* 1. bāz (*'torre' in Lat.*); kārpi = bake much.

2. rānd = *Lat. coque.*

Baker, *s.* unḍegār, -rā, *m.*

Bakery, *s.* khorn, -nā, *n.*

Balance, *s.* 1. tāgḍi, -ḍe, *f.*; tārās, -si, *f.*: 'scale of b. = tāgāḍ, -gḍā', *n.*

2. bāki, -ki, *f.* = b. of an account.

Balcony, *s. vlg.* bālkāuñ, -kāvā, *m.*; tsāḍāu, -ḍāvā, *m.* (*H. K.*)

Bald, *a.* 1. boḷmānḍo; boḍko (*mn. also*, without horns *or* bare head); boḷmāteñ (*vlg.*); kesnātullo; *some say* koḍḍo = skull without hair.

Bale, *s.* penḍi, -ye, *f. as* of cloth.

Ball, *s.* 1. guḷo, -ḷeā, *m.* (*mn. ex.* shot, cannon-ball, *and the like*); *fg.* colics. *Dim.* guḷi, -ye, *f.*

2. nāts, -tsā, *m.* = dance.

Balloon, *s.* guḷo, -ḷeā, *m.*

Balm, *s.* pǎrmǎḷātso ros, -sā, *m.* = *l.* good-smelling juice: pǎrmǎḷāčeñ tel, -lā, *n.* = good-smelling oil.

Bamboo, *s.* vāso, -seā, *m.*; kǎṇǎk, -ṇki, *f.*; kirl, -lā, *m.* = tender b.; pieces of b. *used as* ligaments *are called* 'kāmb, -bi,' *f.*

Bamboo-mat, *s.* hātor, -trā, *m.*

Ban, *s.* (of marriage) čiṭ, -ṭi, *f.*

Band, *s.* 1. bāndāp, -dpā, *n.*

2. bireñ, -reā, *n.*, *e.g.* of men.

Bandicoot, *s.* koḷundir, -drā, *m.*

Banditti, *s.* luṭkāri, -riā, *m.* = *l.* making prey.

Banian-tree, *s.* voḍātso ruk, -kā, *m.*

Banish, *v.* 1. gǎḍ pār kǎr; pǎrgāvānt dhāḍ = send to a foreign country.

2. *fg.* bhāir gāl = put out.

3. soḍ = *l.* leave.

Bank, *s.* 1. nǎinči kinār, -ri, *f.* = *l.* shore of a river; vèḷ, -ḷe, *f*; tǎḍi, -ye, *f.* (shore).

2. benk, -kā, *n.*, *fr.*; hunḍisāl, -lā, *n.* = *l.* hall of cheque, *fg.*

3. muṇǎi, -ṇiye, *f.* = a small bench *or* stool.

4. dokko, -keā, *m.* = *l.* beach, dock.

5. bāṭi, -ye, *f.* (a river-bank).

Banker, *s.* sāukār, -rā, *m.*

2. činvār, -rā, *m.*; sǎrāf, -fā, *m.*

Bank-note, *s.* hunḍi, -ye, *f.*

Bankrupt (Become), divāḷi kāḍ.

Banner, *s.* bāuṭo, -ṭeā, *m.*; giāuñ, -āvā, *m.*, *fr.*; bǎnder, -rā, *n.*, *fr.*

Banquet, *s.* *vlg.* bonket, -ti, *f.* (meat and plantains); voḍ jevāṇ, jeuṇā, *n.* = *l.* great dinner.

Banter, *s.* česṭāi, -ye, *f.*

Banter, *v.* česṭāi kǎr.

Baptism, *s.* bāptizm *or* bāutizm, -mā, *m.*, *fr.*

Baptistery, *s.* bāptizm·diunči suāt, -te, *f.*; bāptizmāči pi, -ye, *f.*

Baptize, *v.* bāptizār kǎr (*used in the formula of baptism*); bāutizm di = *l* give b., *vlg.*; vol lāi = *l.* apply oil; 'be baptised = bautizm ghe'.

Bar, *s.* 1. āḷveñ, -veā, *n.*

2. sǎrǎḷ, -ḷā, *m.*, *e.g.* b. of windows.

Barbarity, *s.* 1. heḍpoṇ, -ṇā, *n.*; rānuoṭpoṇ, -ṇā, *n.*

2. niṣ̌ṭurpoṇ, -ṇā, *n.* *or* niṣ̌ṭurāi, -ye, *f.*

Barbarous, *a.* 1. rānuoṭ = *l.* wild.

2. niṣ̌ṭur = *l.* cruel; mhāru.

Barber, *s.* kelši, -šiā, *m.*; mālo, -leā, *m.*

Bare, *a.* ugto = *l.* open, *fg.*

Barefaced, *a.* lăzbanḍgo *or* lăzbanḍo; mostitso.

Bargain, *s.* 1. kărār, -rā, *m.*; sāṭo, -ṭeā, *m.*

Bark, *s.* 1. sāl, -li, *f.* (of trees).
2. dóṇ, -ṇi, *f.* (boat).

Bark, *v.* 1. bòb mār = *l.* beat crying.
2. ghonk (*or* bhonk)=*Lat. latra.*

Barley, *s.* bārli, -le, *f.*

Barn, *s.* 1. tupeñ, -peā, *n.*
2. ugrāṇ, -ṇā, *n.* (a sort of godown).

Barometer, *s.* vāreāčeñ māp, -pā, *n.* = *l.* measure of the air, (vāreāzăḍāyemāp, -pā, *n.* = mea. of the pressure of the air), *n. u.*

Barque, *see* **Bark.**

Barrack, *s.* barāk, -kā, *n. or* barkăs, -sā, *n.*

Barrel, *s.* pīp, -pā, *n.*

Barren, *a.* 1. vānz, *pr.* (*esp. appl. to women*); goḍḍu, *pr.* (*esp. appl. to irrational animals*); bănjer (*place*).
2. *fg.* foḷ dinātullo, *fg.* = *l.* not giving fruit; nirfoḷ.

Barrier, *see* **Bar.**

Barrister, *s.* văkil, -lā, *m.*

Barter, *v.* bădăl, (*e. g.* bar. one thing for another).

Base, *a.* 1. uṇo=*l.* less, *used fg.*; hălko; *see* **Abject.**
2. săkăilo (b. voice).

Base, *s.* bunyād, -di, *f.*

Basement, *s.* dărn, -ni, *f.* (lowest story of a building).

Bashful, *a.* 1. lăjiṣṭ.
2. bizuḍ = *l.* timid; bhiyātso; phukkela = very timid.

Bashfulness, *s.* 1. lăz, -je, *f.*
2. bheñ, bhiyā, *n.* = *l.* fear.

Basil, *s.* tuḷăs, -ḷsi, *f.*

Basilica, *s.* mukhya igărz, -je, *f.* (m. devăstān, -nā, *n.*)

Basin, *s.* tăst, -tā, *n. mn.* vessel for washing in, *etc.*; vāṭli, -ṭle, *f.* = a sort of plate to eat rice from; guḷāmb, -ḷmbā, *n.* (for curry); pokāli, -le, *f.* = a vessel to draw water with.
2. tăḷeñ, -ḷeā, *n.* = *l.* tank.
3. phalkeñ, -keā, *n.* = *l.* valley.

Basket, *s.* kānṭ, -ṭi, *f.* (larger kind); bāṭi, -ye, *f.* (smaller); kurpāṇo, -ṇeā, *m.*, *or* kurveñ, -veā, *n.* (still smaller); peṭāro, -reā, *m.* = wicker-basket; dāli, -ye, *f.*; pānṭli, -le, *f.*; kurpoṇ, -ṇi, *f.*

Basket-maker, *s.* korgār, -rā, *m.* (name of a caste specially employed in making baskets, *etc.*)

Bass-relief, *s.* kāntoṇetso vāur, -rā, *m.* = *l.* work of an engraver.

Bastard, *a.* bāpuinātullo = *l.* without father; (*not, perhaps, an exact equivalent, but the following are commonly terms of abuse*); vāreātso = *l.* aerial; rānḍetso *or* bodkitso = child of a widow; lăunḍitso = child of an unmarried woman; dasiro (*vlg.* desātso) = child of a maid-servant.

Baste, *v.* pōnt mār (*mn.* sew with long stitches).

Bat, *s.* 1. toṇko, -keā, *m.* (cudgel).
 2. pāko, -keā, *m.* animal (larger kind).
 3. vāguḷ, -gḷā, *n.* (smaller).

Bath, *s.* nāṇ, -ṇā, *n.*; snān, -nā, *n.*

Bathe, *v.* 1. nā, *n. v.* (*var.* nāñ): nāṇāi, *c. v.*
 2. bizāi = *l.* make wet.

Bathing-room, *s.* nāṇi, -ye, *f.*

Baton, *s.* 1. vār, -ri, *f.* (mostakāči) = *l.* stick (of a commander), *fr.*
 2. betkaṭi, -ṭe, *f.* = *l.* sceptre.
 3. dānḍo, -ḍeā, *m.*; *all three words mn.* a stick used as a sign of honour or command: *the last one may also be* for common uses.

Battalion, *s.* pāṭlām, -mi, *f.* (*corruption of the English word*).

Batter, *v.* nāḷiniñ mār = *l.* beat with guns.

Battery, *s.* (nāḷintso) mēḷ, -ḷā, *m.*

Battle, *s.* zuz, -zā, *n.* = war; lāḍāi, -ye, *f.* = *l.* fighting.

Bay, *s.* (dāryāčeñ) koḷ, -ḷā, *n.*

Bayonet, *s.* 1. bāndukeči bhāli, -ye, *f.* = *l.* arrow of the firelock; sānin, -ne, *f.*, *n. c.*

Bazaar, *s.* pēnṭ(è), -ṭe, *f.*

Be, *v.* 1. āsā, *to denote: a*) existence in a place, *b*) mere existence, *c*) exterior quality *or* relation, *e. g.* 'the door is open', *and the like.*
 2. vortautā *or* zāun vortautā, *denoting* quality; *in this 2nd mn. the verb is very often omitted* (*see* Gram. p. 102).

Beach, *s.* dākko, -keā, *m.* (*viz.* shore prepared for landing boats *etc.*)

Beacon, *see* Lighthouse.

Bead, *s.* māṇi (*or* móṇi), -yā, *m.*; sāri, -ye, *f.*

Beadle, *s.* pedo, -dea, *m.*

Beak, *s.* bonts, -či, *f.*

Beam, *s.* 1. āḍeñ, -ḍeā, *n.* (small b.); pākāso, -seā, *m.* (rafter); tirānt, -te, *f.* (big b.); tóḷ, -ḷā, *m.* (upon which the roof rests); kāḍi, -ye, *f.* (small slices *or* pieces of wood); pāṭi, -ye, *f. is used sometimes instead of* 'kāḍi' *for* 'beam' (small); rip, -pā, *n.*, *e. g.* the pieces used to connect the planks of a door, *etc.*
 2. dānḍo, -ḍeā, *m.* (b. of a balance).
 3. isāḷeñ, -ḷeā, *n.* = b. of a cart.
 4. kirn, -nā, *n.* = *l.* ray.

Bean, *s.* bogḍo, -ḍeā, *m.* (b. of Kanara); āḷsāndo, -deā, *m.*; āuro, -reā, *m.*

Bear, *s.* 1. āsvel, -lā, *n.*
 2. *fg.* rāṇuoṭ mānis, -nsā, *m.* = a wild man.

Bear, *v.* 1. zăḍāi dăr = *l.* keep the weight.
2. sos = *l.* suffer.
3. bāḷānt (*or* porsut) zā = bring forth.
4. zălmăi = beget, *c. v. of* zălma (*more commonly only* zălma, *ch. cs.*)
5. āsā = is *e. g.* b. a name, *ch. cs.*
6. di = *l.* give, *e. g.* give fruit.

Beard, *s.* khāḍ, -ḍā, *n.*; dāḍi, -ye, *f.*: 'seize by the b. = kh. dhăr *or* kh. hālăi'.

Bearer, *s.* 1. hămāl, -lā, *m.* (*only* of palanquin *and* manchil); boi, -yā, *m.*
2. vortso mănis, -nšā, *m. general term* = *l.* carrying man.

Beast, *s.* monzāt, -ti, *f.*; *see* **Animal.**

Beat, *v.* 1. măr; phophāi; dāḍāi *or* pēṭ(ė), *mn.* beat in order to make hard, *e. g.* roads; kānḍ = b. paddy (thrash the 1st time); fărāi, *i. e.* beat rice (thrash the 2nd time); boḍāi, *e. g.* b. on a wall.
2. dāunḍāi = *l.* cause to run (defeat).
3. uḍ = *l.* palpitate, jump (the heart); 'b. down (*e. g.* fruits) = zăḍāi'.

Beatific, *a.* bhāgevont kărtso *or* sukhi kărtso.

Beatification, *s.* bhāgevont moṇṇeñ, -ṇeā, *n.*

Beatify, *v.* bhāgevont moṇ.

Beatitude, *s.* sukh, -khā, *n.*; bhāg, -gā, *n.*; visou, -sovā, *m.* (eternal b.)

Beautiful, *a.* sobit; sundăr; tshănd (*H. K.*)

Beautify, *v.* sobăi, *c. v. of* sob.

Beauty, *s.* sobitāi, -ye, *f. or* sobāi, -ye, *f.*; sundărāi, -ye, *f.*

Becalm, *v.* fuslāi; nidān kăr; thănḍ kăr.

Because, *conj.* kiteāk, *or* keteāk moḷeār *or* kiteāgāi moḷeār = *l.* to what if I said; dekun (*put at the end*); pāsun *or* pāsvot, *postp.* (*with the participle*); kiteāk . . . . dekun (*see* Gram. p. 302, *seq.*) *e. g.* he has not come b. he is sick = to yeunk nāñ, *a*) k. m. to piḍest; *b*) piḍest dekun; *c*) piḍest āsčeā pāsvot; *d*) k. to piḍest dekun.

Becharm, *see* **Charm.**

Beck, *see* **Nod.**

Become, *v.* zā = fit; vāzbi zāun āsā = *l.* is convenient, proper.

Becoming, *a.* măryāditso (decent); boreā nădteātso = *l.* of good character.

Bed, *s.* khăṭleñ, -leā, *n.*; māntso, -čeā, *m.*; āntuḷn, -nā, *n.* (a low poor bed): 'āntuḷnār āsā = is sick'.
2. hindḷo, -ḷeā, *m.* = hammock.

Bedstead, *s.* polăng, -gā, *n.*; māntso, -čeā, *m.*

Bee, *s.* movātso mus, -sā, *m.* = *l.* fly of honey.

Beef, *s. vlg.* gāičeñ (*or* vākāčeñ) mās, -sā, *n.*

Beehive, *s.* movāčeā musāntso guḍ, -ḍā, *m.*

Beer, *s.* bīr, -ri, *f.*, *fr.*

Beetle, *s.* 1. zărlo, -leā, *m.* = *Lat. scarabeus.*

2. gungurlo, -leā, *m.* (the droning beetle); bovor, -vrā, *m.*

Befall, *v.* 1. găḍ = happen.

2. zā = become; 'tākā kiteñ zāleñ = what befell him?'

Before, *ad., prep.* 1. ādiñ, *ad.* (*of time*) *and postp.*

2. poilo (-i, -eñ) *a.* = *Lat. prior* (poileñ *postp.*).

3. hujir = *Lat. coram:* 'Devā hu. = *coram Deo*'.

4. mukār (*from* 'muk = face'): 'mukār vots = go b.'

5. fuḍeñ, *e.g.* yeā fuḍeñ = after this (in future).

6. prăs, *with the comparat., if it means* 'more than' (*see* Gram. p. 64, *seq.*)

Beforehand, *ad.* ādiñ *or* poilo (poilots) = *l.* before, *or* first; *see* **Advance.**

Befoul, *v.* mheḷăi *or* mheḷo kăr.

Beg, *v.* māg = request: 'I b. pardon = māf kăr *or* māf māgtāñ = *l.* make forgive ness, *or* I ask forgiveness.

2. bhīk māg = *l.* beg alms.

Beget, *v.* zălmăi (*bet. use* zălma = be generated, *ch. cs.*)

Beggar, *s.* 1. (bhīk) māgtolo, -leā, *m.*

2. bhikāri, -riā, *m.*

Begin, *v.* 1. suru kăr, *G. F.* = make beginning.

2. suru zātā, *n. v.*, *G. F.* = *l.* beginning is done; lāg, *Dat.* = *l.* be applied, *e. g.* vāurāk lāg = b. to work; 'to moṇunk lāglo = he began to say'.

Beginning, *s.* suru, -ve, *f.*: 'in the b. = suruvent *or* suruver'; 'from the b. = suru thāun *or* suruver thāun'; ărămb, -bā, *m.* = origin; mūḷ, -ḷā, *n.* = *l.* root, *e. g.* b. of wisdom (*fg.*).

Begone, *v.* (*Lat. apage*) tsăl, vóts = *l.* walk, go.

Beguile, *v.* mōs kăr = *l.* make deceit.

Behalf, (on b. *or* in b. of), 1. pāsun, khātir (*Lat.* '*pro*' *or* '*propter*').

2. *G.* pāḍtin = on the part of, *fr.*; păkṣen = on the side of.

Behave, *v.* tsăl = *l.* walk, *fg.*; tsăm.

Behaviour, *s.* tsăl, -li, *f.*; năḍteñ, -teā, *n.* = *l.* character; tsămkānḍ, -ḍā (*or* tsămkāṇ, -ṇā), *n.*

Behead, *v.* tăkli (*or* māteñ) kātăr = *l.* cut the head; sis kāp = *l.* cut the head.

Behind, *ad. prep.* 1. pāṭleān, *ad. postp.*

2. pāṭi, *ad.*

Behold, *v.* 1. poḷe *or* poḷei.

2. disṭ ghāl = *l.* put sight (*2nd Loc.*).

Behold, *int.* poḷe (*or* obḷe, *vlg. corrupt. of* oh poḷe).

Being, *s.* 1. văstų, -tu, *f.* = *l.* thing. 2. āsāp, āspā, *n.* = existence.

Belching, *s.* dénk, -kā, *m.*

Belfrey, *s.* ghānṭiči tōr (ó), -ri, *f.* = *l.* tower of bells (*var.* ghānṭitso tōr, -rā, *m.*).

Belie, *v.* 1. lipăi = *l.* conceal. 2. *see* **Calumniate.**

Belief, *s.* 1. nămbgăṇeñ, -ṇeā, *n.* 2. āločen, -ni, *f.* = *l.* opinion; ghăṭ ā. = firm persuasion. 3. bāvāḍt, -tā, *m. mn.* divine faith; šāstir, -rā, (*or* šāstrų, -trā), *n.* = religion.

Believe, *v.* 1. sătmānd = *l.* esteem truth, *used esp. of divine faith* (*with 2nd Loc.*, *e. g.* Devāčer sătmānd). 2. pātiye = *l.* trust (*with 2nd Loc.*), *or* pātiyeṇi dóvór = *l.* keep confidence, *or* nămbgā *or* nămboa (nămgā, *vlg.*). 3. čint = *l.* think.

Believer, *s.* sătmāndtolo, -leā, *m.*; kristāuñ, -tāvā, *m.*; bāvāḍti, -tiā, *m.*

Bell, *s.* 1. ghānṭ, -ṭi, *f.*: 'ring the b. = ghānṭ mār'. 2. kāmpiṇ, -ṇi, *f.* = small bell, *fr.*; ghānṭleñ, -leā, *n.* (*bigger than* 'kāmpiṇ').

Bellow, *v.* āmbe (*Lat.* '*mugi*', *used of cows and bullocks*).

Bellows, *s.* bhāto, -teā, *m.*: 'blow the b. = bhāto funk'; sidi, -de, *f.*, *n.c.* (*some understand* 'sidi' *as meaning a vessel like* 'koḷso', *but smaller*; *but the Tulu for* 'bellows' *is also* 'sidi').

Belly, *s.* pòṭ, -ṭā, *n. pr.*, *fg.*, *e.g.* of a vessel; kănvăṭ (round of the belly).

Belong, *v.* 1. fāvo zā; *where it signifies*, 'be the property of', *it is translated by the Gen. case of the noun governed by* 'of'; *see* Gram. p. 223. *seq.* 2. lāg, *Dat. mn.* concern, *l.* be attached, *e.g.* yeñ mākā lāgānāñ = this does not belong to me, it does not concern me.

Beloved, *a.* mogāḷ *or* mogātso; ăpurbāyetso; prititso *or* pritimogātso.

Below, *ad. prep.* 1. săkal *ad. and postp.* 2. uṇo = *l.* less, *fg. e. g.* look on everything worldly as being b. you = săkăṭ săuñsārāčeo văstu tuje uṇeo moṇ čint. 3. ponda = *l.* beneath. 4. khāl.

Belt, *s.* 1. munz, -ji, *f.*; pāṭo, -ṭeā, *m.* 2. kămbărband, -dā, *n.*; *see* **Girdle.**

Bemoan, *v.* răḍ; *see* **Groan.**

Bench, *s.* bānk, -kā, *m.* (*e.g.* a school-bench), *fr.*; băska, -ke, *f.*; muṇăi = stool; syăsăṇ, -ṇā, *n.* (*e.g.* seat of a judge).

Bend, *v.* 1. bāgāi, *c. v. of* bāgā, *n. v.*
2. portā = *l.* turn.
Bending, *s.* bāu, bāve, *f.*
Beneath, 1. săkal; ponda.
2. *fg.* năiñzāllo = *l.* unbecoming.
Benediction, *s.* 1 besāuñ, -sāvā, *n.*, *fr.*; āširvād, -dā, *n. or* āširvazan, -nā, *n.*
Benefactor, *s.* upkārkārtolo, -leā, [*m.*
Benefice, Benefit, *s.* upkār, -rā, *m.*; ādāi, -yā, *m.* = *l.* advantage.
Benefit, *v.* upkār; upkārāk pód.
Beneficial, *a.* upkāratso *or* ādāyātso.
Benevolence, *s.* 1. borepoṇ, -ṇā, *n.*; bori khuši, -še, *f.*; upkārpoṇ, -ṇā, *n.*; mōg, -gā, *m.* = *l.* love.
Benevolent, *a.* upkārkārtolo, *or* mogātso, *or* boro, *or* bore khušetso.
Bent, *a.* 1. bāgoun *or* bāgvāllo, *or* vānkḍo: 'b. forward = mukār b.'
2. *fg.* lāgullo = *l.* attached.
Bent, *s.* *see* **Bending.**
Bequeath, *v.* testamentār dovor = *l.* keep *or* put on will, *fr.*; *see* **Will.**
Bequest, *s.* testamentāčeñ deṇeñ, -ṇeā, *n.* = *l.* a gift of will, *fr.*
Bereave, *v.* 1. tsukăi, *c. v. of* tsuk = be missing; kāḍ.
Berry, *s. approx.* dākṭeñ foḷ, -ḷā, *n.* = *l.* small fruit.

Beseech, *v.* 1. māg, *Cm. Prs.*
Beset, *v.* veḍo ghāl *or* v. mār.
Beside, *prep.* lāgiñ; kăḍe; săršiñ.
Besides, *prep.* šivāi; khărit; *both these words are used in the formation of many tenses, those chiefly which are introduced by the conj.* nisi, quin; *see* Gram.
Besides, *ad.* teā šivāi = *Lat. praeterea.*
Besiege, *v.* veḍo ghāl, *or* v. mār.
Besieging, *s.* veḍo, -ḍeā, *m.*
Besmear, *v.* 1. lāi = apply; ('lāi' *should govern in the Acc. the name of the stuff used for smearing*).
2. mhéḷăi = befoul.
Besom, *s.* sāruṇ, -ṇe, *f.*
Bespeak, *v.* 1. poilits hukum di = *l.* give order beforehand.
2. bāḍeāk kāṇe = *l.* take at hire.
3. *Cm.* lāgiñ ulăi = *l.* speak with.
Besprinkle, *v.* *see* **Sprinkle.**
Best, *a.* 1. bhou boro.
2. uttăm *or* uttim.
Best, *ad.* bhou boreñ.
Bestial, *a.* monzātitso, *pr. fg.*
Bestow, *v.* di = *l.* give; *see also* **Expend.**
Bestride, *v.* bos = *l.* seat, *2nd Loc.*
Bet, *s.* pōnt, -tā, *m.*
Bet, *v.* pōnt mār = *l.* beat a bet.
Betake, *v. n.* 1. lāg = *l.* apply.
2. āsro kāṇe = take refuge: 'b. yourself to the carriage = gāḍiyer tsăḍ'; *see* **Recourse.**

Betel, *s.* pānānči vāl, -li, *f.*

Betel-nut, 1. fopāḷ, -pḷā, *n.*; supāri, -re, *f.*

2. pān foḍ = *l.* nut of betel, (*exact mn.* b. n. and leaves); pān supāri, -re, *f.*

Bethink (oneself), *v.* āṭou kăr *or* ugḍās kār *or* motint hāḍ *or* čint.

Betimes, *ad.* vegiñ; fānteār; 'early in the morning = bhou f. *or* bhou săkāḷiñ'.

Betoken, *v.* dākāi = *l.* show; gurtų āsā = *l.* sign is.

Betray, *v.* 1. ghāt kăr, *G. M.*; mōs kăr, *G. M.*

2. ugto kăr = *l.* make open, (reveal).

Betrayal, *s.* ghāt, -tā, *m.*; mōs, [-sā, *m.*

Betroth, *v.* săirik kār; 'bāpāin āple duvek Pedruk săirik keleā = the father has betrothed his daughter to Peter'; *in pass.* săirik zā.

Betrothal, *s.* mudi ghālči = *l.* putting the ring; săirik, -ke, *f.*

2. uloṇeñ, -ṇeā, *n.*, *n. c.* = *l.* speaking, *fg.*

Betrothed, *see* **Bride** *and* **Bridegroom.**

Between, *prep.* modeñ (*vlg.* modegăt) = *l.* in the middle; bitār = *l.* in, *Lat. inter.*

Bewail, *v.* răḍ = *l.* weep, *ch. cs.*; pirngā = *l.* groan.

Beware, *v.* kăbārdār rāu; tsātrāi kāṇghe.

Bewitch, *v.* bhul ghāl; ghāḍi kăr.

Beyond, *prep.* 1. póltăḍi (*opp. to* 'āltăḍi = on this side').

2. viṇeñ = *l.* without, *Lat. sine.*

3. bhāir (*or. adj.* bhāilo), *e.g.* b. my duty, b. the years of; šivāi.

Bible, *s.* păvitrų pustak, -kā, *n.* = *l.* sacred book; purāṇ, -ṇā, *m.*, *n. c.*; grānt, -tā, *m.*, *n. c.*

Bid, *v.* 1. formāi = *l.* command.

2. māg = *l.* request.

3. sāng = *l.* tell.

4. (offer a price) tsăḍăi = *l.* increase (price).

Bier, *s.* tūmb, -bā, *m.* (a frame for carrying corpses on to the grave).

Big, *a.* 1. vóḍ *or* vóḍlo.

2. gărbest (*vlg.* guruār) = *l.* pregnant.

Bigamist, *a.* dogi potiṇintso.

Bile, *s.* pīnt, -tā, *n.*

Bill, *s.* 1. bonts, -či, *f.* = beak.

2. čīṭ, -ṭi, *f.*, *e.g.* b. of expense; lēk (è), -kā, *n.* = *l.* account, statement.

3. zāmin, -ne, *f.* = *l.* security.

4. istyār, -rā, *m.*; *see* **Advertisement.**

5. nāi, -yā, *m.* = *l.* law.

Billet, *s.* čīṭ, -ṭi, *f.*

Bill-hook, *s.* koito, -teā, *m.*

Bind, *v.* 1. bānd.

2. formāi = *l.* command.

3. čents = *l.* crush, *fg.* (check).

Biographer, *s.* jiṇiboreitolo.

Biography, *s.* jiṇiyebărāp (*or* -borāp), -rpā, *n.*

Bird, *s.* sukṇeñ, -ṇeā, *n.*

Birdlime, *s.* bendăr, -dri, *f.*

Birth, *s.* 1. zólm, -mā, *m.* (zălm); porsutpoṇ, -ṇā, *n.* = *Lat. partus*; bāḷntyor (*or* bāḷnter), -rā, *m.*; zălmātso dis = *l.* day of birth; zăllo dis.
2. kuṭām, -ṭmā, *n.* = *l.* family, descent.
3. ărămb, -bā, *m.* = *l.* origin.

Birthplace, *s.* zăllo gāuñ, -gāñvā, *m.*; vilāyet, -ti, *f.*

Biscuit, *s.* biskut, -te, *f.*, *fr.*; don pāuṭi bāzụllo (unḍo).

Bishop, *s.* bisp, -pā, *m.*, *fr.* ('sāib = Lord' *is usually added*); *var.* bismụ, -mā, *m.*

Bishopric, *s.* bispāčeñ rāz, -jā, *n.* = *l.* kingdom of the Bishop, *fg.*; bispāpoṇ, -ṇā, *n.* = office of the Bishop.

Bissextile, *a.* upari (moino, vors).

Bit, *s.* 1. lăgām, -mā, *n.* = *Lat. frenum.*
2. kuḍko, -keā, *m.* = *l.* piece.

Bitch, *s.* kolgeñ, -geā, *n.*

Bite, *v.* tsāb.
2. *fg.* zăḷ, *n. v.* = *l.* be burning, *fg.*; dukăi = *l.* cause sorrow.

Bite, *s.* gās (*or* ghās), -sā, *m.* = *l.* mouthful.

Bitter, *a.* 1. koḍu, *pr.* *fg.*
2. *fg.* kăṣṭāntso = *l.* difficult; dukountso = *l.* causing pain; niṣṭur.

Bitterness, *s.* koḍsāṇ, -ṇe, *f.* *pr. and fg.*, *e.g.* b. of words.

Bitumen, *s.* tār, -rā, *n.* *not ex.*; kātrāṇ, -ṇā, *n.*

Black, *adj.* 1. kāḷo.
2. *fg.* khăntiṣṭ *or also* kāḷo, *e.g.* b. days.

Blacken, *v.* kāḷo kăr.

Blacksmith, *s.* kāmār, -rā, *m.*; lovār, -rā, *m.*

Blackwood, *s.* bīṭ, -ṭi, *f.*

Blade, *s.* 1. kăṇās, -ṇsi, *f.* (*Lat. spica*).
2. dhār, -ri, *f.* = edge, (of a knife, of an oar, *etc.*).

Blame, *v.* durvăi, *c. v. of* duruā, *n. v.* = reproach; dūr di (complain); gunyāukār kăr = *l.* make guilty; păsănd kăr (*with neg. particle*) = *l.* approve, *or bet.* nāpăsănd kăr; besṭăi = *l.* reproach.

Blame, *s.* gunyāuñ, -vā, *m.* = *l.* fault; nāpăsănd, -dā, *n.* = *l.* not approval, disapproval; dūr, -rā, *n.*

Blameless, *a.* gunyāuñnātullo = *l.* not having fault; nenṭo = innocent (*l.* ignorant).

Blank, *s.* khāli = *l.* empty, *viz.* paper *or* place.

Blank, *a.* khāli.

Blanket, *s.* kāmboḷ, -bḷi, *f.*; bănāt, -ti, *f.* (a better kind of bl.)

Blaspheme, *v.* blasfem ulăi = *l.* say bl., *fr.*; dēuninda ulăi = *l.* say injuries against God.

Blasphemy, *s.* blasfem, -mā, *m.* *fr.*; dēuninda, -de, *f.* *or* devaninda = *l.* injuries to God, *n. c.*

Bleed, *v.* 1. răgat kāḍ = *l.* draw blood; sir mār = *l.* beat vein.

2. răgat vāutā = *l.* blood flows, *e.g.* the nose bleeds = nākāntleñ răgat vāutā.

Bleeding, *s.* sirmārneñ, -neā, *n.* *or* sir mārāp, -rpā, *n.*

Blemish, *s.* tsūk, -ki, *f.* = *l.* mistake; ăib, -bā, *n.* = *l.* fault, flaw; khăt, -tā, *n.* = *l.* stain.

Bless, *v.* besāuñ di = *l.* give blessing, *fr.* *or* āširvād di.

2. boreñ kăr = *l.* make good.

3. benjār (*or* besment) kăr = consecrate, *e.g.* water, houses, *fr.*

4. ārgāñ di = *l.* give thanks, *or* glorify God.

5. vrăddi kăr = *l.* make prosperous.

Blessed, *a.* besāvāntso, *fr.*; āširvād meḷullo (= he who was *or* is blessed).

2. sukhi = *l.* happy, *or* bhāgevont.

3. sānt; *used of the saints and the blessed in heaven, fr.*

Blessing, *s.* 1. besāuñ, -sāvā, *n.* *e.g.* give me your bl. = besāuñ diyā, *fr.*; āširvād, -dā, *or* āširvazan, -nā *n.*; vardhan, -nā, *n.*

2. borepoṇ, -ṇā, *n.* = *l.* benefit, prosperity; bărkăt, -tā, *n.* = prosperity.

Blind, *a.* 1. kuḍḍo; ăndăḷo *or* ăndḷo; disṭnātullo, *or* disānātullo: 'he is b. = tākā doḷe disānānt = *l.* to him the eyes do not appear'.

2. *fg.* somzānātullo *or* būd nātullo.

Blindness, *s.* kuḍḍepoṇ, -ṇā, *n.*

Bliss, *see* **Happiness.**

Blister, 1. fōḍ, -ḍā, *m.* = *l.* bladder; bokko, -keā, *m.* (*esp. H. K.*)

2. *ol.* plastar, -rā, *m.*, *fr.*; lēp (é), -pā, *m.*

Blood, *s.* 1. *pr.* răgat, -gtā, *n.*

2. *fg.* kuṭām, -ṭmā, *n.* = *l.* house, descent; 'măntanāčeñ răgat = noble blood': 'every man's b. was up for revenge = sămestānčeñ răgat fārikpoṇ kāṇeunk utsāmboḷ zāun āsăl-leñ'.

Bloodless, *a.* răgat nātullo, *e. g.* b. man.

2. răgtāviṇ = *l.* without blood, *e.g.* b. victory.

Bloodshed, *s.* răgtāvikrāp, -pā, *n.*

Bloody, *a.* răgtātso.

Bloom, *s.* ful, -lā, *n.*

Bloom, *v.* ful.

Blossom, *s.* ful, -lā, *n.*

Blossom, *v.* ful.

Blot, *v.* 1. mhèḷo kăr.

2. pus = *l.* obliterate; 'b. out = čittu kāḍ'.

Blot, *s.* čittu, -tā, *n.*

Blotting-paper, *s.* čiṭčeñ kāgād, -gdā, *n.*

Blow, *s.* 1. mār, -rā, *m.*; pēṭ (é), -ṭā, *m.*
2. *fg.* nāṣṭ, -ṭā, *n.* = *l.* loss.

Blow, *v.* 1. funk, *tr.*, *n. v.*
2. ye = *l.* come, *e. g.* vāreñ yetā = wind blows.
3. vāz = *l.* sound.
4. ful = *l.* blossom.

Blow-pipe, *see* **Bellow.**

Blue, *ad.* niḷso *or* nīḷarongātso. *or* nīḷrongātso.

Blue, *s.* niḷso rong, -gā, *m. or* nīḷ, -ḷi, *f.* = *l.* blue colour.

Blunder, *s.* voḍ tsūk, -ki, *f.* = *l.* great mistake.

Blunder, *v.* tsūk.

Blunt, *a.* 1. dhārnātullo = *l.* not sharp, *pr.*, *or* daḍḍo.
2. *fg.* somzāṇātullo = *l.* not understanding; *or* daḍḍo = dull.
3. ăḍadiḍi = roughly frank.

Blush, *v.* loje; lăz; lăz dis-tā.

Bluster, *v.* hāk mār.

Bluster, *s.* hāk, -ki, *f.*

Boa-constrictor, *s.* hār, -rā, *m.*

Boar, *s.* rāndukor, -krā, *m.* = wild swine.

Board, *s.* 1. foḷeñ, -ḷeā, *n.* = *l.* plank.
2. foḷi, -ye, *f.* = black-board.
3. mēz (è), -zā, *n.* = *l.* table.
4. khāṇ, -ṇā, *n.* = *l.* food.
5. dhāzăṇ, -ṇā, *n.* = a body of men, *l.* 10 persons; *or perh.* mēḷ (é), -ḷā, *m.*
6. bāṇi, -ye, *f.* (the rail of a ship); 'go on board a ship = tāruñ tsăḍ *or* tārvār ts.'; 'be on b. a ship = tārvār āsā'.

Boarder, *s.* biḍārgār, -rā, *m.*, *n. c.*; jeuṇāk rāullo = remaining at dinner; 'boarding house = jeuṇāčeñ ghăr, -rā, *n.* = *l.* house of dinner'; 'boarding school = biḍār āsṷlli sāḷ, -ḷe, *f.*'

Boast, *s.* ăbbār, -rā, *n.*

Boast, *v.* 1. ăhănkār kăr *or* ăbbār kăr = *l.* make pride, vanity; băḍāi kăr, *Dat.*
2. ănănd pāu = *l.* reach glory; *with* 1*st Loc.*, *or* thăiñ *e. g.* to mănis grestkāyent *or* grestkāye thăiñ ănănd pāutā = he boasts of riches.

Boat, *s.* dōṇ, -ṇi, *f.*

Boatman, *s.* 1. doṇigār, -rā, *m.* *or* doṇkār, -rā, *m.*
2. kăḍougār, -rā, *m.* (*or* kăḍoukār).

Bodily, *a.* kūḍitso.

Body, *s.* 1. kūḍ, -ḍi, *f.* (*used also for* 'matter'); šărir, -rā, *n.*; āng, -gā, *n.*, *used only in some instances*, *e. g.* 'āngār poḍ = assault'.
2. *fg.* mēḷ(é), -ḷā, *m.* = collection, *or* zomo, -meā, *m.* = multitude.

Bog, *s.* kòḷ, -ḷā, *n.* (*var.* kuḷ, -ḷā, *n.*)

Boil, *v.* 1. sizăi, *c. v. of* siz, *n. v.*; kărpi (*tr.*) *or* kărpā (*n.*) = boil too much; umăḷ, (*n. v.*) *pr.*, *fg.*
2. ukăḍ, *tr.*, *n. v.*; khătkăt, *n. v.*

Boil, *s.* 1. fōḍ, -ḍā, *m.*; făil, -lā, *n.* (bigger); kesoḷi, -ḷe, *f.* (smaller).

Boisterous, *a.* 1. tufānātso *or* vādāḷātso.
2. tănṭălmāri = *l.* turbulent.

Bold, *a.* 1. dhăirāvont = *l.* courageous.
2. hănkārātso *or* gărvi = *l.* proud.
3. khăḍākăḍ (b. in a good sense, resolute).

Boldly, *ad.* dhăirāvont zāun *or* dhăirān.
2. gărvān *etc.*

Boldness, *s.* 1. dhăir, -rā, *n.*
2. (lekā) vorteñ dhăir = *l.* courage above limit.
3. gărv, -vā; *n. or* hănkār, -rā, *m.* = *l.* pride, vanity.

Bolster, *s.* ušeñ, -seā, *n.* (pillow).

Bolt, *s.* 1. khiḷ, -ḷi, *f. Lat. pessulus.*
2. bhāli, -ye, *f.* = *l.* arrow.

Bolt, *v.* khiḷ ghāl.

Bomb, *s.* ujeātso guḷo, -ḷeā, *m.* = *l.* ball of fire (*or* ujeāguḷo).

Bombard, *v.* guḷeāniñ mār = *l.* batter with bombs.

Bombardment, *s.* guḷeāmārneñ, -neā, *n.*, *n. u.*

Bombastic, *a.* hănkārātso = *l.* conceited; dăndi; āunṭi.

Bond, *s.* 1. bānd, -dā, *m.* = *l.* tie.
2. dăstevoz, -zā, *n.* = *l.* deed (legal document).
3. (*in pl.*) băndi, -di, *f.* = prison.

Bondage, *s.* gulāmpoṇ, -ṇā, *n.*

Bone, *s.* hāḍ, -ḍā, *n.*

Bonnet, *s.* topi, -ye, *f.*

Book, *s.* 1. liuru, -rā, *m.*, *fr.*; pustak, -kā, *m.*; grănt, -tā, *m.*, *n. c.*
2. vānṭo, -ṭeā, *m.* = *l.* division.

Bookbinder, *s.* pustaksiuntolo, -leā, *m.*

Bookseller, *s.* pustakviknār, -rā, *m.*

Boon, *s.* deṇeñ, -ṇeā, *n.* = *l.* gift; kurpā, -pe, *f.* = grace; upkār, -rā, *m.* = *l.* benefit.

Boor, *s.* nāḍkār, -rā, *m.* = *l.* villager, *fg.* (uneducated).

Boot, *see* **Shoe.**

Booty, *s.* lūṭ, -ṭi, *f.*

Border, *s.* 1. pònd, -dā, *n.*, *e. g.* of a dress.
2. dēg (è), -ge, *f.*, *e. g.* of a well; kāmb, -bi, *f.* (*H. K.*).
3. găḍ, -ḍi, *f.* = *l.* limit.

Border, *v.* găḍ āsā = *l.* limit is, *ch. cs.*, *e. g.* Canara borders on Malabar = Kanaḍāči găḍ Malabārā kăḍe āsā.

Bore, *v.* top; dompḷo kăr = *l.* make a hole.
2. kărkār kăr = *l.* make trouble.

Bore, *s.* 1. burāk, -kā, *m.* = *l.* hole, *fr.*; dompḷo, -ḷeā, *m.*
2. kărkāri, -riā, *m.* = *l.* botherer.

Borer, *s.* burmo, -meā, *m.*; rum, -mā, *n.*; *see* **Auger.**

Born (Be), zălma; ubza (*used also for the* Divine Son).

Borough, *s.* māg-ṇeñ, -ṇeā, *n.* *strictly*, a village to which other less important villages called 'grāmāñ' are subject).

Borrow, *v.* 1. ušṇo (-ṇi, -ṇeñ) ghe=*l.* take loan, *pr.*, *fg.*, *e.g.* b. words; māgunghe=*l.* asking take.

Borrowing, *s.* ušṇeñ, -ṇeā, *n.*

Bosom, *s.* 1. hărdeñ, -deā, *n.*; kūs, -si, *f.*=*l.* side, *but used also for* bo. *as* Mărieči k.; *in some cases* 'usko' *may be used; yet it mn. ex.* lap.
2. *fg.* 1st *Loc. e.g.* in the bo. of the earth=mātiyent.
'Bo. friend=kāḷzātso išṭ, -ṭā, *m.*'

Botany, *s.* rukzāḍāñvidya, -ye, *f.*=*l.* science of plants.

Botch, *s.* 1. suz, -ji, *f.*=swelling.
2. *fg.* făḍpoši vāur, -rā, *m.*=*l.* clumsy work.

Botch, *v.* făḍpoši kăr.

Both, *pron. con.* 1. dogi (*fem.* dogāiñ, *n.* doniñ).
2. *when it means* 'and' *it is translated by* i (=also) *added to both the connected words.*

Bother, *v.* kărkăr kăr *or* bezār kăr=*l.* make botheration.

Botheration, *s.* kărkăr, *pl. m.*

Bottle, *s.* bòtlụ, -tli, *f.*, *fr.*; sisli, -le, *f.*; siso, -seā, *m.*; ḍăbbo, -beā, *m.* (of leather); ḍăbbi, -be, *f.*

Bottle, *v.* botlint bhor, *e.g.* bo. soro bh.=b. wine.

Bottom, *s.* gunḍi, -ye, *f.* (*or* gunḍāi, -ye, *f.*); pond, -dā, *n.*, *e.g.* bo. of a chest; thăḷ, -ḷā, *n.*; ăḍi, -i, *f.*; thāu, -vā, *n.*
'From the bo. to the top = thăḷā thāun voir legun'; 'he was at the bo. of that plan = to te āločeničeñ kārāṇ'.

Bound, *v.* 1. dóvór=*l.* keep.
2. dāmp=*l.* shut.

Bound, *see* **Limit.**

Boundary, *s.* sărhăddụ, -de, *f.*; găḍ, -ḍi, *f.*; mēr, -re, *f.* (of a field); četurgăḍ, -ḍi, *f.*

Boundless, *a.* găḍnātullo.

Bountiful, *a.* udār.

Bountifully, *ad.* udārpoṇān.

Bounty, *s.* 1. upkār, -rā, *m.*; udārpoṇ, -ṇā, *n.*
2. inām, -mā, *n.*=*l.* reward.

Bouquet, *s.* ghos, -sā, *m.* (fulāntso).

Bow, *v.* 1. *tr.* bāgāi.
2. *n.v.* bāga (*also*, show respect).

Bow, *s.* 1. ārk, -kā, *n. fr.*; gòmprụ, -prā, *m.* (of a church).
2. doṇuñ, -ṇvā, *n.*: 'doṇu poḍlāñ = a rainbow appeared'.
3. găz, -zā, *m.* (of a violin).

Bowels, *s.* 1. ānkiṭi, -ṭe, *f.*, *pr.*
2. *fg.* bităṛleñ, -leā, *n.*=what is inside.

Bower, *s.* moḷo, -ḷeā, *m.* (natural); māṭou, -ṭvā, *m.* (artificial).

Bowl, *s.* kop, -pā, *n.*, *fr.*; vāṭli, -le, *f.* (of metal).

Box, *s.* 1. pēṭ (è), -ṭe, *f.* (chest); kornḍo, -ḍeā, *m.*=a small

round box; bul, -li, *f.* (snuff-box).
2. thāpāḍ, -pḍā, *n.* = slap.

Box, *v.* 1. tāpăi (*vlg.* bizăi = *l.* cause to get wet; *or* udāk piyeunk lāi = *l.* apply to drink water).
2. muṭi mār = *l.* fight with fists.

Boy, *s.* 1. burgo, -geā, *m.*; čeḍo, -ḍeā, *m.* (*esp.* a servant boy).
2. čerko, -keā, *m.* = male, *as opposed to* 'čeḍuñ = female'.

Boyhood, *s.* burgepoṇ, -ṇā, *n.* *or* burgipirāi, -ye, *f.*

Brace, *s.* 1. zōḍ, -ḍā, *m.* = *l.* pair.
2. bānd, -dā, *m.* = *l.* fastening.

Bracelet, *s.* 1. kānkāṇ, -kṇā, *n.* (precious b.)
2. tsuḍo, -ḍeā, *m.* (simple b.)

Brackets, *s.* dāmpče giṭ = *l.* shutting lines, *n. u.*

Brackish, *a.* khārso.

Brad, *s.* māteññātullo khiḷo, -ḷeā, *m.*

Brahmin, *s.* 1. bamăṇ, -mṇā, *m.* (christian B.).
2. bhrāmăṇ = a non-christian B.

Brain, *s.* 1. mendu, -dā, *m.*, *pr. and fg.*, *e.g.* tākā m. nāñ.
2. *fg.* mót, -ti, *f.* = *l.* mind.

Bramble, *s.* kānṭi, -ye, *f.* (thorny plants); kānṭeāzāḍ, -ḍā, *n.*

Bran, *s.* kunḍo, -ḍeā, *m.*

Branch, *s.* khāndo, -deā, *m.* (big), (*dim.* khāndi, -ye, *f.*) *used also fg.* br. of science; fānṭo, -ṭeā, *m.* = small, shooting br.; *var.* phānṭo; tāḷi, -ye, *f.*

Branch, *v.* fānṭe; fānṭe phuṭṭāt.

Brand, *s.* 1. kòlit, -ltā, *n.* = a burnt piece of wood.
2. dāg, -gā, *m.* = a mark made by burning.
3. talvār, -ri, *f.* = sword.

Brand, *v.* dāg ghāl.

Brandish, *v.* hālăi; dălăi.

Brandy, *s.* brānd, -di, *f.*, *fr.*

Brass, *s.* pitul, -tḷi, *f.* (*or* pităḷ).

Brave, *a.* dhăirāvont = courageous; ušār = clever; tsurk = active, *n. c.*; sudăḷ = active.

Brave, *v.* *see* **Affront.**

Bravely, *ad.* dhăirāvont zāun *or* dhăirān.

Bravery, *s.* dhăir, -rā, *n.* = *l.* courage.

Bravo, *int.* 1. šābās (a term of encouragement).
2. kāpās (*signifying* approval, *or ironically*, disapproval).

Brazen, *a.* 1. pitultso (*or* pităḷtso).
2. lăzbānḍo.

Bray, *v.* bób mār.

Breach, *s.* moḍāp, -ḍpā, *n.* = *l.* rupture; dhāḷ, -ḷi, *f.* (*esp.* in a wall); fuṭ, -ṭe, *f.*; yer, -ri, *f.* = small br.

Bread, *s.* 1. unḍo, -ḍeā, *m.* (made of wheat).
2. poḷi, -ye, *f.* = any kind of rice-cakes, *subdivided into:* *a*) poḷo, -ḷeā, *m.* = the usual round rice-bread; *b*) sāndāṇ *or* sānnu, -nā, *n.* = the same as *a.* but boiled; *c*) bibik, -kā, *n.* = the same as *b.* but smaller;

d) pātoḷi, -ḷe, *f.* = a cake covered with a leaf of saffron; *e*) voḍo, -ḍeā, *m.* round cakes, *etc.*

3. bākri, -re, *f.* = any kind of toasted bread.

4. 'pāpḍe' *or* 'pāple' *are of a thin round shape, like hosts, without any rice in them.*

5. *fg.* grās, -sā, *m.* = *l.* food.

Bread-fruit, *s.* divitso (diutso) poṇos, -ṇsā, *m.* = *l.* jack-fruit of Diu.

Breadth, *s.* rundāi, -ye, *f.*

Break, *v.* 1. mōḍ (ó) (*tr.*) *or* moḍ (ò) (*n.*).

2. foḍ, *tr. v.* = *Lat.* '*frange,*' *used of* fragile things, *e.g.* a plate, *also* a plank (*pass.* fuṭ).

3. pīnd, *tr.*, *n. v.* = *l.* tear, rend, *e.g.* clothes.

4. tuṭāi, *c. v. of* tuṭ, *n. v. used when speaking of* ropes *and the like.*

5. suṭāi, *c. v. of* suṭ, *used of* planks *and* breaches in walls, (get loose).

6. *in fg. mn.* mōḍ, *e.g.* b. the force, the order.

7. ăskăt zā = get weak.

B. silence = gărje šivāi ulăi.

B. fast = jinzvār mōḍ; upās mōḍ.

B. rest = soukāsāi pāḍ kăr.

'Day is breaking = uzuāḍ zātā' *or* 'uzuāḍtā'.

B. asunder = kuḍkeān kuḍke kăr.

B. down = mōḍn ghāl.

B. in = sādo kăr, *e.g.* a horse.

B. into = boḷān rig.

B. in pieces = kuḍkeān kuḍke kăr.

B. loose = zā *or* uṭ.

B. off = 1. mōḍ, *e.g.* a marriage; mōḍn kāḍ.

2. rāu = stop.

B. open = foḍ.

B. out = bhāir săr.

B. up = usti, *e.g.* b. up earth; pūḍ kăr.

B. upon = ādāḷ.

B. with = nāi kăr = *l.* make discord.

Break, *s.* āsor, -rā (*or* -srā), *m.* (in the weather).

Breakfast, *s.* 1. nāšṭo, -ṭeā, *m.* = *l.* tiffin; săkāḷinčeñ jevāṇ, -jeuṇā, *n.* = *l.* meal of the morning; ālmăs, -sā, *n.*, *fr.*; *vlg.* pēz (è), -je, *f.* = *l.* conjee.

Breakfast, *v.* nāšṭo kāṇe = *l.* take br.; *see the subst.*; pēz jeu.

Breaking, *s.* moḍāp, -ḍpā, *n. see* **Breach.**

Breast, *s.* 1. hărdeñ, -deā, *n.* *Lat. pectus.*

2. čiuñ, -ve, *f. Lat. uber;* pāno, -neā, *m.* (*ex.* milk given to children); momo, -meā, *m.* (*low word*).

Breath, *s.* 1. usvās, -sā, *m.*

2. dăm *or* dom, -mā, *m.* = *l.* rest, *e.g.* take a little rest.

3. *fg.* jiṇi, -ye, *f.* = *l.* life.

Breathe, *v.* usvās sărtā = *l.* br. goes out.
2. u. soḍ = *l.* leave br.
3. *fg.* soukāsāi kāṇe *or* dăm k. = *l.* take rest; utsăr = *l.* express.
B. in = usvās kāṇe.
B. out = usvās soḍ, *pr.*
B. upon = funk.

Breathless, *a.* 1. usvāsnātullo.
2. mello.

Breeches, *s.* 1. izăr, -rā, *n.*
2. puḍveñ, -veā, *n.* (native br.)
3. *if with a border:* toḍop, -ḍpi, *f.* (native br.)
4. guḍgi, -ge, *f.* (drawers.)

Breed, *v.* 1. zălmăi, *c. v. of* zălmā (*bet. use only* zălmā); gărb sămbāvăi = *l.* conceive; *c. v. of* sămbāva.
2. pos = raise a breed.

Breeding, (good b. = politeness), *s.* măriyāḍ, -di, *f.*

Breeze, *s.* vāreñ, -reā, *n.*
Sea b. = bhăileñ *or* dăryāčeñ v.; land b. = tăḍiye v.

Breviary, *s.* ophis, -phsā, *m.*, *fr.*

Brevity, *s.* moṭvepoṇ, -ṇā, *n.*; sănkṣep, -pā, *n.*, *n.c.*

Bribe, *s.* lonts, -tsā, *m.*: 'take a br. = lon. khā, *l.* eat a br.' *or also* lon. kāṇe = take a br.'

Bribe, *v.* lonts di = give br.

Briber, *s.* lontsāgăr, -rā, *m.*

Brick, *s.* iṭṭo *or* hiṭṭo, -ṭeā, *m.*

Brick-maker, *s.* hiṭṭegăr, -rā, *m.*

Bridal, *s.* kăzăr, -rā, *n.*

Bridal, *a.* kăzărătso.

Bridal-dress, *s.* săḍo, -ḍeā, *m.* (săḍi, -ye, *f.* = common female dress).

Bride, *s.* vokăl, -kle, *f.* (*diff. from* vokăl, -klā, *and* vokil, -kilā); tsăli, -ye, *f.* = *l.* girl, *fg.* (*H. K. esp.*)

Bridegroom, *s.* nouro, -reā, *m.* horet, -tā, *m.*; tsălo, -leā, *m.* = *l.* boy.

Bridge, *s.* sānkou, -kvā, *m.*; pāmpāḷeñ, -ḷeā, *n.* (small, of logs of wood, *etc.*)

Bridle, *s.* lăgām, -mā, *n.* = *Lat. frenum.*

Brief, *a.* moṭvo.

Brief, *s.* 1. sănkṣep, -pā, *n.* = *l.* abridgment.
2. nămbrăčeñ sănkṣep, -pā, *n.*

Brier, *see* **Bramble.**

Brigade, *s.* foujivānṭo, -ṭeā, *m.*

Brigadier, *s.* foujivānṭeāčeñ mostak, -kā, *n.*

Brigand, *see* **Bandit.**

Bright, *a.* 1. părzăḷik; nităḷ = *l.* pure, clean.
2. bărik = *l.* witty.

Brighten, *v.* 1. părzăḷ, *n. v.*
2. părzăḷăi, *c. v.*

Brightness, *s.* 1. uzvăḍ, -ḍā, *m.* = *l.* light; părzăḷăi, -ye, *f.* *or* părzăḷ, -ḷā, *m.* = *l.* splendour; prăkăš, -šā, *m.*, *n. c.*

Brilliant, *see* **Bright.**

Brim, 1. dēg(è), -ge, *f.* of a precipice.
2. kănṭ, -ṭā, *m.*, *e.g.* of a vessel; 'up to the br. = kănṭ păriyānt'.

Brine, *s.* khār udāk, -dkā, *n.* = *l.* salt water.

Bring, *v.* 1. hāḍ *or* āḍ; vāvoi = *l.* cause to flow; *but used also for* 'carry.'
2. vór.
B. up (educate) = vāḍăi.
Often cs. must be changed, e.g. b. a man to an opinion = somzăi.
B. about = kărăi, *c. v., e.g.* b. a. peace = sollo kărăi, *or* kārāṇ āsā = is cause; tirsi = conclude, finish.
B. back = paṭi hāḍ.
B. before = mukār ghāl.
B. down = săkal vor.
B. forth = 1. bāḷānt zā, *Acc.*; porsut zā, *Acc.*
2. bhāir kāḍ = *l.* take out.
3. di.
B. out = bhāir vor.

Brinjal, *s.* vāingeñ, -geā, *n.*

Brink, *s.* dēg(è), -ge, *f.*

Brisk, *a.* tsurk.

Broad, *a.* vistārlolo = *l.* extended; [rund.

Broil, *s.* zăgḍeñ, -ḍeā, *n.*

Broker, *s.* dălāl, -lā, *m*; *see* **Interpreter.**

Bronze, *s.* kāšeñ, -šeā, *n.*; (*approximately*) păntslāuñ, -lāvā, *n.* = a mixture of five metals.

Bronze, *a.* kāšeātso.

Brooch, *s.* 1. motiñ, -tiyā, *n.* = *l.* pearl.
2. kānṭo, -ṭeā, *m.* (māteātso), *i. e.* hair and head-dress pins.

Brood, *s.* 1. pilāntso hinḍ, -ḍā, *m.* = *l.* a flock of little ones.
2. *fg.* săntăt, -ti, *f.* = *l.* posterity, *or* kuṭām, -ṭmā, *n.* = *l.* family.

Brood, *v.* 1. rovāṇeñ bos.
2. *fg.* niyāḷ = *l.* meditate.

Brook, *s.* vāḷ, -ḷā, *m.*

Broom, *s.* sāruṇ, -ṇe, *f.*

Broth, *s.* kāld, -dā, *m.* = *Lat. jus, fr.*; kăsāi, -yā, *m.*

Brothel, *s.* čeḍiyāñghăr, -rā, *n.*

Brother, *s.* bhāu, -āvā, *m.*: 'elder brother = bāb'; 'bāb' *is the form used when addressing him*; 'younger brother = dākṭo bhāu'.

Brother-in-law, *s.* meuṇo (*or* miuṇo), -ṇeā, *m., used only to denote the relationship of* br.-in-law; bāvoji, -ji, *m., term of address*; kugnād, -dā, *m. not generally used.*

Brotherly (love), *a.* moya (mog).

Brow, *s.* āsḍi, -ḍe, *f.* = eye-brow.
2. kopāl, -lā, *n.* = *l.* forehead.

Browbeat, *v.* besṭāi.

Brown, *v.* kāḷso.

Browse, *v.* khā.

Bruise, *v.* vāṭ (by grinding); dāḍāi (*in any way except by grinding*); mār.

Bruise, *see* **Contusion.**

Brush, *s.* 1. brus, -sā, *m., fr.*
2. kăpāi, -ye, *f.* (for bullocks).

Brush, *v.* dūḷ kāḍ = *l.* take away the dust; pus.

Brutal, *a.* niṣṭur = *l.* cruel; monzātitso = *l.* of beasts: mhāru = *l.* cruel; rānvoṭ = *l.* wild.

Brutality, *s.* niṣṭurāi, -ye, *f.*; monzātipoṇ, -ṇā, *n.*; mhārupoṇ, -ṇā, *n.*; rānuoṭkāi, -ye, *f.*; *see adj.*

Brutally, *ad.* niṣṭurāyen; monzāti bări *or* monzātiče jinsiñ.

Brute, *s.* monzāt, -ti, *f.*

Bubble, *s.* fōḍ, -ḍā, *m.*

Buck, *s.* (male of certain animals). *If the English word have no special Konkani equivalent,* 'dādlo' *may be used; see* Gram. p. 47.

Bucket, *s.* koḷso, -seā, *m.*, *dim.* koḷsulo; sidi, -di, *f.*

Bud, *s.* kȍḷo, -ḷeā, *m.*; bongo, -geā, *m.*; ānkri, -re, *f.*

Bud, *v.* bongo fuṭṭā.

Budget, *s.* lēk(è), -kā, *n.* (sărkārāčeñ) = *l.* account (of the state).

Buffalo, *s.* reḍo, -ḍeā, *m.*, *fem.* mosụ, -si, *f.*

Buffet, *v.* muṭi mār = *l.* beat with b.

Buffoon, *s.* nāḍgo, -geā, *or* nāḍigār, -rā, *m.*

Bug, *s.* bikoṇ, -kṇā, *m.*

Bugbear, *s.* biyānkuḷāi, -ye, *f.* *mn.* frightening thing.

Build, *v.* 1. bānd.

2. *fg.* pātiye = *l.* trust, *2nd Loc.*

Building, *s.* bāndāp, -dpā, *n.* = edifice; ghăr, -rā, *n.* = house; bănglo, -leā, *m.* = palace; bāndāvoḷ, -ḷi, *f.*

Bulk, *s.* mukhya = *l.* main; *see* **Trunk, Size.**

Bull, *s.* 1. pāḍo, -ḍeā, *m.*: 'small b. = pāḍko, -keā, *m.*'

2. govo, -veā, *m.* = wild bull, bison.

3. *fg.* nākāzālli văstụ, -tu, *f.* = *l.* nonsensical thing.

4. Bull (of the Pope) = (Pāp Sāibāčeñ) tirpā kāgād, -gdā, *n.*

Bullock, *s.* 1. boil, -lā, *m.*

2. pāḍo, -ḍeā, *m.* = a young b. *or* a rather large calf.

Bully, *a.* 1. lăḍāi kărtso = *l.* quarrelling.

2. tănṭălmāri = *l.* turbulent.

Bulwark, *s.* pāgār, -rā, *m.*; koṭeñ, -ṭeā, *n.* = *l.* castle; rākčeñ bāndāp, -dpā, *n.* = *l.* defending building.

Bunch (of fruits), *s.* ghós, -sā, *m.*; *see also* **Bundle.**

Bundle, *s.* 1. poṭli, -le, *f.* (of clothes *and the like*).

2. gānṭ, -ṭi, *f.* = *l.* knot, *fg. used for* b. of money.

3. mouḷi, -ḷe, *f.*, *e.g.* b. of firewood.

4. kāṭ, -ṭā, *m.* = *l.* pack.

5. bhoro, -reā, *m.* (*the same as* 'kāṭ'); borkuṭi, -ṭe, *f.*

Bungle, *v.* 1. făḍpoši kăr = *l.* do clumsily.

2. tsūk = *l.* mistake.

Buoy, *v.* thirăi = *l.* cause to be firm, *or bet.* thir kăr; kāḍn dor.

Buoyancy, *s.* hāḷvāi (?), -ye, *f.* =lightness.

Burden, *s.* vojeñ, -jeā, *n.* = *l.* load, cargo.
2. beroz, -zā, *m.* = *l.* tax.
3. vozăn, -nā, *n.* = capacity of a ship.
4. *fg.* ākānt, -tā, *m.* = anxiety; kărkăr, -rā, *m.* = trouble.

Burden, *v.* 1. bhor = *l.* load.
2. *fg.* dăgdăi = *l.* oppress.

Burdensome, *a.* kărkărātso = *l.* annoying, troublesome.

Burial, *s.* mórn, -nā, *n.*; nikṣep, -pā, *n. ol.*; purāp, -rpā, *n. ol.*

Burlesque, *a.* hāstso.

Burn, *v.* 1. lās, *tr. and n. v., it mn. also* injure by fire; ujeānt ghāl = put into fire.
2. zăḷ, *n. v., mn.* be alight.
3. *fg.* zăḷ = *l.* burn, *e.g.* rāgān zăḷ = burn with anger; mor = *l.* die, *e.g.* āsen mor = die out of desire; bhorlā = has been filled, *e.g.* durguṇān = with passion (*in a bad mn.*)

Burning (taste), *n.* kār, -rā, *m.*

Burrow, *s.* fănjer, -rā, *n.*; dol, -li, *f.*

Burst, *v.* foḍ (*pass. and n.* fuṭ); soḍ (*pass.* suṭ = be disjoined); *see* **Break.**

Bury, *v.* pūr; mātiyek pāvoi = *l.* cause to arrive to earth; nikepi, *ol. rl.*

Bush. *s.* 1. kānṭi, -ye, *f.* (thorny plant).
2. boleñ, -leā, *n.*

Bushel, *s.* 1. kăḷsi, -se, *f.*
2. ser = $\frac{1}{14}$ of kăḷsi; *see Appendix.*

Business, 1. kām, -mā, *n., a very common word, used very broadly; e.g. for* office, employment, duty, *etc.*

Bust, *s.* runḍ, -ḍā, *n.*

Busy (Is), kāmār (āsā) = *l.* (is) on work; *or* tākā kām āsā = *l.* to him is business.

But, *prep. conj.* 1. šivāi *or* khărit, *postp.* = *l.* except.
2. puṇ = *Lat. sed*; părānt.
3. băgār, *used antithetically, e.g.* not only, but...
4. mātrụ = only.
5. *often omitted, chiefly if equivalent in Lat. to* '*sed*', '*at*'.
6. *In the sentence* 'there is hardly a day but he comes', *and the like, ch. cs. chiefly by using the neg. ger. in* 'ānāñ'; *see in the 3rd Appendix of the* Gram. 'Quin'.

N. B. The English 'but' *frequently cannot be translated by* 'sed': *in such cases, except where* 'šivāi' *may be used, the form of the sentence should be changed, and some other conjunction employed.*

Butcher, *s.* kăsāi, -yā, *m. or* kăsāigār, -rā, *m.*

Butler, *s.* mezātsākor, -krā, *m.*

Butter, *s.* 1. tūp, -pā, *n.* (melted and then preserved; ghee).
2. loṇiñ, -yā, *n.* (not melted).

Butterfly, *s.* pisoḷeñ, -ḷeā, *n.*

Buttermilk, *s.* tāk, -kā, *n.*
Button, *v.* butāuñ ghāl.
Button, *s.* butāuñ, -tāvā, *m. fr.*; gubbi, -be, *f.*
Button-hole, *s.* kāz, -zā, *n.*
Buy, *v.* molāk kāṇe = *l.* take at price.
Buyer, *s.* molāk kāṇetolo.
By, *prep.* 1. *by Instr. e.g.* higher by a foot.
2. lāgiñ = *l.* near, close.
3. *Dat. or Acc. or Or., if used with expressions of time (e.g.* by the ides of April).
4. pāsun (in adjurations) = *l. Lat. propter; see* Grammar Syntax. Instrument.
By the bye, *ad.* voilebar.
By and by, thoḍeñ-thoḍeñ.

C

Cabal, *s.* tănḍ, -ḍā, *m.* = *l.* faction; *or* kuṭ, -ṭā, *n.* = *l.* plot.
Cabbage, *s.* kob, -bi (*or* -be), *f.*
Cabin, *s.* tārvāči, koṭri, -re, *f.* = *l.* a bed-place, a berth, *n. c.*
Cabinet, *s.* 1. (dākṭeñ) kuḍ, -ḍā, *n.* = (small) room.
2. dhāzăṇ, -ṇā, *n., e.g.* ca. of a kingdom; măntriñsăbha, -bhẹ, *f.* = council of ministers.
Cable, *s.* ālāt, -tā, *m.*
Cacophony, *s.* pāḍ tāḷo, -ḷeā, *m.* = *l.* bad sound; *bet.* pāḍ vāzāp, -zpā, *n.*
Cadence, *s.* poḍneñ, -neā, *n. or* deuṇeñ, -ṇeā, *n.* (tāḷeāčeñ po.), *or bet.* -poḍāp, -ḍpā, *n.*
Cadet, *s.* dākṭo put, -tā, *m.*
Cadjan, *s.* mòḍăl, -ḍlā, *n.*
Cage, *s.* pāndro, -reā, *m.* (*Lat. cavea*); guḍ, -ḍā, *m.*; *chiefly,* c. for beasts.
Cajole, *v.* fuslāi.
Cake, *s.* 1. bākri, -re, *f.* = toasted bread; roṭṭi, -ṭe, *f.*; poḷi, -ye, *f.* (*general name for all* rice cakes). [cake).
2. ból, -lā, *m.* (*a kind of* coarse
3. pātoḷi, -ḷe, *f.*
Calamity, *s.* kăṣṭ, -ṭāñ, *pl. m.*; ăpād, -dā, *m.* (apāt?); ākānt, -tā, *m.*; dăgd, -dā, *m.* (*used in pl.*); vig-nụ, -nā, *n.*
Calculate, *v.* 1. lēk(è) = *l.* count; lēk(è) kăr = *l.* make the account.
2. āločen kăr = *l.* make consideration, take into con.
3. riyāt kăr = take into (kind) consideration (*l.* make favorable attention).
Calculation, *s.* 1. lēk (è), -kā, *n.*
2. riyāt, -ti, *f.* = (favorable) attention: 'āuñ tuji riyāt măgtāñ = please take into your kind consideration'.

Caldron, *s.* 1. kăḍāi, -ye, *f.* 2. hānḍo, -ḍeā, *m.* (*of the larger sort*).

Calendar, *s.* 1. pănčăng, -gā, *n.* 2. păṭṭi, -ṭe, *f.* = list.

Calf, *s.* 1. vāsruñ, -srā, *n.* = very small calf. 2. pāḍo, -ḍeā, *m.* = male calf; pāḍi, -ye, *f.* 3. *fg.* daḍḍo = *l.* stupid, *or* reḍo.

Calibre, *s.* 1. rundāi, -ye, *f.* breadth, *e.g.* of a gun. 2. *fg.* somzikāi, -ye, *f.* = *l.* understanding.

Caligraphy, *s.* (sobit) bărāp, -rpā, *n.*

Call, *v.* 1. āpoi (summon); ulo kăr = give a call, invoke, call upon. 2. moṇ (by name): 'tumiñ ākā kiteñ moṇtāt = what do you call this?'

C. aside, *v.* vingăḍ dóvór = *l.* keep aside.

C. away, *v.* kāḍ.

C. on, *v.* bheṭ = *l.* visit.

Calling, *s.* 1. āpouṇeñ, -ṇeā, *n.*; ulo, -leā, *m.* 2. bhes, -sā, *m.* = vocation.

Callosity, *see* **Corn.**

Calm, *a.* 1. nidān (quiet); thănḍ = *l.* cold, *fg.*; soukāsāyetso = *l.* of peace.

Calm, *s.* soukāsāi, -ye, *f.* (*also for* c. of the sea); sămādhān, -nā, *n.* nidānāi, -ye, *f.*

Calm, *v.* *expressed by the adj. with* kăr; *see* **Allay.**

Calmly, *ad.* soukāsāyen *or* nidānāyen.

Caloric, *s.* uzo, -jeā, *m.* = *l.* fire; *or* ujeātso ărămb, -bā, *m.* = origin of fire, *or* gărmetso ărămb, *or only* gărmi, -me, *f.*

Calumniate, *v.* 1. tsāḍio săng = *l.* say detractions; bădlām ghāl = *l.* put calumnies; b. ghe = get calumnies; ninda kăr = *l.* make c.; ăprād ghāl, *Prs. 2nd Locat.*

Calumny, *s.* tsāḍi, -ye, *f.*; ninda, -de, *f.*; bădlām, -me, *f.* (*exactly* calumny); ăprād, -dā, *m.* (*var.* uprād).

Camel, *s.* kăreñ, -reā, *n.*

Camp, *s.* kāmp, -pā, *n.*, *fr.*; măidān, -nā, *n.* = *l.* plain.

Camphor, *s.* kāpur, -rā, *m.*

Can, *v.* (mākā) tānktā, *Dat. Prs.* *or* tānk āsā = *l.* is ability; *expressed by the pot. mood; see* Gram. Verb P. II. IV.

Often ch. cs., e.g. I cannot but exclaim = bob mārn sāngizāi, *or* bob mārn sānginăstanāñ rāunk nozo.

Canal, *s.* tōḍ, -ḍā, *m.*

Canary-bird, *s.* kanaričeñ sukṇeñ, -ṇeā, *n.*

Cancel, *v.* 1. măr, *e.g.* in writing. 2. *fg.* răddu pāḍsi, *or* răddu kăr = c. an order, *l.* annul.

Cancer, *s.* mānpuḷi, -ye, *f.* (disease). 2. kurli, -le, *f.* = crab.

Candid, *a.* sādo = *l.* simple; nīz = *l.* sincere; niškăpṭi, *from* niš *and* kăpăṭ; mōskărnātullo = *l.* not deceiving.

Candidate, *s.* umeduār, -rā, *m.* (*ex.* volunteer).

Candidly, *ad.* nīz zāun *or* sādeñ *or* sādo zāun.

Candle, *s.* vāt, -ti, *f.* *or fully*, meṇāči vāt.

Candlemas-day, *s.* vāti benjār kărtso dis, -sā, *m.* = *l.* day (on which) candles are blessed.

Candlestick, *s.* kastisăl, -lā, *n.*

Cane, *s.* 1. čivo, -veā, *m.* (*ex.* reed); boḍi, -ye, *f.* (*ex.* stick); bèt, -tā, *n.* (*ex.* stick); ròt, -tā, *n.*, *fr.*

Canister, *s.* 1. kornḍo, -ḍeā, *m.*
 2. *see* **Basket.**

Cannibal, *a.* mănšakhāugi (*or* khāuni).

Cannon, *s.* nāḷ, -ḷi, *f.* 'c. ball = nāḷitso guḷo, -ḷeā, *m.*'; 'charge a c. = nāḷ bhor'; 'let off a c. = nāḷ mār, *l.* beat a c.', *or* 'fār mār = *l.* beat a shoot'.

Canoe, *s.* dōṇ, -ṇi, *f.*

Canon, *s.* 1. kānun, -nā, *n.* = law; kāido, -deā, *m.* = rule.
 2. kaneg, -gā, *m.* *or* kānungār, -rā, *m.*, *or as some say*, konik, -kā, *m.* (*Lat. canonicus*).

Canonization, *s.* sānt moṇčeñ, *n. u.*

Canonize, *v.* 1. bhāgevont moṇ pāsār; sānt moṇ.

Canopy, *s.* pāl, -li, *f.*

Cantharides, *s.* foḍ kāḍtso mus, -sā, *m.*

Canticle, *s.* kăntig, -ge, *f.* (sacred).

Cantonment, *s.* čāvăṇi, -ṇe, *f.* (paṭlāmiči), *n. c.*; *vlg.* bārak, -kā, *n.*

Canvas, *s.* 1. daḍḍeñ lugāṭ, -gṭā, *n.* = *l.* coarse cloth.
 2. siḍ, -ḍā, *n.* = *l.* sail.

Cap, *s.* 1. topi, -ye, *f.*
 2. kēp (è), -pā, *n.* (gun-cap), *fr.*

Capability, *see* **Capacity.**

Capable, *a.* trāṇ āsullo (*bet. rs.*; *or*) zānṭo = clever; šăktivont = able.

Cape, *s.* dărnitso muḷo, -ḷeā, *m.*

Capacity, *s.* 1. māp, -pā, *n.*, *e.g.* c. of a vessel.
 2. trāṇ, -ṇā, *n.*; tānk, -ki, *f.* = *l.* ability (*Lat. facultas*); săkăt, -kti, *f.*

Capillary, *a.* bhou ăšir = *l.* very narrow; *sometimes* bhou ăšir năḷiyetso.

Capital, *a.* 1. mukhya = principal.
 2. mornātso = *l.* of death.
 3. uttim = *l.* excellent.
 4. voḍlo = *l.* great (c. letter).

Capital, *s.* 1. (chief town), *perhaps*, poileñ šer *or* mukhya šer, -rā, *n.*
 2. (in money) gāṇṭ, -ṭi, *f.* = (a petty sum), *l.* knot; *it being a custom here to carry money in a knot of the handkerchief;* punji, -je, *f.* = *l.* heap (of money).

3. ăsăl, -slā, *n.* (*in connexion with* vāḍ = interest).
4. c. of a pillar = māteñ, -teā, *n.* = *l.* head.

Capitulate, *v.* āpṇāk vopsun di = *l.* surrender, consign thyself.

Caprice, *s.* vāiṭ mărji, -je, *f.*

Capricious, *a.* 1. thirnātullo, *ex.* not constant.
2. vāiṭ mărjetso.

Capriciously, *ad.* thirnāstanāñ; vāiṭ mărjen *etc.*

Captain, *s.* kopit, -tā, *m.* (of soldiers, of a ship); mostăk, -kā, *n.* = *l.* head; nāyak, -kā, (*also* c. of a ship); tānḍel, -lā, *m.* (of a pattimar); mālim, -mā, *m.*, *e.g.* of a ship.

Captious. *a.* mosātso (*from* mōs = deceit).

Captivate, *v.* 1. pisăi *or* piso kăr = *l.* make mad, *fg.*
2. bhulăi = charm. [attraction.
3. voḍniñ hāḍ, *G. N.* = *l.* bring
4. món voi kăr = conciliate, *l.* make heart yes.

Captive, *s.* băndivan, -nā, *m.*; gulām, mā, *m.* = slave.

Captivity, *s.* gulāmpoṇ, -ṇā, *n.*; băndi, -di, *f.*

Capture, *s.* 1. dărneñ, -neā, *n.* *or bet.* dhărāp, -rpā, *n.*
2. pāg-ṇeñ, -ṇeā, *n.* (c. of fishes), *or* pāgāp, -gpā, *n.* = draught.

Car, *s.* bănḍi, -ye, *f.*; sărāṭ, -ṭā, *n.*; răth, -thā, *m.* (*used for parading an idol on certain occasions*).

Caravan, *s.* poiṇāreāñmēḷ(é), -ḷā, *m.* = *l.* assemblage of travellers. [cious stone).

Carbuncle, *s.* kèmp, -pā, *n.* (pre-

Carcass, *see* Corpse.

Card, *s.* 1. dāṭ kāgād, -gdā, *n.* = *l.* thick paper.
2. čiṭ, -ṭi, *f.* (*mn.* ticket).
3. kāgād (playing card): 'play cards = kāgdāñ khéḷ' *or*, *if for money*, 'k. jugār kheḷ'.

Cardinal, *a.* mukhya.

Cardinal, *s.* kārdiāl, -lā, *m.*, *fr.*; igărjevaṭo, -ṭeā, *m.*, *n. u.*

Care, *s.* 1. zătān, -tne, *f.*, *e. g.* of a charge *or* trust; tsătrăi, -ye, *f.* = attention, observation; zāgrutăi, -ye, *f.* = being awake.
2. husko, -keā, *m.* = anxiety, *Lat. sollicitudo.*
3. lăkša, -še, *f.*: 'I don't care = lăkša kărinañ, *or* voḍnăiñ'.
4. bezārăi, -ye, *f.* = *l.* anxiety.
5. zogasāṇ, -ṇe, *f.* *or* zogeñ, -geā, *n.*; porva, -ve, *f.*

Care, *v.* 1. *one of the above nouns with* kāṇe *or* kāṇghe *or* kăr; partiboḷ (*bet.* prătipāḷ) kăr, *or* harbār kāṇe, *e. g.* take care of children; părveša kăr.
2. āḍn (āṇ) di = *l.* bringing give, provide.

Career, *s.* 1. *pr.* dāuñ, -ve, *f.*
2. *fg.* jiṇi, -ye, *f.* = life, *or also*, dāuñ, *or* bhes, -sā, *m.* = state of life.

Careful, *a.* 1. zāgrut = *l.* attentive, awake.
2. budivont = *l.* prudent.
3. *One of the nouns given under* 'care' *with* a participle.
4. sārko = *l.* exact; *ad.* sārkeñ.

Careless, *a.* 1. bepārvi = *l.* negligent; tsătrāinātųllo.
2. fădpoši = good for nothing, clumsy.
3. *One of the* nouns *given under* 'care' *with* 'nātųllo'.

Caress, *v.* 1. fuslāi, *pr.* (as a mother caresses her child); prītkăr = *l.* love; bhulăi (*in bad mn.*)

Caress, *s.* fuslāuṇeñ, -ṇeā, *n.*

Cargo, *s.* vojeñ, -jeā, *n.* (*or* vozăn, -nā, *n.*)

Caricature, *s.* năkăl, -klā, *n.* = *l.* copy, *fg.*

Carious, *a.* pokăḷ = *l.* hollow.

Carmel, *s.* karmiṇ, -ṇi, *f.*; 'karmiṇiči bentiṇ, -ṇi, *f.* = scapular of M. C.

Carminative, *a.* haḷuāyetso *or* haḷuāi kărtso.

Carnal, *a.* kuḍitso = *l.* of body, *e.g.* c. pleasure.

Carnival, *s.* *approximately*, khéḷ, -ḷā, *m.* = *l.* play; sigmo, -meā, *m.*; intruz, -zā, *m.*; domingord, -dā, *m.*, *fr.*

Carol, *s.* ănănd gāyān, -nā, *n.* = *l.* hymn of praise.

Carousal, *s.* khāugipoṇ, -ṇā, *n.*

Carpenter, *s.* āčāri, -riā, *m.* = *ex.* workman; sutāri, -riā, *m.*; băḍgi, -giā, *m.*, *n. c.*; băḍāi, -yā, *m.*, *n. c.*

Carpet, *s.* 1. jemkān *or* zămkāṇ, -ṇā, *n.* tivāsi, -se, *f.* (fine woollen c.).
2. sumbāči māndri, -re, *f.* = *l.* mat of coir.

Carriage, *s.* 1. gāḍi, -ye, *f.* (gaaḍi).
2. *fg.* mol, -lā, *n.* = *l.* price (of conveying).
3. năḍteñ, -teā, *n.* = *l.* demeanour.

Carry, *s.* vor; vāvoi.
C. away = kăḍ *or* kāḍn vor.
C. back = pāṭi ghāl.
C. forward = mukār tsălăi = *l.* cause to go on, *e.g.* the sacrifice.
C. off = kăḍ.
C. out = 1. pāḷ; 2. kāḍn vor.
C. on = tsălăi.

Cart, *s.* 1. bănḍi, -ye, *f.*
2. tēr(é), -rā, *m.* (*the car used for parading an idol on certain occasions*).

Carve, *v.* 1. kāntăi.
2. kātārn vānṭ = *l.* cutting distribute.

Carver, *s.* guḍgār, -rā, *m.* (*ex.* turner); *sometimes* 'āčāri = *l.* carpenter' *is met with in this sense.*

Carving, *s.* 1. kāntounči sāmārthi, -rthe, *f.*
2. kāntouṇeñ, -ṇeā, *n.*

Cascade, *s.* udkāpoḍāp, -ḍpā, *n.*

Case, *s.* 1. fór, -rā, *m.* (covering); poteñ, -teā, *n.*, *e. g.* of a

sword, scabbard; gousaṇi, -ṇe, *f.* (pillow c.)
2. stiti, -ti, *f.* = condition; *bet. rs.*
3. nămbăr, -brā, *n.* (*e.g.* in the court), *fr.*; vyājyụ, -jyā, *n.*
4. bāb, -be, *f.* = a doubt, a case of conscience.
In case (if perhaps) = păkšek, *used as Postp.*; *see* Gram.
'Tākā nămbăr guṇ (*or* ăuguṇ) zāleñ = the case was decided for (*or* against) him, *l.* to him the case favourable (*or* unfavourable) became'.

Casern, *s.* bărkăs, -sā, *n.*

Cash, *s.* năgdi duḍu, -ḍvā, *m.* = *l.* ready money; bāndụllo duḍu = *l.* bound money, *n. c.*; năgăd, -gdi, *f.*

Cash-book, *s.* lekāčeñ pustak, -kā, [*n.*

Cashew, *s.* kāẓ, -zu, *f.*

Cashier, *s.* mutsudi, -di, *m.*, (matsudi?)

Cashier, *v.* 1. bărtărāp kăr = deprive, *e.g.* of an office.
2. nāš kăr = ruin.

Cask, *s.* pīp, -pā, *n.*

Cassock, *s.* lōb, -bā, *m.*, *fr.*; pāyāngoḷ văstur, -rā, *n.*

Cast, *v.* 1. uḍăi *or* kāḍn uḍăi.
2. soḍ = *l.* leave (suffer to fall).
3. ghāl = *l.* put.
C. down the eyes = doḷe săkal kăr = *l.* make down.
C. out = soḍăi, *e.g.* devils; bhāir ghāl = put out.
C. down, deject = dukăi = *l.* cause to feel pain, sorrow.

Caste, zăt, -ti, *f.*; kuḷi, -ye, *f.* (*or* kul, -lā, *n.*); vorg, -gā, *m.* = *l.* class (*approx.*)

Castle, *s.* koṭeñ, -ṭeā, *n.*

Castor, *s.* (a plant) yenḍi, -ḍe, *f.* (*var.* yerunḍi, -ḍi, *f.*)
C. oil = yerunḍičeñ tēl(è) *or* jenḍičeñ tēl(è) *or only* tēl, -lā, *n. or more comm.* yenḍel tēl.

Casual, *a.* aučit; grātstsārātso; *see* **Accidental.**

Casually, *ad.* āpšents; grātstsārān; aučit.

Cat, *s.* 1. māzār, -zrā, *n.*
2. bokul, -klā, *m*, (male c.)

Cataclysm, *s.* 1. āur, -rā, *n.* = inundation; buḍtugāl, -lā, *n.*

Catacomb, *s.* 1. buyār, -rā, *n.* (*Lat. spelunca*).
2. pātāḷ, -ḷā, *n.* (subterraneous place).

Catafalque, *s.* yes, -se, *f.*

Catalogue, *s.* păṭṭi, -ṭe, *f.* = *l.* list.

Cataract, *s.* udkapoḍāp, -ḍpā, *n.* = *l.* waterfall.

Catastrophe, *s.* 1. sevȯṭ, -ṭā, *m.* = *l.* issue.
2. ădrušṭ, -ṭā, *n.* = misfortune.

Catch, *v.* dhăr, *e.g.* fishes; pāg, *e.g.* fishes.
2. sāmpăḍăi *or* sāmpḍăi, *e.g.* to entrap a person, to c. him in words, *Lat. capere in verbo*; 'dhăr' *is used also for* 'receive'.
'I caught a cold = mākā thănḍ zāleñ'. C. fire = uzo lāg.

Catching, *s.* 1. pāgṇeñ, -ṇeā, *n.* *or* pāgāp, -gpā, *n.* (of fishes). 2. dhărneñ, -neā, *n.* *or* dhărāp, -rpā, *n.*

Catechism, *s.* *vlg.* katekism *or* katesism, -mā, *m.*, *fr.*; dotorn, -ni, *f.* = *Lat. doctrina*, *fr.*

Catechist, *s.* upadesi, -si, *m.*; dotorn sikăitolo.

Catechize, *v.* dotorn sikăi = *l.* teach doctrine; (*sometimes* 'sikăi' *by itself will be found enough*).

Catechumen, *s.* kristāuñ zăuntso.

Categorical, *a.* khănḍit = *l.* positive.

Cathedral, *s.* sāči-igrăz; sădreigărz, -ji, *f.* = *l.* church of chair.

Catholic, *a.* kătholik; sărvu̥ thăiñ vistārlolo *or* săgḷeān v.

Catholicism, *s.* kristāvānčeñ (kătholik) šāstru̥, -trā, *n.*

Cattle, *s.* goruñ, -rvā, *n.* (*or* gordān, -nā, *n.*, *old*).

Causality, *s.* kărčeñ, -čeā, *n.*

Causative, *a.* kărtso.

Cause, *s.* 1. kāraṇ, -ṇā, *n.* 2. nămbăr, -brā, *n.* (legal suit), *fr.*; vyājyu̥, -jyā, *n.* 3. kām, -mā, *n.* = affair.

Cause, *v.* kāraṇ di *or* kāraṇ zā = *l.* give cause *or* become cause; kăr = *l.* do; *expressed by the caus. form of the dependent verb; see* Gram. P. II *ch.* iv.

Caustic, *a.* 1. lāstolo. 2. *fg.* koḍu *or* dukountso.

Caustic, *s.* lāščeñ vokāt, -ktā, *n.*; lāstso fātor, -trā, *m.* = burning stone.

Cauterize, *v.* lās = *l.* burn, *or* lonkḍān lās.

Caution, *s.* bud, -di, *f.* = *l.* prudence, wisdom, advice; zāgrutāi, -ye, *f.* = *l.* attention.

Caution, *v.* bud sāng = *l.* say advice. 2. kăḷăi = *l.* make known (warn).

Cautious, *a.* budivont; zāgrut.

Cautiously, *ad.* budin, *or* zāgrutāyen.

Cavalry, *s.* trupsăvār, -rā, *n.*, *fr.*; goḍeasăvār, -rā, *n.*

Cave, *s.* dhol, -li, *f.*; buyār, -rā, *n.* = *Lat. spelunca*; māṭeñ, -ṭeā, *n.*

Cavil, *v.* 1. ninda ghāl = *l.* put calumny. 2. muḍnāi kăr = *l.* make frivolous objection, sophism.

Cavil, *s.* muḍnāi, -ye, *f.* (*or* -yā, *m.*)

Caviller, *s.* muḍnāyeli, -liā, *or* muḍnāi kărtolo.

Cease, *v.* thāmb; soḍ = *l.* leave; kābār zā = *l.* finish *or* be finished; tirsā; mugdā = come to an end; mănna kăr, *e.g.* God ceased to work on the 7th day; rāu = *l.* stop; năpăints zā = *l.* disappear.

Cedar, *s.* deudār, -rā, *m.*

Cede, *v.* soḍun di, *tr.* = *l.* leaving give, (give up); *see* **Yield.**

Ceiling, *s.* 1. māḷo, -ḷeā, *m.* (*strictly*, loft *or* garret).

Celebrate, *v.* 1. părgăṭzāun hogoḷsi = *l.* praise publicly; pāsār (*or* pātsār), *e. g.* c. the virtue of. . . .
2. kăr, *e.g.* c. a feast; tsălăi, *e.g.* a feast.

Celebrated, *a.* nāvāḍgo = *l.* of name; voḍ = great.

Celebration, *s.* 1. părgăṭ hogḷāp, -pā, *n.* = *l.* public praise.
2. *for* c. of a feast *rs. into v.*

Celebrity, *s.* ănănd, -dā, *m.* = *l.* glory; kirt, -ti, *f.*

Celerity, *s.* jerurāi, -ye, *f.*

Celestial, *a.* sărgintso.

Celibacy, *s.* ānkuārpoṇ, -ṇā, *n.*

Cell, *s.* dākṭeñ kuḍ, -ḍā, *n.* = *l.* small room.

Cellar, *s.* buyār, -rā, *n.* (subterraneous room); ugrāṇ, -ṇā, *n.*; *vlg.* dispens, -sā, *n.*

Cellarer, *s.* mezātsākor, -krā, *m.*

Cement, *s.* gār, -rā, *m.*

Cement, *v.* 1. gārăn gădsi (*or* g. joḍsi).
2. *fg.* meḷăi = *l.* unite.

Cemetery, *s.* simitèr, -ri, *f.*, *fr.*; fonḍāsuāt, -te, *f.*, nikepunči suāt, *or* purtso zāgo, -geā, *m.* = *l.* place of graves; suḍkāḍ, -ḍā, *n.* = *l.* desert of burning, *but this word is used only for* pagan cemeteries; măsăṇ, -ṇā, *n.*

Cenobite, *s.* monj, -jā, *m.* (pagan c.); frad, -di, *m.* = *l.* friar, *fr.*; sangatvāsi, -si, *m.* = *l.* living together, *opp. to* vănavāsi = living alone (anchorite).

Cenotaph, *s.* gōr, -ri, *f.* (gori, -ye, *f.*)

Censer, *s.* turiblu̥, -blā, *n.*, *fr.*; dhupārti, -ti, *f.* (*anal. to H. K.*) *or* dhumpār, -rā, *n.*

Censure, *v.* gunyāukār kăr = *l.* make guilty; *not common* durua; gunyāuñ sāng = *l.* say the faults; *see* **Blame, Criticize.**

Censure, *s.* dūr, -rā, *n.*

Census, *s.* lokānčeñ lēk (è), -kā, *n.* = *l.* counting of people.

Cents, (%) šăkḍo, -ḍeā, *m.*; '4% = šăkḍeăk 4 rupoi lekān'.

Centipede, *s.* vāgoṇi, -ṇi, *f.*

Central, *a.* modeñ āsullo, *or* modlo.

Centralise, *v.* modeñ vor = *l.* bring to a centre, *pr. and fg.*

Centrally, *ad.* modeñ *or* māzānt.

Centre, *s.* māz, -zā, *m.*, *e.g.* of a circle *and the like*; modeñ, -deā, *n.*

Century, *s.* šătamān, -nā, *n.* *or* šăṭăk, -kā, *n.*, *or* šatang, -gā, *n.*

Ceremonious, *a.* 1. dărbār, *or bet.* dobajeātso = *l.* solemn.
2. tsăḍ sārko = *l.* too exact.
3. măryāditso.

Ceremony, *s.* 1. sermoni, -ni, *f.* *e.g.* of the church, *fr.*; kăṭleñ, -leā, *n.* (*H. K.*); rīt, -ti, *f.* (rite), *or* šāstrāči rīt, *or* rivāz, -ji, *f.*; păddăt, -ti, *f.*
2. dobāzo, -jeā, *m.* = *l.* pomp.

Certain, *a.* 1. khăro *or* săt = *l.* true (c. objectively).
2. drăḍ (c. subjectively): mākā. d. āsā.
3. ămko *or* fălāṇo (*Lat. quidam*).
4. khăṇḍit = c. to be obtained; 'āuñ nīz somzātāñ = *or* ā. n. zāṇāñ = I am certain'; 'mākā khărents kăḷtā = *l.* to me is truly known'.

Certainly, *ad.* khărents (*or* khărots); dubāunāstanāñ = *l.* not being doubt; dubāu vorānāstanāñ = *l.* not carrying doubt; drăḍ zāun = surely, to be sure.

Certainty, *s.* 1. thirāsāṇ, -ṇe, *f.* = subjective certainty.
2. săt, -tā, *n.* = *l.* truth; objective [c.

Certificate, *s. vlg.* āsent, -tā, *m. fr.*; zātăk (*or* jātăk), -kā, *n.* (*H. K.*); dāklo, -leā, *m.*: 'get a certificate = āsent kāḍ, *l.* draw a certificate'.

Certify, *v.* 1. drăḍ kăr = *l.* make sure; niščei sāng = *l.* say sincerely; nīz zāun sāng = *l.* say sincerely; kăḷāi.

Certitude, *s.* nirdār, -rā, *m.*

Cerumen, *s.* kānulo, -leā, *m.*

Cessation, *s.* 1. rāvāp, -pā (*or* rāupā), *n.*; soḍni, -ne, *f.* = *l.* leaving; mănnakărni, -ne, *f.*, *or only* mănna, -ne, *f.*
2. *fg.* soukāsāi, -ye, *f.* = *l.* rest.

Cession, *s.* 1. soḍni, -ne, *f.*
2. vopsāp, -pā, *n. from* vopsun di = consign.

Chafe, *v.* 1. gāsun tāpāi = *l.* make warm by rubbing; gās.
2. kāt kāḍ = *l.* take away skin.
3. rāg āḍāi = irritate.
4. rāgār zā = be impatient.

Chaff, *s.* 1. sărl, -lā, *n.*; kunḍo, -ḍeā, *m.*
2. *fg.* kunḍeāpāsṭ.

Chagrin, *s.* 1. kărkăr, -rā, *m.* = trouble; bezārāi, -ye, *f.*
2. rāg, -gā, *m.* = *l.* anger; *see* **Ill-nature.**

Chain, *s.* 1. sānkăḷ, -kḷi, *f.*, *pr.* (big); sărpăḷi, -ḷe, *f.* (small); gop, -pā, *n.* (fine).
2. bănd, -di, *f.* = *l.* prison.
3. hăr, -ri, *f.* = line; kāmp, -pā, *m.*, *e.g.* hārin (*or* kāmpān) tsălā = walk in a line; făngt, -ti, *f.* = line; 'făngtin bosa = sit in a line'.

Chair, *s.* kădel, -lā, *n.*, *fr.*; băska, -ke, *f.*
Arm-chair = hāt āsulli băska = *l.* ch. having arms.

Chairman, *s.* president, -ti, *m.*, *fr.*; *vlg.* pirjent, -ti, *m.*; săbhenāik, -kā, *m.*

Chalice, *s.* kāls, -si, *f.*, *fr.*; pātrụ, -trā, *n.*

Chalk, *s.* europi tsuno, *or* vilāyeti (*or* vilāiti) tsuno, -neā, *m.*

Challenge, *v.* lăḍāyek āpoi = *l.* call to fighting.

Challenge, *s.* lăḍāyek āpouṇeñ, -ṇeā, *n.*

Chamber, *s.* kuḍ, -ḍā, *n.*: 'c. pot = *vlg.* tăst, -tā, *n.*'

Chameleon, *s.* sirli, -le, *f.*

Champion, *s.* vīr, -rā, *m.*; parākrămi, -miā, *m.*, *n. c.*=*l.* doing extraordinary things.

Chance (By), ākăsmăt: 'tō mākā ā. meḷḷo = I met him by c.'; neṇārpoṇān = *l.* unknowingly; aučit=*l.* suddenly; āplestăki = *l.* by itself; āpšents = *l.* by itself.

Chance, *s.* 1. ădrušṭ, -ṭā, *n.*
2. pātiyeṇiñ, -ṇi, *f.*=*l.* trust: 'I have a ch. = pātiyeṇi dovortāñ *or* pātietāñ, *l.* I hope, I trust, *or* āšā āsā'; *see* **Accident.**

Chance, *v.* găḍ=*l.* happen.

Chancellor, *s.* măntri, -ri, *m.*

Change, *s.* bădlāp, -pā, *n.*

Change, *v.* bădăl=alter entirely *or* partially; *also* ch. a dress; vāṭāi, (change money); *as n. v.* bădăl zātā *or only* zātā = becomes, *or* dusro zātā = becomes another, *or* bădal.

Changeable, *a.* bădăl zāuntso *or* bădăltso.

Channel, *s.* tōḍ, -ḍā, *m.* (watercourse); khăṇi, -ye, *f.* (in the fields).

Chapel, *s.* kopel, -lā, *n.*, *fr.*; irmit, -ti, *f.*, *fr.*; *bet.* (dākṭi) igărz, -je, *f.* = *l.* small church; tsăḍāu, -ḍāvā, *n.* (*anal. to H. K.*) = chapel within a church; *vlg.* kapel, -lā, *n.*

Chaplain, *s.* kăpelāuñ, -lāvā, *m.*, *fr.*; dākṭo vigār, -rā, *m. or* dākṭo pādri, -ri, *m.*=*l.* the little vicar *or* father, *vlg.*; kumki guru, -ru, *m.* = assistant priest; sărkāri pādri = military ch.; irmititso pādri, -ri, *m.* = *l.* father of a chapel.

Chaplet, *s.* 1. kònt, -tā, *n.*
2. jelo, -leā, *m.* (crown of flowers); kopèl, -lā, *n.* = *l.* garland; moḷa, -ḷe, *f.* (of flowers).

Chapter, *s.* 1. ăvăsvăr, -rā, *m.* (c. of book).
2. pādrinči (*or* mādrinči) săbha, -bhe, *f.* = *l.* meeting of friars (*or* of nuns).
3. konegāñmēḷ (é), -ḷā, *m.* = body of canons.

Character, *s.* 1. ăkšer, -rā, *n.* = *l.* a letter.
2. ābru, -brā, *m.* = honour: 'măryāditso (*or* ābrātso) monis, -nšā, *m.* = man of c.'; măryād, -di, *f.* = *l.* honesty; mān, -nā, *m.* = *l.* honour, reputation.
3. vóndouṇi, -ṇi, *f.* = *l.* inclinaation, *e.g.* what is the c. of that man? năḍteñ, -teā, *n.*; sobāuñ, -bāvā, *m.* = temper, nature; guṇ, -ṇā, *m.* = characteristic; *by Gen. see* Gram. p. 223, *seq.*
4. vès, -sā, *m.* = *l.* mask; *as in the phrase*, 'he assumes the c. of = to ves ghāltā'.

Characteristic, *see* **Character.**

Characterize, *v.* vondouṇ *or* vondauṇeñ săng = *l.* say the character of; guṇ sāng *or* sobāu sāng; kăḷit kăr *or* kăḷăi = cause to be known; somzăi, *c. v.* = *l.* give to understand.

Charcoal, *s.* ingḷo, -ḷeā, *m.*; 'burning c. = kènḍ, -ḍā, *n.*'

Charge, *v.* 1. bhor = *l.* fill, *e.g.* a cart.

2. āngār poḍ = *l.* fall on body, attack.

3. lēk(é) = *l.* account, *ch. cs.*

4. gunyāukār kăr = *l.* make guilty (accuse); lāi; ghāl; *see* **Ascribe.**

5. formāi *or* hukum di = *l.* give order.

6. vopsun di = *l.* give in care (charge with the care of).

7. nemsi = *l.* appoint.

8. zătăn kāṇe = *l.* take care, *ch. cs.*

9. bānd = *l.* bind, *e.g.* mol bānd = *l.* bind a price (*Konk.*), *Acc.*

N. B. The form of the Eng. expression is often changed, e.g. 'tākā ghăr rākunk sānglāñ = I charged him to look after the house'; 'how much do you charge me = mol kiteñ? *or* kiteñ māgtāi? 'I do not like to charge any body = koṇāk kărkărātso zāunk khušivornāñ, *l.* I don't like to get annoying to any body'.

Charge, *s.* 1. vojeñ, -jeā, *n.* *or* vozăn, -nā, *n.* (load).

2. hukum, -kme, *f.* = *l.* order.

3. kāido, -deā, *m.* = *l.* duty.

4. kām, -mā, *n.* = *l.* business.

5. firiyād, -di, *f.* = accusation.

6. mòl, -lā, *n.* = *l.* price.

7. zulum, -lme, *f.* = *l.* attack.

Chariot, gāḍi, -ye, *f.*; sărāṭ, -ṭā, *n.*

Charitable, *a.* kākuḷtitso *or* kākuḷdār = *l.* merciful; dhărmiṣṭ; mogāḷ = *l.* dear, *not ex.* charitable, *but expressing an attribute springing from* charity; *used fg.*

Charitably, *ad.* kākuḷtin; dhărmān; mogān; mogāḷzāun.

Charity, *s.* 1. mōg, -gā, *m.*: 'Divine ch. = Devātso mōg'.

2. moya mōg = fraternal ch.

3. izmāl, -lā, *n.* = *l.* alms, *fr.*; dhărm, -mā, *m.*

Charlatan, *s.* borboro, -reā, *m.* (boḍboḍo); *vlg.* loṭṭebira, -rā, *m.*

Charm, *s.* 1. tăntrụ, -rā, *n. pr.* *or* măntrụ, -rā, *n.* *or* nimit, -tā, *n.*

2. *fg.* voḍni, -ne, *f.* = *l.* attraction.

3. sundărāi, -ye, *f.* = *l.* beauty.

Charm, *v.* 1. tăntrañ kăr = *l.* make ch., *pr.*

2. piso kăr, (please very much, *l.* make mad); *in the passive,* săntos bhōg = *l.* enjoy pleasure; voḍniñ di = *l.* give inclinations; tsăḍ mānuă = *l.* please very much.

Chase, *v.* 1. šikār kăr.
2. kāntăi = *l.* engrave.

Chase, *s.* sikār, -re, *f.*

Chaste, *a.* niskăḷ; nităḷ.

Chastise, *v.* 1. šikša di *or* š. lāi = *l.* give *or* apply punishment.
2. kăšṭ di *or* kăšṭăi = *l.* give pain.

Chastity, *s.* niskăḷăi, -ye, *f.*, *or* niskăḷkāi, -ye, *f.*; nităḷpoṇ, -ṇā, *n.* *or* nităḷăi, -ye, *f.*

Chasuble, *s.* kāzul, -lā, *n.*, *fr.*; vestiment, -tā, *m.*, *fr. vlg.*; *prh.* misāči nesoṇ, -ṇi, *f.*

Chat, *v.* ulăi = *l.* speak, *Cm. Prs.*; găzāli măr (say things of no importance).

Chat, *s.* găzāl, -li, *f.*; rāmāiṇ, -ṇā, *n.* (long ch.); phāndḷo, -ḷeā, *m.*

Chattel, *s.* sāmān, -nā, *m.*

Chatter, *v.* nākāzālleñ ulăi = *l.* say nonsense; *see also* **Gnash.**

Chattering, *s.* nākāzāllo, -leā, *m.*, *or* nākāzālleo văstu, -tuñ, *f.*; găzāli, -li, *f.*; uloṇeñ, -ṇeā, *n.*: 'long chat = lāmb găzāli'; phāndḷo, -ḷeā, *m.*

Cheap, *a.* sovāi (*not to be confounded with* sóvói=custom).

Cheat, *s.* 1. mōs, -sā, *m.*; ṭhăkkụ, -kā, *n.*; dăgo -geā, *m.*; foṭ, -ṭi, *f.* = *ex.* lie.
2. mosāgār, -rā, *m.* = deceiver.

Cheat, *v.* 1. dăgo kăr = *l.* make cheating, *Acc.*
2. foṭăi, *c. v. of* foṭuā = be deceived.

Cheating, *s.* dăgo, -geā, *m.*; *see* **Cheat.**

Check, *v.* 1. rāvoi = *l.* cause to stop, *c. v. of* rāu = stop.
2. bāgāi = *l.* bend, *fg.*; *see also* **Restrain.**
3. bòḷ kăr = *l.* make force.
4. āḍ ye = *l.* come against (*Dat.*)
5. mōḍ(ó) = *l.* break, *fg.*; *see* **Suppress**; tsălăi.
6. mokābilo kăr = *l.* compare, *or* tăn-ki kăr = audit (accounts).

Check, *s.* 1. āḍkăḷ, -ḷi, *f.*
2. in-kāri, -ri, *f.* = *l.* resistance, denial (*or* in-kār, -rā, *n.*); *see* **Hindrance, Rebuff.**
3. (money-order), *see* **Cheque.**

Cheek, *s.* polo, -leā, *m.*; gāl, -lā, *m.* (*ex.* jaw).

Cheek-bone, *s.* dāḍ, -ḍā, *n.*

Cheer, *v.* 1. khušāl kăr = *l.* make cheerful, *or* dādos kăr = *l.* make glad.
2. hogḷāp kăr *or* hogoḷsi = *l.* make praise.

Cheer, *s.* hogḷāp, -pā, *n.*; ulās, -sā, *m.*: 'be of good cheer = dhăir ghe'.

Cheerful, *a.* khusāl, *or* khušāli, *or* khušālāyetso; săntosātso.

Cheerfully, *ad.* khušālāyeñ, *or* khušen.

Cheerfulness, *s.* khušālāi, -ye, *f.*; săntos, -sā, *m.*

Cheese, *s.* čiz, -zi, *f.*, *fr.*; hālvo, *which is sometimes used in this sense, is rather* Arabic

cheese, *or bet.* a sweetmeat, like cheese on the outside.
Chemist, *s.* răsāvidyegār, -rā, *m.*
Chemistry, *s.* răsāvidya, -ye, *f.*
Cheque, *s.* hunḍi, -ye, *f.*
Cherish, *v.* 1. mogān tslăi (*Acc. pers.*) = *l.* rule with love.
2. pos = feed.
3. bhuzăi = comfort.
Cherub, *s.* kerubim, -mā, *m.*, *fr.*
Chess, *s.* četrăng, -gā, *n.*
Chest, *s.* 1. pèṭ, -ṭe, *f.* = *l.* box.
2. hărdeñ, -deā, *n.* (*Lat. pectus*).
Chew, *v.* tsāb; găḷăi (move to and fro), *e.g.* sugar-cane.
Chicane, *see* **Trick, Cavil.**
Chicken, *s.* 1. pīl, -lā, *n.*, *or* kunkḍāčeñ pīl, -lā, *n.*
2. pilo, -leā, *m.* (in the egg).
Chicken-pox, *s.* koṭlo, -leā, *m.*
Chide, *v.* 1. besṭăi = *l.* rebuke.
2. bās khā = *l.* eat a scolding.
Chief, *a.* mukhya; poilo = *l.* first.
Chief, *s.* mukhyest, -stā, *m.*, *or* mostak, -kā, *n.* = *l.* head.
Chiefly, *ad.* mukhyazāun; bhou kărn; ădhik kărn; višes.
Child, *s.* burgeñ, -geā, *n*; bāḷšeñ, -šeā, *n.* = *l.* infant; bāḷ, -ḷā, *n.*, *joined to* burgeñ, *as a term of affection;* bāḷok, -ḷkā, *or* -ḷokā, *m.*, *used of the* Infant Jesus; put, -tā, *or* putrų, -rā, *m.* = *l.* son.
Childhood, *s.* burgipirāi, -ye, *f.* = *l.* age of the children, *or* burgepoṇ, -ṇā, *n.*
Childish, *a.* burgeāntso = pertaining to children; burgeāñ bări = *Lat. puerorum instar; ch. cs.*, *or* burgepoṇātso.
Childishness, *s.* burgepoṇ, -ṇā, *n.*
Childless, *a.* burgiññātullo.
Chill, *s.* thănḍso; šēḷ, -ḷi, *f.*
Chilli, *s.* mirsāng, -ge, *f.*
Chimera, *s. approx.* bhiyankuḷāi, -ye, *f.*; girigiri, -ri, *f.*
Chimney, *s.* duvrāči vāṭ, -ṭe, *f.* = *l.* way of smoke; nāḷi, -ye, *f.* = *l.* tube.
Chin, *s.* khāḍki, -ke, *f.*; bontso, -čeā, *m.*
Chink, *s.* fuṭ, -ṭi, *f.*
Chisel, *s.* irneñ, -neā, *n.*
Chocolate, *s.* čokolad, -di, *f.*, *fr.*
Choice, *s.* vintsāp, -tspā, *n. or* vintsṇeñ, -ṇeā, *n.*
Choice, *a.* uttăm (*var.* uttim) = *l.* excellent; vintsnār; vintsleli (văstų) = *l.* chosen (thing); ămrut = excellent thing (eatable), *also fg.*
Choir, *s.* 1. kór, -rā, *m.*; igărzeči māḷăi, -ḷiye, *f.* (place).
2. kăntāreāntso mēḷ (é), -ḷā, *m.*; gāyāngārāntso mēḷ, -ḷā, *m.* (singers).
Choke, *v.* 1. muḍḍi = *l.* twist the neck round; fugār kăr, *fr.*; gāḷo dāmp = *l.* shut the neck.
2. āḍkāḷ kăr = *l.* make hindrance; ăḍči, *e.g.* choke corn (*in pass.* ăḍtsa).
Cholera (morbus), *s.* sirsiri, -re, *f.*; thănḍ piḍa, -ḍe, *f.* = *l.* cold

sickness; sănni, -ne, *f.* *or* sănnirōg, -gā, *m.*

Choose, *v.* 1. vints; vintsun kāḍ = *l.* selecting take out; sodun kāḍ, = *l.* seeking take out; prăs khuši vor, *e.g.* choose virtue before wealth = grestkāye prăs seguṇ khuši vor; boreñ distā = pleases, seems good.
2. nemsi, *or* nomiyār, *fr.* = *l.* appoint, nominate.

Chop, *v.* 1. tsātsāi; kuḍkeān kuḍke kăr = *l.* make pieces.
2. porta = *l.* turn, *e.g.* the wind changes.

Chop-house, *n.* gutki, -ke = *l.* tavern; biḍār, -rā, *n.* = dwelling, *used fg.*

Chopper, *s.* (voḍli) suri, -ye, *f.*

Chord, *s.* 1. *vlg.* kordāuñ, -dāvā, *n.* *or* *m.* = string (musical).
2. sări, -ye, *f.* (of brass); dori, -ye, *f.*

Chorister, *s.* kăntārist, -tā, *or* kăntāri, -riā, *m.*, *fr.*

Christian, *s.* kristāuñ, -tāvā, *m.*

Christian, *a.* kristāvāntso.

Christianity, *s.* 1. kristāvānčeñ šāstru, -trā, *n.* = *l.* christian religion.
2. (sămest) kristāuñ = (all) Christians.

Chronic, *a.* lāmb = *l.* long; dig *or* digso.

Chronicle, *s.* vărsānčeo kobro, -rāñ, *pl.*; kăta, -te, *f.*

Chronological, Chronologically, *ad.* kālāñ părmāṇe = *l.* according to the time, *ch. cs.*

Chronology, *s.* kālānči vidya *or* kālāñvidya, -ye, *f.* = science of times.

Chronometer, *s.* ghăḍiyāḷ, -ḷā, *n.* (*var.* -ḷi, *f.*) = *l.* clock; kālāmāp, -pā, *n.*, *or* veḷāmāp.

Church, *s.* 1. igărz, -je, *f.*, *or* igrăz, -je *or* igreja, -je, *fr.*; diuḷ, -ḷā, *n.* *used only of* pagan temples; devasthān, -nā, *n.* (*H. K.*), *or* devālăi, -yā, *n.*; devāčeñ ghăr, -rā, *n.*
2. igărz mātā, -te, *f.*, *or* santa mādr igărz (living church).

Church-warden, *s.* fišāli, -liā, *m.* *vlg.*; moktesăr, -rā, *m.*; igărjetso udyogăst, -tā, *m.*

Church-yard, *s.* igărječeñ kāmp, -pā, *n.*; *see* **Cemetery.**

Churl, *s.* nāḍkār, -rā, *m.* = *l.* villager, *fg.*

Churlish, *a.* añmăryāditso, *bet.* ăumăryāditso.

Cicatrize, *v.* ghāi suk = *l.* wound become dry.

Cigar, *s.* čeruṭ, -ṭā, *n.*; iḍi *or* viḍi, -ye, *f.* (a small one): 'smoke a c. = č. voḍ'.

Cinder, *s.* ingḷo, -ḷeā, *m.* = *Lat. carbo; see also* **Ashes.**

Cinnabar, *s.* sindur, -rā, *n.*

Cinnamon, *s.* tikesāl, -li, *f.*

Cipher, *s.* 1. sonneñ, -neā, *n.* *or* pūji, -je, *f.*
2. ănko, -keā, *m.* (arithmetical character).
3. guḍānči bhās, -še, *f.* = *l.* language of secrets.

Circle, *s.* 1. mănḍăḷ, -ḷā, *n.*; suttụ, -tā, *m.*; *also* circuit, compass; phero, -reā, *m.*
2. mēḷ(é), -ḷā, *m.*, *e. g.* a c. of listeners.

Circlet, *s.* vāḷo, -ḷeā, *m.* = an ornament for children.

Circuit, *s.* bounḍi, -ḍe, *f.*; suttụ, -tā, *m.*

Circular, *a.* āḍkulo = round.

Circular, *s.* bounḍekāgād, -gdā, *n.*

Circulation, *s.* bounḍi, -ḍe, *f.*

Circulate, *v.* 1. *n. v.* bountăṇiñ vetā = *l.* goes around; bouñ *or in tr. mn.* bounḍāi (*used also of* books).
2. *tr. v., fg.* părgăṭ kăr = *l.* make public.

N. B. All words beginning with 'circum' *not given here, if translateable literally, are to be translated by* 'bountiñ' *or* 'bountăṇiñ' *and the word which* 'circum' *is compounded with.*

Circumlocution, *s.* utrāñbounḍi, -ḍe, *f.*

Circumspection, *s.* bud, -di, *f.* = *l.* prudence; zāgrutāi, -ye, *f.*

Circumstance, *s.* 1. săngti (*var.* săngăt, -gti), -ti, *f.*; găt, *or* hăkigăt, -ti, *f.* (*about the same mn. as* săngti), *n. c.*
2. stiti, -ti, *f.* = state, condition.
3. tānk, -ki, *f.* = power, *e. g.* according to your circumstances = tānki părmāṇe.
4. thăr, -rā, *m. or* jinos, -nsā, *m.* = kind, quality.

Cistern, *s.* 1. tăḷeñ, -ḷeā, *n.* = tank.
2. bāiñ, bāiñ, *f.* = *l.* well.

Citadel, *s.* koṭeñ, -ṭeā, *n.* = *l.* castle.

Cite, *v.* āpoi = *l.* summon; *see* **Summon** *and* **Quote.**

Citizen, *s.* răit, -tā, *m.* = *l.* subject; šerāgār = *l.* man of the town; gāunkār, -rā, *m.* = *l.* of the place, of the country.

Citron, *s.* māuḷing, -gā, *n.*

City, *s.* šèr, *or* šeār, -rā, *n.*; păṭăṇ, -ṭṇā, *n.*; năgăr, -rā, *n.*

Civil, *a.* 1. păṭṇātso; sărkāri (noukor) = (servant) of the Government; răitāntso = *l.* of the subjects; sādhārn = *l.* common.
2. măryāditso = polite.

Civility, *s.* măryād, -di, *f.* = *l.* politeness; sikāp, -kpā, *n.* = learning, education; tsāltsămkăṇ, -ṇā, *n.*, *used also for* 'politeness'; mānsugi, -ge, *f.*, *e.g.* c. of a gentleman.

Civilize, *v.* tsāltsămkăṇ sikāi.

Claim, *v.* māg = *l.* request, demand, *or* pāṭi māg = ask back, *or* hăkkān māg; hăkkụ āsā moṇ săng = say that there is right, *with or without* thāiñ *preceding* hăkkụ.

Clamour, *s.* hākbob, -be, *f.*, *or also* hāk āni bob.

Clap, *v.* taḷio peṭ = *l.* strike the palms of the hands.

Clapper (of a bell), *s.* ghānṭitso loḷo, -ḷeā, *m. or* guḷo, -ḷeā, *m.*
Clarify, *v.* niuḷāi.
Clash, *v.* ādăḷn āvāz zā, *or only* ādăḷ.
Clasp, *v.* 1. bānd = *l.* bind.
2. veng mār = embrace, grasp.
3. zōḍ(ó), *e.g.* clasp the hands.
Class, *s.* 1. thăr, -rā, *m.* = *l.* kind, quality.
2. vorg, -gā, *m.*
Classic, Classical, *a.* nămuneātso = *l.* of model, *e.g.* cl. author = nă. bărpi *or* nă. kărt; *or* uttim = excellent.
Classify, *v.* zātivār kăr; vilevāri kăr.
Clause, *s.* 1. klam *or* kălăm, -lmā, *n.* = *l.* paragraph.
2. vānṭo, -ṭeā, *m.* = *l.* part, *e.g.* of a sentence.
Claw, *s.* 1. nākuṭ, -kṭā, *n.*
2. dāuli, -le, *f.*
Clay, *s.* āvo, -veā, *m.*, *or* āveāči māti, -ye, *f.*; čikăḍ, -kḍā, *n.*
Clean, *a.* nităḷ.
Clean, *v.* nităḷ kăr = *l.* make c.; gās (*mn.* polish).
Cleanliness, *s.* nităḷpoṇ, -ṇā, *n.*, *or* nităḷāi, -ye, *f.*
Cleanse, *v.* nităḷ kăr = *l.* make clean; dūḷ kāḍ = *l.* take away dust; du = *l.* wash.
Clear, *a.* 1. nităḷ.
2. moḍnāntullo *or* kupāññātullo = *l.* not cloudy (sky).
3. sóṣṭ = distinct, *e. g.* voice; evident.
4. părzăḷik = *l.* shining.
In the meaning of 'not obstructed', *the negat. form* 'nātullo' *may be used, e. g.* clear of grass = tăṇṇātullo. 'The sky is clearing up = moḷāb nităḷ zātā'.
Clear, *v.*, *use the adj.* 'clear' *with the verb required if taken pr.*
Cl. off a debt = riṇ fārik kăr.
Cl. away = kāḍ.
Cl. oneself of a charge = băčāu zā *or* suṭ.
Clearly, *ad.* nităḷ zāun; soṣṭ.
Clearness, *s. see* **Brightness.**
Cleave, *v.* 1. soḍ, *tr. v.; n. v.* suṭ *used of things previously joined;* fuṭ = *l.* burst.
2. lāg = *l.* adhere.
Cleft, *s.* fuṭ, -ṭi, *f.*; moḍāp, -ḍpā, *n.* = *l.* breach.
Clemency, *s.* dăya, -ye, *f.* = *l.* benignity; kākuḷt, -ti, *f.* = *l.* mercy.
Clement, *a.* mogāḷ; kākuḷtitso; dăyāḷ; kanvaḷ.
Clepsydra, *s.* udkăčeñ găḍiyāḷ, -ḷā, *n.* (*or* udkāgăḍiyāḷ).
Clergy, *s.* igărjemuniyāriñmēḷ (é), -ḷā, *m.*, *or* muniyāripoṇ, -ṇā, *n.*; pādriñmēḷ, -ḷā, *m.*
Clergyman, *s.* igărjemuniyāri, -riā, *m.* = minister of the church.
Clerk, *s. or* gumost, -stā, *m.*; bărpi, -piā, *m.*; năkălvis, *or* năkăluis, -sā, *m.*

Clever, *a.* ušār; tsurk = active; zānṭo = skilful; vidvāuñs; sudăḷ.

Cleverness, *s.* ušārpoṇ, -ṇā, *n.*; zānṭepoṇ, -ṇā, *n.*; tsurkāi, -ye, *f.*, *or* tsurkpoṇ, -ṇā, *n.*; sudăḷāi, -ye, *f.*

Client, *s.* kăkḳigār, -rā, *m.*; asāmi, -miā, *m.*

Climate, *s.* hăvo, -veā, *m.*; dešaguṇ, -ṇā, *m.*=*l.* quality of the country, *n. c.*, *Cn.*

Climb, *v.* tsăḍ, *n. v.*, *2nd Loc.*; khāḍuñ ghāln tsăḍ, = *l.* ascend putting a rope.

Cling, *v.* lāg.

Clip, *v.* kāḍ=*l.* take away.; kātăr = *l.* cut.

Cloak, *s.* jibbo, -beā, *m.*

Cloak, *v.* lipăi = *l.* conceal.

Clock, *s.* găḍiyāḷ, -ḷā, *n.* (*more comm.* -ḷi, *f. but* -ḷā *acc. to Mr.*): 'what o'clock is it? = kitle gănṭe?' 'at what o'-clock? = kitleā gănṭeār?'

Cloister, *s. vlg.* koñvent, -tā, *m.*, *fr.*; móṭ, -ṭā, *m.* (*H. K.*)

Close, *v.* 1. dāmp, *or* dānk (*tr. and n. v.*), *e. g.* a door *etc.*
2. tirsi = *l.* finish.

Close, *a.* 1. dāṭ (thick); lāgun = *l.* attached, *or* lāgsilo.
2. găṭ (*or* ghăṭ).
3. guṭātso = *l.* secret.
4. moṭvo = short.
5. imṭo = stingy.

Close, *ad.* lāgiñ; sărsiñ.

Closeness, *s.* dāṭāi, -ye, *f.*; *rs. into ad.*

Closet, *s.* lān kuḍ, -ḍā, *n.*

Clot, *s.* geṭo, -ṭeā, *m.* (*Lat. sanguis coagulatus.*)

Cloth, *s.* lugāṭ, -gṭā, *n.*; bāṇsireñ, -reā, *n.* = rags, used for cleaning kitchen utensils; săklāt, -ti, *f.* (coverlet, *also* broadcloth); mălmăl, -lā, *n.* = muslin.

Clothe, *v.* 1. *pr.* lugṭāñ ghāl = *l.* put clothes; nesăi, *c. v. of* nes, *n. v.*; *pr.* pāngrăi, *e. g.* the poor, *ol. rl.* (*l.* cover).
2. *fg. rs.* the covering thing *with* āsā, *e. g.* some animals are covered with fur=thoḍeañ monzātink kăt āsā; *or the form of the sentence is changed, and someone of the vbs. given above is used.*

Clothes, *s.* lugṭāñ, *n. pl. of* lugāṭ; nesoṇ, -ṇi, *f.* = dress, prepared dress; mustāigi, -ge, *f.*, *used in sing.* (*collective*); văstur, -trā (*or* -rā), *n.*

Cloud, *s.* kup, -pā, *n.*; moḍ, -ḍā, *n.*; 'is it cloudy? = moḍañ tsăḍ ăsātgi?'

Cloudless, *a.* kupnātullo *or* moḍnātullo.

Cloudy, *a.* moḍāntso; kupāsullo; *bet. rs. into* noun.

Clove, *s.* lăvăng, lăungā, *n.*

Clown, *see* Boor.

Club, *s.* 1. toṇko, -keā, *m.* = cudgel.

2. mēḷ (é), -ḷā, *m.* = *l.* assembly.

Clumsily, *ad.* făḍpoši, *e.g.* this table is c. made.

Clumsy, *a.* făḍpoši; karkoṭo, *e.g.* c. bench.

Cluster, *s.* ghós, -sā, *m.* (of grapes, *etc.*); găḍāi, -yā, *m.*; fāṇo, -ṇeā, *m.*

Coach, *s.* gāḍi, -ye, *f.*; *see* **Carriage.**

Coachman, *s.* gāḍiyegār, -rā, *m.*

Coadjutor, *s.* kumki, -kiā, *m.*, *or* kumkigār, -rā, *m.*

Coagulate, *see* **Curdle.**

Coal, *s.* 1. ingḷo, -ḷeā, *m.*
2. kolit, -ltā, *n.* = *l.* brand: 'burning c. = kenḍ, -ḍā, *n.*, *or* uzeātso ingḷo', -ḷeā, *m.*

Coalesce, *v.* meḷ, *n. v.*

Coalition, *s.* mēḷ (é), -ḷā, *m.*; yekoṭ, -ṭā, *m.*

Coarse, *a.* 1. moṭo = *l.* not fine, *e.g.* bran; daḍḍo, *e.g.* food.
2. *fg.* ăumăryāditso = *l.* unpolite.

Coarseness, *s.* 1. daḍḍepoṇ, -ṇā, *n.*
2. ăumăryād, -di, *f.*

Coast, *s.* tăḍ, -ḍi, *f.* (*ex. mn.* shore); véḷ, -ḷe, *f.*; kărāvoḷ, -ḷi, *f.*, *e.g.* of sea.

Coat, *s.* kutāuñ, -āvā, *m.*, *fr.*; băndiyān, -nā, *n.* (a sort of light jacket).

Coax, *see* **Caress.**

Cobra-capella, *s.* nāg, -gā, *m.*

Cock, *s.* kombo, -beā, *m.*

Cockscomb, *s.* šeṇkāreñ, -reā, *n.* (kombeāčeñ š.)

Cockroach, *s.* zărlo, -leā, *m.*

Cocoanut, *s.* nārl, -lā, *m.*, *mn.* ripe c.; bonḍo, -ḍeā, *m.* = tender c.
C. day = dăryāk puja kărtso dis, *l.* day (on which) they do honour to the sea.
C. tree = māḍ, -ḍā, *m.*
C. shell = voṇók, -ṇkā, *m.*; *pl.* voṇăk; kăṭṭi, -ṭe, *f.*
Juice of c. = udāk (water): the white matter inside = kāntoḷi, *or* kāntḷi, -ḷe, *f.*; the fibre of which coir matting is made = kāto, -teā, *m.*; the fibre after preparation = kābḷo, -ḷeā, *m.*

Cod (fish), *s.* tāṭo, -ṭeā, *m.*
C. liver oil = tāṭeāčeñ tēl (è), -lā, *n.*

Code, *s.* kānun, -nā, *n.* = *l.* law.

Codicil, *s.* tāzakălăm, -lmā, *n.*

Co-equal, *a* sărisăma, *e. g.* in age.

Coffee, *s.* kāpi, -ye, *f.*; būndu, -dā, *n.*

Coffee-pot, *s.* pónč, -či, *f.*

Coffer, *s.* pèṭ, -ṭe, *f.*

Coffin, *s.* morṇānči pèṭ, -ṭe, *f.* = *l.* box of dead; tumb, -bā, *m.* = bier (a sort of wooden frame kept in the church and used by the poor for carrying their dead to the grave).

Cohabitation, *s.* sangātrāvāp, -rāupā, *n.*, *or only* sangāt, -tā, *n.*

Coherence, *etc. see* **Connexion.**

Coin, (a piece of money), *s.* nāṇeñ, -ṇeā, *n.*

Coin, *v.* 1. nāṇeñ kăr.
2. *fg.* găḍ, *e.g.* coin words.

Coincide, *v.* 1. săma āsčeñ = *l.* to be equal; săma poḍ.
2. vop = *l.* agree.

Coincidence, *s.* 1. săma poḍāp, -ḍpā, *n.*, *or* săma poḍneñ, -neā, *n.*
2. găḍāp, -ḍpā, *n.* = event.
3. voppigi, -ge, *f.* = agreement.

Cold, *a.* 1. šeḷo, *e.g.* water, *etc.*; thănḍ, *e.g.* weather.
2. *fg.* čappo, *e.g.* cold heart, without affection.

Cold, *s.* hiuñ, hivā, *n.*; 'I am cold = mākā hiuñ khātā, *l.* c. eats me'; šeḷ, -ḷi, *f.*; siñ, siyā, *n.*; 'I caught a cold = mākā thănḍ zāleñ, *or* mākā šéḷ zāli'; 'make cold, *v.* = ṇivăi, *c. v. of* niu'.

Coldly, *ad.* (*fg.*) mòn kuskon = *l.* heart crooked.

Coldness, *s.* 1. bepārvăi, -ye, *f.* = negligence.
2. *see* **Cold.**

Colic, *s.* guḷo, -ḷeā, *m.* (of a complicated kind); *rs. into* pòṭ duktā = *l.* to the belly is pain.

Collapse, *v.* poḍ; bhăsma = get ruined.

Collar, *s.* pāṭo, -ṭeā, *m.* (goḷeātso p.); piḍḍuk, -ke, *f.* (of amethysts).

Colleague, *s.* sāngāti, -tiā, *m.*

Collect, *v.* 1. meḷăi, *c. v. of* meḷ; rās kăr = *l.* make heap, amass, *Acc.*
2. kāḍ = *l.* draw, pick up.
3. luuñ, *e.g.* crop, corn.

Collected, *a.* (not disconcerted), bheñ nātullo = *l.* not having fear; gābrenātullo = *l.* not having confusion.

Collection, *s.* yekṭăi, -ye, *f.*; mēḷ(é), -ḷā, *m.*; zomo, -meā, *m.*

Collector, *s.* kăllekăṭăr, -rā, *m.*

College, *s. vlg.* kolej, -ji, *f.*; vidyesāl, -le, *f.*

Collision, *s.* 1. ādḷāp, -pā, *n.*
2. *fg.* lăḍăi, -ye, *f.* = *l.* fighting.

Colloquial, *a.* (language) tsālti (bhās) = *l.* current.

Colloquy, *s.* uloṇeñ, -ṇeā, *n.*; sămbāšăṇ, -ṇā, *n.*

Collusion, *s.* vănčăn, -ne, *f.* (*or* -nā, *n.*); dăga, -ge, *f.* (dăgo, -geā, *m.*)

Colonel, *s.* kolonel *or* kornel, -lā, *m.*, *fr.*; paṭlāmitso mukhyest, -tā, *m.*

Colossal, *a.* bhou voḍ = *l.* very large.

Colossus, *s.* moṭṭeñ bombeñ, -beā, *n.*; gumṭo, -ṭeā, *m.*

Colour, *s.* 1. rong, -gā, *m.*; *pl.* răng.
2. *fg.* nīb, -bā, *n.* = *l.* pretext.

Colour, *v.* 1. rong lăi = *l.* apply colour.
2. *fg.* ves ghāl = *l.* put the mask.

Column, *s.* khāmbo, -beā, *m.*

Colt, *s.* goḍeāčeñ pīl, -lā, *n.* = *l.* the young of the horse.

Comb, *v.* ugăi; vālăi.

Comb, *s.* dāntoṇi, -ṇe, *f.*

Combination, *s.* 1. mēḷ(é), -ḷā, *m.* = *l.* union.
2. voppigi, -ge, *f.* = *l.* consent, agreement; kărār, -rā, *m.* = *l.* agreement; kuṭ, -ṭā, *n.* = *l.* conspiracy.
3. săngăt, -gti, *f.* = *l.* circumstance.

Combine, *v.* 1. meḷăi, *c. v. of* meḷ = be united.
2. vop = *l.* agree.

Combustible, *a.* lāsāsārko.

Combustion, *a.* lāsāp, -spā, *n.* (*or* lāsṇeñ, -ṇeā, *n.*)

Come, *v.* 1. ye; *past.* āilo; *see* Gram. P. II. ch. iv.; pāu = *l.* arrive.
2. *fg.* găḍ *or* zā = happen.
3. eya, *Lat. 'cia', used in animated appeals.*
Come out = kăḷit zā, *l.* become known.
Come to a resolution = niščeisi, *l.* resolve.
Come at = meḷ, *l.* be found.
Come to, *see* **Amount.**
Come to pieces = kuḍkeān kuḍke zā.
Come together = meḷ. [c. up.
Come up = zā, fuṭ, *e.g.* plants
Come upon (evils) = poḍ.
Come away = nikăḷ, *e.g.* a button comes away.

Comedy, *s.* hāsountso nāṭ, -ṭā, *m.*

Comely, *a.* sundăr = *l.* nice; lāyek = *l.* fit; vāzbi = *l.* becoming.

Comet, *s.* dumaket, -tā, *n.* (*H. K.*)

Comfort, *v.* bhuzăi, *e.g.* c. a man in sorrow; sămādhān (*or* săntos *or* soukāsāi) kăr; dhăir di = *l.* give courage.

Comfort, *s.* bhuzoṇ, -ṇe, *f.*

Comfortable, *a.* soukāsāyetso = *l.* of peace; *used also of place,* iskăḷāyetso = *l.* extended.

Comic, *a.* hāsountso *or* hāstso.

Coming, *s.* yeṇeñ, -ṇeā, *n.*; pāuṇeñ, -ṇeā, *n.* = *l.* arrival.

Command, *v.* 1. formāi, *tr. and n.* (be in command); hukum di = *l.* give order; tākid di = *l.* give order.
2. isiñ āsā = *l.* is in the direction of, *e.g.* the house commands the river.

Command, *s.* formāṇ (*or* fărmāṇ), -ṇā, *n.*; hukum, -kme, *f.*; tākid, -de, *f.* (a particular order); upades, -sā, *m.* (*said of the* Ten Commandments).

Commander, *s.* hukumdār, -rā, *m. rl.*; ădipăti *or* foujiădipăti, -ti, *m.* = c. of an army; formāitolo mănis, -nšā, *m.* = commanding man.

Commemorate, *v.* ugḍās kăr = *l.* make remembrance, *G. M.*; āṭou kăr.

Commemorative, *a.* ugḍās kărtso.

Commence, *v.* suru kăr (*tr.*) *or* suru zā (*n. v.*) = begin.

Commend, *v.* 1. suādin di = *l.* give n the possession of;

vopsun di = deliver; *as* 'he delivered the boy to his care = tāṇeñ burgeāk tāče zātnek vopsun dilo'; hogoḷsi=praise; umedin sāng = *l.* say with aspiration.
2. bud sāng = *l.* say advice; kăntsăi = *l.* impress.

Commendable, *a.* 1. hogḷāpātso *or* hogḷāp fāvozāllo.
2. šipārăs fāvozāllo.

Commendation, *see* **Recommendation.**

Commensurated, *a.*, *rs.* lāyek zātā = is fit, suitable.

Comment, *v.* vivor sāng = *l.* give explanation, *G. M.*; tsătrayo kăr = *l.* make notes; ărth sāng = *l.* say the meaning, *G. M.*

Comment, *s.* 1. vivor, -rā, *m.*; tsătrāi, -ye, *f.*
2. ărth sāngtso, *or only* ărth, -thā, *m.*

Commerce, *s.* vepār, -rā, *m. pr.*: 'there is no commerce = v. tsălnāñ, *l.* commerce does not walk'.

Commercial, *a.* vepārātso.

Commiserate, *v.* kākuḷt kăr = *l.* make mercy, *G. F.*; (mākā) birmot distā, *G. F.* = *l.* compassion appears; tsurtsuro distā, *Dat. Prs. G. thing.*

Commission, *s.* 1. dălāli, -le, *f.*; ugalañ, *n. pl. or* ugalpoṇ, -ṇā, *n.*; păñčāiti, -te, *f.*
2. dhāzăṇ, -ṇā, *n.* = committee; 'in c. = dălāl zāun'.

Commission, *v.* dălāli di.

Commissioner, *s.* 1. dălāl, -lā, *m.*
2. pódvi kāṇghello (mănis).

Commit, *v.* 1. vopsun di = *l.* give, deliver (to the care *or* charge of).
N. B. To express this meaning, the form of the sentence must often be changed. [do.
2. ādār *or* kăr = *l.* perpetrate *or*

Committee, *s.* dhāzăṇ, -ṇā, *n.*; zunt, -tā, *m.*, *fr.*

Commodious, *a.* soukāsāyetso.

Common, *a.* 1. tsālto = *l.* current, ordinary; sādo = usual, ordinary, *e.g.* meal; sădāntso = *l.* of always, *hence* customary, ordinary; *or* tsăḍavot.
2. sămestāntso = of all; sādārṇ.
3. sărkārātso = *l.* of the government.
4. sumār = *Lat. mediocris*, moderate, average.
5. nāḍkār, *mn.* uneducated, *as opposed to* sikpi = educated.

Common, *s.* sărkārātso zāgo, -geā, *m.* = *l.* ground of the government.

Common (In), sāngata = *l.* together.

Commonly, *ad.* tsăḍāvot, *or* tsăḍāvot zāun = *l.* usually, generally; tsālteñ; sādārṇ = mostly, ordinarily; sumār = *Lat. mediocriter.*

Commonwealth, *s.* dhāzăṇăčeñ rāz, -jā, *n.* = *l.* state of ten persons (republic).

Commotion, *s.* 1. hālāp, -lpā, *n.* *or* hālouṇeñ, -ṇeā, *n.*; *see* **Agitation.**
2. kāṭkāi, -ye, *f.* = revolution.

Commune, *s.* 1. māg-ṇeñ, -ṇeā, *n.* (a large c. comprising some smaller communes called 'grāmañ)'.
2. grām, -må, *n.* = a small c. subordinate to a 'māg-ṇeñ'.

Communicate, *v.* 1. di = give, *or* pāvoi = cause to arrive.
2. yekameka ulăi = *l.* speak reciprocally.
3. săḷāvoḷ āsā = is intercourse.
4. *in the sense of* 'is joined to', 'communicates with' *it is translated by* 'lāgtā = *l.* is attached', *e.g.* găr igărzek lāgtā = the house c. with the church; meḷon āsā *or* lāgun āsā.
5. kumgār kāṇe = *l.* receive communion.

Communication, *s.* 1. *rs. v.*; sămănd, -dā, *m.* = *l.* connexion.
2. săḷāvoḷ, -ḷi, *f.*

Communion, *s.* 1. sāngăt, -tā, *m.* = *l.* fellowship.
2. kumgār, -rā, *m.* *or* kommuniāuñ, -āvā, *m.*, *fr.*
3. mēḷ(é), -ḷā, *m.* = a collection, a gathering of people.
4. yekoṭ, -ṭā, *m.* (*or* yektār, -rā, *m.*), *e.g.* c. of saints; *this last word mn. rather* union.

Community, *see* **Communion,** 3. 4.

Commute, *v.* bădăl; bădlāk = instead of. . ., *with the verb required by the meaning*, *e.g.* c. the punishment of death into imprisonment = mornāčea formāṇa bădlāk băndint ghāl. [găṇ.

Compact, *a.* 1. ghăṭ = *l.* strong;
2. lāgun = *l.* attached, *e.g.* a c. company of soldiers.
3. kăntsoun = *l.* pressed, *from* kăntsăi = press.

Compact, *s.* kărār, -rā, *m.* = agreement.

Compactness, *s.* kăntsouṇeñ, -ṇeā, *n.*; dāmbāp, -pā, *n.*

Companion, *s.* sāngāti, -tiā, *m.* *see also* **Partner, Friend.**

Company, *s.* 1. sāngăt, -tā, *m.*
2. mēḷ(é), -ḷā, *m.* = *Lat. coetus.*
3. *sometimes rs. or crc.*

Comparative, *a.* šărtātso = *l.* conditionate, *e.g.* c. advantage.

Comparatively, *ad.* săkăṭ čintun = all thinking, *or* dusreāñ mukār = before others; săr keleār = if you compare.

Compare, *v.* 1. sārko kăr *or* săr kăr *or* săr kărn dākāi = *l.* make equal, *or* making equal show.
2. *in the sense of* 'confronting' *a copy with its original*, mokābilo kăr.

Comparison, *s.* 1. mokābilo, -leā, *m.* (*vid. sup.* **Compare,** 2.)
2. vopār, -re, *f.* = similitude, parable; guṭ, -ṭā, *m.* = *l.* secret, (parable).

In comparison with 'mukăr = *l.* in face'; *the comparative with* prăs.

Compass, *s.* 1. vistăr, -rā, *m.* = *l.* extension; suttu̥, -tā, *m.* = *l.* circumference.

2. băunḍi, -ḍe, *f.* = *l.* circuit.

3. dikkăčeñ āid, -dā, *n.* (mariner's compass).

Compasses, *s.* kovar, -rā, *m.*

Compassion, *s.* kākuḷt, -ti, *f.*; birmot, -ti, *f.* = pity; tsurtsuro, -reā, *m.*

Compassionate, *a.* kākuḷtiso, *or* kākuḷdār.

Compassionate, *v.* kākuḷt kăr, *G. F.*; (măkā) birmot distā, *G.F.* = *l.*(to me) pity appears, *n.*; tsurtsuro distā, *G. M. or* tsurtsur, *e.g.* āuñ tākā tsurtsurtāñ = I pity him.

Compel, *v. may be expressed by the causative form of the verb following, e. g.* compel him to build a house = găr bāndăi; boḷ kăr = *l.* make force, *or* bălătkār kăr; lāi = *l.* apply, induce; 'tākā borounčeāk lāi = c. him to write'; loṭ = push.

Compendium, *s.* sănkšép, -pā, *m.*

Compensate, *v.* 1. fārikpoṇ di = *l.* give satisfaction, payment; fārik kăr = *l.* pay.

2. inām *or* sāmbāḷ di = give reward *or* pay.

3. săma kăr = *l.* make right.

Compensation, *s.* fārikpoṇ, -ṇā, *n.*; inām, -mā, *n.* = *ex.* reward, *but used also for* c.; sāmbāḷ, -ḷā, *m.* = payment.

Compete, *v. see* **Vie.**

Competency, *s.* 1. zāi teñ = *l.* (what) is required that, *e.g.* mākā zāi teñ mākā āsā = what I require I have; udărpošăṇ, -ṇā, *n.*

2. hăkku̥, -kā, *n.* = right.

Competition, *s. rs into v.*

Compile, *v.* 1. kăr *or* borăi = *l.* make *or* write.

2. kāḍn borăi = *l.* drawing out write.

Complacency, *s.* kălpana, -ne, *f.*; khušālāi (*or* kušālāi), -ye, *f.*; *see also* **Pleasure.**

Complain, *v.* 1. šiṇ ulăi (*Lat. queri*) *as in the sent.* 'one complains of the ingratitude of another'.

2. legally, *see* **Accuse**; *see also* **Groan.**

Complainant, *see* **Accuser.**

Complaining, *a.* (full of complaints) kărkărātso = *l.* annoying, *used fg.*

Complaint, *s.* 1. šiṇ, -ṇā, *m.*; firyād, -di, *f.* = legal complaint; dur (*or* dhur), -rā, *n.* (non-legal); dursāṇ, -ṇā, *n.*

2. piḍa, -ḍe = *l.* sickness.

Complement, *s.* bhărti, -te, *f.*

Complete, *a.* bhorn = *l.* full, *or* săgḷo = whole, *or* purto; sămpurṇ = *l.* abundant, perfect.

Complete, *v.* 1. bhor = *l.* fill.

2. kābār kăr = *l.* finish, *fr.*: 'mākā vis vărsañ zāliñ (*or* borliñ) = I have completed my twentieth year'; tirsi.

Completely, *ad.* purteñ; păripurṇ.

Completeness, *s.* sămpurṇāi, -ye, *f.*

Completion, *s.* mugdaṇeñ (*or* mugdoṇeñ), -ṇeā, *n.*

Complex, *a.* zāite doḍo.

Complexion, *s.* 1. năḍteñ, -teā, *n.* = *l.* character.

2. kālet, -ti, *f.*, *e.g.* of body.

Complicate, *v.* gābri kăr = *l.* make confused, intricated; gusăp kăr = *l.* make confusion, *or* guspăḍāi = *l.* cause to get confused.

Complicated, *a.* kăṭiṇ = *l.* difficult.

Complication, *s.* 1. tondre, -reāñ *pl. m.* = *l.* embarrassment.

2. *rs. into v.*

Complicity, *s.* šāmilpoṇ, -ṇā, *n.*

Compliment, *s.* sălām, -mā, *m.*; rekāt, -tā, *m.*

Compliment, *v.* sălām kăr = make salute (*nearest word*).

Comply, *v.* 1. tsălāi, *e.g.* c. with a request; vop = *l.* consent.

2. khuše părmāṇe tsăl = *l.* walk according to the desire.

Comport (with), *v.* 1. zātā: 'their conduct does not comport with their principles = tānčeñ năḍteñ tānčeā pāyāñ părmāṇeñ zāināñ'.

2. tsăl = behave thyself (*pr.* walk).

Compose, *v.* 1. meḷăi = *l.* cause to be together.

2. borăi *or* kăr (books) = *l.* write *or* make.

3. săma kăr = *l.* make right (settle).

4. fuslāi = appease by sweet words: *see also* **Allay.**

5. nidān zā = *l.* become calm: *e.g.* I compose myself.

Composed, *a.* 1. meḷon *or* kello.

2. *fg.* nidān = quiet.

Composer, *s.* kărt, -tā, *m.* = *l.* author; borăitolo = *l.* writer.

Composition, *s.* 1. borăilleñ kām, -mā, *n.* = *l.* written theme, *bet. crc.*; borāp *or* pătrụ, -rā, *n.* = a written thing; ṭhărāvoṇ, -ṇi, *f.*

2. I made a c. for 50 p. c. = sembóranñ bădlāk ponās diunk kărār kelā = *l.* I made an agreement to give 50 instead of 100.

Composure, *s.* nidānāi, -ye, *f.* = *l.* calmness; sosṇigāi (*or* sosṇikāi), -ye, *f.* = patience; măryād, -di, *f.* = *l.* modesty; ghăṭăi, -ye, *f.* = strength; sămādhān, -nā, *n.*

Compound, *n.* meḷăi = *l.* cause to come together; kăr = *l.* make.

Compound, *s.* ităl, -tlā, *n.* = *l.* garden; vāṭăr, -rā, *m.*, *or* vāṭāro, -reā, *m.*

Compound, *a.* *see* **Compose.**

Comprehend, *v.* 1. āṭāpi, *e.g.* 'this

idea comprehends many others'; *c.v. of* āṭāp = is contained.

2. dhăr = catch, *fg.*; somza = *l.* understand, *Nom. or Dat. of Prs.*, *e.g.* mākā soṃzatā, *or* āuñ somzatāñ.

Comprehension, *s.* somzikāi, -ye, *f.* = *l.* understanding.

Comprehensive, *a.* vistārlolo = *l.* extended.

Compress, *v.* dāmb, *e.g.* clothes in a box; dāmp, *e.g.* c. one's lips; kăntsăi, *esp. fg.*'

Comprise, *see* **Comprehend.**

Compromise, *v.* 1. rāji (*or* kobuli) kăr = *l.* make a treaty of peace (*or* consent).

2. riskek poḍ *or* sampăḍ.

Compromise, *s.* rāji, -je, *f.* = *l.* treaty of peace; kobuli, -le, *f.* = *l.* consent.

Compulsion, 1. *pr.* bòḷ, -ḷā, *n.* = *l.* violence; ănkya, -ye, *f.*

2. *fg.* gărz, -je, *f.* = *l.* necessity; *or as in the sent.* 'I acted under c. = boḷvosṭiñ keleñ'.

Compulsory, *a.* bòḷkărtso *or* boḷātso.

Compunction, *s.* duk, -ki, *f.* = *l.* sorrow, *or bet.* ăntăskărnăči duk = *l.* sorrow of the heart; ăntăskărnăče, tsurtsure, *pl. m.*; zăḷ, -ḷā, *m.* = burning, *fg.*

Computation, *s* lèk, -kā, *n.*

Compute, *v.* lèk kăr *or only* lēk(é). 'I cannot c. the amount = mākā lèk nāñ'.

Concatenation, *s.* yekoṭ, -ṭā, *m.*, *e.g.* of events.

Concave, *s.* pokăḷ = *l.* hollow, *or* ākāšarupātso; gunḍ, *or bet.* bāgāllo = bent.

Concavity, *s.* gunḍāi, -ye, *f.* = *l.* depth, *or bet. rs. adj.*

Conceal, *v.* lipăi, *c.v. of* lip; guṭ dovor = *l.* keep the secret, *or* guṭān dovor = *l.* keep with secret.

Concealment, *s.* 1. lipouṇeñ, -ṇeā, *n.*

2. lipči suăt, -te, *f.*

Concede, *v.* di *or* soḍun di; soḍ; răja di = *l.* allow; *by the pot. mood in* yet *of the principal verb;* vop *or* kobuli di = *l.* consent (grant), *Lat. 'concede', opp. to Lat. 'nega'.*

Conceit, *s.* pisāyeči čintna, -ne, *f.* = *l.* a foolish thought; hănkār, -rā, *m.*; săḷ, -ḷā, *n.* = *l.* obstinacy.

Conceited, *a.* hănkārātso *or* hānkāri.

Conceive, *v.* 1. gărb sămbāvăi, *c.v. of* sămbāva; ubzăi, *tr. v.*; gărbest zā; *vlg.* guruār zā, *n. v.*

2. *fg.* čint = *l.* think (imagine, suppose).

Concentrate, *v.* 1. *pr.* modeñ vor, *not used in fg. mn.* = *l.* bring in the middle.

2. meḷăi, *e.g.* c. troops = păṭlām yeka zāgeār vor *or* meḷăi, *l.* collect troops in a place.

3. *fg*. c. the mind upon = bori čit diun čint, *l*. very attentively think; *or* tuji mot yekāčer āsundi = *l*. let your mind be upon one (thing); *or* buḍ = plunge thyself.

Conception, *s*. 1. konsesāuñ, -sāvā, *n*. (the Immaculate C.)
2. gărb, -bā, *m*. = *l*. fetus.
3. guruārpoṇ, -ṇā, *n*.
4. *fg*. čintnā, -ne, *f*. = *l*. thought; năkša, -še, *f*. = plan.

Concern, *s*. 1. kām, -mā, *n*. = *l*. affair.
2. zătăn, -tne, *f*. = *l*. care: 'it is an object of c. to me = āuñ tāči zătăn kāṇetāñ'.

Concern, *v*. lāg = *l*. be attached; 'mākā lāgtā = it concerns me'; 'it does not c. me = mākā lāgānāñ, *or* mojeñ kām năiñ.'

Concerned, be c. in = lāgtā; 'I too am c. in it = āni mākā lāgtā *or* mākāi lāgtā'; *Or*. višyānt kām āsā, *e.g* farmers are c. in the soil.

Concerned with, *Cm*. (mākā) kām āsā = *l*. (to me) business is.

Concerning, *prep*. višyānt = *l*. about.

Concert, *v*. āločeñ kăr = *l*. make deliberation; vop = *l*. agree, consent.

Concert, *s*. kărār, -rā, *m*.; 'by c. = kărārā părmāṇe'; vāzāp, -zpā, *n*.; *or bet*. vāzpāmēḷ, -ḷā, *m*. *used also for* musical concert.

Concession, *s*. kăbuli (*or* kobuli), -le, *f*.

Conch, *s*. šănko, -keā, *m*.

Conciliate, *v*. 1. voḍnio di = give attractions, *G. N. pl*., *n. c*.
2. sămādhān kărāi = *l*. cause peace to be made, *or* fuslāi; mòn voi kăr = *l*. make heart yes; gain the heart of.

Conciliation, *s*. sămādhān, -nā, *n*.

Concise, *a*. moṭvo *or* thoḍeañ utrāntso = *l*. short, *or* of few words; sănkšepātso.

Conclave, *s*. săbhā, -bhe, *f*. (kărdiālānči).

Conclude, *v*. 1. āker kăr = *l*. make a conclusion; tātpărya kăr (*Kn*.); kābār kăr, *or* purteñ kābār kăr = *l*. finish entirely; tirsi.
2. niščeisi = *Lat*. *statue*, draw a conclusion.

Conclusion, *s*. 1. āker, -re, *f*. = *l*. end, *e.g*. of a sermon.
2. tirp, -pā, *n*.; *bet*. niščeisilli văstụ, -tu, *f*. = resolution, *e.g*. of a meeting.
3. tātpărya, -ye, *f*. = deduction.

Concord, *s*. 1. voppigi, -ge, *f*.; sămādān, -nā, *n*.; bănāu, -nāvā, *m*.; soukāsāi, -ye, *f*.
2. sămapoḍāp, -ḍpā, *n*. = *l*. fall together (gram. c.); yekamek, -kā, *n*.

Concourse, *s*. 1. săbār lok, -kā, *m*. *or* lokātso zomo, -meā, *m*.

2. *for all other meanings, use the verb* meḷtā *or* yetā, *etc.*

Concubine, *s.* čeḍi, -ye, *f.*; dovorn ghetulli, -le, *f.*

Concupiscence, *s.* kuḍiči voḍni, -ne, *f.* = *l.* inclination of body, *or bet.* kuḍiči khuši, -še, *f.* (*strictly*); vāiṭ khuši, -še, *f.*; most, -ti, *f.*; kām, -mā, *n.* (*low w.*)

Concur, *v.* 1. mèḷ = *l.* be found, (meet in the same point).
2. pāu = *l.* come, arrive, *e.g.* God concurs with man.
3. vòp = *l.* agree.
4. kumok kăr = *l.* help, *e.g.* in a bad action; vānṭo meḷtā = a portion is received.

Concurrence, *s.* 1. mêḷ, -ḷā, *m.*; săma poḍneñ, -neā, *n.*
2. kăbuli, -le, *f.* = *l.* consent, *bet. rs.*

Concussion, *s.* ādḷāp, -pā, *n.*; *see* **Shock.**

Condemn, *v.* 1. fitvo di = *l.* give sentence (*Dat.*), *also* stigmatise; fitvo zā (*pass.*); mornāčeñ formāṇ di = give order of death, *2nd Loc.*; gunyāukār kăr = *l.* make guilty; gunyāukār zā (*pass.*); *used also in rl. mn. as in Lat.* '*qui non crediderit condemnabitur*'; 'condemned to hell = yemkouḍāntlo dāiji'.
2. *neg. of* păsănd kăr *or* kobul kăr.

Condemnation, *s.* fitvo, -veā, *m.* (civil); šikša, -ṣe, *f.* = *l.* punishment.

Condensation, *s.* kăntsouṇeñ, -ṇeā, *n.*; lāgāp, -gpā, *n.*; găṇụpoṇ, -ṇā, *n.*; dāmbāp, -pā, *n.*

Condense, *v.* kăntsăi (*esp. in fg. mn.*); găṇụ kăr; dāmb = *l.* press; āuḷ"; lāgăi *or* lāgiñ meḷăi; dāṭ kăr, *l.*

Condescend, *v.* 1. puṭua = (*Lat. dignare*) deign.
2. vòp = *l.* agree, consent.
3. *G.* khuše părmāṇe tsăl = *l.* walk according to the will of. . .

Condescension, *s.* puṭuāp, -pā, *n.*; dăya, -ye, *f.* = *l.* clemency; *bet. rs. v.*

Condign, *a.* 1. fāvo (*indecl.*) *or* fāvozāllo.
2. devo = *l.* due; vāzbi = *l.* convenient.

Condiment, *s.* 1. foṇṇụ, -ṇā, *or* fòḍṇụ, -ṇā, *n.* (for seasoning); čăṭṇi, -ṇe, *f.* (*Engl.* chutney).
2. nisteñ, -teā, *n.* = what is taken with meat *etc.*; păkvān, -nā, *n.* (*It. companatico.*)

Condition, *s.* 1. sthiti, -ti, *f.* = *l.* state.
2. săngăt, -gti, *f.* = *l.* circumstance.
3. šért (*var.* šărt), -tā, *n.*, *e.g.* of a contract.
4. kărār, -rā, *m.* = *l.* agreement.

Conditional, *a.* šertātso; *often bet. rs.*

Conditionally, *ad.* šertān *or* šert zāun; *often rs.*

Condole, *v.* bhuzăi = *l.* comfort, *ch. cs.* (*Acc.*); duk-tā = *l.* is sorry *ch. cs.* (pāsun); (āuñ) duk pāutāñ (pāsvot); (mākā) birmot distā (tuje pāsun) = *l.* (to me) pity appears (for thee); kākuḷt kăr, *G. F.* = *l.* make compassion.

Conduce, *v.* poḍ = *l.* fall, *e.g.* to the advantage of; *this verb is the one most frequently used to express* advantage *or* disadvantage; *it may be translated by* sārko, *e.g.* it conduces to move the heart = movaḷāi sārko (zāun āsā); *in subordinate sentences, it may be expressed by the* Imperfect subj.; *see* Gram.

Conduct, *s.* 1. nădteñ, -teā, *n.* (behaviour).
2. *by* tsălăi, *e.g.* under your conduct = tumiñ tsălăitanañ; tsălouṇeñ, -ṇeā, *n.*, *n. c.*; *by* khāl = under, *e.g.* under your c. = tumče kh.

Conduct, *v.* 1. tsălăi, *pr.* = cause to walk, as a mother her child, *and fg.* as a king conducts his kingdom.
2. vor = *l.* bring, as a general conducts soldiers.
3. tsăl = *l.* walk, *fg.* (behave).

Cone, *s. there is no word in Konk. to express the geometrical figure, if not* čip, -pā, *n.* = wedge, *or* bunu; *Mr. Cn. Sans.* šănku, -kā, *m.*

Confection, *s. approx.* miṭāi, -ye, *f.*; dòs, -si, *f.*; hālvo, -veā, *m.*

Confederacy, *s.* sollo, -leā, *m.*; iṣṭăgăt, -ti, *f.* = *l.* friendship.

Confederate, *s*, solleāgār, -rā, *m.*; iṣ̈ṭ, -ṭā, *m.* = *l.* friend.

Confer, *v.* 1. di = *l.* give; kăr = *l.* do.
2. āločen kăr = make deliberation; săbha kăr.
3. *Cm.* ulăi; *G.* bud vitsār = *l.* ask advice of.

Conference, *s.* 1. uloṇeñ, -ṇeā, *n.* = *l.* colloquy; kuṭ, -ṭā, *n.* = *l.* secret (improper, illegal) meeting.
2. budbāḷ, -ḷi, *f.* = *l.* familiar exhortation.
3. mēḷ(é), -ḷā, *m.* = *l.* meeting, reunion.

Confess, *v.* 1. vòp = *l.* acknowledge, grant, consent; kobuli di = *l.* give consent; voḷka = acknowledge; nīz zāun sāng = say sincerely.
2. kumsār kăr = hear confession, *rl.*; kumsārāk bos = *l.* sit for confession.
3. kumsār zā = c. oneself. (*Cm.*)

Confession, *s.* 1. voppigi, -ge, *f.* = *l.* consent; *rs. into v.*
2. kumsār, -rā, *n.* (*rl.*)

Confessional, *s.* kumsăr, -ri, *f.* (*rl.*)

Confessor, *s.* 1. *vlg.* pādri, -ri, *m. or* konfesor, -rā, *m.* (hearing

confession); kumsār kărtolo; 'who is your c.? = koṇa lāgiñ kumsār zātāi ?'
2. bāvāḍt utsārtolo = professing (Christian) faith; *or* konfesor, -rā, *m.*, *fr.*

Confide, *v.* 1. pātiye, *2nd Loc.*, *or* pātiyeṇi dovor = rely on.
2. vopsun di = give over; suādin di = *l.* alienate, *pr. fg.*, *e.g.* a son; tāben di = *l.* give in care.

Confidence, *s.* pātiyeṇi, -ṇi, *f.*: 'in c. = guṭān'.

Confidential, *a.* 1. pātiyeṇitso.
2. guṭātso, *or rs.* guṭ, -ṭā, *m.*

Configuration, *s.* rūp, -pā, *n.*; ākār, -rā, *m.*

Confine, *s.* sărhăddụ, -de, *f.* = boundary; găḍ, -ḍi, *f.* = boundary; mit, -ti, *f.*, *or bet.* mèr, -re, *f.* = boundary.

Confine, *v.* dāmp = *l.* shut; bānd = *l.* tie; băndint ghāl = put into prison.

Be confined to bed = *a*) āntuḷnār āsā; *b*) porsut zā, bāḷānt zā = bring forth.

Confined, *a.* ăšir = *l.* narrow.

Confinement, *s.* bănd, -di, *f.* = *l.* fetters *or* bonds; bālntyor, -rā, *m.* = *Lat. partus*; *rs. into v.*

Confirm, *v.* 1. thir kăr, *pr.*, *fg.*, *e. g.* the Sacraments c. us; *or also* confirm a contract.
2. păsănd kăr *or* kobul kăr; vòp = approve, consent.
3. krizm di, *fr.* = *l.* give confirmation.

Confirmation, *s.* 1. thirāsāṇ, -ṇe, *f.*
2. krizm, -mā, *m.*, *fr.* (*rl.*)

Confiscate, *v.* zăpti kăr (*var.* jepti k.).

Confiscation, *s.* zăpti, -te, *f.*

Conflagration, *s.* voḍ uzo, -jeā, *m.*; lāsāp, -spā, *n.*

Conflict, *s.* 1. lăḍāi, -ye, *f.*; zuz, -zā, *n.* = *l.* war.
2. *fg.* nāi, -yā, *m.* = *l.* discord; zăgaḍneñ, *or* zăgḍeñ, -ḍeā, *n.*

Conflict, *v.* 1. lăḍāi kăr.
2. zăgăḍ = *l.* quarrel.

Conflicting, *a.* virodh āsullo = *l.* contrary, *e. g.* c. words; lāganātullo = *l.* non-cohering; sămapoḍanātullo.

Confluent, *s.* 1. sāngāta vāutolo.
2. năintso phānṭo, -ṭeā, *m.* = branch of a river.

Conform, *v.* rūp di; *see* **Adapt, Accommodate, Comply.**

Conformation, *s.* rūp, -pā, *n.*; *rs. v.*

Conformity, *s.* 1. sămapoḍneñ, -neā, *n.* = *l.* falling right, *fg.*; sārkeñ, -keā, *n.* = *l.* similitude.
2. lāyekpoṇ, -ṇā, *n.* = *l.* suitableness.
3. yekoṭ, -ṭā, *m.* = *l.* conjunction, *e.g.* c. with the will of God, (*see* **Uniformity**).
4. tents rūp, -pā, *n.* = *l.* the same form.
5. *rs. into* pārmāṇe tsăl = behave according to the. . .

(*or another verb instead of* **tsăl** *may be used, as the mn. requires*).

Confound, *v.* 1. guspaḍăi = *l.* cause confusion, *c. v. of* guspoḍ (*or* guspaḍ); gălibili kăr (gābri k.) = *l.* make perplexed; *pass.* guspoḍ; sāmpăḍăi (*or* sāmpḍăi) = entangle, *c. v. of* sāmpăḍ; širkăi, *c. v. of* širka. 2. borsi *or* meḷăi = *l.* mix, join. 3. lăzăi = *l.* put to shame; *c. v. of* lăz, *n. v.*

Confraternity, *s.* bhāvapoṇ (*or* bhāupoṇ), -ṇā, *n.*, *n. u.*; *vlg.* konfrụ, -ri, *f.*, *fr.*; irmāuñdād, -di, *f.*, *fr.*; 'enter a c. = irmāuñ zā', *n. v.*, *fr.*

Confrère, *s.* irmāuñ, -āvā, *m.*, *fr.*; bhāu, *or* sāngātbhāu, -āvā, *m.*

Confront, *v.* 1. mukār rāu = *l.* remain in face, *n. v.* 2. mokābilo kăr = *l.* make comparison (of a copy with its original); *vlg.* yeñ āni teñ poḷe.

Confuse, *see* **Confound.**

Confusion, *s.* gusāp, -spā, *n. or* guspăḍ, -ḍe, *f.*, *fg.*, *pr.*; gondóḷ, -ḷā, *m.*

Confutation, *s.* solvāp, -pā, *n.*; păḍāu, -ḍāvā, *m.* = *l.* defeat, *fg.*

Confute, *v.* soluăi, *c. v. of* solua; păḍāu kăr, *e. g.* arguments.

Congeal, *v.* kăre kăr (găr kăr?), *tr. v.*; *fg.* bhou thănḍ kăr, *tr. v.*; ghăṭ kăr, *tr. v.*

Congee, (*Anglo-Ind. word*), *s.* pèz, -je, *f.* (boiled rice and water).

Congenital, *a.* săimbātso; zălmātso.

Congestion, *s.* răgtasănkăṭ, -ṭā, *n.* (*var.* -sankaḷ, *agreeing with Mr.*)

Conglomerate, *v.* zomo (*or* rās) kăr.

Congratulate, *v.* părab *or* porāb di, *or* p. kăr; (āuñ) săntos pāutañ (tuje pāsun, ăče thăiñ) = *l.* (I) feel joy (for you, about this); *vlg.* boreñ fest di *or* b. f. māg.

Congratulation, *s.* = părab, -rbe, *f.*

Congregate, *v.* meḷăi, *c. v.*; zomăi *or* zomo kăr; rās kăr = *l.* make heap.

Congregation, *s.* mēḷ(é), -ḷā, *m.*; zomo, -meā, *m.*; lók, -kā, *m.* = *l.* people.

Congress, *s.* săbha, -bhe, *f.*; mēḷ, (é) -ḷā, *m.*; *vlg.* zunt, -tā, *m.*

Congruence, *s.* lāyekpoṇ, -ṇā, *n.*; sămapoḍāp, -ḍpā, *n.*

Congruent, *a.* lāyek; sămapoḍtso.

Congruity, *s.* 1. vāzbipoṇ, -ṇā, *n.* 2. *see* **Congruence.**

Conjecture, *s.* 1. pārkoṇeñ, -ṇeā, *n.* = *l.* guess; parak, -kā, *n.* 2. āločen, -ni, *f.* = *l.* opinion; gunḍhăḷt, -tā, *n.* (rough estimate, *e. g.* of the number of pages in a book at a glance).

Conjecture, *v.* pārki = *l.* guess; āločen kăr; distā = *l.* appear, *ch. cs.*

Conjunction, *s.* 1. mēḷ(é), -ḷā, *m.* (*esp.* state of c.).
2. yekoṭ, -ṭā, *m.* (*esp.* act of conjoining).
3. zomo, -meā, *m.* = *l.* collection.

Conjuncture, *s.* săngăt, -gti, *f.* = *l.* circumstance; sămayo, -yeā, *m.* = *l.* occasion; vēḷ(é), -ḷā, *m.* = *l.* time, opportunity.

Conjuration, *s.* 1. măntrụ, -trā, *n.* (illicit).
2. lāleunčeñ māg-ṇeñ, -ṇeā, *n.* = *l.* longing request; umāḷeāčeñ māg-ṇeñ = *l.* longing request.

Conjure, *v.* 1. măntrụ kăr (in a forbidden way).
2. āṇ māg = ask under oath.
3. lāleun māg = *l.* ask longing.

Connect, *v.* 1. bānd = tie; meḷăi; lāgăi; jodsi *or* gădsi *or* sóndăi, *e.g.* two planks.
2. kăntsăi (connect by dovetailing, *etc.*, *n. c. in pr. mn.*).

Connection, *s.* 1. yekoṭ, -ṭā, *m.* = *l.* union; bāndāp, -dpā, *n.* = *l.* binding.
2. *fg.* săirik, -ke, *f.* = *l.* affinity (*abstr.*); săiro, -reā, *m.* (*concrete*).
3. *fg.* sămănd, -dā, *m.* = *l.* relation.
4. *fg.* sălgi, -ge, *f.* = *l.* intimacy; iṣṭăgăt, -ti, *f.* = *l.* friendship.
5. kām, -mā, *n.*, *e. g.* I have no c. with him = mākā tāčekāḍe kām nāñ; *see* **Intercourse.**

Connive, *v.* šāmil zā = *l.* become accomplice; poḷeun poḷeinātụllea bări kăr (*or another equivalent verb in place of* kăr); doḷe dāmp = *l.* shut eyes, *fg.*

Connivance, *s.* šāmilpoṇ, -ṇā, *n.*

Conquer, *v.* 1. jik = *l.* gain, *fg.*; zăit vor, *2nd Loc.*
2. (zulmen) kāṇe, *e.g.* a town, *l.* take (violently); solvăi, păḍāu kăr = defeat.
3. *fg.* āḍ ye = *l.* come against, *e. g.* passions; inkār kăr (*Acc.*) = *l.* resist, *e.g.* passions; mōḍ (ó) = *l.* break, *e.g.* passions; palvoi = *l.* quench, *e.g.* passions. [vortolo.

Conqueror, *s.* jikpi, -piā, *m.*; zăit

Conquest, *v.* jikāp, -kpā, *n.*; zăit, -tā, *n.* = *l.* victory.

Consanguinity, *s.* (bāpā isili) săirik, -ke, *f.* = *l.* relation on the side of the father.

Conscience, *s.* ăntăskărn, -nā, *n.*; *some use* konsert, -tā, *n.*; hărđeñ, -deā, *n.*; 'case of c. = bāb, -be, *f.*'; 'remorse of c. = ăntăskărnātso kiḍo, -ḍeā, *m.*' *or* 'tsurtsuro, -reā, *m.*'

Conscientious, *a.* nitivont *or perh.* ăntăskărnātso; ăntăskărnā părmāṇe tsăltolo; sārko = *l.* exact; nāzuk ăntăskărnātso; *vlg.* konserti.

Conscientiousness, *s.* nīt, -ti, *f.*; nāzuk ăntăskărn, -nā, *n.*; ābru, -rā, *m.* = *l.* character; *see* **Conscience.**

Conscious, *a.* motir āsullo = *l.* being on mind (in possession of one's senses) = voḷkontso, *e.g.* of a fault.

Be c. of = voḷkā, *l.* recognize; kăḷtā, *Sb. Dat.*

Consciousness, *s.* mot, -ti, *f.* = *l.* mind; *rs. into v. or adj.*

Consecrate, *v.* 1. păvitrụ kăr = *l.* make sacred.

2. bheṭăi = *l.* dedicate (Devāk); *see* **Offer**; somorpi; konsekrār kăr, *fr.*; benjār kăr, *fr.*, *e.g.* water, a cemetery; bezment kăr, *fr.*, *e.g.* houses.

Consecrated, *a.* păvitrụ; *vlg.* benjār keḷḷo (*var.* benjer k.).

Consecration, *s.* 1. bheṭouṇeñ, -ṇeā, *n.*; somorpouṇeñ, -ṇeā, *n.*; *or* sămărpoṇ, -ṇā, *n.*

2. bezment, -tā, *n.*; konsekrasāuñ, -sāvā, *n.*, *fr.*; (at mass) păvitrụpoṇ, -ṇā, *n.* *or* păvitrụ kărni, -ne, *f.* *or bet.* păvitrụ kărčeñ; *rs. v.*

Consecutive, *a.* 1. māgirtso = *l.* which is after.

2. pāṭlo = *l.* which is behind; pāṭleān yeuntso = coming after.

Consent, *s.* kobul, -li, *f.*, *or* koblāt, -ti, *f.*; voppigi, -ge, *f.*

Consent, *v.* 1. kobul kăr; vop = *l.* consent, *e.g.* to a proposal, to temptation, *etc.*

2. khuši vor = *l.* desire, *e.g.* c. to temptation; (mākā) metsvātā (teñ) = *l.* (to me) is approved (that); metsoṇi kăr.

Consequence, *s.* 1. fóḷ, -ḷā, *m.* = *l.* effect, what follows.

2. sevoṭ, -ṭā, *m.* = *l.* issue; *rs. into* zātā = is done, *or* happens.

In c. of = pāsun *or* pāsvot *or* dekun; *see* Gram.

Consequent, *see* **Consequence.**

Consequently, *ad.* tăr; dekun; teā pāsun.

Conservation, *s.* sāmbaḷāi, -ye, *f.* *or* sām̃baḷāp, -ḷpā, *n.*; rākṇeñ, -ṇeā, *n.*; *bet. rs. v.*

Conservative, *a.* sāmbāḷtolo (ādleo sovoyo).

Conserve, *see* **Preserve.**

Conserves, *s.* miṭāi, -ye, *f.*; hālvo, (*or* ālvo), -veā, *m.*

Consider, *v.* 1. niyāḷ; āločen kăr; (boreñ kărn) čint; dhyān kăr; prestāu kăr, *e.g.* what sin is.

2. zătăn kăr = *l.* take care, *e.g.* c. your own well-being.

3. lėk, *e.g.* I c. him a friend.

Considerable, *a.* bhou = much, *or* čikke (*or* tikke) voḍ.

Considerate, *a.* tsătrāyetso; budivont; zāgrut.

Consideration, *s.* 1. niyāḷ, -ḷā, *m.*; dhyān, -nā, *n.*; prestāu, -tāvā, *m.*, *e.g.* about God.

2. zătăn, -tne, *f.* = *l.* care tsătrāi, -ye, *f.* = attention, care.

3. āločen, -ni, *f.* = *l.* opinion, deliberation, reason, regard; vitsār, -rā, *m.*
4. măryād, -di, *f.* = *l.* honesty, honour.
5. zăbāb, -bi, *f.* = *l.* motive.
Take into c. = āločenik kāṇe; riyāt kăr.

Considering, *prep.* čintun = *l.* by thinking; *rs. into* părmāṇe, *ch. cs.*

Consign, *v.* vopsun di; tāben di.

Consignment, *s.* vopsāp, -pā, *n.* *or bet.* vopsoṇeñ, -ṇeā, *n.*

Consist, *v.* 1. meḷon āsā; kello āsā.
2. zātā = agrees, is in accordance.

Consistence, Consistency, *s.* 1. dāṭāi, -ye, *f.* = *l.* thickness; ghăṭāi, -ye, *f.*
2. *fg.* nidānāi, -ye, *f.* = *l.* equability; *or also* thirguṇ, -ṇā, *m.* = *l.* constancy.

Consistent, *a.* 1. thir = *l.* firm.
2. yekameka lāgtso = *l.* attached reciprocally, *or* sāma poḍtso, *e.g.* c. sermon; *or bet. rs. with* vāṇṭe lāgtāt = the parts are attached.

Consistory, *s.* săbha, -bhe, *f.*

Consolation, *s.* 1. bhuzoṇ, -ṇe, *f.* (*esp.* of persons in sorrow).
2. săntós, -sā, *m.* = joy; ulās, -sā, *m.* = joy, *etc.*

Console, *v.* 1. bhuzăi, *c. v.*
2. *one of the above* Nouns *with* di.

Consolidate, *v.* ghăṭ kăr.

Consonance, *s.* 1. voppigi, -ge, *f.* = *l.* consent.
2. sămapoḍāp, -ḍpā, *n.*

Consonant, *s.* sāngāta utsārčeñ (akṣer, -ra, *n.*), *or the Mr.*, *Cn.*, *Sans.* vyanjan (venjan), -nā, *n.*

Consort, *s.* 1. sāngāti, -tiā, *m.*; sāngātiṇ, -ṇi, *f.*
2. ghărkār, -rā, *m.*; ghărkārn, -ni, *f.*; poti, -ti, *m.*; potiṇ, -ṇi, *f.*, *etc.*: *see* **Husband.**

Conspicuous, *a.* 1. distso = *l.* appearing; diṣṭik poḍtso = *l.* visible; drăṣṭitso, *n. c.*
2. nāvāḍdik *or* nāvāḍlolo (*var.* nāvāḍgo).

Conspicuously, *ad.* bhāirăng; *see* **Conspicuous.**

Conspiracy, *s.* kuṭ, -ṭā, *n.*

Conspirator, *s.* kuṭāgār, -rā, *m.*

Conspire, *v.* 1. kuṭ kăr = *l.* make a plot.
2. vop = *l.* agree, *ch. cs.*
3. petsāḍ = *l.* try, *ch. cs.*; *see* **Vie.**

Constable, (policeman), *s.*, *vlg.* pholisman, -nā, *m.*; *see* **Policeman.**

Constancy, *s.* thirāsāṇ, -ṇi, *f.* *or* thirguṇ, -ṇā, *m.*; ghăṭāi, -ye, *f.*

Constant, *a.* thir; *rs.* khăḷānāstānāñ, = *l.* without interruption; sădāntso = *l.* of always, *or bet. rs. into* sădānts.

Constellation, *s.* neketrānči rās, -si, *f.*

Consternation, *s.* bheñ, bhiyā, *n.* = *l.* fear; ākānt, -tā, *m.* = *l.* distress; gusăp, -spā, *m.* = *l.* confusion.

Constipated (Be), *vlg.* utkāḍe bănd zā; kuntăṇ.

Constipation, *s.* kuntăṇāp, -pā, *n.*, *n. c.*; săit, -tā, *n.*

Constitute, *v.* 1. niščeisi (*var.* niččeisi) = *l.* establish.
2. kăr = *l.* do (compose), *or bet. rs.* meḷon āsā, *ch. cs.*; săimb āsā = *l.* nature is, *ch. cs.*
3. nemsi = *l.* appoint.

Constitution, *s.* 1. kāleti (*var.* kālet, -ti), -ti, *f.* (bodily c., good bodily c.); kuḍitso guṇ, -ṇā, *m.* = *l.* quality of body.
2. (rājā-)kāide, = *l.* laws (of the state); (rājā-)rūp, -pā, *n.* = *l.* form (of government); *see* **Foundation.**

Constitutional, *a.* kāideā părmāṇe āsullo, *or prh.* kāideātso.

Constrain, *v.* bòḷ kăr = *l.* make violence; lāi = *l.* apply, *e.g.* c. to do.

Constrained, *a.* tònḍātso = *l.* of the mouth, *e.g.* c. laugh; āḍetso, *e.g.* walk, *etc.*

Constraint, *see* **Compulsion.**

Construct, *v.* bānd = *l.* build; kăr = *l.* dó.

Construction, *s.* 1. bāndāp, -dpā, *n.* = *l.* building.
2. the act of constructing, *rs. into v.*
3. rūp, -pā, *n.* = *l.* form; ākār, -rā, *m.* = *l.* figure.
4. (utrānči) mānḍāvoḷ, -ḷi, *f.* = *l.* arrangement (of words).
5. ărthu̥, -thā, *m.* = *l.* meaning.
6. găḍāvoḷ, -ḷi, *f.* (*used with* hāḍānči).

Construe, *v.* 1. (utrāñ) mānḍ = *l.* arrange (words).
2. ărthu̥ sāng = *l.* say meaning.

Consul, *s.* 1. *approx.* ădhikāri, -ri, *m.*, *or* ădhipăti, -ti, *m.*; konsul, -lā, *m.*, *fr.*
2. *in modern mn.* sărkārātso văkil, *or* -dălāl, -lā, *m.*

Consult, *v.* 1. bud kāṇe; măslăt kăr (illegally); āločen kăr = *l.* make opinion (deliberation).
2. zătăṇ kāṇe = *l.* take care, *G.F.*

Consultation, *s.* āločenimēḷ(é), -ḷā, *m.*, *e. g.* of ministers; măslăt, -ti, *f.* (illegal); āločen, -ni, *f.* = *l.* deliberation; bud, -di, *f.* = *l.* advice.

Consulter, *s.* bud sāngtolo.

Consume, *v.* 1. nāš kăr, *Acc.* = *l.* make ruin; vibāḍ kăr.
2. lās = *l.* burn, *tr.*, *n. v.*
3. pind = *l.* tear (a dress); *see* **Wear.**
4. mugdi = *l.* put an end; *c. v. of* mugda, *n. v.*
5. khărči = *l.* expend; veṭ, *e.g.* money.
6. hóstu̥ kāṇghe, *rl. mn.*

Consummate, *v.* 1. tirsi, *c. v. of* tirsa (finish).

2. sămpurṇ kăr; bhorn kăr.

Consummate, *a.* sămpurṇ = *l.* perfect.

Consummation, *s.* 1. tirsāp, -pā, *n.*

2. sevoṭ, -ṭā, *m.* = *l.* issue.

Consumption, *s.* kevād, -di, *f.* (disease).

Consumptive, *s.* kevādi, -diā, *m.*

Consumptive, *a.* kevāditso.

Contact, *s.* āpḍāp, -pā, *or* āpoḍṇeñ, -ṇeā, *n.*, *bet. rs. v.* āpoḍ; *or still bet.* lāi *or* lāg.

Contagion, *s.* voso, -seā, *m.*

Contagious, *a.* voseātso; *rs. into* lāg = *l.* be attached.

Contain, *v.* 1. dăr, *e.g.* this box contains gold; āṭāpi, *c. v. of* āṭāp, *n. v.*, *pr. fg.*, *e.g.* the ten commandments are contained in two precepts.

2. *fg.* mōḍ = *l.* break, *fg.* (check); bāgāi = *l.* bend, *fg.*, *c. v.* of bāgā *or* bāgo; čents = *l.* crush, *fg.*

Contaminate, *v.* khătāi = violate; băṣṭāi = violate; mheḷo kăr, *or* mheḷāi, *pr. fg.*; ăḷšik kăr; čikol kăr.

Contamination, *s.* khătouṇeñ, -ṇeā, *n.*, *or* khătounčeñ, *or* khăt, -tā, *n*; ăḷšik văstụ, -tu, *f.* = *l.* ugly thing, *fg.*; ăḷšik-poṇ, -ṇā, *n.*, čikol, -klā, *m.*, *fg.*, *see* **Impurity.**

Contemplate, *v.* niyāl, *or* niyāḷ kăr; dhyān kăr (*more ex. than* niyāḷ); tòp kăr, *h. w.*; topāk bos = *l.* sit for contemplation.

Contemplation, *s.* tòp, -pā, *n.*; dhyān, -nā, *n.*; vorto niyāḷ, -ḷā, *m.*

Contemplative, *s.* tòp kărtolo; *in its widest sense* niyāḷi, -ḷiā, *m.*

Contemporarily, *ad.* teāts veḷār; soveñ.

Contemporary, *a.* teāts veḷātso, *or* t. kālātso; yekăts veḷātso, *or* yekăts kālātso; *bet. rs. into adv.*

Contempt, *s.* bepārvo, -veā, *m.* *or* bepārvāi, -ye, *f.*; ăsăḍḍụ, -ḍā, *n.*

Contemptible, *a.* bepārvo fāvozāllo *or* bepārveātso; hălko, *or* ăṇvo = *l.* low; uṇo = *l.* inferior, *fg.*; thoḍeā lekātso; *rs.* mol bānd.

Contend, *v.* 1. zăgăḍ = *l.* quarrel; ārenji; lăḍāi kăr = *l.* fight.

2. inkār kăr = *l.* resist (*Acc.*).

3. petsăḍ = *l.* try, vie; prăyătăn kăr = make effort.

4. khănḍit săng = *l.* say positively.

Content, *s.* dādosāṇ, -ṇe (-ṇi), *f.* *or* dādoskāi, -ye, *f.*; săntos, -sā, *m.*; khušālāi, -ye, *f.*; ulās, -sā, *m.*

Content, *a.* dādos; săntosātso *etc.*

Contention, *s.* 1. zăgḍeñ, -ḍeā, *n.*; lăḍāi, -ye, *f.* = *l.* fight; nāi, -yā, *m.* = *l.* discord.

2. prăyătăn, -tnā, *n.* = *l.* effort; petsāḍneñ, -neā, *n.* = *l.* effort, emulation.

Contentious, *a.* zăgḍontso, (*bet.* zăgăḍtso), *or* lăḍāi kărtso, *or* nāyeḷi.

Contentment, *see* **Content.**

Contents, *s.* năg, -gā, *m.* = *l.* article; dărleleo văstu = *l.* things contained.

Conterminous, *a.* lāgsilo *or* lāgtso, *or rs.* lāgiñ; *rs.* mit (*or* mitmer) āsā *or* lāg.

Contest, *v.* 1. *see* **Contend.**
2. sāmbāḷ = *l.* defend, *e. g.* c. rights.

Contest, *s.* *see* **Contention.**

Context, *s.* 1. utrānči māndāvoḷ, -ḷi, *f.*; utrāntso sămănd, -dā, *m.*; mătlăb, -bā, *m.* (*or* -be, *f.*), *e. g.* of a passage.
2. ărth, -thā, *m.* = *l.* meaning.

Contiguity, *s.* lāgāp, -gpā, *n.*; *bet. rs. into v. or adj.*

Contiguous, *a.* lāgiñ āsullo *or* lāgsilo; lāgtso; *bet. rs. into adv. or into* lāg.

Continence, *s.* 1. sāmbāḷoṇeñ, -ṇeā, *n. or* sāmbāḷāp, -ḷpā, *n.*; nidānāi, -ye, *f.*; sudăḷāi, -ye, *f.* = self-control.
2. *fg.* niskăḷāi, *or* niskăḷkāi, -ye, *f.* = *l.* chastity.

Continent, *a.* 1. seguṇi; nidāni; āpṇāk sāmbāḷtolo; sudăḷ.
2. niskăḷ.

Continent, *s.* (suki) buiñ, -iṇ, *f. or* (suko) gāun, -āvā, *m.*

Contingency, *s.* găḍāp, -ḍpā, *n.*; *by Pot. Mood.*

Contingent, *a.* ākăsmătātso; aučit; grātsārātso; *rs. Pot. Mood.*

Continual, *a.* khālinātullo (*var.* khăḷānātullo); sădāntso, *bet. rs. into* sădānts, *or* rāvanāstānāñ *etc.*

Continually, *ad.* khăḷānāstānāñ; rāvanāstānāñ; sădānts.

Continuation, *s.* mukārtsăloùṇeñ, -ṇeā, *n.*; mukārtsălāp, -lpā, *n.*; *bet. rs.*

Continue, *v.* 1. mukār tsălăi, *c. v. of* mukār tsăl, *n. v.*
2. mukār vetā, *n. v.*
3. (thir) rāu.
4. āni vāido di = give more time.

Continuity, *s.* 1. nāñkhāli, -li, *f.*
2. nāñrāvāp, -rāupā, *n.*
3. *rs. into v.*

Continuous, *a.* khăḷānātullo.

Contortion, *etc.*, *see* **Wreath.**

Contraband, *s.* tsoriyehăḍāp, -ḍpā, *n.*, *n. c.*; 'make c. = tsoriye vor; sunk tsukăi'.

Con'traband, *a.* (kāideān) mănna kello, *or bet.* tsoriyetso.

Contract, *s.* kărār, -rā, *m.*; guttigeñ, -geā, *n.*; gutto, -teā, *m.*
C. of marriage = kărār, *or rs. into* săirik, *or* mudi ghālči.

Contract, *v.* 1. kărār (*or* gutto) kăr.
2. uṇo (*or* ăšir) kăr = *l.* diminish, make narrow; ăširăi, *c. v. of* ăšir, *n. v.*, *n. u.*

3. zātā = is produced, *or* lāgtā = is attached, *Sb. Dat.*, *e.g.* a disease.
4. kăr = do, *e.g.* c. a friendship.
5. mirio ghāl = *l.* make folds, *pass.* m. poḍ; vānkḍo kăr, *e.g.* the face.
6. zoḍn ghe, *e.g.* c. an obligation.

Contracted, *a.* 1. ăšir; moṭvo; dākṭo.
2. *fg.* somzanātullo.

Contraction, *s.* šănkšep, -pā, *n.* = *l.* abridgment; moṭvepoṇ, -ṇā, *n.*

Contractor, *s.* gutteagār, -rā, *m.*

Contradict, *v.* 1. *Dat.* āḍ ulăi; inkār kăr (*Acc.*).
2. *neg. of* lāg, *e.g.* you c. yourself; *Dat.* virodh āsā; *neg. of* săma poḍ.

Contradiction, *s.* 1. inkār, -ri, *f.* (*var.* -rā, *n.*) = *l.* resistance; āḍuloṇeñ, -ṇeā, *n.*
2. virodhăi, -ye, *f.* = inconsistency; nākāzāllo, -leā, *m.* = *l.* absurdity, nonsense; *rs. into neg. form of* lāg.

Contradictory, *a.* virodh (āsullo); lāganātullo; samāpoḍānātullo.

Contrariety, *s.* virodhăi, -ye, *f.*

Contrary, *a.* 1. porto; virodh āsullo *or* virodh vetso.
2. *fg.* ăuguṇātso = *l.* unfavourable; sămapoḍānātullo.

Contrary to, *see* **Against.**

On the c. = porteñ.

Contrast, *s.* tăfāvot, -ti, *f.*, *e.g.* of white and black, good and evil; bhēd(é), -dā, *m.* = *l.* difference.

Contrast, *v. Dat.* āḍ āsā; *see* **Differ.**

Contravene, *v.* mōḍ(ó) = *l.* break, *fg.*, *e.g.* c. a law; *Dat.* āḍ vetā.

Contravention, *s.* moḍāp, -ḍpā, *n.* (kāideā m.); āḍyeuṇeñ, -ṇeā, *n.*, *n. c.*, *e. g.* c. of an order.

Contribute, *v.* pāu; kumok kăr; tsăḍăi = *l.* increase, *ch. cs.*

Contribution, *s.* 1. pāunčeñ, *or* pāvāp, pāupā, *n.*; kumok, -mke, *f.*
2. vānṭo, -ṭeā, *m.* = *l.* portion; *often rs. v.*

Contrite, *a.* dukest *or* dukitso.

Contrition, *v.* Dēvmogāči duk, -ki, *f.*, *rl.*; *speaking broadly* (pātkānči) duk.

Make an act of c. = dukitso ākt kăr.

Contrivance, *s.* upāi, -yā, *m.*; hikmăt, -ti, *f.*; čămătkār, -rā, *m.*; nāḍ, -ḍi, *f. see* **Plan.**

Contrive, *v.* 1. sodun meḷ = *l.* by seeking be found, *ch. cs.*; sodun kāḍ = *l.* by seeking take; čint = *l.* think; nāḍ kăr *or* n. tsălăi = play a trick.
2. kăr, *e.g.* c. schemes = hikmăt kăr.

Control, *v.* tsălăi = *l.* govern; sāmbāḷ = *l.* defend, guard; rāk = *l.* guard; melbăndobăst poḷe; kăbărdāri kāṇe (take care of).

Control, *s.* melbăndobăst, -ti, *f.* kăbărdāri, -re, *f.*

Lose (one's) self-c. = utsāmboḷ zā.

Controversy, *s.* 1. tărk, -kā, *n.* = *l.* discussion; čărtso, -čeā, *m.*

2. nămbăr, -brā, *n.* = legal case, *fr.*; vyājyụ, -jyā, *m.*; nāi, -yā, *m.* = *l.* discord.

Controvert, *v.* tărk kăr.

Controvertible, *a.* tărkātso.

Contumacious, *a.* săḷiṣṭ; dhāruṇ.

Contumacy, *s.* săḷ, -ḷā, *n.*; dhāruṇāi, -ye, *f.*

Contumelious, *a.* ăkmānātso *or* ăpamānādik; gāḷi sountso.

Contumely, *s.* ăkmān, -nā, *m.*, *or* ăpamān, -nā, *m.*; gāḷ, -ḷi, *f.*

Contuse, *see* **Bruise.**

Contusion, *s.* dāḍāuṇeñ, -ṇeā, *n.*; loḷo. -ḷeā, *m.*

Convalescence, *s.* guṇ, -ṇā, *m.*; *rs.* boro zātā.

Convalescent, *a.* guṇātso; *bet. rs.* (tākā) guṇ zātā; *or* boro zātā.

Convene, *v.* meḷăi; āpoi; 'c. a meeting = meḷāk āpoi; zuntāk āpoi,' *fr.*

Convenience, *s.* 1. vāzbipoṇ, -ṇā, *n.*

2. săndrāp, -pā, *m.* = *l.* opportunity.

3. lāyekpoṇ, -ṇā, *n.* = suitableness.

4. soukāsāyetso zāgo, -geā, *m.* soukāsāi, -ye, *f.*

Convenient, *a.* 1. vāzbi; fāvo.

2. lāyek; upkārāk poḍtso.

3. soukāsāyetso.

4. *rs.* zāi, *Lat. decet.*

5. *by the* Necess. Mood *of the principal verb.*

Convent, *s.* koñvent, -tā, *n.*, *fr.*; moṭ, -ṭā, *m.*, *used only for* pagan c. adjoining temples.

Conventicle, *s.* kuṭ, -ṭā, *n.*

Convention, *s.* 1. mēḷ (é), -ḷā, *m.* = *l.* assembly.

2. kărār, -rā, *m.* = *l.* agreement.

3. rivāz, -ji, *f.* = *l.* fashion.

Conventional, *a.* kărārātso.

Converge, *v.* bāga = *l.* bend; meḷ = *l.* meet.

Convergency, *s.* konso, -seā, *m.*; bāgoṇeñ, -ṇeā, *n.*; bāu, bāve, *f.* = *l.* bending.

Convergent, *a.* bāgontso; yeke suātent vetso; meḷtso.

Conversation, *s.* 1. uloṇeñ, -ṇeā, *n.*; găzāli, -li, *f.*

2. năḍteñ, -teā, *n.* = *l.* behaviour; tsāl, -li, *f.*

Converse, *v.* yekameka ulăi = speak one to another; găzāli mār = *l.* beat a chat.

Conversely, *ad.* porteñ.

Conversion, *s.* portouṇeñ, -ṇeā, *n.*; bădlāp, -pā, *n.*; novi jiṇi, -ye, *f.*

Convert, *v.* 1. bădāl = *l.* change (*tr.*); bădāl (*n.*); *obj. with* thăiñ, *pr. fg.*

2. porti = *l.* turn, *c. v. of* porta, *n. v.*, *pr. fg.*, *e. g.* be converted to God; boro kăr, *pass.* b. zā.

Convert, *s.* novo kristāuñ, -tāvā, *m.* = new Christian; Devāk portillo (mănis) = (a man) converted to God.

Convex, *a. vlg.* ubār; *rs.* ărdo guḷo *or* ărdeā guḷea rupātso.

Convexity, *s.* ubārāi, -ye, *f.*, *or bet.* ubār āng, -gā, *n.*; *rs. into adj. or* ărdeāguḷeāčeñ rūp, -pā, *n.*; ărdoguḷo, -ḷeā, *m.*

Convey, *v.* 1. vor; vāvoi; sāgsi.
2. (păra) suādin kăr; 'c. an idea = *rs.* ărth āsā,' *ch. cs.*

Conveyance, *s.* băṇḍi, -ḍe, *f.*; gāḍi, -ye, *f.*; sărăṭ (*or* sărāṭ), -ṭā, *n.*

Convict, *v.* gunyāukār kăr.

Conviction, *s.* 1. gunyāukārpoṇ, -ṇā, *n.* = *l.* state of being guilty.
2. āločen, -ni, *f.* = *l.* opinion.
3. *rs. into v.*

Convince, *v.* somzoun di *or* somzăi; somzaso kăr; dākăi; *see also* **Convict.**

Convincing, *a.* somzountso *or* somzasārko.

Convocation, *s.* 1. mēḷ (é), -ḷā, *m.* = meeting; zunt, -tā, *m.*, *fr.* = meeting.
2. āpouṇeñ, -ṇeā, *n.*; meḷouṇeñ, -ṇeā, *n.*, *or* meḷounčeñ.

Convoke, *v.* āpoi = *l.* summon; meḷăi; zomo kăr.

Convoy, *s.* pāre, *pl. m.*; *see* **Caravan.**

Convulse, *v.* voḍi kăr, *n. c.*

Convulsion, *s.* voḍ, -ḍi, *f.*; kāmp, -pi, *f.*; morlugi piḍa (epilepsy).

Cook, *v.* rānd; sizăi (by boiling).

Cook, *s.* rāndpi, -piā, *m.*; *vlg.* kusinier (*or* kuzner), -rā, *m.*, *fr.*

Cool, *a.* 1. thănḍ, *or bet.* thănḍso, *pr. fg.*; šeḷo.
2. *fg.* nidān = *l.* quiet.
3. *fg.* bepārvi *or* făḍpoši = *l.* careless.

Cool, *s.* šeḷ, -ḷi, *f.*; thănḍāi, -ye, *f.*

Cool, *v.* 1. thănḍ kăr, *pr. fg.*, *e. g.* appease; nivăi, *c. v. of* niv, *pr. fg.*, *e. g.* appease.
2. vāreñ ghe = *l.* get a breeze.
3. *fg. also* nidān kăr, *tr. v.*
4. *fg.* săḍil zā = *l.* get lax; rāg niutā = *l.* anger ceases.

Cooly, *s.* kulkār, -rā, *m.*; mānāi, -yā, *m.*; vāurāḍi, -ḍiā, *m.*; begāri, -riā, *m.*; āḷ, -ḷā, *m.*

Co-operate, *v.* 1. pāu, *e. g.* God co-operates with man.
2. părmāṇe tsăl *with the Or. case* = *l.* walk according to, *e. g.* c. with grace.
3. kumok kăr = *l.* help.
4. sāngātā vāur kăr *with the Or. case; or bet.* sāngātā *with the Or. case and the verb expressing the kind of co-operation, e. g.* c. in the defence of; *or* -i = also, *affixed to a Noun, with the required verb.*

Co-operation, *s.* kumok, -mke, *f.*; pāvāp, pāupā, *n.*; săhāi, -ye, *f.*; *rs. into v.*

Cope, *s.* kāp, -pā, *m.* (a kind of priestly vestment), *rl.*

Copious, *a.* sămpurṇ; bhou, *or* tsăḍ = *l.* much; dādos.

Copiousness, *s.* sămpurṇāi, -ye, *f.*; dādospoṇ, -ṇā, *n.*

Copper, *s.* tāmbeñ, -beā, *n.*

Copper, *a.* tāmbeātso.

Copper-money, *s.* khurḍo, -ḍeā, *m.*

Copper-pot, *s.* hāṇḍo, -ḍeā, *m.*

Copper-smith, *s.* tāmbṭi, -ṭiā, *m.*

Copper-wire, *s.* tāmbeāči ārām, -me, *f.*

Copy, *s.* 1. năkăl, -klā, *n.*
2. nămuno, -neā, *m.* = *l.* model.

Copy, *v.* 1. năkăl kāḍ.
2. *fg.* năkăl kăr.

Copyist, *s.* gumost, -tā, *m.*; bărpi, -piā, *m.*; năkălvis, -sā, *m.*

Coral, *s.* pouḷeñ, -ḷeā, *n.*

Cord, *s.* rāzu, -zvā, *m.* (strong, long c.); ālāt, -tā, *m.* (stronger, thicker than 'rāzu'); dori, -ye, *f.* (a common c.); sumb, -bā, *n.* (c. of cocoanut fibre).

Coriander, *s.* kăn-pir, -re (*or* -ri), *f.*

Cork, *s.* guḍḍi, -de, *f.*; buč, -či, *f.*, *n. c.*

Corn, *s.* 1. dāni, -ye, *f.* = *l.* grain; bhāt, -tā, *n.* (*ex.* paddy).
2. khiṇ, -ṇā, *n.* (horny excrescence of the skin).

Corner, *s.* konso, -seā, *m.*, *pr. fg.*; c. stone = konseātso fātor.

Corn-field, *s.* gādo, -deā, *m.*

Cornice, *s.* kangór, -rā, *m.*

Corollary, *s.* fóḷ, -ḷā, *m.*; sevóṭ, -ṭā, *m.* = *l.* issue; *bet. rs.*, *e.g.* tantleān zātā.

Coronation, *s.* 1. pāṭār bosouṇeñ, -ṇeā, *n.*; *or bet. rs. into* pāṭār bosăi.
2. mukuṭ -ṭā, *m.* = *l.* crown.
3. kurou, -rovā, *m.*, *fr.* (*rl. mn.*)

Corporal, *a.* kuḍitso.

Corporation, *s.* mēḷ(é), -ḷā, *m.*

Corpse, *s.* moḍeñ, -ḍeā, *n.*

Corpulence, *s.* moṭāi, -ye, *f.*

Corpulent, *a.* moṭo (*emph.* moṭṭo); puṣṭi.

Corpuscle, *s.* kuskuṭ văstụ, -tu, *f.*

Correct, *a.* săma; sārko; suddụ, *n. c.*

Correct, *v.* 1. kăr *with the above adj.*
2. bud săng = *l.* say advice; šikṣa di = *l.* give punishment; besṭāi (beṣṭāi).

Correction, *s.* *rs. into v.*, *or* suddụkărni, -ne, *f.*, *n. c.*

Corrector, *s.* 1. săma kărtolo.
2. besṭāitolo.

Correctness, *s.* 1. suddụpoṇ, -ṇā, *n.*
2. šikṣa, -ṣe, *f.*

Correlative, *a.* lāgtso; sămănd āsụllo.

Correspond, *v.* 1. săma poḍ; săma āsā.
2. (yekāmekā) zātāt.
3. săḷāvoḷ āsā = *l.* intercourse is.

4. ărth āsā.
5. *rs. into Or. of noun, with* bări = as.

Correspondence, *s.* 1. sămapoḍāp, -ḍpā, *n.*
2. săḷāvoḷ, -ḷi, *f.* = *l.* intercourse; sălgi, -ge, *f.* = *l.* familiarity; dosti, -te, *f.* = *l.* favour.

Correspondent, *s.* kobro ditolo (of a journal).

Corroborate, *v.* thir kăr; bòḷ di.

Corroboration, *s.* bòḷ, -ḷā, *n.*; thirpoṇ, -ṇā, *n. or* thirāsāṇ, -ṇe, *f.*; *rs. into v.*

Corrode, *v.* tarye, *n. v.* (*n. c.*), *e.g.* worms c. timber; surye, *n. v.*, *ch. cs.*; kuskus, *n. v.*

Corrosion, Corrosive, *rs. v.*

Corrupt, *v.* kusăi, *c. v. of* kus, *n. v.*, *pr. fg.*; pāḍ kăr; *see* **Falsify, Contaminate, Corrode.**

Corrupted, *p. part. of* Corrupt; *see* **Degraded, Base.**

Corrupter, *s.* kusḍi, -ḍiā, *m.*

Corruption, *s.* 1. kusāp, -spā, *n.*
2. lonts, -tsā, *m.* = *l.* bribe.

Coruscation, *s.* prăkāš, -šā, *m.*; părzăḷ, -ḷā, *m.*

Corvina, *s.* (a kind of fish), dăḍiñ, -ḍiyā, *n.* (*dim.* dăḍiyāro, -reā, *m.*)

Corypheus, *s.* muktesăr, -rā, *or* muktesi, -siā, *m.*

Cosmogony, *s.* 1. săuñsārātso ărămb, -bā, *m.*
2. săuñsārāărămbavidya, -ye, *f.*

Cosmography, *s.* săuñsārātso vivor, -rā, *m.*

Cost, *s.* 1. mòl, -lā, *n.*
2. khărts, -tsā, *m.*
3. luksān, -nā, *n.* = *l.* loss, harm; năšṭ, -ṭā, *m.*

Cost, *v.* (mòl) poḍ, *e.g.* dhā rupoi poḍle; it costs = mòl āsā, (mòl) lāgtā, *e.g.* tin rupoi lāgtāt.

Costive (Is), *a.* kuntăṇ.

Costiveness, *s.* kuntăṇāp, -pā, *n.*; *vlg.* utkāḍeñ bănd zātā.

Costly, *s.* mhārāg; molādik.

Costume, *s.* 1. sóvói, -ye, *f.*; rivāz, -ji, *f.*; dăstur, -ri, *f.*
2. nesoṇ, -ṇi, *f.*

Cot, *see* **Cottage, Hammock.**

Cottage, *s.* kombāṭ, -bṭā, *n.*; guḍsul, -lā, *n.*

Cotton, *s.* kāpus, -psā, *m.*

Cotton-tree, *s.* kāpsiṇ, -ṇi, *f.*

Couch, *s.* khaṭlen, -leā, *n.*; āntāḷn, -nā, *n.* (native c.); mantso, -čeā, *m.* = bedstead.

Couch, *v.* 1. poḍ, *n. v.*
2. lipon bos.

Cough, *s.* khonkli, -le, *f.*; usmoḍ, -ḍi, *f.* (suffocating c.).

Cough, *v.* khonkli yetā; khonk.

Council, *s.* săbha, -bhe, *f.*, *or* āločenisăbha; *vlg.* zunt, -tā, *m. or* mēḷ(é), -ḷā, *m.*

Councillor, *s.* āločenisăbhegār, -rā, *m.*; săbhe(tso) sāndo, -deā, *m.*

Counsel, *s.* bud, -di, *f.*; āločen, -ni, *f.*

Counsel, *v.* bud di; āločen sāng.

Count, *v.* lēk(é) = cast up accounts; mēz(é) = *l.* measure.

Count, *s. nearest w.* prăbu, -bu, *m.*

Countenance, *s.* 1. rūp, -pā, *n.*; tònḍ, -ḍā, *n.*

2. nidānāi, -ye, *f.*; măryād, -di, *f.*

3. guṇ, -ṇā, *m.* = *l.* favour.

Countenance, *v.* 1. mānua = *l.* please, *e. g.* an opinion; vintsun kāḍ = choose, *e.g.* an opinion.

2. guṇātso zāun āsā.

Counteract, *v. Dat.* āḍ ye; inkār kăr. (*Acc.*)

Counterbalance, *v.* 1. *pr.* sămatuk = weigh equally; săma āsā, *ch. cs.*, *e. g.* these virtues were counterbalanced by great vices.

2. *fg.* āḍkăḷ ghāl = *l.* put obstacle.

Counterbalance, *s.* 1. *pr.* sămatuk, -kā, *n.*

2. *fg. rs. into v. or* āḍkăḷ, -ḷi, *f.*

Counterfeit, *v.* kăpăṭ kăr = *l.* make simulation, *e. g.* c. friendship; *Or. of the noun with* bări = *l.* as, *with the required verb*, *e.g.* c. the cry of a bird = suknea bări bob măr; foṭkiro kăr.

C. a document = foṭkireñ dăstevoz borăi.

C. money = foṭkiro duḍu kăr.

Counterfeit, *a.* 1. foṭkiro.

2. kăpṭi.

Counterfeit, *s.* foṭouṇeñ, -ṇeā, *n.*; kăpăṭ, -ṭā, *n.*

Countermand, *v.* (ādli *or* dilli) hukum kāḍ.

Countless, *a.* leknātullo *or* lekāvorto.

Country, *s.* 1. gāuñ, -āvā, *m.*; dēš (é), -šā, *m.*

2. buiñ, -iñ, *f.* = *l.* earth.

3. jillo (*var.* zillo), -leā, *m.* = *l.* district; muluk, -kā, *n.* = *l.* district, *n. c.*

4. nāḍ, -ḍā, *n.* = *l.* village.

Native c. = zăllo gāuñ; vilāyet, -tā, *n.*

Countryman, *s.* 1. gāuntso mănis, -nšā, *m.*

2. nāḍkār, -rā, *m.*, (*used also fg. for* uneducated); *see* **Cultivator.**

Couple, *s.* zoḍi, -ye, *f.*

Couple, *v.* meḷăi; yekoṭ kăr.

Courage, *s.* dhăir, -rā, *n.*; mărdh, -dhā, *n.*

Be of good c. = dhăir ghe.

Courageous, *a.* dhăirādik, *or* dhăirāvont; zobor.

Courier, *s.* 1. pedo, -deā, *m.*

2. dălāyet, -tā, *m.* (of a judge, collector, *and the like.*)

Course, *s.* 1. dāuñ, dāve, *f.* = *l.* running; *also* c. of a river; vāṭ, -ṭe, *f.* = *l.* road, *e.g.* c. of the stars.

2. jinos, -nsā, *m.* = *l.* manner; pārmāṇe (*used only in the Or.*), *e.g.* fāvoteā p. = in the proper manner.

3. păripāt, -ti, *f.*, *e.g.* c. of lectures.
4. prăvăti, -ti, *f.*, *n.c.*; *see also* **Plan.**
5. jinos, -nsā, *m.* = the part of a meal served at one time; *e.g.* a dinner of several courses.

In the c. of = veḷār *with the G.*, *or* modeñ *with the Or. case.*

A matter of c. = săhăz.

Of c. = khărents; tăseñ zāi; săhăz; albăt (*var.* ăblăt); ăvăš zāun = necessarily.

Court, *s.* 1. āngāṇ, -gṇā, *n.* (*also* c. yard of private houses).
2. rāuḷ, -ḷā, *n.* (royal palace); kăčări, -ri, *f.* (public office).
3. nitirāuḷ, -ḷā, *n.* = *l.* palace of justice, *n.c.*; *vlg.* koḍt, -ti, *f.*
4. munsubdār, *or* monsubdār, *or* nitidār, -rā, *m.* = *l.* judge.

Pay court = mān dākăi.

Court, *v.* mān dākăi; fuslăi.

Courteous, *a.* 1. măryāditso.
2. mogāḷ *or* dăyāḷ.

Courtesy, *s.* 1. măryād, -di, *f.*; tsāltsămkăṇ, -ṇā, *n.*
2. mōg, -gā, *m.*; dăya, -ye, *f.*

Cousin, *s.* 1. bāpulbhāu, -āvā, *m.* = brother on the uncle's side.
2. māusibhāu = brother on the maternal aunt's side.
3. bāpulbăiṇ, -ṇi, *f.* = sister on the paternal uncle's side.
4. māusibăiṇ, -ṇi, *f.* = sister on the maternal aunt's side.

Covenant, *s.* kărār, -rā, *m.*

Cover, *v.* 1. dānk (*or* dāmp).
2. *fg.* lipăi.
3. sāmbāḷ.

C. the expenses = khărts bhărti kăr.

Cover, *s.* dāmpṇeñ, *or* dānkṇeñ, -ṇeā, *n.*

Coverlet, *see* **Blanket.**

Covet, *v.* 1. āše *or* apekṣi; āšā kăr, *G.F.*; khuši vor; abla kăr.
2. lāle = long for.

Covetous, *a.* 1. surāti = stingy.
2. apekṣitolo, *etc.*
3. orbosi (c. of food).

Covetousness, *s.* surāt, -tā, *m.* *or* absurāt, -tā, *m.*; abla, -ble, *f.*

Cow, *s.* gāi, gāi, *f.*; vāk, -kā, *n.*, *fr.* (*in the phrase* vākāčeñ mās).

Coward, *a.* poḷkuro; āḷsi; bhiyātso.

Cowardice, *s.* poḷkurepoṇ, -ṇā, *n.*; āḷsāi, -ye, *f.*; bheñ, bhiyā, *n.*; hălkeñ mon, -nā, *n.*

Cowdung, *s.* šeṇ, -ṇā, *n.*

Spread c. = š. kāḍ.

Coxcomb, *s.* 1. šenkāreñ, -reā, *n.*
2. *fg.* hănkārātso mănis, -nšā, *m.*, *or* ăhănkāri, -riā, *m.*; dănḍi, -ḍi, *m.*

Crab, *s.* kurli, -le, *f.* (shell-fish).

Crack, *v.* soḍ = disjoin (suṭ, *n. v.* = be disjoined), *e.g.* beams of a roof; foḍ, *tr. v.* (fuṭ, *n. v.*); yere.

C. jokes = hāsăi *or* čeṣṭāio kăr.

Crack, *s.* 1. fuṭ, -ṭi, *f.*; yer, -ri, *f.* 2. gouji, -je, *f.*

Crack-brained, *a.* piso; vid lāgųllo.

Craft, *s.* 1. hikmăt, -ti, *f.* = artifice; čămătkār, -rā, *m.* = artifice; nāḍgepoṇ, -ṇā, *n.* 2. kām, -mā, *n.* (handicraft); kăsăb, -sbe, *f.* 3. tāruñ, -rvā, *n.*

Cram, *v.* bhor = *l.* fill; sāṇsi = thrust in.

Cramp, *s.* 1. *rs.* šir guspoḍtā, *or* šir vòḍtā; vākuḷ, -kḷā, *n.* 2. voḍi, *pl. f.*

Crane, *s.* dònk, -kā, *n.* (the blue bird, common here, somewhat similar to a crane).

Crapulous, *a.* khāugi; poṭāro; piyeunčeāk lāgųllo *or* piyeunk l.

Crash, *s.* gouji, -je, *f.*

Crater, *s.* tònḍ, -ḍā, *n.*

Cravat, *s.* gomṭeāčeñ lugāṭ, -gṭā, *n.*

Crave, *v.* (lāleun) māg.

Crazy, *a.* 1. piso; vid lāgųllo. 2. ăskăt = weak.

Cream, *s.* 1. sāi, -ye, *f.* 2. *fg.* uttim.

Create, *v.* 1. răts. 2. *fg.* nemsi. 3. găḍ = found.

Creation, *s.* 1. rătsāp, -tspā, *n.*, *or* rātsneñ, -neā, *n.* 2. săuñsār, -rā, *m.* = *l.* world.

Creator, *s.* rătsnār, -rā, *m.*

Creature, *s.* 1. rătsna, -ne, *f.* 2. bāḷ, -ḷā, *n.* (*in pl.*) a term of endearment.

Credentials, *s.* šipārasičeñ kāgād, -gdā, *n.*

Credibility, *s.* pātiyeṇi, -ṇi, *f.*; nămbgăṇi, -ṇe, *f.*; sătmāndčeñ.

Credible, *a.* pātiyeṇitso; nămbgăṇitso; sătmāndtso.

Credit, *s.* 1. boreñ nāuñ, nāvā, *n.*; ābru, -brā, *m.*; mān, -nā, *m.* 2. itbār (*or* hitbār), -rā, *m.* (in commerce). give on c. = hitbārān di; usṇo di; udārāk di.

Creditable, *a.* šipārasitso; mărvāditso.

Creditor, *s.* riṇ dillo (mănis).

Credulous, *a.* (sompeñ) pātiyeuntso; nămbgontso.

Creed, *s.* sătmāndtāñ = I believe, *used also as subst.*

Creep, *v.* tsăr.

Creeper, *s.* vāl, -li, *f.* (plant); bēl(é), -lā, *m.*

Crescent, *a.* voḍ zāuntso (moon).

Crest, *s.* 1. šenkāreñ, -reā, *n.* 2. šenḍi, -ye, *f.* (of a helmet).

Crest-fallen, *a.* khālto *or* kh. kello.

Crevice, *s.* fuṭ, -ṭi, *f.*

Crew, *s.* *see* **Crowd.**

Crib, *s.* 1. morgi, -ge, *f.* = manger; khāvoṇ, khāuṇe, *f.* 2. goṭo, -ṭeā, *m.* = *l.* stable. 3. pāḷneñ, -neā, *n* = *l.* cradle.

Crick, *s.* 1. voḍi, *f. pl.* = *l.* spasm. 2. ghăṭ găḷo, -ḷeā, *m.* = *l.* stiff neck, *ch. cs.*

Cricket, *s.* 1. birmoṭi, -ṭe, *f.* (insect).
2. čenḍāṭ, -ṭā, *m.* (play).
Crime, *s.* ăkrăm, -mā, *n.*; ăprād, -dā, *m.*; voḍ gunyāuñ, -āvā, *m.*; khoṭepoṇ, -ṇā, *n.*; pātak, -tkā, *n.*; pāp, -pā, *n.*
Criminal, *a.* 1. khoṭepoṇātso, *or* khoṭo.
2. firiyāditso.
Criminate, *v.* 1. firiyād di.
2. gunyāukār kăr; zătpi (retaliate), *n. c.*
Cripple, *s.* thonṭo, -ṭeā, *m.*
Crisis, *s.* zăkhmekāl, -lā, *m., n. u.*; tirp, -pā, *n.*, *or* tirpakāl, -lā, *m.*; sevoṭ, -ṭā, *m.*; risk, -ke, *f.*
Criterion, *s.* gurtu, -tā, *m.*; lăkšăṇ, -ṇā, *n.*
Critic, *a.* khoḍi kăḍtso; *see verb.*
Critical, *a.* 1. risketso, *or* zăkhmetso.
2. khoḍi kăḍtso.
Criticize, *v.* 1. *vlg.* khoḍi kăḍ.
2. văiṭ boreñ bhēd (é) kăr; ăibañ bhēd kăr; tsuki sod; duruă.
Critique, *s.* guṇ-ăibañ-părikša, -kše, *f.*
Croak, *s.* 1. mānkeānči bob, -be, *f.*
2. *fg.* siṇ, -ṇā, *m.*
Croak, *v.* 1. bob mār.
2. siṇ ulăi.
Crocodile, *s.* sisăr, -sri, *f.*
Crook, *v.* bāgāi, *c. v.* *of* bāga *or* bāgo.
Crook, *s.* gānts, -tsā, *m.* = hook.

Crooked, *a.* 1. vānkḍo; ḍonku.
2. *fg.* ănnāyātso; kuskon, *pr.* (*used esp. of* a dress stitched wrongly).
Crookedness, *s.* vānkḍepoṇ, -ṇā, *n.* *or* vānkuḍ, -ḍā, *n.*
Crop, *s.* 1. *general terms,* beḷeñ, -ḷeā, *n.*; pik, -kā, *n.*
2. *particular kinds of rice are,* yeṇel, -lā, *n.*, *or* kārti, -ti, *f.* (*1st* crop); suggi, -ge, *f.* (*2nd* cr.); koḷkeñ, -keā, *n.* (*3rd* cr.).
Crop, *v.* tsāb = *l.* bite.
Cross, *s.* 1. kuris, -rsā, *m.*
2. *fg.* kăšṭ, -ṭā, *m.*
Cross, *a.* 1. āḍ āsullo.
2. kărkărāntso.
Cross, *v.* 1. zóḍ, *e.g.* c. the hands.
2. utăr, *e.g.* c. the river; poltăḍi vots.
3. inkār kăr = thwart, *Acc.*
Cross-examination, *s.* aḍḍasăvāl, -li, *f.*
Crossing, *s.* (vāṭāntso) mēḷ (é), -ḷā, *m.*; *bet. rs.*
Crouch, *v.* bāga *or* bāgo.
Croup, *s.* gunṭañ, *pl. n.*
Crow, *s.* 1. kāuḷo, -ḷeā, *m.*, *dim.* kāuḷer, -ri, *f.* (a small bird similar to a cr.).
2. sād, -dā, *m.* (cry of a cock).
Crow, *v.* sād ghāl.
Crowd, *s.* 1. tăḷḷeñ-biḷḷeñ, -ḷeā, *n.* (čilleñ-b.); zomo, -meā, *m.*
2. tănḍ, -ḍā, *m.* = *l.* faction.
Crowd, *v.* zomoun zomoa, *n. v.*
Crowded, *a.* lāgun.

Crown, *s.* 1. mukuṭ, -ṭā, *m.*; kurou, -rovā, *m.* (*rl.*)
2. *fg.* rāzvoṭkāi, -ye, *f.*

Crown, *v.* mukuṭ ghāl.

Crown-prince, *s.* kuvor, -rā, *m.*

Crucible, *s.* kovo, -veā, *m.*

Crucifix, *s.* kursimāz, -ji, *f.* (*var.* imāz kursāver); *vlg.* kuris, -rsā, *m.*; kursār zoḍullo.

Crucifixion, *s.* kursārmārneñ, -neā, *n.*; *rs. into v.*

Crucify, *v.* kursār mār; kursār zóḍ; kursār khiḷāi.

Crude, *a.* 1. jivo; hărvo = not boiled.
2. tărno; pikānātullo.

Cruel, *a.* niṣṭur; mhāru; krūr.

Cruelty, *s.* niṣṭurāi, -ye, *f.*; mhārupoṇ, -ṇā, *n.*

Cruet, *s.* bul, -li, *f.* (*some understand by* 'bul' 'snuff-box'); sisli, -le, *f.* (*not generally accepted*).

Cruise, *v.* (dăryānt) bouñ.

Cruising, *s.* dăryānt bounḍi, -ḍe, *f.*

Crumb, *s.* lān kuḍko, -keā, *m.*

Crumble, *v.* kuḍkeān kuḍke kăr, *tr.*; bhăsma, *n. v.*

Crush, *v.* 1. vāṭ = *l.* pound.
2. mosti = *l.* trample; čents; čiḍḍi (*esp.* with the hand); dāḍāi, *e.g.* stones.
3. jik = *l.* gain (conquer).
4. *fg.* nāš kăr.

Crust, *v.* 1. kāt, -ti, *f.*, *e.g.* of bread.
2. māu, māve, *f.* = *l.* scar.

Cry, *v.* 1. gouji kăr; bob mār.
2. părgāṭ kăr *or* părgāṭāi; bob mārn sāng.
3. răḍ = *l.* weep.

Cry, *s.* 1. bob, -be, *f.*
2. răḍneñ, -neā, *n.*

Crystal, *s.* 1. ārso, -seā, *m.*
2. rūp āsullo fātor, -trā, *m.*; *or the Sans. Mr. Cn.* sfaṭik, -kā, *n.*
3. khăḍo, -ḍeā, *m.* (of salt).

Crystalline, *a.* ārseātso; părzāḷik.

Crystallization, *s.* fātrānčeñ rūp, -pā, *n.*; *or* sfaṭik zāunčeñ, -čeā, *n.*

Crystallize, *v.* rūp meḷ; *or* sfaṭik kăr, *pass.* sf. zā.

Cub, *s.* pīl, -lā, *n.*

Cube, *s.* sătsoukāntso kuḍko, -keā, *m.*; *or the Sans. Mr, Cn.* ghăn, -nā, *m.*
C. root = ghănamūl, -lā, *n.*

Cuckoo, *s.* koguḷ, -gḷi, *f.*

Cucumber, *s.* 1. touseñ, -seā, *n.*
2. gosāḷeñ, -ḷeā, *n.* (Egyptian 'luffa').

Cudgel, *s.* boḍi, -ye, *f.* (small), toṇko, -keā, *m.* (bigger); sonṭo, -ṭeā, *m.*

Cue, *s.* 1. hišāro, -reā, *m.* = hint.
2. mărji, -je, *f.* = humour, caprice.
3. khuši, -še, *f.* = will.

Culpability, *s.* gunyāukārpoṇ, -ṇā, *n.*

Culprit, *s.* gunyāukār, -rā, *m.*

Cultivate, *v.* 1. sāgoḷi kăr; besāi kăr; văsāi.

2. *fg.* zătăn kăr, *G. F.*, *e. g.* the beard; sovoi (*or* ăbyās) kăr = *l.* make practice.

Cultivated, *a.* 1. sikullo *or* sikpi = learned.

2. zătăn kāṇello, *e. g.* language.

Cultivation, *s.* sāgoḷi, -ḷe, *f.*; vomp, -pe, *f.* = *l.* sowing, *fg.* spreading.

Cultivator, *s.* besāikār, -rā, *m.*; buinkār -rā, *m.*; sāgoḷigār, -rā, *m.*

Culture, *s.* 1. *fg.* sikāp, -kpā, *n.*

2. *pr.* sāgoḷi, -ḷe, *f.*

Cumbersome, *a.* 1. bhou zăḍ.

2. tondreātso.

Cumin-seed, *s.* jireñ, -reā, *n.*

Cumulative, *a.*, *rs. into* voṭṭu, *e.g.* c. arguments.

Cunning, *a.* nāḍgo *or* nāḍgiro.

Cunning, *s.* nāḍgepoṇ, -ṇā, *n.*; nāḍ, -ḍi, *f.*

Cup, *s.* tāmblér, -rā, *m.*, *fr.*; kòp, -pā, *n.*, *fr.*; pātrụ, -trā, *n.*; čikrụ, -rā, *n.*

Cupboard, *s. vlg.* ālmār, -ri, *f.*; *no purely Konk. word is used, if not* kantrèl, -lā, *n.* = a kind of cavity or recess made in the wall, used as a c.; khāno, -neā, *m. is used, but not commonly understood, though common in composition with* dăfter.

Cupping-glass, *s.* răgāt voḍčeñ pātrụ, -rā, *n.*

Curate, *see* Vicar.

Curb, *s.* (low wall) doro, -reā, *m.*

Curdle, *v.* dăiñ kăr (*tr. v.*), d. zā (*n. v.*); meḷāi ghāl; dāṭ kăr; māṇke (*ex. mn.* milk turned sour).

Cure, *s.* 1. vokāt, -ktā, *n.*

2. bolāiki, -ke, *f.* = *l.* health.

Cure, *v.* 1. vokāt di; piḍa thāmbāi; boro kăr; guṇ kăr; vās kăr, *n. c.*

2. miṭāk ghāln dovor = *l.* putting to salt keep, *e.g.* meat.

Curiosity, *s.* 1. nāzukāi, -ye, *f.* (a curious thing).

2. ătrégụ, -gā, *m.* = longing desire; kobro āikunči āšā (kobrāñāšā), -še, *f.*

Curious, *a.* 1. nāzuk (worthy to be seen); čămăṭkārātso.

2. kobrānčeā āšetso, *or bet. rs. v.*; tārifetso.

3. zāgrut.

Curl, *v.* jilpañ kăr *or* jilpăi, *c. v.* (hair); pānti ghāl.

Curl, *s.* jilpañ, *pl. n.*; pānti, -ye, *f.*

Currency, *s.* 1. sóvói, -ye, *f.*; rivāz, -ji, *f.*; tsălāp, -lpā, *n.*; *bet. rs. into v.* tsăl.

2. tsălteñ nāṇeñ, -ṇeā, *n.*; tsălto duḍu, -ḍvā, *n.*

Current (Is), *v.* tsăltā; sóvói āsā.

Current, *s.* 1. dāuñ, dāve, *f.*; tsărni, -ne, *f.* (c. of water); *rs. into* vāu = flow; voḷo, -ḷeā, *m.* (c. of a river).

2. vāḷ, -ḷā, *m.* = *l.* stream; năiñ, -iñ, *f.*

3. *fg.* rivāz, -ji, *f.*

Curry, *v.* 1. mālis kăr (rub *or* cleanse horses).
2. kămāi (tan, anneal).

Curry, *s.* kăḍi, -ye, *f.*; āmb, -bā, *n.*

Curry-comb, *s.* khărār, -rā, *n.*

Curse, *v.* širāp ghāl = *l.* put curse; gāḷi sāng = *l.* say abuses; vāiṭ māg = *l.* pray evil; bădlām ghāl = *l.* put calumnies, *fg.*; āṇ di = *l.* give adjuration.

Curse, *s.* širāp, -pā, *m.*; āṇ, -ṇi, *f.* = *l.* adjuration; gāḷ, -ḷi, *f.* = *l.* abuse.

Cursed, *a.* širāp poḍullo.

Cursorily, *ad.* vegiñ *or* voilebār.

Curtail, *v.* moṭvo kăr; kāḍ; kātăr; uṇo kăr.

Curtain, *s.* pordo (*var.* phordo), -deā, *m.*

Curved, *a.* yānkḍo; bâgāllo.

Cushion, *s.* ušeñ, -šeā, *n.*

Custard-apple, *s.* ātu̥, -tā, *n.*

Custody, *s.* 1. rākṇeñ, -ṇeā, *n.*
2. pāro, -reā, *m.* = *l.* guard, satellite.
3. kăid, -dā, *n.* = arrest; *see* **Prison.**
Put in c. = pāreār ghāl.
Keep in c. = kăidānt dovor.

Custom, *s.* 1. sóvói, -ye, *f.*; dăstur, -ri, *f.*; rivāz, -ji, *f.*; rīt, -ti, *f.*
2. sunk, -kā, *n.* = *l.* tax.

Custom-house, *s.* sunkākaṭeñ, -ṭeā, *n.*

Customary, *a.* sóvóyetso *or* sovoye părmāṇe āsullo; sădāntso, *e.g.* c. meal.

Customer, *s.* kekāri, -riā, *m.*; girāiki, -kiā, *m.*

Cut, *v.* kātăr, *pas.* kātār; tās = *l.* hew.; sind; benḍ (grass); bhét (fuel).
C. in two = don kuḍke kăr.
C. off = kāḍ; nāš kăr; yekats phaṛa kāḍ.
C. short = moṭvo kăr.

Cut, *s.* 1. kātrāp, -pā, *n.*; kātro, -treā, *m.* (small c.).
2. ghāi, -yā, *m.*; zăkhăm, -khme, *f.* = wound.
3. mār, -rā, *m.*, pēṭ (ó,) -ṭā, *m.* = *l.* stroke.

Cutler, *s.* suriyegār, -rā, *m.*; surio kărtolo; surio iktolo.

Cutlet, *s.* *vlg.* katleṭ, -ṭi, *f.*

Cut-throat, *s.* khunigār, -rā, *m.*

Cylinder, *s.* āḍkuḷeñ, -ḷeā, *n.*

Cypress, *s.* tsābkātso ruk, -kā, *m.* (*perh. Casuarina*).

D

Dab, *v. see* **Dash, Strike, Slap.**

Dabble, *v.* 1. udkānt khèḷ = *l.* play in water.

2. voilebār, *with* kăr *or some other equivalent verb* = *l.* do on the surface.

Dabbler, *s.* 1. voilebār kărtolo.

2. phăḍpoši, -siā, *m.*

Dagger, *s.* kăṭāri, -re, *f.*

Daily, *a.* dispoḍto: 'dispoḍto grās = daily food'.

Daily, *ad.* disāndis *or* hăryek dis = *l.* every day.

Daintiness, *s.* 1. nāzukāi, -ye, *f.*

2. poṭārpoṇ, -ṇā, *n.* = *l.* gluttony.

Dainty, *a.* 1. nāzuk.

2. ručitso = *l.* tasteful.

Dam, *s.* 1. āvoi, -voi, *f.* = *l.* mother.

2. kāṭ, -ṭā, *m.* (mill d. *etc.*)

Dam, *v.* kāṭ ghāl.

Damage, *v.* 1. luksān (*or* năṣ̌ṭ) kăr = make harm; *or* luksānāk poḍ = *l.* fall to loss, *ch. cs.*

2. vāiṭ kăr = *l.* make evil.

Damage, *s.* 1. luksān, -nā, *n. or* năṣ̌ṭ, -ṭā, *m.*

2. vāiṭ, -ṭā, *n.* = evil.

Damask, *s.* dămāsk, -kā, *n.*

Damn, *v. see* **Condemn.**

Damnation, *see* **Condemnation.**

Damp, *v.* šeḷo kăr (*or* šeḷăi, *n. c.*); šeḷe, *n. v.* = get damp; volo kăr, *e.g.* cloth; bāte = get damp through monsoon-weather.

Damp, *a.* šeḷitso.

Dampness, *s.* šéḷ, -ḷi, *f.*; bāto, -teā, *m.* (d. caused by the monsoon).

Dance, *v.* nāts *or* (*Goa.*) nādtsă.

Dance, *s.* nāts, -tsā, *m.* [*f.*

Dancing (**woman**), *s.* kalvont, -ti,

Danger, *s.* risk, -ke, *f.* (*var.* risk, -kā, *n.*) *perh. fr.*; zăkhām, -khme, *f.*

Be in danger = riskent āsā.

Be out of danger = risk utăr-lea = *l.* risk passed.

Dangerous, *a.* risketso = *l.* of danger; mosātso = *l.* deceitful; luksānātso = *l.* of harm; luksānāk poḍtolo = *l.* falling to loss.

Dangerously, *ad.* zăkhām zāun.

D. sick = bhou tsăḍ piḍest = *l.* very much sick; găḍis vāiṭ kărtso.

Dare, *v.* 1. *tr. v. see* **Challenge.**

2. *n. v.* mākā dhăir āsā *or* āuñ dhăirāvont zāun āsāñ = I have courage.

Dark, *a.* 1. kāḷokātso.

2. kāḷoso *or* kāḷso, *used both of colours and fg., e.g.* d. (sad) days.

3. somzonk nozo āsullo *or only* somzānātullo = *l.* not intelligible; *see* **Abstruse.**

Darken, *v.* kāḷok (*or* kāḷso) kăr = make darkness (*or* dark),

pr., *fg.*; uzvāḍ kāḍ *or* divo kāḍ = take away light.
Darkish, *a.* kāḷso; sāuḷo.
Darkness, *s.* 1. kāḷok (*or* kāḷuk), -kā, *m.*; ăndkār, -rā, *m.*
2. *fg.* guṭ, -ṭā, *m.* = *l.* secret.
Darling, *a.* mogāḷ; ăpurbāyetso.
Darling, *s.* bāḷ, -ḷā, *n.*
Dart, *s.* bhāli, -ye, *f.*
Dash, *v. n.* ādăḷ; *sometimes the Nom. in English to this vb. becomes the Object in Konkani, e.g.* the carriage dashes against the gate = bāgil gāḍiyek ādăḷtā; *see also* **Disappoint.**
Date, *s.* 1. tārik, -rke, *f.*: 'āz kitli tārik? = what date is to-day?'; 'kitle tārker? = at what date (*or* day) of the month?' 'moineāče vis tārker = on the 20th of the month'; tithi, -thi, *f.* (of a lunar month).
2. isvi, -ve, *f. used where there is question of* years, *e. g.* what year are we in now?
3. khāzur, -zrā, *m.* = *Lat. dactylus* (fruit); kharku, -kā, *m.* = dried date.
Date, *v.* 1. *pr.* tārik borăi = *l.* write the date.
2. suru zā = *l.* begin, *e.g.* d. from.
Daughter, *s.* du, -ve, *f.*
Daughter-in-law, *s.* sun, -ne, *f.*
Daunt, *v.* besṭāi; bheñ ghāl = cause fear; bhiyeunk lāi.
Dauntless, *a.* bheññātullo; dhăirāvont *or* dhăirāḍik.
Dawn, *s.* 1. fānteñ, -teā, *n. or* fānteāpār, -rā, *n.*; 'fānteār = at dawn'.
2. uzvāḍ, -ḍā, *m.* = *l.* light: 'uzvāḍ zālo = *l.* light is done'.
Dawn, *v.* uzvāḍ zā *or* uzvāḍ.
Day, *s.* 1. dis, -sā, *m.*; holiday = āitār, -rā, *m.*; *or* sontātso dis *or* sontādis'; 'working-day = vāurātso dis, *or*, *rare*, vāuru kăriyet āsullo dis'; 'in the course of the d. = disā modeñ *or* disāčea veḷār'.
2. uzvāḍ, -ḍā, *m.* = *l.* light, *as in the phrase*: 'it got day = uzvāḍ zālo'.
'The day before yesterday = pór (*to be distinguished from* pur = bury, *and from* poruñ = last year').
'The day after to-morrow = porvāñ'.
'From day to day = disādisa'.
'Every third day = poiro'; 'at every third day = poireān'.
Daybreak, *see* **Dawn.**
Day-labourer, *s.* (cooly) kulkār, -rā, *m.*; vāurāḍi, -ḍeā, *m.*; begāri, -riā, *m.*
Day-light, *s.* uzvāḍ, -ḍā, *m.*
Dazzle, *v.* tòp = *l.* prick, *fg.*, *e.g.* uzvāḍ doḷeānk tòptā.
Deacon, *s.* diāknu, -nā, *m.*, *fr.*
Deaconship, *s.* diāknupoṇ, -ṇā, *n.*, *fr.*
Dead, *a.* 1. mello, *pr. and fg.*
2. *fg.* jīvnātullo.

Dead, *s.* 1. mello, -leā, *m.*
2. ătmo, -meā, *m.* = *l.* soul; *vlg.* kuleñ, -leā, *n.*, *i.e.* apparition; 'raise from the d. = melleāntlo jivont kăr'.

Deadly, *a.* 1. risketso = *l.* of risk; mornātso; jīv kāḍtso = *l.* taking away life; 'deadly wound = jīv kāḍtso ghāi'.
2. koḍu = *l.* bitter, *e.g.* d. hatred.

Deaf, *a.* 1. keppo *pr.* *and* *fg.*; kān-nātullo; bhero.
2. *fg.* āikanātullo, *e.g.* d. to prayers.

Deafen, *v.* 1. keppo kăr.
2. *fg.* kān phuṭṭā, *ch.* *cs.* = *l.* ear is broken.

Deafish, *a.* kepposo.

Deafness, *s.* keppepoṇ, -ṇā, *n.*

Deal, *s.* (a good deal), tsăḍ = *l.* much; bhou; săbār (*all these words are strictly adjectives*).

Deal, *v.* 1. vepār kăr = *l.* make trade.
2. tsăl = *l.* walk, behave, *Cm.* *Prs.*
3. I have to deal with = *Cm.* kām āsā, *l.* to me business is.
4. goḷăi = *l.* handle, *e.g.* d. in money.

Dealer, *s.* vepāri, -riā, *m.* = *l.* merchant.

Dealing, *s.* 1. vepār *or* vyāpār, -rā, *m.* = trade.
2. săḷāvoḷ, -ḷi, *f.* = *l.* intercourse: 'd. with the devil = săitānā lāgiñ săḷāvoḷ'.

Dear, *a.* 1. mogāḷ (*Lat. dilectus*); mogātso; pritimogātso; prititso.
2. mhārăg *or* molădig = *l.* much costing, *opposite to* sovāi = cheap.

Dearness, *s.* 1. mhārgāi, -ye, *f.* = much price.
2. mòl, -lā, *n.* = *l.* price, *used also fg.*, *e.g.* price of virtue.

Dearth, *s.* dukoḷ, -ḷā, *m.* = famine; bărgāl, -lā, *m.* = famine; durbikṣa, -ṣe, *f.*

Death, *s.* morāṇ *or* morn, -nā, *n.*; 'condemn to death = mornāceñ formāṇ di, *l.* give the order of death, *or* mornātso fitvo di'; 'sudden d. = aučit m.'; 'premature d. = āḍečeñ m.'; 'violent d. = voḷvoḷeāčeñ m.'; 'natural d. = săimbāčeñ m.'; 'd.-bed = mornāčeñ āntuḷn'; 'd.-warrant = mornātso dāklo', '*or* -čeñ zatăk'.

Debar, *v.* *see* **Exclude.**

Debase, *v.* *see* **Adulterate** *and* **Disgrace.**

Debate, *v.* 1. tărk kăr = *l.* make discussion; *vlg.* ārment kăr, *corruption of* argument kăr.
2. vivor săng = *l.* say explanation, *G. M.*

Debate, *s.* tărk, -kā, *n.*; čărtso, -čeā, *m.*

Debauch, *v.* kusăi, *c.v.* *of* kus = corrupt.

Debilitate, *v.* ăskăt kăr = *l.* make weak.

Debility, *s.* ăskătkāi, -ye, *f.* = weakness.

Debonair, *a.* 1. mogāḷ.
2. măryāditso.

Debt, *s.* 1. riṇ, -ṇā, *n.* (of money); 'be in d. = riṇ āsā'; 'contract a d. = riṇ kăr'; 'clear off a d. = riṇ fārik kăr'.
2. kāido, -deā, *m.* = duty.
3. tsuk, -ki, *f.* = *l.* mistake.
4. kām, -mā, *n.* = *l.* business.

Debtor, *s.* 1. riṇkāri, -riā, *m.* = d. of money.
2. tsukullo, -leā, *m.* = offender; *bet. rs. v.*

Debut, *s.* suru, -ve, *f.* = *l.* beginning.

Decade, *s.* khăṇ, -ṇā, *m.* (of the rosary): 'rosary of 5 dec. = pānts khăṇānčeñ kont, -tā, *n.*'

Decalogue, *s.* (Devāče) somortiče dhā upades = *l.* the ten commandments of the Divine religion.

Decamp, (flee), *v.* pòḷ.

Decant, *v.* vót = *l.* pour out (*fully,* dusreā āidānānt vót).

Decapitate, *v.* tăkli (*or* māteñ) kātăr = *l.* cut the head; sis kāp = *l.* cut the head.

Decapitation, *s.* tăklekātrāp, -pā, *n.*; sisakāpṇeñ, -ṇeā, *n.*

Decay, *v.* 1. suk = *l.* dry, wither away, *e.g.* a flower decays.
2. *fg.* pòḍ = *l.* fall, *e.g.* a building; *fg.* pāḍ poḍ = *l.* get bad, *e.g.* a state.

Decay, *s.* pāḍpoḍneñ, -neā, *n.*

Decease, *v.* săr.

Deceased, *a.* sărullo; mello; morn pāullo.

Deceit, *s.* 1. mōs, -sā, *m.*; fōṭ, -ṭi, *f.* = lie.
2. dăgo, -geā, *m.*, *or* dăga, -ge, *f.*
3. fituri, -re, *f.*

Deceitful, *a.* mosātso; foṭkiro.

Deceive, *v.* mōs kăr = *l.* make deceit, *Prs. Acc.*; foṭăi, *c. v. of* foṭou, *n. v.*; dăgo kăr; văntsăn kăr (collude); fāls kăr, *fr.*; tsukăi = *l.* deprive.

Decennial, *a.* 1. dhā vărsāntso = of ten years.
2. dhādhāveā vărsāntso = of every tenth year.

Decency, *s.* 1. măryād, -di, *f.*; *vlg.* mān, -nā, *m.* = *l.* honour.
2. māṇsugi, -ge, *f.*

Decent, *a.* 1. măryāditso, *with reference to* exterior deportment; mānātso = respectable.
2. vāzbi = convenient; *vlg.* boro = good.

Decently, *ad.* măryādin.

Deception, *see* **Deceit.**

Decide, *v.* 1. niščeisi, *e.g.* as a judge; tīrp kăr; nīt kăr = *l.* make justice; săma kăr = *l.* make right; phăisăl utsăr = pronounce sentence.
2. ničeu kăr *or* niščeisi, *mn.* make up the mind.

Decided, *a.* 1. bheñ nātųllo = not afraid; thir = firm.
2. tirsillo = *l.* certain, settled; khăndit.

Decidedly, *ad.* 1. dubāvaviṇe = doubtless; khărents = indeed; ălbăt (*var.* ăblăt).
2. thir zāun = *l.* firmly.

Decipher, *v.* vivor săng, *G. M.*; ărth săng, *G. M.*

Decision, *s.* 1. phăisăl, -lā, *n.*; tīrp, -pā, *n.*; tirmāṇ, -ṇā, *n.* = decree *or* judgment delivered.
2. sevoṭ, -ṭā, *m.* = *l.* issue.

Decisive, *a.* tirmāṇātso, *e.g.* d. victory.

Deck, *v.* surungār kăr = *l.* adorn.

Declaim, *v.* 1. unči bhās utsār, = *l.* pronounce a nice language; unči bhās utsārunk ăbyās kăr = *l.* make practice in pronouncing nice language; *or shorter and bet. only* utsār *or* moṇ, *e. g.* declaim a sermon = sermāuñ moṇ; *or still bet.* unči utsār.
2. bob mār = cry.
3. gāḷi sāng = *l.* abuse.

Declamation, *s.* unči utsāraṇ, -ṇā, *n.* = *l.* nice pronunciation.

Declaration, *s.* 1. vivor, -rā, *m.* = *l.* explanation.
2. utsāraṇ, -ṇā, *n.*, *e.g.* d. of our faith.
3. kăḷitāi, -ye, *f.*, *from* kăḷit = known; părgăṭāi, -ye, *f.* = *l.* publication.

Declare, *v.* 1. vivor săng = *l.* explain, *G. M.*
2. utsār = *l.* express.
3. părgăṭāi *or* părgăṭ kăr = *l.* publish; kăḷāi, *c. v.* = make known (inform).
4. vòp = *l.* acknowledge; voḷka.
5. somzāi = *l.* give to understand.
6. khăndit sāng = *l.* say positively; moṇ = say.

Decline, *v.* 1. *pr.* bāgā = bend.
2. *fg.* utăr = *l.* cross; 'dis utărtā = the day is declining'.
3. deuñ = *l.* descend, *e. g.* price.
4. pāḍ poḍ = decay.
5. inkār kăr = *l.* make resistance, refuse; nākā moṇ = *l.* say 'no', refuse.

Decline, *s.* pāḍpoḍāp, -ḍpā, *n.*

Declivity, *s.* devāṇeñ, -ṇeā, *n.* = descent, *or* deuṇi, -ṇe, *f.*

Decoction, *s.* kăsāi, -yā, *m.*; koḍo, -ḍeā, *m.*; nivoḷ, niuḷā, *m.*

Decompose, *v.* 1. kusāi = cause to be rotten, *c. v. of* kus, *n. v.* = rot.
2. vingăḍ kăr = *l.* make aside *or* separate, *tr. v.*; vingăḍ zā = get separate, *n. v.*

Decomposition, *s.* 1. vingăḍ zāunčeñ, -čeā, *n.*
2. kusāp, -spā, *n.*

Decorate, *v.* surungār kăr, *G. M.*; ălănkār kăr, *Cn.*, *G. M.*; neṭāi = adorn.

Decoration, *s.* 1. surungār, -rā, *m.*; ălănkār, -rā, *m.*; nēṭ (è), -ṭe, *f.* (*or* -ṭā, *m.*)
2. măryād, -di, *f.* (*Lat. insignia*).

Decorum, *s.* măryād, -di, *f.*; mān, -nā, *m.*=*ex.* honour; māṇsugi, -ge, *f.*

Decoy, *v.* (dākoun) phoṭăi; voḍ, voḍni di; fuslăi.

Decrease, *v.* 1. *tr. v.* uṇo kăr = *l.* make less; uṇo zā = become less.
2. devoi (*c. v. of* deuñ) = *l.* cause to descend, (abate), *e. g.* d. the price = mòl devoi.

Decree, *s.* 1. hukum, -kme, *f.* = order; formāṇ, -ṇā, *n.* = command.
2. phăisăl, -lā, *n.*=decision, sentence; tīrp, -pā, *n.* = decision; tirmāṇ, -ṇā, *n.* = decision.

Decree, *v.* 1. hukum di; formāi = order.
2. phăisăl utsār = pronounce sentence.
3. nisčeisi = establish.

Decrepit, *a.* bhou mātāro = *l.* very old; zăḍḍo; zărăḍio; mortāñ.

Decrepitude, *s.* mātārepoṇ, -ṇā, *n.*

Decretal, *s.* tīrp, -pā, *n.*; tirmāṇ, -ṇā, *n.*

Dedicate, *v.* bheṭăi = *l.* offer; somorpi *or* sămărpi; *see* **Consecrate.**

Dedication, *s.* bheṭouṇeñ, -ṇeā, *n.* = offering: somorpoṇ (*or* sămărpăṇ), -ṇā, *n.*; *see* **Consecration.**

Deduce, *v.* deuñ = *l.* descend, *ch. cs.*; ye, *ch. cs.* = come; ghe, *ch. cs.* = take; niščeisi; tātpăriya kăr = make a conclusion.

Deduct, *v.* kăḍ = *l.* take away; kăḷvi = subtract.

Deduction, *s.* 1. kăḷvunčeñ, -čeā, *n.*
2. tātpăriya.

Deed, *s.* 1. kărni, -ne, *f.* = action.
2. dăklo, -leā, *m.* = authority, *or* document; dăstevoz, -zā, *n.*
D. of sale = krăičit, -ṭi, *f.*

Deem, *v.* āločen kăr; čint.

Deep, *a.* 1. gunḍ *pr.*, *and fg. also*, *e. g.* thought, meditation, mind; khol; kăntu.
2. *fg.* kăṭiṇ, *e.g.* sleep, matter; nibbor, *e.g.* sleep.
3. săkăilo, *e. g.* voice.
4. guṭātso, *e.g.* questions.
5. ghăṭ = *l.* firm, *e.g.* d. conviction.
Deep silence = āñ-huñ nāñ, *l.* not 'āñ-huñ', *or* găpčip *mn.* very silent, *ch. cs.*, *e.g.* găpčip rāule = they remained very silent.

Deepen, *v.* 1. gunḍ kăr, *tr.*; gunḍ zā, *n. v.*
2. *fg.* tsăḍăi = *l.* increase.

Deeply, *ad.* 1. gunḍ zāun.
2. *fg.* purteñ = totally; bhou tsăḍ = very much.

Deer, *s.* čitāḷ, -ṭlā, *n.*

Deface, *v.* vidrup kăr = *l.* make a fearful figure, *or* without figure.

Defamation, *s.* tsāḍi, -ye, *f.* = backbiting; bădlām, -mi, *f.* *or* -mā, *n.* = calumny; *see* **Calumny**; ninda, -de, *f.*; bēdap, -pā, *m.*; byābru, -rā, *m.* = *l.* no character.

Defame, *v.* boreñ nāuñ (*or* mān) kāḍ = *l.* take away the good name (*or* honour); ninda sāng = say calumnies; bădlām ghāl; bedāp kăr = make defamation; mānār ulăi.

N. B. mān kāḍ *is not quite exact: yet it is used in this mn.*

Default, *s.* 1. nāstanāñ = *l.* not being, *ch. cs.*; *or resolve it into verb* distā = appears, *with* neg. part.

2. găirhāzri, -re, *f.* = absence, *ch. cs.*

Defeat, *v.* 1. zăit vor, *prs. 2nd Loc.* = *l.* gain a victory; dāunḍāi = cause to run (away), *c. v. of* dāuñ; pădāu kăr, solvi, *or* solvăi = defeat.

2. inkār kăr, *e.g.* d. a bill (in Parliament) nirfoḷ kăr = *l.* make fruitless, frustrate.

Defeat, *s.* 1. pădāu, -ḍāvā, *m.* = military d.

2. inkār, -ri, *f.* (*or* -rā, *n.*) = *l.* denial.

Defect, *s.* ăib, -bā, *n.* = *esp.* physical defect.

Defection, *s.* 1 kāṭkāi, -ye, *f.* = *l.* revolution.

2. soḍneñ, -neā, *n.*, *or* soḍni, -ne, *f.* = *l.* leaving.

Defective, *a.* 1. uṇo = *l.* less.

2. ăibātso, *e.g.* not having all (one's) members, *or* with any (esp. physical) fault.

Defence, *s.* 1. sāmbāḷāp, -ḷpā, *n.*, *or* sāmbaḷāi, -ye, *f.*; rākṇeñ, -ṇeā, *n.* = *l.* protection, guard; āšro, -reā, *m.* = refuge; gòp, -pā, *n.* = bosom, *fg.*; ādhār, -rā, *m.* = help.

2. zāp, -pi, *f.* = *l.* answer; *fg. mn.* defence.

3. băčāvi, -ve, *f. mn.* d. of a case by a pleader.

Defenceless, *a.* āšro nātullo: nirādhāri.

Defend, *v.* 1. sāmbāḷ; āšro āsā = is refuge, *ch. cs.*; rāk = *l.* guard, *hence* 'rākoṇboḍvo, -veā, *m.* = guardian angel'; pois kăr = keep far; tsukăi = ward off, *ch. cs.*

2. tsălăi, = *l.* cause to walk, *e.g.* d. a case; băčāvi sòd = *l.* seek defence (of a pleader).

Defendant, *see* **Accused** *under* **Accuser.**

Defensive, *a* sāmbāḷtso.

Defer, *v.* 1. pāṭi ghāl = *l.* put back; māgir kăr = *l.* make afterwards.

2. mān dākăi, = *l.* show honour; *see also* **Comply.**

Deference, *s.* mān, -nā, *m.* = *l.* honour; lăkṣa, -ṣe, *f.*

Deficiency, *s.* uṇepoṇ, -ṇā, *n.*; *by the verb* tsuktā = is missing, *or* nāñ = is not; *or rs. into* thoḍo = a little.

Deficient, *a.* 1. uṇo, *e.g.* d. in virtue.
2. ăibātso; *see* **Defective.**

Defile, *v.* 1. mhèḷo kăr, *or* mhèḷăi = *l.* make dirty; bhăṣṭăi; ăḷṣik pātak ādār = *l.* commit an obscene sin; khătăi = *Lat. viola, contamina.*
2. bòḷ kăr = *l.* make violence, *Lat. stuprare.*

Defilement, *s.* khăt, -tā, *n.* = *l.* stain; burseroṇ, -ṇā, *n.* = impurity; bhăṣṭ, -ṭā, *n.*

Define, *v.* 1. *pr.* găḍi ghāl = put limits.
2. *fg.* vivor săng, *G. M.* = *l.* give explanation; *or* vivorsi, = *l.* explain; săkṭăñ bităr dākăi = *l.* show among all, *i.e.* distinguish; niščeisi = establish; somzăi = give to understand, *c. v. of* somza = understand; ărth săng = say the meaning, *G. M.*; soṣṭ dākăi = show clearly.

Definite, *a.* khănḍit; niščeisillo = *l.* established, decided.

Definition, *s.* 1. măsudo, -deā, *m.*, *e.g.* d. of man.
2. vivor, -rā, *m.* = *l.* explanation; ărth săngtso = saying of the meaning.

Definitive, *see* **Decisive.**

Deform, *v.* băirūp kăr = *l.* make disfigured; rūp pāḍ kăr; ūn kăr; vidrūp kăr.

Deformed, *a.* rūp nātuḷlo; ăḷṣik; vikaṭ.

Deformity, *s.* 1. băirūp (*or* vidrūp), -pā, *n.* = physical d.; ūn, -nā, *n.*
2. văiṭpoṇ, -ṇā, *n.* = moral d.; vikaṭăi, -ye, *f.*, *e.g.* of sin.

Defraud, *v.* mōs(ó) kăr = *l.* deceive.

Defray, *v.* di = give; 'defray the expenses = khărts kăr, *or* fārik kăr, *or* khărts bhorti kăr'.

Defy, *v. see* **Challenge, Despise.**

Degeneracy, *s.* khoṭepoṇ, -ṇā, *n.* = *l.* wickedness; pāḍ zāunčeñ; kusāp, -spā, *n.* = *l.* corruption.

Degenerate, *v.* kus; văiṭ zā; pāḍ zā.

Degradation, *s.* 1. kirkoḷăi, -ye, *f.*; luččepoṇ, -ṇā, *n.*; ăpamān, -nā, *m.* = dishonour.
2. bărtărap, -pā, *n. mn.* removal from a degree, *e.g.* from the priesthood, *etc.*

Degrade, *v.* 1. bărtărap kăr = *l.* make degradation; kāḍ = *l.* take away, *e.g.* kāmāntlo kāḍlo.
2. lăzăi, *c. v. of* lăz = be ashamed, *fg.*
3. hălko kăr = *l.* make low; uṇo kăr.

Degree, *s.* 1. grāu, -āvā, *m. fr.* (*vlg.* tăkli = *l.* head). 'Grāu' *is used in nearly all the mn. of the English* 'degree'.
2. pāṭo, -ṭeā, *m.* = diploma.
3. huddo, -deā, *m.* = *l.* rank.
4. thăr, -rā, *n.* = sort.
By degrees = thoḍeñ thoḍeñ = little by little.
In some d. = tikkeñ = a little.
In a certain d. = thoḍeñ *or* sumār.
In the same d. = tăsents.

Deification, *s.* Devāk sārko kărtso; Devāk sārko zāuntso.

Deign, *v.* puṭua = *l.* condescend, *Sb. Dat., e.g.* mākā puṭuatā; dăya kăr = make kindness; *often omitted.*

Deism, *s.* kēvalēšvaramăt, -tā, *n.* (*Cn. Mr.*)

Deity, *s.* Dēupoṇ, -ṇā, *n.* (*abstract term*); Dēu, Dēvā, *m.* = God.

Deject, *v.* dhăir kāḍ = *l.* take away courage; dukăi (*c. v. of* duk) = *l.* cause to feel sorrow.

Dejected, *a.* dukăillo; dhăir nāṭullo; čintest; dukest.

Dejection, *s.* duk, -ki, *f.*; ăpabărvānso, -seā, *m.*; ăpadhăir, -rā, *n.*

Delay, *v.* 1. pāṭi ghāl = *l.* put back; *vlg.* māgir kăr = make after.
2. toḍou kăr = *l.* make late; khăḷ, *tr., e.g.* vāur kh. = delay a work.
3. soukās kăr = make slowly; soukās vots, *n. v.* = go slowly.

Delay, *s.* toḍou, -ḍovā, *m.*; kāḷau, -ḷavā, *m.*

Delegate, *v.* 1. dūt zāun dhāḍ = send as ambassador; āpleā bădlāk dhāḍ = *l.* send in one's place; āpleā huddeār dhāḍ = *l.* send on one's own dignity.
2. *Dat.* āpli podvi di = *l.* give one's power; vopsun di = *l.* entrust.

Delegate, *s.* bădli, -leā, *m.*; văkil, -lā, *m.*

Delegation, *s.* dilli podvi, -ve, *f.* = *l.* given power.

Deliberate, *v.* 1. poḷe = look; čint = think; tūk = *l.* weigh.
2. tărk kăr = *l.* make discussion; āločen kăr = *l.* make deliberation; *see* **Enquire.**

Deliberate, *a.* 1. budvont (*or* budivont) = *l.* prudent, circumspect; boreñ kărn čintun = well considered; zāgrut = attentive; zāgrutāyen kello.
2. khušetso = *l.* wilful; khušen kello = made with will; tukullo; *or rs.* khušen = wilfully.

Deliberately, *ad.* 1. zāi moṇ; khušen = *l.* with will.
2. zāgrutāyen = *l.* with attention; boreñ kărn čintun = *l.* after having well thought.

Deliberation, *s.* 1. āločen, -ni, *f.*

2. ničeu, -čevā, *m.*, = resolution.
3. *rs. v.*, *or ad.*, *or a.*

Delicacy, *s.* 1. nāzukāi, -ye, *f.*
2. ruts, -ruči, *f.* = *l.* taste.

Delicate, *a.* 1. nāzuk, *e. g.* food; ručitso; sukṣām, *e. g.* d. instrument.
2. risketso = *l.* dangerous.
3. dākṭo = little; ăskăt = *l.* weak.

Delicious, *a.* 1. suādik; khušālāyetso.
2. ručitso = d. to the taste.

Delight, *s.* săntos, -sā, *m.*; khušālāi, -ye, *f.* = *l.* pleasure; sukh, -khā, *n.* = *l.* happiness; ulās, -sā, *m.*

Delight, *v. tr.* 1. săntos (*or* kušālāi) di; săntos bhogăi = *l.* cause to feel joy, *c. v. of* bhog.
2. mānua = *l.* please.
3. *n. v.* săntos (*or* kušālāi) bhog = feel pleasure.

Delightful, *see* **Delicious.**

Delineate, *v.* 1. *fg.* vivor sāng, *G. M.* = *l.* say explanation.
2. *pr.* risko ghāḷ = *l.* put (draw) lines, *fr.*; năkṣa kāḍ.

Delineation, *see* **Sketch.**

Delinquent, *s.* gunyāukār, -rā, *m.*

Delirious, *a.* mót tsukụllo = *l.* deprived of mind; girigiri; mótir nātụllo = *l.* not being in mind; zānkiro.

Delirious (Be), *v.* zānk *or* zāmp.

Delirium, *s. rs.* mót nāñ = *l.* mind not, *or* nāñmót, -ti, *f.*; girigiri, -ri, *f.*

Deliver, *v.* 1. soḍ = *l.* leave; soḍăi = *l.* cause to be left, release; sāmbāḷ = *l.* defend.
2. vopsun di, *or only* di (hand over to), *Prs. Cm.*
3. utsār = *l.* express, *e. g.* d. a speech, a sentence.
4. dhāḍ = *l.* send, *e. g.* a missile; soḍ = discharge, *e. g.* a missile.
5. kumok kăr = *l.* help (to bring forth).
6. nivrāi, *e. g.* from enemies; *for* 'be delivered' *see* **Bring forth.**

Deliverance, *s.* soḍvoṇ, -ṇi, *f.*

Deliverer, *s.* soḍvoṇdār, -rā, *m.* *appl. to our L. J. C.*

Delivery, *s.* 1. pursutpoṇ, -ṇā, *n.* (*Lat. partus*); bāḷnter, *or* bāḷntyor, -rā, *m.*
2. utsāraṇ, -ṇā, *n.*; utsāraṇā-tso jinos, -nsā, *m.* = way of uttering.

Deluge, *s.* 1. āuru, -rā, *n.* = partial d.
2. buḍtugāl, -lā, *n.* = universal d.
3. *fg.* dăryo, -yā, *m.* = *l.* sea, *e. g.* d. of tears; guḍe = *l.* mountains, *e. g.* d. of iniquities.

Deluge, *v.* 1. āuru yetā, *n. v.* = *l.* inundation comes.
2. *fg.* bhor = *l.* fill; dāmp = *l.* cover, *fg.*

Demagogue, *s.* kūṭ kărtso mănis *or* kūṭagār, -rā, *m.* = *l.* a man making revolution; kāṭkāi kărtso mănis *or* kāṭkāyegār, -rā, *m.* = *l.* a man making revolution; tănṭālmāri, -riā, *m.* = troublesome; utsāmboḷāi kărtso mănis = *l.* a man exciting.

Demand, *v.* 1. māg = request; hăkkān māg = *l.* ask with right.
2. zāi = is required, *ch. cs.*

Demand, *s.* 1. māg-ṇeñ, -ṇeā, *n.*
2. vorāt, -tā, *m.* = d. for payment.

Demean, *v.* 1. tsăl = behave thyself; *see* **Behave.**
2. puṭua = deign, *Sb. Dat.*

Demeanour, *s.* tsāl, -li, *f.*; nădteñ, -teā, *n.*

Democracy, *s.* dhāzăṇānčeñ rāz, -jā, *n.*; părječeñ rāz.

Demolish, *v.* 1. nāš kăr; vibāḍ kăr; bósmi; *all three have the same mn.*
2. kāḍn ghāl = abolish, *l.* putting out put.
3. āpṭi.

Demolition, *s.* nāš, -šā, *n.*; vibāḍ, -ḍā, *m.*; bósm, -mā, *m.*

Demon, *s.* bhut, -tā, *m.*; deuñtsār, -rā, *m.*; săitān, -nā, *m.*

Demoniac, *s.* deuntsār lāgullo mănis, -nšā, *m.*; deuntsār āsullo mănis.

Demoniacal, *a.* săitānātso; deuntsărātso.

Demonstrate, *v.* ruzvāt di = *l.* give proof; *or* ruzu kăr; dākăi = *l.* show; vivor săng = *l.* say explanation, *G. M.*; săngun di, *e.g.* in preaching, *ex.* speak, treat; gurtu āsā = *l.* sign is, *ch. cs.*

Demonstration, *s.* ruzvāt, -ti, *f.*; ruzu, *f.* (*mn. also* signature *or* a mark standing for it); vivor, -rā, *m.* = *l.* explanation; dākoṇ, -ṇi, *f.* = *l.* representation; dāklo, -leā, *m.* = *l.* d. by documents; gurtu, -tā, *m.* = *l.* sign.

Demonstrative, *a.* ruzvātitso; thir; ghăṭ.

Demoralization, *s.* 1. kusāp, -spā (*or* -pā), *n.* = *l.* corruption.
2. hălkepoṇ, -ṇā, *n.*

Demoralize, *v.* kusăi = *l.* corrupt, *c. v. of* kus.

Demure, *s. see* **Modest.**

Den, *s.* dol, -li, *f.*; buyār, -rā, *n.*; pănjer, -rā, *n.*

Denial, *s.* inkār, -ri, *f.* (-rā, *n.*)

Denominate, *v.* moṇ = *l.* call, give name, *Dat.*; ulo kăr, *n. c.* = *more com.* call *or* call by name.

Denomination, *s.* 1. nāuñ, -āvā, *n.* = *l.* name; ulo, -leā, *m.*, *n. c. in this mn.*
2. thăr, -rā, *m.* = *l.* kind.

Denote, *v.* dākăi = *l.* show; gurtu āsā = sign is.

Denounce, *v.* 1. somzăi, *c. v.* = *l.* give to understand; părgăṭ kăr, *or* părgăṭăi = *l.* make public; kăḷit kăr, *or* kăḷăi, *c. v.* = *l.* make known.

2. firiyād di = *l.* give accusation (legally); durua (non-legally).

Dense, *a.* kăntsoun = *l.* pressed (*esp. in fg. mn.*); găṇ, *e.g.* d. hair (*superl.* găṇṇu); lāgun = *l.* attached, *e.g.* a company of soldiers; dāṭ = *l.* thick.

Density, *s.* dāṭāi, -ye, *f.*; kăntsouṇeñ, -ṇeā, *n.*; lāgāp, -gpā, *n.* = *l.* contiguity; găṇu-poṇ, -ṇā, *n.*

Dentist, *s.* dāntañvoiz, -zā, *m.*

Denunciation, *s.* 1. *vlg.* noṭis, -sā, *n.* (common advertisement), *fr.*; istyār, -rā, *m. or n.* (by the Government); părgăṭneñ, -neā, *n.* = publication; vātsāp, -tspā, *n.* = *l.* reading.

2. *rs. v. for other mn.*

Deny, *v.* 1. inkār kăr = *l.* make resistance, refuse, *Acc.*

2. nirākărisi.

3. *fg.* d. oneself = visrāi, *l.* cause to forget; *Dat.* āḍ vots = *l.* go against; āpleā ăuguṇāčer zăit vor = *l.* gain victory against one's own vices; *see* **Self-denial.**

4. *pr.* nākā moṇ = *l.* say 'no'; nāñ moṇ; *neg. form of* vop = *l.* agree, grant ('*nega*' *opp. to* '*concede*').

Depart, *v.* bhāirsăr; vetā = goes tsăl, *e.g.* d. from here.

D. this life = săr.

Departed, *a.* sărullo *or* morn-pāullo = dead.

Department, *s.* 1. zillo (*or* jillo), -leā, *m.* = district.

2. ilāko, -keā, *m.*, *e.g.* forest department.

3. *fg.* thăr, -rā, *m.* = *l.* kind, *e.g.* in every d. of studies.

Departure, *s.* 1. bhāirsărāp, -rpā, *n.*, *bet. rs.*

2. morn, -nā, *n.* = *l.* death.

Depend, *v.* 1. umkăḷon āsā, *or* umkăḷ-tā.

2. khālto āsā = be under; tābedār zā = be in care of.

3. fāvo āsā = *l.* belongs.

4. pātiye, *Prs. 2nd Loc.* = *l.* trust.

5. hātānt āsā = is in the hand of, *e.g.* it depends on you to come.

6. *fg.* lāgun āsā, *2nd Loc.* = *l.* is attached, *e.g.* on the life of the king depend the lives of the subjects; *bet. rs. and ch. cs.*

Dependence, *s.* 1. khāltepoṇ, -ṇā, *n.* = *l.* subjection.

2. *fg.* sămănd, -dā, *m.* = *l.* connection.

Dependency, *s.* ādin āsullo gāuñ, -āñvā, *m.* = *l.* subject country; khālgāuñ = *l.* subject country.

Dependent, *a.* khālto.

Depict, *v.* *see* **Paint.**

Depletion, *s.* širmārneñ, -neā, *n.*

Deplorable, *a.* 1. dukountso.
2. rāḍtso; rāḍneñ fāvo zāllo.

Deplore, *v.* bòb mārn rāḍ = *l.* crying weep; *or only* rāḍ.

Depopulate, *see* **Devastate.**

Deport, *v.* 1. găḍ pār kăr = exile; ṭāpāk dhāḍ = confine to a certain place.
2. tsăl = *l.* walk, *fg.* (behave).

Depose, *v* 1. hălko kăr = *l.* make low; nisrāi = *l.* deprive, *e.g.* of an office, *n.c.*; bărtărap kăr, *e.g.* of an office (*the comm. expression*); kāḍ = take away, *e.g.* from an office.
2. sóḍ = *l.* leave, abdicate.
3. sākṣ kăr; sākṣ di = *l.* give evidence.

Deposit, *v.* 1. ămānăt dóvór.
2. dóvór = *l.* keep (save); thăi.

Deposit, *s.* 1. ămānăt, -tā, *n.*
2. āḍou, -ḍvā, *m.*

Depositary, *s.* thavanigār, -rā, *m.*

Deposition, *s.* 1. bărtărap, -pā, *n.* = degradation.
2. vāngmul, -lā, *n.* = written evidence under oath; sākṣ, -ṣi, *f.* = evidence *or* witness.

Depravation, *s.* 1. kusāp, -spā (*or* -pā), *n.*
2. hălkepoṇ, -ṇā, *n.*

Deprave, *v.* kusăi, *c. v. of* kus.

Deprecate, *v.* 1. māg = *l.* pray.
2. *bet.* pois kărunk māg = *l.* pray to keep far.

Depreciate, *v.* 1. bepārvo kăr = *l.* despise, *G. M.;* mol bānd.
2. mān kāḍ.
3. *see also* **Abate** (the price).

Depress, *v.* 1. khālto kăr = *l.* make humble, low.
2. dhăir kāḍ = take away courage.
3. mōḍ(ó) = *l.* break; *fg.* dukăi.

Depression, *s.* khāltepoṇ, -ṇā, *n.*; *see* **Dejection.**

Deprive, *v.* tsukăi, *c. v. of* tsuk = miss; kāḍ = *l.* take away; nisrāi, *e. g.* of an office.

Depth, *s.* gunḍăi, -ye, *f. also fg. e. g.* of mind; kholāi, -ye, *f.*

Deputation, *s.* 1. bădli, -liā, *m.* = *l.* substitute.
2. *bet.* dūt, -tā, *m.*

Depute, *v.* āple suāter . . . dhāḍ; āplea bădlāk dhāḍ = *l.* instead of him send; bădliāk dhāḍ = *l.* send a substitute; dūtāk dhāḍ = *l.* send a messenger; *or* dūtzāun dhāḍ; *see* **Delegate.**

Deputy, *s.* dălāl, -lā, *m.* = agent; bădli, -liā, *m.* = substitute; dūt, -tā, *m.* = messenger.

Derange, *v.* gusăp kăr = *l.* make confusion; guspaḍăi = *l.* confound, *e.g.* the mind.

Deranged, *a.* pisoso; vīd lāguḷlo.

Dereliction, *s.* soḍni, -ne, *f.*; nirādhār, -rā, *m.*

Deride, *v.* hās *or* hāseāk ghāl; yeḍăi = *l.* mock; čeṣṭăi kăr, *G. F.*

Derivation, *s.* ărămb, -bā, *m.* = *l.* origin.

Derive, *v.* 1. *rs. into* āsā, *e.g.* St. Francis derives his name from castle Xavier = Sāuñ Frāñčiskāk Xavier moḷḷeā koṭeāčeñ nāuñāsā.
2. ghe = *l.* receive.
3. yetā = *l.* comes, *ch. cs.*
4. kāḍ = *l.* draw.
5. meḷtā = *l.* is found, *fg.* comes, is derived.
6. nipăzā (*n. v.*).

Derogate, *v.* răddų kăr = *l.* make nullity; *see also* **Disparage, Detract.**

Descend, *v.* 1. *pr.* deuñ, *c. v.* devoi (*or* deunḍăi, *n. c.*); utăr.
2. *fg.* ubzatā, *ch. cs*, *mn.* has origin.
3. puṭua = *l.* deign, *Sb. Dat.*
4. mèḷ = be found, *e.g.* an inheritance, *Sb. Dat.*; pòḍ = fall; ye = come.

Descendant, *s.* săntăt, -ti, *f.* = *l.* posterity.

Descent, *s.* 1. devāṇeñ, -ṇeā, *n.* (deuṇi, -ṇe, *f.*).
2. ărămb, -bā, *m.* = origin; kuṭamb, -bā, *n.*, *or* kuṭām, -ṭmā, *n.*; răgat, -gtā, *n.* = *l.* blood, *fg.*

Describe, *v.* 1. ghāl = *l.* put, *e.g.* d. a circle.
2. vivorsi (*or* vivor sāng) = *l.* give a description.
3. tăpsil sāng, *G. F.* = *l.* say detail.
4. yetaprăkār sāng, *mn.* say the history of, *l.* say as it comes (as it came).

Description, *s.* 1. tăpsil, -li, *f.*; vivor, -rā, *m.*
2. ăbiprāi, -ye, *f.* = *l.* news.
3. thăr, -rā, *m.* = *l.* kind.

Desert, *a.* yekăts = alone; yeksuro = solitary.

Desert, *s.* 1. ărăṇeñ, -ṇeā, *n.*; rān, -ṇā, *n.*; moleñ, -leā, *n.* = *ex.* forest.
2. pun, -nā (*or* puneñ, -neā), *n.* = merit; tsākri, -re, *f.* = *l.* service, *fg.*

Desert, *v.* sóḍ = leave; pòḷ = *l.* run away.

Desert, *s.* soḍāp, -ḍpā, *n.*; soḍni, -ne, *f.*; nirādhăr, -rā, *m.*

Deserve, *v.* (mākā) fāvo zātā, *Dat. Prs.* = *l.* is due; tākā zāi = he deserves it; devo, (-i, -eñ) āsā = is due.

Design, *v.* 1. năkşa kāḍ = draw.
2. sodun kāḍ = *l.* seeking take; borăi = *l.* write.
3. nomiyār = *l.* nominate; čintun borăi = *l.* thinking write.
4. āločen kăr = make intention, have in mind, make a plan.

Design, *s.* bhāu, -āvā, *m.* = conception of the mind, plan; āločen, -ni, *f.* = intention; *see* **Plan.**

Designate, *v.* 1. dākăi = *l.* show.
2. nemsi = *l.* appoint, mokruri kăr.

3. kāḍ = *l.* draw, (select); vintsun kāḍ = select.

Designation, *see* **Appointment.**

Desire, *s.* khuši, -še, *f.*; ăpekša, -kše, *f.*; āšā, -še, *f.* (*or* āše) ruts, -či, *f.* (of food); urbā, -be, *f.* = longing; lāleuṇeñ, -ṇeā, *n.*

Desire, *v.* 1. khuši vor, *G. F.* = wish; āšā kăr, *G. F. or only* āše = wish; ăpekši, apekša kăr; lāle = long for.

2. māg = *l.* request.

Desirous, *a.* 1. khušetso; *bet. rs. into s. or v.*

2. urbest = longing.

Desist, *v.* thāmb = *l.* cease; sóḍ = *l.* leave; rāu = *l.* remain (from doing); mănna kăr = *l.* cease.

Desk, *s.* dākṭeñ mēz, -zā, *n.* = *l.* small table.

Desolate, *a.* 1. yeksuro = solitary.

2. nāš kello = ruined.

3. dukest = *l.* sorry.

D. place = ărāṇeñ, -ṇeā, *n.*

Desolate, *v.* dukăi = *l.* cause sorrow, *c. v. of* duk; *see* **Devastate.**

Desolation, *s.* duk, -ki, *f.* = *l.* sorrow; *see* **Solitude, Devastation.**

Despair, *v.* 1. āšā (*or* āše) sóḍ = *l.* leave desire *or* hope.

2. *neg. form of* pātie = *l.* trust.

Despair, *s.* bebăruānso, -seā, *m.*; ăpabăruānso, -seā, *m.*; nirāšā, -še, *f.*, *e.g.* in d. of life.

Despatch, *v.* 1. dhāḍ = *l.* send; dāṇdi; răvāneñ kăr = send *e.g.* a message.

2. kābār kăr = *l.* accomplish; tirsi; phăḍčā kăr.

3. săma kăr = *l.* settle.

4. *fg.* jiusiñ mār = kill.

Despatch, *s.* 1. dhāḍneñ, -neā, *n. or* dhāḍāp, -ḍpā, *n.*, *n. c.*; răvāneñ, -neā, *n.*

2. kāgād, -gdā, *n.* = *l.* letter.

3. istyār, -rā, *m.* public advertisement.

4. hukum, -kme, *f.* = *l.* order.

Despise, *v.* bepārvo (*or* bepārvāi) kăr, *G. M.* (*F.*)

Despond, *v.* āšā sóḍ = *l.* leave hope.

Despot, *s.* 1. vāiṭ rāi, -yā, *m.* = *l.* bad king; nišṭur rāi, -yā, *m.* = *l.* cruel king; āple iččhadipăti, -ti, *m.*

2. sotăntri, -riā, *m.*, *i. e.* a king with absolute power; āple iččhadikāri, -ri, *m.*

Despotism, *s.* 1. nišṭurāi, -ye, *f.* = *l.* cruelty.

2. sotăntrụ, -rā, *n.* = *l.* absolute power; āple iččhadikār, -rā, *m.*

Dessert, *s.* fòḷhār, -rā, *m.*

Destination, *s.* 1. sevoṭ, -ṭā, *m.* = *l.* aim, end; *bet. rs.*

2. mokruri, -re, *f.* = appointment.

3. māndāvoḷ, -ḷi, *f.* = arrangement.

Destine, *v.* 1. kărn dovór, *mn.* ordain, appoint; nemsi = nominate, appoint.
2. nirmi, *e.g.* God has destined me to die.
3. vintsun kāḍ = select, *e.g.* d. for heaven.

Destiny, *s.* grātstsār, -rā, *m.* = fate (*often* misfortune); nirmāṇeñ (*or* nirmoṇeñ), -ṇeā, *n.*; năsib, -bā, *n.* = lot, *Lat. fortuna.*

Destitute, *s.* durbaḷo, *or* dubḷo = *l.* poor; *bet.* soḍullo = abandoned; vāṭer ghāllo = *l.* put on the way (abandoned); nirbhāgi = *l.* unhappy, wretched; nāstānāñ = not having, *added to the word following*, destitute of; viṇeñ = *l.* without, *ch. cs.*; *or use the neg. form*, *e.g.* d. of feet = pāi nātullo; upāi nātullo; ādhār nātullo = *l.* without money; nirādhāri; gătnātullo; kir koḷ = *l.* wretched.

Destitution, *s.* nirādhār, -rā, *m.*; soḍneñ, -neā, *n. or* soḍni, -ne, *f.*; durboḷpoṇ, -ṇā, *n.* = poverty; durboḷkāi, -ye, *f.* = poverty; ākānt, -tā, *m.* = *l.* misery; kăṣṭ, -ṭā, *m.* = *l.* suffering; *see* **Destitute.**

Destroy, *v.* nāš kăr = *l.* ruin; vibāḍ kăr = ruin; bhăsmi, *c. v. of* bhăsma; *see also* **Demolish, Annul, Consume, Abolish.**

Destructible, *a.* nāš fāvo zāllo; nāš zāuntso.

Destruction, *s.* nisāntān, -nā, *n.*; bhong, -gā, *m.*

Destructive, *a.* luksānātso = *l.* causing loss; nāš kărtso; vibāḍ kărtso.

Desuetude, *s. rs.* sovoi nāñ = *l.* no custom.

Desultory, *a.* krămaviṇ = irregular.

Detach, *v.* 1. *pr.* kāḍ.
2. nikḷāi, *c. v. of* nikăḷ, *e.g.* a button.
3. *fg.* pois″ kăr, pois″ dovór = *l.* separate.
4. vingăḍāi *or* vingăḍ kăr = *l.* separate.

Detachment, *s.* kumpni, -ne, *f.*, *fr.*

Detail, *v.* tăpsil sāng = *l.* say detail, *G. F.*

Detail, *s.* tăpsil, -li, *f.*

Detain, *v.* 1. dovór = keep; pāṭi dovór = keep back.
2. toḍou kăr = make late.
3. rāvoi, *c. v. of* rāu = remain.

Detect, *v.* 1. mèḷ = *l.* be found, *Dat. Prs.*; sodun mèḷ = *l.* seeking be found.
2. tālās kăr, *e.g.* a thief.

Deter, *v.* 1. beṣṭāi = *l.* scold, menace, *hence ch. cs.*; āḍāi = *l.* pre- vent, *e.g.* he deterred him from doing this = tāṇeñ tākā yeñ kărunk āḍāilā.
2. pois″ dovór = *l.* keep far.

Deteriorate, *v.* pāḍ kăr, *tr. v.*; pāḍ zā, *n. v.*

Determination, *s.* 1. tirmāṇ, -ṇā, *n.* = *l.* decision.
2. ničeu, -vā, *m.* = resolution; măṭṭu, -ṭā, *n.*, *n. c.*
3. nirmoṇeñ, -ṇeā, *n.*, *e.g.* d. of a meeting; niščeisilli văstụ, -tu, *f.* = determined thing.

Determine, *v.* 1. vivor săng = *l.* say explanation, *G. M.*
2. niščeisi = *l.* decide; tīrp kărn di.
3. čint = *l.* think (make up one's mind); ničeu kăr; măṭṭu kăr.
4. sămā kăr = *l.* settle.
5. lāi = *l.* apply, *e.g.* d. to write.

Determined, *a.* niščeisillo, *i.e.* fixed; khănḍit.

Detest, *v.* kānṭāḷ; hăgeñ dovór.

Detestable, *a.* kānṭāḷo fāvozāllo; kānṭāḷeātso; hăgeātso.

Detestation, *s.* kāṇṭāḷo, -ḷeā, *m.*; hăgeñ, -geā, *n.*; jiddụ, -dā, *n.*

Dethrone, *v.* pāṭ soḍăi = *l.* cause to leave the throne; pāṭāntlo kāḍ, *n. c.*; pāṭa voilo kāḍ; nisrāi = *l.* deprive (of an office).

Detract, *v.* 1. *pr.* kāḍ.
2. *fg.* durua; mān kāḍ = *l.* take away honor; tsāḍio sāng = *l.* say detraction.

Detraction, *s.* tsāḍi, -ye, *f.*

Devastate, *v.* desvāṭ kăr; nāš kăr; *see* **Ruin.**

Devastation, *s.* desvāṭ, -ṭe, *f.*; nāš, -šā, *m.*

Develope, *v.* 1. *pr.* kāḍ; soḍăi.
2. *fg.* vistārāi = *l.* enlarge; *only* vistār.
3. vivor săng = *l.* give explanation.
4. vāḍăi = *l.* bring up.
5. tsăḍăi = *l.* increase.

Development, *s.* 1. *rs. v.* tsăḍăi = increase.
2. vāḍāu, -ḍāvā, *m.*
3. sevoṭ, -ṭā, *m.* = issue.

Deviate, *v.* 1. portā = *l.* turn, (*imper. sing.* porăt).
2. vāṭ soḍ = *l.* leave the way; vāṭ tsuk = *l.* miss the way.
3. *fg.* pāḍ zā, vāiṭ zā = *l.* get bad.

Deviation, *s.* 1. portouṇeñ, -ṇeā, *n.*
2. tsuk, -ki, *f.* = *l.* mistake, erring; gunyāuñ, -āvā, *m.* = *l.* fault.

Device, *s.* 1. čămătkār, -rā, *m.* = *l.* artifice; hikmăt, -ti, *f.*
2. upāi, -yā, *m.* = *l.* means.

Devil, *s.* săitān, -nā, *m.*; bhut, -tā, *m.*; deuntsār, -rā, *m.*; mhāru, -rvā, *m.*

Devilish, *a.* 1. săitānātso, *pr.*, *fg.*; deuntsārātso, *pr.*, *fg.*
2. *fg.* khoṭepoṇātso = wicked.

Devise, *v.* sodun kāḍ = *l.* seeking draw; čint = *l.* think, frame, imagine; *see* **Bequeath.**

Devolve, *v.* 1. vopsun di, *tr. v.* = *l.* deliver; soḍn di.
2. *n. v.* mèḷ = *l.* be found, *e.g.* property, an inheritance, *etc.*

Devote, *v.* 1. bhāl, *e. g.* d. thyself wholly to; bheṭāi = *l.* offer, *G. M.* (tsākrek).
2. prăyog kăr=*l.* make use, *e.g.* time; *bet.* khărči = expend.
3. lāg = *l.* apply, *e.g.* to studies.

Devoted, *a.*, *rs. v.*; lāgullo = given to, *l.* attached, *fg.*

Devotion, *s.* 1. devăspoṇ, -ṇā, *n.*; bhăktipoṇ, -ṇā, *n.*; bhăkt, -ti, *f.*; săntipoṇ, -ṇā, *n.*
2. *fg.* bhālāp, -pā, *n.*, *n. c.* = *l.* attachment; ăpurbāi, -ye, *f.* = *l.* affection.

Devour, *v.* 1. giḷ = swallow, *pr.*, *fg.*, *e. g.* eat quickly; grāsi (*ol. w.*); bakabaka khā.
2. nāš kăr = *l.* ruin.

Devout, *a.* bhāgevont = *l.* holy; devāgelo; devăspoṇātso, *e.g.* a d. woman.

Dew, *s.* dou, -ovā, *m.*

Dewy, *a.* dovātso; dovān bhorlolo = *l.* filled with dew.

Diadem, *s.* mukuṭ, -ṭā, *m.* = *l.* crown; kurou, -rovā, *m.* = *l.* crown, *rl.*, *fr.*

Diagnosis, *s.* 1. piḍeguṇ = *l.* quality of sickness.
2. piḍepărikṣa = examination of sickness.

Dial, *s.* suryāčeñ găḍiyāḷ, -ḷā, *n.* = *l.* clock of the sun.

Dialect, *s.* tsālti bhās, -se, *f.* = *l.* current language; hălki bhās = *l.* low language.

Dialectic, *s.* tărkāvidya, -ye, *f.* = *l.* science of discussion, reasoning.

Dialogue, *s.* uloṇeñ, -ṇeā, *n.*; găzāl, -li, *f.* = chat; sămbāšeṇ, -ṇā, *n.*

Diameter, *s.* 1. (măndăḷāčeñ) āḍmezāp, -zpā, *n.*, *n. u.*; vyās, -sā, *n.*, *Mr. Cn.*
2. dāṭāi, -ye, *f.* = *l.* thickness.

Diametrically, *ad.* 1. *fg.* purteñ = *l.* entirely; kēvăl.
2. porteñ = *l.* contrarily.

Diamond, *s.* văzrụ, -rā, *n.*

Diaphoretic, *a.* ghāmăitolo = *l.* causing perspiration.

Diarrhœa, *s.* utkāḍe, -ḍeā, *n.*; 'have d. = utkāḍe zā'; *vlg.* poṭāntleñ vetā, *Prs. Dat.*; 'tākā p. vetā'; nirvoḷi, -ḷe, *f.*; jalab, -bā, *n.*

Diary, *s.* disāčeñ pustak, -kā, *n.* = *l.* book of the day; disāvrati pātrụ, -rā, *n.*

Dictate, *v.* 1. formāi = *l.* command; *see* **Command.**
2. vātsun sāng = *l.* reading say; borounčeāk vāts = read for writing, *n. c.*

Diction, *s.* bhāsetso jinos, -nsā, *m.*; *or only* bhās, -se, *f.* = language.

Dictionary, *s.* utrāntso mēḷ(é) *or* utrāñ mēḷ(é), -ḷā, *m.* = *l.* collection of words; utrānčeñ pustak, -kā, *n.*; săbdāñ-ărthapustak; ărthapustak; săbdañ bănḍār, -rā, *n.*

Die, *s.* tsouk *or* čouk, -kā, *m.* = *l.* square, *n. ex.*

Die, *v.* 1. mòr; mòrn pāu; săr = *l.* depart; prāṇ soḍ = *l.* leave the life; prāṇ di = *l.* give life (for another).

2. *fg.* d. (of love, *etc.*) = mòr.

Diet, *s.* 1. khāṇ, -ṇā, *n.* = *l.* food.

2. uṇeñ khāṇ, thoḍeñ khāṇ = *l.* little food; uṇeñ khāunčeñ; *bet.* pòt, -tā, *n.*, *e. g.* of a sick man, *h. w.*

3. săbha, -bhe, *f. Lat. conventus.*

Differ, *v.* 1. săma năiñ = *l.* is not equal; *rs.* bhēd(é) āsā = *l.* difference is (are not equal); tăphāvot āsā.

2. *neg. form of* vop = *l.* agree.

Difference, *s.*, *rs. v.*; *neg. form of* sārkeñ, -keā, *n.* = resemblance; tsăḍuṇeñ, -ṇeā, *n.* = *l.* more or less, *used also as noun*; bhēd(é), -dā, *m.* = *l.* distinction; tăphāvot, -ti, *f.*; vettyās, -sā, *m.*; phorăk, -kā, *m.*; ăntăr, rā, *n.*

Different, *a.* 1. săma nātullo = *l.* not equal; tots năiñ = not the same; yer = *Lat. alius*, *e.g.* they went back to their country by a different road; bădăl *from* bădăltā = changes; dusro = *Lat. alius*, *e.g.* it is not this, but another, *or* it is different from this.

2. veglo = *l.* separated: 'men speak different things = mănis vegḷeo vegḷeo văstu ulăităt'.

Differently, *a.* 1. dusre jinsiñ = *l.* in another manner.

2. nāñ zāleār = *l.* if it does not happen, (else, *Lat. secus*).

Difficult, *a.* kăṭin, *e.g.* the study of a language; kăṣṭāntso = *l.* painful; *sometimes the subst.* kăṣṭ *is used*; ăugăḍ = hard, *e.g.* to God no work is difficult; we walked through difficult ways; sănkăṣṭ.

Difficulty, *s.* 1. kăṣṭ, -ṭā, *m.* = *l.* arduousness, pain; kăṭināi, *or* kănṭināi, -ye, *f.*; *see adj.*

2. ăugăḍāi, -ye, *f. see adj.*

3. ăḍḍi, -ḍe, *f.* = *l.* objection.

4. prăyās, -sā, *n.*, *e. g.* d. of doing something.

5. ākānt, -tā, *m.* = *l.* distress.

Diffidence, *s.* ăpabărvāso *or* bebărvāso, -seā, *m.*; *neg. form of* pātiyeṇi, -ṇe, *f.* = trust; bheñ, bhiyā, *n.* = *l.* fear; nirāša, -še, *f.* = *l.* despair; ăpadhăir, -rā, *n.*; ăpanămbik, -ke, *f.*

Diffident, *a.* pātiyenātullo; ăpanămbigetso.

Diffuse, *v.* 1. vāvoi = cause to flow.

2. vistārāi = *l.* extend, *tr. v.*

3. vāu = *l.* flow, *n. v.*

4. ye = *l.* come, *e.g.* diffuses a sweet smell = pormoḷ yetā, *l.* a good smell comes.

5. fāsḷāi, *e.g.* d. an odour; fāsăḷ, *n. v.*

Diffuse, *a.* 1. vistārlolo = *l.* extended.
2. tsăḍ = much.

Dig, *v.* 1. konḍ.
2. usti = *l.* stir, *e.g.* a grave.

Digest, *v.* 1. săma kăr = *l.* make right (arrange); mānḍ = arrange.
2. jirăi, *c. v. of* jir; jirvoṇ kăr; văгgā; mākā jirtā (food).
3. *fg.* boreñ kărn čint = *l.* think well.

Digestible, *a.* bolāiketso = *l.* healthy.

Digestion, *s.* jirvoṇ, -ṇe, *f.* (of food).

Digestive, *a.* jirvoṇetso.

Digger, *s.* konḍtolo, -leā, *m.*

Digit, *s.* ăngăl, -lā, *n.* (inch).

Dignitary, *s.* huddeagār, -rā, *m.*, *e.g.* a bishop.

Dignity, *s.* 1. podvi, -ve, *f.* = *l.* power, *e.g.* walks with dignity; vodpoṇ, -ṇā, *n.* = *l.* greatness; dăbāzo, -jeā, *m.* = *l.* pomp.
2. stiti, -ti, *f.* = *l.* state; huddo, -deā, *m.* = rank.
3. mān, -nā, *m.* = *l.* honour; mānāčeñ kām, -mā, *n.* = *l.* high office.
4. măryād, -di, *f.* = *l.* decorum, *and also* decorations.

Digress, *v.* 1. sóḍ = *l.* leave, *fg.*; porta = turn (*imper. sing.* porăt).
2. bhāir săr = start, *pr.*

Digression, *s.* *rs.* *v.*; soḍneñ, -neā, *n.*, *or* soḍni, -ne, *f.*; portaṇeñ, -ṇeā, *n.*, *or* portāp, -pā, *n.* = *l.* turning.

Dilapidated, *a.* poḍtso = *l.* falling.

Dilate, *v.* vistārāi, *c. v. of* vistār.

Dilemma, *s.* *vlg.* yeṇeñ ḅāiñ teṇeñ năiñ = *l.* here well there river; kātri bări tărk, -kā, *n.*, *n. c.* = *Lat. argumentum forficis instar.*

Diligence, *s.* zāgrutāi, -ye, *f.* = carefulness; ušārāi, -ye, *f.* = *l.* cleverness; tsătrāi -ye, *f.* = care.

Diligent, *a.* zāgrut; ušār; tsurk = *l.* active; tsătur.

Dilute, *v.* mélăi (*with the word expressing the diluting liquid*) = *l.* mix; pātăḷ kăr = make thin.

Dim, *a.* kāḷoso, *or* kāḷso; kāḷki, *appl. to* night *and* mind; musku.

Dim, *v.* kāḷso kăr.

Dimension, *s.* voḍāi, -ye, *f.* zòk, -kā, *n.* = *l.* measure; mezāp, -zpā, *n.* = measurement.

Diminish, *v.* uṇo kăr, *tr. v.* = *l.* make less; uṇo zā, *n. v.*; devoi = *l.* cause to descend (price).

Diminution, *s.* uṇepoṇ, -ṇā, *n.* = *l.* deficiency, *or rs. v.*

Dimness, *s.* kāḷok, -kā, *m.*

Din, *s.* hāk ani bòb, -be, *f.*, *or* hāk bòb.

Dine, *v.* jeu, *c. v.* jevoi; jevāṇ kāṇe (*or* kāṇghe).

Dining-room, *s.* jeuṇāčeñ kuḍ, -ḍā, *n.*; jeunčeñ kuḍ; jeuṇā-kuḍ.

Dinner, *s.* jevāṇ, jeuṇā, *n.* = meal: 'invite to d. = jeuṇāk āpoi'; 'give d. = vāḍ (serve d.)'.

Diocese, *s.* dios, -sā, *m.*, *or* diosez, -zi, *f.*, *fr.*; bispāčeñ rāz, -jā, *n.*

Dip, *v.* buḍăi, *c. v. of* buḍ; buḍoun bizăi = *l.* plunging wet.

Dip, *s.* buḍāp, -ḍpā, *n.*

Diploma, *s.* pāṭo, -ṭeā, *m.*, *e. g.* doctor's d.

Diplomacy, *s.* tsălounči vidya, -ye, *f.*

Diplomatic, *s.* rāyātso văkil, -lā, *m.*; măntri, -ri, *m.*

Direct, *v.* 1. săma kăr = *l.* make straight.

2. *G.* isileān nīṭ vots = go in the direction of, *ch. cs.*, *e. g.* direct yourself towards = isileān vots.

3. porti = *l.* turn; 'direct the ship towards the shore = tāruñ veḷek porti'.

4. *Or.* părmāṇe kăr = *l.* do according to (regulate); *instead of* kăr, *the meaning may require some other verb.*

5. tsălăi = *l.* cause to walk, *fg.*, rule.

6. *G.* nāvār kāgād borăi = *l.* write the letter in the name of, address; melviḷās borăi = write the address.

7. vor = *l.* bring, lead.

Direction, *s.* 1. *rs. v.*; kārkhāno, -neā, *m.* = *l.* administration.

2. kus, -si, *f.* = *l.* side: 'te kusin = *l.* in that side'; vessi; *only* thăiñ: 'in every direction, everywhere = sărvuṇ thăiñ *or* săgḷeān'.

3. kārbār, -rā, *n.*

4. regrụ, -re, *f.* = *l.* rule, *fr.*; kāido, -deā, *m.*

5. sikoṇ, -ṇe, *f.* = instruction.

Directly, *ad.* 1. nīṭ zāun = straight.

2. ātānts = now.

Director, *s.* 1. tsălăitolo (*joined to the thing or person directed*).

2. kārbāri, -riā, *m.* administrator *or* superintendent of a building, *and the like.*

3. voḍil, -lā, *m.* = *l.* superior.

Directress, *s.* voḍiln, -ni, *f.*; tsălăiteli, -le, *f.*

Dirt, *s.* 1. koir, -rā, *m.*; čikol, -klā, *m.*; bursepoṇ, -ṇā, *n.* filthiness, *pr. fg.*

2. āgruñ, -rā, *n.*, *e. g.* of the feet.

Dirty, *a.* mheḷo; ăḷsik = *l.* ugly; burso (*physic. and moral*); uṣṭo (hands); čiklātso, *e. g.* d. body, d. place, *pr. fg.*

Dirty, *v.* mheḷăi, *c. v. of* mheḷ; mheḷo kăr = make dirty; čikolăi, *n. c.*; čikol kăr.

N. B. Some verbs compounded with dis *not put down here may be expressed by the* negative form *of the* compounded verb.

Disability, *s.* ăšăkt, -ti, *f.*, *e.g.* for an office; *rs.* podvi nāñ = *l.* power not. [weak.

Disable, *v.* ăskăt kăr = *l.* make

Disaccustom, *v.* sovoi kāḍ = *l.* take away the custom, (ādli = anterior *must be sometimes added*).

Disadvantage, *s.* luksān, -nā, *n.*; năšṭ, -ṭā, *n.*: 'luksānāk poḍtā = *l.* it falls to d.'

Disadvantageous, *a.* 1. luksānātso = injurious.
2. ăuguṇātso = unfavourable.

Disaffect, *v.* mòn pois kăr.

Disaffection, *a.* 1. nākhuši, -še, *f.*; ăpaprit, -ti, *f.*, *n. c.*; kānṭāḷo, -ḷeā, *m.* = abhorrence.
2. čappeñ mon, -nā, *n.* = *l.* heart not salted (cold).

Disagree, *v.* 1. *neg. form of* vop = agree.
2. *neg. form of* zā: 'mākā zāināñ = I disagree with this'. 'I disagree with you = mākā āni tukā vettyās āsā'.

Disagreeable, *a.* 1. dukountso = *l.* afflicting; *vlg.* boreñ năiñ = not good; *by the neg. form of the verb* mānua = please, *or of* boreñ distā = it seems well (is nice, pleasant); kărkărāntso = *l.* annoying; bezārāyetso (*or* bejārātso) = troublesome; tondreātso = *l.* embarrassing.
2. ăḷsik (*said of* smell) = *l.* ugly.
3. kăṭiṇ = severe.
4. lăḍāi kărtso = quarrelling.

Disagreeableness, *s.*, *rs. into adj.*; kărkăr, -rā, *m.* = annoyance; bezārāi, -ye, *f.* = *l.* trouble.

Disagreement, *s.* nāñvoppigi, -ge, *f.*, *n. c.*; nyāi, -yā, *m.* = *l.* discord; vetyās, -sā, *m.* (difference of opinion *etc.*).

Disappear, *v.* 1. năpăints zā; māyāk zā.
2. cause to disappear = năpăints (*or* māyāk) kăr.

Disappoint, *v.* āšā khāli kăr, *or* ā. besṭi kăr; āšā tsukăi; pātiyeṇi tsukăi; *vlg.* āmbaḍeñ zāleñ, *or* āmbaḍo di; foṭăi (*not ex.*); mōs(ó) kăr; *vlg.* suḷār ghāl (put on a big stick); kāḍiyer ghāl (put on a small stick).

Disappointment, *s. by the verb;* găḍāi, -yā, *m.* = *l.* cluster, *fg.* (*Konk.*); nirāša, -še, *f.*; mosavoḷok, -ḷki, *f.* = acknowledgment of deceit; tsukmuk, -ki, *f.*

Disapproval, *s.* nāpăsănd (*not decl.*).

Disapprove, *v. neg. form of* păsănd kăr = approve; *or of* kobul kăr = consent; gunyāukār kăr = *l.* make guilty; durva (*ex.* reproach).

N. B. Some verbs compounded with **dis** *not put down here may be expressed by the* **negative form** *of the* **compounded verb.**

Disarm, *v.* hātyārañ kāḍ = *l.* take away the weapons.

Disarrangement, *s.* gusăp, -spā, *n.* = *l.* confusion; ăkrăm, -mā, *n.*

Disaster, *s.* pădāu, -ḍāvā, *m.* = *l.* defeat; (voḍ) kăṣṭ, -ṭā, *m.* = (great) suffering; tsuk, -ki, *f.* = mistake (which has been the cause of disaster); ăpād, -dā, *n.*

Disavow, *v. neg. form of* vop = acknowledge; *or of* kobul kăr, *or of* kobul zā = consent.

Disbelief, *s.* 1. ănbāvăḍt, -tā, *m.* *used for* d. in God.
2. ăpabărvānso, -seā, *m.*; ăpanămbik, -ke, *f.* = distrust; ăpadhăir, -rā, *n.*
3. dubāu, -bāvā, *m.* = doubt.

Disbelieve, *v.* 1. *neg. form of* sătmānd (d. in God).
2. *Neg. form of a)* pātiye, *b)* nămga, *c)* nāmboa = trust.

Disburse, *v.* fārik kăr = *l.* pay; khărči = *l.* expend.

Disc, *s.* mānḍ, -ḍi, *f.* = quoit.

Discern, *v.* bhēd kăr = *l.* make distinction; tăfāvot kăr = *l.* make distinction; somza; kăḷ = get known, *Prs. Dat.*; soṣṭ poḷe; soṣṭ distā = appears clearly, *ch. cs.*

Discernment, *s,* bud, -di, *f.*; budiprăkāš, -šā, *m.*

Discharge, *v.* 1. vojeñ kāḍ = *l.* take off the burden.
2. vāu = *l.* flow *as* rivers, *ch. cs.*
3. vonk = *l.* vomit.
4. soḍ = *l.* leave *or* dismiss, *e.g.* a missile.
5. tsălăi = *l.* perform; pāḷ, *e.g.* duty.
6. mār = *l.* beat, *e.g.* a gun.
7. kăr = *l.* execute, do.

Discharge, *s.* 1. făr, -rā, *m.* (of a gun).
2. pāḷo, -ḷeā, *m.*, of a duty.
3. *rs. v.*

Disciple, *s.* sis, -sā, *m.* = pupil (*var.* sissu̥, -sā, *m.*); siktolo burgo, -geā, *m.* = learning boy; iskulātso burgo, -geā, *m.* = school-boy, *fr.*

Discipline, *s.* 1. sikāp, -kpā, *n.* = *l.* learning; tărbet, -ti, *f.* = education.
2. măryād, -di, *f.* = *l.* modesty, decorum; kăido, -deā, *m.* = *l.* duty, *e.g.* military d. demands sacrifices.
3. tsāl, -li, *f.* = behaviour; năḍteñ, -teā, *n.* = conduct.
4. kăṣṭ, -ṭā, *m.* = *l.* pains.
5. korḍo, -ḍeā, *m.* (instrument).
6. pāḷo (kăideātso), -ḷeā, *m.* = observance (of duty).

Disclose, *v.* 1. *pr.* dānkṇeñ kāḍ = *l.* take away the cover *or* lid; ugto kăr = open.
2. *fg.* părgăṭ kăr, părgăṭăi = *l.*

N. B. Some verbs compounded with dis *not put down here may be expressed by the* negative form *of the* compounded verb.

make public; kăḷit kăr, kăḷăi = *l.* make known.
3. dākăi = *l.* show.

Discolour, *v.* róng kāḍ.

Discoloured, *a.* róng nātullo.

Discomfit, *v.* dāunḍăi = *l.* cause to run away.

Discomfort, *s.* bezārăi, -ye, *f.* = *l.* trouble; husko, -keā, *m.*; kăṣṭ, -ṭā, *m.*; kărkăr, -rā, *m.* = *l.* annoyance; duk, -ki, *f.* = *l.* sorrow; khănt, -ti, *f.* = affliction; ăsămādhān, -nā, *n.*

Discomposure, *s.* 1. gusăp, -spā, *n.*; *see* **Confusion.**
2. ăsămādhān, -nā, *n.*

Disconcert, *v.* 1. mōḍ (ó) = *l.* break, *e.g.* d. plans.
2. guspăḍăi = *l.* confuse; nirfoḷ kăr = make fruitless, *fg.*

Discontent, *see* **Discomfort.**

Discontinue, *see* **Interrupt.**

Discord, *s.* 1. năi, -yā, *m.*; vegḷačai, -ye, *f.*, *more common* vegḷatsăr, -rā, *m.*; dusmānkăi, -ye, *f.* = *l.* enmity; zăgḍeñ, -ḍeā, *n.* = a quarrel *viva voce.*
2. *neg. form of* sămapoḍāp, -ḍpā (*or* -pā), *n.*, *e.g.* d. in music; bebănāu, -nāvā, *m.*, *e.g.* d. among brethren.
3. gālgouji, -je, *f.*, *e.g.* in music, of a meeting *etc.*, *n. c.*: 'create discord = ādḷăi, *l.* cause to dash', *fg.*

Discount, *s.* vāṭāu, -ṭāvā, *m.*; uṇeñ, -ṇeā, *n.* = *l.* less, *ch. cs.* (*or* uṇāu, -ṇāvā, *m.*).

Discount, *v.* kăḷvi.

Discountenance, *v.* lăzăi = put to shame; *neg. form of* păsănd kăr = approve; durva = reproach, blame; kānṭāḷ = abhor, not to like; inkār kăr = *l.* make resistance, *Acc.*; boreñ disanāñ = does not seem good.

Discourage, *v.* 1. dhăir kāḍ *or* dh. tsukăi = *l.* take away courage; ăšā kāḍ = *l.* take away desire, hope.
2. bhesṭăi = *l.* threaten, scold, deter, *ch. cs.*; āḍăi = *l.* prevent, impede.

Discouragement, *s.* ăpadhăir, -rā, *n.*; ăḍḍi, -ḍe, *f.* = *l.* objection; *rs. v.*

Discouraging, *a.* ăuguṇātso *etc.*; dhăir tsukountso.

Discourse, *v.* 1. *Or.* višiănt ulăi = *l.* speak about; tărk kăr = *l.* make a discussion.
2. găzāli mār = have a chat.
3. sămbāšăṇ kăr = *l.* make a dialogue. [kăr.
4. sermāuñ kăr, *fr.*; prăsăng

Discourse, *s.* 1. uloṇeñ, -ṇeā, *n.* = conversation.
2. sermāuñ, -māvā, *m.* = *l.* preaching, *fr.*; prăsăng, -gā, *n.*

N. B. Some verbs compounded with **dis** *not put down here may be expressed by the* **negative form** *of the* **compounded verb.**

3. sămbāšăṇ, -ṇā, *n.*; găzāli, -li, *f.* (chat).

Discourtesy, *s.* ăumăryād, -di, *f.*

Discover, *v.* 1. ukto kăr = make open.
2. părgăṭ kăr, părgăṭăi = *l.* make public.
3. dākăi = *l.* show.
4. sodun mèḷ (*or* kāḍ) = seeking find, find out; *if* an accidental discovery *is meant, then only* (mākā) mèḷ.

Discovery, *see* **Invention.**

Discredit, *v.* 1. ăpanămbiki kăr = *l.* distrustful; mān kāḍ = *l.* take away honour.
2. *neg. form of* nămboa = believe.

Discredit, *s.* ăpamān, -nā, *m.* = *l.* dishonour; pāḍ nāuñ, -nāvā, *n.* = bad name, bad reputation.

Discreet, *a.* 1. budivont = *l.* prudent.
2. mogāḷ = *l.* dear.
3. *by a gerund* (čintun = thinking), *ch. cs.*

Discretion, *s.* 1. bud, -di, *f.* = *l.* prudence.
2. kuši, -še, *f.* = *l.* will, *as*, (leave it) to his discretion = tače khuše părmāṇe, *l.* according to his will (*ch. cs.*); bud *might also be used in the 2nd mn.*

Discuss, *v.* 1. tărk kăr = *l.* make discussion (*vlg.* ārment kăr); čertso kăr = *l.* make discussion; čint = *l.* think; poḷe = *l.* see; tuk = weigh, *fg.*
2. ulăi = speak.
See also **Enquiry.**

Discussion, *s.* tărk, -kā, *n.* = argument; čertso, -čeā, *m.*; *see* **Enquiry.**

Disdain, *v.* bepārvo (*or* bepārvāi) kăr, *G. M.* (*F.*); bepārvāyen soḍ *or* tsukăi = *l.* avoid with contempt; kānṭāḷ = *l.* abhor.

Disdain, *s.* bepārvo, -veā, *m. or* bepārvāi, -ye, *f.* = *l.* contempt; kānṭāḷo, -ḷeā, *m.*; hăgeñ, -geā, *n.* = *l.* abhorrence.

Disease, *s.* piḍa, -ḍe, *f.*, *e. g.* to piḍent poḍlā = *l.* he has fallen into sickness. 'Tākāi piḍa lāgleā = he too got the sickness'. 'Recover from d. = boro zā'. 'Severe sickness = kānṭin *or* nibbor piḍa'. 'To die of a disease = piḍent *or* piḍen morčeñ'. 'Hereditary d. = dāizāntli piḍa'.

Diseased, *a.* piḍest; piḍevont.

Disembarrass, *v.* tondreāntlo tsukāi, *e.g.* a person in perplexity.

Disembark, *v.* 1. *tr. v.* tārvāntlo kāḍ = *l.* take out of a ship; uspi.
2. *n. v.* tārvāntlo deuñ = *l.* descend from the ship.

N. B. Some verbs compounded with **dis** *not put down here may be expressed by the* **negative form** *of the* **compounded verb.**

Disengage, *v.* 1. kāḍ = *l.* draw. 2. veg̣lo kăr, vingăḍ kăr = *l.* make separated. 3 soḍăi, *c. v. of* soḍ = release.

Disengaged, *a.* I am disengaged = mākā kām nāñ, I have no business; āuñ khāli āsāñ = I am without (business); mākā pursot āsā = I have leisure.

Disentangle, *v.* 1. kāḍ = *l.* draw, *e.g.* tākā kăṣṭāntlo kāḍlā = he has been disentangled from his difficulties. 2. păriyār kăr, (*Pass.*) păriyār zā (kāmāntlo p. zālo); tsukăi (*in pass.* tsukon ghe).

Disesteem, *v. neg. form of* mānd; mòl bānd; bepārvo kăr = despise, *G. M.*

Disesteem, *s.* 1. bepārvo, -veā, *m.* 2. pāḍ nāuñ, -nāvā, *n.*

Disfavour, *s.* 1. ăpamān, -nā, *m.*; *vlg.* ăkmān, -nā, *m.* 2. nākhuši, -še, *f.* (disgrace).

Disfigure, *v.* vidrup kăr *or* (băirup kăr); *vlg.* ăḷšik kăr = *l.* make ugly.

Disfigurement, *s.* băirup, -pā, *n.*

Disgrace, *s.* 1. nākhuši, -še, *f.* = *l.* not will, *e.g.* he fell into d. with the king = rāyăče nākhušent poḍlā, *l.* he fell into the not-will of the king. 2. nirbhāgipoṇ, -ṇā, *n.* = wretchedness. 3. ăpamān, -nā, *m.*

Disgrace, *v.* 1. bārtărăp kăr = depose; nisrāi = deprive (of office). 2. ăpamān kăr = *l.* make offence.

Disgraced, *a.* 1. nākhušent poḍullo. 2. măryādnātụllo. 3. bekup (stupid).

Disgraceful, *a.* ăpamānātso *or* ăkmānātso = *l.* ignominious; ăḷšik, *vlg.*; lăjetso = shameful; lăjiṣṭ.

Disguise, *s.* vés, -sā, *m.*, *pr. and fg.* (pretext).

Disguise, *v.* vés ghāl = *l.* put a mask; *Or.* bări (kăr, *or some other verb*) = *l.* (do) as, *e.g.* gouḷia bări tsăltā = *l.* he walks as a shepherd; lip = *l.* conceal.

Disgust, *s.* 1. *by the neg. of* ruts = taste (ruts nāñ). 2. kărkăr, -rā, *m.* = *l.* annoyance: 'mākā kărkăr zātā = I get annoyed (*or bet. in plural* mākā kărkăr zātāt); bezārāi, -ye, *f.* = *l.* trouble, tiredness; *crc., e.g.* mākā puro zāleñ = I have got enough, I am tired. 3. kānṭāḷo, -ḷeā, *m.* = abhorrence (*also of* food); vonkāro, -reā, *m.* = nausea, *fg.*; *neg. form of* khusālāi, khušālāi nāñ; săntos nāñ.

N. B. Some verbs compounded with **dis** *not put down here may be expressed by the* **negative form** *of the* **compounded verb.**

4. ubgoṇ, -ṇi, *f.*, *e.g.* āikon u. āili = I got tired of listening.

Disgust, *v.* 1. *neg. form of* rutstā (*of* food): 'mākā rutsanāñ = I have no appetite.
2. (mākā) puro zātā = I am disgusted, *or* tired; kānṭāḷ = abhor; *neg. form of* mānua = please; vonkāro yetā = *l.* nausea comes.

Disgusting, *a.* 1. rutsanātullo (to the taste), *pr. fg.*
2. āḷšik = *Lat. foedus*; kānṭāḷo fāvozāllo = abominable; kānṭāḷeātso = abominable; vonkāreātso = causing nausea; kārkārātso = *l.* annoying.

Dish, *s. pr.* 1. tăbāk, tăbkā, *n.* (of tin *or* brass); polgāṇ, -ṇā, *n.* = a large plate, tray.
2. tāṭ, -ṭā, *n.* (of a balance).

Dish-cover, *s.* dānkṇeñ, -ṇeā, *n.* = *l.* a covering, lid.

Dishearten, *v.* 1. dhăir (*or* āša) kāḍ *or* dh. tsukāi = *l.* take away courage *or* hope.
2. besṭāi = *l.* cause to fear.

Dishonest, *a.* mān nātullo = *l.* without honour; khoṭo = *l.* wicked; apātiyeṇitso (*or bet.* (bepātiyeṇitso) = *l.* unfaithful; dăgeātso.

Dishonesty, *s.* ăumăryād, -di, *f.* (disposition to cheat, *etc.*); khoṭepoṇ, -ṇā, *n.* = wickedness; mōs (ó), -sā, *m.* = *l.* deceit; *see* **Injustice.**

Dishonour, *s.* ăpamān, -nā, *m.*; *vlg.* ăkmān, -nā, *m.*; lăz, -je, *f.* = shame; beābru, -rā, *m.*

Dishonour, *v.* 1. ăpamān kăr = *l.* make dishonour; mān kāḍ = *l.* take away honour.
2. kăṭai *or* zulum kăr = do violence.

Dishonourable, *a.* ăpamān fāvozāllo; ăkmānātso.

Disinclination, *see* **Aversion.**

Disinfect, *v.* ghāṇ kāḍ = *l.* draw out a bad smell.

Disinherit, *v.* dāiz kāḍ; dāiz tsukāi; dāizā bhāir ghāl; dāiz nivrāi.

Disinter, *v.* mātiyentlo kāḍ.

Disinterested, *a.* 1. I am disinterested = mākā lāgaṇāñ = *l.* to me is not attached, *i.e.* I am not concerned.
2. sămănd nātullo.

Disjoin, *v.* vegḷo kăr = *l.* make separate; soḍ; viṇgăḍ kăr; vingḍāi, *n. c.*

Disjunction, *s.* 1. veglātsār, -rā, *m.*; vingăḍāp, -pā, *n.*
2. suṭ, -ṭi, *f.*, *e.g.* of planks.

Disjunctive, *a.* veglātsār kărtso *or* vegḷo kărtso; vingăḍounṭso, *n. c.*

Disk, *see* **Disc.**

Dislike, *s.* kānṭāḷo, -ḷeā, *m.*; *see* **Antipathy, Disaffection.**

N. B. Some verbs compounded with **dis** *not put down here may be expressed by the* **negative form** *of the* **compounded verb.**

Dislike, *v.* 1. *neg. form of* ruts, *Prs. Dat., e.g.* I dislike this fọod = yeñ khāṇ mākā rutsanāñ.
2. *neg. form of* boro distā = seems good; *neg. form of* mānua = please; *neg. form of* zā.

Dislocate, *v.* tsukăi, *e. g.* sănd tsukăi; hāḍāñ vingăḍ sărtāt = the bones are disjoined.

Dislocation, *s.* hāḍāñ veg̣latsār, -rā, *m.*

Dislodge, *v.* bhāir ghāl.

Dismal, *a.* 1. kāḷso = *l.* darkish; kāḷokātso = *l.* dark; *bet. rs. into* kāḷok pòḍ *or* ye.
2. bhiyānkuḷ.

Dismember, *v.* 1. kuḍke kăr = *l.* make pieces.
2. sānde kātăr = *l.* cut limbs.
3. veg̣lātsār kăr = *l.* separate.

Dismiss, *v.* bhāir ghāl = *l.* put out, *vlg.*; soḍăi = *l.* cause to leave, *or only* soḍ; răja di = give leave; bărtărap kăr, *e.g.* from an office.

Dismissal, *s.* 1. soḍāp, -ḍpā *n.*, *e. g.* of a prisoner.
2. bărtărap, -pā, *n.* = d. from office.

Dismount, *v.* deuñ = *l.* descend; *c. v.* devoi (*or* deunḍăi, *n. c.*)

Disobedience, *s.* miruoṇeñ, -ṇeā, *n.*

Disobedient, *a.* khāltonātullo; voḍilānčeñ utăr āikanātullo.

Disobey, *v.* mirua = *l.* trespass, *fg.*; khālto năiñ = is not obedient; voḍilānčeñ utăr āikānāñ = *l.* does not hear the word of the superiors; voḍilānčea utrāk mān dināñ; voḍilānk mān dināñ; *vlg.* săngụlleñ āikanāñ; *Or.* părmāṇe tsăl, *in neg. form* = walk according to.

Disoblige, *v.* 1. ăpamān kăr = *l.* make an offence; dukăi = *l.* cause sorrow; khuše părmāṇe tsăl, *in neg. form* = walk according to; ăumăryādin tsăl.

Disobliging, *a.* 1. ănupkāri = not making favours.
2. imṭo = *l.* stingy.
3. *rs. v.*

Disorder, *s.* 1. gusăp, -spā, *n.*; confusion; ăkrăm, -mā, *n.* *see* **Confusion**; tsuk, -ki, *f.* = mistake, error; gunyāuñ, -nyāvā, *m.*
2. kuṭ, -ṭā, *n.* = disturbance, plot.
3. piḍa, -ḍe, *f.* = disease.
4. *vlg. rs.* săma năiñ = not arranged (*ch. cs.*)

Disorder, *v.* 1. kăr *with the words given above under* (1) *and* (2).
2. tsuk.

Disorderly, *a.* 1. krămaviṇ.
2. tăuṭālmāri = turbulent.

N. B. Some verbs compounded with dis *not put down here may be expressed by the* negative form *of the* compounded verb.

Disorganisation, *s.* 1. kusāp, -spā, *n.* = corruption.
2. gusăp, -spā, *n.* = confusion.

Disorganise, *v.* 1. *pr.* kusăi, *c. v. of* kus = rot.
2. pāḍ kăr; krămāviṇ kăr.
3. kuḍke kăr = *l.* make pieces; sānde kāḍ = *l.* draw out the limbs; vingăḍ kăr = separate; simpḍāi = *l.* disperse.

Disown, *v. neg. form of* vop = consent.

Disparage, *v.* mān kāḍ = *l.* take away the honour, *or bet.* ăpamān kăr; boreñ nāuñ pāḍ kăr = spoil the good name; mānāk năṣṭ kăr; beābru kăr; mānār ulăi.

Disparagement, *s.* ăpamān, -nā, *m.*; mānānăṣṭ, -ṭā, *n.* = loss of rank *or* honor; beābru, -rā, *m.*

Disparity, *s. rs. into* săma = equal, *with the neg. particle*; tăfāvot = difference; *or* tsăḍuṇeñ, -ṇeā, *n.*; vetyās, -sā, *m.*

Dispassionate, *a.* nidhān = calm; thănḍ = cold, *fg.*; sămādhānātso = of peace; ruppoḷeinātullo = *l.* not looking face (not partial); *see* **Impartial.**

Dispel, *v.* kāḍ = *l.* take away, *e.g.* fear, clouds; bhāir ghāl = *l.* put out.

Dispensary, *s. vlg.* āspătri, -tri, *f.*; gāndsărkāči āngăḍ, -gḍi, *f.* = shop of the apothecary.

Dispensation, *s.* 1. vānṭāp, -ṭpā, *n.* = distribution; băṭvāḍo, -ḍeā, *m.*, *e.g.* of money.
2. săsăi, -ye, *f.* (Devāči) = providence.
3. (Devān dhāḍulleñ) sukduk, -kā, *n.*

Dispense, *v.* 1. vānṭ = *l.* distribute; băṭvāḍo kăr. (*Acc.*)
2. (from a law) răja di = *l.* give leave; *or* soḍăi = *l.* cause to be left; māf kăr.
3. sóḍ = leave, remit.

Disperse, *v.* 1. simpṭăi = scatter, *c. v. of* simp, *e.g.* water; simpḍăi = scatter, *c. v. of* simpăḍ.
2. kāḍ = *l.* take away.
3. dāunḍăi = *l.* cause to run away.
4. *n. v.* dāuñ = *l.* run.
5. uḍăi = *l.* throw.

Dispersion, *s.* simpăḍneñ, -neā, *n.*; *rs v.*

Display, *v.*, *tr. v.* dākăi = *l.* show; ukto kăr = make open (reveal).

Display, *s.* dākoṇ, -ṇi, *f.*

Displease, *v.* 1. dukăi = *l.* cause sorrow, *c. v.*
2. ăpamān kăr = *l.* make offence.
3. kărkăr kăr = *l.* cause annoy-

N. B. Some verbs compounded with **dis** *not put down here may be expressed by the* **negative form** *of the* **compounded verb.**

ance; kărkăr zā = get annoyance; *neg. form of* metsvo = approve, be satisfied; *neg. form of* mānua; nākhušent pòḍ = fall into disgrace.

Displeased (Be), *neg. form of* metsvo; *neg. form of* mānua *etc.*

Displeasure, *s.* 1. duk, -ki, *f.* = *l.* sorrow, pain; nākhuši, -še, *f.* = disgrace.
2. kăṣṭ, -ṭā, *m.* = *l.* suffering, calamity.
3. ăpamān, -nā, *m.*; 'incur any one's displeasure = ăpamān kăr, *or Acc.* dukăi = cause sorrow, *or* nākhušent pòḍ = fall into disgrace'.

Disposal, *s.* 1. māndāvoḷ, -ḷi, *f.* = *l.* arrangement.
2. *rs.* săma kăr = *l.* arrange.
I am at the disposal of = āuñ *Or.* khāl āsāñ = *l.* I am under; *see* **Discretion.**
3. hāt, -tā, *m.*; *e.g.* tujeā hātānt āsā = (he) is in your hand.

Dispose, *v.* 1. săma kăr = *l.* put right *or* in order; mānḍ = arrange.
2. món voi kăr = incline; mót *or* mòn vondăi; vondăi = *l.* incline.
3. mārog ugto kăr = make open the way.
4. *by the* c. form *of the* princ. verb.
5. kăr = do, *as in* 'how shall I d. of this?'
6. ik = sell.
'Hātānt *or* podvent āsā = is in the hand, *or* at the disposal of'.

Disposed (Be), *v.* khuši āsā; soukāsāi āsā; vondaú.

Disposition, *s.* 1. māndāvoḷ, -ḷi, *f.* = arrangement.
2. vondauṇeñ, -ṇeā, *n.* = inclination; voḍni, -ne, *f.*
3. guṇ, -ṇā, *m.* = character.
4. mărji, -je, *f.*

Dispossess, *v.* 1. āst nisrāi; suādin tsukăi = *l.* deprive of possession.
2. kāḍ.

Disproportion, *s.* 1. *rs. into* zātā = is convenient, *in neg. form; or neg. form of* săma mezāp, -zpā, *n.*, *or of* săma māp, -pā, *n.* = right measure; nāñlāyekpoṇ, -ṇā, *n.*; nāñdāmāsāi, -ye, *f.*
2. *neg. form of* sămănd, -dā, *m.*, = *l.* connexion; *see* **Disparity.**

Disproportionate, *a.* săma poḍānātullo; lāyeknātullo.

Disputable, *a.* dubāvātso = *l.* doubtful; tărkātso = controversial.

Disputant, *s.* tărkagār, -rā, *m. or* tărkist, -tā, *m.*

N. B. Some verbs compounded with **dis** *not put down here may be expressed by the* **negative form** *of the* **compounded verb.**

Disputation, *s.* tărk, -kă, *n.*

Dispute, *s.* 1. tărk, -kă, *n.* = *l.* discussion.
2. zăgḍeñ, -ḍeă, *n.* = *l.* quarrel (*viva voce*); năi, -yă, *m.*; vevăr *or* yevăr, -ră, *m.*

Dispute, *v.* 1. tărk kăr.
2. zăgăḍ *or* zăgḍa.
3. dubăvai = *l.* spread doubt (*or* dubăvăk ghăl).

Disqualification, *see* **Disability.**

Disquiet, *see* **Discomposure.**

Disquisition, *see* **Discussion** *and* **Enquiry.**

Disregard, *v.* 1. bepărvo kăr = *l.* make contempt, neglect, *G. M.*; ălăkṣa kăr, *G. M.*; *neg. form of* gumăn kăr, *Acc.*
2. *neg. form of* zătăn kăr, *or* z. kăṇe = take care, *G. F.*; soḍ = leave.

Disregard, *s.* bepărvo, -veă, *m.*; soḍneñ, -neă, *n.* = abandonment; soḍni, -ne, *f.*; ălăkṣa, -ṣe, *f.* = *l.* not care.

Disregardful, *a.* bepărvo kărtso *or* lăkṣa kărnătullo *or* ălăkṣa kărtso.

Disrespect, *s.* ăpamăn, -nă, *m.*

Disrespect, *v.* ăpamăn kăr; *neg. form of* măn di = give honour.

Disrespectful, *a.* 1. ăpamănătso; ăkmănătso.
2. măn dinătullo.

Disruption, *s.* moḍăp, -ḍpă, *n.*; fuṭ, -ṭi, *f.*

Dissatisfaction, *s.* 1. ăsăntos, -să, *m.*
2. *expr. by* dădos năiñ = (I am) not satisfied, *or by neg. form of* dădoskăi, -ye, *f.*
3. *by* duktă = feel pain.
4. duk, -ki, *f.* = *l.* pain.
5. năñmetsvoṇeñ, -ṇeă, *n.* = disappoval.

Dissatisfied (Be), *v. rs.* metsva, *in neg. form, or* dădosnătullo.

Dissect, *v.* kătăr; kuḍkeăn kuḍke kăr.

Dissection, *s.* čirăp, -rpă, *n.*; kătrăp, -pă, *n.*; kătărneñ, -neă, *n.*, *n. c.*

Dissemble, *v.* lipăi = *l.* conceal; *rs. into* poḷăinătuḷleă bări = *l.* as not seeing, *and the other verb required by the context;* lipoun dovor; kăpăṭ kăr.

Disseminate, *v.* 1. vomp, *pr.*, *fg.*; biñ uḍăi.
2. *fg.* vistăr (*or* vomp), *e. g.* d. doctrine.

Dissension, *s.* năi, -yă, *m.*; *expr. by neg. form of* sămădhăn, -nă, *n.*, *or of* soukăsăi, -ye, *f.*; vetyăs, -să, *n.*, *e. g.* of opinion.

Dissent, *v.* 1. *neg. form of* vop.
2. vetyăs ăsă = *l.* difference is, *e. g.* of opinions.

Dissertation, *s.* 1. tărk, -kă, *n.* = *l.* discussion.
2. lămb uloṇeñ, -ṇeă, *n.* = *l.*

N. B. Some verbs compounded with dis *not put down here may be expressed by the* negative form *of the* compounded verb.

long speech; *bet.* vivaraṇeñ, -ṇeā, *n.*

Disserve, *see* **Disoblige.**

Dissever, *see* **Separate.**

Dissimilar, *a.* dusro; bădăl; sărkonātụllo; sămanātụllo.

Dissimilarity, *see* **Difference.**

Dissimulation, *s. rs. neg. form of* poḷe = see, *and* bări = *Lat. instar, e. g.* poḷenātụlleā bări = *Lat. non videntis instar, with another verb in finite mood, as the meaning requires*; kăpăṭ, -ṭā, *n.* = *l.* simulation; *rs.* lipăi = conceal; šāmilpoṇ, -ṇā, *n.* = *l.* connivance, complicity.

Dissipate, *v.* pāḍ kăr = *l.* make bad, spoil; gărje šivāi khărči = *l.* spend without necessity; nāš kăr, *n. ex.*; yeṭ = *l.* pay quickly, *fg.*, *n. c.*, *e. g.* money; bhongăi, *c. v.*, *e. g.* d. money; *see* **Disperse.**

Dissipated, *a.* 1. čintinātụllo = *l.* not thinking; *or bet. rs into* čint *in a finite mood.*

2. vāiṭ khušālāyānk lāgụllo = given to bad pleasures; dăngi, *h. w.*, *n. c.*

3. *rs.* mòn bountā = *l.* heart walks.

Dissipation, *s.* 1. vert khărts, -tsā, *m.* = *l.* vain expenses.

2. bhongostoḷ, -ḷā, *m.*, *e. g.* of money.

3. *rs.* mòn bountā = heart walks.

4. dăngai, -ye, *f.* (irregularity of life), *n. c.*

Dissolute, *see* **Dissipated,** *2nd mn.*

Dissolution, *s.* moḍāp, -ḍpā, *n. etc.*

Dissolve, *v.* 1. kăḍ = *l.* melt; *or bet.* kăḍăi; khirăi, *c. v. of* khir, *e. g.* in water.

2. *fg.* kāḍn ghāl = *l.* abolish.

3. mōḍ(ó) = *l.* break, *e. g.* a contract.

4. meḷăi = *l.* mix.

Dissonance, *s.* gālgouji, -je, *f. see* **Discord;** *bet. rs.* affirm. word.

Dissuade, *v.* bud sāng = *l.* say advice, *ch. cs.*; besṭăi = *l.* cause fear, *ch. cs.*; *vlg.* kărnākā moṇ sāng; mót porti = turn the mind; firăi; *vlg.* kānāk vāingiñ bānd.

Dissuasion, *s.* motiporṭouṇeñ, -ṇeā, *n.*

Distaff, *s.* kirki, -ke, *f.*

Distance, *s.* poiṇ, -ṇā, *n.*; lāmbāi, -ye, *f.*; *rs.* pois = far.

Distant, *a.* 1. pois = *l.* far, *ch. cs.*

2. vegḷo = separated.

Distaste, *s. by* ruts nāñ = no taste (of food); *or* kānṭāḷo, -ḷeā, *m.*

Distasteful, *a.* rutsnātullo; kānṭāḷeātso.

Distemper, *s.* piḍa, -ḍe, *f.* = *l.* disease.

N. B. Some verbs compounded with **dis** *not put down here may be expressed by the* **negative form** *of the* **compounded verb.**

Distend, *v.* 1. vistār = *l.* extend; rundāi = make large; soḍăi, *e.g.* a cloth.
2. suzăi, *c. v. of* suz = swell.

Distention, *s.* vistārāp, -pā, *n. etc.*

Distil, *v.* 1. kāḍ (d. cashew-nut juice, *etc.*); mur = take toddy from the trees; rānd = *l.* cook (d. over the fire).
2. *n. v.* vāutā = *l.* flows.

Distillation, *s.* 1. vāvāp, vāupā, *n.* = *l.* flowing.
2. rāndāp, -dpā, *n.*
3. murāp, -rpā, *n.*

Distillery, *s.* bhăṭṭi, -ṭe, *f.* (of toddy).

Distinct, *a.* 1. bădăl.
2. dusro = *l.* other, different.
3. vegḷo = *l.* separated.
4. višes = peculiar.
5. sošṭ (*or* suăšṭ) = clear, evident.
6. *neg. form of* săma: 'A. is distinct from B. = A. āni B. săma năiñ'.

Distinction, *s.* 1 bhēd (é), -dā, *m.* = *l.* difference, not equality; phorok *or* phărăk, -kā, *n.*; *see* **Difference.**
2. mān, -nā, *m.* = *l.* honour; măryād, -di (*or* -de), *f.* (marks of honour).
3. ănănd, -dā, *m.* = glory.
'Without d. = teāts jinsiñ, *or* bhēd (é) kărnāstanāñ'.

Distinctive, *a.* bhēd kărtso, *or G.* (*see* Gram.) *or rs. noun.*

Distinctly, *ad.* 1. vingăḍ = *l.* separately, aside.
2. sošṭ (zāun) = clearly, expressly.

Distinguish, *v.* 1. bhēd (é) kăr = *l.* make difference; čint = think, *e.g.* we must d. two cases = dón bābo čintizăi.
2. sārkeñ poḷe = *l.* look well.
3. vegḷo kăr = *l.* separate.
4. nāvāḍgo zātā = gets famous.
5. dusreañ prăs ušār zātā = *l.* gets more clever than the others; *or only* zăit vor = gain victory; jik.

Distinguished, *a.* 1. uttăm = *l.* excellent.
2. nāvāḍgo = *l.* famous.

Distort, *v.* vóḷ.

Distortion, *s.* voḷāp, -ḷpā, *n.*

Distract, *v.* 1. *pr.* kāḍ; vōḍ (ó).
2. *neg. form of* čit di = *l.* give attention.
3. āḍāi = prevent.
4. mót bounḍāi = *l.* cause the mind to walk.

Distracted, *a.* 1. *rs. v.*
2. čit dinātuḷlo; *or rs.* mòn bountā = *l.* mind walks; *or* mòn bountolo.

Distraction, *s.* 1. motibounḍi, -ḍe, *f.*, monābounḍi, *n. c.* = *l.* walking of mind.

N. B. Some verbs compounded with dis *not put down here may be expressed by the* negative form *of the* compounded verb.

2. in prayer, *by crc., e.g.* māgṇeñ moṇtānāñ dusri čintnā āili = *l.* while praying other thoughts came; ăḍčintnā, -ne, *f.* = *l.* contrary thought, *n. c.*; bhāili čintnā, -ne, *f.* = exterior thought.

Distress, *s.* kăṣṭ, -ṭā, *m.*; ăprād, -dā, *m.*; ākānt, -tā, *m.*; *see* **Calamity.**

Distress, *v.* kăṣṭ di = *l.* give pain; kăṣṭăi; kărkăr kăr = *l.* annoyance make; bezār kăr = *l.* trouble make.

Distribute, *v.* vānṭ; pāṭăi = *l.* send, *e.g.* gifts; băṭvāḍo kăr, *e.g.* money, letters.

Distribution, *s.* băṭvāḍo, -ḍeā, *m.*; vānṭāp, -ṭpā, *n.*

Distributive, *a.* vānṭo kărtso; vānṭeātso.

District, *s.* 1. jillo, -leā, *m.* (local division of a country, in India).
2. tāluk, -kā, *n.* (subdivision of a 'jillo'); muluk, -kā, *n.*, *n. c.*; vāḍo, -ḍeā, *m.* (of a village); *see* **Country.**

Distrust, *s. rs. into* pātiyeṇi, -ṇe, *f.* = confidence, *in neg. form*; ăpabărvānso, -seā, *m.*; nirāša, -še, *f.*; ăpadhăir, -rā, *n.*

Distrust, *v. neg. form of* pātiye = trust, *Prs. 2nd Loc.*

Distrustful, *a.* 1. pātiyenātullo; ăpātiyeṇitso.
2. dubāuntso *or* dubāvāntso.

Disturb, *v.* 1. dós; răgle kăr; upădrụ di; utsāmboḷ kăr = *l.* excite; bezār kăr, kărkăr kăr = bother *or* annoy.
2. sămādhān kāḍ = *l.* take away peace; gălibili kăr = confound.

Disturbance, *s.* 1. kuṭ, -ṭā, *n. mn.* political disturbance, plot; kāṭkāi, -ye, *f.* = *l.* revolution; utsāmboḷāi, -ye, *f.* = excitement.
2. bezārāi, -ye, *f.* = *l.* anxiety, trouble.

Disunion, *s.* nāi, -yā, *m.*; vegḷātsār, -rā, *m.*; ăsămādhān, -nā, *n.*; nāsoukāsāi, -ye, *f.* = no peace, *com. rs.* soukāsāi nāñ; nāvoppigi, -ge, *f.* = no agreement, *com. rs.* voppigi nāñ.

Disunite, *v.* vegḷo kăr; vingăḍ kăr.

Disuse, *s.* sovoi nāñ = *l.* custom not; ăpaprăyog, -gā, *m.*

Disuse, *v.* 1. *tr. v.* sovoi kāḍ = take away the custom; sovoi mōḍ(ó) = break the custom; sovoi sóḍ, *or* s. soḍăi.
2. sikăilleñ kāḍ = *l.* take away (what has been) learned.

Ditch, *s.* 1. kondok, -kā, (*or* khăndăk, -dkā), *m.*

2. khăṇi, -ye, *f.*, *mn.* ditch by the wayside.

Ditty, *s.* pòd, -dā, *n.*

Divan, *s.* (Turkānči) măntriñ-săbha, -bhe, *f.*

Dive, *v.* 1. buḍăi, *c. v. of* buḍ = *Lat.* '*merge*', *used also fg.*, *e.g.* d. into a science.
2. gunḍāyent rig = *l.* enter into depth; ponda vots.
3. *fg.* niyāḷ = meditate; dhyān kăr = make meditation.

Diverge, *v.* 1. *pr.* vāṭ sóḍ = *l.* leave the way; porta.
2. dusre isileān tsăl = *l.* walk *or* go in another side; vingăḍ zā *or* vegḷo zā = get separated.
3. *neg. form of* vop = agree.

Divergence, *s.* 1. vetyās, -sā, *m.* (of opinion).
2. vingăḍăi, -ye, *f.*, *n. c.*; portouṇeñ, -ṇeā, *n.*, *e.g.* of lines.

Divers, *a.* vegḷo.

Diverse, *a.* 1. vegḷo.
2. bădăl.

Diversion, *s.* 1. *rs. into v.*
2. vegḷātsār, -rā, *m.* = separation; *or bet.* portouṇeñ, -ṇeā, *n.* = *l.* turning, *also fg. for* 'relief'; *or* gămmăt, -tā, *n.* (recreation).

Divert, *v.* 1. porti = turn, *c. v. of* portā, *pr. and fg.*
2. *tr. v.* kāḍ; pois kăr.
3. kušāl kăr = *l.* make cheerful, amuse, *n. v.*; soukāsāi kāṇe = *l.* take peace.

Divest, *s.* 1. nāgḍăi, *more common* nāgḍo kăr = *l.* strip.
2. *fg.* banish (from the mind) = bhāir ghāl, *l.* put out.
3. sóḍ = leave (an office); rāji di = give resignation.

Divide, *v.* 1. vānṭe kăr = *l.* make parts (distribute); bhāg kăr; vānṭ = divide.
2. kuḍke kăr = *l.* make pieces.
3. vingăḍ kăr, *or* vingăḍ dovór = *l.* make aside, separate; vingaḍăi, *c. v.*, *n. c.* = *l.* make aside, separate; vegḷo kăr = *l.* separate.
4. *n. v.* suṭ = *l.* leave; *see also* **Vote.**

Dividend, *s.* vānṭo, -ṭeā, *m.*

Divination, *s.* bolmeñ, -meā, *n.* (*rl.*) nimit, -tā, *n.*

Divine, *s. see* **Theologian.**

Divine, *a.* 1. Devātso; Dēupoṇā-tso; Devāgelo (devout); Deupoṇi, *e. g.* d. nature.
2. *fg.* ăjāpātso = admirable.

Divine, *v.* 1. bolmeñ (*or* nimit) sāng = *l.* say divination, (*rl.*)
2. pārki = *l.* guess (naturally); sumār čint = *l.* think about (*like* pārki).

Diviner, *s.* bolmeāgār, -rā, *m.*; nimitgār, -rā, *m.*

Divinity, *s.* Dēupoṇ, -ṇā, *n.*; Dēu, -vā, *m.*; Devāsămăndi-vidya, -ye, *f.* (*Theol.*)

Divisibility, *s.* vānṭisārkeñ, -keā, *n.*

Division, *s.* 1. vānṭāp, -ṭpā, *n.*

2. vāṅṭo, -ṭeā, *m.* (partition of two places, chapter, section); bhāg, -gā, *m.* (*also* d. of an army).
3. nāi, -yā, *m.* = *l.* discord; vegḷātsār, -rā, *m.*
4. tăṇḍ, -ḍā, *m.*, *i.e.* a division, a company of men, a certain class.

Divorce, *s. by the verb* (bāilek soḍčeñ); bāiletso vegḷātsār, -rā, *m.* = *l.* separation of woman.

Divorce, *v.* bāilek (*or* dādleāk) sóḍ = leave wife (*or* husband).

Divulge, *v.* pārgăṭāi *or* pārgăṭ kăr; kăḷit kăr, *or* kăḷāi, *c. v.*; fāis kăr, *e.g.* news; ukto kăr = *l.* make open, *fg.*

Dizziness, *s.* 1. guvoḷu, -ḷi, *f.* = turning.
2. My head is dizzy = moji tăkli guuntā = *l.* my head is turning.

Do, *v.* 1. kăr, *Past.* kelo, *is used in a great variety of ways, chiefly in the composition of vbs.* 'I have to do with = *Cm.* mākā kām āsā'. 'How do you do? = kăso (*or* kăsi *in f.*) āsāi? = *l. Lat. qualis es*, *or* tujeñ kārbār kăseñ = how are your things?' 'They are doing well = bore tsăltāt, *l.* they walk well'.
2. zātā = is convenient; puro = enough: 'that will do = puro.'

Do away with = kāḍn ghāl, *l.* abolish.

Do without = gărz nān, *l.* no necessity, *or* sóḍ = leave.

Docile, *a.* 1. sikasārko = fit to learn.
2. sādo = tame.
3. khālto (*or* kālto) = *l.* obedient.

Docility, *s.* 1. sikasārkeñ, -keā, *n.*
2. sādepoṇ, -ṇā, *n.*
3. khālteponṇ, -ṇā, *n.*

Dock, *s.* 1. găḍ, -ḍi, *f.*, *or* tăḍ, -ḍi, *f.* (for ships).
2. (băndivānānči) pèṭ, -ṭe, *f.* = *l.* box (of criminals); (băndivānānči) dări, -ye, *f.* = *l.* rail (of prisoners).

Doctor, *s.* 1. dāktér -rā, *m.*, *fr.* (*chiefly* a physician).
2. păṇḍit, -tā, *m.* = a learned man; šāstri, -riā, *m.*

Doctrine, *s.* 1. sikāp, -kpā, *n.* (learning).
2. sikoṇ, -ṇe, *f.* = instruction.
3. dotorn, -ni, *f.* = catechism, *fr.*

Document, *s.* 1. dāklo, -leā, *m.* (deed).
2. dăstevoz, *var.* dăsteivoz, -zā, *n.* (papers).

Doe, *s.* 1. bāileñ meruñ, -rvā, *n.*
2. bāilo soso, -seā, *m.*

Doer, *s.* kărt, -tā, *m.* (*rare in this sense*) *more com.* kărtolo.

Dog, *s.* 1. suṇeñ, -ṇeā, *n.*; kutreñ, -reā, *n.*
2. peṭo, -ṭeā, *m.* = male dog.
3. kolgeñ, -geā, *n.* = female dog, bitch.

Dog-collar,. *s.* gāḷeātso pāṭo, -ṭeā, *m.*

Dogma, *s.* bāvāḍtāči sikoṇ, -ṇi, *f.* = *l.* instruction of the faith; *or* bāvāḍtāči nemsilli sikoṇ = *l.* decided instruction of the faith; *or simply* bāvāḍt, -tā, *m.* = faith.

Dogmatic, *s.* bāvāḍtāči vidya, -ye, *f.*

Dole, *see* **Allowance.**

Dolorous, *a.* 1. dukest, *e.g.* d. mother.

2. khăntiṣṭ = *l.* gloomy.

3. dukountso = *l.* causing pain.

Dolour, *s.* duk, -ki, *f.*

Dolphin, *s.* dăryātso dukor, -krā, *m.* = *l.* pig of the sea.

Domain, *s.* 1. rāz, -jā, *n.*

2. āst, -ti, *f.*; bhuiñ, -iñ, *f.*

Dome, *s.* koḷos, -sā, *m.* (a pointed ornament at the top of the roof); ghumăṭ, -ṭā, *n.* (cupola); *n. c., Mr., Cn.*; găvi, -ye, *f.* = vault; *see* **Cathedral.**

Domestic, *s.* tsākor, -krā, *m.*

Domestic, *a.* 1. gărtso = of home; kuṭmātso = of the family.

2. sādo = tame; 'the domestics = gărčiñ' (*see* Gram. P. IV. ch. i.).

Domesticate, *v.* 1. sovoi kăr, *tr.* = make custom; sovoi zā, *n. v.* = *l.* get accustomed.

2. sādo kăr = *l.* make tame.

Dominate, *v.* 1. rāzvoṭ kăr = reign; tsălăi = rule; formāi = command.

2. ădhikāri zāun āsā = be prevailing, *e. g.* the Liberal party dominates in ....

Dominion, *s.* 1. sotăntrụ, -rā, *n.* (absolute power); poḋvi, -ve, *f.* = power.

2. rāzvoṭkāi, -ye, *f.* = *l.* kingdom; rāz, -jā, *n.*

Donation, *s.* 1. deṇeñ, -ṇeā, *n.*; dān, -nā, *n.*

2. kāṇik, -ke (*or* -ṇke), *f.* (splendid don.)

3. izmăl, -lā, *n. fr.*, bhīk, -ke, *f.* = alms; dhărm, -mā, *m.* = charity (act of relieving), alms.

Donkey, *s.* gāḍāuñ, -ḍvā, *n.* = ass.

Door, *s.* 1. bāgil, -glā, *n.*

2. dārvāṭo, -ṭeā, *m.* = gate.

3. dār, -rā, *n.*

4. kouḍi, -ḍe, *f.* of cadjans.

Door-frame, *s.* dārvónt, -tā, *m.*; *pl.* —vănt.

Doorkeeper, *s.* bāglārākṇo, -ṇeā, *m.*

Dormitory, *s.* nidčeñ kuḍ, -ḍā, *n.* = *l.* sleeping room.

Dose, *s.* 1. mezāp, -zpā, *n.*, māp, -pā, *n.* = measure.

2. părimāṇ, -ṇā, *n.* = quantity; kitleñ = *l.* how much?

Dot, *s.* tibo, -beā, *m.*

Dote, *v.* 1. mogān mòr; lāle.

2. bāḷbud lāgtā = *l.* the reason of a child is attached (to old men when their minds become weak).

Double, *a.* doḍo; dón pāuṭi tsăḍ.

Double, *v.* 1. doḍto kăr; doḍo kăr, *or only* dóḍ; *vlg.* forṇ kăr = cover; *see also* **Fold.**
2. dón päuṭi tsäḍ kăr = make twice as large.
3. portun (kăr *or another v.*) = (make) again.
4. boutăṇiñ vots = go round.

Doubleness, *s.* dupat, -tā, *n.*

Doubt, *v.* 1. dubāu; dubāu čint = *l.* think doubt; dubāu vor = *l.* carry doubt.
2. dubāvăi, *c. v.* = dispute about; *or* dubāvāk ghāl.

Doubt, *s.* dubău, -bāvā, *m.*; săndev, -vā, *m.*

Doubtful, *a.* 1. dubăuntso, dubāvi (subjectively *and* objectively).
2. tărkātso = controversial.

Doubtless, *ad.* dubāvāviṇe, *or* dubăunāstanāñ = *l.* without doubt; dubāu vornātullo; khărents; ălbăt = of course.

Dough, *s.* 1. gondṇ, -dā, *m.* (*ex. mn.* gum).
2. moḷḷeleñ pīṭ, -ṭā, *n.* = kneaded flour.

Dove, *s.* kouḍo, -ḍeā, *m.*

Dovecot. *s.* kouḍeāntso gūḍṇ, -ḍā, *m.* = *l.* cage of doves.

Dowager, *s.* dót āsṇlli vidou, *or only* vidou, -dvi, *f.*

Dower, *s.* 1. dót, -ti, *f.*; dān, -nā, *n.*
2. āndăṇ, -ṇā, *n.* (native paraphernalia).

Down, *s.* pāk, -kā, *n.*

Down, *ad.* 1. săkăl.
2. dărnir = on the ground (lower story).
'Run up and down = voir săkăl dāuñ'.

Down, *a.* săkăilo.
Downwards = săkăileān.

Downcast, *a.* 1. săkăl ghāllo.
2. pondlo; *as in the sentence* pondleāñ doḷeāniñ poḷe = *l.* look (upwards) with downcast eyes. [*n. c.*

Downfall, *s.* săkălpoḍāp, -ḍpā, *n.*,

Downright, *a.* khărots (*emph. of* khăro = true) = *Lat. merus;* kăpăṭaviṇ.

Downright, *a.* niṣkäpăṭi.

Dowry, *see* **Dower.**

Doze, *v.* nid ye, *bet.* āḍ pòḍ (half-sleep); jèm ye = *l.* drowsiness come.

Dozen, *s.* dăzăn, -nā, *n.*, *fr.*

Doziness, *s.* 1. jèm, -mi, *f.*; zóp, -pā, *m.* (-pi, *f.*), *pr. and fg.*
2. *fg.* āḷsāi, -ye, *f.*

Draft, *s.* năkṣa, -ṣe, *f.*

Drag, *v.* vóḍ = *Lat. trahe.*

Dragoman, *see* **Interpreter.**

Drain, *v.* udāk kăḍ = *l.* draw out water (from the land); *see* **Filter, Empty.**

Drake, *s.* dādleñ ās, -sā, *n.*

Drama, *s.* nāṭ, -ṭā, *m.*

Dramatic, *a.* nāṭātso.

Dramatist, *s.* nāṭagār, -rā, *m.*

Drape, *v.* nesăi; pāngrăi.

Draught, *s.* 1. voḍāp, -ḍpā, *n.*
2. piyeunčeñ = *l.* drinking; piyoṇeñ, -ṇeā, *n.*

3. vāreñ, -reā, *n.*; vāreāči dāuñ, -āve, *f.*; *rs. into* vāreñ yetā = *l.* air comes.
4. bonṭi, -ṭe, *f.* (of fishes, birds *etc.*)
5. năkăl, -klā, *n.* = copy.
See **Cheque** and **Levy.**

Draught-board, *s.* gurpāḷeñ, -ḷeā, *n.*

Draw, *v.* 1. vóḍ *mn.* pull steadily; kunti (d. to land).
2. kāḍ (water, a sigh, a sword, a conclusion, a line).
3. risko kāḍ, *fr.*; năkša kāḍ.
D. tears = dukañ găḷăi.
D. near = lāgiñ pāu.
D. round to = zomoun vetā.
D. up = 1) borăi; 2) mānḍ = arrange.

Drawer, *s.* (of a chest of drawers) govet, -tā, *n.*, *fr.*

Drawers, *s.* izār, -rā, *n.* = close under-garment.

Drawing, *s.* 1. pintur, -rā, *n.* (the picture drawn), *fr.*
2. năkša, -še, *f.* = *l.* line; năkša kāḍāp, -ḍpā, *n.*, *n. c. or only* năkša, *or* risko (*nom. pl. f.*)

Dread, *s.* bheñ, bhiyā, *n.*; bhiyānkuḷăi, -ye, *f.*; bhirānt, -ti, *f.*; kāmp, -pi, *f.* = *l.* trembling.

Dread, *v.* bhiye; kāmp = *l.* tremble.

Dreadful, *a.* bhăyănkăr; bhiyānkuḷ; tărtărountso.

Dream, *s.* sopāṇ, -pṇā, *n.* (*or* -ṇā, *n.*)

Dream, *v.* (măkā) sopāṇ pòḍ = *l.* d. fall, *also fg.*; sopṇe.

Dreamer, *s.* sopṇāgār, -rā, *m. pr. and fg.*

Dreary, *a.* bhiyānkuḷ.

Dregs, *s.* măḍḍi, -ḍe, *f.* (sediment of liquor).

Drench, *v.* bizăi; *see also* **Soak.**

Dress, *s.* 1. nesoṇ, -ṇi, *f.*; mustăigi, -ge, *f*; vostru, -trā, *n.* (văstur, -rā); lugāṭ, -gṭā, *n.* = *l.* cloth, *fg. used.*
2. vestiment, -tā, *m.* (sacred vestments), *fr.*
3. kāpāḍ, -pḍā, *n.* (native female dress).
4. kirgi, -ge, *f.* = girl's dress; gāgro, -reā, *m.*
5. āngleñ, -leā, *n.* = child's dress.
6. khopoṇ, -ṇā, *n.* (for dead bodies).

Dress, *v.* 1. nesăi, *c. v. of* nès; pāle (trees).
2. boro kăr, = *l.* make good (cure); guṇ kăr, *e. g.* a wound.
3. tăyār kăr = *l.* prepare (food); rānd = cook.
4. săma kăr, *e.g.* the hair; ugăi, *e.g.* the hair; iṇi ghāl (make tresses); pānti vóḷ; šenḍo bānd (braid women's hair); šenḍi bānd (braid men's hair), *or simply* kès bānd, *which last is a very simple way of dressing women's hair; the others are more elaborate.*

5. (besāyek) tăyār kăr.

Dresser, *s.* voiz, -zā, *m.* (native physician).

Dressing, *s.* tăyārăi, -ye, *f.* = *l.* preparation.

Dried, *a.* sukụllo *or* suko (suki).

Drift, *s.* 1. sevoṭ, -ṭā, *m.* = *l.* aim.
2. rās, -si, *f.* = heap.

Drift, *v.* rāsik meḷăi; rāsik vor; rāsik sāgsi.

Drill, *v.* 1. tóp = pierce.
2. pokăḷ kăr = make hollow.
3. *fg.* sikăi = *l.* teach (a soldier).

Drink, *v.* 1. piye.
2. *vlg.* kòp mār = *l.* beat a cup, (be given to drinking).

Drinkable, *a.* piyeuntso; piyesārko.

Drinker, *s.* piyeunčeāk lāgụllo mănis, -nšā, *m.* = *l.* a man given to drinking.

Drinking, *s.* piyoṇeñ, -ṇeā, *n.*

Drip, *v.* vāu = *l.* flow.

Drip, *s.* văvāp, vāupā, *n.*; tembeāñ văvāp, *n. c.*; *bet. rs. v.*

Drive, *v.* 1. lóṭ = *l.* push; bòḷ kăr = *l.* make violence; bòḷān tsălăi = *l.* cause with force to walk; mukār tsălăi.
2. dāunḍăi = *l.* cause to run, *e. g.* d. a herd of cattle.
3. lăi = *l.* apply, *e.g.* d. stakes into the earth.
4. *n. v.* gāḍiyesăvāri kăr (a carriage), *n. c.*; gāḍiyer boson vots.

Drive about = yeṇeñ teṇeñ hălăi.

Drive out, drive forth = bhāir ghāl.

Drive together = meḷăi.

Drive, *s.* 1. gāḍiyesăvāri, -re, *f.*, *n. c.*
2. gāḍiyesăvāresuāt, -te, *f.*; panth, -thā, *m.*?

Driveller, *s.* piso (mănis); sopṇāgār, -rā, *m.*; harebira (*or* arebira), -rā, *m.*, *vlg.*

Driver, *s.* gāḍiyegār, -rā, *m.*

Droll, *a.* hāstso.

Drone, *s.* 1. dādlò movāntso mus, -sā, *m.*
2. *fg.* āḷsi.

Droop, *v.* 1. umkăḷ = *l.* hang (*n. v.*)
2. bāu = *l.* fade, languish; deuñ = descend, *fg.*; pòḍ = *l.* fall, *e. g.* courage.

Drop, *n.* 1. tembo, -beā, *m.*, *pr.* *and* *fg.*; čiṭ, -ṭi, *f.*; boṭṭu, -ṭā, *m.*
2. mudi, -ye, *f.* = *l.* ring; *bet.* văzrāči mudi = *l.* ring of diamond.
3. *fg.* góṭ, *e. g.* give me some drops of wine.

Drop, *v.* 1. let fall in drops, *crc.*, *e.g.* tembe tembe poḍunk sóḍ *or* t. t. poḍăi *or* tembe zāun găḷăi; *for leaves* zhăḍăi.
2. *fg.* sóḍ = *l.* leave, omit.
D. in = bheṭ, *l.* visit.

Dropsy, *s.* nālkut, -tā, *n.*; *vlg.* āngānt udāk bhòrlañ.

Dross, *s.* koir, -rā, *m.*; *vlg.* gu, guvā, *m.*

Drossiness, *s.* bursepoṇ, -ṇā, *n.*
Drossy, *a.* burso.
Drought, *s.* sukidāḍ, -ḍi, *f.*
Drown, *v.* buḍāi, *c. v. of* buḍ.
Drowsiness, *s.* 1. jèm, -me, *f.*; zóp, -pā, *m.*
2. *fg.* āḷsāi, -ye, *f.*
Drowsy, *a.* 1. *expr. by* jèm yetā = drowsiness comes.
2. *fg.* āḷsi.
Drudge, *v.* 1. kăṣṭa, *n. v.* = *l.* suffer pain.
2. tsākri kărn kăṣṭa.
Drudge, *s.* gulām, -mā, *m.*
Drug, *s.* vokāt, -ktā, *n.*
Druggist, *s.* voktāñ iktolo; găndsărkagār, -rā, *m.*
Drum, *s.* dólụ, -li, *f.*
Drunk, *a.* ămālzāllo, *or* ămālātso, *or* ămālkor; bebdo, *fr.*; soro piyello: 'he got drunk = to bebdo zālo, *or* tākā ămāl zālāñ'.
Drunkenness, *s.* bebdepoṇ, -ṇā, *n.*, *fr.*; ămāl, -lā, *n.*
Dry, *a.* 1. *pr.* suko.
2. bèṭ (gāde), *opp. to* băil (gāde) = wet (fields).
3. *fg.* khušālāinātullo = *l.* not having pleasure; *see* **Thirsty.**
Dry, *v.* 1. sukăi, *c. v. of* suk.
2. d. tears = dukāñ pus.
Dryness, *s. pr.* sukidāḍ, -ḍi, *f.*
Dubious, *a.* dubāuntso; dubāvi; *see* **Doubtful.**
Duck, *s.* ās, -sā, *n.*; ādmānil, -lā, *n.*, *fr.*
Ductile, *see* **Docile.**

Due, *a.* 1. devo; yevo, *e.g.* due to me = mākā yevo.
2. fāvo; fāvo zāllo.
3. *expr. by the* Necess. mood.
Due, *s.* riṇ, -ṇā, *n.* = *l.* debt; *see* **Taxes.**
Duel, *s.* dogānči lăḍāi, -ye, *f.* = *l.* fighting of two; dogāñ bitărli lăḍāi.
Duke, *s.* duk, -kā, *m.*, *fr.*
Dull, *a.* 1. kāḷso (of colour) = *l.* blackish; *see* Gram. p. III. ch. ii.
2. dhārnātụllo = *l.* not sharp, (*said of* cutting instruments).
3. kupāntso = *l.* of clouds (of the sky); *bel.* moḷbār kupañ tsăḍ āsāt.
4. săkăilo (sound).
5. daḍḍo = *l.* stupid; somzānātụllo = *l.* not understanding; phăḍpoši = *l.* faint, *e.g.* d. impression, colour.
6. dukest = *l.* sad, sorry; bezārāyetso.
Dull, *v.* kāḷso kăr; *see* **Blunt.**
Dullness, *s.* phăḍpoši róng, -gā, *m.*; phăḍpošipoṇ, -ṇā, *n.* (of colours).
Duly, *ad.* sārkeñ = *l.* exactly; fāvote jinsiñ; kāideā părmāṇeñ = *l.* according to duty; boreñ = *l.* well.
Dumb, *a.* mono; monko, *n. c.*; poṭṭa.
Dumbness, *s.* monepoṇ, -ṇā, *n.*
Dun, *a.* kāḷso.
Dunce, *a.* piso; *see* **Dull.**

Dung, *s.* 1. šèṇ, -ṇā, *n.* (cow d.). 'Put dung on the floor = šèṇ kāḍ = *l.* draw d.'
2. sāreñ, -reā, *n.* = manure.
3. gu, -uvā, *m.* (*general w.*)

Dung, *v.* sóp ghāl = put manure (to trees, *etc.*).

Dungeon, *s.* zăil, -lā, *n.*, *or* jăil, -lā, *n.*, *fr.*; (kāḷokāčeñ) băndikhān, -nā, *n.* *see* **Prison.**

Dunghill, *s. pr.* sāreāči rās, -si, *f.* = *l.* heap of dung; thāpo, -peā, *m.*

Dupe, *v.* *see* **Cajole.**

Dupe, *s.* vegiñ foṭvontso; ṭhăktso; mōs(ó) pāuntso. [copy.

Duplicate, *s.* năkăl, -klā, *n.* = *l.*

Duplicity, *v.* fālsapoṇ, -ṇā, *n.*; kăpăṭ, -ṭā, *n.*

Durability, *s.* tăgāp, -gpā, *n.*

Durable, *a.* tăgtolo; tăgnār.

Duration, *s.* 1. kāl,-lā, *m.*(of time).
2. tăgāp, -gpā, *n.*

During, *prep.* 1. veḷār = *l.* at the time, *precèded by the participle of the verb denoting the action to which* during *refers, or by the adjective form of the noun governed by it; e. g.* mis săngčea veḷār = during mass *or* when mass is said, *or* misāčea veḷār.
2. *by the* Dat. (*seldom used*).
3. modeñ, *e. g.* disā modeñ = during the day; *see* Gram. ch. *on* Verbs, *and alibi.*

Dusk, *s.* *see* **Twilight.**

Dusky, *a.* kāḷso.

Dust, *s.* 1. dūḷ, -ḷi, *f.*
2. puḍ, -ḍi, *f.*, *e.g.* saw-dust.

Dust, *v.* dūḷ kāḍ = *l.* take away d.

Dusty, *a.* duḷitso.

Dutiful, *a.* 1. khālto.
2. mogāḷ = *l.* dear.

Dutifulness, *s.* khālltepoṇ, -ṇā, *n.*

Duty, *s.* 1. kāido, -deā, *m.* = obligation.
2. kām, -mā, *n.* = *l.* business (*or* thing to be done).
3. tirvo, -veā, *m.*, tergi, -ge, *f.* = tax on the land.
4. sunk, -kā, *n.* = tax on moveable property.

Dwarf, *s.* kuḷḷa, -ḷā, *m.* (*irreg. noun*); khunṭo, -ṭeā, *m.*; khunṭi, -ye, *f.*

Dwarfish, *a.* kuḷḷaso.

Dwell, *v.* 1. rāu = *l.* remain, live.
2. *fg.* niyāḷ; čint.
3. soukās utsār.

Dwelling, *s.* biḍār, -rā, *n.*

Dwindle, *v.* bāu = fade; deuñ = *l.* descend, *fg.*

Dye, *v.* róng lāi = *l.* apply colour.

Dynasty, *s.* pāṭakuṭām, -ṭmā, *n.*; *or bet.* rāyakuṭām; gărāṇeñ, -ṇeā, *n.*

Dysentery, *s.* zărăm utkāḍe, -ḍeā, *n.*; hāgóṇ, -ṇe, *f.*; bhembro, -reā, *m.*

Dyspepsia, *see* **Indigestion.**

E

Each, *a. pron.* 1. dogi, doni = both; *see* Gram. p. 60.
2. hăryek (*adj.*); hăryeklo (*pron.*); yeyek (*adj.*); yeyeklo (*pron.*); *these two last are more common than the preceding; see also* **All.**

Eager, *a.* 1. bhou āšetso *or* āšetolo; lāguḷlo (given to).
2. urbest, *or* urbevont, *e. g.* for the glory of God; umāḷeātso = *l.* fervent.

Eagerness, *s.* 1. (tsăḍ) āšā, -še, *f.* = *l.* much desire.
2. urba, -be, *f.* = *l.* much desire; umāḷo, -ḷeā, *m.* = *l.* fervour.
3. khāugipoṇ, -ṇā, *n.*

Eagle, *s.* gāruḍ, -ḍā, *m.*

Eaglet, *s.* gāruḍāpīl, -lā, *n.*

Ear, *s.* 1. kān, -nā, *m.* (*also* sense of hearing); 'kānānt poḍlāñ = it fell into the ear, I heard'.
2. ear of corn = kāṇās, -ṇsi, *f.*

Ear-ache, *s.* kānāfoḍāpoḍ, -ḍi, *f.*; *rs.* kān duktā = *l.* the ear feels pain; *or* kānāči duk, -ki, *f.*

Earl, *s. has no equivalent in Konkani beyond* prābhu, -bhu = lord.

Early, *a.* 1. *pr.* săkāḷintso.
2. porno = *l.* ancient.
3. suru zāuntso = *l.* commencing.
4. vegintso.

Early, *ad.* 1. săkāḷiñ.
2. vegiñ = *l.* at time, soon. 'Early in the morning = bhou săkāḷiñ.'

Earn, *v.* meḷtā (mākā) = *l.* is found (to me); meḷāi = gather, *tr. v.*; zātā, *ch. cs.*; zóḍ = *l.* obtain; jik = *l.* gain.

Earnest, *a.* 1. khărots (*emph. of* khăro = true) = not in joke, *or* energetic; nīz = *l.* true.
2. *Often crc. or rs. and ch. cs.*
3. umāḷeātso; suḍsuḍāyetso = *l.* fervently, *ch. cs.*
4. tsurkụ = *l.* active.

Earnest, *s.* sănčigār, -rā, *m.* = earnest, *i. e.* part paid beforehand.

Earnestly, in earnest, *ad. Besides the adv. formed from the preceding,* khărots zāun *etc.*
1. thāmbānāstanāñ = without ceasing.
2. monapurvok.
3. măryādin = with gravity.

Earnestness, *a.* 1. suḍsuḍāi, -ye, *f.* = fervour.
2. zāgrutāi, -ye, *f.* = *l.* attention, care.
3. khărits khuši, -še, *f.* = *l.* true will.

Ear-ring, *s.* 1. mudi, -ye, *f.*
2. ārkāt, -tā, *m.*
3. ālko, -keā, *m. These are three different kinds of* e.

Earth, *s.* 1. māti, -ye, *f.* (the soil of the earth).
2. buiñ, -iñ, *f.* (*seems to mean* the globe).
3. săuñsār, -rā, *m.* = *l.* world; pritim, -mi, *f.*, *or* prătvi, -vi, *f.* = world, *ol.*

Earthly, *a.* 1. mātiyetso = *l.* made of earth.
2. săuñsārātso (of this world).

Earthquake, *s.* bhuiñkāmp, -pā, *m.*, *or* bhukāmp, -pā, *m.* = *l.* trembling of the earth.

Ear-wax, *s.* kānulo, -leā, *m.*; kaupo, -peā, *m.* ?

Ease, *s.* 1. soukāsāi, -ye, *f.*
2. măryād, -di, *f.* = *l.* modesty (grace); sobitāi, -ye, *f.* = beauty.
3. sompepoṇ, -ṇā, *n.* = facility; săsārāi, -ye, *f.* = facility.

Easily, *ad.* 1. săsāryen; sompeñ; sompepoṇiñ; sompepoṇān.
2. soukās, *or* soukāsāyen = *l.* slowly *or* with peace.

Easiness, *see* **Ease,** 3.

East, *s.* udenti, -ti, *f.*, *it also mn.* an oriental country; muḍla, -lā, *n.* 'In the e. = udenti (*or* udentint)'.

Easter, *s.* pāskānčeñ fest, -tā, *n.*

Eastern, *a.* udentitso.

Eastern, *s.* udenti, -ti, *f.*

Eastward, *ad.* udenti isileāu.

Easy, *a.* 1. săsār; sompo; sompepoṇātso: kăṣṭnātullo = *l.* not difficult; slob *or* sulob; sărāg.
2. soukāsāyetso, *or* sămādhānātso = *l.* peaceful, comfortable.
3. săimbātso = natural.

Eat, *v.* 1. khā, *past* khelo, *c. v.* khāvoi (*esp.* anything not seasoned).
2. jeu (take a meal).
3. seu (luxuries).

Eatable, *s.* khāunčeo văstu, *pl. f.* = *l.* things to be eaten.

Eating, *s.* khāṇ, -ṇā, *n.* (*mn.* food); *rs. v.*

Eaves, *s.* ḍāmbeñ, -beā, *n.*; pāuḷeo, *pl. f.*; nāḷi, -ye, *f.*

Ebb, *s.* sukti, -te, *f.* (falling *or* low e.); *the opposite of* bhărti, -te, *f.*

Ebb, *v.* sukti yetā *or* āsā.

Ebony, *s.* ābnus, -sā, *n.*; kărimar, -rā, *m.*

Ebriety, *s. see* **Drunkenness.**

Ebullition, *s.* 1. khătkăto, -teā, *m.*; umāḷo, -ḷeā, *m.*
2. *fg.* utsāmboḷāi, -ye, *f.*; *or also* umāḷo, -ḷeā, *m.*

Eccentric, *a.* 1. modeññātullo; māzābhāilo.
2. *fg.* tārifetso = awkward.

Ecclesiastic, *s.* igărjemoṇiyāri, -riā, *m.*

Ecclesiastic, *a.* igărjetso.

Echo, *s.* prătitāḷo, -ḷeā, *m.* = *l.* second voice; porto tāḷo, -ḷeā, *m.* = *l.* again voice; porto āvāz, -zā, *m. or* prătiāvāz, -zā, *m.* = *l.* again sound.

Echo, *v.* 1. *pr.* tāḷo pāṭi ghāl (*or* di *or* kăr).
2. *n. v.* tāḷo pāṭi ye; tāḷo portun zā.

Eclat, *s.* 1. prăkāš, -šā, *m.* = *l.* splendour.
2. *fg.* ănănd, -dā, *m.* = *l.* honour, glory; mān, -nā, *m.* = *l.* honour, glory.

Eclectic, *a.* vintsun kāḍtso.

Eclipse, *s.* 1. grāṇ (*or* girāṇ), -ṇā, *n.* (suryagrāṇ: tsăndragrāṇ).
2. uṇo mān, -nā, *m.*

Eclipse, *v.* 1. kāḷokātso kăr.
2. *fg.* (mānāk) năšṭ kăr = cause loss (to honour); mānār ulăi.

Ecplitic, *s.* suryăči vāṭ, -ṭe, *f.*; grāṇāgīṭ, -ṭā, *m.*

Economic, *a.* lekān khărčitolo = *l.* expending with account; hăḷtān khărčitolo = expending moderately; hăḷtātso; uṇo khărtsuntso; kăšišitso.

Economize, *v.* lekān khărči = *l.* spend with limit; hăḷtān khărči = *l.* spend with moderation.

Economy, *s.* 1. kăšiši, -ši, *f.*; ghărākārkāno, -neā, *m.*; *or* găr tsălounčisāmārti, -te, *f.* *or* gărāsāmārti; săilāb, -bā, *m.*
2. mit, -ti, *f.* = *l.* limit, *fg.*, *n. c.*
3. săsăi, -ye, *f.* (Deyāči) = providence (Divine).

Ecstasy, *s.* dišṭ, -ṭi, *f.* = *l.* apparition, *or* dišṭipoḍāp, -ḍpā, *n.*; 'tākā yek dišṭ poḍli = he fell into an ec.'

Ecstatic, *a.* 1. dišṭipoḍpātso.
2. dišṭpoḍullo = one who has seen an apparition.
3. *fg.* săntosātso.

Ecumenical, *a.* săgḷe igărjetso = of the whole church (council).

Eddy, *s.* bovor, -vrā, *m.*

Edge, *s.* 1. dèg, -ge, *f.* = *l.* brink.
2. dhār, -ri, *f.*, *e.g.* of a knife.

Edict, *s.* 1. hukum, -kme, *f.* = *l.* order; vărtamān, -nā, *n.*; formāṇ, -ṇā, *n.*; upades, -sā, *m.* = commandment, *e.g.* of the church.
2. dāngro, -reā, *m.*: 'd. mārlo'.

Edification, *s.* 1. bori dēk(é), -ki, *f.* = *l.* good example.
2. vrăddipoṇ, -ṇā, *n.* (motičeñ), *n. c.*

Edifice, *s.* bāndāp, -dpā, *n.*

Edify, *v.* 1. bori dēk (é) di = *l.* give good example.
2. vrăddi kăr.

Edit, *v.* 1. părgăṭ kăr, *or* părgăṭăi.
2. săma kărn părgăṭ kăr = *l.* having revised publish (a book).

Edition, *s.* părgăṭouṇeñ, -ṇeā, *n.*; părgăṭpoṇ, -ṇā, *n.*

Educate, *v.* 1. sikăi = *l.* instruct; *or bet.* (Devāče bhirāntint) vāḍăi = *l.* bring up (in the fear of God); *or only* vāḍăi.
2. suddụ kăr = *l.* cleanse, *fg.* *h. w.*

Educated, *a.* măryāditso; mānātso; sikpi; tsāltsămkăṇātso; *or* tsāltsămkăṇ sikullo; *bet. rs. into s.*

Education, *s.* 1. sikāp, -kpā, *n.* = *l.* instruction; tărbet, -ti, *f.* = course of e.
2. măryād, -di, *f.* = *l.* politeness; tsāltsămkăṇ, -ṇā, *n.* = tidiness, civility.

Educe, *v.* kāḍ; bhāir kāḍ.

Eel, *s.* 1. marimuguḍ, -ḍā, *m.* *seems to be the true* eel.
2. puryoḷ, -ḷā, *m. and* pamból, -lā, *m. are animals similar to an* eel.

Efface, *v.* 1. pus, *e.g.* characters.
2. kāḍn ghāl.

Effect, *s.* 1. fóḷ, -ḷā, *m.*; guṇ, -ṇā, *m.* = *ex.* quality, propriety, *fg.* effect.
2. *in pl.* sāmān, -nā, *m.* (chattels).
'In effect = khărents.' 'To the effect of = *Dat.*, *or* pāsun = on account of'.

Effective, Effectual, *a.* 1. bòḷ āsullo = *l.* having force.
2. khărents = *l.* true; guṇātso; guṇāk poḍtso, *ch. cs.*

Effectuate, *v.* kăr = *l.* do; guṇāk pòḍ, *ch. cs.*, *e. g.* vokāt guṇāk pòḍtā.

Effeminacy, *s.* bāilanḍpoṇ, -ṇā, *n.*

Effeminate, *a.* bāilanḍo.

Effervescence, *s.* 1. umāḷo, -ḷeā, *m.*
2. *fg.* utsāmboḷāi, -ye, *f.* = *l.* excitement.

Efficacious, *a.* 1. guṇāk poḍtso; *or rs.* guṇāk pòḍ = *l.* effect fall; *or* guṇ kăr; *or* guṇ zā.
2. ghăṭ; boḷādik; *see* **Effectual.**

Efficacy, *s.* bòḷ, -ḷā, *n.*; podvi, -ve, *f.* = *l.* power; guṇ, -ṇā, *m.* (*first mn.* effect, *second*, efficacy); *rs. adj.*, *e. g.* e. of good example = bori dēk bhou guṇāči.

Efficient, *a.* 1. guṇest = virtuous, *e. g.* man; guṇātso, *e. g.* medicine.
2. lāyek = *l.* fit.

Efflorescence, *s.* foḷvāstu, -tu, *f.* (germination).

Effort, *s.* prăyătăn, -tnā, *n.*; petsāḍāp, -pā, *n.*; minăt, -ti, *f.*

Effrontery, *s.* lăzbanḍpoṇ, -ṇā, *n.*; móst, -ti, *f.*

Effusion, *s.* 1. sindăr, -rā, *m.* (of blood).
2. lōṭ, -ṭā, *m.* (of water).
3. vikrāp, -pā, *n.*
4. voḷāp, -ḷpā, *n.*, *e. g.* of water *or* blood.

Eft, *s.* pāl, -li, *f.*

Egg, *s.* tāntiñ, -tiyā, *n.*; pēr, -ri, *f.* (of fishes).
'Lay eggs = tāntiyañ ghāl *or* dovór'. 'White of an egg = dovo bóḷ, -ḷā, *m.*' 'Yolk of an egg = tāmbḍi munḍoḷ, -ḷi, *f.*'

Egotism, *s.* 1. āplo mōg, -gā, *m.*, *or* āpṇātso mōg, -gā, *m.* = *l. Lat. amor sui.*
2. hănkār, -rā, *m.* = vainglory.

Egotist, *s.* āpṇātso mōgkărtolo mănis, -nšā, *m.*=a man loving himself.

Egregious, *a.* 1. uttăm (*var.* uttim) = *l.* excellent; bhou ušār = *l.* very clever.
2. voḍlo = great.
3. ăprup = *l.* rare, *fg.*

Egress, *s.* bhāirsărāp, -rpā, *n.*

Egyptian luffa, *s.* gosāḷeñ, -ḷeā, *n.*

Eight, *a.* āṭ; *for the numbers compounded with* eight *see* Gram. P. II. ch. ii. art. II.

Either, *a.* vo yā to = *l.* this or that; dontleñ yek.

Either....or, *only* or *is translated, which see.*

Ejaculation, *s.* uskār, -rā, *m.* (pious e.); ăntăskărnăčeñ māg-ṇeñ, -ṇeā, *n.*

Eject, *v.* 1. uḍăi = *l.* throw, *e.g.* food; bhāir ghāl = put out (expel).
2. (āsti) nisrāi = deprive (of property).

Eke out, *v.* urăi.

Elaborate, *v.* 1. kābār kăr = *l.* accomplish, *fr.*; tirsi.
2. zāgrutāyen kăr = *l.* make attentively.

Elaborate, *a.* sārko *or* zāgrutāyen kello = *l.* made attentively.

Elapse, *v.* utrun vetā; pāšār zā, *fr.*; *or only* zā; *the 2nd phrase is more common.*

Elastic, *a.* vistārisārko; votti; jaggi; pāṭivetso; pāṭibāgontso; pāṭiuḍtso.

Elasticity, *s.* pāṭivotsāp, -tspā, *n.*; pāṭibāgoṇeñ, -ṇeā, *n.*; pāṭivoḍāp, -ḍpā, *n.*; pāṭi-uḍāp, -ḍpā, *n.*

Elate, *v.* fugăi (*c. v. of* fug) = *l.* cause to ferment, *fg.*

Elated, *a.* hănkārātso *or* hănkā-ri; gărvi; fugtso.

Elation, *s.* hănkār, -rā, *m.*; gărv, -vā, *n.*; fugāp, -gpā, *n.*

Elbow, *s.* kompor, -prā, *m.*

Elder, *a.* mālgoḍo (eldest); 'elder brother = mālgoḍo bhāu (if the eldest), *or* bāb, -bā, *m.*'; *or* voḍlo (*ex.* elder).

Elect, *v.* 1. vints; vintsun kāḍ = *l.* selecting take; sodun kāḍ = *l.* seeking take.
2. nemsi = *l.* appoint; nomiyār = *l.* nominate, *fr.*

Elect, *a.* 1. nomiyārullo, *fr.*
2. vintsun kāḍullo (*also rl. mn.*)

Election, *s.* vintsāp, -tspā, *n.*; vintsṇeñ, -ṇeā, *n.*, *n. c.*

Elector, *s.* vintsun kāḍtolo *or only* vintstolo, -leā, *m.*

Electricity, *s.* viz, -zā, *m.*; *or* vizāči vidya, -ye, *f.*, *or bet.* čaktividya, -ye, *f.*, *n. c.*

Elegance, *s.* 1. rūp, -pā, *n.* = *l.* figure, of figure.
2. unči bhās, -se, *f.* = *l.* nice language.
3. sobitāi, -ye, *f.* = beauty, grace, refinement; sundărāi, -ye, *f.*; tsăndāi, -ye, *f.*, *H. K.*; *or* unčāi, -ye, *f.*

Elegant, *a.* 1. rūp āsullo = *l.* having form (nice).
2. unči (of language).
3. sobit = *l.* nice; sundăr; tsănd.
4. nităḷ = *l.* pure (*Lat. nitidus*).

Element, *s.* 1. mulātso vānṭo, -ṭeā, *m.* = *l.* radical part; multătvo, -veā, *m.*, *n. c.*; kuḍko, -keā, *m.* = *l.* part, piece; suru, -ve, *f.* = *l.* beginning.
2. poili sikoṇ, -ṇe, *f.* = first instruction; vidyemuḷ, -ḷā, *m.*

Elementary, *a.* 1. *fg.* sādo = *l.* simple.
2. suruetso = beginning.
3. sompepoṇātso = *l.* easy; kăṣṭnātullo = *l.* not difficult, *ch. cs.*

Elephant, *s.* hăst, -ti, *f.*

Elephantiasis, *s.* hăstipāyānči piḍa, -ḍe, *f.* = *l.* sickness of the feet of an elephant.

Elevate, *v.* 1. *pr.* ukol; *or* ubār.
2. *fg.* mān di = *l.* give honour; *or* mānāčeñ kām di = *l.* give high place *or* office *or* honour; băḍti di = promote.

Elevated, *a.* 1. ubār = *l.* high, *pr.*
2. *fg.* gărviṣṭ = *l.* proud.
3. voḍpoṇātso = *l.* great; vorto = sublime.
4. voilo = *l.* being over: (e. voice).

Elevation, *s.* 1. *pr.* ubārāi, -ye, *f.* = *l.* height; uklāp, -pā, *n.* = lifting up.
2. ubār zāgo, -geā, *m.*
3. mātiyeči rās, -si, *f.*
4. gărv, -vā, *n.* = *l.* pride.
5. mān, -nā, *m.*; voḍpoṇ, -ṇā, *n.* = highness *or* greatness; vortepoṇ, -ṇā, *n.* = sublimity.

Elicit, *v.* 1. kāḍ = *l.* extract.
2. dhăr, *e. g.* an act of contrition.

Eligibility, *s.* vintsi sărkeñ, -keā, *n.*

Eligible, *a.* vintsi sărko.

Eliminate, *v.* kāḍ; bhāir ghāl = *l.* put out; *see* **Remove, Rid,** (get r. of).

Elixir, *s.* răsāyan, -nā, *n.*, *Cn. Mr.*

Ellipse, *a.* ăndākrăti, -ti, *f.* (*Geom.*), *Cn. Mr.*; *or* tāntiyā-rūp, -pā, *n.*

Ellipsis, *s.* pădalōp, -pā, *n.*, *Cn.* (*Gram.*); utrāsoḍneñ, -neā, *n.*; *or* săbdāñsoḍneñ, -neā, *n.*

Elocution, *s.* utsārăṇ, -ṇā, *n.*; utrānči păddăt, -ti, *f.*

Elope, *v.* pòḷ.

Eloquence, *s.* unči bhās, -se, *f.* = *l.* nice language; supralāp, -pā, *m.*, *Cn. and Mr.*; *see* **Rhetoric.**

Eloquent, *a. rs. into s.*, *e. g.* unči bhāsen ulăitolo; *or* unči bhās yetā to = *l.* he who e. comes; *or only* unči ulouṇo; supralāpātso, *Cn. Mr.*

Else, *a. ad.* 1. nāñ zāleār = *Lat. secus*, *l.* if this does not happen.
2. āni = *l.* more: 'and nothing else = āni kāiñ nāñ, *l.* and

some thing more no'; 'no one else = āni koṇ nāñ'.

3. dusro = *l.* other: 'somewhere else = dusre suāter *or* yer suāter, *l.* in another place'.

Elsewhere, *ad.* dusre suāter.

Elucidate, *v. fg.* vivor sāng, *G. M.* = *l.* say explanation; soṣṭ kăr = *l.* make elucidation.

Elucidation, *s.* 1. vivor, -rā, *m.* 2. *rs. v.*

Elude, *v.* 1. tsukāi = *l.* avoid, *or* cause to be missing, *or* cause not to be, *e.g.* e. a blow, a person.
2. foṭāi = *l.* deceive.

Emaciate, *v.* bārik kăr = *l.* make thin, meagre, *tr. v.*; bārik zā = *l.* become thin, meagre, *n. v.*; bhāg = become meagre.

Emaciated, *a.* bārik; bhāgeṭo.

Emanate, *v. pr.* bhāir ye = *l.* come out from, *with* -ntlo *affixed to the noun governed by* from; bhāir săr = *l.* go out.

Emanation, *s.* 1. kirlāp, -pā, *n.* (germination).
2. *pr.* (vāiṭ) vāreñ, -reā, *n.* = *l.* (bad) air.
3. ub, -be, *f.*
4. bhāirsărāp, -rpā, *n.*
5. bhāirvāvāp, -vāupā, *n.*

Emancipate, *v.* soḍāi = *l.* cause to leave, deliver; suṭka kăr.

Emancipation, *s.* suṭka, -ke, *f.*

Embalm, *v.* pormoḷāi; kuḍint pormoḷ ghāl = *l.* put balm in the body; kuḍik pormoḷāčeñ tēl(è) lāi = *l.* apply balm to the body; moḍeāk pormoḷāčeñ tēl(è) lāi = *l.* apply balm to the corpse; moḍeñ pormoḷān dovór = *l.* keep the corpse with balm; moḍeñ pormoḷāčeā telān bhór = *l.* fill *etc.*

Embank, *v.* bānd ghāl = *l.* put a tie; kāṭ ghāl.

Embankment, *s.* kāṭ, -ṭā, *m.*

Embargo (Lay an), *v.* āḍāi = *l.* prevent, *i.e.* from going out.

Embark, *v.* 1. *tr.* tārvār tsăḍāi.
2. *n. v.* tārvār tsăḍ = *l.* ascend on the ship.
3. *fg.* lāi = *l.* apply, *e.g.* e. any one on an undertaking.
4. lāg, *n. v.*

Embarrass, *v.* 1. tondre kăr = *l.* make embarrassment; găli-bili (*or* gābri) kăr = *l.* make confusion; gusăp kăr = *l.* make confusion (g. zā = *l.* get c.); *or* guspăḍāi; ṣirkāi, *c. v. of* širka = get entangled.
2. mōḍ(ó) = *l.* break, *fg.* disconcert.
3. āḍāi; ăḍḍi ghāl = *l.* put objection.

Embarrassed, *a.* tondreānt āsuḷlo = *l.* in embarrassment; *see the verb*; guspăḍuḷlo.

Embarrassment, *a.* tondre, -reāñ, *m. pl.*; gusăp, -spā, *n.* = *l.* confusion; širkāuṇeñ, -ṇeā, *n.*; *see the v.*

Embassy, *s.* 1. rāibāri, -riā, *m.*; rāyādūt, -tā, *m.*
2. rājarăvāneñ, -neā, *n.*

Embellish, *v.* sobăi (*c. v. of* sob) = *l.* make nice; surungār kăr; róng di.

Embers, *s.* 1. gobor, -brā, *m.* = ashes.
2. murmuro, -reā, *m.* = burning embers.
3. ujeātso ingḷo, -ḷeā, *m.* = *l.* burning cinder.

Ember-day, *s.* katemp, -pā, *n.*, *fr.*; *here usually they say:* mās khāunk nozo zāllo (*or* āsụllo) dis, -sā, *m.* = day (in which) meat cannot be eaten.

Embezzle, *v.* nāgăi.

Embitter, *s.* dukăi = *l.* afflict; rāg āḍăi = *l.* cause to bring anger (*Dat.*), provoke.

Emblem, *s.* kuru, -ve, *f.*; gurtụ, -tā, *m.* = sign; khuṇa, -ṇe, *f.* = sign; sārkeñ, -keā, *n.* = image.

Embody, *v. fg.* rūp di = *l.* give form.

Embolden, *v.* dhăir di = *l.* put courage; thir kăr = *l.* make firm.

Embowel, *v.* ānkiṭi kāḍ = *l.* draw out the bowels.

Embrace, *v.* 1. poṭlun dhăr, *or* poṭlăi, *or* poṭlun ghe, *e.g.* a mother embraces her child.
2. vèng mār (*in general, even in order to* catch) = grasp.
3. *fg.* vints *or* vintsun kāḍ = *l.* elect, take, *e.g.* an opinion.
4. *fg.* khuši vor = *l.* desire, *G. F.*, *fg.*; mānua = *l.* please (*ch. cs.*).
5. *fg.* ghe *or* kāṇghe = *l.* take, *e.g.* an opportunity.
6. vop = *l.* consent.

Embrace, *s.* vèng, -ge, *f.*; khem, -mā, *n.*

Embrocation, *s.* bizouṇeñ, -ṇeā, *n.*; *or* bizāp, -zpā, *n.*

Embroider, *v.* lugṭār fulāñ ghāl = *l.* put flowers on a cloth.

Embryo, *s.* pilo, -leā, *m. used also fg.*

Emend, *etc. see* **Correct,** *etc.*

Emerald, *s.* māṇik, -ṇkā, *n.*; păčč, -čā, *n.*

Emerge, *v.* 1. (udkāntlo) voir ye = *l.* come (out of the water) above.
2. *fg.* zā = *l.* become, happen.

Emergency, *s.* 1. bhāir yeṇeñ, -ṇeā, *n.*; bhāirsărāp, -rpā, *n.*
2. *fg.* ākăsmăt, -tā, *n.*; zărurāi, -ye, *f.*; gărz, -ẓe, *f.*; vēḷ (é), -ḷā, *m.*

Emetic, *s.* vonkounčeñ vokāt, -ktā, *n.* = *l.* a medicine causing to vomit.

Emigrate, *v.* bhāir săr = *l.* start; părgāvānt rāu = *l.* stop in a foreign country; găḍi bhāir vetā = goes beyond the boundary; găḍpār vetā.

Eminence, *s.* 1. *pr.* ubārāi, -ye, *f.* = *l.* height.
2. *fg.* vóḍ mān, -nā, *m.* = *l.* great honour; vortepoṇ, -ṇā, *n.* = *l.* sublimity.

Eminent, *a. fg.* ăprup = *l.* rare; zăit vortolo=gaining victory, *fg.*; uttim = *l.* excellent; vorto = sublime; nāvāḍdik, *var.* nāvāḍgo, nāvāḍullo = famous.

Emissary, *s.* bedi, -di, *m.* = *l.* spy; guṭātso dūt, -tā, *m.* = *l.* secret envoy.

Emission, *s*, bhāir dhāḍāp, -ḍpā, *n.*; *see* **Sending.**

Emit, *v. pr.* bhāir uḍāi = *l.* throw, *e.g.* Vesuvius emits fire; bhāir sărāi = *l.* cause to go out, *e.g.* e. a sound.

Emmet, *s.* mūi, -ye, *f.*

Emollient, *a.* hāḷu *or* moū kăr-čeñ (vokāt) = *l.* making light *or* soft (medicine); *or only* movāḷountso.

Emolument, *a.* jikāp, -kpā, *n.*; upkār, -rā, *m.*; ādāi, -yā, *m.*; *see* **Advantage.**

Emotion, *s.* 1. movāḷāi, -ye, *f.*
2. voḍṇi, -ṇe, *f.* = *l.* inclination, *fg.*
3. utsāmboḷāi, -ye, *f.* = *l.* excitement.
4. gusăp, -spā, *n.* = *l.* perturbation, confusion.

Emperor, *s.* măharāi, -yā, *m.*; *Cn.*, *n. c.*; vȯḍ rāi = *l.* great king; pādša, -šā, *m.* (*Turkish word*), *n. c.*; sultān, -nā, *m.*, *n. c.*; rāi, -yā, *m.* = king.

Emphasis, *s.* bȯḷ, -ḷā, *n.* = *l.* force, *fg.*; tāḷeābhār, -rā, *m.* = stress of the voice, *fg.*; utrāñ-bhār = *l.* stress of words.

Empire, *s.* rāzvoṭ, -ṭi, *f.* = *l.* kingdom; rāz, -jā, *n.*

Empiric, *s.* ănbovātso, *e.g.* e. science.

Employ, *v.* 1. khărči = *l.* spend; prăyog kăr, *G. M.* = *l.* make use.
2. *tr.* kāmāk lāi = *l.* apply to business; *or* kām di = *l.* give business.
3. *n. v.* lāg = occupy oneself, *l.* apply to, *Dat.*
4. kāmār āsā = *l.* is on duty, in business, is busy; *or* tākā kām āsā.

Employment, *s.* 1. prăyog, -gā, *m.* = *l.* use.
2. kām, -mā, *n.* = *l.* business, occupation.
3. udyog, -gā, *m.* = employment profession.

Emporium, *s.* vepārātso zāgo, -geā, *m.* = *l.* place of merchandise.

Empower, *v.* podvi di = *l.* give power; *or* ădhikār di.

Empowered, *a.* podvi ăsullo.

Empress, *s.* măharāṇi, -ye, *f.*; čăkravărtiṇ, -ṇi, *f.*, *Cn.*; rāṇi. -ye, *f.* = *l.* queen.

Emptiness, *s.* khālipoṇ, -ṇā, *n.*; *bet. rs. adj.*

Empty, *a.* 1. *pr.* khāli, *also fg.*, *e.g.* e. pleasure; rito.
2. *fg. also*, vāreātso = *l.* of air.

Empty, *v.* 1. khāli kăr = *l.* make empty.

2. kāḍ = *l.* take out, discharge.
3. vompti.

Emulate, *v.* uḍḍa *or* urḍa, *e.g.* Pedru ani Pāulu teā kāmāk uḍḍatāt, *or* Pedru Pāulu kăḍe teā kāmāk uḍḍatā; melvoḍsi *or* meloḍḍi (*like* uḍḍa); petsāḍ = *l.* try.

Emulation, *s.* uḍḍāp *or* urḍāp, -pā, *n.*; petsāḍāp -ḍpā, *n.*

Emulous, *s.* petsāḍi; uḍḍatolo.

Enable, *v.* 1. bŏḷ di = *l.* give force.
2. *by Imperf. subj. or by a c. v., e.g.* J. C. sent the H. Ghost to enable the Apostles to preach the Gospel = J. Kristān Spirit Săntāk dhāḍla Apostlāniñ vānjel părgăṭ kăṙiso; *yet, this does not ex. mn.* enable. 'He enabled him to have a house = tāṇeñ tākā găr băndăileñ', *or also the pot. mood might be used.*

Enact, *v.* 1. (kāido) găḍ = *l.* found (a law).
2. păsănd kăr = *l.* approve; kăbul kăr = *l.* consent (*Lat. sancio*); metsvo = *l.* approve.
3. *fg.* vés tsălăi = act a part.

Enamel, *s.* dāntānčeñ rogān -nā, *n.*; dāntānčeñ lukaṇ, -ṇā, *n. entirely Mr.*

Encamp, *v.* tombu mār = *l.* pitch a tent; *or* ṭhāṇeñ kăr.

Enceinte, *a.* gărbest; guruār.

Enchain, *v.* bānd = *l.* bind; *see* **Enchant.**

Enchant, *v.* 1. *pr.* tăntrañ kăr (*or* măntrañ kăr) = *l.* make charms.
2. *fg.* pisăi = *l.* make mad; bānd = *l.* bind, *e.g.* by a sermon, *n. c.*; voḍni di = *l.* give attractions; bhou khušāl kăr = *l.* make very cheerful.

Enchanter, *s.* tăntragār, -rā, *m.*

Enchantment, *s.* 1. *pr.* tăntrụ, -rā, *n.*
2. *fg.* pisouṇeñ, -ṇeā, *n.*

Enchanting, *s. fg.* ăjāpātso = *l.* wonderful; *or* bhou sobit = very nice; *or* pisountso.

Enchantress, *s.* tăntragārn, -ni, *f.*

Encircle, *v.* 1. suttu ghāl (besiege); veḍo ghāl.
2. voi ghāl (enclose, *e. g.* a field with a fence).
3. guṭlăi = *l.* envelop, tie.

Enclosure, *s.* voi, -i, *f.* = fence, *e.g.* voin bānd = *l.* bind by a fence; beli, -li, *f., n. c.*; văṭār, -rā, *m.*

Encomium, *etc. see* **Praise.**

Encompass, *etc. see* **Encircle.**

Encounter, *v.* 1. meḷ = *l.* be found; pŏḍ = *l.* fall, *Prs. 2nd Loc.*
2. mukār rāu = *l.* remain in face (in a hostile manner).
3. *Or.* mukār vots = go in face of, *e. g.* encounter death, dangers.

Encourage, *v.* dhăir di = *l.* give courage; bŭd sāng = *l.* say advice; bòḷ di = *l.* give strength.

Encouragement, *s.* 1. *rs. into v.*
2. dhăir, -rā, *n.*

Encumber, *v.* tondre kăr = *l.* make embarrassments; bhār kăr.

Encyclical, *a. crc.* sămestānk borăillen̄ kāgād, -gdā, *n.* = a letter written to all; *bet.* bounten̄ kāgād.

Encyclopedia, *s.* sărvụvidya, -ye, *f.* = *l.* science of all.

End, *s.* 1. sevoṭ, -ṭā, *m.* = *l.* exit, aim: 'tātso sevoṭ pāula = his end is come'; 'Dēu āmtso sevoṭ = God is our end'.
2. mit, -ti, *f.* = *l.* limit, *n. c.*, *Cn.*; găḍ, -ḍi, *f.* = limit.
3. nimāṇo = *l.* last, *ch. cs.*
4. ănt, -tā, *m.*; āker, -ri, *f.* = *l.* extremity, *e. g.* the end of a letter, of a house.
5. tirmāṇ, -ṇā, *n.*, *n. c.* = decision; tīrp, -pā, *n.* = decision.

End, *v.* 1. *tr.* tirsi, *c. v. of* tirsa; kābār kăr = *l.* accomplish, *fr.* (*pass.* kābār zā = *l.* get accomplished); mugdi (*c. v. of* mugda = be ended) = bring to an end, *e. g.* labours.
2. thāmb = *l.* cease; mănna kăr.
3. sóḍ = *l.* leave.
4. sevoṭ āsā = *l.* there is an end, issue, (turns out).
5. ăntăr: 'to ăntărlo = he died'.

Endanger, *v.* 1. *tr. v.* riskent ghāl = *l.* put in danger.
2. *n. v.* riskent āsčen̄ = to be in danger; mosānt ghāl; mosānt āsčen̄.

Endear, *v.* mogāḷ kăr = make dear; *or* mọg(ò) kărăi = cause to love; *or* bānd = *l.* bind.

Endearment, *s.* fuslāuṇen̄, -ṇeā, *n.* = *l.* caresses.

Endeavour, *v.* prăyătăn kăr = make an effort.

Endeavour, *s.* prăyătăn, -tnā, *n.*

Endorse, *v.* pāṭir borăi.

Endow, *v.* 1. di = *l.* give; bhór = *l.* fill, *fg.*
2. dót di = *l.* give dowry.

Endowed, *a.* āsullo, *e. g.* e. with wisdom = bŭd āsullo; bhorlolo = *l.* filled.

Endurance, *s.* 1. sosṇikāi, -ye, *f.* = patience.
2. *in other mn. ch. cs. or rs.*

Endure, *v.* 1. *tr.* sós, bhóg = *l.* suffer.
2. *n. v.* thir zāun rāu = *l.* remain constant.
3. tăg = *l.* last.

Enduring, *a.* 1. *rs. into v.*
2. sosṇik.
3. tăgtolo.

Enemy, *s.* dusmān, -nā, *m.*; virod (mănis) = adversary; duṣṭ, -ṭā, *m.*; văiri, -ri, *m.*; duršan, -nā, *m.*

Energetic, *a.* tsuṛk = active; šăktivont; ušār; boḷādik.

Energy, *s.* tsurkpoṇ, -ṇā, *n.* = activity; săkăt, -kti, *f.*; bòḷ, -ḷā, *n* = *l.* force; ušārāi, -ye, *f.* = cleverness.

Enervate, *v.* ăskăt kăr = *l.* make weak.

Enervation, *s.* ăskătkāi, -ye, *f.*

Enfeeble, *see* **Enervate.**

Enforce, *v.* 1. bòḷ di = *l.* give force, *e.g.* a law; *in the pass.* b. zā.
2. ghăṭ kăr = make strong; thir kăr.

Engage, *v.* 1. āḍou di = *l.* give a pledge; *bet.* āḍvān bānd (*or some such verb*) = *l.* bind by pledge.
2. utăr di = *l.* give a word (promise), *ch. cs.*; bhāsāi.
3. bāḍeāk kāṇghe = *l.* take to hire (hire); lāi, *e.g.* e. workmen, hire, *or also* occupy.
4. voḍni di = *l.* give an inclination, allure, captivate.
5. āngār pòḍ = *l.* attack, fall on life; zuz mār = *l.* beat a battle.
6. kărār kăr = *l.* make an agreement.
7. āpṇāčer kāṇe = take upon oneself; voisun ghe = take upon oneself.

Engaged (Is), 1. kāmār (āsā).
2. utăr dilāñ = gave word.

Engagement, *s.* 1. zuz, -zā, *n.* = *l.* battle.
2. dilleñ utăr, -trā, *n.* = *l.* given word (promise); (dilli) bās, -se, *f.* = *l.* given word (promise).
3. kărār, -rā, *m.* = *l.* agreement.
4. mokruri, -re, *f.* = *l.* appointment.
5. săirik, -ke, *f.* = *l.* betrothal, exchange of ring; iḍefóḍ, -ḍi, *f.* = exchange of betelnuts *etc.*; *or rs.* săirik zāli = *l.* relation rose (is betrothed).
6. kām, -mā, *n.* = *l.* business.

Engaging, *a.* mogāḷ = *l.* dear; *or* mogātso; voḍneāntso; voḍnio āḍtso; mānuontso = *l.* pleasing; khušālāyetso = *l.* delightful; sobit = *l.* beautiful.

Engender, *v. pr.* zălmăi, *c. v. of* zălma.

Engine, *s.* čăkrụ, -rā, *n.*; yăntrụ, -rā, *n.*

Engineer, *s.* mārgabāndpašāstri, -ri, *m. or only* bāndpi, -piā, *m.*

England, *s.* Ingland, -dā, *n.* Ingleter, -rā, *n. Prtg.*

English, *a.* Inglez.

Engrave, *v.* 1. kāntăi.
2. kātăr = cut.

Engraver, *s.* kāntăitolo, -leā, *m.*

Engraving, *s.* kāntouṇeñ, -ṇeā, *n.*; *or* kāntounči vidya, -ye, *f.* = *l.* the art of engraving.

Engross, *v.* 1. *if it mn.* occupy, *crc. rs.*, *e.g.* my attention is engrossed by the game = săgḷi moji mōt (ó) kheḷā thăiñ āsā; *or* āuñ ātāñ kheḷā visyānt făkăt čintāñ = *l.* (my) whole mind is on the play,

or I think only play; būḍ = be plunged.
2. mōt (ó) bānd = *l.* bind the mind.
3. poilents molāk kāṇe = *l.* take at price before.
4. soṣṭ năkăl kāḍ, *etc.*

Enhance, *v.* 1. tsăḍăi, *c. v. of* tsăḍ = be too much.
2. vāḍăi (*c. v. of* vāḍ) = cause to grow.
3. sobit kăr *or* sobăi = *l.* make fine, beautiful.
4. mhārăg kăr = *l.* make dear (rate highly).

Enhancement, *s.* vistārāp, -rpā, *n.*; tsăḍāp, -ḍpā, *n.*

Enigma, *s.* guṭ, -ṭā, *m.* = *l.* secret; umeṇi, -ṇe, *f.*

Enigmatical, *a.* guṭātso.

Enjoin, *v.* formăi, *or* hukum di = order; *see* **Command.**

Enjoy, *v.* 1. bhóg = *Lat. fruere.*
2. prăyog kăr = *l.* use, *G. M.*
3. upkārāk pōḍ (ò), *preceded by* Dat. *of the person* = *l.* falls to advantage.

Enjoyment, *s.* 1. bhogāp, -gpā, *n.*
2. khuṡālăi, -ye, *f.* = *l.* pleasure.

Enlarge, *v.* vistār = *l.* extend; tsăḍăi, *c. v. of* tsăḍ = *l.* increase, *not ex.*; rundăi.

Enlargement, *s. rs. into v.*; vistār, -rā, *m.*

Enlighten, *v.* uzvāḍ kăr, *or* uzvāḍăi, *pr.*, *fg.*, *e. g.* mind; peṭăi; *or* uzvāḍ di; u. lăi.

Enlist, *v.* 1. păṭṭer borăi; nāuñ borăi = *l.* write the name; meḷăi = *l.* collect.
2. bāḍeāk kāṇe = *l.* hire.

Enliven, *v.* uṡār kăr, *e.g.* a conversation.

Enmity, *s.* dusmān-kăi, -ye, *f.*; hăgeñ, -geā, *n.* = hatred; jiddu, -dā, *n.*: 'cherish enmity = jiddu (*or* dusmān-kăi) dovór'; năi, -yā, *m.* = *l.* discord; lăḍăi, -ye, *f.* = *l.* contention, war; zăgḍeñ, -ḍeā, *n.* = *l.* quarrel; virodăi, -ye, *f.* = *l.* contrariety.

Ennoble, *v.* 1. măntăn meḷăi, *tr. v.*; m. mèḷ, *n. v.*
2. *fg.* vorto kăr.

Enormity, *s.* 1. khoṭepoṇ, -ṇā, *n.* = *l.* wickedness.
2. niṣṭurăi, -ye, *f.* = *l.* cruelty.

Enormous, *a.* 1. khoṭo.
2. niṣṭur.
3. bhou vóḍ = very large.

Enough, *a.* puro: 'not enough = pāvanāñ = *l.* does not reach'.

Enquire, *v.* 1. vitsār (*or* itsār), *Prs. Cm.*; māg = *l.* request (respectfully).
2. tăn-ki kăr; dăriyāft kăr.

Enquiry, *s.* 1. săvāl, -le, *f.* = question, *also* matter of investigation.
2. vitsārāṇ, -ṇā, *n.* (into a case); *or* vitsār, -rā, *m.*
3. tăn-ki, -ke, *f.* = *l.* examination; dăriyāft (*or* dăryāpt), -ti, *f.*

Enrage, *v.* rāg āḍăi = *l.* cause to be offended; utsāmboḷ kăr = excite.

Enraged, *a.* rāgiṣṭ; *or* rāgār zāllo.

Enrich, *v.* 1. *pr.* grestkāi di = *l.* give riches; grest kăr.
2. *fg.* bhór = fill.

Enrol, *v.* păṭṭer nāuñ borăi = *l.* write the name in the list.

Enslave, *v.* gulām kăr.

Ensnare, *v.* 1. nāḍint dhăr = *l.* catch in the snare; širkāi, *c. v. of* širka = be entangled.
2. pāsānt ghāl = *l.* put into a snare (birds).
3. *fg.* voḍni di = *l.* give inclination.
4. *fg.* pisăi = *l.* cause to get mad, *n. c.*

Entail, *v.* 1. *fg.* (-ntleān) zā = (from it) become, *ch. cs.*
2. hāḍ = bring; ittillo zā (*the legal term, but more commonly used in the mn. of* referring a case to a higher authority).

Entangle, *v.* 1. guspăḍāi, *c. v. of* guspăḍ = get confounded; sāmpăḍāi, *e.g.* a person in his words.
2. dhăr = *l.* catch, *e.g.* in a net.
3. gònd, *e.g.* thread; reuḍāi, *c. v. of* revòḍ; vòḷ.

Enter, *v.* 1. rig, 1*st. Loc.*; bităr vots = *l.* go in.
2. suru zā = *l.* begin (time).
Enter a confraternity = irmāuñ zā, *l.* become an associate.
E. on the priesthood = pādri (*or* sāserdot) zā, *l.* become Father (*or* Priest).
E. on office = kāmāk rig.
E. in a book = dākăl kăr.

Enterprise, *s.* kărtuveñ, -veā, *n.* (măha k.)

Enterprising, *a.* tsurk = *l.* active; dhăirāvont = courageous.

Entertain, *v.* 1. biḍār di = *l.* give hospitality; kāṇghe = *l.* receive.
2. khušāl kăr (*or* khušālăi, *c. v., n. c.*) = *l.* make cheerful, (amuse); 'I entertain a wish, a hope = āšā āsā', *ch. cs.*

Entertainment, *s.* 1. biḍār, -rā, *n.* = *l.* hospitality.
2. khušālāi, -ye, *f.* = pleasure; upačār, -rā, *m., n. c.*

Enthrone, *v.* 1. bisp kăr = *l.* make bishop.
2. pāṭār bosăi = *l.* seat on the throne.

Enthusiasm, *a.* 1. immoderate e.: pišepoṇ, -ṇā, *n.* = *l.* madness.
2. *in general mn.* suḍsuḍāi, -ye, *f.* = *l.* fervour; *or* umāḷo, -ḷeā, *m.*; urba, -be, *f.*; tsăḍ āšā, -še, *f.*
3. utsāmboḷāi, -ye, *f.* = excitement.

Enthusiastic, *a., rs. into s.,*
1. urbevont = *l.* fervent.
2. utsāmboḷist.

3. phontăjigār = *l.* a man of fancy.
4. gărmetso = hot, *fg.*

Entice, *v.* voḍni di = *l.* allure (give inclination); foṭăi = *l.* deceive; nāḍint dhăr = *l.* catch in a net; mosānt ghāl; fuslăi; pisăi *or* piso kăr = *l.* cause to get mad; vóḍ = *l.* draw.

Enticement, *s.* voḍni, -ne, *f.*; mōs, -sā, *m.*; fuslāuṇeñ, -ṇeā, *n.*

Enticing, *a.* 1. mosātso, foṭkiro = *l.* deceitful.
2. voḍnetso = *l.* of inclination; fuslāuntso.

Entire, *a.* săgḷo.

Entirely, *ad.* purteñ = *l.* fully, altogether; păripūrṇ; sompurnāyen = with fullness.

Entitle, *v.* 1. hăkkų di = *l.* give a right.
2. E. a book = pustăkāk nāuñ dovór = *l.* give the name to a book.

Entity, *s.* 1. āsāp, -spā, *n.* = being.
2. văstų, -tu, *f.* = *l.* thing.

Entrails, *s.* ānkiṭi, -ṭe, *f.*

Entrance, *s.* 1. rig, -ge, *f.*
2. răja, -je, *f.* = leave.
3. bāgil, -glā, *n.* = *l.* door.
He has entrance to the king = rāyā lāgiñ votsunk tākā răja āsā.

Entrance-fee, *s.* sănčigār, -rā, *m.*; mungăḍ, -ḍā, *n.*

Entrap, *v.* 1. *pr.* kātăr mānḍ = prepare the trap.
2. kātrin dhăr = catch in a trap; *see* **Ensnare.**

Entreat, *v.* lāleun māg = *l.* beg with longing; āṇ diun māg = beg adjuring.

Entreaty, *s.* ăntăskărnāčeñ māgṇeñ, -ṇeā, *n.* = *l.* a request from the heart.

Entrust, *v.* vopsun di = *l.* deliver; tāben di = *l.* give in care; sóḍ = *l.* leave; *G.* hātānt di = *l.* give into the hand of.

Entry, *s.* 1. rig, -ge, *f.*
2. make an e. in a book = pustakār borăi, *or* dākăl kăr.

Entwine, *v.* revoḍ; vóḷ; bānd.

Enumerate, *v.* 1. lēk (é); mēz (é).
2. moṇ = *l.* recite.

Enumeration, *s.* 1. lēk, -kā, *n.*
2. mezāp, -zpā, *n.*

Enunciate, *v.* sāng = *l.* say; utsār = *l.* pronounce.

Envelope, *s.* lokaṭo, -ṭeā, *m.* (*var.* lakoṭo), *e.g.* of a letter.

Envelope, *v.* guṭlăi, *e.g.* e. in a cloth.

Envenomed, *a. fg.* bhou khoṭo = *l.* very wicked; vikāḷ, *fg.*

Enviable, *a.* ăšā fāvo zāllo *or* ăšā kărtso *or* ăšeuntso = desirable; ăpurbāyetso = *l.* lovely.

Envious, *a.* mosri; niskutsārātso; niskutsāri; kusḍo; an envious person = āgio, *l.* a cobra, *fg.*

Environs, *s.* sărhăddu, -di, *f.*; bountănitso gāun, -gāñvā, *m.* = *l.* the country which is around.

Envoy, *s.* dūt, -tā, *m.*

Envy, *s.* niskutsār, -rā, *m.*; mosor, -srā, *m.*

Envy, *v.* niskutsār kăr, *G. M.*

Epic, *a.* vīrātso: 'e. poetry = v. slók'.

Epidemic (disease), *s.* 1. voso, -seā, *m*; *or* voseāči piḍa, -ḍe, *f.*
2. lokāči piḍa, -ḍe, *f.* = disease of the people.

Epigram, *s.* borāp, -rpā, *n.*

Epilepsy, *s.* morlugi piḍa, -ḍe, *f.*; girāvu, -vā, *n.*

Episcopal, *a.* bispātso.

Episcopate, *s.* bispapon, -ṇā, *n.* (dignity); bisparāz, -jā, *n.* (diocese).

Episode, *s.* āḍkātha, -the, *f.* = *l.* cross-story, *n. c.*

Epitaph, *s.* mornāčeñ bărāp, -rpā, *n.*

Epitome, *s.* sănkšep, -pā, *m.*

Epitomize, *v.* sănkšep kăr.

Epoch, *s.* kāl, -lā, *m.* (occasion *and* era).

Equability, *s.* nidānāi, -ye, *f.*

Equable, *a.* nidāni *or* nidān = calm.

Equal, *a.* 1. săma; sārko = similar.
2. lāyek = *l.* suitable.

Equal, *v.* săma āsā.

Equality, *s.* săr, -ri, *f.*, *e.g.* e. of two lines.

Equally, *ad.* 1. *rs. into adj.*
2. bări = *Lat. instar*, *e.g.* love thy neighbour eq. with thyself = tuje bări peleātso mōg kăr; teāts jinsiñ = in the same way.

Equator, *s. has no proper equivalent*; sămabhāgāgiṭ, -ṭā, *m. or Mr. Cn.* višuvavrăt, -tā, *n.*; buiñmodlogiṭ, -ṭā, *m.*, *anal. to Cn. Sans.*

Equilibrium, *s.* 1. sărituk, -kā, *n.*
2. *fg. rs.* săma.

Equinox, *s.* rātikdisāksăr, -ri, *f.*; *Mr. Cn.* višuv, -vā, *n.*

Equip, *v.* tăyār kăr = *l.* make ready.

Equipage, *s.* 1. zuzasāmān, -nā, *m.*
2. dărbār, -rā, *n.* (retinue).

Equipoise, *s.* sămabhār, -rā, *m.*; săma tūk, -kā, *n.*

Equity, *s.* nīt, -ti, *f.*

Equivalent, *a.* 1. săma = equal.
2. yekātukātso; yekābhārātso.

Equivocal, *a.* dubāvātso *or* dubāvi; *see* **Ambiguous.**

Equivocation, *s.* dubāu, -bāvā, *m.* = *l.* doubt; *or* dubāvāčiñ utrañ, *pl. f.* = doubtful words; *see* **Ambiguity.**

Equivocate, *v.* guḍārtān ulăi.

Era, *s.* kāl, -lā, *m.*

Eradicate, *v.* 1. humbol; (rukāčiñ pāḷañ) kāḍ = *l.* draw out (the roots of a tree).
2. *fg.* kāḍn ghāl; *see* **Destroy.**

Erase, *v.* 1. pus = cancel.

2. čittu kād = remove a blot.
Erasure, *s.* 1. *rs. v.*
2. pusāp, -spā, *n.*
Erect, *a.* 1. nīṭ = straight.
2. ubo = *l.* standing.
Erect, *v.* 1. ukól = lift up.
2. bānd = *l.* build.
Erection, *s.* 1. bāndāp, -dpā, *n.* (*Lat. aedificium*).
2. *rs. into v. or adj.*
Err, *v.* 1. tsuk: 'vāṭ tsukli = I went astray, *l.* the way has been missed'. 'Tsuklā = he made a mistake, a sin (*subj. constr.*).
2. foṭua = be deceived.
3. pārpoḷ zāun bouñ *or only* bouñ = be vagabond.
Erratic, *a.* 1. pārpoḷ.
2. krămaviṇ = irregular.
Erroneous, *s.* fāls, *fr.*; foṭkiro; sătāviṇ = not true; *rs. into* noun.
Error, *s.* 1. tsuk, -ki, *f.*
2. pātak, -tkā, *n.* = *l.* sin.
Eructation, *s.* dénk, -kā, *m.*
Erudition, *s.* sikāp, -kpā, *n.*
Eruption, *s.* 1. eruption of a volcano, ujeāvónk, -ki, *f.*
2. fóḍ, -ḍā, *m.* (a suppurating tumour).
3. mumbār, -brā, *n.* = a pimple.
Erysipelas, *s.* daddurόg, -gā, *m.*, *n. c.*
Escape, *v.* 1. pòḷ = flee; *or* pòḷn vots.
2. tsukăi = *l.* avoid; *or* tsukoun ghe.
3. lip = *l.* hide; (-ntlo) păriyār zā = get rid of.
4. bhāir săr = *l.* go out, *e.g.* water.
Escape, *s.* 1. poḷāp, -ḷpā, *n.* = *l.* flight.
2. iḍeñ, -ḍeā, *n.* = a small hole, *e.g.* in a cask of wine.
3. *often rs. into v.*, *e. g.* there is no escape from death.
Escort, *v.* pāryār vor.
Escort, *s.* 1. pāro, -reā, *m.*
2. dărbār, -rā, *m.*
Esculent, *see* **Eatable.**
Esoteric, *a.* guṭātso.
Especial, *a.* mukhya = *l.* principal; višes.
Especially, *ad.* mukhyazāun; bhou kărn; ădik kărn; tsăḍzāun; višes.
Espionage, *s.* bedipoṇ, -ṇā, *n. from* bedi, -di, *m. pr.* = spy.
Esplanade, *s.* măidān, -nā, *n.*
Esquire, *s.* săib, -bā, *m.*
Essay, *s.* 1. prăyătăn, -tnā, *n.* = *l.* effort.
2. părikṣā, -ṣe, *f.* = *l.* trial, examination.
3. dākṭeñ borāp, -rpā, *n.*; *see* **Pamphlet.**
Essence, *s.* săimb, -bā, *n.* = nature; sār, -rā, *m.* = *l.* extract, *fg. used also for* e. *in phil. mn.*
Essential, *a.* mukhya = *l.* principal; sārātso, *e.g.* e. quality of.

Establish, *v.* 1. găḍ = *l.* found; stāpăn kăr *or* stāpsi, *e.g.* a college, *n. c.*
2. niščeisi = *l.* decide, determine; nemsi = *l.* appoint.

Establishment, *s.* 1. kārkhāno, -neā, *m.*
2. bāndāp, -dpā, *n.* = *l.* a building.

Estate, *s.* 1. āst, -ti (*or* āsti, -te), *f.* = landed property; buiñ, -iñ, *f.*
2. stiti, -ti, *f.*; bhés, -sā, *m.*; huddo, -deā, *m.* = rank; thăr, -rā, *m.* = kind, class. The second *and* third estate *here have no better equivalents than* măntănāntlo = noble, *or* grest = rich; *and* khāunk jeunk āsullo = having to eat, *or* dublo = poor, *respectively.*

Esteem, *s.* boreñ nāuñ, -nāvā, *n.* = *l.* a good name; mān, -nā, *m.* = *l.* honour; măntăn, -nā, *n.* = *l.* nobility.
He is in great e. = to bou boreñ nāuñ bhógtā.

Esteem, *v.* 1. čint = *l.* think.
2. mānd = *Lat. magnifac;* boreñ čint; mān dākăi = show honor; ăpurbāi kăr, *G. F.* = *l.* make affection; prīt kăr = *l.* love, *G. F.* mòl kăr = make price, appreciate, *Acc.*; lăkṣa kăr = *l.* make care, *Acc.*

Estimate, *s.* 1. lēk (ė), -kā, *n.* = *l.* account; ăndāz, -zā, *m.* (*or* ăndāzo, -zeā, *m.*), *e.g.* of the cost.
2. āločen, -ni, *f.* = judgment, opinion.

Estimate, *v.* lēk(ė) kăr; ăndāz kăr, *G. M.*

Estrange, *v.* mòn pois kăr = *l.* make the heart far.

Estuary, *s.* 1. āḷveñ, -veā, *n.* (the mouth of a river).
2. dăryākuḷ, -ḷā, *n.*

Eternal, *a.* sāsṇātso; ăgāṇit = *l.* infinite; sădāntso; mornāviṇ.

Eternally, *ad.* sāsṇāčeā sāsṇāk; *or* sădānkāl.

Eternity, *s.* sāsăṇ, -sṇā, *n.*; sădānkāl, -lā, *m.* = *l.* epoch of always.

Ethic, *a.* tsālitso.

Ethics, *s.* tsālišāstru, -rā, *n.*

Etiquette, *s.* tsāltsămkăṇ, -ṇā, *n.*; măryād, -di, *f.*; măryādiči dăstur, -re, *f.*

Etymology, *s.* 1. săbdāñvidya, -ye, *f.*
2. (šăbda-) mūl, -lā, *n.*

Etymon, *s.* săbda- (*or* săbdāñ-) mūḷ, -ḷā, *n.*

Eucharist, *s.* săntisim săkrāment, -tā, *m.*; kumgār, -rā, *m.*, *and* komuniāuñ, -āvā, *m.* *are used not uncommonly by the people for* euch.

Eunuch, *s.* khozo, -jeā, *m.*

Euphonic, *a.* boro vāztolo.

Euphony, *s.* boreñ vāzāp, -zpā, *n.*

Evacuate, *v.* 1. khāli kăr = *l.* make

empty; vót *or* vomti=pour; uspi.
2. kāḍ = *l.* take out.
3. sóḍ=*l.* leave, *e.g.* a country.
4. hāg (go to stool).
Evacuation, *s.* 1. utkāḍe, -ḍeā, *n.*; hāgoṇ, -ṇi, *f.*
2. *fg.* soḍni, -ne, *f.*
Evade, *v.* 1. tsukăi = *l.* avoid.
2. pòḷ = *l.* get away; *see* **Escape.**
Evanescent, *a.* 1. năpăints zāuntso.
2. *fg.* khāli; foṭkiro.
Evangelical, *a.* evanjel sikăitā to; *or* evanjelān sikăillo. 'Evangelical counsels=evanjelānt sāngụlleo budi (*or* sikoṇeo); Durboḷkăi, Ānkuārpoṇ, Khālteapoṇ *are the* three e. counsels).
Evangelist, *s.* evanjelist, -tā, *m.* *fr.*; suvārtamānagār, -rā, *m.*, *n. u.*
Evangelize, *v.* evanjel părgăṭ kăr; suvărtamān p. k.
Evaporate, *v.* (vāreānt uḍon vetā = *l.* (in the air) flying goes; ub.
Evasion, *s.* 1. tsukāp, -kpā, *n.*
2. nību, -bā, *n.* = *l.* pretext.
Evasive, *a.* tsukountso.
Eve, *s.* vijil, -lā, *m.* (of a feast), *fr.*; (festātso) ādlo dis, -sā, *m.* = previous day (of the feast). 'We are on the eve of war = zuz lāgiñ āsā'.
Even, *a.* 1. telto=smooth; sārko.
2. *fg.* nidān=calm.
E. number=fāḍeñ, -ḍeā, *n.*
Even, *ad.* legun; săit; pāriyant; *these words are placed after the word modified*; *see* **Also.**
Not even (*Lat. ne quidem*) = i *with neg. particle, or* păriyant *in neg. f.*, *see* Gram.
Evening, *s.* sānz, -je *f.* 'In the evening=sānjer *or* sānječeñ'.
Evenness, *s.* 1. telteapoṇ, -ṇā, *n.*
2. *fg.* nidānāi, -ye, *f.* = equanimity.
Event, *s.* 1. gāḍāp, -ḍpā, *n.*
2. sevoṭ, -ṭā, *m.* = *l.* issue.
At all events = puṇi, kăseñi zāundi.
In the e. of = zārtăr, if.
Eventual, *a. rs.* sekiñ; kăḍetso; tirsountso; *bet. rs.*
Ever, *ad.* 1. sădānts = always.
2. thāmbanāstanāñ=incessantly.
3. kăiñ(puṇi), *as in the sentence*, 'did he ever commit such a thing?'; kăiñ; *by the conting. fut. or Potential Mood.*
For ever = sāsṇāčeā sāsṇāk.
In neg. sentences it is joined to the verb.
'No mortal has e. been able to attain so much = mānšāk titleñ kedints tānklenāñ'. 'Are friends ever to be preferred to old men? = iṣṭānk mātāreāñ prās kăiñ" vintsun kāḍi zāigi?'
Everlasting, *a.* sāsṇātso; sădānts tăgtso.

Evermore (For), *ad.* sădānts.
Every, *a.* 1. hăryek; yeyek; kăsoloi = *Lat. quivis*; hăr.
2. jinsañ.
Everybody, *pron.* hăryeklo; yeyeklo; kăsoloi mănis, -nšā, *m.*; *or* koṇi.
Every-day, *ad.* disāndis.
Every-day, *a.* disadisātso, dispoḍto.
Everything, *s.* săkăṭ.
Every-way, *s.* 1. sărvụ kusin.
2. purteñ = altogether; păripūrṇ = altogether.
Everywhere, *a.* săgḷeān; săgḷe kăḍe; sărvụ thăiñ, *ol.*
Evidence, *s.* 1. uktepoṇ, -ṇā, *n.* = *l.* being open, *fg.*, *n. c.*; *rs.* soşṭ = evident.
2. ruzvāt, -ti, *f.*
3. sākş, -şi, *f.* (*Lat. testimonium*). 'Give e. = sākş sāng'.
Evident, *a.* sóşṭ; ukto.
Evidently, *ad.* soşṭzāun.
Evil, *s.* 1. văiṭ (*s. and adj.*), -ṭā, *n.*
2. khoṭo (*adj.*); pāḍ. 'Speak e. = văiṭ ulăi'. 'Wish e. = v. māg'.
Evil-doer, *s.* văiṭ kărtolo.
Evil-minded, *a.* 1. mosor kărtolo = *l.* envious.
2. *rs.* tākā khuši nāñ = *l.* he is not willing.
Evil-speaking, *s.* 1. tsāḍiyegār, -rā, *m.* = *l.* backbiter.
2. gāḷi sāngtolo = *l.* abusing.
3. tsāḍi, -ye, *f.*
4. gāḷ, -ḷi, *f.*

Evince, *v.* soşṭ kăr = make clear; dākăi = *l.* prove, show.
Eviscerate, *v. pr.* ānkiṭi kāḍ = *l.* take out the bowels.
Evoke, *v.* -ntlo āpoi.
Evolve, *v.* 1. soḍăi; kāḍ.
2. *fg.* soşṭ kăr.
Ewe, *s.* bokri, -re, *f.*, *n. u.*; *vlg.* gāṭāči bokḍi, -ḍe, *f.*; *see* **Sheep**.
Ex-, as part of the title of one who has been in office,
1. māji—if he has left the office lately;
2. kăḷḷa (thief)—if degraded from it.
Exacerbate, *v.* utsāmbóḷ kăr = *l.* make excited; dukăi (*c. v. of* duk) = *l.* cause sorrow.
Exact, *v.* 1. (hăkkān) māg = *l.* request.
2. formāi = *l.* command, *ch. cs.*
3. vărāt kăr = *l.* make a demand.
Exact, *a.* 1. sārko; zāgrut = *l.* attentive; krămātso = *l.* regular; *or* krăm ăsụllo.
2. săma.
3. bărābăr = *l.* exact, right, equal; *as,* I found the accounts e.
Exaction, *s.* 1. vărāt, -tā, *m.*
2. bòḷ, -ḷā, *n.* = violence.
Exactly, *ad.* 1. sārkeñ.
2. ex. so = tăsents.
Exactness, *s.* zāgrutāi, -ye, *f.*
Exaggerate, *v.* 1. tsāḍăi = *l.* increase.

2. tsăḍ sāng = *l.* say too much; tsăḍoun sāng; *vlg.* goppe mār; kuvāḷe kātăr; tsouḷio mār. (*Konk.*)

Exaggeration, *s.* tsăḍouṇ, -ṇe, *f.*; *vlg.* goppo, -peā, *m.* (*in the pl.* goppe).

Exalt, *v.* 1. *fg.* hogoḷsi = *l.* praise; hoglăi; uboḷsi.

2. băḍti di (promote to a higher office); mānāčeñ kām di = *l.* give high office; vorto kăr, *e.g.* e. humble men; voir kāḍ; mān di = *l.* give honour.

3. vorni = exalt, *e.g.* e. God; tārif kăr, *G. F.*, *n.c.*

Exaltation, *s.* 1. *fg.* hogḷāp, -pā, *n.* = *l.* praise; tārif, -fe, *f.*, *n.c.*; mān, -nā, *m.* = *l.* honour.

2. vortepoṇ, -ṇā, *n.* = sublimity.

3. băḍti, -te, *f.* = promotion to a higher office.

Examination, *s.* 1. părikṣa, -še, *f.*, *e.g.* in the school; vitsārăṇ, -ṇā, *n.* = *l.* inquisition; tănki, -ke, *f.* = *l.* inquisition; dăriyāft, -ti, *f.*

2. ugḍās, -sā, *m.* = *l.* remembrance: 'e. of conscience = pātkāntso ugḍās = *l.* remembrance of sins'; *or* ăntăskărnătănki, -ke, *f.* = inquisition of the heart.

Examine, *v.* 1. părikṣa kăr, *G. F.*, *pass.* p. di.

2. vitsār = *l.* investigate.

3. (ăntăskărn) tănki kăr; dăriyāft kăr; pātkāutso ugḍās kăr = *l.* make memory of sins.

4. poḷe (*or* poḷei) = *l.* see, inspect.

Examiner, *s.* părikṣa kărtolo; părikṣegār, -rā, *m.* = *also* he who is examined, *whereas* părikṣa ditolo = *only* examined.

Example, *s.* 1. dēk (é), -ki, *f.* (bori dēk = good example, edification, *e.g.* e. of saints).

2. dāklo, -leā, *m.* = a short story; drăṣṭānt, -tā, *n.*, *n. c.*; kăta, -te, *f.* = history.

3. vopār, -re, *f.* = a parable.

4. nămuno, -neā, *m.* = *l.* pattern, sample.

For example = kăseñgi moḷeār = *l.* as if you say; drăṣṭāntāk.

Exasperate, *v.* rāg āḍăi = *l.* cause anger; utsāmboḷ kăr = *l.* excite; dukăi, *c. v.* = *l.* afflict; koḍu kăr.

Exasperated, *a.* rāgiṣṭ, *etc. see v.*

Exasperating, *a.* dukountso; koḍu.

Exasperation, *s.* 1. rāg, -gā, *m.* = anger.

2. dukouṇeñ, -ṇeā, *n.*

Excavate, *v.* 1. pokăḷ kăr = *l.* make hollow; pokór.

2. konḍ = *l.* dig.

Excavation, *s.* pokăḷāp, -pā, *n.* *or* pokăḷăi, -ye, *f.*, *n. c.*; fónḍ, -ḍā, *m.* = grave; kònḍ, -ḍā, *n.*

Excavator, *s.* konḍtolo, -leā, *m.*

Exceed, *v.* 1. tsăḍ = too much, *with the verb showing the kind of excess;* mirua = *l.* trespass; mikua: 'he exceeds his limits = podvek mikvatā, *l.* trespasses power'; tsăḍ = *l.* be too much.
2. zăit vor = *l.* gain a victory.
3. *by the* comparative.

Exceedingly, *ad.* bhou = much; *or* bhou tsăḍ = very much.

Excel, *v.* 1. jik = *l.* gain, *e.g.* Peter excels Paul; zăit vor = *l.* gain victory, *Prs. 2nd Loc.*; uttim zāun vortautā = *l.* is excellent; *by the comparative.*
2. boro zāun vortautā (*with superl. or compar.*) *or, instead of* boro, *some other adj. as the meaning requires.*

Excellence, *s.* vorteponn, -ṇā, *n.*; ăprupāi, -ye, *f.* = rarity, *fg.*

Excellent, *a.* uttim *or* uttăm; bhou boro; vorto; ăprup.

Excellently, *ad.* bhou boreñ.

Except, *prep.* šivāi, *postp.*; khărit, *postp.*; *by the gerund. neg. in* tanāñ, *or by the neg. conditional.*

Exception, *s.* virodāi, -ye, *f.* = contrariety, *n. u.*; ăprupāi, -ye, *f.* = rarity; ăpavād, -dā, *m.*, *Cn. Mr.*; *bet. rs. ad. or* virod āsā.

Exceptional, *a.* ăprup = *l.* rare; virodāyetso; *see* **Exception.**

Excess, *s.* 1. tsăḍāu, -ḍāvā, *n.*
2. nigutāi, -ye, *f.*
3. tsuk, -ki, *f.* = *l.* error; miruoṇeñ, -ṇeā, *n.* ăkrăm, -mā, *n.* = *l.* disorder.

Excessive, *a.* 1. tsăḍāvot, *e. g.* e. anger, heat.
2. krămaviṇ; miruontso.

Exchange, *v.* 1. bădăl; ădălbădăl kăr.
2. vāṭāi = *l.* e. money.
Exchange places = yere suāter vots, *l.* go to another place, *or also* suāt bădăl.

Exchange, *s.* bădlāp, -pā, *n.*

Exchequer, *s.* khăzāno, -neā, *m.*

Excise, *s.* sunk, -kā, *n.*; *see* **Tax.**

Excitability, *s.* utsāmboḷāi, -ye, *f.*; *or* utsāmboḷa sārkeñ, -keā, *n.*

Excitable, *a.* utsāmboḷātso, utsāmboḷā sārko.

Excite, *v.* 1. utsāmboḷ kăr.
2. ubzăi = cause to become excited.
3. uṭāi, *e. g.* e. your hearers to penance; huskāi, *e. g.* a dog against.
4. kāṇṭe vor = *l.* bring thorns, *i. e.* instigate.
5. bòḷ di = *l.* give force.
6. lāi = *l.* apply.
7. bud săng = give advice.
8. *by the c. v.*, *e. g.* ex. laughter = hāsāi.
Ex. compassion = movāḷāi; kākuḷt dhărăi, *or rs.* kākuḷt distā *or* k. kăr.

Excitement, *s.* utsāmboḷāi, -ye, *f.*; umāḷo, -ḷeā, *m.* = *l.* boiling; *fg.*, *e. g.* e. to sin.

Exclaim, *v.* bòb mār = *l.* beat noise; sāng = *l.* say (in speaking); bòb mārn sāng = crying say; *commonly the form of the sentence must be changed.*

Exclamation, *s.* bòb, -be, *f.* = *l.* crying.

Exclude, *v.* 1. pois dovór = *l.* keep far.
2. bhāir ghāl = *l.* put out; kāḍ = *l.* take out; bhāir dānk, *or* bhāir ghāln dānk.

Exclusion, *s.* bhāir gālāp, -pā, *n.*, *n. c.*; *rs. v.*

Exclusive, *a.* 1. yeksuro = *l.* solitary.
2. *by the emph.* -ts; *rs. into* khărit *or* šivāi = except.

Exclusively, *ad.* mātrụ, făkăt *or* făkt = *l.* only; *rs.* khărit *or* šivāi; *by* -ts *emph.*, *e.g.* that is not the fault of old age e. = utăr pirāyečits ti tsuk năiñ.

Excommunicate, *v.* 1. igărjentlo bhāir ghāl, *or* igărje bhāir ghāl.
2. zāti bhāir ghāl = *l.* put out of the caste.

Excommunication, *s.* eskomuniāuñ, -āvā, *m.*, *fr.*; sărgiñ širāp, -pā, *m.* = the curse of heaven; igărješirāp, -pā, *m.*; *or rs. v.*

Excrement, *s.* gu, -vā, *m.*; lăddi, -de, *f.* = horse-dung; šeṇ, -ṇā, *n.* = cow-dung.

Excrescence, *s.* dunkuṭụ, -ṭā, *n.*

Excruciate, *v.* 1. kăṣṭăi; iza di; dukăi; voḷvoḷāi.
2. dukin jīu vetā = *l.* by pain life goes.

Excruciating, *a.* kănṭin; kăṣṭountso; dukountso; voḷvoḷountso; ijetso; dăgdountso.

Exculpate, *v.* 1. gunyāunātullo dākăi = show innocent; udāraṇ sāng; niraprādi kăr.
2. nīb sāng = say excuse.

Exculpation, *s.* udārăṇ, -ṇā, *n.*, *or rs. v.*

Excursion, *s.* 1. pāsăi, -ye, *f.* (*Lat. deambulatio*); bounḍi, -ḍe, *f.*
2. săvāri, -re, *f.* = a riding e.

Excusable, *a.* māf fāvo zāllo, *or rs. v.*

Excuse, *v.* 1. *tr.* māf (*or* māp) kăr, *or* m. di = *l.* make *or* give pardon; bogsi = forgive.
2. māf māg = beg pardon.
3. nīb sāng = *l.* exculpate, say excuse.

Excuse, *s.* 1. māf, -fe, *f. or* -fā, *n.*, *but bet. indecl.*; bogsāṇeñ, -ṇeā, *n.*
2. nīb, -bā, *n.* = pretext.

Execrable, *a.* širāpātso; khoṭeponātso; kānṭāḷo fāvo zāllo; kānṭāḷeātso.

Execrate, *v.* 1. kānṭāḷ = *l.* abhor; širāp ghāl = *l.* put a curse.
2. băṣṭăi = defile.

Execration, *s.* 1. širāp, -pā, *m.*
2. *rs. v.*

Execute, *v.* 1. kăr = *l.* do; sovoi kăr, *G. F.*, *e.g.* a good resolution.
2. pāḷ = *l.* perform, *e.g.* a duty, a promise.
3. tsălăi = *l.* cause to walk.
4. jāri kăr, *e.g.* a will.

Execution, *s.* 1. kărni, -ne, *f.*, *bet. rs. into v.*; jāri, -re, *f.*
2. mornāči šikṣa, -ṣe, *f.*
3. āsteikāp, -kpā, *n.*

Executioner, *s.* mhār = a pariah, *only such people being employed in this office;* jāri kărtolo, -leā, *m.*; fāsi ghāltolo.

Executor (of a will), *s.* = (testament) jāri kărtolo.

Executive, *a.* jārikărtso.

Exegesis, *s.* vivorsāngči vidya, -ye, *f.*

Exemplar, *s.* 1. nămuno, -neā, *m.* = pattern, sample, *used also fg.*
2. dēk (ė), -ki, *f.*, *e.g.* J. C. is our exemplar.

Exemplary, *a.* dēk (ė) kāṇeunk fāvo zăllo = *l.* worthy of taking (from it) an example; uttim = *l.* excellent; nămuneātso.

Exemplify, *v.* dēk (ė) (*or* dāklo) di; dākleāniñ dākăi.

Exempt, *a.* viroit: 'exempt from sin = pātkañ viroit'; *often ch. cs.*

Exempt, *v.* 1. rāja di = *l.* give leave, *ch. cs.*; māf kăr.
2. sóḍ = *l.* leave.

Exemption, *s.* 1. māf, -fā, *n.*, *e.g.* from a law.
2. suṭka, -ke, *f.*, *e.g.* from sin; sóḍni, -ne, *f.*

Exercise, *s.* 1. ăbyās, -sā, *m.*
2. kām, -mā, *n.* = *l.* business, theme.
3. boundi, -ḍe, *f.* = walking ex.
4. kāido, -deā, *m.* = *l.* duty, *e.g.* daily ex.
5. sovoi, -ye, *f.* = practice, custom.
6. veḷār, *as in the phrase,* 'in the exercise of his office = kām kărčeā veḷār'.
7. *rs.* (kām) tsălăi = exercise (an office).
8. kovāt, -tā, *n.* (military exercise).

Exercise, *v.* 1. tsălăi, *c. v.* = *l.* cause to walk, *e.g.* an office.
2. sovoi kăr = *l.* make habit; ăbyās kăr.
3. părikṣa kăr = *l.* make examination, try, *e.g.* patience.
4. kovāt sikăi = drill.

Exercised, *a. rs.* tākā ăbyās āsā, *or* kăḷtā = hẹ has practice, *or* he knows; ăbyās āsullo.

Exercises, *s.* (vorsātso) kāido = retreat = *l.* (yearly) exercise; riṭrīṭ, -ṭi, *f.*, *or* riter, -ri, *f.*, *fr.*; ătmeātso (*or* devasponātso) ăbyās, -sā, *m.*; tòp, -pā, *n.* = the hearing of God's voice; contemplation.

Exert, *v.* 1. vāur″ = make effort;

2. prăyătăn kăr = *l.* make an effort.
3. dākăi = *l.* show.

Exertion, *s.* prăyătăn, -tnā, *n.* (*var.* -tne, *f.*)

Exhalation, *s.* 1. pormóḷ, -ḷā, *m.* (a good smell).
2. ub, -be, *f.* = *l.* vapour.
3. ghāṇ, -ṇi, *f.* = a bad smell.

Exhale, *v.* 1. bhāir ghāl = *l.* put out, *ch. cs.*; bhāir sărăi.
2. bhāir săr = come out

Exhaust, *v.* 1. *tr.* mugdi, *c. v. of* mugda = finish; khărči = *l.* expend; tirsi = *l.* finish, *e.g.* e. a question.
2. ăskăt kăr = make weak; dăṇsi = make tired; dăṇvăi.

Exhausted, *a.* puro zăllo = tired, *l.* got enough; văṭer poḍso = *l.* falling on the way; dăṇvăllo.

Exhaustion, *s.*, *rs. into v.*; (tsăḍāvot) ăskătkăi, -ye, *f.* = *l.* (excessive) weakness; dăṇsoṇeñ, -ṇeā, *n.*

Exhibit, *v.* 1. dākăi = *l.* show, dis-[play.
2. doḷeāñ mukār ghāl = put before the eyes.

Exhibition, *s.* dākoṇeñ, -ṇeā, *n.* (*or* dākoṇi, -ṇe, *f.*)

Exhilarate, *v.* khušālăi, *c. v. of* khušāl, *n. c.*, *or* khušāl kăr.

Exhilaration, *s.* khušālăi, -ye, *f.* cheerfulness.

Exhort, *v.* bori bud sāng = *l.* say good advice; budbāḷ sāng; uṭāi; *see* **Encourage.**

Exhortation, *s.* 1. bud, -di, *f.* = *l.* advice.
2. budbāḷ, -ḷi, *f.* = *l.* a kind of familiar preaching.
3. sermāuñ, -āvā, *m.* = preaching, *used also for* exhortation, *fr.*

Exigency, *s.* gărz, -je, *f.*; kăšṭ, -ṭā, *m.*

Exile, *s.* 1. părdesi, -siā, *m.*; părdes, *a.* = foreign.
2. găḍpār, -rā, *m.* = *Lat.* '*exul*' *and* '*exilium*', *n. c.*; părdespoṇ, -ṇā, *n.* = *Lat. exilium*; dēsantăr, -rā, *n.*

He is in exile = părgāvānt bhāir ghālā, *or* părdesi zāun āsā.

Exile, *v.* găḍpār kăr; păradešāk dhāḍ = send to a foreign country; *or* gāvāñ bhāir ghāl = put out of the country.

Exist, *v.* āsā.

Existence, *s.* 1. āsāp, -spā, *n.*, *n. c.*
2. jiṇi, -ye, *f.* = *l.* life.

Existent, *a.* 1. jiyeuntso = living; hāzăr = present.
2. ātāntso = *l.* of now.

Exit, *s.* 1. bhāir sărāp, -rpā, *n.* = departure.
2. ăkāḍo, -ḍeā, *m.* = a narrow footpath; iḍeñ, -ḍeā, *n.* = a small opening, *e.g.* in a door.

Exonerate, *v.* hāḷuāi; *see also* **Exculpate.**

Exorbitant, *a.* bhou tsăḍ, *or* tsăḍāvot = *l.* excessive.

Exorcise, *v.* deuntsārāk soḍăi = *l.* cause the devil to leave.

Exorcism, *s.* 1. bhutasoḍouṇi, -ṇe, *f.*, *n.c.*
2. bhutasoḍouṇeamāg-ṇeñ,-ṇeā *n.*

Exordium, *s.* suru, -ve, *f.*; tăyārăi, -ye, *f.*

Exoteric, *a.* părgăṭ = *l.* public; ugto = *l.* open, *fg.*

Exotic, *a.* bhāilo = *l.* exterior.

Expand, *v.* 1. vistār.
2. sóḍăi, *e.g.* flowers e. their leaves; ghāl = *l.* put.

Expansion, *s.* vistārāp, -rpā, *n.*

Expatiate, *v.* lāmbāi ulăi; vistārn ulăi.

Expatriate, *see* **Exile.**

Expect, *v.* 1. rāk, *e.g.* I expect you to-morrow; e. a letter, payment, *etc.*
2. rāu, *n.v.* = *l.* wait.
3. pātiye = *l.* hope, trust; āšā āsā, *ch. cs.*
4. čint = *l.* think.

Expectation, *s.* 1. băruāso, -seā, *m.*, *e.g.* I was disappointed in my e.; pātiyeṇi, -ṇi, *f.* = *l.* hope, trust; āšā, -še, *f.*
2. āločen, -ni, *f.* = *l.* opinion.

Expectorate, *v.* khānkār.

Expediency, *s.* vāzbipoṇ, -ṇā, *n.* upkār, -rā, *m.*; upāi, -yā, *m.*

Expedient, *s.* 1. fāvo = *l.* due; vāzbi = *l.* convenient.
2. upkārātso = *l.* advantageous.
3. *by* zāi = it is e., *Lat. decet.*

Expedition, *s.* 1. ausăr, -rā, *m.* = haste.
2. (phoujičeñ) dhāḍāp, -ḍpā, *n.* = the sending of an army; *or* phoujipoiṇ, -ṇā, *n.*

Expel, *v.* bhāir ghāl = *l.* put out; bhāir dhāḍ = *l.* send out; nivrāi = *l.* deprive; *or* bărtărap kăr = dismiss.

Expend, *v.* khărči.

Expenditure, *s.* khărts, -tsā, *m.*

Expense, *s.* khărts, -tsā, *m.*; ḳust, -tā, *n.* (*in 2nd Loc.*), *only in the phrase* at my ex.

Expensive, *a.* khărtsātso; mhārăg = *l.* dear; molādig = of price.

Experience, *s.* 1. ănbou, -bovā, *m.*, *or.* ănbhóg, -gā, *m.*
2. părikša, -še, *f.* = *l.* examination, a trial, a specimen.

Experience, *v.* 1. sós, bhóg = *l.* suffer, feel.
2. părikša kăr = *l.* make trial, *G.F.*; *or* poḷe = *l.* look.
3. sik = *l.* learn.

Experienced, *a.* ănbhógi; *or* ănbovātso.

Experiment, *s.* părikša, -še, *f.*; păryătăn, -tnā, *n.*, *e.g.* physical e.

Expert, *a.* ušār; zānṭo; *see* **Skillful.**

Expiate, *v.* 1. prāčit kăr = *l.* make penance, *G. N.*
2. fārikpoṇ di = *l.* give satisfaction.

Expiation, *s.* 1. prāčit, -tā, *n.* 2. fārikpoṇ, -ṇā, *n.* = *l.* satisfaction.

Expiatory, *a.* 1. prāčitātso. 2. fārikpoṇātso.

Expiration, *s.* 1. usuās, -sā, *m.* (*ex.* usuāsāči sóḍne, -ne, *f.* 2. ănt, -tā, *m.* = end; *rs.* zātā: 'on the e. of 5 years = pānts vorsañ zāun'.

Expire, *v.* prāṇ sóḍ = *l.* leave life, die.

Explain, *v.* 1. sóḍāi = *l.* unfold. 2. *fg.* vivor sāng, *G. M.* = *l.* say explanation; dākoun di = *l.* show, *as* in preaching; somzăi = *l.* give to understand.
3. ărth sāng = *l.* say the meaning.

Explanation, *s.* 1. vivor, -rā, *m.*, *e.g.* of doctrine.
2. ărth, -thā, *m.* = *l.* meaning.
3. udārăṇ, -ṇā, *n.*, *e.g.* e. of one's own proceedings.

Explicit, *a.* sošṭ; khănḍit = *l.* positive.

Explicitly, *ad.* sošṭ (zāun).

Explode, *v.* mār, *e.g.* a gun. Ex. an opinion = yek āločen kāḍn uḍăi.

Exploit, *s.* vorti kărni, -ne, *f.* = great action; dhăirāvont kāryeñ, -yeā, *n.*; *or* măha kărtuveñ, -veā, *n.*

Explore, *v.* 1. sódna kăr; sód; părikša kăr; poḷe (*or* poḷei).
2. vitsārăṇ kăr = make inquiry.

Explosion, *s.* fār, -rā, *m.*

Explosive, *a.* fārātso; *or* fār zăisārko.

Export, *v.* răft kăr; bhāir vor.

Exportation, *s.* răft, -tā, *n.*, *Hind.*

Expose, *v.* 1. bhāir dovór, bhāir ghāl *or* mukār ghāl = *l.* place out, *or* before.
2. ugto ghāl = *l.* place open, *e.g.* to a danger; părgăṭăi = publish.
3. dākăi = *l.* exhibit.
4. riskent ghāl = *l.* put in danger; 'he exposed himself to death = mornāče riskent pòḍlo'.

Exposed, *a.* ukto ghāltso *or* pòḍtso (*e.g.* to a danger); *bet. rs.* khāl, *e.g.* riske kh. = e. to risk; pātka kh. = e. to sin.

Exposition, *s.* 1. vivor, -rā, *m.* = *l.* explanation; dākouṇeñ, -ṇeā, *n.* (*or* dākoṇ, -ṇe, *f.*)
2. lēk(è), -kā, *n.* = a statement.
3. Sakramentāčeñ besāuñ, -sāvā, *n.* = e. of the Blessed Sacrament, *fr.*; Sakramentāčeñ dākouṇeñ, -ṇeā, *n.*

Expostulate, *v.* šiṇ ulăi = *l.* speak a complaint; durva = *l.* blame; gunyāukār kăr = *l.* make guilty; hăkkān māg = ask with right.

Exposure, *s.* kăšṭ, -ṭā, *m.* = *l.* difficulty, pain; *see* **Expose.**

Expound, *see* **Explain.**

Express, *v.* 1. pīḷ = squeeze.

2. utsār = *l.* give expression in words to, pronounce; pātsār.
3. dākăi = *l.* show.
4. ulăi = *l.* speak.

Express, *a.* -ts *emph.*, *i.e.* exact, very.

Express, *s.* răvāni, -niā, *m. or n.*

Expression, *s.* 1. utsār, -rā, *m.*
2. utrāñ = *l.* words, sentences.
3. rūp, -pā, *n.*, *e.g.* e. of the face.

Expressive, *a.* 1. *rs. into* gurtụ āsā=*l.* is a sign; *or* dākăitā.
2. rūpātso, soṣṭ, *e.g.* e. face.
3. bòḷ āsụllo = *l.* having force.
4. somzontso = intelligible.

Expressly, *see* **Explicitly.**

Expulsion, *s.* bhāir ghālāp, -lpā, *n.*, *n.c.*; *or rs. v.*

Expunge, *v.* pus; čittụ kāḍ.

Expurgate, *v.* săma kăr; nităḷ kăr; nitḷăi.

Exquisite, *a.* 1. uttăm = *l.* excellent; vintsụllo, *or* vintsnār, *e.g.* e. pain, e. food; bhāri, *e.g.* benefit.
2. niṣṭur = cruel, *e.g.* e. pain.
3. ručitso = tasteful (food); nāzuk = *l.* delicate.

Exquisite, *s.* nāzukgār = a delicate, elegant man.

Exquisiteness, *s.* 1. nāzukăi, -ye, *f.* = delicacy.
2. vortepoṇ, -ṇā, *n.* = sublimity.

Extant, *a.* urtā to = remaining; āni āsā to.

Extempore, *ad.* 1. yekats fāra=*l.* at once, *ch. cs.*; aučit.
2. tăyārnāstanāñ = *l.* not being prepared, *ch. cs.*; *rs.* utrāñ tonḍār āsāt = *l.* words are on the mouth, *i.e.* he can speak extempore.

Extend, *v.* 1. vistār.
2. lāmb kăr = *l.* make long.
3. kāḍ.
4. rundăi *or* rund kăr, *e.g.* a road.
5. āni di = *l.* give more (*e.g.* time).
6. pāu = reach.

Extension, *s.* vistārāp, -rpā, *n. or* vistār, -rā, *m.*; lāmbăi, -ye, *f.* = *l.* length; zāgo, -geā, *m.* = *l.* space, place; *rs. into* kitlo = how much.

Extensive, *a.* 1. *pr.* vistārlolo.
2. tsăḍ.

Extent, *s.* vistārāp, -rpā, *n.*

Extenuate, *v.* 1. māf kăr = *l.* excuse.
2. lān kăr = *l.* make little, *e.g.* ext. a fault; uṇo kăr = *l.* make less.
3. ăskăt kăr = *l.* make weak; bòḷ mōḍ(ô) = break the force.

Exterior, *a.* 1. bhāilo.
2. sămănd nātullo = *l.* not having connexion.

Exterminate, *v.* kāḍn ghāl = *l.* drawing put; nāš kăr, vibāḍ kăr = *l.* make ruin.

Extermination, *s.* nāš, -šā, *n.*; vibāḍ, -ḍā, *m.*

External, *a. see* **Exterior.**

Extinct, *a.* săruḷlo *or* mòrn pāullo.

Extinction, *s.* 1. nāš, -šā, *n.* bhăsm, -mā, *m.*; vibāḍ, -ḍā, *m.*
2. ănt, -tā, *m.* = *l.* end, *e. g.* of a family.

Extinguish, *v.* pālvoi, *c. v. of* pālva (a candle, anger, *etc.*)

Extinguisher, *s.* pālvounčeñ kuṭ-ṭeñ, -ṭeā, *n.*

Extirpate, *v.* kāḍ; kāḍn ghāl; humboḷ = root out, *pr. and fg.*

Extort, Extract, *v.* kāḍ.

Extortion, *s.* zulum, -lme, *f.*

Extra, *s.* 1. kusri, -ri, *f.* = *l.* supplement, addition, *e.g.* what is given over and above in selling.
2. višes = *l.* special.

Extract, *s.* 1. sār, -rā, *m.*, *e.g.* e. of fruits.
2. sănkšep, -pā, *n.* = abridgment.

Extraction, *s.* kuṭām, -ṭmā, *n.*; răgat, -gtā, *n.*

Extra-judicial, *a.* sărkārazāinā-tullo.

Extraneous, *a.* 1. părgāvāntso *or* părgāuntso = of a foreign country; bhāilo = *l.* from outside; părki = foreign.
2. sămănd nātullo = not having connexion.

Extraordinarily, *ad.* ăprup; ăsā-dhārn zāun.

Extraordinary, *a.* ăprup = rare; ăsādhārn.

Extravagance, *s.* 1. ăkrăm, -mā, *n.* = *l.* irregularity; vid, -di, *f.*
2. pisepoṇ, -ṇā, *n.* = *l.* foolishness; girigiri = madness in a small degree; tārifeči văstu, -tu, *f.*

Extravagant, *a.* 1. pisoso; vid lāgullo; ăkrămātso = irregular.
2. fontăjigār = fantastic; tārifetso = awkward.

Extreme, *a.* ākritso = being at the extremity; nimāṇo = last; bhou tsăḍ; ăsādhārn.

Extremity, *s.* 1. mit, -ti, *f.*; *bet.* mitmer, -re, *f.*
2. ākêr, -kri, *f.*
3. tudi, -ye, *f.* = top.
4. pālouñ, -lvā, *m.* (of a dress).
E. of suffering = tsăḍāvot kăšṭ.

Extricate, *v.* 1. sóḍăi, *e. g.* from debt.
2. săma kăr = *l.* make right; kāḍ = draw.
Extricate out of difficulties = tsukon ghe *or* păriyār zā.

Extrinsic, *see* **Exterior.**

Exuberance, *s.* sămpurnāi, -ye, *f.*

Exuberant, *a.* bhorn, *or* puskăḷ.

Exude, *v.* dike, *from* dik, -kā, *m.* = juice, exudation.

Exult, *v.* (āuñ) ănănd pāutāñ = *l.* (I) arrive to exultation; săntos bhóg = feel joy.

Exultation, *s.* ănănd, -dā, *m.*; ulās, -sā, *m.*; sukh, -khā, *n.* = happiness.

Eye, *s.* doḷo, -ḷeā, *m.*

Eye-brow, *s.* āsḍi, -ḍe, *f.*

Eye-glass, *s.* voklụ, -klā, *n.*, *fr.*; diṣṭičākrụ,-rā,*n.* (*H. K.*); *see* **Spectacles.**

Eyelid, *s.* doḷeāčeñ dāmpṇeñ, -ṇeā, *n.*; pāpḍeñ, -ḍeā, *n.*

Eye-witness, *s.* poḷāillo sākṣigār, -rā, *m.*

F

Fable, *s.* 1. kāṇi, -ye, *f.*
2. vopār, -re, *f.* = a parable.

Fabric, *s.* 1. bāndāp, -dpā, *n.* = *l.* an edifice; kārkhāno, -neā, *m.* = *l.* an establishment.
2. lugāṭ, -gṭā, *n.*; văstur, -rā, *n.* = *l.* cloth (manufactured).

Fabrication, *s.* fóṭ, -ṭi, *f.*; kălpana, -ne, *f.*, *n. c.*

Fabulous, *a.* *neg. of* khăro = true; kălpanetso; fóṭkiro = *l.* false; fóṭ (*in composition*); kāṇiyetso, *or bet. rs.* kāṇiye bări.

Face, *s.* muk, -kā, *n.*; mukambòḷ, -ḷā, *n.*, *rarer than* muk; rūp, -pā, *n.* = *l.* figure, features, countenance; tònḍ, -ḍā, *n.*
In the face = mukār. Face to face = mukār, *or* rubrub. To mukār poḷeitā = he looks you in the face, *Lat. facie ad faciem.*

Face, *v.* 1. mukār rāu = *l.* remain in face; mukār vots = go in face of, *e.g.* f. dangers, death.
2. *fg.* poḷe, *e.g.* the window faces the street, *n. c.*; *G.* isileān āsā.

Facetious, *a.* česṭāyetso; česṭāi kărtso; năklañ kărtso = *l.* making copy, *fg.* mocking.

Facetiousness, *s.* česṭāi, -ye, *f.*; tomāso, -seā, *m.*; bārikāi, -ye, *f.* = *l.* wit.

Facilitate, *v.* 1. sompo kăr.
2. haḷu kăr = *l.* make light; uṇo kăr = *l.* make less.

Facility, *s.* 1. sompepoṇ, -ṇā, *n.*; săsārāi, -ye, *f.*
2. săndrāp, -pā, *n.* = *l.* an opportunity.

Fac-simile, *s.* năkăl, -klā, *n.*

Fact, *s.* 1. kāryeñ, -yeā, *n.*
2. văstụ, -tu, *f.* = *l.* thing.
3. kărni, -ne, *f.* = *l.* action; kărtuveñ, -veā, *n.* = *l.* action.
4. găḍāp, -ḍpā, *n.* = *l.* event.
In fact = khărents, *emphatic of* khăreñ = true; *or* nīz zāun, *or* ălbăt.

Faction, *s.* 1. kuṭ, -ṭā, *n.* = plot.
2. tănḍ, -ḍā, *n.* = party.

Factious, *a.* kuṭātso; tăndḍātso tănṭălmāri = *l.* turbulent.

Factitious *a.* čămătkārātso; *or bet.* hikmătitso = *l.* artificial, produced by art; kăpăṭi.

Factor, *s.* dălāl, -lā, *m.* = agent; bădli, -leā, *m.* = *l.* acting for; kārbāri, -reā, *m.*

Factory, *s.* kārkhāno, -neā, *m.*

Faculty, *s.* 1. podvi, -ve, *f.* = power.
2. săkăt, -kti, *f.*, *e.g.* a faculty of the soul.
3. sāmārthi, -the, *f.* = ability; *see* **Ability.**
4. vidya, -ye, *f.*, *or* šāstru, -rā, *n.*, *e.g.* theological f.

Fade, *v.* suk (*not to be confounded with* sukh); bāu.

Fag, *v.* kăšṭa, *c. v.* kăšṭāi; kăšṭān vāur kăr; minătin vāur".

Fagot, *s.* mouḷi, -ḷe, *f.* = a small bundle of firewood; bhoro, -reā, *m.* (a large one); *dim.* bhorkuṭi, -ṭe, *f.*

Fail, *v.* 1. tsuk; bepārvo kăr = neglect, *G. M.*
2. khăḷ = neglect, *e. g.* sāḷ khăḷḷi; uṇo āsā = is less, *e.g.* he failed in going to church, *or also* the light failed me.
3. foṭāi.
4. divāḷi kāḍ = make bankrupt.
5. sóḍ = leave.
6. *neg. of* jik, *e.g.* părikša jikunk nāñ; pāḍ zā, *used for* failing in a law-suit.

Fail (Without), *s.* tsukanāstanāñ.

Failure, *s.* 1. tsuk, -ki, *f.* = *l.* error.
2. *often by* nāñ *prefixed, e. g.* f. in strength = nāñ bolāiki.
3. gunyāuñ, -āvā, *m.*

Fain, *ad.* I would f. die = morān zāleār boreñ.

Faint, *a.* puro zāllo = *l.* tired; bāuntso = languishing; ăskăt = weak, *used also fg., e.g.* f. remembrance; illots (illits, illents) = only a little.

Faint, *v.* 1. puro zā = *l.* get enough.
2. vāṭer pòḍ = fall on the way.
3. jint măr = swoon.

Faintness, *s.* 1. guvoḷ, -ḷi, (*or* guuḷi), *f.*
2. ăskătkāi, -ye, *f.* = weakness.
3. *rs.* mót tsuktā = *l.* mind is not.

Fair, *a.* 1. sobit, sundor; unči; goro (*said of* Europeans *as opposed to* natives); părzăḷik = shining; nităḷ = pure; kupaññātullo = unclouded.
2. guṇātso = favourable; *or* lāyek, *e.g.* a fair wind.
3. nitivont = just.
4. sumār = moderate, *or* sumārātso.
5. boro = good.

Fair, *s.* sānt, -ti, *f.*; jātro, -reā, *m.* = *l.* a Hindu feast.

Fairness, *s.* 1. sobitāi, -ye, *f.*; sobāi, -ye, *f.*; sundărāi, -ye, *f.*
2. nīt, -ti, *f.*

Faith, *s.* 1. bāvāḍt, -tā, *m* (divine faith).
2. nămgăṇeñ, -ṇeā, *n.*, *or* nămgăṇi, -ṇe, *f.* (human faith).
3. dilleñ utar, -trā, *n.*=*l.* given word.
4. pātiyeṇi, -ṇi, *f.* = *l.* confidence, faithfulness.
5. šāstrụ, -rā, *n.* = religion.
In faith = khărents; bāvāḍtiñ *or* bāvāḍtān.

Faithful, *a.* 1. bāvāḍti (he who believes in God).
2. pātiyeṇitso = trustful.

Faithfulness, *s.* nămgăṇi, -ṇe, *f.*; pātiyeṇi, -ṇe, *f.*

Fakeer, *s.* făkir, -rā, *m.* (a Mussulman mendicant).

Falcon, *s.* păkkisaḷo, -ḷeā, *m.*; giḍgo, -geā, *m.*

Fall, *v.* 1. pōḍ (ò), *used also for* be slain, decrease, decline from a state; seuṭā.
2. deuñ = *l.* descend, *pr. and fg.*, *e.g.* the price, the wind falls.
3. vibāḍ zā = get destroyed.
F. asunder = mòḍ(ó) = break.
F. at a man's feet = *G.* pāyāñ pōḍ(ò).
F. away = 1. săr; sóḍ.
2. bārik zā = *l.* get lean; bhāg.
F. back = pāṭi ye, *or* portun ye = come back.
F. foul of = 1. ādăḷ = dash.
2. gāḷi sāng.
F. headlong = vompto pòḍ.
F. into = vāu = flow.
F. in with = mèḷ = *l.* be found, meet; săma pòḍ = agree.
F. off = 1. nisăr = slip.
2. pāḍ zā.
3. pòḍ, *e.g.* f. from a high state.
F. on = āngăr pòḍ = *l.* fall on life, attack; tārker pòḍtā = falls on the day; pòḍ = *l.* fall, *e.g.* evils f. upon bad men; *Or.* visyānt āileñ (*or* pòḍleñ) = *l.* came about, *e.g.* the conversation; mākā āilāñ *or* poḍlāñ (dāiz) = *l.* there fell (an inheritance) to me.
F. out = 1. zā, *or* găḍ = *l.* happen.
2. zăgăḍ = *l.* quarrel.
F. short = tsuk; uṇo zā.
F. sick = piḍent pòḍ.
F. under = *Or.* khāl pòḍ, *or* khāl zā.
F. among robbers = tsorāñ bităr pòḍ.

Fall, *s.* 1. pòḍāp, -ḍpā, *n.*; deuṇi, -ṇe, *f.*, *or* devāp, deupā, *n.*, *also for* a f. in the revenue.
2. vibāḍ, -ḍā, *m.* = ruin.

Fallacious, *a.* fóṭkiro; dăgeātso; mosātso.

Fallacy, *s.* mōs, -sā, *m.*; dăgo, -geā, *m.*

Fallibility, *s.* tsukasārkeñ, -keā, *n.*

Fallible, *a.* tsukon poḍāyet āsụllo, *or* tsukon poḍtso, *or* tsukasārko.

Falling, *a.* pòḍtso. 'F. sickness = morlugi piḍa, -ḍe, *f.*'

Falling off, *s.* kāṭkāi, -ye, *f.* = revolution.

Fallow, *a.* bănjer; bănjer zāgo, -geā, *m.* = f. ground; pădil z.

False, *a.* 1. fāls, *or* phāls, *fr.*; sătaviṇ = not true.
2. *neg.* *of* khăro, *or of* nīz; fóṭkiro = *l.* deceiving, *e. g.* f. gods, coin; loṭik, *e. g.* f. witness, *ol.*

Falsehood, *s.* fóṭ, -ṭi, *f.*

Falsify, *v.* 1. bădăl kăr, *or bet.* borsi = *l.* mix.
2. fóṭkiro kăr = make false.
F. a document = fóṭkireñ dăstevoz borăi.
F. money = fóṭkiro duḍu kăr.

Falter, *v.* gāge; rāun rāun ulăi = *l.* speak stopping stopping; kāmpon ulăi = *l.* speak trembling.

Fame, *s.* 1. kobro = *l.* news, *pl. f. from* kobăr.
2. ănănd, -dā, *m.* = glory; boreñ nāuñ, -āvā, *n.* = *l.* good name; mān, -nā, *m.* = honour; kīrt, -ti, *f.*

Familiar, *a.* 1. iṣṭ, -ṭā, *m.* = *l.* friend; *rs.* sălgi kăr.
2. *rs.* voḷok āsā, *ch. cs.* = *l.* is acquaintance.
Grow f.: sovói zā = custom get, *ch. cs.*
Be on f. terms with = *Cm.* sălgi āsā.

Familiarity, *s.* 1. sălgi, -ge, *f.*
2. săḷāvoḷ, -ḷi, *f.*

Family, *s.* 1. gărčiñ = *Lat. domestici.*
2. kuṭām, -ṭmā, *n.*
3. gărāṇeñ, -ṇeā, *n.*, *e. g.* the family of the Bourbons.
4. răgat, -gtā, *n.* = blood.

Family-name, *s.* ālkugn, -gnā, *n.*, *fr.*; kuṭmāčeñ nāuñ, -āvā, *n.*

Famine, *s.* dukoḷ, -ḷā, *m.*; bărgāl, -lā, *n.*

Famous, *a.* nāvāḍgo *or* nāvāḍullo *or* nāvāḍdik; kīrt pāullo = *l.* arrived fame.

Fan, *s.* āiṇo, -ṇeā, *m.*

Fanatic, *s.*, *a.* utsāmboḷist, -tā, *m.* = *l.* an excited man; pisoso *or* vid lāguḷlo, *n. c.*; *vlg.* săvăi budivont, -tā, *m.* = *l.* 1¼ wise; fontăsigār, -rā, *m.* = a fantast, *fr.*

Fanaticism, *s.* utsāmboḷāi, -ye, *f.*; pisepoṇ, -ṇā, *n.* = foolishness; tsăḍāvot urba, -be, *f.*

Fanciful, *a.* fontăzitso; sopṇetso; kălpănetso (mănis, -nšā, *m.*).

Fancy, *s.* 1. kălpăna, -ne, *f.* = *l.* fiction.
2. girigiri, *mn.* half-foolishness, *fg.*; pisepoṇ, -ṇā, *n.* = *l.* foolishness, *fg.*
3. mărji, -je, *f.* = caprice.

Fancy, *v.* kălpana kăr, *n. c.*; *vlg.* čint.

Fantastic, *s.* fontăzigār, -rā, *m.*

Fantastic, *a.* kălpanetso.

Far, *ad.* pois.
As far as = păriyănt, *nom.*
As far as I can = măkā tāṇktā

titleñ, *or* mākā tānktā tăseñ; moje tānki părmāṇe.
Far the most diligent = sărivin ušār.
So far, thus far = titleñ.
How far = kitleñ.

Fare, *s.* 1. khāṇ, -ṇā, *n.* = food.
2. mòl, -lā, *n.* = *l.* price.

Farewell, *s.* Dēu boreñ kăruñ = God make good; sukhu zāuñ = *l.* be happiness.

Farm, *s.* itāl, -tlā, *n.*; zămin, -ne, *f.*; āst, -ti, *or* āsti, -te, *f.* = property; gādo, -deā, *m.* = a field.

Farm, *v.* 1. besāi kăr.
2. bāḍeāk kāṇghe = hire (*l.* take to hire).
3. bāḍeāk di = *l.* give to hire.

Farmer, *s.* 1. vokāl, -klā, *m.*
2. buinkăr, -rā, *m.* = cultivator; sāgoḷigār, -rā, *m.* = cultivator.

Farther, *ad.* mukār; *a.* mukāvelo.

Farthing, *s.* 1. farding, -gā, *n.*, *fr.*
2. tār, -re, *f.* = two pies, *if the £ = exactly* 10 *Rs.*

Fascinate, *v.* bolmeñ sāng = *l.* say incantation; ghāḍi kăr; bhul ghāl.

Fascination, *s.* 1. bhul, -li, *f.*; ghāḍi, -ḍi, *f.*; bolmeñ, -meā, *n.*; tăntru, -rā, *n.*; măntru, -rā, *n.*
2. *fg.* voḍni, -ne, *f.*; pisepoṇ, -ṇā, *n.*; fuslāuṇeñ, -ṇeā, *n.*

Fascine, *s.* mouḷi, -ḷe, *f.*; *see* **Fagot.**

Fashion, *s.* rivāz, -ji, *f.*; mādri, -ri, *f.*, *n. c.*; sovói, -ye, *f.* = habit; dăstur, -re, *f.*; 'go out of f. = ātāñ rivāz nāñ'.

Fashion, *v.* kăr; rūp di.

Fast, *a.* 1. ghăṭ = strong; ărnun.
2. thir = firm.
Make fast = 1. ghăṭ kăr = make strong.
2. bānd = bind.
3. bīg ghāl = put a lock.
4. dāmp = shut.

Fast, *ad.* ghăṭ *or* ghăṭ zāun; *or* thir zāun.

Fast, *v.* jinzvār kăr, (*or* -dhăr), *fr.*; *see* **Abstinence;** upās rāu = *l.* remain abstaining.

Fast, *s.* jinzvār, -rā, *m.*, *fr.*; upās, -sā, *m.*
Break a f. = upās mōḍ(ó).
Declare a f. = upās formāi.

Fasten, *v.* 1. ghăṭ kăr.
2. meḷăi = *l.* annex; bānd = *l.* tie; sirkāi (f. with hooks); (butāuñ) ghāl, *fr.*, (gubbi) ghāl = *l.* put a button.

Fastening, *s.* 1. bāndāp, -dpā, *n.*; bāndni, -ne, *f.*, *n. c.*
2. bāndpās, -sā, *m.*, *e. g.* for shoes; sutli, -le, *f.*; fint, -tā, *n.*; dori, -ye, *f.* = a rope.

Fastidious, *a.* 1. bezārāyetso; dostso; bezāri; kărkărātso.
2. nāzuk = delicate, never content.

Fastidiousness, *s.* 1. bezārāi, -ye, *f.*

2. kărkăr, -rā, *m.*, *used more frequently in the plural.*
3. nāzukāi, -ye, *f.*

Fasting, *s.* upās, -sā, *m.*; *see* **Fast.**

Fasting, *a.* 1. khāṇnātụllo=without food; upāsi; jeunk khāunk nātụllo = not having to eat.
2. *rs.* khāināstanāñ rāu.

Fat, *s.* vòs, -se, *f.*; tsărāb, -rbe, *f.*

Fat, *a.* 1. moṭo; 'very fat=moṭṭo'; puṣṭi.
2. iṭātso (f. soil).

Fatal, *a.* 1. grātstsărātso.
2. risketso; jīvkāḍtso; ădruṣṭātso.
3. bhou luksānātso = *l.* very hurtful.

Fatalism, Fate, *s.* 1. grātstsār, -rā, *m.*; ădruṣṭ, -ṭā, *n.*
2. ākānt, -tā, *m.* = *l.* difficulty; *see* **Calamity.**

Father, *a.* bāpui, -pāi, *m.*; Bāp, -pā, *m. used for the* First Person of the B. Trinity; pāi, pāi, *m. used only partially;* bāb, -bā, *m.*, ān, -nā, *m. used chiefly as the term of address;* pādri, -ri, *m.* = *l.* a priest.

Father of the church = igărz mātetso bāp.

Father-in-law, *s.* māuñ, -āvā, *m.*

Fathom, *v.* gunḍāi mēz(é)=sound the depth.

Fathom, *s.* 1. vāuñ, vāvā, *n.* (*Lat. ulna* = 6 ft. *about*).
2. gunḍāi, -ye, *f.*; thăḷ, -ḷā, *n.* = bottom, depth.

Fathomless, *s.* thăḷ mèḷānātụllo.

Fatigue, *s.* minăt, -ti, *f.*; tsăḍ kām, -mā, *n.* = *l.* much work; kăṣṭ, -ṭā, *m.* (*in pl.*).

Fatigue, *v.* 1. puro kăr = make tired, *pr.*; dăṇvăi, *c. v.*, *n. c.*
2. puro zā = get tired.

Fatigued, *a.* 1. puro zāllo; dăṇvallo.
2. bāullo = languishing.

Fatness, *s.* 1. moṭāi, -ye, *f.*
2. iṭ, -ṭā, *m.* (*or* iṭāi, -ye, *f.*) = f. of soil, *l.* manure, *fg.*

Fatten, *v.* moṭāi, *c. v.*, *n. c.*; *bet.* moṭo kăr.

Fatuity, *s.* pisepoṇ, -ṇā, *n.*; *see* **Folly.**

Fault, *s.* tsuk, -ki, *f.*; gunyāuñ, -āvā, *m.*; ăprād, -dā, *m.*; pātak, -tkā, *n.*; ăib, -bā, *n.* (physical f., flaw); ūṇ, -ṇā, *n.*, *or* uṇepoṇ, -ṇā, *n.*

Faultless, *a.* gunyāvaviṇe, *or* gunyāuñ nātụllo.

Faulty, *a.* tsuk; săma nātụllo.

Favour, *s.* 1. dosti, -te, *f.*, *e.g* he enjoys the f. of the king = rājāče dostent āsā.
2. upkār, -rā, *m.* = a benefit.
3. mōg, -gā, *m.* = love; *or rs. into* mogāḷ.
4. ādhār, -rā, *m.* = help.
5. dăya, -ye, *f.* = *l.* clemency.

In favour of = khātir, *or* vināt, *or* pāsun (*Postp.*).

Restore to f. = *rs.* portun dost

zā *or* ādli dosti mèḷ. Enter into the f. of = dostint rig. Lose the f. of = nākhušent pòḍ.

Favour, *v.* upkār kăr = make favour; dăya kăr = please! (*usually*, dăya kărn); guṇātso zā = become favorable; kumok di.

Favourable, *a.* 1. guṇātso = propitious, *e.g.* f. answer.
2. ādāyātso = advantageous; upkārātso = beneficial.
3. lāyek = fit, suitable, *e.g.* f. wind.
4. dăyāḷ = clement, kind; dostitso.

Favourite, *s.* dóst, -stā, *m.*, *e.g.* f. of the king.

Favourite, *a.* mogāḷ.

Fawn, *v.* fuslāi = flatter; pāṭleān vots = *l.* go behind, show affection.

Fear, *s.* bheñ, bhiyā, *n.*; bhirānt, -ti, *f.*: 'fear of God = Devāči bhirānt'; *see* **Dread, Alarm.**

Fear, *v.* bhiye; bheñ distā.

Fearful, *a.* 1. bhiyātso; phukkela (very much afraid); bizuḍ = timid, shy.
2. bhiyānkuḷ (causing fear); bhăyănkăr, *n. c.*

Fearfulness, *s.* bheñ, bhiyā, *n.*; bhiyāčeñ mòn, -nā, *n.*

Fearless, *a.* bheññātullo.

Fearlessness, *s.* dhăir, -rā, *n.* = courage.

Feast, *s.* fèst, -tā, *n. fr.*; părāb, -rbe, *f.*; sónt, -tā, *m.* = saint's day, not a mere Sunday. I wish you a happy feast = boreñ fèst māgtāñ.

Feather, *s.* pāk, -kā, *n.*

Feathered, *a.* pākañ āsullo; *or* pākañ fuṭullo.

Feature, *s.* 1. rūp, -pā, *n.*; *bet.* tonḍāčeñ rūp; tònḍ, -ḍā, *n.*
2. guṇ, -ṇā, *m.* = character; năḍteñ, -teā, *n.*; *see* **Dress.**

Feculence, *s.* čikol, -klā, *m.*; măḍḍi, -ḍe, *f.* = sediment; bursepoṇ, -ṇā, *n.*

Feculent, *a.* čiklātso; burso.

Federal, *a.* solleātso.

Fee, *s.* 1. sāmbāḷ, -ḷā, *m.* = payment; kūl, -li, *f.* = wages.
2. tergi, -ge, *f.* = *l.* a tax.

Feeble, *a.* 1. ăskăt; bòḷnātullo = *l.* not having strength; bolāikinātullo = unhealthy.
2. phăḍposi = faint, languid, *e.g.* f. impression.
3. kāḷso = darkish.

Feebleness, *s.* ăskătkāi, -ye, *f.*; nāboläiki, -ke, *f.* = *l.* unhealthiness.

Feed, *v.* 1. *tr.* pós (*c. v.* posăi); khāunk di = *l.* give to eat.
2. khā = eat, *c. v.* khāvoi.
3. jeu = eat (take a meal); seu = eat (delicacies).
4. tsărăi, *c. v. of* tsăr = graze.
5. *fg.* udāk di, *e.g.* rivers feed the sea.

Feel, *v.* 1. bhóg.
2. āpoḍ = touch.

3. hāt ghāl = *l.* put the hand; *or* hāt lāi.
4. sós = *l.* suffer.

F. glad = săntos bhóg. F. sorry = dukhụ distā. This table feels smooth = yeñ mèz telteñ lāgtā. He felt it deeply = boreñ lāglāñ *or* boreñ riglāñ.

Feeler (of an insect), *s.* mišio, *pl. f.* = *l.* mustaches, *fg.* (*sing.* miši, -še).

Feeling, *s.* 1. bogt, -ti, *or* bogti, -ti, *f.*, *e.g.* f. of humility; bhogāp, -gpā, *n.*; *or* bogtipoṇ, -ṇā *n.*; voḍni, -ne, *f.* = *l.* inclination; mănšapoṇ (*or* mănšepoṇ), -ṇā, *n.* = tender heart, civility, politeness.
2. āločen, -ni, *f.* = an opinion.

Feign, *v.* 1. kăpăṭ kăr = *l.* make simulation, *e. g.* f. friendship.
2. dākăi, *with* fóṭkiro *added to* what is feigned; *Or.* bări kăr = do as.

F. tears = fóṭkiriñ dukañ gāḷāi.'

Feigning, Feint, *s.* kăpăṭ, -ṭā, *n.*

Felicitation, *s.* pŏrāb, -rbe, *f.* 'P. ditāñ = I offer (my) felicitations'.

Fell, *v.* 1. kātrun ghāl; porti, *or* portun ghāl, *e.g.* a tree.
2. kāḍnụ ghāl.

Fell, *s.* 1. porvót, -tā, *m.* = high land.
2. kāt, -ti, *f.* = skin.

Fellow, *s.* 1. săngāti, -tiā, *m.*; išṭ, -ṭā, *m.* = friend; sāndo, -deā, *m.* = *l.* member, *e. g.* of a university.
2. mănis, -nšā, *m.* = *l.* a man.
3. lutstso, -uččea, *m.* = (a bad f., a rascal).

Fellow-citizen, *s.* (āpleā) gāuntso = of (one's own) country; *or* (āpleā) šerāntlo = of (one's own) town; săngātirăit, -tā, *m.*

N.B. In the same way, all other words, not put down here, compounded with fellow, *may be translated.*

Fellow-prisoner, *s.* săngātibāndivān, -nā, *m.*

Fellow-soldier, *s.* săngātisipāi, -yā, *m.*

Fellowship, *s.* 1. săngāt, -tā, *m.* = company; yekoṭ, -ṭā, *m.* = community, union.
2. išṭagăt, -ti, *f.* = friendship.
3. *fg.* sămănd, -dā, *m.* = connexion.
4. of a university, *rs.* 'Got a f. = sāndo zālo, *or* meḷāilo'.

Felt, *s.* burnās, -sā, *m.*; *comm.* = good for nothing, *but in Mr. it mn.* felt.

Female, *s.* bāil, -le, *f.*; bāili văstụ, -tu, *f.* = a female being; bāilmănis, -nše, *f.*; čeḍuñ, -ḍvā, *n.* = *l.* girl, *as opposed to* boy.

Female, *a.* bāilo *or* bāili *according as the word to which* *it is joined is* masc. *or* fem.; *see* Gram. p. 47.

Feminine (gender), *a.* bāilo; bāilāntso.

Fence, *s.* voi, -i, *f.*; beli, -li, *f.*, *n. c.*; veḍo, -ḍeā, *m.* = surrounding.

Fence, *v.* voi ghāl = *l.* put a fence, *or* voi bānd = *l.* bind a fence.

Fennel, *s.* bădišep, -pi, *f.*

Ferment, *s.* 1. fug, -gi, *f.*
2. *fg.* umāḷo, -ḷeā, *m.* = *l.* boiling; utsāmboḷāi, -ye, *f.*

Ferment, *v. fg.* sizăi, *c. v. of* siz.

Fermentation, *s.* fug, -gi, *f.*

Ferocious, *a.* 1. niṣṭur; mhāru.
2. khoṭeponātso.

Ferocity, *s.* 1. niṣṭurāi, -ye, *f.* = cruelty; mhārupoṇ, -ṇā, *n.*
2. khoṭepoṇ, -ṇā, *n.*

Ferret, *v.* bhāir kāḍ.

Ferruginous, *a.* lonkḍātsoso.

Ferrule, *s.* 1. kăṭ, -ṭā, *m.* (a metal ring fastened to the end of a common stick).
2. āṇăs, -ṇsi, *f.* = an iron ring fastened to the end of a pestle.

Ferry, *s.* kăḍou, -ḍvā, *m.* (the part of a river over which passengers are carried).

Ferry-boat, *s.* kăḍvăči doṇ, -ṇi, *f.*

Ferry-man, *s.* doṇigār (*or* doṇkār), -rā, *m.* = a boatman; kăḍvāgār, -rā, *m.* = the owner of the boat.

Fertile, *a.* fòḷ diuntso = *l.* giving fruit; *or* fòḷādik; fòḷābărit; iṭāl *or* iṭātso.

Fertility, *s.* iṭ, -ṭā, *m.* = *l.* manure, *used freq. fg. for* f.; săr, -rā, *m.*; foḷābăritpoṇ, -ṇā, *n.*; *vlg.* bhărtigāi, -ye, *f.*; *vlg. rs. crc.*

Fervent, *a. pr. & fg.* suḍsuḍāyetso = *l.* active; urbevont = zealous; umāḷeātso.

Fervently, *ad.* suḍsuḍāyen; āšen; umāḷeān.

Fervour, *s.* 1. umāḷo, -ḷeā, *m.*, *pr. and fg.*
2. suḍsuḍāi, -ye, *f.* = *l.* activity.
3. āšā, -še, *f.* = *l.* desire.

Festival, *s.* 1. răja, -je, *f.* = *l.* leave.
2. săḷ nātullo dis, -sā, *m.* = *l.* the day on which there is no school; fèst, -tā, *n.*, *fr.*; părāb, -rbe, *f.*; sónt, -tā, *m.*

Festive, *a.* 1. festātso.
2. ănăndātso = *l.* of joy.

Festivity, *see* **Feast.**

Festoon, *s.* fulāñ, *pl. n.*; ărk, -kā, *n.* = arch (of flowers), *fr.*; gòmpru, -rā, *n.*; tòrn, -nā, *n.*

Fetch, *v.* āpoun hāḍ, *or only* hāḍ = *l.* bring, *or* vor. [kāḍ.
Fetch a sigh = uskār sóḍ *or* u.

Fetid, *a.* 1. ghāṇiero.
2. *fg.* vonkāreātso = *l.* causing vomiting.

Fetter, *s.* 1. sānkḷi, *pl. f. from* sānkăḷ.
2. băndi, -i, *f.* = *Lat. vincula,* prison.

Fetter, *v.* 1. băndint ghāl = *l.* put in fetters.
2. *fg.* āḍāi = *l.* prevent.

Fetus, *s.* 1. gărb, -bā, *m.*
2. pilo, -leā, *m.* = *strictly,* embryo.

Feud, *s.* zăgḍeñ, -ḍeā, *n.*; nāi, -yā, *m.* = discord.

Fever, *s.* tāp, -pā, *m.*; zór, -rā, *m.*
'He has fever = tākā tāp yetā = *l.* fever comes to him; *or* āng un zātā = *l.* life gets warm, (is slightly feverish). 'Get free from fever = tāp sóḍ (mākā), *or* (mozo) tāp suṭ.

Feverish, *a.* tāpātsoso.

Few, *a.* thoḍe, *pl. from* thoḍo = a little; 'a few more = aniki thoḍe'.

Fibre, *s.* 1. kāto, -teā, *m.* (cocoanut f.).
2. nār, -rā, *m.* (f. *in general*).

Fickle, *a.* thirnātullo; ăthir; bădăltso.

Fickleness, *s.* ăthirpoṇ, -ṇā, *n.*

Fiction, *s.* 1. fālsapoṇ, -ṇā, *n.*; *see* **Feign.**
2. kăpăṭ, -ṭā, *n.* = simulation.
3. kălpana, -ne, *f.* = imagination; kāṇi, -ye, *f.* = *l.* fable, story.

Fictitious, *a.* kălpanetso = fantastic; kāṇiyetso.

Fiddle, *s.* rebek, -kā, *n.*; sarăng, -gā, *n.* (*H. K.*)

Fiddle-string, *s.* kordāuñ, -dāvā, *m.*, *fr.*; *bet.* dori, -ye, *f.*

Fidelity, *s.* pātiyeṇi, -ṇi, *f.*; nămgăṇi, -ṇi, *f.*

Fiduciary, *s.* (ămānăt) dovórtolo; tābedār, -rā, *m.*

Fie, *int.* čhi; *or* čhā.

Field, *s.* 1. gādo, -deā, *m.*
2. zāgo, -geā, *m.* = a place, ground.
3. kāmp, -pā, *n.*, *fr.*; *bet.* măidān, -nā, *n.*
4. lăččil, -lā, *n.* = a meadow.
5. tsorovātso zāgo, -geā, *m.* = pasture.
Wet f. = băil gādo. Dry f. = beṭgādo.

Field-marshal, *s.* mukhya ădhipăti, -ti, *m.* = *l.* chief commander.

Fiend, *s.* bhut, -tā, *m.* = devil.

Fierce, *a.* 1. kănṭin; niṣṭur; mhāru.
2. bhou rāgiṣṭ; rānvoṭ = wild.

Fierceness, *s.* 1. kănṭinăi, -ye, *f.*; niṣṭurāi, -ye, *f.*; mhārupoṇ, -ṇā, *n.*
2. rānvoṭpoṇ, -ṇā, *n.* = wildness.

Fiery, *a.* ujeātso; utsāmboḷasārko *or* utsāmboḷ zāuntso; utsāmboḷ.

Fife, *s.* pirluk, -ke, *f.*

Fig, *s.* ānjur, -rā, *n.*; rumbāḍ, -bḍā, *n.* (country fig).

Fight, *v.* 1. lăḍāi kăr = *l.* make fighting.
2. zăgḍa.
3. zuz kăr; zuz.

Fighting, *s.* 1. zuz, -zā, *n.*
2. lăḍāi, -ye, *f.*

3. zăgḍeñ, -ḍeā, *n.*

Figure, *s.* 1. ākār, -rā, *m.*; rūp, -pā, *n.* (*also* a statue *or* picture on a wall *etc.*)
2. pintur, -rā, *n.* = picture, *fr.*; rupṇeñ, -ṇeā, *n.*; čitrụ, -trā, *n.*
3. sămăndi utăr, -trā, *n.* = connected expression (rhet. f.)

Figure, *v.* čint = think.

Figurative, *a.* sămăndi, *or* sămăndiărthātso.

Filch, *v.* guṭān tsór = steal secretly, *or only* tsór; nāgăi.

File, *s.* 1. hār, -ri, *f.*, of soldiers, of papers; kāmp, -pā, *n.*
2. păṭṭi, -ṭe, *f.* = a list.
3. kāṇăs, -ṇsi, *f.*=a carpenter's tool.
Hāri āsāt = there are lines; harin = in files; *see* Line.

File, *v.* 1. hārin ghāl.
2. kāṇsin ghās; kāṇăs ghāl.
3. *fg.* nităḷ kăr; suddụ kăr.

Filial, *a.* burgeā bări, *ch. cs.* = as a child; *or* burgeātso.

Filings, *s.* tsuro, -reā, *m.*; *or* puḍ, -ḍi, *f.*
N. B. Care should be taken to pronounce the ḍ *in* puḍ *distinctly palatal.*

Fill, *v.* 1. bhór, *pr. and fg.*, *e.g.* jails, pipes, camps. Fill with emotion, graces *etc.*
2. *Intr.* bhórn zā; bhór, *e. g.* the vessel fills with water.

Filled, *a.* 1. bhorụllo, *or* bhorlolo; bhórn.
2. dādos = *l.* satisfied.

Filter, *v.* gāḷ.

Filter, *s.* găḷčeñ āidān, -nā, *n.*, *or* gāḷni, -ne, *f.*

Filth, *s.* 1. koir, -rā, *m.*
2. mheḷāp (*or* mheḷóp), -ḷpā, *m.*; *or* mheḷepoṇ, -ṇā, *n.*, *pr. and fg.*; ăḷšikpoṇ, -ṇā, *n.*, *pr. and fg.*; čikol, -klā, *m.*; bursepoṇ, -ṇā, *n. pr. and fg.*

Filthy, *a.* mheḷo; ăḷšik; burso; čiklātso.

Fin, *s.* šempaṭo, -ṭeā, *m.*

Final, *a.* ākăir *or* ākritso; kăḍetso; nimāṇo = last.

Finally, *ad.* sekiñ; kăḍek *or* kăḍer.

Finance, *s.* 1. irsāl, -lā, *n.* (a remittance of money).
2. huṭṭavoḷ, -ḷi, *f.* (income).

Find, *v.* 1. mèḷ, *Dat. Prs.* = *l.* be found (to me).
2. sik = learn, *e.g.* I find from what you say; kăḷ = get known.
3. bhóg=enjoy, *e.g.* f. pleasure.
4. distā = *l.* appears, *e. g.* f. guilty = gunyāukār moṇ distā.
F. fault = durva.
F. by experience = ănbhóg.

Find out=sodun kăḍ=*l.* seeking take out.

Fine, *a.* 1. bārik = thin.
2. nāzuk=delicate, *e.g.* f. taste in drawing.
3. sobit = nice.

4. boro, *e.g.* fine flour, gold; *or* boreā jinsātso (*or* b. thărātso).
5. molādik = precious.
6. rūp āsullo = having form.
7. borsinātullo = not mixed.
8. suddụ = purified.
9. unči, *e.g.* f. cloth.

Fine, *s.* julmān, -nā, *m.*, *or* julmāno, -neā, *m.*; sikṣ̌a, -ṣ̌e, *f.* = punishment; dănḍ, -ḍā, *m.* = *Lat. mulcta.*

Fine, *v.* di *with one of the above substantives.*

Fineness, *s.* 1. bārikāi, -ye, *f.*
2. nāzukāi, -ye, *f.*

Finger, *s.* bòṭ, -ṭā, *n.*
The names of the five fingers are: *a*) ākanḍo = thumb; *b*) dākounčeñ bòṭ = forefinger; *c*) modleñ bòṭ = middle finger; *d*) mudiyečeñ bòṭ = ring-finger; *e*) kirokoḷičeñ bòṭ = little finger.

Finish, *v.* 1. *tr.* kābār kăr, *or* kābār zā, *n. v.*, *fr.*; phăḍča kăr; tirsi, *tr. v.*; tirsā, *n. v.*
2. mugdi, *c. v. of* mugda.
3. *n. v.* ăntăr = end.
4. thāmb = cease; mănna kăr.
5. zā (zāleñ = done) = *l.* get.

Finite, *a.* 1. *rs. by* ănt āsullo; găḍ āsullo.
2. khănḍit (certain, fixed).
3. mit āsullo = having limit.

Fire, *s.* 1. uzo, -jeā, *m.*, *also* a conflagration.
2. divo, -veā, *m.*=*l.* lamp, light.
3. fār, -rā, *m.* = a discharge of artillery.
4. *fg.* bòḷ, -ḷā, *n.*; *or also* uzo, -jeā, *m.*, *e. g.* rāgān uzo zātā.
5. suḍsuḍāi, -ye, *f.*
Of fire = ujeātso. Be on fire = lās. Set on fire = lāsāi *or* uzo lāi. Take f. = pèṭ *or* uzo lāgtā.

Fire-box, *s.* ujeāči pèṭ, -ṭe, *f.*

Fire-brand, *s.* kolit, -ltā, *n.*

Fire-engine, *s.* ujeāčākrụ, -rā, *n.*

Fire-fly, *s.* kāzulo, -leā, *m.*

Fire-lock, *s.* bănduk, -ke, *f.*

Fire-pan, *s.* 1. kāili, -le, *f.* (a pot-sherd).
2. kāil, -li, *f.* (of pot-stone).
3. tondor, -rā, *m.* (for cakes).

Firewood, *s.* lānkuḍ, -kḍā, *n.*

Fire-work, *s.* dursupoṇ (dursabāṇ), -ṇā, *n.*, *or* ākāšabāṇ, -ṇā, *n.*; čămātkārātso uzo, -jeā, *m.* = *l.* fire of artifice; *or* hikmătitso uzo; fugeteo, *f. pl.* = crackers; khăzneñ, *pl. of* khăzno, -neā, *m.* = a small sort of cannon.

Firm, *a.* 1. ghăṭ; hālnātụllo = not moving.
2. thir.
Be firm = thir zāun rāu.
Make firm = thir kăr, *or* bòḷ di, *or* ghăṭ kăr.

Firmament, *s.* moḷāb, -ḷbā, *n.*; ăntrăḷ, -ḷā, *n.*; ākās, -sā, *n.*

Firmly, *ad.* ghăṭ zāun; thir zāun.

I am f. convinced = āuñ thir āločen kărtāñ.

Firmness, *s.* 1. bòḷ, -ḷā, *n.* = *l.* force.

2. ghăṭāi, -ye, *f.* = *l.* strength.

3. thirāsāṇ, -ṇe, *f.* = *l.* constancy.

First, *a.* 1. poilo, in time, place, rank, *etc.*

2. mukhya = *l.* principal.

First, *ad.* 1. poile suāter = in the first place, first of all.

2. poilo.

3. ādiñ = before.

First-born, *a.* mālgoḍo *or* poilo zălmollo.

First-fruits, *s.* poiliñ fòḷañ.

Fiscal, *s.* sărkāri khăzāno, -neā, *m.*; rāyāčeñ băndār, -rā, *n.*

Fish, *s.* māsḷi, -ḷe, *f.* (*vlg.* māhaḷi).

Fish, *v.* 1. māsḷi dhăr; māsḷi pāg.

2. *fg.* sārkeñ vitsăr *or* sód = *l.* ask exactly *or* seek.

Fisherman, *s.* 1. khārvi, -viā, *m.* (a certain caste).

2. mogór, -grā, *m.* (a caste slightly different from khārvi).

3. (māsḷi) pāgtolo, -leā, *m.* (*gener. term*); găriyegār, -rā, *m.* = an angler.

4. māsḷegār, -rā, *m.* (fish-seller), *n. c.*

Fish-hook, *s.* gări, -ye, *f.*

Fishing, *s.* māsḷepāgāp, -gpā, *n.*

Fish-pond, *s.* kòḷ, -ḷā, *n.*

Fist, *s.* muṭ, -ṭi, *f.* *or* guddu, -dā, *m.* = a blow with the f.

G. mār = buffet.

Fit, *s.* jórụ, -rā, *m.*, *e.g.* a f. of anger; *used also for* a fit of sickness.

Fit, *a.* 1. lāyek.

2. *rs. into* zā = be fit, fit for, *Dat.*

3. zānṭo = wise; šăktivont = able; *rs. into potent. mood.*

Fit, *v.* 1. mānḍ = *l.* put in order, *e.g.* f. one with a hat.

2. ghāl = put; *or* săma ghāl = put right.

3. lāyek kăr = make fit.

4. tăyār kăr = make ready.

5. lăg = (fit together) *l.* be attached.

Fitness, *s.* lāyekpoṇ, -ṇā, *n.*

Five, *a.* pānts.

Fix, *v.* 1. lāi *or* lāgāi, *c. v. of* lāg.

2. ghăṭ kăr = make firm.

3. nemsi = appoint; mokruri kăr = make an appointment; niščeisi = resolve.

4. kărār kăr = make an agreement.

Fix in the memory = motint khăntsāi *or* boro ugḍās dovór.

Fixed, *a.* 1. nomiyārlolo; niščeisillo; sārko.

2. khănḍit.

3. rāuntso = *l.* remaining, *e.g.* f. stars.

Flabby, *a.* băutso; sădiḷ = *l.* loose.

Flag, *s.* bonder, -rā, *n.* = a banner, *fr.*; giāuñ, -āvā, *m.* = a blessed b., *fr.*; bāuṭo, -ṭeā, *m.* = a signal-flag.

Flag, *v.* bāu = languish, fade, *fg. used*; uṇo zā = get less, deuñ *or* pòḍ, *e.g.* the conversation flags.

Flagellate, *v.* (jerbāndāniñ) mār.

Flagellation, *s.* jerbāndanče mār.

Flaggy, *a.* bāgontso; bāutso; ăskăt.

Flagitious, Flagrant, *a.* khoṭo.

Flag-staff, *s.* bāutokaṭo, -ṭeā, *m.*

Flail, *s.* băitāḍ, -ḍā, *n.* (the native flail).

Flambeau, *s.* tsuḍ, -ḍi, *f.*, *or* diuṭi, -ṭe, *f.* = a torch.

Flame, *s.* ujeāčeñ kènḍ, -ḍā, *n.*; āgṭeñ, -ṭeā, *n.* (ujeāčeñ ā. = a great fire).

Flannel, *s.* flanel, -lā, *n.*, *vlg.*; lovečeñ lugāṭ, -gṭā, *n.* = woollen cloth.

Flap, *v.* (pākāṭe) phāpuḍ.

Flash, *s.* porzăḷ, (*or* părzăḷ), -ḷā, *m.*

Flash, *v.* porzăḷ.

Flask, *s.* kodrād, -dā, *m.* = a square bottle, *fr.*; siso, -seā, *m.*; *dim.* sisli, -le, *f.*; botlu̥, -li, *f.* = a bottle, *fr.*

Flat, *a.* 1. săma = even, *e. g.* s. zāgo.
2. čeṭṭo (*esp.* stones, nose).
3. telto = smooth.
4. vistārlolo = extended.
5. *fg.* rutsnātu̥llo = without taste, *e.g.* a flat joke; bārik năiñ āsullo, *e.g.* not witty; čappo = *l.* not salted, *fg.*
6. *fg. as in* to tell a flat lie, to give a flat denial, *by the emphatic* -ts.
7. bhou săkăilo = *l.* very low, *as* a voice, a sound.

Flat, *s.* 1. săma suvāt, -te, *f.*, *or s.* zāgo, -geā, *m.* = an even place; măidān, -nā, *n.*
2. māḷăi, ḷiye, *f.* = a story.
3. ărdo gurtu̥, -tā, *m.* = *l.* half a note.

Flatter, *v.* 1. hogoḷsun fòṭăi; fuslăi; pāṭleān bouñ = *l.* walk after, *fg.*
2. F. oneself = āšā dhăr = *l.* entertain hope.

Flatterer, *s.* fuslăitolo, *or bet.* fòṭkiro hogoḷsoṇegār, -rā, *m.*; *or* fuslăuṇeagār, -rā, *m.*

Flattery, *s.* foṭkireñ hogḷāp, -pā, *n.*; tònḍāčeñ hogḷāp, -pā, *n.*; fuslăuṇeñ, -ṇeā, *n.*

Flatulence, *s.* vāi, -ye, *f.*

Flaunt, *v.* 1. bouñ.
2. ub = *l.* fly, *fg.*

Flavour, *s.* suād, -dā, *m.*; ruts, -či, *f.*

Flaw, *s.* ăib, -bā, *n.* = a physical fault; tsuk, -ki, *f.* = *l.* a mistake.

Flawless, *a.* ăibnātullo.

Flax, *s.* nār, -rā, *m.* (*a generic term*); *perh.* sòṇ, -ṇā, *m.*

Flay, *v.* kāt vòḍ; tsāmbḍeñ vòḍ.

Flea, *s.* 1. čiru, -ue, *f.*

2. kirănṭ, -ṭi, *f.* (a bullock-flea).
3. hulku, -ke, *f. found esp. on dogs, cats and fowls*).

Fledged, *a.* pākañ fuṭullo.

Flee, *v.* 1. pòḷ = escape, *or* pòḷn vots; dāuñ = run.
2. tsukăi = avoid; sóḍ = leave.
3. (-ntlo) bhāir vetā, *or only* vetā = goes out; *fg.* năpăints zā = disappear.

Flee to = *Cm.* āsro kāṇe = *l.* take refuge.

Fleer, *s.* čeṣṭăi, -ye, *f.*; năkăl, -klā, *n.*; yeḍāuṇeñ, -ṇeā, *n.*

Fleet, *s.* tārvañ = *l.* ships.

Fleet, *a.* ăuñsări; vegintso = swift.

Flesh, *s.* 1. mās, -sā, *n.*
2. *fg.* kuḍ, -ḍi, *f.* = *l.* body.

Fleshy, *a.* māsāḷ.

Flexibility, *s.* bāgasārkeñ, -keā, *n.*, *pr. and fg.*; *or* bāgoṇeñ, -ṇeā, *n.*, *pr. and fg.*; sădiḷăi, -ye, *f.*, *pr. and fg.*

Flexible, *a.* bāgăiyet āsullo; *or* bāgontso; *or* bāgāsarko.

Flicker, *v.* 1. pākañ hāḷăi; ub, *with the quasi Dim.* -so; *see* Gram. P. III. ch. ii.
2. zăḷkăi, *c. v.*; zăḷka, *n. v.*, *e. g.* tsuḍ zăḷkata = the torch is flickering.
3. hāl, *e.g.* a string.

Flight, *s.* 1. pòḷāp, -ḷpā, *n.*; ubāp, -pā, *n.*; uḍāp, -ḍpā, *n.*; dāuñ, -uve, *f.*; dāvāp, dāupā, *n.*
2. mēḷ, -ḷā, *m.*; zomo, -meā, *m.* = a swarm.

Put to flight = dāunḍăi, *c. v.*

Flimsiness, *s.* bārikăi, -ye, *f.*; pātăḷăi, -ye, *f.*, *n. c.*

Flimsy, *a.* bārik; pātăḷ; ăskăt, *e. g.* f. arguments.

Flinch, *v.* 1. pāṭi săr = go back.
2. inkār kăr *Acc.* = deny.

Fling, *v.* uḍăi.

Flint, *s.* 1. čekmăkātso fātor, -trā, *m.* = *l.* stone of flint.
2. pākāṇ, -ṇā, *n.* (*ex.* granite).

Flirt, *v.* 1. hālăi.
2. uḍăi.

Flit, *v.* bouñ; ub = *l.* fly, *fg.*

Float, *v.* 1. upe = swim.
2. ub = fly; sădiḷ umkăḷ = be hanging loose.

Float, *s.* terpo (*or* teppo), -peā, *m.* = a raft.

Flock, *s.* 1. hinḍ, -ḍā, *m.*
2. jilpañ, *pl. n.* = a lock, *e. g.* of hair.
3. (loventso) punzo, -jeā, *m.* = a little wool.

Flog, *v.* măr.

Flogging, *s.* măr, -rā, *m.*

Flood, *s.* 1. āuruু, -rā, *n.*
2. buḍtugāl (*or* burtugāl), -lā, *n.* = a deluge.
3. *fg.* dăryo, -yeā, *m.* = a sea, *e. g.* f. of tears.

Floor, *s.* 1. nèl, -lā, *n.*; dărn, -ni, *f.*
2. māḷăi, -ḷiye, *f.* = *l.* upstairs.

Floor, *v.* nèl săma kăr (reduce to a level).

Flora, *s.* fulañ (yeka gāunčiñ).
Florid, *a.* 1. vrăddhi.
2. tāmbḍoso = reddish.
3. tāmbḍots = very red.
4. *fg.* ălānkārătso.
Flour, *s.* piṭ, -ṭā, *n.*
Flourish, *v.* 1. fulañ di; kirla.
2. *fg.* vrăddhi zā = *l.* get prosperous.
3. jiye = *l.* live; *see* **Brandish** *and* **Blow.**
Flow, *v.* 1. vāu.
2. sădiḷ zāun umkăḷ.
Flow, *s.* 1. vāvāp, vāupā, *n.*
2. bhărti, -te, *f.* = high water; *see* **Course.**
Flower, *s.* 1. ful, -lā, *n.*
2. *fg.*, *e. g.* f. of nobility, *rs.* mukhya, *or also* ful.
3. surungār, -rā, *m.* = an ornament.
Fluctuate, *v.* 1. yeṇeñ teṇeñ hāl.
2. dubāu, dubāu čint.
3. upe = *l.* float.
Fluency, *s.* sădiḷāi, -ye, *f.*; sădsăḍāi, -ye, *f.*, *n. c.*
Fluent, *a.* sădiḷ; săḍsăḍit.
Fluently, *ad.* sădiḷ; săḍsăḍit.
Fluid, *a.* pātăḷ = *l.* thin, *fg.*
Fluid, *s.* vāunči văstụ = *l.* a fluid thing, *or bet.* pātăḷ văstụ, -tu, *f.*
Flute, *s.* pirluk, -ke, *f.* = a musical pipe.
Flutter, *v.* 1. yeṇeñ teṇeñ ub.
2. *fg.* simpḍāi. *See* **Flicker.**
Flux, *s.* vāvāp, vāupā, *n.* = a flowing.

Fly, *s.* mus, -sā, *m.*, *dim.* musk, -kā, *n.*
Drive away the flies = m. āmboḍ *or* dāunḍāi.
Fly, *v.* 1. ub.
2. pòḷ = *l.* flee.
Foal, *s.* (goḍeāčeñ) pīl, -lā, *n.* = the young of a horse.
Foam, *s.* fenḍ, -ḍā, *m.*
Foam, *v.* fenḍ yetā = *l.* foam comes; fenḍ bortā.
Fob, *s.* dākṭeñ bols, -sā, *n.*
Fodder, *s.* gorvānčeñ khāṇ, -ṇā, *n.* = food of cattle; tsorou, -rvā, *m.*
Fodder, *v.* tsărāi; pós.
Foe, *s.* dusmān, -nā, *m.*
Fog, *s.* 1. duuri, -re, *f.*
2. kāḷok, -kā, *m.* = *l.* darkness.
Foggy, *a.* duuretso.
Foh, *int.* čhi.
Foible, *s.* ăib, -bā, *n.*
Foil, *s.* domosnātụlli tālvār, -ri, *f.*; daḍḍi tālvār, -ri, *f.* = *l.* a blunt sword.
Foil, *v.* nāḍi kăr; yeḍāi; mōs(ó) kăr; vèrt kăr.
Foist, *v.* mosān borāi = *l.* write deceitfully.
Fold, *s.* 1. gòṭo, -ṭeā, *m.* for animals.
2. miri, -ye, *f.* (of a garment).
3. găḍi, -ye, *f.*
Fold, *as an affix*, doḍo; *see* Gram. P. II. ch. ii.
Fold, *v.* 1. dóḍ, *e. g.* a towel; āuḷāi; kovóḷ.
2. găḍi kăr; mirio pòḍ.

Foliage, *s.* 1. pālo, -leā, *m.*, *collective noun.*
2. *pl. of* kholi, -ye, *f.*; *see* **Leaf.**

Follow, *v.* 1. pāṭleān vots = *l.* go after; āik = *l.* hear, *e.g.* f. advice.
2. pāṭlāu kăr = *l.* make following, f. a custom, *G. M.*; *Or.* părmāṇeñ kăr = act according to.
3. sāngāta vots.
4. zā = *l.* become, happen.
5. dék kāṇe = take example.
6. vòp = consent, *e. g.* f. an opinion.
7. *by instr.*, *e.g.* f. anger.
As follows = ăseñ.
F. on = thir rāu.
F. out = tirsi, jāri kăr.

Follower, *s.* sis, -sā, *m.* = a disciple; māndtolo, -leā, *m.*; pāṭlāu kărtolo; pāṭlāugār, -rā, *m.*

Following, *s.* pāṭlāu, -lāvā, *m.*

Following, *a.* 1. dusro = *l.* other; yeuntso = *l.* coming, *e. g.* f. year.
2. pāṭlo = being behind.

Folly, *s.* pisepoṇ, -ṇā, *n.*

Foment, *v.* 1. šék.
2. *fg.* utsāmboḷ kăr = *l.* excite, stir up; bòḷ di = *l.* give force.

Fomentation, *s.* šékų, -kā, *m.*

Fond of, *a.* ăpurbāyetso; *bet. rs. into* ăpurbāi āsā = fondness is; *rs. into* ruts = like (in taste), *sb. Dat.*; lāgųllo = attached, given; *rs.* mōg kăr = love; *rs.* mānua = please.

Fondle, *v.* fuslāi; prīt kăr; lāle.

Fondness, *s.* ăpurbāi, -ye, *f.*; mogāḷpoṇ, -ṇā, *n.* = *l.* dearness; *or* mōg, -gā, *m.*

Font, *s.* bāutizmāči suāt, -te, *f.*

Food, *s.* 1. khāṇ, -ṇā, *n.* = food; ăn, ănnā, *n.*
2. jevāṇ, jeuṇā, *n.* = a meal.
3. grās, -sā, *m.*, *e.g.* dispoḍto grās = daily bread.

Fool, *s.* piso mănis, -nšā, *m.*; budnātullo mănis.

Foolish, *a.* piso; budnātullo.

Foolishness, *s.* pisepoṇ, -ṇā, *n.*; girigiri, -ri, *n.*

Foot, *s.* 1. pāi, -yā, *m.*, *pr. fg.*; čărăṇ, -ṇā, *n.*, *h. K. rl.*; muḷ, -ḷā, *n.* = f. of a mountain; meṭañ = *l.* steps, *e. g.* f. of the altar.
2. khur, -rā, *m.* (of a chest of drawers).
3. fuṭ, -ṭi, *f.* (measure), *fr.*; gèṇ, -ṇā, *n.* = a measure in use in this country, equal to 9 inches about; *see App. to* Konk.-Eng. Dictionary.
On foot = pāivāṭen. Go on foot = pāivāṭen vots *or* tsăl.

Foot-bath, *s.* pāyāñšekāp, -kpā, *n.*

Footing, *s.* 1. ghăṭ nèl, -lā, *n.* = *l.* standing ground.
2. *fg.* stiti, -ti, *f.* = *l.* a condition, a state; *bet. rs. e. g.* on the former f. = ādle bāri.

Footman, *s.* tsăltolo sipāi, -yā, *m.*; *bet.* pāidăḷ, -ḷā, *n.*

Footpath, *s.* ăsir vāṭ, -ṭe, *f.* = *l.* a narrow road; pāivāṭ, -ṭe, *f.*

Footstep, *s.* pāyāntso gurtụ, -tā, *m.* = *l.* a sign of the foot; mèṭ, -ṭā, *n.*

Footstool, *s.* moṇăi, -ṇiye, *n.*

Fop, *s.* dăndi, -ḍi, *m.*; doulăt kărtolo.

For, *prep.* 1. *pr.* pāsun, *or* pāsvot = on account of, *Lat. propter, pro.*

2. vorviñ = through, *Lat. per.*

3. nimtiñ = on account of.

4. khātir = *Lat. pro.*

5. părmāṇeñ = according to *or* considering, *Lat. prae.*

6. bădlāk = instead.

7. *to express* price, *Dat.*

8. *to snow* time, *Acc.*

For, *conj.* 1. kiteāk, *or* kiteāk moḷeār = because.

2. dekun (*put at the end of a clause*), *e. g.* to boro dekun = because he is good.

3. pāsun = on account of (*with the* participle), *e.g.* for God has created us = Devān āmkāñ rătsụllea pāsun.

Forage, *v.* khāṇ (*or* ăn) di *or* hāḍ = give food.

Forage, *s.* khāṇ, -ṇā, *n.*

For as much as, *see* **Because.**

Forbear, *v. rs. into neg. form, e. g.* f. lamentation = šiṇ ulăinākā; sóḍ = leave.

Forbearance, *s.* sosṇikāi, -ye, *f.* = patience.

Forbid, *v.* 1. āḍvār.

2. formāi, *ch. cs.* = *l.* command.

3. *rs. into neg. form of potent. mood.*

Forbidden, *a.* năiñzāllo; āḍvār-lolo.

Force, *s.* 1. bòḷ, -ḷā, *n.*; *or* bolāi-ki, -ke, *f.*

2. săkăt, -kti, *f.* = f. of nature.

3. zulum, -lme, *f.* = violence.

4. sipāi, -yā, *m.* = a soldier (*in the pl.*)

5. păṭlām, -mi, *f.* = a battalion.

6. fouz, -ji, *f.* = an army.

(The law) is in f. = boḷ āsā *or* tsăltā. (The law) has lost its f. = (kānun) tsălnāñ.

Force, *v.* 1. bòḷ kăr = make force. zulum kăr = make violence.

2. lāi = apply, compel.

3. *rs. into c. v.*

4. zulmen rig = enter violently.

F. in = boḷān (*with the verb required by the mn.*)

F. out = kāḍ.

F. a passage through = boḷān rig.

F. out tears = dukañ găḷăı.

Forced, *a.* ăuñsărātso (f. marches); *See* **Constraint.**

Forcible, *a.* boḷān kello (*or* boḷān *with some other vb.*); boḷātso; zulmetso.

Forcibly, *ad.* boḷān.

Ford, *v.* 1. utron vots.

2. pāyāñiñ utron vots; kāḍou utăr.

Ford, *s.* kāḍou, -ḍvā, *m.*

Fore, *a., ad.* mukāvelo; ādiñ.

N. B. **Fore,** *in composition with other words not given here, is to be rendered mostly by* **ādiñ.**

Fore-arm, *v.* (adiñ) tăyār kăr.
Forebode, *v.* mukār (*or* ādiñ) sāng; dākăi; ā. bhóg (feel before); kăḷăi = announce.
Forefather, *s.* mālgoḍo, -ḍeā, *m.*
Forefend, *see* **Forbid.**
Forego, *v.* sóḍ.
Forehead, *s.* kăpāl, -lā, *n.*
Foreign, *a.* 1. păra.
2. părki = a stranger.
3. *fg.* sămăndnātullo = not connected.
Foreigner, *s.* 1. părdesi, -siā, *m.*
2. ātvo, -veā, *m.* = an unknown man.
3. părki, -kiā, *m.*
Foreknow, *v.* ādiñ zāṇāñ.
Foremost, *a.* 1. mukāvelo.
2. mukhya = chief; poilo = first.
Forenoon, *s.* săkāḷiñ; donpārañ [ādiñ.
Fore-ordain, *v.* ādiñ niščeisi; ādiñ vintsun kăḍ.
Fore-runner, *s.* 1. harakāri, -ri, *m.*; *see* **Precursor.**
2. mukār vetso mănis, -nšā, *m.* = a man going before.
Foresee, *v.* ādiñ voḷkatā; *or* ādiñ poḷe.
Foresight, *s.* 1. bārikăi, -ye, *f.* = prudent provision, *l.* thinness.
2. mukăili voḷok, -ḷki, *f.*; bud, -di, *f.*
Forest, *s.* ărăṇeñ, -ṇeā, *n.*; moleñ, -leā, *n.*; rān, -nā, *n.*
Forestall, *v.* ādiñ molāk kăṇe = *l.* buy before.
Forester, *s.* 1. moleagār, -rā, *m.*
2. mălekuḍiyā, -yā, *m.* = a man living in a forest.
Foretaste, *s.* *l.* ādiñruts; *but bet. use simply* ruts, -či, *f.* = taste, *e.g.* God gave him a f. of heaven.
Foretell, *v.* ādiñ sāng = *l.* say before.
Forfeit, *s.* julmān, -nā, *m.*; dănḍ, -ḍā, *m.*
Forfeit, *v.* 1. dănḍ fārik kăr = *l.* pay a fine.
2. tsukăi = *l.* deprive, *ch. cs.*; hogḍāi = *l.* lose.
3. hăkku sānḍ = *l.* abandon a right.
Forfeiture, *s.* hogḍāuṇeñ; -ṇeā, *n.*
Forge, *v.* 1. kăr, *e.g.* f. a bolt, a nail.
2. fóţkiro kăr = *l.* make false.
3. fóţkiro dākăi, *n. c.*
Forge, *s.* kāmārăči sāḷ, -ḷe, *f.* = a big f.; kāmāračeñ kāţeñ, -ţeā, *n.* = a small f.; (kāmārači) āngăḍ, -gḍi, *f.*; kāmārākoḍkeñ, -keā, *n.*
Forger, *s.* fóţkireñ dăstevoz kărtolo.
Forgery, *s.* fóţ dăskăt, -ti, *f.* = a false signature; fóţkireñ dăstevoz, -zā, *n.* = a false document.

Forget, *v.* 1. visăr *or* isăr, *c. v.* visrāi (*fg.* deny oneself).
2. *neg. of* ugḍās āsā *or* u. kăr.
I forgot = *vlg.* ugḍās pāvanāñ, *or* ugḍās nāñ.

Forgetful, *a.* ugḍās nātullo; visărtolo. [*f.*

Forgetfulness, *s.* visăr, *or* isăr, -ri,

Forgive, *v.* bogsi, *e.g.* f. sins; māf di, *or* māf kăr = *l.* excuse; sóḍ = *l.* leave.

Forgiveness, *s.* bogsāṇeñ, -ṇeā, *n.*; māf (*or* māp), -fi, *f.* (*perh.* -fā, *n.*)

Fork, *s.* gārp, -pā, *n.* (a table fork); kānṭo, -ṭeā, *m.* = *l.* a thorn, *fg.*

Forlorn, *a.* vāṭer ghāllo = *l.* put on the way, abandoned; kirkoḷ = wretched; upāinātullo; nirādhāri.

Form, *s.* 1. rūp, -pā, *n.*; nămuno, -neā, *m.* = *l.* a model.
2. rīt, -ti, *f.* = a manner; *or* khănḍit rīt, *e.g.* f. of vows; păddăt, -ti, *f.*, *n. c.*
3. jinos, -nsā, *m.* = a kind.

Form, *v.* 1. kăr, *e.g.* f. the world, a statue, a friendship.
2. săma ghāl = put in order (arrange); mānḍ = *l.* arrange, *e.g.* an army; rūp di.
3. čint = *l.* think (a plan).
4. *ch. cs.* meḷon āsā = *l.* is constituted.

Formal, *a.* -ts, *emphat.*, *e.g.* a formal letter = kāgāduts; *or* khăro = true.

Formally, *ad.* sārkeñ = *l.* exactly; *by* -ts.

Formation, *s. rs. into* kăr *or* zā.

Former, *a.* poilo = first; to = that (*opp. to* vo = this); ādiñ āsullo = being before; ādlo = ancient, anterior.
In former times = ādiñ, ādiñ purviñ *or* ādiñ māgiñ.

Formerly, *ad.* ādiñ; ādiñ purviñ.

Formidable, *a.* bhăyănkărātso; bhiyānkuḷ; tărtărāuntso.

Formless, *a.* rūpnātullo.

Formula, *s.* 1. utrāntso thăr, -rā, *m.* = *l.* a manner of words; păddăt, -ti, *f.*, rīt, -ti, *f.*, *e.g.* a f. of words, a mathematical f.
2. utăr, -trā, *n.* = a word.
3. nămuno, -neā, *m.*

Formulary, *s.* rititso mēḷ (é), -ḷā, *m.*; păddătitso mēḷ (é).

Fornicate, *v.* vebičār kăr.

Fornication, *s.* vebičār, -rā, *n.*

Fornicator, *s.* vebičāri, -riā, *m.*

Forsake, *v.* sóḍ = leave; sānḍ; vāṭer ghāl = *l.* put on the way; sóḍn ghāl.

Forsooth, *a.* 1. khărents; ălbăt.
2. moḷeār = that is to say.
3. -ts *emphat.*, *see* Gram. p. 81.

Forswear, *v.* 1. părmāṇār sóḍ.
2. fóṭ părmāṇ kăr.

Fort, *s.* koṭeñ, -ṭeā, *n.*

Forth, *ad.* bhāir = *Lat. extra. It is sometimes omitted, as,* 'from that day forth = teā disā thāun *or* teā disā lāgāit'. 'And so f. = āni äseñ yer säit'.

Forthcoming, *a.* yeuntso = *l.* coming; distso = *l.* appearing.

Forthwith, *ad.* ätānts; yeā kṣ̌ä-ṇa = in this moment; tovoḷụts = just then; *or* teā kṣ̌äṇa.

Fortification, *s.* 1. koṭeñ, -ṭeā, *n.* = *l.* a castle.

2. pāgār, -rā, *m.* = *l.* a wall.

3. ghäṭāi, -ye, *f.*

Fortify, *v.* ghäṭ kär = *l.* make strong; bòḷ di = give force.

Fortitude, *s.* ghäṭāi, -ye, *f.*; bòḷ, -ḷā, *n.*; dhäir, -rā, *n.* = *l.* courage.

Fortnight, *s.* dón häpte = *l.* two weeks.

Fortress, *see* **Fort.**

Fortuitous, *a.* aučit; grātstsā-rātso; *see* **Accidental.**

Fortunate, *a.* sukhi, bhāgi = happy, *or* a happy man; ädruṣ̌ṭ-vont = lucky.

Fortunately, *ad.* ädruṣ̌ṭān; *often rs. into adj.*

Fortune, *s.* 1. ädruṣ̌ṭ, -ṭā, *n.* = luck; grātstsār, -rā, *m.*

2. bhāg, -gā, *n.* = happiness; sukhụ, -khā, *n.* = happiness.

3. näsib, -bā, *n.* = destiny.

4. äst, -ti, *f.* (*or* āsti, -te) = property; 'a man of fortune = āstivont, *or* āstidār = rich *or* having much property'; grest = rich. [*m.*

Fortune-teller, *s.* 1. ghāḍigār, -rā, *m.*

2. nimitgār, -rā, *m.* = a soothsayer.

Fortune-telling, *s.* nimit, -tā, *n.*

Forum, *s. the nearest equivalent to* the old Roman forum *is perhaps* käčeri, -re, *f.*

Forward, *ad.* mukār = before.

Forward, *a.* 1. vegiñ yetolo; āḍe-tso, *e. g.* f. rain.

2. vortea dhäirātso = *l.* too bold.

Forward, *v.* 1. dhāḍ = send; *or* dānḍi.

2. vopsun di = deliver.

3. kumok di = give help.

4. bäḍti di = *l.* promote (to higher offices).

5. *rs. into* vegiñ yetā; *or* poileñ yetā.

Forwardness, *s.* äumäryād, -di, *f.*; läzbanḍpoṇ, -ṇā, *n.*; móst, -ti, *f.*

Fossil, *a.* konḍụlli (vāstụ).

Foster, *v.* pós.

Foster-father, *s.* poskobāpui, -pāi, *m.* = *l.* the father who feeds.

Foster-mother, *s.* poskiāvoi, -voi, *f.* = *l.* the mother who feeds.

N. B. All other words, compounded with foster, *are to be rendered in the same way as those given here.*

Foul, *v.* mheḷo kär, *or* mheḷāi = make dirty; khätāi = *l.* stain, violate, *n. c.*; čikol kär = make dirty.

Foul, *a.* 1. mheḷo = dirty; čiklā-tso; khätātso.

2. vonkāreātso = *l.* loathsome.

3. khoṭeāpoṇātso; ăumăryādi-tso.
'Fall foul of = ādăl'

Foulness, *see* Dirt.

Found, *v.* 1. găḍ.
2. stāpisi.
3. bānd = *l.* build; ghāl = cast (type), *etc.*

Foundation, *s.* 1. bunyād, -di, *f.*, *used also fg.*
2. garpan, -nā, *n.* = *l.* an institution, an order.
3. ghăr = *l.* house *compounded with some word specifying further the kind of* foundation *referred to.*
4. bānduḷleñ *or* ghăḍuḷleñ ghăr = *l.* a built house.
5. tsouki, -ke, *f.*, *n. c. in this mn.* (*usually* a square).

Founder, *s.* găḍpist, -tā, *m.*

Fountain, *s.* 1. zăr, -ri, *f.*
2. *fg.* muḷ, -ḷā, *n.* = *l.* a root.

Four, *a.* čār.

Fourfold, *a.* čārdoḍo, *or* čār-pāuṭi tsăḍ.

Fowl, *s.* 1. sukṇeñ, -ṇeā, *n.*
2. kunkāḍ, -kḍā, *n.* (a cock, hen, *or* chicken).

Fowl, *v.* sikāri kăr.

Fowler, *s.* sikāregār, -rā, *m.*

Fox, *s.* kòlò, -leā, *m.* (*strictly*, a jackal), *used fg. also for* a cunning person.

Fraction, *s.* 1. kuḍko, -keā, *m.*
2. ăuñš, -šā, *m.* (*math.*), *n. c. Mr. Cn.*, *or* ăuñšo, -šeā, *m.*

Fracture, *s.* moḍāp, -ḍpā, *n.*

Fragile, *a.* 1. mòḍtso, *or* fuṭtso, *or* mòḍāsārko.
2. *fg.* ăskăt.

Fragility, *s.* mòḍasārkeñ, -keā, *n.*

Fragment, *s.* kuḍko, -keā, *m.* = a part (large *or* small); kus-kuṭ, -ṭā, *n.* = *l.* an atom, a very small part.

Fragrance, *s.* pormóḷ, -ḷā, *m.*; suād, -dā, *m.*

Fragrant, *a.* suādik; pormoḷātso.

Frail, *a.* 1. mòḍtso (*pr.*); *or* mò-ḍāsārko (*pr.*)
2. ăskăt, *fg.*

Frailty, *s.* ăskătkāi, -ye, *f.*

Frame, *s.* 1. tsouku, -kā, *m.*, *e. g.* of a window.
2. rūp, -pā, *n.* = shape.
3. *fg.* sobāu, -bāvā, *m.*, *e. g.* of mind.

Frame, *v.* 1. săma meḷăi = *l.* put together regularly; mānḍ = adjust; lāyek kăr = make suitable.
2. nămuno kăr = make a plan.
3. ghăḍ, *e. g.* a law, a rule; kăr = make.
4. sikăi = teach.
5. tsouk kăr.

Frame-work, *s.* tsouk, -kā, *m.*

Franchise, *s.* 1. vót, -tā, *m.* = *l.* a vote, a voice, a right to vote, *fr.*
2. suṭka, -ke, *f.* = liberty.

Frank, *a.* 1. niskăpṭi = sincere; ugto = open.
2. bheññātullo = without fear.

3. sādo = simple.

Frankincense, *s.* lobān, -nā, *n.*

Frankness, *s.* 1. dhăir, -rā, *n.* = courage.

2. nenṭuvāi, -ye, *f.* = candour of mind.

3. sādeñ mòn, -nā, *n.* = *l.* a simple heart.

Frantic, *a.* mót tsukụllo = *l.* deprived of mind; vid lāgụllo; piso.

Fraternal, *a.* moya (mōg) = fraternal (charity).

Fraternity, *s.* bhāupoṇ, -ṇā, *n.*; mēḷ(é), -ḷā, *m.* = an association; *vlg.* confrụ, -ri, *f.*, *fr.*

Fratricide, *s.* 1. bhāvākhuni, -ye, *f.*

2. bhāvākhunigār, -rā, *m.*

Fraud, *s.* mōs, -sā, *m.*; ṭhăkkụ, -kā, *n.*

Fraudulent, *a.* mosātso; fóṭkiro; ṭhăkkagār.

Fray, *s.* zăgḍeñ, -ḍeā, *n.*

Freak, *s.* mărji, -je, *f.* = *l.* a caprice.

Freckle, *s.* ăḷduvi kāt, -ti, *f.*; šib, -bā, *n.*

Free, *a.* 1. săttyātso (*phil.*); băndnātụllo = *l.* not bound by a bond; khālnātụllo, *or* koṇāk (*or* konnāčea) khālnātụllo = *l.* not being under any one; (āpleā) sotăntrār āsụllo, *or* sotăntrātso.

2. viräit = exempt.

3. *rs. into Ger.* nāstanāñ, *ch. cs.*

4. duḍu dināstanāñ = without fee, *or* sāmbāḷ dinātụllo; *bct.* funkeātso = gratuitous.

5. ukto = open.

6. āple podvent = under one's own power.

7. ăumăryāditso = not becoming, not honest.

Man is free = vāiṭ boreñ kărunk mănšāk kāiñ bòḷ kărināñ = *l.* nothing compels man to do evil or good.

Make f. = 1. tsōr (ó).

2. ăumăryādin kăr.

Free, *v.* 1. sóḍ = leave; sānḍ; suṭka di = *l.* give liberty, *e.g.* to a prisoner.

2. kāḍ = draw; viräit kăr = make exempt; tsukăi (make free).

Free-booter, *s.* tsōr, -rā, *m.*

Free-booting, *s.* tsóri, -ye, *f.*

Freedman, *s.* suṭka meḷụllo (mănis, -nšā, *m.*).

Freedom, *s.* 1. suṭka, -ke, *f.*, *e.g.* from a prison.

2. săttya, -ye, *f.*, *e.g.* of doing good.

3. ăumăryād, -di, *f.* = dishonesty.

4. sotăntrụ, -rā, *n.*, *e.g.* āplea sotăntrār āsā = is in his own power.

Freehold, *s.* vărg, -gā, *m.*; svănta zāgo, -geā, *m.*

Freeholder, *s.* văragadār, -rā, *m.*

Freely, *ad.* 1. *rs.* ăḍḍi nāstanāñ = *l.* not having objection; khušen = *l.* with will; monapurvok; zāi moṇ = *l.* that must

be done, *e.g.* commit sin f.; săttyen = *l.* with liberty; zāṇāzāun = *l.* knowingly.
2. ărthā pārmāṇe = *l.* according to the meaning (not literally).
3. sădiḷzāun = *l.* loosely.
4. ăumăryādin = *l.* unbecomingly.

Freeman, *s.* āplea sotăntrār āsullo mănis, *or shorter* sotăntrātso mănis, -nšā, *m.* = *l.* an independent man.

Free-will, *s.* 1. săttya, -ye, *f.*, *n. c.*; khuši, -še, *f.* = *l.* will.
2. sotăntru, -rā, *n.* = *l.* independent power.

Freeze, *v.* kăre zātāt = *l.* hail becomes; gār zātā = *l.* ice becomes; *vlg.* ghăṭ zātā = *l.* gets solid (*e.g.* water freezes).

Freight, *s.* 1. nōr, -rā, *m.*, *e.g.* f. of a vessel; bāḍeñ, -ḍeā, *n.* = *l.* hire.
2. vojeñ, -jeā, *n.* = *l.* a burden.

French, *s. a.* Fransez.

Frenzy, *s.* pisepoṇ, -ṇā, *n.* = *l.* foolishness; vid, -di, *f.*; pisepoṇātso rāg, -gā, *m.* = *l.* the anger of mad men; rāgiṣṭ pisepoṇ, -ṇā, *n.* = *l.* angry madness.

Frequency, *s.* nirăprupāi, -ye, *f.*

Frequent, *a.* 1. tovoḷ tovoḷtso; nirăprup = *l.* not rare.
2. tsăltolo *or* tsaltso = *l.* current; *rs.* săbār pāuṭi zātā, *or* s. p. găḍtā.

Frequent, *v.* vetā *with* -ts, *or only* vetā; săbār pāuṭi vetā.

Frequented, *a.* vetso yeuntso = *l.* going and coming, *e.g.* f. town.

Frequently, *ad.* săbār păuṭi; tovoḷ tovoḷ; găḍiye găḍiye = every moment.

Fresh, *a.* 1. novo; āilevārtso.
2. thănḍ = *l.* cold, *e.g.* f. wind.
3. bolāiketso = untired; bolāikent = *l.* in health, *ch. cs.*
4. sāvo, *e.g.* f. water, not salt.
5. khārnātullo = not impregnated with potash.

Freshen, *v.* thănḍ kăr, nivoi = *l.* make cold.

Fresh-man, *s.* umeduār, -rā, *m.* = *l.* apprentice, novice.

Freshness, *s.* jivāḷ, -ḷi, *f.*

Fret, *v.* 1. tsābun kāḍ = *l.* biting take away.
2. *fg.* kărkăr kăr, bezār kăr = *l.* make trouble; zăḷāi = *l.* tease; dós = trouble.

Fret, *s.* kărkăr, -rāñ, *m. pl.*

Fretful, *a.* kărkărātso.

Friable, *a.* čenčisārko.

Friar, *s. vlg.* frād, -di, *m.*; moṭhavāsi, -si, *m.* = *l.* living in a convent; sănyāsi, -siā, *m.*, *used only for* a pagan f.

Friction, *s.* gāsṇeñ, -ṇeā, *n.*, *n. c.*; gāsāp, -spā, *n.*

Friend, *s.* iṣṭ, -ṭā, *m.*; iṣṭiṇ, -ṇi, *f.*; dost, -tā, *m.* = *l.* a favourite; *see* **Fond, Favourable.**

Friendless, *a.* iṣṭṇātullo.

Friendliness, *s.* mogāḷpoṇ, -ṇā, *n.*; dăya, -ye, *f.*; mănšepoṇ, -ṇā, *n.* = *l.* humanity, *fr.*

Friendly, *a.* 1. mogāḷ = *l.* dear; dăyāḷ = *l.* clement.
2. guṇātso = *l.* favourable.

Friendship, *s.* 1. iṣṭăgăt, -ti, *f.*
2. dosti, -te, *f.* = *l.* favour.
Form a f. = i. kăr.
Intimate f. = kāḷzāči i.

Fright, *s.* bheñ, bhiyā, *n.*; bhiyānkuḷāi, -ye, *f.*
Take f. = bheñ distā, *l.* fear appears, *Prs. Dat.*

Frighten, *v.* beṣṭāi, *c. v.* = cause fear by speaking, scolding; bhiyeunk lāi = cause to fear, *l.* apply to fear.

Frightful, *a.* bhăyănkărātso, *or bet.* bhiyānkuḷ; tărtărountso = *l.* causing trembling.

Frigid, *a.* thănḍ = *l.* cold, *used also fg.*, *e.g.* f. temper.

Frill, *s.* mirio, *pl. f.* = *l.* folds.

Fringe, *s.* rènd, -dā, *n.*

Frippery, *s.* 1. čindi, -de, *f.* = old torn clothes, rags.
2. *fg. see* **Bran.**

Frisk, *v.* nāts (*or* nātsoa) = *l.* dance; uḍ = *l.* jump.

Frith, *s.* dăryā-ăširāi, -ye, *f.* = *l.* a strait; āḷveñ, -veā, *n.* = an estuary.

Fritter, *s. see* **Cake.**

Fritter, *v.* (f. away) = yeṭṭāi (waste); pāḍ kăr = *l.* spoil; khărči = *l.* expend.

Frivolity, *s.* khāli văstụ, -tu, *f.* = *l.* an empty thing; nākazāllo, -leā, *m.* = *l.* nonsense; čillăr văstụ = *l.* a trifling thing.

Frivolous, *a.* khāli = *l.* empty; čillăr = *l.* trifling; nākazāllo (-li, -leñ).

Frizzle, *v.* iṇi ghāl = f. hair.

Fro (To and), yeṇeñ teṇeñ, *or* pāṭi phuḍe = here there, *or l.* behind before.

Frock, *s. approx.* kutāuñ, -tāvā, *m.*; voileñ văstur, -rā, *n.*

Frog, *s.* 1. māṇko, -keā, *m.* = a toad.
2. māṇki, -ke, *f.* = the common f.

Frolic, *s.* mărji, -je, *f.* = *l.* caprice; khêḷ, -ḷā, *m.* = *l.* sport; mărje-khušalāi, -ye, *f.* = *l.* pleasure of caprice.

Frolic, *a.* uḍtso = *l.* jumping.

Frolic, *v.* uḍ = *l.* jump; nāts = *l.* dance.

From, *prep.* 1. *in the meaning of* out of, -ntlo (*to be added to the Loc.*), *e.g.* (J. C. delivers) from hell = yemkăndāntlo.
2. *if signifying distance of time or place*, thāun, *e.g.* from 10 to 12 o'clock = dhā thāun bārā păriant, *or* dărn = taking, *may be used instead of* thāun (dhā dărn....).
3. kăḍtso, *the same almost as* thāun; *it is formed from* kăḍe

= close, *hence* kădtso = which is close; *e. g.* Deva kăḍči kurpa āmkāñ melṭā = from God (which is near to God) we receive graces.

4. lāgāit, *e. g.* from to-day = āz lāgāit, *n. c.*

5. *Instrum. signifying cause, e. g.* he is pale from loss of blood.

6. *Or.* pāsun = on account of.

F. day to day = disa disa.

Front, *s.* 1. muk, -kā, *n. or* mukāveli (*or* mukāvoili *or* mukāili) kus, -si, *f.* (văstu̦, -tu, *f. etc.*) = the front side.

2. *In composition*, mukāvelo *may be used, e. g.* f. door = mukāveleñ bāgil.

3. poilo = first.

In f. = mukār.

Front, *v.* pòḷe = *l.* see, *e.g.* this room fronts the street, *n. c.*; *G.* isileān āsā.

Fronting, *prep.* mukār.

Frontispiece, *s.* 1. muk, -kā, *n.* = *l.* the anterior part, *e. g.* mukār kiteñ boroun āsā = what is written in the f.

2. (pustaka-) ărāmbāčeñ čitru̦, -rā, *n.* = *l.* the figure of the beginning (of a book).

Frost, *s. approx.* kăre, -reāñ, *pl. m.* = hail; gār, -rā, *m.* = *l.* ice; *rs.* dāṭ zā = become thick.

Frosty, *a.* gārātso.

Froth, *see* **Foam.**

Froward, *a.* dhāruṇ; *see* **Obstinate.**

Frown, *v.* tònḍ vānkḍeñ kăr = *l.* make the face crooked; kopalār mirio ghāl = *l.* put folds on the forehead.

Frozen, *a.* 1. ghăṭ = *l.* solid, *or* dāṭ.

2. gārātso = *l.* of ice.

Fructification, *s.* fòḷ, -ḷā, *n.*; *rs. into* fòḷ diunčeñ.

Fructify, *v.* iṭ kăr = *l.* make fertility, (*or bet.* iṭātso kăr); fòḷādik kăr.

Frugal, *a.* hăḷtān khāuntso = *l.* eating moderately; hăḷtān khărtsuntso = *l.* expending moderately.

Frugality, *s.* hăḷt, -tā, *n.*; kăši-ši, -še, *f.* = *l.* economy; *rs.* hăḷtān khā, *or* h. khărči.

Frugally, *ad.* hăḷtān; kăšišen.

Fruit, *s.* 1. fòl, -lā, *n.* = a material fruit.

2. fòḷ, -ḷā, *m., fg. or* effect.

Fruitful, *a.* 1. fòḷādik *or* fòḷdiuntso.

2. iṭāḷ *or* iṭātso = *l.* fertile; fòḷabărit = *l.* fertile.

Fruitfulness, *s.* iṭ, -ṭā, *m.* = *l.* fertility; fòḷādikpoṇ, -ṇā, *n.*; fòḷabăritpoṇ, -ṇā, *n., n. c.*

Fruitless, *a.* nirfòḷ; fòḷdinātullo.

Fruit-tree, *s.* fòḷāntso ruk, -kā, *m.*; fòḷvostutso ruk.

Frustrate, *v.* mōḍ(ó) = *l.* break, *fg.*; nirfòḷ kăr = *l.* make without effect, *fg.*; vèrt kăr; *see* **Disappoint.**

Frustration, *s.* moḍāp, -ḍpā, *n.*, *bet. rs. into v.; see* **Disappointment.**

Fry, *s.* zomo, -meā, *m.* = a swarm.

Fry, *v.* bāz; tāḷ.

Fry, *s.* bāzullen khāṇ, -ṇā, *n.*

Frying-pan, *s.* kāil, -li, *f.*

Fudge, *int.* čhi!

Fuel, *s.* lānkuḍ, -kḍā, *n.*; zoḷou, -ḷvā, *m.*; šéṇ, -ṇi, *f. or* šéṇkuṭ, -ṭā, *n.* (*consisting mostly* of cowdung).

Fugitive, *a.* 1. pòḷtso = *l.* fleeing; phărāri; dāuntso = *l.* running.
2. *fg.* ăthir = *l.* unstable.

Fulcrum, *s.* kuṭṭi, -ṭe, *f.*, *n. c.*; kalăng, -gā, *n.*

Fulfil, *v.* pāḷ, *e. g.* f. a duty, a promise; sāmbāḷ, *e. g.* a command, a vow; tirsi = *l.* carry out; tsălăi = *l.* cause to walk, *fg.*, *e. g.* a duty; fārik kăr = *l.* pay, *e. g.* f. a vow; khărots dākăi = *l.* show true; sampăi, *e. g.* f. a prophecy, *n. c.*; găḍun yetā = *l.* comes happened (is fulfilled), *ch. cs.*

Fulfilment, *s.* pāḷo, -ḷeā, *m.*, *e. g.* of a duty.

Full, *v.* lovečen lugāṭ dāḍăi.

Full, *a.* 1. bhorn; borābor; bhărto; sămpurṇ; pūra.
2. dādos = *l.* satisfied.
3. trāṇi *or* trāṇik (voice).
4. săgḷo.

F. of comfort = (purte) soukāsāyetso.
F. of sorrow = dukin bhorlolo.

Full-moon, *s.* punou, -nvi, *f.*

Fully, *ad.* purto (*decl.*); păripurṇ; sămpurṇāyen.

Fulminate, *v. pr.* zăglāitā = *l.* it lightens.

Fulness, *s.* 1. bhărtipoṇ, -ṇā, *n.*, *e. g.* f. of riches, of colour, *etc.*; bhărti, -te, *f.*
2. sămpurṇāi, -ye, *f.* = abundance.

Fulsome, *a.* 1. kānṭāḷeātso.
2. kirkoḷ = *l.* low; ăṇvo.

Fumble, *v.* sāspi, *tr. v.*; sāspa, *n. v.* (feel for something in the dark).

Fume, *s.* 1. duvór, -vrā, *m.*, *pr.* *fg.*, *e. g.* fumes of anger.
2. ub, -be, *f.* = *l.* vapour, steam.
3. *fg.* gărmi, -rme, *f.* = *l.* heat, *e. g.* fumes of anger.

Fume, *v.* 1. duvór bāirsăr = *l.* smoke go out.
2. *fg.* rāgār zā = *l.* get angry.

Fumigate, *v.* duvór ghāl = *l.* put smoke; *bet.* duvrāk ghāl = *l.* put to smoke; dhumpăi = *l.* incense.

Fun, *s.* čeṣṭăi, -ye, *f.*; tămāso, -seā, *m.*

Make fun = *G. F.* čeṣṭăi kăr.

Function, *s.* 1. kāido, -deā, *m.* = *l.* a duty, an office; bhés, -sā, *m.* = *l.* a vocation; kām, -mā, *n.* = *l.* business.
2. săkăt, -kti, *f.* = *l.* a faculty.

3. guṇ, -ṇā, *m.* = *l.* power.
4. kāryeñ, -yeā, *n.* = *l.* an action.

Functionary, *s.* 1. ădhikāri, -ri, *m.* = *l.* having power.
2. udyogăst, -tā, *m.* = *l.* one employed in a public office.

Fund, *s.* 1. ăsăl, -slā, *n.*
2. *fg.* khăzāno, -neā, *m.* = *l.* a treasury, *fg.*, *e.g.* f. of learning; băndạ̄r, -rā, *n.* = *l.* a treasury.

Fundamental, *a.* 1. bunyāditso = *l.* of foundation, *pr.*, *fg.*
2. *fg.* mukhya = *l.* principal.

Funeral, *s.* mòrn, -nā, *n.*; purāp, -rpā, *n.* = *l.* a burial.

Funeral, *a.* mòrnātso.
F. pile = sāri, -ye, *f.*

Fungus, *s.* āḷmeñ, -meā, *n.* (*perh.* āḷmbeñ, -beā, *n.*)

Funnel, *s.* năḷi, -ye, *f.* = *l.* tube, *is the nearest Konk. equivalent; the Engl. word is commonly used, at least in the large towns.*

Funny, *a.* čeṣṭāyetso; hāstso = *l.* laughable.

Fur, *s.* 1. louñ, -ove, *f.* = *l.* wool.
2. tsāmbḍeñ, -ḍeā, *n.*, *or* lovečeñ tsāmbḍeñ = a woolen skin; *sometimes*, kāt, -ti, *f.* = *l.* a skin.

Furbish, *v.* telto kăr = *l.* make smooth; gās = *l.* rub.

Furious, *a.* rāgār zāllo, *or* rāgān zăḷtolo; piso = *l.* mad, *fg.*; rānuoṭ = *l.* wild, *fg.*

Furl, *v.* revoḍ = *l.* roll, *e.g.* a sail; kovoḷ.

Furlong, *s.* măilaāṭvo vāṇṭo, -ṭeā, *m.* = *l.* $\frac{1}{8}$ of a mile; *vlg.* ulo, -leā, *m.* = *l.* call (as far as one's voice can carry), *or* kombasuāt, -te, *f.* = *l.* the place of a trumpet.

Furlough, *s.* răjā, -je, *f.* = *l.* leave.

Furnace, *s.* 1. *vlg.* khòrn *or* khòzn, -nā, *n.* (for bread).
2. āguṭeñ, -ṭeā, *n.* (*or* agăṭeñ), of goldsmiths.

Furnish, *v.* 1. di = *l.* give.
2. tăyār kăr = *l.* make ready.
3. āṇ di (ăḍn di) = *l.* purchase, procure.

Furred, *part. a.* lovetso *or* louñ āsullo.

Furniture, *s.* sāmān, -nā, *m. or* ghărtso sāmān = *l.* an article of the house; gărvata, -te, *f.*

Furrow, *s.* vorro, -reā, *m.*; tsări, -ye, *f.*; tās, -sā, *n.*, *n. c.*, *Mr. not in use everywhere.*

Furrow, *v.* kós; nāngrāi, *n. c.*

Furrowed, *part. a.* mirio āsullo = *l.* having wrinkles (*Lat. rugosus*).

Further, *ad.* 1. yeā šivāi = *l.* beside this.
2. āni = *l.* and (more), *e.g.* I say nothing f. = āni kāiñ sāngināñ.
3. mukār = *l.* before, *e.g.* go f. = mukār vots.

Further, *v.* vāḍăi = *l.* cause to grow, *also fg.*, *e.g.* f. God's glory; kumok *or* săhāi kăr = *l.* make help.

Furtherance, *s.* kumok, -mke, *f.* = *l.* help; săhāi, -ye, *f.* = *l.* assistance.

Fury, *s.* kōp, -pā, *m.*, *or bet. rs.* rāgān zăḷ=burn with anger; tsăḍāvot rāg, -gā, *m.*=*l.* excessive anger; kród, -dā, *m.*; pisepoṇ, -ṇā, *n.* = *l.* folly, *fg.*

Fuss, *s.* gouji, -je, *f.* = *l.* noise, *fg.*

Future, *a.* yeuntso = *l.* coming; găḍtso = *l.* happening; phuḍlo, *e.g.* phuḍlo kāl = f. time.

Future, *s.* 1. fuḍār, -rā, *m.*; *or* phuḍlo kāl, -lā, *m.*
2. nimit, -tā, *n.* = divination: 'n. vitsār=ask (a fortune-teller) about future things'.
In f. = phuḍeñ.

G

Gabardine, *s.* jibbo, -beā, *m.*

Gabble, *v.* boḍboḍ; găzāli mār = *l.* beat a chat.

Gabbler, *s.* boḍboḍo, -ḍeā, *m.*, *or* borboro, -reā, *m.*

Gabbling, *s.* găzāli, -liñ, *f. pl.*

Gad, *v.* pārpoḷzāun bouñ=*l.* walk roaming; bouñ.

Gadder, *s.* pārpoḷ, -ḷā, *m.*

Gadfly, *s.* kirănṭ, -ṭi, *f.*

Gag, *s.* tònḍăčeñ bīg, -gā, *n.* = *l.* a lock of the mouth, *pr. fg.*

Gag, *v.* tònḍăčeñ bīg ghāl = *l.* put the gag, *pr.*, *fg.*

Gage, *v. see* **Pledge, Engage.**

Gaiety, *s.* ulās, -sā, *m.*; khušālāi, -ye, *f.*; săntós, -sā, *m.*

Gaily, *ad.* khušālāyen.

Gain, *s.* jikāp, -kpā, *n.*; zóḍ, -ḍi, *f.*; ādāi, -yā, *m.*; lāb, -bā, *m.*; fāido, -deā, *m.*; nofo, -feā, *m.*

Gain, *v.* jik (make profit); zōḍ(ó) = acquire; mèḷ = *l.* be found, *e.g.* mākā moineāk čār rupoi mèḷtāt = I gain 4 rupees a month; kăr = *l.* do, *with* some one of the preceding nouns.

G. over: voḍni di = *l.* give inclination; mòn voi kăr = *l.* make the heart yes.

G. the favour of = *G.* dostint rig = *l.* enter into the favour of.

G. a cause: vyājyụ jik, *or Dat.* v. guṇ zātā = *l.* favour becomes to.

Gainful, *a.* ādāyātso; fāideātso, *etc.*

Gait, *s.* tsāl, -li, *f.*

Gala, *s.* dobāzo, -jeā, *m.*=*l.* pomp.

Galaxy, *s.* moḷbamārog, -rgā, *m.* = *l.* the road (which is) on the sky; ākāšagăngā, -ge, *f.*, *Mr. Cn.*, *but not used in Konk.*; dudavāṭ, -ṭe, *f.* (*H. K.*).

Gale, *s.* 1. vāreñ, -reā, *n.* = *l.* wind.
2. vāreāči dāuñ, -ve, *f.* = *l.* a current of air.

Gall, *s.* 1. pīnt, -tā, *n.*, *pr.*, *fg.* *e.g.* *for* anger.
2. *fg.* koḍsāṇ, -ṇi, *f.* = *l.* bitterness.

Gall, *v.* gās = *l.* rub; zezarăi.

Gallant, *a.* 1. sobit = *l.* nice.
2. dhăirāvont = *l.* courageous.
3. măryāditso = *l.* polite.
4. dănḍi = *l.* ostentatious.

Gallant, *s.* vīr, -rā, *m.* = *l.* a hero (a courageous man).

Gallantry, *s.* 1. dhăir, -rā, *n.* = *l.* courage.
2. dănḍipoṇ, -ṇā, *n.* *mn.* vanity in dress and the like.

Galleon, *s.* vóḍ tāruñ, -rvā, *n.* = *l.* a large ship.

Gallery, *s.* 1. *vlg.* bălkāuñ, -kāvā, *m.*, *e.g.* g. of a church; vārānd, -dā, *m.* (*var. n.*); tsăḍāu, -ḍāvā, *m.* (*H. K.*)
2. čitrāñsāl, -lā, *n.* = *l.* hall of pictures.

Gall-nut, *s.* ăḍḍo, -ḍeā, *m.* *used for* ink *and* cement.

Gallop, *s.* khădam, -mā, *n.*

Gallop, *v.* khădamañ ghāl.

Gallows, *s.* găḷaruk, -kā, *m.* = *l.* the tree of a rope; găḷ, -ḷā, *m.*; făšeruk, -kā, *m.* = *l.* the tree of rope; făši, -še, *f.*

Gamble, *v.* jugār khėḷ, yéṭ khėḷ = play for a stake.

Gambler, *s.* jugārkār, -rā, *m.*; yéṭigār, -rā, *m.*

Gambling, *s.* jugār, -rā, *m.*; yéṭ, -ṭi, *f.*

Game, *s.* 1. khėḷ (*or* kyóḷ), -ḷā, *m.*; khušālāi, -ye, *f.* = *l.* pleasure; āṭ, -ṭā, *m.*
2. rānuoṭ = *l.* wild, *i. e.* animals pursued.
Make g. of = *G.* năkāl kăr, *l.* make a copy of.

Game, *v.* khėḷ *or* kyaḷ; *see* **Gamble.**

Gamut, *s.* gāyānamānḍāvoḷ, -ḷi, *f.* = order of music, *n. u.*

Gander, *s.* dādleñ ās, -sā, *n.* = *l.* male of the goose.

Gang, *s.* zomo, -meā, *m.*; čiḷḷeñ-biḷḷeñ, -ḷeā, *n.*, *mn.* a crowd.

Gaol, *s.* *vlg.* zăil *or* jăil, -lā, *n.* *fr.*; *see* **Jail.**

Gangrene, *s.* bogdāḷ, -ḷā, *n.*

Gaoler, *s.* *vlg.* zăiler, -rā, *m.*; *see* **Jailer.**

Gap, *s.* 1. iḍeñ, -ḍeā, *n.*
2. fuṭ, -ṭi, *f.*

Gape, *v.* tònḍ ukteñ kăr = *l.* make the mouth open, *pr.*, *fg.*

Garb, *see* **Dress.**

Garble, *see* **Falsify.**

Garden, *s.* itāl, -tlā, *n.*; moḷo, -ḷeā, *m.* *as* the g. of Gethsemani; voḍt, -tā, *n.* = a small g.; tòṭ (ò), -ṭā, *n.*, *used also for* plantation; bāg, -gā, *n.*

Gardener, *s.* māli, -li, *m.*, *fr.* = he who waters the plants; tòṭagār, -rā, *m.*

Garland, *s.* jelo, -leā, *m.* = a string of flowers; kopel, -lā, *n.*, *fr. used esp. for* a g. of artificial flowers.

Garlic, *s.* losuṇ, -sṇi, *f.*

Garment, *s.* mustaigi, -ge, *f.*; lugāṭ, -gṭā, *n.* = *l.* cloth, *fg.* vǎstur, -turā, *n.*; nesoṇ, -ṇi, *f.*

Garnet, *s.* yākut, -tā, *m.*, *n. u.*, *Mr.*

Garret, *s.* 1. māḷo, -ḷeā, *m.* (*Ital. solajo*).

2. *fg.* biḍār, -rā, *n.* = *l.* an abode; ṭhikāṇeñ, -ṇeā, *n.* = *l.* an abode.

Garrison, *s.* šibǎndi, -de, *f. mn. also* establishment; rākṇeñ, -ṇeā, *n.* = *l.* a guard, a defence.

Garrulous, *a.* boḍboḍo; lāmb jibetso = *l.* of long tongue; phāndḷeāgār.

Garter, *s.* nāḍo, -ḍeā, *m.*

Gas, *s.* vāi, -ye, *f.*, *used com. for* flatulence, *root meaning* gas *as in Cn. & Mr.*; ub, -be, *f.* = *l.* steam; *vlg.* vāreñ, -reā, *n.*

Gash, *s.* vóḍ ghāi, -yā, *m.* = *l.* a large wound; kātrāp, -pā, *n.* = *l.* a cut.

Gash, *v.* kātǎr = *l.* cut.

Gasp, *v.* kǎrše.

Gasp, *s.* kǎrǎs, -rsi, *f.*

Gate, *s.* dārvaṭo, -ṭeā, *m.* = a big door, *also*, *e.g.* a church door; bāgil, -glā, *n.* = a common door.

Gate-keeper, *s.* bāglarākṇo, -ṇeā, *m.*

Gather, *v.* 1. meḷǎi, *c. v. of* mèḷ; yekṭāiñ kǎr = *l.* make gathering, *e.g.* corn; ārāi = g. with hands, *e.g.* what you have swept up.

2. luuñ = reap, *e.g.* g. a crop.

3. pārki = *l.* guess.

4. nisčeisi = *l.* establish, conclude; tātpǎriya kǎr, *n. c.*

5. pule = *l.* suppurate.

G. in = zōḍ(ó).

G. round = *Or.* kǎḍe mèḷ.

Gathering, *s.* meḷounčeñ *or bet.* meḷāp, -ḷpā, *n.*; mēḷ (é), -ḷā, *m.*

Gauge, *v.* mēz(é).

Gauge, *s.* mezāp, -zpā, *n.*

Gauntlet, *s.* luñ, -vā, *n.* = *l.* a glove, *fr.*; *see* **Glove.**

Gay, *a.* 1. khušālāyetso; sǎntosātso.

2. pǎrzǎlik = *l.* bright, *e. g.* colour.

Gaze, *v.* pòḷe *with* -ts, *or* jīv sōḍn poḷe = *l.* look giving up life.

Gaze, *s.* 1. *rs. v.*

2. diṣṭ, -ṭi, *f.* = *l.* sight.

Gazette, *s.* 1. *vlg.* gajet, -ti, *f.*, *fr.*

2. vǎrtamānapǎtrụ, -rā, *n.* = *l.* a writing of news.

Gazetteer, *s.* vǎrtamānapǎtrist, -tā, *m.*, *or* —pǎtrikegār.

Gear, *s.* 1. sāmān, -nā, *m.* = *l.* an article.

2. mustāigi, -ge, *f.* = *l.* a garment.

Gelatine, *s.* 1. ăṇṭu, -ṭā, *m.* = vegetable g.
2. govardān, -nā, *n.* = animal g.

Gelid, *a.* thăṇḍ gār; gārātṣo *or* gārā bări = *l.* like ice.

Gem, *s.* 1. rătăn, -tnā, *n.* = a precious stone.
2. bongo, -geā, *m.*; *see* **Bud.**

Gem, *v. fg.* surungār kăr, *G. M.* = *l.* make an ornament.

Gender, *s.* 1. ling, -gā, *n.* (Gram.)
2. thăr, -rā, *m.* = *l.* kind.

Genealogy, *s.* 1. kuṭmāčeo kobro, *pl., f.* = *l.* news of family.
2. tăkleānči hār, -ri, *f.*

General, *a.* 1. sādhārn = *l.* ordinary.
2. sămestāntso, săkṭāntso = of all.
3. părgăṭ = *l.* public.
4. tsăḍāvot *mn.* common to all (*not com. in this mn.*)
G. confession = jerāl kumsār, -rā, *n., fr.* (*vlg.*)
In g. = voṭṭār; tsăḍāvot zāun.
Become g. = părgăṭ zā, *or only* părgăṭ.

General, *s. vlg.* jeral, -lā, *m., fr.* ădhipăti, -ti, *m.*; ădhikāri, -ri, *m.*; mostak, -kā, *n.* = *l.* head, *fg.*
G. of an army = foujiădhipăti, -ti, *m.*; foujihuddeāgār, -rā, *m.*

Generalise, *v.* sămestānk lāi, *etc.*

Generalissimo, *s.* mukhya ădhipăti, -ti, *m.*

Generality, *s.* 1. sādhārnāi, *or* sādāraṇāi, -ye, *f., n. c.*
2. tsăḍāvot vāṇṭo, -ṭeā, *m.* = *l.* the greatest part; tsăḍāvot lók, *or only* lók, -kā, *m.* = the most people; *bet. rs. into adj.*

Generally, *ad.* 1. tsăḍāvotzāun, *mn.* for the most part.
2. voṭṭār *or* voṭṭu = altogether, not in particular.

Generate, *v.* zălmăi, *c. v. of* zălma; *bet. use the neuter v., ch. cs.*

Generation, *s.* 1. zălm, -mā, *m.*
2. săntăt, -ti, *f.* = *l.* posterity.
3. kuḷi, -ye, *f.*, săst, -sti, *f.* = a tribe.

Generic, *see* **General.**

Generosity, *s.* udārpoṇ, -ṇā, *n.*; vóḍ mòn, -nā, *n.* = *l.* a great heart.

Generous, *a.* udār; voḍa monātso.

Genesis, *s.* ărămb, -bā, *m.*

Genial, *a.* kušălāyetso = *l.* of pleasure; mogāḷ = *l.* dear; bore mărjetso = *l.* of good humour.

Genius, *s.* 1. sobāu, -āvā, *m.* = *l.* a disposition (of mind).
2. dăitpoṇ, -ṇā, *n.*
3. *concrete noun,* dăit (mănis, -nšā, *m.*)

Genteel, *a.* măryāditso; *see* **Polite.**

Gentile, *s.* ănbāvāḍti, -tiā, *m.* = *l.* unbeliever; Hindu *or* Hinduāntso (g. of these places); *the Goanese word* Konkṇo *is used partially also in Canara in this sense.*

mn. only Konkani-speaking gentiles.

Gentle, *a.* 1. măryāditso, *mn.* of good manners.
2. līn = *l.* meek, *n. c.*
3. soukāsāyetso = *l.* of peace, *fg., e.g.* g. wind.

Gentleman, *s.* sărdār, *or* sărdār-băhudār, -rā, *m.*; măryāditso mănis, -nšā, *m.* = *l.* a genteel man; mānātso mănis, -nšā, *m.* = a man of honour; voḍlo mănis = *l.* a great man; sāib, -bā, *m.*; bāb, -bā, *m.*; *see* Gram. P. III. ch. i.

Gentleness, *s.* măryād, -di, *f.*; tsāl-tsămkăṇ, -ṇā, *n.* = politeness.

Gently, *ad.* 1. măryādin.
2. soukāsāyen; thoḍeñ thoḍeñ.

Genuine, *a.* 1. nīz = *l.* sincere, true; khărots = *l.* true (*emph.*)
2. niskăpṭi = *l.* sincere.
3. borsinātullo = *l.* not mixed.
4. sādo = *l.* simple.
5. nigăl, apuṭ, *e.g.* genuine Christian, g. wine.

Geographer, *s.* buiñvivori, -riā, *m.* = *l.* explainer of the earth; buiñšāstri, -ri, *m.* = a man learned as regards the earth; buiñnăkṣegār, -rā, *m.*

Geography, *s.* buiñvivor, -rā, *m.* = *l.* a description of the earth; buiñšāstru̥, -trā, *n.*; buiñ-năkṣa, -ṣe, *f.*

Geographical, *a.* buiñvivorātso *or* —vivorkărtso, *or sometimes only* buintso, *or rs.* buiñ.

G. position = buinči suāt, -te, *f.*

Geological, *a.* buiñărămbātso = *l.* of the origin of the earth, *or bet. rs.* buiñărămba vi-šyānt, *or perh.*—višăyātso.

Geologist, *s.* buiñărămbapănḍit, *or, shorter,* buiñpănḍit, -tā, *m., n. u.*

Geology, *s.* buiñărămbašāstru̥, -rā, *n.*; *perh.* buiñrātsne-šāstru̥, -rā, *n.*

Geometer, *s.* buiñmāpist, -tā, *m.*; rēkhāgăṇitašāstri, -ri, *m.* (*Cn. Mr.*)

Geometry, *s.* buiñmāp, -pā, *n.* = *l.* a measure of the earth; rēkhāgăṇitašāstru̥, -rā, *n.* (*Cn. Mr.*)

German, *s.* 1. săiro, -reā, *m.* = *l.* a relative.
2. bhāu, -āvā, *m. or* bhăiṇ (*or* boiṇ), -ṇi, *f.* = brother *or* sister; bāpulbhāu *or* māusi-bhăiṇ = cousin.

Germinate, *v.* ubzăi, *c. v. of* ubza; kirlăi.

Germination, *s.* kirlāp, -pā, *n.*

Gesticulate, *v.* hāt porti = *l.* turn hands; āngavikṣep kăr (*Cn. Mr.*) = *l.* make a movement of the body; āng porti = *l.* turn the body.

Gesticulation, *s.* hātāñbhās, -se, *f.* = *l.* the language of the hands.

Gesture, *s.* 1. āvăsta, -te, *f.* = an unbecoming g.
2. hātañportouṇeñ, -ṇeā, *n.* = *l.*

a turning of the hands; *see* **Gesticulation.**

Get, *v.* 1. mèḷ = *l.* be found (obtain), *Prs. Dat.*; zóḍ = *l.* obtain, acquire.
2. pòḍ = *l.* fall, *e.g.* g. an inheritance.
3. *by caus. verb*, *e.g.* get done = kărăi.
4. zā = *l.* become, be done.
5. pāu = *l.* reach.
G. abroad = 1. kăḷit zā = *l.* become known, *or* părgăṭ zā.
2. tsăl, *or* tsălto zā = *l.* be current.
G. across = utrăi, *c. v. of* utăr = cross; *or* poltăḍi vor.
G. along = mukār vots = *l.* go further.
G. among = pòḍ = *l.* fall.
G. at = pāu = *l.* reach.
G. away = pòḷ, *or* dāuñ = *l.* flee, run away.
G. back = 1. vāpas ghe *or* vosul kăr, *or* pāṭi ghe.
2. pāṭi vots = go back.
G. clear of = tsukăi; păriyār zā.
G. down = devoi, *c. v. of* deuñ = descend.
G. hold = dhăr.
G. in = yekṭāi kăr; *see* **Gather.**
G. off = kāḍ, suṭ (be acquitted).
G. on = boro āsā = *l.* is well.
G. out = *2nd Loc.* deuñ = *l.* descend from; bhāir vots.
G. ready = tăyār kăr.
G. rid of, *see* G. clear of.
G. through = 1. pāu = *l.* reach.
2. tirsi = *l.* finish.
G. together, *see* **Gather.**
G. up = uṭ.
G. upon = tsăḍ = *l.* ascend.

Gewgaw, *s.* 1. čillăr văstu̩, -tu, *f.* = *l.* a trifling thing.
2. khèḷtso sāmān, -nā, *m.* = a plaything.

Ghastliness, *s.* bhiyānkulāi, -ye, *f.*; mòrnāčeñ pānṭrepoṇ, -ṇā, *n.* = *l.* the paleness of death; *bet. rs.* moḍeā bāri pānṭro.

Ghastly, *a.* 1. kāmpereātso.
2. bhiyānkuḷ = *l.* dreadful.

Ghost, *s.* 1. ātmo, -meā, *m.* = *l.* a soul; kuleñ, -leā, *n.* = a goblin *or* ghost.
2. dușṭakāi, -ye, *f.* (devil); 'dușṭakāyečeñ vokāt, -ktā, *n.* = a medicine against dușṭakāi'.
3. prāṇ, -ṇā, *m.* = life, *e.g.* give up the g. = prāṇ sóḍ.
4. Spirit, -tā, *m.* = *H. G.*

Giant, *s.* 1. rākkos, -ksā, *m.* (*often an abusive term*).
2. pānḍou, -ovā, *m.* = g. of fable.
3. dăit, -tā, *m.* = a tall man, *pr.*, *fg.*

Gibber, *see* **Chatter.**

Gibbet, *see* **Gallows.**

Gibbosity, *s.* pòng, -gi, *f.* (*or* -gā, [*n.*)

Gibbous, *a.* pòngo.

Gibe, *v.* yeḍāi = *l.* mock; hās = *l.* laugh at.

Giblets, *s. has no nearer equivalent than* nākāri văstu̩, -tu, *f.* = *l.* useless parts (of poultry).

Giddiness, *s.* guvoḷ, -ḷi, *f.*; *rs.* tăkli guuntā = the head is turning, *or* mót tsuktā = *l.* the mind is not present.

Giddy, *a.* 1. guvoḷitso.
2. *fg.* budnātullo = *l.* not wise.

Gift, *s.* 1. deṇeñ, -ṇeā, *n.*; kāṇik, -ke, *f.* = a splendid gift; bhèṭ, -ṭe, *f.* = *l.* an offering.
2. săkti, -ti (*or* šakăt, -kti), *f.* = *l.* a power, *e.g.* g. of invention.
'Beḷeñ kāṇik = the present of the first crop to the landlord'.

Gifted, *a.* āsullo, *with the name of what one is gifted with; e.g.* g. with a strong mind = mót āsullo.

Gigantic, *a.* dăitātso, *or* dăita bări; bhou vóḍ = *l.* very great.

Giggle, *v.* amburko hās = *l.* a smiling laugh.

Gild, *v.* bāngār *or* mulām lāi = *l.* apply gold; m. kāḍ.

Gilded, *a.* bāngār *or* mulām lāillo; mulāmātso.

Gilder, *s.* mulāmgār, -rā, *m.*

Gilding, *s.* mulāmāsamarthi, -the, *f.* = *l.* the art of gilding.

Gill, *s.* 1. (¼ of a pint) jil, -lā, *n.*, *fr.*
2. gābḷañ, *pl. n.* (of birds *and also* of men): 'tākā g. deuliñ = he got gills'.

Gimlet, *s.* rum, -mā, *n.*

Gin, *s.* 1. nāḍ, -ḍi, *f.* = *l.* a snare.
2. jin, -nā, *m.*, *fr.* = a liquor so called.
3. kāpsalāṭo, -ṭeā, *m.* = a machine for cleaning cotton.

Gin, *v.* kāpus nităḷ kăr.

Ginger, *s.* āleñ, -leā, *n.*; sunṭ, -ṭi, *f.* (dried g.)

Gipsy, *s.* 1. jipsi, -siā, *m.* = *Lat. zingarus.*
2. *fg.* pārpóḷ = *l.* roaming.

Gird, *v.* 1. revoḍn ghāl, *or only* revoḍ, *or*, *often*, *only* ghāl, *e.g.* g. a sword; *Or.* bountăṇiñ bānd.
2. lāg = *l.* be applied, *e. g.* g. (oneself) to the task = kāmāk lāg.
G. up oneself = tăyār zā.
G. on a sword = penkṭāk tălvār bānd = *l.* bind the sword to the loins.

Girdle, *s.* pāṭo, -ṭeā, *m.*; munz, -ji, *f.* (*gener. term*); nevāḷeñ, -ḷeā, *n. used mostly by* non-catholics; dāb, -bi, *f.*; kămbărbănd, -dā, *n. used by* Mahomedans; bānd, -dā, *n.* = *l.* a tie.

Girl, *s.* čeḍuñ (*var.* čoḍuñ), -ḍuā, *n.*; tsăli, -ye, *f.* (*H. K.*)

Girth, *s.* 1. bānd, -dā, *n.*
2. băunḍi, -ḍe, *f.*; *see* **Circumference.**

Gist, *s.* 1. sār, -rā, *m.* = *l.* substance; mukhya văstu, -tu, *f.* = *l.* the chief thing; mūḷ, -ḷā, *n.* = *l.* a root, *fg.*
2. mulo, -leā, *m.* = *l.* a hinge, *fg.*

Give, *v.* di.
G. a blow = mār lāi, *or bet. only* mār.
G. to understand = somzăi.
G. back = pāṭi di *or* vāpās di (*Lat. restitue*).
G. chase = dāunḍāi = *l.* cause to run.
G. in one's name = dākăl zā (be registered).
G. out (juice) = 1. dike, *or bet.* dik ye.
2. móṇ = say.
3. āšā sóḍ.
4. sóḍ *or* tāmb = *l.* cease.
G. over = vopsun di.
G. up = 1. vopsun di, *viz.* deliver.
2. ghāt kăr = *l.* make deceit.
3. vāṭer ghāl = *l.* put on the way, abandon; sóḍ = *l.* leave.
G. way = 1. păḍāu zā = be defeated.
2. khuše părmāṇe kăr = *l.* do according to the will of.
3. iḍeñ di = *l.* give escape (to a passion); kobuli di = *l.* give consent.
G. place = 1. pois = far, *ch. cs.*
2. vāṭ sóḍ = *l.* abandon the way.
G. a dinner = vāḍ (*of inferiors to superiors*); jevāṇ di.

Glacial, *a.* gārātso = *l.* of ice; bhou šéḷ *or* bhou thănḍ = *l.* very cold.

Glacis, *s.* 1. gārātso zāgo, -geā, *m.* = *l.* a ground of ice.
2. deuṇi, -ṇe, *f.* = *l.* slope.

Glad, *a.* dādos *or* dādosi; săntosātso = *l.* joyful; khušāl = *l.* merry; ănănd āsullo = *l.* having joy.

Gladden, *v.* dādos kăr; khušāl kăr.

Glade, *s. approx.* lăččil, -lā, *n.* = *l.* meadow; moḷeālăččil, -lā, *n.*; tsărovazāgo, -geā, *m.*

Gladiator, *s.* kustigār, -rā, *m.*

Gladly, *ad.* săntosān; dādosizāun; khušālāyen; ănăndān.

Gladness, *s.* săntos, -sā, *m.*; *see* Joy.

Glance, *v.* pòḷe; dišṭ ghāl = *l.* put sight.

Glance, *s.* dišṭ, -ṭi, *f.*; 'cast a g. = d. ghāl.

Glare, *s.* 1. părzăḷ, -ḷā, *m.*, *or* părzăḷāi, -ye, *f.*; prăkāš, -šā, *m.*
2. kirn, -nā, *n.* = *l.* a ray.
3. ulop, -lpā, *m.*; dāu, -āvā, *m.* = heat with light (*also* heat of the body).

Glare, *v.* părzăḷ.

Glass, *s.* 1. ārso, -seā, *m. mn.* mirror, *and also* the substance.
2. tamblér, -rā, *m.*, *Engl.* = tumbler; pātru, -rā, *n.*, *not used.*

Glassy, *a.* ārseātso.

Glaze, *v.* ārso ghāl *or* ā. lāi.

Gleam, *v.* părzăḷ, *pr. fg.*; miṇimiṇi kăr (*Ital. luccicare*) *as the eyes of a cat or as the stars* g.; *or only* miṇmiṇ; jiḷibiḷi kăr.

Gleam, *s.* 1. părzăḷ, -ḷā, *m.*
2. fār, -rā, *m.*
3. *fg.* kirn, -nā, *n.* = *l.* a ray, *as* a g. of hope.

Glean, *v.* 1. vints; băitāčeñ bhāt meḷăi = *l.* collect the paddy of straw.
2. *fg.* bāki.

Glide, *v.* nisăr, *mn.* slip, *and also* run away.

Glimmer, *v.* părzăḷ, *with the quasi-dim.* -so; *see* Gram. P. III. ch. ii.

Glimpse, *s.* 1. diṣṭ, -ṭi, *f.*
2. illo uzvāḍ, -ḍā, *m.* = *l.* faint light; 'get a g. = poḷe'.

Glitter, *v.* părzăḷ; zăgzăg.

Glitter, *s.* părzăḷ, -ḷā, *m.*

Gloat, *v.* jīv sóḍn pòḷe = *l.* look leaving life (*Konk.*).

Globe, *s.* 1. guḷo, -ḷeā, *m.*; *dim.* guḷi, -ye, *f.*
2. buiñ, -iñ, *f.* = *l.* earth.

Globular, *a.* vāḍkulo.

Gloom, *s.* 1. kāḷok, -kā, *m.*, *pr. fg.*, *e.g.* g. of life.
2. *fg.* kăṣṭ, -ṭā, *m.*; khănt, -ti, *f.*

Gloomy, *a.* 1. kāḷso = *l.* blackish; kāḷki, *applied esp. to* night.
2. *fg.* khăntiṣṭ, dukest, čintest = *l.* sorry.
3. lāsulleñ tònḍ = surly.

Glorification, *s.* ănăndpoṇ, -ṇā, *n.*, *or bet.* ănăndbăritpoṇ, -ṇā, *n.*, *n. c.*; *see* **Glory.**

Glorify, *v.* ănănd di, *or* ă. kăr; mān di; mān vāḍăi = *l.* increase the honour, *e.g.* of God; uboḷsi *or* hogoḷsi = *l.* praise.

Glorious, *a.* 1. zăitevont = *l.* victorious.
2. mānādik, *mn.* giving honour; *rs.* mānāk pòḍtso; ănăndbărit = *l.* full of glory.

Glory, *s.* ănănd, -dā, *m.*; mān, -nā, *m.*; hoḍvi, -ve, *f.* = *l.* majesty; măima, -me, *f.* = *l.* majesty; hogḷāp, -pā, *n.* = *l.* praise.

Glory, *v.* ănănd pāu: 'I g. in God = āuñ Devā thăiñ ă. pāutāñ'.

Gloss, *v.* părzăḷ; miṇimiṇi kăr.

Glossary, *s.* utrāntso vivor, -rā, *m.* = *l.* an explanation of words.

Glossy, *a.* părzăḷik.

Glove, *s.* luñ, -uvā, *n.*, *fr.*; hātāñmēi, -yā, *m.* = *l.* stockings of the hands, *fr.*, *n. u.*

Glow, *s.* 1. gărmi, -me, *f.* = *l.* heat, *e.g.* of anger; umāḷo, -ḷeā, *m.*
2. părzăḷ, -ḷā, *m.* = *l.* shining.

Glow, *v.* 1. tāp = *l.* be hot; *c. v.* tāpăi; un zā = *l.* get warm.
2. *fg.* zăḷ = *l.* burn, *e.g.* rāgān z.; umāḷ.

Glowing terms = umāḷeāčiñ utrāñ.

Glow-worm, *s.* kāzulo, -leā, *m.*

Gloze, *v.* fuslāi = *l.* flatter.

Glue, *s.* 1. góndu, -dā, *m.*
2. pānk, -kā, *m.*

Glut, *v.* jīv sódn khā; pòṭ bhór.

Glut, *s.* khāugipon, -ṇā, *n.*; pòṭāčeñ bhorāp, -rpā, *n.*; dādoskāi, -ye, *f.*

Glutinous, *a.* pānkātso.

Glutton, *s.* pòṭāro mănis, -nšā, *m.*; khāugi, -giā, *m.*; orbosi, -siā, *m.*

Gluttonous, *a.* pòṭāro; khāugi.

Gluttony, *s.* pòṭārpon, -ṇā, *n.*; pòṭārd, -dā, *n.*

Gnash, *v.* kiḍkiḍ, *or* kirli.

Gnashing, *s.* dāntāñčābṇeñ, -ṇeā, [*n.*

Gnat, *s.* 1. zăḷār, -re, *f.*
2. musk, -kā, *n.* (a little fly, *dim. of* mus).

Gnaw, *v.* tsābun kāḍ = *l.* biting take away.

Gnomon, *s.* uorānči boḍi, -ye, *f.* = *l.* a stick of the hours; khiḷ, -ḷi, *f.*; kānṭo, -ṭeā, *m.* = *l.* a thorn, *used for the* hand of a watch, *hence perh. for* gn.

Go, *v.* 1. vetā (goes); *Past* gelo; *see* Gram.
2. bhāir săr = *l.* start.
3. zā = *l.* become (turn out); sevoṭ āsā = aim is.
I am going to bed = nidtāñ thāiñ āsāñ; *see* Gram. P. II. ch iv.; the story goes that. . . = kăta tsăltā ki. . . .
Two go for one = donānk yek (āsā).

G. about = 1. bouñ.
2. prăyătān kăr = *l.* make an effort.
G. abroad = bhāir vots, *or* bărpăr vots.
G. astray = tsuk.
G. away = bhāir săr, *or only* vots.
G. back = pāṭi vots.
G. behind = pāṭleān vetā.
G. beyond = poltoḍi vots, *or only* utăr = cross, *or* bărpăr, *or* găḍi bhāir vots, *n. c.*
G. by = 1. lāgiñ vots.
2. pāṭlāu kăr = *l.* make following, *or* dēk(ė) kāṇe = *l.* take example.
G. down = deuñ.
G. for = āpoun hāḍ = *l.* calling bring.
G. forth = bhāir săr.
G. in = rig.
G. off = zā = *l.* become.
Go on = 1. mukār vots = *l.* go forward.
2. găḍ = *l.* happen.
3. jik = *l.* gain, *fg.* succeed; vrăddhi zā = *l.* get prosperous.
G. out = 1. bhāir săr = start.
2. pālvā = *l.* get quenched; thāmb = *l.* cease.
G. over = 1. utron vots = *l.* crossing go.
2. sóḍ = *l.* abandon (revolt).
3. vòp = *l.* consent, *e.g.* g. over to an opinion.
4. voilebār vāts = *l.* read superficially.

G. round; *see* G. about.
G. through = 1. vetā, *with the Instr. in* -ntleān.
2. tirsi = *l.* finish, carry out.
G. to = lāg = *l.* be applied, *e.g.* g. to war.
G. up = tsăḍ = *l.* ascend.
Let go = sóḍ.

Goad, *s.* khiḷo, -ḷeā, *m.* = *l.* a nail (fixed in a stick); ānkuš, -šā, *m.*

Goad, *v.* 1. (khiḷeān) dāunḍāi = *l.* cause to run (with the g.)
2. *fg.* uṭāi = *l.* cause to rise (excite).

Goal, *s.* sevoṭ, -ṭā, *m.* = *l.* aim.

Goat, *s.* gāuntso bokḍo, -ḍeā, *m.*, *or* bokḍi, -ḍe, *f.* = *l.* a sheep of the country; *some say simply* bokḍo, bokḍi; benkreñ, -reā, *n.* = a wild he-goat.

Go-between, *s.* 1. mālo, -leā, *m.* = *l.* barber (g. for arranging a marriage, *a barber formerly being used as such*).
2. dălāl, -lā, *m.* = *l.* an agent; păñčāyetdār, -rā, *m.* = *l.* an arbiter.

Gobble, *v.* jīv sóḍn khā = *l.* eat giving up life (*Konk.*).

Goblet, *s.* *vlg.* kòp, -pā, *n.* *or* tambler, -rā, *m.*, *fr.*; pātrụ, -rā, *or* păñčapātrụ, -rā, (*Cn. Mr.*)

Goblin, *s.* druṣṭakāi, -ye, *f.* (*vlg.* duṣṭakāi); kuleñ, -leā, *n.*; bhut, -tā, *m.* = *l.* a devil.

God, *s.* Dēu, -ēvā, *m.*

God-child, *s.* *vlg.* filiād, -dā, *n.*, *fr.*; dhărmaput, -tā, *m.*, dh. du, -ve, *f.* = a child of charity, *exact w.*

Goddess, *s.* devi, -vi, *f.*

God-father, *s.* *vlg.* podorn, -ni, *m.*, *fr.*; dhărmabāp, -pā, *m.*

Godhead, *s.* Dēupoṇ, -ṇā, *n.*

Godless, *a.* Dēunātullo = *l.* without God; Dēu deuntsār nātullo = *l.* without God or devil (*vlg.*).

Godliness, *s.* bhăkt, -ti, *f.*, *or* bhăktipoṇ, -ṇā, *n.*

Godly, *a.* Devāgelo.

God-mother, *s.* *vlg.* modorn, -ni, *f.*, *fr.*; dhărmamāi, -ye, *f.*

Go-down, *s.* māḷo, -ḷeā, *m.*; ugrāṇ, -ṇā, *n.*

God-send, *s.* măima, -me, *f.* (*also* punishment); sukduk, -kā, *n.*

Goggle, *a.* gugitso = *l.* of an owl, *e.g.* g. eyes; āmbāḍo; āmbāḍeāñ-doḷeāntso.

Goitre, *s.* 1. fòḷụ, -ḷā, *n.* = *l.* fruit (*Ital. pomo d' Adamo*).
2. gunṭ, -ṭā, *n.* (*Ital. gozzo*).

Gold, *s.* bāngār, -rā, *n.*
Some kinds of g. *are* 1. poun; 2. stāmbol; 3. kurzāt.

Golden, *a.* bāngārāčeñ mulām lāillo.

Gold-leaf, *s.* (bāngārāčeñ) tăgăḍ, -gḍā, *n.*; fól, -li, *f.*

Goldsmith, *s.* sonār, -rā, *m.*

Gong, *s.* *perh.* ghānṭ, -ṭi, *f.*, *or* thāli, -ye, *f.*; vāṭli, -le, *f.*

Good, *a.* boro, *applicable in all the senses of the Engl. word* 'good'.
A g. deal = bhou tsăḍ.
Make g. = 1. săma kăr = *l.* make right.
2. fārikpoṇ di = *l.* give satisfaction; bhórn di = *l.* give full, *e.g.* m. g. honour.

Good, *s.* 1. boreñ, -reā, *n.*
2. *pl.* āst, -ti, *f.* = *l.* property; mhāl, -lā, *m.* = *l.* chattels; dăn, -nā, *n.*, *or* dăn văstụ, -tu, *f.*
Do g. = boreñ kăr.

Good-breeding, *s.* tsāltsămkăṇ, -ṇā, *n.*; măryād, -di, *f.*; mănšepoṇ, -ṇā, *n.* = *l.* humanity, *fg.*

Good-bye, *s.* sukhi zāuñ = *l.* be happy.

Good-Friday, *s.* nimāṇo sukrār, -rā, *m.* = *l.* last Fr.

Good-humour, *s.* bori mărji, -je, *f.*

Good-looking, *a.* bolāiketso, *or* bolāikent āsullo; *rs.* boro distā = *l.* appears well.

Good-nature, *s.* mogāḷ sobāu, -āvā, *m.* = *l.* dear character; mogāḷpoṇ, -ṇā, *n.* = *l.* dearness.

Good-natured, *a.* mogāḷ = *l.* dear; sādo = *l.* tame; dăyāḷ = *l.* clement.

Goodness, *s.* borepoṇ, -ṇā, *n.*; boreñ mòn, -nā, *n.* = *l.* good heart; mogāḷpoṇ, -ṇā, *n.* = *l.* dearness.

Goods, *s.* mhāl, -lā, *m.*, sāmān, -nā, *m.* = articles.

Good-temper, *s.* boro sobāu, -āvā, [*m.*

Good-tempered, *a.* boreā sobāvātso, *or* mogāḷ, *or* līn.

Good-will, *s.* bori khuši, -še, *f.*; mōg(ó), -gā, *m.* = *l.* love; dosti, -te, *f.* = *l.* favour.

Goose, *s.* bāileñ ās, -sā, *n.*

Gooseberry, *s.* *approx.* fòḷ, -ḷā, *n.*

Gordian, *a.* *nearest eq.* kăṣṭāntso, *or* kăṭiṇ = *l.* difficult.

Gore, *s.* răgat, -gtā, *n.*; geṭo, -ṭeā, *m.* = clotted blood.

Gore, *v.* hānḍ (stab with horns).

Gorge, *s.* 1. gomṭo, -ṭeā, *m.*; gă-ḷo, -ḷeā, *m.*
2. *fg.* ăširāi, -ye, *f.* = *l.* narrow-[ness.

Gorgeous, *a.* sobit = *l.* nice; surungārātso = *l.* ornamental; dobājeātso = *l.* showy.

Gormandise, *v.* jīv sóḍn khā = *l.* eat leaving life.

Gormandiser, *s.* pòṭāro mănis, -nšā, *m.*; khāugi, -giā, *m.*

Gory, *a.* răgtātso; răgtān bhorlolo.

Gospel, *s.* *vlg.* vanjel *or* evanjel, -lā, *m.*, *fr.*; šubhavārtā, -te, *f.* (*Cn.*, *Mr.*), *or bet.* suvărtamān, -nā, *n.* (*Cn.*, *Tul.*, *Mr.*, *Sans. and Mal.*); J. Kristāči sómórt, -ti, *f.* = *l.* the religion of J. C.; bori kobār, -bre, *f.* = *l.* good news; boreñ răvaneñ, -neā, *n.* = *l.* good message; Devāčeñ utăr, -trā, *n.* = *l.* God's word.

Gossip, *s.* 1. găzāl, -li, *f.* = idle talk; phāndḷo, -ḷeā, *m.* = idle talk.
2. phāndḷeagār, -rā, *m.* = a talkative person.

Gossip, *v.* phāndḷe *or* găzāli mār = *l.* beat chats.

Gourd, *s.* dudiñ, -diyā, *n.*

Gourmet, *s.* nāzuk mănis, -nšā, *m.* *or* nāzukgār, -rā, *m.* = *l.* a delicate man; khāugi, -giā, *m.*

Gout, *s.* vāt, -tā, *m.*

Govern, *v.* 1. tsălăi = *l.* cause to walk, *fg.*
2. rāzvoṭ *or* rāzvoṭkāi kăr (*obj. 2nd Loc.*) = reign.

Governess, *s.* 1. mestiṇ, -ṇi, *f.* = a female teacher, *fr.*
2. voḍāngeli mestiṇ, *Lat. paedagoga*, (a female attendant on children); *bet.* āyā, -yā, *f.*

Government, *s.* 1. sărkār, -rā, *m.* = civil power; ădhikār, -rā, *m.* = *l.* authority (supreme).
2. rāz, -jā, *n.* = *l.* a kingdom.
3. kārkhāno, -neā, *m.* = *l.* an administration.

Governor, *s.* ădhikāri, -ri, *or* ădhipăti, -ti, *m.*

Gown, *s.* lób, -bā, *m.* (of priests), *fr.*; pāyāngol văstur, -rā, *n.*; āngleñ, -leā, *n.* (of native girls); gāgro, -reā, *m.*

Grace, *s.* 1. kurpa, -pe, *f.* (*no pl.*), *e.g.* Divine g.
2. dosti, -te, *f.* = *l.* favour, *e.g.* of a king.
3. māf, -fi, *f.* = *l.* a pardon, an excuse.
4. măryād, -di, *f.* = *l.* honesty, *e.g.* walk with g.
5. ārgāñ, *pl.* *n.* = *l.* thanksgiving.
6. neṭoṇi, -ṇe, *f.* = *l.* an ornament.
7. sāib, -bā, *m.* = *l.* a lord.

Grace, *v.* neṭăi = *l.* adorn; sobăi = *l.* make nice.

Graceful, *a.* măryāditso; sundăr = *l.* nice.

Gracefulness, *s.* măryād, -di, *f.*; sobitāi, -ye, *f.* = *l.* beauty.

Gracious, *a.* guṇātso = *l.* favourable.

Graciousness, *s.* mogāḷpoṇ, -ṇā, *n.*; dăya, -ye, *f.*

Gradation, *s.* krăm, -mā, *n.* = *l.* order, *or* mānḍāvoḷ, -ḷi, *f.*

Grade, *s.* grāu, -āvā, *m.*; huddo, -deā, *m.* = *l.* a rank; thăr, -rā, *m.* = *l.* a kind.

Gradual, *a.* thoḍeñ thoḍeātso; *bet. rs. into ad.*

Gradually, *ad.* thoḍeñ thoḍeñ.

Graduate, *v.* 1. pāṭo di = *l.* give a diploma; *pass.* p. ghe = receive a d.
2. grāu ghāl = *l.* put degrees, *e.g.* to a thermometer; vāṇṭe kăr = make divisions.

Graduation, *s.* 1. grāu, -āvā, *m.* = *l.* a degree.
2. *rs. into v.; see also* **Gradation.**

Graft, *v.* iseḍt kăr, *fr.*; kăsi kăr = *l.* inoculate.

Grain, *s.* dhāni, -ye, *f.*
2. kăṇ, -ṇā, *n.* = a single grain.

Gram, *s.* kuḷit, -ḷtā, *m.*; tsăṇo, -ṇeā, *n.* = Bengal gram.

Grammar, *s.* vyākărăṇ, -ṇā, *n.*

Grammarian, *s.* vyākărăṇist, -tā, *m.*

Grammatical, *a.* vyākărăṇātso, *or bet.* vyākărăṇa părmāṇe āsullo.

Grammatically, *ad.* vyākărăṇa părmāṇe.

Granary, *s.* tupeñ, -peā, *n.*

Grand, *a.* dobājeātso; voḍpoṇātso.

Grand-child, *s.* nātruñ, -trā, *n.*

Grand-daughter, *s.* nāt, -ti, *f.*

Grand-father, *s.* āzo, -jeā, *m.*

Grand-mother, *s.* āji, -je, *f.*

Grand-son, *s.* nātu, -tuā, *m.*
Great grand-father = poṇzo, -jeā, *m.*
Gr. grand-mother = poṇji, -je, *f.*
Gr. grand-son, gr. grand-daughter = ponṭuruṇ, -rā, *n.*

Grandee, *s.* 1. măntănāntlo = *l.* noble.
2. huddeāgār, -rā, *m.* = *l.* dignitary.

Grandeur, *s.* dobāzo, -jeā, *m.*; voḍpoṇ, -ṇā, *n.*

Grange, *s.* năḍ, -ḍā, *n.* = *l.* village, *fg.*

Granite, *s.* pākăṇ, -ṇā, *n.*

Grant, *v.* 1. di; pāṭăi = *l.* send, *e.g.* gr. indulgences, gifts.
2. sóḍ = *l.* permit; vòp = *l.* consent, *e.g.* in argument.

Granulous, *a.* revetso = *l.* sandy.

Grape, *s.* dāk, -ke, *f.* *mn.* a single fruit of the vine.

Graphic, *a.* soṣṭ = *l.* expressive.

Grapnel, *s.* lān nāngor, -grā, *m.* = *l.* a small anchor

Grapple, *v.* 1. dhăr = *l.* seize.
2. lăḍăi kăr = *l.* fight; zăgăḍ = *l.* quarrel.

Grasp, *v.* 1. dhăr, *pr.*, *fg.*, *e.g.* understand.
2. somza = *l.* understand; rig = *l.* enter (in mind), *ch. cs.*; jik = *l.* gain, *fg.* (understand).

Grass, *s.* tăṇ, -ṇā, *n.*

Grass-hopper, *s.* dempo, -peā, *m.*

Grassy, *a.* tăṇātso, *or* tăṇān bhorlolo.

Grate, *s. see* **Grating.**

Grate, *v.* 1. vāṭ = *l.* grind.
2. gās = *l.* rub.
3. zăḷăi = *l.* cause to burn, *fg.* (tease, irritate); utsāmboḷ kăr = *l.* make excited.
4. gărgăr, *mn.* make an unpleasant noise, *e.g.* that of snoring.

Grateful, *a.* 1. upkāri.
2. mānuontso = *l.* pleasing.

Gratefulness, *s.* upkārpoṇ, -ṇā, *n.*

Gratification, *s.* 1. khušālăi, -ye, *f.* = *l.* pleasure.
2. dādoskăi, -ye, *f.* = contentment.

Gratify, *v.* 1. upkār kăr = *l.* make a benefit.
2. dādos kăr = *l.* make content.
3. mănua = *l.* please.

Grating, *s.* 1. gărgăro, -reā, *m.* = *l.* a grating, harsh sound.
2. dări, -ye, *f.* = rails, *e.g.* of a church, of a monastery.

Gratis, *ad.* funkea *or* funkeāče; sāmbaḷ dināstanāñ = *l.* without paying.

Gratitude, *s.* upkārpoṇ, -ṇā, *n.* *or* upkār, -rā, *m.*; upkāri mòn, -nā, *n.* = *l.* a grateful heart; upkārāñugḍās, -sā, *m.*

Gratuitous, *a.* funkeātso = free from fee.

Gratuity, *s.* deṇeñ, -ṇeā, *n.* = *l.* a gift (*or* dān, -nā, *n.*, *n. c.*); ināṃ, -mā, *n.* = *l.* a reward.

Grave, *s.* fònḍ, -ḍā, *m.*

Grave, *v.* *see* **Engrave.**

Grave, *a.* 1. zăḍ = *l.* onerous.
2. *fg.* bhāri, *e.g.* g. man.
3. *fg* săkăilo = *l.* low, *fg.*, *e.g.* g. sound.

Grave-digger, *s.* fonḍkāḍtolo.

Grave-stone, *s.* fonḍātso fātor, -trā, *m.*, *some say* khăḍiyetso fātor, *or* mārblātso fātor, *or* ārseātso fātor; *bet.* gori, -ye, *f.*

Grave-yard, *s.* *vlg.* simiter, -ri, *f.* *see* **Cemetery.**

Gravitate, *v.* zăḍāi kăr = *l.* make heaviness; *vlg.* *rs.* zăḍ zāun āsā = *l.* is heavy.

Gravity, *s.* bhār, -rā, *m.*, *pr.*, *fg.* *mn.* *also* the force of g.

Gravy, *s.* 1. kāld, -dā, *m.*, *fr.*; kăsāi, -yā, *m.*
2. ròs, -sā, *m.* = *l.* juice.

Gray, *a.* gobrā rouṅgātso = *l.* of the colour of ashes; dovoso = *l.* whitish.

Gray-hairs, *s.* pike kès = *l.* ripe hairs; 'of g. = pikeañ kèsāntso'.

Graze, *v.* 1. pòs = *l.* feed; tsărāi = *l.* pasture; *c. v.* *of* tsăr.
2. dărnir pāi lāgoun ub = *l.* fly attaching the feet to the ground (as birds are sometimes said to graze the ground).
3. lāg = *l.* be attached (rase).

Grazing, *s.* tsărou, -ovā, *m.*

Grease, *s.* tsărāb, -rbe, *f.* = *l.* fat.

Grease, *v.* tsărāb lāi.

Great, *a.* 1. *in dignity* vòḍ *or* voḍlo, *used also for* large; tsăḍ = *l.* much, in great quantity; rund = *l.* broad.
2. *fg.* vorto = *l.* sublime, superior.
3. *fg.* bhāri = *l.* grave, *fg.* (important).
'How gr. = kedo'; 'so gr. = tedo'; 'as gr. as = bări vòḍ'; 'rather gr. = voḍso'; 'too gr. = tsăḍ, *or* tsăḍ rund'.

Greatly, *ad.* tsăḍ; bhou.

Greatness, *s.* 1. voḍpoṇ, -ṇā, *n.*, *pr.*, *fg.*; rundāi, -ye, *f.* = breadth.
2. *fg.* vortepoṇ, -ṇā, *n.* = *l.* sublimity.

Greedy, *a.* tsăḍ khušetso, āšetso, urbetso; khāugi, (gr. in the matter of food). *Sometimes* gr. *may be expressed by a noun, as by* khāugi.

Green, *a.* 1. tărno (of fruits) *mn. also* unseasoned.
2. pātsuo.

Green, *s.* 1. tărnepoṇ, -ṇā, *n.*
2. pātsuo róng, -gā, *m.* = *l.* a green colour.

Green-grocer, *s.* rāndvoi iktolo, -leā, *m.*

Greenhorn, *s.* umeduār, -rā, *m.* (a beginner).

Greenness, *see* **Green.**

Greenish, *a.* 1. tărnoso.
2. pātsuoso.

Greet, *v.* sălām kăr, *or* s. sāng = *l.* make compliments; rekād di, *fr.* = *l.* make compliments; besāuñ māg = *l.* ask a blessing (*used by inferiors*), *fr.*

Greeting, *s.* 1. sălām, -mā, *m.*
2. rekād, -dā, *m.*, *fr.*

Grenade, *see* **Bomb.**

Grenadier, *s.* G. moḷḷo sipāi, -yā, *m.*; dăit sipāi = *l.* a giant soldier.

Greyhound, *s.* šikārepeṭo, -ṭeā, *m.*

Gridiron, *s.* bāzči dări, -ye, *f.*

Grief, *s.* duk, -ki, *f.*; kăšṭ, -ṭā, *m.* (*used in pl.*)

Grievance, *s.* šiṇ, -ṇā, *m.* = *l.* a complaint; apam, -mā, *n.*, *n. c.*; duk, -ki, *f.*; kărkăr, -rāñ, *m.* (*pl.*) = *l.* troubles; kăšṭ, -ṭā, *m.*; koḍsāṇ, -ṇi, (-ṇe), *f.* = *l.* bitterness, *fg.*

Grieve, *v.* dukăi, *c. v. of* duk; kăšṭăi, *c. v. of* kăšṭa.

Grievous, *a.* kăšṭāntso = *l.* of pains; dukountso = *l.* afflicting; zăḍ = *l.* heávy, *fg.*; koḍu = *l.* bitter, *fg.*

Grievousness, *s.* koḍsāṇ, -ṇi (-ṇe), *f.* = *l.* bitterness, *etc.*

Grill, *v.* bāz = roast.

Grim, *a.* 1. vānkḍea tònḍātso = *l.* of crooked face, *or only* vānkḍo.
2. mhāru = *l.* cruel; rānuoṭ = *l.* wild.

Grimace, *s.* vānkḍeñ muk, -kā, *n.*, *or* vānkḍeñ tònḍ, -ḍā, *n.*

Grin, *s.* dānt kirkiḍăi; dānt dākăi = *l.* show the teeth; ăumăryādin hās = *l.* laugh immoderately; hāseār ghāl = *l.* put on laughing, *ch. cs.*

Grind, *v.* 1. dóḷ; vāṭ.
2. *fg.* dăgdăi, *c. v.* = *l.* cause sufferings.

Grinder (Tooth), *s.* dāḍi, -ye, *f.*

Grind-stone, *s.* dānteñ, -teā, *n.*; vān, -nā, *n.* (for grinding curry-seeds); sāṇ, -ṇe, *f.* = a stone used for pulverising medicine.

Gripe, *v.* 1. dhăr.
2. muḍḍăi, *c.v.* = cause gripes.

Gripes, *s.* 1. muḍḍoṇeñ, -ṇeā, *n.*, *or* muḍḍoní, -ne, *f.*, *mn. ex.* gr.
2. guḷo, -ḷeā, *m.* = *l.* ball, a disease of a more violent character.

Griping, *part.a.* 1. muḍḍaneātso. 2. *fg.* kăṭiṇ = *l.* severe, *e.g.* hunger.

Grist, *s.* 1. pīṭ, -ṭā, *n.* = flour. 2. dhāni, -ye, *f.* = *l.* corn.

Groan, *v.* răḍ; pirnga.

Groaning, *s.* răḍneñ, -neā, *n.*, *or* răḍāp, -ḍpā, *n.*; pirngoṇi, -ṇe, *f.*

Grocer, *s.* yāri, -riā, *m.*

Groom, *s.* goḍeāgār, -rā, *m.* = a horse-boy.

Groove, *s.* gero, -reā, *m.*, *e.g.* of a column.

Groove, *v.* gero kăr, *e.g.* in a column.

Grope, *v.* sāspi (*tr.*); sāspa (*n.*) = feel with the hand in darkness.

Gross, *a.* 1. dāṭ. 2. *fg.* ăumăryāditso. 3. jumla, -lā, *n.* = the total sum.

Grossness, *s.* 1. dāṭāi, -ye, *f.* 2. ăumăryād, -di, *f.* = *l.* unpoliteness.

Grot, *s.* dol, -li, *f.*

Grotesque, *a.* vidrupātso; tārifetso (awkward).

Ground, *s.* 1. dărn, -ni, *f.* = *l.* soil; nèl, -lā, *n.* 2. zāgo, -geā, *m.* = *l.* ground; zămin, -ne, *f.* = a possession, a farm; suāt, -te, *f.* = *l.* a place. 3. săngti (*or* săngăt, -gti), -ti, *f.*, bāb, -be, *f.* = *l.* point, matter, *e.g.* my argument rests on these grounds. 4. pāṭ, -ṭi, *f.* = *l.* back, (gr. of a picture). 5. kārāṇ, -ṇā, *n.* = *l.* cause; zăvāb, -bi, *f.* = *l.* motive.

Gain gr. 1. jik = *l.* gain, make profit; ādāi mèḷ = *l.* profit be found. 2. vistār = *l.* get spread, *e.g.* news.

Lose gr. = pāḍāu zātā = *l.* defeat takes place; pòḍ.

Grounded (Be well), *v.* boro rombtā = *l.* it goes very deep.

Ground-floor, *s.* dărn, -ni, *f.*

Groundless, *a.* khāli = *l.* empty; kārāṇ nātullo; vèrt = *l.* vain.

Ground-rent, *s.* géṇ, -ṇi, *f.*

Ground-work, *s.* bunyād, -di, *f.*, *pr.*, *fg.*

Group, *s.* zomo, -meā, *m.* = *l.* a collection; mēḷ(é), -ḷā, *m.* = *l.* union (*perh. also* in art).

Group, *v.* mānḍ = *l.* arrange; meḷāi = *l.* collect.

Grove, *s.* phāḍ, -ḍi, *f.*; bòn, -nā, *n.* (*Ital. boschetto*).

Grovel, *v.* tsăr = *l.* creep.

Grow, *v.* 1. fuṭ, *as* plants in the earth. 2. vāḍ, *e.g.* a child grows in stature. 3. zā = *l.* become, *e.g.* he grows pale. 4. ādāi kăr = *l.* make progress. 5. *tr. v.* besāi kăr = *l.* cultivate.

Grown up, vāḍullo *or* vāḍavoḷ, -ḷi, *f.*; mānāi, -yā, *m.*

Growl, *v.* ghonk (as a dog); bòb mār.

Growth, *s.* vāḍ, -ḍi, *f.*, *or* vāḍa-voḷ, -ḷi, *f.* (*this 2nd means also* a district of a village).

Grudge, *v.* 1. mosór kăr, *G. M.* = *l.* make envy; *or* niskutsār kăr, *G. M.*
2. purpur = *l.* grumble.
3. purpurn di = *l.* give grumbling; nākā moṇ = *l.* say no.

Grudge, *s.* mosór, -srā, *m.*, *or* niskutsār, -rā, *m.* = *l.* envy; koḍsāṇ, -ṇe (-ṇi), *f.* = *l.* bitterness, *fg.*; dusmānkāi, -ye, *f.*; jiddu̥, -dā, *n.* = enmity; nākhuši, -še, *f.* = ill-feeling.

Gruel, *s. approx.* āmbil, -lā, *n.*

Gruff, *a.* 1. ăumăryāditso = *l.* unpolite.
2. kăḍḍu̥ = *l.* severe; kăṭiṇ = *l.* severe.

Gruffness, *s.* 1. ăumăryād, -di, *f.*
2. kăṭiṇāi, -ye, *f.* = *l.* rigour.

Grumble, *v.* purpur; pāṭi ulăi = *l.* speak behind; portun ulăi = *l.* speak turning *or* again; šiṇ ulăi = *l.* speak a lament.

Grunt, *v.* gurgur (as a pig), *pr. fg.*

Guarantee, *s.* zāmin, -ne, *f.* (*Lat. vadimonium*).

Guarantee, *v.* zāmin di = *l.* give g.

Guard, *v.* sāmbāḷ; părtibol kăr; pravesa kăr; rāk; pāro kăr = *l.* make an escort.

Guard, *s.* 1. āsro, -reā, *m.* = *l.* a refuge.
2. rākṇo, -ṇeā, *m.* = a guardian; rākṇeñ, -ṇeā, *n.*; ādār, -rā, *m.* = *l.* help.
3. pāro, -reā, *m.* = *l.* an escort.
4. šibāndi, -di, *f.* = *l.* a garrison.
5. muṭ, -ṭi, *f.* = g. of a sword.
Mount g. = rāk.
Be on g. = tsătrāi kāṇe.

Guardian, *s.* rākṇo, -ṇeā, *m.*, *e.g.* a guardian angel; a tutor; kāvălgār, -rā, *m.*

Guardianship, *see* **Guard.**

Guava, *s.* perātso ruk, -kā, *m.* (a tree of this country like a pear tree).

Guess, *v.* 1. pārki; sumār čint; dubāvār sāng = *l.* say on doubt; hăḷtār sāng.
2. bolmeñ sāng = *l.* say an incantation.

Guess, *s.* 1. pārkouṇeñ, -ṇeā, *n.*
2. bolmeñ, -meā, *n.*

Guest, *s.* 1. săiro, -reā, *m.* (*mn. also* g. at an entertainment).
2. vouḷo, -ḷeā, *m.* = g. at a marriage dinner.

Guide, *s.* 1. vāṭ dākăitolo = *l.* showing the way.
2. tsălăitolo = *l.* ruling.
3. sikăitolo = *l.* instructor; rākṇo, -ṇeā, *m.*
4. sikāp, -kpā, *n.*, sikoṇ, -ṇe, *f.* = instruction; bud, -di, *f.* = *l.* wisdom.

Guide, *v.* 1. vāṭ dākăi.
2. tsălăi.
3. sikăi; pāḷ, *n. c.*; *see above.*
4. pāuoi *or* pāvoi = *l.* cause to reach (accompany), *c. v. of* pāu; sāngāt kăr = *l.* make company.

5. sourăkṣăṇ kăr = protect; părtibol kăr = protect.

Guide-post, *s.* vāṭ dākountso fātor, -trā, *m.*; mārgātso fātor, -trā, *m.* = *l.* a stone of the road; khāmbo, -beā, *m.*

Guild, *s.* vānṭeleañ mēḷ(é), -ḷā, *m.* = *l.* an association of partners; *bet. rs. into* vānṭeli, -liā, *m.* = a partner.

Guile, *s.* mōs(ó), -sā, *m.*

Guileless, *a.* sādo = *l.* simple; neṇto = *l.* innocent; niskăpṭi = *l.* not simulating.

Guillotine, *s. near w.* kuḍār, -ri, *f.*

Guilt, *s.* gunyāuñ, -āvā, *m.*; tăppu, -pā, *m.*; ăprād, -dā, *m.*; ăpamān, -nā, *m.* = *l.* an offence.

Guilty, *a.* gunyāukār.
Become g. = g. zā.
Prove g. = g. moṇ kăr.

Guinea, *s.* gini, -ni, *f.*, *fr.*

Guise, *s.* vés, -sā, *m.*; rūp, -pā, *n.* = *l.* figure, appearance; rīt, -ti, *f.* = *l.* fashion, manner.

Gulf, *s. see* **Bay.**

Gull, *s.* 1. mōs(ó), -sā, *m.*
2. *fg.* bomma, -mā, *m.* = a simple fellow.

Gulp, *s.* gās, -sā, *m.* (a single swallow).

Gum, *s.* 1. mòḷa, -ḷe, *f.* (of the teeth).
2. gónd, -dā, *m.* = that which exudes from the tree.
3. dik, -kā, *m.* = the sap of trees; pānk, -kā, *m.*

Gummy, *a.* pānkātso; gondātso, *etc.*

Gun, *s.* 1. nāḷ, -ḷi, *f.* (a big cannon).
2. bănduk, -ke, *f.*, *e.g.* a rifle.

Gunpowder, *s.* dāru, -rve, *f.*

Gurgle, *v.* gāz, as a small stream running over a stony bottom does.

Gurgling, *s.* gāz, -ji, *f.*

Gush, *v.* 1. vāu = *l.* flow (*n. v.*).
2. vót = *l.* empty, clear (*tr. v.*).

Gut, *v.* āntkiṭio kāḍ = *l.* extract the bowels.

Gutter, *see* **Eaves.**

Guttural, *a.* gomṭeāntlo *or* gomṭeātso.

Guzzle, *v.* jīv sóḍn piye; kòp mār (*vlg.*); piyeunčeāk lāgụllo zāun āsā.

Gymnasium, *s.* 1. kăsrătiñghăr, -rā, *n.*
2. vidyesāḷ, -ḷe, *f.* = school of science.

Gymnast, *s.* kăsrăti, -ti, *m.*

Gymnastic, *s.* kăsrăt, -tā, *n.*

H

Haberdasher, *s.* yāri, -riā, *m.*

Habit, *s.* 1. nesoṇ, -ṇi, *f.* = *l.* a dress.
2. sovói, -ye, *f.* = *l.* a custom, a practice; dăstur, -ri, *f.* = *l.* fashion.
3. bolāiki, -ke, *f.* = *l.* health; kaleti, *or* kalet, -ti, *f.* = *l.* constitution (of body).

Habitable, *a.* rāvasārko; vāsasārko, *n. c.*; *rs. into v.*

Habitation, *s.* ghăr, -rā, *n.*; biḍār, -rā, *n.* (not permanent); ṭhikāṇeñ, -ṇeā, *n.*, *or* ṭāṇeñ, -ṇeā, *n.* = *l.* a place of residence.

Habitual, *a.* 1. sovóyetso, *or rs.* sovói āsā.
2. porno = *l.* old.

Habitually, *ad.* sovóye părmāṇe = *l.* according to habit; *rs. into* sovói āsā, *e. g.* do a thing h.

Habituate, *v.* 1. sovói kăr = *l.* make a custom.
2. sādo kăr = *l.* domesticate, make tame.

Hack, *v.* kātăr = *l.* cut; tsātsāi = *l.* chop; kuḍke kăr.

Hack, *s.* bāḍeagoḍo, -ḍeā, *m.* = *l.* a hired horse.

Hackney, *s.* porkoṭo, *e. g.* a h. horse.

Haggard, *s.* kuleñ, -leā, *n.*, *mn.* an old ugly intractable person, *l.* a goblin.

Haggle, *v.* moḍnāi kăr = *l.* make cavillations.

Hail, *s.* 1. kăre, *pl. m.*; kăreāntso pāus, -sā, *m.* = *l.* rain of hail.
2. gār, -rā, *m.* = *ex.* ice.

Hail, *v.* 1. gār pòḍtā *or* kăre pòḍtāt.
2. sălām di; sălām kăr = *l.* give compliments.

Hail-stone, *s.* koro, -reā, *m.* (*var.* kăro, -reā, *m.*); gār, -rā, *m.* = ice.

Hair, *s.* kēsu̥ (ê), -sā, *m.*, *pl.* kès; 'cut the h. = k. kāḍ'.

Hair-cloth, *s.* kesāñčeñ lugāṭ, -gṭā, *n.*; *vlg.* prājitāčeñ lugāṭ = *l.* cloth of penance.

Hairy, *a.* lovetso; săbār kès āsullo.

Half, *a.* ărdo; sāḍe, *e.g.* half past nine = sāḍe nou uorañ; *see* Gram. p. II. ch. ii. Art. ii.

Half-brother, *s.* māusibhāu, -āvā, *m.*, *or* bāpulbhāu *or abbrev.* bābāu.

Half-dead, *a.* ărdo mello; *all other words compounded with* half *not given here may be rendered in the same way as* half-dead.

Hall, *s.* sāl, -lā, *n.*

Hallo, *int.* arĕ (to call attention).

Hallucination, *s.* bhărm, -mā, *n.*; sopāṇ, -pṇā, *n.* = *l.* a dream, *fg.*; tsuk, -ki, *f.* = *l.* an error.

Halo, *s.* 1. disātso mānḍ, -ḍā, *m.*
2. părives̆, -s̆ā, *m.* (*Cn. Mr.*)

Halt, *v.* 1. rāu = *l.* remain; mokām (*or* mokkām) kăr.
2. thonṭo tsăl, *or* kunṭa = *l.* walk lame.
3. dubāu = *l.* doubt (hesitate).

Halt, *s.* rāvāp, rāupā, *n.*

Halter, *s.* găḷ, -ḷā, *m.*, *e.g.* a horse's halter, *n. c.*; pās, -sā, *m. the same as* găḷ, *also* a noose; dóri, -ye, *f.* = *l.* a rope.

Halve, *v.* dón vānṭe kăr = *l.* make two parts.

Ham, *s.* zāngal, -glā, *n.* (thigh).

Hamlet, *s.* 1. grām, -mā, *n.*
2. vāḍo, -ḍeā, *m.*, *a very common word to express* a subdivision of a large village.

Hammer, *s. vlg.* mortel, -lā, *n.*, *fr.*; kudānṭi. -ṭe, *f.* = *strictly* a wooden h.; *may be used also as* a general term; lonkḍāči kudānṭi = iron h.; tutyo, -yeā, *m. is the exact equivalent*; čammaḍi, -ḍe, *f.*

Hammock, *s.* hindḷo, -ḷeā, *m.*

Hamper, *v.* sāmpḍāi = *l.* confound; tondreār ghāl = *l.* put in embarrassment.

Hand, *s.* 1. hāt, -tā, *m.*: 'palm of the h. = tălāt, -tā, *n.*; tăḷvo, -veā, *m.*
2. vorāntso gurtụ, -tā, *m.* = *l.* a sign of hours; kānṭo, -ṭeā, *m.*; gănṭeagurtụ.
Have in h. = hātānt āsā, *ch. cs.*
Clap the hands = tāḷio péṭ.
Lay h. on = hāt ghāl = *l.* put h.
Pass from h. to h. = bounḍāi; hāt bădāl.
Be at h. = 1. lāgiñ āsā = *l.* is near.
2. kumok kăr = help.
3. tăyār āsā = *l.* is ready.
4. I have no money at h. = mojea hātānt kāiñ nāñ.
5. hāzăr āsā = *l.* is present.
Take in h. = hātānt kāṇe.
Be in the hands of = *G.* sotăntrār āsā = *l.* is in the power of, *or G.* hātānt āsā.
On the one h., on the other h. = ye partin, te partin, *or* ye vāṭen, te vāṭen.
On the other h. = zāleāri, *or* puṇ.
Out of h. = hāta bhāir.
Come to h. = hātānt pòḍ.
To live from h. to mouth = āičeñ āz, phāleāčeñ phālea.

Hand, *v.* di, *or* vopsun di = *l.* consign.
H. down = pāṭleān dovór, *e.g.* h. d. an example, a doctrine.
H. round = vānṭ = *l.* distribute.

Hand-bell, *s.* kāmpiṇ, -ṇi, *f.*, *fr.* = any small bell; ghānṭleñ, -leā, *n.*

Hand-bill, *s.* kăikurāḍ, -ḍi, *f.* = a pruning-instrument.

Hand-book, *s.* hātpustak, -kā, *n.*

Hand-breadth, *s.* gèṇ, -ṇā, *n.*

Handcuff, *s.* khòḍò, -ḍeā, *m.* (for prisoners).

Handful, *s.* unḍi, -ye, *f.*; posò, -seā, *m.*; muṭ, -ṭi, *f.*; thoḍo (*a.*) = *l.* a little.

Handicraft, Handiness, *s.* 1. čămătkār, -rā, *m.*

2. hātāñkām, -mā, *n.*

Handkerchief, *s.* lēsụ(é), -sā, *m.*; *pl.* lès.

Handle, *s.* 1. thoruñ, -rvā, *n.*, *e.g.* of a knife; muṭ, -ṭi, *f.*; hātāḷo, -ḷeā, *m.* (of boxes).

2. *fg.* kārāṇ, -ṇā, *n.* = *l.* a cause.

Handle, *v.* 1. tsălăi; goḷăi, *e.g.* h. money.

2. āpoḍ = *l.* touch.

Handsome, *a.* 1. sobit; sundăr.

2. udār = *l.* liberal.

3. dobājeātso = *l.* pompous.

4. vóḍ = *l.* great, much.

Handwriting, *s.* hātbărāp, -rpā, *n.*, *or only* bărāp.

Hang, *v.* 1. umkăḷăi = execute, *or* hang up, *e.g.* clothes, *c. v. of* umkăḷ; lāmbăi, *e. g.* a lamp.

2. fāši ghāl = *l.* put the rope (execute).

Hanging, *s.* 1. umkăḷouṇeñ, -ṇeā, *n.*

2. fāši, -še, *f.* = *l.* a rope (the hangman's rope).

Hangman, *see* **Executioner.**

Hanker, *v.* lāle, *obj. Dat.* = *l.* long for; āšen mòr.

Hankering, *s.* lāleuṇeñ (*or* lālouṇeñ), -ṇeā, *n.*

Hap, *see* **Chance.**

Haply, *ad.* yekādeveḷa; *by potent. mood.*

Happen, *v.* găḍ; zā = *l.* become.

Happily, *ad.* sukhzāun; ădruṣṭān = *l.* by fortune.

Happiness, *s.* sukh, -khā, *n.*; bhāg, -gā, *n.*, *n. c.*; *see* **Joy;** kṣém, -mā, *m.* (*H. K.*).

Happy, *a.* 1. sukhi; bhāgi *or* bhāgevont; khušāl = *l.* joyful; sufoḷ.

2. lāyek = *l.* fit, *e.g.* a h. word.

3. jikpi = *l.* successful.

Harangue, *s.* uloṇeñ, -ṇeā, *n.*

Harangue, *v.* uloṇeñ utsār; *not ex.*; *see* **Preach, Oration.**

Harass, *v.* zăḷăi = *l.* cause to burn, *fg.* (disquiet); dukăi = *l.* cause sorrow; dós; bezār kăr = *l.* make uneasy; kărkăr kăr = *l.* make trouble; kăṣṭăi (*c. v. of* kăṣṭa) = *l.* cause pain; āngār pòḍ = *l.* fall on body (*milit. term*).

Harbinger, *s.* 1. harakāri, -riā, *m.*

2. khuṇa, -ṇe, *f.* = *l.* a sign.

Harbour, *s.* 1. băndăr, -drā, *n.*; āḷveñ, -veā, *n.* = *l.* an estuary, *here used for* h.

2. *fg.* āsro, -reā, *m.* = *l.* refuge.

Harbour, *v.* 1. āsro di, *tr. v.* = *l.* give refuge.

2. āsro meḷtā, *n. v.* = *l.* refuge is found.

Hard, *a.* 1. ghăṭ (to the touch, not flexible); kărkoṭo.
2. kăṣṭountso = *l.* painful (*tr.*); kăṣṭāntso (*n.*); kăṭin = *l.* difficult; prăyāsātso, *n.c.* = *l.* difficult; mănšeponnātullo = *l.* without humanity; kăḍdu (kărd) = *l.* rigorous.

Harden, *v.* ghăṭ kăr, *pr. fg., e.g.* h. to heat, cold.

Hard-hearted, *a.* uṣṭo.

Hardiness, Hardness, *s.* 1. moṭāi, -ye, *f.* = *l.* stoutness.
2. dhăir, -rā, *n.* = *l.* courage.
3. ghăṭāi, -ye, *f.* = *l.* strength.
4. dhāruṇāi, -ye, *f.* = *l.* obstinacy.

Hardly, *ad.* 1. kăṣṭān = *l.* with difficulty.
2. kăṭiṇāyen = *l.* with severity.

Hardship, *s.* upădru, -drāñ, *m. pl.* = *l.* sufferings; kăṣṭ, -ṭā, *m.* = *l.* pain; ākānt, -tā, *m.* = *l.* distress; minătu, -ti, *f.* = *l.* fatigue.

Hardy, *a.* 1. ghăṭ = *l.* firm.
2. dhāruṇ = *l.* obstinate.
3. lăzbanḍo = *l.* impudent.

Hare, *s.* soso, -seā, *m.*

Hark, *int.* čit di; āikre (*or* -go).

Harlequin, *s.* hāšāgār, -rā, *m.*

Harm, *s.* luksān, -nā, *n.*; năṣṭ, -ṭā, *n.*; vāiṭ, -ṭā, *n.* = *l.* evil; kēḍ(é), -ḍā, *m.*

Harm, *v.* 1. kăr = do, *with any of the above nouns.*
2. dukăi = *l.* cause pain.

Harmful, *a.* luksānātso, *or* luksān (*or other nouns*) kărtso *or* luksānāk pòḍtso; vāiṭ.

Harmless, *a.* gunyāunātullo; vāiṭkărinātullo; nentuo (nento).

Harmonious, *a.* 1. yekăts tāḷeātso = *l.* of one voice; tāḷeāñ mėḷātso.
2. *fg.* sămapòḍtso = *l.* falling together, *fg.*

Harmoniously, *ad.* 1. yekăts tāḷeān (?); tāḷeañmeḷān, *or rs.*
2. *fg.* sămādhānān = *l.* with concord; yėkmotin = *l.* with one mind.

Harmonize, *v.* 1. fuslāi = *l.* pacify; thănḍ kăr = *l.* make cold, *fg.* (calm); sămādhān kărāi = *l.* cause to make peace.
2. *fg.* sămapòḍ = *l.* fall right (fit together).

Harmony, *s.* 1. tāḷeañmēḷ(ė), -ḷā, *m., or only* mēḷ; *vlg.* boreñ kantār, -rā, *n., fr.*
2. *fg.* sămādhān, -nā, *n.* = *l.* concord; soukāsāi, -ye, *f.* = *l.* peace.

Harness, *s.* 1. săvārevăstur, -rā, *n.* = *l.* the dress (armour) of a horseman.
2. goḍeāsāmān, -nā, *m.* = *l.* furniture of a horse.

Harp, *s.* kindari, -ri, *f.* (?)

Harpy, *s. fg.* doḷeānt răgatnātullo mănis, -nšā, *m.* = *l.* a man without blood in the eyes (*Konk.*).

Harrow, *s.* gunṭčeñ phoḷeñ, -ḷeā, *n.*

Harrow, *v.* gunṭai.

Harsh, *a.* 1. āmboṭ = *l.* acid.
2. kărkăṭo (to the taste, *or* to the ear); gărgăreātso (voice); gărgări.
3. kăṭiṇ = *l.* difficult, severe; kărkărāntso = *l.* troublesome; *see also* **Grate.**

Harshness, *s.* 1. kărkăṭāi, -ye, *f.* = h. in taste.
2. gărgăro, -reā, *m.* = h. of voice.
3. kăṭiṇāi, -ye, *f.* = *l.* severity.

Harvest, *s.* 1. beḷeñ kātărtso vēḷ (é), -ḷā, *m.*, *or only* beḷeñ, -ḷeā, *n.*
2. beḷeāči luuṇi, -ṇe, *f.* = *l.* gathering of a crop; beḷeāluvāp, -luupā, *n.*
3. luuntso kāl, -lā, *m.* = *l.* the time of gathering.

Hash, *v.* kuḍkeān kuḍke kăr = *l.* make pieces; tsātsāi = *l.* chop.

Hasp, *s.* ānkḍo, -ḍeā, *m.* (the hasp of a door).

Hassock, *s.* (pāyānčeñ) ušeñ, -šeā, *n.* = *l.* cushion (for the feet).

Haste, *s.* ausăr, -rā, *m.* (*var.* auñsăr); *see* **Hurry.**

Haste, *v.* ausăr; vegiñ tsāl (*or* kăr *or other verbs*) = *l.* go quick.

Hastily, *ad.* ausărān; vegiñ.

Hasty, *a.* ausărātso; ausări; vegintso, *n. c.*

Hat, *s.* 1. *vlg.* čepeñ *or* čapeñ, -peā, *n.*; topi, -ye, *f.*; kănḍi, -ḍe, *f.* (of areca leaves).
2. tópụ, -pā, *m.* (of a bishop); take off your h. = t. kāḍ.

Hatch, *v.* rovāṇe bòs.

Hatchet, *s.* kăikurāḍ, -ḍi, *f.*

Hate, *v.* kānṭāḷ = *l.* abhor; hăgeñ *or* jiddụ dovór; mosór kăr = *l.* make hatred (envy), *G. M.*

Hateful, *a.* kānṭāḷeātso, *or* kānṭāḷo făvozāllo; khóṭo = *l.* wicked; khóṭeponātso.

Hatred, *s.* 1. kānṭāḷo, -ḷeā, *m.* = *l.* abhorrence; hăgeñ, -geā, *n.*; niskutsār, -rā, *m.*, mosór, -srā, *m.* = envy, hatred.
2. dusmānkāi, -ye, *f.*; jiddụ, -dā, *n.* = enmity.

Haughtiness, *s.* gărvụ, -vā, *n.*

Haughty, *a.* gărvi; *see* **Proud, Insolent.**

Haul, *v.* vóḍ = *l.* pull, drag.

Haunt, *v.* 1. kăšṭāi, *c. v. of* kăšṭa; dukăi (*c. v. of* duk) = cause pain.
2. vetā = *l.* goes, *with* -ts.

Have, *v.* 1. āsā = *l.* is, *ch. cs.*
2. dovór = *l.* keep.
3. *by c. v., e. g.* have done = kărāi; *by necess. mood, e. g.* have to go = votsāzāi.

Have (the dinner) on (the table) = ghāl = *l.* put.

Haven, *see* **Harbour.**

Havock, *s.* vibāḍ, -ḍā, *m.*, bósmụ, -mā, *m.* = ruin; nāš, -šā, *n.* = destruction; desvaṭ, -ṭe, *f.* = devastation.

Hawk, *s.* giḍgo, -geā, *m.*; păkkisaḷo, -ḷeā, *m.*

Hawk, *v.* 1. khankăr = force up phlegm.
2. yār ik, *e.g.* hawk wares.

Hawker, *s.* bountso yāri, -riā, *m.* = *l.* a walking peddler.

Hay, *s.* tăṇ, -ṇā, *n.*

Hay-cock, *s.* tăṇāči rās, -si, *f.*

Hazard, *s.* ădruṣṭ, -ṭā, *n.* = *l.* a venture; risk, -ke, *f.* = *l.* risk; zăkăm, -kme, *f.*; *by the pot. mood.*

Hazard, *v.* mosānt ghāl = *l.* put into risk.

Hazardous, *a.* mosātso; ădruṣṭātso; *see* **Hazard.**

He, *pron.* to; *see* Gram. P. II. ch. iii.

He, *prefix.* dādlo = *l.* male; *see* Gram. p. 47.

Head, *s.* 1. tăkli, -le, *f.*; boḍko, -keā, *m.*; boḍik, -ḍkā, *n.* (of a fish); māteñ, -teā, *n.*; mostak, -kā, *n. pr.*, *fg.*, *e.g.* h. of a community.
2. mukhyest, -tā, *m.* = *l.* principal, (leader), *e.g.* of a church; siromăṇi, -ṇi, *m.* of a party.
3. tāḷi, -ye, *f.*, *e.g.* h. of a tree (top); *rs. into* voir = upon.
4. somzoṇkāi, -ye, *f.* = *l.* understanding.
5. năg, -gā, *m.* = *l.* an article, *e.g.* ten heads of cloth.
6. mulo, -leā, *m.* = *l.* a hinge, *fg.* (main point); mūḷ, -ḷā, *n.* = *l.* a root, *fg.* (main point).

Two head of cattle = gorvānči zóḍi, -ye, *f.*

Head, *pref.* mukhya, *e. g.* h. master.

Headache, *s.* tăkleči duk, -ki, *f.* *or* kăpalāči duk; tăkleči phoḍāpoḍ, -ḍi, *f.*: 'I have a h. = moji tăkli duktā *or* t. phoḍtā'.

Head-foremost, Headlong, *ad.* 1. *rs.*, *e. g.* plunge h. = buḍ; tăkli săkleān, tăkli săkal kărn = *l.* head downwards.
2. *fg.* ausărān = *l.* hastily.

Headiness, *s.* dhāruṇāi, -ye, *f.* = *l.* obstinacy; săḷ, -ḷā, *n.*

Heading, *s.* mélviḷās, -sā, *m.* = *l.* an address, an inscription.

Headland, *see* **Cape.**

Headless, *a.* māteñ nātullo.

Headman, *s.* 1. gurkār, -rā, *m.*
2. pāṭel, -lā, *m.* (civil h. of a village).
3. moktesăr, -rā, *m.* = leader, (*also* of soldiers, captain).

Headmost, *a.* mukāvelo = *l.* anterior; poilo = *l.* first.

Head-quarters, *s.* mokām, -mā, *n.*

Headsman, *see* **Executioner.**

Headstrong, *a.* āplea vādeātso; āple iččetso.

Heady, *a.* săliṣṭ.

Heal, *v.* 1. boro kăr (*tr.*); boro zā (*n.*); guṇ kăr.
2. *fg.* săma kăr = *l.* make right.

Health, *s.* bolāiki, -ke, *f.*; kṣém, -mā, *m.* (*H. K.*); guṇ, -ṇā, *m.*; kāleti, -ti, *f. mn.* good constitution, *fr.*

Is in good h. = bolāikent āsā.

Drink to health = bolāiki mār.

Healthy, *a.* 1. bolāiketso; bolāikent āsullo = *l.* being in health; bolāiki āsullo = *l.* having health; kṣemātso; *vlg.* boro.

2. *fg.* soukāsāyetso; sămādhānātso, *e.g.* h. place.

Heap, *s.* 1. rās, -si, *f.*; punji, -je, *f.*, *e.g.* of money (punzo, -jeā, *m.* = a big h.); zomo, -meā, *m.* = *l.* an accumulation.

2. muṭeñ, -ṭeā, *n.*, *e.g.* of firewood.

Heap, *v.* rās kăr; zomo kăr, *or* zomăi, *c. v.*

H. reproaches = ăkmānāñ voir ăkmān kăr.

Hear, *v.* 1. āik (*root*: āika; *see* Gram. p. 140, para. 10); *mn. also* hear prayers; pay attention

2. kānānt pòḍ = *l.* fall into the ear; kobār āik = *l.* hear news.

3. kān di *or* čit di, *mn.* listen.

I do not h. well (am a little deaf) = kān āikanāñ = *l.* ear does not hear.

Hearer, *s.* 1. sis, -sā, *m.* = *l.* a disciple.

2. āikatolo.

Hearing, *s.* 1. kān, -nā, *m.* (the sense).

2. bhèṭ, -ṭe, *f.* = *l.* visit (audience).

3. ulo, -leā, *m.*, *mn.* distance within which one can be heard, (a furlong).

Hearken, *v.* guṭān āik = *l.* hear secretly; kān di.

Hearsay, *s.* phukāro, -reā, *m.* = *l.* a rumour.

Hearse, *s.* mornāči gāḍi, -ye, *f.* = *l.* carriage of a funeral.

Heart, *s.* 1. *vlg.* kāḷiz, -ḷzā, *n.* *ex. it mn.* liver, *according to the Mr.*; *yet in Mr. too it is commonly understood of the* heart (*pr. fg.*); kāḷzātso gonḍo, ḍeā, *m.*; unḍ, -ḍā, *m.* = (*this mn. ex.* heart).

2. ăntăskărn, -nā, *n.* (*moral mn.*), *var.* ăntărăng, -gā, *n.*; mòn, -nā, *n.* (*moral mn.*).

3. dhăir, -rā, *n.* = *l.* courage.

4. modeñ = *l.* middle, *e. g.* h. of a tree.

Learn by h. = bāipāṭ kăr; *vlg.* dekor sik, *fr.*

Hearth, *s.* rāndăṇ, -dṇi, *f.* (*var.* rānnu̥, -ni, *f.*)

Heartily, *ad.* kāḷzān; ăntăskărnān *or* ăntăskărniñ; *rs. into adj.*

Hearty, *a.* 1. kālzātso *or* ăntăskărnātso, *see above*; nīz = *l.* sincere.

2. mogāḷ = *l.* dear.

Heaṭ, *s.* 1. gărmi, -me, *f.*, *pr. fg.*; ub, -be, *f.*; vòt, -tā, *n.*; tāp, -pi, *f.* (h. of rainy season);

ulop, -lpā, *m.*, *e.g.* h. causing inflammation, *or* the inflammation itself; khărāi, -ye, *f.* (of the body).
2. *fg.* utsāmboḷāi, -ye, *f.* = *l.* excitement; zāḷ, -ḷā, *m.*; uzo, -jeā, *m.*

Heat, *v.* tāpăi, *c. v. of* tāp, *n. v.*, *e.g.* h. iron, water; un kăr = *l.* make hot, *e.g.* water; gărmi kăr = *l.* make heat; kăḍăi, *e.g.* milk.

Heathen, *s.* ănbāvāḍti, -tiā, *m.*; *vlg.* Hindu, -duā, *m.*; *the Goanese say* Konkṇo, -ṇeā, *m.*, *but this is only a partial term.*

Heathenism, *s.* ănbāvāḍtpoṇ, -ṇā, *n.*

Heating, *s.* tāpouṇeñ, -ṇeā, *n.*; ulop, -lpā, *m.*

Heave, *v.* 1. ukol = *l.* lift.
2. suzăi = *l.* cause to swell; *c. v. of* suz, *n. v.*
3. *fg.* utsāmboḷ zā *or* uṭ, *mn.* get excited.
H. a sigh = uskār kāḍ *or* u. sóḍ.

Heaven, *s.* 1. sărg, -gā, *m.*
2. văinkuṭ, -ṭā, *n.* (paradise); mukti, -ti, *f.*, *ol.*, *mn.* eternal happiness.
3. moḷāb, -ḷbā, *n.* = *l.* sky.
4. *fg.* Dēu, -vā, *m.* = *l.* God; sărgintso lók, -kā, *m.* = people of heaven.

Heavenly, *a.* sărgintso.

Heavenwards, *ad.* sărgā isileān.

Heaviness, *s.* 1. bhār, -rā, *m.*; zăḍāi, -ye, *f.*, *mn. also* physical depression.
2. *fg.* khănt, -ti, *f.* = *l.* distress, *fg.*; duk, -ki, *f.* = *l.* sorrow.
3. ăpadhăir, -rā, *n.* = depression of spirit.
4. dăḍḍepoṇ, -ṇā, *n.* = *l.* dulness (of mind).

Heavy, *a.* 1. zăḍ, *e.g.* air, burden; bhārādik, *pr. fg.*, *e.g.* h. cross.
2. *fg.* āḷsi = *l.* lazy.
3. *fg.* khăntisṭ *or* dukest = *l.* sorry.
4. *fg.* boro = *l.* good, *e.g.* h. rain (*or* boḷvont).
5. *fg.* kăšṭāntso = *l.* difficult, painful.
6. jirnātullo = *l.* not digestible; *or* jiruoṇnātullo.

Hebrew, *s.* yebreu, -revā, *m.*

Hedge, *s.* voi, -i, *f.*; *see* **Fence.**

Heed, *s.* zāgrutāi, -ye, *f.* = *l.* awakening; tsătrāi, -ye, *f.* = *l.* attention.
Take h. = kăbărdār rāu *or* tsătrāi kāṇghe.

Heedless, *a.* tsătrāinātullo.

Heel, *s.* 1. khòṭ, -ṭe, *f.*
2. pònd, -dā, *n.* = *l.* the lower part, *perh. bet.* pāyăčeñ pònd; pāul, -lā, *m.*

Heel, *v.* bāga = *l.* be bent (*as*, the ship heels over).

Heft, *see* **Handle.**

Heifer, *s.* pāḍi, -ye, *f.*

Heigho, *int.* šābās.

Height, *s.* 1. ubārāi, -ye, *f.*, *or* ubār suāt, -te, *f.* = *l.* a high place; untsāi, -ye, *f.*
2. *fg.* voḍpoṇ, -ṇā, *n.* = *l.* greatness; huddo, -deā, *m.* = *l.* rank, high state.

Heighten, *s.* tsăḍăi = *l.* increase; ubār kăr = *l.* make high; *see* **Exaggerate.**

Heinous, *a.* bhou khoṭo, *or* b. khoṭeponātso; bhou kăṭiṇ; kānṭāḷeātso = *l.* abominable.

Heir, *s.* dāiji, -jiā, *m.*
Leave h. by will = *vlg.* testamentār dāiji kăr; *see* **Will.**

Heiress, *s.* dāijiṇ, -ṇi, *f.*

Heirloom, *s.* čarajindigečeñ dāiz, -zā, *n.* = *l.* movable inheritance.

Hell, *s.* 1. yemkòṇḍ, -ḍā, *n.*
2. pātāḷ, -ḷā, *n.*, *mn.* a subterraneous place.

Hellish, *a.* 1. yemkòṇḍātso; yemkòṇḍāntlo; *rs.* yemkòṇḍa bări = *l.* like hell.
2. săitānātso = *l.* devilish.

Helm, *s.* sukhāṇeñ, -ṇeā, *n.* (of a ship).

Helmet, *s.* (lonkḍāči) topi, -ye, *f.* = *l.* hat (of iron).

Help, *s.* 1. kumók, -mke, *f.*; ādhār, -rā, *m.*; āspăd, -dā, *n.*, *or* āspăt, -tā, *n.*; săhāi, -ye, *f.* = *l.* assistance.
2. kākuḷt, -ti, *f.* = *l.* mercy; măzăt, -ti, *f.* = intercession, help.

Help, *v.* kăr *with the above nouns.*
I cannot h. exclaiming = bòbmārn sānginăstanāñ rāunk nozo.

Helpless, *a.* kumoknātullo; upāinātullo; dubḷo = *l.* poor; nirādhāri; kirkoḷ = *l.* wretched; ăskăt = *l.* weak; lāčāri = *l.* reduced.

Helplessness, *s.* lāčāri, -re, *f.* *or* lāčārpoṇ, -ṇā, *n.*; sóḍni, -ne, *f.* = *l.* abandonment; nirādhār, -rā, *m.*

Hem, *s.* pònd, -dā, *n.*, *e.g.* of a dress; dèg, -ge, *f.*

Hem, *v.* 1. pònd siuñ = *l.* stitch a hem.
2. kāṭ ghāl = *l.* put a dam.

Hemisphere, *s.* ărdo guḷo, -ḷeā, *m.* = *l.* half globe.

Hemorrhage, *s.* pāši, -še, *f.*

Hemp, *s.* sòṇ, -ṇā, *m.*; nār, -rā, *m.*

Hen, *s.* 1. kombi, -ye, *f.*; kunkāḍ, -kḍā, *n.*
2. bāilo (-li, -leñ) = *l.* female, *added to some nouns, for which see* Gram. p. 47.

Hence, *ad.* 1. āngā thāun = *l.* from here.
2. āz lāgāit = *l.* from to-day.
3. yeā mukār, yeā phuḍāñ = in future.
4. tăr *or* dekun = *l.* therefore.

Henceforth, *see* **Hence.**

Hen-house, *s.* kunkḍāntso gūḍ, -ḍā, *m.* = *l.* a cage of hens.

Henpecked (husband), *a.* bāilānḍo (dādlo), *n. c. in this mn.*; bāilek bhiyetolo.

Hepatic, *a.* kālzātso.

Heptagon, *s.* sātgiṭāñrūp, -pā, *n.* = *l.* a figure (made) of 7 lines; sātkonseāñrūp, -pā, *n.* = *l.* a figure (made) of 7 angles.

Heptarchy, *s.* sātzăṇānčeñ rāz, -jā, *n.* = *l.* a kingdom of 7 persons, *or bet.* sāt rājāntso-yekóṭ, -ṭā, *m.*

Her, *pron.* titso *or* itso; *see* Gram. P. II. ch. iii.

Herald, *s.* 1. dūt, -tā, *m.*
 2. răvāni, -niā, *m.*; harakāri, -ri, *m.*

Herb, *s.* 1. tăṇ, -ṇā, *n.*
 2. zāḍ, -ḍā, *n.* = *l.* a plant; giḍamulki, -ke, *f.* = a native medicine. (*H. K.*)

Herd, *s.* 1. hinḍ, -ḍā, *m.*, *e.g.* of cattle.
 2. *fg.* čăḷḷeñ-biḷḷeñ, -ḷeā, *n.* (a crowd).

Herdsman, *s.* gouḷi, -ḷiā, *m.*, *pr. fg.*

Here, *ad.* āngā (hāngā, *H. K.*).
 H. and there = 1. isiñ tisiñ, *or* yeusiñ teusiñ, *or* yeṇeñ teṇeñ.
 2. sărvụ dikkān = *l.* in every direction.
 3. tāče uprānt = *l.* after that.

Here-about, *ad.* sumār āngā.

Here-after, *ad.* 1. āče uprānt; yeā mukār; yeā phuḍañ; mukārik.
 2. yék pāuṭi = *l.* one time (once).
 3. meleā uprānt = *l.* after dead (death).

Here-after, *s.* dusri jiṇi, -ye, *f.* = *l.* another life.

Hereby, *ad.* āče vorviñ = *l.* through this.

Hereditary, *a.* dāizāntlo.

Herein, *ad.* āntuñ.

Heresiarch, *s. vlg.* herejinčeñ mostăk, -kā, *n.* = *l.* head of heretics; bāvāḍtavirodhān-čeñ mostăk, -kā, *n.*

Heresy, *s. vlg.* herezi, -zi, *f.*, *fr.*; mătabhēd (é), -dā, *m.* = *l.* difference in religion; bāvāḍ-tavirodhāi, -ye, *f.* = *l.* opposition to faith.

Heretic, *s. vlg.* herej (*or* yerej), -ji, *or* yerod, -dā, *m.*; bāvāḍ-tāk virodhi, -dhiā, *m.*

Heretical, *a.* bāvāḍtāk āḍ āsullo = *l.* being against faith; mă-tabhēdātso.

Hereupon, *ad.* tāče uprānt; tovóḷ = *l.* then.

Herewith, *ad.* āče vorviñ.

Heritage, *see* **Inheritance.**

Hermeneutic, *a.* ărthavivori.

Hermeneutics, *s.* ărthavivor, -rā, *m.*, *or* ărthavivoravidya, -ye, *f.* = *l.* explanation of the meaning, *or* science explaining the meaning.

Hermit, *s. vlg.* anakoret, -tā, *m.*, *fr.*; sănyāsi, -siā, *m.* = a pagan anchorite; vănavāsi, -si, *m.* = *l.* an inhabitant of the desert; yeksuro mănis, -nšā, *m.* = *l.* a solitary man.

Hermitage, *s.* vănavăsti, -te, *f.* (*perh.* vănāvās, -sā, *n.*); mōṭ -ṭā, *m.* = *l.* a convent.

Hero, *s.* vīr, -rā, *m.*; dhăiravont mănis, -nšā, *m.*; poilvān, -nā, *m.* (*used for* a cunning person).

Heroic, *a.* vīrātso; bhou vorto = very high.

Heroine, *s.* vīriṇ, -ṇi, *f.*; poilvāni, -ni, *f.*, *n.c. in this mn.*; *vlg.* ušār ăstri, -re, *f.*

Heroism, *s.* vīrāi, -ye, *f.*, *n. c.*; vorteponṇ, -ṇā, *n.* = *l.* sublimity; ăsādārn dhăir, -rā, *n.* = *l.* extraordinary courage.

Hers, *pron.* titso; *see* Gram. P. II. ch. iii.

Hesitate, *v.* 1. dubāu = *l.* doubt; tondreār āsā = *l.* is in embarrassment.
2. gāge = *l.* stammer.
3. pāṭi phuḍeñ kăr = *l.* do behind and before.

Hesitation, *s.* 1. dubāu, -bāvā, *m.* = *l.* doubt.
2. tondre, -dreañ, *m. pl.*
3. gāg, -gi, *f.* = *l.* a stammering.

Hesperian, *a.* ăstămti, *or* ăstămtitso.

Heteroclite, *a.* krămaviṇ = *l.* irregular; *see also* **Awkward.**

Heterodox, *see* **Heretic.**

Heterogeneous, *a.* 1. dusreā (*or* bădăl) thărātso = *l.* of a different kind.
2. *fg.* sămăndnātullo = *l.* without connexion.

Hew, *v.* tās, *e.g.* a rough plank; kātăr = *l.* cut, *e. g.* h. a branch from the trunk.

Hey, *int.* šābās.

Hiatus, *s.* 1. uktepoṇ, -ṇā, *n.* = *l.* an opening; iḍeñ, -ḍeā, *n.*; fuṭ, -ṭi, *f.*; khāli = *l.* an empty place.
2. pāḍ vāzāp, -zpā, *n.* = *l.* a bad sound; *see* **Exit.**

Hibernate, *v.* pāusātso vēḷ(é) tsălăi = *l.* pass the time of rain.

Hiccup, *s.* keḷni (*or* kăḷni), -ne, *f.*

Hiccup, *v.* kăḷni ye = *l.* h. come.

Hidden, *a.* guṭātso = *l.* secret; lipun *or* lipụllo = *l.* concealed.

Hide, *v.* lipăi, *c. v. of* lip, *n. v.*; guṭān dovór = *l.* keep secretly; dāmp = *l.* cover, shut.

Hide, *s.* kāt, -ti, *f.*; tsămbḍeñ, -ḍeā, *n.* (*esp.* dressed skin, leather).

Hideous, *a.* 1. ăḷsik = *l.* ugly; vidrup = *l.* without form.
2. bhiyānkuḷ; bhăyānkărātso; tărtărountso = *l.* causing trembling; kānṭāḷeātso = *l.* abominable.

Hideousness, *s.* bhiyānkuḷăi, -ye, *f* = *l.* dread; ăḷsikpoṇ, -ṇā, *n.* = *l.* ugliness.

Hiding, *s.* lipouṇeñ, -ṇeā, *n.*

Hiding-place, *s.* lipun rāunči suāt, -te, *f.* = a place for remaining hidden; lipụlli suāt, -te, *f.* = *l.* a hidden place.

Hie, *v.* ausăr; vegiñ tsăl = *l.* walk quickly.

Hierarch, *s.* păvitrụ ădhikāri, -ri, *m.* = *l.* a sacred empowered person.

Hierarchy, *s.* 1. păvitrụ ădhikār, -rā, *m.* = *l.* sacred power.
2. hudde, *pl.*, *m.* = *l.* dignities, ranks, *e.g.* h. of angels.

Hieroglyphic, *s.* 1. guṭăčeñ bărāp, -rpā, *n.* = *l.* secret writing.
2. săričiñ ăkṣerañ, *pl. n.*; săr asăllin akṣerañ, *pl. n.*; sănketăčitrụ, -rā, *n.* (*Mr. Cn.*) = *l.* pictures of signs.

Higgle, *see* **Haggle.**

High, *a.* 1. ubār.
2. huddeātso = *l.* of high state; vóḍ = *l.* great; vorto, voḍlo, voḍpoṇātso; boro, *e.g.* h. opinion.
H. voice = voilo tāḷo *or* unts tāḷo, -ḷeā, *m.*
He aims h. = tātso ševoṭ ubār.

Highland, *s.* 1. porvotāntso gāuñ, -gāñvā, *m.* = *l.* country of mountains.
2. podou, -dvā, *m.* (*ex.* high place).

High-mass, *s.* *vlg.* kāntār mis, -sā, *n.*

High-priest, *s.* voḍlo guru, -ru, *m.*; voḍlo saserdot, -ti, *m.*

High-treason, *s.* rāyāmōs(ó), -sā, *m.*

High-water, *s.* bhărti, -te, *f.*

Hilarity, *s.* kušālāi, -ye, *f.*; *see* **Joy.**

Hill, *s.* guḍo, -ḍeā, *m.*; ghāṭ, -ṭā, *m.*

Hillock, *s.* ghāṭi, -ye, *f.*

Hilly, *a.* guḍeāntso.

Hilt, *s.* muṭ, -ṭi, *f.* = *l.* fist, *fg.* (of a sword).

Himself, *pron.* tots; *see* Gram. P. II. ch. iii.

Hind, *s.* bāileñ meruñ, -ruā, *n.*

Hinder, *a.* pāṭlo.

Hinder, *v.* āḍāi *or* āḍkăḷ kăr = *l.* make objection.

Hindmost, *a.* nimāṇo = *l.* last; dusreānčea pāṭleān yeuntso; sămestañ bităr pāṭlo; ākeritso = *l.* extreme; kăḍetso.

Hindrance, *s.* ăḍḍi, -ḍe, *f.*; hărkăt, -ti, *f.*; āḍkăḷ, -ḷi, *f.*

Hindu, *s.* Hindu *or* Hinduāntso.

Hinge, *s.* (bāglātso) mulo, -leā, *m.*; bizāgrụ, -grā, *m.*; vāto, -teā, *m.* (h. of wood).

Hinge, *v.* (muleār) portatā = *l.* turns upon the hinge.

Hint, *s.* hišāro, -reā, *m.*

Hint, *v.* 1. hišāro di (*or* kăr) = *l.* give a h.
2. mótint hāḍ = *l.* bring to mind; săr kăr = *l.* make allusion.

Hippopotamus, *s.* năintso goḍo, -ḍeā, *m.*

Hire, *s.* mòl, -lā, *n.* = *l.* price; sāmbāḷ, -ḷā, *m.* = *l.* payment; pāg, -gā, *n.* (*n. c.*); bāḍeñ, -ḍeā, *n.*, *e.g.* work for h.

Hire, *v.* 1. bāḍeāk kāṇe.
2. lāi = *l.* apply (h. persons); dhăr = *l.* catch, *fg. used.*

Hireling, *s.* bāḍeāk kāṇello; kulkār, -rā, *m.* = day-labourer.

Hirer, *s.* bāḍeāk kāṇetolo.

Hiring, *s.* bāḍeñ, -ḍeā, *n.*; bāḍeāk kāṇeunčeñ; *rs.*

Hirsute, *a.* lovetso = *l.* of wool.

His, *pron.* tātso; *see* Gram. P. II. ch. iii.; āplo *mn.* his own.

Hiss, *v.* fusfus.

Historian, *s.* kobrangār, -rā, *m.* *or* kobregār; kătegār, -rā, *m.*; kobro sikullo = *l.* learned in news.

History, *s.* 1. kătā, -te, *f.*
2. kāṇi, -ye, *f.*, *mn.* a short story, fable.
3. kobro, *pl. f.* = *l.* news.

Hit, *v.* 1. mār = *l.* beat.
2. pēṭ(é) = give blows.
3. boḍăi = knock, *e.g.* a wall.
H. off = sārko vivor sāng = *l.* say exact explanation.
H. upon = mèḷ = *l.* be found (*Dat. prs.*)
H. the mark = noṭāk lāg.
H. together = ādăḷ = *l.* dash.
H. or miss = kăseñi zāundi.

Hit, *s.* mār, -rā, *m.*; pēṭ, -ṭā, *m.*

Hitch, *s.* 1. ăḍkăḷ, -ḷi, *f.*; ăḍḍi, -ḍe, *f.*
2. tondre, -reāñ, *pl.*, *m.* = *l.* embarrassment; tondreānčeñ kārāṇ, -ṇā, *n.* = *l.* cause of troubles.

Hither, *ad.* āngā. 'H. and thither = yeṇeñ teṇeñ, *or* thăiñ āngā'.

Hitherto, *ad.* 1. yedóḷ; yedoḷ păriyānt; ātāñ păriyānt; yedóḷ moṇasăr.
2. āngā păriyānt = *l.* till here.

Hive, *s.* 1. movāčeñ māleñ, -leā, *n.* (*strictly it mn. only* a nest of bees *or* wasps).
2. movāntso gūḍ, -ḍā, *m.* (wooden box).

Ho, *int.* 1. yé.
2. kăṭakăṭa = alas.

Hoar, *a.* ḍovoso *or* douso = *l.* whitish.

Hoar-frost, *s. approx.* dou, dovā, *m.*

Hoarse, *a.* sărānṭeātso; *rs.* tāḷo pòḍlā = *l.* voice fell.

Hoarseness, *s.* sărānṭo, -ṭeā, *m.*; moṭo tāḷo, -ḷeā, *m.*; tāḷeāčeñ pòḍāp, -ḍpā, *n.*

Hoary, *a.* 1. dovo = *l.* white (hair).
2. dovoso = *l.* whitish (hair); piko = *l.* ripe, *fg.*

Hoax, *v.* play a h. upon = čeṣṭăi kăr; kheḷkuḷañ kăr = mock, *Ital. burlare.*

Hobble, *v.* thonṭozāun tsăl = *l.* walk lamely; kunṭa.

Hobby, *s.* ăṣa, -ṣe, *f.*

Hobby-horse, *s.* 1. lānkḍātso goḍo, -ḍeā, *m.* = *l.* a horse of wood.
2. mogăči āločen, -ni, *f.* = *l.* favourite opinion.

Hobgoblin, *s.* druṣṭakāi, -ye, *f.*

(ghost); kuleñ, -leā, *n.*; bhut, -tā, *m.* = *l.* a devil.

Hobnob, *v.* bolāiki mār = *l.* beat health (drink to the health of); bolāiki kāṇe (*G. F.*).

Hock, *see* **Ham.**

Hoe, *s.* khoreñ, -reā, *n.*; korānṭi, -ṭe, *f.* = a little hoe.

Hog, *s.* dukor, -krā, *m.* (male); dukărn, -ni, *f.* (female).

Hogshead, *s.* pīp, -pā, *n.*

Hold, *v.* 1. dhăr, *e.g.* in order to prevent one falling.

2. vèng mār, *mn.* grasp.

3. somb, *e.g.* a vessel holds water.

4. tsălăi = *l.* cause to walk, *e.g.* h. an office.

5. kăr = *l.* do, *e.g.* an opinion (āločen kăr); čint = *l.* think.

6 dākăi = *l.* show, *e.g.* h. in honour, *ch. cs.*

7. rāu = *l.* stop, *e.g.* h. your tongue = vogo rāu.

8. zā = *l.* be fit (be applicable).

H. back = 1. dhăr = *l.* catch; āḍāi.

2. inkār kăr = *l.* make resistance (show difficulty, hesitate).

H. cheap = bepārvo kăr, *G. M.* = *l.* make contempt; săsār kăr.

H. fast = ghăṭ dhăr.

H. peace = vogo rāu = *l.* remain silent.

H. out = 1. sosṇigāi kāṇe (*or* sosṇikāi k.).

2. di *or* bheṭăi = give *or* offer.

H. in = pāṭi dovór.

H. to, *see* **Apply.**

H. up = 1. ukol, *or* ukoln dhăr.

2. rāu = *l.* remain, *e.g.* if the weather holds up.

H. with = vòp = *l.* consent.

H. your tongue = jib kovóḷ = *l.* roll the tongue.

Hold-fast, *s.* ānkḍo, -ḍeā, *m.* = a hook.

Holding, *s.* geṇisuāt, -te, *f.*, *or* geṇizămin = a land held on lease.

Hole, *s.* burāk, -kā, *m.*; dompḷo, -leā, *m.*; nèm, -mā, *n.* (in the earth); moḍāp, -ḍpā, *n.* = *l.* a rupture; bīḷ, -ḷā, *n.* of a rat and the like.

Holiday, *s.* 1. răjā, -je, *f.* = *l.* leave; khāli = *l.* empty (day).

2. fèst, -tā, *n.*, *or* sónt, -tā, *m.*

Holiness, *s.* sāntipoṇ, -ṇā, *n.*; bhāgevontpoṇ, -ṇā, *n.*

Hollow, *a.* 1. khāli = *l.* empty, vain, *pr. fg.*, *e. g.* vain pleasure.

2. pokaḷ.

H. voice = ḍobḍob tāḷo, -ḷeā, *m.*

Hollow, *s.* dhol, -li, *f.*; *see* **Cave.**

Hollow, *v.* pokaḷ kăr, pokrāi.

Holy, *a.* 1. bhāgevont, *or* bhāgevontpoṇātso (h. man).

2. păvitrụ = sacred (books, sacraments).

3. sānt (title of saints).

4. benjār, *e.g.* h. water, oil, *fr.*

5. *vlg.* sagrad, *fr.*

Holy-water, *s.* āgment, -tā, *n.*, *fr.*; tīrt, -tā, *n.*, the sacred water of the Hindus, used for washing their idols, *etc.* (*H. K.*)

H. water-pot = pī, -ye, *f.* (big).

Homage, *s.* mān, -nā, *m.*

Home, *s.* ghăr, -rā, *n.*: 'go h. = ghăra vots'; 'at h. = ghăra'; ṭhikāṇeñ, -ṇeā, *n.*; ṭhāṇeñ, -ṇeā, *n.* = a residence; biḍār, -rā, *m.* = a dwelling, an abode.

Come h. to any one = lāg.

Homeless, *a.* ghārnātullo.

Homely, *a.* 1. tsălto = *l.* current.

2. sādo = *l.* tame, simple.

3. sādhārăṇ = *l.* ordinary.

4. ăumăryāditso = *l.* unpolite.

Home-sickness, *s.* ghărči činta, -te, *f.*

Homicide, *s.* 1. khunigār, -rā, *m.* (a murderer).

2. khuni, -ye, *f.* (murder).

Homily, *s.* budbāḷ, -ḷi, *f.*

Homogeneous, *a.* yekats thărātso = *l.* of one kind.

Hone, *see* **Whetstone.**

Honest, *a.* 1. măryāditso; appănt; mānādik = *l.* of honour; mānātso; năḍteātso, ābrātso = *l.* of character.

2. sādo = *l.* simple; *vlg.* boro.

Honesty, *s.* 1. măryād, -di, *f.*

2. bori jiṇi, -ye, *f.* = *l.* good life.

3. ābru, -rā, *m.* = *l.* character.

Honey, *s.* 1. mouñ, movā, *n.* (natural), *pr. fg.*

2. mèl, -lā, *n.* (artificial).

Honey-bee, *s.* movātso mus, -sā, *m.*

Honey-comb, *s.* poḷi, -ye, *f.*

Honey-sweet, *a.* movātso, *pr. fg.*

Honorary, *a.* mānādik.

Honorary, *s.* inām, -mā, *n.*

Honour, *s.* 1. mān, -nā, *m.*; boreñ nāuñ, nāvā, *n.* = *l.* good name.

2. niskăḷāi, -ye, *f.*, *or* niskăḷpoṇ, -ṇā, *n.* = *l.* purity, *e. g.* h. of a woman.

3. ănănd, -dā, *m.* = *l.* glory, praise.

4. măryād, -di, *f.* = decorum, *mn. also* distinctions, signs of honour.

5. năḍteñ, -teā, *n.*, ābru, -rā, *m.* = character.

6. huddo, -deā, *m.* = *l.* rank.

7. kāido, -deā, *m.* = *l.* duty, *e. g.* pay the last h. to; mān *may also be used in this mn. e.g.* nimāṇo mān dākăi.

Honour, *v.* 1. mān kăr, *or* mān dākăi; gummān kăr, *G. N.*

2. neṭăi = adorn.

Honorable, *a.* mānādik; *see* **Honest.**

Honorably, *ad.* mānān.

Hood, *s.* 1. topi, -ye, *f.*

2. khòḷ, -ḷā, *n.* = a cloth worn on the head.

3. muski, -ke, *f.* (a covering for the whole body).

Hoodwink, *v.* fóṭăi = *l.* deceive.

Hoof, *s.* gèḷ, -ḷā, *n.* (of bullocks).

Hook, *s.* 1. gări, -ye, *f.*, for catching fishes.
2. ānkḍo, -ḍeā, *m.*, for windows, dresses, etc.; gānts, -tsā, *m.*

Hooked, *a.* 1. vānkḍo.
2. ānkḍo ghāllo, *or* ā. āsụllo = having a hook.

Hooping-cough, *s.* suṇekhonkli, -kle, *f.* = *l.* cough of dogs.

Hoot, *n. v.* (gug) bòbmār.

Hop, *v.* donko ghāl = *l.* put (one) leg.

Hope, *s.* 1. bărvāso, -seā, *m.*, *var.* bărvānso, (theol. virtue *and also in other mn.*, *as*, there is no hope of success).
2. pātiyeṇi, -ṇi, *f.* = *l.* confidence; āšā, -še, *f.*

Hope, *v.* 1. bărvāso dovór (*2nd Loc.*).
2. pātiye (*2nd Loc.*).

Hopeful, *a.* 1. pātiyeṇitso.
2. bărvāso āsụllo.

Hopeless, *a.* pātiyenātullo; nirāšetso; vèrt = *l.* vain, not giving hope; āšā sóḍtso.

Hopelessness, *s.* nirāša, -še, *f.*; nāñpātiyeṇi, -ṇi, *f.*; ăpabărvāso, -seā, *m.*; *vlg.*; vomptea koḷseār udāk = *l.* water in a pail turned upside down.

Horde, *s.* tănḍ, -ḍā, *m.*

Horizon, *s.* 1. dišṭ, -ṭi, *f.* = *l.* sight.
2. moḷbadèg, -ge, *f.* = *l.* brim of the sky; ākāš, -šā, *m.* = sky; moḷāb, -ḷbā, *n.* = firmament.

Horizontal, *a.* āḍ.

Horn, *s.* 1. sing, -gā, *n.*, *e. g.* of a bullock.
2. kómbụ, -bā, *m.* = a trumpet.

Hornblower, *s.* kómbagār, -rā, *m.* = a trumpeter.

Horned, *a.* singañ āsụllo.

Hornet, *s.* kirănṭ, -ṭi, *f.*

Horny, *a.* singātso.

Horologe, *s.* ghăḍiyāḷ, -ḷi, *f.* (*bet.* -ḷā, *n.*).

Horrible, *a.* 1. bhiyānkuḷ; tărtărountso = *l.* causing trembling; bhăyănkăr, *n. c.*
2. *fg.* bhōu ăḷšik = very ugly; khoṭepoṇātso = *l.* wicked.

Horror, *s.* 1. bheñ, bhiyā, *n.*; bhiyānkuḷāi, -ye, *f.*
2. *fg.* kānṭāḷo, -ḷeā, *m.* = an object of abhorrence.

Horse, *s.* 1. goḍo, -ḍeā, *m.*
2. trupsăvār, -rā, *n.* (*corr. from* trupsăvāri?) = cavalry. Ride on horseback = goḍeār bòs.

Horsekeeper, *s.* goḍeāgār, -rā, *m.*; kāskār, -rā, *m.*

Horseman, *s.* 1. goḍeār bòstolo.
2. săvārigār, -rā, *m.* (a cavalryman).

Horserace, *s.* goḍeāñpănth, -thā, *m.*

Horse-shoe, *s.* nāḷ, -ḷi, *f.*

Horse-soldier, *s.* săvārigār, -rā, *m.*, *or* goḍeāsăvār, -rā, *m.*

Horse-culture, *s.* tōṭānčeñ kām, -mā, *n.*; tōṭānči besāi, -ye, *f.*

Hose, *s.* 1. mēi, -yā, *m.*

2. izār, -rā, *n.*
Hospice, *s.* văsti, -te, *f.*
Hospitable, *a.* 1. biḍār diuntso = *l.* giving abode.
2. udār = *l.* liberal.
Hospital, *s.* āspătri, -ri, *f.*
Hospitality, *s.* 1. biḍār, -rā, *n.*
2. udārpoṇ, -ṇā, *n.* = *l.* liberality.
Host, *s.* 1. biḍār ditolo = *l.* giving abode.
2. hostu̥, -tu, *f.* = a consecrated wafer; zomo, -meā, *m.* = *l.* a multitude.
3. fouz, -ji, *f.* = *l.* an army.
Hostage, *s.* zāmindār, -rā, *m.*
Hostess, *s. see* **Host.**
Hostile, *a.* 1. dusmānātso; hăgeātso; jiddātso = of enmity.
2. virodhi = *l.* contrary; ăuguṇātso = *l.* unfavourable.
Hostility, *s.* 1. dusmānkāi, -ye, *f.*; *see* **Enmity.**
2. virodhāi, -ye, *f.* = *l.* contrariety.
3. *In pl.* lăḍāi, -ye, *f.* = *l.* fighting.
Hot, *a.* 1. un, *e.g.* water; khăr, *mn.* very hot (water); tāpāillo = *l.* made warm; votātso = sunny, warm; ubāḷ, *e.g.* hot days; gărmetso (*or* gărmi), *e.g.* day, dress, man (*fg.*); umāḷeātso = *l.* boiling, *fg.* fervent.
2. utsāmboḷ = *l.* excited.
H. bath = un udkāčeñ nāṇ.
Hotel, *s.* 1. musāfări, -ri, *f.* = a traveller's bangalow.
2. jeuṇāmusāfări = a bangalow providing bed and board; puzăt, -tā, *n.*
3. mèzkhān, -nā, *n.* = *l.* mess-house; biḍār, -rā, *n.* = *l.* abode, *fg.*; jeuṇāčeñ ghăr, -rā, *n.*; puzăt, -ti, *f.*; dhărmasāl, -lā, *n.*
Hotchpotch, *s.* khičāḍi (khičḍi), -ḍe, *f.*, *n. c.*
Hound, *s.* (sikāre-) pèṭo, -ṭeā, *m.*
Hour, *s.* 1. uor, -rā, *n.*, *fr.*
2. gănṭo, -ṭeā, *m.*
'What o'clock is it? = kitli uorañ zāliñ? *or* kitle gănṭe?' '¼ h. = yek kāldo'; '½ h. = ărdeñ uor'; '3 hours = pār, -rā, *m.*'
Hour-glass, *s.* reveči ghāḍiyāḷ, -ḷi, *f.* = *l.* a clock of sand.
Hour-hand, *s.* uorāntso gurtu̥, -tā, *m.*; vorāntso kānṭo, -ṭeā, *m.*; *see* **Hand.**
House, *s.* 1. ghăr, -rā, *n.* (*var.* găr); biḍār, -rā, *n.* = *l.* abode, a temporary dwelling-place.
2. gărčiñ, *pl. n.* (persons of the house).
3. ghărāṇeñ, -ṇeā, *n.* = dynasty.
4. hudde, -deāñ, *pl. m.* = *l.* dignities, a legislative body.
House, *v.* 1. biḍār di.
2. āsro di = *l.* give refuge.
H. cattle = goruañ goṭeānt ghāl *or* haṭiyent ghāl.
H. grain = dhāni rās kăr = *l.* heap g.

House-dog, *s.* suṇeñ, -ṇeā, *n.*

Household, *s.* 1. kuṭām, -ṭmā, *n.* = *l.* a family.

2. ghăr, -rā, *n.*

Householder, *s.* ghărkār, -rā, *m.* *used also for* husband.

Housekeeper, *s.* ghărarākṇo, -ṇeā, *m.*

Houseless, *a.* ghărnātullo.

House-maid, *s.* tsākărn, -ni, *f.*

House-rent, *s.* ghărābāḍeñ, -ḍeā, *n.*

House-wife, *s.* ghărkārn, -ni, *f.*

Hovel, *s.* kombāṭ, -bṭā, *n.*; *see* **Cottage.**

Hover, *v.* umkăḷ, *or* umkăḷn āsā; ub = *l.* fly, *fg.*; bouñ = *l.* walk; *see* **Flag, Wander.**

How, *ad.* 1. kăso (*adj.*, *see* Gram. P. II. ch. iii.), *or* kăsòlo (*vlg.* kăhălo).

2. kedo = *l.* how great (kedo vóḍ = how great).

H. many = kitle.

H. much = kitlo *or* kedo.

However, *ad.* tări *or* zāleāri (notwithstanding); kăsălei, jinsiñ = *l.* in any way; zărtăr = if, *with* i *added to the verb* (zătăr keleāri); i *added to the verb will often suffice.*

H. his intentions are good = zāleāri, *etc.*; h. sagacious you may be = kitlo budivont tuñ zāun āsleāri.

Howl, *v.* bòbmār = *l.* beat noise; *see* **Bark.**

Howl, *s.* bòb, -be, *f.*; goroz, -zi, *f.*

Hubbub, *s.* hăk ani bòb, -be, *f.*, *e.g.* an infernal h.

Huckster, *s.* yāri, -riā, *m.*

Huddle, *v.* gălibili zāun zomăi = *l.* collect with confusion (*tr. v.*); *rs. into* ăusărān = hastily, *or* guspon = confusedly.

Hue, *s.* 1. róng, -gā, *m.*

2. tsóráči pāṭ dhărči bòb, -be, *f.* = *l.* a cry for catching the back of a thief.

Hug, *see* **Embrace.**

Huge, *see* **Giant.**

Hulk, *s.* porkoṭeñ tāruñ, -rvā, *n.* = *l.* a spoiled old ship.

Hull, *s.* sāl, -li, *f.* = *l.* a bark.

Human, *a.* 1. mănšātso *or* mănšeponātso, *or* mănšeponi.

2. souñsārātso = *l.* worldly.

Humane, *a.* mănšeponātso (kind); mogāḷ = *l.* dear; kākuḷtitso, dăyāḷ, = merciful, clement.

Humanity, *s.* 1. mănšepoṇ, -ṇā, *n.* (*mn. also* pity); mănšāčeñ săimb, -bā, *n.* = *l.* human nature.

2. boḷepoṇ, -ṇā, *n.* = *l.* clemency; dăya, -ye, *f.*; kākuḷt, -ti, *f.*

Humanize, *v.* mānšugi sikăi = *l.* teach civility.

Humble, *a.* 1. khālto = *l.* subject; līn; măryāditso = *l.* modest.

2. uṇo = *l.* less, low; hălko; kirkóḷ.

Humble, *v.* 1. khālto kăr.

2. mōḍ (ò) = *l.* break, *fg.*; *see* **Check.**

Humbug, *s.* nākāzāllo, -leā, *m.* *or* nākāzālli văstų, -tu, *f.*; zāṅk, -ki, *f.*; ṭhăkkųpoṇ, -ṇā, *n.*, *n. c.*; mōs (ó), -sā, *m.* = *l.* deceit.

Humbug, *v.* ṭhăkkųpoṇ kăr; mōs kăr; khe̥lkuḷañ kăr = hoax.

Humidity, *s.* 1. šèḷ, -ḷi, *f.*
2. bāto, -teā, *m.* (h. of monsoon).
3. bizouṇeñ, -ṇeā, *n.*

Humility, *s.* khālteponṇ, -ṇā, *n.*, *or* khālteñ mòn, -nā, *n.*; līntuvāi (*var.* lenṭuvāi), -ye, *f.*

Humorous, *a.* 1. česṭāi kărtso, *or* česṭāyėtso = *l.* making fun; năklañ kărtso = *l.* making copies, *fg.*
2. bārik = *l.* witty; tārifetso = *l.* awkward; (bore) mărjetso = *l.* of (good) humour; khušāl = *l.* merry.

Humour, *s.* 1. mărji, -je, *f.*
2. sovói, -ye, *f.* = *l.* custom (bad).
3. nădteñ, -teā, *n.* = *l.* character; voḍni, -ne, *f.* = *l.* inclination; sobāu, -bāvā, *m.* = *l.* temper (of mind).

Humour, *v.* fuslāi.

Hump, *s.* pòng, -gā, *n.*

Humped, *a.* pòngo.

Hundred, *a.* sembor, *or* šembor (*in sing.*); señ *or* šeñ (*pl.* siñ *or* šiñ).

Hundred-fold, *a.* sembor pāuṭi *or* semborāni.

Hunger, *s.* bhuk, -ke, *f.*

Hunger, *v.* bhuke; bhuk lāg (*Prs. Dat.*) = *l.* h. be attached.

Hungry, *a.* bhukello *or* bhuk lāgųllo.

Hunt, *v.* šikāri kăr.

Hunt, *s.* šikāri, -re, *f.*; bónṭ, -ṭe, *f.*

Hunter, *s.* šikāri kărtolo, *or* šikāregār, -rā, *m.*; bónṭegār, -rā, *m.*

Hurdle, *s.* 1. tăṭṭi, -ṭe, *f.* (a screen made of cadjan-leaves).
2. voḍāp, -ḍpā, *n.* (a very big 'tăṭṭi').
3. izāi, -ye, *f.* (a screen of bamboo sticks).

Hurl, *v.* sóḍ = *l.* leave, free, *e. g.* missiles; uḍāi = throw, *e. g.* missiles.

Hurrah, *int.* šabās.

Hurricane, *s.* tufān, -nā, *n.*; vādāḷ, -ḷā, *n.* = a storm.

Hurried, *a.* ăusărātso; dărvoḍ kărtso.

Hurry, *s.* ăusăr, -rā, *m.*; dărvoḍ, -ḍā, *m.*
Be in a h. = ăusărār (*or* ăusărānt) āsā.

Hurry, *v.* ăusărāi, *c. v. of* ăusăr, *n. v.*; *more com.* ăusăr kăr; vegiñ kărāi = *l.* cause to be done soon.

Hurt, *s.* 1. luksān, -nā, *n.*
2. ghāi, -yā, *m.* = *l.* a wound.

Hurt, *v.* luksān kăr, (*tr.*); l.-zā, (*n. v.*); năšṭ kăr; dukāi = *l.* cause pain.

Hurtful, *a.* vāiṭ kărtso *or* năṣṭ kărtso, *or* luksānātso, *or* năṣṭātso, *etc.*

Hurtle, *see* **Dash.**

Husband, *s. vlg.* dādlo, -leā, *m.* = *l.* man, male; ghărkār, -rā, *m.* = *l.* householder; góu, govā, *m.* (*a low word*); poti, -ti, *m.*

Husbandman, *s.* buiñkār, -rā, *m.*; sāgoḷigār, -rā, *m.*; *see* **Cultivator.**

Husbandry, *s.* sāgoḷi, -ḷe, *f.*; besāi, -ye, *f.*

Hush, *int.* 1. ye.
2. čap (to command silence).

Hush, *v.* vogo rāvoi = *l.* cause to remain silent; fuslāi = *l.* appease.

Husk, *s.* 1. sāl, -li, *f.*; sărl, -lā, *n.* (of grain).
2. moṭo kunḍo, -ḍeā, *m.* = *l.* thick bran.

Hustle, *v.* komprān mār = *l.* beat with the elbow.

Hut, *see* **Hovel.**

Huzza, *see* **Hurrah.**

Hydraulic, *s.* prăvāhaśāstru̥, -trā, *n.*

Hydrophobia, *s.* udkābhirānt, -ti, *f.* = *l.* fear of water.

Hydropic, *a.* nalkutātso.

Hydrostatics, *s.* udkāsămānda-vidya, -ye, *f.* = *l.* science relative to water.

Hyena, *s.* suṇeñvāgāṭ, -gṭā, *n.* = *l.* a dog-tiger; kăttekurba, -be, *f.* (*var.* -bā, *n.*)

Hygrometer, *s.* śeḷimāp, -pā, *n.* = *l.* a measure of humidity.

Hymn, *s. vlg.* kăntig, -ge, *f.*; ănăndgāyān, -nā, *n.*

Hyperbole, *see* **Exaggeration.**

Hyperborean, *a.* 1. bhou băḍgātso = *l.* very northern.
2. bhou thănḍ = *l.* very cold.

Hypercritic, *a.* bhou koḍikāḍtso (*vlg.*)

Hyphen, *s.* mēḷagurtu̥, -tā, *m.* = *l.* a sign of conjunction.

Hypochondria, *s.* khănt, -ti, *f.*; *see* **Melancholy;** ăpadhăir, -rā, *n.*

Hypocrisy, *s.* kăpăṭ, -ṭā, *n.* = *l.* simulation; bhăktikăpăṭ = *l.* simulation of devotion; fóṭkiri bhăkt, -ti, *f.* = *l.* false devotion.

Hypocrite, *s.* kăpăṭi, -ṭiā, *m.* = *l.* simulating; fóṭkiro mănis -nśā, *m.* = *l.* a deceiving man; fóṭkiri bhăkt dākăitolo.

Hypostasis, *s.* sotăntrāčeñ săimb, -bā, *n.* = *l.* nature in its own power (*Lat. substantia tota*).

Hypostatic, *a.* āpleā sotăntrār āsu̥llo *or* sotăntrātso.

Hypothesis, *s.* śărt, -tā, *n.*, *n. c.*; kălpăna, -ne, *f.* = *l.* imagination, *n. c.*

I.

I, *pron.* ãuñ (hãuñ); *see* Gram. P. II. ch. iii.

Ice, *s.* kăre (kore), *pl. m.* (*perh.* hail); gār, -rā, *m.*

Ice-cold, *a.* thănḍgār, gāra bări thănḍ, *or only* gārabăriso.

Icicle, *s.* udkātso fātor, -trā, *m.* = *l.* a stone of ice.

Idea, *s.* 1. mònabhāu, -āvā, *m.* = *l.* a conception of the mind (*phil.*); čintna, -ne, *f.* = *l.* a thought.
2. voḷok, -ḷki, *f.* = *l.* knowledge.
3. kălpăna, -ne, *f.*, *n. c.*
4. nămuneāči čintna = *l.* an exemplifying thought.

Ideal, *a.* 1. nămuneātso = *l.* of a a model.
2. čintullo = *l.* thought.
3. kălpănetso = *l.* imaginary.

Ideal, *s.* nămuno, -neā, *m.* = *l.* model.

Idealism, *s.* māyā, -ye, *f. Sans. Mr., and partly also Konk. for* māyāk zā = disappear; kălpăna, -ne, *f.* = *l.* imagination.

Identical, *a.* tots = *l.* the same (*see* Gram. P. II. ch. iii.); săma = *l.* equal; sārko = *l.* equal (similar); yekāts = *l.* one thing: '*A* and *B* are identical = *A* ani *B* yekāts'.

Identify, *v.* săr kăr = *l.* make equality; sārko kăr; yekāts moṇ săng = *l.* say that (they are) one.

Identity, *s.* săr, ri, *f.*

Idiom, *s.* 1. (bhāšetso) guṇ, -ṇā, *m.* = *l.* a quality (of the language); bhāserīt, -ti, *f.*
2. tsālti bhās, -se, *f.* = *l.* current language.

Idiomatic, *a.* (bhāše-) guṇātso; *rs.* prătèk = *l.* peculiar; višès; *rs. into the noun.*

Idiot, *s.* neṇār, -rā, *m.* = *l.* ignorant.

Idiotic, *a.* neṇār; tsāltsămkăṇ nātullo = *l.* unpolite; pisoso = *l.* somewhat mad.

Idle, *a.* 1. āḷši; kām nātullo = not busy.
2. khāl = *l.* empty, *e.g.* id. talk = kh. utrañ (*or* găzāli).
3. vèrt = *l.* useless; upkārnātullo, *or* upkārākpòḍnātullo, *e.g.* u. utrañ=useless words.

Be i. = āḷsāi kăr.

Idle, *v.* 1. ālsāi kăr.
2. pāḍ kăr = *l.* make bad (spoil), *e.g.* i. away time.

Idleness, *s.* āḷsāi, -ye, *f.*; jèm, -me, *f.* = *l.* sloth.

Idler, *s.* făḍpoši, -šeā, *m.*, *mn.* good for nothing.

Idol, *s.* 1. bombeñ, -beā, *n.* = *l.* statue, *applied however to* i.; kuḍḍēu, -evā, *m.*; murt, -ti, *f.*

2. *fg*. bhou mogāḷ văstu̦, -tu, *f.* = *l.* a very dear thing.

Idolater, *s.* bombeānk bhăztolo, -leā, *m.*

Idolatry, *s.* bombeāñpuja, -je, *f.* = *l.* worship of idols; kuḍdēvañpuja, -je, *f.* = *l.* worship of idols.

Idolize, *v.* *G.* mogān mòr = *l.* die for love of; lāle = *l.* long for (*Dat.*); *G.* tsăḍāvot ăpurbāi āsā = *l.* is a great affection of.

Idyll, *s.* gouḷeāntso šlōk, -kā, *m.*

If, *conj.* zărtăr; *by the cond. in* -leār; păkšek (*with the participle*) = in the event of, in case that; *see* Gram. p. 251.

Even if = zăritări, *or* zărităr, *or* zărtăr *and* i *added to the verb*; *see* Gram. p. 155.

If not, 1. *by the condit. neg.*, *or* 2. *by* šivāi = *l.* beside, *with the* past participle, *e.g.* yeñkeleā šivāi = if you do not do this.

Ignoble, *a.* uṇo; kirkoḷ; hălko; ăṇvo; *see* **Base.**

Ignominious, *a.* ăḷšik = *l.* ugly, *fg.*; lăjišṭ = *l.* shameful; ăpamānātso = *l.* disgraceful.

Ignominy, *s.* lăz, -je, *f.* = *l.* shame; ăpamān, -nā, *m.* = *l.* an offence, loss of honour.

Ignoramus, *s.* dăḍḍo mānis, -nšā, *m.* = *l.* a stupid man; *vlg.* reḍo, -ḍeā, *m.* = *l.* a buffalo, *fg.*; *or* boil, -lā, *m.*, *or* gāḍāuñ, -ḍvā, *n.*

Ignorance, *s.* neṇārpoṇ, -ṇā, *n.*; neṇtuvāi, -ye, *f.*

Ignorant, *a.* neṇār, *or* sikanātullo, neṇto.

Ignorantly, *ad.* neṇārpoṇān.

Ignore, *v.* 1. neṇāñ; *see* Gram. p. 144.

2. *fg.* sóḍ = *l.* leave, omit.

Ill, *a.* vāiṭ; 'I am i. = mākā vāiṭ kārtā' (*diff. from* āuñ v. kārtāñ).

Fall i. = piḍent pòḍ.

Speak i. = vāiṭ ulāi, *or* vāiṭ kobār ulāi, *or* mānār ulāi.

Ill-affected, *a.* nāñkhušetso.

Ill-bred, *a*, tsāltsămkāṇnātullo, *or* ăumăryāditso.

Ill-breeding, *s.* nāñtsāltsămkăṇ, -ṇā, *n.*, *or* ăumăryād, -ḍi, *f.*

Ill-health, *s.* nāñbolāiki, -ke, *f.*

Illegal, *a.* kāideāvirodhi, *or* kāideā părmāṇe nātullo.

Illegible, *a.* vātsunk nozo āsullo; *bet. rs.*; vātsināñso.

Illegitimate, *a.* 1. ādhārāk zāllo = *l.* become by help; *vlg.* poṭār zāllo = *l.* born on the belly (*low expr.*); khăro bāpui nātullo; vāreātso.

2. krămāviṇ = *l.* irregular; kāideā virodhi = *l.* against law.

Illiberal, *a.* udārnāiñāsullo; surāti; imṭo = stingy.

Illicit, *a.* *by the neg. Pot. Mood; see* Gram.; ănnāyātso.

Illiterate, *a.* sikanātullo.

N. B. All the words compounded with the Lat. **im = not,** *not put down here, are to be formed according to* **Gram. Part III. ch. iv.**

Ill-nature, *s.* kărkărātso, *or* vāiṭ sobāu, -āvā, *m.* = *l.* troublesome nature; bezārāi, -ye, *f.*

Ill-natured, *a.* vāiṭsobāvātso, *etc.*

Illness, *s.* piḍa, -ḍe, *f.*; rōg(ó), -gā, *m.*

Illogical, *a.* nāyāvirodhi.

Ill-temper, *s.* koḍsāṇ, -ṇe (-ṇi), *f.* = *l.* bitterness, *fg.*; *see* **Ill-nature.**

Illuminate, *v.* prăkāsăi, *n. c.*; uzuāḍ kăr = *l.* make light; uzuāḍăi, *c. v. of* uzuāḍ, *n. v.*; dive lāi = *l.* apply lamps.

Illumination, *s.* uzuāḍ, -ḍā, *m. pr. fg.*, *e.g.* of mind; prăkāš, -šā, *m.*

Budiprakāš, -šā, *m.* = use of reason.

Illusion, *s.* bhrăm, -mā, *n.*; tsuk, -ki, *f.* = *l.* an error; fóṭkiri āločen, -ni, *f.* = *l.* a wrong opinion; sopāṇ, -pṇā, *n.* = *l.* a dream, *fg.*

Illustrate, *v.* vivor sāng, *G. M.* = *l.* say explanation; sārko (-ki, -keñ) dākăi = *l.* show exactly; soṣṭ kăr = *l.* make clear, distinct.

Illustration, *s.* vivor, -rā, *m.*; dāklo, -leā, *m.* = *l.* example.

Illustrious, *a.* nāvāḍgo; părzāḷik = *l.* splendid; dobājeātso = *l.* pompous, grand; vóḍ, *or* voḍpoṇātso = *l.* great.

Ill-will, *s.* mosór, -srā, *m.*, niskutsār, -rā, *m.* = *l.* envy.

Image, *s.* 1. imāz, -ji, *f.* = *l.* a statue, *fr.*

2. rejist, -tā, *m.* = a picture, *fr.*; pintụr, -rā, *n.*, *fr.*; rupḍeñ, -ḍeā, *n.*, *or* rupṇeñ, -ṇeā, *n.*; čitrụ, -trā, *n.*

3. sārkeñ, -keā, *n.* = *l.* a similitude.

4. kălpăna, -ne, *f.* = *l.* an imagination.

Imaginable, *a.* činttso, *or* čintuyet asụllo; *bet. rs.*; čintunk tānktā teñ = what can be thought; sărvụ jeñ čintunk tānktā teñ = whatever can be thought.

Imaginary, *a.* kălpănetso, *n. c.*; girigiritso = *l.* of fancy; *rs.* čintun (*or* čintụllo) mātrụ = *l.* only thought; khăro nāiñ āsullo = *l.* not true.

Imagination, *s.* 1. kălpăna, -ne, *f. exact but n. c.*

2. girigiri, -ri, *f.* (half-folly).

3. kălpouneñ, -neā, *n.* (act of the i.); *vlg.* čintna, -ne, *f.*

Imagine, *v.* 1. kălpăna kăr; čint = *l.* think.

2. sódun kāḍ = *l.* seeking take.

Imbecile, *a.* pisoso; ăremārla (*vlg.*); neṇār = *l.* ignorant; vid lāgụllo.

Imbibe, *v.* piye = *l.* drink; *fg.* bhórn zā *or* bhór = *l.* be filled.

N. B. All the words compounded with the Lat. im = not, *not put down here, are to be formed according to* Gram. Part III. ch. iv.

Imbrue, *v.* buḍăi = *l.* plunge; bizăi = *l.* moisten; róng lāi, *or* r. di = *l.* apply colour.
Be imbrued with = bhôrn āsā.

Imitable, *a.* dēk(é) kāṇeyet āsullo, *or* dēk kāṇeuntso; nămuneātso = *l.* exemplary.

Imitate, *v.* 1. *G.* dēk(é)kāṇe = *l.* take example; *G.* pāṭlāu kăr = *l.* make following; ...sārkeñ kăr, *Or.* bări kăr, *Or.* părmāṇe kăr = make similar to.
2. năkāl kāḍ = *l.* take a copy.

Imitation, *s.* 1. paṭlāu, -lāvā, *m.* = following.
2. sārkeñ, -keā, *n.* = *l.* similitude.
3. dēk(é), -ki, *f.* = *l.* an example; *rs. into v.*

Immaculate, *a.* pāpkhătnātullo; niskăḷ = *l.* pure.

Immaterial, *a.* kuḍnātullo = *l.* without body or matter.

Immature, *a.* 1. pikanātullo; tărno = *l.* green (fruits).
2. ăsămpurṇ = *l.* imperfect.

Immediate, *a.* 1. (bhou) lāgsilo = *l.* (very) near, *e.g.* im. cause.
2. *rs. into* ātānts = *l.* just now, *ch. cs.*

Immediately, *ad.* 1. bhou lāgiñ = *l.* very near.
2. teā (*or* yeā) kṣ̌āṇa, *or* teā (yeā) fāra = in that (this) moment.

Immediately after, uprānt teā fāra, *e.g.* im. after death there is the judgment = meleā uprānt teāts fāra zăḍti āsā; uprātăts; *only* fāra, *e.g.* im. after getting up, pray to God = uṭullea fāra Deva lāgiñ māg.

Immemorial, *a.* from time i. = kobro nātullea kālā thāun.

Immense, *a.* 1. māpnātullo, *or* mezāpnātullo = *l.* without measure; găḍ nātullo = *l.* without limit; ăgăṇit = *l.* numberless; lèkāviṇ, *or* lèknātullo; ăntaviṇ = *l.* without end; *vlg.* bhou vóḍ, *or* bhou tsăḍ vistārlolo = *l.* very great *or* extended.
2. dăit = *l.* gigantic (very tall).

Immensity, *s.* nāñmāp, -pā, *n.*; *bet. rs. into adj.*

Immerge, *v.* buḍăi, *c. v. of* buḍ, *n. v.*, *pr.*, *fg.*, *e. g.* im. in business.

Immersion, *s.* buḍāp, -ḍpā, *n.*

Immigrate, *v.* yetā = *l.* comes; părăgāvāntlo yetā.

Imminent, *a.* 1. pòḍtso = *l.* falling, *fg.*
2. bhou lāgšilo, *or* bhou lāgiñ āsullo.

Immoderate, *a.* hălt nātullo; mirvontso = *l.* surmounting; tsăḍāvot.

N. B. All the words compounded with the Lat. **im = not,** *not put down here, are to be formed according to* **Gram. Part III. ch. iv.**

Immoderately, *ad.* hăltnāstanāñ.

Immoderation, *s.* miruoṇeñ, -ṇeā, *n.*

Immodest, *a.* ăumăryāditso; ăḷšik = *l.* ugly, *fg.*, *e. g.* im. sin; lăzbānḍo (*var.* lăzmanḍo), *or* lăz nātullo = shameless.

Immodesty, *s.* ăumăryād, -di, *f.*; lăzbānḍpoṇ, -ṇā, *n.* = *l.* shamelessness.

Immolate, *v.* bheṭăi = *l.* offer.

Immolation, *s.* bheṭouṇeñ, -ṇeā, *n.*; sakrifis, -sā, *m.*, *fr.*

Immoral, *a.* ănnāyātso = *l.* illicit; ăumăryāditso = *l.* immodest; khoṭo = *l.* wicked; lăjist = *l.* shameful; kusullo = corrupted; kānṭāḷeātso = *l.* abominable; vāiṭ tsālitso *or* vāiṭ guṇātso = *l.* of bad morals.

Immorality, *s.* ăuguṇ, -ṇā, *m.*, *or* durguṇ, -ṇā, *m.* = *l.* vice; ănnāi, -yā, *m.*; vāiṭ, kārnio = *l.* bad actions; vāiṭ tsāl, -li, *f.*

Immortal, *a.* mòrnaviṇ; mòrnnātullo; sāsṇātso = *l.* eternal sădānkālātso = *l.* of ever.

Immortalize, *v.* visărnātullo kăr = *l.* make unforgotten; sāsṇāk dovór *or* sāsṇāk urăi = *l.* cause to remain for ever.

Immortality, *s.* amòrāṇ, *or* amòrn, -nā, *n.*, *n. c.*

Immovable, *a.* hālonk nozo āsullo, *or* hālnāso, *or* hālnātullo; *rs. into* rāu = *l.* remain; ghăṭ = *l.* firm; tsālnātullo.

Im. property = stirajindgi, -ge, *f.*

Immunity, *s.* suṭka, -ke, *f.* = *l.* freedom; *see* **Exemption.**

Immutability, *s.* thirasāṇ, -ṇi, *f.*; nāñbădlāp, -pā, *n.*, *n. c.*

Immutable, *a.* bădălzāunknātullo, *or* bădālnātullo; thir; tòts = *l.* the same.

Imp, *s.* 1. druṣṭakāi, -ye, *f.*; bhut, -tā, *m.* = a ghost, a devil.

2. tănṭālmāri, -riā, *m.*

Impair, *v.* pāḍ kăr = spoil; uṇo kăr = *l.* make less; ăskăt kăr = *l.* make weak; kāḍ = *l.* take away, *e. g.* im. honour; mōḍ(ó) = *l.* break, *e. g.* im. one's energy.

Impale, *v.* (suḷiyen) tóp = *l.* transfix (with a pale).

Impalpable, *a.* āpoḍnāñso, *or* āpḍunknozoāsullo; bhou bārik = *l.* very thin.

Impanel, *v.* păṭṭer borăi = *l.* write on the list (a jury).

Impart, *v.* di; vānṭo di = *l.* give a part, communicate.

Impartial, *a.* nitivont = *l.* just; khăḍākhăḍ; rūp (*or* tònḍ) pòḷenātullo = *l.* not looking

N. B. All the words compounded with the Lat. **im = not,** *not put down here, are to be formed according to* **Gram. Part III. ch. iv.**

at the face; păkšapātnātullo, *from* păkša = the side.

Impartiality, *s.* 1. nāñpăkšapāt, -tā, *n.*; nīt, -ti, *f.* = *l.* justice.

Impassable, *a.* utrunknozoāsullo, *or* utranāñso, *or* utrasārko nātullo.

Impassibility, *s.* sosināñsārkeñ, -keā *n.*; *bet. rs.*

Impassible, *a.* sosināñsārko.

Impassioned, *a.* utsāmbóḷ = *l.* excited; rāgān zăḷtso = *l.* burning for anger; umāḷeātso = *l.* boiling, *fg.*

Impatience, *s.* 1. nāñsosṇikāi, -ye, *f.*
2. ăusăr, -rā, *m.* = *l.* haste; dărvóḍ, -ḍā, *m.*

Impatient, *a.* 1. sosṇikāinātullo.
2. ăusărātso = *l.* hasty; āšetso = *l.* eager.
Be im. = sosṇikāi kāṇenāñ.

Impeach, *v.* firiyād di = *l.* give accusation; durva = *l.* blame.

Impeccability, *s.* pātkāntli suṭka, -ke, *f.* = *l.* freedom from sin.

Impeccable, *a.* pātkāntlo viroit = free from sin; pātak ādārunk nozo ăsullo = *l.* impossible to commit sin; pātak nātullo = without sin; pātkāntlo suṭullo = free from sin.

Impede, *v.* 1. āḍāi, *or* āḍkăḷ (*or* ăḍḍi) kăr.
2. toḍou kăr = *l.* make delay.

Impediment, *s.* 1. ăḍḍi, -ḍe, *f.*, *or* āḍkăḷ, -ḷi, *f.*
2. găg, -gi, *f.* = *l.* a stammering.

Impel, *v.* 1. tsălăi = *l.* cause to walk, *c. v. of* tsăl; dāunḍāi = *l.* cause to run, *c. v. of* dāuñ; bòḷ kăr = *l.* make force, violence; lóṭ = *l.* push.
2. lāi = *l.* apply, *e. g.* i. to write = borounčeāk lāi; bud sāng = *l.* say advice; utsāmboḷ kăr = *l.* make excited; uṭāi = *l.* cause to rise, *fg.*, *e. g.* i. to perform a duty; *by the c. v.*

Impend, *v.* 1. umkăḷāi, *c. v. of* umkăḷ, *n. v.*
2. pòḍtso āsā = *l.* is falling (imminent).

Impending, *a.* pòḍtso; bhou lāgiñ āsullo.

Impenetrability, *s.* riganāñsārkeñ, -keā, *n.*

Impenetrable, *a.* riganāñsārko, *or* rigunk nozo āsullo.

Impenitence, *s.* dhāruṇāi = *l.* obstinacy; nāñprājit, *or* ăprājit, -tā, *n.* = *l.* not satisfaction.

Impenitent, *a.* dhāruṇ = *l.* obstinate; prājitkārinātullo.

Imperative, *a.* 1. formāitolo *or* formāuntso.
2. gărjetso = *l.* necessary.

Imperceptible, *a.* āikunk (*or* poḷeunk) nozo āsullo; *bet. rs.*

N. B. All the words compounded with the Lat. im = not, *not put down here, are to be formed according to* Gram. Part III. ch. iv.

āikunk nozo; diṣṭipòḍanātullo = *l.* not falling to sight.

Imperfect, *a.* 1. ăsămpurṇ; tirsinātullo = *l.* not finished.
2. tsuk = *l.* wrong, *or bet.* tsuk āsullo = having faults; ăib āsullo *or* ăibātso = *l.* having imperfections.

Imperfection, *s.* 1. ăsămpurṇāi, -ye, *f.*; ăib, -bā, *n.* = a fault (*esp.* physical).
2. ăskătkāi, -ye, *f* = *l.* frailty; tsuk, -ki, *f.* = a mistake.

Imperial, *a.* 1. maharājātso, *or* maharāyātso.
2. *fg.* rāyābăriso, *or bet. rs.* rāyābări *or* rāyāčea jinsiñ = *l.* in the manner of a king.

Imperious, *see* **Arrogant.**

Imperishable, *a. vlg.* kābārzāunk nozo āsullo, *fr.*; mòrnāviṇ = *l.* immortal; nāšnātullo; sădānkālātso; ăntaviṇ = *l.* without end.

Impermeable, *a.* udkāk dāmpụllo = *l.* shut to water; *see* **Impenetrable.**

Impersonal, *a.* zoṇ dākăinātullo.

Impertinence, *s.* săḷ, -ḷā, *n.*

Impertinent, *a.* săḷiṣṭ.

Imperturbable, *a.* nidān = *l.* calm; thănḍ = *l.* cold, *fg.*; thir = *l.* constant; sămādhānātso = *l.* of concord.

Impervious, *a. see* **Impenetrable.**

Impetuosity, *s.* bòḷ, -ḷā, *n* = *l.* fòrce; zulum, -lme, *f.* = *l.* violence; ăusăr, -rā, *m.* = *l.* haste.

Impetuous, *a.* 1. bòḷiṣṭ, *or* bòḷātso.
2. ăusărātso = *l.* hasty.

Impetus, *see* **Impetuosity.**

Impiety, *s.* 1. nāñbhăkt, -ti, *f.* = *l.* no piety.
2. khoṭepoṇ, -ṇā, *n.* = *l.* wickedness.

Impinge, *see* **Dash.**

Impious, *a.* 1. bhăktnātullo = *l.* not pious; šāstra-āḍāsullo.
2. khoṭo = *l.* wicked.
3. kānṭāḷeātso = *l.* abominable.

Implacable, *a.* movāḷanātullo; dhāruṇ = *l.* obstinate; fārikpoṇ kāṇenātullo = *l.* not receiving satisfaction.

Implant, *v.* 1. lāi.
2. *fg.* kăntsăi = *l.* press, *e.g.* in the mind = mòtint.

Implement, *s.* 1. āid, -dā, *n.* = *l.* an instrument.
2. upāi, -yā, *m.* = *l.* means.

Implicate, *v.* 1. sirkāi = *l.* entangle; tondreānt ghāl = *l.* put in trouble.
2. lāg = *l.* be attached, *ch. cs.*, *e.g.* he is also implicated in it = āni tākā lāgtā; meḷāi = *l.* mix, mingle; *see* **Imply.**

Implication, *s.* (say something by i.) hišāre di = *l.* give hints; *see* **Imply.**

N. B. All the words compounded with the Lat. **im = not,** *not put down here, are to be formed according to* **Gram. Part III. ch. iv.**

Implicit, *a. rs. into* implicate; gupit.

Implore, *v.* māg, *Prs. Cm.*; āṇ diun māg = *l.* ask giving adjuration.

Imply, *v.* 1. somzun yetā = *l.* comes understood.

2. āṭāpi, *c.v. of* āṭāp = contain.

Impolite, *a.* tsāltsămkăṇ nātullo, *or* ăumăryāditso; dăḍḍo = *l.* rough.

Impoliteness, *s.* nāñtsāltsămkăṇ, -ṇā, *n.*; ăumăryād, -di, *f.*; rānuoṭpoṇ, -ṇā, *n.* = *l.* wildness, *fg.*

Impolitic, *a.* 1. budnātullo, budibrăṣṭ.

2. tsălounčeăk āḍāsụllo = *l.* being against governing.

Imponderable, *a.* bhārnātullo.

Import, *s.* ărthụ, -thā, *m.*

Import, *v.* 1. hāḍ = *l.* bring.

2. ărthụ āsā = *l.* meaning is; somzon yetā = *l.* is understood.

3. gărjetso zāun āsā = *l.* is necessary; *see* **Concern.**

Importance, *s.* 1. bhār, -rā, *m.* = *l.* weight, *fg.*; gărz, -je, *f.* = *l.* necessity.

2. huddo, -deā, *m.* = *l.* high state; 'man of im. = voḍlo mănis, *or* podvi asullo, *or* huddeātso mănis, -nšā, *m.*'

Important, *a.* 1. bhāri = *l.* weighty, *fg*; gărjetso = *l.* necessary; āločen kărtso = *l.* making opinion (giving to think).

2. vóḍ *or* voḍlo = *l.* great; podvedăr = *l.* powerful; huddeātso = *l.* of rank.

Importune, *v.* bezār kăr, *or* kărkăr kăr; portun portun māg = *l.* ask again and again.

Importunity, *s.* kărkăr, -rāñ, *pl. m.*; tondre, *pl. m.* = *l.* embarrassment; khanpati, -te, *f.*

Impose, *v.* 1. formāi.

2. fóṭāi = *l.* deceive.

Impossibility, *s.* nāñtānk, -ki, *f.*; *bet. rs. into* nozo.

Impossible, *a.* nozo; tānknātullo.

Impostor, *s.* mōs(ó) kărtolo, *or* mosāgăr, -rā, *m.*

Imposture, *s.* nāḍ, -ḍi, *f.* = *l.* a trick; mōs(ó), -sā, *m.* = *l.* deceit.

Impotence, *s.* ăskătkāi, -ye, *f.* = *l.* weakness.

Impotent, *a.* bhou ăskăt = *l.* very weak.

Imprecate, *v.* māg, *e. g.* vāiṭ māg; sou, *e.g.* gāḷi sou = say injuries (abuse), *also* call nicknames.

Imprecation, *s.* 1. šāp, -pā, *m.*, *n. c.*, *or* širāp, -pā, *m.* = *l.* curse; souvo, -veā, *m.* = a calling (one) bad names; gāḷ, -ḷi, *f.* = *l.* abuse, con-

N. B. All the words compounded with the Lat **im. = not,** *not put down here, are to be formed according to* **Gram. Part III. ch. iv.**

tumely; *vlg.* māldisāuñ, -āvā, *n.*, *fr.*

Impress, *v.* 1. mhor mār = *l.* beat a seal.
2. kăntsăi, *e.g.* on the mind; boro ugḍās kăr = *l.* make good remembrance, *ch. cs.*
3. movāḷāi = *l.* make tender (the heart); rig = *l.* enter, *e. g.* boro riglā = made a good impression; lāg = *l.* be attached: 'sermāuñ boro lāglo'.

Impression, *s.* 1. kăntsouṇeñ, -ṇeā, *n.*
2. mhor, -re, *f.* = *l.* a seal.
3. lāgāp, -gpā, *n.*, *e.g.* upon the mind.
4. utsāmboḷāi, -ye, *f.* = *l.* excitement; *bet. rs. into v.*
I have an im. that..., I am under the im. that... = mākā distā ki...

Impressive, *a.* lāgtso.

Imprint, *see* **Impress.**

Imprison, *v.* băndint ghāl; turingānt ghāl; *vlg.* jăilānt ghāl, *fr.*

Improbable, *a.* 1. sătmāndunk nozoso = almost impossible to be believed.
2. păsănd kărunk fāvonăi āsullo = *l.* not worthy of approval.

Improper, *a.* boronăiñ āsullo; năiñzāllo; ăumăryāditso.

Improperly, *ad.* 1. ăumăryādin = *l.* not decently.
2. tsukon = *l.* wrongly.

Impropriety, *s.* ăumăryād, -di, *f.*

Improve, *v.* 1. kurt kăr = *l.* make improvement (*esp.* material); guṇ kăr = *l.* make improvement(*esp.* immaterial, moral); boro kăr = *l.* make good; vrăddhi kăr = *l.* make prosperous.
2. ādhār kăr = *l.* make help.

Improvement, *s.* kurt, -tā, *m.*, *e.g.* of the ground; guṇ, -ṇā, *m. or* vrăddhi, -dhi, *f.*; *see* **Improve.**

Imprudence, *s.* nāñbud, -di, *f.*; *rs. into* čintināstanāñ = *l.* not thinking (well).

Imprudent, *a.* budnātullo; budibrăṣṭ; tsătrāinātullo; zāgrutāinātullo, *or* zāgrutnātullo.

Impudent, *a.* lăzbanḍo; lăjiṣṭ.

Impugn, *v.* *Dat.* virod ulăi = *l.* speak against; *or* virod vetā.

Impulse, *s.* bòḷ, -ḷā, *n.*, *pr. fg.*, *e. g.* im. of mind.

Impulsive, *a.* 1. *l.* loṭtso.
2. kumketso *or* kumkitso = *l.* helping.

Impunity, *s.* šikṣesuṭka, -ke, *f.* = *l.* freedom from punishment.

Impure, *a.* 1. nităḷnātullo; ăḷšik = *l.* ugly, *fg.*; mheḷo = *l.* dirty; čiklātso = *l.* dirty, *e. g.* water.

2. burso, *pr. fg.* (morally); pozḍo = *l.* profane, dishonest; mostitso = *l.* wanton.
3. borsillo = *l.* mixed.

Impurity, *s.* most, -ti, *f.* = wantonness; pozḍepoṇ, -ṇā, *n.*; kuḍičeo khušio = *l.* bodily pleasures; bursepoṇ, -ṇā, *n.*

Imputation, *s.* firyād, -di, *f.*; *see* **Charge, Blame.**

Impute, *v.* lāi = *l.* apply (ascribe); gunyāukār kăr = *l.* show guilty.

In, *prep.* 1. 1*st.* Loc. *if* place where *is meant*, *e.g.* in India = Indient.
2. *by the 2nd* Loc. *to show* time, place, *e.g.* sānjer = in the evening; păṭṭer = in the list.
3. *by the* Instr. *to show* direction: 'teā kusin vots'.
4. bităr = *l.* in, among.
5. thăiñ = there, as regards; *e.g.* in the soul there are three faculties; *see* Gram. P. IV. ch. ii.

Inability, *see* **Incapability.**

Inaccessible, *a.* votsanāñsārko; votsunk nozo āsullo; votsanāñso.

Inaccuracy, *s.* părāmăši, -še, *f.* = inadvertence; nāñtsătrāi, -ye, *f.*

Inaccurate, *a.* ăšuddụ = not correct, *n. c.*; zāgrutnăiñāsullo; tsătrāinātullo.

Inactive, *a.* āḷsi; kāmnātullo.

Inactivity, *s.* āḷsāi, -ye, *f.*

Inadequate, *a.* kāmāk pòḍanātullo = *l.* not falling to the business; lāyek năiñāsụllo.

Inadvertence, *s.* nāñtsătrāi, -ye, *f.*; părāmăši, -še, *f.*

Inalienable, *a.* părādin kărunk nozo āsụllo; părādin kărināñso.

Inanimate, *a.* jīvnātullo.

Inapplicable, *a.* nāñzāuntso; pòḍanātullo; *bet. rs. into* zāịnāñ.

Inappreciable, *a.* mòl fāvonăiñ āsụllo; mòlnātullo.

Inapproachable, *see* **Inaccessible.**

Inaptitude, *s.* nālāyekpoṇ, -ṇā, *n.*

Inarticulate, *a.* sošṭnātullo, *or* —năiñāsụllo.

Inasmuch, *ad.* dekun = *l.* therefore; teā pāsun = *l.* for that.

Inattention, *s.* nāñčit, -ti, *f.*; nāñtsătrāi, -ye, *f.*

Inattentive, *a.* čit dinātullo; tsătrāinātullo.

Inaugurate, *v.* 1. suru kăr = *l.* make a beginning, *G. F.*
2. benjār kăr = *l.* bless, *fr.*; păvitrụ kăr.
3. dobajeān kāṇe = *l.* take with solemnity; kāmāk rigăi = *l.* cause to enter into an office.

Incalculable, *a.* lèknātullo, *or* lèk kărnozo āsụllo.

Incandescence, *s.* tāpouṇeñ, -ṇeā, *n.*

Incandescent, *a.* tāpăillo.

Incantation, *s.* bolmeñ, -meā, *n.*; bhul, -li, *f.*; ghāḍi, -ḍi, *f.*

Incapability, *s.* ašăkt, -kti, *f.*; ătrāṇ, -ṇā, *n.*; nāñlāyekpoṇ, -ṇā, *n.*

Incapable, *a.* 1. lāyeknātullo, *or* —năiñāsullo.
2. săkătnātullo.

Incarnate, *v.* mănšasăimb ghe = *l.* take human nature; mănis zā = *l.* become man.

Incarnation, *s.* mănšāvatār, -rā, *m.*, *n. c.*; *some say* inkārnasāuñ, -sāvā, *n.*, *fr.*

Incautious, *a.* tsătrāinātullo; budnātullo.

Incense, *s.* 1. dhump, -pā, *m.*
2. lobān, -nā, *n.* = frankincense.

Incense, *v.* dhumpăi, *c. v.*

Incentive, *s.* umāḷāi, -ye, *f.*, *e. g.* to sin; utsāmboḷāi, -ye, *f.* = *l.* excitement; vondouṇeñ, -ṇeā, *n.* = *l.* allurement.

Incertitude, *s.* ănmān, -nā, *m.*, *e. g.* in. of death; dubāupoṇ, -ṇā, *n.*

Incessant, *a.* khăḷanātullo.

Incessantly, *ad.* khăḷnāstanāñ, *or* khăḷnāstanāñ; thāmbanāstanāñ; rāvanāstanāñ; găḍiye găḍiye = *l.* from moment to moment.

Incest, *v.* săireaprăduvār, -rā, *n.*; săireabitărleñ produvār, -rā, *n.*

Inch, *s.* ăngăl, -lā, *n.* *approx.*

Incidence, *s.* pòḍāp, -ḍpā, *n.*

Incident, *s.* găḍāp, -ḍpā, *n.* = *l.* event; săngăt, -gti, *f.*

Incision, *s.* kātrāp, -pā, *n.*; kātro, -treā, *m.* (small, ornamental).

Incisor, *s.* mukāvelo (*or* muklo) dānt, -tā, *m.* (*var.* mukāilo).

Incite, *v.* utsāmboḷ kăr; uskāi (a dog); uṭăi = *l.* cause to rise, *fg.*, *e. g.* to virtue.

Incitement, *see* **Incentive.**

Incivility, *see* **Impoliteness.**

Inclemency, *s.* kăṭiṇāi, -ye, *f.* ăsămādhān, -nā, *n.*, *e. g.* of the weather.

Inclination, *s.* 1. bāgouṇeñ, -ṇeā, *n.*, *or* bāgāp, -pā, *n.*
2. deuṇi, -ṇe, *f.* = *l.* a slope.
3. *fg.* voḍni, -ṇe, *f.*; ăpurbāi, -ye, *f.* = *l.* affection, fondness.

Incline, *v.* 1. bāgāi, *c. v. of* bāgā.
2. *fg.* mòn voi kăr = *l.* make heart yes.
3. vondăi, *c. v. of* vondou, *e. g.* văiṭăk vondoutā = inclines to evil; khuši āsā = *l.* is desire; boreñ distā = *l.* appears good.

Inclined, *part. a.* 1. tăyār = *l.* ready (*not ex.*).
2. -so *quasi-dim.* (*see* Gram. P. III. ch. ii.) *e. g.* in. to white = dovo-so.
3. *rs. into* vondouṇeñ āsā = *l.* inclination is, *e. g.* I am well in. towards N. = N. thāiñ mākā v. ā.

Include, *v.* 1. bităr ghāl = *l.* put inside.

2. āṭāpi = *l.* contain.
3. lék = *l.* count, consider.

Inclusive, *a.* 1. săit = also.
2. āṭāpun = *l.* containing (*n. c.*), *e.g.* from 2 to 13 in. = don thāun tera āṭāpun, *or* don thāun tera păriānt āṭa.

Incognito, *a.* guṭāčea rupān; vès bădlun.

Incoherence, *s.* nāñlāgāp, -gpā, *n.*; *bet. rs. into* lāgānāñ.

Incoherent, *a.* lāgānātullo; sămapòḍnātullo.

Income, *s.* 1. huṭṭavoḷ, -ḷi, *f.*
2. ādāi, -yā, *m.* = *l.* profit.

Incommensurable, *a.* yekăts māpnātullo; *bet. rs.* yekăts māp nāñ = there is not one measure.

Incommodious, *a.* soukāsāinātullo.

Incommunicable, *a.* vāṇto zāuñsārko nātullo, *n. c.*; dina sārko; *bet. rs.*

Incomparable, *a.* sărivin *or* sărkărināñso; sărnātullo.

Incompatible, *a.* 1. vopanātullo = *l.* not agreeing, *or* nāñvoptso.
2. meḷanāñsārko.

Incompetence, *s.* nāñvāzbipoṇ, -ṇā, *n.*

Incompetent, *a.* podvinātullo; vāzbinātullo; hăkkuṇātullo = *l.* not having right; kāmāk pòḍanātullo.

Incomplete, *a.* ăsămpurṇ.

Incompleteness, *s.* ăsămpurṇāi, -ye, *f.*

Incomprehensible, *a.* somzunk nozo āsullo, *or* somzasārkonātullo somzanāñso; păripurṇ somzanāñso = *l.* not fully intelligible.

Inconceivable, *a.* čintisārko nātullo; *bet.* čintunk nozo āsullo.

Inconclusive, *a.* ākernātullo, *n. c.*; ruzu zāunknātullo; tāḷmuḷ nātullo (*n. c.*), *e. g.* i. argument.

Incongruity, *s.* virod, -dā, *n.*

Inconsiderable, *see* **Trifling.**

Inconsiderate, *a.* tsătrāinātullo.

Inconsiderateness, *s.* nañtsătrāi, -ye, *f.*

Inconsistency, *s.* 1. thirnātulleñ mòn, -nā, *n.* = *l.* not firm heart.
2. nāñlāgāp, -gpā, *n.* = *l.* incoherence.

Inconsistent, *a.* 1. thirnātullo = *l.* not firm.
2. nāñvoptso, *or* vopanātullo.
3. lāgānātullo = *l.* not adhering.
4. sămapòḍanātullo = *l.* not falling right.

Inconsolable, *a.* sămādhānnātullo; bhuzăisārkonātullo, *or* bhuzounk nozo āsullo.

Inconstancy, *s.* thirnātulleñ mòn, -nā, *n.*

Inconstant, *a.* thirnātullo, *or* ăthir.

Incontinence, *s.* nāñsāmbāḷouṇeñ, -ṇeā, *n.*, *n. c.*; bursepoṇ, -ṇā, *n.* = *l.* impurity.

Incontrovertible, *a.* dubāunātullo; tărk kărunk nozo āsullo.

Inconvenience, *s.* 1. ăsăndrāp, -pā, *n.*
2. nāñvāzbipoṇ, -ṇā, *n.*

Incorporate, *v.* meḷāi = *l.* mix.

Incorrectness, *s.* ăšuddụpoṇ, -ṇā, *n.*

Incorrigible, *a.* sămazāisārkonātullo.

Incorrupt, *a.* kusanātullo.

Incorruption, *s.* nāñkusāp, -spā, *n.*

Incorruptible, *a.* kusanāñsārko, *or* kusasārkonātullo.

Increase, *v.* 1. tsăḍăi, *c. v. of* tsăḍ, *n. v.*; *bet.* tsăḍ kăr.
2. vrăddhi zā = *l.* get prosperous.

Increase, *s.* 1. tsăḍāp, -ḍpā, *n.*, *or bet.* tsăḍāu, -ḍāvā, *m.*
2. vrăddhi, -dhi, *f.* = *l.* prosperity.

Incredible, *a.* nāmbgasārkonātullo; nāñsātmāndtso, *or* sătmāndināñso; *vlg. rs. into verb.*

Incredulity, *s.* ănbāvāḍt, -tā, *m.*, *or* ănbāvāḍtpoṇ, -ṇā, *n.*; nāñ nāmbgaṇeñ, -ṇeā, *n.*

Incredulous, *a.* ănbāvāḍti; nāmbganātullo; sătmāndinātullo.

Incriminate, *v.* firyād di; *see* **Charge.**

Incrust, *v.* 1. kātin dānk; kāt zā.
2. māu zā.

Incubate, *v.* rovāṇe bòs.

Incubus (nightmare), *s.* hārdeasuḷ, -ḷā, *m.*

Inculcate, *v.* kăntsăi, *e.g.* on the mind; mótint ghāl = *l.* put into mind; sāngun sāng = saying say; portun portun sāng = *l.* again again say.

Inculcation, *s.* porti porti bud, -di, *f.*

Inculpable, *a.* neṇto (*var.* neṇṭuo); gunyāuñnātullo.

Inculpate, *v.* gunyāukār kăr = *l.* make guilty; *see* **Blame.**

Incur, *v.* mèḷ = *l.* be found, *sb. Dat.*

Incurability, *s.* nāñguṇ, -ṇā, *m.*; *bet. rs.*

Incurable, *a.* boro zāunk nozo āsullo; *bet. rs.*

Incursion, *s.* āngār pòḍāp, -ḍpā, *n.*

Indebted, *a.* riṇ āsullo.

Indebted (Be), *v.* 1. devo āsā: 'I am i. to you for one rupee = āveñ tukā yék rupoi devo āsā'; riṇkār zāun āsā = *l.* is debtor, *fg. also, e.g.* for one's health; riṇ āsā = *l.* debt is; riṇāniñ bhòrlolo zāun āsā.
2. *fg. also,* upkār mānd, *or* u. bāuḍ".

Indecency, *s.* ăumăryād, -di, *f.*

Indecent, *a.* ăumăryāditso; lājiṣṭ; ăḷšik.

Indecision, *s.* tondre, *pl. m.*; dubāu, -bāvā, *m.* = *l.* doubt.

Indecisive, *a.* dubāvi *or* dubāuntso, *e.g.* i. victory; tondreātso.

Indeclinable, *a.* rūpnātullo; bădălzăunknātullo; bădalnātullo.

Indecorous, *s.* năiñzăllo; ăumăryāditso.

Indecorum, *s.* ăumăryād, -di, *f.*

Indeed, *ad.* khărents, *mn. also the Lat. quidem*; niz-zăun; ălbăt = of course (*var.* ăblăt); nizgi, *or* khăreñgi, *or* sătgi = *l.* is it true?

Indefatigable, *a.* purozăunknātullo; bezărzăunknātullo.

Indefinable, *a.* ărthụ săngunk nozo āsụllo; vivornātullo = *l.* not having explanation.

Indefinite, *a.* găḍnātullo = *l.* without limit; ăgăṇit = *l.* numberless, *e. g.* ăg. jiṇi = eternal life; dubăuntso, *or* dubāvi = *l.* uncertain; khănḍit năiñ āsullo = *l.* not determined.

Indelicate, *a.* nāzuknăiāsullo; ăumăryāditso.

Indelicacy, *s.* năñnāzukăi, -ye, *f.*

Indemnification, *s.* fārikpoṇ, -ṇā, *n.*

Indemnify, *v.* fārikpoṇ di.

Indemnity, *s.* fārikpoṇ, -ṇā, *n.*; *rs.* năṣṭaviṇ = without harm.

Indent, *v.* kātre ghāl = *l.* put cuts.

Independence, *s.* sotăntrụ, -trā, *m.*

Independent, *a.* 1. āpleā sotăntrār āsụllo (*or* sotăntrātso); (koṇāk) khālnātullo = not being under any one.
2. āple khuše părmāṇe tsăltolo = *l.* walking according to one's own will; *see* **Free.**

Independently, *ad.* 1. sotăntrān.
2. šivăi = *l.* except, *with the Participle, e.g.* ind. of self-denial we do not go to heaven = āpṇāk inkār keleā šivăi, *etc.*
3. tsătrăi dināstanāñ = *l.* not paying attention.
4. āple khuše părmāṇe = *l.* according to one's own wish.

Indestructible, *a.* nāšasārkonātullo, *n. c.*; *bet.* nāš kărnozo āsụllo.

Indeterminable, *a.* niščeisisārkonātullo, *or* niščeisunk nozo āsullo.

Indeterminate, *a.* niščeisinātullo; khănḍit năiñ āsụllo.

Indetermination, *s.* ănmān, -nā, *m.* = incertitude.

Index, *s.* 1. pānāñpăṭṭi, -ṭe, *f.* = *l.* a list of pages.
2. kānṭo, -ṭeā, *m.*; *see* **Hand.**
3. gurtụ, -tā, *m.*

Indian, *a.* Indietso, *or* Hindustānātso.

Indicate, *s.* dākăi; gurtụ āsā = *l.* a sign is, *ch. cs.*; ărthụ āsā = *l.* meaning is, *ch. cs.*

Indication, *s.* 1. gurtụ, -tā, *m.*
2. dākoṇ, -ṇe, *f.*

Indicative, *a.* dākountso.

Indict, *see* **Accuse.**

Indifference, *s.* 1. nidānăi, -ye, *f.* = calmness (ascetic ind.).

2. thănḍ = *l.* cold, *or* thănd mòn, -nā, *n.* = *l.* a cold heart; bepārvo, -veā, *m.* = *l.* neglect (šāstrabepārvo); āḷsāi, -ye, *f.* = laziness.
3. nāñvondouṇeñ, -ṇeā, *n.* = *l.* no inclination.

Indifferent, *a.* 1. nidān = *l.* calm.
2. thănḍ = *l.* cold, *fg.*
3. tsăstrāinātullo = *l.* not giving attention.
4. bepārvi = *l.* neglecting; āḷsi = *l.* lazy; sumārātso = *l.* moderate.
5. vondanātullo = *l.* not inclining; vāiṭ-boronātullo.

I am indifferent to it = mākā yekāts.

Indifferently, *ad.* 1. *see the a.*
2. bhēd (é) kărināstanāñ = *l.* not making difference.

Indigence, *s.* 1. durboḷkāi, -ye, *f.*, *or* durboḷāi, -ye, *f.*
2. kirkoḷāi, -ye, *f.* = *l.* wretchedness.
3. sóḍni, -ne, *f.* = *l.* abandonment; nirādhār, -rā, *m.*
4. gărz, -je, *f.* = *l.* necessity.

Indigenous, *a.* gāuntso = *l.* of the country; *vlg.* āngātso = *l.* of here.

Indigent, *a.* dubḷo; kirkoḷ; sóḍullo, *or* vāṭer sānḍullo; gărjent āsullo = *l.* being in need; upāi nātullo; nirādhāri.

Indigestible, *a.* jiranātullo, *or* jirasārkonātullo.

Indigestion, *s.* ăjirn, -nā, *n.*

Indignant, *a.* rāgiṣṭ *or* rāgār zāllo; kródātso.

Be ind. = rāgār zā, *or* rāgār rāu, *or* rāgān zāḷ.

Indignation, *s.* rāg, -gā, *m.*: 'excite ind. = rāg āḍăi'.

Indignity, *s.* 1. năiñzālli kărni, -ne, *f.* = *l.* an unbecoming action; khoṭepoṇ, -ṇā, *n.* = *l.* wickedness.
2. ăkmān, *or* ăpămān, -nā, *m.* = *l.* offence.

Indigo, *s.* niḷ, -ḷi, *f.*

Indirect, *a.* nīṭnāiñ āsullo = *l.* not straight; vānkḍo = *l.* crooked, *pr.* *fg.*, *e. g.* ind. proof.

Indirectly, *ad.* vānkḍe vāṭen = *l.* in an indirect way.

Indiscreet, *a.* bhēd(é) kărnātullo = *l.* not making difference; budnātullo = *l.* not prudent.

Indiscretion, *s.* nāñbud, -di, *f.*

Indiscriminate, *a.* bhēd(é) kărnātullo = *l.* not making difference.

Indiscriminately, *ad.* bhēd(é) kărināstanāñ.

Indispensable, *a.* bhou gărjetso = *l.* very necessary; bhou zărur = *l.* very urgent; *rs.* ... viṇe (*or* nāstanāñ); rāunk nozo.

Indispose, *v.* *Dat.* āḍ ulăi = *l.* speak against, *ch. cs.*; món ... thāun pois kăr = *l.* make the heart far from...

Indisposed, *a.* 1. *rs.* bolāiki nāñ =

(there is) no health; *or* bolāiki nātullo; *rs.* soukāsāi nāñ.
2. nāñkhušetso = *l.* not willing; *bet. rs.* [*f.*

Indisposition, *s.* 1. nāñbolāiki, -ke, 2. nāñkhuši, -še, *f.* = *l.* no will; *rs.* soukāsāi nāñ.

Indisputable, *a.* dubāunātullo; tărknātullo.

Indissoluble, *a.* veglatsār kărunk nozo āsullo; vingăḍ kărunk nozo āsullo; moḍanātullo.

Indistinct, *a.* 1. soštnātullo, *e.g.* voice.
2. făḍpoši = *l.* faint, *e.g.* colour.

Indistinctly, *ad. rs. into* sošṭ *and* nāñ *affixed to the verb*; *vlg.* guluguḷu.

Indistinguishable, *a.* bhēd(ê) kărunk nozo āsullo; *bet. rs.*

Indite, *v.* borăi = *l.* write.

Individual, *a.* 1. āplo = *l.* own.
2. višes = *l.* particular.
3. yekatso *or* yekleātso = *l.* of one only.
4. vingăḍ = *l.* separated, single.

Individual, *s.* yeklots = *l.* one; vingăḍ zóṇ, -ṇā, *m.* (*or other similar noun*) = *l.* a single person.

Individuality, *s.* (yekleātso) guṇ, -ṇā, *m.*

Indivisibility, *s.* nāñvāṇṭisārkeñ, -keā, *n.*

Indivisible, *a.* vānṭisārkonātullo; vānṭunk (*or* kuḍke kărunk) nozo āsullo.

Indocile, *a.* sikasārko năi ñāsullo.

Indocility, *s.* sikanāñsārkeñ, -keā, *n.*, *or* nāñsikasārkeñ, -keā, *n.*, *n. c.*

Indolence, *s.* āḷsāi, -ye, *f.*; jèm, *or* zèm, -me, *f.* (*var.* jim) = *l.* sloth, sleepiness.

Indolent, *a.* āḷsi; jèmetolo.
Be ind. = jème (*var.* jèm yetā).

Indomitable, *a.* sādo kărunk nozo āsullo = *l.* impossible to make (be made) tame; sādo kărināñsārko, *n. c.*; sādo kărināñso, *n. c.*

Indoor, *a.* ghără bitărlo.

Indubitable, *a.* dubāunātullo.

Induce, *v.* lāi = *l.* apply, *e.g.* ind. to do; *by c. v.*; bud sāng = *l.* say advice; uṭăi = *l.* cause to rise, *fg.*, *e. g.* ind. to act couragoously, *ch. cs.*; fuslāi = *l.* coax, *e.g.* to sin.

Inducement, *s.* voḍni, -ne, *f.* (*var.* voḍneñ, -neā, *n.*), *or bet.* vondouṇeñ, -ṇeā, *n.*; inām, -mā, *n.* = *l.* a reward.

Induct, *v.* *see* **Inaugurate.**

Induction, *s.* tātpărya, -ye, *f.* (logical argument), *n. c.*

Indulge, *v.* 1. soukāsāyen tsălăi = *l.* govern peacefully; soukās tsăl = *l.* walk (behave) slowly, *ch. cs.*
2. iḍeñ di = *l.* give escape, *fg.*, *e.g.* ind. a passion.
3. vòp, *or* vòpun di = *l.* consent *or* consenting give; sóḍ = *l.* permit.

4. khušẹ pǎrmāṇe tsǎl = *l.* walk according to the desire of (comply with); dādos kǎr = *l.* make satisfied.
5. lāgụllo zāun āsā = *l.* is attached (given), *e.g.* to drinking.

Indulgence, *s.* 1. induljens, -sā, *n.*, *fr.* (*rl.*); šikṣemāf, -fi, *f.* = *l.* pardon of punishment.
2. upkār, -rā, *m.* = *l.* favour; soukāsāi, -ye, *f.* = *l.* peace (*opp. to* severity); dādoskāi, -ye, *f.* = *l.* satisfaction; dǎya, -ye, *f.* = *l.* clemency; šāmilpoṇ, -ṇā, *n.* = *l.* connivance, complicity.
Grant ind. = induljens pāṭāi = *l.* send ind.

Indulgent, *a.* mogāḷ = *l.* kind; šāmil = *l.* conniving; soukāsāyen tsǎltolo = *l.* ruling with peace, *G. F.*

Indurate, *v.* ghǎṭ kǎr.

Industrious, *a.* 1. kǎṣṭi = making difficult things; zānṭo; tsurk = *l.* active.
2. prǎyǎtǎn kǎrtolo = *l.* making effort.
3. hikmǎtitso = *l.* of artifice, arts; čǎmǎtkārātso = *l.* of artifice.

Industry, *s.* 1. hikmǎt, -ti, *f.*; čǎmǎtkār, -rā, *m.*
2. minǎt, -ti, *f.* = *l.* an effort.

Inebriate, *v.* ǎmāl kǎr = *l.* make intoxication; ǎmālātso kǎr = *l.* make intoxicated, (*uncommon*).

Ineffable, *a.* utsārunk nozo āsullo *etc.*; *bet. rs.*

Ineffective, *a.* vèrt; guṇāk pòḍanātullo; nirfoḷādik; *rs.* riganāñ = does not enter; bòḷnātullo = *l.* without force.

Inefficacy, *s.* nāñguṇ, -ṇā, *m.*; ǎskǎtkāi, -ye, *f.* = *l.* weakness.

Inelegant, *a.* unčināiñāsullo.

Inelegance, *s.* nāñsobitāi, -ye, *f.*; nāñunčāi, -ye, *f.*, *n. c.*

Ineligibility, *s.* vintsinañsārkeñ, -keā, *n.*; *bet. rs.*

Ineligible, *a.* vintsināñsārko; vintsun kāḍināñso.

Inequality, *s.* nāñsār, -ri, *f*; bhēd (é), -dā, *m.* = *l.* difference.

Inert, *a.* 1. hālnātullo, *or* hālunk nozo āsullo, *or* hālanāñsārko.
2. āḷsi = *l.* lazy.

Inestimable, *a.* ǎmolik (*used esp. of* the Precious Blood of J. C.); bhou molādik = *l.* very precious.

Inevitable, *a.* tsukounk nozo āsullo; tsukanāñso, *or* tsukanāñsārko; ǎvǎš āsullo = *l.* being necessary.

Inexcusable, *a.* māf fāvonāiñ (āsullo).

Inexhaustible, *a.* *vlg.* kābārzāunk nozo āsullo, *fr.*; mugdanātullo = *l.* not finishing; *perh.* tirsanātullo, *but this mn.* which is not to be completed.

Inexorable, *a. rs.* āikanāñ = *l.* does not hear, *or* āikanātullo; fārikpoṇkāṇenātullo = *l.* not taking satisfaction; kăṭiṇ = *l.* rigorous, cruel.

Inexpediency, *s.* nāñvāzbipoṇ, -ṇā, *n.*

Inexpedient, *a.* vāzbi năiñ āsullo; lāyeknātullo = *l.* not fit, not suitable; kāmāk pòḍanātullo; *rs.* zāināñ.

Inexperience, *s.* nāñānbóg, -gā, *m.* (*var.* -bou, -bovā, *m.*); neṇārpoṇ, -ṇā, *n.* = *l.* ignorance; nāñābyās, -sā, *m.*; nāñsovói, -ye, *f.* = *l.* no practice.

Inexplicable, *a.* vivor sāngunk nozo āsullo, *or* vivor sāngināñso, *or* v. sāngināñsārko.

Inextinguishable, *a.* pālvanāñso, *or* pālvanātullo.

Inextricable, *a.* tondreāntso = *l.* embarrassed; suṭanāñso, *or* suṭtso năiñ āsullo.

Infallibility, *s.* nāñtsuk,-ki, *f. n. c.*

Infallible, *a.* 1. tsukon pòḍanātullo.
2. dubāunātullo = not doubtful.

Infamous, *a.* beābrātso = *l.* of no character; ăpamānātso, *or* ăpamānādik = *l.* of no honour; khoṭepoṇātso = *l.* wicked.

Infamy, *v.* beābru, -rā, *m.*; ăpamān, -nā, *m.*; khoṭepoṇ, -ṇā, *n.* = *l.* wickedness.

Brand with inf. = ābru kāḍ, *or* beābru kăr.

Infancy, *s.* bāḷsepoṇ, -ṇā, *n.*

Infant, *s.* bāḷseñ, -seā, *n.*

Infanticide, *s.* 1. burgeakhuṇi, -ye, *f.* = *l.* the killing of a child; bāḷseakhuṇi.
2. bāḷseākuṇigār, -rā, *m.* = the murderer of a child; bāḷseākhuṇigārn, -ni, *f.* = the murderess of a child.

Infantry, *s.* pāidăḷ, -ḷā, *n.*

Infatuate, *v.* pisăi, *c. v. of* pisa, *n. v.*, *or* piso kăr.

Infatuation, *s.* pisepoṇ, -ṇā, *n.*

Infect, *v.* 1. lāi (*tr.*), *or* lāg (*n. v.*) = *l.* attach, *or* be attached; zā = *l.* get (*n. v.*), *e.g.* a sickness, *ch. cs.*
2. *fg.* kusăi = *l.* corrupt; bhor = *l.* fill, *fg.*

Infection, *s.* voso, -seā, *m.*

Infer, *v.* 1. niščeisi; *vlg.* āntuñ sik = *l.* in this learn, *ch. cs.*
2. pārki = *l.* guess.

Inference, *s.* 1. *rs. v.*
2. pārkouṇeñ, -ṇeā, *n.* = a guess.

Inferior, *a.* khāl āsullo = being under, *or* khālto; uṇo = *l.* less, *fg.*

Inferiority, *s.* uṇepoṇ, -ṇā, *n.*; *bet. rs. into adj.*

Infernal, *a.* 1. yemkonḍātso *or* yemkonḍāntlo.
2. yemkonḍa băriso = *l.* as in the hell.

Infertility, *s. rs.* bănjer = not

fertile; čappepoṇ, -ṇā, *n.*, *fg.*; uṇepoṇ, -ṇā, *n.*

Infect, *v.* 1. vòsò lāgăi, *n. c.* 2. băčāvāviṇ kăr = *l.* make not safe.

Infected, *a.* vòsò lāgullo; băčāvāviṇ.

Infidel, *a. s.* ănbāvāḍti, (-tiā, *m.*)

Infidelity, *s.* ănbāvāḍtpoṇ, -ṇā, *n.*

Infinite, *a.* ăgăṇit = *l.* numberless, *e.g.* inf. God; leknātullo = *l.* numberless; ăntaviṇ = *l.* endless; sămpurṇ = *l.* full; sărvụ guṇāniñ sămpurṇ = *l.* full of all perfections; mitnātullo, găḍnātullo = without limit; 'God is i. = Deva thăiñ săkăḍ boreo văstu āsāt'.

Infinitely, *ad.* 1. *see adj.* 2. săriviṇ = *l.* without comparison.

Infinitive, *a.* khănḍitnātullo, niščeisinātullo = not determined.

Infirmary, *s.* piḍestānčeñ kuḍ, -ḍā, *n.*, *or* p. sāl, -lā, *n.*

Infirmity, *s.* ăskătkāi, -ye, *f.* = *l.* weakness.

Inflame, *v. fg.* zăḷăi = *l.* cause to burn (for anger); ulpāi, *c. v. of* ulpa, *n. v.*; utsāmboḷ kăr = *l.* make excited.

Inflamed, *a. fg.* rāgān zăḷtolo, *or* rāgān bhorlolo = *l.* filled with anger; rāgān khătkăttolo = *l.* boiling for anger; utsāmboḷ.

Inflammation, *s.* 1. uzo, -jeā, *m.* *esp. fg.* passion, heat; ulop, -lpā, *m.*, *pr. fg.* 2. vāidamān, -nā, *n.*, *mn.* infl. of the heart. 3. āgruñ, -grā, *n.* (of the tongue).

Inflate, *v.* 1. suzăi = *l.* cause to swell, *c. v. of* suz. 2. *fg.* gărv kăr = *l.* make proud; *fg.* ful (*n. v.*) = get like a flower (proud); *fg.* fugăi (*c. v. of* fug) = get puffed up (proud).

Inflect, *v.* bāgăi.

Inflexibility, *s.* nāñbāgoṇeñ, -ṇeā, *n. or* nāñbāgāp, -pā, *n.*

Inflexible, *a.* bāgānātullo, *or* bāgānāñsārko, *or* bāgānāñso.

Inflexion, *s.* bāgoṇeñ, -ṇeā, *n.*

Inflict, *v.* di, lāi, *e. g.* punishment; mār = *l.* beat.

Influence, *s.* 1. mulādo, -deā, *m.*, *e.g.* infl. of a man with others; bòḷ, -ḷā, *n.* = *l.* force; bhār, -rā, *m.* = *l.* weight, *fg.*; (*also, the same as* mulādo); podvi, -ve, *f.* = *l.* power. 2. săkăt, -kti, *f.* = *l.* ability. 3. upāi, -yā, *m.* = *l.* means, *e. g.* mākā u. nāñ = I have no i. 4. hārbār, -rā, *m.*, *e. g.* divine infl. *or also* care.

Influence, *v.* mulādeāk ghāl = *l.* put to infl.; *pass.* m. pòḍ = *l.* fall to infl.

Influential, *a.* bhāri; podvedār, *or* podvi āsullo; ădhikāri.

Influx, *s.* votóṇ, -ṇe, *f.*

Inform, *v.* 1. kăḷit kăr, *or* kăḷăi, *c. v. of* kăḷ = be known.
2. rūp di, *or* r. kăr = *l.* give form.
Informal, *a.* kăidea părmāṇe nātullo; kăideāk virodhi; rītnātullo = *l.* not having formality.
Information, *s.* 1. kobār, -bre, *f.*; ăbiprāi, -ye, *f.*; vordi, -de, *f.* = *l.* report.
2. uoḷok, -ḷki, *f.* = *l.* knowledge.
Infraction, *s.* 1. moḍāp, -ḍpā, *n.* = *l.* rupture, *fg.*
2. gunyāuñ, -āvā, *m.* = *l.* fault.
Infrequency, *s.* ăprupāi, -ye, *f.*
Infrequent, *a.* ăprup.
Infuriate, *v.* rāgān zăḷăi = *l.* cause to burn for anger.
Infuse, *v.* 1. bităr ghāl = *l.* put in, *pr.*, *fg.*, *e.g.* i. gifts.
2. vót, *e. g.* i. oil in the lamp.
3. *fg.* lābăi, *c. v. of* lāb, *e. g.* i. graces.
Infusion, *s.* 1. bitărghālneñ, -neā, *n.*, *bet. rs. into v.*
2. kăsāi, -yā, *m.* (medic. i.)
Ingenerate, *v.* zălmăi, *c. v. of* zălma.
Ingenious, *a.* 1. kăṣṭi.
2. bārik = *l.* witty; *see* **Industrious.**
Ingenuity, Ingeniousness, *s.* bārikāi, -ye, *f.*; čămătkār, -rā, *m.*, hikmăt, -ti, *f.* = *l.* artifice; ušārāi, -ye, *f.* = *l.* cleverness.
Ingenuous, *a.* niskăpṭi = *l.* sincere; sādo = *l.* simple; ukto = *l.* open, *fg.*
Ingenuousness, *s.* niskăpăṭ, -ṭā, *n.*; sādepoṇ, -ṇā, *n.*
Inglorious, *a.* mānbhoginātullo; ăpamānātso, *or* ăpamānādik; lăjiṣṭ = *l.* shameful.
Ingraft, *see* **Graft.**
Ingrate, *a.* ănupkāri.
Ingratiate, *v.* movāḷāi = *l.* move, make tender; mogāḷ zā = *l.* become dear; mōg(ó) kărăi = *l.* cause to love.
Ingratitude, *s.* ănupkārpoṇ, -ṇā, *n.*
Ingredient, *s.* 1. sāmbār, -rā, *m.* (curry-stuff).
2. āḷeān, -nā, *n.* = all the ingredients for curry.
Ingress, *s.* rig, -ge, *f.*
Ingulf, *v.* giḷ = *l.* swallow.
Inhabit, *v.* 1. āsā.
2. rāu = remain; vās kăr; jiṇi jiye = *l.* live life.
Inhabitable, *a.* rāviet āsullo; biḍār diuntso.
Inhabitant, *s.* lók, -kā, *m.* = *l.* people (*in the sing. mostly*).
Inhale, *v.* usuās kāṇe = *l.* take breath.
Inharmonious, *a.* tāḷeāmēḷ(é) nātullo; sămapòḍanātullo = *l.* not falling together.
Inherent (Be), *v.* lāg.
Inherit, *v.* dāiz pòḍ = *l.* inheritance fall, *Sb. Dat.*; dāiz yetā = *l.* inheritance comes, *Sb. Dat.*; dāiz kāṇe = *l.* inheritance take.

Inheritable, *a.* dāizasārko.

Inheritance, *s.* dāiz, -zā, *n.*; pitrāsti, -te, *f.*

Inheritor, *s.* dāiji, -jiā, *m.*

Inhibit, *v.* āḍvār.

Inhospitable, *a.* biḍār dinātullo = *l.* not giving abode; rāunk" nozo āsullo *or* rāvanāso.

Inhuman, *a.* niṣṭur; mhāru; mănšeponnātullo.

Inhumanity, *s.* nāññmănšepoṇ, -ṇā, *n.*; niṣṭurāi, -ye, *f.*; mhārupoṇ, -ṇā, *n.*

Inimitable, *a.* dēk(é) kāṇeunk nozo āsullo, *or* dēk kāṇeināso; *rs.* dēki voir = *l.* above example, *or perh.* dekivoilo.

Iniquitous, *a.* ănnāyātso.

Iniquity, *s.* 1. ănnāi, -yā, *m.* = *l.* injustice.
2. khoṭepoṇ, -ṇā, *n.* = *l.* wickedness.

Initial, *s.* suruvetso *or* suruver āsullo, *or* suru kărtso.
I. letters = suruvečiñ ăkṣerañ.

Inject, *v.* bităr ghāl *or* b. uḍāi.

Injunction, *s.* hukum, -kme, *f.*; *see* **Order.**

Injure, *v.* luksān kăr, năṣṭ kăr, vāiṭ kăr = make harm; ăkmān kăr = make offence; bòḷ kăr = make violence; dukăi, *c. v. of* duk = afflict.

Injurious, *a.* ăkmānātso; dukountso = *l.* afflicting; luksānāk pòḍtso = *l.* falling to harm.

Injury, *s.* ăkmān, -nā, *m.*; năṣṭ, -ṭā, *m.*, *or* luksān, -nā, *n.* = *l.* harm; vāiṭ, -ṭā, *n.* = harm; duk, -ki, *f.* = *l.* pain, sorrow.

Injustice, *s.* ănnāi, -yā, *m.*; ănīt, -ti, *f.*

Ink, *s.* *vlg.* tint, -tā, *n.*; šāi, -ye, *f.* (*H. K.*); māši, -še, *f.*

Inlay, *v.* kātrāp ghāl (?).

Inkstand, *s.* *vlg.* tintyor, -rā, *m.*; šāidouti, -te, *f.*

Inlet, *s.* rig, -ge, *f.* = ingress; *see* **Estuary.**

Inmate, *s.* 1. lók, -kā, *m.* = *l.* an inhabitant, people.
2. vokāl, -klā, *m.* = a tenant.

Inmost, *a.* bhou bitărlo, *pr. fg.*

Inn, *see* **Hotel.**

Innate, *a.* săimbātso = *l.* natural; săimbān čhāpo ghāllo = *l.* printed by nature.

Innavigable, *a.* tāruñtsălnātullo.

Inner, *a.* bitărlo.

Innkeeper, *s.* mezkhān (*or some such word*) tsălăitolo, *or perh.* mezkhānāgār, -rā, *m.*, *n. c.*; jevaṇagār, -rā, *m.* = *l.* he who gives meals; jevāṇ ditolo.

Innocence, *s.* nenṭepoṇ, -ṇā, *n.* *or* nenṭuvāi, -ye, *f.*; nirāprād, -dā, *m.*; gunyāuññātụlli jiṇi, -ye, *f.* = *l.* life without fault; šāntipoṇ, -ṇā, *n.*, bhāgevontpoṇ, -ṇā, *n.* = sanctity; niskăḷāi, -ye, *f.*, *or* niskăḷpoṇ, -ṇā, *n.* = purity; niskăpăṭ, -ṭā, *n.* = *l.* simplicity.

Innocent, *a.* nenṭo; pātaknātullo, *or* pāpkhātnātullo; gunyāuñ nātullo; bhāgevont; niskăḷ;

vāiṭkārinātullo; niskāpṭi; *see the noun.*

Innocuous, *a.* vāiṭkārnātullo.

Innovate, *v.* novo kăr; bădăl = *l.* change.

Innovation, *s.* bădlāp, -pā, *n.* = *l.* change; novi rīt, -ti, *f.*, novi rivāz, -ji, *f.*, novi măryād, -di, *f.* = a new custom; novi văstu, -tu, *f.* = *l.* a new thing.

Innovator, *s.* nove măryādegār, -rā, *m.*

Innoxious, *see* **Innocuous.**

Innumerable, *a.* lèknātullo, *or* lèkavin (āsullo), *or* lèkavorto.

Inobservant, *a.* bepārvo kărtso = *l.* making neglect, *G. M.*, *or* bepārvı; móḍtso=*l.* breaking, *fg.*

Inoculate, *v.* 1. dāg ghāl = *l.* put vaccine (in medicine).
2. *see* **Graft** (in gardening).

Inodorous, *a.* părmăḷnātullo.

Inoffensive, *a.* ăkmān kărnātullo; *see* **Innocuous.**

Inopportune, *a. rs.* fāvonātullea veḷār = *l.* in not right time; fāvonātullea veḷār āsull.

Inordinate, *a.* krămavin, *n. c.* = *l.* without order; miruontso = *l.* exceeding (the limits); sămanăiñ āsullo = *l.* not right; vāiṭ = *l.* bad; ăumăryāditso = *l.* unbecoming.

Inorganic, *a.* jīvnātullo = *l.* lifeless; gòpnātullo, *n. c.*

Inquest, *s.* vitsārăṇ, -ṇā, *n.*

Inquire, *v. see* **Enquire**; *moreover*, somzun ghe = *l.* take understanding; kobār ghe = *l.* take news.

Inquisition, *s. see* **Enquiry.**

Inquisitive, *a.* vitsāri.

Inroad, *s.* 1. āngārpòḍāp, -ḍpā, *n.* = *l.* a falling on the body.
2. luṭ, -ṭi, *f.* = *l.* prey.

Insalubrious, *a.* boḷāikinātullo.

Insane, *a.* piso; aremarla; vidlāgullo.

Insanity, *s.* 1. pisepoṇ, -ṇā, *n.*
2. vid, -di, *f.*

Insatiable, *a.* dādos kărunk nozo āsullo, *or* dādos zāinānso.

Insatiability, *s.* nāñdādoskāi, -ye, *f.*

Inscribe, *v.* 1. borăi *or* bităr borăi.
2. *G.* nāvār borăi = *l.* write in the name of, (address); melviḷās borăi = *l.* write the address.

Inscription, *s.* melviḷās, -sā, *m.*

Inscrutable, *a.* 1. vitsārunk nozo āsullo, *or* vitsārināñso.
2. guṭātso = *l.* secret.

Insect, *s.* kiḍo, -ḍeā, *m.*; kiḍ, -ḍi, *f.* (of a small kind).

Insensibility, *s.* 1. *rs.* melāso = he seems to be dead.
2. nāñbhogāp, -gpā, *n.*; *bet. rs. into aff.*

Insensible, *a.* 1. visve nātullo = *l.* without senses; bhóginātullo = *l.* not feeling.
2. melloso = *l.* apparently dead;

āng tsukăitolo = *l.* body avoiding: *an expression applied to bullocks, etc. when they will not let themselves be yoked, and fg. applied to people who try to avoid the performance of their religious duties, or are* insensible to religion.

Inseparable, *a.* vingăḍkărunk nozo āsullo, *or* vingăḍ kărinăñso, *etc.*

Inseparability, *s.* vingăḍanāñsārkeñ, *or* vingăḍzăināñsārkeñ, -keā, *n.*; nāñvingaḍāp, -pā, *n.*, *n. c.*

Insert, *v.* bităr ghāl, *or* lāi = *l.* put in *or* apply.

Insertion, *s.* sirkāvăṇi, -ṇe, *f.*, *e.g.* i. in a book, *n. c.*

Inside, *prep.* bităr; *adj.* bitărlo.

Insidious, *a.* mosātso; nāḍitso; fóṭountso.

Insight, *s.* voḷok, -ḷki, *f.*; 'get a thorough i. into = purti voḷok mèḷ'.

Insignia, *s.* gurtụ, -tā, *m.* (ădhikāragurtụ) = *l.* sign.

Insignificant, *a.* 1. ărthụnātullo = *l.* without sense.
2. čillār = *l.* trifling.

Insincere, *a.* kăpṭi.

Insincerity, *s.* kăpăṭ, -ṭā, *n.*

Insinuate, *v.* 1. (vānkḍe vāṭen) rig = *l.* enter (crookedly); thoḍeñ thoḍeñ ghāl = *l.* put little by little; hišāro di = *l.* give a hint.
2. portun portun sikăi = *l.* teach again again; fuslāi = *l.* flatter.

Insinuating, *a.*, *see verb*; mogāḷ = *l.* dear.

Insinuation, *s.* 1. hišāro, -reā, *m.* = *l.* hint; vānkḍiñ utrañ = *l.* crooked words.
2. fuslāuṇeñ, -ṇeā, *n.*; *see the verb.*

Insipid, *a.* čappo = *l.* without salt, *pr.*, *fg.*, *e.g.* i. words; rutsnātullo = *l.* without taste; nākāzāllo = *l.* nonsense.

Insipidity, *s.* čappepoṇ, -ṇā, *n.*; nākāzāllo, -leā, *m.*

Insist, *v.* māgun māg, *or* portun portun māg, *or* māg *with* -ts; thirzāun rāu (*or some other verb instead of* rāu) = *l.* remain constantly.

Insolence, *s.* 1. săḷ, -ḷā, *n.*; gărvụ, -vā, *n.* = *l.* pride.
2. lăzbanḍpoṇ, -ṇā, *n.* = *l.* impudence; hemmeñ, -meā, *n.* = *l.* vanity.

Insolent, *a.* săḷiṣṭ, dhāruṇ = obstinate; gărvi = *l.* proud; āplea vādeātso, *or* āple khuše părmāṇe tsăltolo = *l.* walking according to one's own will.

Insoluble, *a.* 1. kăḍounk nozo āsullo, *e.g.* an i. metal.
2. *fg.* zāb diunk nozo āsullo = *l.* not possible to give an answer; *fg.* suṭanāñso = *l.* not possible to get rid of, *e.g.* an i. question.

Insolvent, *see* **Bankrupt.**

Insomuch, *ad.* titlo...ki = so... that; ăse jinsiñ...ki.

Inspect, *v.* 1. sārkeñ pòḷe = *l.* look exactly; melbăndobăst pòḷe; tănki kăr.
2. rāk = *l.* guard; *see* **Superintend.**

Inspection, *s.* vitsārăṇ, -ṇā, *n.* = *l.* inquisition; tănki, -ke, *f.*; *bet. rs. into v.*; *see* **Superintendence.**

Inspector, *s.* 1. *vlg.* inspekṭăr, -rā, *m.*
2. mélbăndobăst pòḷetolo, *or* părikṣegār, -rā, *m.*

Inspiration, *s.* 1. usvās, -sā, *m.*, *or bet.* usvās kāṇeuntso = *l.* taking (in) breath.
2. hārbār, -rā, *m.* (divine i., d. operation); măima, -me, *f.* (divine i.)
3. Devāgeli čintna, -ne, *f.* = *l.* a thought coming from God (*ascetic mn.*); suāsadeṇeñ, -ṇeā, *n.*; budideṇeñ, -ṇeā, *n.*
4. In. of the Holy Bible, *rs.* Devān mótint ghālleñ; kontsouṇeñ, -ṇeā, *n.* (Devāk-).

Inspire, *v.* 1. uskār vor = draw inspiration; *or bet.* usuās kāṇe = *l.* take breath.
2. mótint ghāl = *l.* put into the mind, *e.g.* the Holy Bible.
3. *only* di *or* ghāl, *e.g.* i. courage = dhăir di; *by c. v.*, *e.g.* i. fear = besṭăi.

Instability, *s.* thirnātulleñ mòn, -nā, *n.* = *l.* an unstable heart; ăthirasāṇ, -ṇe, *f.*

Install, *v.* 1. pāṭār bosăi = *l.* cause to sit on the throne.
2. sădrer bosăi = *l.* cause to sit on the seat; huddo vopsun di; kām dobājeān di = *l.* give employment solemnly; mokrur kăr = *l.* appoint.

Instalment, *s.* 1. mokruri, -re, *f.*; huddeāčeñ vopsāp, -pā, *n.*
2. kisti, -te, *f.* (1st, 2nd, *etc.* i.); vāido, -deā, *m.*

Instance, *s.* 1. zărurāi, -ye, *f.* = *l.* urgency.
2. māg-ṇeñ, -ṇeā, *n.* = *l.* request.
3. dāklo, -leā, *m.* = *l.* example, *e.g.* to give an i.

Instance, *v.* mótint hāḍ = *l.* bring into memory; ugḍās kăr = *l.* make remembrance; niyāḷāk hāḍ = *l.* bring to consideration.

Instant, *a.* 1. zărur = *l.* urgent.
2. pòḍtso = *l.* falling (imminent); lāgiñ lāgiñ āsullo = *l.* being very near.

Instant, *s.* kṣāṇ, -ṇā, *n.*; kiṇ, -ṇā, *n.*

Instantaneous, *a.* yekats fārātso (teāts phārātso); yekats kṣāṇātso; *bet. rs. into ad.*

Instantaneously, *ad.* yekats fārā, yeka kṣāṇā (*or* kiṇa) bitār = in one moment.

Instantly, *ad.* 1. māgun māgun = *l.* asking asking.
2. yekats fārā = at once.

Instead of, *prep.* bădlāk; suāter = *l.* in place, (*with the partic.*), *e.g.* i. of receiving a blessing, he received curses = āširvād mèḷče suāter tākā širāp pòḍlā.

Instep, *s.* pāul, -lā, *n.*

Instigate, *v.* utsāmboḷ kăr = *l.* make excited; huskăi (a dog); *see* **Excite**; kānṭe vor = *l.* bring thorns, *fg.* (*Konkan.*).

Instigation, *s.* utsāmboḷăi, -ye, *f.*

Instil, *v.* (thoḍeñ thoḍeñ) bităr ghāl = *l.* put in (little by little).

Instinct, *s.* săimbāčeñ vondouṇeñ, -ṇeā, *n.* = *l.* natural inclination; *perh.* săimbāči bud, -di, *f.*, *or* s. zāṇvăi, -ye, *f.*

Instinctive, *a.* săimbāvondouṇeātso, *or* săimbāčea vondouṇeā pārmāṇe āsullo.

Institute, *v.* găḍ = *l.* found; stāpisi = *l.* found, *n. c.*; kārn dovór = *l.* appoint, *e.g.* J. C. appointed the Apostles; niščeisi = *l.* establish; nemsi = *l.* appoint; nomiyār = *l.* nominate, *fr.*

Institute, *s.* 1. găḍāp, -ḍpā, *n.* (that which is founded); garpar, -rā, *n.*, *e.g.* a religious order is an i.; kārkhāno, -neā, *m.*; dhārmaštai, -ye, *f.* = i. of charity, *n. c.* (dhārmasāḷ, -ḷe, *f.*); ord, -di, *f.*, *fr.*
 2. bāndāp, -dpā, *n.* = *l.* a building.

Instruct, *v.* 1. sikăi, *c. v. of* sik.
 2. vāḍăi, *c. v. of* vāḍ = *l.* grow, be prosperous.
 3. hukum di = *l.* give an order.

Instruction, *s.* 1. sikāp, -kpā, *n.* *or* sikoṇ, -ṇe, *f.*
 2. hukum, -kme, *f.* = *l.* order.

Instructive, *a.* 1. sikountso.
 2. upkārāk pòḍtso = *l.* falling to benefit; bud diuntso = *l.* giving wisdom.

Instructor, *s.* 1. sikăitolo.
 2. upadesi, -si, *m.*; ăiguḷ, -ḷā, *m.*; mestri, -ri, *m.*, *fr.*

Instrument, *s.* 1. āid, -dā, *n.* (*also* musical i.); čăkru, -rā, *n.* (a machine).
 2. upăi, -yā, *m.* = *l.* means.
 3. dāklo, -leā, *m.* = a deed (a written document).

Instrumental, *a.* kumki = *l.* helping, *e.g.* i. cause, *opp. to* mukhya = principal; *often rs. into* vorviñ = through, *ch. cs.*; āid zāun āsullo.

Insubordinate, *a.* 1. khāltonātullo; miruontso = *l.* surmounting (orders).
 2. kuṭ kārtso = *l.* making plot.
 3. săḷiṣṭ = *l.* obstinate.

Insubordination, *s.* 1. miruoṇeñ, -ṇeā, *n.* = disobedience.
 2. săḷ, -ḷā, *n.* = *l.* obstinacy.
 3. kāṭkăi, -ye, *f.* = *l.* revolution.

Insufficiency, *s.* 1. nāñudārpošaṇ, -ṇā, *n.* = *l.* want of means of living.

2. *rs. into* pāvanāñ = *l.* does not reach.

Insufficient, *a.* pāvanāṭullo; *bet. rs. into* pāvanāñ.

Insular, *a.* kudreāntso, *or* kudreāntlo, *or* kudreā bări.

Insult, *s.* ăkmān, -nā, *m.*; gāḷ, -ḷi, *f.* = *l.* abuse, contumely.

Insult, *v.* ăkmān kăr = *l.* make offence; gāḷi sāng = *l.* say abuses; *see* **Abuse.**

Insulting, *a.* ăpamānātso, *or* ăpamānādik *or* ăkmānātso, *or* ăkmān kărtso.

Insuperable, *a.* 1. jikunk nozo āsullo, *or* jikanāñso, *e.g.* an i. general, rival; zăit vorunk nozo āsullo = *l.* not possible to gain victory.

2. miruonk nozo āsullo = *l.* not to be surmounted, *pr. fg.*; utranāñso *or* utrunk nozo āsullo = *l.* not to be crossed.

3. bāgāunk nozo āsullo, *or* bāgānāñso.

Insupportable, *a.* sosunk nozo āsullo, *or* sosināñso.

Insurance, *s.* zāminetso mēḷ (è), -ḷā, *m.* = *l.* society of i.; băčāvi, -ve, *f.*; bim, -mā, *m.*

Insure, *v.* 1. risknātullo kăr; bim utrăi; băčāvi kăr.

2. zāmindār zā = *l.* become surety, *ch. cs.*; zāmin di = *l.* give surety, *ch. cs.*

Insurgent, *a.* kāṭkāi kărtso; kāṭkāiyetso.

Insurgent, *s.* kāṭkāyegār, -rā, *m.*

Intact, *a.* 1. āpḍunknātullo (*or* āpoḍnātullo) = *l.* not touched.

2. *fg.* khăt nātullo = *l.* stainless; *or* khătoun-nātullo.

3. tots = *l.* the same.

Integer, *s.* purto ănko, -keā, *m.* = *l.* a whole number.

Integral, *a.* purto.

Integrity, *s.* 1. gunyāuñnāṭulli jiṇi, -ye, *f.* = *l.* a blameless life; nenṭuvāi (lenṭuāi), -ye, *f.* = *l.* innocence; măryād, -di, *f.* = *l.* honesty; ābru, -rā, *m.* = *l.* character.

2. ānkuārpoṇ, -ṇā, *n.* = *l.* virginity; niskāḷpoṇ, -ṇā, *n.* = purity.

Intellect, *s.* ginyān, -nā, *n.*; mót, -ti, *f.* = *l.* mind; somzikāi, -ye, *f.* = *l.* understanding.

Intellectual, *a.* mótitso.

Intelligence, *s.* 1. somzikāi, -ye, *f.* (*var.* somzeṇkāi).

2. ginyān, -nā, *n.*

Intelligent, *a.* somzoṇitso, *or* somzatolo; ušār = *l.* clever; bārik = *l.* thin, *fg.* (of sharp mind).

Intelligible, *a.* somzayet āsullo, *or* somzasārko.

Intemperance, *s.* 1. nāñhāḷt, -tā, *n.*

2. poṭārpoṇ, -ṇā, *n.* = *l.* gluttony.

Intemperate, *a.* hăḷtnātullo; miruontso = *l.* surpassing (the proper limit); merebhāilo = *l.* beyond the limits.

Intend, *v.* sevóṭ āsā = *l.* aim is, *ch. cs.*; āločen āsā = *l.* aim is, *ch. cs.*; čint, = *l.* think; niščeisi = *l.* establish.

Intense, *a.* umāḷeātso = *l.* fervent (boiling, *fg.*), *e. g.* i. sorrow; kăṭin; *by the emph.* -ts (*see* Gram. P. III., ch. ii.); *by repeating the word it qualifies.*

Intensity, *s.* umāḷo, -leā, *m.*; kăṭiṇāi, -ye, *f.*

Intent (To the i.), *by the supine*; *by the Dat. of the absol. infin.*

Intent, *a.* lāguḷlo = *l.* given; *rs. into* prăyătăn kăr = *l.* make effort, *ch. cs.*; čit duintso = *l.* giving attention.

Intent, *s.* 1. sevóṭ, -ṭā, *m.*

2. āločen, -ni, *f.*

Intention, *s.* sevóṭ, -ṭā, *m.*; mòn, -nā, *n.* = *l.* heart; khuši, -še, *f.* = *l.* will; āločen, -ni, *f.*; irādo, -deā, *m.* (purpose, aim, object); *vlg.* tesâuñ, -āvā, *n.*, *fr.*

Intentional, *a.* khušen kello = *l.* done willingly.

Intentionally, *ad.* khušen.

Intently, *ad.* čit diun; prăyătăn kărn, petsāḍn = *l.* making efforts.

Inter, *v.* pur; mātiyek pāvoi.

Intercalary, *a.* 1. mirvontso.

2. tsăḍtso; *see* **Bissextile.**

Intercalate, *v.* bităr ghāl.

Intercede, *v.* māg; mădesti kăr = *l.* make mediation; măzăt kăr = *l.* make intercession, help.

Interceder, *s.* mădesti, -sti, *m.*

Intercept, *v.* 1. dhăr = *l.* catch; rāuoi = *l.* stop.

2. ăḍḍi (*or* āḍkāḷ) kăr = *l.* make objection.

3. kāḍ = *l.* take away, *e. g.* light, communication.

Intercession, *s.* māg-ṇeñ, -ṇeā, *n.*; vinăt, -ti, *f. ol.*; măzăt, -ti, *f.*

Intercessor, *s.* mădest, -tā, *m.*

Interchange, *v.* bădāl.

Intercourse, *s.* 1. săḷāvoḷ, -ḷi, *f.* (indifferent *and* bad i.)

2. kām, -mā, *n.* = *l.* business; sămănd, -dā, *m.* = *l.* connexion; iṣṭăgăt, -ti, *f.* = *l.* friendship; tsāl, -li, *f.* (*or* tsālvat), *e.g.* mākā tāče lāgiñ tsāl āsā.

Interdict, *s.* mānnāi, -ye, *f.* = *l.* suspension; āḍvārāp, -rpā, *n.* = *l.* prohibition (*with the addition of some words to specify the* i. *meant*).

Interdict, *v.* 1. āḍvār (*see the noun*) = *l.* prohibit.

2. mānnāi kăr = *l.* make suspension.

Interest, *v.* 1. ādāyātso zāun āsā.

2. voḍni di = *l.* give inclination; bānd = *l.* bind, *fg.*; monāk lāg; *see* **Charm, Please.**

Interest, *s.* 1. ādāi, -yā, *m.* = *l.*

profit; upkār, -rā, *m.* = *l.* benefit; prăyog, -gā, *m.* = *l.* use.
2. kām, -mā, *n.* = *l.* business.
3. voḍni, -ne, *f.* = *l.* inclination; monāklāgāp, -gpā, *n.*; *bet. rs.*
4. čit, -ti, *f.* = *l.* attention.
5. vāḍ, -ḍi, *f.* (i. of a capital).

Interested, *a.* 1. *rs.* lāg = *l.* be attached, *fg.*, *e.g.* tukā lāgtā.
2. hāt āsā (*obj. Dat.*) = *l.* hand is, *e.g.* i. in a business.
3. ādāyātso = *l.* of profit.

Interesting, *a.* 1. ādāyātso.
2. voḍnetso = *l.* of inclination; mònāk lāgtso; mòn bāndtso = *l.* binding the heart, *fg.*, *n. c.*

Interfere, *v.* rig = *l.* enter, *e.g.* in a business; ăḍḍi (*or* āḍkăḷ) kăr = *l.* make objection; mèḷ = *l.* mingle (*in the past tense use* meḷăi).

Interference, *s.* bórsaṇeñ, -ṇeā, *n.* = *l.* mixture; āḍyeṇeñ, -ṇeā, *n.* = *l.* coming against.

Interim, *s.* bitărlo vēḷ(é), -ḷā, *m.* = *l.* time between.

Interim, *ad.* itlea bităr.

Interior, *a.* bitărlo.

Interjacent, *a.* bităr āsullo; modeñ āsullo.

Interlace, *see* **Fold, Twine.**

Interlard, *v.* meḷăi; borsi = *l.* mix; bităr ghāl = *l.* put in *or* between.

Interleave, *v.* pānañ bităr ghāl = *l.* put leaves between.

Interline, *v.* giṭañ bităr borăi = *l.* write between lines.

Interlinear, *a.* giṭañbitărlo.

Interlocutor, *s.* uloṇeagār, -rā, *m.* *or* ulouṇo, -ṇeā, *m.* (bităr).

Interloper, *s.* modeñ āillo (mănis) = *l.* (a man) who came between.

Intermarry, *v.* diun āḍ = *l.* giving bring; *or* hāḍ vor.

Intermediate, *a.* modlo *or* modeñ āsullo, *or rs. into* modeñ.

Interment, *s.* purāp, -rpā, *n.*; mòrn, -nā, *n.*

Interminable, *a.* ăntaviṇ *or* ăntnātullo.

Intermingle, *v.* meḷăi; *see* **Interfere.**

Intermission, *s.* mănna, -ne, *f.*; thāmbouṇeñ, -ṇeā, *n.*

Intermit, *v.* thāmb = *l.* cease; mănna kăr; sóḍ = *l.* leave.

Intermittent, *a.* poireātso = *l.* of the day after to-morrow (*used for all kinds of* i. fever); kāḍto (kārto) vorto (tāp), *n. c.* = *l.* taking bringing (fever); vetso yeuntso = *l.* going coming.

Internal, *a.* 1. bitărlo.
2. āplo = *l.* own.

International, *a.* kuḷietso (kuḷiāntso), *or* kuḷiañbitărlo, *e.g.* i. law.

Internecine, *a.* yekameka jivsiñ mārtso.

Interpolate, *v.* fóṭkiro kăr; pustakānt fāvonăiñ tiñ utrañ ghāl (*or* borăi) = *l.* put not proper words in the book.

Interpose, *v.* 1. bităr ghāl = *l.* put between.

2. mădesti zā = *l.* become intercessor; pănčāyetdār zā = *l.* become arbitrator; măzăt kăr = *l.* make intercession; *see* **Interfere.**

Interpret, *v.* vivor sāng, *G. M.* = *l.* say explanation; ărthụ sāng = *l.* say the meaning, *G. M.*

Interpretation, *s.* vivor, -rā, *m.*; = ărthụ, -thā, *m.* = *l.* meaning.

Interpreter, *s.* munsi, -si, *m.* = a public i. in the civil courts; dubaši, -šiā, *m.* = private i.; ărthavivori, -riā, *m.* = *l.* explaining the meaning, *e.g.* i. of the H. Bible; tărzumo kărtolo = *l.* making translation; (utrāntso) ărthụ sāngtolo = *l.* saying the meaning (of words); (*vlg.*) dón bhāso kăḷtāt to = he who knows two languages.

Interregnum, *s.* rājantrụ, -rā, *n.*, *n. c.*

Interrogate, *v.* vitsār, *or* itsār.

nterrogation, *s.* 1. vitsāraṇ, -ṇā, *n.* = inquiry.

2. săvāl, -li, *f.* = question.

Interrogative, *a.* vitsārtso, *or* vitsārtolo, *or* vitsāri.

Interrupt, *v.* 1. vogo rāuoi = *l.* cause to remain silent, *e.g.* a speaker; ăḍḍi kăr = *l.* make objection; āḍ ulăi = *l.* speak against, *Dat.*; thāmbăi, *or* rāuoi = *l.* cause to cease, to remain.

2. sóḍ = *l.* leave (*or* sóḍăi, *c. v.*)

Interruption, *s.* 1. ăḍḍi, -ḍe, *f.*, *or* āḍkăḷ, -ḷi, *f.* = *l.* opposition.

2. thāmbouṇeñ, -ṇeā, *n.*, mănna, -ne, *f.* = intermission.

Intersect, *v.* modeñ kātăr = *l.* cut between.

Intersection, *s.* (giṭañ) mēḷ(é), -ḷā, *m.* = *l.* union (of lines).

Interstice, *s.* 1. pursot, -ti, *f.* = *l.* leisure.

2. iḍeñ, -ḍeā, *n.*; fuṭ, -ṭi, *f.*

Interval, *s.* 1. bitărlo vēḷ(é), -ḷā, *m.* = *l.* time between; *vlg.* témp, -pā, *m.*, *fr.*

2. poiṇ, -ṇā, *n.* = *l.* distance, *n. c.*; modli suāt, -te, *f.*; lāmbăi, -ye, *f.* = *l.* length.

In the i. = itlea bităr.

At frequent intervals = tovóḷ tovóḷ.

Intervene, *v.* 1. bităr (*or* modeñ) ye = *l.* come between.

2. āḍ ye = *l.* come against; āḍkăḷ kăr = *l.* make opposition; *see* **Interfere.**

Intervention, *s.* *see* **Interference.**

Interview, *s.* uloṇeñ, -ṇea, *n.*; bhèṭ, -ṭe, *f.* = *l.* visit.

Have an i. with = lāgiñ ulăi.

Interweave, *v.* meḷăi; *see* **Weave.**

Intestate, *a.* *vlg.* testament kărināstanāñ; *see* **Will.**

Intestine, *a.* bitărlo.
Intestine, *s.* āntkiṭi, -ṭe, *f.*
Inthrall, *see* **Enslave.**
Intimacy, *s.* iṣṭăgăt, -ti, *f.* = *l.* friendship; sălgi, -ge, *f.* (*used for* proper *and* improper i.)
Intimate, *s.* iṣṭ, -ṭā, *m.* = *l.* friend; sălgegār, -rā, *m.*, *or* sălgist, -tā, *m.*
Intimate, *a.* 1. gunḍ = *l.* deep, *fg.*, *e.g.* i. knowledge.
2. mogāḷ = *l.* dear.
Intimate, *v.* kăḷit kăr, *or* kăḷăi = *l.* make known.
Intimately, *ad.* 1. kāḷzān = *l.* heartily; sălgen = *l.* famil-liarly.
2. gunḍāi păriyānt = *l.* till depth.
Intimation, *s.* kăḷit, -tā, *n.*; păr-găṭouṇeñ, -ṇeā, *n.* = *l.* publi-cation.
Intimidate, *v.* besṭāi (by threats); bhiyeunk lāi = *l.* apply to fear.
Intimidation, *s.* bheñ, bhiyā, *n.*; besṭāuṇeñ, -ṇeā, *n.*
Into, *prep.* 1. thăiñ; *see* Gram. Syntax. ch. II. Art. I.
2. *Dat.*; *see ibid.*
3. *Acc.*; *see ibid.*
Intolerable, *a.* sosunk nozo āsullo, *or* sosinăñso.
Intolerance, *s.* ṅăñsosṇigāi, -ye, *f.*
Intolerant, *a.* sosnikāinātullo, *or* sosinātullo.
Intonation, *s.* tāḷeāči suru, -ve, *f.*, *or bet.* gāyānarig, -ge, *f.* = *l.* ingress into music, song.
Intone, *v.* (gāyān) suru kăr = *l.* begin (the song).
Intoxicate, *v.* ămāl kăr = *l.* make intoxication; ămālātso kăr = *l.* make intoxicated; bebdo kăr = *l.* make intoxicated (*fr.*): 'I got intoxicated = mākā ămāl zāleñ'.
Intoxication, *s.* ămāl, -lā, *n.*; bebdepoṇ, -ṇā, *n.*, *fr.*
Intractable, *a.* tsăloun k nozo āsul-lo, *or* tsăloanāñso, *or* tsă-lăisārkonātullo; tănṭālmāri = *l.* troublesome; săḷiṣṭ = *l.* obstinate; āplea vādeātso = *l.* of one's own will.
Intrench, *v.* khăndăk kăr.
Intrenchment, *s.* khăndăk, -dkā, *m.*
Intrepid, *a.* bhoñnātullo; dhăira-vont.
Intrepidity, *s.* nāñbheñ, -bhiyā, *n.*; dhăir, -rā, *n.*
Intricate, *a.* kăṭiṇ = *l.* difficult; tondreāntso, *or* tondre kārtso = *l.* embarrassing.
Intricacy, *s.* tondre, -reañ, *m.pl.*
Intrigue, *s.* nāḍ, -ḍi, *f.* = *l.* a trick; kuṭ, -ṭā, *n.* = *l.* a plot; mōs, -sā, *m.* = *l.* deceit; fóṭ, -ṭi, *f.*; măslăt, -ti, *f.*
Intriguer, *s.* mosagār, -rā, *m.*; măslătigār, -rā, *m.*
Intrinsic, *a.* bitărlo.
Introduce, *v.* 1. vor = *l.* bring.
2. *in a drama*, tsălāi = *l.* cause to walk, *fg.*

3. dākăl kăr, *e.g.* i. a custom, *or* i. (make known) a person.

Introduction, *s.* 1. vorāp, -rpā, *n.*; *bet. rs. into* vor.

2. šipārăs, -se, *f.* = *l.* recommendation, *e.g.* letter of i.

3. ărămb, -bā, *m.* = *l.* origin; *or* suru, -ve, *f.* = *l.* beginning, *or the Mr.* păribāš *for the* i. of a book, *or perh.* rig = *l.* entrance, *fg.*

4. tăyārāi, -ye, *f.* = *l.* preparation, *Lat. exordium.*

Introductive, *a.* ărămbātso, *or* suruvetso, *or* tăyār kărtso.

Intrude, *v.* prăveš zā; tsora bări rig = enter as a thief.

Intruder, *s.* prăveši, -šiā, *m.*

Intrusion, *s.* ănnāyāči rig, -ge, *f.*, *or rs. into v.*; tsora bărisi rig, *n.c.*; *bet. rs.*; hăkkụnātụlli rig = *l.* entrance without right.

Intrust, *v.* suādin, *or* părasuādin kăr; voisi; *see* **Entrust.**

Intuition, *s.* sošṭ dišṭ, -ṭi, *f.* = *l.* clear sight.

Inundate, *v.* āur yetā = *l.* inundation comes; *see* **Deluge.**

Inundation, *s.* āur, -rā, *n.*

Inure, *v.* sovói kăr (*tr.*), *or* s. zā (*n.v.*); ghăṭ kăr = *l.* make hard, *fg.*, *or* gh. zā (*n.v.*).

Inutility, *s.* nisprăyog, -gā, *m.*

Invade, *v.* āngār pòḍ = *l.* fall on the body; zulmen rig = *l.* enter violently.

Invalid, *a.* 1. ăskăt = *l.* weak; bolāiki nātullo = *l.* without health.

2. răddụ ăsullo = *l.* null; ăthir, *ex. but n.c.*

Invalidate, *v.* 1. răddụ kăr = *l.* make invalid.

2. ăskăt kăr = *l.* make weak.

Invaluable, *a.* 1. ămolik (infinitely precious); molavoilo.

2. bhou molādik = *l.* very precious.

Invariable, *a.* bădăl zāunknātullo.

Invasion, *s.* 1. āngārpòḍāp, -ḍpā, *n.*

2. zulmeči rig, -ge, *f.* = *l.* violent entrance.

3. bòḷ, -ḷā, *n.* = *l.* violence.

Invective, *s.* gāḷ, -ḷi, *f.* = *l.* abuse; ăkmān, -nā, *m.* = *l.* offence.

Inveigh against, *v.* gāḷi sāng = *l.* say abuses; āngār pòḍ = *l.* fall on the body, attack, *fg.*

Inveigle, *v.* fuslāi = *l.* coax; pisāi *or* piso kăr = *l.* make mad (*fg.*)

Invent, *v.* 1. sódun kāḍ = *l.* seeking take.

2. ghăḍ = *l.* found.

Invention, *s.* 1. mèḷāp, -ḷpā, *n.* (*esp.* a chance i.).

2. sódun kāḍneñ, -neā, *n.* (purposely sought i.)

3. novi văstụ, -tu, *f.* = *l.* a new thing.

4. kălpaneči văstu = *l.* a thing of fancy; kălpana, -ne, *f.* = *l.* fancy.

Inventive, *a.* bārik = *l.* thin, *fg.*; kăṣṭi = *l.* industrious.

Inventor, *s.* gădpi, -piā, *m.*

Inventory, *s.* păṭṭi, -ṭe, *f.* = a list.

Inverse, *a.* porto (turned); *rs.* pāṭi fuḍeñ (p. f. zālo).

Inversion, *s.* portouṇeñ, -ṇeā, *n.*

Invert, *v.* porti, *c. v. of* porta.

Invest, *v.* 1. kām di = *l.* give work; mokrur kăr = *l.* make an appointment; nemsi = appoint.
2. veḍo ghāl = *l.* put a siege.
3. băndobăstin dovór = *l.* put in security, *e.g.* money; vāḍik ghāl = *l.* put to interest.

Investigate, *v.* vitsāraṇ kăr.

Investigation, *s.* vitsāraṇ, -ṇā, *n.*

Investiture, *see* **Instalment.**

Inveteracy, *s.* săbār vēḷ(é), -ḷā, *m.* = *l.* much time; *bet. rs. into* săbār kālātso, *or crc.*

Inveterate, *a.* săbār kālātso = *l.* of much time; ādlo = *l.* of before; porno = *l.* old.

Invidious, *a.* mosri.

Invigorate, *v.* bòḷ di = *l.* give force.

Invincible, *see* **Insuperable.**

Inviolability, *s.* 1. ăkmānkărinā-sārkeñ, -keā, *n.*; khătounā-sārkeñ, -keā, *n.*
2. păvitrụ guṇ, -ṇā, *m.* = *l.* a holy character.

Inviolable, *a.* khătounk nozo āsullo, *or* khătounāye āsullo; khătnātullo; păvitrụ = *l.* sacred.

Inviolate, *a.* khătnātullo.

Invisible, *a.* diṣṭi pòḍanātullo; disanātullo.

Invitation, *s.* āpouṇeñ, -ṇeā, *n.*; vouḷik, -ke, *f.* = i. for marriage.

Invite, *v.* 1. āpoi; vouḷik săng, *see the noun.*
2. *fg.* voḍni di = *l.* give inclination; fuslāi = *l.* caress.

Inviting, *a.* voḍnetso; *see* **Attract.**

Invocation, *s.* māg-ṇeñ, -ṇeā, *n.*; ulo, -leā, *m.*

Invoice, *s.* sāmānañpăṭṭi, -ṭe, *f.* = *l.* a list of articles.

Invoke, *v.* māg, *Prs. Cm.*

Involuntary, *a.* khuŝinātullo, *or* khuŝen kărinātullo, *or* nā-khuŝen kello; neṇārpoṇān kello; *bet. rs.*

Involve, *see* **Imply, Implicate.**

Invulnerable, *a.* ghāi ghālunk nozo āsullo, *or* ghāyesārko-nātullo.

Inward, *a.* bitărlo.

Inwardly, *ad.* bităr.

Irascibility, *s.* krodasărkeñ, -keā, *n.*

Iris, *see* **Rainbow.**

Irksome, *a.* kărkărātso, *or* bezā-rāyetso = *l.* troublesome; tondreāntso = *l.* embarrassing.

Irksomeness, *s.* kărkăr, -rāñ, *pl. m.*; tondre, -reañ, *pl. m.* = *l.* embarrassment.

Iron, *s.* 1. lonkāḍ, -kḍā, *n.*
2. pāṭo, -ṭeā, *m.* = *l.* a hoop of iron.

Iron, *v.* istri kăr.
Iron, *a.* lonkḍātso.
Irons, *s.* bănd, -di, *f.*
Ironical, *a.* nănjetso; khelkuḷātso = *l.* mocking.
Ironmonger, *s.* lonkḍāsāukār, -rā, *m.*, *or* —yāri, -riā, *m.*
Irony, *s.* nănji, -je, *f.*; hogḷāpseñ; nāḍihogḷāp, -pā, *n.*; khelkuḷañ, *pl. n.*
Irradiate, *v.* uzvāḍ di = *l.* give light, *or* u. kăr, *or* uzvāḍāi, *c. v.*; prăkāsăi, *c. v.*
Irrational, *a.* 1. budnātullo; ginyānnātullo; somzanātullo. 2. monzātitso = *l.* bestial.
Irrationality, *s.* nāñsomzoṇkāi, *or* nāñsomzikāi, -ye, *f.*
Irreconcilable, *a.* sămādhān kărināsārko, *or* sămādhān kărunk nozo āsullo, *or only* sămādhān nātullo, *etc.*
Irrecoverable, *a.* pāṭimeḷunk nozo āsullo, *or* pāṭimeḷanāñso.
Irrefragable, *a.* zāpdiunknozo āsullo, *or* zāpdināñsārko; *bet. rs.*; ghăṭ = *l.* firm; solvanāso, *or* solvounk nozo āsullo.
Irrefutable, *a.* solvounk nozo āsullo, *or* solvanāñsārko.
Irregular, *a.* 1. krămaviṇ (āsullo); ăkrămātso = *l.* immoral; *vlg.* kāideā părmāṇe nātullo. 2. rupnātullo = *l.* without form. 3. sămanăi āsullo = *l.* not right.
Irregularity, *s.* 1. ăkrăm, -mā, *n.* 2. miruoṇeñ, -ṇeā, *n.* = *l.* excess.
Irrelevant, *a.* kāmākpòḍnātullo; vóḍ nāiñ = *l.* nọt great (no matter), *ch. cs.*; čillar = *l.* trifling.
Irreligious, *a.* šāstrụ nātullo, *or* saštrāk āḍ āsullo; bhăgtiviṇ.
Irremediable, *a.* borozāunk nozo āsullo, *or* sămazāunk nozo āsullo; guṇaviṇ; upāinātullo, *or rs.* upāi nāñ = *l.* no help, no means; upāyaviṇ.
Irreparable, *see* Irremediable.
Irreprehensible, *a.* gunyāuñ nātullo; besṭāunk nozo āsullo, *or* besṭaonāñsārko, *or* besṭāināñso.
Irresistible, *a.* inkār kărunk nozo āsullo, *or* inkār kărināñso.
Irresolute, *a.* dubāvi, *or* dubāuntso, *or* tondreānt āsullo.
Irresolution, *s.* dubāu, -bāvā, *m.*; tondre, -reāñ, *m. pl.* = *l.* embarrassment.
Irreverence, *s.* ăpamān, *or* ăkmān, -nā, *m.*
Irreverent, *a.* ăpamāṇātso, *or* ăkmānātso; mān dinātullo = *l.* not giving honour; ăumăryāditso = *l.* not polite.
Irrevocable, *a.* portun (*with the verb required by the mn.*) nozo āsullo; pāṭi kāḍunk nozo āsullo, *or* pāṭi kāḍināñso, *e.g.* i. words.
Irrigate, *v.* udāk ghāl, *or* u. simp, *or* u. sóḍ.
Irritable, *a.* rāgist *or* rāgār zāi sārko.

Irritate, *v.* rāg hāḍăi.
Irruption, *see* **Inroad.**
Isinglass, *s.* māsḷesār, -rā, *m.*
Island, *s.* kudro, -dreā, *m.*
Islander, *s.* kudreagār, -rā, *m.*
Isolate, *v.* vegḷo kăr; vingăḍ kăr; pois kāḍ.
Isolation, *s.* vingăḍāi, -ye, *f.*, *n.c.*; yeksurpoṇ, -ṇā, *n.*; vegḷatsār, -rā, *m.*
Isothermal, *a.* tets gărmetso.
Issue, *s.* sevóṭ, -ṭā, *m.*; *see* **Exit.**
Issue, *v.* 1. bhāir săr = *l.* come out, *e.g.* i. a decree, *ch. cs.*; părgăṭkăr, *or* părgăṭăi (make public).
2. zā = *l.* become.
Isthmus, *s.* buiñgomṭo, -ṭeā, *m.* = *l.* a neck of the earth.
It, *pron.* teñ *or* yeñ; *see* Gram. P. II. ch. iii.
Italian, *a.* Italitso.
Itch, *s.* khóróz, -rji, *f.*
Itch, *v.* khóróz zā, *or* korza, *e.g.* mozo hāt korzatā.
Item, *s.* răkăm, -kmā, *n.* = kind, sort, *e.g.* books of three kinds; kălăm, -lmā, *n.*; bāb, -be, *f.* = *l.* case.
Iterate, *v.* portun kăr (*or some such verb as* kăr).
Iteration, *s.* porto (-ti, -teñ), *with the required noun*, *e.g.* i. of the same sound = porto tāḷo.
Itinerant, *s.* poiṇāri, -riā, *m.*
Itinerate, *v.* poiṇ kăr.
Itinerary, *s.* poiṇakobrañpustak, -kā, *n.*, *or* poiṇakobro, *pl. f.* = *l.* book of the voyage.
Itinerary, *a.* poiṇātso.
Itself, *pron.* tents; *see* Gram. P. II. ch. iii.
Ivory, *s.* hăstitso dāḍo, -ḍeā, *m.* = *l.* a tusk of the elephant.

J

Jabber, *v. neg. form of* soṣṭ ulăi; *see* **Chatter;** boḍboḍ.
Jackal, *s.* kolo, -leā, *m.*
Jackanapes, *s.* 1. mānkoḍ, -kḍā, *m.*
2. *fg.* tănṭălmāri, -riā, *m.*
Jackass, *s.* 1. dādleñ gāḍāuñ, -ḍvā, *n.*
2. *fg.* dăḍḍa (blockhead), *or also* gāḍāuñ.
Jacket, *s.* băndiyan, -nā, *n.* (*var.* băniyān).
Jack-fruit, *s.* 1. póṇós, -ṇsā, *m.* = the whole ripe fruit; paṇsuli, -le, *f.*, kăḍgi, -ge, *f.*, guzo, -jeā, *m.* (unripe).
2. šèḍ, -ḍā, *n.* (one of the pieces into which the fruit is cut previous to eating).
Jag, *v.* kātre ghāl.

Jaggery, *s.* gòḍ, -ḍā, *n.*; vòrn, -nā, *n.*, khir, -ri, *f.*, *ex.* a sweetmeat made of j.

Jail, *s. vlg.* zăil, -lā, *n.*; băndi, -di, *f.* = *l.* fetters; băndikhān, -nā, *n.*; turing (*var.* turung), -gā, *n.*

Jailer, *s. vlg.* jelăr, -rā, *m.*; băndirākṇo, -ṇeā, *m.* = *l.* a guard of a prison; băndi-ădhipăti, -ti, *m.* = *l.* a commander of a prison (*n. u.*)

Jam, *s.* miṭăi, -ye, *f.*; dòs, -si, *f.*

Jamb, *s.* dārvóntăčo ubo kuḍko, -keā, *m.*

Jangle, *v.* zăgăḍ, *or* zăgḍa.

Jar, *s.* 1. buyāuñ, -yāvā, *n.* = a pot (for pickles *etc.*); bărni, -ne, *f.* (*larger than* buyāuñ).
2. zăgḍaṇeñ, -ṇeā, *n.*, *or* zăgḍeñ, -ḍeā, *n.* = *l.* a quarrel; nāñ-sămapòḍāp, -ḍpā, *n.*
3. gouji, -je, *f.* = *l.* noise.

Jar, *v.* 1. zăgăḍ.
2. gouji kăr = *l.* make noise.

Jasmine, *s.* koḷo (*or* kăḷo), -ḷeā, *m.*

Jaundice, *s.* kāḷkăi, -ye, *f.*

Jaunt, *see* **Excursion.**

Javelin, *s.* bhālo, -leā, *m.* (*or* bhāli, -ye, *f.*)

Jaw, *s.* gāl, -lā, *m.* = the cheek; dāḍam, -mā, *n.* = the jaw-bones.

Jealous, *a.* mosri; niskutsāri; kubdi.

Jealousy, *s.* niskutsār, -rā, *m.*; mosór, -srā, *m.*

Jeer, *v.* yeḍāi.

Jeer, *s.* yeḍauṇeñ, -ṇeā, *n.*; gāḷ, -ḷi, *f.* = *l.* abuse; *see* **Mocking, Irony.**

Jest, *s.* čeṣṭāi, -ye, *f.*; tomāso, -seā, *m.*

Jest, *v.* čeṣṭāi kăr, *G. F.*; năkăl kăr, *G. N.* = *l.* make copy, *fg.* (*or* năklañ kăr); măskă-ri kăr; tomāse kăr; hās (laugh at, *Acc.*) *or* hāseār ghāl.

Jester, *s.* kheḷguḍo, -ḍeā, *m.*

Jesus Christ, Somi Jezu (-zu) Krist, -tā, *m.*

Jew, *s.* Judeu, -devā, *m.*

Jewel, *s.* rătăn, -tnā, *n.*; năg, -gā, *m.*, *vlg.*, *mn.* article, *which see*; moṇi, -yā, *m.*, *vlg.* = beads (of gold); mā-ṇik, -ṇkā, *n.*

Jilt, *s.* pātoḷi, -ḷe, *f.* = *l.* a kind of sweetmeat, *fg.*

Job, *s.* 1. kām, -mā, *n.* = *l.* work; *or* čillăr kām = trifling work.
2. mugdoṇičeñ kām = work by contract (*l.* to be finished, *as opposed to* work by the day).

Jobber, *s.* dălāl, -lā, *m.* = *l.* agent, broker.

Jockey, *s.* 1. gòḍeāpănthāgār, -rā, *m.*
2. goḍeāñdălāl, -lā, *m.* = *l.* a broker of horses.
3. ṭhăkkagār, -rā, *m.* = a deceiving man.

Jocose, *a.* čeṣṭāyetso.

Jog, *v.* hišāro di = *l.* give a hint; doḷe mōḍ(ó) = *l.* break the eyes, *i. e.* give hints by winking with the eye.

Join, *v.* 1. mèḷāi, *c. v. of* mèḷ = *l.* unite; doro (*or* dhāgo) ghāl = j. two pieces of cloth by stitching; kuḍsi = *l.* add, *e.g.* a wing to a house; gădsi, *e.g.* pieces of cloth; joḍsi, *e. g.* planks; *n. v.* kuḍsa.
2. sāngāta vots = *l.* go with, *e.g.* j. bad company; *or also* mèḷ = *l.* be united; iṣṭăgăt kăr = *l.* make friendship.
Join the enemy = dusmāna sāngāta vots, *or* dusmānapăkṣek mèḷ.

Joint, *s.* 1. gānṭ, -ṭi, *f.* (j. of the body).
2. sănd, -dā, *m.*, *e.g.* of a door, of the body, *etc.*

Joist, *see* **Beam.**

Joke, *see* **Jest.**

Jollity, *s.* ulās, -sā, *m.*

Jolly, *a.* khušāl; ulāsātso.

Jolt, *v.* kăskăs, *e.g.* a carriage jolts.

Jostle, *v.* lōṭ(ó) = *l.* push; ādăḷ = *l.* dash.

Jot, *s.* kāiñ = *l.* something: 'he does not know a jot = tākā kāiñ kăḷnāñ; *vlg. rs.* sopṇiñ sirăntiñ (čintunk nāñ = did not think)'.

Journal, *s. vlg.* gajet, -ti, *f.*, *fr.*; dispoḍteñ kāgād, -gdā, *n.*; kobrāñ kāgād; vărtamānapătrik, -ke, *f. or* -pătru, -rā, *n.*

Journalism, *s.* vărtamānapătrānčeñ kām, -mā, *n.* = *l.* business of journalism.

Journalist, *s.* vărtamānapătrist, -tā, *m.*, *or* -pătrikegār, -rā, *m.*; dispoḍte vordegār, -rā, *m* = *l.* a man of daily news.

Journey, *s.* poiṇ, -ṇā, *n.*

Journey, *v.* poiṇ kăr; mărgest zā, *n.c.*

Jowl, *see* **Cheek.**

Joy, *s.* săntos, -sā, *m.*; khušālāi, -ye, *f.*; ork, -kā, *m.*, *rl.*, *ol.*; ulās, -sā, *m.*; sukhu, -khā, *n.*; ănănd, -dā, *m.*

Jubilant, *a.* ulās bhógtso.

Jubilee, *s. vlg.* jubileu, -levā, *m.*

Judge, *s.* munsubdār, -rā, *m.*; nitidār, -rā, *m.*; munsif, -fā, *m.*=native subordinate judge.

Judge, *v.* 1. nīt kăr = *l.* make justice.
2. āločen kăr = *l.* make opinion (think).

Judgment, *s.* 1. nīt, -ti, *f.*, *e.g.* j. pronounced by a judge; phăisăl, -lā, *n.* = *l.* sentence; zăḍti, -te, *f.*, munsub, -be, *f.*, *esp. in rl. mn.*, *e.g.* last j.
2. āločen, -ni, *f.* (logical j.)
3. bud, -di, *f.* = *l.* discernment, *or also* the faculty of judging.

Judgment-day, *s.* nimāṇo dis, -sā, *m.* = *l.* the last day; zăḍtetso dis.

Judgment-hall, *s.* nitisāl, -lā, *n.*
Judicial, *a.* nititso.
Judicature, *s.* 1. nitipodvi, -ve, *f.*; nitiădhikār, -rā, *m.* = *l.* power of judging.
2. sărhăddų, -di, *f.* = jurisdiction.
Judicious, *a.* nitivont.
Jug, *s.* āidān, -nā, *n.*; móg, -gā, *m.*, *fr.*
Juggle, *v.* khèḷ.
Juggler, *s.* khèḷgoḍo, -ḍeā, *m.*; ṭhăkkų, -kā, *m.*; kăṇkăṭgār, -rā, *m.* = one who plays tricks by sleight-of-hand.
Juice, *s.* sār, -rā, *m.* = extract; dik, -kā, *m.*; rós, -sā, *m.*
Jujube, *s.* bòr, -rā, *n.*
Jumble, *v.* rās kăr; gălibili zăun zomăi, *or prh.* gusap kărn meḷăi; borsi = *l.* mix.
Jump, *v.* uḍ; uḍi mār.
Jump, *s.* uḍāp, -ḍpā, *n.*, *or* uḍi, -ye, *f.*
Junction, *s.* mēḷ(é), -ḷā, *m.*; sănd, -dā, *m.* = juncture.
Juncture, *s.* 1. săngăt, -gti, *f.* = a circumstance.
2. sănd, -dā, *m.*
Jungle, *s.* rān, -nā, *n.*; moḷo, -ḷeā, *m.* = a bower, *e.g.* Gethsemani; moleñ, -leā, *n.* = a j. properly so called.
Junior, *a.* dākṭo = *l.* little, *e.g.* j. brother.
Juniper, *s.* jinātso ruk, -kā, *m.*(?)
Junk, *s.* dóṇ -ṇi, *f.*
Jurisconsult, *s.* šāstrazāṇār, -rā, *m.*; văkil, -lā, *m.*
Jurisdiction, *s.* nīt kărči podvi, -ve, *f.*, *or only* podvi, -ve, *f.* = *l.* power; ădhikār, -rā, *m.* = authority, *or* nītiădhikār, -rā, *m.*; sărhăddų, -di, *f.* = *l.* a limit, *fg.*
Jurisprudence, *s.* kāideavidya, -ye, *f.*; nāyăšāstrų, -rā, *n.*
Jurist, *s.* văkil, -lā, *m.*; šāstrazāṇār, -rā, *m.*
Juror, *s.* (pārmāṇār dovórlolo) pănčāyetdār, -rā, *m.*
Just, *ad.* sārkeñ = *l.* exactly; khărents = *l.* truly; mātrų, *or* făkăt = *l.* only. J. now = ātānts. J. before = čikke voḍol.
Justice, *s.* 1. nīt, -ti, *f.*; nāy, -yā, *m.*
2. sāntipoṇ, -ṇā, *n.*, *or* bhāgevontpoṇ, -ṇā, *n.*
Justification, *s.* 1. bhāgevontpoṇ, -ṇā, *n.*
2. udārăṇ, -ṇā, *n.* = an apology.
Justify, *v.* 1. nītivont kăr; bhāgevont kăr.
2. udārăṇ săng = *l.* say an apology.
Jut, *v.* bhāir ye = come out, *e.g.* a rock; mukār póḍ = *l.* fall before, *e.g.* a rock; mukār săr.
Juxtaposition, *s.* lāgāp, -gpā, *n.*

K

Keel, *s.* tārvapònd, -dā, *n.*

Keen, *a.* 1. bārik = *l.* thin, *fg.*, *e.g.* k. sight, mind, *etc.*
2. umāḷeātso, *e.g.* k. sorrow (intense); kăṭiṇ = *l.* severe, bitter, *e.g.* cold.

Keenness, *s.* 1. bārikāi, -ye, *f.*
2. umāḷo, -ḷeā, *m.*; kăṭiṇāi, -ye, *f.*; *see adj.*

Keep, *v.* 1. dovór, (*also* k. order).
2. dhăr = *l.* catch, *e.g.* a falling body.
3. āsā = *l.* is, *sb. Dat.*
4. pós = *l.* feed.
5. sāmbāḷ = *l.* defend, *e.g.* k. promises, vows, order.
6. fārik kăr = *l.* pay, *also* vows.
K. an account = lèk borei.
K. waiting = toḍou kăr, *ch. cs.*
K. a feast = fèst kăr, *or* f. tsălăi.
K. apart = vingăḍ dovór.
K. back = 1. āḍāi; 2. dovór; 3. lipăi.
K. company = pāvoi; sāngāta vots; săngāt kăr.
K. down, *see* **Repress.**
K. off = pois kāḍ, *or* p. kăr, p. dovór; *see also* **Abstain.**
K. together = sāngāta dovór, *or* voṭṭu d.
K. up with = pāṭleān vots = *l.* go after.
K. up = 1. sāmbāḷ, *or* dovór, *e.g.* a custom; 2. dhăir di = *l.* give courage.

Keeper, *s.* rākṇo, -ṇeā, *m.*

Keeping, *s.* 1. sămbaḷāp, -ḷpā, *n.* = *l.* defence; rākṇeñ, -ṇeā, *n.*
2. sămapòḍāp, -ḍpā, *n.* = *l.* a falling together; lāyekpoṇ, -ṇā, *n.* = *l.* fitness.

Kernel, *s.* 1. biñ, -yā, *n.* = *l.* seed.
2. koy, -ye, *f.*, *e.g.* of mangoes; moi, -yā, *m.*

Kettle, *s.* kétlu̥, -li, *f.* (with a spout), *fr.*

Key, *s.* 1. tsāvi, -ye, *f.*; bigahāt, -tā, *m.*
2. *fg.* upāi, -yā, *m.* = *l.* means.

Kick, *s.* khòṭ, -ṭe, *f.*; lāt, -ti, *f.*, of horses *esp.*

Kick, *v.* khoṭen mār, *or* khòṭ mār, *or* khòṭāi.

Kid, *s.* bokḍečeñ pīl, -lā, *n.* = *l.* the young of a she-goat.

Kidnap, *v.* (mānšānk) tsōr(ó) = *l.* steal (men).

Kill, *v.* jivsiñ mār; jīv kāḍ = *l.* take away life.

Kiln, *s.* ăguṭeñ, -ṭeā, *n.* (*or* ăguṣṭeñ).

Kimbo, *a.* vānkḍo; zoḍullo = *l.* clasped; bāgāillo = bent.
Set the arms akimbo = penkṭār hāt dovór.

Kin, *s.* săirik, -ke, *f.*

Kind, *s.* thăr, -rā, *m.*; jinos, -nsā, *m.* (*Instr.* jinsiñ); dinos, -nsā, *m.* (*perh. corr. of* jinos); dărzo, -jeā, *m.*

Kind, *a.* dăyāḷ; mogāḷ; kākuḷti-tso = *l.* merciful.

Kindle, *v.* funk = *l.* blow, *pr. fg.*, *e.g.* the H. Ghost kindled our hearts; 'uzo f. = blow into the fire'; peṭăi, *c. v. of* pèṭ, *e.g.* a candle; uzo *or* uzu-āḍ lāi = *l.* apply fire *or* light; zăḷăi = *l.* cause to burn, *c. v. of* zăḷ, *e.g.* a candle.

Kindliness, *s.* mogāḷpoṇ, -ṇā, *n.*, *or* dăya, -ye, *f.*

Kindly, *ad.* mogān *or* dăyakărn.

Kindly, *a.* mogāḷ, *or* dăyāḷ.

Kindness, *s.* dăya, -ye, *f.*; bore-poṇ, -ṇā, *n.*; mōg(ó), -gā, *m.*, *or* mogāḷpoṇ, -ṇā, *n.*; upkār, -rā, *m.*; kurpa, -pe, *f.* = *l.* grace.

Kindred, *s.* săirik, -ke, *f.*

Kindred, *a.* săiro *or* săiro dāiro. He is of my k. = mākā (săiro) lektā = *l.* to me k. is reckoned.

King, *s.* rāi, -yā, *m.*; rāja, -jā, *m.* (a petty king).

Kingdom, *s.* 1. rāz, -jā, *n.*; rāzvoṭ, -ṭi, *f.*, *or* rāzpāṭ, -ṭā, *n.*; rāzvoṭkāi, -ye, *f.*

2. *fg.* vărg, -gā, *m.* = *l.* class.

Kingly, *a.* 1. rāyabăriso; *bet. rs.* rāyabări = *l.* as of a king.

2. rāyātso = *l.* of a king.

King's-evil, *v.* kănṭmăḷ, -ḷā, *n.*

Kinsfolk, *s.* săiro dāiro.

Kiss, *s.* umo, -meā, *m.*

Kiss, *v.* umo ghe, *or* u. kāṇe.

Kitchen, *s. vlg.* kuzn, -nā, *n.*, *fr.*; rāndpākuḍ, -ḍā, *n.*

Kitchen-work, *s.* rāndpākām, -mā, *n.* (*or* rāndpāčeñ kām).

Kite, *s.* góṇ, -ṇi, *f.*

Kitten, *s.* māzrāčeñ pīl, -lā, *n.*

Knave, *s.* lutstso, -ččeā, *m.*; ṭhăk-kụ, -kā, *m.*

Knead, *v.* móḷ, *e.g.* flour.

Knee, *s.* dimbi, -ye, *f.*; dompār, -prā, *n.*

Kneel, *v.* dimbio ghāl (*or* dimbi gh.) = *l.* put knees; dimbiyer pòḍ = *l.* fall on the knee, *n. c.*

Knife, *s.* 1. suri, -ye, *f.* = a common k.; peskāti, -te, *f.*

2. koito (kuito), -teā, *m.* = a large scythe; koiti, -te, *f.* a small 'koito'; koitul, -lā, *n.* = a still smaller 'koito'.

Knife-maker, *s.* suriyegār, -rā, *m.*

Knight, *s.* 1. *l.* săvārigār, -rā, *m.*

2. *perh. the nearest equivalent for the title is* maharāja, *or the Mr. and Cn.* sărdār bahādūr, (*used sometimes*).

Knit, *v.* 1. vóḷ, *e.g.* k. cadjan leaves = moḍāl vóḷ.

2. iṇi ghāl = *l.* put tresses (braid the hair); *see* **Frown.**

Knock, *v.* 1. boḍăi, *e.g.* at the door, at the walls, *Acc.*; pēṭ(é); tāpuḍ = *l.* tap; lóṭ = *l.* push.

2. āḍăl = *l.* dash.

K. out = boḍoun ghāl.

K. up=kuṭṭi (arouse by touching the head); gongsi (arouse by touching other parts of the body).

K. down = portun ghāl (*or* porti), *e.g.* a wall.

Knot, *s.* 1. gānṭ, -ṭi, *f.*
2. šenḍo, -ḍeā, *m.* = the knot of hair at the back of the head *as arranged by the women of this country*; *in the case of men it is called* šénḍi, -ye, *f.*

Know, *v.* zāṇaṅ; *see* Gram. p. 144; kăḷ = *l.* be known, *sb. Dat.*, *e.g.* a language, an art, a way; kăḷit āsā; gottu āsā (*neg.* gottu nāñ), *vlg.*; voḷka = *l.* recognize; voḷok āsā (*G.F.*) = *l.* knowledge is.

Knowingly, *ad.* zāṇazāun, *or* somzoṇ, *or* monahpurvok.

Knowledge, *s.* 1. zāṇvāi, -ye, *f.*; bud, -di, *f.* = *l.* wisdom; voḷok, -ḷki, *f.*; somzoṇkāi, -ye, *f.*, *or* somzoṇi, -ṇe, *f.*
2. māhet, -ti, *f.*, *e.g.* tākā kāmāči m. āsā.
3. kăḷit, -tā, *n.*

Known, *part. a.* 1. *rs. into v.*
2. nāvāḍgo (well k.); voḍlo = *l.* great, *e.g.* a k. man.

L

La, *inter.* obḷe (*corr. of* o pòḷe).

Label, *s.* mélviḷās, -sā, *m.*; nāuñ, -āvā, *n.* = *l.* a name; čiṭ, -ṭi, *f.* = *l.* a small note, a ticket.

Laborious, *a.* kăṭiṇ (*var.* kănṭin); kăšṭāntso = *l.* painful (*or* kăšṭountso).

Labour, *s.* 1. vāur, -rā, *m.* (vāur″ *is the verb*) = *l.* work; kām, -mā, *n.* = *l.* business.
2. kăšṭ, -ṭā, *m.* = *l.* pain (*used in pl.*); minătu, -ti, *f.* = *l.* fatigue.
3. prăyătăn, -tnā, *n.* = *l.* an effort.

Labour, *v.* 1. vāur kăr *or* vāur″; kām kăr = *l.* make business.
2. kăšṭa, *n. v. of* kăšṭăi (*or* kăšṭăvăi) = *l.* suffer pain; kăšṭ sós = *l.* suffer pain.
3. prăyătăn kăr, petsāḍ = make an effort, try.

Labourer, *s.* vāurāḍi, -ḍiā, *m.*; kulkār, -rā, *m.*; begāri, -riā, *m.*

Lac, *s.* lāk, -kā, *n.*; '100 lacs = kóróḍ, *pl.* korăḍ (*m.*)'.

Lace, *s.* rènd, -dā, *n.*

Lace, *v.* 1. rènd lāi.
2. bānd = *l.* bind.

Lacerate, *v.* ghāi ghāl = *l.* put a wound; bokór = *l.* scratch, as a cat does; pind, *tr.*, *n.* = *l.* tear; *c. v.* pindăi, *e.g.* l. the flesh.

Laceration, *s.* 1. bokrāp, -pā, *n.* 2. pindāp, -dpā, *n.*

Lack, *s.* gărz, -je, *f.* = *l.* necessity; tsukāp, -kpā, *n.*

Lack, *v. rs. into* gărz āsā = *l.* necessity is (*not ex.*); *by the neg. of* āsā; tsuk = *l.* be missing.

Lackey, *s.* tsākór, -krā, *m.*

Laconic, *a.* sănkșépātso = *l.* compendious; thoḍeañ utrāntso = *l.* of few words.

Lad, *s.* burgo, -geā, *m.*; čeḍo, -ḍeā, *m.* (čeḍo burgo).

Ladder, *s.* nisăṇ (*var.* nisoṇ), -sṇi, *f.*; deḷo, -ḷeā, *m.* = a single bamboo with its branches cut short.

Laden, *a.* bhórn, *or* bhorlolo.

Lading, *s.* vojeñ, -jeā, *n.*

Bill of l. = vojeapăṭṭi, -ṭe, *f.*, *or* sāmānarăšid, -de, *f.*

Ladle, *s.* dói, -ye, *f.* = a large wooden utensil for kitchen purposes.

Lady, *s.* 1. sāibiṇ, -ṇi, *f.*, *used almost exclusively for* the Bl. V. Mary.

2. bāi, -ye, *f.* = a native l.; āyi, -ye, *f. is a word used for addressing* an old woman; bibi, -ye, *f. used for* a Mahommedan l., *and also contemptuously.*

Lag, *v. see* **Loiter.**

Laic, *s.* souñsari, -riā, *m.*

Lair, *s.* phănjer, -rā, *n.*; ḍól, -li, *f.*

Lake, *s.* kuḷ, -ḷā, *n.* (*var.* kòḷ); tăḷeñ, -ḷeā, *n.* = a small tank.

Lamb, *s.* bokreāčeñ pīl, -lā, *n.*; šeli, -ye, *f.*, *a generic term used esp. fg. for* J. C., *or for* the faithful.

Lame, *a.* thonṭo.

Lameness, *s.* thonṭepoṇ, -ṇā, *n.*

Lament, *v.* šiṇ ulāi = *l.* say lamentation; răḍ = *l.* weep; pirnga = *l.* groan.

Lamentable, *a.* 1. dukest = *l.* sorry; koḍu = *l.* bitter, *fg.*

2. birmot fāvozāllo = worthy of pity; *or* birmotitso.

Lamentation, *s.* šiṇ, -ṇā, *m.*, *e.g.* l. for ingratitude; răḍneñ, -neā, *n.*, *or* răḍāp, -ḍpā, *n.* = *l.* a weeping; pirngoṇi, -ṇe, *f.* = *l.* a groaning.

Lamp, *s. vlg.* lāmpiāuñ, -āvā, *m.*; divo, -veā, *m.*; diuṭi, -ṭe, *f.* = *l.* a torch; murti, -te, *f.* = a kind of l. used by non-Christian Hindus; pānās, -sā, *m.*

Lampblack, *s.* kāzāḷ, -zḷā, *n.*

Lampoon, *s.* nindečeñ pòtrụ (*or* pătrụ), -rā, *n.*; nindečeñ kāgād, -gdā, *n.*

Lance, *s.* bhālo, -leā, *m.*; bărči, -če, *f.*

Land, *s.* 1. buiñ, -iñ, *f.* = *l.* the earth.

2. zāgo, -geā, *m.* = *l.* a place; zămin, -ne, *f.* = *l.* an estate.

3. gāuñ, gāñvā, *m.* = *l.* a country, *e.g.* the l. of France;

jillo, -leā, *m.* = *l.* a district; muluk, -kā, *n.*; dēš(é), -šā, *m.*, *n.c. except in compounds.*

Land, *v.* (tārva voilo) utrăi, *c. v.* = *l.* cause to come down; (tārva voilo) utăr, *n. v.* = *l.* come down; (tārva voilo) devoi, *c. v.* = *l.* cause to come down; (tārva voilo) deuñ, *n. v.* = *l.* come down.

Landlord, *s.* zămindār, -rā, *m.* (possessor of gardens); bāṭkār, -rā, *m.*; vărgadār, -rā, *m.*; dhăni, -yā, *m.*, khāvănd, -dā, *m.* = a lord.

Landmark, *s.* gādeāči găḍ, -ḍi, *f.* = *l.* a limit of the field; četurgăḍi, -ḍi, *f.* = *l.* a sign of boundaries.

Landlease, *s.* géṇ, -ṇi, *f.*

Lane, *s.* gălli, -le, *f.*; vóṇ, -ṇi, *f.*

Language, *s.* bhās, -se, *f.*; ulounči săkti, -te, *f.* = *l.* a power of speaking.
2. utrañ = *l.* words.
3. jib, -be, *f.* = *l.* a tongue, *fg.*

Languid, *a.* bòḷnātullo = *l.* without strength; ăskăt = *l.* weak; sirpuṭo; bāuntso = *l.* fading, *fg.*; făḍpoši, *e.g.* l. colour.

Languish, *v.* bāu = *l.* fade, *fg.*; pòḍ = *l.* fall, *e.g.* the conversation languishes; uṇo zātā = *l.* becomes less; bòḷ uṇeñ zātā = *l.* force diminishes.

Languor, *s.* bāvāp, -pā, *n.* = *l.* a fading away, *fg.*; ăskătkāi; -ye, *f.* = *l.* weakness.

Lank, *a.* 1. pātăḷ.
2. sădiḷ.

Lantern, *s. vlg.* lāmpiāuñ, -āvā, *m.*, *or* lānṭan, -nā, *n.*, pānăs, -sā, *m.*

Lap, *s.* 1. miri, -ye, *f.* = *Lat. lacinia.*
2. usko, -keā, *m.* = the part of the body from the waist to the knees, *e.g.* burgeñ āuoičea uskeār bostā.

Lapse, *v.* 1. *when* l. of time *is meant*, zā, *e.g.* tīn vorsañ zālea uprānt.
2. nisăr = *l.* glide.
3. tsuk = *l.* err.
4. pòḍ = *l.* fall, *e.g.* a property lapses to...

Lapse, *s.* 1. of time, *rs. into v.*
2. tsuk, -ki, *f.* = *l.* error.
3. nisrāp, -pā, *n.*

Large, *a.* rund = *l.* broad; vóḍ.

Lascivious, *a.* 1. mostitso = *l.* wanton.
2. khusāl = *l.* jolly.

Lash, *s.* 1. čābuk, -bkā, *n.* (*or m.*) = *l.* whip.
2. mār, -rā, *m.* = a blow; pēṭ(é), -ṭā, *m.* = a blow.

Lass, *s.* čeḍuñ, -ḍuā, *n.* = *l.* a girl.

Last, *s.* nămuno, -neā, *m.*, *e.g.* of a shoemaker.

Last, *a.* 1. nimāṇo (of time *esp.*); kăḍetso.
2. ākritso = *l.* extreme (of place).

3. gello = *l.* gone, *e. g.* year; ādlo = previous, of before; kāltso = *l.* of yesterday, *yet used also*, *e.g. in the phrase* l. Sunday.

L. year=poruñ *or* gelleā vorsa.

At last = sekiñ, *or* kăḍek, *or* kăḍer.

Last, *v.* 1. tăg, *e.g.* a house lasts long; ur = *l.* remain, *e. g.* the war lasts a long time; bāḷva; tsăl = *l.* walk, *fg.*, *e.g.* the school lasts 2 hours.

2. pāu = *l.* reach, *fg.*, *or* puro zāun āsā = is enough.

Latch, *s.* khiḷ, -ḷi, *f.*

Latchet, *s.* fint, -tā, *n.*, *fr.*, *e.g.* of shoes; dori, -ye, *f.*; nāḍo, -ḍeā, *m.*

Late, *ad.* 1. toḍou, *a noun, used as an adv.*

2. māgir, *or* uprānt = *l.* after.

Late, *a.* 1. sărlolo = *l.* departed (this life).

2. ādlo = *l.* previous; nimāṇo = *l.* last; māji (late in office).

Lately, *ad.* voḍóḷ; āilevăr; nimāṇeñ.

Lathe, *s.* kăḍčil, -lā, *n.*

Lather, *see* **Foam.**

Latitude, *s.* vistarāp, -pā, *n.* = *l.* extension; rundāi,- ye, *f.* = *l.* breadth.

Latter, *s.* dusro; duyăm; voḍoltso.

Lattice, *s.* tăṭṭi, -ṭe, *f.* = a screen of cadjan leaves; izăi, -ye, *f.* = one made of bamboo-strips; voḍāp, -ḍpā, *n.* = a big 'tăṭṭi'.

Laudable, *a.* hogḷāpātso; *see* **Praise.**

Laugh, *v.* hās.

L. at = čeṣṭāio kăr, *G. F.*; năklañ kăr; khelkulāñ kăr; kebḍāi kăr; *or only* hās *with Acc.*

Laughter, Laughing, *s.* hāso, -seā, *m.*

Laughable, *a.* hāstso.

Launch, *v.* (tāruñ) dăryānt devoi = *l.* cause (a ship) to descend into the sea.

Laundress, *s.* moḍvoḷn, -ni, *f.*

Laundry, *s.* umboḷči suāt, -te, *f.*; duunči suāt.

Laureate, *a.* pāṭo āsullo.

Lavish, *a.* večik; tsăḍ khărčitolo, *or* tsăḍ khārtsuntso.

Lavish, *v.* hăḷtnāstanāñ khărči.

Law, *s.* kāido, -deā, *m.*; kānun, -nā, *n.*

2. nāi, -yā, *m.* = *l.* justice.

Lawful, *a.* 1. vāzbi = *l.* reasonable, convenient.

2. kāideātso, *or* kāidea părmāṇe āsullo; nāyātso; *by the Pot. Mood.*

Law-giver, *s.* kāideāgār, -rā, *m.*

Lawless, *a.* kāideāviṇ *or* kāidonātullo.

Lawn, *s.* laččil, -lā, *n.*

Law-suit, *s.* vevār, -rā, *m.* = a process in law; vyājyụ, -yā, *m.*

Lawyer, *s.* văkil, -lā, *m.*; šāstra zāṇār, -rā, *m.*

Lax, *a.* 1. sădiḷ = *l.* loose, *pr.*, *fg.*, *e.g.* l. conscience; bepārvo kărtso, *or* bepārvi = *l.* neglecting; kāide tsălăinātullo = *l.* not performing duties; āḷsi = *l.* lazy.
2. tsăḍ dăyāḷ = *l.* too clement.

Laxity, *s.* sădiḷăi, -ye, *f.*, *pr.* *fg.*, *e.g.* l. of conscience.

Lay, *v.* 1. ghāl, *or* dovór.
2. bòḷ mōḍ(ó) = *l.* break force.
L. eggs = tāntiañ ghāl, *or* t. dovór.
L. aside = 1. kāḍ, *or* peleān kāḍ = *l.* take away.
2. sāmbāḷn dovór = *l.* preserving keep.
3. zoke dovór = *l.* keep with care.
L. before = mukār ghāl, *e.g.* a truth.
L. down = 1. sóḍ = *l.* leave, *e.g.* weapons.
2. khăṇḍit zāun săng = *l.* say positively.
L. hold = dhăr.
L. in = yekṭāiñ kăr = *l.* make a collection, *Acc.*
L. on = boḷān mār = *l.* beat violently; tāpăi = *l.* cause to get hot, *fg.*
L. open = ugto kăr, *or* u. dovór.
L. out = 1. bhāir ghāl.
2. khărči = *l.* expend.
3. năkṣa kāḍ = *l.* draw a plan.
L. together = sāngata ghāl, *or* voṭṭu dovór.
L. up = 1. dovòr.
2. āntuḷnār āsā = is in bed (ill), *ch. cs.*
L. upon = lāi = impute.
L. waste = piḍḍer kăr, *fr.*; nisăntān kăr; nāš kăr, *or* vibāḍ k.

Layman, *s.* souñsāri.

Laziness, *s.* āḷsāī, -ye, *f.*; bepārvo, -veā, *m.* = *l.* negligence, contempt; jèm, -me, *f.* = *l.* sloth, slumber; dăḍḍepoṇ, -ṇā, *n.*, *n. c.*

Lazy, *a.* āḷsi.

Lead, *s.* siseñ, -seā, *n.*

Lead, *v.* 1. tsălăi = *l.* cause to walk, *c. v.*, *e. g.* a mother leads her child.
2. vor = *l.* bring, *as* a captain leads the way; hāḍ = *l.* bring, carry.
3. vāṭ dākăi = *l.* show the way.
4. mukār vots = *l.* go before.
5. lāi = *l.* apply, induce.
6. khărči = *l.* spend, *e. g.* a life.
7. vetā = *l.* goes, *e.g.* the road leads to; *see also* **Guide.**

Leader, *s.* ădhipăti, -ti, *m.*; tsălăitolo; *see* **General, Influential.**

Leading, *a.* mukhya; *see* **Influential.**

Leaf, *s.* 1. kholo, -leā, *m.* = a green leaf.
2. kholi, -ye, *f.* (a dried l., *or* a small l.)
3. pālo, -leā, *m.* = foliage; sóp, -pā, *m.* = leaf for manuring.

4. pān, -nā, *n.*=*esp. l.* betel leaf, *used also for* a page of a book; fōl, -li, *f.*, *fr.* = l. of a book, of metal.
5. tăgăḍ, -gḍā, *n.* = *l.* of metal.
Plantain-leaf = siroti, -te, *f.* (green); seṇet, -tā, *n.* (dried).
Betel-leaf = kăsăr, -sri, *f.*
Areca-leaf = pouli, -le, *f.*
League, *s.* 1. mēḷ(é), -ḷā, *m.* = *l.* society, company; iṣṭăgăt, -ti, *f.* = *l.* friendship.
2. sollo, -leā, *m.* = *l.* confederacy, alliance; kărār, -rā, *m.* = *l.* agreement.
3. kós, -sā, *m.* (3 miles).
Leak, *v.* (pākeñ) pountā; pāus pòḍtā.
Leak, *s.* fuṭ, -ṭi, *f.*
Lean, *a.* bārik; širpuṭo (very lean); bāgeṭo (so l. as to seem a skeleton).
Lean, *v.* voṇkon bòs (sit leaning); voṇkon ubo rāu (stand leaning).
Leanness, *s.* bārikāi, -ye, *f.*; širpuṭāi, -ye, *f.*
Leap, *v.* uḍ, *or* uḍi mār = *l.* beat a leap.
Leap, *s.* uḍāp, -ḍpā, *n.*, *or* uḍi, -ḍi, *f.*
Leap-year, *s.* upari vărs, -sā, *n.*
Learn, *v.* 1. sik.
2. āik = *l.* hear.
Learning, *s.* sikāp, -kpā, *n.*
Lease, *s.* géṇ, -ṇi, *f.*
L. at will = čālgéṇ, -ṇi, *f.*
Perpetual l. = mulgéṇ, -ṇi, *f.*
On l. = géṇik.
Lease, *v.* géṇik di.
Least, *by the superl. of* lān.
At l. = puṇ, *or* puṇi, *placed after the affected word.*
Not in the l. = kāints nāñ.
Leather, *s.* tsāmbḍeñ, -ḍeā, *n.*
Leather, *a.* tsāmbḍeātso.
Leave, *v.* 1. sóḍ; sānḍ.
2. vopsun di = *l.* give consigned (entrust).
L. off = 1. thāmb *or* rāu; *see* **Cease.**
2. sóḍ, *e. g.* bad habits.
L. out = sóḍ.
Leave, *s.* răja, -je, *f.*
I take l. = r. kāṇetāñ.
With your l. = tumče dăyen.
Leaven, *s.* meḷāi, -ye, *f.*; fug, -gi, *f.*, for bread.
Leaven, *v.* fug, *e. g.* dough by pouring in toddy.
Lecture, *s.* 1. sikouṇeñ, -ṇeā, *n.*; sikoṇ, -ṇe, *f.*
2. besṭāuṇeñ, -ṇeā, *n.* = *l.* a reprimand.
Lecture, *v.* 1. sikouṇeñ di.
2. besṭāi.
Lecturer, *s.* sikouṇegār, -rā, *m.*
Ledger, *s.* lekānčeñ pustak, -kā, *n.* = *l.* a book of accounts.
Leech, *s.* zoḷu, -ḷve, *f.*
Leer, *v.* vānkḍo pòḷe = *l.* look obliquely.
Lees, *s.*, *see* **Dregs.**
Left, *a.* dāvo, *or* dāveahātātso; dāvokuro (dāukuro) = a left-handed man.

Leg, *s.* pāi, -yā, *m.*; khur, -rā, *m.* (of a bench).
Legacy, *s.* mòrnasănăd, -di, *f.* (*H. K.*).
Legal, *a.* kāideātso, *or* kāideān formāillo, *or* kāidea părmāṇe āsullo, *or* kāideasārko.
Legality, *s.* kāido, -deā, *n.*; nīt, -ti, *f.* = *l.* justice.
Legalise, *v.* (kāideān) stāpisi, *n. c.*; (kāideān) thir kăr = *l.* make firm; kāideātso kăr.
Legally, *ad.* kāideā părmāṇe.
Legate, *s.* (rāya) dūt, -tā, *m.*
Legation, *s.* (rāya) răvāneñ, -neā, *n.*
Legend, *s.* 1. melviḷās, -sā, *m.* = *l.* an inscription.
2. kătha, -the, *f.* = *l.* a story.
Legerdemain, *see* **Juggler.**
Legible, *a.* soṣṭ = *l.* distinct; vātsiyet āsullo; vāčisārko.
Legion, *s.* *approx.* pongóḍ, -gḍā, *m.*
Legislation, *s.* 1. kāideagăḍāp, -ḍpā, *n.*
2. kāido, -deā, *m.* = *l.* a law.
Legislative, *a.* kāidegăḍtso.
Legislator, *s.* kāideagār, -rā, *m.*; kāide kărtolo.
Legitimate, *a.* 1. kāidea părmāṇe āsullo, *or* kāideātso; vāzbi = *l.* becoming.
2. nīz = *l.* true.
Leisure, *s.* phursot, -ti, *f.*; khāli = *l.* empty (time); vēḷ(é), -ḷā, *m.*; nāñkām, -mā, *n.*
I find Peter at leisure = Pedru kāmār nātullea veḷār mākā meḷtā, *or* P. khāli āstanāñ...
Not at l. = kāmār.
Lemon, *s.* limbo (*or* tsórlimbo), -beā, *m.*
Lemonade, *s.* limbeāčeñ udāk, -dkā, *n.*
Lend, *v.* usṇo (-ṇi, -ṇeñ) di.
Length, *s.* lāmbāi, -ye, *f.*, *pr. fg.*
At length = sekiñ, *or* kăḍék *or* kăḍér.
Lengthwise, *a.* ubo (-bi, -beñ).
Lengthen, *v.* lāmb kăr.
Leniency, *s.* dăya, -ye, *f.*; kākuḷt -ti, *f.*
Lenient, *a.* dăyāḷ; kākuḷtitso.
Lent, *s.* *vlg.* karezm, -mā, *n.*; *perh.* paskādlo upās, -sā, *m.*; paskafuḍlo upās, -sā, *m.*; paskafuḍlo vēḷ(é), -ḷā, *m.*
Leper, *s.* kòḍkār, -rā, *m.*
Leprosy, *s.* kòḍ, -ḍā, *n.*
Leprous, *a.* kòḍāsullo.
Less, *a.*, *ad.* uṇo.
Less, *affix.* -nātullo, *or* a-, *or* -viṇ, *or* -nis; *see* Gram. P. III. ch. iv.
Lessee, *s.* bāḍeāk kāṇetolo, *or* b. lāitolo; bāḍeagār, -rā, *m.* *mn.* *also* he who gives out to hire.
Lesson, *s.* 1. *vlg.* lisāuñ, -sāvā, *n.*, *fr.*; pāṭ, -ṭā, *m.*; dilleñ kām, -mā, *n.* = *l.* given business.
2. sikoṇ, -ṇe, *f.* = *l.* instruction.
Give lessons = 1. sikāi.
2. bori bud sāng = *l.* say good advice.

Lest, *conj. by the* supine neg. *or by the* imperfect subj. neg. *or by the* neg. participle *with* pāsun; *see* Gram. Appendix I.
Keep him up lest he fall = pòḍanāñ zāunk tākā dovór, *more comm.* pòḍanāso tākā dovór.

Let, *v.* 1. sóḍ (suffer, allow); *by the* imperat. mood, *by the* caus. form.
2. bāḍeāk di = *l.* give to hire.
L. blood = šir mār.
L. down = devoi (deunḍăi, *n.c.*).
L. fall, l. fly, l. go = sóḍ.
L. in = kobuli di; rigăi.
L. off = mār, *e.g.* a gun.
L. slip an opportunity = săndrāp sóḍ.

Lethal, *a.* mòrṇātso, *or* mòrṇasārko.

Lethargy, *s.* gāḍ nid, -de, *f.*; kumbakărnāči nīd, -de, *f.* = *l.* sleep of the god Kumbakărna (a fabulous personage); *rs.* mótir nān = *l.* is not in mind.
2. *fg.* āḷsāi, -ye, *f.* = *l.* laziness.

Letter, *s.* 1. kāgād, -gdā, *n.*, pătrikāgād, -gdā, *n.* (*also* epistle).
2. ăkšar (*var.* ăkšer), -rā, *n.* (l. of the alphabet).
3. sikāp, -kpā, *n.*, *or perh. bet.* sikoṇ, -ṇe, *f.* = *l.* instruction.
To the l. = sārkeñ, *or* săbdañ părmāṇe, *or also* ăkšarañ părmāṇe.

Letting, *s.* bāḍeñ, -ḍeā, *n.*

Levee, *s.* săkāḷintso dărbār, -rā, *m.*

Level, *s.* 1. săma zāgo, -geā, *m.*
2. mòṭ (jălmăṭ), -ṭā, *n.* (an instrument).
3. *fg.* māp, -pā, *n.* = *l.* measure.

Level, *a.* săma; āḍgero, -reā, *m.* = *l.* a horizontal line.

Level, *v.* 1. săma kăr.
2. āḍgero kăr.
3. jălmăṭ kāḍ.

Levelled, *a.* kāpo, *a term used exclusively to express* the levelness of rice or any grain with the brim of a measure.

Lever, *s. approx.* lāṭo, -ṭeā, *m.*

Levigate, *v.* telto kăr.

Levity, *s.* khāli mót, -ti, *f.* = *l.* empty mind.

Levy, *v.* 1. sipāyānk meḷăi, *or* s. yekṭāiñ kăr.
2. ghāl = *l.* put: 'levy a tax = beróz ghāl'.

Lexicon, *s. has no proper equivalent in Konkani: perhaps* utrañbănḍār, -rā, *n. the literal translation of the Mr.* šăbdăkoš, *may be used as such.*

Liable, *a.* pòḍtso; *by the adj. in* -tso, *or* -sārko, *of the principal verb, e.g.* l. to faults = tsukasārko.

Liar, *s.* fóṭkiro mănis, -nšā, *m.*

Libel, *s.* nindepòtrų, -trā, *n.*

Liberal, *a.* 1. uddār, *or* voḍamònātso = bountiful.

2. sămpurṇ = *l.* abundant.
3. ukto = *l.* open, *fg.*
4. *as a term of politics*, novea kālātso = *l.* of the new time, *as opposed to* ādlea kālātso = *l.* of former time, *i. e.* conservative, *may be used. These expressions are commonly used with reference to customs, habits, etc.*

Liberality, *s.* uddārpoṇ, -ṇā, *n.*

Libertine, *s.* 1. čeḍiyāḷo, -ḷeā, *m.* (*fem.* čeḍiyāḷi, -ḷe).
2. móstigār, -rā, *m.*

Libertinism, *s.* most, -ti, *f.*

Liberty, *see* **Freedom.**
Be at l. = l. *by the* pot. mood.
2. mojea sotăntrār āsā.

Libidinous, *a.* móstitso.

Library, *s.* 1. pustakañsāl, -lā, *n.*
2. pustakañ mēḷ(é), -ḷā, *m.* = *l.* a collection of books.

Librarian, *s.* pustakagār, -rā, *m.*; pustakañsālā-ădhikāri, -ri, *m.*

License, *s.* 1. răja, -je, *f.*
2. hukum, -kme, *f.* (legal l.)
3. ăumăryād, -di, *f.*

License, *v.* hukum di.

Licentious, *a.* 1. vāiṭ tsālitso = of bad morals; móstitso.
2. lutstso = *l.* rascal.

Licentiousness, *s.* ăumăryād, -di, *f.*; lăzbandpoṇ, -ṇā, *n.*

Lick, *v.* 1. leuñ.
2. tsāk = *l.* taste.

Lid, *s.* dāmpṇeñ, -ṇeā, *n.*; mānḍ, -ḍi, *f.*; *see* **Eye-lid.**

Lie, *s.* fóṭ, -ṭi, *f.*

Lie, *v.* 1. fóṭi săng, *or* f. mār.
2. āḍ póḍ, *e.g*, l. on the bed; *in other cases only* āsā = is.
3. āḍpóḍun soukāsāi kāṇe = *l.* lying take rest.
4. khăṭleār āsā, *or* āntuḷnār āsā = *l.* is on the bed (sick).
5. āṭāp = *l.* be contained; *see also* **Depend.**
As far as in me lies = mākā tānkta titleñ.
I l. ill = mākā vāiṭ kărtā.
L. in wait = nāḍir āsā.
L. over = pāṭi ghāl = *l.* put behind.

Life, *s.* 1. jīṇ, *or* jiṇi, -ye, *f.* = lifetime; āuk, -kā, *n.*
2. prāṇ, -ṇā, *m.*, *e.g.* J. C. gave His l. for us; jīv, -vā, *m.* = physical and also supernatural l.
3. *fg.* tsurkāi, -ye, *f.*, *or* ušārāi, -ye, *f.* = activity, vivacity.
L. of saints = santānči jiṇi, *or* santānčeo kobro.

Lifeless, *a.* jīvnātullo, *see* **Insensible.**

Lift, *v.* ukoḷ; ubār.

Light, *s.* 1. uzuāḍ, -ḍā, *m.* = *Lat. lux*, *pr. fg.*, *e.g.* l. of mind.
2. divo, -veā, *m.* = *l.* a lamp, *used also for* its light; dipṭi, *or* diuṭi, -ṭe, *f.* = a torch.
Bring to light (secrets) = ukto kăr, *or* părgăṭ kăr.

Light, *a.* 1. uzuāḍātso, *or* prăkāšātso, *pr. fg.*, *e.g.* l. colour.

2. hāḷu (not heavy); hăgur, (*Lat. levis*).
3. bolăiketso = *l.* of health, *e.g.* l. food.
4. čillăr = *l.* trifling.

Light, *v.* peṭăi, *c. v. of* pèt, *e.g.* a candle; divo lāi = *l.* apply light; *perh. bet.* uzuāḍ lāi.
L. upon = mèḷta.

Lighten, *v.* 1. uzuāḍ di, *or* u. kăr, *or* u. lāi.
2. hāḷu kăr = *l.* make not heavy.
3. zăglāitā, *or* zăglaṇeñ yetā = *l.* lightning comes.

Light-house, *s.* bāuṭokaṭo, bāuṭeā-kaṭea, *m.*

Lightly, *ad.* 1. hāḷu zāun.
2. ăusărān, *or* vegiñ = quickly.
3. voilebār = *l.* on the surface.
4. sovāi = *l.* cheap.
5. čintināstanāñ = *l.* not thinking; kārāṇnāstanāñ = *l.* not being cause.
6. ăumăryādin = *l.* unpolitely.

Lightness, *s.* 1. hāḷuāi, -ye, *f.*
2. ăumăryād, -di, *f.* = *l.* unpoliteness.

Lightning, *s.* zăglāṇeñ, -ṇeā, (*var.* zăglāṇ), *n.*, *pr. fg.*, *e.g.* the horse ran like lightning; viz, -zā, *m.* = a thunder-bolt.

Like, *a.*, *ad.* sārko = *l.* similar; săma = *l.* equal; bări = *l.* as, *e.g.* like him = tače b.; pārmāṇe = *l.* according, *e.g.* he acts l. a child = burgeāče sovoye p. tsăltā; jinsiñ = *l.* in the way of (burgeāčea j.).

Like, *v.* 1. ruts = *l.* taste (food), *e.g.* yeñ mākā rutstā.
2. mānua = *l.* please; *vlg.* boro (-ri, -reñ) distā = *l.* seems good; *G.* khuše părmāṇe āsā = is according to the wish of; metsva = *l.* approve of: 'to mākā metsvatā'.
3. *G.* ăpurbāi āsā = *l.* is fondness of.
If you like = khuši āsleār, *or* mānualeār; dăya kărn.

Likely, *a.*, *ad.* *By the* conting. future; sătmāndiso = *l.* which can be believed; metsva-sārko = *l.* which can be approved.

Liken, *v.* săr kăr; *see* **Compare.**

Likeness, *s.* sārkeñ, -keā, *n.*; săr, -ri, *f.*

Likewise, *ad.* legun, *or* săit, *placed after the affected word*; teāts jinsiñ = *l.* in the same way; -i *joined to the word modified*; *see* Gram. P. II. ch. vi.

Liking, *s.* 1. ruts, -či, *f.*
2. *fg.* mărji, -je, *f.* = *l.* caprice; khuši, -še, *f.* = *l.* will.

Lily, *s.* *perh.* kaṇeḷ, -ḷā, *n.*, *Mr.*

Limb, *s.* 1. sāndo, -deā, *m.*, *e.g.* a limb of the body.
2. khāndo, -deā, *m.* = *l.* a branch.

Limbo, *s.* limb, -bā, *n.*; pātāḷ, -ḷā, *n.* = a subterraneous place.

Lime, *s.* tsuno, -neā, *m.*

Lime-stone, *s.* tsuneātso fātor, -trā, *m.*

Limit, Limitation, *s.* găḍ, -ḍi, *f.*; sărhăddu̥, -di, *f.*; mit, -ti, *f.*, *Cn. n. c.*, *except in compounds*; mitmèr, -ri, *f.*; āker, -ri, *f.* = *l.* an extremity; ănt, -tā, *m.* = *l.* an end.
Limit, *v.* găḍ ghāl = *l.* put a limit.
Limited, *part. a.* găḍ āsu̥llo, *or* ănt āsu̥llo.
Limpid, *a.* nităḷ; nirmoḷ; părzăḷik = *l.* shining.
Linch-pin, *s.* khiḷ, -ḷi, *f.*
Line, *s.* 1. giṭ, -ṭā, *m.* (geometrical).
2. fāngt, -ti, *f.* = *esp.* l. of a page, *fg. also*, *e.g.* I write a few lines.
3. vóḷ, -ḷi, *f.*; hār, -ri, *f.*, *e.g.* flowers in a line.
4. gero, -reā, *m.* (drawn line).
5. kus, -si, *f.*, dikku̥, -kā, *m.* = side, direction; *by* isileān = in this side.
6. găḍ, -ḍi, *f.* = *l.* limit.
7. tăkleānči hār, -ri, *f.* = *l.* line of heads (genealogy).
8. *omit and use the Instrum.*; *e.g.* in that line = teṇeñ.
Lineage, *s.* kuṭām, -ṭmā, *n.* = *l.* family; săntăt, -ti, *f.*; răgat, -gtā, *n.*
Lineament, *see* **Feature.**
Linear, *a.* giṭāntso.
Linen, *s.* lugāṭ, -gṭā, *n.* (nārāčeñ lugāṭ).
Linen, *a.* soṇātso (?), nārātso.
Linger, *v.* toḍou kăr; pāṭiphuḍeñ kăr = be not exact at the appointed time.

Linguist, *s.* bhāsañzāṇār, -rā, *m.*; bhāsañpăṇḍit, -tā, *m.*
Linguistic, *a.* bhāsañvidya, -ye, *f.*, *or* bhāsasāmārthi, -the, *f.*
Link, *s.* 1. sānkḷiči mudi, -ye, *f.* = *l.* a ring of a chain; gānts, -tsā, *m.*
2. *fg.* sānkăḷ, -kḷi, *f.* = *l.* a chain, *fg.*
3. bānd, -dā, *m.* = *l.* a tie.
Link, *v.* bānd.
Linseed, *s.* soṇāčeñ biñ, -biyā, *n.*
Lint, *s.* sut, -tā, *n.*
Lion, *s.* siuñ, -ivā, *m.*
Lioness, *s.* siuiṇ, -ṇi, *f.* (bāilo siuñ).
Lip, *s.* 1. vónṭ, -ṭā, *m.*
2. *fg.* dèg, -ge, *f.* = brim, *e.g.* of a pot; kānṭ, -ṭā, *m.*
Liquefy, *v.* kăḍāi, *c. v. of* kăḍ, *n. v.*; pātăḷ kăr.
Liquid, *a.* kăḍāillo; pātăḷ; vāutolo, *or* vāuntso.
Liquid, *s.* vāunči văstu̥, -tu, *f.*, *or* pātăḷ văstu̥.
Liquidate, *v.* fārik kăr.
Liquor, *s.* 1. rōs(ó), -sā, *m.*
2. nibbor soro = *l.* strong country-liquor; soro, -reā, *m.*, *a general name, esp. for* country liquor.
Lisp, *see* **Stammer.**
List, *s.* 1. păṭṭi, -ṭe, *f.*
2. lèk, -kā, *n* = *l.* an account; čiṭ, -ṭi, *f.* = a small note.
3. veḍo, -ḍeā, *m.* = an enclosed field.

Listen, *v.* kān di = *l.* give ear; guṭān āik = *l.* hear secretly.

Listless, *s.* zāgrutnātullo; bāuntso = *l.* fading, *fg.*

Litany, *s.* ladin, -ni, *f.*, *fr.*

Literal, *a.* ăkṣerāñ pārmāṇe āsullo, *or perh.* ăkṣerātso; utrāñ pārmāṇe āsullo.

Literary, *a.* sikpātso.

Literature, *s.* sikāp, -kpā, *n.*; šāstru̥, -trā, *n.*; vidya, -ye, *f.*

Lithography, *s.* fātrac̆hāpo, -peā, *m.*, *n. u.*

Litigant, *s.* zăgăḍtolo.

Litigate, *v.* zăgḍa, *or bet.* zăgăḍ; nāi kăr; arenji.

Litter, *s.* mac̆il (*or* mănc̆il), -lā, *n.*; dól, -li, *f.* = a simple sort of l. used by country people; pālki, -ke, *f.*

Litter, *v.* pilañ kāḍ, *or* p ghāl.

Little, *a.* 1. lān; dākṭo.
2. kirkòḷ = *l.* wretched.
3. moṭvo = *l.* short.

Little, *s.* thoḍo, (-ḍi, -ḍeñ); illo, (-li, -leñ); c̆ikkeñ (*var.* tikkeñ), *dim.* c̆ikkeseñ.

Liturgy, *s.* *vlg.* sermoni, -ni, *f.*; igărjerīt, -ti, *f.*, *or* igărjepăddăt, -ti, *f.*, *or* igărjerivāz, -ji, *f.*; kăṭleñ, -leā, *n.* (*H. K.*)

Live, *v.* 1. jiye; jiṇi khărc̆i = *l.* spend life.
2. jivăn kăr = get a livelihood.
3. rāu, *or* vās kăr.
4. khā = *l.* eat.
5. vānts = be saved, *e. g.* from a sickness, from danger.

Livelihood, *s.* udarpošaṇ, -ṇā, *n.* = sufficiency of means for living; jivăn, -nā, *n.*; khāṇ, -ṇā, *n.*, grās, -sā, *m.* = food; āhār, -rā, *m.*

Liveliness, *s.* bārikāi, -ye, *f.*

Livelong, *a.* 1. săgḷi jiṇi tăgtso, *or* lāmb jiṇiyetso; *vlg.* tīn disāntso = *l.* of three days, *e.g.* tīn dis sermāuñ kelo.
2. *fg.* bezāri, *or* bezārāyetso.

Lively, *a.* ušār; khusāl = *l.* jolly; tsurk.

Liver, *s.* kāḷiz, -ḷzā, *n.*

Livid, *a.* siseātso, *or* siseārăngātso = *l.* of the colour of lead; kāḷso = *l.* rather black, *e.g.* a l. wound.
Become l. = kinḍe (*ex.* become red from a blow).

Living, *a.* jivo.

Living, *s.* 1. udarpošaṇ, -ṇā, *n.*
2. jivit, -tā, *m.*

Lizard, *s.* pāl, -li, *f.*

Lo, *int.* pòḷe, *or* obḷe.

Load, *s.* vojeñ, -jeā, *n.*

Load, *v.* 1. bhór = *l.* fill, *e.g.* a carriage, stomach, gun.
2. (khāndār) ghāl = *l.* put (on the shoulder).
L. with chains = sānkăḷ ghāl.
L. with injuries = ăkmānāniñ bhór.

Loaded, *a.* bhóru̥llo.

Loadstone, *s.* voḍneātso fātor, *or* vóḍtso fātor, -trā, *m.* = *l.* attracting stone; lohāc̆umbak, -kā, *m.*, *Cn. Mr.*, *n.u.*

Loaf, *s.* unḍo, -ḍeā, *m.*=*l.* bread.
Loan, *s* usṇi văstu̥, -tu, *f.* = *l.* a thing lent.
Take a l. = 1. usṇo ghe = *l.* take a loan.
2. riṇ ghe = *l.* take a debt; duḍu usṇo ghe.
Make a l. = riṇ di (give to another).
Loath, *v. neg. form of* ruts; *rs.* vonkāro yetā = *l.* nausea comes; kānṭāḷ = *l.* abhor.
Loathing, *s.* vonkāro, -reā, *m.*
Loathsome, *a.* 1. vonkāreātso.
2.*fg.* bezāri, *or* bezārāyetso.
Local, *a.* zāgeāntlo, *or* gāvāntlo, *or* jilleāntlo; *rs.*
L. disturbances = yekats (*or* thoḍea) gāvāntli kāṭkāi, -ye, *f.*
Locality, *s.* suāt, -te, *f.*; gāuñ, gāñvā, *m.* = *l.* country.
Lock, *s.* 1. bīg, -gā, *n.*
2. kulup, -pā, *n.*
3. jilpañ, *pl. n., e. g.* a lock of hair.
Lock, *v.* 1. bīg ghāl = *l.* put the lock.
2. dāmp = *l.* shut.
Locomotive, *s.* duvrāči gāḍi (durā-gāḍi), -ye, *f.* = *l.* a carriage of smoke.
Locust, *s.* dempo, -peā, *m.*; tolo, -leā, *m.* (*in North Canara*).
Lodge, *v.* 1. rāu = *l.* remain; biḍār āsā = *l.* lodging is; vās kăr = *l.* dwelling make.
2. biḍār di = *l.* dwelling give.
Lodger, *s.* 1. vokāl, -klā, *m.* = a tenant.
2. biḍāri, -reā, *m.*
Lodging, *s.* biḍār, -rā, *n.*; ghăr, -rā, *n.*; *see* **Inn.**
Loft, *s.* māḷo, -ḷeā, *m.*, *an approx. word, such a convenience being unknown here.*
Loftiness, *s.* untsāi, -ye, *f.*; ubā-rāi, -ye, *f.*
Lofty, *a.* 1. unts; ubār.
2.*fg.* vorto, *or* vóḍ.
Logic, *s.* tărkašāstru̥, -rā, *n.*; nāyašāstru̥ (nyāyašāstru̥), -rā, *n.*
Logical, *a.* ruzu kărtso = demonstrative; nāyašāstrātso, *or* tărkašāstrātso.
Logician, *s.* tărkašāstri, -ri, *m.*
Loin, *s.* penkāṭ, -kṭā, *n.*; kruṭ, -ṭā, *n.*
Loiter, *v.* āḷsāi kăr = *l.* make laziness; toḍou kăr = *l.* make late.
Lone, Lonely, *a.* yeksuro.
Long, *a.* 1. lāmb, *e. g.* piece of cloth, time, sermon; dīg.
2. săbār = *l.* much, *e.g.* time.
Long, *ad.* săbār vēḷ(é) = much time; *or* tsăḍ vēḷ = more time.
L. before = săbār veḷa ādiñ; how l. = kitlo vēḷ; how much longer = āni kitlo vēḷ (*vlg.* kitlo témp); so long = titlo, *or* titlo lāmb; too l. = tsăḍ lāmb.
Long, *v.* lāle, *Dat. obj.*; urbā āsā; āšā āsā, *or* āše.

Longish, *a.* lāmbso.

Longitude, *s.* lāmbāi, -ye, *f.*

Look, *v.* 1. pòḷe, *or* pòḷei, *used also for* face in a certain direction, *n. c. in this mn.*; diṣṭ ghāl; tsoi (*H. K.*)
2. distā = *l.* appears, *ch. cs.*, *e.g.* it looks well.
L. about = yeusiñ teusiñ pòḷe, *or* isiñ tisiñ pòḷe.
L. back = pāṭi pòḷe; l. down = săkāl pòḷe.
L. for = sód = *l.* seek.
L. in the face = tòndār pòḷe.
L. out = tsătrāi kāṇge, *or* pāṭi phuḍeñ pòḷe.
L. through = 1. (*Instr.*) pòḷe.
2. diṣṭ ghāl.
L. to = 1. čint.
2. pătiye = *l.* trust.
L. towards = *G.* isileān pòḷe = *l.* look in the direction of.
L. up to = mānd *or* boreñ čint = *l.* think well.

Look, *s.* 1. diṣṭ, -ṭi, *f.*
2. tònḍ, -ḍā, *n.* = *l.* face; rūp, -pā, *n.* = *l.* figure, form.

Looking-glass, *s.* ārso, -seā, *m.*

Loom, *s.* māg, -gā, *m.* (a weaving machine).

Loose, *a.* 1. săḍil, *e. g.* hairs, dress.
2. ghăṭnātullo = *l.* not firm.
3. *fg.* āpleā sotăntrār āsullo = *l.* being in one's own power; āple khušetso = *l.* of one's own will.
4. móstitso = *l.* dissolute.

Loose, *v.* sóḍ, *e. g.* a dress, *or* săḍil kăr; mōḍ(ó) = *l.* break; suṭ, *e. g.* a rope, *n. v.*

Loosely, *ad.* 1. zāgrutāi nāstanāñ, *or* nāñzāgrutāyen.
2. fāḍpoši *or* vāiṭ jinsiñ.

Looseness, *s.* 1. săḍiḷāi, -ye, *f.*
2. utkaḍeñ, -ḍeā, *n.* (sickness); hāgoṇ, -ṇi, *f.*, *see* **Diarrhœa.**
3. móst, -ti, *f.* = *l.* bad morals.

Lop, *v.* kăši kăr.

Loquacious, *a.* 1. boḍboḍo.
2. găzāli mārtso.
Be l. = boḍboḍ.

Loquacity, *s.* boḍboḍneñ, -neā, *n.*; zānk, -ki, *f.* (delirium?).

Lord, *s.* 1. sāib, -bā, *m.*, *used also for* God; suāmi, *or* somi, -yā, *m.*, *used also for* J. C.; sărdār, -rā, *m.*, *used esp. for* European gentlemen; năbāb, -bā, *m.* a Mahomedan prince, *used fg. for* Lord.
2. kărt, -tā, *n.*; dhăni, -yā, *m.*; khāvănd, -dā, *m.* = the master of the house.

Lordship, *s. the title can be rendered only by the common noun* sāib.

Lose, *v.* 1. hogḍāi, *tr. v.*, *or* hogḍaun ghe; ăntăr (*var.* ătra) = *l.* go lost, *e. g.* sărg pātkiāk ăntărtā; *vlg.* bhāir ghāl = *l.* put out; *vlg.* bhāir pòḍ = *l.* fall out, *ch. cs.*
2. pāḍ zā = *l.* be spoiled, *e. g.* the fruit of my work; năšṭ zā = *l.* get loss, *ch. cs.*

3. tsukāi = *l.* deprive.

Loss, *s.* 1. hogḍāuṇeñ, -ṇeā, *n.*
2. luksān, -nā, *n.*, *or* năṣṭ, -ṭā, *m.* = *l.* damage.
3. păḍāu, -ḍāvā, *m.* = *l.* defeat (in a battle).
Be at a l. = (mākā) somzanāñ.

Lot, *s.* 1. soḍti, -te, *f.*, *e.g.* in a raffle.
2. grātstsār, -rā, *m.* = *l.* fate; ădruṣṭ, -ṭā, *n.*; năšib, -bā, *n.*; găt, -ti, *f.*, *e.g.* āmiñ zuzāče gătir āsāuñ.
3. vānṭo, -ṭeā, *m.* = *l.* a portion.
4. (*in pl.*) săbār = *l.* many.

Lottery, *s.* soḍti, -te, *f.*

Loud, *a.* soṣṭ; ghăṭ.

Loudly, *ad.* voḍleān = *l.* by great (voice); soṣṭ = *l.* distinctly; bòb mārn = *l.* crying.

Lounge, *see* **Roam.**

Louse, *s.* vū, -ve, *f.*

Lout, *see* **Boor.**

Love, *s.* 1. mōg(ó), -gā, *m.*; prīt, -ti, *f.*
2. ăpurbāi, -ye, *f.* = *l.* fondness; urbā, -be, *f.*; lāleuṇeñ, -ṇeā, *n.*; āšā, -še, *f.* = a great desire; moyamōg, -gā, *m.* = fraternal love.

Love, *v.* 1. mōg(ó) kăr = *l.* make love, *G. M.*; prīt kăr.
2. săntos bhóg = *l.* enjoy pleasure, *ch. cs.*, *e.g.* love an austere life; boro (-ri, -reñ) distā = *l.* appears good (pleases); metsva = *l.* approve of, *e.g.* to mākā metsvatā = *l.* he is approved to me (I approve of him, I love him).
3. ăpurbāi āsā, *e.g.* mākā tāči ăp. āsā = I love him.

Loveliness, *s.* mogāḷpoṇ, -ṇā, *n.*; ăpurbāi, -ye, *f.*

Lovely, *a.* 1. mōg(ò) fāvozāllo, *or* mogāḷ *or* mogātso; prītitso.
2. sobit.

Loving, *a.* mōg kărtso = *l.* making love; ăpurbāyetso = fond.

Low, *a.* 1. tăpkaṭo, *e.g.* l. place; tăggu (*n. c.*), *or* săklăḍ, *or* săkăilo.
2. hăḷu = *l.* light, *e.g.* l. sound, l. voice; 'with a l. voice = hăḷu *or* lou'.
3. uṇo = *l.* less, inferior, *e.g.* l. man; hălko; ălpo, *e. g.* l. mind, l. place; kirkóḷ; ăṇvo.
4. sovāi = *l.* cheap.
5. bhou ăskăt = *l.* very weak.
6. moṭvo = *l.* short.
L. voice = săkăilo tāḷo, -ḷeā, *m.* (*or see above*).

Low, *ad.* săkăl.

Low, *v.* ambe, *used of* cows *and* sheep.

Lower, *v.* 1. devoi, (*or* deunḍăi, *n. c.*); *c. v. of* deuñ; *also* l. a price.
2. săkăl kăḍ = *l.* take down, *e.g.* the voice.
3. dukest zā = *l.* get sorry.
4. kupañ tsăḍ zātāt = *l.* clouds get many.

Lowliness, *s.* kirkoḷāi, -ye, *f.*; uṇepoṇ, -ṇā, *n.* = *l.* inferiority.

Loyal, *a.* niškăpṭi = *l.* sincere; sādo = *l.* simple; pātiyeṇitso = *l.* trusty; nīz = *l.* true, sincere.

Loyalty, *s.* niškăpăṭ, -ṭā, *n.*

Lozenge, *s.* miṭāi, -ye, *f.*

Lucid, *a.* 1. părzăḷik = *l.* shining; uzuāḍātso = *l.* of light.

2. ṇităḷ = *l.* pure.

3. *rs. into* distā *or* disun āsā = is transparent.

He has l. intervals = thoḍe pāuṭi mótir āsā.

Luck, *s.* grātstsār, -rā, *m.*; ădrušṭ, -ṭā, *n.*; năsib, -bā, *n.*

Luckily, *ad.* ădrušṭān, *or* grātstsārān.

Lucky, *a.* 1. ădrušṭātso.

2. sukhi = *l.* happy; guṇātso = *l.* favourable.

Lucrative, *a.* ādāyātso.

Lucre, *s.* ādāi, -yā, *m.*

Lucubration, *s.* (rātstso) vāur, -rā, *m.* = *l.* work (of night); (rāti kello) vāur.

Luculent, *a.* sošṭ.

Ludicrous, *a.* hāstso, *or* hāsountso = *l.* causing laughter; češṭāyetso = *l.* funny; tārifetso = *l.* awkward, laughable.

Lug, *v.* vōḍ(ó) = *l.* pull; lóṭ.

Luggage, *s.* sāmān, -nā, *m.*

Lugubrious, *a.* dukest = sorry; dukountso = sad.

Lukewarm, *a.* 1. unso; nakši-un; šeḷmoḍo.

2. *fg.* āḷši = *l.* lazy.

Lukewarmness, *s. fg.* āḷsāi, -ye, *f.*; *in pr. mn. rs. into a.*

Lull, *v.* 1. gāṇa gā = compose to sleep by making pleasing sounds; nidāi = *l.* cause to sleep; zomp kāḍ = move the cradle.

2. nidān kăr = *l.* make quiet; thănḍ kăr = *l.* make cold; fuslāi = *l.* appease.

Luminary, *s.* 1. uzuāḍāči văstu, -tu, *f.*

2. ălănkār, -rā, *m.* = *l.* an ornament, *e.g.* the l. of the state.

Luminous, *a.* uzuāḍātso; părzăḷik = *l.* shining.

Lunar, *a.* tsăndremātso.

Lunatic, *a.* pisoso = *l.* a little mad.

Lunch, *s.* phăḷār, -rā, *m.* = a tiffin, collation.

Lung, *s.* popis, -psā, *m.*

Exert the lungs = vāur″.

Lurch, *s.* 1. kăšṭ, -ṭā, *m.*

2. tārvalăkṇeñ, -ṇeā, *n.* (the rolling of a ship); kēp, -pā, *n.*

Leave in the l. = vāṭer ghāl.

Lure, *s.* 1. voḍni, -ne, *f.*; lonts, -tsā, *m.*

2. khāṇ, -ṇā, *n.*; *see* **Bait.**

Lurid, *see* **Ghastly.**

Lurk, *v.* līp = *l.* be concealed.

Lurking-place, *s.* lipči suāt, -te, *f.* = *l.* the place (in which) one can hide; lipṇlli suāt, -te, *f.* = *l.* a hidden place.

Luscious, *a.* tsăḍ ručitso = *l.* too sweet.

Lust, *s.* 1. móst, -ti, *f.* = impure inclination; kām, -mā, *n.*; kuḍiči khuši, -še, *f.* = *l.* bodily desire.
2. āšā, -še, *f.* = *l.* desire.

Lustful, *a.* 1. móstitso.
2. bāilanḍo = *l.* effeminate.

Lustral (water), *s.* 1. āgment, -tā, *n.*, *fr.*
2. tīrt, -tā, *n.* (*H. K.*)

Lustre, *s.* vóḍ kastisăl, -lā, *n.* = *l.* a big candlestick; jumbór, -rā, *m.*

Lusty, *a.* ghăṭ = *l.* strong; bolāikent āsullo = *l.* being in health.

Luxation, *s.* khiḷiñtsukāp, -kpā, *n.*

Luxurious, *a.* móstitso; bāilanḍo; vāiṭ khušiānk lāgullo = *l.* given to bad pleasures.

Luxury, *s.* móst, -ti, *f.*; kuḍičeo khušio = *l.* bodily pleasures; kām, -mā, *n.*; pózḍepoṇ, -ṇā, *n.*, bursepoṇ, -ṇā, *n.* = *l.* dirtiness, *fg.*

Lye, *s.* khār, -rā, *m.*; guḍ, -ḍā, *m.*
Make l. = 1. guḍāk lāi.
2. khārānt ghāl.

M

Mace, *s.* pătri, -re, *f.* (a sort of spice).

Macerate, *v.* 1. bizăi = *l.* make wet.
2. *fg.* kăṣṭăi (*var.* kăṣṭavăi), *c. v. of* kăṣṭa = cause pain.

Machinate, *v.* 1. kuṭañ kăr = *l.* make plots.
2. sódun kāḍ = *l.* seeking take.

Machination, *s.* kuṭ, -ṭā, *n.*; mōs, -sā, *m.* = deceit; măslăt, -ti, *f.*

Machine, *s.* čarăk, -rkā, *n.* (*var.* čerki, -ke, *f.*); yăntru, -rā, *n.*; āid, -dā, *n.* = *l.* an instrument.

Machinist, *s.* čarkañ kărtolo, -leā, *m.*

Mackerel, *s.* bāngḍo, -ḍeā, *m.*

Mad, *a.* piso, *e.g.* man *or* dog; motirnātullo = *l.* not in (one's) mind.
Be m. after = lāle, *Dat.*; mogān mòr = *l.* die out of love; pisau = *l.* be mad.

Madam, *s.* sāibiṇ, -ṇi, *f.*; *vlg.* madām, -mi, *f.*; bāi, -ye, *f.*

Madden, *v.* 1. pisăi, *c. v. of* pisau (*more com.* piso kăr).
2. zăḷăi = *l.* cause to burn (rāgān = for anger).

Mad-house, *s.* piseānčeñ ghăr, -rā, *n.* = *l.* a house of mad persons; piseānči āspătri, -re, *f.*

Madness, *s.* pisepoṇ, -ṇā, *n.*; girigiri, -ri, *f.* = a transient alienation of mind, *n. c.*

Magazine, *s.* 1. dārukhāno, -neā, *m.* (for powder).
2. ugrāṇ, -ṇā, *n.* (for miscellaneous articles).

Magi, *s. pl.* tèg rāi = *l.* three kings.

Magic, *s.* bolmeñ sāngči hikmăt, -ti, *f.* = *l.* the art of saying incantation; măntru̥ (*or* tăntru̥), -rā, *n.*; phitispoṇ, -ṇā, *n.* (*the most common word*); ghāḍi, -ḍi, *f.*; bhul, -li, *f.*; nimit, -tā, *n.*

Magician, *s.* bolmeagār, -rā, *m.*; ghāḍigār, -rā, *m*; tăntragār, -rā, *m.*; phitispoṇagār, -rā, *m.*; nimitgār, -rā, *m.*

Magistrate, *s.* ădhipăti, *or* ădhikāri, -ri, *m.* = a person of public authority.

Magnanimity, *s.* dhăir, -rā, *n.* = *l.* courage; vóḍ mòn, -nā, *n.* = *l.* great heart.

Magnanimous, *a.* vóḍ mònātso; dhăirāvont, *or* dhăirādik.

Magnet, *see* **Loadstone.**

Magnetize, *v.* voḍči săkăt lāi = *l.* apply attracting power.

Magnificence, *s.* dobāzo, -jeā, *m.*; vóḍ mān, -nā, *m.* = *l.* great honour; voḍpoṇ, -ṇā, *n.* = *l.* greatness.

Magnificent, *a.* dobājeātso; voḍpoṇātso.

Magnify, *v.* vorni, hogoḷsi, pāsār = *l.* praise, exalt.

Mahomedan, *s.* musulmān, -nā, *m.*

Maid, Maiden, *s.* čeḍuñ, -ḍuā, *n.* = *l.* a girl; tsăli, -ye, *f.* (*H. K.*); ānkuār, -ri, *f.* = *l.* a virgin; kănyāstri, -re, *f.*; nār, -ri, *f.*

Maid-servant, *s.* tsākārn, -ni, *f.*

Mail, *s.* 1. kăvača, -če, *f.* = a sort of coat of mail, *n. c.*
2. tăpāl, -lā, *n.* (*for* letters *etc.*)
3. tăpālpèdo, -deā, *m.* = a post-peon.

Maimed, *a.* 1. thonṭo = *l.* lame.
2. nātullo *added to the* limb missing.

Main, *a.* mukhya = *l.* principal. Main point = muḷo, -ḷeā, *m.* = *l.* a hinge, *fg.*

Mainly, *ad.* mukhya zāun.

Maintain, *v.* 1. dovór = *l.* keep.
2. tsāl (*with* părmāṇe) = *l.* walk, *fg.*, *e. g.* maintain your dignity.
3. sāmbāḷ = *l.* defend.
4. pós = *l.* feed; jevāṇ di = *l.* give food.
5. khănḍit sāng = *l.* positively say.

Maintenance, *s.* dispoḍto grās, -sā, *m.* = *l.* daily food; dispoḍteñ khāṇ, -ṇā, *n.*; udarpošaṇ, -ṇā, *n.* = sufficiency of means for living.

Majestic, *a.* 1. măimetso; bhou tsāḍ măryāditso; voḍpoṇātso, = *l.* great; mānātso.
2. podvetso = *l.* of power.

Majesty, *s.* 1. măima, -me, *f.*, *e. g.* God's m.; voḍvi, -ve, *f.*; voḍpoṇ, -ṇā, *n.*

2. rāi, -yā, *m.*, *or* rāṇi, -ye, *f.* = king, *or* queen.

Majority, *s.* 1. voḍlo vānṭo, -ṭeā, *m.* = *l.* a great part.

2. pirāi, -ye, *f.* = *l.* age (mănsāči *or some such word being understood*); mānāipoṇ, -ṇā, *n.*, *n. u.*; *bet.* fāvo pirāi *or* vāzbi pirāi, -ye, *f.* = requisite age.

Make, *v.* 1. kăr, *imp.* kelo; *see* Gram., *used especially in composition with a noun; also when we should use* give, *e.g.* kumok kăr = help, *l.* make help (give help).

2. kāḍ, *e.g.* m. the sign of the cross = kursāči kurukāḍ.

3. *by the c. v.*

4. pòḍ, = *l.* fall (contribute); *see also* **Appoint, Form, Constitute, Gain, Represent, Value, Force.**

M. against = āḍkāḷ kăr; āḍ ye; luksānāk pòḍ.

M. amends = fārikpoṇ di = *l.* give satisfaction.

M. as if, *see* **Simulate.**

M. away with = sóḍ = *l.* leave; *see* **Rid, Kill.**

M. for = *G.* isileān (*or* dikkān) vots.

M. free with = ăumăryādin tsăl; *see also* **Filch.**

M. good, *see* **Compensate, Fulfil, Maintain.**

M. light of = bepārvo kăr, *G. M.*, *or* săsār kăr.

M. much of = 1. thăiñ ăpurbāyen tsăl = *l.* proceed with fondness towards.

2. mānd; lăkṣa kăr.

M. haste, *see* **Haste.**

M. over = părādin kăr; vopsun di.

M. out = somza = *l.* understand.

M. ready = tăyār kăr.

M. up = 1. meḷon āsā = *l.* is formed, *ch. cs.*

2. fārikpoṇ di.

3. ničeu kăr = *l.* make a resolution (make up one's mind); niščeisi; *see* **Constitute, Supply.**

M. use of = prăyog kăr, *G. M. n.c.*

M. way = suāt kăr; vāṭ sóḍ.

Make, *s. see* **Figure, Form.**

Maker, *s.* 1. *l.* kărt, -tā, *m.*, *not often used.*

2. -gār *added to the thing made, or by the participle of the verb; see* Gram.

Malapert, *a.* ăumăryāditso; lăzbanḍo *or* lăznātullo.

Malapropos, *a.* 1. lāyeknātullo; kāmāk pòḍanātullo.

2. *rs.* fāvonātulleā veḷār.

Malaria, *s.* vāiṭ vāreñ, -reā, *n.*

Malcontent, *s.* kuṭagār, -rā, *m.* = *l.* a maker of plots.

Male, *a.* 1. dādlo, (-li, -leñ).

2. dādleāntso = *l.* of the male.

Male, *s.* dādlo, -leā, *m.*; čerko, -keā, *m.*, *used in opposition to* girl = čeḍuñ.

Malediction, *s.* širāp, -pā, *m.*; *vlg.* māldisāuñ, -săvā, *n.*, *fr.*

Malefactor, *s.* gunyāukār, -rā, *m.* = *l.* a guilty man; ăkrămātso mănis, -nšā, *m.* = *l.* a man of crimes; vāiṭ kărtolo; ănnāyātso mănis, -nšā, *m.* = *l.* an unjust man; khoṭo mănis = *l.* a wicked man.

Malevolence, *s.* vāiṭ khuši, -še, *f.*; niskutsār, -rā, *m.* = envy; mosór, -srā, *m.* = envy; khoṭepoṇ, -ṇā, *n.* = *l.* wickedness.

Malice, *s.* vikăṭāi, -ye, *f.*, *from* vik = poison, *fg.*; vāitpoṇ, -ṇā, *n.*, *e.g.* m. of sin; khoṭepoṇ, -ṇā, *n.* = *l.* wickedness; nāḍgepoṇ, -ṇā, *n.* = *l.* cunning; mosór, -srā, *m.* = *l.* hatred (envy).

Malicious, *a.* vāiṭ, *etc.*; *see* **Malice.**

Malign, *v.* bădlām ghāl = *l.* put calamities; tsāḍio sāng = *l.* say detractions.

Malignity, *s.* khoṭepoṇ, -ṇā, *n.*, *or* vāiṭpoṇ, -ṇā, *n.*; *see* **Malice.**

Malleable, *a.* móu = *l.* soft.

Mallow, *s.* peṭarlezāḍ, -ḍā, *n.*

Maltreat, *a.* kăṣṭāi, *c. v. of* kăṣṭa; bóng kăr; dăgdāi, *c. v.* = *l.* cause suffering; niṣṭurāi tsălăi, (*2nd Loc.*) = *l.* proceed cruelly.

Maltreatment, *s.* kăṣṭouṇeñ, -ṇeā, *n.*; dăgd, *m. pl.*, *or* dăgdouṇeñ, -ṇeā, *n.*; niṣṭurāi, -ye, *f.*

Man, *s.* 1. mănis, -nšā, *m.*, *or* mănis, -nše, *f. for* a woman (*pl.* mănšañ *for* women).

2. dādlo, -leā, *m.* = male (dādlo mănis).

3. āḷ, -ḷā, *m.* (a cooly).

Mănis *as meaning* mankind *has* mănšañ *in the plural.*

A grown-up man = mānāi, -yā, *m.* (*also* a cooly).

Man, *v.* 1. mănis di = *l.* give men.

2. rāk = *l.* guard, *e. g.* m. the walls.

Man-of-war, *s.* lāmb āgbóṭ, -ṭi, *f.* = *l.* a long steamer; zuzatāruñ, -rvā, *n.* = *l.* a ship of war.

Manacle, *see* **Handcuff.**

Manage, *v.* tsălăi, *e.g.* men *or* beasts; *also* m. a business.

Manageable, *a.* tsălăisārko.

Management, *s.* 1. kārkhāno, -neā, *m.* = *l.* administration; tsălouṇeñ, -ṇeā, *n.*

2. hikmăt, -ti, *f.* = *l.* artifice.

Manager, *s.* tsălăitolo; mostak, -kā, *n.* = *l.* a head, *fg.*; kārkhāneagār, -rā, *m.*, *e.g.* of tiles, *etc.*

Manchil, *s.* mačil, -lā, *n.*

Mane, *s.* māneče kès, -sañ, *pl. m.* = *l.* hair of the neck.

Mange, *s.* 1. khoroz, -rji, *f.*

2. ruñ, ruvā, *n.* (corrupted sores).

Manger, *s*, khāvoṇ, khāuṇi, *f.*

Mango, *s.* āmbo, -beā, *m.*

Mangosteen, *s.* binḍ, -ḍā, *n.*

Mango-stone, *s.* pār, -ri, *f.*

Manhood, *s.* mănšepoṇ, -ṇā, *n.*;

vodli pirāi, -ye, *f.* = *l.* grown-up age.

Mania, *s.* pisepoṇ, -ṇā, *n.*

Manifest, *a.* ugto = *l.* open, *fg.*; sošṭ = *l.* distinct, evident; părgăṭ = *l.* public; *rs. into* kăḷtā = is known, *or* kăḷit āsā.

Manifest, *v.* părgăṭ (*or* ugto) kăr; dākăi = *l.* show.

Manifestation, *s.* părgăṭouṇeñ, -ṇeā, *n.*; gurtu̥, -tā, *m.*

Manifesto, *s.* istyār, -rā, *m.*; *see* **Advertisement.**

Manifold, *a.* 1. tsăḍ doḍo; săbār pāuṭi tsăḍ.
2. vegḷo = *l.* different; *see* **Various.**

Manipulate, *v.* 1. hātāniñ āpòḍ = touch with the hands.
2. hātāniñ kăr = make with the hands.

Mankind, *s.* mănšekuḷ, -ḷā, *n.*

Manliness, *s.* dhăir, -rā, *n.* = *l.* courage; vīrpoṇ, -ṇā, *n.* = *l.* heroism, *n. c.*

Manly, *a.* dhăiravont; vīrātso = *l.* heroic, *n. c.*

Manner, *s.* 1. jinos, -nsā, *m.*; vāṭ, -ṭe, *f.* = *l.* a way, *fg.*; mārog, -rgā, *m.* = a road, *fg.*; părmāṇe = *l.* in the manner (*not used in the nom.*), *e. g.* fāvoteā p. = in due manner; nămuno, -neā, *m.* = *l.* a model, *fg.*; bhās, -se, *f.* = *l.* language, *fg.*
2. măryād, -di, *f.* = *l.* decency.
3. sovói, -ye, *f.* = *l.* custom; poriñ *or* bări (*used as postp.*), *e. g.* teā p. = thus.

Manœuvre, *s.* 1. kovăt, -tā, *n.* (a military exercise).
2. hikmăt, -ti, *f.* = *l.* artifice; čămătkār, -rā, *m.* (*or n.*)

Manse, *s.* pādričeñ ghăr, -rā, *n.*

Mantle, Mantua, *s.* vól, -li, *f.* (a white veil) = the m. of native women.

Manual, *a.* hātāntso; 'm. work = hātānčeñ kām, -mā, *n.*, *or* hātānči kăsăb, -sbe, *f.*'

Manual, *s.* hātpustak, -kā, *n.*

Manufactory, *s.* kārkhāno, -neā, *m.*; kărčeñ ghăr, -rā, *n.* = *l.* house for making, *with the name of* the article manufactured.

Manufacture, *s.* 1. hātān kărčeñ kām, -mā, *n.*
2. hātān kelli văstu̥, -tu, *f.*

Manufacture, *v.* 1. kăr.
2. tăyār kăr = *l.* make ready.

Manure, *s.* šèṇ, -ṇā, *n.* = *l.* cow-dung; iṭ, -ṭā, *m.*; sāreñ, -reā, *n.* = *Lat. laetamen,* dung; sóp, -pā, *m.* = leaves for manuring; gobór, -brā, *m.* = *l.* ashes, *which are used as* manure.

Manure, *v.* sāreñ ghāl.

Manuscript, *s.* hātān boreilleñ (pustak, -kā, *n.*).

Many, *a.* săbār; zāite; tsăḍ; *all these words are used also in sing.*

As m. as = kitlo...titlo, *or only* titlo (*see* Gram. p. 240).
How m. = kitle: so many = title.

Map, *s.* buiññākṣa, -ṣe, *f.*; gāñvaññākṣa, -ṣe, *f.*

Mar, *see* **Spoil, Disconcert.**

Marasmus, *s.* khevād, -di, *f.*

Marauder, *s.* luṭigār, -rā, *m.*; desvoṭ kărtso (*var.* desvăṭ k.) = *l.* making devastation.

Marble, *s.* 1. *no pure Konkani word used*; *we may use the Mr.* sangamaravar, -rā, *m.*
2. (*pl.*) guṭio, *pl. f.* (playing marbles), *from* guṭi, -ye, *f.*

March, *s.* poiṇ, -ṇā, *n.*

March, *v.* poiṇ kăr; tsăl = *l.* walk.

Mare, *s.* goḍi, -ye, *f.*

Margin, *s.* dèg, -ge, *f.*

Marginal, *a.* deger āsullo.

Marine, *a.* dăryātso *or* dăryāntlo.

Marine, *s.* tārvasipāi, -yā, *m.* = *l.* a soldier of a ship.

Mariner, *s.* tārvoṭi, -ṭiā, *m.*; khălāsi, -seā, *m.*

Maritime, *a.* dărya lāgsilo = *l.* being near to the sea; *see* **Marine.**

Mark, *s.* gurtụ, -tā, *m.*; *by the Neut. adj., e.g.* a mark of ignorance = neṇārpoṇāčeñ.

Mark, *v.* 1. gurtụ kăr = *l.* make a sign.
2. borăi = *l.* write; dākăi = *l.* show.
3. čint = *l.* think.
4. bhēd(ė) kăr = *l.* make distinction.
Make out = mēz (ė) = *l.* measure.

Market, *s.* pènṭ, -ṭe, *f.*

Marriage, *s.* kāzār, -rā, *n.*, *fr.*, *but in common use*; vivaha, -vā, *n.*, *or* lăgnụ, -nā, *n.*, *or* vărḍik (*var* vaḍik), -ke, *f.* (*H. K.*); matrimon, -nā, *m.*, *fr.* (*in catech. and eccl. mn.*)
Invitation to m. = vouḷik, -ke, *f.*
Celebrate a m. = kāzār kăr.

Marriageable, *a.* kāzārātso, *or* kāzārāprāyetso; savasini.

Married, *a.* kāzāri, *or* kāzār zāllo.

Marrow, *s.* (āḍāntlo) mendu, -dā, *m.*

Marry, *v.* kāzār kăr, *fr.* = give away in marriage; kāzār zā = *l.* get married, *Prs. Dat.*; rèspèr kăr (*corrup. of* 'receber') = perform the ceremony of marriage at the altar.

Marsh, *s.* tăḷeñ, -ḷeā, *n.*; mădăk, -kā, *n.*; čiklazāgo, -geā, *m.*

Marshal, *s.* mukhya foujiădhipăti, -ti, *m.*

Marshy, *a.* čiklātso.

Martial, *a.* zuzātso, *or* zuzasārko.

Martyr, *s. vlg.* mārtir, -rā, *m.* (-ri, *f.*), *fr.*; răgtasākṣigār, -rā, *m.* = *l.* a witness of blood.

Martyrdom, *s.* răgtasākṣ, -ṣi, *f.* = a witness of blood; răgtasăkšičeñ mòrn, -nā, *n.*; *vlg.* mārtirpoṇ, -ṇā, *n.*, *fr.*

Martyrology, *s.* răgtasākšigārānči păṭṭi, -ṭe, *f.*; mārtirañpăṭṭi, -ṭe, *f.*

Marvellous, *a.* ăjāpātso.

Masculine, *a.* 1. dhăirāvont = *l.* courageous.

2. pullinga = *l.* m. gender.

Mash, *s.* borsouṇeñ, -ṇeā, *n.*

Mask, *s.* vés, -sā, *m.*

Mask, *v.* 1. vés ghāl, *pr. fg.*

2. lipăi = *l.* conceal.

Masquerade, *s.* vésakhéḷ, -ḷā, *m.*

Mason, *s.* fātrāñmèst, -tā, *m.*

Mass, *s.* 1. mis, -sā, *m.* (*rl.*): 'high mass = kăntār mis'; 'low mass = răzār m.'

2. rās, -si, *f.* = *l.* a heap; rūpnātuḷli rās; zomo, -meā, *m.* = *l.* assemblage; '*en masse* = zomoun'.

Massacre, *v.* jivsiñ mār, *or bet.* khuni kăr.

Massacre, *s.* khuni, -ye, *f.*, *or* zomeākhuni = *l.* killing of a crowd.

Mass-book, *s.* misapustak, -kā, *n.*; *vlg.* misāl, -lā, *n.*, *fr.*

Massive, *a.* zăḍ; bhāri.

Mast, *s.* kuvo, -veā, *m.* (of a ship).

Master, *s.* 1. dhăni, -yā, *m.*, *e.g.* m. of the house (*Lat. dominus*); kărt, -tā, *m.*; khăvănd, -dā, *m.*; prăbhu, -bhu, *m.*

2. ghărkār, -rā, *m.* = *l.* a householder (*vlg.* husband).

3. mostak, -kā, *n.* = *l.* head, *fg.*

4. upădeši, -ši, *m.* = a teacher; ăiguḷ, -ḷā, *m.* (a teacher of low classes in village-schools); šeṇăi, -ṇăi, *m.* = *l.* a writer, *mn. also* a village master; *vlg.* mestri, -ri, *m.*, *fr.*, *or* māsṭar, -rā, *m.*, *fr.*

5. kārkhāneagār, -rā, *m.* = *l.* an administrator, director.

6. *fg.* motir āsullo (mănis) = *l.* being in (one's) mind.

7. ădhipăti, -ti, *m.* = *l.* a man of (public) authority.

8. āpṇăčer zăitvortolo = gaining victory against oneself; āpṇāk āḍ yeuntso = *l.* coming against oneself.

Be m. of a science = gunḍăi păriyānt zāṇā = *l.* knows till depth.

Master, *v.* 1. khālto kăr = make subject.

2. purto (-ti, -teñ) zāṇā = *l.* knows fully; boreñ somza = *l.* understands well; gunḍăi păriyānt zāṇā = *l.* knows up to depth.

Masticate, *v.* goḷăi; tsāb; dāntāniñ khāṇ mōḍ(ó) = *l.* break food with teeth, *n. c.*

Mastication, *s.* tsābṇeñ, -ṇeā, *n.*

Mat, *s.* māndri, -re, *f.*

Coir-mat = sumbāči māndri, -re, *f.*

Mat, *v.* vôḷ.

Match, *s.* 1. ujeāči kāḍi, -ye, *f.* = *l.* a stick of fire.

2. kāzārātso kărār, -rā, *m.* = *l.* agreement of marriage.

3. zóḍ, -ḍā, *m.* (equal), *e.g.* not even N. is a m. for them; iḍ, -ḍā, *n.*

Match-box, *s.* ujeāči pèṭ, -ṭe, *f.*

Mate, *s.* sāngāti -tiā, *m.* = *l.* a companion.

Material, *s.* jinos, -nsā, *m.* = *l.* the manner, quality (ingredient); mòp, -pā, *n.* (the wooden material of a house); *as in the sent.* 'Of what material has this house been built?' *often rs. into Instr. or Genit.*; *sometimes* sāmān = *l.* article *may suffice;* sāmbār, -rā, *m.* = the materials for making curry.

Material, *a.* 1. kuḍitso = *l.* of body, *fg.* M. *as opposed to* spiritual, *has no exact Konk. equivalent; a Sans. or Mr. word, as expressing the idea of a false religion, is not suitable, so perhaps the best course will be to use* kuḍitso, *and extend its usual meaning. When* material *is used in reference to* wind *and similar objects, it may perhaps be translated by* kuḍitsoso, *or* murtitso (*perh. ex. Sans. word*).

2. bhāri = *l.* important.

Materialism, *s. has no equivalent in Konkani; the Mr. Cn.* dehātmăvād, -dā, *m. may serve.*

Materials, *s.* sāmān, -nā, *m.*

Maternal, *a.* māyetso *or* āvoitso.

Mathematical, *a.* părimāṇātso.

Mathematics, *s.* părimāṇavidya, -ye, *f.* = *l.* science of quantity; găṇitašāstru̥, -rā, *n.*; găṇitavidya, -ye, *f.*, *Mr.*, *Cn. Sans.*

Matins, *s.* ophis, -phsā, *m.*; săkāḷinčeñ grāṇeñ, -ṇeā, *n.*

Matricide, *s.* 1. āvoikhuni, -ye, *f.*

2. āvoikhuniyegār, -rā, *m.*

Matriculate, *v.* păṭṭer borăi = *l.* write on the list; (vidyesāḷek) meḷăi = *l.* aggregate (into a college).

Matriculation, *s.* (vidyesāḷek) meḷouṇeñ, -ṇeā, *n.*

Matrimony, *see* **Marriage.**

Matron, *s.* āji, -je, *f.*

Matter, *s.* 1. *As opposed to* spirit *it cannot be exactly translated into Konkani: the Sans.* mūrti, -ti, *f.*, *or* kuḍiči văstu̥, -tu, *f.* = *l.* corporal (material) thing, *or only* kuḍ = body, *fg.*, *may be used.*

2. irādo, -deā, *m.* = *l.* object, *e.g.* of a science.

3. văstu̥, -tu, *f.* = *l.* a thing; *by the G.*; *see* Gram. P. IV. ch. ii. Art. ii.; kām, -mā, *n.* = *l.* business, thing.

4. bhār, -rā, *m.* = *l.* gravity, *fg.* (importance).

5. pu, -puvā, *m.*, răši, -še, *f.* = pus.

What is the m. = (tuka) kiteñ?

No m. = voḍ năiñ; čintanāñ.

Matter, *v.* āločen kăr = *l.* make opinion (give to think); gărz āsā = *l.* want is; tsăḍ lāgtā = *l.* much is attached.

It does not m. = āločen kări-nāñ, bisāt nāñ.

Mattock, *s.* pikās, -sā, *n.*, *fr.*; kudoḷ, -ḍḷi, *f.*

Mattress, *s.* găzḍi, -ḍe, *f.*

Mature, *a.* piko, *pr. fg.*, *e.g.* m. man.

Mature, *v.* pikăi, *c. v. pr. fg.*

Maturely, *ad.* boreñ čintun = *l.* after having thought well.

Maturity, *s.* 1. bud, -di, *f.* = *l.* wisdom (of mind).

2. *rs. into* voḍlo = *l.* grown up.

Maudlin, *a.* 1. ămāl zāllo *or* ămā-lātso; soro piyello; bebdo, *fr.*

2. dăḍḍo = *l.* dull.

Maund, *s.* móṇ, -ṇā, *m.* (a measure = 48 seers, *or for* jaggery = 40 seers).

Maw, *s.* gānzo, -jeā, *m.* = *Lat. ingluvies*, the crop of a bird.

Maxim, *see* **Aphorism.**

May, *v. By the Pot. Mood; see* Gram.

May be = zāunk puro; yekā-deveḷa *or* yekāveḷa.

Maze, *see* **Entangle.**

Meadow, *s.* lăččil, -lā, *n.*; tăṇā-čeñ măidān, -nā, *n.*; tsorova-zāgo, -geā, *m.* = a grazing place.

Meagre, *a.* 1. bārik = *l.* thin.

2. suko = *l.* dry, *fg.*

3. bhou lān, thoḍo = little.

Meal, *s.* 1. jevāṇ, jeuṇā, *n.* (dinner).

2. piṭ, -ṭā, *n.* = flour.

Mean, *s.* hăḷt, -tā, *n.* = *l.* moderation.

In the m. = modeñ.

Mean, *a.* 1. modlo, *or* modeñ āsullo.

2. uṇo, hălko, kirkoḷ = low.

3. čillăr = *l.* trifling.

4. imṭo = *l.* stingy.

In the m. time = itlea bităr.

Mean, *v.* 1. sevoṭ āsā = *l.* aim is; čint = *l.* think.

2. ărth āsā = *l.* meaning is, *G. M.*; gurtụ āsā = *l.* sign is; dākăi = *l.* show; somzon yetā = *l.* understood comes.

3. móṇ *or* mhuṇ = *l.* say, call, *e.g.* ākā kiteñ moṇtāt? = how do you call this? (what does it m.?); *see* **Imply.**

Meaning, *s.* 1. ărth, -thā, *m.*

2. sevóṭ, -ṭā, *m.* = *l.* aim; *rs. into v.*

Meanness, *s.* 1. uṇepoṇ, -ṇā, *n.*; kirkoḷāi, -ye, *f.* (low condition).

2. imṭepoṇ, -ṇā, *n.* = stinginess.

Means, *s.* upāi, -yā, *m.*

By no m. = kăseñi nākā; k. năiñ.

Measles, *s.* ururеñ, -reā, *n.*

Measurable, *a.* māpātso, *or* mezi-sārko.

Measure, *s.* 1. māp, -pā, *n.*; hăḷt, -tā, *n.* (right measure, proportion); mezāp, -zpā, *n.*; zòk, -kā, *n.*, *e.g.* of a dress to be made.
2. āločen, -ni, *f.* = *l.* opinion, *e.g.* take measures = āločen kăr, upāi kāṇe; upāi, -yā, *m.* = *l.* means.
In some m. = yeke jinsiñ.
See App. to Konk.-Engl. Dictionary.

Measure, *v.* zòk ghe = *l.* take m., *e.g.* of a dress to be made; mēz(é); vistār = *l.* be extended.
M. out = mēz (ė).

Measured, *a.* vāzbi = *l.* proper; hăḷt āsullo = *l.* moderate.

Measurer, *s.* māpeli, -liā, *m.* (*var.* māpāri, -riā, *m.*).

Meat, *s.* mās, -sā, *n.*

Mechanic, *s.* āčāri, -riā, *m.*

Mechanics, *s.* čākrañsāmārthi, -the, *f.*

Mechanism, *s.* čăkrụ, -rā, *n.* (*or* tsăkr); hikmăt, -ti, *f.* = *l.* artifice.

Medal, *s.* ārluk, -ke, *f.*, *fr.*

Meddle, *v.* rig = *l.* enter; *see* **Interfere.**

Mediate, *v.* mădesti zā = *l.* become intercessor; pănčāyetdār kăr = *l.* make as arbitrator; mădesti zāun fuslāi = *l.* by arbitrating appease.

Mediate, *a.* modlo: 'm. cause = modleñ kārāṇ'; *opp. to* lāgsileñ, *or* lāgčeñ (approximate) *and* poisileñ (remote) kārāṇ.

Mediately, *ad.* dusrea vorviñ = through another; *or* prăspăr; dusrea mukhāntrụ.

Mediation, *s.* vinot, *or* măzăt, -ti, *f.* (*rl.*): 'through his m. = to mădest zāun, *or* tāče vorviñ'.

Mediator, *s.* mădesti, -ti, *m.*

Medical, *a.* 1. boro kărtso, *or* guṇ kărtso = curing.
2. voizātso = *l.* of the physician; văidikātso = m. treatment.
Be under m. treatment = voiza khāl āsā.

Medicate, *v.* vokāt di = *l.* give medicine; boro kăr.

Medicinal, *see* **Medical.**

Medicine, *s.* 1. voizapoṇ, -ṇā, *n.* (science); voktānči vidya, -ye, *f.* (science).
2. vokāt, -ktā, *n.*, *pr. fg.*

Mediocre, *a.* sumār (*or* sumārātso).

Mediocrity, *s.* sumār thăr, -rā, *m.* = *l.* middle kind.

Meditate, *v.* 1. niyāḷ, *or* niyāḷ kăr; dhyān kăr.
2. boreñ čint = *l.* think well.
3. ševoṭ āsā = *l.* aim is.

Meditation, *s.* niyāḷ, -ḷā, *m.*; tòp, -pā, *n.* = contemplation; dhyān, -nā, *n.*

Medium, *s.* 1. modli văstụ, -tu, *f.* = *l.* a thing in the middle.

2. dălāl, -lā, *m.* = *l.* an agent.

Medley, *s.* gusăp, -spā, *n.* = *l.* confusion.

Meek, *a.* boḷo; līn, *n. c.*

Meekness, *s.* boḷepoṇ, -ṇā, *n.*; šāntipoṇ, -ṇā, *n.*; movāḷpoṇ, -ṇā, *n.* = *l.* tenderness.

Meet, *v.* mèḷ, *Sb. Dat.*, *used in nearly all the senses of the Engl.* meet.

Meeting, *s. vlg.* zunt, -tā, *m.*, *fr.*; mēḷ(ê), -ḷā, *m.*; săbha, -bhe, *f.* = a council; kuṭ, -ṭā, *n.* (a secret, illicit m.)

Melancholy, *s.* khănt, -ti, *f.*; duk, -ki, *f.*; sankirnāi, -ye, *f.*

Melancholy, *a.* khăntiṣṭ; čintest; dukhest; *rs.* lāsulleñ tòṇḍ = *l.* burnt face, *fg.*

Mellifluous, *a.* suādik, *or* movabăriso; movātso.

Mellow, *a.* pikots = *l.* very ripe (truly ripe); mou = *l.* soft.

Melodious, *a.* gāyānātso; suādik = *l.* sweet, *fg.*

Melody, *s.* gāyān, -nā, *n.*; gāyānajinos, -nsā, *m.* = *l.* quality of music; tāḷeātso jinos, -nsā, *m.* = *l.* quality of voice; *see* **Harmony.**

Melon, *s.* 1. čipaṭ, -pṭā, *n.*

2. (water-m.) kāḷing, -ḷngā, *n.*

Melt, *v.* 1. kăḍāi, *c. v. of* kăḍ, *n. v.*; kărgi, *c. v. of* kărga, *n. v.*; *vlg.* udāk kăr.

2. movāḷāi = *l.* make soft, *c. v. of* movāḷ.

Member, *s.* 1. sāndo, -deā, *m.*, *pr.*, *fg.*

2. *fg.* vānṭo, -ṭeā, *m.* = *l.* a part, *e.g.* m. of a sentence.

Membrane, *s.* kāt, -ti, *f.* = *l.* skin.

Memorable, *a.* nāvāḍdik = *l.* famous (*used esp. of* things); nāvāḍgo = *l.* famous (*esp. of* persons); nāuñgello = *l.* of name; ugḍās kărtso = *l.* to be remembered.

Memorial, Memorandum, *s.* 1. ugḍās kărči čīṭ, -ṭi, *f.* = *l.* a note for remembering; ugḍās, -sā, *m.*; yādāst, -tā, *m.*

2. ărji, -je, *f.* = *l.* a petition.

Memory, *s.* ugḍās, -sā, *m.*; mót, -ti, *f.* (faculty); yād, -dā, *m.* (*H. K.*).

In the m. of our fathers = āmčeañ mālgoḍeānčea kālār.

Menace, *v.* besṭāi; bheñ ghāl, *n. c.*; *or bet.* bhiyeunk lāi.

Menace, *s.* besṭāuṇeñ, -ṇeā, *n.* (*or* -ṇi, -ṇe, *f.*)

Menagery, *s.* monzātiñsāl, -lā, *n.*; monzātiñzomo, -meā, *m.*

Mend, *v.* săma kăr = *l.* make right; durust kăr; boro kăr = *l.* make good, improve; *see* **Improve.**

Mendicant, *s.* izmòlmāgtolo; dubḷo *or* durbăḷo (mănis) = *l.* a poor (man); bhikāri, -riā, *m.*

Mendicity, *s.* durbăḷkāi, -ye, *f.*

Menial, *a.* 1. tsăkretso = *l.* of service.
2. hălko = *l.* low.

Menstruous, *a.* moineamoineātso.

Mental, *a.* mótitso; ătmea višyānt āsullo; *rs.* ătmea visyānt = *l.* about the soul; ătmeātso = *l.* of the soul.

Mention, *v.* ugḍās kăr, *G. M.* = *l.* make memory; ulăi = *l.* speak; nāuñ moṇ = *l.* say the name of, *G. N.*

Mention, *s.* ugḍās, -sā, *m.*

Mentor, *see* **Guide.**

Mercantile, *a.* vyāpārātso.

Mercenary, *s.* 1. lonts khātolo = *l.* eating bribes.
2. kūl vortolo = *l.* taking payment, *or* kulkār, -rā, *m.*; bāḍeāk kāṇeillo = *l.* a hireling.

Merchandise, *s.* 1. vyār, -rā, *m.*, *vlg.* yār = small things to be sold.
2. vyāpār, -rā, *m.* = saleable articles, *and* trade.

Merchant, *s.* vyāpāri, -riā, *m.*; sāukār, -rā, *m.*

Merciful, *a.* kākuḷtitso, *or* kākuḷdār (*this 2nd is also a noun*); dăyāḷ = kind; līn, *or* boḷo = *l.* meek.

Merciless, *a.* niš̩ṭur; mhāru = cruel; kākuḷtnātullo.

Mercilessness, *s.* niš̩ṭurāi, -ye, *f.*; mhārupoṇ, -ṇā, *n.*; nākākuḷt, -ti, *f.*

Mercurial, *a.* tsurk = *l.* active; ušār = *l.* lively.

Mercy, *s.* kākuḷt, -ti, *f.*; birmot, -ti, *f.*; dăya, -ye, *f.* = *l.* kindness.

Mere, *a. rs.* mātrụ = *l.* only, *or* făkăt; beš̩ṭo, *e.g.* m. water = baji; *by* -ts (*emph.*)

Merge, *v.* buḍăi, *c. v. of* buḍ, *n. v.*

Meridian, *s.* donpārāñmănḍăḷ, -ḷā, *n.*, *n. c.*; donpārāñgīṭ, -ṭā, *m.*

Meridian, *a.* donpārāntso = *l.* of midday.

Merit, *s.* puneñ, -neā, *n.*, *or* pun, -nā, *n.*; punefóḷ, -ḷā, *m.*

Merit, *v.* făvo kărn ghe = *l.* making worthy receive; făvozāun ghe = *l.* becoming worthy receive; făvo zā, *e.g.* mākā inām f. zātā = I m. a prize.

Meritorious, *a.* punevont.
Make m. = făvo kăr = *l.* make due.

Merry, *a.* 1. khušāl.
2. češ̩ṭāyetso = *l.* funny.

Merry-andrew, *see* **Jester.**

Mess, *s.* 1. jevāṇ, jeuṇā, *n.*
2. *vlg. for* m. *in the mn. of* food set on the table at one time, băga *is used*, *e.g.* kitleā băgānčeñ. . . . ? = how many kinds of. . . ?
3. jevāṇ kāṇetolo = a person taking food at; *vlg.* phăngtin bostolo = *l.* sitting in a row, *as is a custom of the country.*
4. gusăp, -spā, *n.* = *l.* confusion.

Mess, *v.* mèzkhānānt jéu; teāts mèzār bòs = *l.* sit at the same table.

Message, *s.* 1. răvāneñ, -neā, *n.*; hukum, -kme, *f.* = *l.* an order.

2. vărdi, -de, *f.*, kăbār, -re, *f.* =news; vărtamān, -nā, *n.* = *l.* an advertisement.

Messenger, *s.* 1. dūt, -tā, *m.* = an ambassador; harakāri, -ri, *m.*; răvāni, -niā, *m.* (any person sent by another).

2. pedo, -deā, *m.* = *l.* a courier.

Mess-house, *s.* mèzkhān, -nā, *n.*

Messmate, *s.* (mèzā-) sāngāti, -tiā, *m.*

Metal, *s.* lōha, -hā, *n.* (*in Mr.* = iron), *n. c.*; *bet.* dhāt, -tā, *m.* (*in Mr.* = metal, *but used fg. for* strength); tāmbeñtāmbāṇ, -ṇā, *n.*

Metamorphosis, *s.* (rupa-) bădlāp, -pā, *n.*

Metaphor, *s.* sămănd-utăr, -trā, *n.* = *l.* related word; sămănd-ărth, -thā, *m.* = *l.* related meaning.

Metaphorical, *a.* sămănd-ărthātso: *sometimes only* sămănd *in composition*, *or* sămănd-āsullo, *or* sămăndi.

Metaphysics, *s.* săimbāpeleñ šāstrụ, -trā, *n.*; săimbabhāileñ šāstrụ, -trā, *n.*

Meteor, *s.* 1. neketrụ, -rā, *n.*; *or the Mr.* ulka, -ke, *f.*

2. ākāšātso čămătkār, -rā, *m.*

Methinks, *v.* distā = *l.* appears.

Method, *s.* krăm, -mā (*vlg.* kărm), *n.* = *l.* order; jinos, -nsā, *m.*; rīt, -ti, *f.*; *see* **Manner.**

Methodic, *a.* krămāntrụ = *l.* regular; *or* krămātso.

Metonymy, *s.* nāvābădlāp, -pā, *n.*

Metre, *s.* slók, -kā, *m.*

Metropolis, *s.* mukhya păṭāṇ, -ṭṇā, *n.*

Metropolitan, *s.* ārčbisp sāib, -bā, *m.*, *fr.* = *l.* lord archbishop.

Mew, *v.* 1. veḍeānt ghāl = *l.* put into an inclosure.

2. myāu kăr, (as a cat).

Miasm, *s.* vāiṭ vāreñ, -reā, *n.* = *l.* bad air (*vlg.*); vāiṭ ub, -be, *f.* = *l.* bad evaporation.

Microscope, *s.* kuskuṭ pòḷeunčeñ āid, -dā, *n.* = *l.* an instrument for seeing small objects.

Microscopic, *a.* bhou lān; kuskuṭ (*or* kuskuṭātso).

Midday, *s.* donpār, -rā, *m.*

Middle, *s.* modeñ, -deā, *n.*; māz, -zā, *m.*, *e.g.* of a circle, (any central point).

In the m. = modeñ.

Middle, *a.* 1. modlo, (which is in the middle).

2. sumār (*or* sumārātso) = *l.* mediocre.

M. class of people = sādārṇ āivozdār.

Middle-aged, *a.* modle pirāyetso.

Middling, *a.* sumār, *or* sumārātso.

Midnight, *s.* modeñrāt, -ti, *f.* (*vlg.* modeān, -ne, *f.*). 'At m. = modeñrātir'; 'from m. = modearāti thāun'; 'of m. = modeñrātitso'.

Midst, *s.* modeñ, -deā, *n.*

Midwife, *s.* voijiṇ, -ṇi, *f.*

Mien, *s.* tònḍ, -ḍā, *n.* = face; rūp, -pā, *n.* = form; tsāro, -reā, *m.* = look, appearance (*It. cera*).

Might, *s.* podvi, -ve, *f.*; bòḷ, -ḷā, *n.* = *l.* force, strength.

Mighty, *a.* podvetso, *or* podvedār, *or* podvi āsụllo.

Migrate, *v.* bhāirsăr; gădpār vetā = *l.* goes beyond the boundaries; *bet.* gădi bhāir vetā.

Milch, *a.* dudātso.

Mild, *a.* 1. nidān = *l.* calm.
2. sămādhānātso, *or* soukāsāyetso = *l.* peaceful, *also of* climate.
3. dăyāḷ = kind; šānti, boḷo, līn = meek.

Mildness, *s.* šāntipoṇ, -ṇā, *n.*, lenṭuvāi, -ye, *f.*; boḷepoṇ, -ṇā, *n.* = meekness; dăya, -ye, *f.* = kindness.

Mile, *s. vlg.* māil, -lā, *n.*; kosatrizāihiso, -seā, *m.* = $\frac{1}{3}$ kós. Three miles = kós, -sā, *m.*; vorāči vāṭ, -ṭe, *f.* = one hour's walk.

Militant, *a.* lăḍāi kărtso; zuztolo.

Military, *a.* foujitso.

Militate, *v.* āsā = *l.* is: 'm. for = pāsun āsā'; 'militate against = āḍ āsā'.

Milk, *s.* 1. dūdụ (*or* dud), -dā, *n.*
2. dăiñ, dăiyā, *n.* = coagulated m., *or* curds.

Milk, *v.* dūdụ kāḍ = *l.* draw milk.

Milk-man, *s.* kauḍigār, -rā, *m.*

Mill, *s.* 1. vāṭtso fātor, -trā, *m.* = *l.* a stone for grinding; vān, -nā, *n.*
2. ghāṇo, -ṇeā, *m. used esp. for grinding cocoanuts and extracting oil.*

Milleped, *s.* koṭārli, -le, *fg.*

Millet, *s.* zăndḷo, -ḷeā, *m.*

Million, *s.* dhā lāk = *l.* ten lacs.

Mimic, *a.* năklañ kărtso = *l.* making copies, *fg.*

Mince, *v.* kuḍkeān kuḍke kăr; tsātsāi = *l.* chop.

Mind, *s.* 1. mót, -ti, *f.*; mòn, -nā, *n.* (*Mr.* mănă); ginyān, -nā, *n.*; somzikāi, -ye, *f.* = *l.* understanding.
2. āločen, -ni, *f.* = *l.* opinion.
3. khuši, -še, *f.* = *l.* wish.

Mind, *v.* 1. čint = *l.* think.
2. zătăn kăr, *G. F.* = *l.* make care; lăkṣa kăr: 'do not mind = lăkṣa kărnākā'; 'I do not m. it = bisāt nāñ = *l.* I have no care'.

Mindful, *a.* ugḍās kărtso.

Mindless, *a.* 1. ugḍāsnātullo = not remembering.
2. zāgrutkāinātullo, tsātrāinātullo = not attentive, careless.

Mine, *s.* bāngārakhăṇi, -ye, *f.* = *l.* a ditch of gold.

Mine, *v.* (bāngār) kónḍ.

Mine, *a.* mozo; *see* Gram. P. II. ch. iii.

Mineral, *s.* *has no pure Konkani equivalent; Sans.* dhātu, -tā, *m.*, *or* lōha, -hā, *n.* = *l.* metal.

Mineralogy, *s.* dhātuvidya, -ye, *f.*

Mingle, *v.* meḷăi; borsi = *l.* mix.

Miniature, *s.* *approx.* lān rūp, -pā, *n.*, *or* lān diṣṭirūp; lān ākārārūp.

Minion, *s.* ăpurbāyetso = *l.* loved; dost, -tā, *m.* = *l.* a favourite.

Minister, *s.* 1. măntri, -ri, *m.*, *e. g.* of a state.
2. moṇiyāri, -riā, *m.* (of the church).
3. tsākor, -krā, *m.* = *l.* a servant; noukór, -rā, *m.*

Minister, *v.* tsākri kăr, *or* seva tsākri kăr, *G. F.*

Ministerial, *a.* 1. măntritso.
2. moṇiyāritso.
3. tsākretso; *see* **Minister.**

Ministry, *s.* 1. seva, -ve, *f.*
2. măntripoṇ, -ṇā, *n.*
3. moṇiyāripoṇ, -ṇā, *n.*; *see* **Minister.**

Minor, *a.* 1. uṇo = *l.* inferior.
2. uṇe prāyetso = of inferior age; prāinātullo = *l.* of no age.

Minority, *s.* uṇi pirāi, -ye, *f.*

Mint, *s.* 1. ortalāuñ, -lāvā, *m.* (a plant).
2. tanksāḷ, -ḷi, *f.* = the place where money is coined.

Minute, *s.* *vlg.* minut, -tā, *m.*; nimiš, -šā, *n.*; kṣăṇ, -ṇā, *n.*, khiṇ, -ṇā, *n.*, ghăḍi, -ye, *f.* = a moment.

Minute, *a.* 1. bhou bārik, *or* bh. lān; čillăr = *l.* trifling.
2. sārko = *l.* exact.

Minute-hand, *s.* kānṭo, -ṭeā, *m.*; voḍlo kānṭo, -ṭeā, *m.*

Minuteness, *s.* 1. bhou lān văstu̧, -tu, *f.* = *l.* a very little thing.
2. bārikāi, -ye, *f.*

Minutiæ, *s.* lān tăpsil, -le, *f.* = *l.* small details; lān vivor, -rā, *m.*

Miracle, *s.* 1. ătsăriyeñ, -yeā, *n.*; ăjāp, -pā, *n.* = *l.* wonder, astonishment (*fg. mn.*); ăjāpāči kărni, -ne, *f.* = *l.* a wonderful action.
2. čămătkār, -rā, *m.* = a wonderful thing; vizmit văstu̧, -tu, *f.*

Miraculous, *a.* ăjāpātso.

Mire, *s.* ubir, -brā, *m.*

Mirror, *s.* ārso, -seā, *m.*

Misanthrope, *s.* sāngāt kānṭāḷtso = *l.* abhorring society.

Misanthropy, *s.* sāngātiākānṭāḷo, -ḷeā, *m.*

Misbehave, *v.* ăumăryādin tsăl.

Misbehaviour, *s.* ăumăryādiči tsāl, -li, *f.*

Misscarriage, *see* **Abortion.**

Miscarry, *v.* 1. voḷăi, *c. v. of* voḷ, *n. v.*; *vlg.* gărb kāḍ.
2. *neg. form of* jik = succeed.

N. B. The words beginning with **Mis-** *signifying* **error, defect,** *and* **the like,** *not put down here, are to be translated in the same manner as* **Misprint,** *viz. by prefixing* **tsukon = mistaking** *or* **mis-,** *to the compounded word.*

3. *neg. form of* pāu = *l.* arrive, *e.g.* a letter; tsuk = *l.* fail.

Miscellaneous, *a.* săbār thărāntso; thără thărāntso; borsillo = *l.* mixed.

Miscellany, *s.* borsouṇeñ, -ṇeā, *n.* = *l.* mixture, *or rs. into a.*

Mischief, *s.* 1 tănṭo, -ṭeā, *m. used esp. in pl.*

2. năşṭ, -ṭā, *m.* = *l.* loss, harm; kēḍ, -ḍā, *m.*

3. ăkmān, -nā, *m.* = *l.* offence.

Mischievous, *a.* 1. tănṭălmāri; pokri.

2. luksānătso = *l.* hurtful.

Misconduct, *s.* pāḍ năḍteñ, -teā, *n.*; pāḍ tsāl, -li, *f.*; beābru, -brā, *m.* = *l.* no character; gunyāuñ, -yāvā, *m.* = *l.* a fault.

Misconstrue, *v.* ărth bădăl = *l.* change meaning.

Miser, *a.* surāti; imṭo (*stronger than* surāti).

Miserable, *a.* kirkoḷ; dubḷo.

Misery, *s.* 1. kirkoḷāi, -ye, *f.* = wretchedness.

2. durboḷkāi, -ye, *f.* = *l.* poverty; bikepoṇ, -ṇā, *n.* = *l.* beggary, *n. c.*

3. kăşṭ, -ṭā, *m.* = *l.* pain; vignu, -nā, *n.*; dăgd, -dāñ, *pl. m.*; dăḷdirpoṇ, -ṇā, *n.*

Misfortune, Mishap, *s.* ădruşṭ, -ṭā, *n.*; nirbhāgipoṇ, -ṇā, *n.* (*var.* nirbhăg, -gā, *n.*); ăpāḍ, -ḍā, *m.*

Misinform, *v.* fóṭkireo kobro ḍi; fóṭkiri ăbiprāi di.

Mislay, *v.* bhāir pòḍ = *l.* fall out, be lost.

Mislead, *v.* fóṭāi *or* mōs(ó) kăr = *l.* deceive; tsukon pòḍāi = = *l.* cause to fall erring; tsukăi = *l.* cause to err.

Misprint, *v.* tsukon chāpo ghāl.

Mispronounce, *v.* tsukon utsār.

Misrepresent, *v.* tsukon kăḷāi; fóṭoun săng.

Miss, *s.* sāibiṇ, -ṇi, *f.*; *see* **Lady.**

Miss, *v.* 1. tsuk, *n. v.*: 'I missed mass = mis tsukloñ'; 'I missed the mark = nōṭ(ó) tsuklo'; *neg. of* āsā: 'one book is missing = yek pustak nāñ'; khăl, *e.g.* (mākā) mis khălleñ.

2. sóḍ = let pass.

3. ăsā āsā = *l.* desire (want) is.

Missal, *s.* misăčeñ pustak, -kā, *n.*

Misshappen, *a.* vidrup = *l.* without form.

Missile, *see* **Arrow.**

Mission, *s.* 1. dhăḍāp, -ḍpā, *n. or* dhăḍneñ, -neā, *n.*

2. răvāneñ, -neā, *n.* = *l.* message; dūtpoṇ, -ṇā, *n.*

3. dūt, *pl. m.* = ambassadors.

Missionary, *s. vlg.* missionār, -rā,

m., *or* pādri, -ri, *m.*; šāstra dūt, -tā, *m.* = a messenger of religion.

Misspell, *v.* tsukon borăi.

Misstatement, *s.* fóṭkireñ sāngṇeñ -ṇeā, *n.*

Mist, *s.* 1. duuri, -re, *f.*
2. *fg.* kāḷok, -kā, *m.* = *l.* darkness.

Mistake, *v.* tsuk, *e.g.* the way.

Mistake, *s.* tsuk, -ki, *f.*; gunyāuñ, -yāvā, *m.* = *l.* fault (moral); ăib, -bā, *n.* (phys. fault); ăprād, -dā, *m.* = *Lat. culpa.*

Mister, *s.* sāib, -bā, *m.*; *see* **Lord.**

Mistress, *s.* 1. sāibiṇ, -ṇi, *f.*; *see* **Lady.**
2. mestiṇ, -ṇi, *f.*, *fr.* = a female teacher; upădešiṇ, -ṇi, *f.*; sikāiteli, -le, *f.*
3. dhăniṇ, -ṇi, *f.* = a house-wife.

Misty, *a.* 1. duuretso.
2. kāḷokātso.

Misunderstand, *v.* tsukon somza.

Misuse, *v.* nisprăyóg kăr.

Mite, *s.* *approx.* kīḍ, -ḍi, *f.* = a small worm.

Mitigate, *etc. see* **Allay,** *etc.*

Mitre, *s.* (bispātso) tōpụ, -pā, *m.*; *vlg.* mitrụ, -rā, *m.*, *fr.*

Mitten, *s.* luñ, luvā, *n.*, *fr.*; hātamēi, -meyā, *m.*

Mix, *v.* borsi; meḷăi.

Mixture, *s.* meḷouṇeñ, -ṇeā, *n.*; mēḷ, -ḷā, *m.*; borsouṇeñ, -ṇeā, *n.*; borsāp, -pā, *n.* (*neut. mn*).

Mnemonics, *s.* ugḍās kărči sāmārthi, -the, *f.*

Moan, *see* **Groan.**

Mob, *s.* zomo, -meā, *m.*; khéṭ, -ṭi, *f.*; čalleñbilleñ, -leā, *n.*; pokreañzomo (*or* pokri zomo), -meā, *m.*

Mob, *v.* zomo kăr.

Mock, *v.* češṭāi kăr, *G. F.*; tomāse kăr = make jokes; hās = *l.* laugh; năklañ kăr = *l.* make copies, *fg.*; măskāri kăr; kebḍāi (*or* -ḍāyo) kăr = *l.* scorn; kheḷkuḷañ kăr; yeḍāi.

Mocking, *s.* yeḍāuṇeñ, -ṇeā, *n.*; kebḍāi, -ye, *f.* = scorn; češṭāi, -ye, *f.*, tomāso, -seā, *m.* = fun; kenḍneñ, -neā, *n.* = an offensive reproach; kheḷkuḷañ, *pl. n.*

Mode, *see* **Manner.**

Model, *s.* 1. nămuno, -neā, *m.*, *pr. fg.*, *e.g.* of virtue.
2. dēk(é), -ki, *f.* = *l.* example.

Model, *v.* kăr, *or* rūp di = *l.* give form.

Moderate, *a.* hăḷt āsullo = *l.* having moderation; sumār = *l.* mediocre; mădyăm; modlo = *l.* middle, *fg.*

Moderate, *v.* 1. tsălăi = *l.* govern, rule.
2. hāḷu kăr = *l.* make light; *see* **Allay.**

Moderation, *s.* hăḷt, -tā, *n.*

Modern, *a.* 1. novo = *l.* new.
2. novea kālātso = *l.* of new time; yeā kālātso = *l.* of this time.

Modest, *a.* niskăḷ; măryāditso.

Modesty, *s.* niskăḷāi, *or* niskăḷkāi, -ye, *f.*, *or* niskăḷpoṇ, -ṇā, *n.*; măryād, -di, *f.*; bhiḍa, -ḍe, *f.*

Modify, *v.* bădăl (bădăl = be modified), *or* bădăl kăr.

Modulate, *v.* (tāḷo) bădăl.

Moist, *a.* šeḷitso; bizăillo.

Moisten, *v.* bizăi; šeḷ kăr.

Moisture, *s.* šeḷ, -ḷi, *f.*; bizāp, -zpā, *n.*, *or* bizouṇeñ, -ṇeā, *n.*

Molar, *a.* *see* **Grinder, Tooth.**

Mole, *s.* 1. tsāmkuḷ, -ḷā, *m.* = a natural spot on the body.
2. kāṭ, -ṭā, *m.* = a dam.

Molecule, *s.* kuskuṭ, -ṭā, *n.*

Molest, *v.* 1. bezār kăr; kărkăr kăr = *l.* trouble; dós.
2. lāsăi = *l.* cause to burn; bhong kăr.

Molestation, *s.* bezārāi, -ye, *f.* *etc.*

Mollify, *v.* mou kăr.

Molten, *a.* kăḍăillo.

Moment, *s.* 1. bhār, -rā, *m.* = *l.* gravity, *fg.* importance.
2. kšăṇ, -ṇā, *n.*; fār, -rā, *m.* = *Lat. ictus*, a stroke; khiṇ, -ṇā, *n.* ghăḍi, -ye, *f.*; tăḍ, -ḍi, *f.*; tăṇ, -ṇi, *f.*, *e.g.* m. of death.

Momentum, *s.* bòḷ, -ḷā, *n.* = *l.* force.

Monarch, *s.* (sotăntrātso) rāi, -yā, *m.* = *l.* (independent) king, *or only* rāi, -yā, *m.*

Monarchy, *s.* rāzvoṭ, -ṭi, *f.*

Monastery, *s.* *vlg.* koñvent, -tā, *m.*, *fr.*; moṭ, -ṭā, *m.*, *H. K.*

Money, *s.* 1. duḍu, -ḍuā, *m.*; dirveñ, -veā, *n.* (much money); *vlg.* poise (*ex.* coins of 4 pies each); *vlg.* rupoi = *l.* rupees; bāngār, -rā, *m.* = *l.* gold.
2. nāṇeñ, -ṇeā, *n.* = *l.* a coin, *also* a golden piece, *or also* a coin = *Lat. 'denarius'*, *thus*: Judas sold J. C. for 30 'nāṇeānk'.
Ready m. = năgdi duḍu.

Money-bag, *s.* thăili, -le, *f.*

Money-changer, *s.* rupoi vāṭăitolo.

Monitor, *s.* 1. upădeši, -si, *m.*
2. tsuki kăḷăitolo, *or* tsuki sāngtolo.

Monk, *s.* frăd, -di, *m.*, *fr.*; vānavāsi, -si, *m.*, *or* *Mr.* moṭavāsi, -si, *m.* = *l.* an inhabitant of solitude, *or* of a monastery.

Monkey, *s.* mānkoḍ, -kḍā, *m.*

Monogamist, *s.* yeke ăstretso (dādlo, -leā, *m.*) = *l.* (the husband) of one wife; yeka potitso.

Monogamy, *s.* yekets ăstre kăḍčeñ vivāha, -hā, *n.*, *n. u.*, *or* yekăts potipoṇ, -ṇā, *n.*

Monogram, *s. l.* yékakšer, -rā, *n.*, *n. u.*

Monomania, *s.* *perh.* bhrăm, -mā, *n.*, *or* bhrānt, -ti, *f.* = *l.* illusion, *n. c.*

Monopolize, *v.* dărkāst kăr.

Monopoly, *s.* dărkāst, -tā, *m.*; gutto, -teā, *m.*

Monosyllabic, *a.* yekakšerātso, *Mr. Cn.*

Monosyllable, *s.* yekakšerašăbdu, -dā, *m.* (*Cn. Mr. Mal.*), *n. u.*; yekakšer, -rā, *n.*, *Mr.*

Monotonous, *a.* yekats tāḷeātso; yeka thărātso; yeka jinsātso; bezārāi kărtso.

Monotony, *s.* 1. yekats tāḷeātso jinos, -nsā, *m.*
2. *fg.* bezārāi, -ye, *f.*

Monsoon, *s.* pāus, -sā, *m.*, *or* pāusātso vēḷ(ė), -ḷā, *m.*, *or* p. kāl, -lā, *m.*, *or* pāusile dis, *pl. m.*

Monster, *s.* 1. vidrup văstu, *or* rūpnātulli văstu, -tu, *f.* = *l.* a thing without form.
2. rākkos, -ksā, *m.* = a wicked person.
3. bhūt, -tā, *m.* = *l.* a devil, *fg.*

Monstrous, *a.* 1. vidrup, *or* rūpnātullo.
2. rāksātso, *or rs.* rāksā bări.

Month, *s.* moino, -neā, *m.*

Monthly, *a.* moineamoineātso, *or* hăryeka moineātso, *or rs.* moineāk yek pāuṭi = once a month.

Monument, *s. perh.* 1. yādagurtu, -tā, *m.* = *l.* a sign for remembrance; ugḍās kărčeñ bāndāp, -dpā, *n.*
2. fónḍ, -ḍā, *m.* = *l.* a grave, *or bet.* gori, -ye, *f.* (a kind of tombstone over a grave).

Mood, *s.* rūp, -pā, *n.* = *l.* form; jinos, -nsā, *m.*

Moody, *a.* 1. rāgišṭ.
2. bezārāyetso = *l.* peevish; *see* **Melancholy.**

Moon, *s.* tsăndrem, -mā, *m.*
New m. = amās, -se, *f.*
Full m. = punou, -nvi, *f.*
Moonlight = tsānneñ, -neā, *n.*

Moor, *s.* 1. revāḷ zāgo, -geā, *m.* = a sandy place.
2. tāḷeñ, -ḷeā, *n.* = *l.* a tank; *see* **Waste.**

Moral, *a.* 1. tsālitso; nāyātso.
2. boro; bhāgevont.
Moral (certitude) = *perh.* tsālti thirasāṇ, -ṇi, *f.* (sovoyeči th.?)
M. theology = nitišāstru, -rā, *n.*

Moral, *s.* 1. tsāl, -li, *f.* = *l.* behaviour.
2. nitišāstru, -rā, *n.*
3. fóḷ, -ḷā, *m.*, *e. g.* m. of a fable.

Morass, *see* **Marsh.**

Morbid, *a.* piḍestso, *n. c.*

More, *ad.* tsăḍ *or* tsăḍtāu: 'bhou tsăḍ = much more, *or* very much'; āni = *l.* and, *e. g.* say something more = āni kāiñ sāng; āniki (some more); ădhik, *for the comparat. of which see* Gram.

Moreover, *ad.* tāče sivāi, *or* teā sivāi.

Moribund, *a.* mortolo, *or* morta thāiñ āsullo.

Morning, *s.* săkāḷiñ: 'very early

in the m. = bhou săkāḷiñ'; 'in the m. = s. *or* săkāḷinčeñ.
Good m. = dēu boro dis diuñ.

Morning, *a.* săkāḷintso.

Morose, *a.* tănṭălmari (mischievous); bezārāyetso (peevish).

Morrow, *s.* fāleā, -leā, *n.*

Mortal, *a.* 1. mornātso (subject to *or* causing death); mortso = who must die; *or* morasārko.
2. mănšātso, *or* săuñsārāntlo (human, worldly).
3. maha (sin).

Mortality, *s.* 1. săbār mòrnañ.
2. mănšepoṇ, -ṇā, *n.* = *l.* humanity.

Mortar, *s.* 1. tsuno, -neā, *m.* = chunam.
2. vān, -nā, *n.*, *esp.* of stone.
3. ruko, -keā, *m.* = a wooden m.; jiḍḍo, -ḍeā, *m.*

Mortgage, *s.* āḍou, -ḍvā, *m.*; īḍ, -ḍā, *n.*

Mortgage, *v.* āḍou di, *or* ā. ghāl.

Mortgagee, *s.* āḍou kāṇetolo.

Mortgager, *s.* āḍougār, -rā, *m.*

Mortification, *s.* 1. *vlg. rs.* mās meleñ = *l.* flesh is dead, *e. g.* an arm; mòrn, -nā, *n.*
2. kuḍiči dănḍon, -ne, *f.* (penance); prājit, -tā, *n.* = *l.* satisfaction.
3. bezārāi, -ye, *f.* = *l.* trouble; duk, -ki, *f.* = *l.* pain, *or* dukouṇeñ, -ṇeā, *n.*; dăgd, -dāñ, *pl. m.* = *l.* sufferings.

Mortify, *v.* 1. morăi *or* jīv mōḍ(ó), *n. u.*; *bet. crc.*
2. (gărvụ) mōḍ(ó) = *l.* break (pride).
3. dukăi = *l.* cause sorrow; dăgdăi = *l.* cause sufferings.
4. āpṇāčer zăit vor = *l.* gain victory against oneself; āpṇāk inkār kăr = *l.* resist oneself; āpṇāk āḍ ye = *l.* come against oneself.

Mosaic, *s.* pănčarăngi kām, -mā, *n.*, (*Mr.*), *n. u.*

Mosque, *s.* măzid, -di, *f.*; păḷḷi, -ḷe, *f.*

Mosquito, *s.* 1. zăḷār, -ri, *f.*
2. musk, -kā, *n.*; kimas, -msā, *n.*

Most, *a.* 1. bhou, *or* săbār, *or* tsăḍ, *or* bhou tsăḍ.
2. tsăḍāvot = *Lat. plerique* = several.
M. of all = mukhya zāun.

Mostly, *ad.* tsăḍāvot *or* ts. zāun; *rs.* voḍlo vānṭo = *l.* a great part.

Mote, *s.* kāḍi, -ye, *f.*; kuškuṭ, -ṭā, [*n.*

Moth, *s.* kiḍ, -ḍi, *f.*; kiḍo, -ḍeā, *m.*, of a large kind; sāṇās, -ṇsi, *f.*

Mother, *s.* 1. māi, -ye, *f.*; māiñ = mother-in-law *is also used, though only partially, for* mother, *but it is properly used only as a term of address for* a mother; āvoi, -voi, *f.* (*pl.* -io).
2. mātā, -te, *f.*, *as in the phrase,* '*Sancta mater ecclesia* = (our) holy mother the church.'

Mother-in-law, *s.* māiñ, -iñ, *f.*
Mother-tongue, *s.* gāunči bhās, -se, *f.* (āpli bhās).
Motion, *s.* 1. hālouṇeñ, -ṇeā, *n.*; bòḷ, -ḷā, *n.* (impulsion).
2. utkaḍe, -ḍeā, *n.* = evacuation.
Motion, *v.* hāt hālăi.
Motive, *s.* săbāb, -bi, *f.*; kārāṇ, -ṇā, *n.* = *l.* cause; āločen, -ni, *f.* = intention; sevoṭ, -ṭā, *m.* = *l.* aim.
Motto, *s.* sāngṇeñ, -ṇeā, *n.* = *l.* saying; gād, -di, *f.* = a proverb; vākya, -yā, *n.* = *l.* a sentence.
Mould, *s.* nămuno, -neā, *m.*
Mould, *v.* rūp di = *l.* give form.
Moulder, *v.* bosma = *l.* get destroyed; nāš zā.
Mouldy (Get), *v.* bāte, (owing to monsoon-weather).
Mound, *s.* 1. (mātyeči) rās, -si, *f.* = *l.* a heap (of earth).
2. guḍi, -ye, *f.* = *l.* a hillock.
Mount, *v.* 1. unts vetā = *l.* goes aloft; tsăḍ.
2. goḍeār bòs = *l.* sit on horse.
M. guard = rāk.
Mountain, *s.* guḍo, -ḍeā, *m.*; pórvót, (*or* părvăt), -tā, *m.*; dóngór, -grā, *m.*
Mountainous, *a.* pórvótāntso.
Mountebank, *see* **Impostor.**
Mounted, *a.* āsullo.
Mourn, *v.* răḍ; *see* **Groan.**
Mournful, *a.* 1. dukest, (sorry).
2. dukountso = *l.* causing sorrow; khăntiṣṭ.

Mourning, *s.* khănt (kănt), -ti, *f.*; duk, -ki, *f.*; răḍneñ, -neā, *n.*; *see* **Melancholy.**
Mouse, *s.* undir, -drā, *m.*
Moustaches, *s.* mišio, *pl. f.*
Mouth, *s.* tònḍ, -ḍā, *n.*, *pr.*, *fg.*, *e.g.* of a vessel.
Move, *v.* 1. hālăi, *c. v. of* hāl, *n. v.*
2. tsălăi (*c. v. of.* tsăl) = cause to walk.
3. sóḍ = *l.* leave, *e.g.* move from a place.
4. *fg.* utsāmboḷ kăr = *l.* make excited; *fg.* movāḷăi = *l.* soften; rīg = *l.* enter, *fg. e.g.* the sermon moved us all deeply, *ch. cs.*
5. *by the c. v.*, *e.g.* m. to work; lāi = *l.* apply, *e.g.* sikčeāk lāi.
M. on = mukār vots.
Moveable, *a.* 1. čărajindgi (property).
2. hālasārko.
Movement, *s.* 1. hālāp, -lpā, *n.* (*neut.*), *or* hālouṇeñ, -ṇeā, *n.* (*causat.*).
2. *fg.* kāṭkāi, -ye, *f.* = *l.* revolution.
Mover, *s.* hālăitolo; *see* **Leader.**
Mow, *v.* kātăr = *l.* cut; luuñ.
Mower, *s.* kātărtolo, *m.*; luuntolo.
Much, *a.* tsăḍ (*used also alone, as pron.*); bhou (*only as adj. or with another word*); zāito; săbār.
Much more = bhou tsăḍ.
As much as = kitlo . . . titlo, *or only* titlo.

How much = kitlo, *or* kedo = how great.
So much = titlo, *or* titlots (*emph.*)
Too much = bhou tsăḍ.
Much less = 1. bhou uṇo (-ṇi, -ṇeñ).
2. năints....băgar = not only ....but also.

Mucilage, *s.* pānk, -kā, *m.*; dīk, -kā, *m.*; gónd, -dā, *m.* = ǵum.

Muck, *s. see* **Dung.**

Mucous, *a.* pānkātso.

Mud, *s.* ubir, -brā, *m.*; kēd, -dā, *m.*; čikol, -klā, *m.*; māti, -ye, *m.*

Muddle, *v.* 1. mheḷo kăr, *or* mheḷăi = *l.* make dirty.
2. guspăḍăi = *l.* confuse; gălibili kăr.
3. *in pass.* be muddled = ămāl zātā = *l.* intoxication becomes.

Muddy, *a.* ubrātso; mātiyetso; čiklātso.

Muff, *s.* hātañčil, -lā, *n.*

Muffle, *see* **Wrap.**

Mug, *s.* mog, -gā, *m.*, *fr.*

Muggy, *a.* šeḷitso.

Mulct, *see* **Fine.**

Mule, *s.* katsār, -rā, *n.*

Muleteer, *s.* katsāragār, -rā, *m.*

Mulish, *see* **Obstinate.**

Multiple, *a.* zāite doḍo.

Multiplication, *s.* tsăḍouṇi, -ṇe, *f.*; guṇākār, -rā, *m.* (*Arith.*)

Multiply, *v.* 1. tsăḍăi, *c. v.*, *or* tsăḍ kăr; *pass.* ts. zā.
2. guṇākār kăr; *bet.* guṇsi.

Multitude, *s.* zomo, -meā, *m.*; rās, -si, *f.*; *by* săbār = many; khêṭ, -ṭi, *f.* = a gathering.

Mummy, *s.* mummi (*a word common to many Oriental languages*); pormăḷăilleñ moḍeñ, -ḍeā, *n.*

Mumps, *s.* 1. keppaṭeñ, -ṭeā, *n.* (sickness).
2. bitărlo rāg, -gā, *m.* = *l.* interior anger.

Municipality, *s.* 1. (šerāntle, *or* šerače) ădhipăti, *pl. m.*
2. šer (*or* šar), -rā, *n.*

Munificence, *s.* uddārpoṇ, -ṇā, *n.*

Munificent, *a.* uddār.

Munition, *s.* pāgār, -rā, *m.* = *l.* a wall; *see* **Fortification.**

Murder, *s.* khuni, -ye, *f.*

Murder, *v.* jivsiñ mār; khuni kăr.

Murderer, *s.* khunigār, -rā, *m.*

Murderous, *a.* khuniyetso.

Murky, *a.* kāḷokātso.

Murmer, *v.* 1. purpur = grumble; măṇamăṇa ulăi.
2. siṇ ulăi = *l.* speak a complaint.

Murrain, *s.* monzātiñpiḍa, -ḍe, *f.*

Muscle, *s.* 1. snāyu (*Sans.*, *Cn. Mr.*), *n. u.*, *or* potra, -re, *f.*
2. *fg.* dhāt, -ti, *f.* = *l.* strength.
3. šindarpi, -pi, *f.* (a shell-fish).

Mushroom, *s.* āḷmbeñ, -beā, *n.*

Music, *s.* 1. gāyān, -nā, *n. used comm. for* vocal m.; *vlg.* kantar, -rā, *n.*, *fr.*
2. vāzāp, -zpā, *n.*, *esp.* instrumental m.

Musical, *a.* gāyānātso; sămapòḍtso = *l.* falling together, *fg.*

Musician, *s.* 1. *vlg.* kăntarist, -tā, *m.*; gāyānagār, -rā, *m.* 2. vāzpi,-piā, *m.* (instrumental).

Musket, *s.* bănduk, -ke, *f.*

Musketry, *s.* băndukañfār, -rā, *m.*

Muslin, *s.* mălmăl, -lā, *n.*

Must, *s.* rōs(ó), -sā, *m.*

Must, *v.* *By the Necess. mood; absolutely,* zăi, *or* gărz āsā.

Mustard, *s.* sāsāuñ, -svā, *n.*

Mustard-plaster, *s.* sāsvātso lēp (é), -pā, *m.*; *vlg.* plaster, -rā, *m.*

Muster, *v.* fouz pòḷe; fouzi meḷoun pòḷe; hāzăr zā = *l.* be present; mèḷ = *l.* be collected. M. up courage = dhăir ghe.

Mustiness, *s.* bāto, -teā, *m.*

Musty, *a.* bātello.

Mutability, *s.* bădlasārkeñ, -keā, *n.*

Mute, *a.* tònḍ yenātullo; mono.

Mutilate, *v.* moṭvo kăr = *l.* make short; uṇo kăr = *l.* diminish; sānde kātăr = *l.* cut members.

Mutineer, *s.* kāṭkāyegār, -rā, *m.*; kuṭagār, -rā, *m.* = *l.* making plots.

Mutinous, *a.* kāṭkāyetso.

Mutiny, *s.* kāṭkāi, -ye, *f.*

Mutiny, *v.* kāṭkāi kăr.

Mutter, *v.* măṇamăṇa kăr; mòna bităr ulăi = *l.* speak within the heart.

Mutton, *s.* bokreāčeñ mās, -sā, *n.* = *l.* meat of sheep.

Mutual, *a.* yekamekātso.

Muzzle, *s.* sonḍi, -ye, *f.*, *e.g.* of a dog; muskār, -rā, *n.*

My, *pron.* mozo.

Myriad, *s.* dhā hāzār.

Myrobalan, *s.* ărḍo, -ḍeā, *m.* (a small fruit).

Myrrh, *s.* *vlg.* mir, -rā, *n.*; *perh.* pormoḷā rōs(ó), -sā, *m.*; musambār, -rā, *n.*

Myself, *pron.* āunts"; *see* Gram. P. II. ch. iii.

Mysterious, *a.* guṭātso.

Mystery, *s.* 1. mistér, -rā, *m.*, *fr.*; guṭ, -tā, *m.* 2. khăṇ, -ṇā, *m.* = a decade of the rosary.

Mystic, *a.* guṭātso; guḍārthavivor sāngtolo; guḍārth vivorsitolo.

Mystify, *v.* dubāun ulăi; mōs(ó) kăr = *l.* deceive; sāmpḍāi = *l.* confound.

N

Nabob, *s.* 1. năbāb *or* năvāb, -bā, *m.* (a Mussulman prince), *used also fg.*, *e.g.* năbāba bări ulăitā = he speaks like a n.
2. duḍuādik = *l.* a man of money.

Nadir, *s.* nadir, -rā, *n.*, *fr. or the Mr.* adhodiša, -še, *f.*, *or* pātāḷabhăg, -gā, *m.*

Nag, *see* **Hack.**

Nail, *s.* 1. năkši, -ṣe, *f.*, of the fingers.
2. khiḷo, -ḷeā, *m.* = a metal spike.

Nail, *v.* khiḷăi, *c.v.*: 'n. to the cross = kursār kh. *or* zóḍ'.

Naive, *a.* sādo; niškăpṭi.

Naked, *a.* viṇgo; nāgḍo; ugto = *l.* open, *fg.*
Make n. = viṇgăi; *bet.* viṇgo kăr.

Nakedness, *s.* nāgḍepoṇ, -ṇā, *n.*; viṇgepoṇ, -ṇā, *n.*

Name, *s.* 1. nāuñ, nāvā, *n.*
2. ālkugn, -gnā, *n.* = family n., *fr.*
3. boreñ nāuñ = *l.* a good name, reputation.
4. utăr, -trā, *n.* = *l.* a word.
5. ulo, -leā, *m.* = *l.* a call, *e.g.* tākā ulo kărtā = he calls him by name.
In my n. = moje nāviñ *or* mojeā nāvār. What is your n. = tujeñ nāuñ kiteñ? What is the name of that thing = tākā kiteñ moṇtāt. Enjoy a good n. = boréñ nāuñ bhóg. Give a name = nāuñ dovór. Hurt the good n. = (boreñ) nāuñ pāḍ kăr.

Name, *v.* 1. moṇ = *l.* say, *Dat. thing*; nāuñ utsār = *l.* pronounce the name; ulo kăr = *l.* call by name; nāuñ dovór = *l.* put a name, *e.g.* in baptism.
2. nemsi = *l.* appoint; nomiyār = *l.* nominate.

Namely, *ad.* moṇje, *or* muṇčeñ = *l.* to say; *or* moḷeār = *l.* if you say.

Namesake, *s.* teāts nāvātso mănis, -nšā, *m.*

Nap, *s.* 1. louñ, -ove, *f.* = *l.* wool.
2. zóp, -pā, *m.* (*var.* -pi, *f.*) = *l.* short *or* half sleep: 'take a n. = lān nīd kāṇe, *or* l. n. kāḍ, *or* āḍpòḍ'.

Nape, *s.* mān, -ne, *f.* = neck.

Napkin, *s. vlg.* tòṇḍātso tuvālo, -leā, *m.*, *fr.*; hāt pusčeñ lugāṭ, -gṭā, *n.*

Narcotic, *a.* nidauntso = *l.* causing to sleep.

Narrate, *v.* sāng, *or* moṇ.

Narration, *s.* kătha, -the, *f.* = *l.* a story; sāng-ṇeñ, -ṇeā, *n.*

Narrow, *a.* ăšir, *e.g.* n. road.

Narrow, *v.* ăšir kăr.

Narrowness, *s.* ăširāi, -ye, *f.*

Nasal, *a.* nākiñ = through the nose.

Nastiness, *s.* mheḷepoṇ, -ṇā, *n. etc.*

Nasty, *a.* ăḷsik; mheḷo; kānṭāḷeātso.

Natal (day), *s.* zălmātso dis, -sā, *m.*

Nation, *s.* părza, -je, *f.*; zāt, -ti, *f.*, kuḷi, -ye, *f.* = a tribe, *used also for* n.; săsăt, -sti, *f.* = *l.* generation.

National, *a.* zātitso *or* kuḷiyetso; gāuntso = *l.* of the country.

Native, *a.* săimbātso = *l.* natural; (yeā) gāuntso = *l.* of (this) country; *vlg.* āngātso = *l.* of here.

N. country = zāllo gāuñ, -gāñvā, *m. vlg.*; vilāyet, -tā, *n.*

Nativity, *s.* zălm, -mā, *m.* = birth.

N. of O. L. J. C. = Natal, -lā, *n.*

N. of the B. V. M. = Montičeñ fèst, -tā, *n.*

Natural, *a.* 1. săimbātso, = not artificial, not violent, *e.g.* death, gifts.

2. nīz, *or* niškăpṭi, *opp. to* affected.

3. ādarāzāllo (put) = a n. son; vāreātso.

Naturalise, *v.* tsălto kăr.

Nature, *s.* săimb, -bā, *n.* (*also in philos. mn.*); guṇ, -ṇā, *m.* = *l.* quality, character; *see* **Character.**

Naughty, *a.* 1. făḍpoši; āḷsi = *l.* lazy.

2. gărjek pòḍanātullo = *l.* not falling to necessity.

3. tănṭălmāri; pāḍ = *l.* bad.

Nausea, *s.* vonkāro, -reā, *m.*

Nauseate, *v.* vonkāro yetā = *l.* nausea comes.

Nauseous, *a.* vonkāreātso; kānṭāḷeātso = *l.* of abhorrence.

Nautical, *a.* tārvāntso; tārvāpoiṇātso; dăryātso = *l.* of the sea.

Navel, *s.* bombli, -le, *f.*

Navigable, *s.* tārvapoiṇasārko; *bet.* tāruñ tsăltso.

Navigate, *v.* tārvār poiṇ kăr, *or* tārvār tsăl.

Navigation, *s.* tārvapoiṇ, -ṇā, *n.* = *l.* travel on ship.

Navigator, *s.* khălāši, -šiā, *m.* = *ex.* sailor; tārvoṭi, -ṭiā, *m.*

Navy, *s.* tārvañ, *pl. of* tāruñ; tārvañmēḷ(é), -ḷā, *m.* = *l.* a collection of ships.

Nay, *ad. rs.* pāvanāñ = *l.* does not reach (suffice); *rs.* năints ... băgar = not only ... but also; porteñ = *l.* on the contrary.

Near, *a.* 1. lāgiñ āsullo, *or* lāgšilo; sărsiñ āsullo, *or* sărsilo; āspās.

2. săiro = *l.* relative.

Near, *ad.* lāgiñ (*emph.* lāgints); āro; 'very near = lāgiñ lāgiñ'.

Near, *prep.* lāgiñ, kăḍe; sărsiñ.

Nearly, *ad.* lāgiñ lāgiñ, *e.g.* n. 30 (less than 30); băhuša, *e.g.* n. 30; tsăḍāvot; tsăḍ-uṇeñ = more or less; sumăr = *l.* about (*Lat. circiter*).

N. related = lāgsilo săiro.

Neat, *s.* goruāñ, *pl. n.* = cattle.

Neat, *a.* nităḷ = *l.* pure; sundăr = *l.* nice; tsănd = *l.* nice, *H. K.*

Neatness, *s.* nităḷpoṇ, -ṇā, *n.*; sundărāi, -ye, *f.*

Necessarily, *ad.* ăvăš zāun = *l.* being necessity; *by the Neces. mood; see* Gram.

Necessary, *a. By the Neces. mood; e.g.* it is n. to go = votsazāi; gărjetso; zāi āsullo; zărur = *l.* urgent.

It is n. = zāi, *Prs. Dat.*

Necessity, *s.* 1. gărz, -je, *f.*

2. ākānt, -tā, *m.* = *l.* distress; kăšṭ, -ṭā, *m.*; dăgd, -dañ, *pl. m.* = sufferings.

Neck, *s.* 1. goḷo (găḷo), -ḷeā, *m.*, *pr.*, *fg.*, *e. g.* of a vessel; gomṭo, -ṭeā, *m.* (*var.* gomṭi, -ṭe, *f.*)

2. gărdān, -nā, *n.* = the 'first stomach' *or* 'shaking-piece' of a cow; *also* the neck itself.

Necklace, *s.* sór, -rā, *m.*, *pl.* sór (*gener.*); goḷeātso mhāl, -lā, *m.*; penḍeñ, -ḍeā, *n.* = a golden n.; pouḷeāñčeñ kònt, -tā, *n.*, of coral; pouḷeāñči sări, -ye, *f.*; piḍḍuk, -ke, *f.*, of golden beads, *or also* of common beads; fugador, -rā, *m.*, with gold and precious stones; tsăkruṣór, -rā, *m.* = a kind of golden n.; kănṭi, -te, *f.* = a golden n.

Need, *see* **Necessity** *and* **Necessary.**

Needful, *a.* gărjetso; gărjevont.

Needle, *s.* suvi, -ye, *f.*

Needy, *a.* dubḷo; *see* **Poor, Indigent.**

Nefarious, *a.* khoṭo.

Negation, *s.* nākā moṇčeñ, *or* nāñ moṇčeñ; *bet. rs.*

Neglect, *v.* bepārvo kăr, *G. M.*; *neg. form of* lăkṣa kăr; ălăkṣa kăr = do not mind; *neg. form of* zătăn kāṇe.

Neglect, *s.* 1. bepārvo, -veā, *m.*, *or* bepārvāi, -ye, *f.*; ălăkṣa, -ṣe, *f.*

2. āḷsāi, -ye, *f.* = *l.* laziness.

Negligence, *s.* udāsiṇ, -ṇā, *n.*

Negligent, *a.* bepārvi; āḷsi; făḍ-poši.

Negotiate, *v.* 1. *Cm.* ulăi = *l.* speak with.

2. kărār kăr = *l.* make an agreement, *Cm.*; kām kăr = *l.* make business; vepār kăr = *l.* make traffic.

Negotiation, *s.* 1. uloṇeñ, -ṇeā, *n.* = *l.* speaking.

2. kărār, -rā, *m.* = *l.* an agreement.

3. vepār, -rā, *m.*

Negotiator, *s.* 1. dūt, -tā, *m.* = *l.* an ambassador.

2. dălāl, -lā, *m.* = an agent; văkil, -lā, *m.* = *ex.* a pleader, *yet apparently used also for* n.

3. vepāri, -riā, *m.* = *l.* a trader.

Neigh, *v.* kiḷikiḷ.

Neighbour, *s.* 1. pelo, -leā, *m.*, *e.g.* love your n.

2. sezāri, -riā, *m.* = one living close to another; dairo sezāri.

Neighbourhood, *s.* lāgsili suāt, -te, *f.*; *bet. rs.*

In the neighbourhood = lāgiñ, *or* āro.

Neighbouring, *a.* lāgsilo, *or* lāgiñ āsullo; lāgun āsullo (*or* lăgti) = *l.* attached; *rs.* bāglāk = at the door.

Neither—nor, *conj.* -i = also, *with the negative particle added to the verb*; *e.g.* he is n. old n. young = to tărnāṭoi năiñ, mātāroi năiñ.

Neither, *a.* toyi nāñ (*or* năiñ), voyi nāñ (*or* năiñ) = *l.* that also not, this also not, (nāñ *or* năiñ *joined to the verb*).

Neophyte, *s.* novo kristāuñ, -tāvā, *m.*

Nephew, *s.* bātso, -čeā, *m.* *is* the n. of a brother *or* sister *only when it is* the child of the sister *or* brother; putnyo, -yeā, *m.* *is* the n. of a brother *or* sister *according as it is* the child of the brother *or* sister; bhāvātso put, *or* boiṇitso put, -tā, *m.*

Nerve, *s.* 1. šir, -re, *f.* = *l.* vein, *is used also for* n. (*in Mr. too*); tănti, -te, *f.*

2. *fg.* bòḷ, -ḷā, *n.* = *l.* strength.

Nervous, *a.* 1. šir āsullo.

2. *fg.* bizuḍ = *l.* shy, of nervous temperament.

3. bòḷādik = *l.* strong.

Nest, *s.* 1. gonṭéru, -rā, *m.*; gūḍ, -ḍā, *m.*

2. *fg.* āsro, -reā, *m.* = *l.* a refuge.

Net, *s.* zāḷ, -ḷā, *n.*

Nettle, *s.* khātkutli, -le, *f.* = *Lat. urtica.*

Nettle, *v.* korzāi, *c. v. of* korza.

Net-work, *s.* kāpča, -če, *f.*

Neutral, *a.* păkšapātnātullo.

Neutrality, *s.* nāñpăkšapāt, -tā, *n.*

Never, *ad.* kedints = ever, *with the neg.* nāñ (*joined to the verb, if there be any*).

N. mind = vóḍ năiñ; čintanāñ.

N. more = āče uprānt (*or* phuḍeñ) kedints. . . . nāñ, *or* āni nāñ.

Nevertheless, *conj.* 1. -i *or* -oi *added to the* conditional, *e.g.* although Peter does not help me, n. I will love him = zărităr Pedru mākā kumok kărināñ āuñ tātso mogui kărtāñ; *or* -i *added to the verb of the protasis suffices, and* n. *is omitted.*

2. zāleāri, *used absolutely.*

New, *a.* novo; voḍol zāllo, *or* voḍoltso, *or* voḍol āil"lo.

N. moon = amās, -si, *f.*

New-comer, *s.* pǎrdeši, -šiā, *m.* = *l.* a foreigner; ātāñ āil'lo = who came now.

Newish, *a.* novoso.

Newly, *ad.* voḍol; āilevar.

News, *s.* kobār, -bre, *f.*; vǎrtamān, -nā, *n.*; vǎrdi, -de, *f.*; ǎbiprāi, -ye, *f.* = information; pukāro, -reā, *m.* = *l.* a report, *Lat. rumor.*

Receive n. = kobār ghe, *or* k. [āik.

I have no n. = mākā kobār nāñ, *mn.* I do not know any thing (about it).

Newspaper, *see* **Journal.**

Next, *a.* lāgsilo *or* lāgiñ āsullo.

N. year = dusreñ vǎrs, *or* phuḍañ, *or* mukārik.

Next, *ad.* 1. lāgiñ, *or* sǎrsiñ.

2. māgir = *l.* afterwards; *often rs. into* uprānt *preceded by a participle*; *see* Gram.

Nib, *s.* pònt, -tā, *n.*, *e.g.* of a pen; domós, -msā, *m.*

Nibble, *v.* khā, *e.g.* a mouse nibbles; *or bet.* tsātsāi.

Nice, *s.* 1. sārko = *l.* exact.

2. tsǎḍ sārko = too exact.

3. nāzuk = exact, too exact, delicate, squeamish, dainty.

4. tsānd = beautiful, *H. K.*; sobit.

5. suādik = tasteful.

6. bezāri = fastidious.

Nicety, *s.* 1. nāzukāi, -ye, *f.*; *see adj.*

2. sobāi, *or* sobitāi, -ye, *f.* = *l.* beauty.

Nickname, *s.* āḍnāuñ, -āvā, *n.* = *l.* against-name; pāḍ nāuñ = *l.* bad name.

Niece, *s.* 1. bāči, -če, *f.*, *or* boiṇiči du, -ve, *f.* = *l.* daughter of a sister.

2. duvḍi, -ḍe, *f.*, *or* bhāvāči du = *l.* daughter of a brother.

Niggard, *a.* surāti; imṭo.

Niggardliness, *s.* surāt, -tā, *m.*; imṭepoṇ, -ṇā, *n.*

Nigh, *see* **Near.**

Night, *s.* rāt, -ti, *f.*

By n. = rātir, *or* rātčeñ, *or* rātčeā veḷār.

Night-mare, *see* **Incubus.**

Nightly, *a.* rāttso.

Nimble, *a.* tsurk; suḍsudit; ušār; *see* **Quick,**

Nimbleness, *s.* suḍsuḍāi, -ye, *f.*; tsurk, -kā, *n.*

Nine, *a.* nóu.

Ninefold, *a.* nóudoḍo, *or* nóu pāuṭi tsǎḍ.

Nip, *v.* 1. čimṭo kāḍ = *l.* give a pinch.

2. kimči = cut off by means of the finger and thumb, *e.g.* a flower.

Nippers, *s.* čimṭo, -ṭeā, *m.*

Nipple, *s.* 1. čiuñ, -ive, *f.*

2. hǎrdeñ, -deā, *n.* = *l.* breast, *fg.*; thān, -nā, *n.*

Nit, *s.* līk, -ke, *f.*

No, *ad.* 1. nāñ *is used to* deny existence, *or* being in a place.

2. nāiñ, *in* denying the possession of some quality.

3. nākā, *in an imperat. and optative mn.*
4. *the whole sentence may be repeated in neg. form, as in Latin, joining the negative to the verb.*

No, *a.* 1. *the affirmative corresponding adj. is used with neg. particle joined to the v.*
2. nāñ, *e.g.* no strength = bòḷ nāñ; kāiñ nāñ = something not.

No more = āni . . . nāñ.
No one, no body = koṇ nāñ.

Nobility, *s.* măntăn, -nā, *n., e.g.* n. of a family; voḍpoṇ, -ṇā, *n.* = *l.* greatness; vortepoṇ, -ṇā, *n., or* vorteñ mòn, -nā, *n.* = sublimity.

Noble, *a.* 1. măntănāntlo, *e.g.* n. family.
2. *fg.* vorto = *l.* sublime; voḍlo = *l.* great.

Nod, *v.* 1. hišāro di = *l.* give a hint; tăkli hālăi = *l.* move the head; tăkli bāgāi = *l.* incline the head.
2. doḷe mōḍ(ò) = *l.* break the eyes, *fg.* give a hint.

Nod, *s.* 1. zèm *or* jèm, -me, *f.* = *l.* sleepiness, drowsiness.
2. *rs. into v.*

Noise, *s.* gouji, -je, *f.*; bòb, -be, *f., or* bobāṭ, -ṭe, *f.*, of crying out, *or* any loud sound; *see* **Grating.**
Make a n. = gouji kăr, *or* bòb mār = cry.

Noisome, *a.* 1. pāḍ; ăḷsik = *l.* dirty; nāñboläiketso.
2. kānṭāḷeātso = disgusting.

Noisy, *a.* gouji kărtso, *or* goujetso; bòb mārtso.

Nomadic, *a.* bountso.

Nomenclature, *s.* 1. săbdāñ bhăndār, -rā, *n.* = *l.* a treasure of words (*anal. to Mr.*).
2. păribhāšika utrañ = *l.* technical words, (*Mr. Cn. Gn.*) *n. u.*

Nominal, *a.* 1. *rs.* utrañ (*or* nāvā) pārmāṇe, *or perh.* nāvātso.
2. utrāntso = *l.* of words.

Nominally, *ad.* bhāileānāts = exteriorly only; *e.g.* bh. dākăitā = he shows exteriorly only; *see* **Nominal.**

Nominate, *v.* moṇ; *see* **Appoint.**

Nomination, *s.* mokruri, -re, *f.* = *l.* appointment.

Nominee, *s.* mokrur kello.

None, *see* **No.**

Nonsense, *s.* nākazāllo, -leā, *m.*; zānk, -ki, *f.*; ărthnātulliñ utrañ = *l.* insignificant words; piseapoṇāčiñ utrañ = foolish words; rāgḷeañ utăr, -trā, *n.* = *l.* a confused word.

Noon, *s.* donpār, -rā, *m.*: 'at noon = donpārāñ'.

Noose, *s.* pās, -sā, *m., e.g.* for birds, *pr., fg.*; gānṭ, -ṭi, *f.* = knot; bāndpās, -sā, *m.*

Noose, *v.* nāḍ kăr = *l.* make tricks (*or.* nāḍ tsālăi).

Nor, *conj.* āni...nāñ; *see* **Neither—nor.**

Normal, *a.* krămāntrụ.

North, *s.* bădg *or* bădăg, -ḍgā, *n.*: 'in the n. = bădgāk'.

Northern, *a.* bădgātso.

Nose, *s.* nāk, -kā, *n.*

Lead by the n. = kānānt simpṭi ghāl; nāk korpi = tease.

Speak through the n. = nākiñ (*var.* nākiañ) ulăi.

Nosegay, *s.* póḍ, -ḍā, *m.*; *see* **Bouquet.**

Nosology, *s.* piḍañšāstrụ, -rā, *n.*

Nostalgy, *s.* (gāunči) āšā, -še, *f.*

Nostril, *s.* nākāčeñ puḍ, -ḍā, *n.*

A man without nostrils = simro, -reā, *m.*

Nostrum, *s.* guṭāvokāt, *or* gupit vokāt, -ktā, *n.*, *or the Hind.*, *Mr.* buṭa *or* buṭi, -ṭi, *f.*

Not, *ad.* nāñ, *or* năiñ *joined to the verb; used also in sentences like this:* who would not wonder?

Notable, *a.* tsătrāyetso, *or* tsătrāi fāvozāllo.

Notary, *s.* māg-ṇeñšānbóg,-gā, *m.*

Notation, *s.* tsătrāi, -ye, *f.*; šāro, -reā, *m.*

Notch, *s.* kātrāp, -pā, *n.*

Note, *s.* 1. gurtụ, -tā, *m.* = *l.* a sign (*it might also be used for* a musical n.)

2. istyār, -rā, *m.* = a public advertisement.

3. tsătrāi, -ye, *f.*, *or* šāro, -reā, *m.*; *see* **Notation.**

4. čiṭ, -ṭi, *f.* = a memorandum.

5. tāḷo, -ḷeā, *m.* = a vocal utterance; *or* tāḷeātso jinos, -nsā, *m.*

Note, *v.* 1. gurtụ kăr = *l.* make a sign.

2. tsătrāi kăr = *l.* make a remark; *or also* pay attention.

Note-book, *s.* tsătrāyečeñ pustak, -kā, *n.*, *or anal. to Cn.* ugḍāsapustak.

Noted, *a.* voḍlo = *l.* great; nāvāḍgo = *l.* famous.

Nothing, *s.* kāiñ nāñ (nāñ *being joined to the verb*): 'he does n. = to kāiñ kărināñ'; *emph.* kāints nāñ.

Once we were n. = āmiñ yék pāuṭi kāints nātulleāuñ.

We should fall into n. if... = āmiñ năpāints zāteāuñ, zărtăr....

Notice, *s.* 1. kobār, -bre, *f.*

2. ăbiprāi, -ye, *f.* = *l.* information.

3. tsătrāi, -ye, *f.*; *see* **Note:** take n. of = tsătrāi kăr; *see* **Advertisement.**

Notice, *v.* kăḷ, *or* kăḷit zā = *l.* get known; tsătrāi kăr; pòḷe = *l.* look.

Notification, *s.* *vlg.* noṭis, -sā, *n.*, *fr.*; *see* **Advertisement.**

Notify, *v.* kăḷăi, *or* kăḷit kăr (make known).

Notion, *s.* 1. ărth, -thā, *m.* = *l.* meaning, *e.g.* nor does any other n. underlie this word.

2. āločen, -ni, *f.* = *l.* opinion, judgment.
3. kobār, -bre, *f.* = *l.* news.
4. sikoṇ, -ṇi, *f.* = *l.* instruction.
5. *for* idea, conception; *see* **Idea.**

Notorious, *a.* părgăṭ.

Notwithstanding, *see* **Nevertheless.**

Noun, *s.* nāuñ, nāvā, *n.*

Nourish, *v.* pós, *also* beasts; jevāṇ di, *or* jevoi; vāḍăi = *l.* cause to grow.

Nourishing, *a.* bolăiketso.

Nourishment, *s.* posāp, -spā, *n.* *or* pōs(ó), -sā, *m.*; *see* **Food.**

Novel, *a.* novo.

Novel, *s.* kătha, -the, *f.*; kāṇi, -ye, *f.* = a fable.

Novena, *s.* noven, -nā, *n.*, *fr.*; sālvi, -ve, *f.*; nou disānčeñ măgṇeñ, -ṇeā, *n.*

Novice, *s.* umeduār, -rā, *m.*; umeduāršāstri, -riā, *n.* (a n. in religion); părikṣer āsullo.

Novitiate, *s.* părikṣekāl, -lā, *m.* = *l.* a time of examination; tănkekāl, -lā, *m.* = *l.* a time of trial.

Now, *ad.* ātāñ, *emph.* ātānts.
N.—n. = thoḍe pāuṭi... thoḍe pāuṭi.
N. and then = thoḍe pāuṭi, *or* tovóḷ tovóḷ.
Nowadays = 1. ātāñ *or* yeāñ disāniñ.
2. yedóḷ, *used more comm. with* păriyānt = till, *e. g.* ātāñ p. = till now.

Nowhere, *ad.* khăiñ" nāñ (*the neg. being joined to the verb*) = *l.* somewhere not.

Noxious, *a.* 1. luksānātso.
2. ăkmānātso = *l.* offensive; vāiṭ (*in 1st and 2nd mn.*), *or bet.* vāiṭ kārtso.

Nugatory, *a.* vèrt; besṭo; čeṣṭāyetso; nisprăyojănātso.

Nuisance, *s.* bezārāi, -ye, *f.*

Null, *a.* 1. *rs.* răddu̥ = nullity, invalidity; *or* răddu̥ āsu̥llo.
2. vèrt = *l.* useless; ăthir, *n. u.*; *see* **Invalid.**

Numb, *a.* isvenātullo = *l.* senseless.
Be n. = jim zā = be struck.

Number, *s.* 1. ănko, -keā, *m.* = arithm. n.
2. zomo, -meā, *m.* = *l.* multitude; săbār = many.
3. slók, -kā, *m.* = *l.* poetry; *or bet.* slókamāp, -pā, *n.* = measure of poetry.

Number, *v.* lēk(é) = count.

Numberless, *a.* lèknātullo; ăgăṇit.

Numbness, *see* **Insensibility.**

Numeral, *a.* ănkeāntso.

Numerator, *s.* 1. lèk kărtolo.
2. ăuñšo, -šeā, *m.*, of a fraction.

Numerous, *a.* săbār, *or* zāito, *or* tsăḍ; *see* **Many.**

Numismatic, *s.* nāṇeañvidya, -ye, *f.*

Nun, *s. vlg.* mādri, -ri (*or* mādru̥, -ri), *f.*; kănyāstri, -re, *f.*, *n.c.*; dēukănya, -ye, *f.*, *n.c.*

Nuncio, *s.* dūt, -tā, *m.* (pāp sāibadūt), of high rank; rāvāni, -niā, *m.*

Nunnery, *s. vlg.* konvent, -tā, *m.*, *or* mādrintso bonglo, -leā, *m.*; (kănyāstreañ) mốṭ, -ṭā, *m.*, *n. u.*

Nuptials, *see* **Marriage.**

Nurse, *s.* 1. āya, -yā, *f.*; *see* **Governess.**

2. dudkārn, -ni, *f.*

Nurse, *v.* 1. vāgāi; *vlg.* čiuo di *or* dud di.

2. *fg.* fuslāi = *l.* fondle.

3. rāk = attend to an invalid.

Nursery, *s.* 1. burgeañkuḍ, -ḍā, *n.*; *vlg.* pāḷneākuḍ, -ḍā, *n.*

2. vāḍounčeñ garpan, -nā, *n.* = *l.* institution for educating, *or the Mr.* pālanasthān, -nā, *n.*, *n. u.*

Nut, *s.* fòḷ, -ḷā, *n.*

Nutmeg, *s.* zāifòḷ, -ḷā, *n.*

Nutriment, *s.* ahār, *or* hār, -rā, *m.*

Nutrition, *s.* posāp, -spā, *n.*, *or* pōs(ó), -sā, *m.*

Nutritive, *a.* póstso.

Nux vomica, *s.* kāzro, -reā, *m.*

O

O, *int.* 1. yé, *used to* invite attention.

2. ah; kāṭakāṭa.

Oak, *s. some say* vrăkṣarāja, -jā, *m.*, *but it is a very uncertain equivalent.*

Oar, *s.* volo, -leā, *m.*

Pull with the oar = v. kāḍ.

Oath, *s.* părmāṇ, -ṇā, *n.*; soput, -tā, *m.* = a private o., *or only* an affirmation, *adding* sāt, *or* khărents.

Keep an o. = p. sāmbāḷ.

Take an o. = p. kăr.

On o. = părmāṇār.

Tender an o. = părmāṇ kărunk lāi.

Obduracy, *s.* sāḷ, -ḷā, *n.*; hāṭ, -ṭā, *n.*

Obdurate, *a.* 1. sāḷiṣṭ.

2. bāgānātullo.

Obedience, *n.* khāltepoṇ, -ṇā, *n.*

Obedient, *a.* khālto.

Be o. = *G.* utăr āik.

Obediently, *ad.* khālto zāun.

Obeisance, *s.* nămăskār, -rā, *m.*

Obey, *v. G.* utăr āik = *l.* hear the word of; khālto zāun āsā; khālto zāun tsāl; (voḍilānčea utrāk mān di; v. u. pāḷo di).

Obituary, *s.* melleānčeñ lèk, -kā, *n.*; melleānči pāṭṭi, -ṭe, *f.*

Object, *s.* 1. irādo, -deā, *m.*, *e.g.* the o. of the sacraments (*Lat. finis* = end); sevóṭ, -ṭā, *m.* (an aim).

2. văstu̥, -tu, *f.* = *l.* a thing, matter.
3. *for* 'object of science' *we can perh. use the obsolete uoun* (*Mr. also*) višăya (*from which the word* višyānt = about *is derived*); *otherwise* irādo.

Object, *v.* 1. āḍāi = *l.* prevent; *or* āḍkăḷ kăr, *or* ăḍḍi kăr; ākšep kăr, *or* ā. hāḍ = bring objection.
2. *neg. of* păsănd kăr = *l.* approve; inkāṛ kăr (*Acc.*) = *l.* make resistance.

Objection, *s.* āḍkăḷ, -ḷi, *f.*; hărkăt, -ti, *f.*; ăḍḍi, -ḍe, *f.*

Objective, *a.* 1. văstuntso = *l.* of the things.
2. bhāilo = *l.* exterior; khărots = real.

Objurgate, *v.* besṭāi.

Objurgation, *s.* besṭāuṇeñ, -ṇeā, *n.*, *or* besṭāuṇi, -ṇe, *f.*

Obligation, *s.* 1. kāido, -deā, *m.* = *l.* a duty.
2. upkār, -rā, *m.* = *l.* a benefit.
Contract an o. = kāido zoḍun ghe.
Be under an o. = *rs.* devo āsā, *Sb. Instrum.* (āveñ tukā devo āsā); *or* (mākā) kāido āsā.

Obligatory, *a. rs. into* kāido āsā; gărjetso; kărizāi āsu̥llo, *or* kărtso.

Oblige, *v.* formāi = *l.* command; lāi = *l.* apply, attach, *fg.*
You will o. me, if = āuñ tukā upkāri zāun vortăutoloñ zărtăr.

Obliging, *a.* mogāḷ; upkāri; voḍnetso, *or* voḍni diuntso = *l.* giving inclination, (sympathetic), *n. c.*; bāndtso = *l.* binding, *fg.*, *n. c.*

Obligingness, *s.* mogāḷpoṇ, -ṇā, *n.*

Oblique, *a.* vānkḍo, *pr. fg.*

Obliquity, *s.* vānkḍepoṇ, -ṇā, *n. or* vānkuḍ, -ḍā, *n.*

Obliterate, *v.* 1. pus = *l.* cancel; mār.
2. *fg.* uṇo zā = *l.* become less, *e.g.* the memory of.

Obliteration, *s.* pusāp, -spā, *n.*

Oblivion, *s.* visăr, -ri, *f.*

Oblivious, *a.* visări; visrāuntso; ugḍāsnātullo.

Oblong, *a.* digso.

Obloquy, *s.* gāḷ, -ḷi, *f.* = *l.* abuse; āḍuloṇeñ, -ṇeā, *n.* = *l.* talk against.

Obnoxious, *a.* 1. pòḍtso = *l.* falling, *e.g.* to risk; ukto ghāllo = *l.* put open, *or only* ukto (*or* ugto); sārko *added to the verb*, *e.g.* pòḍasārko = *l.* ob. to fall.
2. luksānātso = *l.* hurtful.

Obscene, *a.* burso, pòzḍo = dirty, *fg.*; lăjišṭ = *l.* shameful; ăumăryāditso = *l.* unbecoming; ăḷšik = *l.* ugly, *fg.*; kānṭāḷeātso = abominable, *fg.*; móstitso = *l.* luxurious.

Obscenity, *s.* bursepoṇ, -ṇā, *n.*; pòzḍepoṇ, -ṇā, *n.*; ăḷšikpoṇ, -ṇā, *n.*; móst, -ti, *f.*

Obscuration, *s.* kāḷók, -kā, *m.*

Obscure, *s.* 1. kāḷokātso; kāḷso = *l.* somewhat black; uzuāḍnātullo = without light.
2. kăṭiṇ = *l.* difficult; guṭātso = *l.* secret; somzunk nozo āsullo, *or* somzanāñsārko; tăzvizitso = maliciously ob.
3. uṇo *or* hălko = *l.* low; ăṇvo; *see* **Low.**

Obscure, *v.* 1. kāḷok kăr = *l.* make darkness; uzuāḍ kāḍ = *l.* take away light.
2. *fg.* mān kāḍ = *l.* take away honour.

Obscurity, *s.* 1. kāḷok, -kā, *m.*; ăndkār, -rā, *m.*
2. *fg.* ăṇvepoṇ, -ṇā, *n.*; uṇepoṇ, -ṇā, *n.* = a low state.

Obsequious, *a.* 1. mān diuntso.
2. gulām = *l.* slavish, *fg.*

Observance, *s.* 1. pāḷo, -ḷeā, *m.*
2. rivāz, -ji, *f.* = *l.* fashion; lūḷ, -ḷi, *f.*

Observant, *a.* 1. mān diuntso.
2. zāgrut = *l.* careful; tsătrāyetso = attentive; sārko = *l.* exact.

Observation, *s.* tsătrāi, -ye, *f.* = *l.* a note, a remark, attention; šāro, -reā, *m.*

Observatory, *s.* zotišasāl, *or* neketrañpănḍitasāl, -lā, *n.*

Observe, *v.* 1. pòḷe.
2. tsătrāi kāṇge = take care, *or* ts. kăr = make a note.
3. sāmbāḷ, *e. g.* rules, customs.

Obsolete, *a.* porno = *l.* old; ăpṛup, *or* ăprupātso = *l.* rare.

Obstacle, *s.* hărkăt, -ti, *f.*; āḍkăḷ, -ḷi, *f.*; *see* **Objection.**

Obstetric, *a.* voijiṇitso.

Obstinacy, *s.* săḷ, -ḷā, *n.*; dhāruṇāi, -ye, *f.*; murdārpoṇ, -ṇā, *n.*, *n. c.*; *see* **Obduracy.**

Obstinate, *a.* săḷiṣṭ: dhāruṇ; āpleā vādeātso.

Obstruct, *v.* dāmp *or* dānk = *l.* shut; ăḍḍi kăr = *l.* put an obstacle.

Obstruction, *s.* āḍkăḷ, -ḷi, *f.*

Obtain, *s.* 1. zōḍ (ó); ātasi, *n. c.*; māgun ghe; mèḷ = *l.* be found, *Sb. Dat.*; zā = *l.* become, *Sb. Dat.*; jik = *l.* gain.
2. tsăl = *l.* walk, *fg.* be current.

Obtrude, *v.* bòḷ kăr = *l.* make force, compel; *see* **Intrude.**

Obtuse, *a.* 1. dhārnātullo.
2. *fg.* dăḍḍo *or* dăḍḍa = *l.* stupid; somzanātullo.

Obviate, *v.* tsukăi = *l.* avoid; mukār rāu = *l.* remain in face; (-ntlo) păriyār zā = *l.* get rid of; ăḍḍi kăr *or* āḍāi; nivrāi = *l.* deliver, *ch. cs.*

Obvious, *a.* soṣṭ = *l.* evident; pārgăṭ = *l.* public.

Occasion, *s.* 1. sămayo, -yeā, *m.*, *e. g.* of sin.
2. săndrāp, -pā, *m.* = *l.* opportunity.
3. vēḷ(é), -ḷā, *m.* = *l.* time; săngăt, -gti, *f.* = *l.* circumstance.

Occasional, *a.* 1. *rs.* săndrāpa părmāṇe, *or* săndrāpātso.
2. āučit = *l.* casual; āučit găḍtso = *l.* happening casually.

Occident, *see* **West.**

Occupation, *s.* 1. kām, -mā, *n.* = *l.* business; udyóg, -gā, *m.* = *l.* (civil) employment.
2. *rs. into* kāṇe = *l.* take, occupy; *or bet.* zulmen kāṇe = *l.* take violently.

Occupied (Is), *v.* kāmār (āsā) = *l.* (is) on business.

Occupy, *v.* 1. kāṇe = *l.* take.
2. zulmen kāṇe = *l.* take violently.
3. āsā = *l.* is, is in possession, *ch. cs.*
4. vistār = *l.* be extended, *ch. cs.*
5. kāmāk lāi = *l.* apply to work, give work.
6. bhór = *l.* fill, *fg.*, *e.g.* oc. the mind with.

Occur, *v.* 1. zā; găḍ = *l.* happen.
2. mèḷ = *l.* be found, *Sb. Dat.*; mótint ye = come in the mind.

Occurrence, *s.* săngăt, -gti, *f.* = *l.* circumstance.

Ocean, *s.* dăryo, -yeā, *m.*; sămdir, -rā, *m.*; sāgor, -rā, *m. used also fg.*, *e.g.* oce. of graces.

Octave, *s.* 1. *vlg.* oitav, -vā, *m.*, of a feast; āṭvo dis, -sā, *m.* = *l.* eighth day.
2. āṭvo gurtụ, -tā, *m.* (*in* music), *or* āṭvo tāḷo, -ḷeā, *m.*

Oculist, *s.* doḷeāñvoiz, -zā, *m.*

Odd (number), *s.* geḷeñ (*var.* geḍeñ, -ḍeā), -ḷeā, *n.*, *opp. to* fāḍeñ.

Odd, *a.* tārifetso = *l.* awkward.

Odds, *s.* tsăḍuṇeñ, -ṇeā, *n.*, bhēd (ê), -dā, *m.* = difference.
Be at o. = nāi āsā = *l.* discord is.

Ode, *s.* pòd, -dā, *n.* = *l.* a song.

Odious, *a.* kānṭāḷeātso.

Odium, *s.* hăgeñ, -geā, *n.*; *see* **Hatred.**

Odontalgy, *s.* dāntañvidya, -ye, *f.*

Odorous, *a.* părmăḷātso.

Odour, *see* **Scent.**

Œconomy, *see* **Economy.**

Œcumenical, *see* **Ecumenical.**

Of, *prep.* 1. -tso, -či, -čeñ, *or* -lo, -li, -leñ; *see* Gram. P. II. (*Genit.*)
2. višyānt = *l.* about.
3. *Instrum. or Genit. to express the* material of which.
Of late = voḍóḷ, *or* āilevār.
Of old = ādiñ, *or* ādiñ purviñ.

Off, *ad.* 1. pois = far.
2. *for* off *as a particle in compound verbs see such verbs.*
3. tsăl = go; tsăl vots = off with you.
4. mukār = in face, *e.g.* far off the promontory.
5. lāgiñ = *l.* near.
6. vingăḍ = *l.* separated.
Is well off = vrăddhi zāun āsā.

Offence, *s.* 1. ăkmān, -nā, *m.*
2. duk, -ki, *f.* = *l.* sorrow.
3. pāḍ dēk(ê), -ki, *f.* = *l.* bad example.

4. gunyāuñ, -āvā, *m.* = *l.* fault; äprād, -dā, *m.*

Offend, *v.* 1. ăkmān kăr; rāg āḍăi.
2. dukăi, *c. v.* = *l.* afflict.
3. pātak ādār = *l.* commit sin; tsuk = err; mōḍ(ó) = *l.* break, *fg.*, *e. g.* o. against the commandments, *ch. cs.* (*Acc.*)
4. pāḍ dēk(è) di = *l.* give bad example; *see also* **Disgrace.**

Offensive, *a.* 1. ăkmānātso.
2. dukountso.
3. kānṭāḷeātso = *l.* abominable; ăḷšik = *l.* ugly, *fg.*
4. zulmetso = *l.* of violence (o. war), *or* zulum kărtso, *or the Mr. Hind.* čăḍāvātso.

Offer, *v.* 1. bheṭăi (to God *and also* to men), *or* bheṭoun di.
2. somorpi, vopsi, *rl. mn.*
3. di = *l.* give.
4. mótint ye = come in the mind.
5. kăr = *l.* do, *e.g.* o. violence.
6. zā = *l.* become, *e. g.* an occasion.

Offering, *s.* 1. bhèṭ, -ṭe, *f.*; somorpoṇ, -ṇā, *n.*
2. deṇeñ, -ṇeā, *n.* = *l.* a gift.
3. iḍo, -ḍeā, *m.* = a certain o. at the time of marriage.

Office, *s.* 1. kāido, -deā, *m.* = duty.
2. kām, -mā, *n.* = *l.* business; udyóg, -gā, *m.* (civil) employment.
3. upkār, -rā, *m.* = *l.* a benefit, kindness.
4. ophis, -sā, *m.*, *fr.* (eccl. o.)
5. kăčări, -ri, (*or* -re), *f.* = the place where public business is attended to.

Officer, *s.* udyógagār, -rā, *m.* = civil o.; foujisărdār, -rā, *m.* = military o.

Official, *a.* sărkārātso.

Official, *s.* udyógagār, -rā, *m.*, *or* udyógăst, -tā, *m.*

Officiate, *v.* (kām) tsălăi.
O. at the altar = Devāčeñ kām tsălăi.

Officious, *a.* upkāri; mogāḷ; rigtso = *l.* interfering.

Offing, *s.* tăḍi poisileān.

Offscouring, *see* **Bran.**

Offset, *see* **Shoot.**

Offspring, *s.* săntăt, -ti, *f.*; burgiñ, *pl. n.*; kuṭām, -ṭmā, *n.* = *l.* family.

Often, *ad.* săbār pāuṭi; tovóḷ tovóḷ.
As often as = (kitle pāuṭi) title pāuṭi.

Ogle, *v.* vānkḍo pòḷe.

Ogre, *s. perh.* rākkós, -ksā, *m.* = *l.* a monster.

Oil, *s.* tēl(è), -lā, *n.*
Holy o. = *vlg.* benjār tēl; *bet.* păvitrụ t.

Oil-cake, *s.* pēnḍ(é), -ḍi, *f.*

Oilman, *s.* tèlagār (*or* tèlkār), -rā, *m.*; gāṇegār, -rā, *n.*

Oil-mill, Oil-press, *s.* ghāṇo, -ṇeā, *m.*

Ointment, *s.* mulām, -mā, *n.*; pārmāḷāči vāstu̥, -tu, *f.* = *l.* fragrant thing; tēl(è), -lā, *n.* = *l.* oil.

Old, *a.* 1. mātāro, *of persons.*
2. porno, *of things.*
3. ādlo = *l.* anterior.
Elder brother = voḍlo bhāu (mālgoḍo bh. = eldest b.).
Of o. = ādiñ purviñ.
Grow o. = mātāro zā.
O. age = mātāri prāi, -ye, *f.*; *or* utăr p., *or* săbār p., *or* mātārepoṇ, -ṇā, *n.*
O. man = yék mātāro; jabbo; o. woman = yèk mātāri; jabbu.
O. fashioned = ādle rivājitso.

Olden, *a.* ādle sovóyetso = *l.* of former custom; ādle sovóye pārmāṇe āsullo; porno; ādleā kālātso, *or* ādlo.

Oligarchy, *s.* thoḍeāntso ădhikār, -rā, *m.*

Olive, *s.* nāṇelātso ruk, -kā, *m.*; *Sans.* jitaruk; jitafòḷ, -ḷā, *n.*

Omega, *s.* *fg.* ănt, -tā, *m.* = *l.* end.

Omen, *s.* nimit, -tā, *n.*; khuṇa, -ṇe, *f.*; gurtu̥, -tā, *m.* = *l.* a sign; ădrušṭ, -ṭā, *n.*

Omission, *s.* sóḍneñ, -neā, *n.*; nākărni, -ne, *f.*, *n. c.*

Omit, *v.* 1. *neg.* *of* kăr; sóḍ = leave.
2. thāmb = *l.* cease; rāu = *l.* remain; *or bet.* rāu *preceded by Gerund. neg.* *in* tanāñ *of the principal verb*, *e.g.* jevināstanāñ rāu = omit eating.

Omnibus, *s.* tăpālgāḍi, -ye, *f.*

Omnipotence, *s.* sărvu̥podvi, -ve, *f.*

Omnipotent, *a.* sărvu̥podvedār.

Omnipresent, *a.* sărvu̥hāzāri.

On, *prep.* 1. vóir; *or 2nd Loc. to show*, *a*) a local relation, *b*) a logical basis, *e.g.* on that spot, condition.
2. lāgiñ = *l.* close.
3. višyānt = about.
4. *by instrum.*, *e. g.* on a line = hārin; on this side = ye kusin.
Play on the violin = rebek vāz.

On, *ad.* 1. mukār = *l.* forward.
2. rāvanāstanāñ = *l.* not remaining (continually).

Once, *ad.* yék pāuṭi.
At o. = 1. yekāts phara = *l.* in one moment.
2. ātānts = just now.
3. sāngāta = together; soveñ = at the same time.

One, *a.* 1. yék (*cardinal numb. and indef. article*).
2. yeklo = an individual.
3. vo = *l.* this, *in opp. to* to = that, *e.g.* one says...the other...; yeklo *could also be used.*
4. phālāno = a certain (person).
5. *as equivalent to the German* 'man' *it is omitted; or* mānis *or* āmiñ *may be used*, *e.g.* what one wishes one readily believes = āmiñ khuši vor-

tāuñ, teñ āmiñ sompeñ sătmāndtāuñ.

This is the one = vots; at one day = yék pāuṭi; at one time = ādi, *or* ādiñ purviñ; it is all o. = yekăts.

One another = yekameka (*decl.*)

Oneself, *pron.* āpuṇ.

Onion, *s.* piyāu, -yāvā, *m.*

Only, *ad.* mātru; făkăt; *by* -ts; *see* Gram.

Only, *a.* yekăts; *rs. into ad.*

Onset, *s.* 1. zulum, -lme, *f.*; āngārpòḍāp, -ḍpā, *n.*; uprāḷi, -ḷi, *f.*

2. *fg.* gāḷi, *f. pl.* = *l.* abusings.

Onward, *ad.* mukār.

Onward, *a.* mukāvelo.

Opaque, *a.* disanātullo.

Open, *v.* 1. ugto kăr *or* ugăḍ (*used also for* reveal).

2. suru kăr = *l.* make a beginning, *G. F.*

3. kātăr = *l.* cut, *e.g.* a wound; pulāi, *e.g.* a pustule.

4. kăr = *l.* do, *e.g.* o. a way.

O. the bowels = utkāḍe zā.

O. out = vistār, *or* sóḍāi, *e.g.* a cloth.

O. the door = bāgil ugteñ kăr; bāgil kāḍ.

Open, *a.* 1. ugto.

2. votsāyet āsullo = *l.* accessible; rigasārko.

3. părgăṭ = *l.* public.

4. sādo *or* niškăpṭi = *l.* sincere.

5. niščeisinātullo = *l.* not settled.

Opening, *s.* 1. iḍeñ, -ḍeā, *n.*; moḍāp, -ḍpā, *n.* = *l.* a breach; fuṭ, -ṭi, *f.*

2. suru, -ve, *f.* = *l.* a beginning, an inauguration; *see* **Exit.**

Openly, *ad.* sošṭ, *or* părgăṭ zāun; bhăirăng, *or* bhāileān = *l.* exteriorly.

Operate, *v.* bòḷ āsā = *l.* strength is, *ch. cs.*; guṇāk pòḍ = *l.* to improvement fall, *ch. cs.*, *e.g.* a medicine, a sermon; boro rigtā *or* boro lāgtā = *l.* enters *or* is applied well, *are used esp. for* sermons; *see* **Influence.**

Operation, *s.* 1. kărni, -ne, *f.*; kām, -mā, *n.*; kāryeñ, -yeā, *n.*; kărm, -mā, *n.*, *n. c.*; kărtuveñ, -veā, *n.* = *Lat. facinus*, a bad action.

2. kātrāp, -pā, *n.* = *l.* a cutting (in surgery).

Ophthalmy, *s.* doḷeāntso ulóp, -lpā, *m.* = *l.* inflammation of eyes.

Opinion, *s.* 1. āločen, -ni, *f.* = persuasion, judgment, set of tenets, esteem.

2. gād, -di, *f.* = *l.* a saying.

3. ănkul, -lā, *n.* = a good op.

4. vādo, -deā, *m.* = a particular op.

Opium, *s.* āphim, -mā, *n.*

Opponent, *s.* porto; virodhi.

Opportune, *a.* făvoto = *l.* due; lāyek = *l.* suitable; săndrāpātso = *l.* of opportunity;

sāma kālātso = *l.* of right time.

Opportunity, *s.* 1. sāndrāp, -pā, *n.*, pāuṭ, -ṭi, *f.*; sāmayo, -yeā, *m.*; ānkul, -lā, *n.*; sāma kāl, -lā, *m.* = *l.* proper time.
2. upāi, -yā, *m.* = *l.* means.

Oppose, *v.* āḍ ghāḷ = put against; āḍkāḷ kār *or* āḍḍi kār = *l.* make obstacle.

Opposed, *a.* 1. virodh āsullo.
2. porto.
3. mukār āsullo = *l.* being in face; mukāvelo.

Opposite, *a.* 1. mukāvelo.
2. porto.
In the o. direction = porte vāṭen.
Be o. to = *Dat.* porto āsā (*Lat. e regione*).
O. to = mukār.

Opposition, *s.* āḍḍi, -ḍe, *f.*, *or* āḍkāḷ, -ḷi, *f.*; virodhāi, -ye, *f.* (contrariety); virod tānḍ, -ḍā, *m.* = *l.* a contrary part.

Oppress, *v* 1. *pr.* bhārān mōḍ(ó) = *l.* break by heaviness.
2. *fg.* dāgdāi, *c. v.* = *l.* cause sufferings; zulum kār = *l.* make violence; *fg.* rāḍāi = *l.* cause to weep; dukāi = *l.* afflict, cause sorrow; kāṣṭāi = *l.* cause pain; yeṭik dhār, *or* y. lāi = apply to forced work (*Lat. angariare*).
Oppressed with debts = riṇān bhorlolo.

Oppression, *s.* dāgd, -dā, *m.* = suffering; zulum, -lme, *f.*; gulāmpoṇ, -ṇā, *n.* = *l.* slavery; ākmān, -nā, *m.* = *l.* offence.

Oppressive, *a.* dāgdountso; zulum kārtso = *l.* making violence; niṣṭur = *l.* cruel.

Oppressor, *s.* dāgdāitolo, *or* rāḍāitolo; zulmegār, -rā, *m.*

Opprobrious, *a.* lājiṣṭ = *l.* shameful; kānṭāḷeātso = *l.* abominable; āḷšik = *l.* ugly, *fg.*; āpamānādik; beābrātso, *or* ābru kāḍtso.

Opprobrium, *s.* āpamān, -nā, *m.*; lāz, -je, *f.* = *l.* shame; beābru, -brā, *m.*

Oppugn, *v. Dat.* virodh ulāi = *l.* speak against; *Dat.* virodh ye = *l.* come against; *see* **Confute.**

Optative, *a.* āšetso.

Optic, *a.* diṣṭitso; drāṣṭitso, *n. c.*

Optics, *s.* diṣṭividya, -ye, *f.*, *or* drāṣṭividya.

Option, *s.* 1. iččha, -čhe, *f.*; khuši, -še, *f.*
2. vintsāp, -tspā, *n.*, *or* vintsṇeñ, -ṇeā, *n.* = *l.* choice.
I have no op. = mojeā sotāntrār nāñ.

Opulence, *s.* grestkāi, -ye, *f.*; dhān, -nā, *n.*; dirveñ, -veā, *n.* (much money).

Opulent, *a.* (bhou) grest; duḍuādik; dirvest; dhānest.

Or, *conj.* yā *or* va; *it is often omitted.*

Or . . . or = yā (*only one* or *is translated*).
Whether... or = -gi, *e.g.* I do not know w. this is right or not = yeñ sămagi tsuk āuñ neṇāñ, *or* yeñ săma yā tsuk moṇ āuñ neṇāñ; will he come or not? = to yetologi nāñ?

Oracle, *s.* 1. sāṇ, -ṇā, *n.* = a Hindu temple.
2. *for the* o. *itself*, *rs. into* dăršaṇ yeun sāng, *or* (săitān) āngār yeun sāng = *l.* after (the devil) has come in (your) body, say; *perh.* šekun, -nā, *n.*; nimit, -tā, *n.*
3. *fg.* bhou budivont mănis, -nšā, *m.* = *l.* a very wise man.

Oral, *a.* tòṇḍa tòṇḍāntlo = *l.* being from mouth to mouth; tòṇḍpāšiñ.

Orally, *ad.* tòṇḍpašiñ.

Orange, *s.* 1. sonāring (*var.* sonanāring, *or* solnāring, *or* nāring), -rngā, *n.*
2. torenj, -jā, *n.* (*perh.* pompelmous, *Lat. citrus decumana*, *or bet.* the pomilow).

Oration, *s.* *vlg.* sermāuñ, -āvā, *m.*, *fr.*; prăsăng, -gā, *n.*, *n. u.*; uloṇeñ, -ṇeā, *n.*

Orator, *s. has no pure Konk. equivalent; best w.* prăsăngagār, -rā, *m.*; sermāvist, -tā, *m.*, *n. c.*, *fr.*; prăsăngapăṇḍit, -tā, *m.*; săbhañ păṇḍit; uloṇegār, -rā, *m.* = *l.* speaker; *or* ulouṇo, -ṇeā, *m.*

Oratorical, *a.* 1. unči (bhāsetso) = *l.* of nice language.
2. ălănkārātso = *l.* ornamental.

Oratory, *s.* 1. prăsăngavidya, -ye, *f.*; prăsăngpoṇ, -ṇā, *n.*; prăsăngapăṇḍitpoṇ, -ṇā, *n.*; ălănkārăči v.; *see* **Orator.**
2. māg-ṇeñ kărčeñ ghăr, -rā, *n.* = *l.* a house of prayer; *vlg.* kopel, -lā, *n.*, *fr.*; irmit, -ti, *f.*, *fr.*

Orb, *s.* 1. mānḍ, -ḍā, *m.* = disk.
2. guḷo, -ḷeā, *m.* = a globe.

Orbit, *s.* bovāḍo, -ḍeā, *m.*; boun-ḍi, -ḍe, *f.*

Orchard, *s.* (folvostučeñ) tòṭ, -ṭā, *n.*; moḷo -ḷeā, *m.*

Orchestra, *s.* 1. igărjemāḷăi, -ḷiye, *f.*
2. gāyāngārāntso mēḷ(é), -ḷā, *m.* = a body of singers.
3. gāyāngārānčeñ sāl, -lā, *n.* = *l.* a hall of singers.

Ordain, *v.* 1. formāi = *l.* command; nemsi = *l.* appoint.
2. ordinar kăr (*fr.*), *rl.*; păvitrụ ădhikār di = *l.* give sacred power, *or the Mr.* dhărmādhikārăči diha di = *l.* give initiation in religious authority. (*In pass. for* di *put* mèḷ = *l.* be found, received).

Ordainer, *s.* 1. nemsitolo.
2. ordinār kărtolo; dărmādhikārači diha ditolo.

Ordeal, *s.* kăṭiṇ tănki, -ke, *f.* = *l.* a difficult trial.

Order, *s.* 1. mānḍāvoḷ, -ḷi, *f.* =

good disposition; krăm, -mā, *m.* = regularity.
2. hukum, -kme, *f.* = *l.* a command; tākid, -de, *f.* = a special order; formāṇ, -ṇā, *n.*
3. huddo, -deā, *m.* = *l.* rank; thăr, -rā, *m.* = *l.* kind, class.
4. mēḷ(é), -ḷā, *m.* = *l.* a college, society, reunion; yekoṭ, -ṭā, *m.*; *vlg.* òrd, -di, *f.*
5. ord, -di, *f.*, *in rl. mn.*
6. hunḍi, -ye, *f.* = an order for money. [*fr.*
Take holy orders = ordinār zā,

Order, *v.* 1. mānḍ = *l.* arrange; săma ghāl = *l.* put right.
2. hukum (*or* tākid) di = *l.* give order.

Orderly, *ad.* săma; sārkeñ; krămān.

Ordinance, *s.* istyār, -rā, *n.* = an authoritative proclamation.

Ordinarily, *ad.* 1. tsăḍāvot zāun; tsālteñ.
2. sumār (in a common degree).

Ordinary, *a.* sādārṇ; *see* **Common.**

Organ, *s.* sāndo, -deā, *m.* = *l.* a member (*not ex.*); *perh.* āid, -dā, *n.*; gòp, -pā, *n.*, *e. g.* of plants (*l.* bosom, *fg.*)

Organic, *a.* sānde āsullo; gòpātso, *or* gòp āsullo.

Organism, *s.* sāndeamēḷ(é), -ḷā, *m.*; *pl.* sānde = organs.

Organization, *s.* găḍāp, -ḍpā, *n.*; mēḷ(é), -ḷā, *m.*; mānḍāvoḷ, -ḷi, *f.* = *l.* disposition; *bet. rs. into v.*

Organize, *v.* mānḍ = *l.* arrange; rūp di = *l.* give form; meḷăi = *l.* unite; găḍ = *l.* found; săma ghāl = *l.* put right.

Oriel, *see* **Balcony.**

Orient, *see* **East.**

Orifice, *s.* tònḍ, -ḍā, *n.*, *fg.*; *see* **Exit.**

Origin, *s.* 1. ărămb, -bā, *m.*; suru, -ve, *f.* = *l.* a beginning.
2. kuṭām, -ṭmā, *n.* = *l.* a family.
3. mūḷ, -ḷā, *n.* = *l.* a root, *fg.*

Original, *a.* 1. poilo = *l.* first; ărămbātso, *or* suruvetso, *or* surver āsullo; săimbātso = *l.* natural, *e.g.* o. sin; zălmātso = *l.* of nativity.
2. nīz = *l.* true.

Original, *s.* 1. ăsăl, -slā, *n.*, *opp. to* copy.
2. nămuno, -neā, *m.* = a sample.
3. tārifetso mănis, -nšā, *m.* = *l.* a curious man.

Originate, *v.* ărămb āsā = *l.* origin is, *ch. cs.*; nipăzā; kăr = *l.* do; răts = *l.* create; suru kăr = *l.* make a beginning; zălmăi = *l.* beget; zā = *l.* become; ubzăi (*c. v. of* ubza) = *l.* cause to become.

Ornament, *s.* ălănkār, -rā, *m.*, *pr. fg.*; neṭoṇ, -ṇi, *f.*; surungār, -rā, *m.*, *n. c.*

Ornament, *v.* ălānkār kăr, *G. M.* (persons and things); neṭăi, *c. v.* (*esp.* persons).

Ornamental, *a.* ălănkārātso.

Orphan, *a.* pòr (*it means also* any

poor little boy); āvoibāpuinātullo.

Orphanage, *s.* pòrañbiḍār, -rā, *n.*

Orthodox, *a.* āpuṭ = *l.* pure, not mixed, *fg.*; sătevont = *l.* truthful.

Orthodoxy, *s.* āpuṭ sikoṇ, -ṇe, *f.* (*or* āpuṭ bāvāḍt, -tā, *m.*) = *l.* sincere doctrine.

Orthoepy, *s.* săma utsār, -rā, *m.*, *or* săma utsārāp, -rpā, *n.*; šuddu̥ utsār.

Orthography, *s.* săma (*or* šuddu̥) bărāp, -rpā, *n.*

Oscillate, *v.* yeṇeñ teṇeñ hāl; dănḍăḷ.

Oscillation, *s.* hālāp, -lpā, *n.*; dănḍăḷčeñ, -čeā, *n.*, *or* dănḍăḷāp, -ḷpā, *n.*; yeṇeñ teṇeñ hālčeñ.

Osseous, *a.* hāḍāntso.

Ostensible, *a.* dākountso, *or* dākăisārko; pòḷeyet (*or* poḷouyet) āsullo.

Ostentation, *s.* ăbbār, -rā, *n.*; āmsāṇ, -ṇi, *f.*; ăhănkār, -rā, *m.*, băḍāi, -ye, *f.* = vainglory; mizād, -di, *f.* (*var.* mizādki); doulăt, -ti, *f.*; ăunṭu, -ṭā, *m.*

Ostentatious, *a.* dănḍi = showy in dress, *etc.*; ăunṭi.

Ostler, *s.* gāḍiyegār, -rā, *m.*

Other, *a.* 1. dusro; duyăm.
2. āniyek = *l.* one more.
3. yèr = *l.* *Lat. reliquus.*
4. bădăl = *l.* different.
5. thoḍe = *l.* some.
6. āni = *l.* and *or* more, *if* o. *is joined to* some, *e.g.* some o. thing = āni kāiñ.

Other than we wished = yék čintleñ, yék zāleñ (*Konk.*).

Some (cohorts) my brother commanded, others Pomponius = . . . yer . . . . Of beasts, some live on land, others in water = ... thoḍeo. . . . . .

The other part of the body = . . . yèr.

The one is . . . the other . . . . = yeklo . . . . dusro.

No other weapon but = . . bădăl.

Each o. = yekameka.

Otherwise, *ad.* 1. nāñ zāleār (*or some such verb*) = *l.* if it does not happen.
2. dusre jinsiñ = *l.* in another way.
3. *often rs., e. g.* I think you have not yet done it, o. you would have told me = ... kelleñ zāleār măkā săngtoloi āsulloi. A man o. respectable = yek mănis yera višyānt mān fāvo zāllo.

Ottoman, *s.* turik, -rkā, *m.*

Ought, *v. By Neceṣs. mood;* zāi = *l.* is necessary; kāido āsā = *l.* duty is.

Ought, *s.* kāiñ.

Ounce, *s.* ons, -sā, *n.*, *fr.*; *see App. to the Konk.-English Dictionary.*

Our, *a.* āmtso.

Ourselves, *pron.* āmints.

Out, *ad.* 1. bhāir.

N. B. Many words compounded with out, not put down here, may be expressed with the help of a comparative; see Outlast.

2. părgăṭ = *l.* public.
O. of mind = mótir nātullo, *a.*; *or* zāmptso.
O. of my power = moje podve bhāir.
O. of love = mogān.
O. of hell = yemkòṇḍāntlo; *see* Gram. p. 54.
O. of shot = pois (āsā); fārā bhāir.
O. of sport = čeṣṭāyen.
Outbreak, *s.* kāṭkāi, -ye, *f.*; utsāmboḷāi, -ye, *f.* = *l.* excitement.
Outcast, *s. a.* 1. *vlg.* băṣṭāillo; zātibhāilo.
2. păradešānt uḍăillo.
Out-do, *v.* jik; *see* **Surpass.**
Outer, *a.* bhāilo.
Outfit, *s.* sāmān, -nā, *m.*
Outflank, *v. perh.* veḍo ghāl.
Outgrow, *v.* 1. mirvon vāḍ, *or* leka vorto vāḍ.
2. *fg. rs. into* zāinăñ, *or other* [*verb.*
Out-house, *s.* māṭou, -ṭvā, *m.*; govòḷ, -vḷā, *m.*; nāṇi, -ye, *f.*; nāṇiyekoḍkeñ, -keā, *n.*
Outlast, *v.* .... vórn tăg = last more than...
Outlaw, *see* **Outcast.**
Outlay, *s.* khărts, -tsā, *m.*
Outlet, *see* **Exit.**
Outline, *s.* sănkšep, -pā, *n.*; *see also* **Sketch.**
Outlive, *v.* vānts; māgir jiye = *l.* live afterwards.
Outnumber, *v.* ... vórn tsăḍ āsā = is greater than...
Outrage, *s.* ăkmān, -nā, *m.*
Outrage, *v.* ăkmān kăr.
Outrageous, *a.* ăkmānātso.
Outright, *ad.* 1. ātānts; teā kšăṇ.
2. purteñ, *or* păripurṇ = fully.
Outrun, *v.* mukār dāuñ; pāṭi ghāl.
Outset, *s.* suru, -ve, *f.*
Outside, *ad.* bhāir, *ad. postp.*
Outside, *s.* bhāileñ rūp, -pā, *n.* = *l.* exterior form.
Outskirt, *s.* 1. ăkér, -kri, *f.* = *l.* extremity.
2. konso, -seā, *m.* = *l.* a corner.
Outspoken, *see* **Frank.**
Outstanding, *a. rs. into* bāki urtā = *l.* balance remains.
Outstrip, Outvie, *v.* jik = *l.* gain, *fg.*; miruăi = *l.* surpass.
Outward, *a.* bhāilo.
Outward, *ad.* bhāir.
Outweigh, *v.*...vórn tsăḍ tūk = *l.* weigh more than...; miruăi = *l.* surpass.
Outwit, *v.* fóṭăi = *l.* deceive.
Outwork, *s.* bhāilo pāgār, -rā, *m.*; bhāileñ koṭeñ, -ṭeā, *n.*
Oval, *a.* digso; *rs.* ṭāntiya bări.
Oven, *s.* 1. khòrn, -nā, *n.*, *e. g.* o. for bread, *fr.*
2. āguṭeñ (*or* āguṣṭeñ), -ṭeā, *n.* = a sort of brick-kiln.
Over, *prep.* 1. voir, *or* 2nd. *Loc.*
2. prăs tsăḍ = *l.* more than.

3. šivāi = *l.* besides.

Over, *ad.* 1. voir; unts.
2. *G.* veḷār = *l.* in time.
It is all o. = zāleñ, *or* tirsaleñ.
O. and o. again = portun portun.
O. and again = săbār pāuṭi.

Overabound, *v.* tsăḍ, *or* tsăḍ zā.

Overbalance, *see* **Outweigh.**

Overbearing, *a.* săḷiṣṭ.

Overcast, *a.* săbār kupāntso.

Overcharge, *v.* tsăḍ mòl sāng.

Overcome, *v.* zăit vor = *l.* bring victory; jik (surpass); miruăi; khālto kăr.

Overcoat, *s.* kutāuñ, -tāvā, *m.* (native), *vlg.*

Overdo, *v.* tsăḍ kăr (*or* tsăḍ *with some such verb*) = *l.* do too much; miruon kăr.

Overdrink, *v.* miruon piye, *or* miti bhāir p., *or* lekavort p.

Overflow, *v.* bhāir vāu; dèg mirua.

Overfond, *a.* 1. tsăḍ ăpurbāyetso.
2. tsăḍ ăpurbāi kărtso.

Overgrow, *v.* miruon vāḍ, *or* lekavorto vāḍ.

Overhang, *v.* umkăḷāi *or* lāmbăi.

Overhasty, *a.* tsăḍ ăuñsărātso.

Overhead, *ad.* māteā voir.

Overlay, *v.* lāi, *e.g.* with silver; *see* **Smother, Suffocate.**

Overlong, *a.* tsăḍ lāmb.

Overlook, *v.* 1. pòḷe; rāk = *l.* guard.
2. māf kăr = *l.* make excuse.
3. bepārvo kăr = *l.* make contempt, (neglect).

Overpower, *see* **Overwhelm.**

Oversee, *v.* rāk; *see* **Superintend.**

Overseer, *s.* 1. rākṇo, -ṇeā, *m.*; mêlbăndobăst pòḷetolo; muzimdār, -rā, *m.*
2. šeṇăi, -ṇăi, *m.* = a superintendent.

Oversight, *s.* 1. rākṇeñ, -ṇeā, *n.*; *see* **Superintendence;** zătăn, -tne, *f.* = care.
2. sóḍni, -ne, *f.*
3. (doḷeānči) tsuk, -ki, *f.* = *l.* a mistake (of the eyes).

Oversleep, *v.* miruon nīd, *or* lekavorto nīd.

Overspread, *see* **Overlay.**

Overstep, *v.* mirva.

Overtake, *v.* pāṭ dhăr; dhăr; făk kărn dhăr = surprise.

Overtask, *v.* tsăḍ kām di.

Overthrow, *v.* 1. săkal uḍăi.
2. nāš kăr = *l.* make destruction (*Acc.*).
3. păḍāu kăr = *l.* make defeat.

Overtop, *v.* vórn ubār āsā, *or* mirvăi.

Overture, *s.* šărt, -tā, *n.* = a proposal.

Overturn, *v.* 1. vompto ghāl; porti.
2. *fg.* nāš kăr (*Acc.*).

Overvalue, *v.* tsăḍ mòl sāng.

Overwhelm, *v.* zăḍăi kăr = *l.* make gravity, *pr. fg.*; bhār kăr, *e.g.* mótik bh. k. = o. the mind.

Owe, *v.* 1. devo āsā (*Sb. Instr.*) 2. *by Necess. mood; see* **Due.** I o. my life to you = āveñ moji jiṇi tukā devi.

Owl, *s.* nātuk, -kā, *n.* = *ex.* a bird that begins to screech in the evening; gug, -gi, *f.* = a big owl.

Own, *a.* āplo; svănta; khāski, *or* kāski (*in compounds* khās, *e.g.* khās bhāu).

Own, *v.* 1. vop = *l.* acknowledge. 2. āsā = *l.* is, *ch. cs.*

Owner, *s.* dhăni, -yā, *m.*; kărt, -tā, *m.*; khāvănd, -dā, *m.*

Ox, *s.* boil, -lā, *m.*

Oyster, *s.* kāluñ, -lvā, *n.*

P

Pace, *s.* mèṭ, -ṭā, *n.*; băkkār, -rā, *n.*; 'b. dovór = walk with long strides'.

Pace, *v.* 1. tsăl; bouñ. 2. tsăln mēz(é) = *l.* going measure.

Pacific, *a.* nidān; soukāsāyetso; sămādhānātso.

Pacification, *s.* sămādhān, -nā, *n.*, *etc.*, *or rs. into v.*

Pacify, *v.* 1. sămādhān kărăi = *l.* cause to make peace. 2. fuslāi = *l.* caress; *see* **Appease.**

Pack, *s.* 1. kāṭ, -ṭā, *m.*; poṭli, -le, *f.*, of cloth. 2. bireñ, -reā, *n.* = *l.* a faction, set, *e.g.* a p. of thieves.

Pack, *v.* 1. kāṭ bānd = *l.* bind a pack. 2. dāmb = *l.* compress. 3. tsăl *or* vots = *l.* go.

Package, *s.* kāṭ, -ṭā, *m.*; *see* **Pack.**

Packet, *v.* kāṭ bānd; *see* **Pack.**

Paddy, *s.* bhăt, -tā, *n.*

Paddock, *see* **Enclosure.**

Padlock, *s.* bīg, -gā, *n.* = *l.* a lock; khiḷ, -ḷi, *f.* = a wooden bolt.

Pagan, *s.* ănbāvāḍti, -tiā, *m.* = *l.* an unbeliever; Hindu *or* Hinduāntso; Konkṇo, -ṇeā, *m.*, *is sometimes used for* a Konkani p.; *see also* **Idolater.**

Paganism, *s.* ănbāvāḍtpoṇ, -ṇā, *n.*; *see also* **Idolatry.**

Page, *s.* 1. pān, -nā, *n.*, *or* puṭ, -ṭā, *n.*, *n.c.*, of a book. 2. tsākór, -krā, *m.* = *l.* a servant; *perh.* noukór, -rā, *m.*

Page, *v.* pānañ borăi = *l.* write the pages.

Pageant, *s.* 1. dobāzo, -jeā, *m.* = *l.* pomp; doulăt, -ti, *f.* 2. khéḷ, -ḷā, *m.* = *l.* a play, spectacle.

Pagoda, *s.* diuḷ, -ḷā, *n.* = a Hindu temple; băsti, -te, *f.* = a Jain temple; sāṇ, -ṇā, *n.* = a small temple.

Pail, *s.* koḷso, -seā, *m.* = a vessel to carry water in; băldi, -de, *f.* = a leathern vessel to carry water in.

Pain, *s.* duk, -ki, *f.*: 'feel pain = duktā (of the body and soul)'; kăṣṭ, -ṭā, *m.*, *esp.* of the soul; khyāst, -ti, *f.*; khănt, -ti, *f.*; ākānt, -tā, *m.* = *l.* distress; dăgd, -dā, *m.* = suffering; vignu̧, -nā, *n.*; voḷvoḷo, -ḷeā, *m.* = very great pain.

Take pains = vāur"; prăyătăn kăr; minăt kăr.

Pain, *v.* duktā, *Sb. Dat.*; duk distā = *l.* pain appears, *Sb. Dat.*

Painful, *a.* dukitso *or* dukest; dukountso = *l.* causing pain; kăṣṭountso.

Paint, *v.* *vlg.* pintar kăr, *fr.*; čitrăi, *n. u.*; rong lāi; năkṣa kāḍ = draw; *see* **Describe.**

Paint, *s.* róng, -gā, *m.* = *l.* colour; băṇṇu̧, -ṇā, *m.*

Painter, *s.* čitragār, -rā, *m.*, *n. u.*, *vlg.* pintartolo, -leā, *m.*, *fr.*; róng lāitolo, *or* r. kāḍtolo, *or* rongagār, -rā, *m.*, *or* băṇṇagār.

Painting, *s.* 1. čitrāunči vidya, -ye, *f.*, *n. c.*; băṇṇu̧ kāḍči vidya.
2. čitru̧, -rā, *n.*, rejist, -tā, *m.*, *fr.* = a picture.

Pair, *s.* zōḍ(ó), -ḍā, *m.*, *or* zoḍi, -ye, *f.*

Palace, *s.* bănglo, -leā, *m.*; rāuḷer, -rā, *n.* (*dim. of* rāuḷ), *or* *perh.* rāuḷ, -ḷā, *n.* *itself.*

Palanquin, *s.* pālki, -ke, *f.*

Palatable, *a.* ručitso; suādik = *l.* of flavour; gòḍ = *l.* sweet.

Palate, *s.* 1. ruts, -či, *f.* (taste).
2. pompeñ, -peā, *n.*, the roof of the mouth; kopo, -peā, *m.*, *n. c.*

Palaver, *s.* năkazāllo, -leā, *m.* = *l.* nonsense; zănk, -ki, *f.*; čeṣṭāi, -ye, *f.* = *l.* fun; khāli utrañ, *pl. n.* = empty words; găzāli, *pl.*, *f.* = *l.* chat.

Pale, *s.* 1. suḷi, -ye, *f.*; *see* **Stake;** khunṭo, -ṭeā, *m.*
2. phidār; -rā, *n.*; khāmbo, -beā, *m.* (rukātso) = *l.* a pillar (of wood).
3. voi, -i, *f.*, veḍo, -ḍeā, *m.* = *l.* an enclosure.

Pale, *a.* pānṭro; ăḷduvoso.

Paleness, *s.* pānṭrepoṇ, -ṇā, *n.*

Palinode, *s.* (sing a p.) sāngu̧lleñ vāiṭ pāṭi kāḍ; lāganātu̧lleñ uloṇeñ, -ṇeā, *n.*; sāngu̧lleāk āḍ āsu̧lleñ sāng-ṇeñ, -ṇeā, *n.*

Palisade, *s.* suḷiñvoi, -voi, *f.*, *or* khunṭeāñvoi.

Palish, *a.* pānṭroso.

Pall, *s.* 1. kāng, -gi, *f.* = a kind of black cloth. [*etc.*
2. jibbo, -beā, *m.*, of soldiers,
3. vól, -li, *f.*, of native women.
All three only approx.

Pall, *v.* čăppo zā = *l.* become insipid; rutsnātullo zā = *l.* become without taste; *Dat.* puro zā = *l.* get enough, tired.

Pallet, *s.* khaṭleñ, -leā, *n.* = *l.* a bed, a couch; āntuḷn, -nā, *n.*

Palliate, *v.* lipăi, *c. v. of* lip; vés ghāl = *l.* put a mask.

Palliative, *s.* vés, -sā, *m.*

Palm, *s.* 1. māḍ, -ḍā, *m.* = a cocoanut tree; kāvāto, -teā, *m.* = a young p.
2. tsuḍeti, -te, *f.* = a palm-branch.
3. piḍo, -ḍeā, *m.* = the lower part of a palm-branch.
4. gèṇ, -ṇā, *n.* (a measure); vèt, -te, *f.*
Palm of the hand = tăḷăt, -tā, *n., or* tăḷvo, -veā, *m.*
Palm of martyrdom = martirāntso rām, -mā, *m., fr.*; răgtasākṣegurtụ, -tā, *m.*

Palmyra, *s.* 1. tăḷto, -teā, *m.* (tree).
2. irvóḷ, -ḷā, *m.* (fruit).

Palpable, *a.* *rs. into* lāgtā = is attached (*Konk.*); părgăṭ = public; soṣṭ = *l.* evident; vòḍ = *l.* big, *e.g.* p. mistake.

Palpitate, *v.* uḍ = *l.* spring, jump; dăḍdăḍ, *as* the heart.

Palpitation, *s.* dăḍdăḍo, -ḍeā, *m.*

Palsy, *s.* ār, -ri, *f., or* āriči piḍa, -ḍe, *f.*

Palter, *v.* mōs(ó) kăr.

Paltry, *a.* ăṇvo; kirkóḷ; čillăr = *l.* trifling.

Pamper, *see* **Indulge.**

Pamphlet, *s.* dākṭeñ pustak, -kā, *n.*; kăḍtil, -le, *f.* (-lā, *n.*)

Pan, *s.* kāil, -li, *f.*; kunḍleñ, -leā, *n.* = a vessel for making curry in.

Panacea, *s.* sărvụvokāt, -ktā, *n.* = *l.* every medicine.

Pander, *v.* fuslāi.

Pane, *s.* ārso, -seā, *m.* (kiṭke-ārso).

Panegyric, *s.* hogḷāp, -pā, *n.*; hogḷāpāčeñ prăsăng, -gā, *n.*; *vlg.* sermāuñ, -māvā, *m., fr.*

Panegyrist, *s.* hogḷāp kărtso; prăsăngagār, -rā, *m.*

Panel, *s.* foḷeñ, -ḷeā, *n.* (bāgla-foḷeñ; voṇti foḷeñ).

Pang, *s.* 1. voḷvoḷe, *pl., m.* = agony.
2. ākānt, -tā, *m.* = distress.

Panic, *s.* *perh.* ăučit (*or* yekāts pharāčeñ) bheñ, bhiyā, *n.* = *l.* sudden fear; kārāṇ nātulleñ bheñ = *l.* fear without cause.

Pannier, *s.* kurveñ, -veā, *n.*; *see* **Basket.**

Pant, *v.* 1. kărse.
2. *fg.* lāle, *obj. Dat.* = *l.* long; *G.* āšen mòr = *l.* die for desire of.

Panther, *s.* bolpo, -peā, *m.*

Pantomime, *a.* năklañ kărtso = *l.* making copies, *fg.*

Pantry, *s.* ugrāṇ, -ṇā, *n.*

Pap, *see* **Nipple.**

Papal, *a.* pāpsāibātso.

Paper, *s.* 1. kāgād, -gdā, *n.*

2. čīṭ, -ṭi, *f.* = *l.* note, banns.
3. dăstevoz, -zā, *n.* = *l.* a document; dāklo, -leā, *m.* = *l.* a document.
4. vărtamānapătrụ, -rā, *n.* = a newspaper.

Parable, *s.* vopār, -re, *f.*; guṭ, -ṭā, *m.*; guḍ, -ḍā, *n.* = *l.* an ambiguous sentence.

Parabola, *s.* sămakakṣačinnụ, -nā, *n.*, *Cn. Mr.*, *n. u.*

Parade, *s.* 1. kovāt, -tā, *n.* (military).
2. dobāzo, -jeā, *m.* = *l.* pomp.

Paradigm, *s.* nămuno, -neā, *m.*

Paradise, *s.* văinkuṭ, -ṭā, *n.*; *see* **Heaven.**

Paradox, *s.* nozosi āločen, -ni, *f.* = *l.* an opinion which seems to be impossible; sătnăiñseñ = *l.* apparent untruth.

Paragraph, *s.* vānṭo, -ṭeā, *m.*, *or* bhāg, -gā, *m.* = *l.* a division; kălăm, -lmā, *n.*; āvăsvăr, -rā, *m.* = *l.* a chapter.

Parallel, *a.* sămapoisilo; *Mr. Cn.* sămāntrụ, *n. u.*

Parallel, *s.* 1. săr, -ri, *f.*, *or* sārkeñ, -keā, *n.* = *l.* resemblance.
2. sămāntrụ giṭ, -ṭā, *m.*

Parallel, *v. see* **Compare.**

Paralysis, *see* **Palsy.**

Paralyze, *v. fg.* bò̤ḷ mōḍ(ó) = *l.* break force.

Paramount, *a.* 1. mukhya = *l.* principal.
2. sotăntrātso = *l.* independent.

Parapet, *s.* 1. kăṭṭapuṇi, -ṇe, *f.*
2. doro, -rea, *m.* = a kind of parapet crowning a well.

Paraphernalia, *s. approx.* āndāṇ, -ṇā, *n.* = native p., *viz.* a box given to a bride with various little presents in it.

Paraphrase, *s.* ărthātărzumo, -meā, *m.*, *mn.* a translation of the sense.

Parasite, *s.* 1. dusreāñ vorviñ jiyetolo.
2. *Mr.* banḍaguḷ, -ḷā, *n.*, *n. u.*

Parasol, *s.* sătri, -re, *f.*, of cloth; sāteñ, -teā, *n.*, of leaves.

Parcel, *s.* 1. vānṭo, -ṭeā, *m.* = *l.* a portion.
2. kāṭ, -ṭā, *m.* = *l.* a packet.
3. tănḍ, -ḍā, *m.* = *l.* a set, a faction.

Parch, *v.* lās = *l.* burn; *see* **Scorch.**

Parchment, *s.* tsāmbḍeñ, -ḍeā, *n.*

Pardon, *s.* māf, *or* māph, -phā, *n.*: 'beg p. = m. kăr' (*or* kăra, *pl.*); bogsāṇeñ, -ṇeā, *n.*

Pardon, *v.* māf kăr; bogsi, *e.g.* sins (*imperat.* bogós); sóḍ = *l.* remit.

Pare, *v.* 1. kātăr = *l.* cut.
2. uṇo kăr = *l.* make less, diminish.

Parent, *s.* āuoi, -i, *f.*, *or* bāpui, -pāi, *m.*; *in pl.* āuoibāpui = *l.* mother (*and*) father.

Parentage, *s.* kuṭām, -ṭmā, *n.* = *l.* family.

Parenthesis, *see* **Brackets.**

Parhelion, *s.* suryāsārkeñ, -keā, *n.* = *l.* image of the sun, *or the Cn. Mr.* mithyāsuryo, -yeā, *m.*; *or* prătisuryo.

Pariah, *s.* mār, -rā, *m.* (man); *pl.* mārañ (men *and* women); maḍḍuleñ, -leā, *n.*, *or* maḍḍeñ, -ḍeā, *n.* (woman).

P. boy = korlo, -leā, *m.*

P. girl = korleñ, -leā, *n.*

Parish, *s.* 1. *vlg.* firgăz, *or* phirguez, -je, *f.*, *fr.*; *perh.* hinḍ, -ḍā, *m.* = *l.* a flock, *fg.*

2. igărz, -je, *f.* = *l.* a church; mēḷ(é), -ḷā, *m.* = *l.* a congregation.

Parishioner, *s.* *vlg.* firgăjetso; *perh.* šeḷi, -ye, *f.* = *l.* a sheep, *fg.*

Parish-priest, *s.* vigār, -rā, *m.*, *fr.*; gouḷi, -ḷiā, *m.* = *l.* a pastor, *fg.*; mēḷamostak, -kā, *n.* = *l.* the head of a congregation.

Parity, *s.* sārkeñ, -keā, *n.*

Park, *s.* veḍo ghālli suāt, -te, *f.* = *l.* place surrounded; *or only* veḍo, -ḍeā, *m.*

Parliament, *s.* rājasăbha, -bhe, *f.* *or* mēḷ(é), -ḷā, *m.*

Parlour, *s.* ulounčeñ sāl, -lā, *n.*, *or* u. kuḍ, -ḍā, *n.*

Parochial, *a.* *vlg.* firgăjetso; gouḷiātso.

Parody, *s.* năklañ kărtso slók, -kā, *m.* = *l.* poetry making copies, *fg.*

Parole, *s.* bhās, -se, *f.*; utăr, -trā, *n.*

Paroxysm, *s.* bhār, -rā, *m.* = *l.* gravity, *fg.* (of a disease); *see* **Fit.**

Parricide, *s.* 1. bāpāči khuni, -ye, *f.* (crime).

2. bāpātso khunigār, -rā, *m.* (the agent).

Parrot, *s.* kīr, -rā, *m.*

Parry, *v.* tsukăi, *c. v.* *of* tsuk.

Parse, *v.* vākyāče vānṭe sāng.

Parsimony, *v.* hăḷt, -tā, *n.*; *see* **Economy.**

Parson, *see* **Parish-priest.**

Part, *s.* 1. vānṭo, -ṭeā, *m.* (distribution, division).

2. kuḍko, -keā, *m.* = a piece; bhāg, -gā, *m.* = *l.* partition.

3. pāḍt, -ti, *f.* (*in the phrase* tāče pāḍtin = on his part, *fr.*); păkṣa, -ṣe, *f.*

4. kāido, -deā, *m.* = *l.* duty.

5. gāuñ, gāñvā, *m.* = *l.* a country.

6. dikkụ, -kā, *m.*, kus, -si, *f.* = side, direction; *by the Instr.*, *omitting* part.

As for my p. = moje păkṣek; mākā lāgtā.

Play the p. of = 1. *G.* suāter tsāl, *l.* walk (*fg.*) in the place of.

2. vésghāl = *l.* put the mask, *fg.*

Part, *v.* kuḍke kăr = *l.* make pieces; kātăr = *l.* cut; vegḷātsār kăr = *l.* make separation; vegḷo kăr = *l.* make separated.

P. from = sóḍ, = *l.* leave, *e.g.* a wife.

Partake, *v.* (*Or.* sāngāta) vāṇṭo mèḷtā = *l.* part is found with; (vāṇṭo) kāṇe = *l.* take a part; zóḍ = *l.* obtain.

Partial, *a.* 1. tòndār pòḷetolo = *l.* looking in the face; păkṣapātātso; nītnātullo = *l.* unjust; *or* nītivont năiñ āsullo; lònts khāuntso = *l.* eating bribes; vosili kărtso.
2. *rs. into* yêk vāṇṭo = *l.* one part; *or* yeka gāuntso = *l.* of one country, *e.g.* p. disturbances.

Partiality, *s.* vosili, -li, *f.*; păkṣapāt, -tā, *n.*

Particle, *s.* 1. lān kuḍko, -keā, *m.*; kuskuṭ, -ṭe, *f.* = an atom.
2. partikul, -lā, *n.*, *rl. mn.*

Particular, *a.* 1. prātèk; višės, *opp. to* general.
2. sārko = *l.* exact; nāzuk = *l.* delicate, *fg.* curious.
3. ăprup, *or* ăsādhārṇ = extraordinary.

Particular, *s.* 1. yeklo = *l.* one (individual); vingăḍ mănis, -nšā, *m.* = *l.* a separate man.
2. tăpsil, -le, *f.* = *l.* a detail.

Particularly, *ad.* 1. mukhyazāun = *l.* principally; ădhik kărn; višės zāun.
2. *rs. into* tăpsil, *e. g.* t. sāngun.

Partisan, *s.* 1. tănḍagār, -rā, *m.*
2. păkṣegār, -rā, *m.* = adherent; lāgullo (mănis, -nšā, *m.*) = *l.* attached (man).

Partition, *s.* 1. vānṭo, -ṭeā, *m.* = *also* a screen.
2. khăṇ, -ṇā, *m.* = the shelf of a cupboard.

Partitive, *a.* vānṭe kărtso = *l.* making parts; vānṭeātso.

Partly . . . partly, *ad.* ărdo . . . ărdo = *l.* half . . . half; thoḍe . . . thoḍe = some . . . some.

Partner, *s.* vānṭeli, -liā, *m.* = a sharer; sāngāti, -tiā, *m.* = *l.* a companion.

Partnership, *s.* sāngāt, -tā, *m.* = company.

Parturition, *s.* bāḷnter, -rā, *m.* (*var.* bāḷntyór). [tion.

Party, *s.* 1. tănḍ, -ḍā, *m.* = a faction.
2. kuṭ, -ṭā, *n.* = *l.* a plot.
3. virodhi, -dhiā, *m.* = one of two litigant parties.
4. păkṣa, -ṣe, *f.*, *e.g.* in a game, *e.g.* of cards.

Pass, *v.* 1. *vlg.* pašār zā, *fr.*; guzăr.
2. vetā = goes, *with Instr.* -ntleān (*see* Gram.), *e.g.* p. through a town.
3. utăr = *l.* cross, *e.g.* a river.
4. rig = *l.* enter, *e.g.* through an orifice.
5. tsăḍ āsā = is too much; mirua = *l.* surpass.
6. tsălăi = *l.* cause to walk, *fg.*, *e.g.* p. the time; khărči = *l.* spend, *e.g.* life.
7. di = *l.* give, *or* utsār = *l.* pronounce, *e.g.* a sentence.
8. mukār di = *l.* give forward,

e.g. a glass at table; hāt bădăl.

9. kăr = do, *e.g.* a law.

10. păsănd kăr = *l.* make approval; metsva = *l.* be approved (*Sb. Dat.*), *ch. cs.*

11. zā = *l.* be done (is going to be finished); tirsa = *l.* be finished; *vlg.* kābār zā = *l.* finish (*n. v.*), *fr.*

12. bădăl = *l.* change, *ch. cs.*, *e.g.* pass from one place to another.

13. ye = *l.* come, *e. g.* an inheritance.

14. lék = *l.* count, *fg.* (consider), *e.g.* he passes as a great man = voḍlo mănis móṇ tākā léktāt; mānd = *l.* esteem.

Let him pass = vāṭ sóḍ = *l.* abandon the way.

P. away, *e. g.* time = zātā *or* tsăltā, *or* vetā.

P. by = 1. *Or.* lāgiñ vetā = *l.* goes near; *fg.* pāṭlāu kăr = *l.* make following; *fg.* dēk(é) kāṇe = *l.* take an example.

2. sóḍ = *l.* leave, pay no attention; *neg. form of* čit di = *l.* give attention.

3. zātā = *l.* is done, *e.g.* time.

P. over = 1. utăr = *l.* cross.

2. bepārvo kăr, *G. M.* = neglect; sóḍ = *l.* leave.

Come to p. = găḍ *or* zā, *l.* happen, be done.

P. through, *see* **Pass,** 2.

Passable, *a.* 1. sumār = *l.* mediocre.

2. votsayet āsullo.

Passably, *ad.* sumār = *l.* in a mediocre manner.

Passage, *s.* 1. vāṭ, -ṭe, *f.* = *l.* way; khăṇi, -ye, *f.* = a mountain p.; mārog, -rgā, *m.*

2. kaḍou *or* kăḍou, -ḍvā, *m.*, of a river.

3. vānṭo, -ṭeā, *m.* = *l.* a portion, *e.g.* p. of a book.

4. *rs. into the Instr. in* -ntleān; *see* Gram.

Allow a p. = *rs. into poten. mood, or* vāṭ āsā.

Passenger, *s.* vāṭsuro, -reā, *m.*; poiṇāri, -riā, *m.*, *or* poiṇ kărtolo; utari, -riā, *m.* = one who crosses.

Passing-bell, *s.* mòrnāči ghānṭ, -ṭi, *f.* [*mn.*)

Passion, *s.* 1. sosāp, -spā, *n.* (*phil.*

2. durguṇ, -ṇā, *m.* = vice; ăuguṇ, -ṇā, *m.*; vāiṭ voḍni, -ne, *f.* = *l.* bad inclination; *vlg.* paišāuñ, *or* nāḍ paišāuñ, -šāvā, *n.*, *fr.*

3. kăšṭ, -ṭā, *m.* = *l.* pains, *also* p. of our L. J. C.; *vlg.* paišāuñ, -šāvā, *m.*, *also of* J. C., *fr.*

4. rāg, -gā, *m.* = *l.* anger; kród, -dā, *m.*

5. zāḷ, -ḷā, *m.* = *l.* a burning, *fg.* (great internal sorrow, *and also* fury, *but n. u. in this 2nd mn.*).

Predominant p. = mukhya durguṇ, *or anal. to Mr.* rājguṇ, -ṇā, *m.*

Passionate, *a.* 1. *G.* ăpurbăi kărtso = *l.* loving; lāgụllo = *l.* attached, *fg.*; given to; *or rs. into* lāgtā.
2. utsāmboḷāyetso *or* utsāmboḷ = *l.* excited.

Passport, *s.* răhadări, -re, *f.*

Past, *a.* 1. pāṭlo = *l.* of behind, *fg.*; pāṭle jiṇiyetso = *l.* of past life; ādlo = *l.* anterior.
2. zāllo = *l.* done, happened.
Past year = poruñ, *ad.*

Past, *s.* gello kāl, -lā, *m.* = *l.* gone time.

Paste, *s.* 1. moḷḷeleñ pīṭ, -ṭā, *n.* = *l.* kneaded flour.
2. góndụ, -dā, *m.*

Paste-board, *s.* dăḍḍe kāgād, -gdā, *n.* = *l.* coarse paper; dāṭ kāgād = *l.* thick paper.

Pastime, *s.* khéḷ, -ḷā, *m.* = *l.* play, amusement; khušālāi, -ye, *f.* = *l.* pleasure.

Pastor, *s.* gouḷi, -ḷiā, *m.*, *pr. fg.*

Pastoral, *a.* gouḷiātso.

Pastry, *s.* poḷi, -ye, *f.*; miṭāi -ye, *f.*

Pasturage, *s.* tsărou, -rovā, *m.*

Pasture, *v.* tsărăi, *c. v.*

Pat, *v.* thāpuḍ.

Pat, *s.* thāp, -pi, *f.*

Pat, *a.* lāyek = fit; săma = *l.* right; *rs. into* zātā.

Patch, *s.* kuḍko, -keā, *m.*; kopo, -peā, *m.*

Patch, *v.* kuḍke mār, *or* kopo mār.

Pate, *s.* māteñ, -teā, *n.*

Paten, *s.* paten, -nā, *n.*, *fr.*

Patent, *a.* părgăṭ = *l.* public.
Letters-patent = *approx.* răhadări, -re, *f.*

Patent, *s.* pāṭo, -ṭeā, *m.*, *e.g.* p. to teach; *the word in its more usual meaning has no Konk. equivalent.*

Patentee, *s.* pāṭo āsullo.

Paternal, *a.* 1. bāpātso.
2. bāpābăriso.

Paternoster, *s.* āmčea Bāpā.

Path, *s.* ăšir vāṭ, -ṭe, *f.* = *l.* a narrow way; vornku, -kā, *n.*; *see* **Way, Road.**

Pathetic, *a.* movāḷ, *or* movāḷauntso.

Pathos, *s.* 1. bhogāp, *or* bhogtipoṇ, -ṇā, *n.*, *n. c.* = *l.* feeling.
2. kākuḷt, -ti, *f.* = *l.* compassion; movāḷpoṇ, -ṇā, *n.*

Patience, *s.* sosṇigāi -ye, *f.* (*var.* sosṇikāi); pašavai, -ye, *f.*, *n. c.*, *fr.*
Have p. = s. kāṇe.

Patient, *a.* sosṇik = suffering, having patience.

Patient, *s.* piḍest, -tā, *m.*, *or* sosṇik mănis, -nšā, *m.*

Patois, *see* **Dialect.**

Patriarch, *s.* 1. patriark, -kā, *m.* (*add.* sāib = lord).
2. muḷzoṇ, -ṇā, *m.* = *l.* root-person, founder of a family.

Patrimony, *s.* āst, -ti, *f.* = *l.* property; dāiz, -zā, *n.* = *l.* inheritance (*ex.* bāpāčeñ d. = *l.* paternal i.); pitrāsti, -te, *f.*; vatan, -nā, *n.*; vit, -tā, *n.*

Patriot, *s.* vilāyet mōg(ó) kărtso = *l.* loving the fatherland; zāllea gāuntso mōg(ó) kărtso = *l.* loving the fatherland.

Patriotism, *s.* (āplea) gāuntso mōg(ó), -gā, *m.* = *l.* love of (one's own) country.

Patristic, *s.* mătabāpānči vidya, = *l.* science of the fathers of the church.

Patrol, *s.* (sipāyañ) găsti, -te, *f.*, *Cn. Mr.*

Patron, *s.* rākṇo, -ṇeā, *m.*; sāmbāḷtolo = *l.* defending; pālăk, -kā, *m.*; šerati, -tiā, *m.*; *vlg.* patron, -nā, *m.*, *fr.*

Patronage, *s.* rākṇeñ, -ṇeā, *n.*; āsro, -reā, *m.* = *l.* refuge; ādhār, -rā, *m.* = *l.* help.

Patroness, *s.* rākṇi, -ṇe, *f.*; pālakiṇ, -ṇi, *f.*; šerotiṇ, -ṇi, *f.*; šekāi, -ye, *f.*

Patronise, *v.* guṇātso zāun āsā = *l.* is favourable; āsro di = *l.* give refuge; rāk = *l.* guard.

Patter, *v.* dhăḍa dhăḍa zā; daḷadaḷa zā; paṭapaṭa zā, *all onomatopœic words, and the same in Cn., Mr., Konk.*

Pattern, *s.* 1. nămuno, -neā, *m.* 2. *fg.* dēk(é), -ki, *f.* = example.

Paunch, *s.* gānzo, -jeā, *m.* (khānāposkuṭo, -ṭeā, *m.*) = *strictly*, the gizzard of a fowl.

Pauper, *a.* dubḷo; pór = destitute, orphan.

Pause, *s.* soukāsāi, -ye, *f.*; thāmbṇeñ, -ṇeā, *n.* = stoppage, *e.g.* of the blood from a wound.

Pause, *v.* (čikke) rāu = *l.* stop (a little); soukāsāi kāṇe = *l.* take rest; dăm kāṇe.

Pave, *v.* dāḍāi, pēṭ(é) = *l.* beat, *e.g.* a road.

Pavement, *s.* dhărn, -ni, *f.*

Pavilion, *s.* tombụ, -bā, *m.*

Paw, *s.* dāuli, -le, *f.*

Pawn, *s.* āḍou, -ḍvā, *m.*; īḍ, -ḍā, *n.*

Pawn, *v.* āḍou di = *l.* give p.

Pay, *s.* 1. sāmbāḷ, -ḷā, *m.*; pāg, -gā, *m.* (*Mr. too*); tălăb, -lbe, *f.*; kūl, -li, *f.* = wages; măzuri, -re, *f.*
2. inām, -mā, *n.* = reward.

Pay, *v.* fārik kăr, *Acc.*, *e.g.* a debt; sāmbāḷ di = *l.* give pay.
P. penalty = sikṣa sós = *l.* suffer pain.
Farms pay well = fòḷañ ditāt.
P. for = bāḍeāk kāṇe = hire.

Payable, *a.* fārik kărtso.

Payment, *s.* săndāi, -yā, *m.*; *see* Pay.

Peace, *s.* 1. soukāsāi, -ye, *f.*; sămādhān, -nā, *n.* = *l.* concord, peace; săntos, -sā, *m.* = *l.* joy.
2. rāji, -je, *f.*, sollo, -leā, *m.*, *e.g.* p. after war.
Lives in peace = sămādhānānt āsā *or* jiyetā.

Peace, *int.* vogots rāu.

Peaceful, *a.* soukāsāyetso; sămādhānātso; nidān = *l.* calm; šānti = *l.* meek.

Peacock, *s.* mór, -rā, *m.*

Peak, *s.* 1. tudi, -ye, *f.*, *e.g.* p. of a mountain.
2. pònt, -tā, *n.*; domós, -msā, *m.*

Peal, *s.* goróz, -zi, *f.*; āvāz, -zā, *m.* = *l.* sound.

Pearl, *s.* motiñ, -tiyā, *n.*

Pearl-fisher, *s.* motiyañ kāḍtolo.

Peasant, *s.* nāḍkār, -rā, *m.*; *see* **Countryman.**

Pebble, *s.* gunḍo, -ḍeā, *m.*

Peccable, *a.* pātkāk pòḍtso; pātak ādārisārko.

Peccadillo, *s.* lān pātak, -tkā, *n.* = *l.* a little sin.

Peculate, *v.* nāgăi = *l.* steal.

Peculiar, *a.* 1. *by the G.*, *e.g.* p. to men = mănšāčeñ.
2. *by* -ts, *e.g.* a custom p. to you = tumčits rivāz.
3. višés *or* prătėk = *l.* particular; mukhya = *l.* principal; ăsādhārṇ = *l.* extraordinary; ăprup = *l.* rare.

Peculiarity, *s.* višés guṇ, -ṇā, *m.* = *l.* peculiar quality.

Peculiarly, *ad.* *see* **Peculiar**; *moreover*, bhou kărn, *or* ădhik kărn = especially.

Pecuniary, *a.* 1. duḍuātso.
2. *rs. into* duḍua visyānt, *etc.*

Pedagogue, *s.* ăiguḷ, -ḷā, *m.*

Pedant, *s.* 1. doulăt kărtolo, *or* doulătitso = vain; dănḍi; vidyedoulătitso.
2. bezārāyetso.

Pedantry, *s.* 1. (vidye-) doulăt, -ti, *f.* (*or* -doulu, -lā, *m.*, *n.c.*)
2. bezārāi, -ye, *f.*

Peddler, *s.* yāri, -riā, *m.*; bovon viknār, -rā, *m.* = *l.* a walking seller, *n. c.*

Pedestal, *s.* pāi, -yā, *m.*

Pedestrian, *a.* *rs. into* tsăln = walking; *rs.* pāivāṭen = *l.* on foot.

Pedicle, *see* **Stalk.**

Pedigree, *see* **Genealogy.**

Peel, *v.* sāl kāḍ = *l.* take away the bark; sól.

Peel, *s.* sāl, -li, *f.*; sărl, -lā, *n.* = husk.

Peep, *v.* tiḷn pòḷe, *or only* tiḷ; dišṭ ghāl = *l.* put sight; distā = *l.* appears.

Peep, *s.* tiḷneñ, -neā, *n.*, *or* tiḷāp, -ḷpā, *n.*

Peer, *v.* distā = *l.* appears.

Peer, *a.* 1. săma.
2. *approx.* măntănāntlo = *l.* noble.

Peevish, *a.* bezārāyetso, *or* upădrų diuntso, *or* dóstso.

Peevishness, *s.* bezārāi, -ye, *f.*

Peg, *s.* khunṭi, -ye, *f.*, *e.g.* to hang clothes on, *etc.*

Pelf, *s.* duḍu, -ḍvā, *m.*; deuntsār, -rā, *m.* = *l.* a devil, *fg.*

Pelican, *s.* *approx.* hañso, -seā, *m.*; *or Mr.* pāṇakoḷi, -ḷi, *f.*

Pell-mell, *ad.* yeṇeñ teṇeñ.

Pellucid, *a.* distso, *or bet. rs. into* -ntleān distā.
Pelt, *v.* (fātrāniñ) mār.
Pelt, Peltry, *s.* kāt, -ti, *f.* = *l.* skin.
Pen, *s.* 1. *vlg.* pèn, -nā, *n.*, *fr.*; lăkṇik, -ke, *f.*
2. (goruāntso) veḍo, -ḍeā, *m.* = *l.* an enclosure (for cattle).
Penal, *a.* sikṣ̌etso; *bet. rs. into noun.*
Penalty, *s.* sikṣ̌a, -ṣ̌e, *f.*; julmān, -nā, *m.* = *l.* a fine.
Penance, *s.* 1. prājit, -tā, *n.* (*var.* prāčit), *e.g.* for sins; păsča-tāp, -pā, *m.*
2. fārikpoṇ, -ṇā, *n.* = *l.* satisfaction, payment, reparation.
3. (kuḍiči) dănḍoṇ, -ṇe, *f.* (*var.* dănḍoṇi, dănḍouṇcñ, -ṇeā, *n.*, dănḍoun) = *l.* (bodily) mortification; dăgd, -dāñ, *pl. m.* = sufferings.
Pencil, *s. vlg.* pensil, -le, *f.*, *fr.*; siseākhăḍi, -ye, *f.* = *l.* a piece of lead.
Pendant, *s.* mudi, -ye, *f.* = *l.* a ring.
Some kinds of p. *are*: ārkād, -dā, *m.*; pekaḷ, -ḷā, *n.*; gund-lāñ, *pl. n.*; kāp, -pā, *m.*; pāl-vañ, *pl. n.* (*this last kind is bigger*).
Pendant, *a.* umkăḷtolo.
Pendulum, *s.* dăltso bhār, -rā, *m.*, *n. u.*
Penetrable, *a.* rigasārko.
Penetrability, *s.* rigasārkeñ, -keā, *n.*
Penetrate, *v.* 1. rig = *l.* enter, *pr. fg.*, *e.g.* a sermon.
2. *fg.* lāg = *l.* be attached, *fg.*, *e.g.* a word.
3. pārki = *l.* guess.
Penetration, *s.* 1. *fg.* bārikāi, -ye, *f.* = *l.* thinness, *fg.*
2. somzikāi, -ye, *f.* = *l.* understanding.
Penetrative, *a.* bārik; somzoṇitso = *l.* intelligent.
Peninsula, *s.* uḷvo, -veā, *m.*
Penitence, *s. see* **Penance.**
Penitent, *a.* 1. prāčit kărtolo.
2. *rs. into Or.* kăḍe kumsār zātā = *l.* confesses with.
Penitential, *a.* prāčitātso; du-kitso.
Pen-knife, *s.* kānvet, -ti, *f.*, *fr.*; peskati, -te, *f.*
Pennant, Pennon, *s.* giyāuñ, -yāvā, *m.*, *fr.*; *see* **Banner.**
Penny, *s.* penni, -ni, *f.*
Pensile, *a.* umkăḷn.
Pension, *s. vlg.* pènsen, -nā, *n.*; umbăḷi, -ḷi, *f.* (*originally*, a free gift of land); ināma-sāmbăḷ, -ḷā, *m.* = *l.* pay of reward, *or the Mr. Hind.* bouṭāpāg, -gā, *n.*
Pensive, *a.* čintest; khăntiṣṭ.
Pent up, *a.* dāmpụllo.
Pentagon, *s.* pānts konseānčeñ (rūp).
Penultimate, *a.* nimāṇoso; nimā-ṇea poilo, *or* n. ādlo.

Penumbra, *s.* sāuḷisi, -ḷesi, *f.*

Penurious, *a.* 1. ădhārnātullo; upāinātullo.

2. surāti = *l.* stingy.

Penury, *s.* durboḷkāi, -ye, *f.*

Peon, *s.* pedo, -ḍeā, *m.*; uḷgi, -giā, *m.* = a private p.; dălāyet, -tā, *m.* = an official p.; sipāi, -yā, *m.*; dăfedār, -rā, *m.* = a head peon.

People, *s.* 1. lók, -kā, *m.* (*sing.*); mănis, -nšāñ, *m.* = *l.* men.

2. porza, -je, *f.* = *l.* a nation.

3. zāt, -ti, *f.* = *l.* a caste, a tribe; kuḷi, -ye, *f.* = a tribe.

Common p. = ăṇvo lók; čăḷḷeñ-biḷḷeñ (crowd).

People, *v.* vās kăr; lokān bhór = *l.* fill with p.; *rs.* poilots āsā = *l.* is the first.

Peopled, *a.* *rs.* lók āsā.

Pepper, *s.* miriñ, -riyā, *n.*

Peppermint, *s.* voḍtalāuñ, -lāvā, *m.*; pudin, -nā, *m.* (*Mr.*, *Cn.*) *n. u.*

Peradventure, *ad.* ădruṣṭān; grātstsārān.

Perambulate, *v.* bouñ.

Perceive, *v.* 1. pòḷe.

2. kăḷ = become (be) known; voḷka = *l.* know, *Lat.* *cognosce.*

Percentage, *s.* šekḍo, -ḍeā, *m.*

Perception, *s.* voḷok -ḷki, *f.*; kăḷit, -tā, *n.*; somzikāi, -ye, *f.*; *see* Idea.

Perceptive, *a.* voḷkontso.

Perch, *v.* bòs = *l.* sit.

Perch, *s.* kól, -lā, *m.*

Perchance, *ad.* *By the fut. conting. or poten. with* puro; *see* Chance, Peradventure.

Percolate, *v.* găḷăi.

Percussion, *s.* mār, -rā, *m.*; pēṭ(é), -ṭā, *m.*; *bet. rs. v.*

Perdition, *see* Ruin.

Peregrinate, *v.* 1. bouñ.

2. păradeši zāun bouñ.

Peregrination, *s.* (păradešāčeñ) poiṇ, -ṇā, *n.*

Peremptorily, *ad.* khănḍit zāun.

Peremptory, *a.* khănḍit; tirmāṇātso = *l.* decisive.

Perfect, *a.* 1. sămpurṇ; uttim = *l.* excellent; săma = *l.* right.

2. vorto = *l.* sublime; bhāgevont = *l.* holy; nīz = *l.* true, sincere.

Perfect, *v.* sămpurṇ kăr.

Perfection, *s.* 1. sămpurṇāi, -ye, *f.* = *l.* fulness.

2. guṇ, -ṇā, *m.* = *l.* quality (good).

3. vortepoṇ, -ṇā, *n.* = *l.* sublimity.

Way of p. = sămpurṇāyeči vāṭ (ascetic).

God has all perfections = (*vlg.*) Devā thăiñ sărvụ boreo văstu āsāt; D. th. guṇāči sămpurṇāi āsā.

Perfectly, *ad.* *vlg.* bhou boreñ; sămpurṇāyen; kappās, *or* kappās boreñ; purteñ, *or* păripurṇ = fully; gunḍāi păriyant = *l.* till the depth.

Perfidious, *a.* mosātso.

Perfidy, *s.* mōs(ó), -sā, *m.*

Perforate, *v.* tóp; phāpsi = make many wounds; burāk kăr = *l.* make a hole.

Perforation, *s.* topṇeñ, -ṇeā, *n.*; burāk, -kā, *m.*

Perforce, *ad.* bòḷān; *see* **Compulsion.**

Perform, *v.* 1. pāḷ, *e.g.* a duty.

2. tsălăi, *c. v.* = *l.* cause to walk, *fg.*, *e.g.* a duty, a part; kăr = *l.* do.

Performance, *s.* pāḷo, -ḷeā, *m.* (*var.* pāḷ); *bet. rs. into v.*

Perfume, *s.* părmăḷ, -ḷā, *m.*

Perfume, *v.* părmăḷăi, *or* părmăḷ lăi.

Perfunctorily, *ad.* făḍpoši; udāsinān; bepārveān; sămanātullea jinsiñ.

Perfunctory, *a.* făḍpoši; lăkṣanātullo = *l.* careless (not caring).

Perhaps, *ad. By the poten. mood, or by conting. fut.*; *see* Gram.; yekādeveḷa, *or* yekaveḷa; zăunkpuro = *l.* may be, *ch. cs.*; *by the quasi-dim.* -so; *see* Gram. P. III. ch. ii.

Peril, *s. vlg.* risk, -ke, *f.*; zăkhăm, -khme, *f.*; mōs(ó), -sā, *m.*; grātstsăr, -rā, *m.*, ădrušṭ, -ṭā, *n.* = *l.* fate, *fg.*

Period, *s.* 1. vorsañčăkrụ, -krā, *n.* = *l.* wheel of years, *fg.* (*anal. to Mr.*)

2. kāl, -lā, *m.* = *l.* time; *see also* **Circuit.**

3. purteñ vākya, -yā, *n.*, purteñ utsārāp, -rpā, *n.* = a full sentence.

4. vēḷ(é), -ḷā, *m.* (length, duration).

Periodic, *a.* 1. poireān poireātso (tāp); kāḍto vortso, *or* kāḍto urtso (tāp = fever).

2. tovóḷ tovóḷtso = *l.* of then and then.

Periodical, *s.* tovóḷ tovóḷčeñ vărtămānapătrụ, -trā, *n.*

Periphery, *s.* măṇḍăḷ, -ḷā, *n.* = *l.* a circle (*geom.*); suttụ, -tā, *m.*; bounḍi, -ḍe, *f.* (bovāḍo, -ḍeā, *m.*?)

Periphrasis, *see* **Circumlocution.**

Perish, *v.* nāš zā = *l.* ruin get (I p. = āuñ n. zătāñ); bhăsma, *n. v. of* bhăsmi; sāmpăḍ; mòr = die; ăntăr.

Perishable, *a.* nāšzăuntso; sāmpăḍtso; ăntāk pòḍtso.

Periwig, *see* **Peruke.**

Perjure, *v.* fóṭpărmāṇ kăr, *or* fóṭkireñ p. k.; fóṭsoput ghāl (*or* di); fóṭkiro s. gh. (private).

Perjurer, *s.* fóṭpărmāṇagār, -rā, *m.*, *or* fóṭpărmāṇ kărtolo.

Perjury, *s.* fóṭpărmāṇ, -ṇā, *n.*, *or* fóṭkireñ p.; soput, -tā, *m.* (private).

Permanence, *s.* urāp, -rpā, *n.*; rāvāp, rāupā, *n.*, *or* rāunčeñ, -čeā, *n.*; *bet. rs. into v.*

Permanent, *a.* 1. rāuntso, *or* urtso.

2. *fg.* thir = *l.* firm.

Permeable, *a.* rigasārko.

Permeate, *v.* rig = *l.* enter.

Permission, *s.* răja, -je, *f.*; hukum, -kme, *f.* = *l.* an order; *rs. into* sóḍ.

Permit, *v.* răja di; hukum di = *l.* give order; sóḍ; = *l.* leave; kăbuli di = *l.* give consent; vòp = *l.* agree.

Permutation, *s.* bădlāp, -pā, *n.*

Pernicious, *a.* luksānātso; vāiṭ = bad; *or* vāiṭ kărtso.

Peroration, *s.* nimāṇeñ māg-ṇeñ, -ṇeā, *n.*

Perpendicular, *a.* ubo.

Perpetrate, *v.* ādār; kăr.

Perpetual, *a.* sāsṇātso = *l.* eternal; ăntnātullo = *l.* without end; ăgăṇit; *vlg.* kābār zāinātullo = *l.* not finishing; tirsanātullo = *l.* not finishing; *rs. into* rāvanāstanāñ, *or* khăḷanāstanāñ; *rs. into* sădānkāl; găḍiye găḍiye = *l.* every moment.

Perpetuate, *see* **Immortalize.**

Perpetuity, *s.* sāsăṇ, -sṇā, *n.* = *l.* eternity.

Perplexed, *a.* dubāuntso, *or* dubāvi; tondreāntso.

Perplexity, *s.* dubāu, -bāvā, *m.*; tondre, *Nom. pl. m.*

Perquisite, *s.* dusre fāide = *l.* other advantages.

Perron, *s.* meṭāñ, *pl. n.*

Persecute, *v.* 1. dăgdăi = *l.* cause suffering; iza (*var.* hiñsā) di = give torture, *fg.*; kăṣ̌ṭăi = *l.* cause pain; dănḍăi; răḍăi = *l.* cause to weep.
2. dāunḍăi = *l.* cause to run (away).

Persecution, *s.* dăgdouṇeñ, -ṇeā, *n.*, *or* dăgd, *m. pl.*; iza, -ze (hiñsa, -se), *f.*; *see* **Oppression.**

Persecutor, *s.* hiñsegār, -rā, *m.*, *n. c.*; dăgdăitolo = *l.* causing sufferings.

Perseverance, *s.* thirasāṇ, -ṇe, *f.* *or* thirsāṇ, -ṇe, *f.*

Persevere, *v.* thir rāu, *or* thir zāun rāu; āni (*with the req. verb*), *e. g.* p. in writing = āni borăi.

Persevering, *a.* thir; *bet. rs.*

Persist, *see* **Persevere.**

Person, *s.* 1. zoṇ, -ṇā, *m.* (*phil.*) *used also for* a Person of the most H. Trinity; mănis -nšā, *m.*; mānāi, -yā, *m.* = *esp.* a coolie.
2. rūp, -pā, *n.* = *l.* form; vés, -sā, *m.* = *l.* a mask, *fg.*
3. *sometimes omitted*; *e. g.* the keeping of his p. = tāči zătān; my own person = āunts.
4. khudduੁ, *e. g.* kh. pòḷe = see in person, personally.

Personal, *a.* āplo = *l.* own; kāski = *l.* private; zoṇātso (*or* zoṇāntso) = *l.* of person.

Personally, *ad.* khudduੁ.

Personification, *s.* zoṇarūp, -pā, *n.*

Perspective, *s.* 1. diṣ̌ṭ, -ṭi, *f.* = *l.* sight.

2. durbiṇ, -ṇi, *f.*

Perspicacious, *a.* bārik = *l.* thin, *fg.*; somzoṇitso = *l.* intelligent.

Perspicuous, *a.* soṣṭ.

Perspiration, *s.* ghām, -mā, *m.*

Perspire, *v.* ghāme; hume.

Persuade, *v.* 1. somzăi = *l.* cause to understand; *or* somzoun di, *or* somzaso kăr.

2. bud sāng = *l.* say advice.

3. lāi = *l.* apply, *fg.*; movāḷāi = *l.* make soft; mòn voi kăr = *l.* make the heart yes, *fg.* I cannot p. myself = mākā disanāñ.

Persuasion, *s.* ghăṭ āločen, -ni, *f.* = *l.* firm opinion; bud, -di, *f.* = *l.* advice; *by* vorviñ = through, *ch. cs.*

Persuasive, *a.* somzăisārko, *or* somzaso.

Pert, *a.* ăumăryāditso.

Pertain, *v.* 1. fāvozā (fāvo *is indecl.*)

2. lāg = *l.* be attached, *fg.*, *e.g.* tuka lāgtā = it pertains to you.

Pertinacious, *a.* săḷiṣṭ; dhāruṇ; āpleā vādeātso.

Pertinent, *a.* lāyek = *l.* fit; săma = *l.* right; *rs. into* zā (*Lat. facit ad rem*).

Pertness, *s.* ăumăryād, -di, *f.*; lăzbanḍpoṇ, -ṇā, *n.*

Perturb, *v.* tondre kăr.

Perturbation, *s.* tondre, *m. pl.*; bezārāi, -ye, *f.*; ākānt, -tā, *m.* = *l.* distress.

Peruke, *s.* purn, -nā, *n.*; *some say* ṭhăkāri kès, *pl. m.*

Peruse, *v.* zāgrutāyen vāts.

Pervade, *v.* rig = *l.* enter *or* rigun bouñ.

Perverse, *a.* 1. khoṭo; pāḍ; tăn-ṭālmāri, *etc.*

Perversion, *s.* kusāp, -spā, *n.* = *l.* corruption, *fg.*; vāiṭpoṇ, -ṇā, *n.*; (vāiṭ) bădlāp, -pā, *n.* = *l.* (bad) change.

Pervert, *v.* kusăi = *l.* corrupt, *fg.*, *c. v. of* kus; pāḍ kăr.

Pervious, *a.* rigasārko.

Pest, *s.* măr, -ri, *f.*, *pr. fg.* 'măr āili = that troublesome man (pest) came'.

Pester, *v.* kărkăr kăr = *l.* make trouble; *see* **Teaze;** kānānt simpṭi ghāl = *l.* put a tail in the ear (*Konk.*).

Pestilence, *s.* măr, -ri, *f.*; pèst, -ti, *f.*, *fr.*

Pestilential, *a.* 1. măritso, *or* măr lāuntso.

2. bhou luksānātso = very hurtful; nāškārtso = *l.* destructive.

Pestle, *s*, musăḷ, -sḷā, *n.*

Pet, *s.* 1. bhou prītitso burgo, -geā, *m.* (*or* mānis) = a very dear boy; ăpurbāyetso burgo.

2. utsāmboḷāi, -ye, *f.* = *l.* excitement; utsāmboḷasārkeñ, -keā, *n.*

Petal, *s.* pākḷi, -ḷe, *f.*

Petition, *s.* 1. māg-ṇeñ, -ṇeā, *n.*

2. ărji, -je, *f.* = any demand: p. to a superior.
3. firyăd, -di, *f.* = *l.* complaint.
Petition, *v.* ărji di = *l.* give a p.
Petitioner, *s.* ărjegār, -rā, *m.*
Petrifaction, *s.* fātorso, *m.* = *l.* apparent stone.
Petrify, *v.* fātorso kăr.
Petroleum, *s.* fātrāčeñ tēl(è), -lā, *n.*; *vlg.* čimnetēl(è), -lā, *n.*
Pettiness, *s.* hălkeñ mòn, -nā, *n.* = *l.* mean heart.
Pettish, *a.* bezārāyetso.
Petticoat, *s.* gāgro, -reā, *m.* (*ex.* of girls); băniyān, -nā, *n.*
Pettifogger, *s.* čillăr văkil, -lā, *m.*; kāṭvăkil (*vlg.*).
Petty, *a.* dākṭo *or* lān; čillăr = *l.* trifling; hălko *or* ăṇvo = *l.* low; uṇo = *l.* less, inferior.
Petulance, *s.* săḷ, -ḷā, *n.*; ăumăr-yăd, -di, *f.*
Petulant, *a.* sāḷiṣṭ; ăumăryăditso.
Pew, *s.* (igărjentli) băska, -ke, *f.* = *l.* a seat in the church.
Pewter, *s.* doveñ siseñ, -seā, *n.*
Phantasm, *s.* kălpăna, -ne, *f.*; diṣṭ, -ṭi, *f.*; *see* **Fantastic,** *etc.*
Phantom, *s.* sopāṇ, -pṇā, *n.* = *l.* a dream, *fg.*; druṣṭakāi, -ye, *f.* (*vlg.* duṣṭakāi) = *l.* a goblin.
Pharmacy, *s.* găndsărkāči āngăḍ, -gḍi, *f.*
Pharos, *see* **Light-house.**
Phase, *s.* bădlāp, -pā, *n.*; čămăt-kār, -rā, *m.*
Phenomenon, *s.* ākāšačămătkār, -rā, *m.*; disāp, -spā, *n.*

Phial, *s.* šiso, -seā, *m.* (*dim.* sisli, -le, *f.*)
Philologist, *s.* bhāsañpănḍit, -tā, *m.*
Philology, *s.* bhāsañpănḍitpoṇ, -ṇā, *n.*
Philosopher, *s.*, *n. w. u.* ginyāna-sódnār, -rā, *m.* = *l.* a man inquiring into science, *n. u.*
Philosophical, *a.* ginyānātso.
Philosophy, *s.* ginyānasódna, -ne, *f.* = *l.* inquisition of wisdom, *n. u.*; poisileāñ kā-raṇāñvidya, -ye, *f.* = *l.* the science of remote causes.
Phlebotomy, *s.* šir mārči, *f.* = *l.* beating vein.
Phlegm, *s.* 1. timpi, -ye, *f.* = spittle.
2. dărkăl, -lā, *n.*
3. *rs. into* thănḍ = *l.* cold.
Phosphorus, *s.* sukru, -rā, *m.* = the morning star.
Phosphorescence, *s.* părzăḷ, -ḷā, *m.*, *or* prăkāš, -šā, *m.*
Photography, *s.* uzvāḍāntleñ či-tru̥, -rā, *n.* = *l.* picture from the light; *or* uzvāḍāntli năkṣa, -ṣe, *f.*, *n. u.*
Phrase, *s.* utsār, -rā, *m.* = *l.* ex-pression; vākya, -yā, *n.*
Phraseology, *s.* utsārātso jinos, -nsā, *m.* = *l.* manner of ex-pressions; *or* utsārāči rīt, -ti, *f.*, *or only* vākya, -yā, *n.*
Phrenology, *v.* kăpalaguṇānči vidya, *or* kăpalalăkṣăṇavi-dya, -ye, *f.* = science of the

quality of the brain (forehead *ex.*)

Phthisis, *s.* kevād, -di, *f.*

Physic, *s.* vokāt, -ktā, *n.*; bhāiri, -re, *f.* = *l.* a purge.

Physical, *a.* săimbātso = *l.* natural; kuḍitso = *l.* bodily.

Physician, *s.* voiz, -zā, *m.*; păndit, -tā, *m.* = *l.* a learned man, *fg. used for* ph. *as we use* doctor.

Physics, *s.* săimbāči vidya, -ye, *f.*

Physiognomy, *s.* 1. tònḍāčeñ rūp, -pā, *n.*

2. sobāvagurtu̥, -tā, *m.* = *l.* a sign of indications.

Physiological, *a.* prāṇātso.

Physiology, *s.* prāṇavidya, -ye, *f.* = *l.* the science of life.

Piacular, *a.* fārikpoṇātso, *or* fārikpoṇ diuntso.

Pianoforte, *s.* gāyānāči pèṭ, -ṭe, *f.* (*anal. to Cn.*).

Pick, *v.* vints, *or* vintsum kāḍ, *e.g.* something up from the ground; kāḍ.

Pickaxe, *s.* kudòḷ, -dḷi, *f.*; pikās -sā, *n.*, *fr.*

Pickle, *s.* loṇčeñ, -čeā, *n.*

Pickle, *v.* loṇčeñ kăr; fòṇṇu̥ ghāl.

Picture, *s.* rejist, -tā, *m.*, *fr.*; rupḍeñ, -ḍeā, *n.*, *or* rupṇeñ, -ṇeā, *n.*; čitru̥, -rā, *n.* (*H. K.*).

Piece, *s.* 1. kuḍko, -keā, *m.*; kopo, -peā, *m.* (*esp.* a p. of cloth).

2. nāṇeñ, -ṇeā, *n.* = a coin.

3. kuskuṭvar, -rā, *n.* = an atom, *n.c.*, *or* kuskuṭ, -ṭā, *n.*

A p. of ground = dākṭeñ nèl, -lā, *n.*, *or* zāgeakuḍko, -keā, *m.*

Break into pieces = kuḍkeān kuḍke kăr.

Fall to pieces = kuḍke zā.

Be all of one p. = vòp = *l.* agree; yék gānṭ āsā.

Pier, *s.* 1. khāmbo, -beā, *m.* = *l.* pillar.

2. dhăkko, -keā, *m.* (*Mr. Cn.*)

Pierce, *v.* 1. tóp, *e.g.* p. with a sword, *or* a thorn pierces; rig = *l.* enter, *ch. cs.*; phāpsi = *l.* transfix, (make many wounds), wound; burāk kăr = *l.* make a hole.

2. *fg.* dukăi = *l.* afflict.

Piercing, *a.* 1. kăṭiṇ, *e.g.* p. pain; umāḷeātso = *l.* boiling, *fg.* (intense), *e.g.* p. pain.

2. bārik (*also* perspicacious).

3. kindri, *e.g* voice.

Piety, *s.* bhăktipoṇ, -ṇā, *n.*, *or* bhăkt, -ti, *f.*; devaspoṇ, -ṇā, *n.*

Pig, *s.* 1. dukor, -krā, *m.*

2. sológ, -gā, *m.* = a young male pig; lăitāuñ, -tāvā, *m.*

Pigeon, *s.* pārvo, -veā, *m.*

Pigment, *s.* róng, -gā, *m.*

Pigmy, *see* Dwarf.

Pilaster, *s.* khāmbo, -beā, *m.*

Pile, *s.* 1. rās, -ši, *f.* = *l.* a heap.

2. sāri, -ye, *f.* = *l.* a funeral p.

3. rāuḷ, -ḷā, *n.* (*dim.* rāuḷer) = *l.* a palace.
4. suḷi, -ye, *f.* = *l.* a stake.

Pile, *v.* rās kăr.

Pilfer, *v.* kāḍ = *l.* take away; nāgăi = *l.* steal.

Pilgrim, *s.* părdeši, -šiā, *m.* = an exile; poiṇāri, -riā, *m.* = a traveller.

Pilgrimage, *s.* (āngoṇičeñ) poiṇ, -ṇā, *n.* = *l.* journey (votive); părадеšapoiṇ, -ṇā, *n.*

Pill, *s.* guḷi, -ye, *f.* = *l.* a globule (*dim. of* guḷo); mātreñ, -treā, *n.* (*H. K.*)

Pillage, *s.* desvaṭ, -ṭe, *f.*; lūṭ, -ṭi, *f.* = *l.* prey.

Pillage, *v.* desvaṭ (*or* lūṭ) kăr.

Pillager, *s.* luṭkār, -rā, *m.*

Pillar, *s.* 1. khāmbo, -beā, *m.*
2. *fg.* ādhār, -rā, *m.* = *l.* help.

Pillow, *s.* ušeñ, -šeā, *n.*

Pilot, *s.* tāruñ tsălăitolo = *l.* ruling the ship; ārkaṭi, -ṭi, *m.*

Pimple, *s.* mumbār, -brā, *n.*; puḷi, -ye, *f.*

Pin, *s.* ālfinit, -ti, *f.* (*vlg.* ālpinas, -sā, *n.*), *fr.*; *perh.* suvi, -ye, *f.* *might be used also for* pin; *or* māteñ āsụlli suvi.

Pin, *v.* ālfinit tóp.

Pincers, *s.* čimṭo, -ṭeā, *m.*

Pinch, *v.* čimṭo kāḍ; čimṭo ghāl, *n. c.* (*Ital. dare un pizzicone*); kimči = pinch in order to detach *or* cut off.

Pinch, *s.* čimṭo, -ṭeā, *m.*
A p. of snuff = yék čimṭi (-ṭe, *f.*) puḍ, -ḍi, *f.*

Pine, *v.* bhāg; suk, *from consumption*; bārik zā = become thin.

Pine-apple, *s.* aṇās, -ṇsā, *n.*

Pin-hole, *s.* suviyeburāk, -kā, *m.*

Pink, *v.* tóp = *l.* prick.

Pinnacle, *s.* tudi, -ye, *f.* = *l.* top.

Pint, *s.* ărdo siso, -seā, *m.*

Pious, *a.* bhăktivont; devaspoṇātso.

Pip, *v.* 1. kankār, *as* hens p.
2. koke, *as* cocks; sād ghāl = crow (like a cock).

Pipe, *s.* 1. pīp, -pā, *n.* = *l.* a cask, a pipe (*in Mr. also*).
2. pempareñ, -reā, *n.* = a musical p.
3. năḷi, -ye, *f.* = *l.* a chimney.
4. guḍguḍi, -ḍe, *f.* = a pipe for smoking.

Pipkin, *s.* tópleñ, -leā, *n.*; buḍkuḷo, -ḷeā, *m.* = *Lat. olla,* a pot, dish.

Piquant, *a.* 1. tik, *or* tikso; khār.
2. *fg.* bārik = *l.* thin, *fg.*

Pique, *v.* ăbbār kăr = *l.* boast; băḍāi kăr.

Piracy, *s.* dăryāntli tsóri, -ye, *f.*

Pirate, *s.* dăryātsór, -rā, *m.* = a sea-robber.

Pish, *int.* čha.

Pismire, *s.* mūi, -ye, *f.*

Pistol, *s.* lān bănduk, -ke, *f.*; pistòl, -lā, *n.*, *fr.*

Pit, *s.* fónḍ, -ḍā, *m.*; kònḍ, -ḍā, *n.*; *see* **Arm-pit.**

Pit-a-pat, *ad.* dăḍdăḍeān.

Pitch, *s.* 1. tăr, -ri, *f.*; dāmbór, -rā, *m.*
2. kātrāṇ, -ṇā, *n.*; čandan, -nā, *n.*
Highest p. = bhou ubār, *or* bhou vóḍ, *fg.*

Pitch, *v.* 1. borăi = *l.* write, *e.g.* a key-note.
2. mār = *l.* beat, *e.g.* a tent.
3. tār lāi = *l.* apply tar.

Pitched, *a.* (battle), krămāntrụ = *l.* regular.

Pitcher, *s.* sidi, -ye, *f.*

Piteous, *a.* 1. movāḷ; movāḷauntso = *l.* causing pity.
2. dukest = *l.* sorry.

Pith, *s.* 1. benḍu, -ḍā, *m.* (*var.* bonḍu).
2. sār, -rā, *m.* = *l.* substance, essence.
3. tsurkāi, -ye, *f.* = *l.* activity.

Pithy, *a.* 1. benḍu āsullo.
2. *fg.* ărthān bhorlolo, *or perh.* sārātso.

Pitiful, *a.* 1. kākuḷtitso; birmotitso; dăyāḷ = kind; movāḷ = *l.* tender, *or* movāḷountso = *l.* moving.
2. hălko, *or* ăṇvo = *l.* low.

Pittance, *s.* izmăl, -lā, *n.* = *l.* alms, *fr.*; *see* **Alms.**

Pity, *s.* birmot, -ti, *f.*; tsurtsuro, -reā, *m.*; kākuḷt, -ti, *f.*; dăya, -ye, *f.*

Pity, *v.* (mākā) birmot distā, *G. F.* = *l.* pity appears (to me) of; kākuḷt kăr, *G. F.*; *vlg.* pòṭ duktā *or* p. zāḷtā = *l.* my belly feels pain.

Pivot, *s.* moḷo, -ḷeā, *m.*; *see* **Hinge.**

Pix, *s.* piks, -si, *f.*, *fr.*

Placable, *a.* sămādhān kăriyet āsullo = who may be appeased; movāḷ; *bet. rs.*

Placard, *s.* istyār, -rā, *m.*

Place, *s.* 1. suāt, -te, *f.* = a portion of space; zāgo, -geā, *m.*, *mn. also* ground.
2. gāuñ, gāñvā, *m.* = *l.* country.
3. udyóg, -gā, *m.* = a civil employment.
In the first p. = poilents, *or* poile suāter.
If I were in your p. = āuñ tujeñ suāter (*or* tujeā bădlāk) āsleār.

Place, *v.* ghāl = *l.* put; dovór, *more used than* ghāl.
P. in order = mānḍ.
N. B. the compounds of Place *are mostly formed regularly.*

Placid, *a.* nidān *or* soukāsāyetso; *see* **Calm.**

Plagiary, *s.* pustakañtsōr, -rā, *m.*

Plague, *s.* 1. mār, -ri, *f.*; pèst, -ti, *f.*, *fr.*
2. *fg.* kăṣṭ, -ṭā, *m.*
3. kărkăr, -rāñ, *m. pl.* = *l.* troubles.

Plague, *v.* bezār (*or* kărkăr) kăr; dọs.

Plain, *s.* 1. sămagāuñ, -gāñvā, *m.* = *l.* even country; măidān, -nā, *n.* = *Lat. planities.*
2. podou, -dvā, *m.* = a high plain; kāmp, -pā, *n.*

Plain, *a.* 1. sādo = *l.* simple; tsālto = *l.* current.
2. soṣṭ = *l.* clear, evident, distinct; sompò = *l.* easy.
3. nīz = *l.* sincere, true; *often rs.*; *see* **Frank.**

Plaintiff, *see under* **Accuser.**

Plait, *s.* 1. miri, -ye, *f.*: 'make plaits = mirio ghāl, *or* m. kāḍ'; 'mirio pòḍtāt = *l.* plaits fall'.
2. iṇi, -ye, *f.* = tress; *see* **Dress.**

Plait, *v.* *see* **Dress.**

Plan, *s.* 1. nămuno, -neā, *m.* = *l.* sample, model, *fg.*; āločen, -ni, *f.* = *l.* intention, opinion; sevóṭ, -ṭā, *m.* = *l.* aim; nǎkṣa, -ṣe, *f.*, *e.g.* of a building, *pr. fg.*
2. mǎslǎt, -ti, *f.*, *or* kūṭ, -ṭā, *n.* = *l.* a plot.

Plan, *v.* nămuno āsā, *ch. cs.*; sevóṭ āsā, *ch. cs.*; āločen kǎr; nǎkṣa kāḍ.

Plane, *s.* 1. sǎmagāuñ, -gāñvā, *m.* (a level surface).
2. kisuḷ, -ḷe, *f.* (an instrument).

Plane, *v.* tās = *ex.* hew; kisuḷ ghāl.

Planet, *s.* graha, -hā, *n.* (*H. K.*); bounčeñ neketrụ, -rā, *n.* = *l.* a walking star.

Plank, *s.* foḷeñ, -ḷeā, *m.*

Plank, *v.* foḷiñ ghāl.

Plant, *s.* zāḍ, -ḍā, *n.*; ròmpo, -peā, *m.* (a young plant).

Plant, *v.* 1. lāi = *l.* apply, attach (to the earth), *e. g.* ruk lāi.
2. ghāl = *l.* put.
3. gǎḍ *or* stāpisi = *l.* found.

Plantain, *s.* 1. keḷeñ, -ḷeā, *n.*
2. bomgāḷo, -ḷeā, *m.* = a big p. insipid, but good for cooking.
3. nandǎrkāi = p. of Malabar, *the Malayalam name.*

P. tree = 1. khelụmbo, -beā, *m.*
2. moko, -keā, *m.* = a young p. t.

Plantation, *s.* tōṭ, -ṭā, *n.*

Plash, *s.* (udkañ) gouji, -je, *f.*

Plaster, *s.* 1. lēp(é), -pā, *m.*, *e.g.* mustard-plaster.
2. tsuno, -neā, *m.* = *l.* chunam; *or bet.* tsuneātso gār, -rā, *m.*; sāruṇ, -ṇe, *f.*

Plaster, *v.* 1. lēp(é) lāi.
2. tsuneātso gār kāḍ; sāruṇ kǎr.

Plastic, *a.* rūp diuntso.

Plat, *s.* zāgo, -geā, *m.*

Plate, *s.* 1. bosi, -se, *f.*
2. polgāṇ, -ṇā, *n.* = a large hollow plate; *see App. X. to the Konk.-Engl. Dictionary.*

Platform, *s.* 1. sopo, -peā, *m.* = a kind of raised terrace in a house; zǎgli, -le, *f.* (*H. K.*)
2. kāṭeñ, -ṭeā, *n.* = a sort of embankment around trees.

Platinum, *s.* platin moḷḷo dhātu, -tu, *m.*; doveñ rupeñ, -peā, *n.*

Platter, *s.* tǎbak, -bkā, *n.*

Plaudit, *s. rs. into* tāḷio pēṭ (é) = *l.* clasp the hands; metsuoṇeñ, -ṇeā, *n.* = *l.* approval; hogḷāp, -pā, *n.* = *l.* praise.

Plausible, *a.* hogḷāp fāvozāllo, *or* hogḷāpātso; metsvontso.

Play, *s.* 1. khèḷu (*var.* khyóḷ), -ḷā, *m.*; āṭ, -ṭā, *m.*
2. khušālāi, -ye, *f.* = *l.* pleasure.
3. čeṣṭāi, -ye, *f.*; tomāso, -seā, *m.*

Play, *v.* 1. khèḷ *or* khyāḷ.
2. čeṣṭai kăr = *l.* make a joke.
3. săntós bhóg = *l.* enjoy pleasure.
4. vāz, *e.g.* an instrument.

Player, *s.* 1. khèḷagār, -rā, *m.*, in a game.
2. vāztolo, of an instrument; *or* vāzpi, -piā, *m.*

Playful, *a.* 1. khušāl; khèḷgoḍo; ulāsātso = *l.* joyful.
2. čeṣṭāi kărtso = *l.* who makes jokes.

Plea, *s.* 1. nīb, -bā, *n.* = pretext.
2. udārăṇ, -ṇā, *n.*; prătizăvāb, -bi, *f.* = an answer to an accusation.

Plead, *v.* 1. tsălāi = *l.* cause to walk, *fg.*; *e.g.* p. a case.
2. udārăṇ di = give answer to.

Pleader, *s.* văkil, -lā, *m.*

Pleasant, *a.* 1. khušālāyetso, *or* khušāl kărtso; mogāḷ = *l.* dear.
2. sobit = beautiful.
3 čeṣṭāi kărtso = *l.* making jokes.

Pleasantness, *s.* mogāḷpoṇ, -ṇā, *n.* = *l.* affability; khušālāi, -ye, *f.* = *l.* enjoyableness.

Pleasantry, *s.* bārikāi, -ye, *f.*

Please, *v.* 1. mānua, *e.g.* God; *c.v.* mānuăi.
2. metsva = *l.* approve, *ch. cs.* (mākā yeñ metsvatā), *e.g.* the conduct of; păsănd kăr = *l.* make approval; pačuă, *n. c.*; ruts = *l.* be tasteful.
3. khušāl kăr; dăya kăr.
Please give = dăya kărn diyā; upkār kărn diyā.
If you please = mānualeār.
Do as you p. = tuje khuše părmāṇe tsăl.

Pleasure, *s.* 1. khušālāi, -ye, *f.*, *or also* khuši, -še, *f.* (*ex.* will); săntos, -sā, *m.*; ulās, -sā, *m.*; sukhu, -khā, *n.* = *l.* happiness.
2. ruts, -či, *f.* = *l.* taste.

Pleasing, *see* **Please** *and* **Charm.**

Plebeian, *a.* ăṇvo = *l.* low; hīn; zomeātso = *l.* of the people.

Pledge, *s.* āḍou, -ḍvā, *m.*; īḍ, -ḍā, *n.*; zāmin, -ne, *f.* = *l.* security; utăr, -trā, *n.*, *or* bhās, -se, *f.* = *l.* a word, promise.
P. of marriage = āyermān, -nā, *m.*

Pledge, *v.* utăr di, *or* bhāsāi = *l.* give word, *or* promise; zāmin di, *or* āḍou di = *l.* give p.

Plenary, *a.* purto = *l.* full, *e.g.* p. remission.

Plenipotentiary, *s.* sotăntri dūt, -tā, *m.*

Plentiful, *a.* *vlg.* *rs.* *into* rās = *l.* heap, *ch. cs.*; săbār = *l.* much, many; măst; bră-

mānḍ (*H. K.*); puskāḷ; sompurṇāyetso, *n. c.*
Plenty, *s.* sompurṇāi, -ye, *f.*; rās, -si, *f.* = *l.* a heap; *rs.* bhou *or* săbār = much, many, *ch. cs.*
Pleonasm, *s.* tsăḍāu, -ḍāvā, *m.*
Plethora, *s.* răgtabhărti, -te, *f.* = *l.* fulness of blood; tsăḍ răgat, -gtā, *n.* = *l.* much blood.
Pliable, *a.* bāgāuntso, *or* bāgāsārko, *pr. fg.*
Plight, *s.* stiti, -ti, *f.* = *l.* condition, state; *bet. rs., e.g. into the poten. mood.*
Plod, *v.* kăṣṭān vāur" = *l.* endeavour greatly; kăṣṭa = *l.* suffer pain, *n. v. of* kăṣṭāi.
Plot, *s.* 1. kuṭ, -ṭā, *n.*; măslăt, -ti, *f.*
2. dākṭeñ nèl, -lā, *n.*; dākṭo *or* lān zāgo, -geā, *m.* = a small piece of ground.
Plot, *v.* kuṭ kăr.
Plotter, *s.* kutagār, -rā, *m.*
Plough, *v.* kós, nāngrăi.
Plough, *s.* nāngor, -grā, *m.*
Ploughing, *s.* kosāp, -spā, *n.*
Ploughman, *s.* kostolo.
Pluck, *v.* kāḍ, *e.g.* a flower, feathers; khunṭ, *e.g.* leaves.
Plug, *v.* dāmp = *l.* shut.
Plume, *s.* pāk, -kā, *n.*
Plume, *v.* ăbbār, *or* doulăt kăr = boast.
Plump, *a.* 1. puṣṭi, moṭo = stout.
2. făḍposi = clumsy.
Plunder, *s.* desvaṭ, -ṭe, *f.*; lūṭ, -ṭi, *f.* = *l.* prey; nāgoṇ, -ṇi, *f.* = *l.* stealing.
Plunder, *v.* sulvăi; desvaṭ (*or* lūṭ) kăr; zulum tsălăi.
Plunge, *v.* 1. buḍăi, *c. v. of* buḍ *pr. fg., e.g.* into calamities.
2. *n. v.* pòḍ *or* buḍ.
Plunge, *s.* buḍāp, -ḍpā, *n.*
Plurality, *s.* zomo, -meā, *m.*; voḍlo vānṭo, -ṭeā, *m.* = *l.* a great part.
Plus, *ad.* ădhik; tāče vorn.
Plush, *s.* louñ āsulleñ lugāṭ, -gṭā, *n.* = *l.* woolen cloth.
Pluviometer, *s.* pāusamāp, -pā, *n.*
Ply, *v.* 1. lāg = *l.* be applied, attached, *fg.*
2. boreñ kărn tsălăi = *l.* perform, exercise carefully, *etc.*
Pneumatic, *a.* vāreātso, *or* vāreāvelo.
Pocket, *s.* bòls, -sā, *n.*; kiso, -seā, *m.*; čīl, -lā, *n.*; poti, -ye, *f.* = a bag.
Pocket, *v.* nāgăi, *c. v.* = steal.
Pocket-book, *s.* ugḍāsapustak, -kā, *n.*; tsătrāyepustak.
Poem, *s.* slók, -kā, *m.*, *or* slókagăḍāp, -ḍpā, *n.*, *or the Mr.* kāvya, -ye, *f.*
Poet, *s.* slók kărtolo; podañ kărtolo; *or the Mr., Cn., Sans.* kăvi, -vi, *m.*
Poetaster, *s.* ăṇvo kăvi, *or* čillăr kăvi, -vi, *m.*
Poetic, *a.* slókātso, *or the Mr.* kāvyātso.

Poetry, *s.* slók, -kā, *m.*; *or the Mr., Cn., Sans..* kăvita, -te, *f.* *or* kāvya, -ye, *f.*

Poignant, *a.* kóḍu = *l.* bitter, *fg.*; kăṭin = *l.* difficult; dukountso; *perh.* phāpsountso; toptso.

Point, *s.* 1. domós, -msā, *m.*, *e.g.* of an instrument; pònt, -tā, *n.*, *fr.*
 2. bónts, -či, *f.* = beak.
 3. tibo, -beā, *m.* = *l.* a dot.
 4. tăṇ, -ṇi, *f.* = *l.* moment, *e.g.* p. of death.
 5. mukhya văstu̥, -tu, *f.* = *l.* chief thing; *see* **Sting, Object, Stage, Degree, Item.**
 He is on the p. of going = to vetso āsā, *or* vetā thăiñ āsā.
 To such a point = titlo.

Point, *v.* 1. domós kăr.
 2. tibo ghāl.
 3. dākăi = *l.* show.

Pointless, *a.* 1. domósnātullo.
 2. čăppo = *l.* not salted, *fg.*
 3. dăḍḍo = *l.* stupid; jīvnātullo.

Poise, *v.* săma tūk kăr.

Poison, *s.* vik, -kā, *n.*; nănji, -je, *f.*

Poison, *v.* vik ghāl, *or* v. di.

Poisonous, *a.* vikāḷ.

Poke, *v.* kónk *or* tóp.

Poker, *s.* uzo tsaḷči boḍi, -ye, *f.*

Pole, *s.* 1. kōl(ó), -lā, *m.* = *Lat. petrica;* tenkḍi, -ḍe, *f.* = p. to knock down fruits with.
 2. phidār, -rā, *n.*
 3. khāmbo, -beā, *m.* = a pillar, a support.
 4. druv, -vā, *n.* = p. of the earth, *n. u.*

Pole-cat, *s.* rānmāzār, -zrā, *n.*

Polemical, *a.* tărkātso = *l.* controversial.

Police, *s.* gāñvābăndobăst, -ti, *f.* = *l.* safety of the place; *or* krămarākṇeñ, -ṇeā, *n.* = *l.* guard of order.

Policeman, *s. vlg.* pholis, -sā, *m.*; krămarākṇo, -ṇeā, *m.*; gāñvābăndobăstigār, -rā, *m.*

Policy, *s.* (rājā-) kārkhāno, -neā, *m.* = *l.* administration; kārbār, -rā, *n.*, *n. c. in this mn.*

Polish, *v.* telto, săma, *or* suddu̥ kăr = *l.* make smooth, right, *or* correct.

Polished, *a.* telto, săma, *or* suddu̥; sāf; thăḷtăḷit.

Polite, *a.* tsāltsămkăṇ āsullo; măryāditso.

Politeness, *s.* tsāltsămkăṇ, -ṇā, *n.*; măryād, -di, *f.*; mănšepoṇ, -ṇā, *n.* = humanity, *fg.*

Political, *a.* stititso = *l.* of state; rājātso = *l.* of the kingdom; sărkārātso = *l.* of the government.

Politics, *s.* 1. tsălounči sāmārthi, -the, *f.* = *l.* the art of governing.
 2. tsălountso jinos, -nsā, *m.* = way of governing.
 3. stitičeo văstu = *l.* things of the state.

Poll, *s*. 1. nāvāñpăṭṭi, -ṭe, *f*.
2. māteñ, -teā, *n*., tăkli, -le, *f*. = *l*. head.
3. māteāči pāṭ, -ṭi, *f*. = *l*. the back of the head.

Poll, *v*. păṭṭer borăi = *l*. write on the list.

Pollute, *v*. khătăi; bhăṣṭăi; mheḷăi.

Poltroon, *s*. āḷsi, -siā, *m*.

Polygamy, *s*. *anal. to Cn., Mr., Sans.* bhou (*or* săbār) potipoṇ, -ṇā, *n*. = *l*. being many consorts; *bet. rs.* săbār ăstrio āsāt, *or* s. dādle āsāt.

Polyglot, *a*. săbār bhāsāntso.

Polygon, *s*. săbār konseānčeñ (rūp, -pā, *n*.)

Polytheism, *s*. săbār devañšāstrụ, -rā, *n*., *n. c.*; bombeā puza, -je, *f*.

Polytheist, *s*. săbār devañšāstri, -ri, *m*.; *bet*. săbār devānčer sătmāndtolo; bombeañgār, -rā, *m*.

Pommel, *see* **Hilt.**

Pommel, *v*. mār.

Pompous, *a*. 1. dobājeātso = *l*. splendid.
2. doulătitso = *l*. of vanity.

Pond, *s*. tăḷeñ, -ḷeā, *n*.

Ponder, *v*. tuk = *l*. weigh, *fg*.; čint = *l*. think; niyāḷ = *l*. meditate.

Ponderous, *a*. bhāri, *pr*., *fg*.; zăḍ.

Poniard, *see* **Dagger.**

Pontiff, *s*. Pāp, -pā, *m*., *add* saib = lord.

Pontifical, *a*. Pāp sāibātso.

Pontificate, *s*. Pāpsāibārāz, -jā, *n*.

Pony, *s*. ṭānkaṇ, -ṇā, *n*.; poni, -ye, *f*., *fr*.

Pool, *s*. 1. mădăk, -kā, *n*.; tăḷeñ, -ḷeā, *n*.
2. zăr, -ri, *f*. = *l*. a fountain.

Poonwood, *s*. širipoṇṇe, -ṇeā, *n*.

Poor, *a*. dubḷo, *or* durbăḷo; gărīb, *Hind. Mr., yet used sometimes*; pòr = *l*. destitute, orphan; kirkóḷ = *l*. wretched.

Pop, *s*. gouji, -je, *f*.

Pop, *v*. gouji kăr.

Pope, *see* **Pontiff.**

Popinjay, *s*. kīr, -rā, *m*.; *see* **Coxcomb.**

Poppy, *s*. 1. kăskăseātso ruk, -kā, *m*. = *l*. a tree of p., *Mr. Cn.*
2. kăskăso, -seā, *m*. = seed of p. (*in pl.*)

Populace, *see* **Crowd.**

Popular, *a*. 1. lokātso, *or* zomeātso.
2. lokāči dósti bhogtso; lokātso dóst; lokāk mogāḷ.
3. tsālto = *l*. current.

Popularity, *s*. lokāči dósti, -te, *f*. = *l*. favour of the people; lokātso mōg (ó), -gā, *m*. = *l*. love of the people; *bet. rs.*

Populous, *a*. săbār lokātso; lokān bhorlolo.

Porcelain, *s*. čini āidān, -nā, *n*.

Porch, *s*. bălkāuñ, -kāvā, *m*.; tsăḍāu, -ḍāvā, *m*.; varānd, -dā, *n*.; āngāṇ, -gṇā, *n*. = yard of the house.

Porcupine, *s.* sāḷ, -ḷi, *f.*
Porcupine-fish, *s.* mutreñ, -treā, *n.*
Pore, *s.* čīl, -li, *f.*
Pork, *a.* dukramās, -sā, *n.*
Porosity, *s.* rigasārkeñ, -keā, *n.*
Porous, *s.* čili āsullo.
Porpoise, *s.* dăryādukór, -krā, *m.*
Porridge, *s.* āmbil, -lā, *n.* (a kind of p. made of rāgi).
Porringer, *s.* pīr, -ri, *f.*
Port, *s.* 1. bădăr, -drā, *n.* = a quay; āḷveñ, -veā, *n.* = *l.* an estuary.
2. tsāl, -li, *f.*
Portable, *a.* vorasārko, *or* vortso; vāvoisārko.
Portal, *s.* dārvăṭo, -ṭeā, *m.*
Portcullis, *s.* umkăḷtso sānkou, -kvā, *m.* = *l.* a suspended bridge.
Portend, *v.* dākăi = *l.* show, *or* mukār dākăi; gurt āsā = *l.* sign is.
Portend, *s.* 1. gurtu̥, -tā, *m.* = *l.* a sign; khuṇa, -ṇe, *f.*
2. ăjāp, -pā, *n.*, *or* ăjāpāči văstu̥, -tu, *f.* = *l.* a wonder, *or* a wonderful thing; āščăryeñ (*or* ătsăryeñ), -yeā, *n.* = a miracle.
Porter, *s.* bāglarākṇo, -ṇeā, *m.* = *l.* a door-keeper.
Portfolio, *s.* 1. kāgdaññčīl, -lā, *n.*
2. măntrihuddo, -deā, *m.*; măntriudyóg, -gā, *m.* = *l.* the rank of minister.
Portico, *s.* 1. tsouki, -ke, *f.*; tsāuḍi, -ḍe, *f.*
2. sopo, -peā, *m.*; bălkāuñ, -kāvā, *m.*; varānd, -dā, *m.*
Portion, *s.* vānṭo, -ṭeā, *m.*; hiso, -seā, *m.*
Portliness, *s.* ghăn, -nā, *n.*, *e.g.* to ghănān tsăltā = he walks with portliness; bhār, -rā, *m.* = *l.* gravity; bhărm, -mā, *n.* (feigned p.)
Portly, *a.* pušṭi, *etc.*
Portrait, *s.* sārkeñ, -keā, *n.* = *l.* likeness; čitru̥, -rā, *n.*; năkša, -še, *f.* = *l.* a sketch.
Portress, *s.* bāglarākṇi, -ṇe, *f.*
Position, *s.* 1. suāt, -te, *f.* = *l.* a place.
2. stiti, -ti, *f.* = *l.* state, condition; *rs into poten. mood*, *e.g.* I am in a p. to.
Positive, *a.* 1. khănḍit; khăro = *l.* true; *see* **Explicit.**
2. dubāu nātullo.
Possess, *v.* 1. āsā, *Sb. Dat.* = *l.* is; dovór = *l.* keep.
2. *fg.* rig = *l.* enter, *ch. cs.*, *e.g.* p. the mind; bhór = *l.* fill, *e.g.* p. the mind.
3. ănbhóg (*or* bhóg), *e. g.* p. riches.
4. kăḷ = *l.* be known, *e. g.* p. a language, *ch. cs.*
5. pòs kāṇghe = *l.* take possession; 'possessed by the devil = deuntsārān pòs kāṇghello'.
6. sotăntrār dovór (*pass.* s. āsā) = keep in absolute power;

or bet. only sotăntrār āsā, *ch. cs., e.g.* p. a country.

Possession, *s.* 1. āst, -ti, *f.* = *l.* riches; zămin, -ne, *f.*, buin̄, -in̄, *f.* = p. of land; dirven̄, -veā, *n.* (much money); dhăn, -nā, *n.*; dhăn mòn, -nā, *n.* = all that we possess, *l.* property and mind, *as used in the sentence,* we must offer all that we have to God.

2. ănbhou, -bhovā, *m.*, *or* ănbhóg, -gā, *m.*

Possessor, *s.* 1. ănbhógdār, -rā, *m.*

2. dhăni, -yā, *m.* = *l.* master, *Lat. dominus.*

Possibility, *s.* tānk, -ki, *f.*; *rs. into poten. mood.*

Possible, *a.* zāuyet āsullo; *bet. rs. into* zāuyet, *or other verb in the poten. mood.*

Possibly, *ad.* As far as I p. can = mākā tāukta titlen̄.

Post, *s.* 1. (rukātso) khāmbo, -beā, *m.* = *l.* a pillar (of wood); *see* **Stake.**

2. udyóg, -gā, *m.* = civil p.

3. hŭddo, -deā, *m.* = *l.* rank.

4. tăpāl, -lā, *n.* (public service); tăpālgāḍi, -ye, *f.*

5. mokām, -mā, *n.* = *l.* station; ṭhāṇen̄, -ṇeā, *n.*

Post, *v.* 1. (istyār) lāi *or* mār = *l.* attach (a notice).

2. ghāl = *l.* put, *e.g.* troops.

3. tăpalār ghāl = *l.* put on the post, *e.g.* a letter.

4. tăpālgāḍiyer poiṇ kăr = *l.* travel with the post.

5. dākāl kăr = enter (in a book).

Postage, *s.* tăpāldăstur, -re, *f.* = *l.* tax of post; tăpālāčen̄ mòl, -lā, *n.* = *l.* price of post.

Posterior, *a.* pāṭlo = *l.* being behind; māgir āsullo *or* māgirtso = *l.* being after; uprāntlo = *l.* being after.

Posterity, *s.* săntăt, -ti, *f.*; kuṭmātso (kuṭmāčin̄) = *l.* of the family.

Posthumous, *a.* bāpui meleā uprānt zāllo; bāpāik kāḍullo (*a rather offensive expression*).

Postman, *s.* tăpālpedo, -deā, *m.* = a letter-carrier.

Postmaster, *s.* tăpālātso ădhikāri, *or* tăpāla-ădhikāri, -ri, *m.*, *or* tăpālāčen̄ mostak, -kā, *n.*

Post-office, *s.* tăpālkaṭen̄, -ṭeā, *n.*; tăpālkăčeri, -ri, *f.*

Postpone, *v.* pāṭi ghāl.

Postscript, *s.* tāzakălăm, -lmā, *n.*

Posture, *s.* kuḍirīt, -ti, *f.* = *l.* manner of body; kuḍistiti, -ti, *f.* = *l.* state of body; uborāunči rīt, -ti, *f.* = *l.* manner of standing; *bet. rs.*

Pot, *s.* moḍki, -ke, *f.*; āidān, -nā, *n.*; kunḍlen̄, -leā, *n.* = an earthen p. for preparing curry in; buḍkuḷo, -ḷeā, *m.* = a kind of earthen p.; *see App. to Konk.-Engl. Dictionary.*

Potash, *s.* khār, -rā, *m.*

Potato, *s.* 1. băṭaṭo, -ṭeā, *m.*
2. kārāndo, -deā, *m.* = a kind of fruit similar to a p.
3. keno, -neā, *m.* = Telinga p.
Sweet p. = kăṇgi, -ge, *f.*

Potion, *s.* piuṇeñ, -ṇeā, *n.*

Pottage, *s.* kāld, -dā, *m.*, *fr.*; kăsāi, -yā, *m.* = soup, decoction.

Potter, *s.* kumbār, -rā, *m.*

Pottery, *s.* 1. kumbārāčeñ kām, -mā, *n.*
2. kumbārakārkhāno, -neā, *m.* = *l.* workshop of p.

Pouch, *s.* poti, -ye, *f.* = *l.* a bag.

Poultice, *s.* lēp(ê), -pā, *m.*

Poulterer, *s.* kunkḍāñ iktolo = *l.* a seller of fowls; kombe iktolo.

Poultry, *s.* kunkāḍ, -kḍā, *n.*

Pounce (on), *v.* zompāi mār; dhăr, *or* ubon dhăr = *l.* flying catch.

Pounce, *s.* reti, -ye, *f.* = *l.* sand (*used to dry up ink on paper*); *see* **Claw.**

Pound, *s.* 1. rātlụ, -lā, *m.* (weight).
2. veḍo, -ḍeā, *m.* = *l.* an enclosure.
3. paunḍ, -ḍā, *m.* (coin).

Pound, *v.* 1. pūḍ kăr; văṭ, *or* dóḷ (by grinding).
2. dāḍāi, *e.g.* roads.
3. mosti = *l.* trample.
4. veḍeānt ghāl = *l.* put into an enclosure.

Pour, *v.* 1. vót *or* vómti.
2. simp, *e.g.* by watering.
The clouds p. out = kupañ vóttāt.

Pout, *v.* khăntiṣṭ distā = *l.* appears gloomy.

Pout, *s.* bezārāi, -ye, *f.*; *see* **Ill-temper.**

Poverty, *s.* 1. durbăḷkāi, -ye, *f.*, *or* durbăḷpoṇ, -ṇā, *n.*
2. *fg. rs. into* uṇo = *l.* less, *e.g.* p. of courage.

Powder, *s.* 1. pūḍ, -ḍi, *f.*, *e.g.* snuff.
2. dāru, -rve, *f.* = gunpowder.
3. piṭo, -ṭeā, *m.* = thick p. like that into which bamboos are sometimes eaten by worms.
4. kup, -pā, *m.* = sandstone-powder, *n. c.*
5. dhuḷ, -ḷi, *f.* = *l.* dust.

Powder, *v.* pūḍ kăr; *see* **Pound.**

Power, *s.* 1. podvi, -ve, *f.*
2. bòḷ, -ḷā, *n.*; yekthār, -rā, *m.*
3. trāṇ, -ṇā, *n.* = *l.* ability; *see* **Ability**; guṇ, -ṇā, *m.*; sāmārthi, -the, *f.*
According to his p. = tāče tānki pārmāṇe.

Powerful, *a.* podvedār; boḷādik, *or* bòḷ āsullo.

Pox (Small), *s.* boḷnik, -ke, *f.*

Practicable, *a.* kăriet āsullo; kărtso; *bet. rs.*

Practical, *a.* kărneañ višyānt āsullo = *l.* being about actions; *bet. rs. into* kărneañ višyānt; ănbovātso = *l.* of experience; *or* ănbou āsullo; zānṭo = *l.* clever (in action); kāmāk pòḍtso = *l.* falling (fit) to business; upkārāk pòḍtso.

Practically, *ad.* kărčea părmāṇe = *l.* according to what is to be done; kărčeñ pòḷeun = *l.* looking to what is to be done.

Practice, *s.* 1. sovói, -ye, *f.*, *e.g.* p. of a good resolution, *also* exercise, custom.
2. dăstur, -ri, *f.* = *l.* fashion; rūḍ, -ḍi, *f.*; luḷ, -ḷi, *f.*
3. ăbyās, -sā, *m.*, *n. c.* = exercise, *e.g.* of a language; prăyóg, -gā, *m.* = *l.* use.
4. ănbóu, -vā, *m.*, *or* ănbóg, -gā, *m.* = *l.* experience.

Practise, *v.* 1. sovói āsā = *l.* practice is, *ch. cs.*; ăbyās kăr, *or* sovói kăr.
2. tsălăi = *l.* cause to walk, *fg.*, *e.g.* medicine.

Prairie, *s.* lāmb măidān, -nā, *n.* = *l.* a long plain.

Praise, *s.* vornoṇi, -ṇe, *f.*; hogḷāp, -pā, *n.*; ănănd, -dā, *m.* = *ex.* glory.

Praise, *v.* 1. hogoḷsi (*var.* uboḷsi); hogḷāp (*or* ănănd) kăr; pātsăr, *e.g.* the saints; vorni = *l.* exalt.
2. sipārăs kăr = *l.* make recommendation (by praising); tārif kăr.

Praiseworthy, *a.* hogoḷsountso, *or* hogḷāp făvozăllo, *or* hogḷāpātso, *etc.*; *see* **Praise.**

Prance, *v.* 1. uḍ = *l.* spring.
2. *fg.* ăbbār kăr = *l.* make ostentation; *or* ăbbarān tsăl.

Prank, *s.* mărji, -je, *f.* = *l.* caprice; khéḷkuḷañ, -ḷāñ, *n. pl.* = merry tricks.

Prank, *v.* ăbbār kăr.

Prate, *v.* 1. găzāli mār = *l.* beat a chat; phānḍle mār.
2. bās khā = *l.* eat language (get a scolding); bòb mār = *l.* cry; *vlg.* boḍboḍ = *l.* chatter.

Prater, *s.* boḍboḍo, -ḍeā, *m.* (*vlg.*); phānḍleagār, -rā, *m.*

Prating, *s.* găzāl, -li, *f.* (*com. in pl.*)

Pray, *v.* māg-ṇeñ kăr, *or* m. móṇ; prārtăn kăr, *n. c.*; *Cm.* māg; *vlg.* răzār kăr, *fr.*

Prayer, *s.* māg-ṇeñ, -ṇeā, *n.*; *vlg.* răzār, -rā, *n.*, *fr.*; prārtăn, -nā, *n.*; grāṇeñ, -ṇeā, *n.*

Prayer-book, *s.* māg-ṇeāčeñ pustak, -kā, *n.*

Preach, *v. vlg.* sermăuñ kăr; săngon di = *l.* say, speak; prăsăng kăr. (*H. K.*)

Preacher, *s.* sermăvist, -tā, *m.*, *fr.*; pregadór, -rā, *m.*, *fr.*, *n. c.*; sermāuñ kărtolo, *or* pādri, -ri, *m.*, *fr.*; prăsăngagār, -rā, *m.* (*H. K.*)

Preaching, *s. vlg.* sermāuñ, -māvā, *m.*, *fr.*, prăsăng, -gā, *n.* (*H. K.*)

Preamble, *s.* tăyārăi, -ye, *f.* = *l.* preparation; *perh.* rig, -ge, *f.* = *l.* ingress, *fg.*

Precarious, *a.* thirnātullo (*or* stirnātullo) *or* ăthir.

Precaution, *s.* tsătrăi, -ye, *f.* = *l.* care, heed: 'take precautions = ts. kāṇghe'.

Precede, *v. l.* mukār (*or* ādiñ) vetā = goes before; ādiñ *and the verb required by mn., e.g.* study should p. food = jeunčeā ādiñ sikazāi.

Precedence, *s.* 1. mān, -nā, *m.* = *l.* honour.

2. *rs. into v.*

Give the p. to = vórn vintsun kāḍ.

Precedent, *s.* ādlo dāklo, -leā, *m.* = *l.* preceding example.

Precedent, *a.* ādlo *or* poilo; *see* **Precede.**

Precept, *s.* upades, -sā, *m.*; *vlg.* mandament, -tā, *m., fr.* (*rl.*); formāṇ, -ṇā, *n.* = *l.* a command; kāido, -deā, *m.* = *l.* a rule, law; hukum, -kme, *f.* = *l.* an order.

Preceptor, *s.* 1. upadesi, -si, *m.*

2. ăiguḷ, -ḷā, *m.*, *vlg.* = a master of low classes; *see* **Teacher.**

Precinct, *s.* mitmer, -re, *f.*; găḍ, -ḍi, *f.*; sărhăddụ, -di, *f.*

Precious, *a.* 1. molādik, *or* ămolik.

2. mhārăg = *l.* dear, of price.

P. blood (of J. C.) = ămolik răgat.

Precipice, *s.* 1. kăḍso, -seā, *m.* = *l.* declivity; khăndăk, -dkā, *m.*

2. gunḍi, -ye, *f.*

Precipitance, Precipitation, *s.* ăusăr, -rā, *m.* = *l.* haste.

Precipitate, *v.* buḍăi, *c. v. of* buḍ.

Precipitous, *a.* ăusărātso.

Precise, *a.* sārko.

Precocious, *a. rs.*, sămanātullea veḷār; *rs. into* tsăḍ vegiñ yeuntso = coming too soon; *perh.* kāla-ādlo = *l.* before the time.

Precocity, *s.* kāla-ādli bud, -di, *f.*, *or rs. into adj.*

Preconception, *s.* āḍāločen, -ni, *f.*; vānkḍiāločen.

Preconcerted, *a.* ādiñvopụllo, *or* adiñkărār kello.

Precursor, *s.* 1. dūt, -tā, *m.* = *l.* a messenger (*ex.* mukāvelo d.); hărăkāri, -riā, *m.*

2. khuṇa, -ṇe, *f.* = a presage.

Predecessor, *s.* māji (ădhikāri, -ri, *m.*) = *l.* anterior (magistrate).

Predestinate, *v.* (ādiñ) vintsun [kāḍ.

Predestination, *s.* ādiñvintsāp, -tspā, *n.*, *n. c.*

Predetermine, *v.* ādiñ niščeisi; ādiñ lāi = *l.* apply before to (*phil.*)

Predicament, *s.* vărg, -gā, *m.* = *l.* class.

Predicate, *v.* (khănḍit) sāng = *l.* say (positively).

Predict, *v.* ādiñ kăḷăi; ādiñ sāng.

Prediction, *s.* ādiñsāng -ṇeñ, -ṇeā, *n.*; profesi, -si, *f.*, *fr.*

Predilection, *s.* ăpurbāi, -ye, *f.* = *l.* fondness, great affection.

Predispose, *v.* 1. vondăi = *l.* incline; voḍneo di, *or* vondouṇeñ di = *l.* give inclinations; bāgāi = *l.* bend, *fg.*
2. kārāṇ di = *l.* give cause.
3. ādiñ mānḍ = *l.* arrange before.

Predisposition, *s.* 1. ādiñmānḍāvoḷ, -ḷi, *f.* = *l.* before-arrangement.
2. vondouṇeñ, -ṇeā, *n.* = *l.* inclination.

Predominant, *a.* 1. tsălountso = *l.* ruling; zăit vortso = carrying victory.
2. sădāntso = *l.* of always, *e.g.* passion; mukhya = *l.* principal; *see* **Influential.**

Predominate, *v.* . . vórn podvedār zăun āsā = *l.* is more powerful than. . . ; tsălăi = rule; tsăl = *l.* be current.

Pre-eminent, *a.* uttim (uttăm) = *l.* excellent.

Preface, *s.* ādiñsāng-ṇeñ, -ṇeā, *n.*

Prefect, *s.* ădhipăti, -ti, *m.*

Prefer, *v.* vintsun kāḍ = *l.* choosing take, *pr. fg., e.g.* p. true honour to vain honour, *etc.*; khuši āsā, = *l.* will is, *with comparat.*; mānva *or* boro (-ri, -reñ) distā = *l.* pleases, *with comparat.*; mānd = *l.* esteem.

I prefer Rome to Paris = Parisa prās Róm mākā mānvatā; *see also* **Appreciate.**

Preference, *s.* give the p. to: *rs. into* prefer, *v.*

Prefigure, *v. rs.* gurtụ āsā = *l.* is sign; dākăi = *l.* show.

Prefix, *v.* mukār borăi = *l.* write before.

Pregnancy, *s.* gurvārpoṇ, -ṇā, *n.*, *or* guruatsār, -rā, *m.*

Pregnant, *a.* guruār; gărbest.

Prejudice, *s.* 1. vānkḍi āločen, -ni, *f.* = *l.* a crooked opinion; āḍāločen, -ni, *f.* = *l.* a contrary opinion.
2. luksān, -nā, *n.* = *l.* harm.

Prejudice, *v.* luksānāk pòḍ = *l.* fall to p., *ch. cs.*

Prejudicial, *a.* luksānātso = *l.* hurtful.

Prelate, *s.* igārjehuddeagār, -rā, *m.* = dignitary of the church.

Prelection, *s.* sikoṇ, -ṇe, *f.* = *l.* instruction; sikouṇeñ, -ṇeā, *n.*; *see* **Lecture.**

Preliminary, *a.* mukāvelo, *or* mukār vetso; ărāmbātso = *l.* original, of the beginning; poilo = *l.* first.

Prelude, *s.* tăyārāi, -ye, *f.* = *l.* preparation.

Prelude, *v.* tăyār kăr = *l.* make ready, prepare.

Premature, *a. see* **Precocious.**

Premeditate, *v.* ādiñ čint = *l.* think before; ādiñ niyāḷ = *l.* meditate before.

Premise, *v.* ādiñ niščeisi = establish before; ādiñ sāng = *l.* say before.

Premises, *s.* 1. ghăravedo, -deā, *m.*; ghăr āni zāgo = *l.* house and ground.
2. *the Mr., Cn., Sans.* pūrvapăkša, -šā, *m.*

Premium, *s.* inām, -mā, *m.*

Premonish, *v.* ādiñ kăļăi.

Prentice, *see* **Apprentice.**

Pre-occupation, *s.* husko, -keā, *m.* = trouble.

Pre-occupied, *a.* huskeātso = troubled by thoughts.

Pre-occupy, *v.* (dusreāñ ādiñ) kāṇe = *l.* take (before others).

Preparation, *s.* 1. tăyārāi, -ye, *f.*; āitemon, -nā, *n.*
2. sănnāi, -yā, *m.*

Prepare, *v.* tăyār kăr; kăr = *l.* do.

Preponderance, *s.* bhār, -rā, *m.* = *l.* gravity, *fg.*; zăit, -tā, *n.* = *l.* victory, *fg.*

Preponderate, *v.* zăit vor.

Pre-requisite, *a. s. By the Necess. mood and* ādiñ; gărječeo văstu, *or* zāi āsulleo văstu, *pl. f.* = necessary things.

Prerogative, *s.* hăkkų, -kā, *n.*; višes deṇeñ, -ṇeā, *n.*, *or* v. ălănkār, -rā, *m.*

Presage, *s.* gurtų, -tā, *m.*; ādli (*or* mukāveli) volok, -ļki, *f.* = *l.* anterior knowledge (feeling); *bet. rs.* ādiñ bhóg; (ādli) khuṇa, -ṇe, *f.*

Presage, *v.* (ādiñ) dākăi = *l.* show (before).

Prescribe, *v.* formāi = *l.* command.

Prescription, *s.* 1. (*legal*) *perh.* zāizāllo ănbou = *l.* required possession; *or the Mr.* zunivāhivāṭ, -ṭe, *f.*
2. hukum, -kme, *f.* = *l.* an order.
3. voizāčiṭ, -ṭi, *f.* = *l.* a note of the physician; *or* voizā hukum = *l.* an order of the ph.

Presence, *s.* hāzri, *or* hăzări, -re, *f.*; *rs. into* hāzăr = *l.* present.
Real p. = nīz h.
In p. = mukār.
P. of mind = dhăir, -rā, *n.*

Present, *a.* 1. hāzăr (p. in a place).
2. ātāntso = *l.* of now.
For the p. = sădyāk; at p. = ātāñ.

Present, *s.* deṇeñ, -ṇeā, *n.*; kāṇik, -ke, *f.* = a splendid pr.; inām, -mā, *n.*; beļeakāṇik *is* a present of tenants to a landlord.

Present, *v.* 1. bheṭăi = *l.* offer; di = *l.* give.
2. dākăl kăr = *l.* make known, introduce.
3. mukār ghāl = *l.* put before.
P. thyself = mukār ye.
P. (to a living) = *perh.* šipārăs kăr = *l.* recommend.

Presentation, *s.* 1. bheṭouṇeñ, -ṇeā, *n.* = *l.* offering, *e.g.* in the temple.
2. šipārăs, -se, *f.* = *l.* recommendation (to a living).

Presentiment, *s.* *vlg. rs.* mākā ādiñ distā; *see* **Presage.**

Presently, *ad.* *By the Pres. instead of Fut., see* Gram.; ātānts = *l.* just now; yeka khiṇa bitār = *l.* within one moment.

Preservation, *s.* rākṇeñ, -ṇeā, *n.*; zogāsāṇ, -ṇi, *f.*, *e.g.* of health.

Preservative, *a.* rāktso.

Preserve, *v.* rāk; sāmbāḷ = *l.* defend, keep; (sāmbāḷn) dovór, *e.g.* food.

Preserve, *s.* dòs, -si, *f.*; miṭāi, -ye, *f.* = a sweetmeat.

Preside, *v.* tsălăi = *l.* cause to walk, *fg.*; *vlg.* pirjent zāun āsā, *or* kădelār āsā.

Presidency, *s.* 1. tsălouṇeñ, -ṇeā, *n.* = act of one who presides; ădhikār, -rā, *m.*, *or* ădhipătipoṇ, -ṇā, *n.*

2. khāto, -teā, *m.*, *e.g.* the Madras p.

President, *s.* 1. ădhipăti, -ti, *m.*, *e.g.* of a country, of a feast.

2. (săbhe)nāik -kā, *m.*, for a meeting; *vlg.* pirjent, -ti, *m.*, *fr.*

Press, *v.* 1. dāmb (*not to be conf. with* dāmp), *e.g.* with the hand upon clothes; bòḷ kăr = *l.* make force; sāṇsi; čép.

2. čirmuṭāi.

3. lóṭ = *l.* push.

4. gāṇeānt ghāl = *l.* put into the press (*e.g.* to extract oil).

P. one with questions = yeka voir yék vitsārāṇ kăr; săvāli voir săvāl kăr.

P. the enemy = bhāir kăr.

He presses me = to mākā ău-săr kărtā, *or* to m. vāttāi k.

Press, *s.* 1. čhāpkhān (*or* čhāpa-khān), -nā, *n.* (office).

2. gāṇo, -ṇeā, *m.* = the machine.

Pressing, *a.* zărūr.

Pressure, *s.* 1. dāmbāp, -pā, *n.*

2. *fg.* dăgdu̥, *pl.* *m.* = *l.* sufferings.

3. raṭāvóḷ, -ḷi, *f.*, *e.g.* of business.

4. zărurāi, -ye, *f.* = *l.* urgency; tăḍāko, -keā, *m.*, *e.g.* p. of responsibility.

Prestige, *s.* gaujer, -rā, *m.*, *e.g.* p. of a name.

Presume, *v.* 1. *2nd Loc.* tsăḍ pātiye = *l.* trust too much to; ăhănkār kăr = *l.* make pride, *fg.*

2. čint = *l.* think.

Presumption, *s.* 1. ăhănkār, -rā, *m.*

2. gărv, -vā, *n.* = *l.* pride.

Presumptuous, *a.* ăhănkāri, *or* -rātso; gărviṣṭ.

Pretence, *s.* 1. nīb, -bā, *n.* = a pretext.

2. kăpăṭ, -ṭā, *n.* = *l.* simulation.

3. hăkku̥, -kā, *n.* = *l.* right, *or rs. into v.*

Pretend, *v.* 1. (phoṭāun) móṇ = *l.* (deceiving) say.

2. nīb sāng = *l.* say pretext.

3. kăpăṭān tsăl = *l.* proceed with simulation, *ch. cs.*

4. hăkkụ móṇ sāng = *l.* say as a right.

Pretender, *s.* kăpṭi, -tiā, *m.* = *l.* a simulator, *rs. into v.*

Pretension, *s.* 1. hăkkụ, -kā, *n.*, *or bet.* hăkkụšeñ.

2. āločen, -ni, *f.* = *l.* judgment, opinion.

3. doulăt, -ti, *f.* = *l.* vanity; nīb, -bā, *n.* = *l.* a pretext.

Preternatural, *a.* săimbmiruontso *or* -mikontso.

Pretext, *s.* nīb, -bā, *n.*

Pretty, *a.* sobit; gòmṭo (*H. K.*); sundăr; tsănd (*H. K.*)

Pretty, *ad.* sumār = *l.* moderarately.

Prevail, *v.* 1. zăit vor = *l.* carry victory, *fg.*; jik = *l.* gain, *fg.*, prove stronger.

2. dākăl zā, *e. g.* a custom, a fashion; tsăl = *l.* walk, *fg.* (be current), *see* **Influence.**

Prevent, *v.* āḍāi *or* āḍkāḷ kăr; inkār kăr = *l.* make resistance, opposition (*Acc.*).

P. from doing = kărčeāntlo āḍāi, *or* kărināso āḍāi.

Previous, *a.* ādlo, *or* mukāvelo.

Previously, *ad.* ādiñ.

Prey, *s.* 1. lūṭ, -ṭi, *f.*, *e.g.* of soldiers, of wild beasts.

2. khāṇ, -ṇā, *n.* = *l.* food.

3. sikārečiñ sukṇiñ = *l.* birds of hunting.

Prey, *v.* lūṭ kăr.

Price, *s.* 1. mòl, -lā, *n.*

2. kimmăt, -ti, *f.* = *l.* valuation.

Low p. = uṇeñ m.

Prick, *v.* tóp, *e.g.* kānṭo toptā.

Prick, *s.* topṇeñ, -ṇeā, *n.*

Prickle, *s.* 1. kānṭo, -ṭeā, *m.*

2. ghāmāḷeñ, -ḷeā, *n.* (p. caused by heat).

3. muḷo, -ḷeā, *m.*

Pride, *s.* gărvụ, -vā, *n.*; 'to gărvān rāutā = *l.* he remains in pride'; ăhănkār, -rā, *m.*; āmsāṇ, -ṇi, *f.* = acidity, *fg.*, *e.g.* tākā tsăḍ āmsāṇ āsā = he is very proud, *l.* to him much ac. is; doulăt, -ti, *f.* = vanity; ăbbār, -rā, *n.*

Pride (oneself), *v.* ăbbār kăr, *or* gărvụ kăr; băḍāi kăr.

Priest, *s.* pujāri, -ri, *m.*, boṭ, -ṭā, *m.*, *and* guru, -ru, *m. are strictly applicable only to* pagan priests; guru *may perhaps be used also of* Catholic priests; *vlg.* pādri, -ri, *m.*, *fr.*; sāserdót, -ti, *m.*; *vlg.* vigār, -rā, *m.*, *fr.* = *l.* parish-priest, *yet with many equally applicable to all priests.*

Priesthood, *s.* gurupoṇ, -ṇā, *n.*, *n. c.*; sāserdotipoṇ, -ṇā, *n.*, *fr.*; pādripoṇ, -ṇā, *n.*

Priestly, *a.* sāserdotitso, *or* gurutso.

Prig, *s.* dănḍi, -ḍi, *m.*

Prim, *a.* tsăḍ sārko = *l.* too exact.

Primacy, *s.* poilepoṇ, -ṇā, *n.*; sotăntrụ, -rā, *n.* = *l.* independent power.

Primary, *a.* 1. poilo = *l.* first.
2. mukhya = *l.* principal, *or* mukhyest.

Prime, *a.* poilo; mukhya.

Prime, *s.* ful, -lā, *n.* = *l.* flower, *fg.* (the best of); *see also* Dawn.

Primer, *s.* (pāṭa-) poileñ pustak, -kā, *n.* = *l.* first book (of lessons); poileo sikoṇeo = *l.* first instuctions; suruvečeo sikoṇeo = *l.* beginning instructions.

Primitive, *a.* 1. poilo.
2. ărămbātso.

Prince, *s.* kuvor, -rā, *m.*, *e.g.* the son of a king; năbāb, -bā, *m.* = a Mahomedan p.

Princess, *s.* kuvórn, -ni, *f.*

Principal, *a.* mukhya.

Principal, *s.* 1. mukhyest, *e.g.* of a church; mostak, -kā, *n.* = *l.* head; gurkār, -rā, *m.*
2. păṭel, -lā, *m.* = p. of a village, appointed by civil authority with magisterial power.

Principally, *ad.* mukhya zāun, *or* ădhik kărn, *or* bhou kărn.

Principle, *s.* 1. suru, -uve, *f.*, ārămb, -bā, *m.* = *l.* a beginning.
2. văčăn, -nā, *n.* = a fundamental truth; mukya săt, -tā, *n.* = *l.* a fundamental truth; zăr, -ri, *f.* = *l.* a fountain, *fg.*; pāyo, -yeā, *m.*

Print, *v.* 1. čhāpo ghāl *or* čh. mār *or* čh. kăntsăi, *or* čhāpsi.
2. *fg.* kăntsăi = *l.* press, *e.g.* in the mind.

Print, *s.* 1. čhāpkhān, -nā, *n.* = office, *etc.*
2. čhāpo, -peā, *m.* = a (physical) impression.

Printer, *s.* čhāpeāgār, -rā, *m.*, *or* čhāpo ghāltolo.

Printing-office, *s.* čhāpkhān, -nā, *n.*

Printing-press, *s.* čhāpeāyăntrụ, -rā, *n.* *or* —āid, -dā, *n.*, *or* *perh.* —ghāṇo, -ṇeā, *m.*

Prior, *s.* măṭavoḍil, -lā, *m.* = *l.* the superior of a convent, *n.c.*

Prioress, *s.* măṭavoḍiln, -ni, *f.*

Prison, *see* Jail.

Prisoner, *s.* băndivān, -nā, *m.*

Prithee, *int.* dăyā kărn.

Privacy, *s.* yeksurāi, -ye, *f.*, *or* yeksurpoṇ, -ṇā, *n.*

Private, *a.* 1. khāski (kāsgi) = own.
2. yekoḍo (*opp. to* public) = single.
3. yeksuro = *l.* living alone.
4. pātiyeṇitso = *l.* of confidence.
5. vingăḍ = *l.* separated.
6. guṭātso *or* gupit = *l.* secret.

Privation, *s.* 1. tsukouṇeñ, -ṇeā, *n.*, *or* tsukāp, -pā, *n.*, *n. u.*; *rs.*
2. dăgd, *m. pl.* = sufferings.

Privilege, *s.* hăkkụ, -kā, *n.*, *or* višés hăkkụ; višés upkār, -rā, *m.* = *l.* a special benefit.

Privy, *a.* gupit, *or* guṭātso; *rs. into* gottu āsā = *l.* is known.
P. council = măntriñsăbha, -bhe, *f.*

Privy, *s.* kākus, -sā, *m.*, *fr.*; pāikhān, -nā, *n.*, *n. c.*

Prize, *s.* 1. inām, -mā, *n.*
2. luṭ, -ṭi, *f.* = *l.* prey.

Probable, Probability, *see* Likely, *etc.*

Probation, *s.* 1. tănki, -ke, *f.*, *e.g.* of an apprentice.
2. părikṣa, -ṣe, *f.* = *l.* examination.

Probationer, *s.* umedvār, -rā, *m.*

Probity, *s.* bori jiṇi, -ye, *f.* = *l.* good life; ăppăntpoṇ, -ṇā, *n.*; niskăpăṭ, -ṭā, *n.* = *l.* sincerity.
Man of p. = sătātso mănis, -nšā, *m.*

Problem, *s.* 1. săvāl, -lā, *n.* = interrogation, *as* in the catechism.
2. guṭ, -ṭā, *m.* = *l.* a secret.
3. vitsārăṇ, -ṇā, *n.* (*or* vitsārāp, -rpā, *n.*) = *l.* a question.

Problematical, *a.* dubāvi.

Proboscis, *s.* sónḍi, -ye, *f.*

Proceed, *v.* 1. niṭ vots = *l.* go straight.
2. mukār vots = *l.* go forward; mundărsa (*c. v.* mundărsi).
3. *only* vots, *e.g.* I p. now to explain = săngunk vetāñ.
4. zā *or* ubza, *e.g.* fruits from a tree, *and fg. also for* the proceeding of the Second and Third Persons of the most H. Trinity, *e.g.* Putrụ Bāpātso (*or* Bāpāthāun) ubzatā.
5. firiyād di = *l.* give an accusation.

Proceeding, *s.* tsălouṇi, -ṇe, *f.*, *e.g.* of a meeting.

Proceeds, *s.* huṭṭavóḷ, -ḷi, *f.*

Process, *s.* 1. firiyād, -di, *f.*; vevār, -rā, *m.*
2. upāi, -yā, *m.* = *l.* means.
In p. of time = māgir.

Procession, *s.* prosesāuñ (*vlg.* puršāuñ), sāvā, *m.*; meravaṇig, -ge, *f.* (*H. K.*)

Proclaim, *v.* părgăṭ kăr, *or* părgăṭāi; dāngro mār.

Proclamation, *s.* prăgăṭpoṇ, -ṇā, *n.*; formāṇ, -ṇā, *n.*, *or* hukum, -kme, *f.* = *l.* an order.

Procrastinate, *v.* toḍou kăr = *l.* make delay; pāṭi ghāl = *l.* put back, *fg.*

Procrastination, *s.* kaḷau, -ḷavā, *m.*

Procreate, *v.* zălmăi, *c. v. of* zălma.

Proctor, Procurator, *s.* 1. mukthālik, -kā, *m.*
2. dălāl, -lā, *m.* = an agent.

Procure, *v.* 1. kărn di = *l.* doing give, *or* hāḍn di = *l.* bringing give.
2. tăḷās kăr = *l.* make search.

Procurer, *s.* mālo, -leā, *m.* = *l.* a barber, *used also for* p.; dălāl, -lā, *m.* = *l.* an agent.

Prodigal, *a.* 1. tsăḍ khărčitolo,

or ts. khărtsuntso, *or* hăḷt-nāstanāñ khărtsuntso; ve-čik.

2. (bāpāk) sóḍlolo = he who left (the father), the pr. son of the H. Bible.

Prodigality, *s.* večikpoṇ, -ṇā, *n.*, *or* véts, -tsā, *m.* = *ex.* expense.

Prodigious, *a.* ăjāpātso = *l.* wonderful; ăprup = *l.* rare.

Prodigy, *s.* 1. ătsăriyeñ, -yeā, *n.* = *l.* a miracle; ăjāp, -pā, *n.* = *l.* a wonder, miracle.

2. khuṇa, -ṇe, *f.* = *l.* a sign, *Lat. signum.*

Produce, *v.* 1. kăr = *l.* do.

2. *by c. v.*, *e.g.* pr. laughing = hāsăi.

3. mukār ghāl = *l.* put before; hāḍ = *l.* bring.

4. lāmb kăr = make long(er).

Produce, Product, *s.* 1. fóḷ, -ḷā, *m.* = *l.* effect.

2. huṭṭavoḷ, -ḷi, *f.*

Production, *s.* 1. *perh.* dākoṇi, -ṇe, *f.* = *l.* representation.

2. zălmouṇeñ, -ṇeā, *m.*

3. fòḷabăritpoṇ, -ṇā, *n.*; *see* **Fertility.**

See also **Product.**

Productive, *a.* fòḷadik = *l.* fruitful; fòḷabărit.

Profanation, *s.* bhăṣṭ, -ṭā, *n.* (*or* bhrăṣṭ).

Profane, *v.* bhăṣṭăi (*var.* bhăṣṭi, brăṣṭi); pāḍ kăr = *l.* make bad, spoiled.

Profane, *a.* pòzḍo, *e.g.* p. words; văiṭ; pāḍ.

Profess, *v.* 1. utsār = *l.* express, *e.g.* faith; kăḷăi = *l.* make known.

2. tsălăi = *l.* cause to walk, *fg.*, *e.g.* medicine.

3. părgăṭ āngoṇeo kăr = *l.* make public vows.

Profession, *s.* 1. bhés, -sā, *m.* = state, condition.

2. utsăr, -rā, *m.*, *or perh. bet.* utsărăṇ, -ṇā, *n.* = *l.* expression.

3. părgăṭ āngoṇeo, *pl. f.* = *l.* public vows.

Professor, *s.* păṇḍit, -tā, *m.*; vidye-upădesi, -si, *m.* = *l.* a teacher of a science.

Professional, *a.* bhésātso; bhés tsălountso.

Proficiency, *s.* ādāi, -yā, *m.*

Proficient, *a.* ādāi kărtso; kabil.

Profile, *s.* yeka păkṣečeñ rūp, -pā, *n.*; yeka păkṣečeñ čitrụ, -trā, *n.*, *or perh.* păkṣečitrụ; kusičeñ čitrụ.

Profit, *s.* ādāi, -yā, *m.*; jikāp, -kpā, *n.* = *l.* gain, *pr. fg.*; năfo, -feā, *m.*; fāido, -deā, *m.*; lāb, -bā, *m.*

Profit, *v.* 1. ādāyātso zāun āsā; upkār, *or* upkārāk pòḍ = *l.* fall to benefit; ādāi kăr = *l.* make p.

2. prăyòg kăr = *l.* make use, *G. M.*

P. by an opportunity = sănd-rāp kāṇghe.

Profitable, *a.* ādāyātso; upkārātso, *or* upkārāk pòḍtso; prăyojănātso = *l.* of use.

Profligacy, *s.* 1. khoṭepoṇ, -ṇā, *n.* 2. móst, -ti, *f.* = *l.* luxury.

Profligate, *a.* 1. khoṭo; phăṭing. 2. móstitso.

Profound, *a.* 1. gunḍ, *pr.* *fg.* 2. *fg.* vorto = *l.* sublime.

Profundity, *s.* 1. gunḍāi, -ye, *f.* (gunḍi, -ye, *f.*) 2. vortepoṇ, -ṇā, *n.*

Profuse, *a.* tsăḍ khărtsuntso; večik.

Profusion, *s.* sămpurṇāi, -ye, *f.* = *l.* fulness; *see* **Prodigality.**

Progenitor, *s.* malgoḍo, -ḍeā, *m.*; pitra, -rā, *m.*; purvoz, -zā, *m.*

Progeny, *s.* săntăt, -ti, *f.*

Prognostic, *s.* gurtụ, -tā, *m.*; khuṇa, -ṇe, *f.*

Prognosticate, *v.* ādiñ sāng = *l.* say before; ādiñ kăḷ = be known before; pārki = *l.* guess.

Programme, *s.* kărčeātso vivór, -rā, *m.* = *l.* explanation of what is to be done; yād, -dā, *m.* = *l.* remembrance.

Progress, *s.* ādāi, -yā, *m.*; vrăddhi, -dhi, *f.*

Progressive, *a.* 1. mukār vetso = *l.* going forward. 2. ādāyātso. 3. thoḍea thoḍeātso.

Prohibit, *v.* āḍvār; mănna kăr = *l.* suspend, *e.g.* traffic.

Prohibition, *s.* āḍvarāp, -rpā, *n.*; mănnāi, -ye, *f.* = suspension.

Project, *v.* 1. nămuno kăr; āločen kăr. 2. mukār săr = *l.* come before, *Lat.* *eminere*, to stand out.

Project, *s.* nămuno, -neā, *m.*; āločen, -ni, *f.*, *etc.*; *see* **Plan.**

Projectile, *a.* 1. guḷo, -ḷeā, *m.*, a large p. 2. guḷi, -ye, *f.*, small.

Projection, *s.* 1. năkṣa, -ṣe, *f.* 2. mukārsărāp, -rpā, *n.*

Prolix, *a.* lāmb = *l.* long; vistārlolo = *l.* extended; săbārutrāntso = *l.* of many words.

Prolixity, *s.* lāmbāi, -ye, *f.*; săbār utrāñ = *l.* many words, *etc.*

Prologue, *s.* tăyārāi, -ye, *f.*

Prolong, *v.* 1. lāmb kăr. 2. vāido di = *l.* give more time, *e.g.* p. the time. 3. pāṭi ghāl = *l.* put back.

Prolongation, *s.* *rs.* *into* *v.*

Promenade, *s.* bounḍi, -ḍe, *f.*

Prominence, *s.* ubārāi, -ye, *f.*; *see also* **Projection.**

Prominent, *a.* 1. ubār. 2. mukār pòḍtso *or* rāuntso.

Promiscuous, *a.* borsillo = *l.* mixed; thărathărāntso = *l.* of many kinds; *rs.* *into* bhēd kărināstanāñ.

Promise, *s.* utăr, -trā, *n.*; bhās, -se, *f.*

Promise, *v.* 1. utăr di; bhāsāi. 2. *in* *fg.* *mn.*, *e.g.* p. to become good; *rs.*, *e.g.* dista = appears, *or bet.* pātiye = trust, *ch. cs.*

Promissory-note, *s.* vāideāčīṭ, -ṭi, *f.*

Promontory, *s.* bŭiñgāḷo, -ḷeā, *m.* = *l.* a neck of the earth; *or bet.* mulo, -leā, *m.*

Promote, *v.* 1. vāḍāi, *e.g.* the glory of God; tsāḍāi, = *l.* increase.

2. upkārāk pòḍ = *l.* fall to the benefit; ādhār kăr = *l.* make help.

3. băḍti di = *l.* give promotion (to higher offices); voir kāḍ; unts kām di, *n. c.*

Promotion, *s.* băḍti, -te, *f.* = p. to higher offices; *for other mn., rs. into v.*

Prompt, *a.* 1. ušār = *l.* clever, lively; tsurk.

2. tăyār = *l.* ready.

Prompt, *v.* 1. lāi = *l.* apply, determine, *e.g.* kāmāk lāi.

2. bud sāng = *l.* say advice; uṭāi = *l.* excite; sučen di = suggest words, *as*, to a speaker.

Promptitude, *s.* 1. tsurkāi *or* ušārāi, -ye, *f.*

2. tăyārāi, -ye, *f.* = *l.* readiness.

Promptly, *ad.* vegiñ = *l.* quickly.

Promulgate, *v.* pārgăṭ kăr, *or* pārgăṭāi.

Promulgation, *s.* pārgăṭpoṇ, -ṇā, *n.*

Promulgator, *s.* pārgăṭ kărtolo.

Prone, *a.* 1. bāgāllo = *l.* bent.

2. *rs.* pòng pòḍlāñ = *l.* the hump fell.

3. lāgullo = *l.* given, affectionate; vondountso = *l.* inclining, *pr. fg.*, *e.g.* to sin.

Prong, *s.* moḷo, -ḷeā, *m.*; kānṭo. -ṭeā, *m.*

Pronoun, *s.* nāvābădli, -le, *f.*

Pronounce, *v.* 1. utsār; móṇ = *l.* say, *e.g.* a sermon.

2. di, *e.g.* a sentence (fitvo).

Pronunciation, *s.* utsārāp, -rpā, *n.*

Proof, *s.* 1. ruzvāt, -ti, *f.*, *or* ruzu = oral p.

2. dāklo, -leā, *m.* = p. by documents.

3. vivor, -rā, *m.* = *l.* an explanation.

4. tānki, -ke, *f.* = *l.* a trial; părikša -še, *f.* = *l.* an examination.

5. kāšṭ, -ṭā, *m.*, *or* dăgd, *pl. m.* = *l.* pain.

6. tānkenăkăl, -klā, *n.* = *l.* a copy of trial, proof-sheet, *opp. to* tāzānăkăl.

Prop, *v.* zăḍāi vor, *or* z. sāmbāḷ = *l.* carry gravity, *e.g.* a pillar.

Prop, *s.* 1. digo, -geā, *m.*, *e.g.* such as are put to falling houses.

2. khāmbo, -beā, *m.*, *pr. fg.*, *e.g.* p. of a family.

Propagate, *v.* 1. vāḍāi, *c. v. of* vāḍ; tsāḍāi, *c. v. of* tsāḍ = increase; vistārāi = *l.* extend, *c. v. of* vistār.

2. pārgăṭ kăr = *l.* make public.

Propel, *v.* lōṭ = *l.* push; lăkăi (*H. K.*); mukār tsălăi, *or* m. dāunḍāi = cause to go forward.

Propense, *see* **Prone.**

Propensity, *s.* vondouṇeñ, -ṇeā, *n.*, *or* voḍni, -ne, *f.* = *l.* inclination; *rs. into* lāgullo zāun āsā, *or* boro (-ri, -reñ) distā; khuši -še, *f.* = *l.* will; āšā, -še, *f.* = *l.* desire.

Proper, *a.* 1. prăték; višés; *see* **Particular.**
2. āplo = *l.* own; *rs. into* fāvo zātā = *l.* belongs.
3. măryāditso = *l.* becoming.
4. lāyek = *l.* fit, *or rs. into* zātā.
5. *by the G. e.g.* it is p. for man to fail = monšāčén...

Properly, *ad.* 1. sārkeñ = *l.* exactly, *or* boreñ kărn.
2. măryādin = *l.* becomingly.

Property, *s.* 1. guṇ, -ṇā, *m.* = *l.* quality; sobāu, -āvā, *m.*; *rs. into G.* (*see* **Proper,** 5.)
2. āst, -ti, *f.* = *l.* possession; bădik, -dkā, *n.*; dhăn, -nā, *n.*; mhāl, -lā, *m. used rather for* p. in jewels *and the like;* vit, -tā, *n.*

Prophesy, *s. vlg.* profesi, -si, *f.*; mukāili săng-ṇi, -ṇe, *f.*

Prophet, *s.* prophet, -tā, *m.*, *fr.*; dirgadăršī, -ši, *m.*, *n. u.*; mukāvelo săng-ṇār, -rā, *m.*

Prophetess, *s.* prophetiṇ, -ṇi, *f.*; dirgadăršiṇ, -ṇi, *f.*, *n. u.*

Propitiate, *v.* 1. *anal. to Mr.* ănkul kăr, *but n. c. in this mn. although* ănkul *is used;* movāḷāi = *l.* make tender; fuslāi = *l.* appease; fārikpoṇ di = *l.* give reparation.
2. guṇātso kăr = *l.* make favourable.

Propitiation, *s.* fārikpoṇ, -ṇā, *n.* = *l.* satisfaction.

Propitiatory, *a.* fārikpoṇātso; upkārātso *or* upkārāk pòḍtso = *l.* beneficial; *anal. to Mr.* ănkulātso, *but n. c.*

Proportion, *s.* 1. sămapòḍneñ, -neā, *n.*, *or* —pòḍāp, -ḍpā, *n.*; sămamāp, -pā, *n.* = *l.* just measure; dāmasāi, -ye, *f.*; mezāp, -zpā, *n.*, *or* māp, -pā, *n.* = *l.* measure, *e.g.* yeā ghărāk m. nāñ; hăḷt, -tā, *n.*, *e.g.* in preparing food.
2. vānṭo, -ṭeā, *m.* = *l.* portion; părmāṇ, *used only in the abl. case* (părmāṇe).

Proportional, *a. rs.* māpa părmāṇe = *l.* according to measure; vānṭea părmāṇe = *l.* according to portion.

Proportionate, *a.* sămapòḍtso, *or rs. into noun.*

Proportionately, *ad.* dāmasāyečer, *etc.*

Proposal, *s.* 1. *rs. into v.*; nămuno, -neā, *m.* = *l.* a plan, model.
2. āločen, -ni, *f.* = *l.* an opinion, a sentence.

3. šărt, -tā, *n.* = *l.* condition; ăbiprāi, -ye, *f.*

Propose, *v.* 1. (mukār) ghāl = *l.* put (before).

2. šărt kăr = *l.* make (put) a condition; āločen kăr = *l.* make opinion; čint = *l.* think; *vlg.* móṇ = *l.* say.

I have something to p. to the meeting = săbhek yék āločen sāngunk āsā, *or*...utar sāngčeñ āsā.

Proposition, *s.* 1. ăbiprāi, -ye, *f.* (*ex.* ăbhiprāi), *e.g.* to deliberate on.

2. šărt, -tā, *n.* = *l.* condition.

3. bud, -di, *f.* = *l.* advice, suggestion.

4. vākya, -yā, *n.*; utsār, -rā, *m.* (Gram.); *see* **Proposal.**

Propound, *v.* părgăṭ kăr = *l.* make public.

Proprietor, *s.* dhăni, -yā, *m.*; kărt, -tā, *m.*; *see* **Master.**

Proprietorship, *s.* dhănipoṇ, -ṇā, *n.*, *or* yăzmānpoṇ, -ṇā, *n.*

Propriety, *s.* măryād, -di, *f.* = *l.* honesty; *rs. into* zātā teñ = what is proper.

Propulsion, *s.* lōṭ(ó), -ṭā, *m.*

Prorogue, *v.* pāṭi ghāl = *l.* put back.

Proscribe, *v.* găḍ pār kăr = *l.* make out of boundaries; *see* **Exile.**

Prose, *s.* văčăn, -nā, *n.* *Cn.*; *bet.* gāthā, -the, *f.*, *Mr.* (*or* gădya, -yā, *n.*)

Prosecute, *v.* 1. tsălāi = *l.* cause to walk, *fg.*, *c. v. of* tsăl.

2. firiyād di = *l.* give an accusation, *ch. cs.*; vevār kăr = *l.* file a suit.

Prosecution, *s.* 1. tsălouṇeñ, -ṇeā, *n.*

2. firïyād, -di, *f.*, vevār, -rā, *m.* = *l.* an accusation.

Prosecutor, *see* **Accuser.**

Proselyte, *s.* 1. sis, -sā, *m.* = *l.* a pupil.

2. novo kristāuñ, -tāvā, *m.* = *l.* a new Christian; pāṭlāugār, -rā, *m.* = *l.* a follower; mānd-tolo.

Prosody, *s.* slókapăddăt, -ti, *f.* = *l.* a formula for verses; kăvitepăddăt = a formula for verses.

Prospect, *s.* 1. diṣṭ, -ṭi, *f.* = *l.* sight.

2. săngăt *or* săngti, -gti, *f.* = *l.* a circumstance; āšā, -še, *f.* = *l.* chance.

Prospectus, *s.* năkṣa, -ṣe, *f.* = *l.* a sketch, outline, *or* -păṭṭi, -ṭe, *f.*; nămuno, -neā, *m.* = *l.* a plan; risko, *pl. f.* = *l.* lines (outl.), *fr.*

Prosper, *v.* vrăddhi kăr.

Prosperity, *s.* 1. vrăddhi, -dhi, *f.*; bărkăt, -tā, *n.*; sukh, -khā, *n.* = *l.* happiness; borepoṇ, -ṇā, *m.*

2. grestkāi, -ye, *f.* = *l.* riches.

Prosperous, *a.* vrăddi; guṇātso, *or bet. rs. into* guṇ, -ṇā, *m.*, *or into the v., e. g.* nămbăr tākā guṇ zāleñ.

Prostitute, *s.* čeḍi, -ye, *f.*

Prostrate, *v.* 1. săkăl ghāl = *l.* put down; seuṭi.

2. *fg.* bòḷ mōḍ(ō) = break force.

3. sărpòḍ = *l.* fall, *e. g.* upon the ground for praying.

Prostrate, *a.* 1. bòḷnātullo = *l.* without force.

2. sărpòḍlolo, *e. g.* for prayer; vomto.

Prostration, *s.* 1. nāñbòḷ, -ḷā, *n.* = *l.* no force.

2. ăpadhăir, -rā, *n.* = *l.* no courage.

3. sărpòḍāp, -ḍpā, *n.*, *e. g.* in prayer; săṣṭāng, -gā, *n.*

Protect, *v.* 1. rāk; sāmbāḷ = *l.* defend.

2. ādhār kăr = *l.* make help; mozăt kăr.

3. pois kăr = *l.* make far, *e. g.* p. against.

Protection, *s.* rākṇeñ, -ṇeā, *n.*; sāmbāḷoṇeñ, -ṇeā, *n.*, *or* sāmbāḷāp, -ḷpā, *n.*; ādhār, -rā, *m.* = *l.* help; mozăt, -ti, *f.* = *l.* intercession; āsro, -reā, *m.* = *l.* refuge.

Protector, *s.* rākṇo, -ṇeā, *m.*, *or* rākṇār, -rā, *m.*; *see* **Patron.**

Protectress, *s.* rākṇi, -ṇe, *f.*, *or* rākṇārn, -ni, *f.*

Protest, *v.* 1. ăḍḍi ghāl = *l.* put objection; inkār kăr = *l.* make resistance (*Acc.*); *neg. of* păsănd kăr.

2. khănḍit zāun sāng = *l.* say positively; părmāṇār sāng = *l.* say on oath.

Protest, *s.* ăḍḍi, -ḍe, *f.* = *l.* objection, *fg.*; nāñpăsănd, -dā, *n.* = *l.* disapproval; *rs. into v.*, *or* khănḍit sāngṇeñ, -ṇeā, *n.* = *l.* a positive saying.

Protestant, *s.* protestānt, -tā, *m.*

Protract, *v.* lāmb kăr = *l.* make long; urăi = *l.* cause to remain, to last (longer); toḍou kăr = *l.* make delay; kăḷāu kăr.

Protraction, *s. rs. into v.*

Protrude, *v.* mukār lōṭ(ō).

Protrusion, *s.* lōṭ(ō), -ṭā, *m.*, *or* mukārlōṭ.

Protuberance, *s.* 1. gunṭ (gănṭ), -ṭā, *n.*; dunkuṭ, -ṭā, *n.*, *e. g.* from a blow.

2. māskuṭ, -ṭā, *n.*

Protuberant, *a.* mukār sărtso.

Proud, *a.* gărvi (*var.* gărviṣṭ); ăhănkāri.

Prove, *v.* 1. ruzvāt kăr, *or* ruzu k., *G. F.* = demonstrate; dākăi = *l.* show.

2. pòḷe = *l.* look; prăyătăn kăr = *l.* make an effort.

3. tănker ghāl = *l.* put on trial.

Proverb, *s.* gād, -di, *f.*; moṇṇi, -ṇe, *f.*

Proverbial, *a.* gāditso, *or rs.* gādi bări.

Provide, *v.* 1. di *or* hāḍn di, *e. g.* food.

2. tăyār kăr = *l.* make ready.

3. zătăn kāṇghe = *l.* take care, *G. F.*; tsătrāi kāṇghe.
4. formāi = *l.* command.
P. against, *the 3rd followed by the neg. supine, etc.*

Provided, *a.* bhorlolo, *or* bhórn = *l.* filled; āsullo = *l.* having (being).

Provided, *conj. By the cond. tense*; zărtăr = if; *sometimes by the Gerund* -tanāñ; *see* Gram. P. IV. *and* App. I.

Providence, *s.* Devāči săsāi, -ye, *f.*; hārbār, -rā, *m.*

Provident, *a.* zătăn (*or* tsătrāi) kāṇeuntso; budivont = *l.* wise, prudent.

Providential, *a.* Devāče săsāyentlo *or* -yetso.

Province, *s.* 1. jillo (*var.* zillo), -leā, *m.* = a district; *some say* jilli, -le, *f.*, *n. c.*, *probably a diminutive form.*
2. gāuñ, -āñvā, *m.* = *l.* a country.
3. *fg.* kāido, -deā, *m.* = *l.* duty; *or* kām, -mā, *n.*

Provincial, *a.* jilleātso.

Provision, *s.* 1. khāṇ, -ṇā, *n.*; ahār (*var.* hār), -rā, *m.* = food; udărpošăṇ, -ṇā, *n.* = *l.* livelihood.
2. zătăn, -tne, *f.* = *l.* care; tăzviz, -zi, *f.* = prudence, investigation; tăyārāi, -ye, *f.* = preparation; upāi, -yā, *m.* = *l.* measures, means.
3. băndobăst, -ti, *f.* = *l.* security.
4. šărt, -tā, *m.* = *l.* a condition, stipulation; kărār, -rā, *m.* = *l.* a contract.

Provisionally, *ad.* sădyāk = for the present.

Proviso, *s.* šărt, -tā, *n.* = *l.* a condition.

Provoke, *v.* 1. rāg hāḍāi.
2. utsāmboḷ kăr.
3. *by c. v.*

Provocation, *s. rs. into v.*; utsāmboḷāi, -ye, *f.* = *l.* excitement.

Provoking, *a.* utsāmboḷ kărtso; bezārāi kărtso, *or* bezārāyetso, *or* kărkărātso = troublesome.

Provost, *see* **Superintendent.**

Prow, *s.* tārvāmuk, -kā, *n.* = *l.* the face of a ship.

Prowl, *see* **Plunder, Roam.**

Proximate, *a.* lāgiñ āsullo, *or* lāgsilo, *or* lāgtso; 'p. cause = lāgsileñ kārāṇ'.

Proxy, *s.* 1. *rs.* dălāl, -lā, *m.* = an agent; bădli, -liā, *m.*
2. dălālpoṇ, -ṇā, *n.* (*abstr.*)

Prudence, *s.* bud, -di, *f.*; zāṇvāi, -ye, *f.* = *l.* science, *fg.*; šānipoṇ, -ṇā, *n.*; vivék, -kā, *m.*

Prudent, *a.* budivont; zāṇṭo = *l.* clever (in acting); viveki, *n. c.*; šāni.

Prune, *v.* 1. kăsi kăr; boḍkāi.
2. *fg.* kāḍ = *l.* take away; kātăr = *l.* cut (off).

Pruriency, *s.* 1. khoróz, -rji, *f.*
2. *fg.* āšā, -še, *f.* = *l.* great desire.

Pry, *v.* 1. tīḷ, *or* tiḷn pòḷe = peep.
2. sārkeñ pòḷe; portun portun pòḷe = *l.* look again (and) again; sódun pòḷe = *l.* seeking look.
3. gunḍāi păriyānt pòḷe = *l.* look up to the bottom.

Psalm, *s.* sālm, -mā, *m.*, *fr.*; ănăndgāyān, -nā, *n.*

Pseudo, *a.* fóṭkiro, *or as prefix, only* fóṭ-

Pshaw, *int.* čha.

Psychology, *s.* ătmeašāstrụ, -rā, *n.*

Puberty, *s.* (kāzār zāunči) prāi, -ye, *f.*; *rs.* prāyebhărit, *adj.*; *or* nāunk lāgtā = *l.* begins to bathe.

Public, *a.* 1. părgăṭ, *opp. to* secret; prăsiddụ.
2. sărkārātso = *l.* of the government.
3. sărvụlokātso = *l.* of all people (common); sămestāntso.

Public, *s.* lók, -kā, *m.* = *l.* people.

Public-house, *see* **Tavern.**

Publican, *s.* sunkāñguttedār, -rā, *m.*

Publication, *s.* 1. părgăṭouṇeñ, -ṇeā, *n.*
2. pustak, -kā, *n.* = *l.* a book.

Publish, *v.* părgăṭ kăr.

Puck, *s.* druṣṭakāi, -ye, *f.*

Pucker, *s.* miri, -ye, *f.* = *l.* a fold.

Puddle, *s.* ubir, -brā, *m.*; kēd(é), -dā, *m.*; čikól, -klā, *m.*

Puddle, *v.* ubrān bhór *or* čiklān bh.; mheḷāi, *or* mheḷo kăr.

Puerile, *a.* burgeapoṇātso, *or rs. into* burgeā bări.

Puff, *s.* funk, -ki, *f.*

Puff, *v.* 1. funk (*Acc.*).
2. *fg.* gărvụ (*or* ăbbār *or* doulăt) kăr, *or* gărvānt rāu.
3. fugăi = inflate, *fg.*
P. away = funkun uḍăi.

Pug, *s.* 1. mānkoḍ, -kḍā, *m.* = an ape.
2. dākṭo peṭo, -ṭeā, *m.* = *l.* a little dog.

Pugnacious, *a.* lăḍāi kărtso.

Puissant, *a.* podvedār, *or* bòlādik.

Pule, *v.* bòb mār, *or* răḍ.

Pull, *v.* 1. vōḍ(ó) = *Lat. trahe*, draw.
2. kāḍ = *l.* draw, *e. g.* water.
P. up = kāḍ *or* humbóḷ = root out.
P. down = kāḍn ghāl; āḍ porti.

N. B. The other compounds are mostly expressed by one or other of the two given verbs.

Pullet, *s.* tălăg, -lgā, *n.* = *l.* a young hen.

Pulley, *s. approx.* lāṭo, -ṭeā, *m.*; *or Mr.* kappi, -pi, *f.* (*used on board ship*).

Pullulate, *v.* ubza.

Pulp, *s.* (fòḷānčeñ) mās, -sā, *n.* = *l.* flesh (of fruits).

Pulpit, *s. vlg.* pulputrụ, -rā, *n.* (*or m.*); prăsāngasiyāsaṇ, -ṇā, *n.*, *n. u.*

Pulpous, *a.* māsāḷ; tsăḍ māsātso = *l.* of much flesh.

Pulsate, *v.* uḍ.

Pulsation, *s.* uḍāp, -ḍpā, *n.*
Pulse, *s.* 1. nāḍ, -ḍi, *f.*
2. sāng, -ge, *f.* (vegetable).
Pulverise, *v.* puḍ kăr = *l.* make powder; vāṭ; *see* **Grind.**
Pump, *s.* *approx.* lāṭo, -ṭeā, *m.* (a wheel for drawing water), *or the Mr. Cn.* bómb, -bā, *m.* (*perh. from* pump?)
Pump, *v.* 1. lāṭeān . . . kāḍ.
2. kāḍ = *l.* draw out, discover.
Pumpkin, *s.* 1. dudiñ, -diyā, *n.*
2. kuvāḷo, -ḷeā, *m.*
3. bobḷeñ, -ḷeā, *n.* = white p.
Pun, *s.* bārikāi, -ye, *f.* = *l.* wit; čeșṭāi, -ye, *f.* = *l.* fun; nāḍ, -ḍi, *f.* = *l.* a trick, *fg.*; 'to nāḍi kărtā = he makes fun'.
Punch, *s.* 1. pănč, -čā, *n.* = the beverage so called.
2. *approx.* burmo, -meā, *m.* = *l.* auger.
Punch, *v.* tóp = *l.* perforate.
Puncheon, *s.* pīp, -pā, *n.* = *l.* a cask.
Punctilio, *s.* sukșām, -mā, *n.*
Punctilious, *a.* sukșāmi.
Punctual, *a.* sārko; zāgrut; sukșāmi; kāideātso; bărābăr; *rs.*
Punctuality, *s.* krăm, -mā, *m.* = *l.* order; sukșām, -mā, *n.*; zāgrutāi, -ye, *f.*
Punctuate, *v.* gurtụ ghāl = *l.* put signs; tibe ghāl = *l.* put dots.
Puncture, *s.* topṇeñ, -ṇeā, *n.*
Pundit, *s.* pănḍit, -tā, *m.*
Pungency, *s.* kār, -rā, *m.*; kāṇer, -rā, *m.*, *e.g.* p. of mango leaves (to the taste).
Pungent, *a.* 1. toptso = *l.* pricking.
2. *fg.* tik, *as is* a chilli; kāṇerātso.
Punish, *v.* šikșa di, *or* š. lāi; kāșṭ di = *l.* give pains.
Punishment, *s.* 1. šikșa *or* sikša, -še, *f.*
2. kāșṭ, -ṭā, *m.* = *l.* pain.
3. julmān, -nā, *m.* = *l.* a fine.
Undergo p. = šikșa bhóg.
Capital p. = mornāči šikșa.
Liable to p. = šikșek pòḍtso.
Puny, *a.* lān.
Pupil, *s.* 1. sis, -sā, *m.*
2. bāuli (*var.* māuli), -le, *f.* = p. of the eye.
Puppet, *s.* bombeñ, -beā, *n.* = *l.* a statue, *used comm. for* an idol.
Puppy, *s.* 1. (suṇeāčeñ) pīl, -lā, *n.*
2. *fg.* ăhănkāri burgo, -geā, *m.* = *l.* a conceited boy.
Purchase, *v.* mòlāk kāṇe = take at a price; zóḍ = *l.* obtain; hāḍ = *l.* bring; *or* hāḍn di.
Pure, *a.* 1. nităḷ, *pr. fg.*; nirmoḷ.
2. borsinātụllo = *l.* not mixed; nigăḷ; āpuṭ; thēṭ(é).
3. niskăḷ = *l.* chaste.
4. suči = *l.* correct, *n. c.*
5. nirāḷ.
Purgatory, *s.* purgatór, -ri, *f.*; *adj.* purgatorintlo; *see* Gram.
Purge, Purify, *v.* 1. nităḷ kăr.
2. bhāir ghāl = *l.* put out, *ch. cs.*

3. bhāiri kāṇe=*l.* take a purge, *ch. cs.*

Purge, *s.* bhāiri, -re, *f.* =*l.* physic.

Purist, *s.* suddṇ bhāsek lāgullo; sučibhāšegār, -rā, *m.*, *or* bhāsesučigār, -rā, *m.*

Purity, *s.* 1. niskāḷāi (*var.* -ḷkāi), -ye, *f.*; nitāḷpoṇ, -ṇā, *n.*; nirmāḷkāi, -ye, *f.*

2. măryād, -di, *f.* = *l.* modesty.

Purple, *s.* 1. zāmbḷilugāṭ, -gṭā, *n.*

2. zāmbḷiróng, -gā, *m.*

Purport, *s.* ărth, -thā, *m.*; tātpărya, -ye, *f.*; ăbiprāi, -ye, *f.*

Purport, *v.* móṇ=*l.* say, (intend to say); ărth āsā=*l.* meaning is; dākăi = *l.* show.

Purpose, *s.* 1. sevóṭ, -ṭā, *m.* (aim, *Lat. causa finalis*); irādo, -deā, *m.*, *e.g.* of the sacraments; āločen, -ni, *f.* = *l.* opinion, judgment, intention.

2. ničeu, -čevā, *m.* = *l.* resolution, *e.g.* to avoid sin; khuši, -še, *f.* = *l.* will.

3. čintna, -ne, *f.* = *l.* a thought.

4. săbăb, -bi, *f.* = *l.* a motive; tesāuñ, -āvā, *n.* =*l.* an intention, *vlg. fr.*

5. *by the Dat.*, *see* Gram. P. IV. ch. ii. Art. I. *or* Supine.

Purpose, *v.* 1. ničeu kăr.

2. *Dat.* sevóṭ āsā = aim is, *etc.*

Purposely, *ad.* hikmătin = *l.* with industry; zāṇā zāun = *l.* knowingly; zāimoṇ = *l.* freely; khušen = *l.* willingly.

Purse, *s.* (duḍuāčeñ) bòls, -sā, *n.*; (duḍuāči) poti, -ye, *f.*; tăili, -le, *f.*

Pay out of his own p. = āpleā duḍuān fārik kăr.

Purse, *v.* (duḍu) potiyent ghāl.

Pursiness, *see* **Asthma.**

Purslain, *s.* goḷčibāji, -je, *f.*

Pursuance, *s.* (in. p. of) *Or.* părmāṇe.

Pursue, *v.* 1. dāunḍāi = *l.* cause to run, *c. v. of* dāuñ; āngār pòḍ = *l.* fall on the body; bōḷ(ò) kăr = *l.* make violence, press.

2. (mukār) tsălăi = carry forward.

3. sevóṭ āsā = aim is, *ch. cs.*

P. a course, p. study = tsălăi.

Pursuit, *s.* 1. kām, -mā, *n.*

2. dāunḍauṇeñ, -ṇeā, *n.*; āngārpòḍāp, -ḍpā, *n.*, *or* uprāḷi, -ḷiñ, *f. pl.*

3. sevóṭ, -ṭā, *m.*

Purulence, *s.* pu, -vā, *m.*; răši, -še, *f.*; rendi, -ye, *f.*

Purvey, Purveyance, *see* **Provide.**

Pus, *see* **Purulence.**

Push, *s.* 1. lōṭ(ó), -ṭā, *m.*

2. *fg.* prăyătăn, -tnā, *n.* = *l.* an effort.

Push, *v.* 1. lōṭ(ó); lăkăi.

2. utsāmboḷ kăr, uṭăi = excite.

3. tsălăi *or* dāunḍāi = *l.* cause to go.

4. (on) prăyătăn kărn mukār tsăl.

P. away = lōṭun kāḍ; bòḷ kărn kāḍ.

Pushing, *a.* tsurk = *l.* active; *see also* **Push.**

Pusillanimity, *s.* ăpadhăir, -rā, *n.*

Pusillanimous, *a.* ăpadhăirāvont, *or* ăpadhăirātso; bhiyātso.

Pustule, *s.* fŏḍ, -ḍā, *m.*; puḷi, -ye, *f.*; kesoḷi, -ḷe, *f.* (a large p.); phăil, -lā, *n.*

Put, *v.* 1. ghāl; dovór.
2. lāi = *l.* apply.
P. to flight = dāunḍăi.
P. to death = mòrnāči šikṣa lāi.
P. into the heart = mótint ghāl.
P. spirit = dăir di.
P. to trial = tănker ghāl.
P. into the hand = vopsun di, hātānt di.
P. into prison = băndint ghāl.
P. a case = čint; šărt kăr.
P. a question = vitsār.
P. as certain = khăreñ móṇ sāng, *or* kh. m. čint.
P. an end = kāḍn ghāl, *or* sóḍ.
P. in the number of = lēk(é).
P. bounds to = găḍ ghāl.
P. apart = vingăḍ dovór.
P. away = 1. sāmbāḷn dovór (p. safe).
2. sóḍ = *l.* leave, *e.g.* bad habits, a wife.
P. by = 1. *Cm.* dovór = deposit; vopsun di = *l.* deliver.
2. sóḍ = *l.* leave, refuse.
P. down = 1. ghāl, *or* săkăl ghāl; devoi, *c. v. of* deuñ = descend.
2. khālto kăr = humiliate.
3. kāḍ = *l.* take away, *e.g.* reputation; ăṇvo kăr = *l.* make dishonourable.
4. rāvoi = *l.* cause to stop, *e.g.* death puts down envy.
5. sóḍ = *l.* leave (resign).
P. forth = 1. vistār, sóḍăi, *e.g.* a cloth.
2. ye = *l.* come, *e.g.* p. f. shoots, *ch. cs.*; fuṭ; ubzăi = *l.* produce.
3. sāng, *or* utsār = *l.* propose, express, *e.g.* a saying; mukār ghāl = *l.* put before.
4. mār, *e.g.* a cry.
5. sóḍ (muṭ), *e.g.* the fist; ukto kăr = *l.* open, *e.g.* hands.
P. out of = bhāir ghāl.
P. in = bităr ghāl.
P. in mind = mótint hāḍ (*or* m. ghāl).
P. in danger = riskent ghāl.
P. in doubt = dubāvāk ghāl.
P. in a passion = rāg hāḍăi.
P. in array = mānḍ.
P. in order = mānḍ, *or* săma ghāl.
P. in a fright = beṣṭăi, (by scolding, *etc.*); bhiyeunk lāi (in other ways); bhisḍăi.
P. in practice = sovoi kăr.
P. in the way of = mārgār vor.
P. in writing = borăi.
P. in the place of = *G.* bădlāk ghāl.
P. into suspicion = ănmān ghāl.
P. in = rāu = *l.* stop; deuñ = *l.* descend.

P. off = 1. kāḍ = *l.* take away.
2. sóḍ = *l.* resign.
3. pāṭi ghāl = *l.* put back.
4. dovór = keep for.
5. foṭăi = *l.* deceive.

P. on = 1. ghāl, *e.g.* a tax.
2. nès, *e.g.* p. on a dress.

P. out = 1. bhāir ghāl; *see* **Depose.**
2. pālvoi = *l.* quench.
3. kāḍ = *l.* draw out, *e. g.* eyes.
4. gălibili kăr = *l.* confound.
5. părgăṭ kăr = *l.* make public.
6. (vāḍik) ghāl = *l.* put (at interest).

P. to = 1. *Dat. or 2nd Loc.*
2. *by c. v.*; lāi = *l.* apply, determine.

P. to silence = vogo rāvoi.

P. to work = kāmāk lāi.

P. to shame = lăzăi, *or* lăjek ghāl.

P. to sea = dăryā voir kāḍ, *or* dăryānt ghāl; dăryāk devoi.

P. together = sāngāta ghāl, *or* meḷăi, *or* voṭṭu ghāl.

P. up the ears = kān di.

P. up = 1. uṭăi = *l.* excite.
2. mukār ghāl = *l.* put before.
3. sós = *l.* suffer.
4. rāu, *with 2nd Loc. in* -ger (live at).

P. upon = *Dat.*

Putrefaction, *s.* kusāp, -spā, *n.*; kusăḍāi, -ye, *f.*

Putrefy, *v.* kusăi.

Putrid, *a.* kusullo.

Putty, *s.* gurud, -di, *f.*

Puzzle, *v.* tondreār ghāl = *l.* put in embarrassment; dubāvăi, *or* dubāu kăr = cause doubt.

Puzzle, *s.* tondre, *m. pl.*; gusăp, -spā, *m.* = *l.* confusion.

Puzzling, *a.* kăṭin = difficult; tondreātso = of embarrassment; *see also* **Puzzle.**

Pygmy, *s.* kuḷḷa, -ḷā, *m.*; khunṭo, -ṭeā, *m.*

Pyramid, *s. perh.* domsātso khāmbo, -beā, *m.* = *l.* an acuminated pillar.

Pyre, *see* **Pile.**

Pyrotechnics, *s.* hikmăti-ujeāči vidya, -ye, *f.*; ākāsbāṇavidya.

Pyx, *s.* piksid, -di, *f.*, *fr.*; *vlg.* kāls, -si, *f.* = *l.* a chalice.

Q

Quack, *v.* 1. bòb mār = *l.* cry, *as* a duck.

2. ăbbār kăr = *l.* boast; băḍāi kăr.

3. boḍboḍ = speak nonsense.

Quack, *s.* 1. boḍboḍo, -ḍeā, *m.*; zānkero, -reā, *m.*; phāndḷeāgār, -rā, *m.*

2. loṭṭebira, -rā, *m.* (*vlg. word*) = *Lat. circulator.*

Quadragesima, *see* Lent.

Quadrangle, *s.* 1. čār konseānčeñ (rūp, -pā, *n.*).

2. tsouki, -ke, *f.* = a kind of portico of a quadrangular form.

Quadrant, *s.* mănḍălakāldeñ, *or bet.* kāldeñ mănḍăl, -lā, *n.*

Quadratic, *a.* čăččouk.

Quadrilateral, *a.* čārgiṭāntso, *or* čār gerāntso.

Quadruped, *a.* čārpāyāntso.

Quadruple, *a.* čārdoḍo.

Quaff, *v.* jīv sóḍn piye.

Quail, *s.* kenkaṇ, -ṇā, *n.* (of a large kind); lovo, -veā, *m.* (smaller).

Quail, *v.* dhăir sóḍ = *l.* leave courage; bhiyān thărtăr = *l.* tremble for fear.

Quaint, *a.* nāzuk.

Quaintness, *s.* nāzukāi, -ye, *f.*

Quake, *v.* kāmp; thărtăr.

Quake, *s.* kāmp, -pi, *f.*, *or* kāmpero, -reā, *m.*

Qualification, *s.* lāyekpoṇ, -ṇā, *n.* = *l.* suitableness; šărt, -tā, *n.* = *l.* condition.

Qualified, *a.* 1. lāyek.

2. părikša dillo = *l.* (one) who has given examination; *vlg.* pās zāllo, *fr.*

Qualify, *v.* 1. lāyek kăr = *l.* make fit.

2. guṇ (*or* sobāu) sāng = *l.* say the qualities.

3. meḷāi = *l.* mix, *e.g.* q. sharp sounds with flat; *perh.* deunḍāi *or* devoi = *l.* cause to descend, *fg.*, *e.g.* q. joy, language.

Quality, *s.* 1. guṇ, -ṇā, *m.*, *e.g.* q. of a horse; săimb, -bā, *n.* = *l.* nature; sobāu, -bāvā, *m.* = *l.* inclination (natural).

2. thăr, -rā, *m.*, jinos, -nsā, *m.* = *l.* kind.

3. huddo, -deā, *m.* = *l.* rank; săkăt, -kti, *f.* = *l.* power.

4. *by the G.*, *e.g.* it is a q. of the lion = siñvāčeñ. . . .

5. *rs. into adj.* kăso *or* kăsolo.

Qualm, *s.* 1. vonkāro, -reā, *m.*

2. *fg.* tsurtsuro, -reā, *m.*, of conscience.

Qualmish, *a.* bezārāyetso.

Quantity, *s.* 1. părimāṇ, -ṇā, *n.* = a mathematical q.

2. zomo, -meā, *m.* = *l.* a multi-

tude; rās, -si, *f.* = *l.* a heap, a multitude.
3. māp, -pā, *n.* = *l.* a measure (in prosody).
4. bhărtipoṇ, -ṇā, *n.* = fulness.
5. *by* kitle = how many.

Quarrel, *s.* zăgḍeñ, -ḍeā, *n.*; nāi, -yā, *m.* = discord; lăḍāi, -ye, *f.* = *l.* a fight.

Quarrel, *v.* zăgăḍ *or* zăgḍa; arenji; lăḍāi kăr = *l.* fight.

Quarrelsome, *a.* zăgăḍtso; lăḍāi kărtso.

Quarry, *s.* podou, -dvā, *m.* = *l.* high ground where quarries are worked; kălpaṇeñ, -ṇeā, *n.*; tānk, -ki, *f.*

Quart, *s.* siso, -seā, *m.* = a bottle; yék kāldo, -deā, *m.* = one quarter.

Quartan, *a.* poireātso (tāp).

Quarter, *s.* 1. săvāi, *used to express* $2\frac{1}{4}$, $4\frac{1}{4}$, *etc. e.g.* săvāi ikra ghănṭe = a quarter past eleven.
2. pāu, *used to express* $\frac{3}{4}$, $1\frac{3}{4}$, $2\frac{3}{4}$, *etc. e.g.* pāuṇe čār = $3\frac{3}{4}$.
3. kāldo, -deā, *m.*; tsouto vānṭo, -ṭeā, *m.* = *l.* the fourth part; *see* Gram. P.II. ch.ii. Art. II.

Quarter, *v.* 1. čār vānṭe kăr = make four parts.
2. biḍār di = give abode; biḍār sód.

Quarterly, *ad.* titisreā moineāk.

Quarters, *s.* biḍār, -rā, *n.* = *l.* a dwelling; ghăr, -rā, *n.* = *l.* a house.

Quash, *v.* mósti; *see* **Trample,** *see also* **Annul, Subdue.**

Quasi, -so; *see* Gram. P.III. ch. ii.

Quaver, *s.* 1. kāmp, -pi, *f.*
2. āṭvo vānṭo (in music).

Quaver, *v.* (tāḷo) kāmpăi.

Quay, *s.* dhăkko, -keā, *m.*

Queasiness, *s.* vonkāro, -reā, *m.*

Queasy, *a.* 1. vonkāro yetolo = (he) to whom nausea comes.
2. vonkāreātso = *l.* causing nausea.
3. bezārāyetso (fastidious); nāzuk.

Queen, *s.* rāṇi, -ye, *f.*

Queer, *a.* tārifetso; vidrup; hāseagār; hāsountso; phantăzigār, *or* phantăzi kărtso, *fr.*, *n. c.*

Queerness, *s.* tārif, -fe, *f.*

Quell, *v.* 1. khālto kăr = *l.* make subject.
2. rāuoi = *l.* stop, *e.g.* sedition; thāmbăi.
3. fuslāi = *l.* appease; thănḍ kăr = *l.* make cold, *fg.*; nivăi = make cold, *fg.*; sămādhān kărăi = *l.* cause to make peace.

Quench, *v.* 1. pālvoi, *c. v. of* pālva, *pr. fg.*, *e. g.* passion, thirst.
2. *fg.* nivoi = *l.* make cold, *e.g.* a passion; thănḍ kăr.
3. dādós kăr = *l.* make satisfied, *e.g.* thirst.
4. nāš kăr = *l.* destroy.

Querulous, *a.* šiṇ ulountso.

Querist, *s.* tănkegār, -rā, *m.*

Query, *s.* 1. săvāl, -li, *f.*, *e.g.* a q. made with a view to elicit an answer.
2. vitsārăṇ, -ṇā, *n.* = *l.* inquiry, an interrogation.

Quest, *s.* sódna, -ne, *f.* = *l.* inquisition; vitsārăṇ, -ṇā, *n.*

Question, *s.* 1. sódna, -ne, *f.* = *l.* inquisition; vitsārăṇ, -ṇā, *n.*
2. bāb, -be, *f.* = *l.* a case, *e.g.* of conscience.
3. tărk, -kā, *n.* = *l.* a discussion *or* matter of discussion.
4. tănki, -ke, *f.* = *l.* a trial, inquiry.
Call in q. = dubāvăi, *or bet.* dubāvāk ghāl; tărk kăr.

Question, *v.* 1. vitsār = inquire.
2. tărk kăr = *l.* make discussion, dispute.

Questionable, *a.* tărkātso; dubāvi = doubtful.

Quibble, *see* **Cavil.**

Quick, *a.* 1. tsurk = *l.* active; ušār = *l.* clever; somzoṇitso = *l.* intelligent; bārik = *l.* witty.
2. vegiñ *with the required verb*, *e.g.* vegiñ tsăltolo; vegintso, *n. c.*; zăld *or* zăldi; ăusărātso = *l.* hasty.
3. jivo = *l.* living.
4. aučit = sudden; yekats pharātso = *l.* of one moment.

Quicken, *v.* 1. jīv di *or* vāntsăi = give life.
2. uṭăi = *l.* excite; utsāmboḷ kăr.
3. ăusăr kăr = *l.* make haste; ăusărăi, *c. v. of* ăusăr.

Quickly, *ad.* 1. vegiñ, *in time and manner*; zăp kărn; sărāraṅ, *e.g.* he walks q.; ăusărān = *l.* hastily; zăldi (*Hind.*)
2. tsurkāiyen = *l.* actively.

Quickness, *s.* 1. ăusăr, -rā, *m.* = *l.* haste.
2. bārikāi, -ye, *f.* = *l.* wit.
3. ušārāi, -ye, *f.* = *l.* liveliness.

Quicksilver, *s.* pādrós, -sā, *m.*

Quiddity, *s.* sār, -rā, *m.*

Quiescence, *s.* soukāsāi, -ye, *f.*

Quiet, *a.* nidān = calm; soukāsāyetso; thănḍ = *l.* cold, *fg.*
Be q. = 1. vogo rāu = *l.* remaiṇ silent.
2. soukāsāi bhóg = enjoy peace.

Quiet, *s.* soukāsāi, -ye, *f.*; visou, -sovā, *m.*; viśrām, -mā, *n.*; sămādhān, -nā, *n.*

Quiet, *v.* nivăi; thănḍ kăr, fuslāi; *see* **Quell, Calm.**

Quill, *s.* 1. pāk, -kā, *n.*
2. lăkṇik, -ke, *f.*; *vlg.* pèn, -nā, *n.*, *fr.*
3. *for* the q. of a weaver, *perh.* năḷi, -ye, *f.*

Quilt, *s.* găzḍi, -ḍe, *f.* (*It. imbottita.*)

Quintessence, *s.* sār, -rā, *m.*; uttim sār.

Quintuple, *v.* pāntsdoḍo; pānts pāuṭi tsăḍ.

Quip, *s.* bārikāi, -ye, *f.* = *l.* wit, a witty saying; čeṣṭāi, -ye, *f.* = *l.* a joke.

Quire, *s.* tsovis foli, *pr. fg.* = 24 sheets, *fr.*; tsovis pānañ, *pl. n.*; *see* **Choir.**

Quirk, *s.* nīb, -bā, *n.* = *l.* a pretext; nāḍ, -ḍi, *f.* = *l.* a trick; bārikāi, -ye, *f.*; *see* **Cavil.**

Quit, *v.* 1. sóḍ = *l.* leave (free). 2. fārik kăr = *l.* pay (a debt); pāḷ = *l.* fulfil (a duty).

Quit, *a.* suṭụllo;—viṇ (*affixed*). We are quits = săma zāleñ; hăngnātullo (-li, -leñ) zālo = *l.* (he) became without dependence; suṭka zāli.

Quite, *ad.* purteñ; kevăl; văргus; ăgḍi; păripurṇ; -ts, *emph.* *e.g.* q. so = tăsents; dubāunāstanāñ; bhou = very much; kāiñ = any; boreñ = well; sărivin = without comparison.

Quittance, *s.* 1. *rs.* fārik kăr. 2. răsid, -de, *f.* 3. inām, -mā, *n.* (*or m.*) = *l.* reward.

Quiver, *v.* kāmp; thărtăr.

Quivering, *s.* kāmp, -pi, *f.*

Quoit, *s.* mānḍ, -ḍi, *f.*; boḷeñ, -ḷeā, *n.*

Quorum, *s.* zāi title zăṇ, *pl. m.*

Quota, *s.* vānṭo, -ṭeā, *m.*

Quotation, *s.* dāklo, -kleā, *m.*

Quote, *v.* dāklo di; vivorsi.

Quoth, *v.* sāngleñ = (I *or* he) said.

R

Rabbi, *s.* somi *or* suāmi, -yā, *m.*

Rabbit, *s.* soso, -seā, *m.*

Rabid, *a.* 1. piso, *e.g.* a dog. 2. (rāgān) zăḷtso; rāgiṣṭ.

Race, *s.* 1. kuṭām, -ṭmā, *n.* (*var.* kuṭamb). 2. kuḷi, -ye, *f.* (*or* kuḷ, -ḷā, *n.*) = *l.* a tribe; zāt, -ti, *f.* = *l.* a caste, tribe. 3. goḍeañpont, -tā, *m.*, *or* -pănth. R. of life = jiṇi, -ye, *f.*, *or* jiṇiyetso vēḷ(é), -ḷā, *m.*

Race, *v.* 1. petsāḍ = *l.* try, rival. 2. pontāk dāuñ.

Race-course, *s.* pontazāgo, -geā, *m.*

Rack, *s.* 1. ròz, -zā, *n.*, *or* ròd, -dā, *n.* = a wheel; čākrụ, -rā, *n.* 2. kăṭiṇ duk, -ki, *f.* 3. gòṭo, -ṭeā, *m.*

Rack, *v.* 1. iza di; bhóng kăr; dăgdăi. 2. vóḍ = stretch, strain. 3. (mōt) pisi kăr = r. the brains.

Racy, *a.* ručitso; *see* **Pungent.**

Radiance, *s.* părzāḷ, -ḷā, *m.*, *or* părzāḷkāi, -ye, *f.*

Radiant, *a.* părzăḷik.

Radiate, *v.* kirna di; părzăḷ.

Radical, *a.* 1. poilots = *l.* first.
2. *rs.* muḷa thāun = *l.* from the root, *e.g.* a r. reform.
3. mukhya = *l.* principal.

Radius, *s.* kirn, -nā, *n.*

Raffle, *s.* sòḍt, -ti, *f.* (*var.* sóḍti, -te, *f.*)

Raffle, *v.* sòḍt ghāl.

Raft, *s.* terpo, -peā, *m.*; jangăl, -lā, *n.*

Rafter, *s.* păkāso, -seā, *m.*

Rag, *s.* 1. lugāṭ, -gṭā, *n.*
2. *in pl.* čindi lugāṭ; pindkăr nesoṇ, -ṇi, *f.*
3. *infg. mn.* nesoṇ, *e.g.* wisdom is often clad in rags = dubḷe nesoṇent thoḍe pāuṭi zāṇvāi liptā.

Rage, *s.* króđ, -dā, *m.*; zāḷ, -ḷā, *m.* = *l.* burning, *fg.*, *n. c. in this mn.*; *perh. bet.* rāgāzāḷ, -ḷā, *m.*, *n. c.*; utsāmboḷāi, -ye, *f.*, *also* a storm, enthusiasm.
R. of hunger, *rs.* nibbór bhuk.

Rage, *v.* rāgān zăḷ = *l.* burn for anger.

Ragi, *s.* nātno (*var.* nātsno), -neā, *m.* (an inferior kind of grain).

Rail, *v.* 1. vói ghāl = *l.* put a hedge; dări kăr = *l.* make a r.
2. āngār pòḍ = *l.* fall on the body; gāḷi sou.

Rail, *s.* 1. dări, -ye, *f.*; grād, -di, *f.*, *fr.*
2. digo, -geā, *m.* (*ex.* a support).

Raillery, *s.* yeḍauṇeñ, -ṇeā, *n.*; khéḷkuḷāñ, *pl. n.*

Railway, *s.* lohamāróg, -rgā, *m.*, *or* lonkḍātso māróg, -rgā, *m.*, *n. c.*
R. carriage = duvragāḍi, -ye, *f.*, *l.* a carriage of smoke.

Raiment, *s.* nesoṇ, -ṇe, *f.*; văstur, -rā, *n.*

Rain, *s.* pāus, -sā, *m.*; 'strong r. = boro *or* boḷvont p.'

Rain, *v.* pāus pòḍ; vòt = *l.* pour, *n. v.*

Rainbow, *s.* doṇu, -ṇvā, *n.*

Rainy, *a.* pāusātso, *or* pāusilo.

Raise, *v.* 1. ukól *or* ubār.
2. bānd = *l.* build.
3. uṭăi; utsāmbòḷ kăr = excite.
4. măr = *l.* beat (a cry).
5. (melleāntlo) jivont kăr = resuscitate.
6. băḍti di = *l.* give promotion to a higher office; voir kāḍ; mānāčeñ kām di = *l.* give honourable employment.
7. meḷăi = collect, gather, *l.* cause to be found; rās kăr = collect, *l.* make a heap.
8. tsăḍăi = *l.* increase, *c. v. of* tsăḍ.

Raisin, *s.* kismis, -se, *f.*

Rake, *s.* kaipul, -lā, *n.* = an agricultural implement.

Rake, *v.* *see* **Scrape.**

Rally, *v.* 1. meḷăi = *l.* gather.
2. mānḍ = arrange.

3. yeḍāi = *l.* mock; nāklañ kăr = *l.* make copies, *fg.*

Ram, *s.* dādlo bokro, -reā, *m.*

Ram, *v.* boḍăi; sāṇsi; jeḍvi.

Ramble, *v.* pārpoḷ zāun bouñ.

Ramify, *v.* khānde zātāt, *or* kh. fuṭṭāt = *l.* branches become, *ch. cs.*

Ramp, *v.* (zulmen) uḍ = *l.* jump (violently).

Rampant, *a.* mitmèr mirvontso = *l.* exceeding limit; tsăḍāvot.

Rampart, *s.* pāgār, -rā, *m.* = *l.* a fortification.

Ramrod, *s.* góz, -zā, *m.*

Rancid, *a.* 1. āmbóṭ = acid.

2. ghāṇiyero = *l.* stinking; *see* **Pungent, Musty.**

Rancour, *s.* rāg, -gā, *m.* = *l.* anger; mosór, -srā, *m.* = hatred; hăgeñ, -geā, *n.* = hatred; *rs. into* mòn kuskatā = *l.* heart is not right, *not ex.*

Random, *a.* ākăsmăt = *l.* accidental.

At r. = čintināstanāñ *or* tsătrāināstanāñ.

Range, *s.* 1. hār, -ri, *f.* = *l.* a line, a rank.

2. thăr, -rā, *m.* = *l.* a class.

3. vistarāp, -rpā, *n.* = *l.* extension; suttu, -tā, *m.* = *l.* compass.

Range, *v.* 1. mānḍ = *l.* arrange.

2. bouñ = *l.* walk.

Rank, *s.* 1. huddo, -deā, *m.* = *l.* dignity; stiti, -ti, *f.* = state; bhés, -sā, *m.* = *l.* state, vocation.

2. hār, -ri, *f.* = *l.* a line; kāmp, -pā, *n.*

3. thăr, -rā, *m.* = *l.* a class.

Rank, *a.* 1. lekavorto vistārtso.

2. āmboṭ = *l.* acid.

3. tsăḍāvot = excessive.

Rank, *v.* 1. hāriṇ (*or* kāmpān) ghāl.

2. ghāl *or* dovór = *l.* put.

3. lēk(é), *e. g.* as a friend.

Rankle, *v.* 1. kus = *l.* be corrupted.

2. utsāmbóḷ zā = *l.* be excited; zăḷ = *l.* burn, *fg.*, *e.g.* angry feelings; *see* **Suppurate.**

Ransack, *v.* 1. lūṭ kăr = *l.* make prey, m. robbery.

2. sārkeñ sód = *l.* seek exactly.

Ransom, *v.* (gulāmpoṇāntlo) sóḍăi = *l.* deliver (from slavery).

Ransom, *s.* 1. sóḍvoṇ, -ṇi, *f.*; udargăti, -ti, *f.*

2. sóḍvoṇičeñ mòl, -lā, *n.* = *l.* price of r.

Rant, *v.* utsāmboḷ zāun ulăi.

Ranter, *s.* utsāmboḷ uloṇeāgār, -rā, *m.*; *see* **Fanatic.**

Rap, *s.* thāpāḍ, -pḍā, *n.*; thāp, -pi, *f.*

Give a r. = tāpăi.

Rap, *v.* boḍăi, *or* thāp mār (*Dat.*)

Rapacious, *a.* luṭkār.

Rapacity, *s.* bòḷ, -ḷā, *n.*; zulum, -lme, *f.*

Rape, *s.* zulum, -lme, *f.* = *l.* violence; *rs. into* kāḍ.

Rapid, *a.* jeldi; tsurk; vegintso, *or* vegiñ tsăltso.

Rapidity, *s.* tsurkpoṇ, -ṇā, *n.*; ăusăr, -rā, *m.*

Rapier, *see* **Dagger.**

Rapine, *s.* 1. tsóri, -ye, *f.*; nāgoṇ, -ṇi, *f.*
2. luṭ, -ṭi, *f.* = *l.* prey.

Rapt, *v.* jīv sóḍn = *l.* leaving life, *added to the required verb* (*Konk.*)

Rapture, *s.* 1. ulās, -sā, *m.* = *l.* (great) pleasure.
2. dišṭ, -ṭi, *f.* = *l.* a vision.

Rare, *a.* 1. ăprup, *or* ăprupātso.
2. uttim = *l.* excellent.
3. nāzuk = *l.* delicate, fine.
4. ăsādhārn = *l.* extraordinary.

Rarefy, *v.* pātăḷ kăr, *or* pātlăi, *e.g.* air.

Rarity, *s.* 1. ăprupāi, -ye, *f.*
2. pātăḷāi, -ye, *f.* = *l.* thinness.

Rascal, *s.* lutstso, -čeā, *m.*; pokri, -riā, *m.*; ṭhăkkagār, -ra, *or* ṭhăkkụ, -kā, *m.*

Rase, *v.* 1. kāḍ.
2. kāḍn ghāl; *see* **Graze, Erase.**

Rash, *a.* 1. tsătrāinātullo; zāgrutnātullo.
2. khāli = *l.* empty; ănāvăt = *l.* unjust, *e.g.* a r. judgment.
3. ăusărātso = *l.* hasty.
R. judgment = *also* āḍāločen, -ni, *f.*

Rash, *s. see* **Pustule.**

Rashness, *s.* nātsătrāi, -ye, *f.*; utāvóḷ, -ḷi, *f.*

Rat, *s.* undir, -drā, *m.*; čitsondri, -re, *f.* (a smaller kind); čiuḷeñ, -ḷeā, *n.* (a still smaller kind); koḷundir, -drā, *m.* = a big r. *or* bandicoot.
Smell a r. = nāḍitso pormóḷ yetā = *l.* smell of trick comes.

Rat, *v.* 1. ăndāz kăr, *G. M.*; mòl niščeisi; mòl bānd.
2. mānd = *l.* have a high opinion.
3. beṣṭāi = *l.* scold.

Rate, *s.* 1. mòl, -lā, *n.*; dăr, -ri, *f.*, *e.g.* khănče dărin iktāi.
2. lēk (è), -kā, *n.* = *l.* account.
3. jinos, -nsā, *m.* = *l.* manner; *see* **Tax.**
At the r. of five annas an hour = kosāk (ghănṭeāk) pāṇts āṇeāñ lekān.
At any r. = kăseñi zāundi.

Rather, *ad.* 1. prăs, *or* vórn, *or* ki *with the comp.; see* Gram.
2. porteñ = on the contrary.
3. čikke *or* tikke = a little; -so, *quasi dim.*, *see* Gram. P. III. ch. ii.

Ratification, *s.* păsănd, *n.c. as a noun;* metsvoṇeñ, -ṇeā, *n.*; monzur, -re, *f.* = *l.* confirmation; kăbuli, -le, *f.* = *l.* consent.

Ratify, *v.* păsănd kăr; mănjur kăr; thir kăr; kobul kăr.

Ration, *s.* bhāteñ, -teā, *n.* = allowance.

Rational, *a.* 1. somzikāi (*or* bud) āsullo; somzoṇi; budivont.

2. săma = *l.* right; vāzbi = *l.* convenient, proper.

Rationalism, *s. has no recognised equivalent; perh.* budičisi āločen, -ni, *f.* = *l.* an opinion, which has (only) the appearance of reason (wisdom); *or crc. or the Mr.* hetuvāda, -dā, *n.*, *n. u.*

Rationalist, *s.* budivont-so; *see the note above.*

Rattle, *s.* 1. khiḷkuḷo, -ḷeā, *m.* = a toy for children.
2. phoḍpoḍeñ, -ḍeā, *n.* (used in the holy week).

Rattle, *v.* 1. gărgăr.
2. *fg.* găzāli mār.

Ravage, *v.* lūṭ kăr; zulum tsălăi; desvāṭ kăr; vibād (*or* nāš) kăr.

Ravage, *s.* lūṭ, -ṭi, *f.*; zulum, -lme, *f.*; desvāṭ, -ṭe, *f.*; nāš, -šā, *m.*

Ravager, *s.* lūṭkār, -rā, *m. etc.*

Rave, *v.* (rāgān) zăḷ = *l.* burn (for anger).

Raven, *s.* kāuḷo, -ḷeā, *m.*

Raven, *v.* 1. lūṭ kăr; ništurāi tsălăi.
2. găpagăpa khā.
3. kóp = be angry.

Ravenousness, *see* **Gluttony** *and* **Rapacity.**

Ravine, *s.* 1. khăṇi, -ye, *f.* = a gorge made by torrents of water.
2. phalkeñ, -keā, *n.* = *l.* a valley.

Raving, *s.* kóp, -pā, *m.*

Ravish, *v.* 1. zulum kăr = *l.* make violence; khătăi = *l.* violate, stain.
2. bhou khusāl kăr.

Ravishment, *s.* 1. zulum, -lme, *f.* = *l.* violence; bòḷ, -ḷā, *n.*; khătouṇeñ, -ṇeā, *n.*
2. bhou săntos, -sā, *m.*

Raw, *a.* 1. jivo = *l.* living.
2. tărno = *l.* green (not ripe).
3. tăyārnātullo = *l.* not prepared; rāndunknātullo *or* rāndinātullo; surăi (r. rice).
4. neṇār = *l.* ignorant; ănbhounātullo = *l.* inexperienced.
5. kărăḍo = *l.* rough.
6. šeḷitso = *l.* wet, *e.g.* weather.

Ray, *s.* 1. kirn, -nā, *n.*
2. vāgoḷeñ (the animal).

Razor, *s.* vākór, -krā, *m.*

Reach, *v.* 1. vistār = *l.* be extended, *e. g.* a country; lāgun āsā = *l.* is attached.
2. pāu = *l.* arrive.
3. lāgiñ pāu = *l.* reach close to.
4. kānānt pòḍ = *l.* fall into the ears, (hear).
5. di = *l.* give, *or* bhāir di = *l.* give out, *Lat. porrige.*

Reach, *s.* 1. vistārāp, -rpā, *n.* = *l.* extension.
2. săkăt, -kti, *f.* = *l.* capacity.

Re-act, *v.* āḍ ye, *or* pāṭi lōṭ(ó).

Re-action, *s.* pāṭi lōṭ(ó), -ṭā, *m.*; prătikărni, -ne, *f.*

Read, *v.* vāts.

Reader, *s.* vātspi, -piā, *m.*

Reading, *s.* vātsāp, -tspā, *n.*

N. B. Words compounded with **Re-**, *not put down here, are formed by prefixing* **pāṭi** *or* **portun** *to the word compounded with* **Re-**.

Readiness, *s.* tăyārāi, -ye, *f.*; tsurkpoṇ, -ṇā, *n.* = *l.* activity.
Ready, *a.* 1. tăyār.
2. tsurk = *l.* active.
3. bārik = *l.* witty.
4. năgdi, *e.g.* money.
Real, *a.* khărots; nīz.
R. property = zāgo, -geā, *m.*; thir āst, -te, *f.*
Reality, *s.* 1. văstụ, -tu, *f.* = *l.* a thing.
2. săt, -tā, *n.* = *l.* truth.
3. *rs.* khărots.
In r. = khărents, *or* nīz zāun.
Realize, *v.* 1. kăr = *l.* do; jāri kăr = execute.
2. sovói kăr = *l.* make execution.
3. khăro móṇ kăr = *l.* make true; kărniāniñ dākăi = *l.* show with facts; *see also* **Verify.**
Realm, *s.* rāzvoṭkāi, -ye, *f.*; rāz, -jā, *n.*; rāzvoṭ, -ṭi, *f.*
Ream, *s.* rèzm, -mā, *n.*, *Mr.* (*from the Engl.*)
Reap, *v.* 1. (beḷeñ) luuñ; (pīk) kātăr.
2. *fg.* zóḍ = *l.* obtain; *fg.* mèḷ = *l.* be found, *ch. cs.*
Reaper, *s.* luuntolo.
Reaping-hook, *s.* (luunči) koiti, -te, *f.*
Rear, *v.* 1. vāḍăi.
2. pós = *l.* feed.
3. bānd = *l.* build, *e.g.* an altar.
4. pāṭleañ (dón) pāyāniñ-uṭ = *l.* rise with (two) hinder feet.
Rear, *s.* pāṭli fouz, -ji, *f.* = *l.* behind-army.
Reason, *s.* 1. somzikāi, -ye, *f.* = *l.* intelligence; mót, -ti, *f.* = *l.* mind; bud, -di, *f.*, *e.g.* the use of r.
2. ruzvāt, -ti, *f.*, *ex.* ruzu = *l.* a proof.
3. kārāṇ, -ṇā, *n.* = *l.* a cause; săbăb, (*or* săvāb) -bi, *f.* = *l.* a motive.
4. *often rs.*
Without r. (for nothing) = beṣṭeñ.
Reason, *v.* 1. tărk kăr = make discussion, *Lat. ratiocinari*; *vlg.* arment (*corrup. of* argument) kăr, *fr.*
2. budin ulăi = *l.* speak wisely.
Reasonable, *a.* 1. vāzbi = *l.* proper, convenient; săma = *l.* right.
2. budivont = *l.* wise.
3. sumār = *l.* moderate; *see also* **Rational.**
Reasonableness, *s.* bud, -di, *f.* = *l.* wisdom; vāzbipoṇ, -ṇā, *n.*
Reasoner, *s.* tărkagār, -rā, *m.*
Rebec, *s.* rèbèk, -kā, *n.*; sārăngi, -gi, *f.* (*H. K.*)
Rebel, *s.* kāṭkāyegār, -rā, *m.*, *or* kāṭkāi kărtolo; kūṭagār, -rā, *m.*
Rebel, *v.* kūṭ kăr; kāṭkāi kăr.

N. B. Words compounded with **Re-**, *not put down here, are formed by prefixing* **pāṭi** *or* **portun** *to the word compounded with* **Re-**.

Rebellion, *s.* kāṭkāi, -ye, *f.*; kuṭ -ṭā, *n.* = plot, r.; utsāmboḷāi, -ye, *f.* = *l.* excitement.

Rebound, *v.* pāṭi săr, *or* p. pòḍ, *or* portun uḍ.

Rebuff, *v.* inkār kăr = *l.* make opposition; *bet. rs. into* mèḷ, *in neg. form; see also* **Check.**

Rebuff, *s.* inkār, -ri, *f.* (-rā, *n.*)

Rebuke, *v.* beṣṭāi = *l.* scold; *see also* **Blame.**

Rebus, *s.* guḍ, -ḍā, *m.*

Rebut, *v.* 1. pāṭimār = *l.* beat back.
2. săbăb di = *l.* give answer.
3. inkār kăr = *l.* make resistance.

Recall, *v.* 1. pāṭi (*or* portun) āpoi.
2. kāḍ = *l.* take away.
3. răddu kăr = *l.* make nullity.
4. mótint hāḍ = *l.* bring into mind.

Recant, *v.* pāṭi hāḍ = retract, take back, *e.g.* a former declaration.

Recapitulate, *v.* sănkṣ̌ép kăr.

Recapitulation, *s.* sănkṣ̌ép, -pā, *m.*

Recapitulatory, *a.* sănkṣ̌épātso, *or* sănkṣ̌ép-kărtso.

Recast, *v.* 1. portun ghāl, *e.g.* in printing.
2. porteān rūp di = *l.* again give form.

Recede, *v.* pāṭi săr.

Receipt, *s.* 1. rășid, -de, *f.* (*Hind.*) = acknowledgment of: 'acknowledge the r. of = ră. lekun ghe'.
2. pănḍitačīṭ, -ṭi, *f.* = *l.* a note of the doctor.
3. *rs. into* kāṇghe = receive (*or* kāṇghevāp).
4. huṭṭavóḷ, -ḷi, *f.* = income.

Receive, *v.* 1. ge (*ex.* ghe), *past* ghetlo, *or* kāṇghe, *or* kāṇe, (*past* kāṇgelo *or* kāṇelo), *or* kāṇei.
2. bhóg = *l.* feel, *e.g.* r. pleasure.
3. mèḷ = be found, *e.g.* an answer, *ch. cs.*; *see* **Admit.**

Recent, *a.* novo; āilevartso.

Recently, *ad.* voḍól (voḍḍol = some time ago); āilevār.

Receptacle, *s.* dărāp, -rpā, *n.*; āidān, -nā, *n.*

Reception, *s.* kāṇghevāp, -gheupā, [*n.*

Recipe, *s.* pănḍitačīṭ, -ṭi, *f.*

Recipient, *s.* āidān, -nā, *n.*

Recess, *s.* yeksurāi, -ye, *f.*, *or* yeksuri suāt, -te, *f.*

Reciprocal, *a.* yekamekātso.

Reciprocally, *ad.* yekameka.

Recital, *s.* 1. sāng-ṇeñ, -ṇeā, *n.*; *bet.* sāngčeñ.
2. utsārāp, -rpā, *n.*, *or* utsār, -rā, *m.* = *l.* expression, pronunciation.

Recitation, *s.* vātsāp, -tspā, *n.*; *rs. into* sāng *or* móṇ = say.

N. B. Words compounded with **Re-**, *not put down here, are formed by prefixing* **pāṭi** *or* **portun** *to the word compounded with* **Re-**.

Recite, *v.* utsār, *e.g.* a speech; sāng, *e.g.* a speech; móṇ, *e.g.* prayers, *etc.*

Reckless, *a.* foḍposi = good for nothing; tsătrāināttullo = *l.* inattentive.

Recklessness, *s.* nāñtsătrāi, -ye, *f.*; udāsin, -nā, *n.*; utāvoḷ, -ḷi, *f.*

Reckon, *v.* 1. lèk kăr, *or only* lēk(é), *e.g.* accounts, *or also*, *fg.* consider as, *e. g.* as a friend; r. it as a gain = yeñ ādāi móṇ lēk.

2. mēz(é) = count, one by one.

3. čint = *l.* think, *ch. cs.*

R. on = pātiye, *2nd Loc.*, *e.g.* Devāčer pātiye; *see* **Consider.**

Reckoning, *s.* lèk, -kā, *n.*; mè-zāp, -zpā, *n.* = *l.* measure; *see* **Reckon.**

Reclaim, *v.* 1. (pāṭi) māg (*or* vāpās m.) = *l.* ask back; hăkkụ āsā = *l.* right is, *or* h. ā. móṇ sāng.

2. bud sāng = *l.* say advice, *e.g.* r. from crime; *or also* pāṭi kāḍ.

Reclamation, *s.* māg-ṇeñ, -ṇeā, *n.*; *or bet.* pāṭi māg-ṇeñ.

Recline, *v.* 1. bāgāi = *l.* bend, *c. v. of* bāgā.

2. bòs = *l.* sit.

3. āḍpòḍ, *e.g.* on the grass.

4. voṇkon ubo rāu = *l.* lean standing, *or* voṇkon bòs = *l.* sitting l.

Recluse, *s. vlg.* anakoret, -tā, *m.*, *fr.*; sănyāsi, -siā, *m.*, *used only for* a pagan r.; vănavāsi, -si, *m.* = *l.* the inhabitant of a desert.

Recognize, *v.* voḷka; gurt āsā, *e.g.* tātso gurt mākā āsā = I r. him, *l.* his sign is to me.

Recoil, *v.* 1. pāṭi săr (on account of fear).

2. kānṭāl = abhor.

Recollect, *v.* 1. ugḍās kăr, *G. M.*, *or* u. yetā = *l.* memory comes, *ch. cs.*; āṭou kăr, *G. M.*; yād kăr.

2. dusri čintna bhāir ghāl = *l.* put out other thoughts; mòn pāṭi vòḍ.

Recollection, *s.* ugḍās, -sā, *m.*; āṭou, -ṭovā, *m.*; yād, -dā, *m.* (*H. K.*)

Within r. of men = ugḍās āsā titleñ.

Recommence, *v.* portun (*or* porto, *adj.*) *with the required verb;* portun suru kăr.

Recommend, *v.* 1. šipārăs kăr, *e.g.* r. a person to another; umedin sāng, *G. F.*

2. metsva = *l.* approve, *Sb. Dat.*

Recommendable, *a.* 1. šipārăsetso; metsvontso.

2. ăpurbāyetso = *l.* amiable.

3. tārifetso = r. for wit, *n. c. in this mn.*

N. B. Words compounded with **Re-**, *not put down here, are formed by prefixing* pāṭi *or* portun *to the simple word compounded with* Re-.

Recommendation, *s.* 1. šipārăs, -si, *f.*
2. metsvoṇeñ, -ṇeā, *n.* = *l.* approbation, *e.g.* of a superior of his subjects.

Recommendatory, *a.* šipārăsitso *or* šipārăs kărtso.

Recompense, *v.* inām di = *l.* give reward.

Recompense, *s.* inām, -mā, *m.*

Recompose, *v.* 1. portun săma ghāl, *or* p. mānḍ.
2. p. borăi = *l.* write again.
3. thănḍ kăr, *or* fuslāi = *l.* make calm.

Reconcile, *v.* sămādhān kărăi, *c. v.*; fuslāi; thănḍ kăr = *l.* make cold, *fg.*

Reconciliation, *s.* sămādhān, -nā, *n.*; soukāsāi, -ye, *f.*

Recondite, *a.* gupit *or* guṭātso; lipullo = *l.* concealed.

Reconnoitre, *v.* vitsārăṇ kăr; sārkeñ pòḷe, *or* sódna kărn p.

Record, *s.* 1. dāklo, -leā, *m.* = *l.* a document, *e.g.* a volume of records.
2. ugḍās, -sā, *m.* = *l.* memory.
3. dăftèr, -rā, *n.* = a roll of books.
4. *in pl.* (vărsānčeo) khăbro, *pl. f.* = *l.* news (of the years); kătha, -the, *f.* = *l.* history.

Record, *v.* dākăl kăr (enter in a book); urăi = *l.* cause to remain; *bet.* ugḍās urăi.

Recount, *v.* sāng *or* móṇ.

Recourse, *s.* (have r. to) 1. *Cm.* āsro kāṇghe = take refuge in; ādhār māg = *l.* ask help, *Cm.*; kākuḷt māg = *l.* ask mercy, *G. F.*; *only* māg; vetā = *l.* goes.
2. prăyóg kăr = *l.* make use.
3. prăyătăn kăr = *l.* make effort, try.
4. *sometimes omitted*, *e.g.* have r. to flight = dāuñ.

Recover, *v.* 1. văsul ghe, *or* vāpăs ghe = *l.* get back, *e.g.* money.
2. guṇ zātā = *l.* good quality (health) becomes; boro zātā = *l.* becomes good (healthy).
3. vānts = *ex.* survive, *e.g.* kăsăloi jīv vāntsasonāñ = *Lat. non fieret salva omnis caro*, *l.* all flesh would not be saved.
Let me r. = usuās sóḍunk di.

Recovery, *s.* 1. văsuli, -le, *f.*, *e.g.* of money.
2. guṇ, -ṇā, *m.*, *e.g.* of health; sănin, -ne, *f.* (from a fit).

Recreant, *a.* bhiyātso = *l.* fearing; phukki = *l.* coward; dhăirnātullo; *see* **Apostate.**

Recreate, *v.* 1. khušāl kăr (*or* kušālăi, *n. c.*)
2. săntos-bhóg = *l.* enjoy pleasure (*n. v.*).

Recreation, *s.* 1. soukāsāi, -ye, *f.*;

N. B. Words compounded with **Re-**, *not put down here, are formed by prefixing* pāṭi *or* portun *to the simple word compounded with* **Re-**.

khušālāi, -ye, *f.*; gămmăt, -tā, *n.*

2. khušālāyetso vēḷ(é), -ḷā, *m.* = *l.* a time of pleasure; khèḷtso vēḷ = *l.* a time of playing; khéḷ, -ḷā, *m.* = play, amusement.

Recriminate, *v.* tònḍār mār = *l.* beat on the mouth; pāṭi (*or* portun) gunyāukār kăr = *l.* make back guilty; uprāṭeñ ulăi; durva.

Recruit, *s.* novo sipāi, -yā, *m.* = *l.* a new soldier.

Recruit, *v.* 1. novo kăr = *l.* make new.

2. bòḷ di = *l.* give force.

3. bhór = *l.* fill.

Recruiting, *s.* sipāyānčeñ meḷouṇeñ, -ṇeā, *n.*

Rectangle, *s.* sămakonso, -seā, *m.*

Rectification, *s.* suči kărčeñ, -čeā, *n.*; suddụ kărčeñ.

Rectify, *v.* săma kăr; *see* **Correct.**

Rectitude, *s.* nāi, -yā, *m.*

Rector, *s.* voḍil, -lā, *m.* = *l.* a superior; tsălăitolo; kārkhāneagār, -rā, *m.* = *l.* an administrator (*not ex.*, *or only for some cases*).

Recumbent, *see* **Lean, Recline.**

Recuperation, *s.* văsuli, -le, *f.*, *e.g.* of one's own things.

Recur, *v.* 1. māg = *l.* ask, *Cm.*

2. portun ye, *or* pāṭi ye = come again *or* back; póḍ = *l.* fall, *e.g.* a feast; *see* **Recourse.**

Red, *a.* 1. tāmbḍo.

2. zāmbḷi răngātso (a reddish purple).

3. kentso (*said of* hair), light-red, auburn (*It. biondo*).

R. timber = mārtitso ruk (?).

Redden, *v.* tāmbḍo kăr, *tr. v.*; t. zā, *n. v.*

Reddish, *a.* tāmbḍoso, *or* tāmbso.

Redeem, *v.* sóḍăi, *c. v. of* sóḍ = leave; sóḍvoṇ kăr = *l.* make salvation, *G. F.*

Redeemer, *s.* Sóḍvoṇdār, -rā, *m.*; Tārók, -kā, *m.*

Redemption, *s.* sóḍvoṇ, -ṇi, *f.*; udargăti, -ti, *f.*

Red-hot, *a.* tāpăillo; ujeabăriso; zăḷtso = *l.* burning.

Redness, *s.* tāmbḍo róng, -gā, *m.* = *l.* red colour.

Redolent, *a.* *rs.* părmăḷ yetā = *l.* smell comes; părmăḷātso = good smelling.

Redouble, *v.* doḍo kăr = *l.* make double; dón pāuṭi tsăḍ kăr = make twice more.

Redound, *v.* 1. mirua = *l.* exceed, surpass; bhāir vāu = *l.* flow out.

2. *fg.* pòḍ = *l.* fall, *e. g.* upkārāk pòḍtā = *l.* redounds to benefit.

Redress, *v.* 1. pāṭi di = *l.* give back; vāpās di = *l.* give back.

N. B. Words compounded with **Re-**, *not put down here, are formed by prefixing* **pāṭi** *or* **portun** *to the simple word compounded with* **Re-**.

2. bhórn di = *l.* give full, (repair), *e.g.* honour.

Reduce, *v.* 1. *by c. v.*; kăr = do.
2. uṇo *or* bārik *or* ăskăt zātā = gets less, *or* thin, *or* weak.
3. khālto kăr = *l.* make subject, *ch. cs.*
4. urăi = *l.* cause to remain with, *e.g.* Cæsar had been reduced to two legions.
5. pāu = *l.* reach, arrive; zā = *l.* become, *e.g.* reduced to poverty.
6. săma kăr = make right, *e.g.* a dislocation.

Reduction, *s.* 1. *rs. into v.*
2. uṇepoṇ, -ṇā, *n.* = *l.* diminution, *fg.* misery; lăčārpoṇ, -ṇā, *n.*

Redundancy, *s.* tsăḍāu, -ḍāvā, *m.*

Redundant, *a.* tsăḍtso; *see* **Redound.**

Reduplication, *s.* doḍāp, -ḍpā, *n.*

Reed, *s.* čivo, -veā, *m.*; nóḷ, -ḷā, *m.*

Reek, *v.* 1. duvor yetā = *l.* smoke comes, *ch. cs.*
2. ub yetā = *l.* steam comes.

Reel, *v.* kāmp; hāl = *l.* move (*n. v.*).

Refectory, *s.* jeuṇăčeñ kuḍ, -ḍā, *n.*; j. sāl, -lā, *n.*

Refer, *v.* 1. dhāḍ = *l.* send; *bet. crc.*, *e.g.* r. to the letter = kāgād pòḷe móṇ sāng.
2. mukār ghāl = *l.* put before, *e.g.* a thing to a judge.
3. móṇ = *l.* say.
4. lāi = *l.* apply, *fg.* ascribe, *e.g.* r. faults to; gunyāukār kăr = *l.* make guilty, *ch. cs.*
5. săr kărn dākăi = *l.* making comparison show, (allude).
6. *rs.* pāsun = on account of; (to what does this r.? = yeñ kiteā pāsun?); višyānt āsā.

Reference, *s.* (with r. to), višyānt = *l.* about.

Refine, *v.* 1. săma (*or* nităḷ = pure, *or* sămpurṇ = perfect, *or* suddụ = correct) kăr.
2. vrăddhi kăr = *l.* make prosperous.

Refinement, *s.* guṇ, -ṇā, *m.* = *l.* improvement; *rs. v.*

Reflect, *v.* 1. (uzvāḍ) pāṭipòḍăi, -sărăi, -uḍăi = *l.* send back (light).
2. (tujea itleāk *or* portuṇ) čint = *l.* think (with yourself *or* again); āločen kăr = *l.* make judgment; čint = *l.* think.

Reflection, *s.* 1. pāṭipóḍāp, -ḍpā, *n.*; sārkeñ, -keā, *n.* = similitude.
2. niyāḷ, -ḷā, *m.*, *or* prestāu, -tāvā, *m.* = meditation, consideration.
3. tsătrāi, -ye, *f.* = *l.* a note, a remark.
4. (porti) čintna, -ne, *f.* = *l.* (turned) thought (*phil.*)

N. B. Words compounded with **Re-**, *not put down here, are formed by prefixing* **pāṭi** *or* **portun** *to the simple word compounded with* **Re-**.

Reflective, *a. rs. into the* participle of the verb (*see above*).

Reform, *v.* 1. noveñ rūp di = *l.* give a new form.
2. săma *or* sărko (kăr) = *l.* make right, *e.g.* life.

Reformation, *s.* 1. noveñ rūp, -pā, *n.* = *l.* a new form.
2. guṇ, -ṇā, *m.* = *l.* improvement.

Refract, *v.* vānkḍo kăr = *l.* make crooked.

Refraction, *s.* vānkḍepoṇ, -ṇā, *n.*; vănkuḍ, -ḍā, *n.*

Refractory, *a.* dhāruṇ = *l.* obstinate; inkār kărtso = *l.* making opposition; hukum miruontso = *l.* surpassing order.

Refrain, *v.* 1. tsukăi, *c. v.* = *l.* avoid, keep back.
2. (āpṇāk) inkār kăr = *l.* make resistance (to oneself); āpṇāk ăḍ yetā *or* vetā = goes against oneself, *n. c.*; (āpṇāčer) zăit vor = *l.* carry victory (against oneself).
3. sāmbāḷ = *l.* keep, *e. g.* r. the tongue.
I could not r. from ... = ... nāstanāñ rāunk" nozo zāleñ.

Refresh, *v.* 1. soukāsāi di = *l.* give peace.
2. portun ghe, p. di = receive, *or* give again.
3. thănḍ kăr = *l.* make cool (mind and body).

Refreshment, *s.* 1. soukāsāi, -ye, *f.* = *l.* peace.
2. ghăṭāi, -ye, *f.* = *l.* strength.
3. phăḷār, -rā, *m.* = *l.* luncheon.

Refrigeratory, *a.* thănḍ kărtso.

Refuge, *s.* 1. āsro, -reā, *m.*, *pr. fg.*; šărăṇa, -ṇā, *n.*
2. ādhār, -rā, *m.* = *l.* help; săsāi, -ye, *f.*
Take r. in ... = *Cm.* āsro ghe.

Refugee, *s.* šărăṇa sódtso, *old rl.*; āsro sódtso (*or* sodullo); părdeši = *l.* an exile.

Refulgence, *s.* pārzăḷ, -ḷā, *m.*

Refusal, *s.* inkār, -ri, *f.*; *rs.* nākā móṇ = *l.* say not; nāñkobuli, -le, *f.* = *l.* no consent.
I got a r. = mākā inkār zāli.

Refuse, *v.* nākā móṇ; inkār kār (*Acc.*); *neg. of* kobuli di, *or* vòp = consent.

Refutation, *s.* soluāp, -pā, *n.*; păḍāu, -ḍāvā, *m.* = *l.* defeat, *fg.*

Refute, *v.* 1. solvăi, *e.g.* an error; păḍāu kăr = *l.* make defeat, *fg.*
2. tonḍār mār, *or* t. jivsi mār = *l.* beat on the mouth: *ex.* recriminate (in private matters).
3. săṭāviṇ dākăi = *l.* show not true, *n. c.*

Regalia, *s.* rāyāče gurtụ, *m. pl.* = *l.* signs of a king.

Regard, *v.* 1. pòḷe = look; diṣṭ ghāl = *l.* put sight (*2nd Loc.*).

N. B. Words compounded with **Re-**, *not put down here, are formed by prefixing* **pāṭi** *or* **portun** *to the simple word compounded with* **Re-**.

2. čint = *l.* think; lēk(é) = *l.* count, consider.
3. lāg = *l.* be attached, *fg.*, *e.g.* it does not r. me = yeñ mākā lāganāñ; pòḍ = *l.* fall, *or* sămănd āsā = *l.* connexion is, respect, have reference to, be concerned with.

Regard, *s.* 1. zătăn, -tne, *f.* = *l.* care; tsătrāi, -ye, *f.* = *l.* attention.
2. āločen, -ni, *f.* = esteem, opinion.
With r. to = višyānt.

Regardless, *a.* tsătrāinātullo; zătăn kāṇe nātullo; făḍpoši.

Regency, *s.* (rājăčeñ) tsălouṇeñ, -ṇeā, *n.*; (rājātso) kārkhāno, -neā, *n.*=*l.* administration of kingdom; tsălounči săbha, -bhe, *f.* = *l.* a council of regency.

Regenerate, *v.* 1. portun zălmăi.
2. *fg.* novo kăr = *l.* make new.

Regeneration, *s.* 1. novi jiṇi, -ye, *f.* = *l.* a new life.
2. novo zălm, -mā, *m.* = *l.* a new birth.

Regent, *s.* rāz tsălountso; rājakārkhāneagār, -rā, *m.*

Regicide, *s.* rāyakhunigār, -rā, *m.*

Regimen, *see* **Diet.**

Regiment, *s.* foujivānṭo, -ṭeā, *m.* = a portion of an army.

Region, *s.* 1. gāuñ, -āñvā, *m.*; *see* **Country.**
2. suāt, -te, *f.* = *l.* a place.

Register, *s.* 1. dāklo, -leā, *m.* = a record.
2. păṭṭi, -ṭe, *f.* = *l.* a list.
3. ḍăfter, -rā, *n.* = a roll of books.

Register, *v.* dākăl kăr, *tr.*; d. zā, *n. v.*, *e.g.* in a book.

Registrar, *s.* dākle dovórtolo; *vlg.* rijistrār, -rā, *m.*, *fr.*

Registration, *s. rs. into v.*

Regret, *s.* duk, -ki, *f.* = *l.* sorrow; păščatāp, -pā, *m.*

Regret, *v.* duk, *or* duk distā = *l.* sorrow appears, *Sb. Dat.*; păščatāp pāu (āuñ p. pāutāñ).

Regular, *a.* 1. krămāntrụ (*var.* kărmāntrụ), *e. g.* r. habits.
2. sămapòḍtso = *l.* falling right (symmetric); khănḍit = *l.* positive.
3. kāideā părmāṇe tsăltolo, *or* kāide sāmbāḷtolo = *l.* observing duties.

Regularly, *ad.* 1. krăm zāun, *or bet.* krămāntrụ zāun, *or* krămān.
2. fāvoteā părmāṇe = *l.* in due manner.
3. tsukanāstanāñ = *l.* not failing.

Regularity, *s.* 1. krăm, -mā, *n.* = *l.* order.
2. mānḍāvóḷ, -ḷi, *f.* = good arrangement, disposition.

***N. B. Words compounded with* Re-, *not put down here, are formed by prefixing* pāṭi *or* portun *to the simple word compounded with* Re-.**

Regulate, *v.* 1. tsălăi = direct.
2. săma ghāl = *l.* put right; krămār dovór = *l.* put in order.
3. *often the construction of the sentence must be changed.*

Regulation, *s.* 1. *vlg.* règrụ, -re, *f.*, *fr.* = *l.* a rule; hukum, -kme, *f.*
2. kāide, *pl. m.* = *l.* rules, *pr.*; kānun, -nā, *n.*

Rehabilitate, *v.* ādle bări kăr.

Rehearsal, *s.* 1. kătha, -the, *f.* = *l.* a story.
2. sovói, -ye, *f.*, *or* ăbyās, -sā, *m.* = *l.* practice.

Rehearse, *v.* 1. sāng *or* móṇ = *l.* say.
2. sovói (*or* ăbyās) kăr = *l.* make practice.

Reign, *v.* 1. rāzvoṭ (*or* rāzvoṭkāi) kăr, *2nd Loc.*
2. tsălăi = *l.* govern.

Reign, *s.* rāz, -jā, *n.*, *or* rāzvoṭ, -ṭi, *f.*, *or* rāzpāṭ, -ṭā, *n.*, *or* rāzvoṭkāi, -ye, *f.*

Rein, *s.* lāgāp, -gpā, *n.*

Reinforce, *v.* (fouz) tsăḍăi = *l.* increase (an army).

Reinforcement, *s.* tsăḍouṇi, -ṇe, *f.*

Reject, *v.* 1. uḍăi = *l.* throw; sóḍ.
2. inkār kăr = *l.* make resistance, (*Acc.*)
3. bepārvo kăr = *l.* despise, reject, *G. M.*; *neg. of* păsănd kăr, *or* vòp = consent, *or* nāpăsănd kăr; *neg. of* āik: 'māg-ṇeñ āikanāñ'.

Rejection, *s.* inkār, -ri, *f.* (*var.* -rā, *n.*)

Rejoice, *v.* khušāl kăr (*or* khušālăi) = make joyful; săntos di, *tr. v.*, *or* s. bhóg, *n. v.* = *l.* give *or* feel pleasure; ulās di *or* u. bhóg.

Rejoin, *v.* 1. meḷăi, *c. v. of* mèḷ = be united.
2. zāb diun săng = answering say.
3. pāṭi ye, *or* pāṭ dhăr = *l.* come back, *or* keep the back.

Relapse, *v.* portun pòḍ = *l.* fall again.

Relapse, *s.* porteñpòḍāp, -ḍpā, *n.*; *bet. rs. into v.*

Relate, *v.* 1. móṇ; săng = say, tell.
2. tăpsil săng = say details.
3. lāg = *l.* be attached, *fg.*, *e.g.* mākā lāganāñ = it does not concern me.
4. *Or.* višyānt āsā = *l.* is about.

Related, *a.* 1. săiro: 'nearly r. = lāgsilo s.'; lèktso.
2. *fg.* sămănd āsụllo = *l.* connected.
3. višāyātso = *l.* which is about, *e.g.* Deva v. niyāḷ, -ḷā, *m.*, *n. c.*

Relation, *s.* 1. kobār, -bre, *f.* = *l.* news; ăbiprāi, -ye, *f.* = *l.* information.

N. B. Words compounded with **Re-**, *not put down here, are formed by prefixing* **pāṭi** *or* **portun** *to the simple word compounded with* **Re-**.

2. săiro, *or* săiro dairo, -reā, *m.* = *l.* kinsman; lèktso mănis, -nšā, *m.*
3 săirik, -ke, *f.* = *l.* consanguinity.
4. *fg.* sămănd, -dā, *m.* = *l.* connection (*also phil.*).
He is my r. = to mākā săiro lektā.

Relationship, *s.* 1. săirik, -ke, *f.* = *l.* consanguinity *or* affinity.
2. sārkeñ, -keā, *n.* = *l.* resemblance.

Relative, *s.* sămăndi, -diā, *m.* (a distant r.)

Relax, *v.* sóḍ *or* sădiḷ kăr = *l.* lax, *pr.*, *fg.*, *e.g.* get tepid.

Relaxation, *s.* 1. sădiḷāi, -ye, *f.*, *pr.* *fg.*
2. dăm, -mā, *m.* = *l.* rest, breathing; khušālāi, -ye, *f.* = amusement, pleasure; soukāsāi, -ye, *f.*

Relaxed, *a.* sădiḷ, *pr.* *fg.*

Relay, *s.* tăpālgòḍe, *pl. m.* = *l.* horses of post.

Release, *v.* 1. sóḍ, *pass.* suṭ; sădiḷ kăr = *l.* make loose.
2. suṭka kăr = *l.* make delivery.

Release, *s.* 1. suṭka, -ke, *f.* = *l.* liberty.
2. soḍvoṇ, -ṇe, *f.* = *l.* redemption.
3. sădiḷāi, -ye, *f.* = *l.* relaxation.

Relent, *v. perh.* suṭ, *e.g.* his anger relents.

Relic, *s.* relik, -ke, *f.*, *fr.*

Relief, *s.* 1. hāḷvāi, -ye, *f.*, *pr.* *fg.* = *l.* lightness; bhuzoṇ, -ṇe, *f.* = comfort, consolation; sămādhān, -nā, *n.*; dăm, -mā, *m.* = *l.* rest, a taking breath.
2. ādhār, -rā, *m.* = *l.* help; săhāi, -ye, *f.* = *l.* help, assistance.
3. sădiḷāi, -ye, *f.* = *l.* relaxation.
4. kāntouṇečeñ čitrụ, -trā, *n.* = *l.* a carved image.

Relieve, *v.* 1. haḷu kăr, *pr.* *fg.*
2. bhuzăi = *l.* console, *e. g.* the afflicted, *etc.*; sămādhān *or* soukāsāi di.
3. bădăl = *l.* change, (*milit.*).

Religion, *s.* šāstrụ, -rā, *n.* (*var.* šāstir, -rā, *n.*); sămoḍt, -ti, *f.*

Religious, *a.* 1. sămoḍtitso *or* šāstrātso.
2. devasponātso = *l.* devout; bhăktivont = devout; bhāgevont = *l.* holy.

Religious, *s.* šāstri, -ri, *m.*; moṭavāsi, -si, *m.* = *l.* an inhabitant of a convent, *n. u.*; *vlg.* frād, -di, *m.*, *or* pādri, -ri, *m. fr.*

Relinquish, *v.* sóḍ *or* sānḍ.

Reliquary, *s.* 1. relike korndo, -ḍeā, *m.* = *l.* a box of relics, *fr.*; relike pèṭ, -ṭe, *f.* = *l.* a box for relics.
2. urku, -kā, *n.* = a native form of r. for private use only.

N. B. Words compounded with **Re-**, *not put down here, are formed by prefixing* **pāṭi** *or* **portun** *to the simple word compounded with* **Re-**.

Relish, *v.* ruts = *l.* taste, *Sb. Dat.*; tsākun pòḷe = *l.* tasting see; *or* tsāk.

Relish, *s.* 1. ruts, -či, *f.* = *l.* taste.
2. nisteñ, -teā, *n.*, what is commonly eaten with rice to make it more palatable.

Reluctance, *s.* nāñkhuši, -še, *f.*, *or rs.* khuši nāñ.

Reluctant, *a.* khušinātullo.

Rely, *v.* pātiye, *obj. 2nd Loc.*; *or* pātiyeṇi dovór.

Remain, *v.* rāu; ur, *e. g.* dón bāṭio urlyāt = two baskets remained (of food).

Remainder, *s.* 1. bāki, -ki, *f.*, *e.g.* of a debt.
2. urta teñ = *l.* what remains.
3. ušṭeñ, -ṭeā, *n.* (of eatables).

Remains, *s.* moḍeñ, -ḍeā, *n.* = *l.* a corpse.

Remark, *s.* tsătrāi, -ye, *f.*; šăro, -reā, *m.* = annotation.

Remark, *v.* tsătrāi kăr *or* ts. kāṇge; pòḷe = *l.* look, *fg.*; kān di = *l.* give ear; mótint ghāl = *l.* put in mind.

Remarkable, *a.* 1. tsătrāyetso, *or* tsătrāi fāvozāllo; pòḷeuntso = *l.* to be seen.
2. nāvāḍdik = *l.* famous; nāvāḍgo; lăkša fāvozāllo = *l.* to which care, attention, respect, must be paid; bhāri = *l.* important; ăsādhārṇ = *l.* extraordinary; ăprup = *l.* rare.
3. ăjāpātso = *l.* wonderful, *etc.*

Remedy, *s.* 1. upāi, -yā, *m.* = *l.* means; vokāt, -ktā *n.* = *l.* medicine, *pr. fg.*, *e.g.* against vices.
2. āsro, -reā, *m.* = refuge; ādhār, -rā, *m.* = help.

Remedy, *v.* 1. boro *or* săma kăr; guṇ kăr = *l.* make improvement.
2. upāi di = *l.* give means.

Remember, *v.* ugḍās (*or* āṭou) kăr, *G. M.*; yād kăr; ugḍās yetā *or* u. āsā = *l.* memory comes, *or* is, *G. M.*; mótint yetā.

Remembrance, *s.* ugḍās, -sā, *m.*; āṭou, -ṭovā, *m.*; yād, -dā, *m.*

Remind, *v.* 1. mótint hāḍ, *or* m. ghāl = *l.* put into mind; ugḍās kăr = *l.* make memory; niyāḷāk hāḍ = *l.* bring to consideration.
2. bud sāng = *l.* say advice.

Reminiscence, *see* **Remembrance.**

Remiss, *a.* āḷsi = *l.* lazy; făḍpoši = negligent, good for nothing; sădiḷ = *l.* loose, *fg.*

Remission, *s.* 1. sădiḷāi, -ye, *f.* (a being loose).
2. bogsāṇe, -ṇeā, *n.* = *l.* pardon.

Remit, *v.* 1. bogsi = *l.* pardon; sóḍ, *e. g.* a fine; suṭ, *n. v.*; māf kăr = *l.* excuse.

N. B. Words compounded with **Re-**, *not put down here, are formed by prefixing* **pāṭi** *or* **portun** *to the simple word compounded with* **Re-**.

2. deuñ = *l.* descend, *e.g.* fever.
3. dhāḍ *or* dhāḍn di = *l.* send; pāvoi = *l.* cause to reach.
4. vopsun di = *l.* consign; *see also* **Refer.**

Remittance, *s.* dhāḍullo duḍu, -ḍuā, *m.* = *l.* sent money; *the Cn.* hunḍi, -ye, *f. commonly used.*

Remittent, *a.* vetso-urtso *or* vortokāḍto (fever); poireātso (fever).

Remonstrance, *see* **Protest.**

Remonstrate, *v.* 1. beṣṭāi = *l.* scold; bud sāng = say advice; durva = *l.* expostulate.
2. ăḍḍi kăr = *l.* make opposition.

Remorse, *s.* tsurtsuro, -reā, *m.* *e. g.* r. of conscience; ăntăskărnātso kiḍo, -ḍeā, *m.* = *l.* a worm of the heart; mònatsābṇi, -ṇe, *f.*

Remote, *a.* poisilo = which is far; *rs. into* pois.

Remotely, *ad.* pois.

Removal, *s.* bhāirsărāp, -rpā, *n.* = *l.* starting; *see* **Degradation, Deposition.**

Remove, *v.* 1. kāḍ, *or* pelān k. *or* p. vor = take away.
2. tsukāi = *l.* avoid, *Acc.*
3. vots mòṇ = *l.* say 'go'.
4. bhāir săr = *l.* start; *see* **Degrade.**

Remunerate, *v.* inām di, *etc.*

Remuneration, *s.* 1. inām, -mā, *n.*
2. kūl, -li, *f.* = wages.

Rend, *v.* pind, *e.g.* cloth; mōḍ(ó) = *l.* break; fóḍ, *e.g.* a tree.

Render, *v.* 1. di = *l.* give, *e.g.* an account.
2. tsălăi, *e. g.* r. what is due to.
3. kăr = *l.* make.
4. tărzumo kăr = *l.* make version.
5. pāṭi (*or* vāpăs) di = *l.* give back; bhórn di = *l.* give full, *e.g.* honour.

Rendezvous, *s.* meḷasuāt, -te, *f.* (*or* meḷči suāt) = *l.* a place of reunion.

Renegade, *s.* 1. bāvāḍt sóḍullo = *l.* one who left faith.
2. lutstso, -čeā, *m.* = *l.* a rascal.

Renew, *v.* 1. portun kăr = *l.* make again.
2. novo kăr = *l.* make new.
3. săma kăr = *l.* make right.

Renewal, *s.* porto, *joined to the req. noun, or rs. into* portun kărčeñ.

Rennet, *s.* meḷāi, -ye, *f.*; irzāṇ, -ṇā, *n.* (buttermilk, *commonly used here as* rennet).

Renounce, *v.* 1. pāṭ kăr (pāṭi kăr = send back).
2. sóḍ = *l.* abandon, *e. g.* an office.

Renovate, *see* **Renew.**

Renowned, *a.* părbăl; *see also* **Famous.**

N. B. Words compounded with **Re-**, *not put down here, are formed by prefixing* **pāṭi** *or* **portun** *to the simple word compounded with* **Re-**.

Rent, *s.* 1. bāḍeñ, -ḍeā, *n.* = r. of a house.
2. géṇ, -ṇi, *f.* = *l.* a lease, *used also for* r.; 'géṇik kāṇe = *l.* take at r.'
3. vāḍ, -ḍi *f.* = *l.* interest (of a capital).
4. fóḷ, -ḷā, *m.* = effect.
5. moḍāp, -ḍpā, *n.*; fuṭ, -ṭi, *f.* = *l.* a chink.

Rent, *v.* 1. bāḍeāk di = *l.* let on lease.
2. bāḍeāk kāṇe = *l.* take on lease.

Renunciation, *s.* sóḍni, -ne, *f.*; rāji, -je, *f.*

Repair, *v.* 1. săma kăr.
2. fārikpoṇ di = *l.* give reparation; bhórn di = *l.* give full (r. honour); *see also* **Recourse.**

Reparation, *s.* 1. fārikpoṇ, -ṇā, *n.* = *l.* satisfaction.
2. *for other mn. rs. into v.*

Repast, *s.* jevāṇ, jeuṇā, *n.* = *l.* dinner.

Repeal, *v.* răddu̦ kăr = *l.* make nullity, *e. g.* a law; kāḍn ghāl.

Repeal, *s.* răddu̦, -dā, *n.*

Repeat, *v.* portun, *with the req. verb*; p. kăr.

Repeatedly, *ad.* portun portun.

Repel, *v.* 1. pāṭi kăr, *or* p. ghāl = *l.* put back.
2. inkār kăr = *l.* resist, (*Acc.*).
3. pāṭi mār = *l.* beat back; pāṭi lōṭ(ó) = *l.* push back.

Repent, *v.* duk distā, *Sb. Dat* = *l.* sorrow appears; d. dhăr = *l.* catch sorrow.

Repentance, *s.* duk, -ki, *f.*; păščatāp, -pā, *m.*; tsurtsuro, -reā, *m.*; zāḷ, -ḷā, *m.* = *l.* a burning, *fg.*

Repertory, *s.* bănḍār, -rā, *n.*

Repetition, *s. rs. into v.*

Repine, *v.* šiṇ ulăi.

Repining, *s.* šiṇ, -ṇā, *m.*

Replace, *v.* 1. *G.* suăter ghāl.
2. ādle suăter ghāl.

Replevy, *v.* zāminer pāṭi kāṇe.

Reply, *v.* zăvāb (*or* prătizăvāb) di; pāṭi ulăi, *or* pāṭi portun u.

Reply, *s.* (prăti-) zăvāb, -bi, *f.*; pāṭi-utăr, -trā, *n.*, *n. c.*

Report, *v.* kăḷăi = *l.* make known, *c. v. of* kăḷ; kăbār hāḍ = *l.* bring news.

Report, *s.* 1. phukāro, -reā, *m.* = *l.* rumour; kăbār, -bre, *f.* = *l.* news.
2. mān, -nā, *m.* = *l.* honour.
3. lèk, -kā, *n.* = an account; vivor, -rā, *m.* = *l.* an explanation, a statement.

Repose, *s.* soukāsāi, -ye, *f.*; dăm, -mā, *m.* = *l.* breath, *fg.*

Repose, *v.* soukāsāi (*or* dăm) kāṇe.
R. your hope on = 2*nd Loc.* pātiyeṇi dovór.

N. B. Words compounded with **Re-**, *not put down here, are formed by prefixing* **pāṭi** *or* **portun** *to the simple word compounded with* **Re-**.

Repository, *s.* dovórči suāt, -te, *f.*
Reprehend, *v.* beṣṭāi; *see* **Blame.**
Reprehension, *s.* beṣṭāuṇeñ, -ṇeā, *n.*
Represent, *v.* 1. hāzăr kăr = *l.* make present.
2. mukār ghāl = *l.* put before.
3. *G.* suāter āsā = is in the place of; *G.* rūp dākăi = *l.* show the form of; *G.* vẻs ghāl = put a mask; *or only* dākăi = *l.* show.
4. niyāḷāk hāḍ = *l.* bring to consideration.
5. čint = *l.* think.
Representation, *s.* 1. dākoṇ, -ṇi, *f.*, *e.g.* of the Passion of J. C.
2. sārkeñ, -keā, *n.* = *l.* resemblance; rūp, -pā, *n.* = *l.* form.
3. ărji -je, *f.* = *l.* a petition.
Representative, *s.* *G.* rūp dākăitolo, *etc.*
Repress, *v.* 1. bȯḷ mōḍ(ó) = *l.* break force.
2. nivăi; thāmbăi, rāvoi, *e.g.* a revolution.
Repression, *s.* *rs. into v.*
Reprieve, *v.* 1. pāṭi ghāl.
2. (phăisăl) pāṭi kāḍ.
Reprimand, *v.* 1. beṣṭāi.
2. nāpăsănd kăr = *l.* make disapproval.
Reproach, *v.* 1. beṣṭāi = *l.* scold.
2. lăzăi = *l.* cause to blush.
3. gāḷi sāng, *or* g. sou = *l.* say abuses.
4. gunyāukār kăr = *l.* make guilty.
5. kénḍ; *see* **Blame.**
Reproach, *s.* 1. dur, -rā, *n.*
2. beṣṭāuṇeñ, -ṇeā, *n.*
3. ăpamān, -nā, *m.* = *l.* disgrace; lăz, -je, *f.* = *l.* shame.
Reprobate, *v.* širāp ghāl, *or* š. pȯḍăi.
Reprobation, *s.* sóḍni, -ne, *f.*, *or rs. v.*
Reproduce, *v.* 1. portun ubzăi = *l.* produce again.
2. p. dākăl kăr = *l.* introduce again, *e.g.* a custom.
Reproof, *see* **Disapproval.**
Reprove, *see* **Reprimand.**
Reptile, *s.* jivāḷ, -ḷi, *f. n. c.*; jiudāḷ, -ḷi, *f.*; tsărči jiudād, -di, *f.* = *l.* a creeping animal.
Republic, *s.* dhāzăṇānčeñ rāz, -jā, *n.* = *l.* reign of 10 persons; părječeñ rāz = *l.* reign of the people.
Repudiate, *v.* (bāilek) sóḍ.
Repugnance, *s.* nāñkhuši, -še, *f.*; inkār, -ri, *f.* (*var.* -rā, *n.*) = *l.* opposition; vonkāro, -reā, *m.* = *l.* nausea.
Have r. to = boreñ disanāñ, *or* khuši nāñ, *or* vonkāro yetā, *e.g.* to food.
Repugnant, *a.* khušinātullo.
Repulse, *see* **Repel, Refusal.**
Repulsion, *s.* āḍlōṭ(ó), -ṭā, *m.*
Repulsive, *a.* āḍlóṭtso.

N. B. Words compounded with **Re-**, *not put down here, are formed by prefixing* **pāṭi** *or* **portun** *to the simple word compounded with* **Re-**.

Reputation, *s.* boreñ nāuñ, -nāvā, *n.* = *l.* good name; mān, -nā, *m.*, ābru, -rā, *m.* = honour; bori āločen, -ni, *f.* = *l.* good opinion; kirt, -ti, *f.*
Enjoy a good r. = boreñ nāuñ bhóg.
Injure, impair the r. = boreñ nāuñ (*or* mān) kāḍ; b. n. (*or* m.) pāḍ kăr.

Request, *v.* māg, *Cm.*

Request, *s.* māg-ṇeñ, -ṇeā, *n.*
At the request of = māglelea (*or* māgčea) pāsun.
Grant a r. = māg-ṇeñ āik.

Require, *v.* 1. zāi = *l.* is necessary, *Sb. Dat.*; gărjetso zāun āsā = is necessary; *or* gărz āsā.
2. māg = *l.* request.

Requisite, *s.* gărječi văstu̥, -tu, *f.* = *l.* a necessary thing; zāi teñ.

Requisition, *s.* 1. māg-ṇeñ, -ṇeā, *n.*
2. āpouṇeñ, -ṇeā, *n.* = *l.* a call.

Requital, *s.* inām, -mā, *n.* = *l.* a reward; sāmbāḷ, -ḷā, *m.* = *l.* pay; (fārik, *or*) fārikpoṇ, -ṇā, *n.* = *l.* satisfaction.

Requite, *v.* inām di *or* fārik kăr.

Rescind, *v.* răddu̥ kăr = *l.* make nullity.

Rescission, *s.* răddu̥, -dā, *n.*

Rescript, *s.* hukum, -kme, *f.*

Rescue, *v.* kāḍ = *l.* take out, *e. g.* from danger; sóḍ = *l.* deliver, *or bet.* sóḍāi, *c. v.*; suṭkā kăr = *l.* make delivery.

Research, *s.* vitsārăṇ, -ṇā, *n.*; dăriyāft, -ti, *f.* = judicial r.; tānki, -ke, *f.* = *l.* a trial.

Research, *v.* kăr *with one of the above nouns.*

Resemblance, *s.* sārkeñ, -keā, *n.*; săr, -ri, *f.*

Resemble, *v.* sārko zāun āsā (tāče sārko; *but* Devāk sārko); *Or.* bări zāun āsā = is like; *Dat.* săma zāun āsā = is like.

Resent, *v.* vāiṭāk voṛ = *l.* take to evil; păščatāp kāṇghe = *l.* take sorrow; *vlg.* bontso fultā = *l.* the bill flowers (he makes long faces), *n. c.*

Resentment, *s.* nāñkhuši, -še, *f.*, *or rs. into v.*

Reservation, *s. rs. v.*

Reserve, *v.* āpṇāk dovór = keep for oneself; sāmbāḷn dovór, *e. g.* food.

Reserve, *s.* guṭātso sobāu, -bāvā, *m.* = *l.* a mysterious inclination, *or rs. into* vogo rāutā.

Reserved, *a.* guṭātso; *vlg.* thărātso.

Reservoir, *s.* 1. tāḷeñ, -ḷeā, *n.* = a tank.
2. bāiñ, bāiñ, *f.* = *l.* a well.
3. mădăk, -dkā, *n.* = *l.* a marsh.
4. kāṭ, -ṭā, *m.* = a dam to keep water in channels.

N. B. Words compounded with **Re-**, *not put down here, are formed by prefixing* **pāṭi** *or* **portun** *to the simple word compounded with* **Re-**.

Reside, *v.* rāu, *or* āsā, *or* vās kăr.

Residence, *s.* 1. ṭhikāṇeñ *or* ṭāṇeñ, -ṇeā, *n.*, *also* of a bishop; biḍār, -rā, *n.* = *l.* dwelling; bonglo, -leā, *m.*, *fr.*
2. rāvāp, rāupā, *n.* = (the act of) remaining.

Resign, *tr. v.* sóḍ = *l.* abandon; vopsun di = *l.* give over; rāji di.

Resign, *n. v.* sosṇikāi kāṇe = keep patience; sămādhān dovór = *l.* keep peace; *rs.* Devāče khuše părmāṇe tsăl.

Resignation, *s.* 1. sosṇikāi, -ye, *f.* = *l.* patience.
2. yekoṭ, -ṭā, *m.* = *l.* union, *e.g.* his r. to the will of God = tātso yekoṭ Devāče khušek.
3. rāji, -je, *f.* = r. of an office.
4. khāltepoṇ, -ṇā, *n.* = *l.* subjection.

Resin, *s.* dāmbor, -rā, *m.*; ărbastāni gónd, -dā, *m.* = Arabic gum; čăndan, -nā, *n.*

Resist, *v.* 1. inkār kăr, *Acc.*; ăḍḍi (*or* āḍkăḷ) kăr = *l.* make objection.
2. mukār rāu = *l.* remain in the face.
3. porto zāun āsā = is contrary (*Dat.*); *Dat.* āḍ zāun āsā = is against.
4. āḍ ulăi = speak against.

Resistance, *s.* 1. inkār, -ri, *f.* (*var.* -rā, *n.*)
2. ăḍḍi, -ḍe, *f.*, *or* āḍkăḷ, -ḷi, *f.* = *l.* obstacle.
3. bòḷ, -ḷā, *n.* = *l.* force.

Resolute, *a.* 1. dhăiravont *or* dhăiradik; thir = *l.* firm; bheñ nātullo = *l.* not afraid; khăḍākhăḍ.
2. tăyār = *l.* ready.

Resolution, *s.* 1. ničeu, -čevā, *m.*, *e.g.* to avoid sin.
2. dhăir, -rā, *n.* = *l.* courage.
3. āločen, -ni, *f.* = *l.* opinion.
4. nirmaṇeñ, -ṇeā, *n.*, *e.g.* of a meeting; *or bet.* niščeisilli văstu, -tu, *f.*

Resolve, *v.* 1. niščeisi = determine, pass a resolution.
2. vivor sāng, *G. M.*, *or* vivorsi = *l.* explain; ărth sāng = *l.* say meaning.
3. vingăḍ kăr = *l.* separate.

Resort, *v.* 1. vetā, *with* -ts; *see* Gram. P. III. ch. ii.; săbār pāuṭi vetā = goes many times.
2. āsro kāṇghe = *l.* take refuge; prăyóg kăr, *G. M.* = *l.* make use; *see* **Use**.

Resound, *v.* 1. tāḷo (*or* āvāz) pāṭi pòḍăi = *l.* send back voice.
2. *fg.* hogoḷsi = *l.* praise, *ch. cs.*; bòb mār = *l.* cry.
The house resounds with uproar = ghăr goujen bhórlāñ.

Resource, *s.* ādhār, -rā, *m.* = help; săhāi, -ye, *f.* = assistance; upāi, -yā, *m.* = means.

N. B. Words compounded with **Re-**, *not put down here, are formed by prefixing* **pāṭi** *or* **portun** *to the simple word compounded with* **Re-**.

Respect, *v.* 1. mān di, *or* mān kăr; mānd.
2. lāg = *l.* be attached, *fg.* (concern); *see* **Regard.**

Respect, *s.* 1. mān, -nā, *m.*; măryād, -di, *f.* = honesty.
2. sămănd, -dā, *m.* = relation, connexion.
3. jinos, -nsā, *m.* = *l.* manner.

Respectability, *s.* 1. măryād, -di, *f.*, *or* mān, -nā, *m.*
2. măryāditso mănis, -nšā, *m.*

Respectable, *a.* 1. mānātso *or* ābrātso *or* măryāditso.
2. sumār = moderate.

Respected, *a.* mān bhógtso.

Respectful, *a.* mān kărtso, *or* mān diuntso; măryāditso.

Respecting, *prep.* višyānt.

Respective, *a.* āplo = *l.* one's own; svănta = own, *n. c.*; hăryék = *l.* each.
Every man has his r. faults = yeyekleāk tāčeo tāčeo tsuki āsāt.
Appoint a captain to each legion respectively = yeyeka tănḍāk yeyék moktesăr nemsi.

Respiration, *s.* 1. *rs. into* usuās kāṇe, *or* usuās, -sā, *m.*
2. *fg.* dăm, -mā, *m.*

Respire, *v.* usuās sóḍ = breathe [out.

Respite, *v.* dăm kāṇe.

Respite, *s.* dăm, -mā, *m.*; toḍou, -ḍovā, *m.*

Response, *see* **Answer.**

Responsibility, *s.* zăvābdāri, -re, *f.*

Responsible, *a.* 1. zăvābdār.
2. āst āsullo, *or* āstitso = *l.* rich.
Is r. = z. zātā *or* z. zāun āsā; āpṇāčer voisun ghetā = *l.* takes upon oneself.

Rest, *s.* 1. nīd, -de, *f.* = *l.* sleep.
2. soukāsāi, -ye, *f.*; dăm, -mā, *m.*, *e.g.* after having worked; visou, -sovā, *m.*, *e.g.* eternal r. in heaven.
3. digo, -geā, *m.* (anything serving as a prop or support).
4. bāki, -ki, *f.* = *l.* remainder; urta teñ.
Find r. = soukāsāi bhóg.
Take r. = soukāsāi (*or* dăm) kāṇe.

Rest, *v.* 1. soukāsāi bhóg.
2. *neg. of* hāl = *l.* move (*n. v.*); rāu = be not moving.
3. *fg.* pātiye = *l.* trust, *2nd Loc.*; *see* **Lean.**

Resting-place, *s.* kāṭeñ, -ṭeā, *n.* (a dam around trees used as a r.); soukāsāi kāṇeunči suāt, -te, *f.*

Restitution, *s.* pāṭi diunčeñ *or* vāpās d.; fārikpoṇ, -ṇā, *n.* = *l.* satisfaction.

Restless, *a.* utsāmbóḷ = *l.* excited; soukāsāinātullo.

Restlessness, *s.* nāñsoukāsāi, -ye, *f.*; utsāmboḷāi, -ye, *f.*

Restoration, *s. see* **Restitution.**

N. B. Words compounded with **Re-**, *not put down here, are formed by prefixing* **pāṭi** *or* **portun** *to the simple word compounded with* **Re-**.

Restorative, *a.* ghăṭāi diuntso = *l.* strengthening.

Restore, *v.* 1. pāṭi (*or* vāpăs) di.
2. ădle bări kăr (*or some similar verb*) = *l.* make as before.
3. portun dākăl kăr = *l.* introduce again, *e.g.* customs.
4. guṇ kăr = *l.* make improvement, (r. to health); boro kăr = r. to health.
5. portun = again, *with the required verb.*

Restrain, *v.* 1. sāmbāḷ = *l.* keep, *e. g.* the senses; dāmpun dovór = *l.* keep shut, *e. g.* the eyes, a sigh, anger, *etc.*
2. āḍāi *or* ăḍḍi kăr = put objection.
3. mōḍ(ó) = *l.* break, *fg.* check.

Restraint, *s.* 1. sāmbāḷouṇeñ, -ṇeā, *n.* (self-restraint); sudaḷāi, -ye, *f.*
2. āḍkăḷ, -ḷi, *f.* = *l.* an obstacle.

Restrict, *v.* 1. mit (*or* mitmèr) ghāl = *l.* put a limit.
2. uṇo kăr = *l.* make less, diminish; ăšir kăr = *l.* make narrow; āvaḷăi.
3. dādós āsā = is satisfied, *e.g.* I r. myself to saying, *ch. cs.*

Restricted, *a.* 1. ăšir, *pr. fg.* = *l.* narrow; găḍ āsullo.
2. *fg.* lān = *l.* little.

Restriction, *s.* 1. mit, -ti, *f.* = *l.* a limit.
2. šărt, -tā, *m.* = *l.* a condition.

Mental r. = *perh.* guḍ, -ḍā, *m.* *or* guḍart, -tā, *m.*

Result, *v.* zā = *l.* become; găḍ = *l.* happen; sevóṭ āsā = *l.* issue is, *ch. cs.*

Result, *s.* fóḷ, -ḷā, *m.* = *l.* effect; sevóṭ, -ṭā, *m.* = *l.* issue.
Be the r. of = zā.

Resume, *v.* 1. portun kāṇghe = *l.* again take.
2. portun lāg = *l.* again be attached, *fg.*, *e.g.* r. studies, *Dat.*
3. portun *with the required verb.*

Resurrection, *s.* jivontpoṇ, -ṇā, *n.* (kuḍičeñ j. = r. of the body).

Resuscitate, *v.* (melleāntlo) jivont kăr.

Retail, *v.* (sell by r.) tsungḍi (*or* čillăr) ikāp, -kpā, *n.*

Retail, *s.* tsungḍi (*or* čillăr).

Retailer, *s.* čillăr vepāragār, -rā, *m.*

Retain, *v.* 1. dovór; *Cm.* āsā; ănbhóg.
2. pós = *l.* feed.

Retaliate, *v.* fārikpoṇ ghe = take revenge, *G. N.*

Retard, *see* **Delay.**

Retch, *v.* vonkāro yetā = nausea comes.

Retention, *s.* 1. pāṭidovórčeñ.
2. rāvāp, rāupā, *n.*

Retentive, *a.* ghăṭ = *l.* firm (memory).

***N. B. Words compounded with* Re-, *not put down here, are formed by prefixing* pāṭi *or* portun *to the simple word compounded with* Re-.**

Retentiveness, *s.* ugḍās, -sā, *m.*

Reticence, *s.* bitărlo guṭ, -ṭā, *m.*; monepoṇ, -ṇā, *n.* = *l.* dumbness, *fg.*, *n.c.*; *bet. rs.*

Reticulated, *a.* zāḷabăriso.

Reticule, *s.* dākṭeñ zāḷ, -ḷā, *n.*

Retina, *s.* doḷeāčeñ zāḷ, -ḷā, *n.*

Retinue, *s.* părivār, -rā, *m.*; sāngāt, -tā, *m.* = *l.* company; dărbār, -rā, *n.*, of a prince.

Retire, *v.* 1. pāṭi săr.
2. vetā = *l.* goes.
3. vingăḍ vetā = *l.* goes aside; yeksure suāter vetā = goes to a solitary place.
4. *G.* kusin vetā = goes in the direction of.
5. sóḍ = *l.* leave, *e.g.* r. from an office, town; rāji di, from an office; bhāirsăr = go out.

Retired, *a.* yeksuro = solitary; vingăḍ = separated.

Retirement, *s.* 1. yeksurāi, -ye, *f.*, *or* yeksurpoṇ, -ṇā, *n.*
2. pāṭisărāp, -rpā, *n.* = *l.* going back.

Retort, *v.* pāṭi măr; uprāṭeñ durva (recriminate); tonḍār măr = *l.* beat on the face.
R. abuse = pāṭi gāḷi sou.

Retort, *s.* 1. pāṭizăvāb, -bi, *f.* = *l.* against answer.
2. năḷi, -ye, *f.* = *l.* a tube.

Retouch, *v.* săma kăr = *l.* make correct.

Retrace, *v.* (āil″le vāṭen) pāṭi vetā.

Retract, *v.* pāṭi kāḍ = *l.* take back, *e. g.* words; fārikpoṇ di = *l.* give satisfaction.

Retractation, *s.* *rs. into v.*

Retreat, *v.* 1. pāṭi săr.
2. sóḍ = *l.* leave, *ch. cs.*

Retreat, *s.* 1. āsro, -reā, *m.* = *l.* refuge.
2. yeksurāi, -ye, *f.*, *or* yeksuri suāt, -te, *f.* = solitude.
3. *in ascet. mn. perh.* tòp, -pā, *n.*; *it mn. ex.* hearing in silence God's voice; *or* ătmeātso ăbyās, -sā, *m.* = *l.* exercise of the soul; (ătmeāči) yeksurāi = *l.* solitude (of the soul); *vlg.* reter, -rā, *n.*, *fr.*

Retrench, *v.* uṇo kăr = *l.* make less, *e.g.* expenses.

Retribution, *s.* inām, -mā, *n.*

Retrograde, *a.* pāṭitsăltso, *fg.*

Return, *v.* 1. pāṭi (*or* vāpăs) di.
2. r. a kindness = titlo upkār kăr *or* prătiupkār kăr.
3. lèk di (*or* vivor di) = *l.* give a statement.
4. pāvoi = *l.* cause to reach, *fg.*
5. pāṭi vetā.

Return, *s.* 1. *rs. into v.*
2. lèk, -kā, *n.* = *l.* account.
3. prătiupkār, -rā, *m.*; pāṭi *with the required noun*, *e.g.* r. of kindness = pāṭi-upkār; fārikpoṇ, -ṇā, *n.* = *l.* pay, *e.g.* of an injury.
4. huṭṭavóḷ, -ḷi, *f.* = *l.* revenue.

N. B. Words compounded with **Re-**, *not put down here, are formed by prefixing* **pāṭi** *or* **portun** *to the simple word compounded with* **Re-**.

Reunion, *s.* porto yekóṭ, -ṭā, *m.*; sămādhān, -nā, *n.* = *l.* peace.

Reunite, *v.* 1. portun meḷăi = *l.* unite again.
2. *fg.* sămādhān kărăi = reconcile; *see* **Join.**

Reveal, *v.* ugto kăr = *l.* make open; *or* ugăḍ; ugḍāpeñ kăr; kăḷit kăr, *or* kăḷăi = *l.* make known; părgăṭ kăr *or* pārgăṭăi = publish; dākăi = *l.* show.

Revel, *s.* khāugipoṇ, -ṇā, *n.*

Revel, *v.* 1. jīv sóḍn séu.
2. vāiṭ khusiānk lāg.

Revelation, *s.* 1. părgăṭouṇeñ, -ṇeā, *n.* = *l.* publication.
2. ugḍāpeñ kelleo văstu = *l.* revealed things; u. kelleñ šāstrụ, -trā, *n.*; bāvāḍt, -tā, *m.* = *l.* faith.

Reveller, *s.* khāugi, -giā, *m.*

Revenge, *v.* fārikpoṇ ghe, *G. N.*

Revenge, *s.* fārikpoṇ, -ṇā, *n.*

Revenue, *s.* 1. huṭṭavoḷ (*var.* huṭuăḷ), -ḷi, *f.*; ādāi, -yā, *m.*
2. beroz, -zā, *m.*; văsuli, -le, *f.*

Reverberate, *v.* pāṭi mār, *or* pāṭi poḍăi, *e.g.* voice; pāṭi uḍ; āvāz, *e.g.* this church reverberates the voice = yi igărz āvāztā; *bet. rs.* prătitāḷo zātā.

Reverberation, *s.* pāṭi uḍāp, -ḍpā, *n.*, *or rs. into v.*; prătitāḷo, -ḷeā, *m.*

Reverence, *v.* mān dākăi, *or* m. kăr, *or* m. di; nămăskār kăr = r. by prostration, *but by the Hindu-Konkans it is used for* r. *in general;* bāgā = *l.* bend oneself.

Reverence, *s.* mān, -nā, *m.*; nămăskār, -rā, *m.*; šărăṇ, -ṇā, *n.*, *n. c.*
Your r. = tumiñ sāibāno, *or* pādri sāib.

Reverend, *a.* mān (*or* nămăskār) fāvozăllo; *vlg. rs.* sāib.

Reverie, *s.* sopāṇ, -pṇā, *n.* = *l.* dream, *fg.*; bhrăm, -mā, *n.* = illusion; girigiri = fancy.

Reverse, *v.* 1. porti, *or* portun dovór.
2. bădăl = *l.* change.
3. răddụ kăr = *l.* make nullity.

Reverse, *s.* 1. bădlāp, -pā, *n.* = *l.* change.
2. portouṇeñ, -ṇeā, *n.* = *l.* turning.
3. păḍāu, -ḍāvā, *m.* = *l.* defeat.
4. pāṭ, -ṭi, *f.* = *l.* back.

Review, *v.* 1. pòḷe = *l.* look.
2. portun tănki kăr = *l.* again make inquiry; *see* **Criticize.**

Review, *s.* (porti) tănki, -ke, *f.*

Revile, *v.* gāḷi săng, *or* g. sou = *l.* say abuse; vāiṭ ulăi = *l.* speak ill; širāp ghāl = *l.* put cursing.

Reviler, *s.* gāḷi soutolo.

N. B. Words compounded with **Re-**, *not put down here, are formed by prefixing* **pāṭi** *or* **portun** *to the simple word compounded with* **Re-**.

Reviling, *s.* gāḷ, -ḷi, *f.*; širāp, -pā, *m.* = *l.* malediction.

Revise, *v.* portun pòḷe; săma kăr *or* suddu̥ kăr = correct.

Reviser, *s.* tănkegār, -rā, *m.*

Revision, *s.* (porti) tănki, -ke, *f.*

Revive, *v.* 1. portun jiye = *l.* live again.
2. *fg.* dhăir di = *l.* give courage; portun suru zā = *l.* again begin.

Revocation, *s.* răddu̥, -dā, *n.* = *l.* nullity; *rs. into v.*

Revoke, *v.* răddu̥ kăr = *l.* make nullity; pāṭi kāḍ = *l.* take back, *e.g.* a promise, contumely.

Revolt, *v.* kāṭkāi kăr = *l.* make revolution; kuṭ kăr = *l.* make plots.

Revolt, *s.* kāṭkāi, -ye, *f.*; kuṭ, -ṭā, *n.*; utsāmboḷāi, -ye, *f.* = *l.* excitement.

Revolution, *s.* 1. bou̥nḍi, -ḍe, *f.* = *l.* a going round.
2. bădlāp, -pā, *n.* = *l.* change; *see* **Revolt.**

Revolutionary, *s.* kāṭkāyegār, -rā, *m.*; *or* kuṭagār, -rā, *m.*

Revolve, *v.* 1. bouñ = *l.* go round, *n. c.*; *or* bountāṇiñ vetā.
2. bounḍăi, *c. v.* = cause to go round; porti = *l.* turn, *c. v.* *of* porta.
3. čint = *l.* think; *or* niyāḷ = meditate.

Reward, *s.* ināṁ, -mā, *m.*; kūl, -li, *f.* = *l.* wages.

Reward, *v.* ināṁ di; *pass.* in. mèḷ.

Rhapsody, *s.* krămaviṇ utrañ; răgḷea-utrañ, *pl. n.*; borsillo slók, -kā, *m.*

Rhetoric, *s.* unči bhās, -se, *f.* = *l.* nice language, eloquence; ălănkārāči sāmārthi, -the, *f.*; *see* **Oratory.**

Rheum, Rheumatism, *s.* vāt, -tā, *m.*

Rhyme, *s.* sămapòḍneñ, -neā, *n.*

Rhythm, *s.* māp, -pā, *n.* = *l.* measure.

Rib, *s.* bór, -ri, *f.* = *Lat. costa.*

Ribald, *s.* lutstso, -čeā, *m.*

Ribald, *a.* khoṭo.

Ribaldry, *s.* khoṭepoṇ, -ṇā, *n.*

Ribband, *s.* fint, -tā, *n.*, *fr.*; *approx.* sutli, -le, *f.* = *It. nastro;* nāḍo, -ḍeā, *m.*, *e.g.* of shoes.

Rice, *s.* 1. bhāt, -tā, *f.* = *l.* paddy.
2. tānduḷ (*var.* tāndu, *in the nom. only*), -dḷā, *m.* = raw rice: *Some kinds of rice are,* *a*) jirsāḷ (fine rice); *b*) surăi; *c*) ukḍo; *d*) măskăti; *e*) kozo; *f*) suggi.
3. sit, -tā, *n.* = cooked rice.

Rice-water, *s.* nis, -sā, *m.* (conjee-w.)

Rice-milk, *s.* khir, -ri, *f.* (a sweetmeat of jaggery and rice).

Rice-gruel, *s.* pèz, -je, *f.*

Fried r. = čirmuli, -le, *f.*

Rich, *a.* 1. grest, *or* grestātso; duḍuātso; dhănvănt; āst āsullo, *or* āstin bhorlolo.
 2. *fg.* bhórn = *l.* full.
 3. dobājeātso = *l.* splendid, pompous.
 4. iṭāḷ *or* iṭātso = *l.* fertile, fat; fòḷ diuntso = *l.* fruitful.

Riches, *s.* 1. grestkāi, -ye, *f.*; ănkul, -lā, *n.*; duḍu, -ḍvā, *m.* = *l.* money; dirveñ, -veā, *n.* = much money (treasure); āst, -ti, *f.* = *l.* property; sămpăt, -tā, *n.*
 2. *fg.* sămpurṇāi, -ye, *f.* = *l.* fulness.

Richness, *s.* 1. sămpurṇāi, -ye, *f.*
 2. dobāzo, -jeā, *m.* = *l.* pomp.

Rick, *s.* rās, -si, *f.* = *l.* a heap.

Rickets, *s.* morlukeči piḍa, -ḍe, *f.*

Rid (get r. of), *v.* tsukon ghe; păriyār zā, *e.g.* yeā kāmāntlo p. zālo; pois kăr = *l.* make far.

Riddle, *s.* 1. umeṇi, -ṇe, *f.*; guṭ, -ṭā, *m.* = *l.* a secret; guḍ, -ḍā, *n.*
 2. tsāḷni, -ne, *f.* (*approx.*) = a sieve; gāḷni, -ne, *f.*

Riddle, *v.* 1. guṭān ulăi = *l.* speak with r.
 2. umeṇi pārki = *l.* guess a r.
 3. papsi = *l.* pierce (full of holes).

Ride, *v.* goḍeār bòs.

Rider, *s.* 1. săvārigār, -rā, *m.*; goḍeār bòstolo.
 2. tsăḍāvot kălăm = *l.* additional clause.

Ridge, *s.* pāṭ, -ṭi, *f.* = *l.* back; pāṭos, -sā, *m.*, of a roof.

Ridicule, *s.* hāsči văstu, -tu, *f.* = *l.* a ridiculous thing; tārifeči văstu; năkăl, -klā, *n.* = *l.* a copy, *fg.*

Ridicule, *v.* năklañ kăr = *l.* make copies, *fg.*; hās (*Acc.*) = *l.* laugh at; čeṣṭāio kăr = *l.* make fun, *G. F.*; tomāse kăr = *l.* make fun; yeḍāi = *l.* mock; kheḷkuḷañ kăr.

Ridiculous, *a.* hāstso (hāsso); tārifetso.

Rifle, *see* **Plunder.**

Rift, *s.* fuṭ, -ṭi, *f.* = *l.* a chink.

Rig, *v.* tăyār kăr = *l.* make ready, (a ship).

Right, *a.* 1. săma; rāsti (r. measure).
 2. nītivont = *l.* just.
 3. sārko = *l.* exact.
 4. uzvo, *e.g.* r. hand.
 5. nīṭ = *l.* straight.
 6. bhou = very, (R. Reverend).

Right, *s.* 1. hăkkụ, -kā, *n.* = *Lat. jus.*
 2. nīt, -ti, *f.* = *l.* justice; nāi, -yā, *m.* = *l.* justice.

Right, *v.* săma ghāl, *or* mānḍ.

Righteous, *a.* nītivont.

Righteousness, *s.* nīt, -ti, *f.*

Rigid, *a.* 1. kăḍḍụ, (kărdụ), *e.g.* r. officer; kăṭiṇ.
 2. niṣṭur = *l.* cruel.

Rigidity, *s.* 1. kăṭiṇāi, -ye, *f.*; kărdāi, -ye, *f.*
2. niṣṭurāi, -ye, *f.*

Rigmarole, *s.* guḍ, -ḍā, *n.* (*Lat. ambages*).

Rigour, Rigorous, *see* **Rigid.**

Rim, *s.* dèg, -ge, *f.*

Rime, *s.* dou, dovā, *m.*

Rind, *s.* sāl, -li, *f.*

Ring, *s.* mudi, -ye, *f.*
Exchange the r. = mudi ghāl; săirik zātā = *l.* relation becomes: *this 2nd expresses rather the effect of* exchanging the r.

Ring, *v.* mār (bells).

Ring-finger, *s.* mudiyečeñ bòṭ, -ṭā, *n.*

Ring-leader, *see* **Leader.**

Ringlet, *see* **Dress.**

Ringworm, *s.* dād, -di, *f.*

Rinse, *v.* du = *l.* wash.

Riot, *s.* 1. kuṭ, -ṭā, *n.* = *l.* a plot.
2. vāiṭ jiṇi, -ye, *f.* = *l.* a bad life; miruoṇeñ, -ṇeā, *n.* = *l.* excess; khāugipoṇ, -ṇā, *n.* = *l.* excess in eating; ăkrăm, -mā, *n.* (*var.* kărm) = *l.* disorder.
3. luṭ, -ṭi, *f.* = *l.* prey, plunder.

Riotous, *a.* 1. kuṭagār.
2. khāugi.
3. vāiṭ jiṇiyetso.

Ripe, *a.* piko.
Almost r. = amborpiko.

Ripen, *v.* pikăi, *c. v. of* pik, *n. v.*

Ripeness, *s.* pikāp, -kpā, *n.*

Rise, *v.* 1. unts vetā = *l.* goes aloft; tsăḍ = *l.* ascend, *e.g.* a barometer rises.
2. uṭ = *l.* get up; ubār.
3. ude, *e.g.* the sun rises.
4. jivont zā = *l.* become in life (from death).
5. *fg.* vrăddhi zā = *l.* get prosperous.
6. zā *or* ubzā = *l.* become, proceed, happen.
7. mèḷ = be found, *e.g.* an opportunity.
8. suru zātā, *G. F.*, *or* yetā = *l.* beginning is done *or* comes, *e.g.* a wind rises.
9. tsăḍ zā = *l.* become more, *e.g.* anger, wind.
10. kāṭkāi kăr = *l.* make revolution.
11. băḍti zātā = *l.* promotion becomes.
12. pāu = *l.* reach, arrive.
13. miruăi = *l.* surpass (r. above).
14. distā = *l.* appears.

Rise, *s.* 1. *rs. v.*
2. tsăḍāp, -ḍpā, *n.*
Give r. to = ărămb di, *or* kāraṇ di, *or by c. v.*

Rising, *s.* 1. *rs. v.*
2. kāṭkāi, -ye, *f.* = *l.* revolution.

Risk, *s.* risk, -ke, *f.*, *fr.*; mōs(ó) -sā, *m.* = *l.* deceit (*used esp. for* moral r.); zăkăm, -kme, *f.* = wound, *yet used for any* bodily r.
Run a r. = riskent pòḍ.

Risk, *v.* riskent (risker) ghāl.

Rite, *s. vlg.* sermoni, -ne, *f.*, *fr.*; (igărje-) rīt, -ti, *f.* (*not fr.*) = *l.* manners (of the church); kăṭleñ, -leā, *n.* (*H. K.*) (igărje-) păddăt, -ti, *f.* = *l.* formula (of the church).

Ritual, *s.* ritičeñ pustak, -kā, *n.*

Rival, *v.* 1. petsāḍ = *l.* try, make effort (in competition with); uḍḍa (*ex. w.*)

2. mosór kăr, *G. M.* = *l.* make hatred, *ch. cs.*

Rival, *s.* 1. petsāḍtolo *or* petsāḍi, -ḍiā, *m.*, *or* uḍḍatolo.

2. mosri, -riā, *m.*

Rive, *v.* fóṭăi.

River, *s.* năiñ", -iñ, *f.*

River-bed, *s.* năiñtăḷ, -ḷā, *n.*

Rivet, *s.* khiḷo, -ḷeā, *m.*

Rivulet, *s.* dākṭi năiñ", *f.*; tōḍ(ò), -ḍā, *m.*

Road, *s.* māróg, -rgā, *m.*; vāṭ, -ṭe, *f.*; răsto, -teā, *m.* (*Cn. Mr. also*).

On the r. = mārgār *or* poiṇ kărtana, *or* vetana.

Bad r. = khărkoṭo mārog.

Easy r. = iskăḷ m.

Make a r. = m. kātăr.

Out of the r. = vāṭe bhāir, *but comm. a crc. is used.*

Roam, *v.* bouñ (pārpoḷ zāun b. = lead a roaming wandering life.

Roaming, *a.* pārpoḷ.

Roan, *a.* činčerongātso = *l.* of the colour of tamarind; tāmbḍoso = reddish.

Roar, *v.* goróz mār, *or* gărza, *as* a lion, tiger, *etc.*; gouji kăr, *or* bòb mār.

Roar, *s.* goróz, -zi, *f.*

Roast, *v.* 1. bāz.

2. *fg.* ẓăḷăi = *l.* cause to burn (for anger).

Rob, *v.* 1. luṭ; tsōr(ó) = *l.* steal (zulmen ts.).

2. *fg.* kāḍ; tsukăi = deprive; *see* **Plunder.**

Robber, *s.* luṭkār, -rā, *m.*; zulmegār, -rā, *m.* = *l.* a maker of violence; tsōr(ó), -rā, *m.*

Robbery, *s.* luṭ, -ṭi, *f.*; tsóri, -ye, *f.*; nāgoṇ, -ṇi, *f.*

Robe, *s.* lugaṭ, -gṭā, *n.* = *l.* cloth.

Robust, *a.* ghăṭ = *l.* strong; dānḍgo; puşṭi = *l.* stout, fat, fleshy; boḷadik, *or* bòḷ āsullo, *or* boḷişṭ; dinḍo.

Robustness, *s.* ghăṭăi, -ye, *f.*; dānḍgepoṇ, -ṇā, *n.*; *rs.* puşṭi = *l.* stout; bòḷ, -ḷā, *n.*

Rock, *s.* khăḍāp, -ḍpā, *n.*; pāz, -je, *f.*

Rock, *v.* hālăi, zómp kāḍ, dălăi, pāḷneñ hālăi = lull a child to sleep.

Rocket, *s.* hikmătitso uzo, -jeā, *m.* = *l.* fire of artifice; ākāsbāṇ, -ṇā, *n.*

Rocky, *a.* fātrāntso; khăḍpāntso; khăḍpañ āsullo.

Rod, *s.* boḍi, -ye, *f.*; bèt, -tā, *n.*; dānḍo, -ḍeā, *m.*

Rodomontade, *s.* khāli băḍăi, -ye, *f.*

Rodomontade, *v.* khāli bădḍāi ulăi; *see* **Bombastic.**

Roe, *s.* bāileñ čitāḷ, -tḷā, *n.*

Rogation, *s.* grāṇeñ, -ṇeā, *n.*

Rogue, *a.* vāiṭ.

Rogue, *s.* lutstso, -čeā, *m.*; ṭhăk-kagār, -rā, *m.*; lăbāḍi, -ḍiā, *m.*

Roguery, *s.* luččepoṇ, -ṇā, *n.*

Roll, *v.* 1. lòḷ, *n. v.*; lolăi, *c. v.*, *e.g.* on the ground.

2. kovóḷ, *e.g.* paper.

Roll, *s.* kouḷo, -ḷeā, *m.*, *e.g.* a r. of paper; lōr, -rā, *m.*

Roller, *s.* păṭṭi, -ṭe, *f.*

Rolling-pin, *s.* lāṭo, -ṭeā, *m.*

Roman, *a.* romātso.

Romance, *s.* kāṇi, -ye, *f.*; kăl-paneči kătha, -the, *f.* = *l.* a fantastic story.

Romantic, *a.* kălpanetso; čămăt-kārātso = *l.* curious.

Romp, *v.* 1. uḍ = *l.* jump.

2. ăumăryādin khèḷ = *l.* play immodestly, rudely.

Romp, *s.* 1. uḍāp, -ḍpā, *n.* = *l.* jump.

2. ăumăryāditso khéḷ, -ḷā, *m.* = rude immodest play.

Rood, *s.* 1. kāldo ekro, -reā, *m.* = the fourth part of an acre.

2. kris (kuris, -rsā), -sā, *m.* = *l.* a cross.

Roof, *s.* pākeñ, -keā, *n.*

Roof, *v.* pākeñ ghāl.

Rook, *s.* *approx.* kāuḷo, -ḷeā, *m.*

Room, *s.* 1. kuḍ, -ḍā, *n.* (r. of a house).

2. zāgo, -geā, *m.* = *l.* a place, ground, space.

3. suāt, -te, *f.*, *l.*, *e.g.* in the r. of N. = N. suāter; bădlāk = instead of.

No r. for mercy = kākuḷt kăr-tso vēḷ(é) nāñ.

Roomy, *a.* vistārlolo = *l.* extended; iskăḷ.

Roost, *s.* kól, -lā, *m.* = *Lat. pertica*; tenkḍi, -ḍe, *f.*

Root, *s.* pāḷ, -ḷā, *n.*; mūḷ, -ḷā, *n.*, *pr. fg.*

Root, *v.* pāḷañ fuṭ.

R. out = humboḷ; umṭi.

Rooted, *fg.* = lāgụllo = *l.* attached, *e.g.* motik l. = r. in the mind; r. to the earth = dăr-nik lāgụllo.

Become rooted = ghăṭ zā.

Rope, *s.* dori, -ye, *f.*; sumb, -bā, *n.* = a r. of cocoanut fibre; yenṭo, -ṭeā, *m.* = a r. of straw; rāzu, -zvā, *m.* = a thick r.; ālāt, -tā, *m.* = a still thicker r.

Ropy, *a.* lāgtso = *l.* attaching; pānkātso = *l.* glutinous.

Rosary, *s.* 1. kònt, -tā, *n.* (*esp.* the material r.).

2. térs, -sā, *m.* = r. prayer of five decades.

3. rozāi, -ye, *f.* = r. prayer of 15 decades.

Rose, *s.* 1. gulób, -bā, *m.*

2. gònḍo, -ḍeā, *m.* (yellow r.?)

3. butāuñgònḍo, -ḍeā, *m.* (*not ex.* r. *but* a red flower similar to a r.

Rostrum, *s.* 1. bónts, -či, *f.* (of birds).
2. tārvajīb, -be, *f.* (of a ship).
Rosy, *a.* gulobirongātso.
Rot, *v.* kusăi, *c. v. of* kus, *n. v.*; pāḍ kăr, *tr. v.*; p. zā, *n. v.*
Rot, *s.* kusāp, -spā, *n.*
Rotate, *v.* bouñ *or* bountăṇiñ vots.
Rotation, *s.* bounḍi, -ḍe, *f.*
Rote, *s.* (learn by r.) bāipāṭ kăr.
Rotten, *a.* kusullo; *vlg.* pāḍ.
Rottenness, *see* **Rot.**
Rotundity, *s.* vāḍkuḷepoṇ, -ṇā, *n.*
Rough, *a.* 1. dăḍḍo, *e.g.* cloth.
2. moṭo = *l.* not fine, *e.g.* flour.
3. khărkăṭo, *e.g.* road, table, (not even).
4. kăṭin = *l.* severe, *e.g.* weather.
5. kărăḍo, *e.g.* paper.
6. tsāltsămkăṇ nātullo = *l.* unpolite.
7. utsāmboḷ = *l.* excited, *e.g.* r. sea.
Rough-draught, *s.* kărăḍi năkṣa, -ṣe, *f.*; *see* **Sketch, Outline.**
Roughness, *s.* 1. dăḍḍepoṇ, -ṇā, *n.*
2. moṭāi, -ye, *f.*
3. khărkăṭepoṇ, -ṇā, *n.*
4. kăṭināi, -ye, *f.*
5. kărăḍepoṇ, -ṇā, *n.*
6. nāñtsāltsămkăṇ, -ṇā, *n.*
7. utsāmboḷāi, -ye, *f.*
For the precise meaning of all these words, see the corresponding adjectives.

Round, *v.* 1. vāḍkuḷo (*var.* āḍkuḷo) kăr.
2. *fg.* sămpurṇ kăr = *l.* make perfect.
Round, *a.* 1. vāḍkuḷo.
2. *by the emph.* -ts; *see* Gram.; purto = *l.* full.
Round, *ad.* bountăṇiñ.
Go r. = bouñ.
Round, *s.* 1. suttu, -tā, *m.* = *l.* a circle; *or* măndăḷ, -ḷā, *n.*
2. bounḍi, -ḍe, *f.* = *l.* rotation.
3. pāunḍo, -ḍeā, *m.* = r. of a ladder.
After a long r. of years = săbār vărsañ zāleā uprānt.
Roundabout, *a. rs.* teṇeñ yeṇeñ, *or* bountăṇiñ.
Roundness, *s.* vāḍkuḷepoṇ, -ṇā, *n.*
Rout, *v.* dāunḍāi = *l.* cause to run, *c. v. of* dāuñ; păḍāu kăr = *l.* make defeat; soluoi.
Rout, *s.* gouji, -je, *f.* = *l.* noise; gusăp, -spā, *n.* = *l.* confusion; čăḷḷeñ biḷḷeñ = *l.* a crowd.
Route, *s.* mārog, -rgā, *m.*; dikkụ, -kā, *n.* = *l.* direction.
Routine, *s.* sovoi, -ye, *f.*, *or* rivāz, -ji, *f.*
Rove, *see* **Wander.**
Row, *s.* hār, -ri, *f.* = *l.* a line, *Lat. series:* 'hārin tsălā = go in a line'; kāmp, -pā, *m.*; *see also* **Mess.**
Row, *s.* zăgḍeñ, -ḍeā, *n.*; lăḍāi, -ye, *f.*
Row, *v.* volo kāḍ *or* v. mār.

Royal, *a.* 1. rāyātso = *l.* of the king.
2. *rs.* rāyabārī = as of a king; voḍpoṇātso = *l.* great.
Royalty, *see* **Reign.**
Rub, *v.* 1. gās.
2. rāgăḍ, *e.g.* r. oil on the body.
R. out = gāsun kāḍ.
Rubber, *see* **Whetstone.**
Indian r. = răbbăr, -rā, *n. fr.*
Rubbing, *s.* gāsāp, -spā, *n.*
Rubbish, *s.* kăčro, -reā, *m.*; năkāri sāmān, -nā, *m.* = useless articles.
Rubric, *s.* 1. tāmbḍi māti, -ye, *f.* = *l.* red earth; tāmbḍiñ ākṣerañ, *pl. n.* = *l.* red letters.
2. (sermoni-) kāide = *l.* rules (of ceremonies); (šāstrāčeañ kāmañ-) kāide.
Ruby, *a.* tāmbḍoso *or* tāmbso.
Ruby, *s.* māṇik, -ṇkā, *n.*; kèmp, -pā, *n.*
Ruck, *see* **Fold.**
Rudder, *s.* sukhāṇeñ, -ṇeā, *n.*
Ruddy, *a.* tāmbḍots.
Rude, *see* **Rough.**
Rudiment, *s.* poileo sikoṇeo = *l.* first instructions; survečeo s. = *l.* initial in.; ādipāṭ, -ṭā, *m.*; ărămb, -bā, *m.*, *or* suru, -ve, *f.* = *l.* a beginning.
Ruffian, *s.* luṭkār, -rā, *m.*; lutstso, -čeā, *m.*; *see* **Murderer.**
Ruffle, *see* **Plait, Fold.**
Rug, *s.* kāmboḷ, -bḷi, *f.*
Rugged, *a.* 1. khărkăṭo; *see* **Rough.**
2. kărkărātso = *l.* troublesome.
Ruin, *s.* 1. vibāḍ, -ḍā, *m.*; bosm, -mā, *m.*; nāš, -šā, *m.*
2. kusāp, -spā, *n.* = *l.* corruption.
3. kuḍke, *or bet. rs. into v.* (3.)
Ruin, *v.* 1. vibāḍ (*or* nāš) kăr; bosmi, *c. v. of* bosma.
2. bòl kăr = *l.* make violence (r. morally).
3. pāḍ pòḍ = *l.* fall spoiled, *e.g.* a house, *n. v.*
Ruinous, *a.* 1. luksānātso = *l.* hurtful.
2. pòḍtso = *l.* falling, *e.g.* a house; bosmāk bāgontso = *l.* inclining to ruin.
Rule, *s.* 1. *vlg.* règruṇ, -re, *f.*, *fr.*; nēm(é), -mā, *n.*; kāido, -deā, *m.*, *e.g.* r. of christian life.
2. tsālouṇeñ, -ṇeā, *n.* = *l.* government.
3. kòl, -lā, *m.* = an instrument for drawing lines, *etc.*
Rule, *v.* 1. tsālāi = govern, *c. v. of* tsāl.
2. rāzvoṭkāi kăr = reign, *obj. 2nd Loc.*
3. tsāl, *n. v.*, *e.g.* a custom.
Ruler, *s.* 1. kòl, -lā, *m.*
2. ădhikāri, -ri, *m.*, *or* tsālāitolo = *l.* governing.
Rumble, *s.* gouji, -je, *f.*
Rumble, *v.* gouji kăr, *or* bòb mār.
Ruminate, *v.* 1. rovond (*or* ruvonts) kāḍ.
2. portun portun čint = think again again.

Rummage, *v.* sód = *l.* seek.
Rumple, *see* **Plait.**
Rumour, *s.* phukāro, -reā, *m.*; kobār, -bre, *f.* = *l.* news.
Run, *v.* 1. dāuñ, *c. v.* dāundāi.
2. vāu = *l.* flow, *c. v.* vāvoi.
3. pòḷ = *l.* flee.
4. vetā = *l.* goes, *e. g.* a way runs to.
R. after = pāṭleān vots.
R. about = bouñ.
R. foul of = ādāḷ.
R. high = tsāḍ = *l.* ascend.
R. into destruction = bosmāk tsāl.
R. out = 1. bhāir pòḍ = *l.* fall out.
2. zā (come to an end); mugda.
R. together = mèḷ = *l.* be found *or* joined.
R. against = āngār pòḍ (attack).
Run, *s.* dāuñ, dāve, *f.*
Runaway, *a.* poḷullo.
Rundlet, *s.* lān pīp, -pā, *n.* = *l.* a small pipe.
Runlet, *see* **Rivulet.**
Rupee, *s.* rupoi, -piyā, *m.*
Rupture, *s.* 1. moḍāp, -ḍpā, *n.*; vingḍāp, -pā, *n.* = *l.* separation.
2. *fg.* nāi, -yā, *m.* = *l.* discord.
Rural, *a.* nāḍātso.
Ruse, *s.* nāḍ, -ḍi, *f.* = *l.* a trick; nāḍgepoṇ, -ṇā, *n.* = *l.* cunningness.
Rush, *v.* 1. *perh.* sākleān pòḍ, *or* s. boḷān pòḍ; dāḍadāḍu dāuñ.
2. buḍ = *l.* be plunged.
3. rig = *l.* enter.
R. into mischief = tānṭe kār; gunyāvānt pòḍ; tsukon pòḍ.
Rush, *s.* boḷiṣṭ dāuñ, dāve, *f.*
Rust, *s.* māti, -ye, *f.* = *l.* earth, *fg.*
Rust, *v.* māti mānḍ; lonkḍe.
Rustic, *s.* nāḍkār, -rā, *m.*, *pr. fg.*; bondro, -reā, *m.*
Rusticate, *v.* nāḍānt soukāsāi bhóg.
Rusticity, *s.* nāñtsāltsāmkāṇ, -ṇā, *n.*
Rusty, *a.* māti lāgullo; *see* **Rough.**
Rye, *s.* lān gouñ, -ovā, *m.*
Ryot, *s.* rāit, -tā, *m.*

S

Sabbath, *s.* sabat, -tā, *m.*
Sabre, *s.* tălvār, -ri, *f.*
Sacerdotal, *a.* saserdotitso, *fr.*; gurutso.
Sack, *s.* 1. goṇi, -ye, *f.*; poti, -ye, *f.* (bag); poteñ, -teā, *n.* = *l.* a bag of leather.
2. desvaṭ, -ṭe, *f.*; *see* **Plunder.**
Sack, *v.* 1. goṇiyent ghāl, *or* g. bhór.
2. desvaṭ kăr; *see* **Plunder.**
Sack-cloth, *s.* dăḍḍeñ lugāṭ, -gṭā, *n.* = *l.* coarse cloth; prājitāčeñ văstūr, -rā, *n.* = *l.* a penitential dress; kāmbóḷ, -bḷi, *f.* = a rough blanket.
Sacrament, *s.* sakrament, -tā, *m.*
Sacred, *a.* 1. păvitrụ, *or* păvitrụ kello = *l.* made sacred.
2. *vlg.* benjār, *or* benjār kello; konsekrār kello = *l.* consecrated.
Sacrifice, *s.* 1. sakrifis, -sā, *m.*, *fr.*; bheṭouṇeñ, -ṇeā, *n.*, *or* bhèṭ, -ṭe, *f.* = *l.* an offering.
2. *fg.* dăgdụ, *pl. m.* = sufferings.
3. sóḍni, -ne, *f.* = *l.* renunciation; *bet. rs. into* sóḍ.
Sacrifice, *v.* 1. bheṭăi = *l.* offer; sămărpi; vopsi.
2. prāṇ di = *l.* give life.
3. vopsun di = *l.* give up; sóḍ, *e.g.* give up enmities.
Sacrilege, *s.* păvitrānčeñ bhăṣṭpoṇ, -ṇā, *n.*; păvitrānči tsóri, -ye, *f.*, *n. u.*; sakrilej, -jā, *m.*, *fr.*
Sacrilegious, *a.* păvitrụ (văstu) bhăṣṭountso; fóṭkiro = *l.* deceitful, *e. g.* s. confession; *or* pāḍ.
Sacristan, *s.* miroṇ, -rṇi, *m.*, *fr.*; *perh.* igărjerākṇo, -ṇeā, *m.* = *l.* the guardian of a church.
Sacristy, *s. vlg.* sankrist, -ti, *f.* (*or* sankest); *perh.* igărjekuḍ, -ḍā, *n.* = *l.* a room of the church.
Sad, *a.* khăntiṣṭ = sorry; dukest; dukountso = *l.* afflicting; kăṣṭāntso = *l.* painful; čintest = *l.* thinking, *but fg.*
Sadden, *v.* dukăi, *c. v. of* duk, *n. v.*; kăṣṭăi = *l.* cause pain, *c. v. of* kăṣṭa, *n. v.*
Saddle, *s.* jīn, -nā, *n.*
Saddle, *v.* jīn ghāl.
Sadness, *s.* khănt, -ti, *f.*; ākānt, -tā, *m.* = *l.* distress; duk, -ki, *f.* = *l.* sorrow; āpad, -dā, *n.* = *l.* calamity.
Safe, *s.* 1. ghăṭ pèṭ, -ṭe, *f.* = *l.* a strongbox; *or* băndobăstiči p.
2. băndobăstiči suāt, -te, *f.* = *l.* a place of security.
Safe, *a.* 1. risknātullo = *l.* without danger; băndobăstitso = *l.* of security; ghăṭ = *l.*

strong; *or* thir; băčāvetso; năṣṭaviṇ = *l.* without harm; sălămătitso.

2. pātiyeṇitso = *l.* trusty.

Safe-conduct, *s.* zāmin, -ne, *f.* = *l.* security.

Safe-guard, *s.* upāi, -yā, *m.* = *l.* means; sāmbāḷouṇeñ, -ṇeā, *n.*; rākṇeñ, -ṇeā, *n.* = *l.* a guarding.

Safety, *s.* băčāvi, -ve, *f.*; nāñrisk, -ke, *f.*

Saffron, *s.* hăḷăd, -ḷdi, *f.*

Sagacious, *a.* tsurk = *l.* active; budivont = *l.* wise; bārik = *l.* thin, *fg.*; nāḍgo = *l.* cunning.

Sagacity, *s.* bud, -di, *f.*; nāḍgepoṇ, -ṇā, *n.*; bārikāi, -ye, *f.*; ušārāi, -ye, *f.*; *l.* tsurkpoṇ, -ṇā, *n.*; *see adj.*

Sago, *s.* sāgu, -gā, *m.*

Sail, *s.* sīḍụ, -ḍā, *n.* (of a ship); parand, -dā, *n.*

Sail, *v.* 1. ankār; siḍañ sóḍ.

2. tārvapoiṇ kăr.

Sailer, *s.* tāruñ, -rvā, *n.*; năg, -gā, [*m.*

Sailor, *s.* kălāsi, -siā, *m.*; năgagār, -rā, *m.*

Saint, *s.* sānt, -tā, *m.* *fr.*

Saintly, *a.* bhāgevont.

Sake, *s.* (for the sake of) pāsun *or.* pāsvot = *Lat. propter*, nimtiñ; khātir; mogān = out of love for.

Salad, *s.* salād, -di, *f.*, *fr.*; kărāmb, -bi, *f.* = a kind of s.

Salaam, *s.* sălām, -mā, *m.*

Salary, *s.* sāmbāḷ, -ḷā, *m.*; pāg, -gā, *m.*; kūl, -li, *f.* = *l.* wages; saskār, -rā, *n.*

Sale, *s.* 1. ikāp, -kpā, *n.*, *or* vikāp, -kpā, *n.*

2. lăilāuñ, -lāvā, *n.* = *l.* an auction.

Salient, *a.* *fg.* mukhya.

Saline, *a.* khār.

Saliva, *s.* timpi, -ye, *f.* (*var.* simpi).

Sallow, *a.* hăḷduvo.

Salmon, *s.* seuṭo, -ṭeā, *m.*

Salt, *s.* 1. mīṭ, -ṭā, *n.*

2. *fg.* bārikāi, -ye, *f.* = wit.

Salt, *v.* miṭāk ghāl.

Saltish, *a.* khārso.

Salt-mine, *s.* miṭākhăṇi, -ye, *f.*

Salt-pit, *s.* kòḷ, -ḷā, *n.*; āgor, -rā, *m.*

Saltpetre, *s.* pòṭlemīṭ, -ṭā, *n.*

Salubrious, *a.* 1. bolāiketso.

2. *fg.* ādāyātso = *l.* advantageous.

Salutary, *a.* upkārāk pòḍtso = beneficial; *see* **Salubrious.**

Salutation, *s.* sălām, -mā, *m.*; nămăskār -rā, *m.* (*H. K.*); mān, -nā, *m.*

Salute, *v.* sălām kăr, *or* s. di; rekat kăr, *or* r. di = give compliments; nămăskār kăr, *or* mān kăr, *e. g.* a person of distinction; *vlg.* besāuñ māg = *l.* ask blessing (for an inferior), *fr.*; besāuñ di = *l.* give blessing (for a superior), *fr.*; itsār, *e. g.* salute for me N. = N. itsārlāñ móṇ sāng.

Salvation, *s.* sóḍvoṇ, -ṇi, *f.*; băčāvi, -ve, *f.*; sălvasāuñ, -sāvā, *n.*, *fr.*; udargăti, -ti, *f.*

Salve, *s.* mulām, -mā, *n.*; părmăḷāčeñ vokāt, -ktā, *n.*

Same, *a.* tots; *see* Gram. p. II. ch. iii.

Sample, *s.* nămuno, -neā, *m.*

Sanctification, *s.* 1. bhāgevontpoṇ, -ṇā, *n.*

2. *for the act*, *rs. into v.*

Sanctify, *v.* 1. bhāgevont kăr = *l.* make holy.

2. păvitrụ kăr = make sacred, consecrate; *vlg.* benjār kăr.

Sanction, *s.* metsvoṇeñ, -ṇeā, *n.*; păsănd, -dā, *n.*, *n. c. as noun*; kobuli, -le, *f.* = *l.* consent; *or* voppigi, -ge, *f.*

Sanction, *v.* metsva, *Sb. Dat.*; păsănd kăr; kobuli di; *or rs.* kobul āsā = *l.* consent is, *ch. cs.*

Sanctity, *s.* sāntipoṇ, -ṇā, *n.*; bhāgevontpoṇ, -ṇā, *n.*

Sanctuary, *s.* păvitrụ zāgo, -geā, *m.* = *l.* a sacred place; kirtiči igărz, -je, *f.*

Sand, *s.* rèuñ, -eve, *f.*

Sand, *v.* rèuñ lāi; reven dāmp.

Sandal, *s.* vāṇ, -ṇe, *f.*; kāḍāu, -ḍāvā, *n.* (of wood).

Sandy, *a.* revāḷ.

Sane, *a.* 1. bolāikent āsullo, *or* bolāiketso.

2. mótir āsullo, săma mótitso = of s. mind.

Sanguinary, *a.* răgtātso = *l.* of blood, *e.g.* victory; niṣṭur = *l.* cruel.

Sanguine, *a.* 1. răgtāṇ bhorlolo, *or* răgtabărit.

2. umāḷeātso, *e.g.* s. hope = umāḷeāči āšā.

Sanity, *s.* săma mót, -ti, *f.* = *l.* right mind.

Sap, *s.* rōs(ó), -sā, *m.*; dik, -kā, *m.*; sār, -rā, *m.*

Sap, *v.* . . . khāl kónḍ = *l.* dig under.

Sapid, *a.* ručitso.

Sapient, *a.* budivont; vidyevont.

Sapless, *a.* 1. diknātullo.

2. *fg.* čappo.

Sapphire, *s.* nīl, -lā, *n.*

Sarcasm, *s.* khéḷkuḷañ, *pl. n.* (*not ex.*) = banter, raillery; khebḍāi, -ye, *f.* = biting mockery.

Sarcophagus, *s.* mornāči pēṭ(è), -ṭe, *f.*

Sardine, *s.* tārlo, -leā, *m.*

Sardonic, *a.* tònḍātso, *or* tònḍapurto, *e.g.* laugh; fóṭkiro = *l.* deceitful.

Sardonyx, *s.* gomedik, -kā, *n.*

Sash, *see* **Belt.**

Satan, *s.* săitān, -nā, *m.*; deuntsār, -rā, *m.*; bhut, -tā, *m.*

Satanic, *a.* săitānātso.

Sate, Satiate, *v.* dādós *or* -si kăr; bhór = *l.* fill.

Satellite, *s.* 1. upăgrăha, *astron.*, *Cn. Mr.* (*H. K.*)

2. pāro, -reā, *m.* = *l.* a guard; pedo, -deā, *m.*, sipāi, -yā, *m.* = a peon.

Satiety, *s.* dādoskāi, -ye, *f.*

Satin, *s.* satin răsim, -smā, *n.*

Satire, *s.* 1. năkăl, -klā, *n.* = *l.* copies, *fg.*; khebḍāi -ye, *f.* = *l.* mocking.
2. năklañ kărtso slók, -kā, *m.*

Satiric, *a.* năklañ kărtso; khebḍāyetso.

Satisfaction, *s.* 1. fārikpoṇ, -ṇā, *n.* = *l.* payment, *fg.*
2. prājit, (*var.* prāčit), -tā, *n.*, *e.g.* for sin; părihār, -rā, *n.*, *e.g.* for sin.
3. săntos, -sā, *m.* = *l.* joy; pleasure in; dādoskāi, -ye, *f.* = pleasure in.

Satisfactorily, *ad.* 1. dādoskāyen.
2. sumār = *l.* moderately.

Satisfactory, *a.* 1. dādos kărtso.
2. lāyek = *l.* fit; sumār = *l.* moderate; kāmāk pòḍtso = *l.* falling to use; purto = *l.* sufficient.

Saturate, *v.* bhór = *l.* fill.

Sauce, *s.* *vlg.* sòs, -sā, *n.*, *fr.*; *approx.* čeṭni, -ne, *f.*

Saucer, *s.* pīr, -ri, *f.*

Saucy, *a.* săḷiṣṭ.

Sausage, *s.* lingis, -sā, *n.* (*It.* *salsiccia*).

Savage, *a.* 1. rānvoṭ, *pr.fg.*
2. *fg.* monzāti băriso, *or only* monzātitso = bestial; bhou rāgiṣṭ = *l.* very angry; niṣṭur = *l.* cruel.
3. sikāpnātullo = *l.* ignorant; tsāltsāmkăṇ nātullo = *l.* unpolite.

Savageness, *s.* 1. rānvoṭpoṇ, -ṇā, *n.*
2. niṣṭurāi, -ye, *f.* = *l.* cruelty.

Save, *v.* 1. rāk = *l.* guard, keep; sāmbāḷ = *l.* defend; sāmbāḷn dovór, *e.g.* food for.
2. sóḍvoṇ kăr, *G. F.* = *l.* make delivery; băčău kăr, *e.g.* s. the soul; sālvār kăr, *fr.*

Save, *prep.* sivāi = *l.* except; *see* **Unless.**

Saving, *a.* *perh.* zāminetso = *l.* of security, *e.g.* s. clause.

Saving, *s.* 1. kăšiši, -še, *f.* = *l.* economy.
2. ādāi, -yā, *m.* = *l.* profit.

Savings-bank, *s.* *perh.* (duḍu) rākčeñ sāl, -lā, *n.*, *or* (duḍu) sāmbāḷn dovorčeñ sāl.

Saviour, *s.* Sóḍvoṇdār, -rā, *m.*, *rl.*; Tāròk, -kā, *m.*, *rl.*

Savour, *s.* suād, -dā, *m.*; ruts, -či, *f.*

Savour, *v.* ruts, *Sb. Dat.*: 'mākā yeñ rutstā'.
This savours of sedition = kāṭkāyeči ruts āsā.

Savoury, *a.* suādik; ručitso.

Saw, *s.* korvont, -tā, *m.*; gărgas, -sā, *m.*

Saw, *v.* čīr; phāḷ (*ex.* cut).

Saw-dust, *s.* puḍ, -ḍi, *f.*; *or* duḷ, -ḷi, *f.*

Saw-fish, *s.* isvoṇ, -ṇā, *m.*

Say, *v.* sāng; móṇ (*or* mhuṇ *or*

mhóṇ), *past* moḷo = *l.* recite, narrate, relate, say; utsăr = *l.* express.

I mean to say = moṇje, *or* moḷeăr.

Saying, *s.* 1. găd, -di, *f.*, *e.g.* sayings of Solomon; săngṇeñ, -ṇeă, *n.*

2. săr, -ri, *f.* = *l.* similitude.

Scab, *s.* khóróz, -rji, *f.*

Scabbard, *s.* poteñ, -teă, *n.*, of a sword.

Scabby, *a.* khórjitso, *or bet.* khorzuvăḷo.

Scaffold, *s.* făšeruk, -kă, *m.* = *l.* a tree of the rope (for hanging); făšekhămbo, -beă, *m.*

Scald, *s.* ujeătso fóḍ, -ḍă, *m.*

Scale, *s.* 1. tăgăḍ, -gḍă, *n.* = dish of a balance.

2. *in the pl.* tăgḍi, -ḍe, *f.*, tărăs, -si, *f.* = a balance.

3. *fg.* huddo, -deă, *m.* = *l.* rank, *e.g.* scale of society.

4. khăvăḷ, khăuḷă, *n.* = s. of a fish.

5. măp, -pă, *n.*, *or* mezăp, -zpă, *n.* = *l.* measure.

6. grău ăsulleñ ăid, -dă, *n.* = *l.* an instrument having degrees.

7. săptasvăra, -ră, *m.* (*Sans.*) = the gamut, *l.* seven notes; *or* găyanamănḍăvoḷ, -ḷi, *f.*

Scale, *v.* 1. khăuḷañ kăḍ = *l.* take away the scales (of fishes).

2. nisṇiniñ tsăḍ = *l.* climb on the ladders; tsăḍn kăṇghe = *l.* ascending take.

Scalene, *a.* săma nătullea giṭăntso = *l.* of not equal sides; višăm, *Cn. Mr.*

Scalp, *s.* măteăči kăt, -ti, *f.*

Scaly, *a.* khăuḷăntso, *or* khăuḷañ ăsullo.

Scamp, *s. see* **Rascal.**

Scamper, *v.* pòḷn vetă.

Scamper, *s.* pòḷăp, -ḷpă, *n.*

Scan, *v.* măpa părmăṇe văts = *l.* read according to quantity.

Scandal, *s.* 1. păḍ dēk(é), -ki, *f.* = *l.* bad example.

2. lăz, -je, *f.* = *l.* shame.

3. bădlăm, -me, *f.* = *l.* calumny.

Scandalise, *v.* 1. păḍ dēk(é) di: *in pass.* ninda bhóg, *or* păḍ d. ghe.

2. dhaḍăi = shock, *fg.*

Scandalous, *a.* păḍ dēk(é) diuntso, *or* păḍ dékitso; ăpamănătso; lăjišṭ = *l.* shameful.

Scanty, *a.* 1. moṭvo = *l.* short, *e.g.* a gown; lăn = *l.* small, *e.g.* s. number.

2. ăprup = *l.* rare.

3. ăšir = *l.* narrow, *fg.*

4. imṭo = *l.* stingy.

Scantiness, *s.* moṭvepoṇ, -ṇă, *n.*; imṭepoṇ, -ṇă, *n.*; uṇepoṇ, -ṇă, *n.*; *see* **Scanty.**

Scapegrace, *see* **Rascal.**

Scapular, *s.* bentin, -ni, *f.*, *fr.*

Scar, *s.* mău, -ăve, *f.*

Scarce, *a.* 1. uṇo = *l.* less.

2. ăprup = *l.* rare.

Scarcely, *ad.* kāṣṭān = with difficulty.
I had s. arrived when = āil''lea pharāk; *see* **After.**

Scarcity, *s.* 1. uṇepoṇ, -ṇā, *n.*
2. ăprupāi, -ye, *f.*

Scare, *v.* beṣṭāi; bhiyeunk lāi.

Scarf, *s.* šelo, -leā, *m.* (loose vesture hanging upon the shoulders; lēsụ, -sā, *m.* (native s.)

Scarify, *v.* bokorn (*or* bokrun) răgat kāḍ.

Scarlet, *a.* bhou tāmbḍo.

Scathless, *a.* năṣṭaviṇ = *l.* safe; băčāvetso.

Scatter, *v.* 1. simpḍāi = disperse, *pr. fg.*
2. simp, *e.g.* water.

Scavenger, *s.* mārog zāḍtolo = *l.* he who sweeps roads, *pr. fg.*

Scene, Scenery, *s.* 1. āṭasāl, -lā, *n.* = *l.* a hall of drama.
2. diṣṭ, -ṭi, *f.* = *l.* sight.

Scent, *s.* părmăḷ, -ḷā, *m.* = *l.* fragrance.

Scent, *v.* părmăḷ kāṇe; p. lāi = *l.* apply fragrance.

Sceptic, *s.* sătmāndinātullo; ăpanămbiketso, *or* nămbganātullo.

Scepticism, *s.* ăpanămbiki, -ke, *f.*

Sceptre, *s.* bètkāṭi, -ṭe, *f.*; (rāyăčeñ) bèt, -tā, *n.* = *l.* the stick (of a king).

Schedule, *s.* čiṭ, -ṭi, *f.*; păṭṭi, -ṭe, *f.* = *l.* a list.

Scheme, *s.* nămuno, -neā, *m.* = *l.* plan; năkṣa, -ṣe, *f.* = *l.* sketch; risko, *pl. f.* = *l.* lines, *fr.*; āločen, -ni, *f.* = *l.* opinion.

Schism, *s.* mătabhēd(é), -dā, *m.* = *l.* difference in religion; igărjentleñ vingḍāp, -pā, *n.* = *l.* separation from the church; tănḍ, -ḍā, *m.* = *l.* faction.

Schismatic, *a.* mătabhēdātso.

Scholar, *s.* 1. *vlg.* iskolātso burgo, -geā, *m.*; sis, -sā, *m.* = *l.* a disciple; siktolo = *l.* learning.
2. sikụllo = *l.* he who is learned, *e.g.* Sanskrit s.; pănḍit, -tā, *m.* = *l.* a doctor.
3. māndtolo, *n.c.* = *l.* a follower; pāṭlāugār, -rā, *m.* = *l.* a follower.

Scholastic, *a.* vidyesāḷetso.

School, *s.* 1. sāḷ, -ḷe, *f.*; *vlg.* iskol, -lā, *n.*, *fr.*
2. pāṭlāugār, -rā, *m.* = *l.* follower.
3. pāṭlāu, -lāvā, *m.* = *l.* a following.
4. siktso zāgo, -geā, *m.* = *l.* a place in which one learns; *e.g.* s. of wickedness.

Sciatic, *s.* penkṭaduk, -ki, *f.*

Science, *s.* 1. vidya, -ye, *f.*, šāstrụ, -rā, *n.* = a system.
2. zāṇvāi, -ye, *f.* = *l.* knowledge; voḷok, -ḷki, *f.*; sāmārthi, -the, *f.*

Scientific, *a.* vidyetso; vidyevont.

Scimitar, *see* **Guillotine.**
Scintillate, *v.* kirnañ di, *or* uzvāḍ di; miṇmiṇ; kiḍi pòḍ, *ch. cs.*
Sciolist, *s.* čillăr sikpi, -piā, *m.*, *or* sikpiso.
Scion, *s.* 1. ānkri, -re, *f.*
2. *fg.* săntătitso.
Scissors, *s.* kātăr, -tri, *f.*
Scoff, *v.* năklañ kăr = *l.* make copies, *fg.*; hās = *l.* laugh at, *Acc.*; yeḍāi; *see* **Mock.**
Scoff, *s.* năklañ, *pl. n.*; khebḍāi, -ye, *f.*
Scold, *v.* beṣṭāi; bās khā; gădḍăḷ kăr.
Scolding, *s.* beṣṭauṇeñ, -ṇeā, *n.*
Scolopendra, *s.* vāgoṇi, -ṇe, *f.*
Scoop, *v.* pokaḷ kăr, *or* pokor.
Scope, *s.* 1. sevoṭ, -ṭā, *m.*
2. suāt, -te, *f.* = *l.* a place.
Scorch, *v.* ulpāi, *e. g.* the sun scorches; sukāi = *l.* make dry.
Score, *s.* 1. gurtu̦, -tā, *m.* = *l.* sign; giṭ, -ṭā, *m.* = *l.* a line.
2. lèk, -kā, *n.* = *l.* an account.
3. kóḍ, -ḍi, *f.* = twenty.
Score, *v.* 1. gurtu̦ (*or* giṭ) kăr.
2. lāi = *l.* apply, attach, impute, *etc.*
Scoria, *s.* koir, -rā, *m.*; *vlg.* gu, -vā, *m.*
Scorn, *s.* bepārvo, -veā, *m.*; khebḍāi, -ye, *f.*
Scorn, *v.* bepārvo (*or* khebḍāi) kăr, *G. M.* (*F.*); yeḍāi = *l.* mock.
Scorpion, *s.* itsu, -tsā, *m.* (*var.* vitsu).
Scot, *see* **Tax.**
Scotch, *s.* kātrāp, -pā, *n.*
Scoundrel, *s. see* **Rascal.**
Scour, *v.* 1. gās.
2. ăusăr = *l.* hasten.
Scourge, *v.* korḍe mār; (jerbandāniñ) mār.
Scourge, *s.* 1. sileñ, -leā, *n.* = a s. of thorns; čābuk, -bkā, *m.* = a whip; korḍo, -ḍeā, *m.* = a discipline.
2. *fg.* šikṣa, -ṣe, *f.* = *l.* punishment; mār, -ri, *f.* = *l.* pest, *fg.*, *Lat. flagellum*, a great punishment, *n. c. in this mn.*
Scout, *s.* bédi, -di, *m.*
Scout, *v.* 1. béd pòḷe; béd kāṇe.
2. *fg.* bepārveān sóḍ.
Scowl, *see* **Frown.**
Scraggy, *a.* kărkoṭo.
Scramble, *v.* petsāḍ, *or rs.*; *crc.*
Scrap, *s.* kuḍko, -keā, *m.*
Scrape, *s.* tondre, *Nom. pl. m.* = perplexity.
Scrape, *v.* kānt.
Scraper, *s.* kāntneñ, -neā, *n.* = an instrument for scraping.
Scraping, *s.* kāntāp, -tpā, *n.*
Scratch, *v.* 1. bokor, *as* a cat with its nails.
2. phāpsi = *l.* pierce in many places; ghāi ghāl = *l.* put a wound.
3. korpi, *e. g.* a sore with the hands; *see* **Erase.**
Scrawl, *v.* giči.

Scream, *s.* bòb, -be, *f.*; kiḷănts, -či, *f.*, of young children.
Scream, *v.* kiḷănts măr; bòb măr.
Screech, *see* **Scream.**
Screen, *s.* 1. răkṇeñ, -ṇeă, *n.*
2. *fg.* ăsro, -reă, *m.* = *l.* refuge.
3. pordo (*or* poḍdo), -deă, *m.*, *e. g.* to separate rooms with; izăi, -ye, *f.* = a screen of bamboo sticks.
Screen, *v.* răk.
Screw, *s.* iskur, -ră, *m.*, *fr.*
Scribble, *v.* gičči.
Scribe, *s.* skrib, -bă, *m.* (of the Bible). *In other mn. see* **Notary, Copyist.**
Scrip, *s.* 1. čīṭ, -ṭi, *f.* = *l.* a note, a small piece of writing.
2. thăili, -le, *f.* = *l.* a bag.
Scripture, *s.* Păvitrụ Pustak, -kă, *n.* = *l.* Holy Book (Bible).
Scrofula, *s.* kănṭmăḷ, -ḷă, *n.*
Scroll, *s.* kouḷo, -ḷeă, *m.* = a roll of paper.
Scrub, *v.* găs.
Scruple, *s.* 1. dubău, -bāvă, *m.* = *l.* doubt, *or bet.* kăṣṭountso dubău, *or perh. bet.* tondre, *pl. m.* = *l.* perplexity.
2. băb, -be, *f.* = *l.* case (of conscience), *n. ex.*; tsurtsuro, -reă, *m.* = pain of heart.
3. skruplụ, -lă, *m.* = a measure of weight, *fr.*
Scruple, *v.* dubău; tondreănt ăsă = *l.* is in perplexity.
Scrupulous, *a.* dubăvi; tondreăntso, *or* tondreănt ăsullo.
Scrutiny, *s.* vitsărăṇ, -ṇă, *n.*; nimit, -tă, *n.* = *l.* inquiry (into the future); părikṣa, -ṣe, *f.* = *l.* an examination.
Scud, *v.* văreăn loṭun vetă = *l.* goes pulled by the wind.
Scuffle, *s.* zăgḍeñ, -ḍeă, *n.*
Scuffle, *v.* zăgăḍ *or* zăgḍa.
Scull, *see* **Skull.**
Sculptor, *s. vlg.* ăčări, -riă, *m.*; šilpi, -piă, *m.*, *n. u.*, *but good w.*; *rs.* kăntouṇitso văur kărtolo, *or* kăntouṇegăr, -ră, *m.*
Sculpture, *s.* kăntouṇeñ, -ṇeă, *n.*, *or* kăntounči vidya, -ye, *f.*
Sculpture, *v.* kăntăi.
Scum, *s.* koir, -ră, *m.* = s. of metals; *see* **Foam.**
Scurf, *s.* khărbeñ, -beă, *n.*
Scurrile, *a.* lăzbanḍo; ăṇvo.
Scurrility, *s.* bursepoṇ, -ṇă, *n.*; lăzbanḍpoṇ, -ṇă, *n.*
Scurvy, *s.* păši, -še, *f.*
Scutcheon, *s.* kuṭmătso gurtụ, -tă, *m.*; ḍălu (*Cn.*), *n. u.*
Scythe, *s.* koito, -teă, *m.*, *or if smaller*, koiti, -te, *f.*, *or if very small*, koitul, -lă, *n.*
Sea, *s.* dăryo, -yeă, *m.*; săgăr, -ră, *m.*; sămudrụ, -dră, *m.*, *or* sămdir, -ră, *m.*
An arm of the s. = khări, -ye, *f.*
On s. and land = dăryănt ăni buinčer.
Put to s. = ăḷveñ sóḍ = *l.* leave harbour.
Be at s. = tărvăr poiṇ kăr.

A s. of troubles = kărkărañ-dăryo.

Sea, *a.* dăryātso *or* dăryāntlo.

Seal, *s.* 1. mhor, -re, *f.*, the instrument *and also* the impression; hostu̥, -tu, *f.* = *l.* a wafer.

2. *fg.* guṭ, -ṭā, *m.* = *l.* a secret.

Keep under s. = mhore bităr dovór, *or* mhor mārn dovór.

Seal, *v.* 1. mhor măr, *or* mh. ghāl.

2. *fg.* dānk *or* dāmp = *l.* shut.

3. *fg.* thir kăr = *l.* confirm, *e.g.* with blood.

Sealing-wax, *s.* lāk, -ki, *f.*

Seam, *s.* sivoṇ (*or* sioṇ), siuṇi, *f.* (*It. cucitura*).

Sear, *v.* ulpāi; sukāi.

Search, *v.* sód = *l.* seek; sărkeñ pòḷe = *l.* look, inspect carefully; vitsār, *or* vitsārăṇ kăr = *l.* make inquiry; tănki kăr, nimgi = *l.* make inquiry; dăriyāft kăr = *l.* make inquiry (judicially).

Searching, *s.* sódna, -ne, *f.*; *see* **Enquiry.**

Season, *s.* 1. (vărsātso) kāl, -lā, *m.*; (vărsātso) vānṭo, -ṭeā, *m.*

2. vēḷ(é), -ḷā, *m.* (due time).

Season, *v.* 1. fòṇṇu (*var.* fòḍnu̥) ghāl = *l.* put condiment.

2. tăyār kăr = *l.* make ready.

3. ghăṭ kăr = *l.* make strong.

4. meḷāi = *l.* mix.

Seasonable, *a. rs.* fāvoteā veḷār = *l.* at due time; lāyek = *l.* suitable.

Seasonableness, *s.* lāyekpoṇ, -ṇā, *n.*; fāvoto vēḷ(é), -ḷā, *m.*

Seasoning, *s.* 1. nisteñ, -teā, *n.* = what is eaten with food as a relish.

2. āḷeān, -nā, *n.* = all the spices commonly used in seasoning.

Seasoned, *a.* 1. fòḍnu̥ ghāllo.

2. tăyār.

3. ghăṭ, *see the verb.*

Seat, *s.* 1. siyāsaṇ, -ṇā, *n.* = s. of authority, *e.g.* in a church; băska, -ke, *f.* = a common s.; *vlg.* bānk, -kā, *m.*, *or* kădel, -lā, *n.*, *fr.*

2. suāt, -te, *f.* = *l.* a place, *or* rāunči suāt; ṭāṇeñ, -ṇeā, *n.*, biḍār, -rā, *n.* = a residence.

Have a seat in . . . = hăkku̥ āsā, *l.* right is.

Seat, *v.* bòsāi, *c.v. of* bòs, *n.v.*

Seated, *a. rs.* āsā = is.

Secede, *see* **Recede.**

Seclude, *v.* dhāmp, *or* bhāir ghāln dhāmp.

Seclusion, *s.* 1. bhāiṛ ghālneñ, -neā, *n.*

2. yeksurāi, -ye, *f.* (yeksurpoṇ, -ṇā, *n.*) = *l.* solitude.

Second, *a.* dusro; duyăm (*Hind. w.*); 'duyăm tāḷo = echo'.

S.-hand clothes = porneñ văstur.

Second, *s.* khiṇ, -ṇā, *n.*

Second, *v.* guṇātso zāun āsā = *l.* is favourable; kumok kăr = *l.* make help; *or* ādhār k.

Secondary, *a.* uṇe gărjetso = *l.* less necessary; mukhyanātullo = *l.* not principal; *or bet.* mukhyanăiñzāllo.

Secondly, *ad.* dusre suāter = in the 2nd place.

Secrecy, *s.* 1. guṭ, -ṭā, *m.*
2. yeksurpoṇ, -ṇā, *n.* (*or* yeksurāi, -ye, *f.*) = *l.* solitude.

Secret, *a.* 1. gupit, *or* guṭātso; lipullo = *l.* concealed.
2. yeksuro = *l.* solitary.
3. guḍātso, *e.g.* s. alphabet.

Secret, *s.* guṭ, -ṭā, *m.*

Secretary, *s.* 1. munsi, -si, *m. a general term.*
2. părdāni, -niā, *m.* = s. of a king.
3. seristedār, -rā, *m.* = s. of a judge or tahsildar and the like.
4. sekretar, -rā, *m.*, *vlg.*, *fr. esp.* of a bishop.

Secrete, *v.* lipăi, *c. v. of* lip, *n. v.*

Secretly, *ad.* guṭān; ăntrăngān, *n. c.*

Sect, *s.* 1. tănḍ, -ḍā, *m.* = faction.
2. mătabhēd(é), -dā, *m.* = *l.* difference in religion; vegḷo vānṭo, -ṭeā, *m.* = *l.* a separated portion.

Sectary, *s.* tănḍagār, -rā, *m.*

Section, *s.* vānṭo, -ṭeā, *m.*; bhāg, -gā, *m.*, of a book.

Secular, *a.* săuñsāri = of the world, *or* in the w.; săuñsārātso = worldly.

Secularise, *v.* tsāltea kāmāk lāi = *l.* apply to common use.

Secure, *a.* 1. soukāsāyetso = *l.* peaceful.
2. risknātullo; băčāvetso; năṣṭaviṇ = without harm.
3. ghăṭ = strong, *e.g.* a s. box; băndobăstint āsullo (*or other verb*) = *l.* being in security.
4. *in the mn. of* certain to be obtained, *etc.*, *rs.* dubāu nāstanāñ = doubtless *with the verb required by the mn.; or* khănḍit.
5 khăro = *l.* true.

Secure, *v.* riske bhāir ghāl = *l.* put out of risk; *or* riskeviṇ kăr; băndobăstin dovór = *l.* keep (put) in security; băčāu kăr = *l.* make safe; dămp = *l.* shut.

Security, *s.* 1. zāmindār, -rā, *m.* = he who gives s.
2. zāmin, -ne, *f.*, *var.* zāmini, -ne, *f.* = security (itself).
3. soukāsāi, -ye, *f.* = *l.* peace.
4. rākṇeñ, -ṇeā, *n.* = *l.* protection, guard.
5. nāñrisk, -ke, *f.*; băndobăst, -ti, *f.*

Sedan, *s.* pālki, -ke, *f.*

Sedate, *v.* thănḍ kăr, *or* nidān kăr; *see* **Appease.**

Sedateness, *s.* nidānāi, -ye, *f.*

Sedative, *a.* haḷu kărtso = *l.* making light, *fg.*; *see also v.*

Sedentary, *a.* bòstso (bòsso), *e.g.* s. life.

Sediment, *s.* măḍḍi, -ḍe, *f.*; mūr, -ri, *f.*; măḷpi, -pe, *f.*

Sedition, *s.* kāṭkāi, -ye, *f.*

Seditious, *a.* kāṭkāyetso, *or* kāṭkāyegār.

Seduce, *v.* 1. pisăi, *or* piso kăr = *l.* make mad, *fg.*; nāḍi kăr = *l.* make tricks, (tempt); voḍni di = *l.* give inclination, allure; fuslăi.
2. kusăi = *l.* corrupt; pāḍ dēk (ė) di = *l.* give bad example.

Seducer, *s.* kusḍi, -ḍiā, *m.*; fuslāitolo, *etc.*; *see the verb.*

Seduction, *s.* fuslāuṇeñ, -ṇeā, *n.*; nāḍ, -ḍi, *f.* = *l.* a trick, temptation; mōs(ó), -sā, *m.* = *l.* deception; ṭhăkkụ, -kā, *n.* = *l.* fraud, simulation.

Seductive, *a.* nāḍitso, *or* fóṭkiro, *or* fuslāuntso; *see verb.*

Sedulity, *s.* tsurkpoṇ, -ṇā, *n.*; zāgrutāi, -ye, *f.* = care; *rs. into* tsuk *in neg. form.*

Sedulous, *a.* zāgrut = careful; ušār; tsuknātullo = not failing.

See, *v.* 1. pòḷe, *or* pòḷei; tsói (*H. K.*); diṣṭ ghāl = *l.* put sight, *obj. 2nd Loc.*
2. somza = *l.* understand, *or* kăḷ = be known.
See to = zătăn kāṇe = *l.* take care, *G. F.*
Go to see, visit = bhèṭ.
Seeing that = dekun *or* pāsvot, *etc.*; *see* Gram. p. 270, *seq.*

See, *s.* siyāsăṇ, -ṇā, *n.*

Seed, *s.* 1. biñ, biyā, *n.*; zun b. (seasoned s.); rov, -vā, *m.*
2. *fg.* săntăt, -ti, *f.* = *l.* posterity.

Seek, *v.* 1. sód, *e.g.* a lost thing.
2. prăyătăn kăr = *l.* make effort.
3. āšā kăr = *l.* make desire, *G. F.*, *or* āše; lāle = *l.* long for (*Dat.*).
4. sevoṭ āsā = *l.* aim is; *or* irādo āsā, *or* āločen āsā.

Seem, *v.* distā.

Seemliness, *s.* 1. rūp, -pā, *n.* = *l.* form.
2. măryād, -di, *f.* = *l.* decency, grace.
3. lāyekpoṇ, -ṇā, *n.* = *l.* fitness.

Seemly, *a.* 1. lāyek = *l.* fit; kāmāk pòḍtso.
2. sundăr = *l.* nice; măryāditso = graceful.

Seer, *see* **Prophet.**

Seeth, *see* **Boil.**

Segment, *s.* (*geom.*) măndăḷabhāg, -gā, *m.*

Segregate. *v.* 1. vegḷo *or* vingăḍ kăr; vegḷo (*or* vingăḍ) dovór = take aside.
2. vintsun kāḍ = *l.* choose; vints = *l.* separate, *e.g.* many things one from the other.

Seine, *s.* vóḍ zāḷ, -ḷā, *n.* = *l.* a large net.

Seize, *v.* 1. dhăr = *l.* catch.
2. lāg = *l.* be attached, *fg.*, *e.g.* fire, disease, *ch. cs.* (*Dat. obj.*)

3. zăpti kăr = distrain; āngār pòḍ = *l.* fall on the body; zompăi mār = pounce.

Seizing, *s.* dhărāp, -rpā, *n.*

Seldom, *a.* ăprup.

Select, *v.* vints *or* vintsun kāḍ = *l.* segregating take; sódun kāḍ = *l.* seeking take.

Select, *a.* uttim = *l.* excellent; vintsnār.

Selection, *s.* vintsāp, -tspā, *n.*, *or* vintsneñ, -neā, *n.*

Self, *s.* -ts, *see* Gram. P. II. ch. iii. *Emph. Pron.*

Selfish, *a.* āpṇātso mōg(ó) kărtolo.

Self-control, *s.* sudaḷăi, -ye, *f.*

Self-denial, *s.* āpli-inkāri, -re, *f.*; āpli visăr, -ri, *f.* = *l.* forgetfulness of oneself, *n. c.*; ătmeāči dănḍon, -ne, *f.*

Sell, *v.* ik *or* vik.

Seller, *s.* iknār, -rā, *m.*, *bet.* iktolo.

Selling, *s.* ikāp, -kpā, *n.*; *see* **Sale.**

Selvage, *s.* lugṭadèg, -ge, *f.* = *l.* edge of cloth.

Semblance, *s.* 1. sārkeñ, -keā, *n.* 2. *fg.* sāuḷi, -ḷe, *f.* = *l.* shadow, *fg.*

Semicircle, *s.* ărdeñ mănḍăḷ, -ḷā, *n.*

Seminary, *s.* *vlg.* seminār, -ri, *f.*, *fr.*

Semitone, *s.* ărdo tāḷo, -ḷeā, *m.*, *or* ărdeñ vāzāp, -zpā, *n.*

Senate, *s.* rājasăbha, -bhe, *f.*

Senator, *s.* rājasăbhesāndo, -deā, *m.*; măntri, -ri, *m.*

Send, *v.* 1. dhāḍ, *or* dhāḍn di = *l.* sending give; pāṭăi, *used esp. fg. for* grant (graces); peṭăi (*H. K.*)

2. răvāne kăr = *l.* make a message, (send a message).

3. sóḍ = *l.* leave free, *e. g.* a missile.

S. for = āpoi *or* āpoun āḍ.

S. forth = bhăir sóḍ.

S. away = bhăir ghāl, *or* sóḍăi = *l.* cause to leave.

S. in the place of = *G.* bădlāk dhāḍ.

S. up = ubzăi = *l.* cause to become, *e. g.* sprouts, *or* fuṭ = come out, *ch. cs.*

Senior, *s.* mālgoḍo.

Sensation, *s.* bhogāp, -gpā, *n.* (*phil.*).

Make a s. = lăg = *l.* get attached, *or* rig = enter, *fg.*, *or* ăjāp zātā = *l.* wonder becomes, *ch. cs.* (*or* ăjāptā).

Sense, *s.* 1. isvo, -veā, *m.* (*or* visvo), of the body; indro, -reā, *m.* (*H. K.*)

2. bud, -di, *f.* = *l.* wisdom.

3. săma mót, -ti, *f.* = *l.* a sane mind.

4. ărth, -thā, *m.* = *l.* meaning.

The five senses are: diṣṭ, kān, părmăḷ, ruts, āpoḍneñ.

Sensible, *a.* 1. distso (disso) = *l.* appearing.

2. isve āsullo = *l.* having senses.

3. budivont = *l.* wise.

4. bārik = *l.* penetrating.

Sensitive, *a.* 1. isve āsullo = *l.* having senses.
2. birmotvont = *l.* feeling pity; movāḷ = *l.* tender; movāḷasārko = fit to be moved.

Sensibility, *s.* 1. isve, *pl. m.* = senses.
2. bhógči săkăt, -kti, *f.* = *l.* the faculty of feeling (bhógāp, -gpā, *n.*); movāḷpoṇ, -ṇā, *n.*, *or* movāḷa sārkeñ; *see adj.*

Sensual, *a.* 1. isveāntso = *l.* of senses.
2. kuḍitso = *l.* bodily, *e.g.* sensual pleasures; móstitso, *or* burso = impure; vāiṭ khušeānk lāgullo = impure.

Sensuality, *s.* móst, -ti, *f.*; kuḍičeo khušio = *l.* bodily pleasures; bursepoṇ, -ṇā, *n.*; pozḍepoṇ, -ṇā, *n.*; ăḷšikpoṇ, -ṇā, *n.* = *l.* ugliness, *fg.*; *vlg.* (vāiṭ) kām, -mā, *n.* = *l.* (bad) things.

Sentence, *s.* 1. phăisăl, -lā, *n.* = s. of a judge; tīrp, -pā, *n.* = *l.* a decision; tirmāṇ, -ṇā, *n.*; nirṇăi, -yā, *n.*
2. vākya, -yā, *n.* (Gram.); utsăr, -rā, *m.* = *l.* an expression.
3. gād, -di, *f.* = *l.* a proverb.
4. āločen, -ni, *f.* = *l.* opinion.

Sentence, *v.* phăisăl sāng, *etc.*; *see noun.*

Sententious, *a.* gādibhărit.

Sentiment, *s.* 1. bhógt, -ti, *f.* (*or* bhógāp, -gpā, *n.*?), *or* bhógtipoṇ, -ṇā, *n.* = *l.* feeling.
2. mòn, -nā, *n.* = *l.* heart, mind.
3. āločen, -ni, *f.* = *l.* opinion.
4. mănšepoṇ, -ṇā, *n.* = *l.* humanity, good s.

Sentimental, *a.* bhógtso; movāḷountso = *l.* moving; movāḷ *or* movāḷasārko = tender *or* fit to be moved.

Sentinel, Sentry, *s.* rākṇo, -ṇeā, *m.*; pāreagār, -rā, *m.*; pāro, -reā, *m.*

Separable, *a.* vingăḍ kărtso, *or* vingăḍsisārko, *or* vegḷo kări sārko.

Separability, *s.* vingăḍsisārkeñ, -keā, *n.*, *or* vegḷa-, *n. c.*

Separate, *a.* vingăḍ; vegḷo.

Separate, *v.* 1. vingăḍ kăr, vegḷo kăr; *fg.* bhēd(é) kăr = *l.* make difference.
2. vānṭe kăr, *or* kuḍke kăr = *l.* make parts.
3. pois dovór, *or* pois kăr = keep far.

Separately, *ad.* vingăḍ zāun, *or* vingăḍ vingăḍ.

Separation, *s.* vegḷatsăr, -rā, *m.* (*var.* vegḷatsāi, -ye, *f.*); vingăḍāp, -pā, *n.*

Sepulchre, *s.* 1. fónḍ, -ḍā, *m.*
2. sepulkru, -rā, *m.*, of J. C.
3. gori, -ye, *f.*; *ex.* a monument over a grave.

Sequence, *s.* 1. pāṭlāu, -lāvā, *m.*
2. fóḷ, -ḷā, *m.* = *l.* effect; *see* Series.

Sequestration, *s.* zăpti, -te, *f.*

Seraph, *s.* serāphim, -mā, *m.*

Serenade, *s.* rātčeñ gāyān, -nā, *n.*
Serene, *a.* 1. kupaññātullo; nitāḷ = *l.* pure.
2. *fg.* nidān.
Serenity, *s.* 1. nitāḷāi, -ye, *f.*; nitāḷ moḷāb, -ḷbā, *n.* = *l.* pure sky.
2. *fg.* nidanāi, -ye, *f.*; soukāsāi, -ye, *f.* = calmness.
Serf, *s.* tsākór, -krā, *m.*; gulām, -mā, *m.* = *l.* a slave.
Sergeant, *s.* havăldār, -rā, *m.*
Series, *s.* 1. hār, -ri, *f.*, *e.g.* s. of statements; kāmp, -pā, *m.* = a line, *e.g.* kāmpān tsălā = go in a line.
2. *fg.* zomo, -meā, *m.* = *l.* a multitude; sānkăḷ, -kḷi, *f.* = *l.* a chain, *fg.*, *e.g.* s. of words, events.
Serious, *a.* 1. gărjotso = *l.* necessary; bhāradik = *l.* grave, *fg.*, important, looking s.; bhāri; āločen kărtso = *l.* giving to think.
2. găḍis, *e.g.* s. sickness; nibbor = *l.* strong, *e.g.* s. sickness.
3. khăro = *l.* true, (not in jest).
Seriously, *ad.* *see adj.;* monahpurvok, *e.g.* say something not in jest.
Seriousness, *s.* bhār, -rā, *m.*
Serpent, *s.* jiudāḷ, -ḷi (*or* jiudād, -di), *f.*; soróp, -rpā, *m.* = a kind of s., *used sometimes generally;* serpentiṇ, -ṇi, *f.*, the s. of Genesis, *ol.*
Serpentine, *a.* sorpabăriso.
Serried, *part. a.* lāgun = *l.* attached, *fg.*, *e.g.* a s. phalanx.
Serum, *s.* tāk, -kā, *n.*
Servant, *s.* 1. tsākor, -krā, *m.*; sevok, -kā, *m.*; dāsi, -si, *f.* = a maid-servant; noukor, -krā, *m.* = a public s.
2. gulām, -mā, *m.* = a slave.
Serve, *v.* 1. tsākri (*or* seva ts.) kăr, *G. F.*
2. upkār, *or* upkār kăr, *or* upkārāk (*or* kāmāk) pòḍ = *l.* be useful.
3. tsălăi = *l.* manage, *e.g.* s. guns.
4. *G.* suāter āsā = is in the place of.
Service, *s.* 1. tsākri, -kre, *f.*, *or* seva tsākri.
2. upkār, -rā, *m.* = *l.* advantage; prăyóg, -gā, *m.* = *l.* use.
3. kām, -mā, *n.* = *l.* office.
4. kāido, -deā, *m.* = *l.* duty.
Divine S. šāstrāčeñ kām, -mā, *n.*; kăṭleñ, -leā, *n.* = *l.* ceremony. (*H. K.*)
Serviceable, *a.* ādāyātso = *l.* profitable; upkārāk (*or* kāmāk) pòḍtso; prăyógātso = *l.* useful.
Servile, *a.* 1. tsākretso.
2. hălko, uṇo = low, mean.
S. work = tsākrečeñ kām; *but commonly* āitārātso vāur = work of Sunday *is used.*
Servility, *s.* gulāmpoṇ, -ṇā, *n.* = *l.* slavery.

Session, *s. vlg.* zunt, -tā, *m.*, *or bet. rs. into* zuntāk bòstāt = they sit for the meeting; mēḷ (é), -ḷā, *m.* = *l.* a union, meeting.

Set, *a.* 1. khăndit = *l.* definite, positive.
2. kāideā părmāṇe (āsullo) = (being) according to rules.

Set, *s.* 1. tănḍ, -ḍā, *m.*, *e.g.* a s. of bearers.
2. rompo, -peā, *m.* = *l.* a young plant.

Set, *v.* 1. ghāl *or* dovór = *l.* put.
2. lāi = *l.* apply, *e.g.* a tree, (plant), an emerald.
3. săma kăr = *l.* make right, *e.g.* a watch, a limb.
4. buḍ, stăm, *e.g.* the sun.
5. gurtu ghāl = *l.* put a sign (set to music), *or bet.* borăi = write.
6. nemsi = *l.* appoint.
S. in order = mānḍ *or* săma kăr.
S. in motion = hālăi.
S. about = suru kăr = begin.
S. against = 1. virodh āsā = is against, *ch. cs.*
2. săr kăr = make comparison.
S. apart, s. aside = vingăḍ dovór, *or* sāmbāḷn dovór.
S. before = mezār ghāl = *l.* put on the table.
S. down = borăi.
S. forward = bhāir săr = start.
S. in = suru zā = begin; lāg = *l.* be attached, *fg.*
S. on = 1. huskāi, *e.g.* a dog; kānṭe lāi = *l.* apply thorns, (excite).
2. zăḷăi = *l.* cause to burn (tease).
3. āngār pòḍ = *l.* fall on the body.
S. forth = 1. mukār ghāl; bhāir săr = start.
2. vistār = *l.* extend.
S. off = 1. hogoḷsi = *l.* praise.
2. surungār kăr = *l.* adorn.
S. on fire = lās (*or* lāsăi, *c. v.*); uzo lāi.
S. over = *Dat.* dovór = *l.* put to, *e.g.* a governor.
S. round = veḍo mār.
S. up = 1. ubo kăr = *l.* make standing, *e.g.* a pillar.
2. *fg.* ukto kăr = *l.* make open, *fg.*

Setting, *s.* (of the sun), ăstămti, -te, *f.*

Settle, *v.* 1. săma kăr = *l.* make right, *e.g.* a quarrel; vòp = *l.* consent, agree.
2. thir kăr = *l.* confirm; nišcei-si = *l.* establish, make certain; dovór = *l.* put, *e.g.* a minister.
3. fārik kăr = *l.* pay, *e.g.* debts.
4. kāzār kăr = *l.* marry, *tr. v.*
5. bòs = *l.* sit, *e.g.* birds s. upon trees.
6. ghăr kărn rāu = *l.* making house stop, colonize; biḍār (*or* ṭhikāṇeñ) kăr = *l.* make

abode; ghărvāsi zā = *l.* making house inhabit.
7. săkăl (*or* pondāk) pȯḍ = *l.* fall to the bottom of.

Settled, *a.* khănḍit; niščeisillo.

Settlement, *s.* 1. vās, -sā, *n.* = *l.* dwelling.
2. āndăṇ, -ṇā, *n.*, (native paraphernalia); dót, -ti, *f.* = *l.* dowry.
3. kărār, -rā, *m.* = *l.* agreement; voppigi, -ge, *f.* = *l.* consent (mutual agreement); *rs. into v.*

Settler, *s.* novo vāsi, -si, *m.* = *l.* a new inhabitant, *n. c.*

Seven, *a.* sāt.

Sever, *v.* vints; *see* **Separate.**

Several, *a.* thoḍe (*pl. of* thoḍo); săbār = many.

Severe, *a.* kăḍḍu, (kărd), *see* **Rigid;** kăṭin, *also for* s. season; găḍis.

Severity, *s.* kăṭinăi, -ye, *f.*; *see* **Rigidity.**

Sew, *v.* siuñ.

Sewer, *s.* čiklātȯḍ(ó), -ḍā, *m.*

Sex, *s.* zāt, -ti, *f.*

Sexton, *see* **Sacristan.**

Shabbiness, *s.* 1. *perh.* durboḷkăi, -ye, *f.* (of clothes).
2. imṭepoṇ, -ṇā, *n.* = *l.* stinginess.

Shabby, *a.* 1. čindi.
2. imṭo = *l.* stingy.

Shade, Shadow, *s.* 1. sāuḷi, -ḷe, *f.* = *Lat. umbra.*
2. *fg.* kāḷok, -kā, *m.* = *l.* obscurity.
3. druṣṭakăi, -ye, *f.* = *l.* goblin kuḷeñ, -ḷeā, *n.*
4. *in pl.* pātāḷ, -ḷā, *n.* = *l.* infernal regions.
5. pordo, -deā, *m.* = *l.* a screen.
6. yeksurăi, -ye, *f.* = *l.* solitude; yeksurpoṇ, -ṇā, *n.*
7. āsro, -reā, *m.* = *l.* refuge.

Shade, *v.* 1. rāk = *l.* guard.
2. sāuḷi kăr.

Shaft, *s.* 1. bhāli, -ye, *f.* = a missile.
2. thoruñ, -rvā, *n.* = *l.* a handle.
3. khāmbo, -beā, *m.* = *l.* a pillar.
4. isāḷeñ, -ḷeā, *n.* = s. of a carriage.

Shag, *s.* kāmboḷ, -bḷi, *f.*; lovečeñ lugāṭ, -gṭā, *n.*

Shake, *v.* 1. hālăi, *c. v. of* hāl, *n. v.*
2. kāmpăi = *l.* cause to tremble.

Shall, *v. By fut. or Necess. mood; see* Gram.

Shallow, *a.* gunḍnăiñ āsullo = *l.* not deep.

Shallow, *s.* gunḍnăiñ āsulli suāt, -te, *f.*

Sham, *s.* fóṭ, -ṭi, *f.*, *or* kăpăṭ, -ṭā, *n.*, *or* ṭhăkkụ, -kā, *n.* = simulation.

Sham, *a.* fóṭkiro, *or* fóṭ *in compounds.*

Shambles, *s.* kăsāigārāči āngăḍ, -gḍi, *f.*

Shame, *s.* lăz, -je, *f.*, *pr. fg.*; ăpamān, -nā, *m.* = *l.* dishonour.

Shame, *v.* lăz distā = *l.* shame appears, *Sb. Dat.*; lăje, *Sb. Nom.*; šerme.
Shameful, *a.* lăjišṭ *or* ăpamānātso *or* ăpamānădik; ăḷšik = ugly, *fg.*
Shameless, *a.* lăzbanḍo.
Shamelessness, *s.* lăzbanḍpoṇ, -ṇā, *n.*
Shampoo, *v.* răgăḍ.
Shank, *s.* pāi, -yā, *m.* = the whole joint from the knee to the ancle.
Shape, *s.* 1. nămuno, -neā, *m.* = *l.* a sample, form, model.
2. rūp, -pā, *n.*
3. form, -mā, *n.*, *fr.* = *l.* mould.
Shape, *v.* 1. rūp di = *l.* give form; kăr = *l.* do.
Shapeless, *a.* rūpnātullo.
Shard, *s.* kăili, -le, *f.* = *Lat. testa*; kăilekuḍko, -keā, *m.*
Share, *s.* 1. vānṭo, -ṭeā, *m.*
2. zăgăl, -gle, *f.* = share of a plough.
Share, *v.* 1. vānṭe kăr = *l.* make parts, *tr. v.*
2. ... sāngāta mèḷ = *l.* be found (received) with others, *ch. cs.*; bhóg = *l.* possess; vānṭo mèḷ.
Shark, *s.* 1. mogór, -grā, *m.*
2. *fg.* mosagār -rā, *m.*; ṭhăkkagār, -rā, *m.*
Sharp, *a.* 1. dhār āsullo = having edge.
2. domsātso = *l.* pointed, *or rs. into* domós.
3. *fg.* bārik = *l.* thin (penetrating), *e.g.* s. mind, eyes.
4. āmboṭ = *l.* acid.
5. dukountso, *or* kăṭin = *l.* severe, *e.g.* words, wind.
Sharpen, *v.* 1. sāṇik dăr = *l.* hold to the whetstone; pāz = sh. with sandstone.
2. bārik kăr, *see adj.*
Sharper, *s.* ṭhăkkagār, -rā, *m.* = *l.* a cheating fellow.
Sharpness, *s.* 1. dhār, -ri, *f.* = edge.
2. domós, -msā, *m.* = point *or* tip.
3. *fg.* bārikāi, -ye, *f.*, *e.g.* of mind.
4. kăṭināi, -ye, *f.* = severity.
Shatter, *v.* 1. kuḍkeān kuḍke kăr = *l.* make into pieces.
2. *fg.* khālto kăr = *l.* make subject; mōḍ(ó) = *l.* break, *fg.* (pull down).
Shave, *v.* kāpṇi kăr; khāḍ kāḍ = *l.* take away the beard.
Shaving, *s.* kāpṇi, -ṇe, *f.*
Shawl, *s.* šelo, -leā, *m.*
She, *pron.* ti; *see* Gram. P. II. ch. iii.
Sheaf, *s.* (bundle), penḍi, -ye, *f.*, of paddy; suḍi, -ye, *f.*; mouḷi, -ḷe, *f.*
Shear, *v.* (louñ) kātăr = *l.* cut (wool).
Shears, *s.* kātăr, -tri, *f.*
Sheath, *s.* poteñ, -teā, *n.*
Sheath, *v.* poteānt ghāl.
Shed, *s.* māṭou, -ṭvā, *m.*; govóḷ,

goulā, *m.* (with sloping roof); măntăp, -pā, *n.*

Shed, *v.* 1. vāuoi = *l.* cause to flow, *c. v. of* vāu; gāḷāi, *e. g.* tears.
2. vikrāi, *e. g.* blood.
3. zăḍ, *n. v.*, zăḍăi, *tr. v.*, *e. g.* leaves.
4. birki.

Sheep, *s.* 1. bokro, -reā, *m.*, *or* kāmbḷibokro; šeḷi, -ye, *f.*, *used also fg.*
2. *fg.* bokro = stupid.

Sheep-fold, *s.* hăṭṭi, -ṭe, *f.*

Sheepish, *a.* dăḍḍo *or* bokro = *l.* stupid.

Sheer, *a.* 1. deuṇi; kòḍso; 's. place = deuṇi, -ṇe, *f.*'
2. -ts *emph.* (mere).

Sheet, *s.* 1. āntulči vól, -li, *f.*; dupaṭo, -ṭeā, *m.*
2. fôl, -li, *f.*; pān, -nā, *n.*, *n. c.*; kāgād, -gdā, *n.*

Shelf, *s. vlg.* ālmār, -ri, *f.*, *fr.*; *see* **Cupboard;** čouk, -kā, *m.*

Shell, *s.* 1. simpi, -ye, *f.* (of fishes); kongo, -geā, *m.* (s. of molluscs).
2. kăṭṭi, -ṭe, *f.* (of fruits).
3. kărl, -lā, *n.* (of an egg).

Shell, *v.* simpi kāḍ, *etc.*

Shell-fish, *s.* khubo, -beā, *m.* = a kind of s.

Shelter, *s.* 1. māṭou, -ṭvā, *m.*
2. *fg.* āsro, -reā, *m.*; rākṇeñ, -ṇeā, *n.*; gòp, -pā, *n.* = *l.* bosom, *fg.*; ādhār, -rā, *m.*, *or* săhāi, -ye, *f.* = help.

Shelter, *v.* 1. rāk, *or* sāmbāḷ = defend.
2. ādhār kăr, *etc.* = help.
3. āsro kāṇe = *l.* take refuge, *ch. cs.*

Shelving, *see* **Sloping.**

Shepherd, *s.* gouḷi, -ḷiā, *m.*, *pr. fg.*

Shield, *s.* 1. hărdeāčeñ karaṇeñ, -ṇeā, *n.*, for defence; hărdeāčeñ rākṇeñ, -ṇeā, *n.*
2. *fg.* āsro, -reā, *m.* = refuge.

Shift, *v.* 1. bădăl = *l.* change.
2. yeṇeñ teṇeñ hāl = *l.* move here and there.
3. petsāḍ = *l.* try.

Shift, *s.* 1. upāi, -yā, *m.* = *l.* means; hikmăt, -ti, *f.* = *l.* industry, device.
2. tsoḷi, -ye, *f.* (of native women).

Shifty, *a.* hikmătitso.

Shin, *s.* pāyāntso noḷo -ḷeā, *m.*; pāi, -yā, *m.*

Shine, *v.* kirnāñ di = *l.* give rays; părzăḷ; prăkāš di; uzăḷ; zăḷzăḷ.

Shingle, *s.* pākeāčeñ foḷeñ, -ḷeā, *n.*; foḷi, -ye, *f.* (*n. u. in this mn.*)

Shining, *a.* zăḷzăḷit.

Ship, *s.* tāruñ, -rvā, *n.*; năg, -gā, *m.*

Ship, *v. see* **Embark.**

Shipwreck, *s.* tārvāčeñ fuṭāp, -ṭpā, *n.*

Shipwreck, *v.* tāruñ fuṭṭā = *l.* ship gets broken.

Shirt, *s.* komis, -msā, *n.* (*also Cn. Mr. Tul., Mal.*)

Shiver, *v.* 1. mōḍ(ó), *or* fóḍ = *l.* break, *tr. v.*
2. kāmp *or* thărtăr = *l.* tremble.
Shivering, *s.* 1. moḍāp, -ḍpā, *n.*
2. kāmpero, -reā, *m.*
Shoal, *s.* 1. zomo, -meā, *m.*; rās, -si, *f.*
2. gunḍ năiñāsụlli suāt, -te, *f.*
Shock, *v.* dāḍāi, *c. v. of* dāḍā, *n. v.*, *pr. fg.*; ādḷāi = *l.* cause to dash, *c. v. of* ādăḷ.
Shock, *s.* āngkāḍneñ, -neā, *n.*
Shocking, *a.* 1. dāḍauntso.
2. dukountso = *l.* afflicting; kānṭāḷeātso = *l.* disgusting, abominable.
Shoe, *s.* 1. motso, -čeā, *m.*; pāpus, -sā, *m.* (Indian half s.); vāṇ, -ṇe, *f.* = *l.* sandal.
2. nāḷ, -ḷi, *f.* = s. of horses, *or* bullocks.
Shoe, *v.* nāḷ mār.
Shoe-maker, *s.* tsāmār, -rā, *m.*; močeagār, -rā, *m.*
Shoot, *v.* 1. sóḍ = discharge.
2. sikāri kār = *l.* make hunting.
Shoot, *s.* ānkri, -re, *f.* (of a plant); *see also* **Twig.**
Shop, *s.* āngăḍ, -gḍi, *f.*; găḍāng, -gā, *n.* = *l.* a tavern; kārkhāno, -neā, *m.* (s. of a smith).
Keep a s. = ā. dovór *or* ā. ghāl.
Shop-keeper, *s.* āngăḍgār, -rā, *m.*
Shore, *s.* véḷ, -ḷe, *f.* [vèḷ, -ḷe, *f.* = carmine colour; vēḷ(é), -ḷā, *m.* = time]; tăḍ, -ḍi, *f.*

Short, *a.* moṭvo; lān = *l.* little, *or* dākṭo = small; thoḍo = *l.* few.
Fall s. = *neg. of* pāu = *l.* reach; *neg. of* mèḷ = *l.* be found.
Short-hand, *a.* (writing), móḍi.
Short-sighted, *a.* lāgsiledișṭitso.
Short-sightedness, *s.* lāgsilidișṭ, -ṭi, *f.*
Shortcoming, *s.* uṇepoṇ, -ṇā, *n.*
Shorten, *v.* moṭvo (*or* uṇo) kăr.
Shortly, *ad.* 1. vegiñ = soon.
2. thoḍeañ utrāniñ = *l.* in a few words.
Shortness, *s.* moṭvepoṇ, -ṇā, *n.*
Shot, *s.* 1. guḷi, -ye, *f.* = *l.* a small ball; *vlg.* monisāuñ, -sāvā, *m.*
2. fār, -rā, *m.* = *Lat. ictus*, a stroke.
Out of s. = fārā bhāir.
Should, *imp. of* **Shall.**
I should like to do = kărtoñ *or* kărin.
You should do = kărizāi distā; *see* Gram. p. 270, *seq.*
Shoulder, *s.* khānd, -dā, *m.*
Shoulder-blade, *s.* bhuz, -zā, *n.*
Shout, *s.* bòb, -be, *f.*; hāk, -ki, *f.*
Raise a s. = bòb mār.
Shout, *v.* bòb mār; hāk āni bòb mār; bòb mārn sāng = *l.* crying say.
Shove, *v.* 1. lōṭ(ó) = *l.* push.
2. mukār dāunḍāi = *l.* cause to run before.
Shovel, *s. approx.* kāilāto, -teā, *m.* = a small s. of iron.

Show, *v.* 1. dākăi *or* dākoun di. 2. tsăl = *l.* walk, *fg.* (behave), *e. g.* s. yourself good = boro tsăl. 3. kăr = *l.* do, *e. g.* s. mercy = kākuḷt kăr. 4. sikăi = *l.* teach; kăḷăi = *l.* notify; somzăi = *l.* cause to understand. S. forth = soṣṭ kăr *or* kăḷăi.

Show, *s.* 1. diṣṭ, -ṭi, *f.* = *l.* sight. 2. dākoṇ, -ṇe, *f.* = representation. 3. dobāzo, -jeā, *m.* = *l.* pomp. 4. disāp, -spā, *n.* = *l.* appearance.

Shower, *s.* 1. pāus, -sā, *m.* = *l.* rain; zhóḍ, -ḍā, *m.*; šéṇ, -ṇi, *f.* 2. săbār = *l.* many; lóḷ, -ḷā, *m.* *e. g.* a s. of tears = dukāntso lóḷ.

Shower, *v.* 1. udārpoṇān di = *l.* give liberally. 2. pāus pòḍtā = rain falls.

Showy, *a.* 1. ăhănkāri = *l.* ambitious; ăṭṭās kārtso = vain, proud. 2. dobājeātso = *l.* pompous.

Shred, *v.* tsātsāi, *tr. v.*, *or* tsur kăr.

Shrew, *s.* zăgăḍči ăstri, -re, *f.* = *l.* a quarrelling woman.

Shrewd, *a.* bārik.

Shrewdness, *s.* bārikāi, -ye, *f.*

Shriek, *s.* kiḷănts, -či, *f.*; kindri, -re, *f.*

Shrill, *a.* voilo = *l.* high, *e.g.* voice; bārik = *l.* thin.

Shrimp, *s.* 1. gālmbi, -be, *f.* = a small s.; sunkaṭ, -kṭā, *n.* (bigger), a kind of crustacean. 2. kuḷḷa, -ḷā, *m.* = *l.* a dwarf.

Shrine, *s.* pèṭ, -ṭe, *f.*

Shrink, *v.* 1. doḍăi = *l.* make double, *used also for* s., *c. v. of* dòḍ; *more comm.* āuḷăi, *or* guṭli kăr. 2. *fg.* pāṭi săr = *l.* go back, *or* kovaḷ.

Shrivel, *v.* (tònḍ) vānkḍeñ kăr = *l.* make (face) crooked; mirio pòḍăi = *l.* cause to fall (make) folds, *n. c.*

Shroud, *s.* khopoṇ -ṇā, *n.*

Shroud, *v.* guṭlăi, *e.g.* in smoke.

Shrub, *s.* zāḍkuṭ, -ṭā, *n.*

Shrug, *v.* bhuz ukoḷ.

Shudder, *v.* thărtăr; kāmp; āng kāḍ = *l.* draw the body.

Shudder, *s.* kāmp, -pi, *f.*; kāmpero, -reā, *m.*

Shuffle, *v.* 1. borsi (cards). 2. guspăḍăi = *l.* confound. 3. nāḍi kăr (*or* n. tsălăi) = make tricks. 4. vānkḍo tsăl = *l.* walk crooked.

Shun, *v.* tsukăi, *c. v. of* tsuk; *or* tsukon kāṇghe; kānṭāḷn tsukăi = *l.* avoid abhorring.

Shunning, *s.* tsukāp, -kpā, *n.*, *or* tsukouṇeñ, -ṇeā, *n.*

Shut, *v.* 1. dāmp (dāmb = press) *or* dānk; bīg ghāl = *l.* put the lock.

2. veḍo mār = *l.* surround; voi" ghāl = *l.* put a hedge.

Shutters, *s.* dār, -rā, *n.*; zănelāčiñ (*or* kiṭkečiñ) bāglañ, *pl. n.* = *l.* doors of a window.

Shy, *a.* bizuḍ; bhiyātso; lăjiṣṭ.

Shy, *v.* bheñ distā.

Shyness, *s.* bheñ, bhiyā, *n.*

Sib, *s.* săiro dāiro, -reā, *m.*

Sibilant, *a.* fusfustso.

Sick, *a.* piḍest; văiṭ kărtolo.
He is s. = tākā văiṭ kărtā.
He fell s. = to piḍent pòḍlo.
He is s. of. . . = to bezār zālo = he got tired.

Sicken, *v.* bezārāi kăr = trouble.

Sickle, *s.* koiti, -te, *f.*

Sickly, *a.* bolāikinātullo; piḍestso (*vlg.* tikke piḍest).

Sickness, *s.* piḍa, -ḍe, *f.*; rōg(ó), -gā, *m.*, *n. c.*; nāñbolāiki, -ke, *f.* = *l.* no health.

Side, *s.* 1. păkṣa, -ṣe, *f.*; kus, -si, *f.*; dikkụ, -kā, *n.*; *rs.* isileān, *or* tisileān = *l.* in the direction of.
2. kăḍvăḷ, -ḷā, *n.*, *ol.* (s. of J. C.); kusāḷ, -ḷā, *n.*
3. tănḍ, -ḍā, *m.* = *l.* faction.
On this s. = āltăḍi; on that s. = poltăḍi.
On one s.—on the other s. = yeka dikkān—dusreā dikkān.
Is on the s. of = *G.* păkṣek āsā.
On the s. of the father = bāpāi isileān, *e.g.* consanguinity.

Sideboard, *s.* sāmānānčeñ mèz, -zā, *n.*; kăpaṭ, -ṭā, *n.*

Sidelong, *a.* vānkḍo.

Siege, *s.* veḍo, -ḍeā, *m.*
Lay s. = veḍo mār; raise s. = v. kāḍ.

Siesta, *s.* (donpārānči) soukāsāi, -ye, *f.*

Sieve, *s.* tsāḷn, -ne, *f.* (*var.* tsāḷni, -ne, *f.*)

Sieve, *v.* tsāḷ.

Sigh, *s.* 1. uskār, -rā, *m.* (*var.* uskāro, -reā, *m.*) *joined usually to* āskār = sob.
2. usvās, -sā, *m.* = *l.* breath.

Sigh, *v.* uskār (*or* usvās) sóḍ = *l.* discharge a s.

Sight, *s.* 1. diṣṭ, -ṭi, *f.*; 'keen s. = bārik d.'
2. rūp, -pā, *n.* = *l.* form.

Sign, *s.* gurtụ, -tā, *m.*; kuru, -rve, *f.* = s. of the cross; khuṇa, -ṇe, *f.* = a portent.

Sign, *v.* 1. gurtụ kăr.
2. nāuñ borāi = *l.* write name; dăskăt ghāl = *l.* put (your) signature; ruzu ghāl.

Signal, *s.* nišāni, -ne, *f.*; *see also* **Sign.**

Signal, *v.* gurtụ kăr.

Signal, *a.* vóḍ = *l.* great; tsătrāifāvozāllo = *l.* considerable.

Signalize (oneself), *v.* nāuñ pāu (āuñ nāuñ pāuloñ) = *l.* reach (to) name.

Signature, *s.* dăskăt, -ti, *f.*; ruzu, zu, *f.*; nāuñ, nāvā, *n.* = *l.* a name.

Signet, *s.* mhòr, -re, *f.*, *or* mhòreči mudi, -ye, *f.* = *l.* a ring of seal.
Significant, *a.* 1. ărth āsullo. 2. bhāri = important.
Signification, *s.* ărth, -thā, *m.*
Signify, *v.* 1. ărth āsā = *l.* meaning is; somzoṇ yetā = *l.* understanding comes; dākăi = *l.* show. 2. bhār āsā = importance is.
Silence, *s.* 1. vogeñ rāvāp, -rāupā, *n.*; *bet. rs. into v.* vogo rāu, *or into neg. of* ulăi = speak. 2. monepoṇ, -ṇā, *n.* = *l.* dumbness, *fg. and only in some sentences.*
Silence, *v.* vogo rāvoi, *c. v. of* v. rāu, *n. v.*; găpčip rāu = be very silent.
Silent, *a.* vogo (văgo); găpčip.
Silently, *ad.* 1. vogo rāun". 2. guṭān = secretly.
Silhouette, *see* **Profile.**
Silk, *s.* răsim, -smā, *n.*
Silk, *a.* răsmātso.
Silk-worm, *s.* răsmākiḍ, -ḍi, *f.*
Sill, *s.* bāglapònd, -dā, *n.*
Silliness, *s.* pisepoṇ, -ṇā, *n.* = folly.
Silly, *a.* piso.
Silt, *v.* (ubrān) bhór.
Silver, *s.* rupeñ, -peā, *n.*
Silver, *a.* rupeātso.
Silver, *v.* rupeāmulām kāḍ.
Similar, *a.* 1. sārko; bări = *l.* as, *with Or. preceding*; *see* Gram.; *vlg.* tākā āni ākā yék gānṭ = *l.* to this and that one knot (is), *i. e.* are similar, agree. 2. *vlg.* tākā āni ākā yék kāpāḍ, (*an indecent expression*).
Similarity, *s.* sārkeñ, -keā, *n.*; săr, -ri, *f.*; surup, -rpā, *n.*, *e.g.* s. with God.
Simile, Similitude, *s.* vopār, -re, *f.*
Simmer, *see* **Boil.**
Simony, *s.* păvitrānčeñ vikāp, -kpā, *n.*
Simper, *v.* (ăumăryādin) hās.
Simple, *a.* 1. sādo, *e.g.* s. boy. 2. tsālto = *l.* ordinary, current. 3. yekoḍo = *l.* not double. 4. pisoso = a little mad; *see* **Sheer.**
Simpleton, *a.* pisoso.
Simplicity, *s.* sādepoṇ, -ṇā, *n.*, *etc. see adj.*
Simplify, *v.* sošṭ kăr = *l.* make clear.
Simulate, *v.* kăpăṭān tsăl = behave with simulation; fóṭoun dākăi = *l.* show deceiving (*or other verb*); fóṭăi = deceive; nāḍi kăr *or* n. tsălăi.
Simulation, *s.* kăpăṭ, -ṭā, *n.*; ṭhăkkụ, -kā, *n.*; nāḍ, -ḍi, *f.* = *l.* trick; *vlg. some say* fālsapoṇ, -ṇā, *n.*
Simultaneous, *a. rs.* teāts veḷār = at the same time; soveñ, *e.g.* soveñ Māri ani Jezu tānkāñ meḷḷiñ = they found simultaneously J. and M.

Sin, *s.* pātak, -tkā, *n.*; pāp, -pā, *n.*; ăprād, -dā, *m.* = a fault; tsuk, -ki, *f.* = *l.* a mistake; gunyāuñ, -āvā, *m.*

Sin, *v.* pātak ādār, *or* p. kăr.

Since, *prep. ad.* 1. thāun = from; lāgāit, *e. g.* from to-day = āz l., *Hind. n. c.*
 2. pāsvot, *or* dekun, *or* kiteāk moḷeār = because; *see* Gram.
 3. uprānt = after.

Sincere, *a.* 1. niskăpṭi; sādo.
 2. nīz = *l.* true.
 3. suṭavo, *e.g.* s. confession.

Sincerity, *s.* niskăpăṭ, -ṭā, *n.*; sādepoṇ, -ṇā, *n.*

Sinecure, *s.* tsākrinātụlleñ kām, -mā, *n.*, *or* -lo sāmbāḷ, -ḷā, *m.* = *l.* office or pay without service.

Sinew, *s.* 1. šir, -re, *f.* = *l.* vein, nerve; *see also* **Nerve, Tendon.**
 2. bòḷ, -ḷā, *n.* = *l.* force.
 3. *fg.* prăyătăn, -tnā, *n.* = *l.* effort.

Sinful, *a.* āḍvārlolo = *l.* prohibited; vāiṭ = *l.* bad; khoṭo = *l.* wicked; pātak zāun āsullo = *l.* which is sin; *or* pātkātso.

Sinfulness, *s.* khoṭepoṇ, -ṇā, *n.*

Sing, *v.* 1. gāyān kăr; *vlg.* kăntār kăr, *fr.*; gā.
 2. *fg.* hogoḷsi, *or* vorni = *l.* praise.

Singe, *v.* ulpāi, *c. v.* = scorch.

Singer, *s.* kăntarist, -tā, *m.*; gāyān kărtolo.

Singing, *s.* gāyān, -nā, *n.*; *vlg.* kăntār, -rā, *n.*, *fr.*

Single, *a.* yekăts.
 I have not a s. pie = moze kăḍe khāints nāñ.

Single out, *v.* vintsun kāḍ.

Singly, *ad.* vingăḍ.

Singular, *a.* 1. yekăts = only one.
 2. ăprup = *l.* rare.
 3. ăsādārṇ = *l.* extraordinary.
 4. tārifetso = *l.* curious, original.

Singularity, *s.* 1. *rs. into adj.*
 2. ăprupāi, -ye, *f.*, *etc.*
 3. tārif, -fe, *f.*

Sinister, *a.* ăuguṇātso; ădrušṭātso.

Sink, *v.* 1. buḍăi, *c. v. of* buḍ, *n. v.*, *pr. fg.*, *e.g.* into sin.
 2. devoi, *c. v. of* deuñ = *l.* lower *e.g.* price.
 3. pòḍăi = *l.* cause to fall, *c. v. of* pòḍ.
 4. *fg.* rig = *l.* enter, *e. g.* a sword.
 5. pāḍ pòḍ = *l.* fall spoiled (be in a declining state); *see also* **Squander, Invest.**

Sink, *s.* burseponātso fònḍ, -ḍā, *m.* = *l.* a grave of dirt; bursi suāt, -te, *f.* = *l.* a dirty place.

Sinless, *a.* pātak nātullo, *or* pāp khăt nātullo *or* gunyāunātullo.

Sinner, *s.* pātki, -kiā, *m.*, *f.*; pāpi, -yā, *m.*; pāpiṇ, -ṇi, *f.*

Sip, *v.* gòṭ; burki.

Sip, *s.* kuskuṭ, -ṭā, *n.*; burko, -keā, *m.*
Siphon, *s.* nāḷi, -ye, *f.*
Sir, *s.* sāib, -bā, *m.*, *in voc.* sāibā, *or* sāibāno; *see* **Esquire**; *see* Gram. P. III. ch. i.
Sire, *s.* măharāi, -yā, *m.*
Siren, *s.* fuslāunči (ăstri); pāṭoḷi, -ḷe, *f.* = a coquette.
Sirrah, *s.* lutstso, -ččeā, *m.*
Sirocco, *s.* fugār kărčeñ vāreñ, -reā, *n.* = *l.* suffocating wind; sirȯk, -kā, *n.*
Sister, *s.* bāiṇ, -ṇi, *f.*
Sister-in-law, *s.* 1. miuṇi, -ṇe, *f.* (a sister of the wife).
2. bāvoz, bāuje, *f.* (the wife of a brother); voni, -ye, *f.* *used in addressing* the wife of a brother.
Sit, *v.* 1. bȯs.
2. zuntār bȯs = *l.* sit on the meeting, *fr.*
3. āḷsāi kăr = *l.* make laziness.
4. săma zā = *l.* become right, *e.g.* a dress; *or* hăḷt zā.
5. răvāṇe bȯs = hatch.
S. down = bȯs.
S. up = zāgo rāu.
Sitting, *s.* zunt, -tā, *m.*, *fr.*; mēḷ (ė), ḷā, *m.* = *l.* reunion.
Situated, (is s.), *v.* āsā.
Situation, *s.* 1. suāt -te, *f.*
2. udyóg, -gā, *m.*, *or* kām -mā, *n.* = *l.* office.
Six, *a.* să.
Size, *s.* voḍāi, -ye, *f.* = volume; vistār, -rā, *m.* = *l.* extension; lāmbāi, -ye, *f.* = *l.* length; părimāṇ, -ṇā, *n.* = *l.* quantity, *n.c.*; māp, -pā, *n.* = *l.* measure.
Skate, *v.* nisăr.
Skate, *s.* nisărtso motso, -čeā, *m.*
Skeleton, *s.* 1. hāḍānči găḍāvoḷ, -ḷi, *f.*; hāḍānts = *l.* only bones.
2. *fg.* bhāgeṭo, -ṭeā, *m.* = a very thin man.
Sketch, *s.* 1. năkṣa, -ṣe, *f.* = a draught; risko, *pl. f.*, *fr.*; măsudo, -deā, *m.*
2. moṭvo vivor, -rā, *m.* = *l.* a short explanation.
Skiff, *s.* dākṭi dóṇ, -ṇi, *f.*
Skilful, *a.* 1. kăṣṭi = *l.* industrious; zāṇto = clever; *or* ušār; hikmătitso, čămātkārātso = artificial, curious; năḍgo = *l.* cunning; *vlg.* boro, *e.g.* he is s. in playing = to boro vhāztā.
2. sikpi = *l.* versed, learned.
3. ănbog (*or* ănbou) āsullo = experienced.
4. *often rs. into v. or ad.*
Skill, *s.* 1. zāṇtepoṇ, ṇā, *n.*, *or* zāṇtigāi, -ye, *f.*
2. čămătkār, -rā, *m.* = artifice.
3. săkăt, -kti, *f.* = *l.* ability; trāṇ, -ṇā, *n.*; tsoturāi, -ye, *f.*
Skim, *v.* 1. fénd kāḍ.
2. voilebār ulăi = *l.* speak on the surface, (touch upon).
Skimmer, *s.* doyi, -ye, *f.*

Skin, *s.* kāt, -ti, *f.*; tsāmbḍeñ, ḍeā, *n.* = leather.

Skin, *v.* kāt kāḍ.

Skinflint, *s.* imṭo mănis, -nšā, *m.*

Skinny, *a.* bārik = *l.* thin; bhāgeṭo.

Skip, *s.* uḍāp, -ḍpā, *n.*

Skip, *v.* uḍ; mirua = *l.* cross.

Skirmish, *s.* lān lăḍāi, -ye, *f.*; lăḍāisi.

Skirt, *s.* văstrapònd, -dā, *n.*; dèg, -ge, *f.*, *or* kāmb, -bi, *f.* = the ornamental border of a dress.

Skittish, *a.* 1. bhiyātso.
 2. lăzbanḍo = *l.* wanton.

Skulk, *v.* lip.

Skull, *s.* kăṭṭeñ, -ṭeā, *n.*; koḍḍo, -ḍeā, *m.*

Sky, *s.* 1. moḷāb, -ḷbā, *n.*; ākāš, -šā, *n.*; āsmān, -nā, *n.*, *n. c.*
 2. vāreñ, -reā, *n.* = *l.* wind, *fg.*

Slab, *s.* 1. mārblātso fātor, -trā, *m.*
 2. dākṭeñ foḷeñ, -ḷeā, *n.*

Slack, *a.* 1. sădiḷ = *l.* loose.
 2. *fg.* āḷsi = *l.* lazy; făḍpoši; bepārvi.

Slackness, *s.* 1. sădiḷāi, -ye, *f.*
 2. āḷsāi, -ye, *f.*

Slag, *s.* koir, -rā, *m.*; ligiṭ, -ṭā, *n.*; *vlg.* lonkḍāgu, -vā, *m.*

Slake, *v.* 1. rāvoi, thāmboi = cause to cease, *e.g.* thirst; pālvoi = *l.* quench (*also for* thirst).
 2. mou kăr = *l.* make soft, *e.g.* lime.

Slander, *s.* 1. bădlām, -me, *f.* = *l.* calumny; vāiṭ kăbār, -bre, *f.* = *l.* bad news.
 2. ninda, -de, *f.* = abuse, blame.
 3. gunyāuñ, -āvā, *m.* = *l.* fault; ăpamān, -nā, *m.*

Slander, *v.* bădlām ghāl = *l.* put calumny; ninda kăr = *l.* say blame, accusation; bedap kăr = *l.* make defamation; mānār ulăi.

Slanderer, *s.* bădlāmegār, -rā, *m.*

Slanderous, *a.* ăpamānātso, *or* bădlāmetso; *see* **Slander.**

Slang, *s.* hălki bhās, -se, *f.* = *l.* low language.

Slant, *a.* vānkḍo = *l.* oblique.

Slap, *s.* 1. thāp, -pi, *f.* = a heavy s.
 2. thāpāḍ, -pḍā, *n.* = a slight s.

Slap, *v.* tāpăi.

Slash, *v.* 1. kātăr = *l.* cut.
 2. tsātsāi = *l.* chop.

Slate, *s.* fātrāči foḷi, -ye, *f.* = *l.* a sheet of stone; borountso fātor, -trā, *m.* = *l.* a stone for writing on.

Slaughter, *s.* (zomeā-) khuni, -ye, *f.*; desvaṭ, -ṭe, *f.* = *l.* plunder; păḍāu, -ḍāvā, *m.* = *l.* defeat.

Slave, *s.* gulām, -mā, *m.*

Slave, *v.* gulāmāčeñ kām kăr = *l.* do work of a slave.

Slaver, *s.* lāḷ, -ḷi, *f.*

Slavery, *s.* gulāmpoṇ, -ṇā, *n.* *pr. fg.*

Slavish, *a.* gulāmpoṇātso.

Slay, *v.* 1. khuni kăṛ = *l.* make homicide, *fg.*; jivsi mār =

kill; jīv kāḍ = *l.* take away life.
2. solvăi, păḍāu kăr = defeat.
Slayer, *s.* khunigār, -rā, *m., etc.*
Slaying, *s.* khuni, -ye, *f., or rs. into v.*
Sledge, *s.* 1. nisărči gāḍi, -ye, *f.* = *l.* a slipping cart; čăkrañ nātulli gāḍi, -ye *f.*
2. kāmārakudănṭi, -ṭe, *f.* = *l.* the hammer of a smith.
Sleek, *a.* telto, *e.g.* s. beast.
Sleep, *s.* nīd, -de, *f.*
Deep s. = bori n.
Get s. = nidāi, *c. v.*
Half s. = zóp, -pi, *f.* (*var.* -pā, *m.*), *or* jèm (*var.* zèm),-me, *f.*
Sleep, *v.* nīd; nīd yetā = s. comes *or* nīd pòḍtā = *l.* s. falls, *more used for* taking a doze, a nap.
I cannot keep from sleeping = dòḷe ugte kărnozo.
Go to s. = nidunk vots.
S. off = nidon niuḷāi (drunkenness) = *l.* get clear by sleeping.
Sleepiness, *s.* jèm, -me, *f.*
Sleepless, *a.* nīďnātullo.
Sleeplessness, *s.* nāññīd, -de, *f.* (*vlg.* nīd nāñ).
Sleepy, *a. rs.* jèm yetā *or* zopir āsā; nidrest.
Sleet, *s.* bārik kăre, -reāñ, *pl. m.*
Sleeve, *s.* lobātso (*or other* garment) hāt, -tā, *m.* = hand of gown.
Laugh in the sleeves = guṭān hās.
Sleight, *s.* nāḍ, -ḍi, *f.* = *l.* trick; hikmăt, -ti, *f.*; čămătkār, -rā, *n.* = *l.* a curious thing.
Slender, *a.* ăskăt = *l.* weak; bārik = *l.* thin; uṇo = *l.* less; bhāgeṭo = very s.
Slenderness, *s.* ăskătkāi, -ye, *f.*; bārikāi, -ye, *f.*; *see adj.*; uṇepoṇ, -ṇā, *n.* = *l.* diminution.
Slice, *s.* 1. pāti, -ye, *f.*, kāp, -pā, *n.* = a s. of bread.
2. kuḍko, -keā, *m.* = *l.* a piece; souli, -le, *f.* = a small piece of wood.
Slice, *v.* tsātsāi.
Slide, *v.* nisăr.
Slide, *s.* nisrāp, -pā, *n.*
Slight, *a.* lān; thoḍo; haḷu = *Lat. levis*; bhārnātullo = unimportant.
Slight, *s.* bepārvo, -veā, *m.* = *l.* contempt; ălăkṣa, -ṣe, *f.*
Slight, *v.* bepārvo kăr, *or* ălăkṣa kăr; sóḍ = *l.* abandon, let go.
Slime, *s.* ubir, -brā, *m.* = *l.* mud.
Sling, *v.* uḍāi = *l.* throw; sóḍ = *l.* discharge, leave (free).
Sling, *s.* gopiṇ, -ṇi, *f.*
Slink, *v.* pòḷ = *l.* flee, run away secretly.
Slip, *v.* 1. nisăr; găḷ.
2. sóḍ = *l.* leave, *e.g.* let s. an opportunity.
3. guṭān vor = *l.* bring secretly.
S. away = pòḷ = *l.* flee.
S. out of the memory = ugḍās visăr (*Sb. Dat.*)

Slip, *s.* 1. nisrāp, -pā, *n.*
2. tsuk, -ki, *f.* = *l.* a mistake.
3. khāndi, -ye, *f.* = *l.* a small branch.
4. tīr, -rā, *m.* = a long narrow piece of paper or cloth.

Slipper, *s.* 1. činel, -lā, *n.*
2. pāpās, -sā, *m.* = a shoe (Indian half s.)

Slippery, *a.* 1. dubāuntso = *l.* doubtful; risketso = *l.* perilous.
2. nisrasārko = *l.* on which one can slip; nisărtso.

Slit, *v.* kātăr = *l.* cut.

Slit, *s.* kātrāp, -pā, *n.*

Sloop, *s.* *approx.* pātmār, -ri, *f.*

Slop, *s.* 1. simpu̥lleñ udāk, -dkā, *n.* = *l.* water thrown about.
2. soro, *mn.* liquor; *bet.* rās soro, -reā, *m.*, *or* urak, -kā, *n.*, *or* găngaro, -reā, *m.*
3. tăyār văstrañ, *pl. n.* = ready clothes.
4. rās, -si, *f.* = *l.* a heap, number.

Slope, *s.* deuṇi, -ṇe, *f.*

Slope, *v.* deuñ = *l.* descend, *e.g.* the roof slopes.

Sloping, *a.* deuntso.

Sloth, *s.* 1. āḷsāi, -ye, *f.*
2. jèm (*var.* zèm), -me, *f.* = *l.* slumber.

Slothful, *a.* āḷsi; *see* **Coward**; făḍpoši.
Be s. = jème, *var.* zème (āuñ jèmetāñ); jèm ye, *ch. cs.*

Slouch, *s.* 1. bāgāp, -pā, *n.* = *l.* bending; bāu, bāve, *f.*; pòng, -gā, *n.* = *l.* a hump.
2. vānkḍi tsāl, -li, *f.* = *l.* clownish gait.

Slough, *s.* kònḍ, -ḍā, *n.* (čiklā-čeñ k.) = *l.* a deep place (of mire).

Sloven, *a.* tsāltsămkăṇ nātulloso, *n. u.*; *vlg.* burso = *l.* dirty.

Slow, *a.* 1. soukās, *or* soukās tsăltolo.
2. āḷsi = *l.* lazy.

Slowly, *ad.* soukās *or* soukāsā-yen.

Slowness, *s.* soukāsāi, -ye, *f.*

Sluggard, *see* **Slothful.**

Sluice, *s.* tumb, -bā, *m.*

Slumber, *s.* jèm, -me, *f.*; zóp, -pi, *f.* (*var.* -pā, *m.*)

Slumber, *v.* jème; zopir āsā = *l.* is in half-sleep.

Slur, *see* **Spot.**

Slut, *s.* bursi ăstri, -re, *f.* = *l.* a dirty woman.

Sluttish, *a.* burso.

Sly, *see* **Cunning.**

Smack, *v.* 1. umo di = *l.* give a kiss.
2. tāpăi = *l.* slap.
3. čābuk hālăi = *l.* move the whip.
It smacks of heresy = mătabhe-dāči ruts āsā.

Smack, *s.* 1. pātmār, -ri, *f.*, dóṇ, -ṇi, *f.* = vessel.
2. gouji, -je, *f.* = *l.* noise.
3. ruts, -či, *f.* = *l.* taste.
4. thāp, -pi, *f.* = *l.* a slap.

Small, *a.* 1. dākṭo, *esp. used of* material things; lān, *pr. fg.*
2. haḷu = *l.* light, *e.g.* voice.
3. uṇo = *l.* less, *e.g.* s. resources.
4. čillăr = *l.* trifling.
5. somzanātullo = *l.* not understanding, *e.g.* s. mind.
Make s. = kuḍkeān kuḍke kăr.
S. coin = khurdo, -deā, *m.*; čungḍi duḍu, -ḍvā, *m.*

Smallness, *s.* lānāi, -ye, *f.*

Small-pox, *s.* boḷṇik, -ke, *f.*

Smalt, *see* **Enamel.**

Smart, *v.* kăṭiṇ duk bhóg = pain much; tsurtsure bhóg = *l.* suffer (interior) pains; zăḷ = *l.* burn, *fg.*; *vlg.* pòṭānt duk.

Smart, *s.* kăṭiṇ duk, -ki, *f.*; zăḷ, -ḷā, *m.*; tsurtsuro, -reā, *m.*
S. money = fārikpoṇātso duḍu, -ḍvā, *m.* = *l.* money of reparation; *or* julmān, -nā, *m.* = fine.

Smart, *a.* 1. dukountso = *l.* afflicting; zăḷountso = *l.* burning, *fg.*, *or* zăḷtso.
2. bārik = *l.* thin, *fg.* acute, *e.g.* mind; tsurk, *or* ušār = clever; suḍuk.
3. nāzuk, = *l.* fine, delicate.
4. părzăḷik = *l.* shining, *e.g.* s. colour.
5. kăṭiṇ = *l.* severe, *e.g.* s. pain.

Smartness, *s.* 1. zăḷ, -ḷā, *m.* = burning interior pain; kăṭiṇ duk, -ki, *f.* = *l.* bitter pain.
2. bòḷ, -ḷā, *n.* = *l.* force (impetuosity).
3. tsurkpoṇ, -ṇā, *n.* = *l.* activity; bārikāi, -ye, *f.* = *l.* acuteness, *fg.*, *e.g.* of mind.
4. ăṭṭās, -sā, *m.* = showiness; *see also* **Smart.**

Smash, *v.* 1. mōḍ(ó) = *l.* break; puḍ kăr = *l.* make powder.
2. vāṭ = *l.* pound.

Smatter, *v.* 1. voilebār sik = learn superficially.
2. voilebār ulăi = *l.* talk sup.; nākazālleñ sāng = *l.* say nonsense.

Smatterer, *s.* zāṇārso = *l.* an apparently learned (man); *vlg.* ărdokuro sikpi, -piā, *m.* = *l.* half learned.

Smear, *v.* 1. (tsărāb *or* tèl) lāi = *l.* apply (fat *or* oil).
2. lēp(é) lāi = *l.* apply plaster.

Smell, *s.* 1. părmăḷ, -ḷā, *m.* (good s.), *mn. also* the sense of s.
2. ghāṇ, -ṇi, *f.* (bad s.); imsāṇ, -ṇi, *f.* (fishy s.); hunga, -ge, *f.*

Smell, *v.* părmăḷ ghe (*or* ghāṇ ghe) = *l.* take smell, *G. M.* (*G. F.*), *e. g.* s. a flower; părmăḷ (*or* ghāṇ) yetā, *G. M.* (*G. F.*), *or* părmăḷtā *or* ghāṇtā.

Smelling, *a.* 1. părmăḷātso (good s.)
2. ghāṇiero (bad s.).

Smile, *v.* amburko (hāso) hās.

Smile, *s.* amburko hāso, -seā, *m.*

Smirk, *s.* āḍetso hāso, -seā, *m.* =*l.* an unnatural laugh; fóṭkirohāso.

Smite, *v.* ādḷāi = *l.* cause to dash, *c. v. of* ādăḷ.

Smith, *s.* 1. āčāri, -riā, *m.*, in iron or wood.
2. lovār, -rā, *m.* = a blacksmith.
3. sonār, -rā, *m.*, in silver, gold.

Smock, *s.* tsóḷi, -ye, *f.*

Smoke, *v.* 1. vōḍ (čiruṭ v.)
2. duvor lāi = *l.* apply smoke, *bet.* duvrāk ghāl = *l.* a. to s., *ch. cs.*
3. duvor bhāir sărtā = s. comes out, *ch. cs.*
4. *fg.* sódun kāḍ = *l.* seeking take.

Smoke, *s.* duvor, -vrā, *m.* (*var.* dur, -rā).

Smooth, *a.* 1. telto = *l.* polished.
2. kèsnātullo = *l.* without hair.
3. nidān = *l.* calm, equable; thănḍ = *l.* cold, *fg.* equable, *e.g.* s. man, s. sea.
4. săma = *l.* right, *e.g.* s. speech.
5. mogāḷ = *l.* dear; fuslāuntso = *l.* caressing.

Smooth, *v.* 1. telto kăr = *l.* make polished.
2. fuslāi = *l.* soothe.
3. hāḷu kăr = *l.* make light.
4. săsār kăr = *l.* make easy.
5. nīb sāng = *l.* say pretext, *ch. cs.*

Smoothly, *ad.* soukāsāyen.

Smoothness, *s.* 1. teltepoṇ, -ṇā, *n.*; *bet.* telsāṇ, -ṇi, *f.*
2. nidānāi, -ye, *f.*
3. fuslāuṇeñ, -ṇeā, *n.*, *see adj.*

Smother, *v.* 1. fugār kăr, *fr.*
2. pālvoi = *l.* quench, *e.g.* fire.
3. dāmpun dovór = *l.* keep shut, *e.g.* a sigh.

Smoulder, *v.* bitărle bităr lās.

Smug, *see* **Neat, Spruce.**

Smuggle, *v.* tsóriye vor.

Smut, *s.* găs, -si, *f.*; găirăm, -mā, *m.*; kăstăḷ, -ḷā, *n.* = *l.* dirt.

Smutty, *a.* 1. găirāmātso = *l.* of smut.
2. *fg.* burso = *l.* dirty, impure.

Snack, *s.* (go s. with) săma vāṇte ghe = receive equal parts.

Snaffle, *see* **Bridle.**

Snail, *s.* pikuḷ, -ḷā, *m.*

Snake, *s.* soróp, -rpā, *m.*, *pl.* sorăp; *see* Gram. Parergon; jiudāḷ, -ḷi, *f.* = a reptile.

Snap, *v.* 1. fóḍ = *l.* break (*pass.* fuṭ), *e.g.* glass; mōḍ(ó) = *l.* break (*pass.* mòḍ).
2. vhāzāi = *l.* cause to sound (s. fingers); čiṭki măr.
S. up, 1. giḷ = *l.* swallow.
2. tsukon rāvoi = *l.* interrupt abusively.

Snappish, *a.* tsābkór; tsābasārko, *or* tsābčeāk lāgullo = given to biting.

Snare, *s.* 1. nāḍ, -ḍi, *f.* = *l.* a trick.

2. pās, -sā, *m.*, for birds.
Snare, *v.* 1. nāḍi kăr = *l.* make tricks.
2. sāmpḍāi = *l.* catch; *see* **Ensnare.**
Snarl, *v.* gurgur, *as* an angry dog.
Snatch, *v.* dhăr; kāṇe.
S. away = kāḍ.
S. down = săkăl dovòr.
Sneak, *v.* tsăr = creep.
S. away = pòḷ.
Sneer, *v.* bepārveān hās = *l.* laugh (at) with contempt; yeḍāi = *l.* mock.
Sneeze, *s.* sink, -ke, *f.*
Sneeze, *v.* sink kāḍ.
Sniff, *v.* (nākān) vóḍ; nākān usvās vóḍ.
Snip, *v.* (tudi) kātăr = *l.* cut (the extremity).
Snivel, *v.* kirmeñ vāutā.
Snore, *v.* gore.
Snoring, *s.* goroṇi, -ṇe, *f.*
Snout, *s.* sonḍi, -ye, *f.*
Snow, *s.* *approx.* dou, -ovā, *m.* = dew, *fg.*
Snow, *v.* dou pòḍ.
Snub, *v.* 1. pònt (*or* domós) kātăr = *l.* cut the point; kimči = nip.
2. rāvoi = *l.* stop (interrupt).
3. ălăkṣa kăr = disregard.
Snub-nose, *s.* čeṭṭeñ nāk, -kā, *n.*
Snuff, *s.* 1. kāzvo, -veā, *m.* = a burnt candle-wick.
2. puḍ, -ḍi, *f.* = tobacco powder.

Snuff, *v.* 1. puḍ vóḍ = *l.* draw powder.
2. kāzvo kāḍ = *l.* take away burnt wick.
S. out = pālvoi, *c. v.*
Snuff-box, *s.* bul, -li, *f.*
Snuffle, *v.* nākiañ ulăi.
Snug, *a.* 1. guṭlāun = wrapped up.
2. lipullo = concealed; yeksuro = *l.* solitary.
3. soukāsāyetso = *l.* peaceful.
So, *ad.* 1. itlo *or* titlo (*decl.*) = *l.* as much, *used with* ki, *e. g.* itlo...ki = so...that; ăseñ *or* tăseñ (*also decl.*) *used with* ki (ăseñ...ki = so ... that); ăse jinsiñ=in such (this) way, *also with* ki.
N. B. ăseñ *etc. may be used also absolutely*, *e. g.* ăseñ āsā = it is so.
2. teā pāsun = for that; tăr = therefore.
As...so = kăso (*or* zăso)... tăso; kedo...tedo, *or* kedo vóḍ...tedo vóḍ.
So that (= in order that), *by Supine*, *or Imperf. Subj.*, *or* pāsun.
So (= provided), *by the condit. or by* zărtăr; *see* Gram.
And so on = āni yer săit, *or* āni ăseñ.
So to say = yeke jinsiñ = in a certain way.
So called = moḷḷo.
So far as = itlo *or* titlo, *e. g.*

so far as depends on me = moje pārtint āsā titleñ, mākā tānktā te jinsiñ.
So far from = moje thāun pois, *or* m. sărsiñ thāun pois.
And so forth = āni tăsăleñ.
So small = tedo lān.
So great = tedo vóḍ.
So so = sumār.
So often = title pāuṭi.
So soon = itle vegiñ.
So then = tăr.

Soak, *v.* 1. mou kăr = *l.* soften; bizăi = *l.* make wet; séḷ kăr = *l.* make wet.
2. *fg.* bebdo zāun āsā, *or* soro piyelā = is drunk.

Soaking, *s.* bizouṇeñ, -ṇeā, *n.*

Soap, *s.* sābu, -bā, *m.*

Soap, *v.* sābān gās (*or* s. du).

Soapnut, *s.* ringo, -geā, *m.*

Soar, *v.* 1. unts vetā = *l.* goes aloft.
2. *fg.* guuñ, *e.g.* the mind soars.
S. above (excel) = jik *or* zăit vor.

Sob, *v.* uskăr.

Sob, *s.* uskăr, -rā, *m.* = a convulsive sigh in sorrow.

Sober, *a.* 1. hăḷtān piyeuntso = *l.* drinking moderately; ămăl zāinātullo = *l.* not drunk.
2. mótir āsullo = *l.* on mind; săma mótitso = *l.* of right mind.
3. nidān = *l.* equable, quiet; sādo = tame; simple.
4. bhāri = grave, *fg.*

Sobriety, *s.* 1. hăḷt, -tā, *n.*; **hăḷtān piyeunčeñ; nāñămāl, -lā,** *n.*
2. săma mót, -ti, *f.*
3. bhār, -rā, *m.*
4. nidānāi, -ye, *f.*, *see adj.*; sāmbāḷouṇeñ, -ṇeā, *n.*, *bet.* sāmbāḷāp, -ḷpā, *n.*

Sociability, *s.* 1. sāngātpoṇ, -ṇā, *n.*
2. *fg.* mogāḷpoṇ, -ṇā, *n.* = *l.* amiability.

Sociable, *a.* 1. sāngātpoṇātso.
2. *fg.* mogāḷ = dear.

Social, *a.* kuḷiāntso = *l.* of nations.

Socialism, *s.* āsteyekoṭ, -ṭā, *m.* = *l.* common union of property.

Society, *s.* 1. sāngāt, -tā, *m.*
2. mēḷ(é), -ḷā, *m.* = *l.* reunion, meeting.
3. sălgi, -ge, *f.* = *l.* familiarity.

Sock, *s.* lān mēi, -yā, *m.*

Socket, *s.* (kastisala) burāk, -kā, *m.*

Soda, *s.* khār, -rā, *m.*

Sodalist, *s.* *vlg.* irmāuñ, -āvā, *m.*, *fr.* = *l.* confrère; bhāupoṇist, -tā, *m. ex.*, *but n. u.*

Sodality, *s.* irmindād (*var.* irmaudād), -di, *f.*, *fr.*; bhāupoṇ, -ṇā, *n.*, *n. u.*; *see* **Confraternity.**

Soever, *see* Gram. P. II. ch. iii.

Sofa, *s.* kóč, -či, *f.*; khăṭleñ, -leā, *n.* = *l.* a bed; sopo, -peā, *m.* = a long seat made of mud or earth; māntso, -čeā, *m.*

Soft, *a.* 1. mou.
2. *fg.* movāḷ.
3. mogāḷ = *l.* dear.
4. nāzuk = delicate.
5. fuslāuntso = alluring.
6. lăzbanḍo = *l.* wanton.
7. telto = even, smooth.
8. soukāsāyetso = peaceful.
9. haḷu = *l.* light (voice).

Soften, *v.* 1. mou kăr.
2. movāḷāi.
3. haḷu kăr.
4. fuslāi; *see adj.*
5. uṇo kăr = make less, diminish, *e.g.* a crime.
6. sādo kăr = make tame.

Softly, *ad.* soukāsāyen.

Softness, *s.* 1. mousāṇ, -ṇi, *f.*
2. *fg.* soukāsāi, -ye, *f.*
3. movāḷpoṇ, -ṇā, *n.*

Soho, *int.* ye! *or* ah!

Soil, *s.* 1. zāgo, -geā, *m.* = ground; dărn, -ni, *f.*, *e.g.* dărnir pòḍlo = he prostrated himself.
2. zāllo gāuñ, -āvā, *m.* = native country.
3. găliz, -zā, *n.* = *l.* dirt.
4. khăt, -tā, *n.* = *l.* a stain.

Soil, *v.* 1. mhèḷo kăr, *or* mhèḷāi = *l.* make dirty.
2. *fg.* pāḍ kăr, *e.g.* s. the reputation of; bhăṣṭāi = stain.

Soiled, *a.* mhèḷo, *or* ăḷšik, *or* burso, *or* khătăillo, *etc.*

Sojourn, *v.* rāu; biḍār kăr; vās kăr.

Sojourn, *s.* rāvāp, rāupā, *n.*; biḍār, -rā, *n.*; vās, -sā, *n.*

Sojourner, *s.* 1. părdeši, -šiā, *m.*
2. vāsi, -si, *m.*

Solace, *v.* bhuzăi, *c. v.*

Solace, *s.* bhuzoṇ, -ṇe, *f.*

Solder, *v.* meḷăi = *l.* unite; pāntsăi; yekoṭ kăr = *l.* make union.

Soldier, *s.* sipāi, -yā, *m.*

Sole, *s.* aṭṭeñ, -ṭeā, *n.*

Sole, *v.* aṭṭeñ ghāl.

Solecism, *s.* 1. bhāsetsuk, -ki, *f.*
2. *fg.* ăumăryād, -di, *f.* = *l.* unpoliteness.

Solemn, *a.* dobājeātso, *or* dărbārātso; vóḍ, găddăḷ, *e.g.* feast; festātso = *l.* festival.

Solemnity, *s.* 1. dărbār, -rā, *n.*; dobāzo, -jeā, *m.* = *l.* pomp; vóḍpoṇ, -ṇā, *n.* = *l.* greatness; găddăḷ, -ḷā, *n.*
2. părāb, -rbe, *f.*, fèst, -tā, *n.* = a feast.

Solemnize, *v.* fèst kăr, *or* vóḍpoṇān kăr, *or* dobājeān kăr.

Solicit, *v.* 1. māg = *l.* request, *or* āṇ diun māg; porāt.
2. fuslāi = *l.* attract, allure, *ch. cs.*; pātak ādārunk lāi = *l.* induce to sin; nāḍi kăr = *l.* make tricks, (tempt).
3. lāle (*Dat.*) = *l.* long for.

Solicitation, *s.* 1. māg-ṇeñ, -ṇeā, *n.* = a request.
2. lāleuṇeñ, -ṇeā, *n.* = a longing for.
3. fuslāuṇeñ, -ṇeā, *n.*, nāḍ, -ḍi, *f.* = a temptation.

Solicitude, *s.* 1. čintna, -ne, *f.*;

porva, -ve, *f.*; lăkšā, -še, *f.*; *see* **Care.**
2. husko, -keā, *m.* = uneasiness.

Solicitor, *s.* văkil, -lā, *m.*

Solid, *a.* 1. ghăṭ, *pr. fg.*
2. bhórn = *l.* full.
3. borsinātullo, āput, nigăḷ = not mixed, *e.g.* s. metal, doctrine.
4. khărots = *l.* true.
5. bolāiketso = *l.* healthy, *e.g.* s. food.
6. tīn jinsāniñ vistārlolo = extended in three ways.
7. gunḍ = *l.* deep, *fg.*, *e.g.* s. erudition.

Soliloquy, *s.* āplea itleāk ulouṇeñ, -ṇeā, *n.*; yekleāčeñ ulouṇeñ, -ṇeā, *n.*, *or* yeklea -uloṇeñ, -ṇeā, *n.*

Solitary, *a.* 1. yeksuro = unfrequented, living alone.
2. khăntišṭ = gloomy.
3. lóknātullo = without people.
4. vingăḍ = separated.

Solitary, *s.* vănavāsi, -si, *m.*

Solitude, *s.* yeksurāi, -ye, *f.*, *or* yeksuri suăt, -te, *f.*; ărăṇeñ, -ṇeā, *n.* = *l.* a desert; yekānt, -tā, *m.* *is used by some, but Cn.*

Solo, *s.* yekăts tāḷo -ḷeā, *m.* = *l.* one voice.

Solstice, *s.* sănkrānt, -ti, *f.*

Solubility, *s.* kăḍasārkeñ, -keā, *n.*, *or* khirasārkeñ.

Soluble, *a.* kăḍasārko, *or* khirasārko.

Solution, *s.* 1. kăḍāp, -ḍpā, *or* khirāp, -rpā, *n.*, *or rs. into v.*
2. tīrp, -pā, *n.* = a decision; tirmāṇ, -ṇā, *n.*; tirsouṇeñ, -ṇeā, *n.* = a completion.
3. pārkouṇeñ, -ṇeā, *n.*, *e.g.* of a riddle.
4. zăvāb, -bi, *f.* = *l.* an answer.

Solve, *v.* 1. kăḍăi *or* khirăi.
2. pārki = guess.
3. ukto kăr, *or* ukto kărn dākăi, *e.g.* a case.

Solvent, *a.* 1. fārik kărisārko = *l.* able to pay.
2. kăḍtso = *l.* which dissolves.

Sombre, *a.* 1. kāḷso = *l.* a little dark.
2. khăntišṭ = *l.* gloomy.

Some, *a.* 1. thoḍo (-ḍi, -ḍeñ), *e.g.* some bread, some men; illo (-li, -leñ) = *l.* a little; tikke *or* čikke = *l.* a little.
2. ămko = *l.* certain, *Lat. quidam.*
3. koṇyek = *Lat. aliquis*, *e.g.* koṇyek mănis = s. man.
4. yeko, *e.g.* s. times = yeke pāuṭi, *n.c.* (yék yék ?).

Something = kāiñ *or* kiteñ.

Somewhat = illo, *or* thoḍo, *or* čikke, *or by* -so; *see* **Some.**

Somebody = koṇ yeklo, *or only* koṇ.

Somehow or other = kăsogi (*decl.*).

Somehow = kăseñ puṇi.

Some time = yék pāuṭi (*past or*

future); ādiñ *or* ādiñ purviñ *or* ā. māgiñ = formerly.
Some time ago = voḍḍol (*emph. of* voḍol).
Somewhere = khăingi.
Somewhere else = khăingi dusre kăḍe.
Sometimes = thoḍe (*or* yêke) pāuṭi.
S. . . s. = thoḍe pāuṭi. . . th. p.

Somerset, *s.* lăg, -gā, *m. or* lăgmuḍi, -ye, *f.*; 'l. mār = *l.* beat a s.'

Somnambulism, *s.* sopṇānt tsălāp, -lpā, *n.*

Somnolence, *s.* jèm, -me, *f.*; zóp, -pi, *f.*; nidči khuši, -še, *f.*

Somnolent, *a.* nidrest.

Son, *s.* putrụ, -rā, *m.*, *or* put, -tā, *m.*; burgeñ, -geā, *n.* = *l.* a child; săntătitso = (one) of posterity.
Eldest s. = mālgoḍo p.

Son-in-law, *s.* zāvoiñ, zāuñyā, *m.*

Sonata, *s.* vhāzāp, -zpā, *n.*

Song, *s.* pòd, -dā, *n.* = *esp.* a profane s.; kăntig, -ge, *f.* = *esp.* a religious s., *fr.*; gāyān, -nā, *n.*
Sing a s. = pòd mhóṇ.

Sonless, *a.* nirputrụ, *n. c.*; burgiññātullo.

Sonorous, *a.* vhāztso.

Soon, *ad.* vegiñ; ăusărān = hastily; ātāñ = *l.* now, *yet used by some for* soon.
As s. as = phuḍeñ, *with the participle*; *see* **After.**
Do as s. as possible = tāukta title vegiñ kăr.
I would as soon be a slave as a soldier = sipāi zāunčea prăs gulām zāin.

Soot, *s.* găirăm, -mā, *m.*; găs, -si, *f.*

Sooth, *s.* săt, -tā, *n.*

Soothe, *v.* haḷu kăr = *l.* make light; fuslāi; thănḍ kăr = *l.* make cold, *fg.* (appease); nivăi = make cold, *fg.*, *e.g.* anger; voḍni di = *l.* give attraction.

Soothsayer, *see* **Fortune-teller.**

Sooty, *a.* găirămātso.

Sop, *v.* bizăi.

Sop, *s.* bizăillo kuḍko, -keā, *m.* = *l.* a soaked piece.

Sophism, *etc. see* **Cavil,** *etc.*

Soporific, *a.* nidauntso.

Soprano, *s.* voilo tāḷo, -ḷeā, *m.*

Sorcerer, *s.* ātsār kărtolo; phitispoṇagār, -rā, *m.*; bolmeagār, -rā, *m.*; tăntragār, -rā, *m.*; ghāḍigār, -rā, *m.*

Sorceress, *s.* ghāḍigārn, -ni, *f.*; *see* **Sorcerer.**

Sorcery, *s.* phitispoṇ, -ṇā, *n.*; bolmeñ, -meā, *n.*; ghāḍi, -di, *f.*; bhul, -li, *f.*; *see* **Charm.**

Sordid, *a.* imṭo, (very stingy); ăḷšik = *l.* ugly, *fg.*; hălko, *or* ăṇvo = *l.* low, abject; kirkoḷ; kānṭāḷeātso, *etc.*

Sordidness, *s.* imṭepoṇ, -ṇā, *n.*; ăḷšikpoṇ, -ṇā, *n.*; kirkoḷpoṇ, -ṇā, *n.*

Sore, *s.* ghāi, -yā, *m.*; zăkăm, -kme, *f.*

Sore, *a.* kăṣ̌ṭountso; dukountso = *l.* causing sorrow, pain; dukest = painful; khăntiṣ̌ṭ = gloomy; kărkărātso = troublesome; movāḷ = *l.* tender.

Soreness, *s.* kăṣ̌ṭ, -ṭā, *m.*; zāḷ, -ḷā, *m.*

Sorites, *s.* tărkarās, -si, *f.*, *or* tărkamēḷ, -ḷā, *m.* = *l.* a heap of syllògisms.

Sorrel, *a.* ăḷduvoso = *l.* yellowish.

Sorrow, *s.* duk, -ki, *f.*, of body and of soul; kăṣ̌ṭ, -ṭā, *m.*, *esp.* of soul; păščatāp, -pā, *m.* = displeasure; zāḷ, -ḷā, *m.* = burning, *fg.* (interior pain), *e.g.* for the death of relatives, *esp.* for sin; tsurtsuro, -reā, *m.* = *l.* remorse, *and also* interior pain; khănt, -ti, *f.* = melancholy.

Sorrow, *v.* duktā, *or* duk distā = pain appears; păščatāp pāu (āuñ p. pāutāñ); kăṣ̌ṭa; tsurtsuro bhóg, *etc.*

Sorrowful, *a.* khăntiṣ̌ṭ; *see* **Sore.**

Sorry, *a.* dukest; khăntiṣ̌ṭ; dučit, *etc.*; *see* **Sore.**

Be s. = duk distā; *see* **Sorrow.**

Sort, *s.* 1. thăr, -rā, *m.*; jinos (*or* dinos), -nsā, *m.*

2. *omit and express by the Genitive.*

Sort, *v.* 1. zātivār kăr = *l.* make classes; bhēd(é) kăr = *l.* make difference.

2. zā = *l.* become (agree with), *e.g.* yeñ mākā zātā.

3. ...sāngāta mèḷ = receive with.

Sortie, *s.* bhāirsărāp, -rpā, *n.*; āngārpòḍāp, -ḍpā, *n.*

Make a s. = bhāir săr.

Sot, *a.* 1. piunčāk lāguḷlo = *l.* given to drinking.

2. piso = foolish.

Sottish, *a.* 1. ămāl zāllo, *or* ămāl piyello = drunk.

2. dăḍḍo = *l.* stupid.

Soul, *s.* 1. ătmo, -meā, *m.*; prāṇ, -ṇā, *m.*, *esp.* as the principle of life; mòn, -nā, *n.*, *e.g.* *Lat. exultavit spiritus* = my soul hath exulted.

2. *fg.* bunyād, -di, *f.* = *l.* foundation.

3. bāḷ, -ḷā, *n.* *as* a term of endearment.

Sound, *s.* 1. vhāzāp, -zpā, *n.*, *or* āvāz, -zā, *m.*

2. tāḷo, -ḷeā, *m.* = *l.* voice, *used also for* the sound of instruments.

3. bòb, -be, *f.* = *l.* a cry.

4. gouji, -je, *f.* = *l.* noise.

5. gāyān, -nā, *n.*, *esp.* a musical oral sound.

Sound, *v.* 1. vhāz (*or* āvāz zā), *tr.*, *n. v.*

2. mār = *l.* beat, *tr. v.*, *esp. used for* other than wind-instruments, *e.g.* bells.

3. *fg.* părikṣa (*or* tănki) kăr = make examination.
4. *fg.* hogoḷsi = *l.* praise.

Sound, *a.* 1. boro, *e.g.* s. sleep.
2. guṇātso = *l.* favourable.
3. bolāiketso = *l.* healthy; bolāikent āsullo = being in health.
4. nibbor *or* gădis = severe, strong; kăṭiṇ = severe.
5. bărābăr, *e.g.* s. argument.
6. āpuṭ = *l.* sincere, *e.g.* s. doctrine; khăro *or* nīz = true, sincere.
7. nāzuk = *l.* delicate, fine, pure.

Soundness, *s.* 1. bolāiki, -ke, *f.* = *l.* health.
2. săma mót, -ti, *f.* = *l.* right mind.
3. dāṭāi, -ye, *f.* = *l.* thickness (of wood).
4. bhār, -rā, *m.* = gravity, *e.g.* of arguments.
5. āpuṭāi, -ye, *f.* = *l.* sincerity; *see* **Sound, Validity.**

Sounding, *a.* vhāztso.

Soup, *s.* kāld, -dā, *m., fr.*; kăsāi, -yā, *m.*; kāṭ, -ṭā, *n.* (of gram).

Sour, *a.* 1. āmboṭ, *pr. fg.*
2. *fg.* kărkărātso = *l.* troublesome.

Sour, *v.* 1. āmboṭ kăr.
2. *fg.* zăḷăi, *or* rāg hāḍăi, *or* dukăi.

Source, *s.* 1. zăr, -ri, *f.*
2. *fg.* kārāṇ, -ṇā, *n.* = *l.* cause; *fg.* ărămb, -bā, *m.* = *l.* origin; mūḷ, -ḷā, *n.* = a root, *fg.*; *rs. into* vorviñ = through; *or* pāsun = on account of, *ch. cs.*

Sourish, *a.* āmboṭso; āmbso.

Sourness, *s.* āmsāṇ, -ṇi, *f.*

Souse, *v.* 1. udkānt buḍăi = *l.* plunge into water.
2. lončeñ ghāl = *l.* put pickle.
3. buḍon dhăr = plunging catch.

South, *s.* tènk, -kā, *n.*, *or* tènka, -kā, *n.*

Sovereign, *s.* sotăntri, (*var.* sosăntri); *see* **King.**

Sovereign, *a.* 1. sotăntrātso = *l.* independent.
2. uttim = *l.* excellent; *see* **Influential.**

Sow, *s.* dukărn, -ni, *f.*

Sow, *v.* biñ uḍăi = *l.* throw seed; vómp = *l.* scatter, *e.g.* seed.

Sowing, *s.* 1. *rs. into v.*
2. biñ, biyā, *n.* = *l.* seed.

Sower, *s.* vómptolo.

Space, *s.* 1. zāgo, -geā, *m.*; suāt, -te, *f.* = a place.
2. vistārāp, -rpā, *n.* = *l.* extension (local).
3. vēḷ(é), -ḷā, *m.* = *l.* time; phursót, -ti, *f.* = *l.* leisure.

Spacious, *a.* vistārlolo; iskăḷ; rund = *l.* broad.

Spade, *s.* khoreñ, -reā, *n.* (*It. badile*); mammaṭi, -ṭe, *f.*

Span, *v.* gèṇañ ghāl.

Span, *s.* 1. gèṇ, -ṇā, *n.* (the measure); vèt, -te, *f.*
2. *fg.* moṭvepoṇ, -ṇā, *n.* = *l.* shortness.

Spangle, *s.* (bāngārāčeñ) tăgăḍ, -gḍā, *n.* = *l.* a leaf (of gold).

Spare, *a.* 1. bārik = thin.
2. urta to = which remains, *e.g.* time.

Spare, *v.* 1. kăšiši kăr = *l.* make economy; hăḷtān khărči = *l.* expend moderately.
2. kăšiši kărn meḷăi (*or* yekoṭ kăr) = *l.* by economising gather (*or* make union); *or bet.* k. kărn rās kăr.
3. tsukăi = *l.* avoid.
4. mogān tsăl = *l.* proceed with love.
5. dovór = *l.* keep, *e.g.* food for to-morrow; *or* keep in life, *e.g.* in a slaughter; bačău kăr = *l.* make salvation (do not kill).

Spark, *s.* kiṭ, -ṭi, *f.*

Sparkle, *v.* părzăḷ = *l.* shine; u-zuăḍ di = *l.* give light; kiṭi pòḍtāt = *l.* sparks fall, *ch. cs.* jiḷibiḷiñ zā, *ch. cs.*, like stars.

Sparrow, *s.* girboji, -je, *f.*

Sparrow-hawk, *s.* păkkisāḷo, -ḷeā, *m.*

Sparse, *a.* 1. ăprup = *l.* rare.
2. simpḍăillo = *l.* dispersed.

Spasm, *s.* kāmp, -pi, *f.*, *or* kām-pero, -reā, *m.* = *l.* a trembling, (kāmp, -pā, *m.* = a row, series); *bet.* voḍi, *pl. f.* = *l.* convulsions; morlugi piḍa, -ḍe, *f.*

Spasmodic, *a.* 1. voḍintso = *l.* of convulsions; kāmpountso = *l.* causing trembling.
2. *fg.* kăṭiṇ = *l.* severe.

Spatter, *v.* dāmp = *l.* cover.

Spatterdashes, *s.* voile mēi, -yāñ, *m. pl.* = over-stockings.

Spattle, Spatula, *s.* koranṭi, -ṭe, *f.*

Speak, *v.* ulăi; utsār = *l.* ex-press; săngun di = *l.* saying give, *i.e.* preach, have a speech, reason.
S. against = *2nd Loc.* vāiṭ ulăi; gāḷi sou.
S. out = nīz săng.
S. together = găzāli măr = chat; săngātā ulăi.

Speaker, *s.* 1. uloṇeagār, -rā, *m.*, *or* uloṇo, -ṇeā, *m.*
2. prăsăngagār, -rā, *m.* = *l.* a preacher.

Spear, *s.* bhālo, -leā, *m.*; bhāli, -ye, *f.* (*dim.*)

Special, *a.* 1. prăték; višes.
2. mukya = principal.

Speciality, *s.* guṇ, -ṇā, *m.*; *by Gen.*; *see* Gram. p. 223, *seq.*

Specially, *ad.* bhou kărn; ădhik-kărn; mukhya zāun; višes *or* v. zāun.

Specie, *s.* nāṇeñ, -ṇeā, *n.* = *l.* current coin.

Species, *s.* thăr, -rā, *m.*; vărg, -gā, *m.* = *l.* a class; zāt, -ti, *f.* = *l.* a caste; *by Gen.*

Specific, *a.* 1. višes *or* prătek; *by Gen.*; *see* Gram. p. 223, *seq.*

2. khăṇḍit = *l.* positive.

Specific, *s.* višes vokāt, -ktā, *n.*

Specify, *v.* tăpsil sāng = *l.* say details; thăr (*or* zāt *or* vărg) sāng; sārkeñ sāng = *l.* say exactly.

Specimen, *s.* 1. dāklo, -leā, *m.* = *l.* an example.

2. nămuno, -neā, *m.* = *l.* a sample.

Specious, *a.* boro distso.

Speck, *s.* khăt, -tā, *n.*; *see* **Spot.**

Spectacle, *s.* diṣṭ, -ṭi, *f.*

Spectacles, *s.* *vlg.* voklu̥, -lā, *n.*; diṣṭičākru̥, -rā, *n.*; kănăḍak, -kā, *n.* (*H. K.*)

Spectre, *s.* druṣṭakāi, -ye, *f.* = *l.* a goblin; kuleñ, -leā, *n.*

Speculate, *v.* 1. dhyān kăr = *l.* make great attention; niyāḷ = *l.* meditate.

2. kăšišen vyāpār kăr = *l.* trade economically; jikčeāk lāg *or* lābāk lāg = be attached to gaining.

Speculation, *s.* 1. dhyān, -nā, *n.*

2. kăšišetso vepār, -rā, *m.* = *l.* economical trade.

Speculative, *a.* dhyānātso.

Speculator, *s.* 1. dhyāni, -niā, *m.*

2. lābāk lāgtolo.

Speech, *s.* 1. ulounči săkăt, -kti, *f.*; bhās, -se, *f.* = *l.* language; utăr, -trā, *n.* = *l.* a word.

2. uloṇeñ, -ṇeā, *n.*; prăsāng, -gā, *n.* = *l.* preaching; *vlg.* sermāuñ, -māvā, *m.* = preaching, *fr.*

Speed, *s.* zărurāi, -ye, *f.* = *l.* urgency, *fg.*; ăusăr, -rā, *n.* = *l.* haste.

Speed, *v.* vrăddhi zā = *l.* become prosperous; *vlg.* besāuñ zāuñ; guṇātso zā = *l.* become favourable, *ch. cs.*

Speedy, *a.* tsurk.

Spell, *s.* măntru̥, -rā, *n.*; *see* **Charm.**

Spell, *v.* ăkṣerañ utsār.

Spelling, *s.* ăkṣerāntso utsār, -rā, *m.*

Spend, *v.* 1. khărči, *pr. fg.*, *e. g.* time, life.

2. *fg.* tsălăi, *e.g.* time.

3. yêṭ = *l.* pay quickly (*also* waste).

Spendthrift, *s.* khărčik *or* večik.

Sphere, *s.* 1. guḷo, -ḷeā, *m.*

2. *fg.* ilāko, -keā, *m.* = *l.* department, *fg.*; bovāḍo, -ḍeā, *m.* = *l.* compass; mitmer, -ri, *f.* = *l.* limit.

Spheroid, *s.* guḷoso, -seā, *m.*

Spice, *s.* părmăḷāči văstu̥, -tu, *f.*; gărămmăsālo, -leā, *m.*; āḷean, -nā, *n.* = a mixture of the spices commonly used in seasoning, condiment; fòḍnu̥, -nā, *n.* (*var.* fòṇṇu̥, -ṇā, *n.*)

Spice, *v.* fòḍnu̥ ghāl.

Spices, *s.* sāmbār, -rā, *m.* (curry-stuff).

Spider, *s.* sāḷiyo, -yā, *m.*

Spigot, *s.* guḍḍi, -de, *f.*

Spike, *s.* kăṇās -ṇsā, *n.* = an ear of corn, *Lat. spica.*

Spill, *v.* simp, *e. g.* s. water; vomti; simpḍāi.

Spin, *v.* 1. vóḷ.
2. guunḍāi = *l.* agitate round, *c. v. of* guuñ.
3. *fg.* lāmb kăr = *l.* make long.

Spinage, *s.* vāḷčebāji, -je, *f.*

Spindle, *s.* sut voḷči gāḍi, -ye, *f.*, *or* čāt, -tā, *n.*, *Mr.*

Spine, *s.* kăṇo, -ṇeā, *m.*

Spiral, *s.* revoḍ, -ḍā, *m.*

Spire, *s. approx.* koḷos, -sā, *m.*, *e.g.* s. of a church.

Spirit, *s.* 1. ătmo, -meā, *m.* = *l.* soul; mòn, -nā, *n.* = *l.* mind, soul, *considered expressly as* spiritual, *e. g.* my spirit praises God; mòn *cannot be used as an equivalent in all cases for* spirit; *perh.* kuḍivoilo sotăntri, -riā, *m.*; spirit, -tā, *m.*, *fr.*
2. kuleñ, -leā, *n.* = a ghost.
3. *fg.* dhăir, -rā, *n.* = *l.* courage.
4. *fg.* tsurkpoṇ, -ṇā, *n.* = *l.* activity; sudaḷāi, -ye, *f.*
5. sevoṭ, -ṭā, *m.* = *l.* aim; săvab, -bi, *f.* = *l.* motive; irādo, -deā, *m.* = aim.
6. guṇ, -ṇā, *m.*, *e.g.* he is led by a good s.; nădteñ, -teā, *n.* = *l.* character.
7. soro, -reā, *m.*, *or vlg.* dobrād *or* tibrād (soro) = *l.* double *or* triple liquor (arrack).

Spirited, *a.* dhăiravont; ušār.

Spiritless, *a.* jīvnātullo; āḷsi.

Spiritual, *a.* 1. ătmeātso = *l.* of the soul, relating to the soul; devasponātso = *l.* devout; păvitrụ = *l.* sacred.
2. kuḍnātullo = *l.* without body (immaterial); nirākāri = *l.* without form.
3. igărjetso = *l.* of the church.
For s. *in philosophical mn. perh.* kuḍivoilo, *or* kuḍivoilea sotăntrātso.

Spirituality, *s.* kuḍivoileñsotăntrụ, -rā, *n.*

Spit, *s.* thimpi, -ye, *f.*

Spit, *v.* thimpi uḍāi.

Spite, *v.* dukāi = afflict; kăṣṭāi = *l.* cause pain.

Spite, *s.* mosór, -srā, *m.* = *l.* envy; niskutsār, -rā, *m.*; nāñkhuši, -še, *f.* = *l.* ill-will.
In s. of = zăritār = although, *ch. cs.*; mosrān = by hatred, bepārvo kărn = despising; jikon = conquering; virodh = *l.* against.

Spiteful, *a.* mosri; nāñkhušetso; koḍu = *l.* bitter; *see* **Spite.**

Spittle, *s.* thimpi, -ye, *f.*

Spittoon, *s.* pikdāni, -ne, *f.*; thimpiyečeñ āidān, -nā, *n.*

Splash, *v.* (ubrān) čiklāi = *l.* make dirty (with mud).

Splash, *s.* čikol, -klā, *m.*; ubir, -brā, *m.*

Spleen, *s.* 1. pint, -tā, *n.* (*probably this is* gall; (plīhā, *Mr. Cn. is perh.* spleen).

2. *fg*. vāiṭ mărji, -je, *f*. = *l*. ill-temper.

Splendid, *a*. voḍpoṇātso = *l*. grand; dobājeātso = *l*. pompous; părzăḷik = *l*. shining; uttim = *l*. excellent.

Splendour, *s*. părzăḷ, -ḷā, *m*. = *l*. brilliancy; dobāzo, -jeā, *m*. = *l*. pomp; voḍpoṇ, -ṇā, *n*. = *l*. greatness.

Splice, *v*. meḷăi, *or bet*. găḍsi = *l*. join together; sondăi, *e.g*. ropes, planks, *etc*.

Splint, *s*. kuḍko, -keā, *m*.; souli, -le, *f*. = a piece of wood.

Split, *v*. kātăr = *l*. cut; čīr = *l*. saw.

Split, *s*. fuṭ, -ṭi, *f*.; moḍāp, -ḍpā, *n*.

Split, *a*. fuṭụllo.

Splutter, *v*. găḍbăḍen ulăi = speak hastily and confusedly; gāge = *l*. stammer.

Spoil, *v*. 1. nisrăi = *l*. deprive.
2. pāḍ kăr = *l*. make bad; kusăi = *l*. corrupt; năš kăr = *l*. ruin.
3. luṭ kăr = *l*. make prey.
4. beḷse, *n. v*., *e.g*. food.

Spoil, *s*. luṭ, -ṭi, *f*. = *l*. prey.

Spoke, *s*. khunṭo, -ṭeā, *m*.

Spokesman, *see* **Orator.**

Sponge, *s*. dăryāčeñ āḷmbeñ, -beā, *n*. = *l*. mushroom of the sea (used for expunging stains); dăryāči jīb, -be, *f*. = *l*. a tongue of the sea, (a spongy substance used for polishing).

Sponge, *v*. (āḷmbeān) pus.

Sponsor, *see* **God-father, God-mother.**

Spontaneous, *a*. khušetso; *bet. rs. into* āpsents, *or* āple khušen; săimba pārmāṇe āsụllo.

Spoon, *s*. kuler, -rā, *n*., *fr*.; săunṭu, -ṭā, *n*. (*H. K.*); *some say* čămčo, -čeā, *m*.

Spoonful, *a*. kulerbhór, *fr*.

Sporadic, *a*. ăprup = rare.

Sport, *s*. 1. khušālăi, -ye, *f*. = *l*. pleasure; khéḷ, -ḷā, *m*. = *l*. play; āṭ, -ṭā, *m*.
2. năkăl, -klā, *n*. = *l*. a copy, *fg*. (mockery).

Sport, *v*. khèḷ.

Sportive, *a*. khéḷ kărtso = *l*. playing; khušālāyetso = *l*. pleasant; čeṣṭāyetso = *l*. funny.

Spot, *s*. 1. suāt, -te, *f*.
2. gurtụ, -tā, *m*. = *l*. a sign, *or bet*. khăt, -tā, *n*., *e.g*. a s. on the body; čiṭi, -ṭiñ, *pl. f*.; lāseñ, -seā, *n*.
On the s. = ātāntso; teā kṣăṇ = in the very moment.

Spotless, *a*. khătnātullo, *pr. fg*.

Spotty, *a*. khăt āsullo.

Spouse, *s*. poti, -ti, *m*.; potiṇ, -ṇi, *f*.; gărkār, -rā, *m*.; gărkārn, -ni, *f*.; dādlo, -leā, *m*.; bāil, -le, *f*. = a wife; gou, govā, *m*. = *l*. a husband (*a low word*).

Spout, *s*. tònḍ, -ḍā, *n*. = *l*. mouth, *fg*. (of a vessel).

Spout, *v*. bhāir săr = *l*. go out.

Sprain, *v*. vóḍ.

Sprawl, *v.* tānḍ.

Spray, *s.* zhoḍ, -ḍā, *m.*, *ex.* the fine rain driven, *e.g.* inside a verandah by the wind.

Spread, *v.* 1. āntuḷ, *e.g.* clothes; soḍăi = unfold.
2. vistār = *l.* extend, propagate.
3. părgăṭăi *or* părgăṭ kăr = publish.
Be s. = fāis zā.

Sprightly, *a.* tsurk; ušār.

Spring, *s.* 1. kămān, -nā, *n.*, of a carriage, for papers.
2. *for* the season, *see App. to the Konk.-Engl. Dictionary.*
3. zăr, -ri, *f.* = *l.* source; čilmbi, -be, *f.*
4. uḍāp, -ḍpā, *n.* = *l.* a jump; uḍi, -ye, *f.*
5. *fg.* ful, -lā, *n.* = *l.* a flower, *fg.*, *e.g.* s. of life.

Spring, *v.* 1. kirla, *e. g.* corn; ubza; yetā = *l.* comes.
2. uḍ = *l.* jump.

Sprinkle, *v.* uḍăi = *l.* throw, *e.g.* water.

Sprout, *v.* vāḍ = *l.* grow; kirla.

Sprout, *s.* ānkri, -re, *f.* (of trees); mungo, -geā, *m.* (of seed).

Spruce, *a.* 1. nităḷ = *l.* pure, clean.
2. dănḍi = *l.* foppish.

Spume, *s.* fênḍ, -ḍā, *m.*

Spur, *s.* *vlg.* spor, -rā, *n.*, *fr.*, *perh.* kānṭo, -ṭeā, *m.* = s. for horses.

Spur, *v.* sporān (kānṭeān) tóp.

Spurious, *a.* 1. *neg. of* khăro *or* nīz = true.
2. borsillo = *l.* mixed.
3. vāreātso (son).

Spurn, *v.* bepārvo kăr, *G. M.* = despise, *or* (bepārveān) sóḍ = leave (with contempt).

Spurt, *v.* bhāir săr.

Sputter, *v.* lāḷ vāutā = *l.* saliva flows.

Spy, *s.* bédi, -di, *m.*

Spy, *v.* béd kāṇe.

Squadron, *s.* 1. săvārāntso zomo, -meā, *m.*, *or* săv. vānṭo, -ṭeā, *m.*; trupsăvārañzomo, *fr.*
2. tārvañ = ships.
3. fouz, -ji, *f.* = *l.* an army.

Squalid, *a.* burso = *l.* dirty; kirkoḷ = *l.* wretched.

Squalidity, *s.* bursepoṇ, -ṇā, *n.*; kirkoḷăi, -ye, *f.*

Squall, *s.* 1. tufān, -nā, *n.*; vādāḷ, -ḷā, *n.*
2. bòb, -be, *f.* = *l.* a cry.

Squall, *v.* bòb măr = *l.* cry.

Squander, *v.* pāḍ kăr = *l.* spoil, *e. g.* money; nāš kăr = *l.* ruin; *rs.* hăḷtnāstanāñ khărči; véṭ.

Squanderer, *s.* khărčik *or* večik mănis, -nšā, *m.*

Square, *s.* tsouk *or* tsók, -kā, *m.*; *it mn.* any thing of a square form.

Square, *a.* tsoukātso *or* čār konseāntso.

Square, *v.* 1. tsouk kăr.

2. *fg*. săma kăr = *l*. make right, settle (accounts).
3. zātā = *l*. is done, agrees with.

Squash, *see* **Crush.**

Squat, *v*. 1. guṭli kărn bòs = *l*. sit on the hams; ukăḍyañ bòs.
2. lipun bòs = *l*. sit concealed.

Squeak, *v*. kirkir.

Squeamish, *a*. nāzuk.

Squeamishness, *s*. nāzukāi, -ye, *f*.

Squeeze, *v*. pīḷ; rōs(ó) kāḍ = *l*. take out juice.

Squib, *s*. ākāsbāṇ, -ṇā, *n*. = a kind of small firework.

Squint, *v*. tirso pòḷe.

Squinting, *a*. tirso.

Squirrel, *s*. 1. tsāni, -ye, *f*. = a s. that frequents the roofs of houses.
2. rān-tsāni, -ye, *f*. = *l*. a wild s.

Stab, *s*. suriyetso mār, -rā, *m*.

Stab, *v*. tóp = *l*. pierce; phāpsi = *l*. pierce with many wounds.

Stability, *s*. ghăṭāi, -ye, *f*.; stiraguṇ, -ṇā, *m*., *or* sthirpoṇ, -ṇā, *n*. = *l*. constancy; thirasāṇ, -ṇi, *f*.

Stable, *a*. thir; ghăṭ.

Stable, *s*. goṭo, -ṭeā, *m*.; haṭṭi, -ye, *f*., for cows and buffaloes; lāi, -ye, *f*., *or* tăbeli, -le, *f*., for a horse.

Stack, *s*. rās, -si, *f*. = *l*. a heap; muṭeñ, -ṭeā, *n*., *as* of straw; punzo, -jeā, *m*.; zomo, -meā, *m*. = *l*. a multitude, number.

Stack, *v*. rās kăr (*Acc*.); zomo kăr *or* zomăi.

Staff, *s*. 1. bèt, -tā, *n*. = *l*. a stick.
2. digo, -geā, *m*. = *l*. a support (wooden).
3. phoujimostakāntso mēḷ(ê), -ḷā, *m*. = *l*. an assemblage of chief commanders.
4. šibăndi, -de, *f*., *e.g*. s. of policemen.

Stag, *s*. dādleñ meruñ, -rvā, *n*.

Stage, *s*. 1. sopo, -peā, *m*., *or* zăgli, -le, *f*.
2. māḷăi, -ḷiye, *f*. = *l*. a story.
3. zāgo, -geā, *m*. = *l*. a place.
4. āṭasuāt, -te, *f*. = *l*. a place for drama.

Stage-coach, *s*. ṭăpālgāḍi, -ye, *f*., *or* gāḍiyeṭăpāl, -lā, *n*.

Stagger, *v*. kămp = *l*. tremble; lăk = *l*. walk as a drunken man; lăkon tsăl; yeṇeñ teṇeñ hālăi, *c. v*. = *l*. move here and there.

Stagnant, *v*. 1. *fg. neg. form of* tsăl, *e.g*. commerce stagnates = vyāpār tsălănāñ.
2. *pr. neg. form of* vāu; *or* vāvanāstanāñ rāu.

Staid, *a*. *see* **Serious, Grave.**

Stain, *s*. 1. khăt, -tā, *n*., *pr. fg*.
2. *fg*. ăkmān, -nā, *m*. = *l*. offence; *bet*. ăpamān, -nā, *m*.; lăz, -je, *f*.

Stain, *v*. khătăi, *c. v*. = *l*. cause stain; bhăšṭ kăr; mheḷăi, *c. v*. = *l*. make dirty.

Stainless, *a.* 1. khătnātullo; nítăḷ = *l.* pure.
2. *fg.* pāpkhătnātullo = *l.* without stain of sin.

Stair, *s.* māḷiyečeñ meṭañ, *pl. n.* = *l.* steps of the story; mèṭ, -ṭā, *n.* = *l.* a step.

Staircase, *see* **Stair.**

Stake, *s.* 1. kól, -lā, *m.* = *l.* a pole.
2. khāmbo, -beā, *m.* = a piece of wood, *e.g.* driven into the earth.
3. suḷi, -ye, *f.* = *l.* a pointed s. of wood; khunṭo, -ṭeā, *m.* = *l.* a stick, *e.g.* of a tent; khunṭ, -ṭā, *m.*
4. *fg.* āḍou, -ḍvā, *m.* = *l.* a pledge.

Stake, *v.* 1. pónt mār = wager.
2. āḍou ghāl = *l.* put a pledge; *see* **Impale.**

Stale, *a.* porno = *l.* old.

Stalk, *s.* dénṭ, -ṭā, *m.* = the stem of a leaf; sărvo, -veā, *m.* (of cut paddy).

Stalk, *v.* gărvān tsăl.

Stall, *s.* băska, -ke, *f.* = *l.* a seat; *vlg.* bānk, -kā, *m.*; *see* **Stable.**

Stammer, *v.* gāge; kāmpun ulăi.

Stammerer, *s.* gāgio, -giyā, *m.*; luḍbo, -beā, *m.*

Stamp, *s.* 1. mhòr, -re, *f.*, for sealing, *or* the impression itself; gurtụ, -tā, *m.* = *l.* a sign.
2. čīṭ, -ṭi, *f.* (of letters); *bet.* ṭăpālčīṭ, -ṭi, *f.*
3. *fg.* thăr, -rā, *m.* = *l.* kind.

Stamp, *v.* mhòr mār.

Stanch, *v.* (răgat) rāvoi.

Stand, *v.* 1. ubo rāu = *l.* remain standing; ubo āsā = *l.* is standing.
2. āsā = *l.* is, *e.g.* so stands the matter.
3. rāu = *l.* remain.
4. sós = *l.* suffer, *e.g.* I cannot s. it.
5. tsăl = *l.* walk, *fg.*, *e.g.* stands as a rule.
S. by, 1. lāgiñ āsā = is near.
2. săhāi kăr = help.
3. sāmbāḷ = *l.* keep, *e.g.* promises.
S. about = āḷsāi kăr = *l.* make laziness.
S. aloof = pois rāu.
S. good = tsăl = *l.* walk, *fg.*
S. in, *see* **Cost.**
S. on dignity = huddo sāmbāḷ.
S. out = -ntleān distā.
S. still = rāu.
S. to, *see* S. by.

Stand, *s.* rāvāp, rāupā, *n.*

Standard, *s.* 1. bāuṭo, -ṭeā, *m.*; giyāuñ, -yāvā, *m.*, *fr.* = a big flag, *e. g.* of a church; bondèr, -rā, *n.* = *l.* a small flag, *fr.*
2. vărg, -gā, *m.* = *l.* a class; mezāp, -zpā, *n.*, *or* māp, -pā, *n.* = *l.* a measure; nămuno, -neā, *m.* = *l.* a model.

Standing, *s.* 1. rāvāp, rāupā, *n.*
2. huddo, -deā, *m.* = *l.* rank.

Stanza, *s.* 1. slók, -kā, *m.*

2. pòd, -dā, *n.*

Staple, *s.* 1. vepār, -rā, *m.* = *l.* merchandise; yār, -rā, *m.* = things sold.

2. gānts, -tsā, *m.* = *l.* an iron loop.

3. pènṭ, -ṭe, *f.* = *l.* a market.

Star, *s.* neketrụ, -rā, *n.*, *pr. fg.*

Starch, *s.* gănji, -je, *f.* = *Lat. amydum*; khăḷ, -ḷi, *f.*

Starch, *v.* gănji (*or* khăḷ) ghāl.

Stare, *v.* jīv sóḍn pòḷe.

Stark, *a.* ghăṭ.

Stark, *ad. see* **Quite.**

Start, *v.* 1. kāmp = *l.* tremble.

2. bhāir săr = depart.

3. găḍ = *l.* found; stāpisi = *l.* found.

4. āng kāḍ = recoil.

Start, *s.* 1. āngkāḍneñ, -neā, *n.* = a sudden fit.

2. suru, -ve, *f.* = *l.* beginning.

3. bāirsărāp, -rpā, *n.* = *l.* departure.

Starvation, *s. perh.* bhukečeo voḍi, *pl. f.*, *or* bhuketso zāḷ, -ḷā, *m.*; *bet. rs. v.*

Starve, *v.* 1. bhuken mòr = *l.* die for starvation.

2. šéḷ zāli = *l.* cold became, *sb. Dat.* (suffer from cold).

State, *s.* 1. stiti, -ti, *f.* = condition, rank; titi, -ti, *f.*

2. bhés, -sā, *m.* = *l.* vocation; huddo, -deā, *m.* = *l.* rank.

3. săngăt, -gti, *f.* (*var.* săngti, -ti, *f.*)

4. voḍpoṇ, -ṇā, *n.* = *l.* greatness.

State, *v.* sāng *or* móṇ = *l.* say, *or* khănḍitzāun sāng.

Stately, *a.* voḍpoṇātso.

Statement, *s.* lèk, -kā, *n.* = *l.* an account; vivor, -rā, *m.* = *l.* an explanation.

Statesman, *s.* măntri, -ri, *m.*

Statics, *s.* sămatukavidya, -ye, *f.*, *or Cn.* stitišāstrụ, -rā, *n.*

Station, *s.* 1. suāt, -te, *f.* = *l.* a place.

2. huddo, -deā, *m.* = *l.* rank.

3. estasāuñ, -sāvā, *n.*, *as in* the Way of the Cross.

4. mokām, -mā, *n.*, *e.g.* of soldiers; ṭāṇeñ, -ṇeā, *n.*

Station, *v.* 1. mokām kăr (soldiers), *or* ṭāṇeñ kăr.

2. nemsi = *l.* appoint.

3. mānḍ = *l.* arrange.

Statistics, *s.* lokānčeñ lèk, -kā, *n.*; lokānčea lèkāvidya, -ye, *f.*

Statuary, *s.* šilpi, -piā, *m.*; kāntoṇegār, -rā, *m.*

Statue, *s. vlg.* imāz, -ji, *f.*, *fr.*; bombeñ, -beā, *n.*, *ex. but used comm. for* idol; murt, -ti, *f.* (*best word*).

Stature, *s.* voḍāi, -ye, *f.*, *or* lāmbāi, -ye, *f.*; ubārāi, -ye, *f.*

Statute, *s.* kāido, -deā, *m.*; kānun, -nā, *n.*

Stave, *s.* 1. (pipa-) foḷeñ, -ḷeā, *n.* = *l.* a plank (of a cask).

2. gāyānagīt, -tā, *m.*, *or the Mr.* kaḍaveñ, -veā, *n.* (line of music).

Stave, *v. see* **Burst.**

Stay, *s.* 1. rāvāp, rāupā, *n.*, *or* rāuṇeñ, -ṇeā, *n.* = *l.* abode; ṭikāṇeñ, -ṇeā, *n.*; biḍār, -rā, *n.*

2. digo, -geā, *m.* = *l.* a support (wooden), a prop.

Stay, *v.* rāvoi, *c. v. of* rāu, *n. v.* = stop.

S. for = rāk.

S. with = *2nd Loc.* (-ger) rāu.

Steadfast, *a.* thir; ghăṭ.

Steadfastness, *s.* stirpoṇ, -ṇā, *n. or* stiraguṇ, -ṇā, *m.*; ghăṭāi, -ye, *f.*; thirāsāṇ, -ṇi, *f.*

Steady, *a.* thir *or* sthir; ghăṭ; hālnātullo.

Steak, *s. approx.* (māsātso) lòḍò, -deā, *m.* = *l.* a piece (of meat).

Steal, *v.* tsōr(ó); nāgăi; fār; kāḍ.

S. over = guṭān ye = *l.* come secretly, *or rs.*

Stealing, *s.* tsóri, -ye, *f.*

Steam, *s.* ub, -be, *f.*

Steam, *v.* ub yetā, *or* ùb bhāir sărtā = *l.* s. comes out.

Steamboat, Steamer, *s.* āgbóṭ, -ṭi, *f.*, *fr.* (*from* āg = fire, *and* bóṭ *corrup. of* boat); duuratāruñ, -rvā, *n.* (*used also*); āgtāruñ, -rvā, *n.* = *l.* a ship with fire, *n. u.*

Steel, *s.* 1. tikeñ, -keā, *n.*; milāuñ, -lāvā, *n.*

2. *fg.* tălvār, -ri, *f.* = *l.* a sword.

Steel, *v.* ghăṭ kăr = *l.* make strong.

Steep, *a.* deuṇetso (*or* deuṇi), *e. g.* s. place; kăḍso, *e. g.* s. mountain.

S. place = deuṇi, -ṇe, *f.*

Steep, *v.* bizăi.

Steeple, *s.* tór, -ri, *f.*; koḷos, -sā, *m.* = *l.* cupola, spire (?), *or the Mr.* suḷaka, -kā, *m.*

Steepness, *s.* deuṇi, -ṇe, *f.*

Steer, *s.* pāḍo, -ḍeā, *m.*

Steer, *v.* tsălăi = *l.* rule, govern.

Steersman, *s.* tsălăitolo; sukāṇeagār, -rā, *m.*

Stem, *v.* 1. *Dat.* virodh vots = *l.* go against; rāvoi.

2. *fg.* inkār kăr (*Acc.*)

Stem, *s.* khāndi, -ye, *f.* (of a tree).

Stench, *s.* ghāṇ, -ṇi, *f.*

Stenography, *s.* sănkṣepāčeñ bărāp, -rpā, *n.*

Step, *s.* 1. mèṭ, -ṭā, *n. used also for* pace.

2. pāul, -lā, *n.* = s. of a foot.

3. pāunḍo, -ḍeā, *n.* = a round *or* step of a ladder.

4. *fg.* upāi, -yā, *m.* = *l.* means, *or rs. into v.*, *e. g.* kiteñ kărčeñ? = what steps must be taken?

Step, *v.* 1. tsăl = *l.* walk.

2. rig = *l.* enter.

Step-mother, *s.* māusi, -se, *f.*

Stereotype, *s.* thir ăkṣerāntso.

Sterile, *a.* 1. vānz, *or* nirputrụ,

or burgiññātullo = *l.* without children.
2. *fg.* fòḷ dinātullo = *l.* fruitless; bănjer.

Sterility, *s.* 1. vānzpoṇ, -ṇā, *n.*
2. bănjerpoṇ, -ṇā, *n.*; uṇepoṇ, -ṇā, *n.* = scarcity.

Stern, *s.* (tārvātso) pāṭlo bhāg, -gā, *m.*; pāṭ, -ṭi, *f.* = *l.* back, *fg.*

Stern, *a.* *see* **Rigid.**

Sternness, *s.* *see* **Rigidity.**

Stew, *v.* (lān ujeān) sizăi = *l.* boil (with a small fire).

Stew, *s.* čeḍiyañghăr, -rā, *n.*

Steward, *s.* 1. kārbāri, -riā, *m.* = *l.* a superintendent.
2. ugrāṇagār, -rā, *m.* = *l.* a purveyor.
3. āmin, -nā, *m.* = *l.* a bailiff, *n. c.*

Stewardship, *s.* kārbārpoṇ, -ṇā, *n.*

Stick, *s.* 1. bèt, -tā, *n.* = a common stick, *e.g.* to be carried when walking; toṇko, -keā, *m.* (big); danḍo, -ḍeā, *m.*, *e.g.* s. of a canopy; boḍi, -ye, *f.* (small).
2. ir, -rā, *m.* = the midrib of a palm-leaf, a bundle of which, when dried and bound together, serves as a broom.
3. vār, -ri, *f.*

Stick, *v.* 1. lāi *or* lāgăi, *tr. v.* = *Lat. affigere*, to fasten to.
2. lāg = *l.* be attached, *pr. fg.*, *n. v.*
3. guspoḍ = *l.* be confounded, *e.g.* in speaking.
S. at nothing = kāiñ bhiyenākā.
S. to justice = nīt sāmbāḷ.
S. up (a notiçe) = lāi.

Stickle, *v.* *see* **Contend.**

Sticky, *a.* pānkātso *or* lāgtso.

Stiff, *a.* ghăṭ; *vlg. rs into* lānkuḍ, *e.g.* hāt l. zātā = *l.* the hand becomes (like) wood; *see* **Formal.**

Stiffness, *s.* ghăṭāi, -ye, *f.*; *see adj.*

Stifle, *v. fg.* dāmpun dovór, *e.g.* a feeling; *see* **Suffocate.**

Stigma, *s.* 1. dāg, -gā, *m.* (a brand which natives make on their newly-born children).
2. *fg.* ăpamān, -nā, *m.*

Stigmatize, *v.* ăpamān kăr.

Stiletto, *s.* kăṭāri, -re, *f.*

Still, *a.* nidān.

Still, *ad.* 1. āniki, *or* āni, *or* āni...i, *e. g.* are you s. here? = tuñ āniki āngā āsāi? yedoḷ *or* yedoḷi, *e.g.* yedoḷ tujeñ kām kărunk nāiñ? *or* yedoḷi kiteñ kărtāi? zāleāri = however; tări = yet, nevertheless.
2. sădānts = always.

Examples: I have still one request = āni yek māg-ṇeñ āsā. While he was s. in bed = āniki niddon āstanāñ; s. greater difficulties = āni tsăḍ kăṣṭ *or* tānče prās tsăḍ kăṣṭ.

Stillness, *s.* nidānāi, -ye, *f.*; soukāsāi, -ye, *f.*

Stilts, *s.* rukātso pāi, -yā, *m.* = *l.* a wooden foot.

Stimulate, *v.* 1. utsāmboḷ kăr, *or* utsāmbolăi, *c. v.*; zăḷăi = *l.* cause to burn, (tease).

2. uṭăi = *l.* cause to rise, *fg.*; kānṭe vor = *l.* bring thorns (*Konk.*).

Sting, *v.* tóp.

Sting, *s.* 1. kus, -sā, *n.*

2. *fg.* tsurtsuro, -reā, *m.* = *l.* remorse.

Stinginess, *s.* surāt, -tā, *m.*; imṭepoṇ, -ṇā, *n.* = meanness.

Stingy, *a.* surāti; imṭo (*this 2nd is very offensive*).

Stink, *v.* ghāṇ yetā = *l.* s. comes; *or* ghāṇtā.

Stink, *s.* ghāṇ, -ṇi, *f.*

Stinking, *a.* ghāṇiero, *or* ghāṇitso.

Stint, *s.* uṇepoṇ, -ṇā, *n.*

Stint, *v.* ăšir kăr = *l.* make narrow, *pr.*; mitmer ghāl = *l.* put a limit.

Stipend, *s.* sāmbāḷ, -ḷā, *m.*; *see* **Pay.**

Stipulate, *v.* kărār kăr = *l.* make agreement; vòp = *l.* consent, agree.

Stipulation, *s.* 1. kărār, -rā, *m.*; voppigi, -ge, *f.* = *l.* consent; guttigeñ, -geā, *n.*, *n. c.*

2. šèrt, -tā, *n.* = *l.* condition (of a contract).

Stir, *s.* kāṭkāi, -ye, *f.* = *l.* a revolution; kuṭ, -ṭā, *n.* = *l.* a plot; utsāmboḷāi, -ye, *f.* = *l.* excitement.

Stir, *v.* 1. kăr, *with the above nouns*; uṭăi.

2. hālăi = *l.* move; kiḍăi; usti, *e. g.* s. the fire; tsāḷ, *e. g.* s. the fire, coffee.

Stirrup, *s.* rikāb, -bā, *n.*

Stitch, *v.* siuñ.

Stitch, *s.* suviyetso pónt, -tā, *m.*

Stock, *s.* 1. duḍu, -ḍvā, *m.* = *l.* money, funds.

2. kuṭām, -ṭmā, *n.* = *l.* family.

3. sămpurṇāi, -ye, *f.* = *l.* abundance.

4. gorvāñ = *l.* cattle.

5. khānḍi, -ye, *f.* = the trunk of a tree.

6. *fg.* dăḍḍo mănis, -nšā, *m.* = *l.* a dull man; *see also* **Sheep** *and* **Fund, Capital.**

Stock, *a.* tsālto = *l.* current.

Stock, *v.* hāḍn di, *or only* di; bhór = *l.* fill.

Stocking, *s.* mēi, -yā, *m.*, *fr.*; čil, -lā, *n.*, *or* pāyāčil, *n. u.*

Stock-still, *see* **Immovable.**

Stock-fish, *s.* suki māsḷi, -ḷe, *f.* = *l.* dry fish.

Stoical, *a.* bhóginăso = *l.* seeming not to feel, *or Mr.* udās.

Stoker, *s.* ujeārākṇo, -ṇeā, *m.*

Stole, *s.* estol, -lā, *n.*, *fr.*

Stolid, *a.* dăḍḍo *or* somzanātullo; piso; *see* **Sheep.**

Stolidity, *s.* dăḍḍepoṇ, -ṇā, *n.*; pisepoṇ, -ṇā, *n.*

Stomach, *s.* 1. poskaṭo, -ṭeā, *m.*; pòṭ, -ṭā, *n.* = *l.* belly, *used also for* s.
2. *fg.* ruts, -či, *f.* = *l.* taste.
3. *fg.* gărvu̥, -vā, *n.* = *l.* pride.

Stone, *s.* 1. fātor, -trā, *m.*; čiro, -reā, *m.* (*for* building).
2. biñ, biyā, *n.*, *or* moi, moyā, *m.* = seed *or* nut of stone-fruit.
Precious s. = rătăn, -tnā, *n.*
S. of mango = 1. pār, -ri, *f.*
2. koi″, koye, *f.* = the interior part of 'pār'.

Stone, *v.* fātrāniñ mār.

Stone-fish, *s.* pālu, -lvā, *m.*

Stony, *a.* fātrāntso.

Stool, *s.* 1. moṇăi, -ṇiye, *f.* (a low seat), *or* pāimoṇăi.
2. kākus, -sā, *m.*, *vlg.*, *or bet.* pāikāneāči băska, -ke, *f.*
3. utkāḍe, -ḍeā, *n.* = *l.* motion.

Stoop, *v.* 1. mukār bāgā = *l.* bend oneself before.
2. *fg.* puṭua = *Lat. dignari*, to condescend.

Stop, *v.* 1. rāvoi, *c. v. of* rāu, *n. v.*; thāmbăi, *c. v.*
2. dhăr = *l.* catch.
3. dāmpun dovór, *e.g.* a sigh.
4. āḍăi = *l.* prevent.
5 mănna kăr = *l.* cease.

Stop, *s.* 1. rāvāp, rāupā, *n.*; thāmbouṇeñ, -ṇeā, *n.*
2. āḍkāḷ, -ḷi, *f.* = *l.* obstacle; ăḍḍi, -ḍe, *f.* = *l.* obstacle.
3. virāmagurtu̥, -tā, *m.* = *l.* the sign of 'virāma' (a full s.).

Stopple, *s.* guḍḍi, -de, *f.* (*or* gurdi).

Store, *s.* 1. sămpurṇăi, -ye, *f.* = *l.* abundance.
2. dāstān, -nā, *n.*

Store, *v.* rās kăr, yekṭāiñ kăr = *l.* collect; tupeānt ghāl = *l.* put in the granary.

Storehouse, *s.* 1. tupeñ, -peā, *n.* = granary.
2. ugrāṇ, -ṇā, *n.* = *l.* dispensary, pantry.

Store-keeper, *s.* ugrāṇi, -ṇiā, *m.*

Stork, *see* **Crane.**

Storm, *s.* 1. vādāḷ, -ḷā, *n.*; tufān, -nā, *n.*
2. uprāḷi, *pl. f.*; *Mr.* hălla.

Storm, *v.* 1. zulmen kāṇe = *l.* take violently, *e.g.* a town; hălla kărn kāṇe.
2. āngār pòḍ = *l.* fall on body.

Stormy, *a.* 1. tufānātso.
2. *fg.* kuṭ kărtso = *l.* rebelling.

Story, *s.* 1. kāṇi, -ye, *f.* = a fable.
2. kătha, -the, *f.* = narration, history.
3. māḷăi, -ḷiye, *f.*

Stout, *a.* moṭo, *superl.* moṭṭo; pu̥ṣṭi; dinḍo.

Stoutness, *s.* moṭăi, -ye, *f.*

Stove, *s.* āguṭeñ, -ṭeā, *n.*

Stow, *see* **Store.**

Straddle, *v.* pāi pindun tsăl; băkkār dovorn tsăl.

Straggle, *v.* pārpoḷ zāun bouñ.

Straight, *a.* nīṭ, *e.g.* road; sārko = *l.* exact; săma = *l.* right;

modleān = through the middle.

Straighten, *v.* nīṭ (*or* sāma) kăr, *etc.*; *see adj.*

Strain, *v.* 1. gāḷ, *e. g.* a liquid.
2. *for* s. *in the mn. of* injure by over-exertion, *the following are samples of the way in which it may be translated: a*) lekavort kăr = make over the measure; *b*) săkăt miruăi = *l.* exceed power; *c*) boḷān vóḍ, *or* tsăḍ vóḍ = *l.* draw too much *is the* literal version.

Strain, *s.* prăyătăn, -tnā, *n.* = *l.* effort.

Strainer, *s.* gāḷṇi, -ṇe, *f.*; kurpoṇ, -ṇi, *f.* = str. for rice.

Strait, *s.* 1. (dăryāči) ăširāi, -ye, *f.* = *l.* narrowness (of the sea); dăryātso sănd, -dā, *m.* = juncture of the sea.
2. *fg.* kăṣṭ, -ṭā, *m.*; tondre, *pl. m.*

Strait, *a.* ăšir, *e. g.* s. road.

Strand, *s.* tăḍ, -ḍi, *f.*

Strand, *v.* tăḍik ādăḷ.

Strange, *a.* 1. păr *or* păra, *e. g.* părgāvānt *or* păragāvānt = in a s. country.
2. părdeši = *l.* exiled.
3. *fg.* sămăndnātullo = *l.* not connected.
4. *fg.* ăsādhărn = *l.* extraordinary; ājāpātso = *l.* wonderful; čămătkārātso = *l.* curious.
5. novo = *l.* new.

Stranger, *s.* 1. părdeši, -šiā, *m.* = *l.* an exile.
2. părki, -ki, (-kiā), *m.* = *l.* an unknown man.
3. nāñgărtso -čeā, *m.* = *l.* not of the family, *n. c.*

Strangle, *v.* (găḷo) muḍḍi = *l.* suffocate; *bet.* g. dāmp; phāsi ghāl = *l.* put a rope (round the neck); (găḷeāk) pās ghāl = *l.* put a rope.

Strangulation, *s. rs. v.*

Strap, *s.* tsāmbḍeātīr, -rā, *m.*

Stratagem, *s.* 1. năḍ, -ḍi, *f.*; hikmăt, -ti, *f.*; năḍgepoṇ, -ṇā, *n.*
2. upāi, -yā, *m.* = *l.* means.

Strategic, *a.* 1. hikmătitso, *etc.*
2. zuzasāmārthetso = *l.* of the art of war.

Strategy, *s.* zuzasāmārthi, -the, *f.*

Straw, *s.* 1. kărăḍ, -rḍā, *n.*; sukeñ tăṇ, -ṇā, *n.*; bāteṇ, -ṇā, *n.* (of paddy).
2. *fg.* mòlnātulli văstu, -tu, *f.* = *l.* a thing of no price.

Stray, *v.* 1. vāṭ tsuk = *l.* mistake the way.
2. bouñ = walk.

Streak, *s.* pāṭo, -ṭeā, *m.* (on the skin); dori, -ye, *f.* = *l.* rope (on cloth).

Stream, *s.* 1. vāḷ, -ḷā, *m.*; năiñ", năiñ, *f.* = *l.* a river.
2. lóṭ, -ṭā, *m.* = the current, *e. g.* of a river.
3. *fg.* dāuñ, dāve, *f.*; sānkăḷ, -kḷi, *f.* = *l.* a chain, *fg.*

Streamer, *s.* *see* **Pennant.**

Streamlet, *s.* dākṭo vāḷ, -ḷā, *m.*; tōḍ(ó), -ḍā, *m.*

Street, *s.* mārog, -rgā, *m.* (large); bīd, -di, *f.*, kēr, -ri, *f.*; gălli, -le, *f.*, *e.g.* in a town.

Strength, *s.* 1. ghăṭāi, -ye, *f.*; dhātụ, -ti, *f.* = *l.* metal, *fg.*, *but not used in the lit. mn.*; bòḷ, -ḷā, *n.*, *or* bolāiki, -ke (*var.* -ki), *f.*
2. trāṇ, -ṇā, *n.*, *or* săkăt, -kti, *f.* = *l.* ability.
3. thiraguṇ, -ṇā, *m.* = *l.* firmness.

Strengthen, *v.* 1. ghăṭ kăr; *pass.* ghăṭ zā; bòḷ di = *l.* give force; *pass.* bòḷ meḷtā.
2. tsăḍāi = *l.* increase, *c. v. of* tsăḍ; thir kăr.

Strenuous, *a.* dhăiravont; tsurk = *l.* active, *or* ušār; sudāḷ.

Strenuousness, *s.* dhăir, -rā, *n.*; tsurkpoṇ, -ṇā, *n.*, *or* ušārāi, -ye, *f.*; sudāḷāi, -ye, *f.*

Stress, *s.* zăḍāi, -ye, *f.* = *l.* heaviness; dāmbāp, -pā, *n.* = *l.* pressure; bhār, -rā, *m.* = *l.* gravity; bòḷ, -ḷā, *n.* = *l.* force.

Stretch, *v.* 1. kāḍ, *or bet.* sóḍāi, *e.g.* a piece of cloth; vistār = *l.* extend.
2. vóḍ = strain.
3. *fg.* miruăi = *l.* surpass, *c. v. of* mirua; mikva = *l.* surpass, *e.g.* s. his power; *see* **Exaggerate.**

Stretch, *s.* 1. prăyătăn, -tnā, *n.* = *l.* effort; petsāḍneñ, -neā, *n.*, *or* petsāḍāp, -ḍpā, *n.*
2. vistārāp, -rpā, *n.* = *l.* extension.

Stretching, *s.* 1. sóḍouṇeñ, -ṇeā, *n.*
2. vóḍāp, -ḍpā, *n.*

Strew, *v.* bhór = fill, *e.g.* with sand; vómp = *l.* disperse; simpḍāi = *l.* disperse; dāmp = *l.* cover.

Stricken, *a.* 1. ghāyello = *l.* wounded; mārlolo = *l.* beaten.
2. utăr prāyetso = *l.* of advanced age.

Strict, *a.* 1. nāzuk = *l.* delicate.
2. khănḍit = *l.* peremptory.
3. sārko, *or* zāgrut = *l.* careful.
4. bhou = much, *e.g.* in strict confidence = bhou guṭān; *see* **Rigid.**

Strictness, *s.* zāgrutāi, -ye, *f.*, *etc.*; *see* **Rigidity** *and adj.*

Stride, *v.* lāmb pāi kāḍ.

Strike, *v.* 1. mār, *e.g.* the hours, an instrument; vāz = *l.* play (sound).
2. boḍāi, *e.g.* on the door, on a wall.
3. devāi = *l.* lower, *e.g.* a sail.
4. čhāpo ghāl = *l.* print.
5. kāḍ, *e.g.* fire.
6. săma kăr = *l.* make right, equal, *e.g.* a measure.
7. (dhāni) kātăr = *l.* cut away (corn).
S. a balance = bāki fārik kăr.

S. with surprise = ăjāpăi, *n. c.*, *or* jim zā, *ch. cs.*
S. with awe = bhiyeunk lāi; jim zā.
S. a bargain = sāṭo kăr.
The clock strikes = găḍiyāḷ mārtā.
S. together, *see* **Clasp.**
S. up = 1. lāg *or* suru zā.
2. (dostint) rig.
S. out = kāḍ; sodun kāḍ.

Striking, *a.* ăjāpātso = *l.* wonderful.
2. bhou sārko = *l.* very exact, *e.g.* a portrait.
3. somzasārko = *l.* fit to be understood (convincing).

String, *s.* kordāuñ, -dāvā, *m.*, *fr.* = ribbon, cord (*also* of an instrument), *fr.*; dori, -ye, *f.*; sări, -ye, *f.* (of metal).

String, *v.* gunt, *e.g.* beads of a rosary.

Strip, *v.* 1. nāgḍăi, *or bet.* nāgḍo kăr; nesoṇ kāḍ.
2. nisrāi = *l.* deprive.

Strip, *s.* tīr, -rā, *m.*

Stripe, *s.* 1. pāṭo, -ṭeā, *m.*, on the skin; dori, -ye, *f.*; vāl, -li, *f.* = creeping line, *fg.*; bóṇ, -ṇā, *m.* (*l.* colour), *not ex.*
2. gānd, -di, *f.*, from a blow with a stick.

Stripling, *s.* burgo, -geā, *m.*

Strive, *v.* prăyătăn kăr; minăt kăr; petsāḍ.
S. after = *Dat.* lāle.
S. against = *Dat.* āḍ vots.

Striving, *s.* petsāḍne, -neā, *n.*, *or* petsāḍap, -ḍpā, *n.* = *also* emulation; prăyătăn, -tnā, *n.* = *l.* effort.

Stroke, *s.* 1. măr, -rā, *m.*; măr făr, *pl. m.*; pēt(é), -tā, *m.*; dumko, -keā, *m.* (with the fist); bukko, -keā, *m.*
2. phāngt, -ti, *f.* = a written line.

Stroke, *v.* poše, *e.g.* the beard *or* a beast with the hand.

Stroll, *v.* bouñ.

Strong, *a.* 1. ghăṭ, *e.g.* voice.
2. boḷadik, *e.g.* s. man; *some say also* foḍt, *e.g.* s. coffee.
3. bhāradik = *l.* grave, *fg.*
4. bārik = *l.* thin, *fg.*, *e.g.* sight.
5. bărābăr, *e.g.* argument.
6. kăṭiṇ, *e.g.* wind, words, bad smell, remedy.
7. boro = *l.* good, *e.g.* light, rain, good smell, memory.
8. moṭo *or* voḍlo, *e.g.* voice.
9. somzasārko = *l.* fit to be understood.
10. podvedār = *l.* powerful; *or* podvi āsullo.
Get s. = boro zā.
Is s. = boro āsā.

Structure, *s.* 1. găḍāp, -ḍpā, *n.* *or* găḍāu, -ḍāvā, *n.*, *or* găḍāvoḷ, -ḷi, *f.*, *e.g.* s. of body.
2. bāndāp, -dpā, *n.* = *l.* building.
3. mānḍāvoḷ, -ḷi, *f.* = *l.* arrangement.

4. rūp, -pā, *n.* = *l.* form.

Struggle, *v.* 1. lăḍāi kăr = *l.* fight.
2. inkār kăr (*Acc.*) = *l.* resist.
3. prăyătăn kăr, petsāḍ = make effort.

Struggle, *s.* 1. petsāḍneñ, -neā, *n.*, *or* petsāḍap, -ḍpā, *n.*; prăyătăn, -tnā, *n.* = an effort.
2. lăḍāi, -ye, *f.* = *l.* a fight.

Strut, *v.* gărvān tsăl.

Stubborn, *a.* āpleā vādeātso; dhāruṇ; săḷiṣṭ.

Stubbornness, *s.* dhāruṇāi, -ye, *f.*; săḷ, -ḷā, *n.*

Stucco, *s.* sāruṇ, *or bet.* nāzuk sāruṇ, -ṇe, *f.*

Stud, *s.* gubbekhiḷo, -ḷeā, *m.*

Student, *s.* siktolo; *vlg.* iskolātso burgo, -geā, *m.*, *fr.*

Studied, *a.* 1. tăyār kello.
2. khušetso = *l.* of will.
3. zāgrut = *l.* exact.

Studious, *a.* 1. āšetso = *l.* desirous.
2. sikčeāk lāguḷlo = *l.* given to study.

Study, *v.* 1. sik, *or* sikčeāk (*or* sikpāk) lāg.
2. tănki kăr = *l.* make inquiry.
3. tăyār kăr = *l.* make ready, *e.g.* a sermon.

Study, *s.* 1. sikāp, -kpā, *n.*
2. lāgāp, -gpā, *n.* = *l.* application.
3. sikčeñ kuḍ, -ḍā, *n.* = *l.* a room for study.

Stuff, *s.* 1. sāmān, -nā, *m.* = *l.* an article.
2. lugṭañ = *l.* pieces of cloth.
3. văstu = *l.* thing.

Stuff, *v.* bhór = *l.* fill.

Stumble, *v.* 1. ādăḷ = *l.* dash, strike against.
2. mèḷ = *l.* be found, *Sb. Dat.*, *e.g.* I stumbled on the man.

Stump, *s.* kuti, -ye, *f.* = the part of a tree remaining in the earth after the trunk has been cut down.

Stun, *v.* kān fóḍ = *l.* break ears; kān keppo kăr = *l.* make ears deaf.

Stunt, *v. neg. form of* vāḍonk sóḍ = *l.* allow to grow; kăši kăr = *l.* prune (*and thereby* stunt).

Stupefaction, *s.* *l.* jim, -mā, *n.*, *n. c.*

Stupefy, *v.* ăjāp zā; jim zā; piso kăr.

Stupendous, *a.* ăjāpātso.

Stupid, *a.* dăḍḍo; murk; heḍḍu; bekuf (*abusive*); somzanātullo; piso.

Stupidity, *s.* dăḍḍepoṇ, -ṇā, *n.*; murkpoṇ, -ṇā, *n.*; heḍḍupoṇ, -ṇā, *n.*; pisepoṇ, -ṇā, *n.*

Stupor, *s.* jim, -mā, *n.*, *n. c.*; ăjāp, -pā, *n.*

Sturdy, *a.* 1. ghăṭ.
2. dhāruṇ = *l.* obstinate.

Stutter, *see* **Stammer.**

Sty, *s.* dukraguḍ, -ḍā, *m.*

Style, *s.* 1. bhāsejinos, -nsā, *m.*

2. (borounči) khăḍi, -ye, *f.* = *l.* a kind of pencil made of lead, formerly in use, (for writing with).
3. rīt, -ti, *f.*, *or* rivāz, -ji, *f.* = *l.* manner.

Style, *v.* móṇ.

Suasion, *s.* bud, -di, *f.*

Suavity, *s.* 1. goḍsāṇ, -ṇi, *f.* = *l.* sweetness; suād, -dā, *m.*, *pr. fg.*
2. *fg.* mogāḷpoṇ, -ṇā, *n.*
3. *fg.* soukāsāi, -ye, *f.*=*l.* peace, indulgence.

Subaltern, *a.* ...khāl āsullo; tāben āsullo = *l.* being in care.

Subaltern, *s.* khālto udyogăst, -tā, *m.*, *or* khāl-udyogast.

Subdivide, *v.* portun vānṭ, *or* āniki vānṭe kăr.

Subdivision, *s.* āniki vānṭo, -ṭeā, *m.*; vānṭeātso vānṭo.

Subdue, *v.* khālto kăr *or* kh. dovór; tābe kăr, *n. c.*; mōḍ(ó) = *l.* break; jik = *l.* gain, overcome; zăit vor = *l.* carry victory.

Subject, *a.* 1. khālto *or* khāl āsullo.
2. pòḍtso = *l.* exposed, *e. g.* to sickness.

Subject, *s.* 1. părza, -je, *f.* (*or* prăza) = *l.* nation; răit, -tā, *m.*, *e.g.* s. of a king.
2. irādo, -deā, *m.* = *l.* object, *e.g.* of a sermon.
3. kărtru, -rā, *m.* (in Gram.)

Subject, *v.* khālto kăr.

Subjection, *s.* khālteporṇ, -ṇā, *n.*; ādhin, -nā, *n.*

Subjective, *a.* āločeni părmāṇe āsullo = *l.* being according to the opinion; mótint āsullo = *l.* which is in mind; kălpănetso = *l.* imaginary.

Subjoin, *v.* kuḍsi.

Subjugate, *see* **Subdue.**

Subjunctive, *a.* šertātso, săuñšăyātso.
S. mood = săuñšăyāčeñ rūp, -pā, *n.*, *n. u.*

Sublime, *a.* 1. unts = *l.* aloft.
2. *fg.* vorto; voḍpoṇātso = *l.* great; uttim = *l.* excellent.

Sublimity, *s.* 1. untsāi, -ye, *f.*, *n. u.*
2. *fg.* vorteporṇ, -ṇā, *n.*; voḍpoṇ, -ṇā, *n.*

Submarine, *a.* dăryapondlo.

Submerge, *v.* buḍăi, *c. v. of* buḍ.

Submersion, *s.* buḍāp, -ḍpā, *n.*

Submission, *s.* khālteporṇ, -ṇā, *n.*

Submissive, *a.* khālto; utăr āikuntso.

Submit, *v.* 1. khālto kăr, *tr. v.*; kh. zā, *n. v.*
2. dākăi = *l.* show; *or* mukār ghāl = put before.
3. puṭua = *l.* condescend.

Subordinate, *a.* 1. *rs.* khāl; *see* **Subaltern.**

Subordinately, *ad.* khāl, *e.g.* s. to the will of God = Devāče khuše khāl.

Subordination, *s.* 1. khāltepoṇ, -ṇā, *n.*
2. vărgabhēd(é), -dā, *m.* = *l.* difference of classes.

Suborn, *v.* 1. lonts di = *l.* give a bribe; kusăi = *l.* corrupt.
2. nāḍ = *l.* tempt.

Subornation, *s.* fituri, -re, *f.*

Subpœna, *see* **Summon.**

Subscribe, *v.* nāuñ borei = *l.* write name; dăskăt ghāl = *l.* put signature.

Subscriber, *s.* văntigegār, -rā, *m.*

Subscription, *s.* văntigi, -ge, *f.*; vărāḍo, -ḍeā, *m.*

Subsequent, *a.* pelo *or* dusro.

Subserve, *v.* kumok kăr = *l.* help; upkārāk (*or* kāmāk) pòḍ, *or* prăyogāk pòḍ = *l.* fall to use.

Subside, *v.* 1. uṇo zā = *l.* become less; thāmb = *l.* cease, *e. g.* a wound.
2. thănḍ zā = *l.* get cold (calm); nidān zā = *l.* become calm; niu = *l.* get cold, *fg.* (calm), *n. v. of* nivăi.
3. deuñ = *l.* descend, *fg.*, *e. g.* fever, anger.

Subsidiary, *a.* kumki, *or* kumketso.

Subsidy, *s.* kumok, -mke, *f.*; săhāi, -ye, *f.*

Subsist, *v.* 1. āni āsā = *l.* is still; tăg = *l.* last.
2. *phil. perh.* āpleā sotăntrār āsā = *l. Lat. est sui juris, est in potestate sui ipsius,* he is his own master.

Subsistence, *s.* 1. udărpošaṇ, -ṇā, *n.* = *l.* livelihood; jivănaupāi, *or* jiyeuntso upāi, -yā, *m.*
2. āsāp, -spā, *n.* = *l.* existence.
3. *phil. perh.* sotăntrāčeñ āsāp = *l.* independent existence, *see adj.*, *or* sotăntrāčeñ săimb, -bā, *n.* = *l. Lat. natura sui juris* (*tota*), virtue of its own right.

Subsistent, *a. phil.* āpleā sotăntrār āsullo.

Substance, *s.* 1. *phil.* sār, -rā, *m.* = *also* solid body, bulk; ăsăl, -slā, *n.*
2. mukhya guṇ, -ṇā, *m.* = *l.* chief quality; săimb, -bā, *n.* = *l.* nature (*phil.*).
3. āst, -ti, *f.* = *l.* property.
4. *rs.* khărots = *l.* true, real.
5. văstu̥, -tu, *f.* = *l.* a thing.
6. rōs(ó), -sā, *m.* = *l.* juice; dik, -kā, *m.*

Substantial, *a.* 1. sārātso (*phil.*)
2. āst āsullo = *l.* having property; grest = *l.* rich.
3. bhāri = *l.* important.
4. khărots = *l.* true, real.
5. ghăṭ = *l.* strong.
6. bolāiketso = *l.* healthy; puṣṭi, *e. g.* s. food.

Substantiate, *v.* 1. khăreñ móṇ dākăi = *l.* show true.
2. ruzu kăr = *l.* prove.

Substantive, *s.* nāuñ, -āvā, *n.* (Gram.)

Substitute, *v. G.* suāter ghāl = *l.*

put in the place of; *G.* bădlāk dovór = *l.* put in the place of; bădăl = *l.* change.
Substitute, *s.* 1. bădli, -liā, *m.*
2. dălāl, -lā, *m.* = *l.* an agent.
Substitution, *s.* bădlāp, -pā, *n.*
Subterfuge, *s.* 1. nīb -bā, *n.* = *l.* pretext.
2. nāḍgepoṇ, -ṇā, *n.* = *l.* cunning; nāḍ, -ḍi, *f.*
Subterranean, *a.* pātāḷātso, *or* pātāḷāntlo; mātiyebitărlo, *or* dărnipondlo, *or* buintlo.
S. place = pātāḷ, -ḷā, *n.*
Subtile, *a.* 1. bārik, *pr. fg.*
2. pātāḷ.
Subtilty, *s.* pātāḷāi, -ye, *f.*, *n. c.*, *or* bārikāi, -ye, *f.*
Subtle, *a.* nāḍgo; bārik.
Subtlety, *s.* 1. bārikāi, -ye, *f.*
2. nāḍgepoṇ, -ṇā, *n.* = *l.* cunning.
Subtract, *v.* kāḍ; kăḷvi, *e.g.* s. an account = lèk k.
Subtraction, *s.* kāḍāp, -ḍpā, *n.*
Suburb, *s.* păṭṇa-kăḍčeñ, -bhāileñ, -lāgčeñ; sărhăddụ, -di, *f.*
Subversion, *s.* nāš, -šā, *m.*
Subvert, *v.* nāš kăr (*Acc.*); kāḍn ghāl.
Succeed, *v.* 1. pāṭleān yetā, *or* pāṭlo zāun āsā = *l.* comes after, *or* is successor to; *G.* bădlāk bòs = *l.* sit instead of. . .
2. jik = *l.* gain, *fg.*, *e.g.* s. in an affair; vrăddhi zā = *l.* become prosperous.
3. zā = *l.* turn (out), *e.g.* an affair.
Success, *s.* 1. jikāp, -kpā, *n.*, *e.g.* in an affair.
2. zăit, -tā, *n.* = *l.* victory, *fg.*
Successful, *a.* vrăddhi = *l.* prosperous; *rs. into v.*
Succession, *s.* 1. pāṭlāu, -āvā, *m.*
2. hār, -ri, *f.* = *l.* a line, row.
3. sānkăḷ, -kḷi, *f.* = *l.* a chain, *fg. e.g.* s. of events.
4. piḷavoḷ, -ḷi, *f.*; *in other mn.rs.*
Successive, *a.* thāmbanātullo = *l.* not ceasing, *or rs. into* khăḷanāstanāñ = without interruption.
Successor, *s.* pāṭlāugār, -rā, *m.* bădli, -liā, *m.* = *l.* a substitute.
Succint, *a.* sănkṣepātso.
Succour, *s.* kumok, -mke, *f. or* săhāi, -ye, *f.*
Succour, *v.* kumok, kăr; săhāi kăr.
Succulence, *s.* sār, -rā, *m.*
Succulent, *a.* sār āsullo, *or* sārātso.
Succumb, *v.* 1. păḍāu zā = *l.* defeat take place; sóḍ = *l.* leave, abandon; sōlua, *n. v. of* solvăi = defeat.
2. mòr = *l.* die.
Such, *a.* tăsolo *or* tăso.
Suck, *v.* 1. čiuñ, as a child; *vlg.* piye.
2. lunts, as an animal.
Suckle, *v.* vāgăi (*refined w.*); duduụ di.
Suckling, *s.* čiuntolo; dudātso burgo, -geā, *m.*

Sudden, *a.* 1. ăučit.
2. yekats pharātso = *l.* of one moment.
3. gupit = *l.* secret; *yet used for* s. death, *also bet. rs. into ad.*

Suddenly, *ad.* ăučit *or* yekăts phara; *see adj.* phăk kărn.

Sudorific, *a.* ghāmăitolo.

Suds, *s.* sābāčeñ udāk, -dkā, *n.* = *l.* water of soap; khārāčeñ udāk = *l.* water of soda.

Sue, *v.* 1. māg = *l.* request; porāt; lāleun māg = *l.* longing ask.
2. firiyād di = give accusation; vevār kăr = *l.* file a suit.

Suffer, *v.* 1. sós *or* bhóg (*or* dăgda, *n. c.*); dăgd bhóg *or* d. sós = *l.* feel pains.
2. sóḍ = *l.* permit.

Suffering, *s.* kăṣṭ, -ṭā, *m.*; dăgd, -dāñ, *m. pl.*; upădru̥, *pl. m.*; duk, -ki, *f.* = *l.* pain, *etc.*

Suffice, *v.* purto āsā = *l.* is sufficient; *or* puro = (is) enough; pāu = *l.* reach, arrive, *fg.*

Sufficiency, *s.* dādoskāi, -ye, *f.*, *from* dādos = satiated, content; zāi titleñ = *l.* what is required; purosāṇ, -ṇi, *f.*; udărpošăṇ, -ṇā, *n.* = *l.* livelihood.

Sufficient, *a.* purto *or* zāi titlo.

Suffocate, *v.* (găḷo) muḍḍi = *l.* turn neck; găḷo dāmp = *l.* shut the neck; *vlg.* fugār kăr, *fr.*

Suffocation, *s.* fugārāi, -ye, *f.*; *rs. v.*

Suffrage, *s. vlg.* vôt, -tā, *m.*, *e.g.* in a meeting; voppigi, -ge, *f.* = *l.* consent; kobuli, -le, *f.* = *l.* consent.

Suffuse, *v.* 1. bhór = *l.* fill, *e. g.* with tears.
2. borsi = *l.* mix.

Sugar, *s.* sākăr, -kri, *f.*

Sugarcane, *s.* kobu, -bā, *m.*; us, -sā, *m.*, *n. c.*

Suggest, *v.* 1. kānānt ghāl = *l.* put into the ears; mótint ghāl = *l.* put into the mind.
2. hišāro di, (words); sučăn di = prompt.

Suggestion, *s.* hišāro, -reā, *m.* = *l.* a hint; bud, -di, *f.* = *l.* advice.

Suicide, *s.* 1. ātmāghāt, -tā, *m.* = self-murder, *n. u.*; āplo jīv kāḍtso.
2. ātmāghātist, -tā, *m.* = self-murderer; āplo jīv kāḍn ghetolo, -leā, *m.*

Suit, *s.* 1. firiyād, -di, *f.* (in criminal cases); vevār, -rā, *m.*; vyājyu̥, -yā, *m.*; kăifet, -ti, *f.* (in civil cases).
2. ărji, -je, *f.* = *l.* a petition; māgṇeñ, -ṇeā, *n.* = *l.* a request.

File a s. = vevār kăr, *or* kăifet ghāl, *or* k. dākăl kăr; *or* firiyād di.

Suit, *v.* 1. tsākri kăr = *l.* serve, be fit; zā = be suitable, adapted; săma pòḍ = *l.* fall right.

2. mānḍ = *l.* arrange; *or* săma kăr = make right; *see* **Please.**

Suitable, *a.* lāyek; săma = *l.* right; (kāmāk) pòḍtso; *rs. into v.* [*n.*

Suitableness, *s.* 1. lāyekpoṇ, -ṇā, 2. sămapòḍneñ, -neā, *n.*, *or* sămapòḍāp, -ḍpā, *n.*

Suite, *s.* 1. săngāti, -tiañ, *m. pl.* = *l.* companions; pāṭlāugār, -rañ, *m. pl.*

2. rākṇeñ, -ṇeā, *n.* = guard (*abstr.*); rākṇe, *pl. m.* (*concrete*).

3. dărbār, -rā, *m.*; părivār, -rā, *m.*, *n. c.*

4. sānkăḷ, -kḷi, *f.* = *l.* a chain, *fg.*, *e.g.* of rooms; hār, -ri, *f.* = *l.* a line, *e.g.* of rooms.

Suiter, *s.* ărjegār, -rā, *m.*; *see* **Plaintiff.**

Sulky, *a.* 1. kărkărātso = *l.* troublesome.

2. čintest, khăntiṣṭ = gloomy.

3. săḷiṣṭ = *l.* obstinate; āpleā vādeātso.

Sullen, *a.* 1. khăntiṣṭ, čintest = gloomy.

2. bezār kărtso = *l.* troublesome.

Sullenness, *s.* 1. khănt, -ti, *f.*; duk, -ki, *f.* (sorrow).

2. bezārāi, -ye, *f.*

Sully, *v.* khătāi, *pr. fg.*; mheḷāi, *or* mheḷo kăr; *fg.* pāḍ kăr = *l.* spoil.

S. the reputation = boreñ nāuñ kāḍ.

Sulphur, *s.* gondóp, -pā, *m.*

Sulphureous, *a.* gondópātso

Sultan, *s.* sultān, -nā, *m.*

Sultaness, *s.* sultānin, -ni, *f.*

Sultry, *a.* fugār kărtso = *l.* suffocating, *vlg.*; *see* **Suffocate.**

Sum, *s.* 1. lèk, -kā, *n.*; zomo, -meā, *m.*; mēḷ(é), -ḷā, *m.* = *l.* collection; răkăm, -kmā, *n.* = *l.* amount; ăivoz, -zā, *n.* = a sum of money.

2. sănkṣep, -pā, *n.* = *l.* abridgment.

Sum, *v.* 1. lèk kăr.

2. sănkṣep kăr = *l.* make an abridgment, voṭṭu kăr = *l.* make together.

Summarily, *ad.* 1. sănkṣep zāun = *l.* compendiously.

2. ăusărān = *l.* hastily; vegiñ = *l.* quickly.

Summary, *a.* 1. sănkṣepātso.

2. ăusărātso = *l.* hasty.

Summer, *s. see App. to the Konk.-Engl. Dictionary.*

Summer, *v.* gim tsălāi (pass the summer).

Summit, *s.* tudi, -ye, *f.*, *e.g.* of a mountain; *by* voir *or* voilo = above; tăkli, -le, *f.* = *l.* head, *fg.*

Summon, *v.* 1. āpoi = *l.* call.

2. tākid di = *l.* give an order (s. judicially).

S. up courage = dhăir ghe.

S. up energy = prăyătān kăr.

Summons, *s.* 1. āpouṇeñ, -ṇeā, *n.*

2. tākid, -di, *f.*; *see verb.*

N. B. **Super,** *in composition with words not put down here, is to be rendered by* **the superlative form** *of the word it is compounded with, or by* **voilo.**

Sumptuary, *a. rs.* kărčea visyānt; kărčea visyānt āsullo.

Sumptuous, *a.* dobājeātso; vodponātso; tsăd khărtsuntso.

Sumptuousness, *a.* 1. tsăd khărts, -tsā, *m.* = *l.* too much expense.
2. dobāzo, -jeā, *m.* = *l.* pomp.

Sun, *s.* 1. dis, -sā, *m.*; suryo, -yeā, *m.*
2. vòt, -tā, *n.* = *l.* heat of the sun.

Sun, *v.* vòtāk ghāl.

Sunbeam, *s.* kirn, -nā, *n.*

Sunburnt, *a.* ulpallo.

Sunset, *s.* ăstămti, -te, *f.*
It is s. = ăstămtā.

Sunder, *v.* vingăd kăr.

Sunny, *a.* vòt pòdtso.

Sunshine, *s.* = vòt, -tā, *n.*

Sup, *v.* rātčeñ jevān kāne; rātčeñ jeu.

Superabound, *v.* tsăd; ur = *l.* remain; mirua = *l.* exceed.

Superabundance, *s.* sămpurnāi, -ye, *f.*; tsădāu, -dāvā, *m.*

Superb, *a.* 1. ăttās kărtso.
2. *fg.* vodponātso; dobājeātso.

Supercargo, *s.* 1. tārvakārbāri, -riā, *m.*
2. tārvāvyāpārakārbāri.

Supercilious, *a.* sălişt, *or* gărvişt = *l.* obstinate, *or* proud.

Supererogation, *s.* kāideabhāileñ kām, -mā, *n.*

Supererogatory, *a.* kāideabhāilo.

Superficial, *a.* 1. voilebār āsullo = *l.* being on the surface.
2. untslo = aloft.
3. *fg.* uno = *l.* less; *fg.* cillăr = *l.* trifling.

Superficies, *s.* mēlbhāg, -gā, *m.*, *n. c.*; voileñ āng, -gā, *n.*

Superfine, *a.* uttim.

Superfluous, *a.* gărznātullo = *l.* not necessary; gărjebhāilo = *l.* being beyond necessity.

Superfluity, *s.* 1. nāñgărz, -je, *f.* = *l.* no necessity.
2. gărjebhāili văstu, -tu, *f.* = *l.* a thing beyond necessity.

Superhuman, *a.* mănšavoilo.

Superintend, *v.* rāk = *l.* guard; pòle = *l.* look, *or* melbăndobăst pòle.

Superintendence, *s.* melbăndobăst, -ti, *f.*

Superintendent, *s.* melbăndobăst poletolo; kārbāri, -riā, *m.*; šenāi, -nāi, *m.* = *l.* a writer, keeper of accounts, *yet used also for* s.

Superior, *s.* 1. vodil, -lā, *m.*; mostak, -kā, *n.* = *l.* a head; gouli, -liā, *m.* = *l.* a pastor, *fg.* (eccl. sup.)
2. *fg.* jiktolo, *or* zăit vortolo = *l.* victorious, *bet. rs. into v.*
Be s. = jik *or* zăit vor.

Superior, *a.* 1. vorto.
2. voilo.

Superioress, *s.* vodiln, -ni, *f.*

Superiority, *s.* 1. voḍilpoṇ, -ṇā, *n.* 2. *fg.* vortepoṇ, -ṇā, *n.*

Superlative, *a.* bhou tsăd.

Supernatural, *a.* săimbavorto (*Lat. supernaturalis*); săimbabhăilo = *l.* beyond nature, *Lat. praeternaturalis.*

Superscription, *s.* melviḷās, -sā, *m.*, *e.g.* of a letter; bărāp, -rpā, *n.*; nāuñ, -āvā, *n.* = *l.* a name; rupḍeñ, -ḍeā, *n.* = *l.* a figure, *e.g.* on a coin.

Supersede, *v.* gărz nātullo kăr; *Or.* suāter dākăl zā = *l.* be introduced instead of; *see* **Depose.**

Superstition, *s.* ātsār, -rā, *m.*, *or* ātsārāči kărni, -ne, *f.*, *or* ātsārāči tsāl, -li, *f.*; *vlg. rs.* băṭa (*or* pujāri) kăḍe itsār = ask the Hindu priest.

Superstitious, *a.* ātsārātso.

Supervision, *see* **Superintendence.**

Supine, *a.* 1. pāṭir āḍ pòḍtso; udāro pòḍtso. 2. *fg.* āḷsi = *l.* lazy.

Supper, *s.* răččeñ jevāṇ, jeuṇā, *n.*

Supperless, *a. vlg. rs. into* jevināstanāñ.

Supplant, *v.* uklāi, *e.g.* to mākā kāmānṭlo uklāitā; *G.* suāter nāḍin ye = *l.* come in the place of. . . by trickery; kāḍ = *l.* take away.

Supplement, *s.* 1. tsăḍouṇi, -ṇe, *f.* 2. kusri, -re, *f.* = something above measure.

Supplicate, *v.* māg, *or* māgṇeñ kăr; *see* **Entreat.**

Supplication, *s.* māg-ṇeñ, -ṇeā, *n.*

Supply, *v.* bhór = *l.* fill; di = *l.* give; sărbarāi kăr, *e.g.* food.

Supply, *s.* 1. sāmpurṇāi, -ye, *f.* = *l.* abundance. 2. bădli, -liā, *m.* = *l.* a substitute.

Support, *v.* 1. zăḍāi vāvoi = *l.* carry pressure *or* weight. 2. sós = *l.* suffer, *e.g.* a persecution. 3. săhāi kăr = *l.* make assistance. 4. pós = *l.* feed; jevoi = give to eat. 5. guṇātso zāun āsā = *l.* is favourable.

Support, *s.* 1. kumok, -mki, *f.*; săhāi, -ye, *f.*, *or* ādhār, -rā, *m.* 2. digo, -geā, *m.* = *l.* a pillar (wooden), *e.g.* for supporting a falling house. 3. guṇ, -ṇā, *m.* = *l.* favour.

Supportable, *a.* sósiyet āsullo; *bet. rs. into v.*

Supporter, *s.* kumkigār, -rā, *m.* *or* kumok kărtolo.

Suppose, *v.* 1. šărt kăr = *l.* make a condition (supposition); čint = *l.* think; āločen kăr = *l.* make opinion. 2. sătmānd = *l.* believe.

Supposing that = zārtăr; păkšek; -i, *see* Gram. P. IV.; *by the condit. tense.*

Supposition, *s.* šărt, -tā, *n.* (*var.* šèrt); āločen, -ni, *f.* = *l.* opinion; *rs. into v.*

Supposititious, *a.* fôṭkiro = deceitful; nīz năiñ āsullo = not sincere, not true; borsillo = mixed; *see* **Illegitimate.**

Suppress, *v.* 1. răddu̥ kăr = *l.* make nullity.

2. dāmpun dovór = *l.* covering keep, *e.g.* a sigh.

3. rāvoi *or* thāmboi = *l.* stop, *e.g.* a revolution; nivăi, *or* thănḍ kăr = *l.* make cold (calm).

Suppression, *s.* răddu̥, -dā, *n.* = *l.* nullity; *rs. into v.*

Suppurate, *v.* pu deuñ = *l.* pus descend; pik = *l.* get ripe; pu zā = *l.* become pus; pu mānḍ; puletā = pus is formed.

Suppuration, *s.* 1. puvadevāp, -deupā, *n.*

2. pu, -vā, *m.*

Supremacy, *s.* poilepoṇ, -ṇā, *n.* = *l.* primacy; sotăntru̥, -rā, *n.* = absolute power; sărvu̥ ă-dhikār, -rā, *m.* = power over all; rāyāči podvi, -ve, *f.* = power of a king.

Supreme, *a.* 1. vorto, *pr. fg.*; Sărvesvăr, *used of* God; sămestāñvoilo = above all; ăpārimit.

2. *fg.* voḍpoṇātso *or* voḍlo.

Sure, *a.* 1. khăro = *l.* true; dubāunātullo = *l.* doubtless.

2. dhrăḍ = *l.* certain (c. *subjectively*), *e.g.* I am s. of it.

3. riskeviṇ; băčāvetso = safe; *see* **Safe.**

Surely, *ad.* 1. dhrăḍzāun (*subj.*)

2. niz-zāun (*obj.*).

Surety, *s.* 1. zāmindār, -rā, *m.* (man).

2. zāmin, -ne, *f.* (state).

Surf, *s.* vòt, -tā, *n.*; ulóp, -lpā, *m.*

Surface, *see* **Superficies.**

On the s. = voileān *or* voilebār.

Surfeit, *v.* jīv sóḍn khā = *l.* eat leaving life; jīv sóḍn piye = *l.* drink leaving life; miruon khā, *or* m. piye.

Surfeit, *s.* miruoṇeñ, -ṇeā, *n.*; khāugipoṇ, -ṇā, *n.*; dādoskăi, -ye, *f.*

Surge, *see* **Surf.**

Surgeon, *s.* vóiz, -zā, *m.*; pănḍit, -tā, *m.*; ghāi guṇ kărtolo.

Surgery, *s.* voizāpoṇ, -ṇā, *n.*; *see* **Medicine.**

Surliness, *s.* lāsu̥lleñ tònḍ, -ḍā, *n.* = *l.* burnt mouth (*Konk.*), *fg.*

Surly, *a.* lāsu̥llea tònḍātso.

Surmise, *s.* pārkouṇeñ, -ṇeā, *n.* = *l.* conjecture; āločen, -ni, *f.* = *l.* an opinion.

Surmise, *v.* pārki = *l.* guess; āločen kăr = *l.* make opinion.

Surmount, *v.* 1. utăr = cross; poltăḍi vòts = *l.* go beyond; mirua, *pr. fg.*

2. *fg.* tsukăi, *e.g.* s. difficulties; *fg.* păriyār zā, *e.g.* s. diffi-

culties (*obj.* -ntlo); jik = *l.* conquer, *e.g.* a difficulty.

Surmountable, *a.* miruasārko, *or* jikasārko, *etc.*; *see verb.*

Surname, *s.* 1. *vlg.* ālkugn, -gnā, *n.*, *or* ālkunz, -zā, *n.*; kuṭmāčeñ nāuñ, -āvā, *n.* = *l.* family-name.

2. vāiṭ nāuñ, -āvā, *n.* = *l.* bad name.

Surpass, *v.* jik = *l.* gain, be over, *e. g.* s. a school-fellow; *by the comparat.*; zăit vor (*obj. 2nd Loc.*) = *l.* carry victory, *fg.*; mirua.

Surplice, *s.* kòtu̦, -tā, *n.*

Surplus, *s.* urtā teñ = *l.* what remains; bāki, -ki, *f.*; tsăḍāu, -ḍāvā, *n.*

Surprise, *v.* 1. ăjāp kăr, *or* ăjāp kărunk lāi = *l.* cause admiration.

2. (ăučit) dhăr = *l.* catch suddenly; āngār pòḍ = *l.* fall on the body.

Surprise, *s.* ăjāp, -pā, *n.*

Surrender, *v.* 1. vopsun di = *l.* give over; sóḍn di.

2. vòp = *l.* agree.

Surreptitious, *a.* mosātso = *l.* deceitful; pāṭi dovorlolo = *l.* kept back; guṭātso = *l.* secret.

Surround, *v.* veḍo ghāl, *or* v. mār; suttu ghāl; bountăṇi vots.

Surtout, *s.* *approx.* jibbo, -beā, *m.*

Survey, *see* **Superintend.**

Surveyor, *s.* muzimdār, -rā, *m.*

Survive, *v.* 1. vānts, *e.g.* to piḍentlo vāntslo.

2. uprānt jiye = *l.* live after...

Susceptibility, *s.* 1. nāzukāi, -ye, *f.* = delicacy, *fg.*; movāḷāi, -ye, *f.* = *l.* tender heart.

2. săkăt, -kti, *f.* = *l.* ability; trāṇ, -ṇā, *n.*

3. *by the poten. mood.*

Susceptible, *a.* 1. nāzuk guṇātso movāḷ, *or* movāḷasārko.

2. *by the poten. mood.*

Suspect, *v.* 1. dubāu, *or* d. čint = *l.* think doubting.

2. čint *or* āločen kăr = *l.* make opinion.

Suspend, *v.* 1. lāmboi (a lamp); umkăḷāi, *e.g.* a cloth.

2. mināi kăr, *e. g.* business, a man from his office; kāḍ = *l.* take away, *e. g.* s. from mass = mis kāḍ.

3. pāṭi ghāl = *l.* put back, delay.

Suspension, *s.* 1. umkăḷāp, -pā, *n.*, *or* umkăḷouṇeñ, -ṇeā, *n.*

2. mināi, -ye, *f.*

3. *rs. into v.*

Suspicion, *s.* dubāu, -bāvā, *m.*, *or* khāli dubāu; săuñšāi, -yā, *m.* (*var.* săuñsyo).

Suspicious, *a.* 1. dubāvi, *e.g.* a s. man, one who entertains suspicion.

2. dubāvāk ghāltso = *l.* causing doubt; dubāuntso = doubting.

Sustain, *v.* 1. dovór = *l.* keep.
2. sós = *l.* suffer.
3. pós = *l.* feed.
4. tsălăi = *l.* cause to walk, *fg.*, *e.g.* s. the part of.

Sustenance, *s.* 1. udărpošăṇ, -ṇā, *n.* = *l.* livelihood; khāṇ, -ṇā, *n.* = *l.* food.
2. săhāi, -ye, *f.* = *l.* support.

Sutler, *s.* foujiāngḍigār, -rā, *m.*

Suture, *s.* sivoṇ, siuṇi, *f.*

Swab, *s.* sāruṇ, -ṇe, *f.*

Swab, *v.* nităḷ kăr; du = *l.* wash; zāḍ = *l.* sweep.

Swaddling clothes, *s.* āngoteo, *pl. f.*

Swagger, *v.* ăbbār kăr.

Swain, *s.* nāḍkār, -rā, *m.*

Swallow, *v.* 1. giḷ.
2. *fg.* sós = *l.* suffer, put up with.

Swallow, *s.* pākoḷi, -ḷi, *f.*, *Mr.*, *n. u.*

Swamp, *s.* *see* **Marsh.**

Swamp, *v.* buḍăi = *l.* plunge.

Swan, *s.* hăuñs, -sā, *m.*, *Mr.*, *n. u.*; āḍou, -ovā, *m.*

Sward, *s.* tăṇātso zāgo, -geā, *m.* = *l.* a place of grass.

Swarm, *s.* hinḍ, -ḍā, *m.* = *l.* a flock; khéṭ, -ṭi, *f.* = *l.* a multitude; mēḷ(é), -ḷā, *m.*

Swarm, *v.* 1. bhāir săr = *l.* go out.
2. mèḷ = *l.* come together.

Swarthy, *a.* kāḷso = *l.* a little dark; ulpallo = *l.* scorched.

Swath, *s.* guṭlāuṇeñ, -ṇeā, *n.*

Swathe, *v.* 1. guṭlāi.
2. bānd.

Sway, *v.* 1. tsălăi = *l.* rule; podvi tsălăi = *l.* exercise power.
2. dălăi = *l.* move to and fro; *see* **Influence.**

Sway, *s.* 1. tsălouṇeñ, -ṇeā, *n.* = *l.* ruling.
2. ădhikăr, -rā, *m.* = *l.* authority; *see* **Influence.**

Swear, *v.* 1. pārmāṇ kăr; soput ghāl; săt kăr = *l.* make truth; săt sāng, *n. c.*
2. širāp ghāl = *l.* put abuse, curse.

Swearing, *s.* 1. pārmāṇ, -ṇā, *n.*; soput, -tā, *m.*; *see v.*
2. gāḷ, -ḷi, *f.* = *l.* abuse.

Sweat, *s.* 1. ghām, -mā, *m.*, *pr. fg.*
2. *fg.* kăšṭ, -ṭā, *m.* = *l.* pain; vāur, -rā, *m.* = *l.* work.

Sweat, *v.* 1. ghāme, *c. v.* ghāmăi.
2. *fg.* kăšṭa (*var.* kăšṭava).
3. dik yetā, *or* d. vāutā = *l.* juice flows, *ch. cs.*

Sweep, *v.* 1. zāḍ; ārāi = gather what has been swept.
2. *fg.* kāḍ = *l.* take away; năpāints kăr = *l.* cause to disappear.

Sweepings, *s.* kăstăḷ, -ḷā, *n.*

Sweet, *a.* 1. góḍ; sāveñ (udāk) = not salt (water).
2. suādik = *l.* of flavour, *pr. fg.*; dulob, *ol.*, *rl.*

Sweeten, *v.* góḍ kăr.

Sweetmeat, *s.* 1. miṭāi, -ye, *f.*, of sugar; poḷi, -ye, *f.*, of rice.
2. dòs, -si, *f.* = a kind of s.

Sweetness, *s.* 1. goḍsāṇ, -ṇi (-ṇe), *f.*, *pr. fg.*
2. suād, -dā, *m.* = *l.* flavour, *pr. fg.*
3. mousāṇ, -ṇi, *f.*

Swell, *v.* 1. suzăi, *c. v. of* suz, *n. v.* (*esp.* wounds); subăm zā, (*esp.* rivers and the like).
2. *fg.* bhór = *l.* fill, *e. g.* with pride = gărvān bhorlolo.

Swelling, *s.* suz, -ji, *f.*

Swerve, *v.* tsuk.

Swift, *a.* 1. tsurk = *l.* active.
2. vegintso, *or bet.* vegiñ tsăltolo = walking quickly; zărur tsăltolo.

Swiftness, *s.* zărurāi, -ye, *f.* (*var.* zăruri, -re, *f.*); suḍsuḍāi, -ye, *f.*, *n. c.*; tsurkpoṇ, -ṇā, *n.* = *l.* activity.

Swill, *v.* jīv sóḍn piye.

Swim, *v.* upe; kăḷkăḷ, as fishes.

Swimming, *s.* upeuṇeñ, -ṇeā, *n.*

Swindle, *see* **Cheat.**

Swine, *s.* dukor, -krā, *m.*; dukorn, -ni, *f.*

Swing, *v.* yeṇeñ teṇeñ hālăi, *tr. v.*; dăl = *Lat. oscillare*, *n. v.*

Switch, *s.* aḍār, -rā, *n.*

Swoon, *v.* *Dat.* jhinṭ mār; tăkli guuntā = *l.* head is turning; tăkli guvon pòḍtā = *l.* head turning falls; mọ́t tsukon pòḍ.

Swoop, *see* **Attack.**

Sword, *s.* 1. tălvār, -ri, *f.*
2. desvaṭ, -ṭe, *f.* = *l.* ruin.

Sycophancy, *s.* 1. tsāḍi, -ye, *f.* = *l.* detraction.
2. gulāmpoṇ, -ṇā, *n.* = *l.* servitude; fuslāuṇeñ, -ṇeā, *n.*

Sycophant, *s.* 1. fuslāuṇeagār, -rā, *m.*
2. tsāḍiyegār, -rā, *m.*

Syllable, *s.* ăkṣer, -rā, *n.*, *or bet.* ăkṣerañmēḷ(é), -ḷā, *m.*, *n. u.*; pădang, -gā, *n.*, *Cn.*, *Tul. Mal.*, *n. u.*

Syllogism, *s.* tărk, -kā, *n.*, *or the Mr.* nāy, -yā, *m.*, *or* tīn vākyāñ tărk, -kā, *n.*

Symbol, *s.* 1. gurtụ, -tā, *m.* = *l.* a sign.
2. bāvāḍta sănkṣep, -pā, *n.* = *l.* an abridgment of the faith.
3. nămuno, -neā, *m.* = a model, sample.

Symmetric, *a.* sămapòḍtso = *l.* falling together.

Symmetry, *s.* 1. sămapòḍneñ, -neā *n.*, *or*—poḍāp, -ḍpā, *n.*
2. mānḍāvoḷ, -ḷi, *f.* = *l.* order.

Sympathize, *v.* vonda *or* vondau = *l.* be inclined; (thăiñ) vondouṇeñ āsā; mōg(ó) kăr = *l.* love; birmot distā (*Sb. Dat.*) = *l.* pity appears.

Sympathy, *s.* vondouṇeñ *or* voḍneñ, -neā, *n.* = *l.* inclination; kākuḷt, -ti, *f.*; birmot, -ti, *f.* = pity.

Symphony, *s.* mēḷ(é) *or* vāzpamēḷ, -ḷā, *m.*
Symptom, *s.* gurtu, -tā, *m.*; guṇ, -ṇā, *m.*; khuṇā, -ṇe, *f.*
Synchronism, *s.* *rs.* teāts veḷār găḍ.
Syncopate, *v.* ăkšeraṅ kāḍ.
Syndic, *s.* văkil, -lā, *m.*
Synecdoche, *s.* upalăkšăṇ, -ṇā, *n.* (*Mr.*)
Synod, *s.* săbha, -bhe, *f.*
Synonym, *a.* yekāts ărthātso.
Synopsis, *s.* sănkšép, -pā, *n.*
Syntax, *s.* utrānči mānḍāvoḷ, -ḷi, *f.* = *l.* arrangement of words; utrāñprăyóg, -gā, *m.*
Synthesis, *s.* meḷouṇeñ, -ṇeā, *n.*, *or* sañyojăn, -nā, *n.* (*Mr. Cn.*)
System, *s.* āločen, -ni, *f.* = *l.* opinion; (sikouṇea) mānḍāvoḷ, -ḷi, *f.* = *l.* arrangement of doctrines; dăršăna, -nā, *n.*, *Cn. Sans.*; rīt, -ti, *f.* = *l.* order, method.

T

Tabby, *a.* săbār rāṅgātso = *l.* of many colours.
Tabernacle, *s.* 1. mănṭăp, -pā, *n.* (*H. K.*); *vlg.* sakramentāči pèṭ, -ṭe, *f.*
2. tombu, -bā, *m.* = *l.* a tent.
Table, *s.* 1. mèz, -zā, *n.*: 'mezār āsā = is at table'.
2. jevāṇ, jeuṇā, *n.* = *l.* meal.
3. foḷeñ, -ḷeā, *n.* = *l.* a plank; păṭṭi, -ṭe, *f.* = *l.* a list.
Tablecloth, *s.* *vlg.* mezātso tuvālo, -leā, *m.*, *fr.*; mezāčeñ lugāṭ, -gṭā, *n.*
Tableland, *s.* podou, -dvā, *m.*; măidān, -nā, *n.*
Tacit, *a.* lipullo, *or* gupit.
Taciturn, *a.* vogo, *or* vogo rāutolo; mono, *fg.* = dumb.
Taciturnity, *s.* vogeñrāvāp, -rāupā, *n.*; *bet. rs.*; monepoṇ, -ṇā, *n.* = dumbness, *fg.*
Tack, *v.* kopo mār.
Tack, *s.* dākṭo khiḷo, -ḷeā, *m.* = *l.* a small nail.
Tackling, *s.* tārvasāmān, -nā, *m.* = *l.* articles of a ship.
Tact, *s.* trāṇ, -ṇā, *n.* = *l.* ability, *which see;* bud, -di, *f.* = *l.* wisdom; sāmārthi, -the, *f.*
Tactics, *s.* (fouz) mānḍči vidya, -ye, *f.* = *l.* the art of arranging (an army).
Taffeta, *s.* tafeta, -tā, *n.*, *or* lāgčeñ lugāṭ, -gṭā, *n.* = *l.* attaching cloth.
Tag-rag, *see* **Crowd.**
Tail, *s.* simpṭi, -ṭe, *f.*
Tailor, *s.* dărji, -ji, *m.*; siunkār, -rā, *m.*, *or* sivoṇgār, -rā, *m.*

Taint, *v.* pāḍ kăr = *l.* spoil; mheḷăi, *c. v.* = *l.* make dirty; kusăi, *c. v.* = *l.* corrupt.

Taint, *s.* kusāp, -spā, *n.*; khăt, -tā, *n.* = *l.* stain.

Take, *v.* 1. kāṇe *or* kāṇghe, *or* ghe (*see* Gram. p. 136).
2. vor = *l.* carry, fetch.
3. dhăr = *l.* catch.
4. lék = consider; čint = *l.* think.
5. sós = *l.* suffer.
6. zāi = *l.* is required, *e. g.* it takes two hours, *ch. cs.*
7. bāḍeāk kāṇe = *l.* hire.
8. vetā = *l.* goes.
9. guṇāk pòḍtā = *l.* effect falls (operates), *ch. cs.*; *see also* **Succeed.**

T. care = zătăn kāṇe, *G. F.*, *e. g.* of the subjects.
T. courage = dhăir ghe.
T. God's name in vain = Devāčeñ nāuñ beṣṭeñ kāḍ.
T. heed, t. care = kăbărdār rāu (*Hind.*), *or* tsătrăi kāṇghe.
T. pleasure in = khuši vor.
T. by the ears = kānāk dhăr.
T. by the hand = hātāk dhăr.
T. an opportunity = săndrāp kāṇghe.
T. command = ădhikār kāṇghe.
T. fire = uzo lāgtā = *l.* fire is attached, *ch. cs.*
T. an oath = părmāṇ kăr.
T. leave = răja kāṇe.
T. sleep = nīd.
T. in a bad sense = vāiṭāk vór, vāiṭ ărth kăr.
T. effect, *see above.*
T. off the hat = topi kāḍ.
T. offence = duk.
T. pity = kākuḷt kăr, *G. F.*; *vlg.* pòṭ duktā *or* p. zăḷtā = feel sorry for others.
T. to pieces = kuḍkeān kuḍke kăr.
T. up with = vintsun kāḍ.
T. a bribe = lónts khā.
T. root = 1. pāḷañ fuṭṭāṭ.
2. *fg.* ghāṭ zātā.
T. a walk = bouñ.
T. hold of = dhăr.
T. ship = tārvār tsăḍ.
T. away, t. out = kāḍ.
T. after = sārko zāun āsā.
T. again = pāṭi (*or* portun) kāṇghe.
T. before-hand = ādiñ kāṇghe.
T. down = devăi; voilo kāḍ, *or* săkăl kāḍ.
T. for = čint *or* lék.
T. in = 1. kāṇghe = *l.* receive, entertain.
2. dăr = *l.* keep, contain, *e.g.* a vessel contains.
3. fôṭăi = *l.* deceive.
T. off = 1. kāḍ.
2. deuñ = *l.* descend (price).
3. năkăl kăr = *l.* make a copy.
T. on = siṇ ulăi = *l.* speak complaint.
T. round = bountăṇi vóḍ.
T. to, *see* **Betake.**
T. to oneself, *see* **Assume.**

T. up = 1. ukol.
2. suru kăr = *l.* begin.
3. portun sāng = *l.* say in reply.
4. beṣṭāi = *l.* scold.
5. dhăr = *l.* arrest.
6. lāg = *l.* be attached, *fg.*, *e.g.* don voraň lāgtāt = *l.* two hours are attached (required).

T. upon oneself = āpṇāčer văisun kāṇe.

Tale, *s.* kāṇi, -ye, *f.*

Talebearer, *s.* tsāḍiyegār, -rā, *m.*; tsāḍiyāḷo, -ḷeā, *m.*

Talent, *s.* 1. talent, -tā, *n.* (coin).
2. somzoṇi, -ṇi, *f.*, *or* somzoṇkāi *or* somzikāi, -ye, *f.*; săkăt, -kti, *f.* = *l.* power; sāmārthi, -the, *f.*, *or* sāmārthkāi, -ye, *f.*
3. mòt, -ti, *f.* = *l.* mind.

Talk, *s.* uloṇeň, -ṇeā, *n.*; găzāli, -li, *f.* = *l.* a chat; phānḍḷo, -ḷeā, *m.* = idle talk.

Talk, *v.* ulăi; găzāli mār = chat.
T. over = ugteň kărn sāng.

Talkative, *a.* boḍboḍo; phānḍleagār.

Talker, *s.* uloṇeagār, -rā, *m.*, *or* ulouṇo, -ṇeā, *m.*

Tall, *a.* ubār; lāmb = *l.* long, *used also for* t.

Tallness, *s.* ubārāi, -ye, *f.*; lāmbāi, -ye, *f.*

Tallow, *s.* tsărāb, -rbe, *f.*

Talon, *see* **Claw.**

Tamarind, *s.* āmsāṇ, -ṇi, *f.*; sòlụ, -lā, *n.* = white t.

Tamarind-tree, *s.* 1. činčetso ruk (*or* činčeruk), -kā, *m.*
2. vonṭāntso (*or* vonṭitso) ruk, -kā, *m.* = white t.

Tame, *a.* sādo.

Tame, *v.* sādo kăr.

Tameness, *s.* sādepoṇ, -ṇā, *n.*

Tamer, *s.* sādo kărtolo.

Tamper, *v.* 1. rig = *l.* enter interfere, meddle; mèḷ = *l.* be mixed; interfere.
2. nāḍi kăr = *l.* make tricks.
3. fuslāi, *or* voḍni di = *l.* allure, attract.

Tan, *v.* 1. tsāmbḍeň hăda kăr, *or* kămāi.
2. kāḷso kăr = *l.* make brown.

Tangent, *s.* āpòḍtso gīṭ, -ṭā, *m.* = *l.* a touching line; *or* spăršareṣa, -ṣe, *f.*; *or* sămpātarekha, -khā, *f.* (*Cn. Mr. Sans.*)

Tangle, *see* **Entangle.**

Tank, *s.* tāḷeň, -ḷeā, *n.*; kòḷ, -ḷā, *n.*

Tankard, *s.* (piyeuntso) tāmbler, -rā, *m.*, *or* (piyeunčeň) āidān, -nā, *n.*

Tanner, *s.* (tsāmbḍeň) hăda kărtolo.

Tantamount, *a.* săma.

Tap, *s.* thāp, -pi, *f.*

Tap, *v.* thāp mār, *or* thāpuḍ.

Tape, *s.* fint, -tā, *n.*, *fr.*; *see* **Riband.**

Taper, *s.* bārik vāt, -ti, *f.*

Taper, *a.* *perh.* domsātso.

Taper, *v.* domos zāun ăntăr = *l.* finish into a point.

Tapestry, *s.* poḍḍo (*or* pordo), -deā, *m.*, *for* windows; *or the Mr. Cn.* buṭedār, -rā, *n.* (*used also in the bazaar*).

Tape-worm, *s. approx.* dónt,-tā, *m.*

Tar, *s.* tār, -ri, *f.* (*or* -rā, *n.*), *or* ḍāmăr, -rā, *m.*, *used by some; perh.* ḍāmăratēl(é), -lā, *n.*

Tardiness, *s.* soukasāi, -ye, *f.*; toḍou, -ḍovā, *m.*

Tare, *s.* nāliyo, -yeā, *m.*

Target, *see* **Shield.**

Tariff, *s.* nirăk, -kā, *n.*

Tarnish, *v.* 1. kāḷokātso kăr = *l.* make dark.

2. pāḍ kăr = *l.* spoil; kusăi = *l.* corrupt.

Tarry, *v.* rāu; vās kăr; *see* **Abide.**

Tart, *a.* 1. āmboṭ = *l.* acid.

2. koḍu = *l.* bitter; *see* **Pungent.**

Tartness, *s.* āmsāṇ, -ṇi, *f.*

Task, *s.* kām, -mā, *n.*

Task, *v.* kām di.

Taste, *s.* 1. ruts, -či, *f.* (*also* the sense of t.), *pr. fg.*; suād, -dā, *m.* = *l.* flavour.

2. *fg.* somzoṇkāi, -ye, *f.* = *l.* intelligence.

Taste, *v.* 1. pòḷe = *l.* look, *or bet.* tsākon pòḷe, *pr. fg.*; tsāk, *pr. fg.*

2. ruts, *Sb. Dat.*

3. părikša kăr = *l.* make examination.

Tasteful, *a.* ručitso (*subj.*), *or* ručik (*object.*); suādik.

Tasteless, *a.* rutsnātullo, *pr. fg.*; čappo, *pr. fg.*

Tatter, *s.* čindi lugāṭ, -gṭā, *n.*

Tattle, *v.* găzāli mār.

Taunt, *s.* ăpamān, -nā, *m.* = *l.* offence; lăz, -je, *f.* = *l.* shame.

Taunt, *v.* 1. lăzăi (*c. v. of* lăz) = cause to be ashamed.

2. beṣṭāi = *l.* reproach; āṇki.

Tavern, *s.* gutki, -ke, *f.*; găḍăng, -gā, *n.*

Tavern-keeper, *s.* găḍăngagār, -rā, *m.*, *or* găḍăng dovórtolo.

Tawdry, *a.* dispātso.

Tawny, *a.* kāḷso.

Tax, *s.* 1. sunk, -kā, *n.*, *esp.* on movable property.

2. beróz, -zā, *m.*, *or* tirvo, -veā, *m.*, *or* tergi, -ge, *f.*, *esp.* on landed property.

Tax, *v.* beróz ghāl.

Tax-collector, *s.* sunk văsul kărtolo.

Tea, *s.* čā, čāve, *f.* (*var.* čāu, čāve, *f.*)

Teach, *v.* 1. sikăi, *c. v. of* sik.

2. kăḷit kăr, *or* kăḷăi = *l.* inform.

3. dākăi = *l.* show.

Teacher, *s.* upădeši, -ši, *m.*, *esp.* religious, *ex. but not c. w.*; ăiguḷ, -ḷā, *m.*, *esp.* of profane knowledge; *used now for* t. of low schools; šeṇăi, -ṇăi, *m.* = *ex.* a keeper of accounts (in the villages); sikăitolo; *vlg.* mestri, -ri, *m.*, *fr.*

Teaching, *s.* sikoṇ, -ṇi, *f.*, *or* sikouṇeñ, -ṇeā, *n.* = lecture.

Teak-tree, *s.* sāulo, -leā, *m.*

Team, *s.* (goḍeañ-) zóḍ, -ḍā, *m.*

Teamster, *s.* gāḍiyegār, -rā, *m.*

Tear, *s.* duk, -kā, *n.*; 'shed tears = dukañ gāḷāi'.

Tear, *v.* tuṭāi, *esp.* ropes; pind, *esp.* clothes.

Tear, *s.* tuṭāp, -ṭpā, *n.*; pindāp, -dpā, *n.*

Tease, *v.* kărkăr kăr = *l.* trouble; dós; răgḷe kăr; bezār kăr = *l.* trouble; zăḷăi = *l.* cause to burn.

Teat, *s.* čiuñ, čive, *f.*; bomb, -bā, *m.*

Technical, *a.* vidyetso = *l.* proper to science; sāmărthetso; *by the Gen. of the* affected word, *e.g.* this is a t. term in mathematics = părimāṇavidyečeñ utăr.

Tedious, *a.* bezārāyetso *or* bezār kărtso, *or* kărkărātso; lāmb = *l.* long.

Teem, *v.* bhorn āsā = *l.* is full.

Tegument, *s.* dāmpṇeñ, -ṇeā, *n.*

Telegraph, *s.* tăntiṭāpāl, *or* săriyeṭāpāl, -lā, *n.* = *l.* post of wire.

Telescope, *s.* durbīṇ, -ṇi, *f.*

Telinga-potato, *s.* keno, -neā, *m.*

Tell, *v.* mhoṇ *or* sāng = *l.* say; hukum di = *l.* give order.

Temerity, *s.* utāvoḷ, -ḷi, *f.*; zobordost, -ti, *f.*

Temper, *v.* 1. *for* t. metals = hăda kăr; *vlg.* udāk di.

2. haḷu kăr = *l.* make light, *fg.*; uṇo kăr = *l.* make less.

3. yekoṭ kăr, *e.g.* t. dignity with affability; borsi = *l.* mix; meḷăi = *l.* mix; hăḷtān = moderately, *with the req. verb.*

Temper, *s.* 1. sobāu, -bāvā, *m.*, *e.g.* t. of mind; guṇ, -ṇā, *m.* = *l.* quality; năḍteñ, -teā, *n.* = *l.* character; mărji, -je, *f.* = *l.* humour.

2. yekoṭ, -ṭā, *m.* = *l.* union (*whereby* t. *is produced*).

Temperament, *s.* 1. kālet, -ti, *f.*, of the body.

2. sobāu, -bāvā, *m.*, *etc.*; *see* **Temper.**

Temperance, *s.* hăḷt, -tā, *n.* = *l.* moderation; nidānāi, -ye, *f.*; t. in eating *has no proper equivalent:* alpahuson, -nā, *n. is used in the Goanese Catechism, but not here:* mit, -ti, *f.* = a limit, hăḷtān khāunčeñ, *or* khāunčeānt māp, -pā, *n.*, *or* khāunčeānt hăḷt *are the most intelligible though not elegant renderings.*

Temperate, *a.* 1. sămādhānātso, *e.g.* climate; nidān = *l.* quiet, calm, observing the proper measure in every thing; thănḍ = *l.* cold, *fg.*

2. hăḷtān khāuntso = *l.* eating moderately.

Temperature, *s.* hăvo, -veā, *m.*; hăveamāp, -pā, *n.* = *l.* measure of climate.

Tempered, *a.* hăda, *e. g.* iron.

Tempest, *s.* tufān, -nā, *n.*; vādăḷ (*or* vādāḷ), -ḷā, *n.*

Temple, *s.* 1. igărz, -je, *f.*, *fr.*; Devāčeñ ghăr, -rā, *n.* = *l.* God's house; Dēvālăi, -yā, *n.* (*contr.* diuḷ) = *l.* house of God, *n. c.*
2. sāṇ, -ṇā, *n.*; koḍkeñ, -keā, *n.*; guḍi, -ye, *f.* (*Hindu*).
3. kānsul, -lā, *n.* = a part of the head.

Temporal, *a.* 1. săuñsārātso = *l.* worldly; *or* săuñsāri.
2. păvitrụ năiñ āsullo = *l.* not sacred, *n. u.*
T. possession = āst, -ti, *f.*

Temporary, *a.* thoḍo vēḷ(é) tăgtolo *or* thoḍea kālātso; moṭvo = *l.* short; *or only* kālātso; *vlg.* don disāntso.

Temporize, *v.* 1. vēḷ(é) pòḷe = *l.* consider time (opportunity).
2. pāṭi ghāl = *l.* delay.

Tempt, *v.* 1. nāḍ, *e.g.* the devil tempts; voḍni *or* vondoṇeo di = *l.* allurements give; tāḷnio āḍ = *l.* bring temptations; *pass.* t. yetāt; *vlg.* tentar kăr.
2. prăyătăn kăr = *l.* make trial.

Tempter, *s.* tāḷnio āḍtolo; tāḷnegār, -rā, *m.*

Temptation, *s.* tāḷni, -ne, *f.*; nāḍ, -ḍi, *f.* = *l.* trick; voḍni, -ne, *f.* = *l.* allurement.

Ten, *a.* dhā.

Tenacious, *a.* 1. dhāruṇ = *l.* obsti- [nate.
2. thir = *l.* firm, constant; sāmbāḷtolo = *l.* keeping, observing.
3. pānkātso = *l.* glutinous; lāgtso = *l.* which remains attached.

Tenacity, *s.* sthir guṇ, -ṇā, *m.* = *l.* constancy; lāgasārkeñ, -keā, *n.*

Tenant, *s.* văkāl, -klā, *n.* (vokāl, -kle, *f.* = a bride).

Tend, *v.* 1. rāk = *l.* guard; zătăn kăr, *G. F.* = *l.* make care.
2. sevoṭ āsā = *l.* aim is, *ch. cs.*

Tendency, *s.* vondouṇeñ, -ṇeā, *n.*

Tender, *a.* 1. mou, *materially so.*
2. movāḷ (of heart); mogāḷ = *l.* dear, *fg.*
Become t. = 1. movāḷ, *fg.*
2. mou zā (*pr.*).

Tender, *s.* dărkāst, -tā, *m.*

Tender, *v.* 1. bheṭăi = *l.* offer.
2. dărkāstāk ărji di.
3. mukār ghāl = *l.* put before.
T. an oath = pārmāṇ kărunk lāi.

Tenderness, *s.* 1. movāḷăi, -ye, *f.* *or* movāḷ mòn, -nā, *n.*
2. ăpurbăi, -ye, *f.* = *l.* fondness, great affection.

Tendon, *s.* šir, -re, *f.*

Tenement, *s.* 1. ghăr, -rā, *n.*
2. geṇizāgo, -geā, *m.*, *or* geṇik kāṇgello zāgo.

Tenet, *s.* 1. gād, -di, *f.* = *l.* a proverb.
2. (ghāṭ) āločen, -ni, *f.* = *l.* firm opinion.

Tenfold, *a.* dhā pāuṭi tsăḍ, *or* dhādoḍo.

Tennis, *s.* (game of t.), čenḍāñ-khéḷ, -ḷā, *m.*

Tenor, *s.* 1. dusro tāḷo, -ḷeā, *m.* = *l.* 2nd voice; duyăm tāḷo.
2. jinos, -nsā, *m.* = *l.* manner.
3. ărthų, -thā, *m.* = *l.* meaning.

Tense, *s.* kāl, -lā, *m.*

Tension, *s.* 1. voḍāp, -ḍpā, *n.*
2. *fg.* prăyătăn, -tnā, *n.*

Tent, *s.* tombu, -bā, *m.*
Pitch a t. = t. mār.

Tentacle, *s.* dākṭeñ sing, -gā, *n.* = *l.* a little horn.

Tentative, *a.* părikṣa kărtso, *or* prăyătăn kărtso.

Tenth, *a.* dhāvo.

Tenuity, *s.* 1. pātaḷāi, -ye, *f.* = *l.* thinness; bārikāi, -ye, *f.*
2. uṇepoṇ, -ṇā, *n.* = *l.* scarcity.

Tenure, *s.* 1. ănbhogtso jinos, -nsā, *m.* = *l.* manner of holding.
2. géṇ, -ṇi, *f.*
T. of life = jiṇi, -ye, *f.*

Tepid, *a.* 1. unso, *or* čikke un, *or* nākši-un, *or* šeḷmoḍo (*pr.*)
2. uṇe bhăktitso.

Tepidity, *s.* 1. *rs. adj.*
2. *fg.* uṇibhăkt, -ti, *f.*

Tergiversate, *v.* nīb sāng = *l.* say pretexts; tsukon kāṇge = *l.* take avoiding; āng tsukāi.

Term, *s.* 1. āker, -kri, *f.* = *l.* extremity; mitmer, -ri, *f.* = *l.* limit.
2. utăr, -trā, *n.* = a word; utsār, -rā, *m.* = *l.* expression.
3. vāido, -deā, *m.* = *l.* space of time.
4. šèrt, -tā, *m.* = *l.* condition.
I am on good terms with = *Cm.* boreponān āsāñ.

Term, *v.* móṇ = *l.* call.

Termagant, *s.* tānṭālmāri, -riā, *m.*; rākṣiṇ, -ṇi, *f.* = a female monster.

Terminal, *a.* ākritso.

Terminate, *v.* 1. tirsi = *l.* finish, accomplish, *c. v. of* tirsa; *vlg.* kābār kăr, *fr.*; puro kăr.
2. mitmer ghāl = *l.* put a limit.

Termination, *s.* 1. ănt, -tā, *m.* = *l.* end; tirsouṇeñ, -ṇeā, *n.*
2. tīrp, -pā, *n.* = decision.
3. sevóṭ, -ṭā, *m.* = *l.* issue, exit.

Terminology, *s.* săbdajinos, -nsā, *m.*, *or only* săbd, -dā, *m.*

Terrace, *s.* 1. mātiyeči rās, -si, *f.* = *l.* a heap of earth; doro, -reā, *m.*; *see* **Parapet.**
2. bosčeñ pākeñ, -keā, *n.* = *l.* a roof for sitting on; māḷiye bāriseñ pākeñ, *n. u.*, *or bet.* ugti māḷāi, -ḷiye, *f.*

Terrene, Terrestrial, *a.* săuñsārā-tso; buintso.

Terrible, *a.* bhiyānkuḷ; bhăyăn-kărātso; tărtărountso = *l.* causing trembling.

Terrify, *v.* tărtărāi = cause trembling; beṣṭāi, by words; bhiyeunk lāi = *l.* apply to fear.

Terror, *s.* bheñ, bhiyā, *n.*; kāmpero, -reā, *m.*; biyāukuḷāi, -ye, *f.*; bhăyăkăr, -rā, *n.*

Terse, *a.* 1. nităḷ = *l.* pure.
2. moṭvo = *l.* short; sănkṣepātso.

Tertian, *a.* poireātso; *see* **Intermittent.**

Testaceous, *a.* (ghăṭ) simpiyetso.

Testament, *s.* 1. mòrnapătrụ, -trā, *n.*,—šāsăn, -nā, *n.* (*H. K.*); *vlg.* testament, -tā, *m.*, *fr.*
2. kărār, -rā, *m.*, *or* sollo, -leā, *m.* = an alliance.

Tester, *s.* mòrnapătrụ kărtolo.

Testify, *v.* 1. sākṣ sāng = *l.* say witness; s. zāun sāng = *l.* say as w.
2. khănḍit zāun sāng = *l.* say positively.

Testimonial, *s.* šipārăsičeñ kāgād, -gdā, *n.* = *l.* a letter of recommendation; *see* **Certificate.**

Testimony, *s.* sākṣ, -ṣi (*or* -ṣe), *f.*

Tetanus, *s.* săndvāi, -ye, *f.*

Tether, *see* **Halter.**

Tetter, *s.* dād, -di, *f.*

Text, *s.* 1. mulagrănth, -thā, *n.* = *l.* root-book.
2. vākya, -kyā, *n.* = *l.* a sentence; utsār, -rā, *m.*

Textile, *a.* voḷụllo.

Texture, *s.* voḷụlleñ lugāṭ, -gṭā, *n.*

Than, *conj.* prăs *or* vórn; ki; *see* Gram. P. II. ch. ii *Art.* iii.

Thank, *v.* upkār mānd = *l.* honour benefice; u. bāuḍ″; ārgāñ di (*rl.*); *vlg.* Dēu boreñ kăruñ.

Thankful, *a.* upkāri *or* upkār māndtso.

Thankfulness, *s.* upkārpoṇ, -ṇā, *n.*

Thanks, *s.* upkār, -rā, *m.*; ārgāñ, *pl. n.*; *see* **Thank.**

Thanksgiving, *s.* ārgāñ diunčiñ.

That, *adj. pron.* to; *see* Gram. P. II. ch. iii.

That, *rel. pron.* zo.

That, *conj.* móṇ, *or* moḷḷeñ; ki; *omitted; see* Gram. P. IV. ch. iii.

Thatch, *s.* kărăḍ, -rḍā, *n.*

Thatch, *v.* kărăḍ ghāl; čhāvāṇi kăr.

Thaw, *v.* 1. kăḍāi, *c. v.* = *l.* melt.
2. khirăi = *l.* dissolve.

The, *art. Omit.*, *or* to; *see* Gram. Parergon.

Theatre, *s.* 1. (native th.) vāiṭ khéḷ (-ḷā, *m.*) āni nāts (-tsā, *m.*) = *l.* bad play and dance; baguonṭakhéḷ, -ḷā, *m.*
2. āṭasāl, -lā, *n.* = *l.* a hall of play; nāṭakasāl, -lā, *n.* = *l.* a hall of drama, *Cn.*, *Mr.*, *Sans.*
3. dākoṇ, -ṇi, *f.* = *l.* representation.
4. *fg.* suāt, -te, *f.*, *with the participle of the verb showing what is performed.*

Theft, *s.* tsori, -ye, *f.*

Theme, *s.* 1. kām, -mā, *m.* (dilleñ k.)
2. irādo, -deā, *m.* = *l.* object, aim, *e. g.* th. of a sermon.

Then, *ad.* 1. tovóḷ = *l.* at that time; tedaḷa *or* tedaḷār; teā veḷār.
2. māgir, *or* uprānt = *l.* afterwards.
3. tăr = *l.* hence, therefore.
4. teā šivāi = *l.* besides that.

Thence, *ad.* thăiñ thāun; tāntleān.

Theologian, *s.* Devasămăndišāstri, -striā, *m.*, *n. u.*

Theological, *a.* Devasămăndi, *n. u.*

Theology, *s.* Devasămăndišāstrụ, -rā, *n.*, *n. u.*

Theorem, *s.* prămeya, -yā, *n.*, (*Sans.*, *Mr.*) = proposition to be proved; tărkāčeñ vākya, -yā, *n.* = a sentence to be discussed.

Theory, *s.* sikoṇ, -ṇi, *f.*, *or* sikāp, -kpā, *n.* = *l.* doctrine; zāṇvāi, -ye, *f.* = *l.* science; *rs.*, *e. g.* in theory this is easy, but in practice difficult = yeñ vingăḍ čintun săsār, puṇ sovoi săsār năiñ.
T. and practice = sikāp ani ănbou.

Therapeutics, *see* **Medicine.**

There, *ad.* thăiñ.

Thereabout, *ad.* 1. thăiñ lāgiñ.
2. sumār.

Thereafter, *ad.* māgir.

Thereby, *ad.* tāče vorviñ.

Therefore, *ad.* 1. teā pāsun (*or* tāče p.); teā dekun (*rare*).
2. tăr (*illative particle*).

Thermometer, *s.* gărmečeñ māp (gărmemāp), -pā, *n.*; *or* gărmi pòḷeunčeñ āid, -dā, *n.*

Thesis, *s.* khănḍit vākya, -yā, *n.*; khănḍit utsār, -rā, *m.*

Theurgy, *see* **Magic.**

Thew, *see* **Nerve.**

They, *pron.* te, teo, tiñ; *see* Gram. P. II. ch. iii.

Thick, *a.* 1. dāṭ, *e. g.* paper, liquids.
2. lāgun = *l.* attached, pressed, *e. g.* in a church; găṇ = dense, *e. g.* hair.
3. ghăṭ, *e. g.* liquids.
4. moṭo = *l.* fat, *e. g.* voice.

Thicken, *v.* 1. kăr *with one of the above adjectives.*
2. āṭăi, *c. v.*, *e. g.* soup by boiling; āṭ, *n. v.*

Thickness, *s.* 1. dāṭāi, -ye, *f.*; *see adj.*
2. moṭāi, -ye, *f.*; *see adj.*
3. ghăṭāi, -ye, *f.*; *see adj.*

Thickset, *a.* lāgun.

Thief, *s.* tsōr(ó), -rā, *m.*

Thieve, *v.* tsōr(ó).

Thigh, *s.* zāng, -ge, *f.*; zāngal, -glā, *n.*

Thimble, *s.* didāl, -lā, *n.*

Thin, *a.* 1. pātāḷ = not thick, not dense; bārik = not thick, acute, *pr. fg.*; săpur (*H. K.*).
2. ăprup = *l.* rare, not dense.

T. voice = bārik tāḷo.

Thin, *v.* pātāḷ kăr *or* bārik kăr; *see adj.*

Thing, *s.* 1. văstu, -tu, *f.*
2. sāmān, -nā, *m.* = *l.* chattels.
3. kām, -mā, *n.* = *l.* matter, business.
4. vyār (*or* yār), -rā, *m.* = t. to be sold.

Think, *v.* 1. čint.
2. āločen kăr = *l.* make opinion, (be of o.); distā = *l.* appears, *Sb. Dat.*
3. sevoṭ āsā = *l.* aim is, *ch. cs.*; *see* **Meditate, Suppose, Imagine.**

Thinker, *s.* čintolo.

Thinness, *s.* bārikāi, -ye, *f.*, *pr. fg.* (wit); pātāḷāi, -ye, *f. n. c.*; *see* **Thin.**

Third, *s.* trizāihiso, -seā, *m.*

Thirst, *s.* tān, -ne, *f.*

Thirst, *v.* tāne; tān lāgtā = *l.* th. is attached, *Sb. Dat.*

Thirsty, *a.* tānello *or* tān lāgullo.

This, *pron.* o (uo) *see* Gram. P. II. ch. iii.
On this side and that side = yeṇeñ teṇeñ, *or* yeusin teusin.
T. way = yeṇeñ; that way = teṇeñ.

Thistle, *s.* kānṭi, -ye, *f.* = a small th.; kānṭeāñzāḍ, -ḍā, *n.* (larger).

Thither, *ad.* thāiñ.

Thong, *s.* tīr, -rā, *m.* = a strip.

Thorn, *s.* kānṭo, -ṭeā, *m.*

Thorny, *a.* kānṭeāntso.

Thorough, *a.* khărots = *l.* true (*emph.*); sămpurṇ = *l.* perfect, full; *by* -ts.

Thoroughly, *ad.* purteñ; *see* **Fully.**

Thou, *pron.* tuñ; *see* Gram. P. II. ch. iii.

Though, *conj.* zărităr, *or* -i; *see* **Although.**

Thought, *s.* 1. čintna, -ne, *f.*; čintăn, -tnā, *n.*
2. činta, -te, *f.* (trouble).
3. āločen, -ni, *f.* = *l.* opinion, judgment.
4. mót, -ti, *f.* = *l.* mind (faculty of thinking).

Thoughtful, *a.* čintest (*mn. also* gloomy), *or* čintolo; budivont = *l.* wise.

Thousand, *a.* hăzār *or* sās.

Thrall, *s.* tsākor, -krā, *m.*; gulām -mā, *m.*

Thrash, *v.* boḍăi, *e.g.* t. paddy; mār = *l.* beat.

Thread, *s.* 1. sut, -tā, *n.*; dhāgo, -geā, *m.* = a single t.
2. zāṇveñ, -veā, *n.* (the sacred t. of the Hindus).

Thread, *v.* sut ghāḷ.

Threadbare, *a.* čindi, *or* porno, *or* jezārlolo.

Threat, *s.* bešṭauṇeñ, -ṇeā, *n.*

Threaten, *v.* 1. bešṭāi (in words); bhiyeunk lāi = *l.* apply to fear.
2. lāgiñ āsā = *l.* is near, *Lat. imminet.*
3. *rs. into* móṇ sāng = *l.* say

that *and the future of another verb expressed or implied*, *e. g.* they threatened him with the prison = băndint ghāltele móṇ sāngleñ; *or also* bhiyeunk lāi *with the object of fear preceding it may be used in this example.*

Three, *a.* tīn *or* tèg; *see* Gram. P. II. ch. ii.

Threshold, *s.* 1. taḷvoṭi, -ṭe, *f.*; humbor, -brā, *m.*
 2. *fg.* ărămb, -bā, *m.*, suru, -ve, *f.* = a beginning.

Thrift, *s.* borepoṇ, -ṇā, *n.* = vrăddhi, -dhe, *f.*

Thrifty, *a.* 1. vrăddhi.
 2. kăšišetso = *l.* economical.

Thrill, *v.* 1. kāmpăi, *c. v.* = *l.* cause to tremble.
 2. āng kāḍ = feel a shivering sensation: 'āuñ ā. kāḍtāñ'.

Thrill, *s.* āngkāḍāp, -ḍpā, *n.*; *see verb, also* **Trill.**

Thrive, *v.* vrăddhi zā; *vlg.* boro zā.

Throat, *s.* gomṭo, -ṭeā, *m.*; gāḷo, -ḷeā, *m.* = neck.

Throb, *see* **Palpitate.**

Throne, *s.* 1. pāṭ, -ṭā, *m.*; siyāsăṇ, -ṇā, *n.* = *l.* seat, tribunal.
 2. *fg.* rāzvoṭkāi, -ye, *f.* = *l.* kingdom.

Throng, *s.* khéṭ, -ṭi, *f.*; *rs.* săbār = *l.* many.

Throng, *v.* khéṭ zāun vetā; hāri hārin vetā = *l.* in rows goes.

Throttle, *see* **Suffocate.**

Through, *prep.* 1. *By the Instr.* (*esp. by the Instr. of the derived adj.; see* Gram. p. 212), *e. g.* he passed th. the town = šerāntleān (*or* šerān) gelo; th. here = āngāčeān.
 2. mārifăt, *or* kărna.

Throughout, *ad.* săgḷeān = everywhere; *see* **Through.**

Throw, *v.* 1. uḍăi, *c. v. of* uḍ, *n. v.*
 2. sóḍ = *l.* leave.
 Th. down = săkăl uḍăi.
 Th. the eyes = dišṭ ghāl.
 Th. away, th. aside = bhāir uḍăi.
 Th. at, *see* **Aim.**
 Th. off = săkăl ghāl, *e. g.* a horseman.
 Th. out = bhāir ghāl.
 Th. out of window = zănelāntleān (kiṭkentleān) bhāir uḍăi.

Thrust, *v.* tóp = *Lat. trude;* bităr mār.

Thumb, *s.* akănḍo, *or* akănḍeāčeñ bòṭ, -ṭā, *n.*

Thump, *v.* mār *or* tāpăi = slap.

Thump, *s.* mār, -rā, *m.*, *or* thāpāḍ, -pḍā, *n.*

Thunder, *s.* goḍgoḍo, -ḍeā, *m.*

Thunder, *v.* guḍguḍtā, *or* goḍgoḍo yetā.

Thunderbolt, *s.* viz, -zā, *n.*; *vlg.* goḍgoḍo, -ḍeā, *m.*

Thunderstruck, *s.* jim, -mā, *n.*

Thus, *ad.* ăseñ, *or* tăseñ (*decl.*), *or* ăse jinsiñ.

Thwack, *see* **Blow, Beat.**

Thwart, *v.* inkār kăr = *l.* resist (*Acc.*); āḍāi = *l.* prevent, impede; *Dat.* āḍ yetā *or* āḍ vetā = *l.* comes *or* goes against.

Thwart, *ad. prep.* = āḍ *or* virodh (*Dat.*).

Thy, *pron.* tuzo; *see* Gram. P. II. ch. iii.

Thyme, *s.* tumbo, -beā, *m.*

Tiara, *s.* mukuṭ, -ṭā, *m.* = *l.* a crown.

Tick, *s.* kiḍ, -ḍi, *f.* = *l.* an insect; ulku, -ke, *f.*; *see* **Credit.**

Ticket, *s.* čiṭ, -ṭi, *f.*

Tickle, *v.* 1. *fg.* voḍni di, *or* fuslāi.
2. muye, *n. v.*

Tide, *s.* 1. bhărti, -te, *f.* = high t.
2. sukti, -te, *f.* = low t.

Tidiness, *s.* 1. nităḷāi, -ye, *f.* = *l.* cleanness.
2. mānḍāvoḷ, -ḷi, *f.* = *l.* order.

Tidings, *s.* kobār, -bre, *f.*; vordi, -de, *f.*; *see* **News.**

Tie, *v.* bānd; ghăṭ kăr = *l.* make firm; yekoṭ kăr = *l.* make union; meḷāi = *l.* unite.

Tie, *s.* 1. bāndāp, -dpā, *n.*, *or* bănd, -di, *f.*, *or* băndpoṇ, -ṇā, *n.*; yekoṭ, -ṭā, *m.* = *l.* union.
2. bāndpās, -sā, *m.*
3. gānṭ, -ṭi, *f.* = *l.* a knot.
4. fint, -tā, *n.*, *fr.*, *e.g.* for shoes.

Tier, *see* **Row.**

Tiger, *s.* vāg, -gā, *m.*; *dim.* vāgaṭ, -ṭā, *n.*; bolpo, -peā, *m.* = a big t.

Tight, *a.* ghăṭ; ărn.

Tighten, *v.* ghăṭ (*or* ărn) kăr; ărnun bānd.

Tightly, *ad.* ărnun.

Tile, *s.* năḷo (nòḷo), -ḷeā, *m.*

Tile, *v.* năḷe ghāl.

Tiler, *s.* năḷeagār, -rā, *m.*

Till, *ad.* moṇasăr (*put at the end of the phrase it modifies*, *e.g.* āuñ yetāñ moṇasăr); săr (*added to the root of a verb*, *e.g.* săkăḍ văstu găḍasăr); ittun; păriyānt, *used both as conj. and as postp.*; *both may govern a noun.*

Till, *v.* besāi kăr = *l.* cultivate, *which see.*

Till, *s.* duḍuāči pèṭ, -ṭe, *f.*

Tillage, *see* **Cultivation.**

Tilt, *s.* pākeñ (*strictly* the covering of a boat, *but referable to* a carriage *or* cart *also*); tòp, -pā, *n.*, *fr.* for a cart.

Timber, *s.* 1. rukāḍ, -ḍā, *n.*
2. mòp, -pā, *n.* = t. material for building a house.

Time, *s.* 1. vēḷ(é), -ḷā, *m.*; *esp.* for opportunity; phursăt, -ti, *f.* = *l.* leisure; kāl, -lā, *m.*, *esp.* for duration.
2. pāuṭi, (*indecl.*) *n.*, *e.g.* three times.
3. sămăyo, -yeā, *m.* = *l.* opportunity; săndrāp, -pā, *n.*

4. vāido, -deā, *m.* = space of time, *e.g.* give me t.
5. *fg.* māp, -pā, *n.*, *or* mezāp, -zpā, *n.* = *l.* measure, *e.g.* in music.
6. ghănṭo, -ṭeā, *m.* = *l.* hour, *e.g.* what is the t.?
7. *fg.* dăm, -mā, *m.* = *l.* breath, rest.
At a proper t. = fāvoteā veḷār.
At the same t. = soveñ.
At the t. of our fathers = āmčeāñ bāpānčea kālār.
Time, *v.* 1. vēḷ(é) pòḷe (dis pòḷe), *or* v. mēz(é), *or* v. sāng.
2. vēḷ nemsi = *l.* appoint the time.
Time-honoured, *a.* porno.
Timely, *ad.* vegiñ; poilots (*decl.*) = *l.* first.
Timepiece, *s.* gădiyāḷ, -ḷā, *n.* (*var.* -ḷi, *f.*) = *l.* watch, clock; kālamāp, -pā, *n.* = *l.* measure of time; kāla-āid, -dā, *n.* = *l.* an instrument of time; kālačăkrụ, -rā, *n.*
Timid, *a.* bizuḍ, *or* bhiyātso.
Timidity, *s.* bheñ, bhiyā, *n.*; bizuḍpoṇ, -ṇā, *n.*
Tin, *v.* kălăi kāḍ.
Tin, *s.* 1. tăgăḍ, -gḍā, *n.* = a sheet of t.
2. toureñ, -reā, *n.* = a lump of tin.
Tincture, *s.* 1. rong, -gā, *m.* *or* *rs. into* rong lāi.
2. *in medic. mn. rs.*; niškărš, -šā, *n.* (*Mr. Sans.*)
Tinder, *s.* (māḍăčeñ) dūdụ, -dā, *n.*
Tinge, *v.* rong lāi.
Tingle, *n. v.* zăḷ = *l.* burn, *fg.*
Tinkle, *v.* muye.
Tinner, *s.* kălăigār, -rā, *m.*
Tinsel, *s.* begăḍ, -gḍi, *f.*
Tip, *s.* pònt, -tā, *n.*, *e.g.* of a knife; domós, -msā, *m.*
Tip, *v.* domós (*or* pònt) kăr.
Tippet, *s.* khāndavăstur, -rā, *n.*
Tipple, *v.* jīv sóḍn piye.
Tipsy, *a.* ămālzāllo; bebdo, *fr.*
Tiptoe, *s.* (pāya-) boṭăčeñ pònt, -tā, *n.*, *or* boṭănči tembeṭi, -ṭe, *f.*
Stand on t. = boṭănčer ubo rāu, *or* boṭănče tembeṭer rāu.
Tirade, *s.* lāmb uloṇeñ, -ṇeā, *n.*
Tire, *s.* 1. pāṭo, -ṭeā, *m.*, of the fellies of wheels.
2. mukuṭ, -ṭā, *m.*
Tire, *v.* puro kăr, *tr. v.*; dăṇsi, *c. v. of* dăṇsa, *n. v.*; puro zā, *n. v.*; *Dat.* văddăḍ, *n. v.*, *fg. esp.*, *e. g. Lat. laxati sumus in via iniquitatis* = we are tired in the way of sin.
Tired, *a.* puro zāllo, *Dat.*
I became t. = măkā puro zāleñ; āuñ dăṇsalāñ.
Tiresome, *a.* kăṣṭāntso; puro kărtso, *or* dăṇsountso; kărkărāntso *or* kărkăr kărtso; bezārāyetso, *or* bezār kărtso; ăugăḍ = *l.* difficult.

Tiro, *s.* umedvār, -rā, *m.*; novo (mănis).

Tissue, *s.* 1. voḷuḷleñ lugāt, -gṭā, *n.*; lugāṭ, -gṭā, *n.*

2. voḷāp, -ḷpā, *n.*

Titbit, *s.* ămrut, -tā, *n.*

Tithe, *s.* dhāntleñ fòḷ, -ḷā, *n.* = *l.* fruit out of ten.

Titillate, *see* **Tickle.**

Title, *s.* 1. melviḷās, -sā, *m.* = *l.* an inscription.

2. nāuñ, -āvā, *n.* = *l.* a name.

3. hăkkṳ, -kā, *n.* = *l.* right.

4. huddo, -deā, *m.* = *l.* rank.

Titter, *v.* guṭān hās.

Tittle-tattle, *s.* găzāli, -li, *f.*

Titular, *a.* 1. *rs.* nāvāts părmāṇe; nāvāts părmāṇe āsullo,

2. nāvāčeñ (fèst).

To, *prep.* 1. *By Dat.* (*see* Syntax, *Dat.*), *e. g.* to the north = băḍgāk.

2. thăiñ, kăḍeñ, lāgiñ (*see* Syntax, *Com.*)

3. . . . . isleān, *or* dikkān, *or* kusin = *l.* in the direction of . . .

4. *2nd. Loc.* (*see 2nd Loc. in* Gram.), *e. g.* teā veḷār = to that time.

5. sumār = *l.* about, *e.g.* to the number of 1000.

6. mukār = *l.* in face, (compared to), *e. g.* nothing to Persius.

As to . . . = visyānt.

To and fro = yeṇeñ teṇeñ.

Toad, *s.* māṇko, -keā, *m.*; bebo, -beā, *m.*; *see* **Park.**

Toast, *v.* 1. bāz, *e. g.* bread; torār kār, *fr.*

2. bolāiki mār = *l.* beat health (drink to the health of. . .).

Tobacco, *s.* dumṭi, -ṭe, *f.*; duvrapān, -nā, *n.*; năṭṭi d. = a kind of t.; suḍsuḍi d. = a kind of t.

To-day, *ad.* āz.

Toddy, *s.* douḷi, -ḷe, *f.*; sūrṳ, -re, *f.* = common t.; niro, -reā, *m.* = sweet t.

Toe, *s.* bòṭ, -ṭā, *n.*

Toga, *s.* pāyangoḷ văstur, -rā, *n.*

Together, *ad.* 1. sāngāta = in company with.

2. kăḍe, *or* lāgiñ; *see* Syntax, *Com. case.*

3. soveñ, teāts veḷār = at the same time.

All t. = voṭṭu.

Toil, *s.* 1. kām, -mā, *n.*

2. kăšṭ, -ṭā, *m.* = *l.* pain; vāur, -rā, *m.* = *l.* work; *see* **Net, Snare.**

Toil, *v.* vāur kăr, *or* vāur".

Toilette, *s.* neṭon, -ni, *f.* = *l.* ornament; *or* neṭounčeñ.

Toilsome, *a.* kăšṭāntso.

Token, *s.* gurtṳ, -tā, *m.*

Tolerable, *a.* 1. sosiyet āsullo.

2. sumār = *l.* mediocre; *bet. rs.*

Tolerance, *s.* sosṇigāi, -ye, *f.*; sosāp, -spā, *n.*; *see* **Connivance.**

Tolerant, *a.* sosṇik.

Tolerate, *v.* 1. sós.

2. vòp = *l.* consent; sósun (*or*

kăṣṭān) vòp = *l.* agree suffering; sóḍ = *l.* leave, permit.

Toll, *s.* sunk, -kā, *n.*

Toll, *v.* ghānṭ soukās mār.

Tomb, *s.* 1. fóṇḍ, -ḍā, *m.* = a grave.

2. gori, -ye, *f.* = a tombstone.

Tome, *s.* pustak, -kā, *n.* = a book, *fg.*

To-morrow, *ad.* phālea.

Tone, *s.* 1. gāyānajinos, -nsā, *m.*

2. rivāz, -ji, *f.* = *l.* fashion.

Tone, *s.* 1. tāḷo, -ḷeā, *m.*, *or* tāḷeātso jinos, -nsā, *m.*

2. *fg.* bòḷ, -ḷā, *n.*

3. *fg.* jinos, -nsā, *m* = *l.* manner.

Tongs, *s.* čimṭo, -ṭeā, *m.*

Tongue, *s.* 1. jīb, -be, *f.*

2. bhās, -se, *f.* = *l.* language.

Tonsure, *s.* *vlg.* kurou, -rovā, *m.* = *l.* a crown.

Too, *ad.* legun *or* săit (*placed after the affected word*); i (*affixed to the affected word*).

T. much = tsăḍ *or* bhou tsăḍ.

T. far = tsăḍ pois.

Tool, *s.* 1. ăid, -dā, *n.*; sāmān, -nā, *m.* = article.

2. hătyār, -rā, *n.* = *l.* weapon.

3. *fg.* moṇiyāri, -ri, *m.* = *l.* minister.

Tooth, *s.* dānt, -tā, *m.*, *pr.*, *fg.*, *e.g.* of a comb.

Incisor t. = muklo d.

Molar t. = dāḍi, -ye, *f.*

Toothache, *s.* dāntānci duk, -ki, *f.*

Toothless, *a.* dāntnātullo; bontsḍo = an old man.

Top, *s.* māteñ, -teā, *n.* = *l.* head, *fg.*; tăkli, -le, *f.* = *l.* head, *fg.*; tudi, -ye, *f.*, *e.g.* of a mountain; *by* voir, *or by 2nd Loc.*, *or by* voilo; *see* Gram. p. 227.

Top, *v.* 1. miruăi, *c. v.* = *l.* surpass.

2. kăsi kăr = *l.* prune.

Tope, *v.* jīv sóḍn piye.

Topic, *s.* văstu̥, -tu, *f.* = *l.* a thing; săngăt, -gti, *f.* = circumstance.

Topsyturvy (Turn), vomto udāro (ghāl).

Topography, *s.* gāuntso (*or* buintso) vivor, -rā, *m.*; gāvanăkṣa, -ṣe, *f.*

Torch, *s.* tsuḍ, -ḍi, *f.*

Torment, *s.* dăgd, -dañ, *m. pl.*; hiñsa (*var.* hiza), -se, *f.* = *l.* torture, persecution; kăṣṭ, -ṭā, *m.* = *l.* pain.

Torment, *v.* kăṣṭăi (*var.* kăṣṭavăi), *c. v. of* kăṣṭa, *n. v.*; dăgdăi, *c. v. of* dăgda.

Torn, *a.* tirkoṭo; pindkăr.

Tornado, *see* **Whirlwind.**

Torpid, *a.* 1. *perh.* tsăitan nātullo; jemtolo, *or* jemetolo = *l.* sleepy, *pr. fg.*

2. *fg.* āḷsi.

Torpor, *s.* 1. jèm, -me, *f.* = *l.* sleepiness.

2. *fg.* āḷsăi, -ye, *f.*

Torrent, *s.* vhāḷ, -ḷā, *m.* (udkātso)

lòṭ, -ṭā, *m.*, *pr. fg.*, *e. g.* a torrent of rain; lòḷ, -ḷā, *m.*; (*ex.* rolling).

Torrid, *a.* uṣṇu (gāuñ) = *l.* hot (country).

Torso, *s.* runḍ, -ḍā, *n.*

Tortoise, *s.* kāsou, -svā, *m.*; kāsăi, -ye, *f.* (of a larger kind).

Torture, *s.* iza, -ze, *f.*; dăgd, *Nom. pl. m.*; kăṣṭ, -ṭā, *m.* = *l.* pain.

Torture, *v.* iza di; dăgdăi; vòḍn kāḍ.

Toss, *v.* hālăi, *c. v.* (yeṇeñ teṇeñ h.)

Total, *s.* jumla, -lā, *n.* = sum; voṭṭu lèk, -kā, *n.*

Total, *a.* săgḷo.

Totality, *s.* sămest = *l.* all.

Totter, *see* **Vacillate.**

Touch, *v.* 1. āpoḍ; hāt lāi = *l.* apply hand (*obj. 2nd Loc.*).

2. *fg.* rig = *l.* enter, *e.g.* a sermon (monānt riglā); *fg.* movāḷăi = *l.* make soft, *c. v. of* movāḷ; lāg = *l.* be attached, *fg.*, *e.g.* words.

3. prăstāp sāng = mention, *G. M.*

T. at = lāg, *e.g.* a steamer.

T. upon, *see above*, 3.

Touch, *s.* āpoḍneñ, -neā, *n.*

Touching, *prep.* visyānt = *l.* about.

Touching, *a.* lāgullo = *l.* attached, *fg.*; *bet. rs. into v.*

Touch-stone, *s.* 1. verountso fātor, -trā, *m.*; orkal, -lā, *m.*

2. *fg.* gurtu̥, -tā, *m.* = *l.* a sign.

Touchy, *a.* toptso = easily excited.

Tough, *a.* 1. *approx.* mou = *l.* soft.

2. bāgasārko, *or* bāgontso.

Toughness, *s.* mousāṇ, -ṇi, *f.*

Tour, *s.* 1. bovāḍ, -ḍā, (*var.* bovāḍo, -ḍeā), *m.*, *or* bounḍi, -ḍe, *f.*

2. poiṇ, -ṇā, *n.*

Tourist, *s.* poiṇāri, -riā, *m.*

Tow, *v.* (tāruñ) doriyāniñ vòḍ.

Toward, *prep. Dat.*, *e.g.* igărjek vetāñ; thăiñ, *pr. fg.*, *e.g.* duties t. parents; isileān *or* dikkān *or* kusin = in the direction of.

Toward, *a.* 1. sikasārko.

2. sādo = *l.* tame, simple.

Towardliness, *s.* 1. sikasārkeñ, -keā, *n.*

2. sādepoṇ, -ṇā, *n.*

Towel, *s. vlg.* tuvālo, -leā, *m.*, *fr.*; āng pustso kuḍko, -keā, *m.*

Tower, *s.* tór, -ri, *f.* (*of Sans. orig.*); burz, -zā, *n.*

Tower, *v.* unts vetā.

Town, *s.* šèr, -rā, *n.* (*var.* šār); păṭăṇ, -ṭṇā, *n.*; băndăr, -drā, *n.* = a maritime t.; năgăr, -grā, *n.* (*ol.*)

Toy, *s.* 1. khèḷtso sāmān, -nā, *m.*

2. čillăr văstu̥, -tu, *f.*

Trace, Track, *s.* mèṭ, -ṭā, *n.*; gurtu̥, -tā, *m.*; *see* **Pace.**

Trace, Track, *v.* meṭāñ mezun vetā, *or* m. pòḷeun v.

Tract, *s.* 1. gāuñ, -āñvā, *m.* = *l.* a country.
2. kaḍtil, -li (*or* -le), *f.* = *l.* a pamphlet.

Trade, *s.* vepār *or* vyāpār, -rā, *m.*

Trade, *v.* vepār (*or* vyāpār) kăr.

Trader, *s.* vepārist *or* vepāri, -riā, *m.*

Tradition, *s.* mốṇṇi, -ṇe, *f.*; sāng-ṇi, -ṇe, *f.*; tòndpāši sikāp, -kpā, *n.* = *l.* oral instruction; kătā, -te, *f.*

Traduce, *v.* boreñ nāuñ kāḍ = *l.* take away good name.

Traffic, *s.* vepār, -rā, *m.*

Traffic, *v.* vepār kăr.

Tragedy, *s.* dukounči dākoṇi, -ṇe, *f.*; dukounčeñ nāṭak, -kā, *n.*; *see* **Calamity.**

Tragical, *a.* *fg.* dukountso.

Trail, *see* **Track.**

Train, *v.* 1. vāḍăi, *c. v.*, *e. g.* a child; tărbet kăr = *l.* make the course of education (*Acc.*); sikăi = *l.* teach.
2. ăbyās (*or* sovoi) kărăi = cause to make practice.

Train, *s.* 1. hār, -ri, *f.* = *l.* series.
2. duuragāḍi, -ye, *f.* = *l.* a cart of smoke.
3. dobāzo, -jeā, *m.* = *l.* pomp.
4. dărbār, -rā, *m.* = *l.* retinue.
5. nāḍ, -ḍi, *f.*, *or* čămătkār, -rā, *m.* = *l.* stratagem.
6. simpṭi, -ṭe, *f.* = *l.* tail, *fg.*, *e. g.* of a bishop.
7. krăm, -mā, *n.* = *l.* order, process, *n. c.*; *see* **Caravan.**

Training, *s.* tărbeti, -ti, *f.*; sikoṇ, -ṇe, *f.*

Trait, *see* **Feature.**

Traitor, *s.* ghātki, -kiā, *m.*; mosagār, -rā, *m.*; vikrit kărtolo.

Traitorous, *a.* mosātso.

Trammel, *s.* 1. pās, -sā, *m.*
2. āḍkăḷ, -ḷi, *f.*
3. kokkeñ, -keā, *n.*, for hanging vessels over the fire.
4. zāḷ, -ḷā, *n.* = *l.* a net.

Trample, *v.* mosti; guḍḍāi, with the feet; čiḍḍi.

Trance, *s.* diṣṭ, -ṭi, *f.* = *l.* vision.

Tranquil, *a.* nidān, *or* thănḍ = *l.* cold, *fg.*

Tranquillity, *s.* nidānāi, -ye, *f.*, *or* nidān, -nā, *n.*; soukāsāi, -ye, *f.*; thănḍāi, -ye, *f.* = *l.* coldness, *fg.*; sămādhān, -nā, *n.* = *l.* concord.

Tranquillize, *v.* nivăi *or* thănḍ kăr = make cold, *fg.*; fuslāi, *etc.*; *see* **Calm.**

Transact, *v.* kăr = *l.* do; tsălăi = *l.* cause to walk, *fg.*

Transaction, *s.* 1. kām, -mā, *n.* = *l.* business.
2. tsălouṇeñ, -ṇeā, *n.* = management; *bet. rs. into v.*

Transcend, *v.* mirua.

Transcendent, *a.* 1. miruontso.
2. *fg.* uttim = *l.* excellent.

Transcribe, *v.* năkăl kāḍ = *l.* take a copy.

Transcript, *s.* năkăl, -klā, *n.*

Transfer, *v.* 1. vòr = *l.* bring.
2. *fg.* ghāl = *l.* put, *or some such verb as the fg. mn. requires.*
3. părādin kăr = *l.* make over, *e. g.* a property.
4. vărgavărgi (*or* vărg) kăr, *e. g.* t. a man from one office to another; 'he has been transferred = ṭākā vărg zālo'.

Transfer, *s.* vărg, -gā, *m.*; *see verb.*

Transfiguration, *s.* rūpabădlāp, -pā, *n.*

Transfigure, *v.* (ākār) bădăl, *pass.* bădāl; dusro autār kāṇe = *l.* take another form.

Transfix, *v.* tóp = *l.* pierce; fāpsi (*var.* phāpsi) = *l.* make many wounds.

Transform, *v.* (rūp) bădăl.

Transformation, *s.* (rupāčeñ) bădlāp, -pā, *n.*; *rs. into v.*

Transfuse, *v.* 1. (mótint) ghāl; lāi = *l.* cause to be attached, *fg.*
2. *pr.* vót.

Transgress, *v.* mōḍ(ó) = *l.* break, *fg.*, *e.g.* an order; bepārvo kăr, *G. M.*; tsuk = *l.* err (*Acc.*).

Transgression, *s.* (kāidea-) móḍāp, -ḍpā, *n.*; *more comm.* bepārvo, -veā, *m.*; pātak, -tkā, *n.* = *l.* sin; gunyāuñ, -yāvā, *m.*, tsuk, -ki, *f.* = *l.* error.

Transgressor, *s.* (kāido) móḍtolo, *or* (k.) miruotolo; gunyāu kār, -rā, *m.*

Transient, *a.* ăthir *or* thirnătullo.

Transit, *s. see* **Passage.**

Transition, *s.* 1. *rs. into* transfer.
2. bădlāp, -pā, *n.* = *l.* change.

Transitive, *a.* săkărmăka (*Cn. Mr.*)

Translate, *v.* tărzumo kăr = *l.* make translation; ărth sāng = *l.* say the meaning, *G. M.*

Translation, *s.* tărzumo, -meā, *m.*; ărth, -thā, *m.* = *l.* meaning.

Transmarine, *a.* dăryeapelo.

Transmigrate, *v.* găḍi bhāir vetā; păragāvānt vetā; găḍpār vetā, *n. c.*

Transmit, *v.* 1. dhāḍ = *l.* send.
2. sóḍ = *l.* omit, leave.

Transparent, *a.* distso; *bet. rs. into v.*

Transplant, *v.* dusre suvāter lāi.

Transport, *v.* 1. (dusre suāter) vor.
2. ṭāpāk dhāḍ (as penalty), *var.* ṭăppu dh.; găḍ pār kăr.
3. sărivin săntos bhóg = *l.* enjoy incomparable joy (as in heaven), *n. v.*, *ch. cs.*

Transport, *s.* 1. vyāpāradoṇ, -ṇi, *f.* = *l.* a boat of trade.
2. gāḍi, -ye, *f.* = *l.* a carriage.
3. sărivin săntos, -sā, *m.*

Transverse, *a.* āḍkăḷtso, *or* āḍ āsullo.

Transversely, *ad.* āḍ, *Dat.*

Transubstantiation, *s.* sārābădlāp, -pā, *n.*

Trap, *s.* 1. kātăr, -tri, *f.*, *for* mice; pās, -sā, *m.*, *for* birds, *pr. fg.*

2. *fg.* suḷi, -ye, *f.* = *l.* a pointed stick, *fg.*, *e. g.* suḷiyer ghāl = *l.* put on a stick, (deceive).

3. *fg.* nāḍ, -ḍi, *f.* = *l.* trick.

Trash, *s.* čillăr văstụ, -tu, *f.* = *l.* a trifling thing.

Trashy, *a.* čillăr.

Travel, *s.* poiṇ, -ṇā, *n.*

Travel, *v.* poiṇ kăr.

Traveller, *s.* poiṇāri, -riā, *m.*, *or* poiṇ kărtolo.

Traverse, *v. Instr.* -ntleān vetā = goes through.

Tray, *s.* tăbak, -bkā, *n.*

Treacherous, *a.* mosātso *or* mós kărtolo; dăgeātso; ghātātso, *or* ghāt kărtso; pātiyeṇi făvonăiñ āsullo; pātiyeunk nozo āsullo.

Treachery, *s.* mōs(ó), -sā, *m.*; ghāt, -tā, *m.*

Tread, *v.* 1. tsăl = walk; meṭāñ ghāl = *l.* put paces.

2. mósti = *l.* crush; *pass.* mòsta *or* mòston yetā.

Treason, *s.* (rāyăčer) mōs(ó), -sā, *m.*; rājadróh, -hā, *m.* (*Cn. Mr.*), *n. u.*

Treasure, *s.* 1. băndār, -rā, *n.*, *pr. fg.* (repertory); thovo, -veā, *m.*; toušekhān, -nā, *n.* (much money, *also belonging to* a private man); dirveñ, -veā, *n.*; āst, -ti, *f.* = *l.* property.

2. *fg.* sămpurṇăi, -ye, *f.* = *l.* abundance.

Treasurer, *s.* mutsudi, -di, *m.* (*n. c.*); tizrer, -rā, *m.*, *fr.*; khăzāneagār, -rā, *m.*, *or* khăzāneādhikāri, -ri, *m.*, of Government.

Treat, *v.* 1. dākoun di = *l.* showing give; sāngon di = *l.* saying give, preach.

2. tsălăi = manage (*Acc.*) *or* tsăl (*Cm.*), *e. g.* mākā mogān tsălăi = t. me with love; *or also* manage a business.

3. (*medic.*) guṇ kăr, *or* vās kăr, *or* vokāt di.

4. tărk kăr *or* čărče kăr = *l.* discuss.

5. kāṇge = *l.* receive.

Treatise, *s.* 1. pustak, -kā, *n.*, *or* grănth, -thā, *n.*

2. kăḍtil, -li, *f.* = *l.* a pamphlet.

3. tărk, -kā, *n.* = *l.* a discussion.

Treatment, *s.* 1. tsălouṇeñ, -ṇeā, *n.*

2. zătăn, -tne, *f.* = *l.* care, *e.g.* of the doctor.

3. văidik, -kā, *n.* (medical t.).

Treaty, *s.* 1. kărār, -rā, *m.* = *l.* agreement.

2. yekamekačeñ uloṇeñ, -ṇeā, *n.*

T. of peace = 1. sollo, -leā, *m.*; rāji, -je, *f.*

2. solleāči tăyārăi, -ye, *f.*

Treble, *a.* tīn pāuṭi tsăḍ, *or* tīn doḍo.

Tree, *s.* ruk, -kā, *m.*

Trellis, *see* **Lattice.**

Tremble, *v.* kāmp; tărtăr=shiver.

Tremble, *s.* kāmp, -pi, *f.*, *or* kāmpero, -reā *m.*; tărtăro, -reā, *m.*

Tremendous, *a.* bhiyānkuḷ; tărtărountso; bhăyănkărātso.

Trench, *s.* khăṇi, -ye, *f.* = a deep trench; khăndok, -kā, *m.* = *l.* a deep trench.

Trencher, *s.* 1. lānkḍăči bosi, -se, *f.*
2. mèz, -zā, *n.* = *l.* a table; khāṇ, -ṇā, *n.* = *l.* food.

Trepan, *s.* rum, -mā, *n.*, to bore wood with; burmo, -meā, *m.*, to bore iron with.

Trepidation, *s.* bheñ, bhiyā, *n.*; kāmp, -pi, *f.*, *or* kāmpero, reā, *m.* = trembling.

Trespass, *v.* mirua = *l.* surpass, *fg.*, *or* miruon tsăl, *e.g.* on his own power; mikua (*var.* mikăi).

Tress, *s.* iṇi, -ye, *f.*; *see* **Dress.**

Tressel, *s.* tīn pāyānčeñ āid, -dā, *n.*

Trial, *s.* 1. tănki, -ke, *f.*, *pr. fg.*; părikṣa, -ṣe, *f.*
2. prăyătăn, -tnā, *n.* = *l.* effort.
3. *fg.* kăṣṭ, -ṭā, *m.* = *l.* pain.
Put on t. = tănker dovór, *or* părikṣer d.

Triangle, *s.* trikonso, -seā, *m.*; tīn konseānčeñ rūp, -pā, *n.*; tīn muleānčeñ rūp.

Tribe, *s.* kuḷi, -ye, *f.*, *or* kul, -lā, *n.*; săsăt, -sti, *f.* = generation; zāṭ, -ti, *f.* = *l.* caste.

Tribulation, *s.* dăgd, -dāñ, *m. pl.*; kăṣṭ, -ṭā, *m.*; mār, -ri, *f.* = *l.* pest, *fg.*

Tribunal, *s.* sădri, -re, *f.*, *e.g.* tr. of a judge; siyāsăṇ, -ṇā, *n.* = *l.* seat, *fg.*; hazur (superior tr.)

Tribune, *see* **Pulpit.**

Tributary, *a.* kăppo diuntso = *l.* giving tribute; khālto = *l.* subject.

Tribute, *s.* 1. kăppo, -peā, *m.*; dām, -mā, *m.*; kist, -te, *f.*; sunk, -kā, *n.* = *l.* tax; *see* **Tax.**
2. *fg.* mān, -nā, *m.* = *l.* honour.

Trick, *s.* nāḍ, -ḍi, *f.*; mōs(ó), -sā, *m.*; ṭhăkkų, -kā, *n.*; hātañčămătkār, -rā, *m.* = *l.* artifice of hand.

Trickle, *v.* thembe ghāl = *l.* put drops.

Trickster, *s.* mŏsagār, -rā, *m.*, *or* ṭhăkkagār, -rā, *m.*

Trident, *s.* tripul, -lā, *n.*

Trifle, *s.* čillăr văstų, -tu, *f.*, *or* bhārnātulli v. = an insignificant thing; năkāri văstų = *l.* a useless thing.

Trifling, *a.* čillăr; albo; năkāri = *l.* useless.

Trigonometry, *s.* trikonseañmāp, -pā, *n.*

Trill, *s.* tāḷeakāmp, -pi, *f.* = *l.* trembling of voice.

Trim, *a.* 1. sǎma = right.
2. sobit = nice.

Trim, *v.* 1. boḍkāi = *l.* prune; kǎsi kǎr = prune.
2. sǎma kǎr; *see* **Dress, Adapt.**

Trinity, *s.* (Most. H.) Trinidād, -di, *f.* (*vlg.* Trindād), *fr.*

Trinket, *s.* 1. nǎg, -gā, *m.*; mhāl, -lā, *m.*
2. kheḷtso sāmān, -nā, *m.*

Trio, *s.* tīn tāḷeānčeñ gāyan, -nā, *n.*

Trip, *s.* 1. nisrāp, -pā, *n.*; *or* nisrouṇeñ, -ṇeā, *n.*
2. bounḍi, -ḍe, *f.*; pasǎi, -ye, *f.*
3. khép, -pi, *f.*, *e.g.* of a vessel.

Tripe, *s.* ānkiṭi, -ṭe, *f.*

Triple, *a.* tīn doḍo, *or* tīn pāuṭi tsǎḍ.

Tripod, *s.* (tīn pāyānči) moṇǎi, -ṇiye, *f.*

Trireme, *s.* tīn voleānčeñ tāruñ, -rvā, *n.*

Trite, *a.* 1. tsālto = *l.* current, common.
2. *pr.* vāṭtso.

Triturate, *v.* vāṭ; *see* **Pound.**

Triumph, *s.* zǎit, -tā, *n.*

Triumph, *v.* zǎit vor.

Triumphal, *a.* zǎitevont.

Trivet, *s.* tīn pāyānčeñ āid, -dā, *n.*

Trivial, *a.* hǎlko, ǎṇvo = low, mean; lān = little; čillǎr = trifling.

Triviality, *s.* hǎlkepoṇ, -ṇā, *n.*

Troop, *s.* 1. zomo, -meā, *m.* = *l.* a multitude.
2. foujivānṭo, -ṭeā, *m.* = *l.* a part of an army.
3. *in pl.* fouz, -ji, *f.*; lǎskār, -rā, *n.*; *vlg.* paṭlām, -mi, *f.* = an army.

Trope, *s.* ǎrthabǎdlāp, -pā, *n.*; *see* **Figure.**

Trophy, *s.* zǎit, -tā, *n.*

Tropical, *a.* uṣṇ.

Trot, *s.* uḍkāṇ, -ṇā, *n.*

Trot, *v.* uḍkāṇañ ghāl.

Troth, *s.* 1. sǎt, -tā, *n.*
2. pātiyeṇi, -ṇi, *f.*

Trouble, *s.* 1. kǎrkǎr, *pl. m.*, tondre, *pl. n.*, bezārāi, -ye, *f.* = vexation.
2. tǎnṭo, -ṭeā, *m.* = *l.* mischief (*in pl.*).
3. ǎnvār, -rā, *n.*, *n.c.* = calamity.
4. minǎt, -ti, *f.* = *l.* fatigue, *e.g.* he took much t. to pass the examination.

Trouble, *v.* 1. kǎr, *with one of the nouns under the above*, 1; zǎḷǎi = *l.* cause to burn, *fg.* (tease); utsāmboḷ kǎr = excite.
2. tǎnṭe kǎr = make mischief.
3. kāṭkāi kǎr = *l.* make revolution.
4. kǎṣṭāi = *l.* cause pain.

Troubler, *s.* 1. kāṭkāyegār *or* kuṭagār, -rā, *m.* = revolutionist.
2. tǎnṭālmāri, -riā, *m.*

Troublesome, *a.* 1. kǎrkǎrāntso, *or* kǎrkǎri, *or* kǎrkǎr kǎrtso;

bezārāyetso, *etc.*; tondreāntso.
2. tăṇṭălmāri; kărmātso; pokri; *see* **Rascal.**

Trough, *s.* mărgi, -ge, *f.*

Trousers, *s.* 1. izār, -rā, *n.*
2. guḍgi, -ge, *f.* (drawers used by natives).
3. kalsāuñ, -sāvā, *n.*, *fr.* (European t.)

Trow, *v.* čint.

Trowel, *s.* *vlg.* kuler, -rā, *n.* *fr.*; tāpi, -ye, *f.*

Truce, *s.* moṭvo sollo, -leā, *m.* = *l.* a short peace; zuzamokupi, -pe, *f.* = *l.* a suspension of war; lăḍāyerāvāp, -rāupā, *n.* = *l.* stop of fight.

Truck, *v.* *see* **Exchange.**

Truck, *s.* dākṭi gāḍi, -ye, *f.*

Trudge, *v.* kăṣṭān tsăl.

True, *a.* 1. khăro, *opp. to* false.
2. sătevont, *opp. to* telling lies.
3. nīz = *l.* sincere, real.
4. āpuṭ, *or* borsinātullo = *l.* not mixed.

Truly, *ad.* khărents.

Trumpet, *s.* kómbụ, -bā, *m.* = Indian t.; tuturi, -re, *f.* = European t.

Trumpet, *v.* părgăṭ kăr = *l.* publish; dāngro mār.

Trumpeter, *s.* kombagār, -rā, *m.*

Truncheon, *s.* dānḍo, -ḍeā, *m.*; bètkāṭi, -ṭe, *f.*; *see* **Staff.**

Trunk, *s.* 1. khānḍi, -ye, *f.*, of a tree.
2. peṭāro, -reā, *m.* = a box *or* chest.
3. sonḍi, -ye, *f.*, of an elephant; zoḷu, -ḷve, *f.*
4. runḍ, -ḍā, *n.*, of the body.

Truss, *s.* bānd, -dā, *m.*; *see* **Tie, Bundle.**

Trust, *s.* 1. pātiyeṇi, -ṇi, *f.*; nămbgăṇeñ, -ṇeā, *n.*, *or* nămbiki, -ke, *f.*
2. tāben dovórleli văstụ, -tu, *f.* = *l.* a thing put in care.

Trust, *v.* 1. pātiye, *obj.*, *2nd Loc.*; pātiyeṇi dovór; nămbga, *n. c.*
2. tāben di.

Trustee, *s.* pārpātgār, -rā, *m.*; moktyār, -rā, *m.*

Trusty, *a.* pātiyeṇitso, *or* pātiyeṇi fāvozāllo.

Truth, *s.* săt, -tā, *n.*
In t. = khărents *or* săt.

Truthful, *a.* sătevont.

Try, *v.* 1. prăyătăn kăr = *l.* make an effort; petsāḍ; vāur"; pòḷe = *l.* look.
2. părikṣa kăr = *l.* make examination; tănki kăr.
3. tănker dovór = put on trial.
4. tsākon pòḷe, *e.g.* food.

Tub, *s.* mărgi, -ge, *f.* (*dim.* mărgul, -lā, *n.*)

Tube, *s.* năḷi, -ye, *f.*

Tubercle, *s.* fóḍ, -ḍā, *m.* = *ex.* pustule; suz, -ji, *f.*; *see* **Protuberance.**

Tuberous, *a.* *see* **Protuberance.**

Tuck, *v.* ukol.

Tuck, *s.* *see* **Fold.**

Tuft, *see* **Lock.**

Tumble, *v.* loḷon pòḍ; gădgădon pòḍ, *said esp. of* stones.

Tumbler, *s.* tambler, -rā, *m., fr.*; pātrụ, -rā, *n.*; āidān, -nā, *n.*

Tumour, *s.* fóḍ, -ḍā, *m.* = pustule; māskuṭ, -ṭā, *n.* = non-suppurating t.; suz, -ji, *f.*

Tumult, *s.* kūṭ, -ṭā, *n.* = *l.* a plot; kāṭkāi, -ye, *f.* = *l.* a revolution; gouji, -je, *f.* = *l.* noise; utsāmboḷāi, -ye, *f.* = *l.* excitement.

Tumultuous, *a.* kuṭ kărtso, *or* kāṭkāyetso, goujetso, *etc.*, *see above*; tănṭălmāri.

Tun, *s. approx.* pīp, -pā, *n.*

Tune, *s.* 1. yekāts tāḷo, -ḷeā, *m.* = one voice; gāyān, -nā, *n.* = *l.* music; pòd, -dā, *n.*; vāzāp, -zpā, *n.* = *l.* a sound.
2. *fg.* sămapòḍneñ, -neā, *n.* = *l.* harmony.

Tunic, *s.* lób, -bā, *m., fr.*; pāyangoḷ văstur, -rā, *n.*; kutāuñ, -tāvā, *m.* = native long dress, *fr.*; ānglen, -leā, *n.* = tunic of children under seven years.

Tunnel, *s.* 1. duvranăḷi, -ye, *f.*
2. năḷi, -ye, *f.* = a funnel.
3. pātaḷamārog, -rgā, *m., n. u.*, *or* dărnipondlo mārog.

Turban, *s.* urmāl, -lā, *m.*; pokḍi, -ḍe, *f.*

Turbid, *a.* nităḷ nāiñ āsullo; ăḷšik, *e.g.* water; kădvāḷ, *e.g.* water.

Turbulence, *s.* 1. gusăp, -spā, *n.* = *l.* confusion.
2. kāṭkāi, -ye, *f.* = *l.* revolution; utsāmboḷāi, -ye, *f.* = *l.* excitement.

Turbulent, *a.* tănṭălmāri; pokri; kāṭkāyetso.

Turf, *s.* tăṇātso zāgo, -geā, *m.* = *l.* a place of herb.

Turgid, *a.* 1. suztso.
2. *fg.* fugtso.

Turkey, *s.* peruñ, -rvā, *n.*, the fowl.

Turmoil, *see* **Tumult.**

Turn, Turning, *s.* 1. bounḍāp, -pā, *n., n. u., or* bounḍi, -ḍe, *f.*, *also* a short walk.
2. guvāp, guupā, *n., e. g.* of the head, of a mill.
3. bovāḍo, -ḍeā, *m., e. g.* t. of the road.
4. bădlāp, -pā, *n.* = *l.* change, *e. g.* of life, vicissitude.
5. vondouṇeñ, -ṇeā, *n.* = *l.* inclination; sobāu, -bāvā, *m.*
6. bāgoṇeñ, -ṇeā, *n.* = *l.* inclination, *e. g.* of the scale.
7. pāsăi, -ye, *f.* = a short walk.
8. rūp, -pā, *n.* = *l.* form, *e. g.* turns of expressions.
By turns = yekā pāṭi yék; sărten.
Good t. = upkār, -rā, *m.*

Turn, *v.* 1. bădăl = *l.* change (*obj. with* thāiñ).
2. *G.* upkārāk kăr = make for the advantage of; meḷāi = *l.* cause to be found (to be applied to).

3. **guunḍāi**, *c. v. of* guuñ, *e.g.* a wheel.
4. kăḍčilăk ghāl = put to the lathe.
5. bountăṇi bounḍāi = *l.* move round, *c. v. of* bouñ.
6. porti, *or* portun dovór, *e.g.* a box.
7. zātā = *l.* becomes (has an issue).
8. bāgāi = *l.* incline.

T. against = virodh rāu, *or* *Dat.* porto rāu.
T. aside = porti.
T. away = pois kăr, *or* tsukăi.
T. over = 1. vomto ghāl.
2. čint *or* āločen kăr.
T. out = 1. bhāir ghāl.
2. zā = have an issue.
3. sevoṭ āsā = *l.* aim is.

Turner, *s.* guḍgār, -rā, *m.*; kāntpi, -piā, *m.*

Turpitude, *s.* ăḷšik văstų, -tu, *f.*, *or* ăḷšikpoṇ, -ṇā, *n.*; lăz, -je, *f.* = *l.* shame, *Lat. dedecus;* ăpamān, -nā, *m.* = dishonour.

Turtle, *s.* kāsou, -svā, *m.* (*smaller than* kāsăi).

Tusk, *s.* dāḍo, -ḍeā, *m.*

Tutelar, *a.* rāktso *or* sāmbāḷtso.

Tutor, *s.* rākṇo, -ṇeā, *m.*

Tweezers, *s.* čimṭo, -ṭeā, *m.*

Twig, *s.* 1. āḍār, -rā, *n.*; boḍi, -ye, *f.*
2. bēl, -lā, *m.* = t. of a creeper.

Twilight, *s.* čiḷibiḷiñ (*indecl.*); jiḷiñbiḷiñ; tinsān, -ni, *f.* (of the evening).

Twin, *s.* zouḷo, -ḷeā, *m.*

Twine, *v.* vóḷ.

Twinge, *s.* zāḷ, -ḷā, *m.*; tsurtsuro, -reā, *m.*; kăṭiṇ duk, -ki, *f.*

Twinkle, *see* **Glitter.**

Twist, *v.* revòḍ, *n. v.*; reuḍāi, *tr. v.*; vóḷ, *tr. v.*

Twit, *v.* bešṭāi.

Twitch, *v.* čimṭo kāḍ.

Two, *a.* don, dòg; *see* Gram. P. II. ch. iii. Art. ii.

Type, *s.* 1. nămuno, -neā, *m.* = *l.* a model.
2. gurtų, -tā, *m.* = *l.* a sign.
3. ăčči, -če, *f.* (a font of type); tās, -sā, *n.*, *n. c.*
4. ăkšer, -rā, *n.* = *l.* a letter.

Typography, *see* **Printing-office.**

Tyrannical, *a.* nišṭur *or* mhāru.

Tyrannize, *v.* dăgdāi, *c. v.*; nišṭurāi tsălăi(*or* nišṭurāyen tsăl); zulum kăr = *l.* make violence.

Tyranny, *s.* nišṭurāi, -ye, *f.*; mhārupoṇ, -ṇā, *n.*; zulum, -lme, *f.*

Tyrant, *s.* zulmegār, -rā, *m.*; nišṭur rāi; nišṭurāi tsălăitolo.

U

N. B. Words beginning with un, *not put down here, are formed regularly; see* Gram. *or the note on* Im-, Engl.-Konk. Dict.

Udder, *s.* vonṭi, -ye, *f.*

Ugliness, *s.* 1. vidruppoṇ, -ṇā, *n.* 2. *fg.* ăḷšikpoṇ, -ṇā, *n.* = *l.* dirt, *fg.*; văiṭpoṇ, -ṇā, *n.*, *e.g.* u. of sin.

Ugly, *a.* 1. vidrup, *or* rūpnātullo; sobitnăi āsullo.
2. *fg.* ăḷšik = *l.* dirty; văiṭ.

Ulcer, *s.* ruñ, -uvā, *n.*

Ulcerate, *v.* ruñ kăr.

Ulterior, *a.* 1. pelo *or* poltăḍi āsullo.
2. māgirtso.

Ultimate, *see* **Last.**

Umbrage, *s.* sāuḷi, -ḷe, *f.*
Take u. = văiṭāk vór.

Umbrella, *s.* sătri, -tre, *f.*, of cloth; săteñ, -teā, *n.*, of leaves; ghurām, -rmā, *n.* = a sort of leaf-covering for the head and back, much used by work-people.

Umpire, *see* **Arbiter.**

Un, *as prefix, neg.* 1. nātullo, *or bet.* năiñ āsullo *affixed to adj.*
2. nāñ *prefixed to subst.*; *see* Gram. P. III.

Unable, *s.* tānknātullo; *bet. rs. into v.*

Unaccomplished, *a.* tirsinātullo.

Unaccountable, *a.* sāngunk nozo āsullo.

Unaccustomed, *a.* sovoinātullo; *bet. rs.* sovoi nāñ.

Unacquainted (Is), *v.* neṇār zāun āsā; kăḷanāñ *or* kăḷnāñ.

Unanimous, *a.* yéke mótitso; yekameka vòptso; vòptso *or* vòptolo.

Unapproachable, *a.* lāgiñ votsanāñso, *or* lāgiñ votsunk nozo āsullo.

Unapt, *a.* lāyek năiñ āsullo; kāmāk pòḍanātullo; *rs. into* tānkanāñ, *Sb. Dat.*

Unaptness, *s.* nāñlāyekpoṇ, -ṇā, *n.*

Unarmed, *a.* hătyārañnātullo.

Unaware, *a.* āučit; *rs.* čintināstanāñ *or* kăḷanāstanāñ.

Unbar, *v.* ugto kăr = *l.* make open, *fg.*

Unbecoming, *a.* năiñzăllo; fāvonăiñāsullo = *l.* unworthy.

Unbelief, *s.* ănbāvāḍtpon, -ṇā, *n.*

Unbeliever, *s.* ănbāvāḍti, -tiā, *m.*

Unbiassed, *a.* nītivont; *see* **Impartial.**

Unbind, *v.* sóḍ.

Unblemished, *a.* ăibnātullo; niskăḷ = pure; nităḷ; -viṇ *affixed to the required word.*

Uncertain, *a.* dubāuntso, *or* dubāvātso, *or* dubāvi (*subj. and object.*); ăumānātso.

N. B. Words beginning with **un**, *not put dawn here, are formed regularly; see* **Gram.** *or the note on* **Im-, Engl.-Konk. Dict.**

Uncertainty, *s.* dubāu, -bāvā, *m.*; ănmān, -nā, *m.*

Unchain, *v.* sānkăḷ sóḍ.

Unchangeable, *a.* bădlasārkonātullo *or* bădălnāñso.

Uncharitable, *a.* mōg(ó) nātullo.

Unchaste, *a.* nităḷ nāiñ āsullo; • niskăḷkāyeviṇ; *see* **Impure.**

Uncivilized, *a.* ăumăryāditso; nāḍkār; tsāltsămkăṇ nātullo; rānvoṭ = *l.* wild, *fg.*

Uncle, *s.* mām, -mā, *m.* = mother's brother; bāppu, -pu, *m.* = father's brother (*used when addressing them*); bāplyo, -lyā, *m.* = paternal u.; māuḷo, -ḷeā, *m.* = maternal u.

N. B. mām *is used also as a sign of respect when addressing persons of one's acquaintance, e. g.* māmā khăiñ vetāi?

Unclean, *a.* ăḷšik; mheḷo; burso; čikḷātso.

Unclouded, *a.* kupaññātullo.

Uncommon, *a.* ăprup = *l.* rare; ăsādhārṇ = *l.* extraordinary.

Unconditional, *a.* ăšărtātso.

Unction, *s.* mākap, -pā, *n.*, *n. u.*; *rs. into* **Anoint.**

Extreme u. = extrema unksāuñ, -sāvā, *n.*; *vlg.* săntesāuñ.

He speaks with u. = tāčiñ utrañ rigtāt.

Uncovered, *a. see* **Naked.**

Uncultivated, *a.* 1. rutakărnātullo (ground).

2. nāḍkār = *l.* unpolite; neṇār = *l.* ignorant.

3. bepārvo kello = *l.* neglected; zătănkāṇenātullo; vrăddhikărnātullo.

Undecided, *a.* dubāvātso *or* dubāvi, *e.g.* victory; tondreāntso = *l.* embarrassed; niščeisinātullo = *l.* not decided.

Under, *prep.* săkăl; khāl; taḷa; pònda; *see* Gram. p. 294, *seq.*

Underline, *v.* pònda gīṭ ghāl.

Undergo, *v.* sós.

Undermine, *v.* 1. pònda kónḍ.

2. pāḍ kăr = spoil.

Underminister, *s.* voḷamăntri, -ri, *m.*

N. B. the prefix voḷa *is used to translate* under *in all compound words not given here.*

Underneath, *ad.* pònda.

Understand, *v.* somza (āuñ somzatāñ; *or* măkā somzatā); *c. v.* somzāi; kaḷ = *l.* be known, *Sb. Dat.*; gom, *Sb. Dat.*; āik = *l.* hear, *fg.*

Understanding, *s.* 1. somzoṇ, -ṇi, *f.*, *or* somzoṇkāi, -ye, *f.* (*var.* somzikāi).

2. ginyān, -nā, *n.* = the faculty of u.; mót, -ti, *f* = *l.* mind, *or* memory.

N. B. Words beginning with **un**, *not put down here, are formed regularly; see* **Gram.** *or the note on* **Im-, Engl.-Konk. Dict.**

Undertake, 1. suru kăr = *l.* begin, *G. F.*
2. voisun ghe = *l.* consigned take, *e. g.* a case; lăg = *l.* be applied.

Undertaking, *s.* kām, -mā, *n.*; kărni, -ne, *f.* = *l.* an action; kărtueñ, -eā, *n.* = a great action, *Lat. facinus.*

Undivided, *a.* čīrnātullo = *l.* not sawn; vingăḍnātullo = *l.* not separated; kuḍke kărnātullo; vānṭinātullo.

Undo, *v.* sóḍ, *e. g.* a knot; *see* **Ruin.**

Undoubtedly, *ad.* dubāvaviṇe, *or* dubāu nāstanāñ.

Undress, *v.* viṇgo kăr; nāgḍo kăr (*or* nāgḍăi, *n. c.*); nesoṇ kăḍ, *e. g.* for sleeping.

Undulate, *v.* dăl.

Undulation, *s.* dălāp, -lpā, *n.*

Uneasiness, *s.* nāñbolāiki, -ke, *f.*; husko, -keā *m.*

Uneasy, *a.* bolāikinātullo.

Unedifying, *a.* bore dekitso, *in neg. sent.*; bori dēk(é) dinātullo.

Uneducated, *a.* sikanātullo, *or* neṇăr, *or* nāḍkăr; tsăltsămkăṇ nātullo, *or* ăumăryăditso.

Unemployed, *a.* kām nātullo; *bet. rs.* khăli āsā.

Unequal, *a.* sămanātullo.

Uneven, *a.* telto năiñāsullo, *or* săma năiñāsullo.

Unexpected, *a.* āučit.

Unfair, *a.* nītnātullo.

Unfaithful, *a.* pātiyeṇi nātullo; ăpanămbigetso.

Unfasten, *v.* sóḍ.

Unfavourable, *a.* ăuguṇātso.

Unfit, *see* **Unapt.**

Unfold, *v.* usăi, *e. g.* a map, a sail; sóḍăi.

Unfortunate, *a.* nirbhāgi.

Unfrequency, *s.* ăprupāi, -ye, *f.*

Unfrequent, *a.* ăpruр, *or* ăprupātso.

Unfrequented, *a.* yeksuro; *see also* **Frequented.**

Unfruitful, *a.* nirfóḷ; fóḷ dinātullo.

Ungovernable, *a.* tsălounknozo āsullo.

Ungrateful, *a.* ănupkāri.

Unhappy, *a.* nirbhāgi.

Unhealthiness, *s.* nāñbolāiki, -ke, *f.*

Unhealthy, *a.* bolāikinātullo; piḍest.

Unheard of (Is), *a.* kedints āikunknāñ.

Uniform, *a.* yekăts jinsātso.

Uniform, *s.* yekăts thărăči nesoṇ, -ṇi, *f.*; tits nesoṇ = *l.* the same dress.

Uniformity, *s.* 1. yekăts jinos, -nsā, *m.* = *l.* one mode.
2. yekoṭ, -ṭā, *m.* = *l.* union, *e.g.* u. with the will of God = y. Devăče khuše thăiñ, *or rs.*

N. B. Words beginning with **un**, *not put down here, are formed regularly; see* **Gram.** *or the note on* **Im-, Engl.-Konk. Dict.**

into Devāče khuše părmāṇe tsăl.

Unimpaired, *a.* pāḍzāunk nātullo.

Unimpeachable, *a.* gunyāuñnātullo.

Union, *s.* 1. mēḷ(é), -ḷā, *m.* = *l.* a college, assembly, union *also*; yekoṭ, -ṭā, *m.*, *or* yektār, -rā, *m.*
2. zomo, -meā, *m.* = *l.* multitude.
3. sămādhān, -nā, *n.* = *l.* concord.
4. voppigi, -ge, *f.* = *l.* consent.

Unique, *a.* sărivin = *l.* without comparison.

Unison (In u.), *s.* yekăts tāḷeān.

Unit, *s.* yék.

Unite, *v.* 1. yekoṭăi, *c.v. of* yekoṭ, *n. c.*; yekoṭ kăr = *l.* make junction (u.) with, *Dat.* *or* *Cm.*; meḷăi = join.
2. *fg.* kăntsăi = *l.* cause to adhere by pressure, *fg. pr.*
Man united with God = Devāk meḷullo mănis.

Unity, *s.* 1. yekoṭăi, -ye, *f.*
2. *fg.* sămādhān, -nā, *n.* = *l.* concord.

Universal, *a.* 1. săgḷeān (*or* sărvu kăḍe) vistārlolo = extended everywhere.
2. tsăḍāvot = which usually happens.
3. sādhārṇ = ordinary.
4. sămestāntso = of all; sămestānk fāvo zāuntso = *l.* belonging to all; sămestānk zāuntso = *l.* suiting all, *e.g.* notion.

Universality, *s.* sămest = *l.* all, *ch. cs.*

Universe, *s.* săuñsār, -rā, *m.*

University, *s.* sărvuvidyesāḷ, -ḷe, *f.*

Unjust, *a.* ănnăigār, *or* nītnātullo, *or* ănnāyātso.

Unkind, *a.* mogāḷnăiñ āsullo.

Unkindness, *s.* nāñmōg(ó), -gā, *m.* nāñdăya, -ye, *f.*

Unknown, *a.* *rs.* *into* kăḷtā, *or* uoḷkatā *in neg. form.*

Unlawful, *a.* kāideāk āḍ āsullo; văiṭ = *l.* bad; *by the neg. poten. mood.*

Unlearned, *a.* sikāp nātullo; sikonk nātullo.

Unless, *conj.* *By* šivāi: 'yeñ kelea šivāi = u. he does this'; verit *with the partic.*

Unlike, *a.* sārko nātullo, *or* sămanātullo.

Unlikely, *see* **Improbable.**

Unlimited, *a.* lekavorto; mitivin.

Unload, *v.* (vojeñ) kāḍ, *or* sămān kāḍ.

Unlock, *v.* khiḷ kāḍ.

Unlucky, *see* **Unhappy.**

Unmarried, *a.* ānkuār, -rā, *m.*, (-ri, *f.*); kāzārnātullo, *or* kāzārzāunknātullo; ānkuārli (*applied to* a woman), *n. c.*

Unmask, *v.* vés kāḍ.

N. B. Words beginning with un, *not put down here, are formed regularly; see* Gram. *or the note on* Im-, Engl.-Konk. Dict.

Unmerciful, *a.* niṣṭur; kākuḷtnātullo.

Unmindful, *a.* ugḍāsnātullo; čintinātullo.

Unmixed, *a.* ăpuṭ; nigăḷ; borsinātullo.

Unnatural, *a.* 1. săimbāk āḍāsullo. 2. rāksātso = monstrous. 3. āḍetso, *i.e.* premature, *e.g.* cleverness. 4. tonḍātso = *l.* of the mouth, *e.g.* u. laugh.

Unnecessary, *a.* gărznātullo.

Unnoticed, *a. rs.* tsătrāi kărunknāñ, *or* čintunk nāñ (it passed u.).

Unoccupied, *a.* 1. kāmnātullo. 2. lóknātullo (gāuñ); *see* **Waste** (land).

Unpleasant, *v.* mānuanātullo.

Unpopular, *a.* (lokāk) mānuanātullo.

Unqualified, *a. vlg.* părikṣa pāšar zāunknātullo; lāyeknātullo = *l.* not fit.

Unravel, *v.* soṣṭ kăr = *l.* make clear.

Unreasonable, *a.* vāzbināiñ āsullo.

Unrestrained, *a.* tsălounk nozo āsullo.

Unrighteous, *a. see* **Unjust.**

Unripe, *a.* tărno = *l.* green (fruits); pikanātullo; hărvo.

Unripeness, *s.* tărnepoṇ, -ṇā, *n.*

Unroll, *v.* sóḍăi, *or* usăi.

Unsafe, *a.* risketso, *or* riskent āsullo.

Unsalted, *a.* čappo (food).

Unsatisfactory, *a.* dādos kărnātullo; dādosi năiñ āsullo; *bet. rs.*

Unseal, *v.* ukto kăr; mhòr fóḍ.

Unseasonable, *a.* 1. bhou ādiñ yeuntso; vēḷ (è) tsukoun yeuntso. 2. *rs. into* zātā, *in neg. form.*

Unserviceable, *a.* kāmāk pòḍanātullo, *or* upkārāk p.; nākāri = *l.* useless.

Unsettle, *v.* 1. dubāvăi = *l.* cause doubt; dubāvāk ghāl. 2. guspăḍăi = *l.* confound.

Unshaken, *a.* hālnātullo.

Unsheath, *v.* pòteñ kāḍ.

Unskilled, *a.* ănbounātullo = without experience; neṇār = *l.* ignorant.

Unsociable, *a.* yeksuro = *l.* solitary; sāngātnātullo.

Unsound, *a.* 1. pāḍ = bad, spoiled. 2. ăskăt = weak. 3. apuṭ năiñ āsullo = *l.* not sincere.

Unstable, *a.* ăthir; thir năiñ āsullo.

Unstained, *a.* khătnātullo, *or* khătăinātullo.

Unsteady, *see* **Unstable.**

Unstitch, *v.* sivoṇ sóḍăi.

Unsuitable, *a. see* **Unapt.**

Untainted, *a.* 1. kusanātullo.

2. khătnātullo; nitāḷ.

Until, *see* **Till.**

Untamed, *a.* rānuoṭ.

Untie, *v.* sóḍ.

Unusual, *a.* ăsādhārṇ.

Unwell (I am), *a.* (mākā) vāiṭ kărtā = *l.* (to me) ill does; bārkoṇ zāleā.

Unwilling, *a.* khušinātullo.

Unwind, *see* **Disentangle.**

Unworthy, *a.* fāvo năiñ āsullo.

Up, *ad.* voir.

U. to this = ātāñ păriyānt, *or* ā. moṇasăr, *or* yedoḷ păriyānt, *or* y. moṇasăr.

Upbraid, *v.* beṣṭāi; bās khā.

Uphold, *see* **Support.**

Upon, *ad.* 1. voir, *or 2nd Loc.*, *e.g.* sit u., u. this condition.

2. višyānt = about.

3. uprānt = after.

Upper, *a.* voilo; vorto, *pr. fg.* (sublime); unts = *l.* aloft, (*var.* untslo).

Upper-dress, *s.* bāzu, -zve, *f.* (of girls).

Uppermost, *a.* bhou untslo, *or* bh. ubār.

Upright, *a.* 1. nītivont = just.

2. ubo, *e.g.* u. columns.

Uprightness, *s.* 1. nīt, -ti, *f.*

2. *rs. adj.*

Uproar, *s.* kuṭ, -ṭā, *n.*; utsāmboḷāi, -ye, *f.*; kāṭkāi, -ye, *f.*

Uproot, *v.* humboḷ.

Upset, *v.* 1. vompto ghāl, *tr. v.*

2. vompto pòḍ, *n. v.*

Upshot, *see* **Issue.**

Upside, *ad.* (turn u.) = vompteñ udāreñ kăr.

Upstart, *s.* āučit grest zāllo (mănis, -nšā, *m.*); āḍegrest zāllo; novo bāb, -bā, *m.*, *n. c.*

Upwards, *ad.* 1. voileān.

2. . . . prās tsăḍ = more than.

Urchin, *s.* tănṭălmāri, -riā, *m.*

Urge, *v.* 1. bòḷ kăr; bòḷ kărn sāng; utsāmboḷ kăr; uṭāi; mukār tsălăi; (āplea) mukār ghāl, *or* m. dāunḍāi.

2. vorāt kăr, *e.g.* u. to remain.

Urgency, *s.* 1. zărurāi, -ye, *f.*; turt, tā, *n.*, *e. g.* turtāčeñ kām.

2. gărz, -je, *f.*

3. vorāt, -tā, *m.* = *l.* demand, *fg.*

Urgent, *a.* 1. zărur, *or* bhou gărjetso.

2. vorātātso.

3. turtātso.

4. *rs.* ăvăš zāun = being necessary.

Urgently, *ad.* ăvăš zāun, *etc.*

Urine, *s.* mūt, -tā, *n.*

Urn, *s.* kăḷmbi, -be, *f.* = a large vessel for keeping rice and other eatables in, in the kitchen.

Usage, *s.* boḷsoṇeñ, -ṇeā, *n.* (*var.* boḷsouṇe).

Use, *s.* 1. prăyóg, -gā, *m.*, *or* prăyojăn, -nā, *m.*

2. *fg.* ādāi, -yā, *m.* = *l.* advantage.

Of what u.? = kiteāk (upkārtā)?

U. of reason = budi-prăkās, -sā, *n.*

Use, *v.* prayóg kăr, *G. M.;* boḷši, *c. v. of* boḷsa, *n. v.*; upăyóg-si, *tr. v.*, *n. c.*; tsălăi = *l.* cause to walk, *fg.*, *e. g.* u. means.

Useful, *a.* upkārāk pòḍtso; pră-yógātso; prăyojănātso.

Usefulness, *see* **Use**

Useless, *a.* upkārāk (*or* kāmāk) pòḍanātullo; năkāri; nirfóḷ = fruitless; nisprăyojănātso; vèrt, beşṭo = which is for nothing.

Uselessly, *ad.* beşṭeñ.

Usher, *s.* naib, -bā, *m.* (*used also*).

Usher, *v.* bităr vor.

Usual, *a.* tsālto = current; sā-dhārṇ = ordinary; sădāntso = of always; sovoye părmāṇe āsullo, *or* sovoyetso.

Usually, *ad.* tsăḍāvot (zāun); tsālteñ zāun, *etc.*

Usufruct, *s.* géṇ, -ṇi, *f.*

Usurer, *s.* tsăḍ vāḍ kāṇetolo.

Usurp, *v.* zulmen kāṇe, *or* boḷān k.; ănnāyān kāṇe.

Usurpation, *s.* 1. *rs. into v.* 2. zulum, -lme, *f.*, *or* bòḷ, -ḷā, *n.* = *l.* violence, force.

Usurper, *s.* zulmen (*or* boḷān) kāṇetolo.

Usury, *s. vlg.* tsăḍ vāḍ, -ḍi, *f.* = *l.* too much interest.

Utensil, *s.* gărvatā, -tā, *n.*; mhāl, -lā, *m.* = articles; āid, -dā, *n.* = an implement.

Utility, *s.* upkār, -rā, *m.*; ādāi, -yā, *m.*

Utmost, *a.* bhou tsăḍ, *or* sāriviṇ *etc.*; *see* Gram. p. 223.

Utter, *a.* săkăḍ *or* sāgḷo = whole; *see* **Full.**

Utter, *v.* utsār.

Utterance, *s.* utsār, -rā, *m.*

Utterly, *ad.* purteñ; *see* **Fully.**

Uttermost, *see* **Utmost.**

Uvula, *s.* poḍjīb, *or* palijīb, -be, *f.*

V

Vacancy, *s.* 1. khāli = *l.* empty, (emptiness), *e. g.* in a post; *see also* **Time.**
2. phursot, -ti, *f.* = *l.* leisure.

Vacant, *a.* khāli = *l.* empty; kāmnātullo; *see* **Waste.**

Vacate, *v.* khāli āsā = *l.* empty is, *ch. cs.*

Vacation, *s.* răja = *l.* leave.

Vaccinate, *v.* dāg ghāl = *l.* put vaccine; boḷnikeče dāg ghāl = *l.* put vaccine of small-pox.

Vaccine, *s.* dāg, -gā, *m.*

Vacillate, *v.* yeṇeñ teṇeñ hāl = *l.* move here and there; dăl = *l.* undulate; pòḍ *with the quasi-dim.* -so; kāmp = *l.* tremble.

Vacillation, *s.* dălneñ, -neā, *n.*; lăkṇi, -ṇe, *f.*

Vade-mecum, *s.* hātapustak, -kā, *n.*; sāngātpustak.

Vagabond, *a.* pārpoḷ, bevāris.

Vagary, *s.* mărji, -je, *f.*; girānt, -ti, *f.*

Vagrancy, *s.* pārpoḷpoṇ, -ṇā, *n.*

Vague, *a.* 1. vāreātso = *l.* windy, *fg.*
2. dubāvi = *l.* doubtful; khănḍitnāiñ āsullo = *l.* undecided; soṣṭ nāiñ āsullo = *l.* not clear.

Vain, *a.* 1. beṣṭo; vèrt; nirfòḷ = fruitless.
2. duvrātso (durātso) = of smoke, *fg. e.g.* v. humour.
3. dănḍi = ostentatious; doulăt kărtso; ăṭṭās kărtso = *l.* proud; ăhănkāri = *l.* proud.

Vain-glorious, *see* **Vain,** 3.

Vain-glory, *s.* băḍāi, -ye, *f.*; ăbbāř, -rā, *m.*; doulăt, -ti, *f.*, *or* doul, -lā, *m.*; hemmeñ, -meā, *n.*; ăhănkār, -rā, *m.*; gărv, -vā, *n.* = *l.* pride.

Vainly, *ad.* beṣṭeñ; *old*, ăḍadăḍi.

Valid, *a.* 1. ghăṭ = strong; boḷadik.
2. thir, *e.g.* v. testament; sind.
3. purto = sufficient.

Validity, *s.* 1. ghăṭāi, -ye, *f.*, *or* bhār, -rā, *m.* = importance.
2. thirpoṇ, -ṇā, *n.*, *e. g.* of a will; sindāi, -ye, *f.*, *n.u. but good word.*

Valley, *s.* phalkeñ, -keā, *n.*

Valour, *s.* dhăir, -rā, *n.*

Valuable, *a.* mòlādik, *or* mòlātso.

Value, *s.* 1. mòl, -lā, *n.*, *pr. fg.*; kimmot, -te, *f.* = v. of a property; ăndāzo, -jeā, *m.* = estimate.
2. ărthu, -thā, *m.* = *l.* meaning.

Value, *v.* 1. mòl bānd = *l.* bind the value.
2. ăndāzo kăr.
3. *fg.* mòl uoḷka = *l.* acknowledge the price.
4. mānd = honour.

Valve, *s.* kăvăḍ, kăuḍā, *n.*, of a door.

Van, *s.* foujimukāvelo vānṭo, -ṭeā, *m.*, *or* foujimuk, -kā, *n.* = the front of an army, *or* mukāili fouz, -ji, *f.*; *see* **Fan, Waggon.**

Vane, *s.* vāreābāuṭo, -ṭeā, *m.*

Vanish, *v.* năpăints zā = disappear; *neg.* *of* dis.

Vanity, *s.* doulăt *or* dăvălăt, -ti, *f.*; khāli văstụ, -tu, *f.* = *l.* an empty thing; ăhănkār, -rā, *m.*; ghăn, -nā, *n.*, *e.g.* to ghănān tsăltā; duvor, -vrā, *m.* = *l.* smoke, *fg.*; văstuntso fóṭkiro mōg(ó), -gā, *m.* = *l.* a deceiving love of things; dobāzo, -jeā, *m.* = *l.* pomp, *fg.*

Vanquish, *v.* jik, *2nd Loc.*; zăit vor, *2nd Loc.*

Vapid, *a.* 1. pāḍ zāllo = *l.* spoiled.
2. rutsnātullo = tasteless.

Vapour, *s.* ub, -be, *f.*

Vapour, *v.* ub bhāir săr.

Variable, *a.* bădăltso, *or* bădăl zāuntso.

Variableness, *s.* bădlāsārkeñ, -keā, *n.*

Variance, *s.* 1. bădlāp, -pā, *n.* = *l.* change; bhēd(é), -dā, *m.* = *l.* difference.
2. nāi, -yā, *m.* = *l.* discord.
Be at v. = vop *in neg. f.*

Varicose, *a.* suzụllo.

Variegate, *v.* veglo răng lāi = *l.* apply different colours; thărāvoḷ rong lāi.

Variety, *s.* bădlāp, -pā, *n.* = *l.* change (*not ex.*); thărāvoḷ, -ḷe, *f.*

Various, *a.* vegḷo; bădăl; thăra thărāntso = *l.* of many kinds.
Men speak v. things = lók bădăl bădăl ulăitā, *or* lók thărāvoḷ ulăitā.

Varlet, *s.* 1. tsākór, -krā, *m.* = a servant.
2. lutstso, -ččeā, *m.* = a rascal; pokri, -riā, *m.*

Varnish, *s.* rogān, -nā, *n.* (*also Mr. Cn.*)

Vary, *v.* bădăl; *pass.* bădāl.

Vase, *see* **Vessel.**

Vassal, *s.* răit, -tā, *m.*

Vast, *a.* 1. sóḍụllo = abandoned (*obs.*).
2. vistārlolo = extended.
3. tsăḍ = much.

Vastness, *s.* vistărāp, -rpā, *n.* *etc.*; *see adj.*

Vat, *s.* moṭeñ pīp, -pā, *n.* = *l.* a large cask (*Mr. too*).

Vaticinate, *v.* mukār (*or* ādiñ) sāng.

Vault, *s.* 1. găvi, -ye, *f.*, *e.g.* of a room.
2. gumăṭ, -ṭā, *n.* = *l.* a drum of this form.

Vaunt, *v.* ăbbār kăr.

Vaunting, *s.* ăbbār, -rā, *m.*; *see* **Boast.**

Vedette, *see* **Sentinel.**

Veer, *see* **Turn.**

Vegetable, *s.* 1. rāndoi (*var.* rāndvoi), -ye, *f.*, for table; sāng, -ge, *f.* (of a special kind); bājisāngo, *pl. f.*
2. zāḍ, -ḍā, *n.* = *l.* a plant.

Vegetate, *v.* vāḍ = *l.* grow; kirla = *l.* germinate.

Vegetation, *s.* fòḷvost, -tu, *f.* (*It. fiorescenza*).

Vehemence, *s.* 1. bòḷ, -ḷā, *n.*; *by* -ts.
2. umāḷo, -ḷeā, *m.*, *e.g.* v. of sorrow; kăṭiṇāi, -ye, *f.* = *l.* severity, *e.g.* of sorrow.
3. utsāmboḷāi, -ye, *f.* = *l.* excitement.

Vehement, *a.* bòḷ kărtso, *or* bòḷātso, *or* boḷvont; bòḷadik; utsāmboḷ = *l.* excited; umāḷeātso; kăṭiṇ; *see noun.*

Vehicle, *s.* gāḍi, -ye, *f.*

Veil, *s.* 1. vev, -vā, *m.*, *esp. of* European *or* Eurasian ladies, *fr.*; vol, -li, *f.*, *esp. of* native women, *fr.*; muski, -ke, *f.* = *l.* a v. covering the whole person; tuvālo, -leā, *m.*, *fr.*
2. *fg.* vês, -sā, *m.* = *l.* a mask.

Veil, *v.* ghāl *with one of the above nouns.*

Vein, *s.* 1. sir *or* šir, -re, *f.*
2. *fg.* săkăt, -kti, *f.* = ability.

Vellum, *see* **Parchment.**

Velocity, *s.* zărurāi, -ye, *f.*; dāuñ, -āve, *f.* = *l.* a running.

Velvet, *s.* ilud, -di, *f.*, *fr.*; măkmal, -lā, *n.* (*Cn. Mr.*)

Venal, *a.* lónts khātolo = *l.* eating bribes, *fg.*

Venality, *s.* lónts khāunčeñ, -čeā, *n.*; kusāp, -spā, *n.*

Veneer, *v. Mr.* fărdăzoḍāni kăr, *n. u.*

Venerable, *a.* mān fāvozāllo, *or* mānātso.

Venerate, *v.* mān di, *or* mānd; vorni = exalt; šaraṇaye.

Veneration, *s.* mān, -nā, *m.*; šaraṇa, -ṇā, *n.*; nămăskār, -rā, *m.*

Vengeance, *s.* fārikpoṇ, -ṇā, *n.*

Venial, *a.* uñ (pātak).

Venom, *s.* vik, -kā, *n.*

Venomous, *a.* vikāḷ.

Vent, *s.* 1. burāk, -kā, *n. or m.*, *fr.*; dompḷo, -ḷeā, *m.* = a hole.
2. iḍeñ, -ḍeā, *n.* = escape way.

Ventilate, *v.* 1. vāreñ ghāl.
2. *fg.* tărk kăr = *l.* make discussion.

Ventricle, *s.* poti, -ye, *f.*

Venture, *s.* mōs(ó), -sā, *m.*; ădrușț, -ṭā, *n.*; risk, -ke, *f.*; zăkăm, -kme, *f.*

Venture, *v.* 1. riskek pòḍ, *n. v.* = *l.* fall (be exposed) to risk.
2. mosānt ghāl, *tr. v.*
3. dhăir āsā = *l.* courage is.

Venturesome, *a.* dhăirāvont.

Veracious, *a.* 1. sătevont = truthful.
2. pātieṇitso = trusty; nămbgontso.

Veracity, *s.* 1. săt, -tā, *n.*

2. pātiyeṇi, -ṇi, *f.*; nămbgoṇeñ, -ṇeā, *n.*, *or* nămbiki, -ke, *f.*
Veranda, *s.* vărānd, -dā, *n.*; tsāuḍi, -ḍe, *f.*; balkāuñ, -āvā, *m.*, *fr.*; sopo, -peā, *m.* (of a house); tsouki, -ke, *f.* = an open veranda.
Verb, *s.* kriyāpăda, -dā, *n.* (*Mr. Cn.*)
Verbal, *a.* 1. tònḍpāši = oral.
2. *rs.* utrañ părmāṇe.
3. kriyāpădātso (*Gram.*).
Verbosity, *s.* boḍboḍčeñ.
Verdant, *a.* fultso.
Verdict, *s.* (pănčāyetdārañ-) phăisăl, -lā, *n.*, *or* pănčāitiphăisăl.
Verdigris, *s.* kălămb, -bi, *f.*
Verdure, *s.* 1. fòḷvostu̧, -tu, *f.*
2. tărnepoṇ, -ṇā, *n.*
Verge, *s.* *see* **Edge, Brink.**
Verge, *v.* deuñ = *l.* descend; bāgā = *l.* be bent.
Verification, *s.* 1. ruzvāt, -ti, *f.*; (sătā-) ruzvāt.
2. *rs.* *into v.*
Verify, *v.* 1. mokābilo kăr = *l.* make comparison (of a copy with the original).
2. ruzvāt kăr *or* ruzu kăr = *l.* make demonstration; khăreñ móṇ dākăi = *l.* show true; *see also* **Fulfil.**
Verily, *ad.* nīzzāun.
Verisimilar, *a.* *see* **Probable.**
Veritable, *a.* khăro.
Vermin, *s.* kīḍ, -ḍi, *f.*
Vernacular, *a.* gāuntso.
Versatile, *a.* 1. (bountăṇiñ) hāltso = moving around; ăthir = *l.* not firm; dănḍăltso = *l.* undulating.
2. bădăl zāuntso *or* bădāltso = *l.* changing.
Verse, *s.* slók, -kā, *m.*; slokavānṭo, -ṭeā, *m.*; slokafāngt, -ti, *f.* = *l.* a line of poetry.
Versed, *a.* sikuḷlo.
V. in = kăḷta, *Sb. Dat.* = *l.* he knows.
Versify, *v.* slók kăr.
Version, *s.* tărzumo, -meā, *m.*
Vertebra, *see* **Joint.**
Vertex, *see* **Summit.**
Vertical, *a.* ubo; voḷmbo = *ex.* the instruments masons use for finding the vertical.
Vertigo, *see* **Giddiness.**
Very, *ad.* bhou = *l.* much; tsăḍ.
Very, *a.* tots = the same; -ts *added to the affected word.*
Vesicle, *s.* suz, -zi, *f.*
Vesper, *s.* 1. sānz, -je, *f.* = *l.* evening.
2. sānjenekétru̧, -trā, *n.* = evening star.
Vespers, *s.* *vlg.* vespru̧, -rā, *n.* (*var.* besp, -pā, *n.*)
Vessel, *s.* 1. āidān, -nā, *n.* = *l.* a pot.
2. tāruñ, -rvā, *n.* = *l.* a ship.
3. mănji, -je, *f.* = a coasting vessel.
4. šir, -re, *f.* = *l.* a vein.
Vest, *s.* nesoṇ, -ṇi, *f.*
Vest, *v.* nesăi, *c. v.*

Vestibule, *s.* rig, -ge, *f.* = *l.* an entrance; zăgli, -le, *f.*

Vestige, *s.* gurtụ, -tā, *m.*; mèṭ, -ṭā, *n.*

Vestment, *s.* 1. mustāigi, -ge, *f.*; nesoṇ, -ṇi, *f.*

2. vestiment, -tā, *n.* = sacred v., *ol. fr.*

Vestry, *s.* *vlg.* sakrist, -ti, *f.*; igărjekuḍ, -ḍā, *n.*

Veteran, *a.* 1. mātāro = old.

2. ănbovātso *or* ănbou āsullo = *l.* experienced.

3. lāmb tsākri kello.

Veto, *see* **Protest.**

Vex, *v.* zăḷāi, *c. v. of* zăḷ; dós; dukăi, *c. v. of* duk; kărkăr (*or* tondre) kăr; rāg hāḍăi.

Vexation, *s.* bóng, -gā, *m.*; zăḷ, -ḷā, *m.* (*com.* great sorrow); kărkăr, -rāñ, *m. pl.*

Viaticum, *s.* 1. mārgakhărts, -tsā, *m.*

2. kumgār, -rā, *m.* = *l.* communion.

Vibrate, *v.* kāmp = *l.* tremble, *n. v.*; dăl = *l.* undulate, *n. v.*; yeṇeñ teṇeñ hālăi = *l.* move here and there, *c. v.*

Vicar, *s.* 1. bădli, -li, *m.* (*low w.*) = a substitute; dălāl, -lā, *m.* = *l.* an agent; vés tsălăitolo.

2. *in the com. mn.*, vigār, -rā, *m.*, *fr.*; gouḷi, -ḷiā, *m.* = *l.* a pastor.

Vice, *s.* ăuguṇ, -ṇā, *m.*; durguṇ, -ṇā, *m.*; gunyāuñ, -āvā, *m.* = *l.* fault; tsuk, -ki, *f.*; ăib, -bā, *n.* = *l.* imperfection (physical *esp.*)

Vice, *as in* vice-admiral, *etc.*, *is rendered by* tsălăitolo *added to the equivalent of the word it is compounded with, which precedes it.*

Viceversa, *ad.* porteñ.

Vicious, *a.* ăuguṇātso; pāḍ; vāiṭ *or* vāiṭ tsālitso.

Vicissitude, *s.* bădăl, -dlā, *n.*, *or* bădlāp, -pā, *n.*

Victim, *s.* bheṭoṇ, -ṇi, *f.*; băli, -ye, *f.* (*H. K.*)

Victor, *s.* zăit vortolo.

Victorious, *a.* zăitevont.

Victory, *s.* zăit, -tā, *n.*; jikāp -kpā, *n.*

Gain a v. = z. vor.

Victual, *v.* khāṇ hāḍn di.

Victuals, *s.* khāṇ, -ṇā, *n.*; grās, -sā, *m.*; hār, -rā, *m.*

Vie, *v.* uḍḍa: 'Pedru āni Pāulu teā kāmāk uḍḍatāt'; petsāḍ = *l.* try, make effort, *ch. cs.*

View, *s.* 1. diṣṭ, -ṭi, *f.*

2. āločen, -ni, *f.* = *l.* opinion.

3. sevóṭ, -ṭā, *m.* = aim.

Vigil, *s.* 1. *vlg.* bèsp, -spā, *n.* = v. of a feast; ādlo dis, -sā, *m.* = the previous day.

2. zāgrutāi, -ye, *f.* = *l.* watching; *bet.* zāgo rāunčeñ.

Vigilance, *s.* zāgrutāi, -ye, *f.*; tsătrāi, -ye, *f.*

Vigilant, *a.* zāgrut; tsătur.

Vigorous, *a.* ghăṭ; bòḷādik *or* bòḷ āsullo.

Vigour, *s.* boḷāiki, -ke (*var.* -ki), *f.*, *or* bòḷ, -ḷā, *n.*; ghăṭăi, -ye, *f.*

Vile, *a.* hălko; hīn; *see* **Coward.**

Vileness, *s.* hălkepoṇ, -ṇā, *n.*; *see* **Cowardice.**

Vilify, *v.* hălko kăr; *see* **Defame.**

Villa, *s.* nāḍ, -ḍā, *n.* = *l.* a village, *fg.*

Village, *s.* nāḍ, -ḍā, *n.*; hăḷḷi, -ḷe, *f.*; grām, -mā, *n.* = a small v.; māgṇeñ, -ṇeā, *n.* = a large v. comprising several grāmañ as subdivisions; gāuñ, -āvā, *m.* = *l.* a country, *fg.*

Villager, *s.* nāḍkār, -rā, *m.*; hăḷḷegār, -rā, *m.*

Villain, *s.* khoṭo mănis, -nšā, *m.*; lutstso, -ččeā, *m.*; *see* **Rascal.**

Vindicate, *v.* 1. sāmbāḷ = *l.* defend; hăkkụ dākăi *or* h. sāmbāḷ.
 2. fārikpoṇ kāṇeunk lāi.

Vine, *s.* dākānči vāl, -li, *f.* = *Lat. vitis.*

Vineyard, *s.* dākānčeñ tòṭ, -ṭā, *n.*

Vinegar, *s.* sirko, -keā, *m.*

Vinous, *a.* dākañ-rosātso.

Vintage, *s.* (folānčeñ) kaṭāu, -āvā, *n.*; beḷeñ, -ḷeā, *n.*

Violate, *v.* 1. mōḍ(ó) = *l.* break, *e. g.* v. an order.
 2. bòḷ (*or* zulum) kăr = make violence; ăkmān (*or* ăpamān) kăr = *l.* make offence; pāḍ kăr = *l.* corrupt, make bad; băṣṭăi = defile.

Violation, *s.* ăkmān *or* āpamān, -nā, *m.*; bòḷ, -ḷā, *n.*, *or* zulum, -lme, *f.* = violence; miruoṇeñ, -ṇeā, *n.* = *l.* excess.

Violator, *s.* 1. ăkmān kărtolo; băṣṭăitolo.
 2. (kāido) móḍtolo = *l.* he who breaks (a law).

Violence, *s.* bòḷ, -ḷā, *m.*; zulum, -lme, *f.*; jāsti, -te, *f.*; zobordosti, -te, *f.*

Violent, *a.* boḷādik, *or* bòḷ kărtso, *or* bòḷ āsullo; zulmetso.

Violet, *a.* zāmbḷirongātso; *vlg.* róš, *fr.*

Violin, *s.* rèbèk, -kā, *n.*; sārang, -gā, *n.* (*H. K.*)

Violinist, *s.* rèbèk vāztolo.

Viper, *s.* 1. *approx.* āgio, -giā, *m.*
 2. *fg.* dušṭ mănis, -nšā, *m.*, *or also* āgio.

Virago, *s.* 1. mănša thāun āil''li.
 2. zuzāriṇ, -ṇi, *f.*
 3. zăgḍeāči ăstri, -re, *f.* = *l.* a quarrelling woman.

Virgin, *s.* ānkuār, -rā, *m.*; ānkuār, -ri, *f.*

Virginity, *s.* ānkuārpoṇ, -ṇā, *n.*

Virtual, *a. rs.* guṇa pārmāṇe, *or* săkti pārmāṇe.

Virtue, *s.* 1. seguṇ, -ṇā, *m.*
 2. niskăḷkāi, -ye, *f.* = *l.* purity.
 3. guṇ, -ṇā, *m.* = *l.* power, effect, *e. g.* of a medicine.

Virtuous, *a.* seguṇi, *or* seguṇātso, *or* guṇest; niskāḷ = *l.* chaste; boro = *l.* good.

Virulence, *s.* koḍsāṇ, -ṇi, *f.* = *l.* bitterness, *fg.*; vik, -kā, *n.* = *l.* venom.

Virus, *s.* nănji, -je, *f.* = poison.

Visage, *s.* rūp, -pā, *n.*; muk, -kā, *n.*; tònḍ, -ḍā, *n.*

Viscera, *s.* ānkiṭi, -ṭe, *f.*

Viscid, *a.* lāgtso; pānkātso.

Viscidity, *s.* pānk, -kā, *m.*; lāgā sārkeñ, -keā, *n.*

Visibility, *s.* diṣṭi sārkeñ, -keā, *n.*

Visible, *a.* distso; diṣṭik pòḍtso; drăša, *ol.*

Vision, *s.* 1. diṣṭ, -ṭi, *f.* = faculty of v., *also* an apparition.
2. kuḷeñ, -ḷeā, *n.* = *l.* a goblin; druṣṭakāi, -ye, *f.*
3. sopāṇ, a -pṇā, *n.* = *l.* a dream, *fg.*

Visionary, *see* **Enthusiast.**

Visit, *s.* bhèṭ, -ṭe, *f.*; *see* **Inspection.**

Visit, *v.* bhèṭ kăr, *or* bhèṭ; milākăt kăr; pòḷe = *l.* look, *fg.*

Visitor, *s.* 1. bhèṭ kărtolo.
2. melbăndobăst kărtolo = *l.* inspector; melbăndobăst kāṇetolo.

Vista, Visual, *s.* diṣṭ, -ṭi, *f.*; diṣṭi-dikkụ, -kā, *m.*

Vital, *a.* 1. jivātso, *pr. fg.*
2. bhou bhāri = very important.

Vitals, *s.* prāṇasānde = *l.* vital organs.

Vitiate, *v.* 1. pāḍ kăr; kus.
2. răddụ kăr = make nullity; ăthir kăr = make invalid.

Vitreous, *a.* *see* **Glassy.**

Vitriol, *s.* 1. măiltuttu, -tā, *n.* = blue v.
2. irākṣ, -ṣi, *f.* = green v.

Vituperate, *v.* duruăi, *c. v. of* durua; beṣṭāi.

Vituperation, *s.* dur, -rā, *n.*; beṣṭāuṇeñ, -ṇeā, *n.*

Vivacity, *s.* ušārāi, -ye, *f.*; tsurkāi, -ye, *f.*; ulāspoṇ, -ṇā, *n.*

Vivid, *a.* 1. părzāḷik.
2. sošṭ, *e.g.* imagination.

Vivify, *v.* vāntsāi.

Vixen, *s.* zăgḍeāči ăstri, -re, *f.* = *l.* a quarrelling woman.

Vocabulary, *s.* săbdañbănḍār, -rā, *n.* (*by anal. to the Mr.* săbda-koš) = *l.* a treasury, a repertory of words.

Vocal, *a.* tònḍpasiñ.

Vocation, *s.* 1. bhès, -sā, *m.*
2. huddo, -deā, *m.* = *l.* rank; āpouṇeñ, -ṇeā, *n.* = *l.* a call.

Vocative, *a.* āpountso.

Vociferate, *v.* bòb măr.

Vociferation, *s.* bòb mărči; bòb, -be, *f.*

Vogue, *s.* rivāz, -ji, *f.*

Voice, *s.* 1. tāḷo, -ḷeā, *m.*
Base v. = săkăilo t.
Tenor v. = modlo t.
Soprano v. = voilo t.; *see also* **Strong, Thin.**
2. vot, -tā, *m.* = *l.* suffrage, *fr.*; kobuli, -le, *f.* = *l.* consent.

Void, *a.* 1. khāli = *l.* empty.

2. ăthir = *l.* invalid, *n. u.*; răddu̥ kello, *or* răddu̥ āsullo.
3. *by neg. Ger. in* -tanañ ; viṇ *affixed to the word it refers to, e.g.* void of reason = motiviṇ; nātullo, *or* nāiñ āsullo *affixed; see also* **Vacant.**

Void, *v.* 1. vót; khāli kăr = make empty.
2. răddu̥ kăr = *l.* make nullity.

Volatile, *a.* ubtso; ub zāuntso.

Volcano, *s. Mr.* jvālāmukhi părvót, -tā, *m.*; *Konk.* ujea-muk, -kā, *n.* = *l.* a mouth of fire, *n. c.*

Volley, *s.* făr, -rā, *m.*

Volubility, *s.* 1. loḷasārkeñ, -keā, *n.*
2. *fg.* mărji, -je, = *l.* caprice.

Volume, *s.* 1. voḍāi, -ye, *f.* = dimension.
2. pustak, -kā, *n.*, *or* grănth, -thā, *n.* = *l.* a book.
3. (pustăkātso) vānṭo, -ṭeā, *m.* = *l.* part (of a book).
4. *see* **Roll.**

Voluminous, *a.* vistārlolo; vóḍ; rund.

Voluntary, *a.* khušen kello, *or* khušetso; zāi moṇ kello = made freely.

Volunteer, *s.* umeduār, -rā, *m.*

Voluptuary, *a.* khušālāyetso.

Volute, *s. approx.* mukuṭ, -ṭā, *m.* = *l.* a crown, *fg.*

Vomit, *s.* vónk, -ki, *f.*

Vomit, *v.* 1. vònk; vónk yetā = *l.* v. comes, *Sb. Dat.*
2. vonkāro yetā = nausea (an inclination to vomit) comes.

Vomitive, *a.* vònkounčeñ.

Voracious, *a.* giḷtso = *l.* swallowing, *fg.*; khāugi = *l.* very greedy of food.

Voracity, *s.* khāunči khuši, -še, *f.*; khāugipoṇ, -ṇā, *n.*

Vortex, *see* **Whirl.**

Vote, *s.* vót, -tā, *m.*, *e. g.* in a meeting, *fr.*; voppigi, -ge, *f.*; kobuli, -le, *f.*, *or* koblāt, -ti, *f.*

Vote, *v.* vòp = *l.* consent (*Dat.*).

Voting-table, *s.* āngoṇiči foḷi, -ye, *f.*

Votive, *a.* āngoṇetso.

Vouch, *v.* 1. sākṣ̌ di (*or* sāng) = *l.* give witness.
2. sākṣ̌ kāṇe = *l.* take witness.
3. zāmindār zā = *l.* become security.
4. sākṣ̌zāun māg; *see* **Evidence.**

Voucher, *s.* 1. sākṣ̌igār, -rā, *m.* = a witness.
2. zāmindār, -rā, *m.* = security (person).
3. zāmin, -ne, *f.* = security (state).

Vouchsafe, *v.* puṭva = *Lat. dignari*; dăya kăr *or* upkār kăr, *com. used in the gerundial form, e. g.* d. kārn gărānt riga.

Vow, *s.* āngoṇ, -ṇe, *f.*, *or* āngoṇ sāngoṇ, -ṇe, *f.*

Keep a v. = ā. sāmbāḷ, *or* ā. fārik kăr.

Vow, *v.* āngoṇ kăr.
Vowel, *s.* jivākṣer, -rā, *m.*
Voyage, *s.* poiṇ (*or* pāiṇ), -ṇā, *n.*
Voyage, *v.* poiṇ kăr.
Vulgar, *a.* 1. tsālto = *l.* current; sādo = simple; sovoyetso = customary; sādhārn = ordinary.
2. hălko = low.
Vulgar, *s.* zomo, -meā, *n.*; *see* **Crowd.**
Vulture, *s.* gīd, -dā, *m.*

W

Wad, *s.* tsumboḷ, -bḷi, *f.* = *ex.* a bundle of cloth *or* straw, (*It. imbottita*).
Wad, *v. see* **Stuff.**
Waddle, *v.* lăk; dăl; *see* **Vacillate.**
Wade, *v.* (udak) utăr (pāyāniñ); udkāntleān tsăln utăr.
Wafer, *s. vlg.* hostụ, -tu, *f.*
Waft, *v.* 1. upeun vór.
2. upe = *l.* float.
Wag, *v.* yeṇeñ teṇeñ hālăi.
Wag, *s. see* **Jester.**
Wage, *v.* kăr, *e.g.* w. war.
Wager, *v.* pónt măr.
Wager, *s.* pónt, -tā, *m.*
Waggery, *s.* bārikāi, -ye, *f.*
Wages, *s.* kūl, -li, *f.*; măzuri, -re, *f.*; sāmbāḷ, -ḷā, *m.*
Waggon, *s.* (čār čăkrānči) gāḍi, -ye, *f.*
Wainscoat, *s.* (kuḍāčiñ) foḷiñ, *pl. n.*
Waist, *s.* kămbăr, -rā, *n.*
Waistcoat, *s.* āngāčeñ văstur, -rā, *n.*; bănian, -nā, *n.*; kăpča, -če, *f.* (*also* mail, network).
Wait, *v.* 1. rāu = stop.
2. rāk = wait on.
Wait, *s.* nāḍ, -ḍi, *f.*; *see* **Ambush.**
Waiter, *s.* 1. tsākor, -krā, *m.*
2. tăbăk, -bkā, *n.* = a dish.
Waiting, *s.* 1. rāvāp, rāupā, *n.*
2. tsākri, -re, *f.*; rākčeñ (rākṇeñ, -ṇeā, *n*).
Waive, *v.* sóḍ; pāṭi ghāl.
Wake, *v.* 1. uṭăi, *c. v. of* uṭ = *l.* cause to rise.
2. zāgo kăr = *l.* make awake.
Wake, *s.* zāgrutāi, -ye, *f.*
Wakeful, *a.* zāgo.
Wakefulness, *s.* zāgrutāi, -ye, *f.*
Walk, *v.* 1. tsăl = move on the feet.
2. bouñ = *Lat. ambulare* = to take a walk.
Walk, *s.* bounḍi, -ḍe, *f.*; tsăl, -li, *f.*
Walk, *s.* tsăltolo.
Wall, *s.* 1. voṇot, -ṇti, *f.*, *also* round a town; doro, -reā, *m.*

2. pāgār, -rā, *m.* (*esp.* round a town).
Wall, *v.* ghăṭ kăr.
Wallet, *s.* poti, -ye, *f.*
Wallow, *v.* loḷ.
Walnut, *s.* ākruṭ, -ṭā, *n.*
Walrus, *s.* dăryāgòḍo, -ḍeā, *m.*
Wan, *a.* pānṭro.
Wand, *see* **Stick, Rod, Twig.**
Wander, *v.* pārpoḷ zāun bouñ = to lead the life of a vagrant; bouñ.
Wanderer, *s.* pārpoḷ mănis, -nšā, *m.* = a vagrant.
Wandering, *s.* pārpoḷpoṇ, -ṇā, *n.*
Wane, *v.* uṇo zā; deuñ.
Want, *s.* 1. gărz, -je, *f.*
2. *fg.* ākānt, -tā, *m.* = *l.* distress.
3. *by the neg. form, e.g.* w. of health = nāñbolāiki.
Want, *v.* 1. zāi = *l.* is required, *Sb. Dat.*; 'what do you w. = tukā kiteñ zāi?'
2. ăpekši, khuši vor, āše = desire.
Wanton, *a.* móstitso; lăzbanḍo; bāilanḍo; vāiṭ khuseānk lāgullo.
Wantonness, *s.* most, -ti, *f.*; lăzbanḍpoṇ, -ṇā, *n.*; bāilanḍpoṇ, -ṇā, *n.*
War, *s.* 1. zuz, -zā, *n.*
2. lăḍāi, -ye, *f.* = *l.* a fight.
Warble, *v.* gāyān kăr.
Ward, *v.* tsukăi; pois kăr, *or* p. dovór.
Ward, *s.* 1. tsukouṇeñ, -ṇeā, *n.*
2. rākṇeñ, -ṇeā, *n.*
Warden, *s.* rākṇo, -ṇeā, *m.*
Warder, *s.* pāro, -reā, *m.*, *or* pāreagār, -rā, *m.*
Wardrobe, *s.* mustāigekuḍ, -ḍā, *n.*
Wardship, *s.* rākṇeñ, *or* rākoṇeñ, -ṇeā, *n.*
Ware, *s.* 1. vèpār, -rā, *m.*; yār, -rā, *m.*
2. sāmān, -nā, *m.*; mhāl, -lā, *m.*
Warehouse, *s.* bănḍsāḷ, -ḷi, *f.*
Warfare, *s.* zuz, -zā, *n.*
Wariness, *s.* zāgrutāi, -ye, *f.*
Warlike, *a.* zuzātso.
Warm, *a.* 1. un, *e.g.* water; khăr (very hot, *used esp. of* water); tāpoillo = made warm, *e.g.* iron, water; ubetso, *e.g.* cloth; gărmetso, *e.g.* weather, cloth, *fg. said also of* men.
2. *fg. rs.* ujea bări (very angry), *n.c.*
I am w. = mākā ukḍaitā.
Warm, *v.* 1. un kăr, *etc.*
2. tāpăi, *e.g.* meat, iron, *etc.*; *also fg.*, give a slap.
Warmth, *s.* 1. gărmi, -me, *f.*, *e.g.* of the sun; vòt, -tā, *n.*, of the sun; ub, -be, *f.*
2. *fg.* uzo, ujeā, *m.*
Warn, *v.* 1. bud săng.
2. kăḷăi = *l.* notify.
3. hišāro di = *l.* give a hint.
Warning, *s.* 1. bud, -di, *f.* = *l.* advice.
2. hišāro, -reā, *m.* = *l.* a hint.
Warrant, *s.* 1. zāmin, -ne, *f.*
2. hukum, -kme, *f.*

3. zāminetso kărār, -rā, *m*.

Warrant, *v*. 1. nīz zāun sāng; khăro (-ri, -reñ) móṇ dākăi.
2. thir kăr = *l*. confirm.
3. zāmin zā = *l*. become security; zăvābdār zā.

Warrior, *s*. zuzāri, -riā, *m*.

Wart, *s*. tsāmkuḷ, -ḷā, *m*.

Wary, *a*. pāṭi phuḍeñ pòḷeuntso; budivont,

Wash, *v*. 1. du; *c. v*. duvoi.
2. umboḷ (w. clothes).

Washerman, *s*. moḍvoḷ, -ḷā, *m*.; dobi, -bi, *m*.

Wasp, *s*. gāndil, -dlā, *m*.

Wasp-nest, *s*. māleñ, -leā, *n*.

Waste, *a*. 1. făḍpu; 'w. land = făḍpustăḷ'.
2. yeksuro = *l*. solitary.
3. pāḍ zāllo = spoiled.

Waste, *s*. nāš, -šā, *m*.

Waste, *v*. 1. nāš kăr; pāḍ kăr.
2. véṭ = w. money; hăḷtaviṇ khărči.
3. desvaṭ kăr.

Wasteful, *a*. desvaṭetso, *or* desvaṭ kărtso.

Watch, *v*. 1. rāk.
2. zāgo rāu.

Watch, *s*. 1. ghăḍiyāḷ, -ḷā, *n*. (*var*. -ḷi, *f*.)
2. zāgrutāi, -ye, *f*.

Watchful, *a*. 1. zāgo.
2. zāgrut.

Watchman, *s*. rākṇo, -ṇeā, *m*., *or* rāktolo, -leā, *m*.

Water, *s*. udāk, -dkā, *n*.

Water, *v*. udāk ghāl, *or* u. simp.

Watered, *a*. bizăillo.

Water-fall, *s*. udkāpoḍneñ, -neā, *n*., *or* —poḍāp, -ḍpā, *n*.

Water-proof, *a*. udāk riganāso, *n. c*.

Watery, *a*. 1. udkātsoso.
2. udkātso.

Wattle, *s*. 1. āḍār, -rā, *n*.
2. tăṭṭi, -ṭe, *f*.; izăi, -ye, *f*.
3. gānzo, -jeā, *m*. (of fowls).

Wattle, *v*. *see* **Weave.**

Wave, *s*. lār, -rā, *n*.

Wave, *v*. 1. dăl = *l*. undulate, *n. v*.
2. hālăi, *c. v*. *of* hāl = *l*. move.

Waver, *v*. 1. dălun dălun yetā.
2. dubāu; dănḍăḷ; tondreār āsā.
3. pòḍ *with affix* -so.

Wax, *s*. mèṇ, -ṇā, *n*.

Wax, *v*. meṇān dāmp (*or* dānk).

Wax-taper, *s*. bārik vāt, -ti, *f*.

Way, *s*. 1. vāṭ, -ṭe, *f*.; mārog, -rgā, *m*.
2. *fg*. jinos, -nsā, *m*.

Waylay, *v*. vāṭer lipon bòs.

Wayward, *a*. săḷiṣṭ.

Waywardness, *s*. săḷ, -ḷā, *n*.

We, *pron*. āmiñ; *see* Gram. P. II. ch. iii.

Weak, *a*. 1. ăskăt; bolāiki nātullo.
2. ghăṭnātullo; ălbo, *e.g*. prop, support.

Weaken, *v*. 1. ăskăt kăr; bārik kăr.
2. *fg*. mōḍ(ó) = *l*. break; uṇo kăr.

Weakness, *s.* ăskătkāi, -ye, *f.*
Weal, *s.* bori kāleti, -ti, *f.*; sukh, -khā, *n.*; borepoṇ, -ṇā, *n.*
Wealth, *s.* 1. grestkāi, -ye, *f.*
2. sămpurṇāi, -ye, *f.*
3. borepoṇ, -ṇā, *n.*; vrăddhi, -dhi, *f.*
Wealthy, *a.* grest; dhănvăst; duḍuādik; āst āsụllo.
Weapon, *s.* hătyār, -rā, *n.*; āid, -dā, *n.*
Wear, *v.* 1. (gāsun) pāḍ kăr.
2. dor (dovór), *e.g.* a dress; nès = wear clothes.
3. tăg = *l.* last.
4. zăr = spoil, *e.g.* a cloth.
Wearied, *a.* puro zāllo; bezār.
Weariness, *s.* dăṇsouṇeñ, -ṇeā, *n.*, *bet. rs. adj.*; jhinṭ, -ṭi, *f.*, *or* zhinṭ.
Wearisome, *a.* kăṣṭountso, *or* kăṣṭāntso.
Weary, *v.* puro kăr; dăṇsi (*H. K.*)
Weary, *a.* *see* **Wearied.**
Weasel, *s.* mungăs, -gsā, *n.*
Weather, *s.* hăvo, -veā, *m.*; vēḷ(é) -ḷā, *m.*; vāreñ, -reā, *n.*
Weather, *v.* pār zā (vādaḷāntleñ).
Weathercock, *s.* vāreabāuṭo, -ṭeā, *m.*
Weave, *v.* vóḷ.
Weaver, *s.* sālio, -yā, *m.*; voḷtolo.
Weaving, *s.* voḷāp, -ḷpā, *n.*
W. machine = măg, -gā, *m.*
Web, *s.* 1. năv, -vā, *m.*, *n. c.*
2. lugaṭ -gṭā, *n.*
3. zāḷ, -ḷā, *n.*, of a spider.
Wedded to, *a.* (*fg.*) lāgụllo, bhalụllo = wholly devoted to.
Wedding-day, *s.* kāzārātso dis, -sā, *m.*, *fr.*; *vlg.* resperātso dis, *fr.*
Wedge, *s.* čip, -pā, *n.* (*perh. not Konk.*); bunu, -nā, *m.*; khiḷ, -ḷi, *f.*
Wedge, *v.* čip mār.
Wedlock, *see* **Marriage.**
Weed, *s.* 1. nālio, -liyā, *m.*
2. mornāčeñ văstur, -rā, *n.*
Week, *s.* hăpto, -teā, *m.*; somān, -nā, *m.*, *fr.*
Week-day, *s.* somānāče dis, *pl. m.*
Weekly, *a.* hăptea hăpteātso.
Ween, *see* **Think.**
Weep, *v.* răḍ; pirnga = *l.* groan; dukañ găḷāi.
Weeping, *s.* răḍneñ, -neā, *n.*, *or* răḍāp, -ḍpā, *n.*; pirngoṇi, -ṇe, *f.*
Weevil, *s.* ṭeko, -keā, *m.* (*anal. to Mr.*), *n. u.*
Weigh, *v.* 1. tuk.
2. zăḍ āsā.
Weight, *s.* 1. tuk, -kā, *n.*
2. bhār, -rā, *m.*; zăḍāi, -ye, *f.*
Weighty, *a.* vozănātso; bhārātso; zăḍ *or* zăḍāyetso.
Welcome, *a.* boro pāullo.
Welfare, *s.* sukh, -khā, *n.*; borepoṇ, -ṇā, *n.*; vrăddhipoṇ, -ṇā, *n.*, *n. c.*
Welkin, *s.* ākāš, -šā, *m.*
Well, *s.* bāiñ, -iñ, *f.*; čilmbi, -be,

f. = a small w.; zăr, -ri, *f.* = *l.* a fountain.

Well, *ad.* 1. boreñ *or* boreñ kărn; săma; sobitāyen.

2. bhou = very.

Well-affected, *a.* bore khušetso; mogāḷ; guṇātso.

Well-born, *a.* măntănāntlo.

Well-bred, *a.* măryāditso; tsāltsămkăṇ āsullo.

Welter, *v.* loḷ.

Wen, *s. perh.* gunṭ, -ṭā, *n.*, *or* māskuṭ, -ṭā, *n.*

Wench, *s.* 1. čeḍuñ, -ḍvā, *n.*; tsăli, -ye, *f.*

2. čeḍi, -ye, *f.*

Wend (one's way), *v.* vetā.

West, *s.* faḍla, -lā, *n.*, *or* ăstămti, -ti, *f.*

Wet, *a.* 1. volo.

2. băil (gādo) = a w. (field).

Wet, *s.* šéḷ, -ḷi, *f.*; 'I got w. = mākā š. zāleā'.

Wet, *v.* bizăi, *c. v. of* biz.

Wetness, *s.* šéḷ, -ḷi, *f.*

Wettish, *a.* šéḷitsoso; volso.

Whale, *s.* māso, -seā, *n.*

Wharf, *s.* dăkko, -keā, *m.*; băndăr, -drā, *n.*

What, *pron.* 1. kiteñ (*inter. and compound rel. pron.*).

2. . . . .teñ.

Whatever, *a.* kăsăleñi; kiteñi.

Wheat, *s.* gouñ, -ovā, *m.*

Wheaten, *a.* govātso.

Wheedle, *v.* fuslăi; *see* **Coax, Flatter.**

Wheel, *s. vlg.* ròd, -dā, *n.*, *or* ròz, -zā, *n.*; čăkru̥, -rā, *n.*

Wheel, *v.* guuñ, *c. v.* guunḍăi.

Wheeze, *v. see* **Pant.**

When, *ad.* 1. kăiñ; kerna (*used only partially*); jedvañ; kedaḷa.

2. zărtăr = if; *by the cond.*; *by the Ger. in* -tanañ.

Where, *ad.* 1. khăiñ.

2. *if correl. of* there, *often omitted.*

Where—there = khăiñ—thăiñ.

Whereas, *see* **Because, Since.**

Whereby, *ad.* zăče vorviñ.

Wherefore, *ad.* kiteāk; zăče (*or* zănče) pāsun.

Wherein, *ad.* zāntuñ.

Whereof, *ad.* zăče višyānt.

Whereso, *ad.* 1. kiteāk.

2. zāka.

Whereupon, *ad.* tăče uprānt.

Wherever, *ad.* khăiñ".

Wherry, *s.* dóṇ, -ṇi, *f.*

Whet, *v.* 1. sāṇik dăr; pāz = sharpen with sandstone.

2. *fg.* zăḷăi, *or* rāg hāḍăi.

Whether, *conj.* -gi, *e.g.* ask w. he came = to ăilogi vitsăr.

I do not know w. this is right or not = yeñ sămagi năiñ ăuñ neṇañ; I do not know w. this is right or wrong = yeñ sămagi tsuk ăuñ neṇañ.

Whether—or, zăuñ—zăuñ, *e. g.* boro zăuñ, pāḍ zăuñ, *or* zăuñ boro, zăuñ pāḍ.

Whetstone, *s.* sāṇ, -ṇi, *f.*, *or* sāṇitso fātor, -trā, *m.*

Which, *a.* kontso *or* kăintso (*from* koṇ, *or* kăiñ); kăsălo; khăintso (*from* khăiñ); kiteñ; koṇ to; *see* Gram. P. II. ch. iii., P. IV. ch. ii., Art. iii.

Whiff, *s.* funk, -ki, *f.*

While, *ad.* veḷār *preceded by part.; by Ger. in* -tanañ.

While, *s.* phursot, -ti, *f.* = leisure.

A little w. = thoḍents.

While away (the time), *v.* = tsălăi.

Whim, *s.* mărji, -je, *f.*

Whimper, *v.* pirnga; bòb mār.

Whimsical, *a.* mărjetso.

Whine, *see* **Whimper.**

Whip, *s.* čabuk, -bkā, *m.*

Whip, *v.* čabkān mār.

Whirl, *s.* guvāp, guupā, *n.*; bovór, -vrā, *m.*

Whirl, *v.* guuñ, *n. v.*; *see* **Wreath.**

Whirlpool, *s.* bovór, -vrā, *m.*

Whirlwind, *s.* tufān, -nā, *n.*; iḷ, -ḷi, *f.*

Whisk, *s.* sāruṇ, -ṇe, *f.*

Whiskers, *s.* gālmišo, *pl. f.*

Whisper, *v.* voḷu ulăi; kānānt ulăi.

Whisper, *s.* voḷu gouji, -je, *f.*, *or rs. v.*

Whistle, *s.* šeḷoni, -ne, *f.*

Whistle, *v.* šeḷoni ghāl.

Whit, *s.* (not a w.) = kăints (nāñ).

White, *a.* dovo; goro, *used esp. of* Europeans *as opposed to* natives.

White-ant, *s.* vāḷăi.

Nest of white-ants = rovoḷn, -ni, *f.*, *or* roiṇ, -ṇi, *f.*

Whiten, *v.* dovo kăr.

Whiteness, *s.* dovo rong, -gā, *m.*

Whitewash, *v.* dovo kăr; tsuno kāḍ; voṭvās kāḍ.

Whither, *ad.* khăiñ.

Whitish, *a.* dovoso *or* dòuso.

Whiz, *v.* fusfus.

Who, *pron.* kōṇ(ò).

Whosoever, *pron.* zokoṇ; *see* Gram.

Whole, *a.* săgḷo; săkăḍ; *see* **All.**

Whole, *s.* săgḷo, -ḷeā, *m.*

Wholesale, *s.* vikāp, -kpā, *n.*, *or* vikro, -reā, *m.*; sāṭo, -ṭeā, *m.*

Wholesome, *a.* bolāiketso, *e. g.* food, climate.

Wholly, *ad.* purteñ; săgḷots; păripurṇ.

Whoop, *s.* bòb, -be, *f.*

Why, *ad.* kiteăk (*var.* kiteā), *or* kiteā pāsun.

Wick, *s.* vāt, -ti, *f.* (*also* a candle).

The burnt part of the w. = kāzuo, -zueā, *m.*

Wicked, *a.* khoṭo.

Wickedness, *s.* khoṭepoṇ, -ṇā, *n.*

Wicker, *s.* vāl, -li, *f.*

Wickerwork, *s.* gòlgo, -geā, *m.*, *or* janga, -gā, *m.*, *or* kăḍo, -ḍeā, *m.*, for storing rice in, as is customary here.

Wide, *a.* rund = *l.* broad; vistărlolo; poisilo, *e.g.* a wide interpretation.

Widen, *v.* vistăr (*tr. n. v.*).

Width, *s.* rundăi, -ye, *f.*

Widow, *s.* vidou, -dvi, *f.*, *Sans.*; rănḍ, -ḍe, *f.* (*dim.* rănḍgi, -ge), *but here in South Canara this is an offensive word;* boḍki, -ke, *f.* (*l.* bald).

Widower, *s.* vidou, -ovă, *m.*; rănḍgo, -geă, *m.*; *see note on* **Widow.**

Wield, *v.* tsălăi, *c. v. of* tsăl.

Wife, *s.* băil, -le, *f.* (*vlg.*); savat, -ti, *f.*; potiṇ, -ṇi, *f.*; gărkărn, -ni, *f.* = *l.* a housewife, *fg.*; ăstri, -re, *f.* = *l.* a woman.

Wig, *s. see* **Peruke.**

Wild, *a.* rănuoṭ (*also* uncultivated); răn *in composition.*

W. beast = murg, -gă, *n.*

Wilderness, *s.* răn, -nă, *n.*, *or* ărăṇeñ, -ṇeă, *n.* = *l.* a desert; moleñ, -leă, *n.* = *l.* a forest; yeksuri suăt, -te, *f. or* yeksurăi, -ye, *f.* = *l.* solitude.

Wildness, *s.* rănuoṭpoṇ, -ṇă, *n.*

Wile, *s.* mōs(ó), -să, *m.*

Wile, *v.* mōs(ó) kăr.

Wilful, *a.* 1. dhăruṇ.

2. khušen kello (*or other participle*); zăimoṇ kello; khušetso; monahpurvok kello.

Wilfully, *ad.* 1. dhăruṇăyen.

2. khušen; zăimoṇ; monahpurvok.

Wilfulness, *s.* dhăruṇăi, -ye, *f.*

Wiliness, *s.* năḍgepoṇ, -ṇă, *n.*; mōs(ó), -să, *m.*

Will, *s.* 1. khuši, -še, *f.*; iččha, -čhe, *f.*; ăšă, -še, *f.*

2. mornapătrụ, -ră, *n.*; mornašăsăn, -nă, *n.*; *vlg.* testament, -tă, *m.*, *fr.*

Will, *v.* *Dat.* khuši ăsă = *l.* desire (*or* will) is; ăše, *or* ăšă kăr (*G. F.*), *or* ăpekṣi; khuši vor.

Willing, *a. rs. into v.*

Willingly, *ad.* khušien, *or* khušen; khušălăyen = with pleasure.

Willingness, *s.* khuši, -še, *f.*; khušălăi, -ye, *f.*; săntos, -să, *m.*

Wily, *a.* năḍgo; mosătso; ṭhăkkagăr.

Wimple, *s.* vôl, -li, *f.*

Win, *v.* jik; zăit vor, *obj. 2nd Loc.*; zóḍ = *l.* obtain.

Wince, *v.* păṭi săr.

Wind, *s.* 1. văreñ, -reă, *n.*

2. văi, -ye, *f.* = *l.* flatulence, (gas?).

Wind, *v.* 1. văz, an instrument; funk.

2. porti = *l.* turn, *c. v. of* porta, *n. v.*; bounḍăi, *c. v. of* bouñ.

3. vôḷ.

W. up (a watch) = tsăvi di = *l.* give the key, *ch. cs.*

Windlass, *s. approx.* čăkrụ, -ră, *n.*

Windmill, *s.* văreadănteñ, -teă, *n.*

Window, *s.* *vlg.* zănèl, -lā, *n.*, *fr.*; kiṭki -ke, *f.* (*H. K.*)

Window-shutters, *s.* *vlg.* zănelāčiñ bāglañ, *pl. n.*; dār, -rā, *n.*

Windpipe, *s.* soknăḷi, -ḷe, *f.*

Windy, *a.* vāreātso.

Wine, *s.* dākāntso rós, -sā, *m.*; Vilāyetātso soro, -reā, *m.*; *some say only* soro = arrack; *vlg.* vāin *or* văin *or* voin, -nā, *m.*

Be given to w. = kòp mār.

Wing, *s.* 1. pākāṭo, -ṭeā, *m.*

2. *fg.* vānṭo, -ṭeā, *m.*

3. *fg.* (of a building), ăntăr kuḍ, -ḍā, *n.* = *ex.* a side-room.

Wink, *s.* 1. kšăṇ, -ṇā, *n.* = a moment.

2. hišāro, -reā, *m.* = a hint.

Wink, *v.* dòḷe mōḍ (ó); hišāro di.

Winnow, *v.* 1. vāreāk di; v. dhăr; vāsuḍ; kāṭāi.

2. *fg.* părikša kăr.

Winter, *s.* *see App. to the Konk.-Engl. Dictionary.*

Wipe, *v.* pus.

Wire, *s.* tănti, -te, *f.* = thick w.; ārām, -mi, *f.* = thin w.; sări, -ye, *f.*

Wisdom, *s.* bud, -di, *f.*; zāṇvāi, -ye, *f.*; somzoṇi, -ṇi, *f.*, *or* somzoṇkāi, -ye, *f.*; ginyān, -nā, *n.*

Wise, *a.* budivont; vidyevont; zānṭo; săktivont.

Wiseacre, *s.* kapas budivont (*iron.*); dăḍḍo.

Wish, *s.* khuši, -še, *f.*; āšā, -še, *or* ăpekši, -še, *f.*

Wish, *v.* khuši vor; āše; āšā kăr, *or* ăpekši; khuši āsā, *Sb. Dat.*

Wisp, *s.* muṭ bhór, (*indecl.*); *see* **Bundle.**

Wistful, *a.* jīv sóḍn āšetolo.

Wit, *s.* 1. somzoṇkāi, -ye, *f.*

2. bārikāi, -ye, *f.* = *l.* thinness, *fg.*

To w. = moṇje.

Witch, *s.* ghāḍigārn, -ni, *f.*

Witchcraft, *s.* ghāḍi, -ḍi, *f.*; bhul, -li, *f.*; phitispoṇ, -ṇā, *n.*; bolmeñ sāngči sāmārthi, -the, *f.*

With, *prep.* 1. sāngāta (in company).

2. kăḍe *or* lāgiñ (*Lat. apud*).

3. *Instr. or 2nd Loc., to show manner.*

4. *Instr. to show instrument.*

5. *sometimes it is omitted and expressed by the Dat., e. g.* I agree w. you = āuñ tukā voptāñ.

Withal, *ad.* săit.

Withdraw, *v.* 1. kāḍ, *tr. v.*

2. pāṭi săr, *n. v.*

Wither, *v.* sukăi, *c. v. of* suk, *n. v.*; ulpāi = *l.* scorch.

Withhold, *v.* pāṭi dovór; nākā móṇ.

Within, *prep.* 1. bităr.

2. āltăḍi = (*Lat. citra*) on this side.

Within, *ad.* bităr; bităarleān; *see* Gram.

Without, *prep.* 1. bhāir (*var.* bāir *but more correct* bhāir).
2. viṇ *or* viṇe.
3. šivāi; khărit, *e.g.* w. necessity; viroit, *e.g.* Deva Putra viroit kāints" rătsunk nāñ.
4. *by the neg. Ger. in* -tanāñ (*with verbs*), *e. g.* w. doing this = yeñ kărināstanañ; *by the neg. conditional.*

Withstand, *v.* 1. inkār kăr (*Acc.*)
2. *Dat.* āḍye.

Withy, *see* **Wicker.**

Witness, *s.* sākṣigār, -rā, *m.* (the person); sākṣ, -ṣi, *f.* (the act); šāidi, -de, *f.*; govāi, -ye, *f.*, *ol.*

Witness, *v.* sākṣ kăr *or* s. di.

Witticism, *s.* bārikāisi.

Witty, *a.* bārik; čeṣṭāi kărtso *or* čeṣṭāyo kărtso.

Wizard, *s.* ghāḍigār, -rā, *m.*; phitisponagār, -rā, *m.*

Woe, *s.* 1. (sărgiñ) širāp, -pā, *m.*; māldisāuñ, -sāvā, *n.*, *fr.*
2. duk, -ki, *f.*

Woful, *a.* dukest.

Wolf, *s.* suṇeñvāgăṭ, -ṭā, *n.*; koḷsundeñ, -deā, *n.*

Woman, *s.* ăstri, -re, *f.*; bāil, -le, *f.*; bāilmănis, -nše, *f.* (*pl.* -šañ), *vlg.*

Womb, *s.* kus, -si, *f.* (*used for the* w. of the Bl. Virgin); pòṭ, -ṭā, *n.*

Wonder, *s.* ăjāp, -pā, *n.*; āščăryeñ, -yeā, *n.* (*var.* ătsăryeñ).

Wonder, *v.* ăjāp zā (*Acc.*).

Wonderful, *a.* ăjāpātso.

Wont, *s.* sovoi, -ye, *f.*; rivāz, -ji, *f.*

Wont, *a. rs. Dat.* sovoi āsā; sovoyetso.

Wood, *s.* 1. lānkuḍ, -kḍā, *n.* = fire-wood.
2. rukāḍ, -ḍā, *n.* = timber.
3. rān, -nā, *n.*, *or* ărăṇeñ, -ṇeā, *n.*; moleñ, -leā, *n.*

Wooden, *a.* lānkḍātso; rukātso.

Wool, *s.* louñ, love, *f.*

Word, *s.* 1. utăr, -trā, *n.* = a promise *also*; sobd, -dā, *m.*
2. bhās, -se, *f.* = a promise.
3. răvāneñ, -neā, *n.* = *l.* a message.
Send w. = kăḷăi.

Work, *s.* 1. vāur, -rā, *m.*
2. kărni, -ne, *f.*; kăryeñ, -yeā, *n.*; kărtuveñ, -veā, *n.*; kām, -mā, *n.*

Work, *v.* vāur kăr, *or* vāur"; kām kăr; goḷ; kăr; tsăḷăi.

Workman, *s.* 1. vāurāḍi, -ḍiā, *m.*; begāri, -riā, *m.*; mānāi, -yā, *m.*; kulkār, -rā, *m.* = a coolie.
2. āčāri, -riā, *m.* = an artisan; lovār, -rā, *m.*, in iron.

Workshop, *s.* mānḍ, -ḍā, *m.*

World, *s.* 1. săuñsār, -rā, *m.*
2. *fg.* mănšekuḷ, -ḷā, *n.*

Worldly, *a.* săuñsārātso *or* săuñsārāntlo.

Worm, *s.* 1. kiḍo, -ḍeā, *m.*; kiḍ, -ḍi, *f.*, small.
2. dónt, -tā, *m.* = w. found in [men.
3. gāinḍoḷ, -ḷā, *m.*

Worm, *v.* w. out a secret = kăḍ.

Worry, *v.* zăḷăi, *c. v.; see* **Tease.**
Worse, *a. comparat. of* pāḍ (ădhik p., *etc.*); pāsṭ.
Worship, *s.* nămăskār, -rā, *m.*; puză, -je, *f.*, *used esp. of* idols.
Worship, *v.* nămăskār kăr; puza kăr *or* băz, *used esp. of* idols.
Worshipper, *s.* nămăskār kărtolo.
Wort, *s.* tăṇ, -ṇă, *n.*
Worth, *a.* fāvo (*indecl.*), *or* fāvoto (*decl.*), *or* fāvo zāllo; vāzbi = *l.* convenient.
Is w. = mòl āsā, *or* mòl pòḍtā, *ch. cs.*, *or* lāgtā = *l.* is attached, *ch. cs.*
Worthily, *ad.* fāvote jinsiñ.
Worthless, *ad.* mòlnātullo; *see* **Useless.**
Wound, *s.* ghāi, -yā, *m.*; zăkhăm, -khme, *f.*
Wound, *v.* 1. ghāi (*or* zăkhăm) kăr; ghāye, *n. v.*
2. *fg.* dukăi.
Wrangle, *v.* zăgăḍ.
Wrap, *v.* guṭlăi = envelop; bităr ghāl; dāmp.
Wrapper, *s.* 1. poteñ, -teā, *n.*
2. mokfardo, -deā, *m.* (of paper).
Wrath, *s.* tsăḍāvot rāg, -gā, *m.*; kród, -dā, *m.*
Wreak (vengeance), *v.* (fārikpoṇ) kāṇe.
Wreath, *v.* revóḍ ghāl, *or* reuḍāi; vóḷ.
Wreath, *s.* kopèl, -lā, *n.* = garland, *which see.*
Wreck, *v.* fóḍ (*pass.* fuṭ).
Wreck, *s.* tārvāčeñ fuṭāp, -ṭpā, *n.*
Wrench, *v.* 1. kāḍ; vóḍ.
2. reuḍāi.
Wrest, *v.* 1. kāḍ.
2. reuḍāi.
Wrestle, *v.* zăgăḍ; prăyătăn kăr.
Wretched, *a.* 1. dubḷo, *or* durbăḷo, *or* nirbhāgi, *or* bhikāri, *or* kirkoḷ *or* upāināṭullo.
2. pāḍ.
Wretchedness, *s.* bhikārpoṇ, -ṇā, *n.*, *used esp. of* moral wr.; kirkoḷāi, -ye, *f.*, *etc.*; nirbhāgpoṇ, -ṇā, *n.*
Wriggle, *v.* reuḍāi.
Wring, *v.* revoḍ ghāl.
Wrinkle, *s.* miri, -ye, *f.*
Wrist, *s.* monkuṭ, -ṭā, *n.*
Writ, *s.* pòtrụ, -trā, *n.*; bărāp, -rpā, *n.*
Holy Writ = păvitrụ pustak, -kā, *n.*
Write, *v.* bărăi.
Writer, *s.* 1. bărpi, -piā, *m.*, *or* bărăitolo.
2. gumăst, -tā, *m.* = a clerk; šeṇăi, -ṇăi, *m.* = an account-keeper.
3. grănthakărt, -tā, *m.* = an author.
Writing, *s.* 1. bărāp, -rpā, *n.*
2. pătrụ, -trā, *n.*

Wrong, *a.* sămanātullo; tsuk; you are wr. = tuji tsuk.
Wrong, *s.* 1. tsuk, -ki, *f.*
2. bādăk, -kā, *n.* = *l.* harm.
3. ăkmān, -nā, *m.* = *l.* offence.
4. nāñhăkku, -kā, *n.*
Wrong, *v.* ăkmān kăr.
Wroth, *a.* (rāgān) zăḷtso; bhou rāgiṣṭ.
Wry, *a.* vānkḍo.

Y

Yacht, *s.* khušālāyečeñ tāruñ, -rvā, *n.*
Yam, *s.* čineñ, -neā, *n.*
Yard, *s.* 1. āngāṇ, -gṇā, *n.* = a courtyard.
2. vār, -ri, *f.*, a measure.
3. kāmp, -pā, *n.*, *e.g.* a churchyard, *fr.*
Yarn, *s.* 1. sut, -tā, *n.* = *l.* thread.
2. *fg.* lāmb kătha, -the, *f.*
Yawn, *s.* zāmbāi, -ye, *f.*
Yawn, *v.* zāmbāi kāḍ.
Ye, *pron.* tumiñ.
Yea, *ad.* voi"; *see* **Nay.**
Year, *s.* 1. vărs, *or* vors, -sā, *n.*
2. isvi, -ve, *f. used only of* the years after Christ.
Last y. = poruñ, -ruñ.
The y. before last = poruñ.
This y. = ăunduñ, *or* ānduñ, -duñ.
Next y. = phuḍāñ, -ḍāñ.
Yearly, *a.* vărsavărsātso.
Yearly, *ad.* vărsavărsa.
Yearn, *v.* lāle, *Dat.*
Yearning, *s.* lāleuṇeñ, -ṇeā, *n.*
Yeast, *see* **Ferment.**
Yell, *v.* bòb mār.
Yell, *s.* bòb, -be, *f.*
Yellow, *a.* 1. ăḷduvo.
2. pānṭro.
Yellowish, *a.* ăḷduvoso.
Yelp, *see* **Bark.**
Yeoman, *s.* vokāl, -klā, *m.*
Yes, *ad.* 1. voi" (oi").
2. zăit = *l.* it will be done, very well.
3. *repeat the sentence or merely the verb as in Latin.*
Yesterday, *ad.*, *a.* kāl, *ad.*; kāltso, *a.*; 'kāltso āitār = last Sunday'.
The day before y. = pór.
Yet, *conj. ad.* 1. āni, -i; *see* Gram.
2. zāleāri; tări; *see* **Gram.**; ăzun; *often omitted.*
Yield, *v.* 1. di.
2. soḍun di.
3. *by c. v.*
4. pāṭi săr.
Yielding, *see* **Comply.**
Yoke, *s.* zuñ, zuvā, *n.*
Yoke, *v.* bānd.

Yonder, *a.* to.
Yonder, *ad.* thăiñ; lāgints.
Yore (of y.), *ad.* ādiñ, *or* ādiñ purviñ, *or* ādiñ māgiñ.
You, *pron.* tuñ (*sing.*), tumiñ (*pl.*).
Young, *a.* tărnaṭo.
Young, *s.* pīl, -lā, *n.*
Your, *pron.* tuzo (*sing.*), tumtso (*pl.*).
Youth, *s.* 1. tărṇaṭi pirāi, -ye, *f.* 2. burgo, -geā, *m.*; tărṇaṭo mănis, -nšā, *m.*

Z

Zeal, *s.* urbā, -be, *f.*; umāḷo, -ḷeā, *m.* = *l.* fervour, *fg.*; suḍsuḍāi, -ye, *f.*, *n. c.*; āšā, -še, *f.*
Zealous, *a.* urbevont, *or* urbest; āšetso.
Zenith, *s.* kḥamadya, -yā, *m.*, *n. u.* (*Sans. Mr. Cn.*); untssuāt, -te, *f.*
Zero, *s.* sonneñ, -neā, *n.*
Zinc, *s.* kăpursuttụ, -tā, *n.*
Zone, *s.* 1. bānd, -dā, *m.*; *see* **Girdle.** 2. bhāg, -gā, *m.* = *l.* division.

APPENDIX I.

SOME OF THE PRINCIPAL MEDICINES OF THIS COUNTRY.

Abrus precatorius, gunji *or* gurgunji.
Acacia arabica, khairāruk *or* kātzuruk.
Acajou, kāz.
Acalipha betulina, dudiyāčeñ pān.
Acalipha indica, kāreteñ.
Achie, pātsu.
Achiranthes aspera, kānṭomogro.
Acorus calamus, voikănḍ.
Ailanthus excelsa, kămăl.
Allium sativum (Garlic), losuṇ.
Aloes littoralis, loḷisăr.
Alum, păṭki (*vlg.* phăṭki) *or* păṭikār.
Ammonia, Hydrochlorate of, năvasāgre.
Anamirta cocculus (*Fr. Coque du Levant*), kākāi phăḷ.
Andrachne cadishaw, gaḍphăḷ ruk.
Andropogon nardus, takatăṇ.
Andropogon muricatus, 1. bannala; 2. karmaḷo.
Andropogon shoenanthus, gāṇiereñ tăṇ.
Aniseed, šep.
Antimonium, surmāuñ.
Arakalekai, kārekai.
Arakalekai mirobalan, ărḍo.
Arakalekai emblic, āvāḷo.
Argemone, dutreāčeñ zāḍ, *or* dutro.
Aristolochia, sāpsikaḍul, *or* kaḍupāḷ.
Arrow-root, kuveā piṭ.
Arsenicum, sănkpāšaṇ.
Aspalathus indica, buiññāring.
Asparagus sarmentosus, šatāvăr.
Assa fœtida, hing.
Barleria longifolia, niruko.
Basilic, tuḷăs.
Bassia longifolia, naṇel.
Bent-grass (*Fr. Chiendent*), kărki.
Bergera Koenigii, karbeñ (karbeu?).
Bismuth, kăpursut.
Bole (Armenian), kāvi fātor, *or* sangāu.
Borax, daunkār.
Bryona, phălsā phăl.
Bryonia grandis, čirpuṭli *or* čirpuṭ.
Butea frondosa, mutak.
Cachou, kătsu.
Calomel, roskărpur.
Calophyllum inophillum, hăngăni?
Calyptranthes, zomli săl.
Camphora, kāpur.
Cardamomum, veḷ *or* yêḷ.

Cassia, kākae.
Cassia alata, agšé.
Cassia tora, kādu-kuli.
Cassia auriculata, nānkèr.
Castor-oil, yenḍečeñ tèl.
Citrus medica, limbo.
Cleome, khāulo.
Clove, lăvăng.
Coloquintides, săngmī.
Convolvulus, čikāi.
Copper-sulphate, măiltut.
Coriander, kănpir *or* kotomir.
Crataeva marmelos, vonḍo kuḍo.
Creyat, jiretā kāḍi.
Croton, yāpal
Cubeba piper, găndmeṇās, *or* bālmiriñ.
Cucurbita citrullus, kuvāḷo.
Cuminum, jireñ.
Curculigo, tigḍe
Curcuma, ălăt.
Cynanchum, kasal.
Dalbergia, samui.
Date, khāzur.
Datura, dutăr, *or* dutro.
Dolichos, poit kāzurkuli.
Eryothroxylon, deudar, *or* tup-deudar.
Euphorbia, nivalkanḍeñ, *or* kăḷḷi.
Flacourtia, salispătrụ.
Foenum graecum, meti.
Gardenia, mărg.
Gentiana, nelbeu.
Ginger, sunṭ, *or* āleñ.
Guilandina, gazug, *or* găzgo.
Gum, gond, *or* dendiga meṇ.
Helleborus, kāṭukārohiṇ.
Hibiscus, sāuri ruk.
Hyperanthera, mogga ruk.
Laurus cassia, (*Fr. Cannelle*), dālčini; *or* tikkesāl.
Linseed, sóṇ.
Magnesia, bāirečeñ mīṭ.
Pomegranate, dāḷimb.
Saffron, hăḷăd.
Silver-nitrate, kāḍikār.
Sulphur, găndop.
Tamarind, āmsāṇ.
Tea, čā.
Tobacco, durāpān.

APPENDIX II.

CERTAIN DISEASES.

Apoplexy, răgtăči piḍā, *or* răgat sărleñ.

Asthma, lăs, -si, *f.*

Boil, 1. fóḍ, -ḍā, *m.*
 2. kesoḷi, -ḷe, *f.*

Burns, ulópụ, -lpā, *m.*

Cancer, mānpuḷi, -ḷe, *f.*

Chicken-pox, koṭle, -leāñ, *m. pl.*

Cholera, sirsiri, -re, *f.*

Congestion, răgtāsănkăṭ, -ṭā, *n.*

Constipation, Costiveness, *expressed by* 'bănd = bind'.

Consumption, khevāḍ, -ḍi, *f.*

Contusion, *expr. by* 'jezār', *see also Dictionary.*

Convulsions, kāmp, -pi, *f.*; voḍi, -ḍiñ, *f. pl.*

Cough, khonkli, -le, *f.*; usmóḍ, -ḍi, *f.* (suffocation).

Croup, gunṭañ, *pl. n.*

Diarrhœa, utkaḍe, -ḍeā, *n.*

Dislocation, 1. *by the v.* āḍañ vingăḍ sărleānt.
 2. khiḷi-nikăḷči.

Dropsy, nalkut, -tā, *n.*

Dysentery, răgtăčeñ zărām, -rmā, *n.*

Elephantiasis, ăsti pāi.

Fainting, jinṭ (tākā jinṭ mārli).

Fever, tāp, -pā, *m.*, *or* zór, -rā, *m.*

Giddiness, guvoḷ, guuḷi, *f.*

Gout, vākḷañ, *pl.*, *n.*

Gripes, muḍḍoṇeñ, -ṇeā, *n.*

Headache, tăkleči foḍāpoḍ, -ḍi, *f.*

Inflammation, ulóp, -lpā, *m.*

Itch, khoróz, -rji, *f.*

Jaundice, kāḷkăi, -ye, *f.*

King's evil, kănṭmăḷ, -ḷā, *n.*

Leprosy, kòḍ, -ḍā, *n.*

Looseness, hāgoṇ, -ṇi, *f.*

Measles, urureñ, -reā, *n.*

Mumps, keppaṭeñ, -ṭeā, *n.*

Palsy, āriči piḍā, -ḍe, *f.*, *or* ār, -ri, *f.*

Rheumatism, 1. keḷči piḍā.
 2. vāt, -tā, *m.*

Ring-worm, dād, -di, *f.*

Small-pox, boḷnik, -ke, *f.*

Snake-bite, mār, -rā, *m.*

Tetanus, săndvāi, -ye, *f.*

Tooth-ache, dāntāči duk, -ki, *f.*, *or* dāntaduk.

Worms, dónt, -tā, *m.*

Wound, ghāi, -yā, *m.*

APPENDIX III.

NAMES OF RELATIONSHIP.

1. **Father,** bāpui; -pāi, *m.*
2. **Mother,** āvoi, -voi, *f.*
3. **Son,** putru̥, -rā, *m.*, *or* put, -tā, *m.*
4. **Daughter,** du, -ve, *f.*
5. **Brother,** bhāu, bhāvā, *m.*
6. **Sister,** boiṇ, -ṇi, *f.*
7. **Grand-father,** āzo, -jeā, *m.*
8. **Grand-mother,** āji, -je, *f.*
9. **Nephew,** putnyo, -yeā, *m.* (son of a brother); bātso, -čeā, *m.* (son of a sister).
10. **Niece,** duuḍi,-ḍe, *f.* (daughter of a brother), bāči, -če, *f.* (daughter of a sister).
11. **Grand-nephew,** nātu, -tuā, *m.*
12. **Grand-niece,** nāt, -ti, *f.*
13. **Uncle,** bāplyo, -yeā, *m.* (a brother of the father); māulo, -ḷeā, *m.*, *or* mām, -mā, *m.* (a brother of the mother).
14. **Aunt,** māvoḷn, -ni, *f.* (a sister of the father); māusi, -se, *f.* (a sister of the mother); māmi, -ye, *f.* (the wife of a maternal uncle).
15. **Cousin,** *m.* (bāpul) bhāu, -vā, *m.* (the child of a brother); māusi bhāu = the child of a sister.
16. **Cousin,** *f.* māusi boiṇ, -ṇi, *f.*
17. **Father-in-law,** māuñ, -āvā, *m.*
18. **Mother-in-law,** māiñ, -āiñ, *f.*
19. **Son-in-law,** zāvoiñ, -viyā, *m.*
20. **Daughter-in-law,** sunu̥, -ne, *f.*
21. **Brother-in-law,** miuṇo, -ṇeā, *m.*
22. **Sister-in-law,** năṇănd, nănḍe, *f.* (a sister of the husband); miuṇi, -ṇe, *f.* (a sister of the wife).
23. Yei, -yā, *m.*, *or* Yeṇ, -ṇi, *f.* = the father *or* mother of a bride and bridegroom.
24. Sāḍu, -ḍvā, *m.* = the husband of a sister-in-law.
25. Nănḍayo, -yeā, *m.* = the husband of 'năṇănd'.
26. Bāvoz, bāuje, *f.* = the wife of a brother.
27. Bāvo, -veā, *m.* = an elder brother of the husband.
28. Dēru̥, -rā, *m.* = a younger brother of the husband.
29. Fāgur māuñ = a brother of the father-in-law.
30. Fāgur māiñ = the wife *or* sister of 'fāgur māuñ'.
31. **Great-grandchild,** poṇṭur, -rā, *n.*
32. **Great-great-grandchild,** seṇṭur, -rā, *n.*
33. **The child of 'seṇṭur,'** kātrur, -rā, *n.*

APPENDIX IV.

THE MOST COMMON CHRISTIAN NAMES.

Adam, Adauñ, -uñ.
Agatha, Agdu, -du.
Alexander, Alexandăr, -dri, *or* Alešendru, -ri.
Alexis, Ales, -sā, *vlg.* Also, -seā.
Ambrose, Ambroz, -zā.
Anastasia, Anastin, -ni, *f.; if a girl*, -nā, *n.*
Anastasius, Anast, -stā.
Andrew, Andru, -ru.
Angelina, Anjeñ, -jeā.
Anna, Anne, -ne, (-neā), *or* Anni, -ni.
Antonia, Antone, -ne; *girl*, -neā.
Anthony, Anton, -ni.
Augustine, Agustin, -ni; *vlg.* Gustin, -ni, *or* Gusto, -teā.
Balthasar, Bāltu, -tu.
Barnabas, Bornu, -nu.
Basil, Bajil, -lā.
Benjamin (Beniamin), *vlg.* Benjmi, -mi.
Bernard, Bernārd, -dā.
Bonaventure, Intru, -ru, *or* Bovintru.
Cajetan, Kăitān, -nā.
Camil, Kāmil, -lā.
Catharine, Katarin, -ni, (*girl*, -nā); *vlg.* Kottru, -tru.
Cecilia, Sesil, -lā.
Celestine, Selestin, -nā.
Clara, Klār, -ri, (*girl*, -rā); *vlg.* Kalār, -rā.
Conception, Končesāuñ, -sāvā; *vlg.* Končes, -si, (*girl*, -sā).
Cyprian, Sipriān, -nā.
Daniel, Dannel *or* Daniel, -li.
David, Dāvid, -dā.
Diego, Dieg, -gā (*or* Diggu, -gu).
Dominga, Dumgi, -ge, *or* Dumgen, -ni (*girl*, -nā).
Domingo, Doming, -gā.
Dulcina, Dulbeñ, -be; *girl*, -beā.
Emilian, Miliān, -ni; *girl*, -nā.
Esperance, Esperās, -sā.
Elia, Elias, -sā.
Emmanuel, Manuel, -li.
Eve, Yev, -ve.
Faustin, Faustin, -nā, *or* -ni.
Feliciana, Felišan, -nā.
Florina, Flor, -rā, *or* Fula, -lā.
Francis, Frask, -skā; *vlg.* Forso, -seā.
Francisca, Frānčiskā, *or* Forsi, -si, *f.*
Gabriel, Gabriel, -lā; *vlg.* Gabru, -bru.
Gaspar, Gaspār -ri.
Gracia, Gorsu, -su; *if joined to* Mary = Gras Māri, -rie.
Gregory, Gregor, -rā, *or* -ri.
Helena, Helen, -nā.
Ignatia, Insu, -su.
Ignatius, Inās, -sā.
Iliana, Iliān, -ni, (-nā), *or* Ilu, -lu.

Isabel, Zăbel, -li, (*girl*, -lā).
James, Jākob, -bā, *or* Jāku, -ku.
Jane, Zuăn, -ni, (*girl*, -nā).
Joachim, Jākki, *or* Jokki, -ki, *f.*
John, Zuāuñ, -uñ.
Joseph, Zoze, -ze.
Lazarus, Lazar, -rā; *vlg.* Lādru, -dru.
Laurence, Lorso, -seā, (-čeā), *or* Lores, -sā.
Lewis, Luis, -sā.
Lucy, Lus, -si, (-sā), *vlg.* Lujeñ, -jeā.
Louisa, Luisā, -se.
Magdalen, Magdalen, -ni; *vlg.* Mornel (*shortened from* Mary Magdalen).
Mary, Mări, -ye, (*girl*, -yā).
Martha, Martu, -tu.
Martin, Mortin, -ni.
Matthew, Motes, -sā.
Merciana, Mersen, -ni (*girl*, -nā).
Michael, Mingel, -li.
Monica, Monku *or* Moku, -ku.
Natalia, Nătu, -tu; Natāl, -lā.
Nicholas, Niklāuñ, -āuñ, *or* Niku, -ku.
Pascoal, Pāsku, -ku.
Pascoala, Paskeñ, -ke, (*girl*, -keā).
Paul, Paul, -lu, *or* -lā.
Peter, Pedru, -ru.
Philip, Filip, -pā.
Philippa, Filpi, -pi (*girl*, -pe).
Rachel, Rakel, -li, (*girl*, -lā).
Regina, Rejin, -ni, (*girl*, -nā).
Rita, Ritu, -tu (*girl*, -tā).
Roque, Rokki, -ki.
Rose, Roz, -zi (*girl*, -zā).
Rosario, Rozār, *or* Ruzār, -ri.
Sabina, Sobin, -nā.
Salvador, Salvador, -rā; *vlg.* Saldor, -rā.
Sebastian, Sebastiauñ, -uñ, *or* Bastiauñ, -uñ.; *vlg.* Bostu.
Sebastiana, Bastian, -ni.
Seraphina, Serpin, -ni, (*girl*, -nā).
Sylvester, Šila, -lā.
Simon, Simāuñ, -uñ.
Thomas, Thomas, -sā.
Valentine, Valentin, -nā.
Xavier, Saver, -rā.

7

ERRATA.

General Corrections.

1. The past participle ending in -llo preceded by u, should have ụ instead of u.

2. The sign *G.M.*, *G.F.*, or *G.N.* has sometimes been omitted. Whenever, in translating the Konkani verb literally, we should use the Genitive, as a rule the sign should have been inserted; *see* Gram. p. 53, n. 6.

3. The Infinitive in -aunk should be -aunk″.

4. Thăiñ should be always thăiñ″.

5. Năiñ always năiñ″ (no).

6. The nasal sound ñ is missing in some words, especially in neuter nouns.

7. Oi *or* voi should be voi″ (yes).

8. Pois should be pois″ (far).

Particular Corrections.

		Errata:	*Corrige:*
Under	Abbey	*converts*	*convents*
,,	Abscond	*n. u.*	*n. v.*
,,	Accordance	părmāṇe āsā	părmāṇe
,,	Acerbity	āmsāṇi	āmsāṇ
,,	Addicted	piyeuṅk = *l.*	piyeunk l. =
,,	Aerometer	vereāmāp	vāreamāp
,,	Agent	*m. G.*	*m.*
,,	,,	suăter tsăltolo	*G.* suăter tsăltolo
,,	Aggregate	if	is

		Errata:	*Corrige:*
Under	Alarm, *s.*	ākāntiči	ākāntāči
„	Alter, 2.	*or* bădăl	*or* bădāl
„	Anxiety	čintnā	čința
After Ascetic insert	Ascribe, *v.* 1. lāi, *e.g.* a crime. 2. gunyāu-kăr kăr. 3. gāl.		
Under	Ashamed	šermetāñ	šerme
„	Ashore	tāḍi	tăḍi
„	Baptize	*vlg.*;	; *vlg.*
„	Because	keteāk	kiteāk
„	Blister, 2.	*ol.*	*vl.*
„	Brown	*v.*	*a.*
„	Burial	mórn	mòrn
„	Castor	jenḍičeñ	yenḍečeñ
		yenḍel tēl	yenḍēl
„	Chance	pātiyeṇiñ	pātieṇi
„	Changeable	bădăltso	bădāltso
„	Chase, *s.*	sikār	šikār
„	Cherish	tslăi	tsălăi
„	Condense	āuḷ"	auḷăi, *c. v. of* āuḷ"
„	Depress	; *fg.*	, *fg.*;
„	Devote	*G. M.*	*belongs to* prăyog kăr.
„	Disinherit	nivrāi	nisrāi
„	Dissatisfaction	feel pain.	feels pain.
		disappoval	disapproval
„	Distress, *s.*	ăprād	ăpād
„	Doubtless	dubāu vornātullo	dubāuvornāsta-nāñ
„	Earnest, *a.*	fervently, *ch. cs.*	fervent.
„	Efficacious	effect	to effect
„	Endear	mōg(ò)	mōg(ó)
„	Event	zărtăr, if.	zărtăr = if.
„	Ewe	bokri	bāilo bokro
„	Exercises	exercise	duty
„	Expel	nivrāi	nisrāi
„	Experiment	păryătăn	prăyătăn
„	Expiration	sóḍne	sóḍni

		Errata:	*Corrige:*
Under	Fickle	bădăltso	bădāltso
,,	Fill, 2.	bhór	bhòr
,,	Firework	khăzneñ	khăzne
,,	Firmament	ākās	ākāš
,,	Flabby, Flaggy	bāutso	bāuntso
,,	Flagstaff	-ṭeā	bāuṭeakaṭeā
,,	Fluently	sădiḷ; sădsădit.	sădiḷ zāun; săḍsăḍit zāun.
,,	Go (Go abroad)	bărpăr	găḍpār
,,	Grown up	vāḍavoḷ, -ḷi, *f*.	vāḍavoḷ
,,	Homeless	ghăr—	ghăr—
,,	Immediately after	uprātăts	uprāntăts
,,	Indifferent, 3.	tsăstrāinātullo	tsătrāinātullo
,,	Indulgent	*G. F.*	*omit it*
,,	Inexcusable	—nāiñ	—năiñ
,,	Infatuate	*of* pisa	*of* pisau
,,	Inflate	get puffed up	puff up
,,	Landlord	(possessor of gardens);	; (possessor of gardens)
,,	Malign	calamities	calumnies
,,	Marry	*Prs. Dat.*	*Prs. Cm.*
,,	Material, *a*.	*as expressing the idea of a false religion*	*omit*
,,	Milleped	*fg*.	*f*.
,,	Misshappen	Misshappen	Misshapen
,,	Molest	lāsāi	zăḷăi
,,	Necklace	*pl*. sór	*pl*. sòr
,,	Paunch	-poskuṭo	-poskāṭo
,,	Perjury	soput	foṭsoput
,,	Physiognomy	indications.	inclinations.
,,	Pole	*petrica*	*pertica*
,,	Porch	tsăḍāu, -ḍāvā, *m*.	tsāuḍi, -ḍe, *f*.
,,	Prate	get	give
,,	Recant	hāḍ	kāḍ
,,	Recommend	*G. F.*	*belongs to* šipārās kăr

		Errata:	*Corrige:*
Under	Refuge	săsāi	săhāi
„	Retail	*v.*	*s.*
„	„	*s.*	*a.*
„	Rule	nēm (é)	nēm (è)
„	Smack, *v.*	di = *l.* give	kāṇghe = *l.* take
„	Solicitude	čintna, -ne	činta, -te
„	Spot	ātāntso	ātānts
„	Stair	māḷiyečeñ	māḷiyečiñ
„	Steamer	āg	ag (ni)
„	Strain, *v.*	lekavort kăr	lekavorto kăr *or* tānḍ
„	Tepidity	uṇibhăkt	*vlg.* āḷsāi, -ye, *f.*
„	Terror	bhăyăkăr	bhăyănkăr

„ Tinkle, muye *belongs to* Tingle, *and for* Tinkle *put* ghăṇghăṇ.

„	Trouble	tondre, *pl. n.*	tondre, *pl. m.*
„	Unchangeable	bădălnāñso	bădālnāñso
„	Year	The year before the last = poruñ.	The year before last = poraruñ.